# YEARBOOK OF AMERICAN & CANADIAN CHURCHES 2007

D0167340

S

# Previous Issues

| Year of Publication | Title | Editor |
|---|---|---|
| 1917 | Federal Council Year Book | H. K. Carroll |
| 1918 | Yearbook of the Churches | C. F. Armitage |
| 1919 | Yearbook of the Churches | C. F. Armitage |
| 1920 | Yearbook of the Churches | S. R. Warburton |
| 1922 | Yearbook of the Churches | E. O. Watson |
| 1923 | Yearbook of the Churches | E. O. Watson |
| 1925 | Yearbook of the Churches | E. O. Watson |
| 1927 | The Handbook of the Churches | B. S. Winchester |
| 1931 | The New Handbook of the Churches | Charles Steizle |
| 1933 | Yearbook of American Churches | H. C. Weber |
| 1935 | Yearbook of American Churches | H. C. Weber |
| 1937 | Yearbook of American Churches | H. C. Weber |
| 1939 | Yearbook of American Churches | H. C. Weber |
| 1941 | Yearbook of American Churches | B. Y. Landis |
| 1943 | Yearbook of American Churches | B. Y. Landis |
| 1945 | Yearbook of American Churches | B. Y. Landis |
| 1947 | Yearbook of American Churches | B. Y. Landis, G. F. Ketcham |
| 1949 | Yearbook of American Churches | G. F. Ketcham |
| 1951 | Yearbook of American Churches | G. F. Ketcham |
| 1952 | Yearbook of American Churches | B. Y. Landis |
| 1953 | Yearbook of American Churches | B. Y. Landis |
| 1954 | Yearbook of American Churches | B. Y. Landis |
| 1955 | Yearbook of American Churches | B. Y. Landis |
| 1956 | Yearbook of American Churches | B. Y. Landis |
| 1957 | Yearbook of American Churches | B. Y. Landis |
| 1958 | Yearbook of American Churches | B. Y. Landis |
| 1959 | Yearbook of American Churches | B. Y. Landis |
| 1960 | Yearbook of American Churches | B. Y. Landis |
| 1961 | Yearbook of American Churches | B. Y. Landis |
| 1962 | Yearbook of American Churches | B. Y. Landis |
| 1963 | Yearbook of American Churches | B. Y. Landis |
| 1964 | Yearbook of American Churches | B. Y. Landis |
| 1965 | Yearbook of American Churches | B. Y. Landis |
| 1966 | Yearbook of American Churches | C. H. Jacquet |
| 1967 | Yearbook of American Churches | L. B. Whitman |
| 1968 | Yearbook of American Churches | L. B. Whitman |
| 1969 | Yearbook of American Churches | C. H. Jacquet |
| 1970 | Yearbook of American Churches | C. H. Jacquet |
| 1971 | Yearbook of American Churches | C. H. Jacquet |
| 1972 | Yearbook of American Churches | C. H. Jacquet |
| 1973 | Yearbook of American & Canadian Churches | C. H. Jacquet |
| 1974 | Yearbook of American & Canadian Churches | C. H. Jacquet |
| 1975 | Yearbook of American & Canadian Churches | C. H. Jacquet |
| 1976 | Yearbook of American & Canadian Churches | C. H. Jacquet |
| 1977 | Yearbook of American & Canadian Churches | C. H. Jacquet |
| 1978 | Yearbook of American & Canadian Churches | C. H. Jacquet |
| 1979 | Yearbook of American & Canadian Churches | C. H. Jacquet |
| 1980 | Yearbook of American & Canadian Churches | C. H. Jacquet |
| 1981 | Yearbook of American & Canadian Churches | C. H. Jacquet |
| 1982 | Yearbook of American & Canadian Churches | C. H. Jacquet |
| 1983 | Yearbook of American & Canadian Churches | C. H. Jacquet |
| 1984 | Yearbook of American & Canadian Churches | C. H. Jacquet |
| 1985 | Yearbook of American & Canadian Churches | C. H. Jacquet |
| 1986 | Yearbook of American & Canadian Churches | C. H. Jacquet |
| 1987 | Yearbook of American & Canadian Churches | C. H. Jacquet |
| 1988 | Yearbook of American & Canadian Churches | C. H. Jacquet |
| 1989 | Yearbook of American & Canadian Churches | C. H. Jacquet |
| 1990 | Yearbook of American & Canadian Churches | C. H. Jacquet |
| 1991 | Yearbook of American & Canadian Churches | C. H. Jacquet, Alice M. Jones |
| 1992 | Yearbook of American & Canadian Churches | Kenneth B. Bedell, Alice M. Jones |
| 1993 | Yearbook of American & Canadian Churches | Kenneth B. Bedell |
| 1994 | Yearbook of American & Canadian Churches | Kenneth B. Bedell |
| 1995 | Yearbook of American & Canadian Churches | Kenneth B. Bedell |
| 1996 | Yearbook of American & Canadian Churches | Kenneth B. Bedell |
| 1997 | Yearbook of American & Canadian Churches | Kenneth B. Bedell |
| 1998 | Yearbook of American & Canadian Churches | Eileen W. Lindner |
| 1999 | Yearbook of American & Canadian Churches | Eileen W. Lindner |
| 2000 | Yearbook of American & Canadian Churches | Eileen W. Lindner |
| 2001 | Yearbook of American & Canadian Churches | Eileen W. Lindner |
| 2002 | Yearbook of American & Canadian Churches | Eileen W. Lindner |
| 2003 | Yearbook of American & Canadian Churches | Eileen W. Lindner |
| 2004 | Yearbook of American & Canadian Churches | Eileen W. Lindner |
| 2005 | Yearbook of American & Canadian Churches | Eileen W. Lindner |
| 2006 | Yearbook of American & Canadian Churches | Eileen W. Lindner |

Seventy-fifth Issue  Annual

# YEARBOOK OF AMERICAN & CANADIAN CHURCHES 2007

Edited by Eileen W. Lindner

Prepared and edited for the
National Council of the Churches of Christ in the U.S.A.
475 Riverside Drive, New York, N.Y. 10115-0050

Published and distributed by
Abingdon Press
Nashville

YEARBOOK OF AMERICAN & CANADIAN CHURCHES 2007

For permission to duplicate any of the material found in the *Yearbook* contact the
Office of the Yearbook of American & Canadian Churches, 475 Riverside Drive,
Room 880, New York, N.Y. 10115-0050.

Telephone: (212) 870-2031

Fax: (212) 870-2817

E-mail: yearbook@ncccusa.org

Printed in the United States of America
ISBN-13: 978-0-687-33569-5
ISSN 0195-9034

Library of Congress catalog card number
16-5726

---

Preparation of this *Yearbook* is an annual project of the National Council of the Churches of Christ in the United States of America.

This is the seventy-fifth edition of a yearbook that was first published in 1916. Previous editions have been entitled: *Federal Council Yearbook* (1916-1917), *Yearbook of the Churches* (1918-1925), *The Handbook of the Churches* (1927), *The New Handbook of the Churches* (1928), *Yearbook of American Churches* (1933-1972), and *Yearbook of American & Canadian Churches* (1973-2006).

**Eileen W. Lindner**          *Editor*
**Marcel A. Welty**            *Associate Editor*
**Tenny Thomas**               *Assistant Editor*

# Contents

Editor's Preface ................................................................. vii

## I
### PERSPECTIVES ON AMERICA'S RELIGIOUS LANDSCAPE
Trends & Developments, 2006 ................................................. 9
Asuza Street at 100: A Century of Pentecostal Ascendance ..............15
 —Eileen W. Lindner, Ph.D.

## II
### DIRECTORIES
1. United States Cooperative Organizations, National ..................... 21
2. Canadian Cooperative Organizations, National ......................... 52
3. Religious Bodies in the United States .................................... 60
 Religious Bodies in the United States Arranged by Family.......... 179
4. Religious Bodies in Canada ............................................. 182
 Religious Bodies in Canada Arranged by Family.....................212
5. Sources of Religion-Related Research ...................................214
 I. Directory of Selected Research Organizations..................... 214
 II. Directory of Selected Faith Traditions in America ................ 221
6. United States Regional and Local Ecumenical Bodies................ 233
 Index of Select Programs for U.S. Regional and
 Local Ecumenical Bodies................................................. 269
7. Canadian Regional and Local Ecumenical Bodies .................... 292
8. Theological Seminaries and Bible Colleges in the United States ..... 295
9. Theological Seminaries and Bible Colleges in Canada ............... 317
10. Religious Periodicals in the United States ............................ 323
11. Religious Periodicals in Canada ....................................... 346
12. Church Archives and Historical Records Collections ................. 353

## III
### STATISTICAL SECTION
Guide to Statistical Tables ................................................... 363
1. Membership Statistics in Canada ....................................... 364
2. Membership Statistics in the United States ........................... 371
3. Membership Statistics for the National Council of the
 Churches of Christ U.S.A................................................384
4. Selected Statistics of Church Finances—Canadian Churches ......... 386
5. Selected Statistics of Church Finances—United States Churches ..... 388
Trends in Seminary Enrollment ............................................. 394

## IV
### A CALENDAR FOR CHURCH USE
A Calendar for Church Use, 2007–2010 ................................... 397

## V
### INDEXES
Organizations ................................................................. 401
Individuals ................................................................... 411

# Editor's Preface

This seventy-fifth edition of the *Yearbook of American & Canadian Churches* marks an anniversary that affirms the remarkable service this resource has played in preserving a fascinating record of our ever-changing religious institutions. We are especially conscious of the intense labors of previous editors and contributors who shaped this annual compilation of data in earlier years, and we are grateful to maintain their legacy. This 2007 edition is accessible in both hardcopy and electronically over the Internet using the unique pass code printed on inside the back cover of this volume. Updated information is reflected in the electronic edition twice during the year. In addition, a compact disc exists of data dating from 1916 through 2000, and brings these longitudinal data into ready availability.

*Recognizing the Contributions of Many*

The field of church statistics is complex and, of necessity, filled with inconsistencies. In recent years, electronic reporting has enabled greater amounts of time at each data collection level to raise questions and to recalculate and refine reports. We at the *Yearbook* are pleased to take our place in this important task of annually capturing a snapshot of American religious life. Reflection upon such findings tells us much about ourselves as well as the institutional religious life in a country that has been referred to as a "nation with the soul of a church."

Our colleagues in the compilation of each edition of the *Yearbook* are the thousands, perhaps tens of thousands, of individuals who keep church records. We rely and build upon the efforts of church pastors, deacons, secretaries and vestrymen and women who carefully review and report church membership statistics and financial giving. We acknowledge the contributions of those at congregational, regional and especially denominational levels who respond with good cheer (most of the time!) and expeditiously (at least at our second request!) in furnishing us with the detailed data we require in the format that we request. We hope that being a part of the record and analysis offered by the *Yearbook* contributes to their sense of satisfaction for a job well done.

For various chapters of the *Yearbook* we are indebted to specific individuals for their assistance in gathering, analyzing and corroborating the information we publish. As she has for the last several years, Nancy Merrill of the Association of Theological Schools in the United States and Canada has furnished us with the data and analysis concerning seminary enrollments. Our colleague, Shanta Premawardhana of the National Council of Churches USA keeps stewardship over our *Directory of Selected Faith Traditions in America*. Our colleague Tracy DeLuca, Librarian of the Interchurch Center in New York is a regular and reliable consultant to us. Likewise, Seth Kasten, Librarian at the Burke Library of Union Theological Seminary in New York is ever ready to offer able assistance and counsel. Cathy Lavendar of the United States Census Bureau assured that the Statistical Abstract remains current with *Yearbook* data.

Annual production of the *Yearbook* requires a variety of skills and commitments within our own editorial offices. Associate Editor Marcel A. Welty gives leadership and prodigious effort to the logistics of researching, requesting, compiling, confirming, correcting, formatting and preparing data for analysis. Earl Davis is invaluable as the Editor's Assistant, aiding in confirming data and preparing the theme chapter text for publication. Newest to our staff is Tenny

Thomas, a doctoral candidate in theology who stepped into our production cycle at a particularly busy juncture, yet has proved especially creative and efficient in organizing a prodigious mountain of information quickly and accurately. Almost as closely associated with us as those we see each day are our colleagues and friends of long standing, John and Sylvia Ronsvalle, of the *empty tomb, inc.* Nationally recognized for their steadfast attention to the patterns of church giving, the Ronsvalles are unfailingly gracious in providing expert assistance and in enabling our own analysis.

On behalf of our readers, we extend our gratitude for the wisdom, skill, patience and generosity of those we acknowledge here. No small group of individuals could hope to have the knowledge needed to compile a text as far ranging as the *Yearbook.* Our efforts strengthened by the contributions of all those named above have led to the 75th edition of the *Yearbook of American & Canadian Churches*; we wish to express our deepest thanks to each of them.

*The 2007 Edition Highlights*

- Reports on an all-time-record high of 224 reporting national church bodies, which itself is reflective of a remarkably robust immigrant history and the cultural and constitutional freedom of religion so characteristic of the United States.
- Signals that churches reporting in *Yearbook* statistics reflect continued overall growth of church participation, and account for the religious affiliation of almost 166 million Americans.
- Reports on 224 national church bodies including brief histories, leadership and headquarter information, broadly inclusive of the varieties of American Christianity.
- Ranks the 25 largest churches by membership. Three of the top ten are "mainline" protestant churches. Reports the fastest growing churches in this group as: the Catholic Church, Assemblies of God, and the Church of Jesus Christ of Latter-day Saints.
- Offers a special focus on the growth of Pentecostal groups, whose ascendance is unique in American church history, noting Pentecostalism's advent and growth occurred during a time of modern, statistical record keeping.
- Analyzes the financial data from 65 churches representing almost 48 million members and more than $34 billion dollars.
- In this day of increasing awareness of religious pluralism the *Yearbook* offers an updated Directory of Selected Faith Traditions in America.
- Continues to offer the only accurate and inclusive directory of U.S. local and regional ecumenical bodies with program and contact information.
- Provides listings of theological seminaries and bible schools, religious periodicals and guides to religious research including church archive listings.
- Accurate and timely information through the *Yearbook*'s Internet edition, in its fifth year. As personnel change, area codes and old e-mail addresses are replaced with new ones, and any new information is submitted to the *Yearbook.* Our readers are kept current with those changes through two regular electronic updates throughout the year.

*Eileen W. Lindner*
Editor
New York, 2006

# I

# PERSPECTIVES ON AMERICA'S RELIGIOUS LANDSCAPE

## Trends and Developments, 2006

*Methodological Considerations*

The *Yearbook of American & Canadian Churches* reports annually on data gathered from national religious bodies that reflect the religious affiliations and financial giving patterns of hundreds of millions of Americans. However, these data generally represent information gathered two calendar years prior to the year of publication. For instance, data reported in this 2007 edition of the *Yearbook* reflects information for 2005 that was collected by national church structures in 2006 and reported to the *Yearbook* at the end of 2006 for publication in the 2007 *Yearbook*. This "lag time" often leads our readers to ask if such data is out of date by the time it is printed. In response we would give a qualified "no". Massive national agencies such as the churches reporting through the *Yearbook* move in their institutional lives at nearly imperceptible rates of speed. Moreover, given the vast size and complexity of such diverse organizations, partial data reported more frequently might well have the unintended effect of conveying a sense of "trend" to momentary or regionally isolated patterns of reporting, affiliation and/or financial giving. Now in the 75th edition, the *Yearbook* believes that an annual review of data continues to provide an appropriate interval for tracking the changes in institutional patterns.

No single standard for data collection exists to apply across the variety of ecclesiastical structures reported in the *Yearbook*. Moreover, the definitions of membership and related terms differ widely from one church structure to another. This lack of universal definition and collection methodology has frequently led to questions about the validity and reliability of self-reported data. Recognizing the limitations of the data reported herein, we continue to have confidence in the overall value of trends and other findings based on these figures and this methodology. While church data collection and analytical practices differ across various institutional and organizational margins, they tend to be remarkably consistent *within* specific organizations over time. (Where we are made aware of changes in a particular church's reporting methods, we will note them for the reader.) This consistency within organizations brings a greater degree of confidence to the relative data of a given church over time. For the same reason the *relative* size of one church to another as reported here, we believe, provides an accurate picture even while lacking a degree of absolute precision of membership statistics, particularly over time. Thus, we believe that the Southern Baptist Convention is roughly twice the size of the United Methodist Church, for example, and that changes relative to each other over several years are probably an accurate reflection of actual membership trends. Moreover, these data are the most exacting figures presently available, and thus serve as the national standard.

The first eight decades of record-keeping represented by the *Yearbook of American & Canadian Churches* is contained on a comprehensive Historic Archive on CD-ROM (which contains membership and financial data from 1916-1999). This CD provides a longitudinal backdrop for the analysis that follows. Only through such a longitudinal study of growth and decline in membership are we able to capture and analyze the emerging patterns. Our annual trends analysis should be regarded as a snapshot taken at a discrete moment in history. The meaning of the figures within that snapshot will best be given definition by the larger and longer context of which they are a part.

The reader is invited to utilize both the current edition and the *Yearbook of American & Canadian Churches'* historic CD to test and amplify the analysis that follows. To obtain the Historic Archive on CD-ROM call 1-888-870-3325 or visit www.electronicchurch.org.

**Table 1  Longitudinal Inclusive Membership**

This Table represents a longitudinal view of aggregated membership totals for all churches reporting to the *Yearbook*. These data do not reflect the entirety of national church membership since some churches either do not gather such data or do not report them to the *Yearbook*. These figures moreover do not include membership of independent congregations including megachurches. Substantial numbers of church members, therefore, are not accounted for in nationally-gathered membership data. With well over

### Table 1
### INCLUSIVE MEMBERSHIP 1890–2005

| Year | Membership | Source | Year | Membership | Source |
|------|-----------|--------|------|-----------|--------|
| 1890 | 41,699,342 | CRB | 1968 | 128,469,636 | YBAC |
| 1906 | 35,068,058 | CRB | 1969 | 128,505,084 | YBAC |
| 1916 | 41,926,852 | CRB | 1970 | 131,045,053 | YBAC |
| 1926 | 54,576,346 | CRB | 1971 | 131,389,642 | YBAC |
| 1931 | 59,268,764 | CH | 1972 | 131,424,564 | YBAC |
| 1932 | 60,157,392 | CH | 1973 | 131,245,139 | YBAC |
| 1933 | 60,812,624 | CH | 1974 | 131,871,743 | YBAC |
| 1934 | 62,007,376 | CH | 1975 | 131,012,953 | YBACC |
| 1935 | 62,678,177 | CH | 1976 | 131,897,539 | YBACC |
| 1936 | 55,807,366 | CRB | 1977 | 131,812,470 | YBACC |
| 1936† | 63,221,996 | CH | 1978 | 133,388,776 | YBACC |
| 1937 | 63,848,094 | CH | 1979 | 133,469,690 | YBACC |
| 1938 | 64,156,895 | YBAC | 1980 | 134,816,943 | YBACC |
| 1940 | 64,501,594 | YBAC | 1981 | 138,452,614 | YBACC |
| 1942 | 68,501,186 | YBAC | 1982 | 139,603,059 | YBACC |
| 1944 | 72,492,699 | YBAC | 1983 | 140,816,385 | YBACC |
| 1945 | 71,700,142 | CH | 1984 | 142,172,138 | YBACC |
| 1946 | 73,673,182 | CH | 1985 | 142,926,363 | YBACC |
| 1947 | 77,386,188 | CH | 1986 | 142,799,662 | YBACC |
| 1948 | 79,435,605 | CH | 1987 | 143,830,806 | YBACC |
| 1949 | 81,862,328 | CH | 1988 | 145,383,739 | YBACC |
| 1950 | 86,830,490 | YBAC | 1989 | 147,607,394 | YBACC |
| 1951 | 88,673,005 | YBAC | 1990 | 156,331,704 | YBACC |
| 1952 | 92,277,129 | YBAC | 1991 | 156,629,918 | YBACC |
| 1953 | 94,842,845 | YBAC | 1992 | 156,557,746 | YBACC |
| 1954 | 97,482,611 | YBAC | 1993 | 153,127,045 | YBACC |
| 1955 | 100,162,529 | YBAC | 1994 | 158,218,427 | YBACC |
| 1956 | 103,224,954 | YBAC | 1995 | 157,984,194 | YBACC |
| 1957 | 104,189,678 | YBAC | 1996 | 159,471,758 | YBACC |
| 1958 | 109,557,741 | YBAC | 1997 | 157,503,033 | YBACC |
| 1959 | 112,226,905 | YBAC | 1998* | 150,105,525 | YBACC |
| 1960 | 114,449,217 | YBAC | 1999* | 151,161,906 | YBACC |
| 1961 | 116,109,929 | YBAC | 2000* | 152,134,407 | YBACC |
| 1962 | 117,946,002 | YBAC | 2001 | 158,952.292 | YBACC |
| 1963 | 120,965,238 | YBAC | 2002 | 161,202,780 | YBACC |
| 1964 | 123,307,449 | YBAC | 2003 | 163,128,935 | YBACC |
| 1965 | 124,682,422 | YBAC | 2004 | 163,432,280 | YBACC |
| 1966 | 125,778,656 | YBAC | 2005 | 165,878,323 | YBACC |
| 1967 | 126,445,110 | YBAC | | | |

†1936 Note CRB and CH data were published seperately
*Note: The total membership figure for this year excludes the membership of the National Baptist Convention, U.S.A., Inc.

CRB—Census of Religious Bodies, Bureau of the Census, Washington
CH—*The Christian Herald*, New York
YBAC—*Yearbook of American Churches*, New York
YBACC—*Yearbook of American and Canadian Churches*, New York

165 million adherents, the churches collectively continue to maintain a substantial organizational and institutional presence within the United States.

**Table 2   U.S Membership Church Ranking**
This table allows comparison in size as determined by membership of the largest twenty-five churches in the nation. Dwarfing any single other church is the Catholic Church, reporting over 69 million adherents. The remainder of the top 25 are Protestant churches with three exceptions; the Greek Orthodox Archdiocese which is ranked 16th, The Orthodox Church in America which is ranked 24th and the Jehovah's Witnesses which is ranked 25th.

The patterns of affiliation reflected in this table offer a numerical view and summary of American church history. Protestantism has, since the founding of the republic and until the present moment, enjoyed cultural hegemony accompanied throughout by a consistent substantial Catholic presence.

Three of the twenty-five largest churches are Pentecostal in belief and practice. Strong figures from the Assemblies of God suggest a continuing overall Pentecostal growth, increase in numbers of

| Denomination Name | Current Ranking (2006 Edition) | Inclusive Membership | Percentage Increase Decrease |
|---|---|---|---|
| **Table 2** U.S. MEMBERSHIP CHURCH RANKING: Largest 25 Churches | | | |
| The Catholic Church | 1(1) | 69,135,254 | 1.94% |
| Southern Baptist Convention | 2(2) | 16,270,315 | 0.02% |
| The United Methodist Church | 3(3) | 8,075,010 | -1.36% |
| The Church of Jesus Christ of Latter-day Saints | 4(4) | 5,690,672 | 1.63% |
| The Church of God in Christ | 5(5) | 5,499,875 | *0.00%* |
| National Baptist Convention, U.S.A., Inc. | 6(6) | 5,000,000 | *0.00%* |
| Evangelical Lutheran Church in America | 7(7) | 4,850,776 | -1.62% |
| National Baptist Convention of America, Inc. | 8(8) | 3,500,000 | *0.00%* |
| Presbyterian Church (U.S.A.) | 9(9) | 3,098,842 | -2.84% |
| Assemblies of God | 10(10) | 2,830,861 | 1.86% |
| African Methodist Episcopal Church | 11(11) | 2,500,000 | *0.00%* |
| National Missionary Baptist Convention of America | 11(11) | 2,500,000 | *0.00%* |
| Progressive National Baptist Convention, Inc. | 11(11) | 2,500,000 | *0.00%* |
| The Lutheran Church—Missouri Synod (LCMS) | 14(14) | 2,440,864 | -0.93% |
| Episcopal Church | 15(15) | 2,247,819 | -1.59% |
| Churches of Christ | 16(16) | 1,639,495 | 9.30%* |
| Greek Orthodox Archdiocese of America | 16(16) | 1,500,000 | *0.00%* |
| Pentecostal Assemblies of the World, Inc. | 16(16) | 1,500,000 | *0.00%* |
| The African Methodist Episcopal Zion Church | 19(19) | 1,440,405 | 0.53% |
| American Baptist Churches in the U.S.A. | 20(20) | 1,396,700 | -1.97% |
| United Church of Christ | 21(21) | 1,224,297 | -3.28% |
| Baptist Bible Fellowship International | 22(22) | 1,200,000 | *0.00%* |
| Christian Churches and Churches of Christ | 23(23) | 1,071,616 | *0.00%* |
| The Orthodox Church in America | 24(24) | 1,064,000 | *0.00%* |
| Jehovah's Witnesses | 25(25) | 1,046,006 | 1.56% |
| **TOTAL** | | **149,222,807** | **0.82%** |

*Percentages in italics and bold signify that no membership report was submitted for the 2007 edition of the Yearbook.*
*\*This percent increase reflects growth since last reported for 1999.*

| Last Year's Ranking | |
|---|---|
| Denomination Name | Inclusive Membership Figures Reported in Last Year's *Yearbook* |
| The Catholic Church | 67,820,833 |
| Southern Baptist Convention | 16,267,494 |
| The United Methodist Church | 8,186,254 |
| The Church of Jesus Christ of Latter-day Saints | 5,599,177 |
| The Church of God in Christ | 5,499,875 |
| National Baptist Convention, U.S.A., Inc. | 5,000,000 |
| Evangelical Lutheran Church in America | 4,930,429 |
| National Baptist Convention of America, Inc. | 3,500,000 |
| Presbyterian Church (U.S.A.) | 3,189,573 |
| Assemblies of God | 2,779,095 |
| African Methodist Episcopal Church | 2,500,000 |
| National Missionary Baptist Convention of America | 2,500,000 |
| Progressive National Baptist Convention, Inc. | 2,500,000 |
| The Lutheran Church—Missouri Synod (LCMS) | 2,463,747 |
| Episcopal Church | 2,284,233 |
| Churches of Christ | 1,500,000 |
| Greek Orthodox Archdiocese of America | 1,500,000 |
| Pentecostal Assemblies of the World, Inc. | 1,500,000 |
| American Baptist Churches in the U.S.A. | 1,432,795 |
| African Methodist Episcopal Zion Church | 1,424,840 |
| United Church of Christ | 1,265,786 |
| Baptist Bible Fellowship International | 1,200,000 |
| Christian Churches and Churches of Christ | 1,071,616 |
| The Orthodox Church in America | 1,064,000 |
| Jehovah's Witnesses | 1,029,902 |
| **TOTAL** | **148,009,649** |

## Table 3
### PATTERNS OF U.S. MEMBERSHIP CHANGE OF SELECTED LARGE CHURCHES 2002-2005

| Denomination | 2002 Membership Change | Percentage Change | 2003 Membership Change | Percentage Change | 2004 Membership Change | Percentage Change | 2005 Membership Change | Percentage Change |
|---|---|---|---|---|---|---|---|---|
| The Catholic Church | 1,136,661 | 1.74 | 852,663 | 1.28 | 561,065 | 0.83 | 1,314,421 | 1.94 |
| Southern Baptist Convention | 84,816* | 0.53* | 67,314* | 0.42* | 62,444* | 0.39* | 2,821 | 0.02 |
| The United Methodist Church | 315 | 0.004 | 133 | 0.002 | -64,921 | -0.79 | -111,244 | -1.36 |
| Evangelical Lutheran Church in America | -61,871 | -1.21 | -53,081 | -1.05 | -54,496 | -1.09 | -79,653 | -1.62 |
| The Church of Jesus Christ of Latter-day Saints | 99,946 | 1.88 | 92,648 | 1.71 | 95,985 | 1.74 | 91,495 | 1.63 |
| Presbyterian Church (U.S.A.) | -48,623 | -1.41 | -166,020 | -4.87 | -51,736 | -1.60 | -90,731 | -2.84 |
| The Lutheran Church—Missouri Synod | -27,331 | -1.08 | -23,778 | -0.95 | -25,189 | -1.01 | -22,883 | -0.93 |
| Assemblies of God | 60,337 | 2.30 | 42,196 | 1.57 | 49,533 | 1.81 | 51,766 | 1.86 |
| American Baptist Churches in the U.S.A. | 41,467 | 2.87 | -51,216 | -3.45 | -8,235 | -0.57 | -28,140 | -1.97 |

*Note: These figures reflect corrections discussed in the 2006 edition.

## Table 4
### U.S. FINANCIAL SUMMARIES 1998-2005

| Year | Number Reporting | Full or Confirmed Members | Per Capita Inclusive Members | Inclusive Members | Total Contributions | Per Capita Full or Confirmed Members | Total Congregational Contributions |
|---|---|---|---|---|---|---|---|
| 1998 | 62 | 44,574,101 | $528.24 | 49,679,497 | $26,242,626,313 | $588.74 | $22,202,379,038 |
| 1999 | 62 | 44,288,906 | $548.77 | 49,196,965 | $26,997,610,588 | $609.58 | $22,801,548,715 |
| 2000 | 65 | 44,401,451 | $599.14 | 49,178,675 | $29,464,889,024 | $663.60 | $24,475,897,453 |
| 2001 | 62 | 45,359,589 | $622.98 | 49,828,003 | $31,041,852,581 | $684.35 | $26,587,142,109 |
| 2002 | 59 | 43,694,611 | $658.63 | 47,773,814 | $31,465,090,286 | $720.11 | $26,908,804,274 |
| 2003 | 63 | 44,211,342 | $667.34 | 48,266,164 | $32,269,713,588 | $725.78 | $27,723,558,838 |
| 2004 | 63 | 43,823,753 | $694.12 | 47,850,712 | $33,214,186,254 | $757.90 | $28,294,047,495 |
| 2005 | 65 | 43,565,587 | $713.05 | 47,922,181 | $34,170,801,942 | $784.35 | $29,002,718,319 |

| Year | Per Capita Full or Confirmed Members | Per Capita Inclusive Members | Total Benevolences | Per Capita Full or Confirmed Members | Per Capita Inclusive Members | Benevolences as a Percentage of Total Contributions |
|---|---|---|---|---|---|---|
| 1998 | $498.10 | $446.91 | $4,040,247,275 | $90.64 | $81.33 | 15% |
| 1999 | $514.84 | $463.47 | $4,197,087,981 | $94.77 | $85.31 | 16% |
| 2000 | $551.24 | $497.69 | $4,988,352,266 | $112.35 | $101.43 | 17% |
| 2001 | $586.14 | $533.58 | $4,510,947,817 | $99.45 | $90.53 | 15% |
| 2002 | $615.84 | $563.25 | $4,555,191,495 | $104.25 | $95.35 | 14% |
| 2003 | $627.07 | $574.39 | $4,748,202,343 | $107.40 | $98.38 | 15% |
| 2004 | $645.63 | $591.30 | $4,921,921,435 | $112.31 | $102.86 | 15% |
| 2005 | $665.73 | $605.20 | $5,168,083,623 | $118.63 | $107.84 | 15% |

adherents, though it is impossible to state unequivocally from this table since the other two Pentecostal churches in this ranking have not reported in some years. The reader might consult the table in the Theme Chapter on page 18 for another perspective regarding the growth in Pentecostal churches. The three largest Pentecostal churches are: The Church of God in Christ, Assemblies of God, and the Pentecostal Assemblies of the World, Inc.

The ranking of churches on the basis of membership remains stable as indicated by the first column of numbers in Table 2. The last column presents increases (decreases) as a percentage change from last reported membership figures. While the Church of Christ is shown to have grown the fastest, by 9.30%, note that this figure reflects growth that occurred since this group last reported in 1999. The large churches that experienced growth include: the Catholic Church; the Assemblies of God; and, the Church of Jesus Christ of Latter-day Saints.

The top fifteen churches, those with membership exceeding two million members, reflect the constancy of the Historic Black Churches. Six of the fifteen largest churches (The Church of God in Christ, National Baptist Convention USA, National Baptist Church of America Inc., National Missionary Baptist Convention of America, Progressive National Baptist Convention, African Methodist Episcopal Church) are predominately African American churches. This of course is reflective of the historic strength of the church within the African American community, the largest of which (the Church of God in Christ) is also Pentecostal.

In the last quarter-century there has been much analysis and debate concerning the decline of "mainline" Protestantism. Whatever the specific rates of growth or decline may be for individual mainline denominations, this ranking illustrates their significant aggregate presence in the American religious landscape. Of the top ten largest churches three are mainline protestant (United Methodist, Evangelical Lutheran, and Presbyterian Church USA). In the top twenty-five churches six are mainline protestant, and all of them report an overall loss of membership for the latest reporting year. In addition to the three noted above the mainline churches ranked in the top twenty-five include: the Episcopal Church, the American Baptist Churches and the United Church of Christ.

### Table 3    Patterns of Membership Gains and Losses

Table 3 offers longitudinal data on rate of growth or loss of church membership of a selected group of large churches for four years, 2002-2005.

The three large churches with the biggest growth measured by percentage of membership are: the Catholic Church (1.94%), the Assemblies of God (1.86%), and the Church of Jesus Christ of Latter-day Saints (1.63%).

Churches experiencing the highest rate of membership loss are: the Presbyterian Church (USA) (-2.84%), the American Baptist Churches (-1.97%), and the Evangelical Lutheran Church in America (-1.62%). For each of these churches, these latest figures represent a rate of membership decline consistent with their respective patterns in previous years.

### Table 4    Financial Trends

Second only to the interest in membership trends is the interest of media and the church world alike in the financial trends reported in the *Yearbook*. While not all churches report their financial information to the *Yearbook* 65 churches have provided full data for the 2007 edition providing an important glimpse into United States church giving. More than $34 billion dollars are accounted for in the reports of these churches and this, of course, is but a portion of the whole of church giving.

The financial reporting for this 2007 *Yearbook* is based on the financial income reports of the 65 churches reporting figures. The records of those 65 reporting churches are reported in Table 4. The nearly 48 million inclusive members contributed a total of over $34 billion, marking an increase in the total amount of income to the churches of almost $957 million. It is particularly useful to view this increase in its per capita terms. The $713 contributed per person is an increase of $18.93 per person from the previous year. The 2.7% increase in per capita giving does not exceed the official inflation figure for 2005, and it must be remembered that some individuals will be contributing to parishes with a declining number of members. In such settings the combined effect of two adverse trends will significantly increase the financial loss associated with membership decline and rising prices.

Benevolence giving for 2005 in our sample of United States churches reporting stands steady at 15%. This ratio of benevolence to total giving is consistent with the figures for the previous two years. An interesting comparison can be made with benevolence reported by Canadian churches. While admittedly reporting on a far smaller sample and reflecting a much lower level of total giving, the percentage of benevolence giving for Canadian churches is consistently in the 18%-20% range compared to the U.S. figure of 15%. This year's figures probably reflect in some measure the ongoing generosity of donations to help persons affected by September 11 and the Tsunami disaster. The churches response to Katrina is not yet reflected in these data.

This year's 15% percent U.S. benevolence giving is consistent with previous patterns, but at the low end in the range of benevolent giving over the period of the last decade. This level of giving for benevolence will be the source of sober reflection for some. The overall increase in giving to the churches, at this reporting, is occurring simultaneously with a stagnant posture in benevolence as a percentage. The churches that seek generosity from their supporters have not, at least in this sample, matched that generosity with an increase in their own benevolence giving. The practical consequences of such a decline continues to translate in local settings to less support for church-sponsored day care, fewer soup-kitchen meals, less emergency help to persons with medical problems, or reduced transportation to the elderly.

No one has given greater attention to church giving patterns than John and Sylvia Ronsvalle. For a fulsome discussion of the giving patterns of churches, see their *The State of Church Giving* series of publications, by writing empty tomb, inc. P.O. Box 2404, Champaign, IL 61825, or through www.emptytomb.org.

14

# Azusa Street at 100: A Century of Pentecostal Ascendance

Eileen W. Lindner, Ph.D.

As 2006 comes to a close, we mark the conclusion of the centennial year of that uniquely America-born expression of Christianity known as Pentecostalism. As Dr. Darrin Rodgers, Director of the Flower Pentecostal Heritage Center, convincingly demonstrates in this year's guest theme essay, Pentecostalism has deep roots and a long history. Yet, both scholars and popular understandings recognize the summer of 1906 and the tiny renewal meeting on Azusa Street in Los Angeles as a watershed event for the Pentecostal movement. That movement, in turn, has forever altered the Christian landscape both in North America and especially around the world.

Anniversaries, in general, and centennial anniversaries in particular, offer opportunities for reflection and assessment. At the *Yearbook of American & Canadian Churches*, celebrating our own 75th anniversary, we recognize that our primary task of monitoring the denominational landscape of American religious life has been greatly influenced by growth in Pentecostal churches throughout our shared history. The *Yearbook's* first report of Pentecostal church membership appeared in the 1925 edition for which the Assemblies of God provided membership figures totaling 50,386. In this year's edition of the *Yearbook*, the same church reports a membership of 2,830,861 within the United States. The accompanying chart, "Growth Since First Report in the *Yearbook*" demonstrates numerically the rapid growth in the Pentecostal movement in the U.S. This chart was drawn from the *Yearbook* statistics and was developed in this format by the Association of Religions Data Archives (ARDA).

The remarkable total growth in Pentecostalism and the respective growth in the respective churches provide a snapshot of Pentecostal growth. World growth is beyond the purview of this volume but is more remarkable still. The Pentecostal growth in Canada has not been as well documented by the *Yearbook of American & Canadian Churches* and provides a rich area for further research.

Each year in the theme chapter we seek to identify new research areas to our colleagues. So, too, this year we acknowledge Pentecostal institutions offer a rich area for further research and study.

# The Place of Azusa Street in Pentecostal Origins

## by Darrin J. Rodgers

The modern Pentecostal movement did not suddenly appear at the outset of the 20th century. Rather, it was forged in the crucible of history, emerging from a complex interaction of theologies and personalities in the Holiness and evangelical movements. An earlier awakening (beginning in 1901) in the Midwest, led by Charles Parham, provided the doctrinal framework for the Azusa Street revival. Azusa Street leader William Seymour, a student of Parham, promoted Parham's identification in Scripture of speaking in tongues as the initial evidence of spirit baptism. Parham's formulation, initially embraced by several thousand followers in his Apostolic Faith band throughout the Midwestern states, was catapulted before a worldwide audience with the advent of the Azusa Street revival.

Parham and Seymour were part of a larger story. Throughout the latter half of the 19th century, evangelical Protestants from various backgrounds began to ask themselves why their churches did not seem to exhibit the same vibrant, faith-filled life as those in the New Testament. Many of these believers joined Holiness or evangelical churches, engaged in ardent prayer and personal sacrifice, and earnestly sought God. It was in this context that people began experiencing biblical spiritual gifts.

The earliest Pentecostal historians were careful to catalog instances of what they deemed to be Pentecostal gifts—usually tongues-speech and divine healing—throughout church history. These Pentecostal outbursts seemed to escalate starting in the mid-1800s, culminating in the early 1900s in what became the Pentecostal movement. In the U.S., scattered reports existed of believers who experienced Pentecostal gifts prior to 1900, in places such as New England, Ohio, Minnesota, North Dakota, South Dakota, North Carolina, Tennessee, and Arkansas.

The emerging Pentecostal revival was of global proportions, though, and similar events occurred elsewhere, including in Finland among the Laestadians, in India at Pandita Ramabai's mission, and in Armenia. Pentecostals were restorationists, believing that God was restoring the gifts of the New Testament church. They identified themselves in the tradition of other reformers and revivalists, such as Martin Luther, John Wesley, and D. L. Moody. [1]

The Pentecostal movement spread quickly, often building upon established networks. Charles H. Mason, a gifted black preacher in the Mississippi Holiness movement, visited Azusa Street and spoke in tongues. Mason returned home and, with part of his old network, founded the Church of God in Christ, which he built into the largest black Pentecostal denomination in the United States. North Carolina Holiness evangelist Gaston B. Cashwell, after visiting Azusa Street in 1906, led significant portions of the Fire-Baptized Holiness Church, the Pentecostal Holiness Church, the Free Will Baptist Church, and the Church of God (Cleveland, Tenn.) into the movement. Chicago, which rivaled Los Angeles as an early Pentecostal center, was home to William H. Durham's North Avenue Mission and William H. Piper's Stone Church, both of which published influential periodicals. Pentecost spread in a similar fashion worldwide, to Brazil, Britain, Canada, China, India, Japan, Liberia, Mexico, Nigeria, Norway, South Africa, Sweden, and elsewhere. Often, people in each new area told their own version of how Pentecostalism began, giving significance to the historical or theological emphases important in their context.

Should the Azusa Street revival be viewed as the beginning of the Pentecostal movement? Some of the earliest Pentecostals would have answered no, claiming that the movement developed from multiple theological and historical strands.

Since the 1960s, various historians have argued alternatively that Parham, Seymour, or both should be viewed as the movement's founder. Prominent historian Walter Hollenweger, for instance, viewed Seymour as the movement's founder because he preferred Seymour's racial inclusivity over Parham's racist views.

Most recently, scholars have wrestled with defining the contours of Pentecostalism in light of its rapidly-growing non-Western varieties. The typical Pentecostal is now a poor female living in the developing world. While most Pentecostals reside in non-Western nations, scholars lack enough up-to-date information to begin to form a comprehensive picture of the movement. Most scholarship relies largely on Western (North American) sources.

However, not all Pentecostal outbreaks can be traced to North America. Gary McGee demonstrated that Pentecostalism in India predated Topeka by at least 40 years, and Juan Sepúlveda argued that the sizable Pentecostal movement in Chile developed independently from events at Azusa Street. Allan Anderson noted that some Pentecostals in England date the movement's beginning to the 1904-05 Welsh revival. African historians Ogbu Kalu and Inus Daneel suggested that many indigenous groups employ identity markers other than those associated with Western Pentecostal churches.

Azusa Street was prominent in Pentecostal histories, particularly in Western accounts. It may even have been the focal point of the emerging Pentecostal movement. However, recent scholarship has emphasized the need to better understand the broader context before making such judgments about the place of Azusa Street in the story of Pentecostal origins.[2]

Reprinted with permission from *Assemblies of God Heritage,* Winter 2005-06. Darrin J. Rodgers, M.A., J.D., is director of the Flower Pentecostal Heritage Center and editor of *Assemblies of God Heritage* magazine.

The Flower Pentecostal Heritage Center is one of the world's largest Pentecostal archives and research centers. Free access to its online catalog and over 200,000 pages of searchable digitized periodicals and books is available on its website: www.AGHeritage.org.

## Bibliography

Burgess, Stanley M. and Eduard M. Van der Maas, eds. *The New International Dictionary of Pentecostal and Charismatic Movements.* Grand Rapids: Zondervan, 2001.

Dempster, Murray W., Byron D. Klaus and Douglas Petersen, eds. *The Globalization of Pentecostalism: A Religion Made to Travel.* Irvine, Calif: Regnum Books, 1999.

Hunter, Harold D. and Cecil M. Robeck, Jr., eds. *The Azusa Street Revival and its Legacy.* Cleveland, Tenn. Pathway Press, 2006.

Robeck, Cecil M., Jr. *The Azusa Street Mission and Revival: The Birth of the Global Pentecostal Movement.* Nashville: Thomas Nelson, 2006.

---

[1] B. F. Lawrence, *Apostolic Faith Restored* (St. Louis, Mo.: Gospel Publishing House, 1916); Henry H. Ness, *Demonstration of the Holy Spirit as Revealed by the Scriptures and Confirmed in Great Revivals of Wesley, Finney, Cartwright, Whitfield, Moody, etc.* (Seattle, Wash.: Hollywood Temple, 1940s?); Stanley H. Frodsham, *With Signs Following* [rev. ed.] (Springfield, Mo.: Gospel Publishing House, 1946); Darrin J. Rodgers, *Northern Harvest: Pentecostalism in North Dakota* (Bismarck, N.D: North Dakota District Council of the Assemblies of God, 2003).
[2] Edith Blumhofer, "Azusa Street Revival," *Christian Century* (Mar. 7, 2006): 20-22.

Table 1
GROWTH SINCE FIRST REPORT IN *YEARBOOK*

| Pentecostal Body | Year First Reported | Membership First Reported | Latest Year | Latest Reported Membership |
|---|---|---|---|---|
| Apostolic Faith Mission | 1935 | 125 | 1936 | 2,288 |
| Apostolic Faith Mission Church of God | 1982 | 2,600 | 2005 | 10,730 |
| The Apostolic Faith Mission of Portland, Oregon | | NA | | NA |
| Apostolic Overcoming Holy Church of God | 1935 | 5,000 | 2001 | 10,714 |
| Assemblies of God | 1925 | 50,386 | 2005 | 2,830,861 |
| Assemblies of God, International Fellowship (Independent/Not Affiliated) | 1962 | NA | | NA |
| Bethel Ministerial Association | 1970 | 2,500 | 1983 | 3,500 |
| The Bible Church of Christ, Inc. | 1976 | 930 | 1993 | 6,850 |
| Bible Standard, Inc. | | NA | | NA |
| Bible Way Churches of Our Lord Jesus Christ World Wide, Inc. | 1957 | 15,000 | 1970 | 30,000 |
| Calvary Pentecostal Church, Inc. | 1940 | 12,000 | 1975 | 983 |
| Church of Christ (Holiness), USA | 1935 | 6,844 | 2003 | 10,460 |
| Church of God | 1940 | 20,000 | 1946 | 77,926 |
| Church of God (Abrahamic Faith) | 1940 | 5,295 | 1970 | 6,800 |
| Church of God (Apostolic) | 1935 | 3,053 | 1954 | 600 |
| Church of God in Christ | 1935 | 200,470 | 1991 | 5,499,875 |
| Church of God in Christ Colored | 1933 | 200,470 | | NA |
| The Church of God | 1942 | 20,065 | 1978 | 75,890 |
| The Church of God by Faith | 1957 | 4,000 | 2004 | 35,000 |
| The Church of God in Christ, International | 1970 | 500,000 | 1982 | 200,000 |
| Church of God of the Mountain Assembly, Inc. | 1970 | 3,500 | 2005 | 7,200 |
| Church of our Lord Jesus Christ of the Apostolic Faith, Inc. | 1952 | 50,000 | 1954 | 45,000 |
| Church of the Full Gospel Church | 1940 | 355 | | NA |
| Church of the Living God, the Pillar and Ground of Truth | 1935 | 18,000 | 1937 | 18,625 |
| Church of the Lord Jesus Christ of the Apostolic Faith | | NA | | NA |
| Churches of God, Holiness | 1935 | 3,940 | 1965 | 25,600 |
| Congregational Holiness Church | 1935 | 2,083 | 2005 | 25,000 |
| Elim Missionary Assemblies | 1961 | 4,000 | 1995 | 21,038 |
| Emmanuel Holiness Church | 1953 | 902 | 1955 | 1,200 |
| Evangelistic Church of God | 1953 | 774 | | NA |
| Fire Baptized Holiness Church | 1940 | 6,000 | 1958 | 988 |

## Table 1
### GROWTH SINCE FIRST REPORT IN *YEARBOOK* (continued)

| Pentecostal Body | Year First Reported | Membership First Reported | Latest Year | Latest Reported Membership |
|---|---|---|---|---|
| Free Church of God in Christ | 1935 | 874 | | NA |
| Full Gospel Assemblies, International | 1978 | 2,800 | 2002 | 3,075 |
| Full Gospel Church, Inc. | 1978 | 2,800 | | 2,800 |
| Full Gospel Fellowship of Churches and Ministers, International | 1980 | 59,100 | 2005 | 414,100 |
| General Conference of the Evangelical Baptist Church, Inc. | | NA | | NA |
| House of God Which is the Church of the Living God, the Pillar and Ground of the Truth | 1956 | 2,350 | | NA |
| House of God Which is the Church of the Living God, the Pillar and Ground of the Truth  House of God Which is the Church of the Living God, the Pillar and Ground of the Truth  Without Controversy | 1937 | 5,000 | | NA |
| House of God, Holy Church of the Living God, the Pillar and Ground of the Truth, House of Prayer for All People | 1936 | 200 | | NA |
| House of the Lord | 1936 | 302 | | NA |
| Independent Assemblies of God, International | 1962 | NA | | NA |
| International Church of the Four-square Gospel | 1935 | 252,380 | 2003 | 326,614 |
| International Pentecostal Assembly | 1936 | 6,333 | 1971 | 10,000 |
| International Pentecostal Church of Christ | 1977 | 11,659 | 2003 | 4,961 |
| King David's Spiritual Temple of Truth Association | | NA | | NA |
| Mount Sinai Holy Church of God U.S.A. | 1937 | 5,000 | | NA |
| Open Bible Evangelistic Association | | NA | | NA |
| Open Bible Standard Churches, Inc. | 1952 | 25,000 | 2005 | 39,000 |
| The (Original) Church of God | 1935 | 2,597 | 1971 | 20,000 |
| Pentecostal Assemblies of Jesus Christ, Inc. | 1936 | 16,070 | 1942 | 17,000 |
| Pentecostal Assemblies of the World | 1935 | 7,850 | 2005 | 1,500,000 |
| Pentecostal Church of Christ | 1955 | 937 | 1975 | 1,659 |
| Pentecostal Church of God in America | 1936 | 4,296 | 2001 | 102,000 |
| Pentecostal Church of God, National and International | 1960 | 213 | 1961 | 229 |
| Pentecostal Church, Inc. | 1937 | 20,000 | 1944 | 20,000 |
| Pentecostal Fire-Baptized Holiness Church | 1940 | 1,655 | 1996 | 223 |
| Pentecostal Holiness Church | 1929 | 8,096 | 2001 | 209,922 |
| The Church of God of Prophecy | 1953 | 31,956 | 2004 | 114,476 |

19

## GROWTH SINCE FIRST REPORT IN *YEARBOOK* (continued)

| Pentecostal Body | Year First Reported | Membership First Reported | Latest Year | Latest Reported Membership |
|---|---|---|---|---|
| United Holy Church of America | 1939 | 31,500 | 1960 | 28,980 |
| United Pentecostal Church | 1950 | 100,000 | 1994 | 550,000 |
| Universal Christian Spiritual Faith and Churches for All Nations | NA | NA | | NA |

This compilation of Pentecostal Family churches is used with permission: The Association of Religious Data Archives

**Note:** Figures may be missing for various reasons: some groups never reported figures, others may have reported figures in time, others may no longer exist under the same name, or merged into new or existing groups. Some churches may have reported consistently for some years, but stopped reporting. Concise histories of these transitions are available at www.TheARDA.com.

# II

# DIRECTORIES

# 1. United States Cooperative Organizations, National

The organizations listed in this section are cooperative religious organizations that are national in scope. Regional cooperative organizations in the United States are listed in Directory 7, "United States Regional and Local Ecumenical Bodies."

## The Alban Institute, Inc.

The Alban Institute is an independent, not-for-profit cradle of learning, grounded in faith and devoted to helping American congregations become greater communities of faithfulness, health, creativity, hospitality and leadership. Alban is the largest congregational resource and advocacy membership organization in the United States, reaching hundreds of thousands of congregants across all faith traditions with our signature of congregation-building known as The Alban Way. From Alban's groundbreaking consulting practice, to original research, publications and seminars on leadership, conflict, planning and transitions, The Alban Institute knows what it takes to build vital, enduring communities of faith. Alban draws on a vast reservoir of congregational know-how and wisdom born on the firing line. Clergy and lay leaders seek guidance from the most respected problem solvers, strategists and teachers in the business.

### Headquarters
2121 Cooperative Way, Suite 100, Herndon, VA 20171 Tel. (800)486-1318
Media Contact, Director of Research, Dr. Ian Evison

### Officers
Pres., The Rev. James P. Wind, Ph.D.

## American Bible Society

In 1816, pastors and laymen representing a variety of Christian denominations gathered in New York City to establish an organization "to disseminate the Gospel of Christ throughout the habitable world." Since that time the American Bible Society (ABS) has continued to provide God's Word, without doctrinal note or comment, wherever it is needed and in the language and format the reader can most easily use and understand. The American Bible Society is the servant of the denominations and local churches.

The American Bible Society is committed to promoting personal engagement with the Holy Scriptures with the goal of changed lives. A special emphasis is placed upon advocacy for the Bible cause, partnerships with like-minded churches and para-church organizations, and with provision of Scripture. Today the ABS serves more than 100 denominations and agencies, and its board of trustees is composed of distinguished laity and clergy drawn from these Christian groups.

The American Bible Society played a leading role in the founding of the United Bible Societies, a federation of 140 national Bible Societies around the world that enables global cooperation in Scripture translation, publication and distribution in more than 200 countries and territories. The Bible Society contributes generously to the support provided by the United Bible Societies to those national Bible Societies which request support to meet the total Scripture needs of people in their countries.

The work of the American Bible Society is supported through gifts from individuals, local churches, denominations and cooperating agencies.

### Headquarters
National Service Center, 1865 Broadway, New York, NY 10023 Tel. (212)408-1200
Media Contact: Senior Manager, Media Relations, Roy Lloyd, Tel. (212)408-8731 Fax (212) 408-1456, Email: rlloyd@americanbible.org

### Officers
Chpsn., Rev. R. Lamar Vest
Vice Chpsn., Dennis Dickerson
Pres., Rev. Dr. Paul G. Irwin
Vice President for Development, Robert L. Briggs
Vice President and Executive Director for Bibles.com, John Cruz
Senior Vice President for Domestic Ministries, Rev. Emilio Reyes
Vice President and General Counsel, Peter Rathbun

21

Vice President for Corporate Services and CFO, Richard Stewart

Dean, Nida Institute for Biblical Scholarship, Dr. Robert Hodgson

Director of Internal Audit, Donald Cavanaugh

Director for Publishing Services, Bibles.com, Thomas Durakis

Director for Finance and Production Services, Bibles.com., Gary Ruth

DEPARTMENT HEADS

Chief Communications Officer, Denise London

Assistant to Vice President of Finance, Stephen King

Director of Operations, Cheryl Berlamino

Director of Building Management Services, John Colligan

Director of Research, Dr. Joseph Crockett

Chief Technology Officer, Nicholas Garbidakis

Director of Operations, Bibles.com, Dr. John Greco

Editorial and Publications Manager, Charles Houser

Director of Direct Response Programs, H. Lee Manis

Controller, Stephen Sharp

Director of Investments, Nicholas Pagano

Director of Human Resources, Sharon Roberts

Director of Church Relations, David Ramos

Director of Programs, Karina Lucero

Director of Sales and Marketing, Bibles.com, Brian Sherry

Director of Development, Melinda Trine

Director of Relationship Development, Karmen Wynick

## American Council of Christian Churches

The American Council of Christian Churches is a Fundamentalist multidenominational organization whose purposes are to provide information, encouragement, and assistance to Bible-believing churches, fellowships, and individuals; to preserve our Christian heritage through exposure of, opposition to, and separation from doctrinal impurity and compromise in current religious trends and movements; to protect churches from religious and political restrictions, subtle or obvious, that would hinder their ministries for Christ; and to promote obedience to the inerrant Word of God.

Founded in 1941, The American Council of Christian Churches (ACCC) is a multi-denominational agency for fellowship and cooperation among Bible-believing churches in various denominations—fellowships, Bible Presbyterian Church, Evangelical Methodist Church, Fellowship of Fundamental Bible Churches (formerly Bible Protestant), Free Presbyterian Church of North America, Fundamental Methodist Church, Independent Baptist Fellowship of North America, Independent Churches Affiliated, along with hundreds of independent churches. The total membership nears 2 million. Each denomination retains its identity and full autonomy, but cannot be associated with the World Council of Churches, National Council of Churches or National Association of Evangelicals.

### Headquarters
P.O. Box 5455, Bethlehem, PA 18015 Tel. (610) 865-3009 Fax (610)865-3033
Media Contact, Exec. Dir., Dr. Ralph Colas

### Officers
Pres., Dr. John McKnight
Vice Pres., Rev. Randy Ardis
Exec. Sec., Dr. Ralph Colas
Sec., Rev. Craig Griffith
Treas., Rev. John Yessa
Commissions: Chaplaincy; Education; Laymen; Literature; Missions; Radio & Audio Visual; Relief; Youth

## American Friends Service Committee

Founded, 1917; Regional offices, 9. Founded by and related to the Religious Society of Friends (Quakers) but supported and staffed by individuals sharing basic values regardless of religious affiliation. Attempts to relieve human suffering and find new approaches to world peace and social justice through nonviolence. Work in 20 countries includes development and refugee relief, peace education, and community organizing. Sponsors off-the-record seminars around the world to build better international understanding. Conducts programs with U.S. communities on the problems of minority groups such as housing, employment, and denial of legal rights. Maintains Washington, D.C. office to present AFSC experience and perspectives to policymakers. The Quaker United Nations offices in New York City and Geneva, Switzerland arrange seminars, testimony before UN committees and behind-the-scene discussions with UN delegates. Seeks to build informed public resistance to militarism. A co-recipient of the Noble Peace Prize. Programs are multiracial, non-denominational, and international. Divisions, Community Relations Unit, International Programs, Peace-building Unit.

### Headquarters
1501 Cherry St., Philadelphia, PA 19102 Tel. (215)241-7000 Fax (215)241-7275
Dir. of Media Relations, Janis Shields, Website: www.afsc.org

### Officers
Presiding Clerk, Paul Lacey
Treas., James Fletcher
General Secretary, Mary Ellen McNish

## The American Theological Library Association

The American Theological Library Association (ATLA) is a library association that works to improve theological and religious libraries and librarianship by providing continuing education, developing standards, promoting research and experimental projects, encouraging cooperative programs and publishing and disseminating research tools and aids. Founded in 1946, ATLA currently has a membership of over 245 institutions and 550 individuals.

**Headquarters**
250 S. Wacker Dr., Suite 1600, Chicago, IL, 60606-5889 Tel. (312)454-5100 Fax (312) 454-5505
Media Contact, Jonathan West

**Officers**
Pres., Paul Schrodt, Methodist Theological School in Ohio, 3081 Columbus Pike, P.O. Box 8004, Delaware, OH 43015-8004
Vice Pres., Paul F. Stuehrenberg, Yale University Divinity School Library, 409 Prospect St., New Haven, CT 06511
Sec., Anne Womack, Vanderbilt University Divinity Library, 419 21st Ave., South, Nashville, TN 37240-0007
Exec. Dir., Dennis A. Norlin, ATLA, 250 S. Wacker Dr., Suite 1600, Chicago, IL 60606-5889

## American Tract Society

The American Tract Society is a nonprofit, interdenominational organization, instituted in 1825 through the merger of most of the then-existing tract societies. As one of the earliest religious publishing bodies in the United States, ATS has pioneered in the publishing of Christian books, booklets and leaflets. The volume of distribution has risen to more than 35 million pieces of literature annually. For free samples or a free catalog contact 1-800-54-TRACT.

**Headquarters**
P.O. Box 462008, Garland, TX 75046 Tel. (972) 276-9408 Fax (972)272-9642
Media Contact, V.P. Evangelism/Outreach, David Leflore

## The American Waldensian Society

The American Waldensian Society (AWS) promotes ministry linkages, broadly ecumenical, between U.S. churches and Waldensian (Reformed)-Methodist constituencies in Italy and Waldensian constituencies in Argentina-Uruguay. Founded in 1906, AWS aims to enlarge mission discovery and partnership among overseas Waldensian-Methodist forces and denominational forces in the U.S.

AWS is governed by a national ecumenical board, although it consults and collaborates closely with the three overseas Waldensian and Waldensian-Methodist boards.

The Waldensian experience is the earliest continuing Protestant experience.

**Headquarters**
American Waldensian Society, VistaCom, Ste. #1, 1902 Vultee St., Allentown, PA 18103-2958 Tel. (866)825-3373 Fax (610)797-9723, Email: info@waldensian.org,
Website: www.waldensian.org
Media Contact, Jack Ferlino

**Officers**
Pres., The Rev. Francis Rivers, '05 PC(U.S.A.)
Vice Pres., The Rev. Gabriella Lettini, '05 WC
Sec., Ms. June Rostan, '06

## Appalachian Ministries Educational Resource Center (AMERC)

The mission of AMERC is to promote contextual, cross-cultural education for theological students, faculties, ministers, and other Christian leaders. Working through an ecumenical consortium of theological schools and denominational judicatories, AMERC supports experiential learning about the theological, spiritual, social, economic and environmental aspects of Appalachian culture, especially for rural and small-town settings for ministry.

Since 1985 AMERC, has provided quality educational programs and learning experiences for seminaries and other religious leaders interested in ministry in Appalachia and other rural areas. The centerpiece of these programs has been and continues to be in-depth, contextually based dialogue with local people engaged in creative ministries, exploring with them social, economic, political, ecological, cultural, and religious issues. Intense theological reflection is used to understand these issues through the eyes of faith, equipping students and other leaders for ministry in the Appalachian context.

In the new millennium AMERC's form of ministry has changed. AMERC is now supporting its consortium of members by providing program grants, technical and library support, and leadership consultation. The consortium seminaries and other groups, in turn, design and offer an even wider variety of experiential programs in rural and small-town ministry in the context of Appalachia. Both seminary, for-credit, and continuing education courses are offered. In 2000 AMERC launched its Grants Program for members of the consortium. Since that time AMERC has funded twenty-four winter and summer travel seminars, a spring course with an immersion component, a Seminary Faculty Immersion experience and a summer intern program. A consultation and six continuing education events with grants of up to $15,000.

**Headquarters**
298 Harrison Rd., Berea, KY 40403 Tel. (859) 986-8789 Fax (859)986-2576, Email: loliver@amerc.org, Website: www.amerc.org

Media Contact, Rev. Dr. Lon D. Oliver, Executive Director

Executive Assistant, Marsha Baker

**Officers**

Chair, Rev. Dr. Leon Carroll, Columbia Theological Seminary

Vice Chair, Rev. Dr. Bill J. Leonard, Wake Forest University Divinity School

Secretary, Ms. Tena Willemsma, Commission on Religion in Appalachia

Treasurer, Mr. Jim Strand, Berea College

## The Associated Church Press

The Associated Church Press was organized in 1916. Its membership includes periodicals and Web sites of major Protestant, Catholic, Orthodox, and ecumenical groups in the U.S., Canada and abroad; individual members who supply publishing services on a freelance or student basis; and affiliate members who supply the Christian press with news, information, and vendor services. It is a professional Christian journalistic association seeking to promote excellence among editors and writers, recognize achievements, and represent the interests of the religious press. It sponsors seminars, conventions, awards programs, and workshops for editors, staff people, and business managers. It is active in postal rates and regulations on behalf of the religious press.

**Headquarters**

Media Contact, Exec. Dir., Mary Lynn Hendrickson, 1410 Vernon St. Stoughton, WI 53589-2248 Tel.(608)877-0011 Fax (608)877-0062, Website: www.theacp.org

**Officers**

Exec. Dir., Mary Lynn Hendrickson, 1410 Vernon St. Stoughton, WI 53589-2248, Tel. (608)877-0011 Fax (608)877-0062, Email: acpoffice@earthlink.net

Pres., Jerry Van Marter, Presbyterian News Service, 100 Witherspoon St., Louisville, KY 40202-1396, Tel. (502)569-5493 Fax (502)569-8073, Email: jvanmart@ctr.pcusa.org

Vice Pres., Terry DeYoung, *The Church Herald*, 4500-60th St. SE, Grand Rapids, MI 49512-9642, Tel. (616)698-7071 Fax (616)698-6606, Email: tdeyoung@rca.org

Past Pres., Victoria A. Rebeck, *The Minnesota Connect*, 122 W. Franklin, Ste. 400, Minneapolis, MN 55404-2472, Tel. (612) 870-0058 x 232 Fax (612)870-1260, Email: victoria.rebeck@mnumc.org

Treas., Silvia Chavez, *The Lutheran*, 8765 W. Higgins Rd., Chicago, IL 60631-4189, Tel. (773)380-2543 Fax (773)380-2751, Email: schavez@elca.org

## The Associated Gospel Churches

Organized in 1939, The Associated Gospel Churches (AGC) endorses chaplains primarily for strong evangelical independent Baptist and Bible churches to the U.S. Armed Forces. The AGC has been recognized by the U.S. Department of Defense for 65 years as an endorsing agency, and it supports a strong national defense. The AGC also endorses Veterans Administration chaplains, police, correctional system and civil air patrol chaplains.

The AGC provides support for its constituent churches, seminaries, Bible colleges and missionaries.

The AGC believes in the sovereignty of the local church, the historic doctrines of the Christian faith and the infallibility of the Bible.

The AGC is a member of the National Conference on Ministry to the Armed Forces (NCMAF) and the Endorsers Conference for Veterans Affairs Chaplaincy (ECVAC).

**Headquarters**

Media Contact, Pres., Billy Baugham, D.D., National Hdqt., P.O. Box 733, Taylors, SC 29687 Tel. (864)268-9617 Fax (864)268-0166

**Officers**

Commission on Chaplains, Pres. and Chmn., Billy Baugham, D.D.

Vice Pres., Rev. Chuck Flesher

Sec.-Treas., Eva Baugham

Executive Committee, Chaplain (Captain) James Poe, USN Member

## Association of Catholic Diocesan Archivists

The Association of Catholic Diocesan Archivists, which began in 1979, has been committed to the active promotion of professionalism in the management of diocesan archives. The Association meets annually; in the even years it has its own summer conference, and in the odd years it meets in conjunction with the Society of American Archivists. Publications include Standards for Diocesan Archives, Access Policy for Diocesan Archives, and the quarterly Bulletin.

**Headquarters**

Archives & Records Center, 711 West Monroe, Chicago, IL 60661 Tel. (312)831-0711 Fax (312)736-0488

Media Contact, Brian P. Fahey

**Officers**

Episcopal Mod., Most Rev. Thomas J. Paprocki, Auxiliary Bishop, Archdiocese of Chicago

Pres., Joseph w. Coen, Diocese of Brooklyn, 310 Propspect Park West, Brooklyn, NY 11215

Vice Pres., Audrey Newcomer, Diocese of St. Louis, 20 Archbishop May, St. Louis, MO 63119

Treas., John J. Treanor, Archdiocese of Chicago, 711 West Monroe St., Chicago IL 60661

Sec., Lori Vodden, Diocese of Peoria, 417 NR Monroe Avenue, Peoria IL 601603

Newsletter Editor, Brian P. Fahey, Diocese of Charleston, 114 Broad Street Rear Building, Charleston, SC 29402

## ADRIS—Association for the Development of Religious Information Services

The Association for the Development of Religious Information Services was established in 1971 to facilitate coordination and cooperation among information services that pertain to religion. Its goal is a worldwide network that is interdisciplinary, inter-faith and interdenominational to serve both administrative and research applications. ADRIS publishes a blog and provides internet consulting services.

### Headquarters

ADRIS Newsletter Office, P.O. Box 210735, Nashville, TN 37221-0735 Tel. (615)429-8744

Media Contact, Editor, Ed Dodds, P.O. Box 210735, Nashville, TN 37221-0735 Tel. (615) 429-8744

Website: www.adris.org
ICQ: 49457096
AIM: ed1dodds
SKYPE: ed_dodds_skype
JABBER: Ed_Dodds@jabber.org
GoogleTalk: ed.dodds@gmail.com
Yahoo: ed_dodds
MSN: ed_dodds@hotmail.com

## Association of Gospel Rescue Missions

The Association of Gospel Rescue Missions (AGRM), formerly the International Union of Gospel Missions, is an association of 300 rescue missions and other ministries that serve more than 7 million homeless and needy people in the inner cities of the U.S., Canada, and overseas each year. Since 1913, AGRM member ministries have offered emergency food and shelter, evangelical outreach, Christian counsel, youth and family services, prison and jail outreach, rehabilitation, and specialized programs for the mentally ill, the elderly, the urban poor, and street youth. The AGRM operates RESCUE College, an Internet-based distance education program to prepare and train rescue mission workers. The AGRM sponsors Alcoholics Victorious, a network of Christian support groups. AGRM is affiliated with the City Mission World Association, representing over 500 City Missions around the world.

### Headquarters

1045 Swift, Kansas City, MO 64116-4127 Tel. (816)471-8020 Fax (816)471-3718

Media Contact, Exec. Dir., Rev. Stephen E. Burger or Phil Rydman

### Officers

Exec. Dir., Rev. Stephen E. Burger

Pres., Mr. Rick Alvis, Box 817, Indianapolis, IN 46206 Tel. (317)635-3575 Fax (317)687-3629

Sec., Rev. James Harriger, 205 Commercial St., Springfield, MO 65803, Tel. (417)831-9980 Fax (417)831-9980

Vice Pres., Mr. Tom Zobel, Box 461, Salem, OR 97308, Tel. (503)362-3983 Fax (503)399-8673

NATIONAL PROGRAM UNITS AND STAFF
Education, Rev. Michael Liimatta
Exec. Asst., Tammy Sharp
Newsletter and Magazine, Stephen E. Burger; Philip Rydman
Convention, Stephen E. Burger
Business Admn., Len Conner
Historian, Delores Burger
Communications, Phillip Rydman
Expansion, Gary Meek
Development, Ken Fast

## Association of Statisticians of American Religious Bodies

This Association was organized in 1934 and grew out of personal consultations held by representatives from The Yearbook of American Churches, The National (now Official) Catholic Directory, the Jewish Statistical Bureau, The Methodist (now The United Methodist), the Lutheran and the Presbyterian churches.

ASARB has a variety of purposes: to bring together those officially and professionally responsible for gathering, compiling, and publishing denominational statistics; to provide a forum for the exchange of ideas and sharing of problems in statistical methods and procedure; and to seek such standardization as may be possible in religious statistical data.

### Headquarters

c/o John P. Marcum, Presbyterian Church (U.S.A.), 100 Witherspoon St., Rm. 2069, Louisville, KY 40202-1396 Tel. (502)569-5161 Fax (502)333-7161

Media Contact, Sec.-Treas., John P. Marcum

### Officers

Pres., Mary Gautier, Center for Applied Research in the Apostolate, Georgetown University, Washington, DC 20057 Tel. (202) 687-8086 Fax (202)687-8083 Email: gautierm @georgetown.edu

Immediate Past Pres., Rich Houseal, Church of the Nazarene, 6401 The Paseo, Kansas City, MO 64131 Tel. (816)333-7000 x 2473 Fax (816)361-5202 Email: rhouseal@nazarene.org

First Vice Pres., Major Diana E. Smith, The Salvation Army, 440 West Nyack Road, Box C-635, West Nyack, NY 10994-1739 Tel. (845)620-7382 Fax (845)620-7777 Email: Diana_Smith@use.salvationarmy.org

Second Vice Pres., John O'Hara, Lutheran Church-Missouri Synod, 1333 S. Kirkwood Road, St. Louis, MO 63122 Tel. (314)965-9917 Fax (314)996-1133 Email: john.ohara@lcms.org

MEMBERS-AT-LARGE
Carl Royster, 21st Century Christian, 2809 12th Ave. S., P.O. Box 40526, Nashville, TN 37204

25

Tel. (615)383-3842 Fax (615)292-5983,
Email: royster@21stcc.com

Destiny Shellhammer, United Church of Christ, 700 Prospect Ave, Cleveland, OH 44111 Tel. (216)736-2149 Fax (216)736-2276, Email: shellhad@ucc.org

## The Association of Theological Schools in the United States and Canada

The Association of Theological Schools in the United States and Canada (ATS) is a membership organization of more than 250 graduate schools that conduct post-baccalaureate professional and academic degree programs to educate persons for the practice of ministry and for teaching and research in the theological disciplines. The ATS Commission on Accrediting accredits schools and approves the degree programs they offer.

### Headquarters

10 Summit Park Drive, Pittsburgh, PA 15275-1103 Tel. (412)788-6505 Fax (412)788-6510

Media Contact, Dir. of Comm., Nancy Merrill, Tel. (412)788-6505 x 234

### Officers

Pres., Donald Senior, Catholic Theological Union, Chicago, IL

Vice Pres., John Kinney, Samuel Delwitt - Proctor - School of Theology of Virginia Union University

Secretary, Leland V. Eliason, Bethel Theological Seminary, St. Paul, MN

Treasurer, Thomas R. Johnson, Kirkpatrick & Lockhart Nicholson Graham, Pittsburgh, PA

Executive Director, Daniel O. Aleshire

## Blanton-Peale Institute

Blanton-Peale Institute is dedicated to helping people overcome emotional obstacles by joining mental health expertise with religious faith and values. The Blanton-Peale Graduate Institute provides advanced training in marriage and family therapy, psychotherapy and pastoral care for ministers, rabbis, sisters, priests and other counselors. The Blanton-Peale Counseling Centers provide counseling for individuals, couples, families and groups. Blanton-Peale also offers a nationwide telephone support service for clergy, social service agencies, and other employers and promotes interdisciplinary communication among theology, medicine and the behavioral sciences. Blanton-Peale was founded in 1937 by Dr. Norman Vincent Peale and psychiatrist Smiley Blanton, M.D.

### Headquarters

3 W. 29th St., New York, NY 10001 Tel. (212) 725-7850 Fax (212)689-3212

### Officers

Chpsn., John Allen

Vice Chpsn., Arthur Caliandro

Sec., Janet E. Hunt

Treas., Mary McNamara

Pres. & CEO, Dr. Holly Johnson

## Bread for the World

Bread for the World is a non-profit, nondenominational Christian citizen's movement of 55,000 members, including 2,500 local churches, that advocates specific hunger policy changes and seeks justice for hungry people at home and abroad. Founded in 1974, Bread for the World is supported by more than 45 Protestant, Catholic and Evangelical denominations and church agencies. Rooted in the gospel of God's love in Jesus Christ, its 55,000 members write, call and visit their members of Congress to win specific legislative changes that help hungry people, and place the issue of hunger on the nation's policy agenda.

Bread for the World works closely with Bread for the World Institute. The Institute seeks to inform, educate, nurture and motivate concerned citizens for action on policies that affect hungry people.

### Headquarters

50 F St., NW, Ste. 500, Washington, DC 20001 Tel. (202)639-9400 Fax (202)639-9401

Media Contact, Shawnda Eibl

### Officers

Pres., Rev. David Beckmann

Bd. Chpsn., Matthew McHugh.

Bd. Vice Chpsn., Eleanor Butt Crook

## Campus Crusade for Christ International

Campus Crusade for Christ International is an interdenominational, evangelistic and discipleship ministry dedicated to helping fulfill the Great Commission through the multiplication strategy of "win-build-send." Founded in 1951 on the campus of UCLA, the organization now includes 60 plus ministries and special projects reaching out to almost every segment of society. There are more than 27,000 staff members and 226,000 trained volunteers in 190 countries.

### Headquarters

100 Lake Hart Dr., Orlando, FL 32832 Tel. (407) 826-2000 Fax (407)826-2120

Media Contact, James Woelbern

### Officers

Chmn. & Pres., Steve Douglass

Chief Operating Officer, J. Roger Bruehl

Chief Financial Officer, Roger L. Craft

## Center for Applied Research in the Apostolate (CARA)

CARA—the Center for Applied Research in the Apostolate is a not-for-profit research organization of the Roman Catholic Church. It operates on the premise that not only theological principles but also findings of the social sciences must be the basis for pastoral care.

CARA's mission since its founding in 1964 has been "To discover, promote, and apply modern techniques and scientific informational resources for practical use in a coordinated and effective approach to the Church's social and religious mission in the modern world, at home and overseas."

CARA performs a wide range of research studies and consulting services. Since its roots are Roman Catholic, many of its studies are done for dioceses, religious orders, parishes, and the United States Conference of Catholic Bishops. Interdenominational studies are also performed. Publishes *The CARA Report*, a research newsletter on Catholic Church-related topics, four times a year and *The Catholic Ministry Formation Directory*, a guide and statistical compilation of enrollments for Catholic seminaries, diaconate formation programs, and lay ministry formation programs.

### Headquarters
Georgetown University, Washington, DC 20057-1203 Tel. (202)687-8080 Fax (202)687-8083, Email cara@georgetown.edu
Media Contact, Executive Director, Mary E. Bendyna, RSM, Ph.D.

### Officers
Bishop John J. Leibrecht, Chair, CARA Board of Directors

PERIODICAL
*The Catholic Ministry Formation Directory*

## Center on Conscience & War

CCW(formerly NISBCO), formed in 1940, is a nonprofit organization supported by individual contributions and related to more than thirty religious organizations. Its purpose is to defend and extend the rights of conscientious objectors to war. CCW provides information on how to register for the draft while documenting one's convictions as a conscientious objector, how to cope with penalties if one does not cooperate, and how to qualify as a conscientious objector while in the Armed Forces. It also provides information for counselors and the public about conscientious objection, military service and the operation of the draft. It provides information to and support for conscientious objectors in other countries.

As a national resource center it assists research in its area of interest including the peace witness of religious bodies. Its staff provides referral to local counselors and attorneys and professional support for them. Through publications and speaking, CCW encourages people to decide for themselves what they believe about participation in war and to act on the basis of the dictates of their own informed consciences.

### Headquarters
1830 Connecticut Ave. NW, Washington, DC 20009-5732 Tel. (202)483-2220 Fax (202) 483-1246
Media Contact, Exec. Dir., J.E. McNeil

### Officers
Exec. Dir., J.E. McNeil
Chpsn., David Miller
Sec., James Feldman
Treas., Jean Martensen

## Center for Parish Development

The Center for Parish Development is an ecumenical, non-profit research and development agency whose mission is to help church bodies learn to become faithful expressions of God's mission in today's post-modern, post-Christendom world. Founded in 1968, the Center brings to its client-partners a strong theological orientation, a missional ecclesial paradigm with a focus on faithful Christian communities as the locus of mission, research-based theory and practice of major change, a systems approach, and years of experience working with national, regional, and local church bodies.

The Center staff provides research, consulting and training support for church organizations engaging in major change. The Center is governed by a 12-member Board of Directors.

### Headquarters
1448 East 53rd St., Chicago, IL 60615 Tel. (773)752-1596 Fax (773)752-5093
Media Contact, Office Manager, Beatrice Vansen

### Officers
Chpsn., John Rottenberg, 2047 Fawnwood Drive SE, Kentwood, MI 49508
Vice Chpsn., Stephen B. Bevens, 5401 S. Cornell Avenue, Chicago, IL 60615
Sec., Delton Krueger, 10616 Penn Ave. South, Bloomington, MN 55431
Managing Directors, Raymond Schulte and Dale Ziemer

## Chaplaincy of Full Gospel Churches

The Chaplaincy of Full Gospel Churches (CFGC) is a unique coalition of 1500 nondenominational churches and networks of churches united for the purpose of being represented in military and civilian chaplaincies. Since its inception in 1984, CFGC has grown rapidly. Today CFGC represents over 7.5 million American Christians. Additionally, we are connected with another 144 fellowship groups consisting of another 7.5 million members, which gives CFGC the potential of representing a total 15 million.

Churches, fellowships and networks of churches which affirm the CFGC statement of faith that "Jesus is Savior, Lord and Baptizer in the Holy Spirit today, with signs, wonders and gifts following" may join the endorsing agency. CFGC represents its member-networks of churches (consisting of over 90,000 churches nationwide) before the Pentagon's Armed Forces Chaplains Board, the National Conference of Ministry to the Armed Forces, Endorsers Conference for Veterans Affairs Chaplaincy, Federal Bureau of Prisons, Association of Professional Chaplains, and other groups requiring professional chaplaincy endorsement (State/County/City Correctional, Healthcare, Law Enforcement, Workplace). The organization also ecclesiastically credentials professional counselors.

### Headquarters

2715 Whitewood Dr., Dallas, TX 75233-2713
Tel. (214)331-4373 Fax (214)333-4401
Media Contact, Rev. Dr. E. H. Jim Ammerman

### Officers

Pres., Rev. Dr. E. H. Jim Ammerman

## Christian Churches Together in the U.S.A.

Christian Churches Together in the U.S.A. (CCT) is a new forum growing out of a deeply felt need to broaden and expand fellowship, unity, and witness among the diverse expressions of Christian faith today. The purpose of Christian Churches Together is to enable churches and national Christian organizations to grow closer together in Christ in order to strengthen our Christian witness in the world. Christian Churches Together in the U.S.A. welcomes churches, Christian communities, and national Christian organizations that: "believe in the Lord Jesus Christ as God and Savior according to the Scriptures; worship and serve the One God, Father, Son, and Holy Spirit; and seek ways to work together in order to present a more credible Christian witness in and to the world."

CCT is inclusive of the diversity of Christian families in the United States—Evangelical, Orthodox, Roman Catholic, Pentecostals, historic Protestant, Racial and Ethnic churches.

Christian Churches Together provides a context—marked by prayer, theological dialogue and fellowship—in which churches can develop relationships with other churches with whom they presently have little contact. This is one response to our Lord's Prayer that all who believe in Him might be one with God and with one another so that the world would believe in Him as God and Savior.

### Administration

Wes Granberg-Michaelson, Steering Committee Moderator, 4500 60th Street, SE, Grand Rapids, MI 49512
Sharon VanGelderen, Administrative Assistant, 4500 60th Street, SE, Grand Rapids, Michigan 49512 Tel. (616)698-7071 x 315 Email: svangelderen@rca.org

Jean Stromberg, Executive Administrator, Tel. 646-784-3478, Email: jsstromber@aol.com

### Steering Committee

Bishop Stephen Blaire, Catholic Diocese of Stockton
Archbishop Demetrios, Greek Orthodox Archdiocese of America
Rev. Jeff Farmer, Open Bible Churches
Rev. Wesley Granberg-Michaelson, Reformed Church in America
Steve Haas, World Vision
Bishop Roger Haskins, Free Methodist Church of North America
Archbishop Cyril Karim, Syrian Orthodox Church of Antioch
Father Leonid Kishkovsky, Orthodox Church in America, President
Cardinal William Keeler, Catholic Church, Archdiocese of Baltimore, President
Bishop James Leggett, International Pentecostal Holiness Church, President
Rev. Larry Pickens, The General Commission on Christian Unity & Interreligious Concerns, The United Methodist Church
Ann Marie Pineda, Catholic Church, U.S. Catholic Conference of Bishops
Rev. Ron Roberson, Catholic Church, U.S. Conference of Catholic Bishops
Rev. Dr. Seung Koo Choi, Korean Presbyterian Church in America
Dr. William Shaw, National Baptist Convention, U.S.A., President
Rev. Ronald J. Sider, Evangelicals for Social Action
Ms. A. Bowie Snodgrass, The Episcopal Church
Dr. Stephen Thurston
Rev. Dr. Daniel Vestal, Cooperative Baptist Fellowship
Rev. Don Dixon Williams, Bread for the World

## Christian Council on Persons with Disabilities

Created in 1988, the Christian Council on Persons with Disabilities (CCPD) is a coalition of churches, non-profit organizations, and individuals advocating an evangelical perspective concerning people with disabilities and their place in God's world. The coalition provides a national voice for Christians involved in disability ministry, framing the Christian community's response to issues relating to disability.

CCPD provides information and responses on issues specifically relating to the church such as accessibility, disability theology, and outreach; as well as disability-related issues of concern to the general public such as genetic research, end-of-life care and cloning.

Advocacy, professional development, networking and education are all part of the coalition's activities. Annual conferences (both national & regional), chapter groups, and mentoring programs are part of the coalition's strategy in strengthening the network of disability ministry.

301 E. Pine St. Suite 150, Orlando, FL 32801, Tel. (407)210-3917, Email: ccpd@ccpd.org, Website: www.ccpd.org

### Officers
Exec. Dir., Jim Hukill
Pres., Gary Wagner, Of Camp Verde, Ariz.
Treas., Stan Higgins, of Rohnert Park, Calif.

## Christian Endeavor International

Christian Endeavor International is a Christ-centered, youth-oriented ministry which assists local churches in reaching young people with the gospel of Jesus Christ, discipling them in the Christian faith, and equipping them for Christian ministry and service in their local church, community and world. It trains youth leaders for effective ministry and provides opportunities for Christian inspiration, spiritual growth, fellowship, and service. Christian Endeavor International reaches across denominational, cultural, racial and geographical boundaries. All materials are on the internet at www.teamce.com

### Headquarters
424 E. Main St., P.O.. Box 377, Edmore, MI 48829, Tel. (989)427-3737 Fax (989)427-5530, Email: contact@teamce.com
Media Contact, Luke Sawyer

### Officers
Chief Executive Officer, Timothy Eldred

## Christian Management Association

Christian Management Association (CMA) provides leadership training, management resources and strategic networking relationships for leaders and managers of Christian organizations and growing churches. Its membership represents leaders and managers from more than 1,500 Christian organizations and larger churches in the U.S. CMA publishes *Christian Management Report* magazine, *CMA Management Monthly* e-newsletter, *Total Compensation Survey Report for Christian Ministries*, www.CMAonline.org website, CMA Management Tape Library and many other resources.

CMA provides management training, resourcing and networking opportunities through its annual conference for Christian organizations and churches, CEO Dialogues one-day roundtables, chapters in selected cities, online Job Market, and many other programs. It also features annually the Best Christian Places to Work finalists and the CMA Management Award. Membership is open to Christian organizations, ministries and churches. Businesses that provide products or services for Christian organizations and churches may apply for a business membership. For complete membership information, go to www.CMAonline.org and click on "Membership."

### Headquarters
P.O. Box 4090, San Clemente, CA 92674 Tel.(800)727-4262 Fax (949)487-0927
CEO, John Pearson, Email: John@CMAonline. org
Director of Management Resources, DeWayne Herbrandson, Email: DeWayne@CMAonline. org
Senior Consultant, Marketing, Dick Bahruth, Email: Dick@CMAonline.org
Director of Conferences & Meetings, Marsha Lyons, Email: Marsha@CMAonline.org
Director of Administration/COO, Suzy West, Email: Suzy@CMAonline.org

### Officers
Chairman, Mark G. Holbrook, Pres./CEO, ECCU
Vice Chairman, C.E. Crouse, Managing Partner, Capin Crouse, LLP
Treas., Robert T. Lipps, Lockton Insurance Brokers of San Francisco
Sec., Mark A. Bankord, Managing Principal/ Chairman, Cap Trust Asset Management

## A Christian Ministry in the National Parks

This ministry is recognized by over 40 Christian denominations and extends the ministry of Christ to the millions of people who live, work and vacation in our National Parks. Ministry staff members conduct services of worship in the parks on Sundays. The staff are employed by park concessionaires and have full-time jobs in which their actions, attitudes, and commitment to Christ serve as witness. Room and board are provided at a minimal cost; minimum commitment of 90 days needed.

### Officers
Dir., The Rev. Richard P. Camp, Jr.
Deputy Director, Gordon Compton

## Church Growth Center—Home of Church Doctor Ministries

The Church Growth Center is an interfaith, nonprofit, professional organization which exists to bring transformational change of the Christian church toward the effective implementation of the Lord's Great Commission, to make disciples of all people. This effort is done through consultations, resources, and educational events.

Founded in 1978 by leader Kent R. Hunter, the Church Growth Center offers more than 17 different consultation services, including church consultations by experienced consultants, cutting-edge resources through The Church Doctor™ Resource Center, and by providing educational events at churches and organizations in the way of providing speakers and resources at seminars, workshops, and conferences. The bi-monthly e-newsletter is the *Church Doctor Report*.

P.O. Box 145, 1230 U. S. Highway Six, Corunna, IN 46730 Tel. (800)626-8515 Fax (260)281-2167, Website: www.churchdoctor.org

Media Contact, assistant to president, Cindy Warren

**Officers**

President, Dr. Kent R. Hunter, D.min, Ph.D.

Vice Pres., Jim Manthei

Treas., Wayne Register

## Church Women United in the U.S.A.

Church Women United in the U.S.A. is a racially, culturally, theologically inclusive Christian women's movement, celebrating unity in diversity and working for a world of peace and justice. Founded in 1941, Church Women United is a movement representing Protestant, Roman Catholic, Orthodox and other Christian women; biblically based, shared Christian faith; organized into more than 1200 state and local units working for peace and justice in the United States and Puerto Rico; supported by constituents in state and local units and denominational women's organizations; impassioned by the Holy Spirit to act on behalf of women and children throughout the world; and recognized as a non-governmental organization by the United Nations.

**Headquarters**

475 Riverside Dr., Ste. 1626, New York, NY 10115 Tel. (800)CWU-5551 or (212)870-2347 Fax (212)870-2338, Office manager, Julie Drews, Email: juliedrews@churchwomen.org

**LEGISLATIVE OFFICE**

CWU Washington Office, 100 Maryland Ave. NE, Rm. 100, Washington, DC 20002 Tel. (202)544-8747 Fax (202)544-9133

Legislative Dir., Wash. Office, Patricia Burkhardt, Email: pburkhardt@churchwomen.org

**Officers**

Pres., Gail Mengel, Independence, Mo.

Vice Pres., Vera Zander, Tucson, Ariz.

Secretary, Carol Kolsti, Austin, Texas

Treasurer, Ann Kohler, Baldwinsville, N.Y.

Regional Coordinators, Central, Susan Becker, Madison, Wisc.; East Central, Margaret Tweet, Rock Island, Ill.; Mid-Atlantic, Blanche Simmons, Landover, Md.; Northeast, Vivian Love-Jones, Newburg, N.Y.; Northwest, Betty Luginbill, Boise, Id; South Central, Martha Moody Boone, Keithville, La.; Southeast, Pat Zangmeister, Tamarac, Fla.; Southwest, Jenny Ladefaged, Alisa Viego, Calif.

## Churches Uniting in Christ

Churches Uniting in Christ (CUIC) was inaugurated on January 20, 2002, in Memphis, Tennessee as a new relationship among nine communions that agreed to start living more fully into their unity in Christ. CUIC is the successor to the Consultation on Church Union (COCU) which was in 1962 organized to explore the formation of a uniting church. At the 1999 COCU Plenary the nine member communions affirmed eight "Marks" of Churches Uniting in Christ and agreed to move into the new relationship of covenanted communion to be called Churches Uniting in Christ. Following confirmation actions by each of the communions, all nine communions officially constituted Churches Uniting in Christ. The nine member communions are: The African Methodist Episcopal Church, the African Methodist Episcopal Zion Church, the Christian Church (Disciples of Christ), the Christian Methodist Episcopal Church, The Episcopal Church, the International Council of Community Churches, the Presbyterian Church (U.S.A.), the United Church of Christ, and the United Methodist Church. Also participating at present are two Partners in Mission and Dialogue, the Evangelical Lutheran Church in America and the Moravian Church (Northern Province). The Catholic Church participates as an observer. Other communions are exploring various possibilities for relating to CUIC.

CUIC is a bold venture, expressed through the participating communions' covenant to seek to live a new relationship that bears witness to a church that is truly catholic, truly evangelical, and truly reformed. Among the goals for bearing witness to that unity are two very challenging endeavors: to heed the "emphatic call to 'erase racism' by challenging the system of white privilege that has so distorted life in this society and in the churches themselves;" and to provide a foundation for the mutual recognition and reconciliation of ordained ministry by the members of Churches Uniting in Christ by the year 2007. Notably, the commitment to address racism is named as a hallmark of the new relationship. Following the Inaugural ceremony, on Dr. Martin Luther King, Jr. Day, January 21, 2002, the Heads of Communion signed an Appeal to the Churches to work together for the eradication of racism.

The Ecumenical Officers of each of the communions will carry major responsibility for the engagement of their congregations and members in the CUIC relationship. Neighboring congregations are encouraged to celebrate the Eucharist together; invite the participation of each in services of baptism, ordinations, and installation as well as other special events in the congregations' lives; and to discover ways in which they might witness together in combating social injustices, especially racism. In addition to the representational Coordinating Council, three task forces will work to enhance the collaborative endeavors of CUIC: Ministry, Racism, and Local and Regional Ecumenism.

The Rev. Dr. Bertrice Y. Wood serves as the Director of CUIC with the office located at 700 Prospect Avenue, Cleveland, OH 44115-1100, Tel. (216)736-3294. The Rev. C. Dana Krutz is President of the Coordinating Council.

**Headquarters**
700 Prospect Ave., Cleveland, OH 44115-1100 Tel.(216)736-3294 Fax (216)736-3296 Email: cuicwood@ucc.org or cuic@ucc.org
Media Contact, The Rev. Dr. Bertrice Y. Wood

**Officers**
Dir., The Rev. Dr. Bertrice Y. Wood, 700 Prospect Ave., Cleveland, OH 44115-1100
President of the Coordinating Council, The Rev. C. Dana Krutz (The Episcopal Church), 660 N. Foster Dr. Ste. A-225, Baton Rouge, LA 70806
Vice Pres., Bishop E. Earl McCloud, Jr. (African Methodist Episcopal Church)
Sec., Mr. Abraham Wright, (International Council of Community Churches)
Trea., Elder James N. Tse (Presbyterian Church U.S.A.)

**COORDINATING COUNCIL REPRESEN-TATIVES FROM MEMBER COMMUNIONS**
African Methodist Episcopal Church, Bishop E. Earl McCloud, Jr.
African Methodist Episcopal Zion Church, The Rev. Dr. Harrison Bonner
Christian Church (Disciples of Christ), The Rev. Dr. Suzanne Webb
Christian Methodist Episcopal Church, Bishop Ronald Cunningham
The Episcopal Church (U.S.A.), The Rev. C. Dana Krutz
International Council of Community Churches, Mr. Abraham Wright
Presbyterian Church (U.S.A.), Elder James N. Tse
United Church of Christ, The Rev. Lydia Veliko
The United Methodist Church, Bishop Albert F. Mutti
Email: cuic@ucc.org

## Day 1/Episcopal Media Center

Day 1/Episcopal Media Center is an ecumenical organization dedicated to producing media resources from a mainline Protestant point of view. The flagship productions are the weekly radio show, "Day 1," formerly "The Protestant Hour," and the "Day 1" television program (produced in association with Faith & Value Media) airing Sunday mornings on the Hallmark Channel. The Web site www.day1.net provides sermon transcripts and audio resources. Day 1 features preachers from the Cooperative Baptist Fellowship, Episcopal Media Center, Evangelical Lutheran Church in America, Presbyterian Church (U.S.A.), United Church of Christ, and the United Methodist Church. The Web site www.Day1.net provides sermon transcripts and audio resources, and www.episcopalmedia.org

offers audio and video resources for churches and individuals.

**Headquarters**
644 West Peachtree St, Suite 300, Atlanta, GA 30308-1925 Tel. (404)815-9110 Fax (404) 815-0258
Media Contact, Nan Ross

**Officers**
Bd. Chpsn., The Rt. Rev. Charles Duvall
Vice Chpsns., Ms. Harriet Tumlin Jobson, Ms. Nancy Zintak
Pres., The Rev. Canon Louis C. Schueddig
Vice Pres., The Rev. Peter M. Wallace
Treas., William F. Law, Jr.
Sec., Laurin M. McSwain, Esq.

## Evangelical Council for Financial Accountability

Founded in 1979, the Evangelical Council for Financial Accountability has the purpose of helping Christ-centered, evangelical, nonprofit organizations earn the public's trust through their ethical practices and financial accountability. ECFA assists its over 1,200 member organizations in making appropriate public disclosure of their financial practices and accomplishments, thus materially enhancing their credibility and support potential among present and prospective donors.

**Headquarters**
440 W. Jubal Early Drive Ste. 130, Winchester, VA 22601-6319 Tel. (540)535-0103 Fax (540) 535-0533
Media Contact, Pres., Ken Behr

**Officers**
Pres., Ken Behr
Vice Pres., Dan Busby

## Evangelical Press Association

The Evangelical Press Association is an organization of editors and publishers of Christian periodicals which seeks to promote the cause of Evangelical Christianity and enhance the influence of Christian journalism.

**Headquarters**
P.O. Box 28129, Crystal, MN 55428 Tel. (763) 535-4793 Fax (763)535-4794
Media Contact, Exec. Dir., Ronald Wilson

**Officers**
Pres., David Neff, *Christianity Today*, 465 Gundersen Dr., Carol Stream, IL, 60188
Pres-Elect, Terry White, *Inside Journal*, P.O. Box 17429, Washington, DC 20041-0429
Treas., Lamar Keener, *Christian Times*, P.O. Box 2606, El Cajon, CA 92021
Sec., Jeanette Thomason, *Aspire*, 107 Kenner Ave., Nashville, TN 37205
Advisor, Dean Ridings, *Christian Camp & Conference Journal*, P.O. Box 62189, Colorado Springs, CO 80962-2189

Advisor, Brian Peterson, New Man, 600 Rinehart Rd., Lake Mary, FL 32746
Exec. Dir., Ronald Wilson

## Faith & Values Media

*(See also National Interfaith Cable Coalition, Inc.)*

Faith & Values Media is a nation's largest coalition of Jewish and Christian faith groups dedicated to media production, distribution and promotion. It is a service of the National Interfaith Cable Coalition, Inc., established in 1987.

Faith & Values Media member association includes more than 40 faith groups and religious organizations representing 200,000 congregations and 120 million congregants. Its mission is to use television and other media to promote the vitality of religious experience in everyday life.

Award-winning programming from Faith & Values Media is available on the Hallmark Channel and on www.faithstreams.com

### Headquarters

74 Trinity Place, Suite 1550, New York, NY 10006 Tel. (212)406-4121 Fax (212)406-4105
Media Contact, Christine Luzano

### Officers

Chair, Dr. Daniel Paul Matthews
Vice Chair, Elder Ralph Hardy Jr., Esq.
Secretary, Rabbi Daniel Freelander
Treasurer, Betty Elam

### Staff

President and CEO, Edward J. Murray
Exec. Vice President, Beverly Judge

## Federation of Christian Ministries

The Federation of Christian Ministries (FCM) is an ecumenical faith community founded in 1968. FCM stresses inclusiveness, opening its membership to women and men of varying faith backgrounds who share its vision of an ecumenical, nondenominational community. Its ministers work in many ways: pastoring house churches or congregations/parishes; serving as chaplains in nursing homes, correctional facilities, hospitals; offering healing ministries; promoting groups dedicated to peace and justice. FCM is a member of the International Council of Community Churches and a faith group member of the Association for Clinical Pastoral Education. Its educational branch, Global Ministries University, offers online degree completion, both undergraduate and postgraduate, for adult learners in the field of ministry.
Contact: GlobalMinistriesUniversity.com.

### Headquarters

1905 Bugbee Rd., Ionia, MI 48846-9663 Tel. (800)538-8923 or (616)527-0419 Fax (616)527-0419, Email: info@FederationofChristian Ministries.org

Media Contact, Co-president, Eileen Mackin, Tel.(303)740-7665, Email: cdewall@pcisys.net

### Officers

Chairperson(s): Jan & Paul Reithmaier, 7415 K Triwoods Dr., Shrewsbury, MO 63119-4456, Tel. (314)962-6220, Email: p.reithmaier@worldnet.att.net
President(s): Eileen Mackin & Clem DeWall, 11298 E. Maplewood Pl., Englewood, CO 80111-5808. Tel. (303)740-7665, Email: cdewall@pcisys.net
Treasurer: Roger J. Fecher, 8330 Catamaran Dr., Indianapolis, IN 46236-9585, Tel. (317) 826-8940, Email: rjfecher@aol.com.
Secretaries/Central Office: Edward & Judy Kalmanek, 1905 Bugbee Rd., Ionia, MI 48846-9663, Tel. (616)527-0419, Email: ejkalmanek@home.ionia.com.
Development Directors: Frederick A. Mason, 12830 Paulina St. Ste 2E, Calumet Park, IL 60827-5951, Tel. (708)589-3357, Email: Mcrincorg@sbcglobal.net.
Bonnie J. McCulley, 3818 Eagle Ridge Dr., Cape Giradeau, MO 63701-1703, Tel. (573) 332-1228, Email: bjmc27@aol.com.
Member at Large: William Manseau, 12 Catherwood Rd., Tewksbury, MA 01876-2620. Tel. (978)851-5547

REGIONAL VICE PRESIDENTS:
Pacific Region: Peggy & Phil Ripp, 2869 Donizetti Ct., San Jose, CA 95132-2310. Tel. (408)272-8184, Email: philandpeg@sbcglobal.net.
Mountains & Plains: Rebecca David, 624 E. Dover St., Davenport, IA 52803-2611. Tel. (563)323-5740, Email: irishblue03@earth-link.net
Great Lakes: Pamela Spence, P. O. Box 204, Ostrander, OH 43061-0204, Tel. (740)666-3204, Email: allespen@midohio.net.
Southern: Eleonora V. Marinaro and David Gaboury, 10231 Oakhill Dr., Port Richey, FL 34668-3291, Tel. (727)697-2763, Email: elly@helpwithdreams.com
Northeast: Michaelita & Thomas Quinn, 93 Post Rd., Danbury, CT 06810-8367. Tel (203)792-6968, Email: quinnems@aol.com.

## Foundation for a Conference on Faith and Order in North America

Foundation for a Conference on Faith and Order is a not-for-profit organization dedicated to promoting the unity of the North American churches by keeping before the churches the gospel call to unity in Faith and Order. It engages in educational studies and programs that relate to issues affecting Faith and Order, and promotes, plans, and administers conferences on Faith and Order in North America. The purpose of these conferences is to encourage and promote the unity of the churches in Faith and Order.

**MEMBERS OF THE BOARD**
Bishop Vinton Anderson
Dr. Wallace M. Alston, Jr.
Dr. Susan E. Davies
Archbishop Demetrios
Dr. Robert M. Franklin
Dr. Donna Geernaert, SC
The Right Rev. Richard F. Grein
Dr. Robert W. Jenson
Dr. Cheryl Bridges Johns
William Cardinal Keeler
Dr. Kevin W. Mannoia
The Rt. Rev. Victoria Matthews
Bishop Donald J. McCoid
Dr. Richard Mouw
Dr. Willam G. Rusch
Dr. George Vandervelde
Dr. Eldin Villafane
The Rev. Portia Turner Williamson

## Friends World Committee for Consultation (Section of the Americas)

The Friends World Committee for Consultation (FWCC) was formed in 1937. There has been an American section as well as a European section from the early days and an African section was organized in 1971. In 1974 the name, Section of the Americas, was adopted by that part of the FWCC with constituency in North, Central, and South America and in the Caribbean area. In 1985 the Asia-West Pacific Section was organized. The purposes of FWCC are summarized as follows: to facilitate loving understanding of diversities among Friends while discovering together, with God's help, a common spiritual ground; and to facilitate full expression of Friends' testimonies in the world.

**Headquarters**
Section of the Americas Headquarters
1506 Race St., Philadelphia, PA 19102 Tel. (215) 241-7250 Fax (215)241-7285 Email: americas @fwcc.quaker.org, Website: www.quaker.org/ fwcc/americas/americas.html
Media Contact, Exec. Sec., Margaret Fraser
Latin American Office, Guerrero 223 Pte., Zona Centro, Cd. Mante, TAM 89800 Mexico

**Officers**
Exec. Sec., Margaret Fraser

## The Fund for Theological Education, Inc.

Begun in 1954 with the goal of supporting excellence in the profession of ministry, the Fund for Theological Education has enjoyed a long and rich history, providing gifted women and men with nearly 5000 fellowships and generating innovative new programs for support of persons preparing for ministry and theological teaching. Supported by individuals and grants from a group of U.S. foundations, FTE envisions new and imaginative programs to encourage diversity and excellence in the churches and seminaries of North America.

**Headquarters**
825 Houston Mill Rd., Suite 250, Atlanta, GA 30329 Tel. (404)727-1450 Fax (404)727-1490 Websites: www.thefund.org, www.exploreministry.org
Email: fte@thefund.org

**Officers**
President, Ann Svennungsen
Vice Pres. For Advancement, Jack Gilbert
Dir., Expanding Horizons Partnership, Dr. Sharon Watson Fluker
Dir., Partnership for Excellence, Melissa Wiginton

## Glenmary Research Center

The Research Center is a department of the Glenmary Home Missioners, a Catholic society of priests and brothers. The Center was established in 1966 to serve the rural research needs of the Catholic Church in the United States. Its research has led it to serve ecumenically a wide variety of church bodies. Local case studies as well as quantitative research is done to understand better the diversity of contexts in the rural sections of the country. The Center's statistical profiles of the nation's counties cover both urban and rural counties.

**Headquarters**
1312 Fifth Ave. North, Nashville, TN 37208 Tel. (615)256-1905 Fax (615)251-1472

**Officers**
Pres., Rev. Daniel Dorsey, P.O. Box 465618, Cincinnati, OH 45246-5618
1st Vice Pres., Rev. Robert Poandl, P.O. Box 465618, Cincinnati, OH 45246-5618
2nd Vice Pres., Rev. Dominic Duggins, P.O. Box 465618, Cincinnati, OH 45246-5618
Treas., Ms. Saney Wissel, P.O. Box 465618, Cincinnati, OH 45246-5618
Dir., Kenneth M. Sanchagrin, Ph.D. Email: ksanchagrin@glenmary.org
Assoc. Dir., Fr. Wil Steinbacher, 1312 5th Ave.N., Nashville, TN 37208 Email: wjsteinba @aol.com

## Graymoor Ecumenical & Interreligious Institute (GEII)

Graymoor Ecumenical & Interreligious Institute has its roots in the Graymoor Ecumenical Institute which was founded in 1967 by the Franciscan Friars of the Atonement, to respond to the Friars' historical concern for Christian unity in light of the theological and ecumenical developments arising from the Second Vatican Council.

In 1991, in response to developments in both the Institute and the wider ecumenical scene, the Graymoor Ecumenical Institute was expanded into an information and service organization with a mission of Christian Unity and interreligious dialogue. Today, the Graymoor Ecumenical & Interreligious Institute employs several means to accomplish this goal. Among these is the annual Week of Prayer for Christian Unity, "a worldwide observance initiated in 1908 by the Rev. Paul Wattson, co-founder of the Society of the Atonement," the theme and text of which are now chosen and prepared by the Pontifical Council for Promoting Christian Unity and representatives of the World Council of Churches. The Institute publishes the monthly journal *Ecumenical Trends* to keep clergy and laity abreast of developments in the ecumenical and interreligious movements; provides membership in, and collaboration with, national and local ecumenical and interreligious organizations and agencies; and cooperates with individuals engaged in ecumenical and interreligious work. A new website, www.geii.org has been launched and will continue to be developed as a resource for ecumenical and interreligious research.

Over the years, the Graymoor Ecumenical & Interreligious Institute has sponsored and cosponsored meetings, colloquia, and workshops in areas of ecumenical and interreligious dialogue.

### Headquarters

475 Riverside Dr., Rm. 1960, New York, NY 10115-1999 Tel. (212)870-2330 Fax (212) 870-2001

### Officers

Dir., Desk for Interreligious Affairs, Rev. James Loughran, SA, Tel. (212)870-2330, Email: jlgeii @aol.com

Assoc. Director, Sr. Lorelei Francis Fuchs, SA, Desk for Ecumenical Affairs, Tel. (212)870-2331, Email: lorgeii@aol.com

Assoc. Dir., Ecumenical Research Desk, Rev. Wilfred L. Tyrrell, SA, Tel.(212)870-2332, Email: wltgeii@aol.com

Editor, Ecumenical Trends, Rev. James Loughran SA., Graymoor, Route 9, P.O. Box 300, Garrison, NY 10524-0300 Tel. (845)424-3671 x 3323, Email: jloughran@atonementfriars.org

Business Manager, Week of Prayer for Christian Unity Office, Mrs. Veronica Sullivan, Graymoor, Rt. 9, P.O. Box 300, Garrison, NY 10524-0300 Tel. (800)338.2620 x 2109 or (845)424-2109 Fax (845)424-2163, Email: rsullivan@atonementfriars.org

## InterVarsity Christian Fellowship of the U.S.A.

InterVarsity Christian Fellowship is a non-profit, interdenominational student movement that ministers to college and university students and faculty in the United States. InterVarsity began in the United States when students at the University of Michigan invited C. Stacey Woods, then General Secretary of the Canadian movement, to help establish an Inter-Varsity chapter on their campus. InterVarsity Christian Fellowship-U.S.A. was incorporated two years later, in 1941.

InterVarsity's uniqueness as a campus ministry lies in the fact that it is student-initiated and student-led. InterVarsity strives to build collegiate fellowships that engage their campus with the gospel of Jesus Christ and develop disciples who live out biblical values. InterVarsity students and faculty are encouraged in evangelism, spiritual discipleship, serving the church, multiethnicity, righteousness, vocational stewardship, and world evangelization. The Urbana triennial missions convention has long been a launching point for missionary service. For more detials on urbana please visit www.urbana.org.

### Headquarters

6400 Schroeder Rd., P.O. Box 7895, Madison, WI 53707 Tel. (608)274-9001 Fax (608)274-7882, Email: info@intervarsity.org, Website: www.intervarsity.org

Media Contact, Gordon Govier

### Officers

Pres. & CEO, Alec Hill

Vice Pres., C. Barney Ford; Robert A. Fryling; Karon Morton, Jim Lundgren, Paula Fuller, Jim Tebbe

Bd. Chpsn., Donald Kolowsky

Bd. Vice Chpsn., E. Kenneth Nielson

## Interfaith Impact for Justice and Peace

Interfaith Impact for Justice and Peace is the religious community's united voice in Washington. It helps Protestant, Jewish, Muslim and Catholic national organizations have clout on Capitol Hill and brings grass-roots groups and individual and congregational members to Washington and shows them how to turn their values into votes for justice and peace.

Interfaith Impact for Justice and Peace has established the following Advocacy Networks to advance the cause of justice and peace: Justice for Women; Health Care; Hunger and Poverty; International Justice and Peace; Civil and Human Rights. The Interfaith Impact Foundation provides an annual legislative briefing for its members.

Members receive the periodic action alerts on initiatives, voting records, etc., and a free subscription to the Advocacy Networks of their choice.

### Headquarters

100 Maryland Ave. N.E., Ste. 200, Washington, DC 20002 Tel. (202)543-2800 Fax (202)547-8107

Media Contact, Jane Hull Harvey

Chpsn. of Bd., Jane Hull Harvey, United Methodist Church

MEMBERS
African Methodist Episcopal Church
African Methodist Episcopal Zion Church
Alliance of Baptists
American Baptist Churches, U.S.A., Washington Office; World Relief Office
American Ethical Union
American Muslim Council
Center of Concern
Christian Methodist Episcopal (CME) Church
Christian Church (Disciples of Christ)
Church of the Brethren
Church Women United
Commission on Religion in Appalachia
Episcopal Church
Episcopal Urban Caucus
Evangelical Lutheran Church in America
Federation of Southern Cooperatives-LAF
Federation for Rural Empowerment
Graymoor Ecumenical and Interreligious Institute
Jesuit Social Ministries
Maryknoll Fathers and Brothers
Moravian Church in America
National Council of Churches of Christ, Church World Service; Washington Office
National Council of Jewish Women

NETWORK
Peoria Citizens Committee
Presbyterian Church (U.S.A.)
Progressive National Baptist Convention
Presbyterian Hunger Fund
Reformed Church in America
Rural Advancement Fund
Society of African Missions
Southwest Organizing Project
Southwest Voter Registration-Education Project
Toledo Metropolitan Ministries
Union of American Hebrew Congregations
Unitarian Universalist Association
Unitarian Universalist Service Committee
United Church of Christ, Bd. for Homeland Ministries; Bd. for World Ministries; Hunger Action Ofc.; Ofc. of Church in Society
United Methodist Church, Gen. Bd. of Church & Society; Gen. Bd. of Global Ministries Natl. Div.; Gen. Bd. of Global Ministries Women's Div.; Gen. Bd. of Global Ministries World Div.
Virginia Council of Churches
Western Organization of Resource Councils

## Interfaith Worker Justice

Interfaith Worker Justice is a network of sixty interfaith groups and people of faith who educate and mobilize the U.S. religious community on issues and campaigns to improve wages, benefits and working conditions for workers, especially low-wage workers. The organization rebuilds relationships between the religious community and organized labor.

The organization supports and organizes local interfaith worker justice groups around the country, publishes *Faith Works* six times a year providing congregations resources and updates on religion-labor work, coordinates the Poultry Justice project to improve conditions for poultry workers, and promotes healthy dialogue between management and unions in religious-owned or-sponsored health care facilities.

**Headquarters**
1020 West Bryn Mawr, 4th floor, Chicago, IL 60660-4627. Tel. (773)728-8400 Fax (773) 728-8409
Media Contact, Bob Hulteen, Email: bhulteen @iwj.org

**Board of Directors**
President: Rev. Nelson Johnson, Pulpit Forum of Greensboro and Faith Community Church
Vice President: Bishop Gabino Zavala, Archdiocese of Los Angeles
Finance Chair: Rev. Dr. Paul Sherry, National Council of Churches
Fundraising Chair: Rev. Jim Sessions, United Methodist Church
Action Committee Chair: Ms. Edith Rasell, UCC Minister for Labor Relations
Education Committee Chair: Ms. Evely Laser Shlensky,* Commission on Social Action of Reform Judaism (URJ & CCAR)
Board Development Chair: Imam Mahdi Bray, Muslim American Society Freedom Foundation
Dr. Charles Amjad-Ali, Luther Seminary
Mr. Hussam Ayloush, Council on American-Islamic Relations - Southern California
Mr. John Boonstra, Washington Association of Churches
Ms. Linda Chavez-Thompson, AFL-CIO
Ms. Marilyn Clement, Campaign for a National Health Program NOW
Rev. Darren Cushman-Wood, Speedway United Methodist Church
Mr. Robert DeRose, Barkan+Neff
Bishop William DeVeaux, African Methodist Episcopal Church
Dr. Mary Heidkamp, Dynamic Insights International
Ms. Karen Herrling, Catholic Legal Immigration Network, Inc
Ms. Karen McLean Hessel, Justice for Women, National Council of Churches
Rev. Clete Kiley, Bishop's Committee, U.S. Conference of Catholic Bishops
Mr. Jeffry Korgen, The Roundtable
Rabbi Mordechai Liebling, Shefa Fund
Rev. Christopher Lockard, Jesuit Refugee Service
Ms. Linda Lotz, American Friends Service Committee

Rabbi Robert Marx,** Congregation Hakafa

Ms. Cynthia Nance,* University of Arkansas

Rev. J. Herbert Nelson, Liberation Community Church/Mid-South Interfaith Committee for Worker Justice

Rev. Sinclair Oubre, Catholic Labor Network

Mr. Mark Pelavin, Religious Action Center of Reform Judaism

Ms. Rosalyn Pelles, Union Community Fund

Sister Mary Priniski, OP, Catholic Committee of the South

Rev. Meg Riley, Unitarian Universalist Association of Congregations

Rev. Michael Rouse,* St. Catherine AME Zion Church

Mr. Chris Sanders, Political Consultant, UFCW

Mr. Thomas Shellabarger, U.S. Conference of Catholic Bishops

Honorable Charles Steele, Southern Christian Leadership Conference

Rev. Ron Stief, UCC Justice and Witness Ministries Public Life and Social Policy

Mr. Monroe Sullivan, Retired Businessman/ Social Activist

Rev. Phil Tom, Urban Ministry Office, Presbyterian Church (U.S.A.)

Rev. Mark Wendorf, McCormick Theological Seminary

Rev. Bennie Whiten, Jr., United Church of Christ

Special Advisors

Bishop Jesse DeWitt,** Retired, United Methodist Church

Rev. Jim Lawson, Holman United Methodist Church

Rev. Joseph Echols Lowery, Southern Christian Leadership Conference

Rev. Addie Wyatt, Vernon Park Church of God

Executive Director, Kim Bobo

* Former Board Officer

** Former Board President

## Interreligious Foundation for Community Organization (IFCO)

IFCO is a national ecumenical agency created in 1966 by several Protestant, Roman Catholic and Jewish organizations, to be an interreligious, interracial agency for support of community organization and education in pursuit of social justice. Through IFCO, national and regional religious bodies collaborate in development of social justice strategies and provide financial support and technical assistance to local, national and international social-justice projects.

IFCO serves as a bridge between the churches and communities and acts as a resource for ministers and congregations wishing to better understand and do more to advance the struggles of the poor and oppressed. IFCO conducts workshops for community organizers and uses its national and international network of organizers, clergy and other professionals to act in the interest of justice.

Churches, foundations and individual donors use IFCO services as a fiscal agent to make donations to community organizing projects. IFCO's global outreach includes humanitarian aid shipments through its Pastors for Peace program to Cuba, Haiti, Nicaragua, Honduras, and Chiapas, Mexico.

### Headquarters
402 W. 145th St., New York, NY 10031 Tel. (212)926-5757 Fax (212)926-5842

Media Contact, Dir. of Communications, Gail Walker

### Officers
Pres., Rev. Schuyler Rhodes

Vice President & Treasurer, Marilyn Clement

## The Kairos Institute, Inc.

The Kairos Institute provides quality support, consultation and in-depth educational opportunities to the professional, medical, mental health and religious communities and promotes assistance, consultation, education and care to families of exceptional children. Its clergy consultation service provides care to many denominations and clergy. "Career Path" offers candidate assessment for ordination and consultation for clergy in transition.

### Headquarters
107 Green Ave., Madison, NJ 07940 Tel. (973) 966-9099 Fax (973)377-8509

### Officers
Executive Director, Kathryn (Penny) Vennard Clark, MSW, LCSW

Clergy Services: The Rev. Dr. Dan Bottorff & The Rev. Dr. Richard Crocker

## The Liturgical Conference

The Liturgical Conference works to renew liturgy within the churches for the reunion of the Body of Christ for the life of the world.

As an ongoing movement with the ecumenical church, founded in 1944, it seeks to provide an ecumenical forum for articulating standards of liturgical excellence and for supporting persons who have a common interest and concern for the liturgical life and the liturgical arts of the church. It is the publisher of the journals Liturgy and Homily Service.

### Headquarters
P.O. Box 31, Evanston, IL 60201

### Officers
Pres., E. Byron Anderson

Vice Pres., Todd Johnson

Sec., Craig Mueller

Treas., Victor Cinson

## Lombard Mennonite Peace Center

The Lombard Mennonite Peace Center (LMPC) is a nonprofit organization with the mission "to proclaim Christ's good news, the gospel of peace and justice—and to be active in the sacred ministry of reconciliation." With an emphasis on equipping clergy and churches to function in healthy ways, LMPC offers training in conflict transformation and in a family systems approach to church leaders' management of themselves and their congregations.

One- and two-day educational workshops and a five-day "Mediation Skills Training Institute for Church Leaders" are offered throughout the U.S. Ongoing clergy clinics provide church leaders with regular opportunities to reflect on their own functioning. LMPC also provides educational events, consultation and mediation services for congregations and judicatories of all denominations, as well as consultation for individual clergy.

Founded in 1983 as a ministry of a local congregation, LMPC became an independent, 501(c)3 corporation in 1997.

**Headquarters**

101 W. 22nd St., Suite 206, Lombard, IL 60148
Tel. (630)627-0507 Fax (630)627-0519,
Email: Admin@LMPeaceCenter.org, Website: www. LMPeaceCenter.org

**Officers**

Exec. Dir., Richard G. Blackburn

## The Lord's Day Alliance of the United States

The Lord's Day Alliance of the United States, founded in 1888 in Washington, D.C., is the only national organization whose sole purpose is the preservation and cultivation of Sunday, the Lord's Day, as a day of rest and worship. The Alliance also seeks to safeguard a Day of Common Rest for all people regardless of their faith. Its Board of Managers is composed of representatives from 25 denominations. It serves as an information bureau, publishes a magazine, *Sunday*, and furnishes speakers and a variety of materials such as pamphlets, videos, posters, radio spot announcements, cassettes, news releases, articles for magazines and television programs.

**Headquarters**

2930 Flowers Rd. S., Atlanta, GA 30341-5532
Tel. (770)936-5376 or (800)746-4422 x 376 Fax (770)936-5385, Email: tnorton@1dausa.org, Website: www.sundayonline.org
Media Contact, Exec. Dir. & Ed., Rev. Timothy A. Norton

**Officers**

Pres., Dr. Roger A. Kvam
Pres. Emeritus, Paul J. Craven
Senior Vice Pres., Wendell J. Schaal
Vice Pres., Brian W. Hanse, David C. McNair, Eugene J. Nicodemus, W. David Sapp, William B. Shea
Sec., Donald R. Pepper

Asst. Sec., Betty Jo Craft
Trea., E. Larry Eidson

## Lutheran World Relief

Lutheran World Relief (LWR) is an overseas development and relief agency based in Baltimore which responds quickly to natural and man-made disasters and supports more than 160 long-range development projects in countries throughout Africa, Asia, the Middle East and Latin America.

As its mission, Lutheran World Relief works with partners in 50 countries to help people grow food, improve health, strengthen communities, end conflict, build livelihoods, and recover from disasters.

**Headquarters**

700 Light Street, Baltimore, MD 21230-3850
Tel. (410)230-2700 Fax (410)230-2882

**Officers**

Pres., Kathryn F. Wolford

## The Mennonite Central Committee

The Mennonite Central Committee is the relief and service agency of North American Mennonite and Brethren in Christ Churches. Representatives from Mennonite and Brethren in Christ groups make up the MCC, which meets annually in June to review its program and to approve policies and budget. Founded in 1920, MCC administers and participates in programs of agricultural and economic development, education, health, self-help, relief, peace and disaster service. MCC has about 1000 workers serving in 55 countries in Africa, Asia, Europe, Middle East and South, Central and North America.

MCC has service programs in North America that focus both on urban and rural poverty areas. There are also North American programs focusing on such diverse matters as community conciliation, employment creation and criminal justice issues. These programs are administered by two national bodies—MCC U.S. and MCC Canada.

Contributions from North American Mennonite and Brethren in Christ churches provide the largest part of MCC's support. Other sources of financial support include the contributed earnings of volunteers, grants from private and government agencies and contributions from Mennonite churches abroad. The total income in FYE 2004, including material aid contributions, amounted to $69.4 million (U.S. dollars).

MCC tries to strengthen local communities by working in cooperation with local churches or other community groups. Many personnel are placed with other agencies, including missions. Programs are planned with sensitivity to locally felt needs.

37

**Headquarters**

21 S. 12th St., P.O. Box 500, Akron, PA 17501-0500 Tel. (717)859-1151 Fax (717)859-2171

Canadian Office, 134 Plaza Dr., Winnipeg, MB R3T 5K9 Tel. (204)261-6381 Fax (204)269-9875

Media Contact, Larry Guengerich, P.O. Box 500, Akron, PA 17501 Tel. (717)859-1151 Fax (717)859-2171

**Officers**

Exec. Directors., Intl., Ronald J.R. Mathies; Canada, Donald Peters; U.S.A., Rolando Santiago

## National Association of Ecumenical and Interreligious Staff

NAEIS is an association of professional staff in ecumenical and interreligious work. Founded as the Association of Council Secretaries in 1940, the Association was widened to include program staff in 1971, and renamed the National Association of Ecumenical Staff. It has included staff of any faith engaged in interreligious work since 1994. NAEIS provides means for personal and professional growth, and for mutual support, through national and regional conferences, a newsletter and exchange among its membership.

NAEIS was established to provide creative relationships among them and to encourage mutual support and personal and professional growth. This is accomplished through training programs, exchange and discussion of common concerns at conferences, and the publication of the *Corletter*, in collaboration with National Council of Churches Ecumenical Networks.

**Headquarters**

Janet Leng, Membership Officer, P.O. Box 7093, Tacoma, WA 98406-0093 Tel. (253)759-0142, Email: naeisjan@aol.com

**Officers**

Pres., 2005-2007: The Rev. Samuel Muyskens, Interfaith Ministers–Wichita, 820 North Market Street, Wichita, KS 67214-1157 Tel. (512)451-2062

Vice Pres., 2005-2007: Mr. Marcus White, Exec. Dir., Interfaith Conference of Greater Milwaukee, 1442 N. Farwell Ave., Ste 200, Milwaukee, WI 53202 Tel. (414)276-9050

Immediate Past Pres.: Barbara White, Social Services, Church of God in Christ, 3500 W. Mother Daniels' Way, Milwaukee, WI 53209 Tel. (414)466-1800 Email: uniquebarbara@hotmail.com

Sec., 2005-2007: The Rev. Dr. Clark Lobenstine, Exec. Dir., Interfaith Conference of Metropolitan Washington, 1426 Ninth St. NW, 2nd Floor, Washington, DC 20001-3330 Tel. (202)234-6300

Treas., 2005-2007: Ms. Lisa H. Mitchell, Grand Rapids Center for Ecumenism.

## The National Association of Evangelicals

The National Association of Evangelicals (NAE) is a voluntary fellowship of evangelical denominations, churches, organizations and individuals demonstrating unity in the body of Christ by standing for biblical truth, speaking with a representative voice, and serving the evangelical community through united action, cooperative ministry and strategic planning.

The association is comprised of approximately 45,000 congregations nationwide from 52 member denominations and fellowships, as well as several hundred independent churches. The membership of the association includes over 250 parachurch ministries and educational institutions. Through the cooperative ministry of these members, NAE directly and indirectly benefits over 30 million people. These ministries represent a broad range of theological traditions, but all subscribe to the distinctly evangelical NAE Statement of Faith. The association is a nationally recognized entity by the public sector with a reputation for integrity and effective service.

The cooperative ministries of the National Association of Evangelicals demonstrate the association's intentional desire to promote cooperation without compromise.

**Headquarters**

NAE-Washington, 701 G. St., SW, Washington, DC 20024 Tel. (202)789-1011 Fax (202)842-0392

Media Contact, Rev. Rich Cizik, Tel. (202)789-1011

**Officers**

Interim President, Rev. Leith Anderson

Vice President of Governmental Affairs, Rev. Rich Cizik

**MEMBER DENOMINATIONS**

Advent Christian General Conference
Assemblies of God
Association of Vineyard Churches
Baptist General Conference
The Brethren Church
Brethren in Christ Church
Christian & Missionary Alliance
Christ Community Church
Christian Church of North America
Christian Reformed Church in Noth America
Christian Union
Church of God, Cleveland, Tenn
Church of God, Mountain Assembly
Church of the Nazarene
United Brethren in Christ Church
Churches of Christ in Christian Union
Congregational Holiness Church
Conservative Baptist Assoc. of America
Conservative Congregational Christian Conf.
Conservative Lutheran Association
Elim Fellowship
Evangelical Church of North America

**U.S. COOPERATIVE ORGANIZATIONS**

Evangelical Congregational Church
Evangelical Free Church of America
Evangelical Friends Intl.-North America
Evangelical Mennonite Church
Evangelical Methodist Church
Evangelical Presbyterian Church
Evangelistic Missionary Fellowship
Fellowship of Evangelical Bible Churches
Fire-Baptized Holiness Church of God of the Americas
Free Methodist Church of North America
General Association of General Baptists
Intl. Church of the Foursquare Gospel
Intl. Pentecostal Church of Christ
Intl. Pentecostal Holiness Church
Mennonite Brethren Churches, U.S.A.
Missionary Church, Inc.
Open Bible Standard Churches
Pentecostal Church of God
Pentecostal Free Will Baptist Church
Presbyterian Church in America
Primitive Methodist Church, U.S.A.
Reformed Episcopal Church
Reformed Presbyterian Church of N.A.
Salvation Army
Regional Synod of Mid-America (Reformed Church in America)
Wesleyan Church
Worldwide Church of God

## National Bible Association

The National Bible Association is an autonomous, interfaith organization of lay people who advocate regular Bible reading and sponsors National Bible Week (Thanksgiving week) each November. Program activities include public service advertising, distribution of nonsectarian literature and thousands of local Bible Week observances by secular and religious organizations. The Association also urges constitutionally acceptable use of the Bible in public school classrooms, i.e. the study of the Bible in literature. All support comes from individuals, corporations and foundations.

Founded in 1940 by a group of business and professional people, the Association offers daily Bible readings in several English and Spanish translations on its website and has the IRS non-profit status of a 501(c)(3) educational association.

### Headquarters
1865 Broadway, New York, NY 10023 Tel. (212)408-1390 Fax (212)408-1448
Media Contact, Pres., Thomas R. May

### Officers
Cpsn., Philip J. Clements
Vice Cpsns.; Robert Cavalero; John W. Pugsley; John M. Templeton, Jr., M.D.
Pres., Thomas R. May
Treas., Paul Werner
Sec., J. Marshall Gage

## The National Conference for Community and Justice

The National Conference for Community and Justice, founded in 1927 as the National Conference of Christians and Jews, is a human relations organization dedicated to fighting bias, bigotry and racism in America. The NCCJ promotes understanding and respect among all races, religions and cultures through advocacy, conflict resolution and education.

Programmatic strategies include interfaith and interracial dialogue, youth leadership workshops, workplace training, human relations research, and the building of community coalitions. NCCJ has 65 regional offices staffed by approximately 350 people. Nearly 200 members comprise the National Board of Advisors and members from that group form the 27-member National Board of Directors. Each regional office has its own Regional Board of Directors with a total of about 2,800. The National Board of Advisors meets once annually, the National Board of Directors at least three times annually.

### Headquarters
328 Flatbush Ave., Brooklyn, NY 11217 Tel. (718)783-0044 Fax (718)783-4143
Media Contact, Dir. of Communications, Diane Powers

### Officers
Pres. & CEO, Sanford Cloud, Jr.

## National Conference on Ministry to the Armed Forces

The Conference is an incorporated civilian agency. Representation in the Conference with all privileges of the same is open to all endorsing or certifying agencies or groups authorized to provide chaplains for any branch of the Armed Forces.

The purpose of this organization is to provide a means of dialogue to discuss concerns and objectives and, when agreed upon, to take action with the appropriate authority to support the spiritual ministry to and the moral welfare of Armed Forces personnel.

### Headquarters
4141 N. Henderson Rd., Ste. 13, Arlington, VA 22203 Tel. (703)276-7905 Fax (703)276-7906
Media Contact, Jack Williamson

### Officers
Chpsn., David Peterson
Chpsn.-elect, Robert Jemerson
Sec., Lemuel Boyles
Treas., John Murdoch

STAFF
Coord., Jack Williamson
Admn. Asst., Maureen Francis

U.S. COOPERATIVE ORGANIZATIONS

39

## National Council of the Churches of Christ in the U.S.A.

The National Council of the Churches of Christ in the U.S.A. is the preeminent expression in the United States of the movement toward Christian unity. The NCC's 35 member communions, including Protestant, Orthodox and Anglican church bodies, work together on a wide range of activities that further Christian unity, that witness to the faith, that promote peace and justice and that serve people throughout the world. Over 45 million U.S. Christians belong to churches that hold Council membership. The Council was formed in 1950 in Cleveland, Ohio, by the action of representatives of the member churches and by the merger of 12 previously existing ecumenical agencies, each of which had a different program focus. The roots of some of these agencies go back to the nineteenth century.

### Headquarters

475 Riverside Dr., New York, NY 10115, Tel. (212)870-2141

Media Contact, Director of Media Relations, The Rev. Daniel Webster, Tel. (212)870-2252

### General Officers

Pres., The Rev. Michael Livingston

Gen. Sec.,The Rev. Dr. Robert W. Edgar

Pres. Elect, Bishop Vicken Aykazian

Immediate Past Pres., Bishop Thomas L. Hoyt, Jr.

Sec., vacant

Vice Pres., Ms. Betty Voskuil

Vice Pres. at Large, The Rev. Dr. Randall R. Lee

Vice Pres. at Large, The Rev. Dr. Thelma Chambers-Young

### THE GENERAL SECRETARIAT

General Secretary, The Rev. Dr. Robert W. Edgar, Tel. (212)870-2141 Fax (212)870-2817

Assist. to the Gen. Sec., Ms. Vicki Manning, Tel. (212)870-2025

### ADMINISTRATION AND FINANCE

Controller, Ms. Karen Wang, Tel. (212)870-3351

Assist. Dir. of Administration and Human Resources, Ms. Joan Gardner, Tel. (212)870-3112

### DEVELOPMENT

Dir. of Development, Mr. John A. Briscoe, Tel. (212)870-2923

Assist. Dir. of Development, Ms. Claire McCurdy, Tel. (212)870-2350

### RESEARCH AND PLANNING

Deputy Gen. Sec. for Research and Planning, The Rev. Dr. Eileen W. Lindner, Tel. (212)870-2333

Assoc. Dir. for Research and Planning, The Rev. Marcel A. Welty, Tel. (212)870-2379

### YEARBOOK OF AMERICAN & CANADIAN CHURCHES

Editor, The Rev. Dr. Eileen W. Lindner, Tel. (212)870-2031

Assoc. Ed. and Technical Coord., The Rev. Marcel A. Welty, Tel. (212)870-2379

Asst. Ed., Mr. Tenny Thomas, Tel. (212)870-2031 Fax (212)870-2817

Asst. to the Ed., Mr. Earl Davis, Tel. (212)870-2333

### WASHINGTON OFFICE

110 Maryland Ave. NE Washington, D.C. 20002, Tel. (202)544-2350 Fax (202)543-1297

Assoc. Gen. Sec. for Justice and Advocacy and Dir. Wash. Office, The Rev. Brenda Girton-Mitchell, Esq.

Assoc. Dir. for Justice and Advocacy, The Rev. Leslie C. Tune, Tel. (202)544-2350 Fax (202)543-1297.

### COMMUNICATION COMMISSION

Associate General Secretary for Communication, Mr. Wesley M. Pattillo, Tel. (212)870-2227 Fax (212)870-2030

Director of Media Relations, The Rev. Daniel Webster, Tel. (212)870-2252

Dir., Interpretation Resources, Mr. Philip E. Jenks, Tel. (212)870-2228

Coord. of Television Programming, Ms. Shirley W. Struchen, Tel. (212)870-2227

FaithfulAmerica.org Electronic Advocacy Program, Dir., Mr. Vince Isner, Tel. (202)544-2350

### EDUCATION AND LEADERSHIP MINISTRIES COMMISSION

Assoc. Gen. Sec. for Education and Leadership Ministries, The Rev. Garland Pierce, Tel. (212) 870-2267

### FAITH AND ORDER COMMISSION

Assoc. Gen. Sec. For Faith and Order, Dr. Ann K. Riggs, Tel. (202)544-2350

Post Doctoral Fellow, Dr. Keelan Downton, Tel. (202)481-6933

### INTERFAITH RELATIONS COMMISSION

Assoc. Gen. Sec. for Interfaith Relations, The Rev. Dr. Shanta D. Premawardhana, Tel. (212) 870-2560

### JUSTICE AND ADVOCACY COMMISSION

Assoc. Gen. Sec. for Justice and Advocacy, The Rev. Brenda Girton-Mitchell, Esq., Tel. (202) 481-6924

Assoc. Gen. Sec. for International Affairs and Peace, Dr. Tony Kireopoulos, Tel. (212)870-3422

Eco-Justice Programs, Dir., Ms. Cassandra Carmichael, Tel. (202)481-6928

Program Associate, Ms. Karen Galles, Tel. (202) 481-6943

Justice for Women, The Rev. Leslie C. Tune, Tel. (202)481-6927

Mobilization to Overcome Poverty, Coord., The Rev. Dr. Paul Sherry, Tel. (216)736-3710

### RELATED ORGANIZATIONS

Agricultural Missions, The Rev. Joseph D. Keesecker, Exec. Dir., Tel. (212)870-2554

Interfaith Center for Corporate Responsibility, Interim Exec. Dir., The Rev. Michael Hoolahan, Tel. (212)870-2295

Natl. Farm Worker Ministry, Exec. Dir., Ms. Virginia Nesmith, 438 N. Skinner Blvd., St. Louis, MO 63130, Tel. (314)726-6470

### CHURCH WORLD SERVICE AND WITNESS

Chair, Betty Voskuil

First Vice Pres., Jennifer Riggs

Second Vice Pres., Deborah Bass

Treasurer, John Paterakis

Secretary, George Flowers

Immediate Past Chair, Patrick Mauney

CEO and Exec. Dir., The Rev. John L. McCullough, Tel. (212)870-2175

Deputy Dir., Operations and CFO, Ms. Joanne Rendall, Tel. (574)264-3102 x 332

Deputy Dir., Programs, Mr. Donald (Rick) Augsburger, Tel. (212)870-2798

Chief Development Officer, vacant, Tel. (574) 264-3102 x 470

Dir., Human Resources, Bernard Kirchhoff, Tel. (574)264-3102 x 346

Dir., Mission Relationships & Witness Program, Mr. David Weaver, Tel. (212)870-2818

Dir., Education & Advocacy for International Justice & Human Rights, Ms. Rajyashri Waghray, Tel. (212)870-2497

Dir., Social and Economic Development, Mr. Chris Falco, Tel. (212)870-2372

Dir., Emergency Response, Ms. Donna Derr, Tel. (212)870-3154

Dir., Immigration & Refugee Program, The Rev. Joseph Roberson, Tel. (212)870-2178

Dir., Marketing and Communications, Ann Walle, Tel. (212)870-2654

### CONSTITUENT BODIES
(with membership dates)

African Methodist Episcopal Church (1950)

African Methodist Episcopal Zion Church (1950)

The Alliance of Baptists in the U.S.A. (2000)

American Baptist Churches in the U.S.A. (1950)

Armenian Apostolic Church, Diocese of the (1957)

Christian Church (Disciples of Christ) (1950)

Christian Methodist Episcopal Church (1950)

Church of the Brethren (1950)

Coptic Orthodox Church (1978)

The Episcopal Church (1950)

Evangelical Lutheran Church in America (1950)

Friends United Meeting (1950)

Greek Orthodox Archdiocese of America (1952)

Hungarian Reformed Church in America (1957)

Intl. Council of Community Churches (1977)

Korean Presbyterian Church in America, Gen. Assembly of the (1986)

Malankara Orthodox Syrian Church, Diocese of America (1998)

Mar Thoma Church (1997)

Moravian Church in America, Northern Province, Southern Province (1950)

National Baptist Convention of America, Inc. (1950)

National Baptist Convention, U.S.A., Inc. (1950)

National Missionary Baptist Convention of America (1995)

Orthodox Church in America (1950)

Philadelphia Yearly Meeting of the Religious Society of Friends (1950)

Polish Natl. Catholic Church of America (1957)

Presbyterian Church (U.S.A.) (1950)

Progressive Natl. Baptist Convention, Inc. (1966)

Reformed Church in America (1950)

Russian Orthodox Church in the U.S.A., Patriarchal Parishes of the (1966)

Serbian Orthodox Church in the U.S.A. & Canada (1957)

The Swedenborgian Church (1966)

Syrian (Syriac) Orthodox Church of Antioch (Archdiocese of the U.S. and Canada) (1960)

Ukrainian Orthodox Church of the U.S.A.(1950)

United Church of Christ (1950)

The United Methodist Church (1950)

## National Institute of Business and Industrial Chaplains

NIBIC is the professional organization for workplace chaplains that includes members from a wide variety of faith groups and work settings, including corporations, manufacturing plants, air and sea ports, labor unions and pastoral counseling centers. NIBIC has six membership categories, including Certified, Clinical, Professional, Affiliates and Organizational.

NIBIC works to establish professional standards for education and practice; promotes and conducts training programs; provides mentoring, networking and chaplaincy information; encourages research and public information dissemination; communicates with business leaders and conducts professional meetings. NIBIC publishes a quarterly newsletter and co-sponsors *The Journal of Pastoral Care and Counseling*. A public membership meeting and training conference is held annually. NIBIC provide certification for qualified clinical members.

### Headquarters

1900 St. James Place, Suite 880, Houston, TX 77056 Tel. (713)266-2456 Fax (713)266-0845

Media Contact, Rev. Diana C. Dale, 1900 St. James Place, Suite 880 Houston, TX 77056 Tel. (713)266-2456 Fax (713)266-0845

### Officers

Executive Dir., Rev. Diana C. Dale, D.Min.

41

President, Rev. Robert L. Lewis, Jr., STM
Vice Pres., Rev. Dr. Juliette Jones
Treas., Rev. Gregory Edwards
Board Member, Rev. Timothy Bancroft, D.Min.

## National Interfaith Cable Coalition, Inc. (NICC)

The National Interfaith Cable Coalition, Inc. (NICC) was formed as a not-for-profit 501(c)3 corporation, in December 1987, and is currently comprised of more than 40 faith groups and organizations from the Jewish and Christian traditions.

In September 1988, NICC launched a religious cable network called VISN (Vision Interfaith Satellite Network), later known as the Odyssey Network. Now known as the Hallmark Channel, it is owned and operated by Crown Media Holdings, Inc., in which NICC is a strategic investor. NICC provides regular and prime-time special programming on the network.

In 2000, NICC adopted Faith & Values Media as its service mark and expanded its mission to include a significant Web presence, www.FaithStreams.com, which features streaming video and video-on-demand service.

### Headquarters

74 Trinity Place, Ste. 1550, New York, NY 10006 Tel. (212)406-4121 Fax (212)406-4105
Media Contact, Christine Luzano

### Officers

Chair, Dr. Daniel Paul Matthews
Vice Chair, Elder Ralph Hardy Jr., Esq.
Secretary, Rabbi Daniel Freelander
Treasurer, Betty Elam

### Staff

President and CEO, Edward J. Murray
Exec. Vice President, Beverly Judge

## National Interfaith Coalition on Aging

The National Interfaith Coalition on Aging (NICA), a constituent unit of the National Council on Aging, is composed of Protestant, Roman Catholic, Jewish and Orthodox national and regional organizations and individuals concerned about the needs of older people and the religious community's response to problems facing the aging population in the United States. NICA was organized in 1972 to address spiritual concerns of older adults through religious-sector action.

Mission Statement—The National Interfaith Coalition on Aging (NICA), affiliated with the National Council on the Aging (NCOA), is a diverse network of religious and other related organizations and individual members which promotes the spiritual well being of older adults and the preparation of persons of all ages for the spiritual tasks of aging. NICA serves as a catalyst for new and effective research, networking opportunities, resource development, service provision, and dissemination of information.

### Headquarters

c/o NCOA, 1910 L Street, NW, 4th Floor, Washington, DC 20036 Tel. (202)479-6655 Fax (202)479-0735
Media Contact, Rita Chow, Ed.D.

### Officers

Chpsn., Rev. Ronald Field
Chpsn.-Elect, Beth Schwartz
Past Chpsn., Jane Stenson
Sec., Donald R. Koepke
Dir., Dr. Rita K. Chow

## National Religious Broadcasters

National Religious Broadcasters is an association of Christian communicators, 1,500 organizations which produce religious programs for radio and television and other forms of electronic mass media or operate stations carrying predominately religious programs. NRB member organizations are responsible for more than 75 percent of all religious radio and television in the United States, reaching an average weekly audience of millions by radio, television, and other broadcast media.

Dedicated to the communication of the gospel, NRB was founded in 1944 to safeguard free and complete access to the broadcast media. By encouraging the development of Christian programs and stations, NRB helps make it possible for millions to hear the good news of Jesus Christ through the electronic media.

### Headquarters

9510 Technology Drive, Manassas, VA 20110. Tel. (703)330-7000 Fax (703)330-7100
Media Contact, Pres., Dr. Frank Wright

### Officers

Chmn., Ron. L. Harris
1st Vice Chmn., Janet Parshall
2nd Vice Chair, John Fuller
Sec., Richard Bott
Treas., Roger Kemp

## National Woman's Christian Temperance Union

The National WCTU is a not-for-profit, non-partisan, interdenominational organization dedicated to the education of our nation's citizens, especially children and teens, on the harmful effects of alcoholic beverages, other drugs and tobacco on the human body and the society in which we live. The WCTU believes in a strong family unit and, through legislation, education and prayer, works to strengthen the home and family.

WCTU, which began in 1874 with the motto, "For God and Home and Every Land," is organized in 58 countries.

### Headquarters

1730 Chicago Ave., Evanston, IL 60201 Tel. (708)864-1396

Media Contact, Sarah F. Ward, Tel. (765)345-7600

**Officers**

Pres., Sarah F. Ward, 33 N. Franklin, Knightstown, IN 46148 Email: sarah@wctu.org
Vice Pres., Rita Wert, 2250 Creek Hill Rd., Lancaster, PA 17601
Promotion Dir., Nancy Zabel, 1730 Chicago Ave., Evanston, IL 60201-4585
Treas., Faye Pohl, P.O. Box 739, Meade, KS 67864
Rec. Sec., Dorothy Russell, 18900 Nestueca Dr., Cloverdale, OR 97112

MEMBER ORGANIZATIONS

Loyal Temperance Legion (LTL), for boys and girls ages 6-12
Youth Temperance Council (YTC), for teens through college age

## North American Baptist Fellowship

Organized in 1964, the North American Baptist Fellowship is a voluntary organization of Baptist Conventions in Canada and the United States, functioning as a regional body within the Baptist World Alliance. Its objectives are, (a) to promote fellowship and cooperation among Baptists in North America and (b) to further the aims and objectives of the Baptist World Alliance so far as these affect the life of the Baptist churches in North America. Its membership, however, is not identical with the North American membership of the Baptist World Alliance. Church membership of the Fellowship bodies is more than 28 million.

The NABF assembles representatives of the member bodies once a year for exchange of information and views in such fields as evangelism and education, missions, stewardship promotion, lay activities and theological education. It conducts occasional consultations for denominational leaders on such subjects as church extension. It encourages cooperation at the city and county level where churches of more than one member group are located.

**Headquarters**

P.O. Box 6412, Falls Church, VA 22040
Media Contact, Dr. Alan Stanford, Gen. Sec., Tel. (703)655-9696

**Officers**

Pres., Dr. David Emmanuel Goatley, 300 I Street, NE, Suite 104, Washington D.C. 20002
Vice Pres., Dr. Derrick Harkins, 4606 16th St. NW, Washington, DC 20011
Vice Pres., Mrs. Bertha Williams, 13520 Corby Rd., Cleveland, OH 44120
Vice Pres., Dr. Ken Belous, 414-195, The West Mall, Etobicoke, ON M9C5K1, Canada
Vice Pres., Dr. Don Sewell, 333 N. Washington St., Dallas, TX 75246-1798

MEMBER BODIES

American Baptist Churches in the U.S.A.
Baptist General Conference
Canadian Baptist Federation
General Association of General Baptists
National Baptist Convention of America
National Baptist Convention, U.S.A., Inc.
Progressive National Baptist Convention, Inc.
Seventh Day Baptist General Conference
North American Baptist Conference
Southern Baptist Convention

## Oikocredit-Ecumenical Development Cooperative Society

Based in the Netherlands, EDCS is often called "the churches' bank for the poor." EDCS borrows funds from churches, religious communities and concerned individuals and re-lends the funds to enterprises operated by low-income communities. Launched in 1975 through an initiative of the World Council of Churches, EDCS is organized as a cooperative of religious institutions and is governed by annual membership meetings and an elected board of religious leaders and development and financial professionals.

An international network of 15 EDCS Regional Managers is responsible for lending funds to cooperative enterprises and microcredit institutions. At the present time over $260 million is at work in coffee shops, fishing enterprises, handicraft production, truck farming, and many other commercial ventures owned and operated by poor people.

EDCS is represented in the United States by the Ecumenical Development Corporation-U.S.A. (EDC-U.S.A.), a 501(c)3 non-profit corporation. American individuals and congregations can invest in EDCS by purchasing one-, three-, and five-year notes paying 0-2% interest that are issued by EDC-U.S.A..

**U.S. Headquarters**

P.O. Box 11000, Washington, DC 20008, Tel. (202)265-0607 Fax (202)265-7029, Email: office.us@oikocredit.org, Website: www.oiko credit. org
Media Contact, Regional Manager for North America, Rev. Terry Provance

**Officers, EDCS-U.S.A.**

Exec. Dir., Rev. Terry Provance
Chair, John Paarlberg
Treas., Richard Gist

## Parish Resource Center, Inc.

Parish Resource Center, Inc. promotes, establishes, nurtures and accredits local Affiliate Parish Resource Centers. Affiliate centers educate, equip and strengthen subscribing congregations of all faiths by providing professional consultants, resource materials and workshops. The Parish Resource Center was founded in 1976. In 2006, there were four free-standing affiliates located in Lancaster, Pa.; Long Island, N.Y.;

43

Denver, Co.; and New York City. These centers serve congregations from 49 faith traditions.

### Headquarters
633 Community Way, Lancaster, PA 17603 Tel. (717)299-2223 Fax (717)299-7229
Media Contact, Pres., Dr. D. Douglas Whiting

### Officers
Chair, Dr. Robert D. Webber
Vice Chair, Rev. Sidney Lovett
Sec./Treas., David P. Harrison
Pres., Dr. D. Douglas Whiting

## Pentecostal-Charismatic Churches of North America

The Pentecostal-Charismatic Churches of North America (PCCNA) was organized October 19, 1994, in Memphis Tenn. This organizational meeting came the day after the Pentecostal Fellowship of North America (PFNA) voted itself out of existence in order to make way for the new fellowship.

The PFNA had been formed in October 1948 in Des Moines, Iowa. It was composed of white-led Pentecostal denominations. The move to develop a multiracial fellowship began when the PFNA Board of Administration initiated a series of discussions with African-American Pentecostal leaders. The first meeting was held July 10-11, 1992, in Dallas, Tex.. A second meeting convened in Phoenix, Ariz., January 4-5, 1993. On January 10-11, 1994, 20 representatives from each of the two groups met in Memphis to make final plans for a Dialogue which was held in Memphis, October 1994.

This racial reconciliation meeting has been called "The Memphis Miracle." During this meeting the PFNA was disbanded, and the PCCNA was organized. The new organization quickly adopted the "Racial Reconciliation Manifesto." Subsequent meetings were held in Memphis (1996), Washington (1997), Tulsa, (1998), and Hampton, Va. (1999).

In an effort to further increase the spirit of reconciliation, the PCCNA meeting of 2000 was held during the North American Renewal Service committee (NARSC) Conference in St. Louis, Mo.. Furthermore, the PCCNA acted as host for the 19th Pentecostal World Conference held in Los Angeles, Calif., May 2001.

### Headquarters
1445 N. Boonville Ave., Springfield, MO 65802 Tel. (417)862-2781 x 3010 Fax (417)683-6614 Email: PCCNA@ag.org
Media Contact, Dr. Charles Crabtree

### PCCNA EXECUTIVE BOARD
Chairperson, Dr. Charles T. Crabtree, General Council of the Assemblies of God, 1445 N. Boonville Ave., Springfield, MO 65802 Tel. (417)862-2781 x 3010 Fax (417)683-6614, Email: PCCNA@ag.org

Co-Chairperson, Bishop Jerry Macklin, Church of God in Christ, 1027 W. Tennyson Rd, Hayward, CA 94544 Tel. (510)783-9377 Fax (510)783-8673, Email: PastorJWM@aol.com
Secretary, Dr. R. Lamar Vest, Church of God, P.O. Box 2430, Cleveland, TN 37320-2430, Tel. (423)478-7308 Fax (423)478-7334
Treasurer, Bishop Randy Howard, Church of God of Prophecy, P.O. Box 2910, Cleveland, TN 37320-2910 Tel. (423)559-5203 Fax (423)472-5037, Email: wmcogop@aol.com

EXECUTIVE COMMITTEE MEMBERS-AT-LARGE
Dr. Ron Carpenter, International Pentecostal Holiness Church, P.O. Box 12690, Oklahoma City, OK 73157
Rev. Daniel de Leon, Templo Calvario, 261 W. 5th St, Santa Ana, CA 92703
Rev. Jeff Farmer, Open Bible Churches, 2020 Bell Ave, Des Moines, IA 50315
Rev. Art Gray, International Church of the Foursquare Gospel, 1910 W. Sunset Blvd; Ste 200, Los Angeles, CA 90026
Bishop Clyde Hughes, International Pentecostal Church of Christ, P.O. Box 439, London, OH 43130
Dr. William Morrow, Pentecostal Assemblies of Canada, 2459 Milltower Ct., Mississauga, ON L5N 5Z6
Bishop Elijah Williams, The United Holy Church of America, 901 Briarwood St., Reidsville, NC 27320

## Project Equality, Inc.

Project Equality is a national, non-profit, interfaith program for affirmative action and equal employment opportunity. Through a Buyer's Guide that is provided to sponsoring organizations and individuals, Project Equality serves as a registry for suppliers of goods and services who commit to equal employment practices. This allows members and friends to economically support those who practice equality and justice with their employees. Project Equality also provides consultation and training for workplace diversity, does EEO audits, and is a resource for Human Resource practices. Project Equality is a leader in creating inclusive and just communities.

### Headquarters
7132 Main St., Kansas City, MO 64114-1406 Tel. (816)361-9222 Fax (816)361-8997

### Officers
Board Chair, Salvador Mendoza
Interim Executive Director, Cathleen D. Cackler-Veazey, Ph.D.

SPONSORS-ENDORSING ORGANIZATIONS
American Baptist Churches in the U.S.A.
American Friends Service Committee
American Jewish Committee
Assoc. Of Junior Leagues, Intl.

Central Conference of American Rabbis
Church of the Brethren
The Episcopal Church
Evangelical Lutheran Church in America
National Council of Churches of Christ in the U.S.A.
National Education Association
Presbyterian Church (U.S.A.)
Reorganized Church of Jesus Christ of Latter-day Saints
The United Methodist Church
Unitarian Universalist Association
United Church of Christ
United Methodist Assoc. of Health & Welfare Ministries
YWCA of the U.S.A.

## Religion In American Life, Inc.

Religion In American Life (RIAL) is a unique cooperative program of some 50 major national religious groups (Catholic, Eastern Orthodox, Jewish, Protestant, Muslim, etc.). It provides services for denominationally-supported, congregation-based outreach and growth projects such as the current Invite a Friend program. These projects are promoted through national advertising campaigns reaching the American public by the use of all media. The ad campaigns are produced by a volunteer agency with production-distribution and administration costs funded by denominations and business groups, as well as by individuals.

Since 1949, RIAL ad campaign projects have been among the much coveted major campaigns of The Advertising Council. This results in as much as $35 million worth of time and space in a single year, contributed by media as a public service. Through RIAL, religious groups demonstrate respect for other traditions and the value of religious freedom. The RIAL program also includes seminars and symposia, research and leadership awards and produces a weekly syndicated radio broadcast, "SpiriTalk".

### Headquarters
250 E 87th St., Suite 12F, New York, NY 10128-3116 Tel. (203)355-1220 Fax (203)355-1221
Media Contact, Exec. Admin., Martha Mesiti Tel. (203)355-1220

#### EXECUTIVE COMMITTEE
Natl. Chpsn., Thomas S. Johnson, Chairman & CEO, Greenpoint Bank, NY
Chpsn. of Bd., Rev. Dr. Gordon Sommers
Vice Chpsns., Bishop Khajag Barsamian, Primate (Armenian Church of America); Most Rev. William Cardinal Keeler, (Archbishop of Baltimore); Rabbi Ronald B. Sobel, (Cong. Emanu-El of the City of N.Y.)
Sec.,Timothy A. Hultquist (Morgan Stanley Dean Witter)
Treas., Robertson H. Bennett (Smith Barney)

#### Staff
Pres. & CEO, Robert B. Lennick, Rabbi, D.Min.

Exec. Admin., Martha Mesiti

## The Religion Communicators Council, Inc.

RCC is an interfaith, interdisciplinary association of professional communicators who work for religious groups and causes. It was founded in 1929 and is the oldest non-profit professional public relations/communications organization in the world. RCC's more than 600 members include those who work in communications and related fields for church-related institutions, denominational agencies, non-and interdenominational organizations, and communications firms that primarily serve religious organizations.

Members represent a wide range of faiths, including Presbyterian, Baptist, United Methodist, Lutheran, Episcopalian, Mennonite, Roman Catholic, Seventh-day Adventist, Jewish, Salvation Army, Brethren, Bahá'í, Disciples, Muslim, Latter-Day Saints and others.

On the national level, RCC sponsors an annual three-day convention, and has published seven editions of a *Religious Public Relations Handbook* for churches and church organizations, and a videostrip, *The Church at Jackrabbit Junction*. Members receive a quarterly newsletter (Counselor). There are 13 regional chapters.

RCC administers the annual Wilbur Awards competition to recognize high quality coverage of religious values and issues in the public media. Wilbur winners include producers, reporters, editors and broadcasters nationwide. To recognize communications excellence within church communities, RCC also sponsors the annual DeRose-Hinkhouse Awards for its own members.

In 1970, 1980, 1990, 2000, and in planning from April 7–10, 2010 (www.rccongres2010. org). RCC initiated a global Religious Communications Congress bringing together thousands of persons from western, eastern and third-world nations who are involved in communicating religious faith.

### Headquarters
475 Riverside Dr., Rm. 1355, New York, NY 10115 Tel. (212)870-2985 Fax (212) 870-2171
Media Contact, Exec. Dir., Shirley Whipple Struchen, Tel. (212)870-2402, Email: SSTRUCHEN@RCN.COM, Website: www.religioncommunicators.org

#### Officers
President., Philip Poole, Exec. Dir., University Communications, Samford Univ., 800 Lakeshore Dr., Birmingham, AL 35229 Tel. (205)726-2823 Fax (205)726-4044 Email: ppoole@samford.edu
Vice Pres., Ellen W. Price, Asst. Dir., Com-munications, U.S. Bahai National Center, 1233 Central St., Evanston, IL 60201, Tel. (847) 733-3559 Fax (847)733-3430, Email: Eprice @usbwc.org

Sec., Barry Creech, Coordinator, Information & Planning, Presbyterian Church (U.S.A.), 100 Witherspoon St., #5430, Louisville, 40202-1396 Tel. (502)569-5127 Fax (502)569-8099 Email: barry.creech@pcusa.org

Treas., Dan Gangler, Director of Communications, Indiana Area UMC, 1100 West 42nd St., #210 Indianapolis, IN 46208 Tel. (317)924-1321 x 18 Fax (317)924-4859 Email: dgangler @inareaumc.org

## Religion News Service

Religion News Service (RNS) has provided news and information to the media for over 70 years. Owned by Newhouse News Service, it is staffed by veteran jounalists who cover stories on all of the world religions as well as trends in ethics, morality and spirituality.

RNS provides a daily news service, a weekly news service, and photo and graphic services. The daily service is also available via the AP Data Features wire, or e-mail. The weekly report is available by wire or e-mail. RNS's Photos Service features stock images, news photography and related graphics. RNS also offers Religion Press Release Services, which distributes press releases and advisories to religion editors. RNS is syndicated in the United States by Universal Press Syndicate and in Canada by Canadian Press.

### Headquarters

1101 Connecticut Ave. NW, Ste. 350, Washington, DC 20036 Tel. (202)463-8777 Fax (202) 463-0033, Email: info@religionnews.com, Website: www.religionnews.com

### Officers

Editor, Kevin Eckstrom

## Religion Newswriters Association and Foundation

Founded in 1949, the RNA is a professional association of journalists who write and edit about religion in the general circulating news media. It sponsors annual contests, conferences, online tools and rreligion links. It also offers the Lilly Scholarships in Religion to journalists in the U.S. and Canada to take religion courses of their choice. Annual meetings are held in the fall.

Our Mission: to promote excellence in religion reporting in the news media.

Our Vision: RNA will achieve its mission by providing education and other resources for its members by raising awareness of the importance of religion coverage in the secular media.

### Headquarters

P.O. Box 2037, Westerville, OH 43086 Tel. (614) 891-9001 Fax (614) 891-9774, Email: mason @RNA.com, Website: www.RNA.org, www.religionlink.org

Media Contact, Exec. Dir., Debra Mason

## Religions for Peace-U.S.A., Inc.

Religions for Peace-U.S.A., formerly the United States Conference of Religions for Peace, began in the 1970's as a program area and chapter of the World Conference of Religions for Peace (now known simply as Religions for Peace), the world's largest representative interreligious organization. Today, the organization is separately incorporated and registered as an independent 501(c)(3) and focuses its mandate on U.S.-based issues, while retaining a strong link to the international work of the Religions for Peace. As the largest and most broadly based representative multi-religious forum in the United States, RFP-U.S.A. engages the religious leaders and experts in interreligious affairs and peace and justice of more than 50 religious traditions. By building on the spiritual, human, and institutional resources of these communities, RFP-U.S.A. establishes cooperative efforts among them to address shared challenges. Primary areas of concern for the organization include building interreligious relationships, creating mutual understanding amidst the country's increasing diversity, and advocating for the responsibility of the U.S. as a citizen of the global community, with particular regard to peace, human rights, and development.

### Headquarters

RFP-U.S.A., 777 United Nations Plaza, 9th Floor, New York, NY 10017 Tel. (212)338-9140 (212)983-0566

### Officers

Sec. Gen./Executive Dir., Rev. Bud Heckman, Email: bheckman@rfpusa.org

Moderator, The Very Rev. Leonid Kishkovsky

## Religious Conference Management Association, Inc.

The Religious Conference Management Association, Inc. (RCMA) is an interfaith, non-profit, professional organization of men and women who have responsibility for planning and/or managing meetings, seminars, conferences, conventions, assemblies, or other gatherings for religious organizations.

Founded in 1972, RCMA is dedicated to promoting the highest professional performance by its members and associate members through the mutual exchange of ideas, techniques and methods.

Today RCMA has nearly 3,400 members who plan over 17,000 conventions and meetings that annually attract 13.2 million attendees.

The association conducts an annual conference and exposition that provides a forum for its membership to gain increased knowledge in the arts and sciences of religious meeting planning and management.

RCMA publishes a bi-monthly magazine, *Religious Conference Manager*; a conference daily, RCMA Highlights; plus a monthly e-newsletter.

One RCA Dome, Ste. 120, Indianapolis, IN 46225 Tel. (317)632-1888 Fax (317)632-7909, Website: www.RCMAWEB.org
Media Contact, Exec. Dir., Dr. DeWayne S. Woodring

**Officers**
Pres., Rev. Thomas M. Jackson, United Pentecostal Church International, 8855 Dunn Rd., Hazelwood, MO 63042
Vice Pres., Ms. Marcia Bullock, Jamaica Tourist Board, 5201 Blue Lagoon Dr., Ste. 670, Miami, FL 33126
Sec.-Treas., Dr. Melvin Worthington, Natl. Assoc. of Free Will Baptists, 4878 Ayden Golf Club Rd., Ayden, NC 28513
Exec. Dir., Dr. DeWayne S. Woodring

## The Seminary Consortium for Urban Pastoral Education (SCUPE)

Founded in 1976, SCUPE is an interdenominational agency committed to the development of individuals, congregations, and organizations for leadership in urban ministry. For individuals, we offer four accredited graduate-level academic programs, the semester- and/or summer-term Graduate Theological Urban Studies program for seminary students; an M.A. in Community Development degree developed in partnership with North Park University; Nurturing the Call, a year-long sequence of graduate courses in theology and ministry for urban pastors who have not previously attended seminary; and Center for African American Theological Studies, an Africentric 3-year M.Div program.

SCUPE also consults to other ministries and urban institutions, providing specially-designed training programs around issues including diversity, strategic planning, leadership development, and human resource mobilization. We operate an urban ministry resource center and publish the *Resource Review*, as well as other occasional materials, as a service to the urban church. Every two years, SCUPE also organizes the Congress on Urban Ministry as a training and networking event for those in urban ministry.

**Headquarters**
200 N. Michigan Ave., Suite 502, Chicago, IL 60601 Tel. (312)726-1200 Fax (312)726-0425
Media Contact, President, Dr. David Frenchak; Director of Development, Nancy Renick

**Officers**
Chair, Rev. Donald Sharp
Vice Chair, Ms. Cheryl Hammock
Treasurer, Mr. Lamont Change
Secretary, Dr. Bill VanWyngaarden

**Lead Program Staff**
President, Dr. David Frenchak
Co-Directors, M.A. in Community Development, Rev. Carol Ann McGibbon & Dr. Arthur Lyons
Director, Graduate Theological Urban Studies, Glenn Martin Klaassen
Director, CAATS, Rev. Dernard Newell
Associate Director of Graduate Studies, Cynthia Milsap
Registrar, Dody Finch

## Transnational Association of Christian Colleges and Schools

Transnational Association of Christian Colleges and Schools (TRACS). TRACS was established in 1979 to promote the welfare, interests, and development of postsecondary institutions whose mission is characterized by a distinctly Christian purpose, as defined in our Foundational Standards. TRACS is a voluntary, non-profit, self-governing organization that provides accreditation to Christian postsecondary institutions offering certificates, diplomas, and/or degrees. TRACS is recognized by the United States Department of Education, the Council for Higher Education Accreditation, and the International Network for Quality Assurance Agencies in Higher Education as a national accrediting body for Christian institutions, colleges, universities, and seminaries. The geographic territory of TRACS currently consists of the United States and its territories.

**Headquarters**
P.O. Box 328, Forest, Virginia 24551 Tel. (434)525-9539 Fax (434)525-9538, Email: info@tracs.org, Website: www.tracs.org
Media Contact: Exec. Dir., Dr. Russell G. Fitzgerald

**Officers**
Accreditation Commission Chairman, Dr. Boyd C. Rist
Exec. Dir., Dr. Russell G. Fitzgerald
Assoc. Exec. Dir., Dr. Jeff McCann

## United Ministries in Higher Education

United Ministries in Higher Education is a cooperative effort to provide religious programs and services to those engaged in higher-education ministries.

**Headquarters**
7407 Steele Creek Rd., Charlotte, NC 28217 Tel. (704) 588-2182 Fax (704) 588-2182
Media Contact, Res. Sec., Linda Danby Freeman, Email: linda_freeman@msn.com

**Officers**
Treas., Dennis Landon, 11477 Olde Cabin Rd., Suite 310, St. Louis, MO 63141-7130
Personnel Service, Kathy Carson, 117 Alicia Circle Ct., Ballwin, MO 63021
Resource Center, Linda Danby Freeman

PARTICIPATING DENOMINATIONS
Christian Church (Disciples of Christ)
Presbyterian Church (U.S.A.)
United Church of Christ

## United Religions Initiative

The purpose of the United Religions Initiative is to promote enduring, daily interfaith cooperation, to end religiously motivated violence, and to create cultures of peace, justice, and healing for the earth and all living beings.

The United Religions initiative is a growing, global community of over 130 Cooperation Circles, involving thousands of people around the world. The URI is inspired by the leadership potential inherent in every individual, leadership that is discovered and deepened through dialogue with others when dreams are shared and cooperative destinies are realized. The individuals who make up the URI network are committed to interfaith peacebuilding, recognizing that for peace to prevail on earth, "peace must begin with me." They believe that by talking with others who come from different faiths, cultures or spiritual traditions all involved can begin to better understand their own beliefs and recognize their common bonds.

The URI seeks to create safe spaces throughout the world where these interfaith partnerships can be seeded, and the ideas and initiatives that they spark can be practically applied. With the mandate in the URI Charter that each Cooperation Circle represents at least three different faith traditions, the very act of coming together builds peace by creating interfaith cooperation among neighbors and within communities where it may never before have been possible. The Charter "Guidelines for Action" affirm the "essentially self-organizing nature" of the Cooperation Circles and empowers CC participants to "choose what they want to do" while providing guidance for community building. The Guidelines assure that all URI activities and actions demonstrate the following heartfelt considerations, (a) sharing the wisdom and cultures of different faith traditions; (b) nurturing cultures of healing and peace; (c) upholding human rights; (d) supporting the health of the entire earth; (e) integrating spirituality in issues of economic justice; and (f) providing grassroots support for all URI activities.

The initial vision for the United Religions Initiative began in 1993 with a dream by its founder, Bishop William Swing. He writes that it came with "a sudden realization that religions, together, have a vocation to be a force for good in the world." In just seven years, tens of thousands of people in more than sixty countries around the world have responded to this vision with a resounding, "Yes!" Their affirmations have taken on a myriad of forms. For example, during the 72 Hours Project at the turn of the millennium, over a million people in 40 countries participated in 200 projects for peace. Highlights included a 12-day interfaith pilgrimage across Pakistan and the celebration of 1 million-signature on a petition to ban handguns in Rio de Janeiro.

### Headquarters
P.O. Box 29242, San Francisco, CA 94129-0242
Tel. (415)561-2300 Fax (415)562-2313
Media Contact, Kristin Swenson

### Staff
Executive Director, Rev. Cn Charles P. Gibbs
Peacebuilding, Barbara H. Hartford, Sarah Talcott
Global Fundraising, Philanthropy, Jennifer Kirk, LaTonya Trotter
Membership and Organizational Development, Sally Mahe, Cory Robertson
Visions for Peace Among Religions Project, Nancy Nielsen
Annual Giving and Knowledge Management, Sarah Talcott
Financial Manager, Ray Signer

GLOBAL COUNCIL
President and Founding Trustee, Bishop William Swing
AFRICA
Malawi, Joyce N'goma
Uganda, Despina Namwembe
Mozambique, Sabapath Alagiah
ASIA
Pakistan, James Channan
Korea, Jinwol Lee
India, Mohinder Singh
EUROPE
Netherlands, Annie Imbens
United Kingdom, Deepak Naik
Germany, Karimah Stauch
LATIN AMERICA AND THE CARIBBEAN
Argentina, Rosalia Guiterrez
Mexico, Jonathan Rose
Chile, Gerado Gonzalez
MIDDLE EAST
Israel, George Khory
Israel, Yehuda Stolov
Egypt, Mohamed Mosaad
MULTI-REGIONAL/NON-GEOGRAPHIC
Yoland Trevino
Jack Lundin
Munirah Shahidi
NORTH AMERICA
United States of America, Don Frew
United States of America, Kay Lindhal
United States of America, Heng Sure
THE PACIFIC
New Zealand, George Armstrong
Philippines, Bonifacio Quirog
Philippines, Shakuntala Moorjani-Vaswani
TRANSITION ADVISORY COMMITTEE
Iftekhar Hai
Rita Semel
Bob Walter

## Vellore Christian Medical College Board (U.S.A.), Inc.

The Vellore Christian Medical College Board (U.S.A.) supports the wide range of programs at Christian Medical College (CMC), Vellore, Tamil Nadu, India, by securing contributions for its major capital equipment and construction goals; grants for program educational, research and health care programs; and funds to support scholarships for medical nursing and allied health students at Vellore and senior faculty study outside of India. The Board also facilitates opportunities for North Americans to volunteer at CMC and fosters working relationships between CMC and institutions in the U.S. Print, DVD and electronic materials about MC's 100-plus years as a leading medical college and hospital are available as part of the Board's public education program. A capital campaign to raise one million dollars toward a new campus is now underway.

### Headquarters

475 Riverside Dr., Rm. 243, New York, NY 10115 Tel. (212)870-2640 Fax (212)870-2173
Media Contact, President, Dr. Louis L. Knowles
Email: usaboard@vellorecmc.org

### Officers

Pres., Dr. Louis L. Knowles
Chair, Mrs. Edwina Scudder-Youth, 211 Blue Ridge Dr., Levittown, PA 19057
Vice Chair, Mr. Anish Mathai, 475 Riverside Dr., Rm. 243, New York, NY 10115
Sec., Dr. Alexander Kuruvila, 2063 Gainsborough Dr., Riverside, CA 92606
Treas., Mr. Richard L. Vreeland, 182 Ameren Way, Ballwin, MO 63021

## World Council of Churches, United States Office

The United States Conference of the World Council of Churches was formed in 1938 when the WCC itself was still in the "Process of Formation." Henry Smith Leiper, an American with many national and international connections, was given the title of "Associate General Secretary" of the WCC and asked to carry out WCC work in the U.S. After the World Council of Churches was officially born in 1948 in Amsterdam, Netherlands, Leiper raised millions of dollars for WCC programs.

Today the U.S. Conference of the WCC is composed of representatives of U.S. member churches of the worldwide body. The U.S. Office of the WCC works to develop relationships among the churches, advance the work of WCC and interpret the council in the United States.

### Headquarters

475 Riverside Dr., Rm. 1371, New York, NY 10115 Tel. (212)870-3260 Fax (212)870-2528

### Officers

WCC President from North America and Moderator: The Rev. Dr. Bernice Powell Jackson
Moderator, U.S. Conference for the WCC: The Very Rev. Leonid Kishkovsky, Orthodox Church in America
Vice Moderator: Bishop McKinley Young, African Methodist Episcopal Church
Vice Moderator and Treasurer: The Rev. Ashley Seaman, Presbyterian Church (U.S.A.)

### Staff

Program Executive for the U.S., Deborah DeWinter, Tel. (212)870-2522
Office Admn., Gloria Feliciano, (212)870-3260

## World Day of Prayer International Committee

World Day of Prayer is an ecumenical movement initiated and carried out by Christian women in 170 countries who conduct a common day of prayer on the first Friday of March to which all people are welcome. There is an annual theme for the worship service that has been prepared by women in a different country each year. For 2007 the women of Paraguay prepared a worship service on the theme, United Under God's Tent. The offering at the WDP is gathered by each WDP National or Regional Committee and given to help people who are in need.

### Headquarters

World Day of Prayer International Comm., 475 Riverside Dr., Rm. 729, New York, NY 10115 Tel. (212)870-3049 Fax (212)864-8648, Email: wdpic@worlddayofprayer.net
Media Contact, Exec. Dir., Eileen King

World Day of Prayer U.S.A., 475 Riverside Dr., Rm. 1626A, New York, NY 10115 Tel. (212) 870-2466 Fax (212)870-2456, Email: wdpusa@churchwomen.org, Website: www.wdpusa.org
Media Contact, Executive Coordinator (U.S.A.): Elizabeth Calvin

### Officers

Chairperson, Sylvia Lisk Vanhaverbeke
Treasurer, Karen Prudente
Africa, Suzie Bayiha II, Assah E. Mgonja
Asia, Junko Matsuura, Woranut Pantupong
Caribbean and North America, Waveney Benjamin; Annette Poitier
Europe, Inge Lise Lollike; Ewa Walter
Latin America, Elisabeth Delmonte, Ormara Nolla
Middle East, Laila Carmi; Nadia Menes
Pacific, Vaieli Fuiono Piita; Joanna S. Matagi-Vilitama
Member at Large for Orthodox Churches, Marija Ciceva-Aleksic

## World Methodist Council—North American Section

The World Methodist Council, one of the 30 or

49

so "Christian World Communions," shares a general tradition which is common to all Christians.

The world organization of Methodists and related United Churches is comprised of 76 churches with roots in the Methodist tradition. These churches found in 132 countries have a membership of more than 40 million.

The Council's North American Section, comprised of ten Methodist and United Church denominations, provides a regional focus for the Council in Canada, the United States and Mexico. The North American Section meets at the time of the quinquennial World Conference and Council, and separately as Section between world meetings. North American Churches related to the World Methodist Council have a membership of approximately 16 million and a church community of more than 30 million.

### Headquarters
P.O. Box 518, Lake Junaluska, NC 28745 Tel. (828)456-9432 Fax (828)456-9433
Media Contact, Gen. Sec., George H. Freeman

### Officers
General Sec., Dr. George H. Freeman

## World Vision
World Vision is a Christian relief and development organization dedicated to helping children and their communities worldwide reach their full potential by tackling the causes of poverty. Motivated by our faith in Jesus, we serve the poor as a demonstration of God's unconditional love for all people. World Vision works with communities in nearly 100 countries to develop long-term solutions that alleviate poverty, provides emergency assistance to children and families affected by natural disasters and civil conflict, and advocates for justice on behalf of the poor. World Vision U.S.—one of 52 national offices in the World Vision Partnership—serves in key United States metropolitan areas, providing intervention for challenged youth, tools that equip strong community leaders, and storehouses that provide essentials for living.

World Vision's Church Relations department facilitates chuch partnerships, connecting U.S. congregations with critical ministry among people in need locally and internationally. Church opportunities include partnerships with international projects, volunteer options through U.S. programs, and educational programs, including youth-oriented 30 Hour Famine and One Life Revolution, and child sponsorship.

### Headquarters
P.O. Box 9716, Federal Way, WA 98063-9716 Tel. (253)815-1000
Church Relations Vice President, Steve Haas, Tel. (253)815-2698
Media Contact, Dean Owen, Tel. (253)815-2158

### Officers
President, Richard Stearns

Senior Vice Presidents, Joan Mussa, Lawrence Probus, Julie Regnier, Atul Tandon, George Ward, Michael Veitenhans

## YMCA of the U.S.A.
The YMCA is one of the largest private voluntary organizations in the world, serving about 30 million people in more than 100 countries. In the United States, more than 2,000 local branches, units, camps and centers annually serve more than 14 million people of all ages, races and abilities. About half of those served are female. No one is turned away because of an inability to pay.

The Y teaches youngsters to swim, organizes youth basketball games, and offers adult aerobics. But the Y represents more than fitness—it works to strengthen families and help people develop values and behavior that are consistent with Christian principles.

The Y offers hundreds of programs including day camp for children, child care, exercise for people with disabilities, teen clubs, environmental programs, substance abuse prevention, family nights, job training, and many more programs from infant mortality prevention to overnight camping for seniors.

The kind of programs offered at a YMCA will vary; each is controlled by volunteer board members who make their own program, policy, and financial decisions based on the special needs of their community. In its own way, every Y works to build strong kids, strong families, and strong communities.

The YMCA was founded in London, England, in 1844 by George Williams and friends who lived and worked together as clerks. Their goal was to save other live-in clerks from the wicked life of the London streets. The first members were evangelical Protestants who prayed and studied the Bible as an alternative to vice. The Y has always been nonsectarian and today accepts those of all faiths at all levels of the organization.

### Headquarters
101 N. Wacker Dr., Chicago, IL 60606 Tel. (312) 977-0031 Fax (312)977-9063
Media Contact, Media Relations Manager, Arnie Collins

### Officers
Board Chairman., Daniel E. Casey
Exec. Dir., Niel Nicoll
(Int.) Public Relations Assoc., Arnold Collins

## YWCA of the U.S.A.
The YWCA of the U.S.A. is comprised of 313 affiliates in communities and on college campuses across the United States. It serves one million members and program participants. It seeks to empower women and girls to enable them, coming together across lines of age, race, religious belief, economic and occupational status to make a significant contribution to the elimination

of racism and the achievement of peace, justice, freedom and dignity for all people.

**Headquarters**

1015 18th St. Suite 1100, Washington, DC 20036. Tel. (202)467-0801 Fax (202)467-0801

Media Contact, Khristina Lew, Email: info@ywca.org

**Officers**

National Pres., Leticia Paez
Sec., Carol O. Markus
Chief Exec. Officer, Margaret Tyndall

## Youth for Christ—U.S.A.

Founded in 1944, as part of the body of Christ, our vision is to see every young person in every people group in every nation have the opportunity to make an informed decision to be a follower of Jesus Christ and become a part of a local church.

There are 220 locally controlled YFC programs serving in cities and metropolitan areas of the United States.

YFC's Campus Life Club program involves teens who attend approximately 58,236 high schools in the United States. YFC's staff now numbers approximately 1,000. In addition, nearly 10,000 part-time and volunteer staff supplement the full-time staff. Youth Guidance, a ministry for nonschool-oriented youth includes group homes, court referrals, institutional services and neighborhood ministries. The year-round conference and camping program involves approximately 200,000 young people each year. Other ministries include DC Ministries, World Outreach, Project Serve, and Teen Moms. Independent, indigenous YFC organizations also work in 127 countries overseas.

**Headquarters**

U.S. Headquarters, P.O. Box 228822, Denver, CO 80222 Tel. (303)843-9000 Fax (303)843-9002

Canadian Organization, 2540 - 5th Ave, NW, Calgary, AB T2N 0T

Media Contact, Pres., Dan Wolgemuth

**Officers**

United States, Pres., Dan Wolgemuth
Intl. Organization, Pres., David Wright
Canada, Natl. Dir., Barry Bowater

# 2. Canadian Cooperative Organizations, National

In most cases, the organizations listed here work on a national level and cooperate across denominational lines. Regional cooperative organizations in Canada are listed in Directory 8, "Canadian Regional and Local Ecumenical Bodies."

## Alcohol and Drug Concerns Inc.

Alcohol and Drug Concerns is a registered, non-profit, charitable organization that has a long association with the Christian Church. The organization's mission is to empower youth to make positive lifestyle choices relating to alcohol, tobacco, and other drugs.

The organization was granted a national charter in 1987, moving from an Ontario charter dating back to 1934. Among its services are Choices F.I.T. (Fostering Independent Thinking)—a substance abuse prevention resource for grade 4 to 8 teachers; an Institute on Addiction Studies; Making the Leap—a substance abuse prevention resource for grade 7 to 8 teachers created by high school students; Drug and Alcohol Game Show for grades 6 to 9—a classroom activity; education and awareness courses for clients of the Ontario Ministry of Corrections.

### Headquarters
4500 Sheppard Ave. E, Ste. 112, Toronto, ON M1S 3R6 Tel. (416)293-3400 Fax (416)293-1142
Media Contact, Robert Walsh, CEO

### Officers
Pres., Jean Desgagne, Toronto
Treas., Peter Varley, Toronto
Vice Pres., Nanci Harris, Toronto
Vice Pres., Valerie Petroff, Oak Ridges
Vice Pres., Heidi Stanley, Orillia
Past Pres., Larry Gillians, Napanee
CEO, Robert Walsh

## Canadian Bible Society

The Canadian Bible Society is a non-denominational and inter-confessional organization that exists to translate, publish, distribute and encourage the use of the Scriptures, without doctrinal note or comment. Bible Society work was begun in Canada in 1804 by the British and Foreign Bible Society. In 1906, the various auxiliaries of the British and Foreign Bible Society joined together to form the Canadian Bible Society. Today, the Canadian Bible Society has 16 district offices across Canada, a Scripture Translation Office in Kitchener, a French Services Office in Montreal, and a National Support Office in Toronto. Additionally, the Bermuda Bible Society is constituted as an Associate District of the Canadian Bible Society. The Society holds quarterly board meetings involving one elected representative from each of the districts and from the francophone sector. About 90% of the Society's revenue comes through the generosity of Canadian supporters in the form of donations, bequests and annuity income. Through the Canadian Bible Society's membership in the United States Societies' fellowship, over 67.5 million Bibles, Testaments and Portions were distributed globally in 2004. The complete Bible has been published in over 420 languages, with at least one book of the Bible available in 2,377 languages.

### Headquarters
C.B.S. National Support Office, 10 Carnforth Rd., Toronto, ON M4A 2S4 Tel. (416)757-4171 Fax (416)757-3376

### Officers
National Director, Rev. Phyllis M. Nesbitt, 10 Carnforth Rd., Toronto, ON M4A 2S4, Tel. (416)757-4171 Fax (416)757-1292, Email: pnesbitt @biblesociety.ca
Director of Fonance, Mr. Nesa Gulasekharam, 10 Carnforth Rd., Toronto, ON M4A 2S4, (416) 757-4171 Fax (416)757-3376, Email: ngulasekharam @biblesociety.ca
Director of Scripture Translation, Mr. Hart Wiens, Frederick Mall (2nd Floor), 385 Frederick Street, Kitchener, ON N2H 2P2, Tel. (519)741-8285 Fax (519)741-8357, Email: hwiens @biblesociety.ca
Directeur du Secteur francophone, Mr. Serge Rhéaume, 4050 avenue du Parc-Lafontaine, Montreal, QC H2L 3M8, Tel. (514)524-7873 Fax (514)524-6116, Email: srheaume@societe-biblique. ca
Director of Donor Support & Development, Mr. Erwin van Laar, 10 Carnforth Rd., Toronto, ON M4A 2S4, Tel. (416)757-4171 Fax (416) 757-3376, Email: evanlaar@biblesociety.ca
Production Manager, Ms. Nelly Safari, 10 Carnforth Rd., Toronto, ON M4A 2S4, Tel. (416)757-4171 Fax (416)757-3376, Email: nsafari @biblesociety.ca
Human Resources Manager/Volunteer Program Coordinator, Ms. Meggy Kwok, 10 Carnforth Rd., Toronto, ON M4A 2S4, Tel. (416)757-4171 Fax (416)757-3376, Email: mkwok @biblesociety.ca

## Canadian Centre for Ecumenism

The Centre has facilitated understanding and cooperation among believers of various Christian traditions and world religions since 1963. An active interdenominational Board of Directors meets annually.

*ECUMENISM*, a quarterly publication, develops central themes such as Rites of Passage, Sacred Space, Interfaith Marriages, Care of the Earth, etc. through contributions from writers of various churches and religions in addition to its regular ecumenical news summaries, book reviews, and resources.

A specialized library is open to the public for consultation in the areas of religion, dialogue, evangelism, ethics, spirituality, etc.

Conferences and sessions are offered on themes such as Ecumenism and Pastoral Work, Pluralism, World Religions, Prayer, and Unity.

### Headquarters

2065 Sherbrooke St. W. Montreal, QC H3H 1G6
Tel. (514)937-9176 Fax (514)937-4986
Email: ccocce@oecumenisme.ca
Website: www.oecumenisme.ca

### Officers

Media Contact, Bernice Baranowski
Exec. Dir., Dr. Stuart Brown
Assistant Director, Adèle Brodeur

## The Canadian Council of Churches

The Canadian Council of Churches was organized in 1944. Its basic purpose is to provide the churches with an agency for conference and consultation and for such common planning and common action as they desire to undertake. It encourages ecumenical understanding and action throughout Canada through local councils of churches. It also relates to the World Council of Churches and other agencies serving the worldwide ecumenical movement.

The Council has a Governing Board that meets semiannually and an Executive Committee. Program is administered through two commissions—Faith and Witness, Justice and Peace.

### Headquarters

47 Queen's Park Crescent East, Toronto, ON M5S 2C3 Tel. (416)972-9494 x 22 Fax (416) 927-0405
Media Contact, Rev. Dr. Karen Hamilton
Email: Hamilton@ccc-cce.ca
Website: www.ccc-cce.ca

### Officers

President, Professor Richard Schneider, 47 Queen's Park Crescent East, Toronto ON M5S 2C3, Tel. (416)972-9494, Email: rschneid@yorku.ca
Vice Presidents, The Rev. Dr. James Taylor Christie, 47 Queen's Park Crescent East, Toronto ON M5S 2C3, Tel. (416)972-9494, Email: sperocontraspem@rogers.com; Ms. Sandra Demson, 47 Queen's Park Crescent East, Toronto ON M5S 2C3, Tel. (416)972-9494 Fax: (416)922-9328, Email: srd@idirect.com ; The Rev. Dr. J. Daniel Gibson, 47 Queen's Park Crescent East,

Toronto ON M5S 2C3, Tel. (416)972-9494, Email: gibsond@execulink.com
Treasurer, Mr. Don Taylor, 47 Queen's Park Crescent East, Toronto ON M5S 2C3 Tel. (416)972-9494, Email: maryanddontaylor@sympatico.ca
General Secretary, The Rev. Dr. Karen Hamilton, 47 Queen's Park Crescent East, Toronto ON M5S 2C3, Tel. (416)972-9494 x 22, Email: hamilton@ccc-cce.ca

### MEMBER CHURCHES

Anglican Church Canada
Archdiocese of Canada of the Orthodox Church in America
Armenian Orthodox Church—Diocese of Canada
Baptist Convention of Ontario and Quebec
British Methodist Episcopal Church of Canada*
Canadian Conference of Catholic Bishops
Canadian Yearly Meeting of the Religious Society of Friends, Quakers
Christian Church (Disciples of Christ)
Christian Reformed Church in North America-Canadian Ministries
Coptic Orthodox Church of Canada
Ethiopian Orthodox Church in Canada
Evangelical Lutheran Church in Canada
Greek Orthodox Metropolis of Toronto (Canada)
Mennonite Church Canada
Old Catholic Church Union of Utrecht
Presbyterian Church in Canada
Regional Synod of Canada–Reformed Church in America
The Salvation Army—Canada and Bermuda
The United Church of Canada
Ukrainian Orthodox Church of Canada
*Associate Member

## Canadian Evangelical Theological Association

In May 1990, about 60 scholars, pastors and other interested persons met together in Toronto to form a new theological society. Arising out of the Canadian chapter of the Evangelical Theological Society, the new association established itself as a distinctly Canadian group with a new name. It sponsored its first conference as CETA in Kingston, Ontario, in May 1991.

CETA provides a forum for scholarly contributions to the renewal of theology and church in Canada. CETA seeks to promote theological work which is loyal to Christ and his gospel, faithful to the primacy and authority of Scripture and responsive to the guiding force of the historic creeds and Protestant confessions of the Christian Church. In its newsletters and conferences, CETA seeks presentations that will speak to a general theologically-educated audience, rather than to specialists.

CETA has special interest in evangelical points of view upon and contributions to the wider conversations regarding religious studies

53

and church life. Members therefore include pastors, students and other interested persons as well as professional academicians. CETA currently includes about 100 members, many of whom attend its annual conference in the early summer. It publishes the *Canadian Evangelical Review* and supports an active internet discussion group, which may be accessed by e-mailing ceta-l@egroups.com.

### Headquarters

Prof. David Guretzki, Briercrest College, Caronport, Saskatchewan, S0H 0S0
Email: dguretzki@briercrest.ca
Media Contact, Prof. David Guretzki

### Officers

President, Prof. David Guretzki
Secretary-Treasurer, Rev. Dr. Archie Pell
Editor, *Canadian Evangelical Review*, Dr. Archie Spencer
Executive Members-at-large, Nicholas Jesson, Adrian Langdon, and Randal Rauser

## Canadian Tract Society

The Canadian Tract Society was organized in 1970 as an independent distributor of gospel leaflets to provide Canadian churches and individual Christians with quality materials proclaiming the gospel through the printed page. It is affiliated with the American Tract Society, which encouraged its formation and assisted in its founding, and for whom it serves as an exclusive Canadian distributor. The CTS is a nonprofit international service ministry.

### Headquarters

P.O. Box 2156, LCD 1, Brampton, ON L6T 3S4
Tel. (905)457-4559 Fax (905)457-0529
Media Contact, Mgr., Donna Croft

### Officers

Director-Sec., Robert J. Burns
Director, John Neufeld
Director, Patricia Burns

## Canadian Society of Biblical Studies-Société Canadienne des Études Bibliques

The object of the Society is to stimulate the critical investigation of the classical biblical literatures, together with other related literature, by the exchange of scholarly research both in published form and in public forum.

### Headquarters

Media Contact, Exec. Sec., Michele Murray, Dept. of Religion, Bishop's University, Lennoxville, PQ J1M 1Z7, Email: mmurray@ubishops.ca, Website: www.ccsr.ca/csbs

### Officers

Pres., Mary Rose D'Angelo, Dept. of Theology, University of Notre Dame, Notre Dame, IN 46556, Tel. (219)631-7040 Fax (219)631-6842

Vice Pres., J. Glen Taylor, Wycliffe College, 5 Hoskin Ave., Toronto, ON M57 1H7, Tel. (416)946-3541 Fax (416)946-3541, Email: glen.Taylor@utoronto.ca
Exec. Sec., Michele Murray, Dept. of Religion, Bishop's University, Lennoxville, QC J1M 1Z7, Tel. (819)822-9600 Fax (819)822-9661, Email: mmurray@ubishops.ca
Treas., Robert A. Derrenbacker, Jr., Regent College, 5800 University Blvd, Vancouver, BC, V6T 2E4, Tel. (604)221-3349 Fax (604) 224-3097, Email: rderrenbacker@regent-college.edu
Prog. Coord., Christine Mitchell, St. Andrews College, 1121 College Dr., Saskatoon, SK S7N 0W3, Email: ckm365@duke.usask.ca
Comm. Officer, Richard Ascough, Queens' Theological College, Kingston, ON K7L 3N6, Tel. (613)533-6000 Fax (613)533-6879, Email: rsa@post.queensu.ca
Student Liason Officer, Derek Suderman, Emmanuel College, 11739 McCowan Rd., Stouffville, ON L4A 7X5, Email: derek.suderman@utoronto.ca

## The Church Army in Canada

The Church Army in Canada has been involved in evangelism and Christian social service since 1929.

### Headquarters

105 Mountain View Dr., Saint John, NB E2J 5B5
Tel. (888)316-8169 Fax (506)642-4005
Email: bsmith@churcharmy.com
Media Contact, National Dir., Capt. R. Bruce Smith

### Officers

National Dir., Capt. R. Bruce Smith
Bd. Chmn., Mr. Peter Bloom

## The Churches' Council on Theological Education in Canada, an Ecumenical Foundation

The Churches' Council (CCTE,EF) maintains an overview of theological education in Canada on behalf of its constituent churches and functions as a bridge between the schools of theology and the churches which they serve.

Founded in 1970 with a national and ecumenical mandate, the CCTE,EF provides resources for research into matters pertaining to theological education, opportunities for consultation and cooperation and a limited amount of funding in the form of grants for the furtherance of ecumenical iniatives in theological education.

### Headquarters

47 Queen's Park Cres., E., Toronto, ON M5S 2C3 Tel. (416)928-3223 Fax (416)928-3563
Media Contact, Exec. Dir., Robert Faris
Website: www.ccte.ca
Email: director@ccte.ca

### Officers

Bd. of Dir., Chpsn., Dr. Richard C. Crossman, Waterloo Lutheran Seminary, 75 University Ave. W., Waterloo, ON N2L 3C5

Bd. of Dir., Vice Chpsn., Dr. Dorcas Gordon, Knox College

Treas., Mr. Brian Cox

Exec. Dir., Robert Faris

### MEMBER ORGANIZATIONS

The General Synod of the Anglican Church of Canada

Canadian Baptist Ministries

The Evangelical Lutheran Church in Canada

The Presbyterian Church in Canada

The Canadian Conference of Catholic Bishops

The United Church of Canada

## Evangelical Fellowship of Canada

The Fellowship was formed in 1964. There are 31 denominations, 124 organizations, 1,200 local churches and 11,000 individual members.

Its purposes are, "Fellowship in the gospel" (Phil. Ch.1 v.5), "the defence and confirmation of the gospel" (Phil. Ch.1 v.7) and "the furtherance of the gospel" (Phil. Ch.1 v.12). The Fellowship believes the Holy Scriptures, as originally given, are infallible and that salvation through the Lord Jesus Christ is by faith apart from works.

In national and regional conventions the Fellowship urges Christians to live exemplary lives and to openly challenge the evils and injustices of society. It encourages cooperation with various agencies in Canada and overseas that are sensitive to social and spiritual needs.

### Headquarters

Office, 600 Alden Rd. Ste. 300, Markham, ON L3R 0E7 Tel. (905)479-5885 Fax (905)479-4742

Mailing Address, M.I.P. Box 3745, Markham, ON L3R 0Y4

Media Contact, Pres., Dr. Gary Walsh, 600 Alden Rd., Ste. 300, Markham, ON L3R 0E7 Tel. (905)479-5885 Fax (905)479-4742

### Officers

Pres., Dr. Gary Walsh

Chair, Dr. Paul Magnus

Vice Chair, Dr. Rick Penner

Treas., Lt. Col. David Luginbuhl

Past Pres., Dr. Brian Stiller

### EXECUTIVE COMMITTEE

Rev. Scott Campbell; Rev. Carson Pue; Ms. Ruth Andrews; Rev. Stewart Hunter; Ms. Jacqueline Dugas; Dr. Rick Penner; Lt. Col. David Luginbuhl; Dr. Ralph Richardson; Rev. Abe Funk; Rev. Gillis Killam; Dr. Paul Magnus; Rev. Winston Thurton

Task Force on Evangelism—(Vision Canada), Interim Chair, Gary Walsh

Social Action Commission, Chpsn., Dr. James Read

Education Commission, Chpsn., Dr. Glenn Smith

Women in Ministry Task Force, Chpsn., Rev. Eileen Stewart-Rhude

Aboriginal Task Force, Co-Chairs, Ray Aldred; Wendy Peterson

Religious Liberties Commission, Chpsn., Dr. Paul Marshall

Task Force on Global Mission, Chpsn., Dr. Geoff Tunnicliffe

## Inter-Varsity Christian Fellowship of Canada

Inter-Varsity Christian Fellowship is a non-profit, interdenominational student movement centering on the witness to Jesus Christ in campus communities, universities, colleges, and high schools and through a Canada-wide Pioneer Camping program. It also ministers to professionals and teachers through Nurses and Teacher Christian Fellowship.

IVCF was officially formed in 1928-29 by the late Dr. Howard Guinness, whose arrival from Britain challenged students to follow the example of the British Inter-Varsity Fellowship by organizing themselves into prayer and Bible study fellowship groups. Inter-Varsity has always been a student-initiated movement emphasizing and developing leadership on the campus to call Christians to outreach, challenging other students to a personal faith in Jesus Christ and studying the Bible as God's revealed truth within a fellowship of believers. A strong stress has been placed on missionary activity, and the triennial conference held at Urbana, Ill.. (jointly sponsored by U.S. and Canadian IVCF) has been a means of challenging many young people to service in Christian vocations. Inter-Varsity works closely with and is a strong believer in the work of local and national churches.

### Headquarters

Unit 17, 40 Vogell Rd., Richmond Hill, ON L4B 3N6 Tel. (905)884-6880 Fax (905)884-6550

Media Contact, Gen. Dir., Rob Regier

### Officers

Gen. Dir., Rob Regier

## Interchurch Communications

Interchurch Communications is made up of the communication units of the Anglican Church of Canada, the Evangelical Lutheran Church in Canada, the Presbyterian Church in Canada, the Canadian Conference of Catholic Bishops (English Sector), and the United Church of Canada. ICC members collaborate on occasional video or print coproductions and on addressing public policy issues affecting religious communications.

### Headquarters

3250 Bloor St. W., Etobicoke, ON M8X 2Y4

Media Contact, Pres. Keith Knight, Presbyterian Church in Canada, 50 Wynford Drive, Don

Mills, Ontario, M3C 1J7 Tel. (416)441-1111 Fax (416)441-2825 Email: kknight@presbyterian.ca

**Members**

Mr. William Kokesch, Canadian Conference of Catholic Bishops, 90 Parent Ave., Ottawa, ON K1N 7B1 Tel. (613)241-9461 Fax (613)241-8117, Email: kokesch@cccb.ca

Pres., Keith Knight, Presbyterian Church in Canada, 50 Wynford Dr., Don Mills, ON M3C 1J7 Tel. (416)441-1111 Fax (416)441-2825, Email: kknight@presbyterian.ca

Religious Television Associates, 3250 Bloor St. W., Etobicoke, ON M8X 2Y4 Tel. (416)231-7680 Fax (416)232-6004

## John Howard Society of Ontario

The John Howard Society of Ontario is a registered non-profit charitable organization providing services to individuals, families and groups at all stages in the youth and criminal justice system. The Society also provides community education on critical issues in the justice system and advocacy for reform of the justice system. The mandate of the Society is the prevention of crime through service, community education, advocacy, and reform.

Founded in 1929, the Society has grown from a one-office service in Toronto to 17 local branches providing direct services in the major cities of Ontario and a provincial office providing justice policy analysis, advocacy for reform, and support to branches.

**Headquarters**

6 Jackson Pl., Toronto, ON M6P 1T6 Tel. (416)604-8412 Fax (416)604-8948
Media Contact, Exec. Dir., William Sparks

**Officers**

Pres., Susan Reid-MacNevin, Dept. of Sociology, Univ. Of Guelph, Guelph, ON N1G 2W1
Vice Pres., Richard Beaupe, 4165 Fernand St., Hamner, ON B3A 1X4
Treas., Jack Battler, Waterloo, ON
Sec., Peter Angeline, OISE, 252 Bloor St. W., Toronto, ON
Exec. Dir., William Sparks

**LOCAL SOCIETIES**

Collins Bay; Hamilton; Kingston; Lindsay; London; Niagara; Oshawa; Ottawa; Peel; Peterborough; Sarnia; Sault Ste. Marie; Sudbury; Thunder Bay; Toronto; Waterloo; Windsor

## Lutheran Council in Canada

The Lutheran Council in Canada was organized in 1967 and is a cooperative agency of the Evangelical Lutheran Church in Canada and Lutheran Church-Canada.

The Council's activities include communications, coordinative service, and national liaison in social ministry, chaplaincy and scout activity.

**Headquarters**

302-393 Portage Ave., Winnipeg, MB R3B 3H6 Tel. (204)984-9150 Fax (204)984-9185
Media Contact, Pres., Rev. Ralph Mayan, 3074 Portage Ave., Winnipeg, MB R3K 0Y2 Tel. (204)895-3433 Fax (204)897-4319

**Officers**

Pres., Bishop Raymond Schultz
Sec., Rev. Leon C. Gilbertson
Vice Pres., Rev. Ralph Mayan

## Mennonite Central Committee Canada (MCCC)

Mennonite Central Committee Canada was organized in 1964 to continue the work which several regional Canadian inter-Mennonite agencies had been doing in relief, service, immigration, and peace. All but a few of the smaller Mennonite groups in Canada belong to MCC Canada.

MCCC is part of the Mennonite Central Committee (MCC) International which has its headquarters in Akron, Pa., from where most of the overseas development and relief projects are administered. In 2000-2001 MCCC's income was $25 million, about 47 percent of the total MCC income. There were 408 Canadians out of a total of 867 MCC workers serving in North America and abroad during the same time period.

The MCC office in Winnipeg administers projects located in Canada. Domestic programs of Voluntary Service, Native Concerns, Peace and Social Concerns, Food Program, Employment Concerns, Ottawa Office, Victim-Offender Ministries, Mental Health, and Immigration are all part of MCC's Canadian ministry. Whenever it undertakes a project, MCCC attempts to relate to the church or churches in the area.

**Headquarters**

134 Plaza Dr., Winnipeg, MB R3T 5K9 Tel. (204)261-6381 Fax (204)269-9875
Communications, Rick Fast, 134 Plaza Dr., Winnipeg, MT R3T 5K9 Tel. (204)261-6381 Fax (204)269-9875

**Officers**

Exec. Dir., Donald Peters

## Project Ploughshares

Project Ploughshares is an ecumenical peace centre of the Canadian Council of Churches, established in 1976 to implement the churches' imperative to seek and pursue peace. Project Ploughshares works with churches, governments, and non-governmental organizations, in Canada and internationally, to identify, develop, and advance approaches that build peace and prevent war, and promote the peaceful resolution of political conflict. Project Ploughshares is sponsored by eight national Canadian churches and is affiliated with the Institute of Peace and Conflict Studies, Conrad Grebel University

College, University of Waterloo. Publications include *The Ploughshares Monitor* (quarterly), *The Armed Conflicts Report* (annually), Briefings and Working Papers (occasional).

### Headquarters
Project Ploughshares, 57 Erb Street West, Waterloo, ON, Canada N2L 6C2 Tel. (519)888-6541 Fax (519)888-0188, Email: plough@ploughshares.ca, Website: www.ploughshares.ca
Media Contact: Director, John Siebert, Tel. (519) 888-6541 x 702, Email: jsiebert@ploughshares.ca

### Officers
Executive Director, John Siebert
Associate Director, Nancy Regehr
Chair, Moira Hutchinson
Treasurer, Philip Creighton
Secretary, Rev. Dr. Martin Rumscheidt

### SPONSORING ORGANIZATIONS
Anglican Church of Canada
Canadian Catholic Organization for Development & Peace
Canadian Unitarian Council
Canadian Voice of Women for Peace
Canadian Yearly Meeting, Religious Society of Friends
Evangelical Lutheran Church in Canada
Mennonite Central Committee Canada
Presbyterian Church in Canada
United Church of Canada

## Religious Television Associates

Religious Television Associates was formed in the early 1960s for the production units of the Anglican, Baptist, Presbyterian, Roman Catholic Churches and the United Church of Canada. In the intervening years, the Baptists have withdrawn and the Lutherans have come in. RTA provides an ecumenical umbrella for joint productions in broadcasting and development education. The directors are the heads of the Communications Departments participating in Interchurch Communications.

### Headquarters
c/o The United Church of Canada, 3250 Bloor St. W., Etobicoke, ON M8X 2Y4 Tel. (416)231-7680 x 4076 Fax (416)231-3103
Media Contact, Shane Chadden

### Officers
The Anglican Church of Canada
Canadian Conference of Catholic Bishops
The Canadian Council of Churches
The Evangelical Lutheran Church in Canada
The Presbyterian Church in Canada
The United Church of Canada

## Scripture Union

Scripture Union is an international interdenominational missionary movement working in 130 countries.

Scripture Union aims to work with the churches to make God's good news known to children, young people and families and to encourage people of all ages to meet God daily through the Bible and prayer.

In Canada, a range of daily Bible guides are offered to individuals, churches, and bookstores from age four through adult. Sunday School curriculum and various evangelism and discipling materials are also offered for sale.

Children's ministry is offered to churches through summer sports camps and training for sports outreach programs.

### Headquarters
1885 Clements Rd., Unit 226, Pickering, ON L1W 3V4 Tel. (905)427-4947 Fax (905)427-0334
Media Contact, President, John Irwin, Email: jirwinc617@rogers.com

### Officers
Chair of the Board, Harold Murray, 216 McKinnon Pl. NE, Calgary, AB T2E 7B9 Tel. 403-276-4716, Email: hjmurray@home.com
President, Robert Szo, 1885 Clements Rd., Unit 226, Pickering, ON L1W 3V4, Email: robert@scriptureunion.ca

## Student Christian Movement of Canada

The Student Christian Movement of Canada was formed in 1921 from the student arm of the YMCA. It has its roots in the Social Gospel movements of the late 19th and early 20th centuries. Throughout its intellectual history, the SCM in Canada has sought to relate the Christian faith to the living realities of the social and political context of each student generation.

The present priorities are built around the need to form more and stronger critical Christian communities on Canadian campuses within which individuals may develop their social and political analyses, experience spiritual growth and fellowship and bring Christian ecumenical witness to the university.

The Student Christian Movement of Canada is affiliated with the World Student Christian Federation.

### Headquarters
310 Danforth Ave., Toronto, ON M4K 1N6 Tel. (416)463-4312 Fax (416)466-6854
Media Contact, Natl. Coord., Sheilagh McGlynn

### Officers
Natl. Coord., Sheilagh McGlynn, Email: info@scmcanada.org

## Women's Inter-Church Council of Canada

Women's Inter-Church Council of Canada is a national Christian women's council that encourages women to grow in ecumenism, to strengthen ecumenical community, to share their spirituality and prayer, to engage in dialogue about women's concerns and to stand in solidarity with one another. The Council calls women to respond to national and international issues affecting women and to take action together for justice. WICC sponsors the World Day of Prayer and Fellowship of the Least Coin in Canada. Human rights projects for women are supported and a quarterly magazine *Making Waves* distributed.

### Headquarters
47 Queen's Park Cres. E, Toronto, ON M5S 2C3 Tel. (416)929-5184 Fax (416)929-4064
Media Contact, Communications Coordinator, Gillian Barfoot

### Officers
Pres., Claire Heron
Exec. Dir., Pat Allinson

CHURCH MEMBER BODIES
African Methodist Episcopal, Anglican Church of Canada, Canadian Baptist Ministries, Christian Church (Disciples of Christ), Evangelical Lutheran Church in Canada, Mennonite Central Committee, Presbyterian Church in Canada, Religious Society of Friends, Roman Catholic Church, The Salvation Army in Canada, United Church of Canada

## World Vision Canada
World Vision Canada is a Christian humanitarian relief and development organization. Although its main international commitment is to translate child sponsorship into holistic, sustainable community development, World Vision also allocates resources to help Canada's poor and complement the mission of the church.

World Vision's Reception Centre assists government-sponsored refugees entering Canada. The NeighbourLink program mobilizes church volunteers to respond locally to people's needs. A quarterly publication, *Context*, provides data on the Canadian family to help churches effectively reach their communities. The development education program provides resources on development issues. During the annual 30-Hour Famine, people fast for 30 hours while discussing poverty and raising funds to support aid programs.

### Headquarters
1 World Dr., Mississauga, ON L5T 2Y4 Tel. (905)821-3030 Fax (905)821-1356
Media Contact, Philip Maher, Tel. (905)567-2726

### Officers
Pres., Dave Toycen
Vice Pres., Intl. & Govt. Relations, Linda Tripp; Natl. Programs, Don Posterski; Fin. & Admin., Charlie Fluit; Donor Development Group, Brian Tizzard

## Young Men's Christian Association in Canada
The YMCA began as a Christian association to help young men find healthy recreation and meditation, as well as opportunities for education, in the industrial slums of nineteenth-century England. It came to Canada in 1851 with the same mission in mind for young men working in camps and on the railways.

Today, the YMCA maintains its original mission, helping individuals to grow and develop in spirit, mind and body, but attends to those needs for men and women of all ages and religious beliefs. The YMCA registers 1.5 million participants in 250 communities that are served by 64 autonomous associations across Canada.

The program of each association differs according to the needs of the community, but most offer one or more programs in each of the following categories; health and fitness, child care, employment counseling and training, recreation, camping, community support and outreach, international development, and short-term accommodation.

The YMCA encourages people of all ages, races, abilities, income and beliefs to come together in an environment which promotes balance in life, breaking down barriers and helping to create healthier communities.

### Headquarters
42 Charles St. E., 6th Floor., Toronto, ON M4Y 1T4 Tel. (416)967-9622 Fax (416)967-9618
Media Contact, Sol Kasimer

### Officers
Chpsn., Ray Mantha
CEO, Sol Kasimer

## Young Women's Christian Association of-du Canada
The YWCA of-du Canada is a national voluntary organization serving 44 YWCAs and YM-YWCAs across Canada. Dedicated to the development and improved status of women and their families, the YWCA is committed to service delivery and to being a source of public education on women's issues and an advocate of social change. Services provided by YWCAs and YM-YWCAs include adult education programs, residences and shelters, child care, fitness activities, wellness programs and international development education. As a member of the World YWCA, the YWCA of-du Canada is part of the largest women's organization in the world.

### Headquarters
80 Gerrard St. E., Toronto, ON M5B 1G6 Tel. (416)593-9886 Fax (416)971-8084
Media Contact, Int. CEO, Margaret MacKenzie

### Officers
Pres., Ann Mowatt

## Youth for Christ—Canada

Youth For Christ is an interdenominational organization founded in 1944 by Torrey Johnson. Under the leadership of YFC's 11 national boards of directors, Youth For Christ-Canada cooperates with churches and serves as a mission agency reaching out to young people and their families through a variety of ministries.

YFC seeks to have maximum influence in a world of youth through high-interest activities and personal involvement. Individual attention is given to each teenager through small-group involvement and counseling. These activities and relationships become vehicles for communicating the message of the gospel.

**Headquarters**

822-167 Lombard Ave., Winnipeg, MB R3B 0V3
Tel. (204)989-0056 Fax (204)989-0067

**Officers**

Natl. Dir., Randy L. Steinwand

# 3. Religious Bodies in the United States

The United States, with its staunch constitutional stance on religious freedom and successive waves of immigrants over the last three centuries, has proved to be a fertile soil for the development of varied Christian traditions. In the directory that follows some 224 distinct church traditions are represented. Many of these groups represent the processes of dividing and re-uniting that are a hallmark of American religious life. Many churches listed here represent those with a long tradition in Europe, Africa, or Asia predating their American tenure. Others are American-born churches. The researcher may be helped by consulting the churches grouped by tradition at the end of this directory in the section entitled, "Religious Bodies in the United States Arranged by Families." In this section, all the Baptists bodies are listed together, all the Lutheran bodies, Methodists, etc.

The following directory information is supplied by the national headquarters of each church. Each listing contains a brief description of the church, followed by the national headquarters contact information, which includes a mailing address, telephone and fax numbers, email and website addresses (when available), and the name of the media contact. After the headquarters, there are data regarding the church officers or leaders, including names, titles, and contact information (when contact information differs from the headquarters). There is a staggering array of churches, each with its own form of organization; not all of them refer to their leaders as "officers." In some places, the reader will find the term "Bishops," "Board Members," or "Executives" in place of "Officers." Finally, when applicable, each entry contains a list of the names of church publications.

The churches are printed in alphabetical order by the official name of the organization. There are a few instances in which certain churches are more commonly known by another name. In such cases, the reader is referred incidentally within the text to the appropriate official name. Churches that are member communions of the National Council of the Churches of Christ in the U.S.A. are marked with an asterisk (*).

Other useful information about the churches listed here can be found in other chapters or directories within the book: Statistical information for these churches can be found in the tables toward the end of this book in Chapter III. Further, more extensive information about the publications listed in this directory can be found in section II, 10, "Religious Periodicals in the United States."

The organizations listed here represent the denominations to which the vast majority of church members in the United States belong. It does not include all religious bodies functioning in the United States. The Encyclopedia of American Religions (Gale Research Inc., P.O. Box 33477, Detroit MI 48232-5477) contains names and addresses of additional religious bodies.

## Advent Christian Church

The Advent Christian Church is a conservative, evangelical denomination which grew out of the Millerite movement of the 1830s and 1840s. The members stress the authority of Scripture, justification by faith in Jesus Christ alone, the importance of evangelism, disciple-making, and world missions and the soon visible return of Jesus Christ.

Organized in 1860, the Advent Christian Church maintains headquarters in Charlotte, N.C., with regional offices in Rochester, N.H., Princeton, N.C., Ellisville, Mo., Sumas, Wash., and Lenoir, N.C. Missions are maintained in India, Nigeria, Ghana, Japan, Liberia, Croatia, New Zealand, Malaysia, the Philippines, Mexico, South Africa, Namibia, Honduras, China, Kenya, Malawi, Mozambique, Congo, Romania, and Memphis, Tenn.

The Advent Christian Church maintains doctrinal distinctives in three areas—conditional immortality, the sleep of the dead until the return of Christ, and belief that the kingdom of God will be established on earth made new by Jesus Christ.

### Headquarters

P.O. Box 23152, Charlotte, NC 28227, Tel. (704)545-6161 x 202 Fax (704)573-0712

Media Contact, Exec. Director, Ronald P. Thomas, Jr.

Email: acpub@adventchristian.org

Website: www.adventchristian.org

### Periodicals

*Advent Christian News; Maranatha; Advent Christian Witness; Prayer & Praise; Henceforth;* Weekly E-newsletter; www.ACGC.us Books published recently: *Hymns of Heritage and Hope, Who Will Go for Us?, Resurrection Hope* (Spanish edition).

## African Methodist Episcopal Church*

This church began in 1787 in Philadelphia when persons in St. George's Methodist Episcopal Church withdrew as a protest against color segregation. In 1816 the denomination started, led by Rev. Richard Allen, who had been ordained deacon by Bishop Francis Asbury and was subsequently ordained elder and elected and consecrated bishop.

## Headquarters

3801 Market St., Suite 300, Philadelphia, PA 29204, Tel. (215)662-0506
Email: cio@ame-church.com
Website: www.AME-Church.com

### Officers

Senior Bishop, Bishop Philip Robert Cousin, Presiding Bishop, Fourth Episcopal District, African Methodist Episcopal Church, 404 East 41st Street, Suite 114, Chicago, IL 60653, Tel. (773)373-6587 Fax (773)373-8356
Chief Ecumenical & Urban Affairs Officer, Bishop E. Earl McCloud, African Methodist Episcopal Church, P.O. Box 310043, Atlanta, GA 31131-0043, Tel. (770)475-2966, Email: emccloudjr@aol.com
Pres., Gen. Bd., Bishop McKinley Young, 101 East Union Street, Jacksonville FL 32202. Tel., 904-355-8262; Fax, 904-356-1617.
Pres. Council of Bishops 2005-2006, Bishop Preston Warren Williams II, 110 Pisgah Church Road, Columbia, SC 29203, Tel. 803-935-0500, Fax. 803-935-0830.

### GENERAL OFFICERS

Dr. Clement W. Fugh; Dr. Richard Allen Lewis; Dr. Daryl B. Ingram; Dr. Johnny Barbour; Jr., Dr. George F. Flowers; Dr. Dennis C. Dickerson; Dr. Jerome V. Harris; Dr. James Wade; Dr. Calvin H. Sydnor, III; Bishop E. Earl McCloud, Ecumenical Officer/Chaplains; Bishop Richard Franklin Norris (First Episcopal Dist.); Bishop Adam Jefferson Richardson, Jr. (Second Episcopal Dist.); Bishop Robert Vaughn Webster (Third Episcopal Dist.); Bishop Philip Robert Cousin, Sr. (Fourth Episcopal Dist.); Bishop John Richard Bryant (Fifth Episcopal Dist.); Bishop William Phillips DeVeaux (Sixth Episcopal Dist.); Bishop Preston Warren Williams, II (Seventh Episcopal Dist.); Bishop Cornal Garnett Henning, Sr. (Eighth Episcopal Dist.); Bishop Theodore Larry Kirkland (Ninth Episcopal Dist.); Bishop Gregory Gerald McKinley Ingram (Tenth Episcopal Dist.); Bishop McKinley Young (Eleventh Episcopal Dist.); Bishop Richard Allen Chappelle, Sr. (Twelfth Episcopal Dist.); Bishop Vashti Murphy McKenzie (Thirteenth Episcopal Dist.); Bishop David Rwhynica Daniels, Jr. (Fourteenth Episcopal Dist.); Bishop Samuel Lawrence Green, Sr. (Fifteenth Episcopal Dist.); Bishop Carolyn Tyler Guidry (Sixteenth Episcopal Dist.); Bishop Paul Jones Mulenga Kawimbe (Seventeenth Episcopal Dist.); Bishop Sarah Frances Davis (Eighteenth Episcopal Dist.); Bishop James Levert Davis (Nineteenth Episcopal Dist.); Bishop Wilfred Jacobus Messiah (Twentieth Episcopal District)

### Periodicals

*The A.M.E. Review,* Editor, Dr. Dennis Dickerson, 500 8th Avenue, South, Nashville, TN 37203
*The Christian Recorder*, Editor, Dr. Calvin Sydnor, 512 8th Avenue, South, Nashville, TN 37203
*Journal of Christian Education*, Editor, Dr. Daryl Ingram, 500 8th Avenue, South, Nashville, TN 37203
*Women's Missionary Magazine*, Editor, Dr. Rosa Baxter, 4079 Summit Crossing Drive, Decatur, GA 30034
*Secret Chamber*, Editor, Dr. James Wade, 280 Hernando Street, Memphis, TN 38126
*Voice of Missions*, Editor, Dr. George Flowers, 1578 Savannah Highway, Charleston, SC 29407-6014

## The African Methodist Episcopal Zion Church*

The A.M.E. Zion Church is an independent body, having withdrawn from the John Street Methodist Church of New York City in 1796. The first bishop was James Varick.

### Headquarters

Dept. of Records & Research, 3225 West Sugar Creek Rd., Charlotte, NC 28269, Tel. (704)599-4630 Fax (704)688-2549, Email: j1gsa@aol.com
Media Contact, Gen. Sec.-Aud., Dr. W. Robert Johnson, III
Email: rojohnson@amezhqtr.org; eljohnson@amezhqtr.org

### Officers

Sr. Bishop, Bishop George W.C. Walker, Sr.

### BOARD OF BISHOPS OFFICERS

*Pres., James E. McCoy, 808 South Lawrence Street, Motgomery, AL 36104, Tel. (334)269-6365 Fax (334)269-6369; Email:alflamez@bellsouth.net
Sec., Clarence Carr, 2600 Normandy Dr., Greendale, MO 63121, Tel. (314)727-2931 Fax (314)727-0663; Office: 2645 Hord Ave., St. Louis, MO 63136, Tel. (314)867-8067
Asst. Sec., Kenneth Monroe, P.O. Box 26403, Fayettville, NC 28318, Tel. (910)843-8274 Fax (910)843-8702
Treas., George Washington Carver Walker, Sr., 3225 W. Sugar Creek Rd., Charlotte, NC 28269, Tel. (704)599-5630; Mailing Address: P.O. Box 26770, Charlotte, NC 28221
*Note: Presidency rotates every six (6) months according to seniority.

### ACTIVE MEMBERS

George Edward Battle Jr., 18403 Dembridge Lane, Davidson, NC 28036, Tel. (704) 895-2236, Email: gebenced@bellsouth.net; Office: Two Wachovia Center, 301 South Tryon St., Ste. 1755, Charlotte, NC 28202, Tel. (704)332-7600 Fax (704)343-3745
Warren Matthew Brown, 22 Crowley Dr.,

**U.S. RELIGIOUS BODIES**

61

Randolph, MA 02368, Tel. (781)961-2434 Fax (781)961-2939

Clarence Carr, 2600 Normandy Dr., Greendale, MO 63121, Tel. (314)727-2931 Fax (314)727-0663; Office: 2645 Hord Ave., St. Louis, MO 63136, Tel. (314)867-8067

Samuel Chuka Ekemam, Sr., Office-Mail: A.M.E. Zion Church Area Headquarters, 1 Zion Hill Plaza, (Ugwu Orji), Okigwe Road, P. O. Box 8000, Owerri, Imo State, Nigeria West Africa; Home Phone from U.S.: (1pm-5pm est) 011-(234)83-231-303, Alt. Quick Phone: 011-(234)803-301-8280; Office fax from U.S.: 011-(234)83-232-271, Email: chukaekemam @hotmail.com

Roy A. Holmes, 22071 Sunset Dr., Richton Park, IL 60471, Tel. (708)748-3725 Fax (708)748-3726

Louis Hunter, Sr., 4255 Laurel Grove Trace, Suwanee, GA 30244, Tel. & fax (678)714-1566, Email: louishunter3@aol.com

Nathaniel Jarrett, Jr., 18031 S. Pheasant Lake Dr., Tinley Park, IL 60477, Tel. (708)802-9873 Fax (708)429-3911

James E. McCoy, 808 S. Lawrence St., Montgomery, AL 36104-5055, Tel. (334)269-6365 Fax (334)269-6369, Email: aflamez@ aol.com

Kenneth Monroe, P.O. Box 26403, Fayettville, NC 28318, Tel. (910)843-8274 Fax (910)843-8702

Richard Keith Thompson, P.O. Box 55458, Washington, DC 20040, Tel. (202)723-8993 Fax (202)722-1840

George Washington Carver Walker, Sr., 3225 W. Sugar Creek Rd., Charlotte, NC 28269, Tel. (704)599-4630 Fax (704)688-2540; Mailing Address: P.O. Box 26770, Charlotte, NC 28221

### RETIRED MEMBERS

William Alexander Hilliard, 690 Chicago Blvd., Detroit, MI 48202

Cecil Bishop, 2663 Oakmeade Dr., Charlotte, NC 28270, Tel. (704)846-9370 Fax (704)846-9371, Email: piedbishop@aol.com

Joseph Johnson, 320 Walnut Point Dr., Matthews, NC 28105, Tel. (704)849-0521; Mailing Address: P. O. Box 608, Matthews, NC 28106, Email: djjjj85@alltel.net

Marshall H. Strickland, I, 2000 Cedar Circle Dr., Baltimore, MD 21228, Tel. (410)744-7330 Fax (410)788-5510

### EPISCOPAL ASSIGNMENTS

Piedmont Episcopal District: Blue Ridge, West Central North Carolina, Western North Carolina, and Jamaica Conferences: Bishop George W. C. Walker, Sr.

Mid-West Episcopal District: Indiana, Kentucky, Michigan, Missouri, Tennessee, Central Africa (Malawi and Mozambique) and South Africa Conferences: Vacant

Eastern West Africa Episcopal District: Central

Nigeria, Lagos—West Nigeria, Nigeria, Northern Nigeria, Rivers, Mainland, Cross River, South Eastern, and Southern Conferences: Bishop Samuel Chuka Ekemam, Sr.

North Eastern Episcopal District: New England, New York, Western New York, and Bahamas Islands Conferences: Bishop George Edward Battle, Jr.

Eastern North Carolina Episcopal District: Albemarle, Cape Fear, Central North Carolina, North Carolina, Virgin Islands, and South Africa (Zimbabwe) Conferences: Bishop Richard Keith Thompson

South Atlantic Episcopal District: Georgia, Palmetto, Pee Dee, and South Carolina Conferences: Bishop Clarence Carr

Mid-Atlantic I Episcopal District: Allegheny, New Jersey, Ohio, Guyana, Trinidad-Tobago, and Barbados Conferences: Bishop Nathaniel Jarrett, Jr.

Mid-Atlantic II Episcopal District: East Tennessee-Virginia, India, London-Birmingham, Manchester-Midland, Philadelphia-Baltimore, Virginia and Angola Conferences: Bishop Warren M. Brown

Western Episcopal District: Alaska, Arizona, California, Oregon-Washington, Southwest Rocky Mountain, and Colorado Conferences: Bishop Roy A. Holmes

Southwestern Delta: Arkansas, Louisiana, Oklahoma, South Mississippi, West Tennessee-Mississippi and Texas Conferences: Bishop Louis Hunter, Sr.

Alabama/Florida Episcopal District: Alabama, Cahaba, Central Alabama, North Alabama, South Alabama, West Alabama, Florida, and South Florida Conferences: Bishop James E. McCoy

Western West Africa: Cote D'Ivoire, East Ghana, Liberia, Mid-Ghana, North Ghana, Togo and West Ghana Conferences: Bishop Kenneth Monroe

### GENERAL OFFICERS AND DEPARTMENTS

Address and telephone number for all Departments (except where indicated) is 3225 West Sugar Creek Rd., Charlotte, NC 28269, Tel. (704)599-4630 and Mailing Address for all Departemnts (except where indicated) is P. O. Box 26670, Charlotte, NC 28221.

Department of Records and Research: W. Robert Johnson, III, Gen. Sec.-Aud., Fax (704)688-2549, Email: j1gsa@aol.com or wajohnson @amezhqtr.org

Department of Finance: Mrs. Shirley Welch, Chief Financial Officer, Fax (704)688-2553, Email: shwelch@amezhqtr.org

*Star of Zion:* Micahel Lisby, Editor, Fax (704)688-2546, Email: editor@starofzion.org.

*A.M.E. Zion Quarterly Review and Historical Society:* James D. Armstrong, Sec.-Editor,

P.O. Box 33247, Charlotte, NC 28233 Fax(704)688-2544, Email: jaarmstrong@amezhqtr.org

Heritage Hall, Livingstone College, Dr. Phyllis Galloway, Dir., 701 W. Monroe St., Salisbury, NC 28144, Tel. (704)216-6094

Department of Overseas Missions and Missionary Seer: Kermit DeGraffenreidt, Sec.-Editor, 475 Riverside Drive, Room 1935, New York, NY 10115, Tel. (212)870-2952 Fax (212)870-2808

Department of Brotherhood Pensions and Ministerial Relief: David Miller, Sec.-Treas., Fax (704)599-4580; Mailing Address: P.O. Box 217114, Charlotte, NC 28221, Email: damiller@amezhqtr.org

Christian Education Department: Raymon Hunt, Sec., Fax (704)688-2550, Email: rehunt@amezhqtr.org

Department of Church School Literature: Mary A. Love, Editor, Fax (704)688-2548, Email: malove@amezhqtr.org

Department of Church Extension and Home Missions: Terrence J. Jones, Sec.-Treas., Fax (704)688-2552, Email: tejones@amezhqtr.org

Bureau of Evangelism: Darryl B. Starnes, Dir., P. O. Box 217258, Charlotte, NC 28221-7258 Fax(704)688-2547, Email: dbstarnesevangel@aol.com

Public Affairs and Convention Manager: George E. McKain, II, Dir., P.O. Box 1417, Summerville, SC 29484, Tel. (843)878-8461 Fax (843)821-1735, Email: zionpagem2 @aol.com; Hqtrs. Tel. (704)599-4630

Department of Health and Social Concerns: Bernard Sullivan, Dir., 292 W. Main Ave., Gastonia, NC 28053, Tel. (704)866-0325 Fax (704)864-7641, Email: bsullivan@successinc.org

A.M.E. Zion Publishing House: David Miller, Interim Gen. Manager, Fax (704)688-2541, Email: damiller@amezhqtr.org

## JUDICIAL COUNCIL

Honorable Adele M. Riley, 625 Ellsworth Dr., Dayton, OH 45426

Rev. Dr. George L. Blackwell, 220 N. Elm St., Williamston, NC 27892

Rev. Dr. E. Alex Brower, 11510-115th Ave., Jamaica, NY 11434-1204

Rev. Dr. Richard Chappelle, 4026 Huron Ct., Cheswick, PA 15024

Ms. Elmira Jackson, Esq., 194 Wood Hollow Lane, New Rochelle, NY 10804

Neville Tucker, Esq., 865 South Figueroa, Ste. 2640, Los Angeles, CA 90017

Rev. Dr. Jewett L. Walker, 910 Bridle Path Lane, Charlotte, NC 28211

Jerome Willingham, Esq.

Rev. Dr. Reid R. White, Jr., 6608 Cartwright Dr., Columbia, SC 29223

## CONNECTIONAL LAY COUNCIL

Pres., David A. Aiken, Sr., 115-21 142nd St., South Ozone Park, NY 11436, Tel. (718) 322-

1893 Fax (718)529-6045, Email: laypresident @att.net

First Vice Pres., Raymond Richmond, Jr., 456 Stillwood Dr., Jackson, MS 39206-5142, Tel. (601)979-2353 or (601)982-7401, Email: raymondrichmond@ccaixjsums.edu

Second Vice Pres., Regina W. Rivera, 9701 Magnolia Pointe Place, Glen Allen, VA 23059, Tel. (804)264-2689 Cell (804)307-6104 Fax (804)264-9777, Email: regrivera@aol.com

Sec., Mary J. Matthews, P.O. Box 3155, Sanford, NC 27331, Tel. (919)499-1187

Treas., Connie B. Williams, 8518 Fansworth, Charlotte, NC 28215, Tel. (704)531-2931 Fax (704)688-2551

Financial Sec., Jerry L. McCombs, P.O. Box 1444, Newton, NC 28658, Tel. (828)464-9609 Fax (828)466-1496, Email: jlmcableman @charter.net

Chaplain, Annie M. Williams, 2416 Heyward Brockington Rd., Columbia, SC 29203-9081, Tel. (803)754-8561 or (803)647-3570

Editor, *The Laity Speaks*, Rhandi M. Stith, Carrington Arms, 33 Lincoln Ave., Apt. 10L, New Rochelle, NY 10801, Tel. (914)235-3596 Fax (914)637-2518, Email: randhim@aol.com

Pres. Emeritus, Betty V. Stith, Carrington Arms, 33 Lincoln Ave., Apt. 10L, New Rochelle, NY 10801, Tel. (914) 235-3596 Fax (914)637-2518

## GENERAL OFFICERS OF THE WOMAN'S HOME AND OVERSEAS MISSIONARY SOCIETY

Gen. Pres., Mrs. Barbara L. Shaw, 4002 Maine Ave., Baltimore, MD 21207, Tel. (410)578-8239 Fax (410)578-0261, Email: bshawmax @comcast.net

First Vice Pres., Mrs. Margie J. Bonner, 12 Eldridge St., Waterbury, CT 06704, Tel. (203) 756-1829

Second Vice Pres., Dr. Sandra L. Gaston, 1808 Heather Hill Ct., Flossmoor, IL 60422, Tel. (708)957-0114 Fax (708)957-4629

Exec. Sec., Mrs. Rosetta J. Dunham, P.O. Box 26846, Charlotte, NC 28221-6846, Tel. (704)599-4630 Fax (704)688-2554; In Rock Hill: Tel. (803)324-5877 Fax (803)980-0759, Email: rodunham@amezhqtr.org

Recording Sec., Mrs. Vivian W. Brown, 3130 Greenvale Way, Decatur, GA 30034, Tel. (770)593-1566

Gen. Treas., Ms. Pamela Valentine, 692 N. Hawkins Ave., Akron, OH 44313, Tel. (330) 864-4890 Fax (330)796-4050

Gen. Coord. of YAMS, Mrs. Sandra B. Crowder, 301 Geranium Lane, Chesapeake, VA 23325, Tel. (757)424-8884

Sec. of Young Women, Mrs. Charlrean B. Mapson, 2214 Oleander Dr., Wilmington, NC 28403, Tel. (910)251-0682 Fax (910)362-9202, Email: ysec@chuckmapson.net

Superintendent of Buds of Promise, Vicki

L. Lewis, 110 S. Bayou St., Mobile, AL 36602, Tel. (251)438-4945

Sec., Bureau of Supplies, Mrs. Henrietta Daniels, 7535 Apache Plume Dr., Houston, TX 77071, Tel. (713)729-3436

Chair, Life Members Council, Mrs. Juletha N. French, 500 State St., Mobile, AL 36603, Tel. (251)438-4096

Editor, Woman's Section, Missionary Seer, Mrs. Ruth J. Stevens, 1080 Lincoln Place, Brooklyn, NY 11213, Tel. (718)604-3681 Fax (718)604-2094, Email: stevens72@msn.com

### Periodicals

*Star of Zion; Quarterly Review; Church School Herald, Missionary Seer, Vision Focus, Evangel*

## Albanian Orthodox Archdiocese in America

The Albanian Orthodox Church in America traces its origins to the groups of Albanian immigrants that first arrived in the United States in 1886, seeking religious, cultural and economic freedoms denied them in the homeland.

In 1908 in Boston, the Rev. Fan Stylian Noli (later Archbishop) served the first liturgy in the Albanian language in 500 years, to which Orthodox Albanians rallied, forming their own diocese in 1919. Parishes began to spring up throughout New England and the Mid-Atlantic and Great Lakes states. In 1922, clergy from the United States traveled to Albania to proclaim the self-governance of the Orthodox Church in the homeland at the Congress of Berat.

In 1971 the Albanian Archdiocese sought and gained union with the Orthodox Church in America, expressing the desire to expand the Orthodox witness to America at large, giving it an indigenous character. The Albanian Archdiocese remains vigilant for its brothers and sisters in the homeland and serves as an important resource for human rights issues and Albanian affairs, in addition to its programs for youth, theological education, vocational interest programs, and retreats for young adults and women.

### Headquarters

523 E. Broadway, S. Boston, MA 02127

Media Contact, Sec., Dorothy Adams, Tel. (617) 268-1275 Fax (617)268-3184

Website: www.oca.org

### Officers

Bishop Nikon, Tel. (617)268-1275

Chancellor, V. Rev. Arthur E. Liolin, 60 Antwerp St., East Milton, MA 02186, Tel. (617)698-3366

Lay Chpsn., William Poist, 40 Forge Village Rd., Westford, MA 01885, Tel. (978)392-0759

Treas., Cynthia Vasil Brown, 471 Capt. Eames Circle, Ashland, MA 01721, Tel. (508)881-0072

## Albanian Orthodox Diocese of America

This Diocese was organized in 1950 as a canonical body administering to the Albanian faithful. It is under the ecclesiastical jurisdiction of the Ecumenical Patriarchate of Constantinople (Istanbul).

### Headquarters

6455 Silver Dawn Lane, Las Vegas, NV 89118, Tel. (702)365-1989 Fax (702)365-1989

Media Contact, His Grace Bishop Ilia

### Officers

His Grace Bishop Ilia, 6455 Silver Dawn Lane, Las Vegas, NV 89118, Tel. (702)365-1989 Fax (702)365-1989

## The Allegheny Wesleyan Methodist Connection (Original Allegheny Conference)

This body was formed in 1968 by members of the Allegheny Conference (located in eastern Ohio and western Pennsylvania) of the Wesleyan Methodist Church, which merged in 1966 with the Pilgrim Holiness Church to form The Wesleyan Church.

The Allegheny Wesleyan Methodist Connection is composed of persons "having the form and seeking the power of godliness, united in order to pray together, to receive the word of exhortation, and to watch over one another in love, that they may help each other to work out their salvation." There is a strong commitment to congregational government and to holiness of heart and life. There is a strong thrust in church extension within the United States and in missions worldwide.

### Headquarters

P.O. Box 357, Salem, OH 44460, Tel. (330)337-9376 Fax (330)337-9700

Media Contact, Pres., Rev. William Cope

Email: awmc@juno.com

### Officers

Pres., Rev. William Cope, P.O. Box 357, Salem, OH 44460

Vice Pres., Rev. David Blowers, 1231 Conser Drive, Salem, OH 44460

Sec., Rev. Ray Satterfield, 31 S. 12th Street, Indiana, PA 15701

Treas., James Kunselman, 1022 Newgarden Ave., Salem, OH 44460

### Periodicals

*The Allegheny Wesleyan Methodist*

## The Alliance of Baptists*

The Alliance of Baptists is an association of individuals and churches dedicated to the preservation of historic Baptist principles, freedoms, and traditions, and to the expression of our ministry and mission through cooperative relationships with other Baptist bodies and the larger Christian community.

From its inception in early 1987, the Alliance has stood for those values that have distinguished the Baptist movement from its beginnings nearly four centuries ago—the freedom and account-ability of every individual in matters of faith; the freedom of each congregation under the authority of Jesus Christ to determine its own ministry and mission; and religious freedom for all in relationship to the state.

### Headquarters
1328 16th St. N.W., Washington, DC 20036, Tel. (202)745-7609 Fax (202)745-0023
Media Contact, Exec. Dir., Rev. Dr. Stan Hastey
Email: jholt@allianceofbaptists.org
Website: www.allianceofbaptists.org

### Officers
Exec. Dir., Rev. Dr. Stan Hastey
Assoc. Dir., Jeanette Holt
Pres., Rev. Jim Hopkins, Oakland, CA
Vice Pres., Kristy Arneson Pullen, Ashburn, VA
Sec., Amy Jacks Dean, Charlotte, NC

### Periodicals
*Connections*

## The American Association of Lutheran Churches
This church body was constituted on November 7, 1987. The AALC was formed by laity and pastors of the former American Lutheran Church in America who held to a high view of Scripture (inerrancy and infallibility). This church body also emphasizes the primacy of evangelism and world missions and the authority and autonomy of the local congregation.

Congregations of the AALC are distributed throughout the continental United States from Long Island, N.Y., to Los Angeles. The primary decision-making body is the General Convention, to which each congregation has pro-portionate representation.

### Headquarters
The AALC National Office, 801 West 106th Street, Ste. 203, Minneapolis, MN 55420-5603, Tel. (952)884-7784 Fax (952)884-7894,
Media Contact, Admn. Asst. to the AALC, Rev Greg Gerendas, 801 West 106th Street, Ste. 203, Minneapolis, MN 55420-5603, Tel. (952) 884-7784 Fax (952)884-7894, Email: revgjg @taalc.com
Email: theaalc@taalc.com
Website: www.taalc.com

### Officers
Presiding Pastor, Rev. Thomas V. Addland, 801 West 106th Street, Ste. 203, Minneapolis, MN 55420-5603, Tel. (952)884-7784 Fax (952) 884-7894, Email: aadland@taalc.com
Asst. Presiding Pastor, Rev. Paul Johansen, P.O. Box 1601, Williston, ND 58801 Tel. & Fax (701)774-3827 Email: Paul@arbsville.us

Sec., to The AALC, Rev. Harold C. Johnson, 7001 San Antonio NE, Ste. S, Albuquerque, NM 87109, Tel. (505) 828-0172, Email: christrayofhope@qwest.net
Treas., Rev. Kurt Luebkeman, Faith Lutheran Church, 6140 NE Stanton Street, Portland, OR 97213, Tel. (503) 288-5397, Email: flpastor @hevanet.com
American Lutheran Theological Seminary (ALTS), Pres., Rev. Franklin Hays, 5238 France Ave. So., Minneapolis, MN 55410, Tel. (952)920-8316

### Periodicals
*The Evangel*

## The American Baptist Association
The American Baptist Association (ABA) is an international fellowship of independent Baptist churches voluntarily cooperating in mis-sionary, evangelistic, benevolent and Christian education activities throughout the world. Its beginnings can be traced to the landmark move-ment of the 1850s. Led by James R. Graves and J.M. Pendleton, a significant number of Baptist churches in the South, claiming a New Testament heritage, rejected as extrascriptural the policies of the newly formed Southern Baptist Convention (SBC). Because they strongly advocated church equality, many of these churches continued doing mission and benevolent work apart from the SBC, electing to work through local associations. Meeting in Texarkana, Texas, in 1924, messengers from the various churches effectively merged two of these major associations, the Baptist Missionary Association of Texas and the General Association, forming the American Baptist Association.

Since 1924, mission efforts have been sup-ported in Australia, Africa, Asia, Canada, Central America, Europe, India, Israel, Japan, Korea, Mexico, New Zealand, South America and the South Pacific. An even more successful domestic mission effort has changed the ABA from a pre-dominantly rural southern organization to one with churches in 48 states.

Through its publishing arm in Texarkana, the ABA publishes literature and books numbering into the thousands. Major seminaries include the Missionary Baptist Seminary, founded by Dr. Ben M. Bogard in Little Rock, Ark.; Texas Baptist Seminary, Henderson, Texas; Oxford Baptist Institute, Oxford, Miss.; and Florida Baptist Schools in Lakeland, Fla.

While no person may speak for the churches of the ABA, all accept the Bible as the inerrant Word of God. They believe Christ was the virgin-born Son of God, that God is a triune God, that the only church is the local congregation of scripturally baptized believers and that the work of the church is to spread the gospel.

### Headquarters
4605 N. State Line Ave. Texarkana, TX 75503, Tel. (903)792-2783

65

Media Contact, Steve Reeves, Public Relations Director

Email: bssc@abaptist.org

Website: www.abaptist.org

### Officers

President, David Butimore, Sr., 197 W. Rialto Ave., Clovis, CA 93612

Vice Presidents, Neal Clark, Rt. 1, Box 48A, Daingerfield, TX 75638; John Owen, P.O. Box 142, Bryant, AR 72089; Donald R. Price, 210 West Mill St., Malvern, 72104

Recording Clerks, Larry Clements, 270 Tracy Dr., Monticello, AR 71655; Lonnie Wiggins, 1114 Occidental St., Redlands, CA 92374

Publications, Editor in Chief, Bill Johnson; Bus. Mgr., Wayne Sewell, 4605 N. State Line Ave., Texarkana, TX 75503

Meeting Arrangements Director, Edgar N. Sutton, P.O. Box 240, Alexander, AR 72002

Sec.-Treas. of Missions, Randy Cloud, P.O. Box 1050 Texarkana, TX 75504

## American Baptist Churches in the U.S.A.*

Originally known as the Northern Baptist Convention, this body of Baptist churches changed the name to American Baptist Convention in 1950 with a commitment to hold the name in trust for all Christians of like faith and mind who desire to bear witness to the historical Baptist convictions in a framework of cooperative Protestantism.

In 1972 American Baptist Churches in the U.S.A. was adopted as the new name. Although national missionary organizational developments began in 1814 with the establishment of the American Baptist Foreign Mission Society and continued with the organization of the American Baptist Publication Society in 1824 and the American Baptist Home Mission Society in 1832, the general denominational body was not formed until 1907. American Baptist work at the local level dates back to the organization by Roger Williams of the First Baptist Church in Providence, R. I. in 1638.

### Headquarters

American Baptist Churches Mission Center, P.O. Box 851, Valley Forge, PA 19482-0851, Tel. (610)768-2000 Fax (610)768-2320

Media Contact, Assoc. Gen'l. Sec. for Mission Resource Development, the Rev. Dr. Leo S. Thorne, Tel. (610)768-2077 Fax (610) 768-2320

Email: richard.schramm@abc-usa.org

Website: www.abc-usa.org

### Officers

Pres., Margaret Johnson

Vice Pres., Arlee Griffin, Jr.

Budget Review Officer, Melva Gray

Gen. Sec., A. Roy Medley; Tel. (610)768-2273; Email: roy.medley@abc-usa.org

Assoc. Gen. Sec.-Treas., Cheryl H. Wade; Tel. (610)768-2280; Email: cheryl.wade@abc-usa.org

### REGIONAL ORGANIZATIONS

Central Region, ABC of, Fred A. Ansell, 5833 SW 29th St. Ste. A, Topeka, KS 66614-5500

Chicago, ABC of Metro, Leonard Thompson, Sr., 8765 W. Higgins Road., Ste. 240, Chicago, IL 60631

Cleveland Baptist Assoc., Dennis E. Norris, 6060 Rockside Woods Blvd., Ste. 317, Cleveland, OH 44131

Connecticut, ABC of, Sarah Hallstrand, Interim, 100 Bloomfield Ave., Hartford, CT 06105-1097

Dakotas, ABC of, Riley H. Walker, 1101 W. 22nd St., Sioux Falls, SD 57105-1699

District of Columbia Bapt. Conv., Jeffrey Haggray, 1628 16th St., NW, Washington, DC 20009-3099

Evergreen Baptist Association, Marcia Patton, 409 Third Ave., South Ste. A, Kent, WA 98032

ABC of the Great Rivers Region, J. Dwight Stinnett, P.O. Box 3786, Springfield, IL 62708-3786

Indiana, ABC of, Larry D. Mason, 1350 N. Delaware St., Indianapolis, IN 46202-2493

Indianapolis, ABC of Greater, Larry D. Sayre, 1350 N. Delaware St., Indianapolis, IN 46202-2493

Los Angeles, ABC of, Samuel S. Chetti, 605 W. Olympic Blvd., Ste. 700, Los Angeles, CA 90015-1426

Maine, ABC of, Alfred Fletcher, 107 Winthrop St., P.O. Box 617, Augusta, ME 04332-0667

Massachusetts, ABC of, Robert Wallace, Interim, 20 Milton St., Dedham, MA 02026-2967

Metropolitan New York, ABC of, James O. Stallings, 475 Riverside Dr., Rm. 432, New York, NY 10115-0432

Michigan, ABC of, Michael A. Williams, 4578 S. Hagadorn Rd., East Lansing, MI 48823-5396

Mid-American Baptist Churches, Marshall Peters, 2400 86th St. Ste. !5., Des Moines, IA 50322-4380

Nebraska, ABC of, Susan E. Gillies, 6404 Maple St., Omaha, NE 68104-4079

New Jersey, ABC of, Lee Spitzer, 3752 Nottingham Way, Ste. 101, Trenton, NJ 08690-3802

New York State, ABC of, William A. Carlsen, 5842 Heritage Landing Dr., East Syracuse, NY 13057-9359

Northwest, ABC of, Charles Revis, 601 S. Ross Point Road, Post Falls, ID 83854-7726

Ohio, ABC of, Robert H. Roberts, Interim, 136 N. Galway Dr., P.O. Box 376, Granville, OH 43023-0376

Oregon, ABC of, W. Wayne Brown, 0245 SW Bancroft St., Ste. G, Portland, OR 97201-4270

Pacific Southwest, ABC of the, Dale V. Salico, 970 Village Oaks Dr., Ste. 101, Covina, CA 91724-3679

Pennsylvania & Delaware, ABC of, Clayton R. Woodbury, 106 Revere Lane, Coatesville, PA 19320

Philadelphia Baptist Assoc., James E. McJunkin, Jr., 100 N. 17th St. 5th floor, Philadelphia, PA 19103-2736

Pittsburgh Baptist Assoc., Lawrence O. Swain, 429 Forbes Ave., #1620, Pittsburgh, PA 15219-1604

Puerto Rico, Baptist Churches of, Cristino Diaz-Montanez, Calle Mayaguez #21, San Juan, PR 00917

Rhode Island, ABC of, Donald R. Rasmussen, P.O. Box 330, Exeter, RI 02822

Rochester-Genesee Region, ABC of, Alan Newton, 151 Brooks Ave., Rochester, NY 14619-2454

Rocky Mountains, ABC of, Desmond Hoffmeister, Interim, 3900 Wadsworth Blvd. Suite 365, Lakewood, CO 80235-2220

South, ABC of the, Walter L. Parrish, II, 5124 Greenwich Ave., Baltimore, MD 21229-2393

Vermont-New Hampshire, ABC of, Z. Allen Abbott, Wheeler Professional Park, One Oak Ridge Rd., Bldg. 3, Suite 4A, West Lebanon, NH 03784-3121

West, ABC of the, Paul D. Borden, 2420 Camino Ramon, Ste. 140, San Ramon, CA 94583-4207

West Virginia Baptist Convention, James E. Lutz, Interim, P.O. Box 1019, Parkersburg, WV 26102-1019

Wisconsin, ABC of, Arlo R. Reichter, 15330 W. Watertown Plank Rd., Elm Grove, WI 53122-2391

BOARDS

American Baptist Assembly, Green Lake, WI 54941; Pres., Kenneth P. Giacoletto

American Baptist Historical Society, 1106 S. Goodman St., Rochester, NY 14620; or P.O. Box 851, Valley Forge, PA 19482-0851; Admn. Archivist, Deborah B. VanBroekhoven; Pres., Esther Irish

American Baptist Men, Pres., Cody Pollington

American Baptist Women's Ministries, Exec. Dir., Virginia Holmstrom; Pres., Lois Chiles

Bd. of Intl. Ministries, Acting Exec. Dir., Charles H. Jones; Pres., Elizabeth Burger

Bd. of Natl. Ministries, Exec. Dir., Aidsand F. Wright-Riggins; Pres., David Blythe

Ministers & Missionaries Benefit Bd., Exec. Dir., Sumner M. Grant; Pres., George Tooze, 475 Riverside Dr., New York, NY 10115

Minister Council, Dir., Carole (Kate) H. Harvey; Pres., Joseph Kutter

### Periodicals
*Tomorrow Magazine; The Secret Place; American Baptist Quarterly; American Baptists In Mission*

## The American Carpatho-Russian Orthodox Greek Catholic Church

The American Carpatho-Russian Orthodox Greek Catholic Church is a self-governing diocese that is in communion with the Ecumenical Patriarchate of Constantinople. The late Patriarch Benjamin I, in an official Patriarchal Document dated Sept. 19, 1938, canonized the Diocese in the name of the Orthodox Church of Christ.

### Headquarters
312 Garfield St., Johnstown, PA 15906, Tel. (814)539-4207 Fax (814)536-4699

Media Contact, Chancellor, V. Rev. Protopresbyter Frank P. Miloro, Tel. (814)539-8086 Fax (814) 536-4699

Email: archdiocese@goarch.org

Website: www.goarch.org

### Officers
Bishop, Metropolitan Nicholas Smisko, 312 Garfield St., Johnstown, PA 15906, Tel. (814)539-4207 Fax(814)536-4699

Chancellor, V. Rev. Protopresbyter Frank P. Miloro, 249 Butler Ave., Johnstown, PA 15906, Tel. (814)539-9143 Fax(814)536-4699, Email: acrod@helicon.net

Treas., V. Rev. Protopresbyter Ronald A. Hazuda, 115 East Ave., Erie, PA 16503, Tel. (814)453-4902

### Periodicals
*The Church Messenger*

## American Evangelical Christian Churches

Founded in 1944, the A.E.C.C is composed of individual ministers and churches who are united in accepting "Seven Articles of Faith." These seven articles are: the Bible as the written word of God; the virgin birth; the deity of Jesus Christ; salvation through the atonement; guidance of our life through prayer; the return of the Saviour; the establishment of the Millennial Kingdom.

The American Evangelical Christian Churches offers the following credentials: Certified Christian Worker, Commission to Preach, Licensed Minister and Ordained Minister to those who accept the Seven Articles of Faith, who put unity in Christ first, and are approved by A.E.C.C.

A.E.C.C seeks to promote the gospel through its ministers, churches and missionary activities.

Churches operate independently with all decisions concerning local government left to the individual churches.

The organization also has ministers in Canada, England, Bolivia, Philippines Thailand, Brazil and South America.

### Headquarters
P.O. Box 47312, Indianapolis, IN 46227, Tel. (317)788-9280 Fax (317)788-1410

Media Contact, Dr. Charles Wasielewski, Sr., 51 Wells Rd, Barton, NY 13734-1818

Email: aeccoffice@infoblvd.net

Website: www.aeccministries.com

## INTERNATIONAL OFFICERS

Mod., Dr. Charles Wasielewski, Box 51, Wells Rd., Barton, NY 13734, Tel. (607)565-4074

Sec., Dr. Gene McClain, 520 Blooming Pike, Morgantown, IN 46160, Tel. (812)597-5021

Treas., Dr. Michael Ward, Sr., 4802 Chervil Ct., Indianapolis, IN 46237, Tel. (317)888-2095

Bd. Member, Dr. Allen Kent, 550 E. Shoeline Drive, Long Beach, CA 90802, Tel. (562)590-7294

Missions Coordinator, Dr. Douglas Schlemmer, P.O. Box 409, Twin Peaks, CA 92391, Tel. (909)338-6495

### REGIONAL MODERATORS

Northwest Region, Rev. Alvin House, P.O. Box 393, Darby MT 59829, Tel.(406)821-3141

Central-West Region, Rev. Charles Clark, Box 314, Rockport, IL 62370, Tel.(217)437-2507

Far West Region, Pastor Richard Cuthbert, 1195 Via Serville, Cathedral City, CA 92234, Tel. (706)321-6682

Lowell Ford, 397 Shamrock Lane, Newark, OH, 43055, Tele. (614)309-3419

Northeast Region, Rev. John Merrill, P.O. Box 183, East Smithfield, PA 18817, Tel.(717)596-4598

East Region, James R. Brown, 17404 W. Washington, Hagerstown, MD 21740, Tel. (301)797-8121

Southeast Region, Rev. James Fullwood, 207 5th Avenue, N.E., Lutz, FL 33549

### STATE MODERATORS

Rev. James Brown, Maryland

Rev. John W. Coats, Delaware

Brenda Osborne, New York

Dr. Berton G. Heleine, Illinois

Rev. R. Eugene Hill, New Jersey

Rev. Kenneth Pope, Washington

Rev. Art Mirek, Michigan

Rev. Charles Jennings, Pennsylvania

Rev. Jerry Myers, Indiana

### FOREIGN OUTREACH MINISTRIES

American Evangelical Christian Churches—Canada

Regional Moderator, Dr. Stephen K. Massey, 730 Ontario street, Suite 709, Toronto, Ontario M4X 1N3, Canada (416)323-9076

Philippine Evangelical Christian Churches

Director, Rev. Alan A. Olubalang, P.O. Box 540, Cotabato City, Philippines 9600

American Evangelical Christian Churches-Philippines

Regional Moderator, Rev. Oseas Andres, P.O. Box 2695, Central Post Office, 1166 Q.C. Metro Manila, Philippines

### Periodicals

*The American Evangelical Christian Churches Newsletter*—Monthly

**American Orthodox Catholic Church—please see Apostolic Orthodox Catholic Church.**

## American Rescue Workers

Major Thomas E. Moore was National Commander of Booth's Salvation Army when a dispute flared between Booth and Moore. Moore resigned from Booth's Army and due to the fact that Booth's Army was not incorporated at the time, Moore was able to incorporate under said name. The name was changed in 1890 to American Salvation Army. In 1913 the current name American Rescue Workers was adopted.

It is a national religious social service agency which operates on a quasimilitary basis. Membership includes officers (clergy), soldiers-adherents (laity), members of various activity groups and volunteers who serve as advisors, associates and committed participants in ARW service functions.

The motivation of the organization is the love of God. Its message is based on the Bible. This is expressed by its spiritual ministry, the purposes of which are to preach the gospel of Jesus Christ and to meet human needs in his name without discrimination. It is a branch of the Christian Church . . . a Church with a mission.

### Headquarters

Operational Headquarters, 25 Ross Street, Williamsport, PA 17701, Tel. (570)323-8693 Fax (570)323-8694

National Field Office, 11116 Gehr Road, Waynesboro, PA 17268-9101, Tel. (717)762-2965

Media Contact, Natl. Communication Sec./Natl Special Services Dir., Col. Robert N. Coles, Rev., Natl. Field Ofc., Fax (717)762-8109

Email: amerscwk@pcspower.net

Website: www.arwus.com

### Officers

Commander-In-Chief & Pres. of Corp., General Claude S. Astin, Jr. Rev.

Natl. Bd. Pres., Col. Sam Astin (Claude S. Astin, III)

Ordination Committee, Chpsn., Gen. Paul E. Martin, (Emeritus) Rev.

Natl. Chief Sec., Col. Dawn R. Astin, NQ-643 Elmira St., Williamsport, PA 17701

### Periodicals

*The Rescue Herald*

**Amish—please see Older Amish Church**

**Anglican Orthodox Church—please see The Episcopal Orthodox Church**

## The Antiochian Orthodox Christian Archdiocese of North America

The spiritual needs of Antiochian faithful in North America were first served through the Syro-Arabian Mission of the Russian Orthodox Church in 1895. In 1895, the Syrian Orthodox Benevolent Society was organized by Antiochian immigrants in New York City. Raphael Hawaweeny, a young Damascene clergyman serving as professor of Arabic language at the

Orthodox theological academy in Kazan, Russia, came to New York to organize the first Arabic-language parish in North America in 1895, after being canonically received under the omophorion of the head of the Russian Church in North America. Saint Nicholas Cathedral, now located at 355 State St. in Brooklyn, is considered the "mother parish" of the Archdiocese.

On March 12, 1904, Hawaweeny became the first Orthodox bishop to be consecrated in North America. He traveled throughout the continent and established new parishes. The unity of Orthodoxy in the New World, including the Syrian Greek Orthodox community, was ruptured after the death of Bishop Raphael in 1915 and by the Bolshevik revolution in Russia and the First World War. Unity returned in 1975 when Metropolitan Philip Saliba, of the Antiochian Archdiocese of New York, and Metropolitan Michael Shaheen of the Antiochian Archdiocese of Toledo, Ohio, signed the Articles of Reunification, ratified by the Holy Synod of the Patriarchate. Saliba was recognized as the Metropolitan Primate and Shaheen as Auxiliary Archbishop. A second auxiliary to the Metropolitan, Bishop Antoun Khouri, was consecrated at Brooklyn's Saint Nicholas Cathedral, in 1983. A third auxiliary, Bishop Basil Essey was consecrated at Wichita's St. George Cathedral in 1992. Two additional bishops were added in 1994, Bishop Joseph Zehlaoui and Bishop Demetri Khoury.

The Archdiocesan Board of Trustees (consisting of 60 elected and appointed clergy and lay members) and the Metropolitan's Advisory Council (consisting of clergy and lay representatives from each parish and mission) meet regularly to assist the Primate in the administration of the Archdiocese. Currently, there are 245 parishes and missions in the Archdiocese.

### Headquarters
358 Mountain Rd., Englewood, NJ 07631, Tel. (201)871-1355 Fax (201)871-7954
Media Contact, Father Thomas Zain, 52 78th St., Brooklyn, NY 11209, Tel. (718)748-7940 Fax (718)855-3608
Email: FrJoseph@antiochian.org
Website: www.antiochian.org

### Officers
Primate, Metropolitan Philip Saliba, 358 Mountain Road, Englewood, NJ 07631— Metropolitan of New York and all North America (210)871-1355
Auxiliary, Bishop Antoun Khouri, 358 Mountain Road, Englewood, NJ 07631- Bishop of Miami and the Southeast (201)871-1355
Auxiliary, Bishop Joseph Zehlaoui, 454 S. Lorraine Blvd., Los Angeles, CA 90020—Bishop of Los Angeles and the West (323)934-3131
Auxiliary, Bishop Basil Essey, 1559 N. Woodlawn, Wichita, KS 67208—Bishop of Wichita and Mid-America (316)687-3169
Auxiliary, Bishop Thomas Joseph, P.O. Box 638,

Ligionier, PA 15658—Bishop of Oakland, PA and the East (724)787-9832
Auxiliary, Bishop Alexander Mufarrij, 10820 Rue La Verdue, Montreal, QC H3L2L9— Bishop of Ottawa, Eastern Canada and Upstate New York, Tel. (514)388-4344

### Periodicals
*The Word; Again Magazine*

# Apostolic Catholic Assyrian Church of the East, North American Dioceses
The Holy Apostolic Catholic Assyrian Church of the East is the ancient Christian church that developed within the Persian Empire from the day of Pentecost. The Apostolic traditions testify that the Church of the East was established by Sts. Peter, Thomas, Thaddaeus and Bartholomew from among the Twelve and by the labors of Mar Mari and Aggai of the Seventy. The Church grew and developed carrying the Christian gospel into the whole of Asia and islands of the Pacific. Prior to the Great Persecution at the hands of Tamer'leng the Mongol, it is said to have been the largest Christian church in the world.

The doctrinal identity of the church is that of the Apostles. The church stresses two natures and two Qnume in the One person, Perfect God-Perfect man. The church gives witness to the original Nicene Creed, the Ecumenical Councils of Nicea and Constantinople and the church fathers of that era. Since God is revealed as Trinity, the appellation "Mother of God" is rejected for the "Ever Virgin Blessed Mary Mother of Christ," we declare that she is Mother of Emmanuel, God with us!

The church has maintained a line of Catholicos Patriarchs from the time of the Holy Apostles until this present time. Today the present occupant of the Apostolic Throne is His Holiness Mar Dinkha IV, 120th successor to the See of Selucia Ctestiphon.

### Headquarters
Catholicos Patriarch, His Holiness Mar Dinkha, IV, Metropolitanate Residence, The Assyrian Church of the East, Baghdad, Iraq
Media Contact, Father Sleiman Shequel, 7201 N. Ashland, Chicago, IL 60626, Tel. (773)465-4777 Fax (773)465-0776
Email: ABSoro@aol.com
Website: www.cired.org/ace

### BISHOPS—NORTH AMERICA
Diocese Eastern U.S.A., His Grace Bishop Mar Aprim Khamis, 8908 Birch Ave., Morton Grove, IL 60053, Tel. (847)966-0617 Fax (847) 966-0012; Chancellor to the Bishop, Rev. Chancellor C. H. Klutz, 7201 N. Ashland, Chicago, IL 60626, Tel. (773)465-4777 Fax (773)465-0776
Diocese Western U.S.A., St. Joseph Cathedral, 680 Minnesota Ave., San Jose, CA 95125, Tel. (408)286-7377 Fax (408)286-1236

Diocese of Canada, His Grace Bishop Mar Emmanuel Joseph, St. Mary Cathedral, 57 Apted Ave., Weston, ON M9L 2P2, Tel. (416)744-9311

Comm. on Inter-Church & Religious Ed., His Grace Bishop Mar Bawai, Diocese of Seattle in Wash., 165 NW 65th, Seattle, WA 98117, Tel. (206)789-1843

## Apostolic Catholic Church

The Apostolic Catholic Church, rooted in the New Testament, affirms the empowerment and the dignity of the poor, the needy, and the oppressed by adopting a preferential option for those who are disenfranchised and marginalized in this society. Apostolic Catholicism is radically committed to the unconditional acceptance of all who are in need.

The special mission of the Apostolic Catholic Church is to be Christ's arms and legs, reaching out to those who suffer and are ignored by the world. We choose to serve others, ever mindful of the example of Christ, who "did not cling to his equality with God, but emptied himself to assume the condition of a slave." (Philippians 2: 6-7)

Member: The Council of North American Old Catholic Bishops, the Florida Council of Churches, and International Council of Community Churches.

### Headquarters

Apostolic Catholic Church

7813 N. Nebraska Avenue, Tampa, FL 33604

Media Contact: Bishop Charles Leigh, Tel. (813)238-6060

Email: Bishop-Chuck@apostoliccatholicchurch. com

Website: www.apostoliccatholicchurch.com

### Missions

Family Counseling Center, Temeous Catholic Worker House, St James Catholic Worker House.

### Periodicals

*The Shofar*

## Apostolic Catholic Orthodox Church

The Apostolic Catholic Orthodox Church (ACOC) is a communion of persons gathered for worship and public ministry outreach within the Christian Apostolic tradition. The ACOC is creedal, renewal-oriented, and is a part of the autocephalous (self-ruling) Old Catholic Movement, which has its origins in the ancient Catholic Church of the Netherlands. The immediate history of the Old Catholic churches comes out of the reform movement that took place after the First Vatican Council (1869-70). The ACOC maintains a friendly relationship with the Old Catholic Church in the Netherlands.

The bishops of the newly forming churches received episcopal consecration in valid apostolic lines from the church of the Netherlands, based in Utrecht, which had been a fully autonomous Catholic church. These churches became known as "Old Catholic" in reference to their insistence upon return to the basic tenets of Apostolic Christianity, and as defined by the seven Ecumenical Councils of the undivided Eastern and Western Christian churches.

The Old Catholic independent church movement came to the United States as early as the 1880's. Bishop DeLandes Berghes, an Austrian nobleman, ordained and consecrated a bishop with valid Old Catholic Apostolic lines, was sent to North America in 1914. Two of the bishops he consecrated in 1916, Carmel Henry Carfora and William Francis Brothers, are from whom the ACOC derives its lines of apostolic succession.

The Apostolic Catholic Orthodox Church finds matters of discipline, administration and pastoral care are governed by discernment about ministry in the Spirit of Christ. Clerical celibacy (which is a matter of discipline) is optional among Old Catholics. In the ACOC, Holy Orders are open to both women and men, single or married. Graduate, seminary and clinical pastoral education are required for candidates for ordination. Decisions pertaining to family planning are left to the concience of married couples, through prayer and counseling.

Matters of faith in the Apostolic Catholic Orthodox Church are the same as in other liturgical churches as formulated in the apostles and Nicene Creeds. The Offices of bishop, priest, and deacon exist for the service of spiritual leadership in facilitating expressions of life with God—in the celebration of the sacraments, counseling and pastoral care, teaching, and public advocacy of gospel values. The sacraments are never denied to any person on grounds of gender, race, or marital status. The Holy Eucharist is the center of worship for the ACOC and all who are baptized are welcomed at the Lord's Table.

The Apostolic Catholic Orthodox Church emphasizes the importance of the life of the church as community, that all may be one in Christ (John 17), through mutual helpfulness, ministering to one another and all creation in love, through the diversity of personal giftedness and sensitivity to the particular needs of those being served. The church values and promotes spiritually based, courageous, and compassionate ministry to both personal and global needs. Ongoing spiritual growth is to be nourished through sacred study and contemplative prayer. The ACOC values ecumenical dialogue as an expression of the life of the church.

### Headquarters

1900 St. James Place, Suite 880, Houston, TX 77056-4129, Tel. (713)266-2456 or (713)977-2855 Fax (713)266-0855

Website: www.apostoliccatholic.org

## Officers

Presiding Bishop, Most Rev. Diana C. Dale, 1900 St. James Place, Suite 880, Houston, TX 77056-41291, Tel. (713)266-2456
Email: dcdale@apostoliccatholic.org
Tresurer, Elizabeth F. Burleigh, J.D., 1770 St. James Place, Suite 550, Houston, TX 77056, Tel. (713)334-0499
Ecumenical Officer, Very Rev. Robert L. Lewis Jr., P.O. Box 10483, Rockville, MD 20849, Tel. (240)401-0178
Register Agent, Rev. Lance Beizer, J.D., P.O. Box 1121, Campbell, CA 9009-1121

## BOARD REGIONAL REPRESENTATIVES

West, Rev. Gale Bellinger, 2033 S.15th St., Centerville, IA 52544-3016
Mid-Continent, Rev. Robert M. Palmer, 871 Stone Blvd. Nolensville, TN 37135
Atlantic, Very Rev. Robert L. Lewis Jr. 2639 Ridge Rd.

## OTHER ORGANIZATIONS:

Institute of Worklife Ministry, 1900 St. James Place, Suite 880, Houston, TX 77056-4129, Tel. (713)266-2456 Fax(713)266-0855
Website: www.apostoliccatholic.org

## Periodicals

*ACOC Quarterly Bulletin; Worklife Quarterly Newsletter*

## Apostolic Christian Church (Nazarene)

This body was formed in America by an immigration from various European nations, from a movement begun by Rev. S. H. Froehlich, a Swiss pastor, whose followers are still found in Switzerland and Central Europe.

## Headquarters

Apostolic Christian Church Foundation, 1135 Sholey Rd., Richmond, VA 23231, Tel. (804) 222-1943 Fax (804)236-0642
Media Contact, Exec. Dir., James Hodges
Email: accf@sprynet.com

## Officers

Exec. Dir., James Hodges

## Apostolic Christian Churches of America

The Apostolic Christian Churches of America was founded in the early 1830s in Switzerland by Samuel Froehlich, a young divinity student who had experienced a religious conversion based on the pattern found in the New Testament. The church, known then as Evangelical Baptist, spread to surrounding countries. A Froehlich associate, Elder Benedict Weyeneth, established the church's first American congregation in 1847 in upstate New York. In America, where the highest concentration today is in the Midwest farm belt, the church became known as Apostolic Christian.

Church doctrine is based on a literal interpretation of the Bible, the infallible Word of God. The church believes that a true faith in Christ's redemptive work at Calvary is manifested by a sincere repentance and conversion. Members strive for sanctification and separation from worldliness as a consequence of salvation, not as a means to obtain it. Security in Christ is believed to be conditional based on faithfulness. Uniform observance of scriptural standards of holiness are stressed. Holy Communion is confined to members of the church. Male members are willing to serve in the military, but do not bear arms. The holy kiss is practiced and women wear head coverings during prayer and worship.

Doctrinal authority rests with a council of elders, each of whom serves as a local elder (bishop). Both elders and ministers are chosen from local congregations, do not attend seminary and serve without compensation. Sermons are delivered extemporaneously as led by the Holy Spirit, using the Bible as a text.

## Headquarters

3420 N. Sheridan Rd., Peoria, IL 61604
Media Contact, Secretary., William R. Schlatter, 14834 Campbell Rd., Defiance, OH 43512, Tel. (419)393-2621 Fax(419)393-2144
Email: Questions@ApostolicChristian.org; wrschlatter@juno.com
Website: www.apostolicchristian.org

## Officers

Sec., Elder (Bishop) William R. Schlatter, 14834 Campbell Rd., Defiance, OH 43512, Tel. (419)393-2621 Fax(419)393-2144

## Periodicals

*The Silver Lining*

## Apostolic Episcopal Church

The Apostolic Episcopal Church on Sept. 23-24, 2000 in New York City signed Concordats of Intercommunion with the following Christian Churches—The Anglican Independent Communion, The Ethiopian Orthodox Coptic Archdiocese of North and South America, The Uniate Western Orthodox Catholic Church, and the Byelorussian Orthodox National Church in Exile under the administration of His Beatitude Yury I.

In effect, the Apostolic Episcopal Church thus became a Uniate Western Rite of the Orthodox Church of the East, using the 1928 Book of Common Prayer. In 1905, under the guidance of Archbishop Tikhon Bellavin (later Patriarch of Moscow), the Holy Synod in St. Petersburg approved the use of the Anglican Liturgy for Western Rite Orthodox Christians. Today this usage is called the Rite of St. Tikhon and is in use among many Orthodox Western Rite Jurisdictions.

This Pilgrimage to Orthodoxy among Anglicans began in 1712 with the Non-Jurors Anglican Hierarchy and faithful. These Non-Jurors were Anglican Clergy who in 1689 refused allegiance to

71

King William III and Queen Mary, the usurpers who had overthrown King James II. In 1712 Metropolitan-Bishop Arsenios of the Alexandrine Patriarchate visited England and received many of these "British Katholicks" into the Orthodox Church.

### Headquarters

World Mission HQS: 80-46 234 St., Jamaica, NY 11427-2116, Attn.: the Rt. Rev. Francis C. Spataro D.D., Tel. (917)529-0585

The Province of Guyana and the Caribbean, c/o The Rev. Lloyd U. Samuel OCR, P.O. Box 10844, Georgetown, Guyana, South America, 630875.

Ohio Vicariate: the V. Rev. Michael B. Reed, St. Peter the Aleut Mission, 3423 Hunter Dr., N. Olmstead, OH 44070, Tel. (216)779-0272

Pennsylvania Vicariate: Rev. Dr. Sam Guido D.D., OCR, St. Paul's Chapel, 620 Main St., Slatington, PA 18080

Shenouda Seminary Dir.: Rev. Dr. Paget Mack, OCR, OSBM, P.O. Box 673, New York, NY 10035

Belarus Home Mission, AWP, 19 Aqueduct St, Ossining, NY 10562 Tel. (914)762-7093

Media Contact, The Rev. S.C. Douglas, M.A., P.O. Box 5016 Athens, GA 30604

Email: apostolic.episcopal@gmail.com

Website: www.apostolic-episcopal.org

### Officers

President, The Rt. Rev. Francis C. Spataro, D.D., OCR, Tel. (718)740-4134 (24-hour number), Email: vil11427@mycingular.blackberry.net

Archbishop of the Central & Western Province, U.S.A., Dr. Wayne Ellis, Ph.D., OCR, Email: wayneellis@charter.net

OCR Primate: The Rt. Rev. Peter P. Brennan, OCR, D.D., Email: ddamdg@aol.com

Vicar for Guyana & the Caribbean: Rev. Lloyd U. Samuel, OCR

Vicar for Ohio: The V. Rev. Michael B. Reed, OCR

Emeritus Primate for the AEC, The M. Rev. Bertil Persson, Th.D., OCR, Archbishop of Scandinavia & Baltic Republics, Illerstigen 22, S-170 71, Solna, Sweden

Pennsylvania Vicariate: Rev. Dr. Sam Guido, D.D. LOC, Email: samsamtheman@aol.com

Shenouda Seminary Dir.: Rev. Dr. Paget Mack, OSBM

Vicar for Belarus: M. Rev. Emigidiusz J. Ryzy, OCR, D.D., Email: amworldpat@aol.com

The Order of Corporate Reunion; The Vilatte Guild/Society of St. Cassian

## Apostolic Faith Mission Church of God

The Apostolic Faith Mission Church of God was founded and organized July 10, 1906, by Bishop F. W. Williams in Mobile, Ala.

Bishop Williams was saved and filled with the Holy Ghost at a revival in Los Angeles under Elder W. J. Seymour of the Divine Apostolic Faith Movement. After being called into the ministry, Bishop Williams went out to preach the gospel in Mississippi, then moved on to Mobile.

On Oct. 9, 1915, the Apostolic Faith Mission Church of God was incorporated in Mobile under Bishop Williams, who was also the general overseer of this church.

### Headquarters

Ward's Temple, 806 Muscogee Rd., Cantonment, FL 32533

Media Contact, Natl. Sunday School Supt., Bishop Thomas Brooks, 3298 Toney Dr., Decatur, GA 30032, Tel. (404)284-7596

### BOARD OF BISHOPS

Presiding Bishop, Donice Brown, 2265 Welcome Cir., Cantonement, FL 32535, Tel. (904)968-5225

Bishop T.C. Tolbert Sr., 226 Elston Ave., Anniston, AL, 36201; Bishop John Crum, 4236 Jackson St., Birmingham, AL, 35217; Bishop Samuel Darden, 25 Taunton Ave., Hyde Park, MA 02136; Bishop James Truss, P.O. Box 495, Lincoln, AL, 35096; Bishop T.C. Tolbert, Jr., 768 Grayton Rd., Ohatchee, AL 36271; Bishop Thomas Brooks, 3298 Toney Drive, Decatur, GA. 30032, Tel: (404)284-7596 Fax (404)284-7173; Bishop Johnny Cunningham, P.O.Box 472 Century, Fla. 32535, Tel: (850)256-2443; Bishop Wayne Smiley, 228 Seville Circle, Mary Ester, FL 32569

### NATIONAL DEPARTMENTS

Missionary Dept., Pres., Rosa Tolbert, Anniston, Ala.

Youth Dept., Pres., Johnny Kennedy, Birmingham, Ala.

Sunday School Dept., Supt., Thomas Brooks, Decatur, Ga.

Mother Dept., Pres., Mother Bessie Davis, 1003 Northeast St., Pensacola, FL 32501

### INTERNATIONAL DEPARTMENTS

Morobia, Liberia, Bishop Beter T. Nelson, Box 3646, Bush Rhode Islane, Morobia, Liberia

### Periodicals

*The Three-Fold Vision*/Published quarterly.

The A.F.M. Church of God Apostolic Bible College/Cantonement, FL 32535

## Apostolic Faith Mission of Portland, Oregon

The Apostolic Faith Mission of Portland, Oregon, was founded in 1907. It had its beginning in the Latter Rain outpouring on Azusa Street in Los Angeles in 1906.

Some of the main doctrines are justification by faith, which is a spiritual new birth, as Jesus told Nicodemus and as Martin Luther proclaimed in the Great Reformation; sanctification, a second definite work of grace; the Wesleyan teaching of holiness; the baptism of the Holy Ghost as experienced on the Day of Pentecost and again poured out at the beginning of the Latter Rain revival in Los Angeles.

Mrs. Florence L. Crawford, who had received the baptism of the Holy Ghost in Los Angeles, brought this Latter Rain message to Portland on Christmas Day 1906. It has spread to the world by means of literature which is still published and mailed everywhere without a subscription price. Collections are never taken in the meetings and the public is not asked for money.

Camp meetings have been held annually in Portland, Ore. since 1907, with delegations coming from around the world.

Missionaries from the Portland headquarters have established churches in Korea, Japan, the Philippines, Romania and many countries in Africa.

### Headquarters

6615 SE 52nd Ave., Portland, OR 97206, Tel. (503)777-1741 Fax (503)777-1743
Media Contact, Superintendent, Darrel D. Lee
Website: www.apostolicfaith.org

### Officers

President, Rev. Darrel D. Lee

### Periodicals

*Higher Way*

## Apostolic Lutheran Church of America

Organized in 1872 as the Solomon Korteniemi Lutheran Society, this Finnish body was incorporated in 1929 as the Finnish Apostolic Lutheran Church in America and changed its name to Apostolic Lutheran Church of America in 1962.

This body stresses preaching the Word of God. There is an absence of liturgy and formalism in worship. A seminary education is not required of pastors. Being called by God to preach the Word is the chief requirement for clergy and laity. The church stresses personal absolution and forgiveness of sins, as practiced by Martin Luther, and the importance of bringing converts into God's kingdom.

### Headquarters

P.O. Box 2948, Battle Ground, WA 98604-2948
Media Contact, Secretary, Ivan M. Seppala
Website: www.apostolic-lutheran.org

### Officers

Chairman, Richard C. Juuti, RRI, Bentley, AB T0C 0J0, Canada
Treas., Ben Johnson, 98920 Keller Rd., Astoria, OR 97103
Secretary, Ivan M. Seppala, 332 Mt. Washington Way, Clayton, CA 94517

### Periodicals

*Christian Monthly*

**Apostolic Orthodox Catholic Church of North America**—*please see* **Holy Synod of the American Diaspora**

## Armenian Apostolic Church of America

Widespread movement of the Armenian people over the centuries caused the development of two seats of religious jurisdiction of the Armenian Apostolic Church in the World—the See of Etchmiadzin, in Armenia, and the See of Cilicia, in Lebanon.

In America, the Armenian Church functioned under the jurisdiction of the Etchmiadzin See from 1887 to 1933, when a division occurred within the American diocese over the condition of the church in Soviet Armenia. One group chose to remain independent until 1957, when the Holy See of Cilicia agreed to accept them under its jurisdiction.

Despite the existence of two dioceses in North America, the Armenian Church has always functioned as one church in dogma and liturgy.

### Headquarters

Eastern Prelacy, 138 E. 39th St., New York, NY 10016, Tel. (212)689-7810 Fax (212)689-7168
Western Prelacy, 6252 Honolulu Ave., La Crescenta, CA 91214; Tel. (818)248-7737; Fax (818)248-7745
Media Contact, Vazken Ghougassian
Email: prelacy@gis.net
Website: www.armprelacy.org

### Officers

Eastern Prelacy, Prelate, Archbishop Oshagan Choloyan
Eastern Prelacy, Chpsn., Jack Mardoian, Esq.
Western Prelacy, Prelate, Archbishop Moushegh Mardirossian
Western Prelacy, Chpsn., Hrair Balian

### DEPARTMENTS

Eastern Prelacy Offices, Executive Director, Vazken Ghougassian
AREC, Armenian Religious Educ. Council, Exec. Coord., Deacon Shant Kazanjian
ANEC, Armenian Natl. Educ. Council, Exec. Coord., Nayira Balanian

### Periodicals

*Outreach*

## Armenian Apostolic Church, Diocese of America*

The Armenian Apostolic Church was founded at the foot of the biblical mountain of Ararat in the ancient land of Armenia, where two of Christ's Holy Apostles, Saints Thaddeus and Bartholomew, preached Christianity. In A.D. 303 the historic Mother Church of Etchmiadzin was founded by Saint Gregory the Illuminator, the first Catholicos of All Armenians. This cathedral still stands and serves as the center of the Armenian Church. A branch of this church was established in North America in 1889. The first church building was consecrated in 1891 in Worcester, Mass. The first Armenian Diocese was set up in 1898 by the then-Catholicos of All

Armenians, Mgrditch Khrimian. Armenian immigrants built the first Armenian church in the new world in Worcester, Mass., under the jurisdiction of Holy Etchmiadzin.

In 1927, the churches and the parishes in California were formed into a Western Diocese, and the parishes in Canada formed their own diocese in 1984. Other centers of major significance of the Armenian Apostolic Church are the Catholicate of Cilicia, now located in Lebanon, the Armenian Patriarchate of Jerusalem and the Armenian Patriarchate of Constantinople.

### Headquarters
Eastern Diocese, 630 Second Ave., New York, NY 10016-4885, Tel. (212)686-0710 Fax (212) 779-3558

Western Diocese, 3325 North Glenoaks Blvd., Burbank, CA 91504, Tel. (818)558-7474 Fax (818)558-6333, Email: mgizlechyan@armenianchurchwd.com

Canadian Diocese, 615 Stuart Ave., Outremont, QC H2V 3H2, Tel. (514)276-9479 Fax (514) 276-9960

Media Contact, Dir., Public Relations, Chris Zakian, Eastern Diocese

Diocesan Council Chpsn., Haig Dadourian, 415 Madison Ave., 7th Fl., New York, NY 10017

Western Diocese, Primate, His Em. Archbishop Vatche Hovsepian, Western Diocese Ofc.

Diocesan Council, Chpsn., Dn. Dr. Varouj Alterbarmakian, 7290 North San Pedro, Fresno, CA 93011

Diocesan Council, Sec., Mr. John Yaldezian, 23221 Aetna St., Woodland Hills, CA 91367, Tel. (818)346-6163

Canadian Diocese, Primate, His Em. Archbishop Hovnan Derderian

Diocesan Council, Chpsn., Mr. Takvor Hopyan, 20 Pineway, Blvd., Willowdale, ON M2H 1A1, Canada, Tel. (416)222-2639

Diocesan Council, Secretary, Mr. Vahe Ketli, 750 Montpellier, #909, St. Laurens, QC H4L 5A7, Canada, Tel. (514)747-1347

Email: mgizlechyan@armenianchurchwd.com
Website: www.armenianchurch.org

### Eastern Diocese
Primate, Archbishop Khajag Barsamian, Eastern Diocese Ofc.

Diocesan Council, Chpsn., Haig Dadourian, 415 Madison Ave., 7th Fl., New York, NY 10017

### Western Diocese
Primate, His Em. Archbishop Vatche Hovsepian, Western Diocese Ofc.

Diocesan Council, Chpsn., Dn. Dr. Varouj Altebarmakian, 7290 North San Pedro, Fresno, CA 93011

Diocesan Council, Sec., Mr. John Yaldezian, 23221 Aetna St., Woodland Hills, CA 91367, Tel. (818)346-6163

### Canadian Diocese
Primate, His Em. Archbishop Hovnan Derderian
Diocesan Council Chpsn, Mr. Takvor Hopyan, 20 Pineway Blvd., Willowdale, ON M2H 1A1, Canada Tel. (416)222-2639

Diocesan Council secretary., Mr. Vahe Ketli, 750 Montpellier, # 909, St. Laurens, QC H4L 5A7, Canada Tel. (514)747-1347

### Periodicals
*The Armenian Church; The Mother Church*

## Assemblies of God
From a few hundred delegates at its founding convention in 1914 at Hot Springs, Ark., the Assemblies of God has become one of the largest church groups in the modern Pentecostal movement with over 50 million adherents worldwide. Throughout its existence it has emphasized the power of the Holy Spirit to change lives and the participation of all members in the work of the church.

The revival that led to the formation of the Assemblies of God and numerous other church groups early in the 20th century began during times of intense prayer and Bible study. Believers in the United States and around the world received spiritual experiences like those described in the Book of Acts. Accompanied by baptism in the Holy Spirit and its initial physical evidence of "speaking in tongues," or a language unknown to the person, their experiences were associated with the coming of the Holy Spirit at Pentecost (Acts 2), so participants were called Pentecostals.

The church also believes that the Bible is God's inspired infallible Word to man, that salvation is available only through Jesus Christ, that divine healing is made possible through Christ's suffering and that Christ will return again for those who love Him. In recent years, this Pentecostal revival has spilled over into almost every denomination in a wave of revival sometimes called the charismatic renewal.

Assemblies of God leaders credit their church's rapid and continuing growth to its acceptance of the New Testament as a model for the present-day church. Aggressive evangelism and missionary zeal at home and abroad characterize the denomination.

Assemblies of God believers observe two ordinances-water baptism by immersion and the Lord's Supper, or Holy Communion. The church is trinitarian, holding that God exists in three persons—Father, Son and Holy Spirit.

### Headquarters
Media Contact: Juleen Turnage, Dir. of Public Relations, Assemblies of God 1445 N. Boonville Ave., Springfield, MO 65802-1894, Tel. (417)862-2781 Fax (417)862-5554
Email: info@ag.org, Statistics@ag.org
Website: www.ag.org/top

### Officers
Gen. Supt., Thomas E. Trask
Asst. Supt., Charles T. Crabtree
Gen. Sec., George O. Wood

Gen. Treas., James E. Bridges

World Missions, Exec. Dir., John Bueno

AG U.S. Missions, Exec. Dir., Charles Hackett

Great Lakes: Charles Crank, P.O. Box 781526, Indianapolis, IN 46278, Tel. (317)217-9498

Gulf: Douglas Fulenwider, P.O. Box 7388, Alexandria, LA 71306, Tel. (318)445-6238 Fax (318)473-9344

North Central: John Palmer, c/o General Secretary's Office, 1445 N. Boonville Ave, Springfield, MO 65802, Tel. (417)862-2781 x 3030

Northeast: H. Robert Rhoden, P.O. Box 690, Gainesville, VA 20156, Tel. (703)753-0300 Fax (703)753-2879

Northwest: Warren Bullock, 3535 Auburn Way S, Auburn, WA 98092 Tel. (253)833-8252 Fax (253)351-2943

South Central: J. Don George, 4401 N. Highway 161, Irving, TX 75038, Tel. (972)261-1919 Fax (972)261-1895

Southeast: Dan Betzer, 4701 Summerlin Rd., Ft. Myers, FL 33919, Tel. (239)936-6277 Fax (239)936-9365

Southwest, Richard Dresselhaus, c/o General Secretary's Office, 1445 N. Boonville Ave, Springfield, MO 65802, Tel. (417)862-2781 x 3030 Fax (417)862-0133

Language Area Spanish, Jesse Miranda, 55 Fair Drive, Costa Mesa, CA 92626, Tel. (714)556-3610 Fax (714)662-5243

Language Area Other, Nam Soo Kim, 130-30 31st Ave., 4th Fl, Flushing, NY 11354, Tel. (718)321-7800 Fax (718)321-9394

Ethnic Fellowship, Zollie Smith, P.O. Box 100, Burlington, NJ 08016, Tel. (609)747-7878 Fax (609)747-9425

#### INTERNATIONAL HEADQUARTERS

Division of the Treasury, Gen. Treas., James E. Bridges

Division of Church Ministries, Executive Liaison, Charles Crabtree

Division of World Missions, Exec Dir., John Bueno

Division of U.S. Missions, Exec. Dir., Alton Garrison

Div. of Publication, Gospel Publishing House, Natl. Dir., Arlyn Pember

#### Periodicals

*Enrichment—A Journal for Pentecostal Ministry; High Adventure; Pentecostal Evangel; Heritage; On Course*

## Assemblies of God International Fellowship (Independent/Not Affiliated)

April 9, 1906 is the date commonly accepted by Pentecostals as the twentieth-century outpouring of God's spirit in America, which began in a humble gospel mission at 312 Azusa Street in Los Angeles. This spirit movement spread across the United States and gave birth to the Independent Assemblies of God (Scandinavian).

Early pioneers instrumental in guiding and shaping the fellowship of ministers and churches into a nucleus of independent churches included Pastor B. M. Johnson, founder of Lakeview Gospel Church in 1911; Rev. A. A. Holmgren, a Baptist minister who received his baptism of the Holy Spirit in the early Chicago outpourings, was publisher of *Sanningens Vittne*, a voice of the Scandinavian Independent Assemblies of God and also served as secretary of the fellowship for many years; Gunnar Wingren, missionary pioneer in Brazil; and Arthur F. Johnson, who served for many years as chairman of the Scandinavian Assemblies.

In 1935, the Scandinavian group dissolved its incorporation and united with the Independent Assemblies of God of the U.S. and Canada which by majority vote of members formed a new corporation in 1986, Assemblies of God International Fellowship (Independent/Not Affiliated).

#### Headquarters

6325 Marindustry Dr., San Diego, CA 92121, Tel. (858)677-9701 Fax (858)677-0038

Media Contact, Exec. Dir. & Ed., Rev. T. A. Lanes

Email: admin@agifellowship.org

Website: www.agifellowship.org

#### Officers

Exec. Dir., Rev. T. A. Lanes

Sec., Rev. George E. Ekeroth

Treas., M. J. Ekeroth

Canada, Sec., Harry Nunn, Sr., 15 White Crest Ct., St. Catherines, ON 62N 6Y1

#### Periodicals

*Fellowship*

## Associate Reformed Presbyterian Church (General Synod)

The origin of the Associate Reformed Presbyterian Church began in Scotland with the Covenanters of the seventeenth century and Seceder movement of the eighteenth. The Covenanters broke from the established Church of Scotland to eventually form separate "praying societies," which led to the Reformed Presbyterian Church of Scotland. The Seceders, about a hundred years later, became the Associate Church of Scotland.

The Associate Reformed Presbyterian Church stems from the 1782 merger of these two groups in America. in 1822 the "Synod of the South" was granted independent status from the national body. It continued to hold to the 1799 constitution of the church with no changes, and probably consisted of around 2,000 members. The present Associate Reformed Presbyterian Church, (General Synod), is the ongoing denomination resulting from that action, the original "General Synod" of the denomination having become a part of the United Presbyterian Church.

The government is by a three-layered court system, the local "Session," the regional

75

"Presbytery," and the national "General Synod," each of which is composed of both ruling and teaching elders. The Standards of the denomination include the Westminster Confession of Faith, the Catechisms and the Forms of Government, Worship and Discipline.

### Headquarters

Associate Reformed Presbyterian Center, One Cleveland St., Greenville, SC 29601-3696, Tel. (864)232-8297 Fax (864)271-3729

Media Contact, Principal Clerk, The Rev. C. Ronald Beard, D.D., 3132 Grace Hill Rd., Columbia, SC 29204, Tel. (803)787-6370.

Moderator, The Rev. William B. Evans, Ph.D., P.O. Box 275, Due West, SC 29639 Tel. (864)379-2570 Email: wbevans@erskine.edu (to June 6, 2006)

Moderator-Elect, Mr. Tom Patterson, P.O. Box 1283, Mooresville, NC 28115-1283 Tel. (704) 663-2611 Email: tpatterson@arpsynod.org

Website: www.arpsynod.org

### AGENCIES AND INSTITUTIONS
#### (In the A.R. Presbyterian Center in Greenville)

Admn. Ser. Dir., Ed Hogan

Covenant Discipleship (Christian Education), Dir., Dr. David Vickery

Outreach North America (Church Extension), Dir., Rev. Alan Avera

Publications, Editor, Sabrina Cooper

Treasurer, Guy H. Smith, III

World Witness, Bd. of Foreign Missions, Exec. Sec., The Rev. P. Frank vanDalen Tel. (864) 833-5226 Email: fvandalen@worldwitness. org

### OTHER INSTITUTIONS

Bonclarken Conference Center, Dir., James T. Brice, 500 Pine St., Flat Rock, NC 28731, Tel. (704)692-2223

Erskine College, Two Washington Street, Due West, SC 29639 President Emeritus, The Rev. John L. Carson, Ph.D.,Tel. (864)379-8759

Erskine Theological Seminary, Two Washington Street, Due West, SC 29639 Vice President, The Rev. H. Neely Gaston (964)379-2171, Dean, Ralph J. Gore, Jr., Ph.D., Due West, SC 26939, Tel. (864)379-8885

### Periodicals

*The Associate Reformed Presbyterian; The Adult Quarterly*

## The Association of Free Lutheran Congregations

The Association of Free Lutheran Congregations, rooted in the northern European revival movements, was organized in 1962 by a Lutheran Free Church remnant that rejected merger with The American Lutheran Church. The original 42 congregations were joined by other like-minded conservative Lutherans, and there has been more than a sixfold increase in the number of congregations. Members subscribe to the Apostles', Nicene and Athanasian creeds; Luther's Small Catechism; and the Unaltered Augsburg Confession. The Fundamental Principles and Rules for Work (1897) declare that the local congregation is the right form of the kingdom of God on earth, subject to no authority but the Word and the Spirit of God.

Distinctive emphases are, (1) the infallibility and inerrancy of Holy Scriptures as the Word of God; (2) congregational polity; (3) the spiritual unity of all believers, resulting in fellowship and cooperation transcending denominational lines; (4) evangelical outreach, calling all to enter a personal relationship with Jesus Christ; (5) a wholesome Lutheran pietism that proclaims the Lordship of Jesus Christ in all areas of life and results in believers becoming the salt and light in their communities; (6) a conservative stance on current social issues.

A two-year Bible school and a theological seminary are in suburban Minneapolis. The AFLC is in fellowship with sister churches in Canada, Brazil, Mexico, and India.

### Headquarters

3110 E. Medicine Lake Blvd., Minneapolis, MN 55441, Tel. (763)545-5631 Fax (763)545-0079

Media Contact, Pres., Rev. Robert L. Lee

Email: webmaster@aflc.org

Website: www.aflc.org

### Officers

Pres., Rev. Robert L. Lee, 3110 E. Medicine Lake Blvd. Minneapolis, MN 55441 Fax (763) 545-0079 Tel. (763)545-5631, Email: president @aflc.org

Vice Pres., Rev. Elden K. Nelson, 8071 Prairie Trail, Rockford, MN 55373-9342, Tel. (763) 545-5631, Email: vpres@aflc.org

Sec., Rev. Brian Davidson, 3110 E. Medicine Lake Blvd., Minneapolis, MN 55441 Tel. (763) 545-5631 Fax (763)545-0079, Email: briand@ aflc.org

### Periodicals

*The Lutheran Ambassador*

## Association of Independent Evangelical Lutheran Churches

The AIELC was established, as a response to the affiliation need of independent missions and churches originally of the Latino community in the U.S.A. and then worldwide, committed to the learning and teaching of Lutheran doctrine and theology. We are a Lutheran denomination that provides support and guidance to independent missions and churches to be better prepared for the work in the Kingdom of God at the light of Lutheran understanding of Confessing Christ. As part of our affiliation process we don't ask those independent missions and churches to surrender their buildings or administrative independency;

and we don't require them to provide financial support to the main denomination itself.

Our current worlwide membership is estimated as approximately 35,000 members with Churches in Scotland, Channel Islands, India, Pakistan, South Africa, Argentina, Ecuador, Colombia, Puerto Rico, Haiti, Chile and the U.S.A.. We have active Concordat with religious bodies in the U.S.A. and abroad, among them the Evangelical Community Church-Lutheran, the Athanasian Catholic Church of the Augsburg Confession, and the Lutheran Orthodox Church. We hold active membership at the Queens Federation of Churches in New York.

### Headquarters
Email: mainoffice@aielc.org
Website: www.associationofindependentevangelicallutheranchurches.org

### Officers
The Rev. Dr. Pedro Bravo-Guzmán, Presiding Bishop, 14-22 27th Ave, Astoria, NY 11102, Tel. (718)932-1633, Email: pbravoguzman@aielc.org

The Rev. Dr. Francis C. Spataro, Bishop Emeritus, 14-22 27th Ave, Astoria, NY 11102, Tel. (718)932-1633, Email: vill1427@mycingular.blackberry.net

The Rev. Dr. Peter P. Brennan, Bishop Visitor, 14-22 27th Ave, Astoria, NY 11102, Tel. (718)932-1633, Email: Ddamdg@aol.com

The Rev. Bishop Louis Marcel Pierre, Bishop for the Caribbean, 14-22 27th Ave, Astoria, NY 11102, Tel. (718)932-1633, Email: louispierre_73@hotmail.com

The Rev. Bishop Louis Mphahlele, Bishop for Africa, 14-22 27th Ave, Astoria, NY 11102, Tel. (718)932-1633, Email: lutheranunited@webmail.co.za

The Rev. Bishop Adolfo Acuña, Bishop for South America, 14-22 27th Ave, Astoria, NY 11102, Tel. (718)932-1633, Email: iclicomunicaciones@yahoo.com.ar

The Rev. Paul Lorentzen, Assistant to the Presiding Bishop, 14-22 27th Ave, Astoria, NY 11102, Tel. (718)932-1633, Email: PAL10314@aol.com

Miss Christine Dobush, Public Relations Director, 14-22 27th Ave, Astoria, NY 11102, Tel. (718)932-1633, Email: cdobush@inch.com

Mr. Antonio Hunneus, Secretary, 14-22 27th Ave, Astoria, NY 11102, Tel. (718)932-1633, Email: aielcsecretariat@aielc.org

Dr. Jeannette Cano-Landivar, M.D., Treasurer, 14-22 27th Ave, Astoria, NY 11102, Tel. (718) 932-1633, Email: jacala@inch.com

## Association of Vineyard Churches
The Association of Vineyard Churches is a worldwide community of 1400 churches committed to building the church and living under the reign of God. It officially started in Southern California in 1982 under the leadership of John Wimber. The Board of Directors is the governing Board for the Association. The form of government is free church and thus the local Vineyards are free to govern as they desire as long as they do not violate the faith or practices of the Vineyard community. The Association consists of eight regions under the direction of a Regional Overseer. Most regions also have Area Pastoral Care Leaders who give oversight to a small group of pastors in a geographic area. The National Director is the CEO of the National Office and works with the National Board to see that the Association achieves its purpose.

### Headquarters
5115 Grove West Blvd., Stafford, TX 77477, Tel. (281)313-8463 Fax (281)313-8464
Email: info@vineyardusa.org
Website: vineyardusa.org

### Officers
National Dir., Berten A. Waggoner, christian@vineyardusa.org
Secretary, Jane Hardesty, janehardesty@vineyardusa.org
Treasurer, Wendell Richardson

### Periodicals
*Cutting Edge*

## Baptist Bible Fellowship International
Organized on May 24, 1950 in Fort Worth, Texas., the Baptist Bible Fellowship was founded by about 100 pastors and lay people who had grown disenchanted with the policies and leadership of the World Fundamental Baptist Missionary Fellowship, an outgrowth of the Baptist Bible Union formed in Kansas City in 1923 by fundamentalist leaders from the Southern Baptist, Northern Baptist and Canadian Baptist Conventions. The BBF elected W. E. Dowell as its first president and established offices and a three-year (now four-year) graduate school) Baptist Bible College.

The BBF statement of faith was essentially that of the Baptist Bible Union, adopted in 1923, a variation of the New Hampshire Confession of Faith. It presents an infallible Bible, belief in the substitutionary death of Christ, his physical resurrection and his premillennial return to earth. It advocates local church autonomy and strong pastoral leadership and maintains that the fundamental basis of fellowship is a missionary outreach. The BBF vigorously stresses evangelism and the international missions office reports 901 adult missionaries working on 110 fields throughout the world.

There are BBF-related churches in every state of the United States, with special strength in the upper South, the Great Lakes region, southern states west of the Mississippi, Kansas, and California. There are seven related colleges and one graduate school or seminary.

A Committee of Forty-Five, elected by pastors and churches within the states, sits as a representative body, meeting in three subcommittees, each chaired by one of the principal officers-an administration committee chaired by the president, a missions committee chaired by a vice-president and an education committee chaired by a vice-president.

### Headquarters

World Mission Service Center:

Baptist Bible Fellowship Missions Bldg., 720 E. Kearney St., Springfield, MO 65803, Tel. (417)862-5001 Fax (417)865-0794

Mailing Address, P.O. Box 191, Springfield, MO 65801

Media Contact, Mission Dir., Dr. Bob Baird, P.O. Box 191, Springfield, MO 65801

Email: csbc@cherrystreet.org

Website: www.bbfi.org

### Officers

Pres., Rev. Bill Monroe, P.O. Box 12809, Florence, SC 29504, Tel. (843)662-0453, WK (417)862-5001

First Vice Pres., Rev. Mike Peper, 4150 Market St., Aston, PA 19014, Tel. (610)497-0700, WK (417)862-5001

Second Vice Pres., Keith Gillming, 3025 N Lindbergh Blvd., St. Louis, MO 63074, Tel. (314)291-6919

Sec., Rev. Don Elmore, P.O. Box 7150, Springdale, AR 72766, Tel. (479)751-4255

Treas., Rev. Ken Armstrong, 2200 Prairie St., Emporia, KS, Tel. (316)342-4142

### Periodicals

*The Baptist Bible Tribune; The Preacher*

## Baptist General Conference

The Baptist General Conference, rooted in the pietistic movement of Sweden during the 19th century, traces its history to Aug. 13, 1852. On that day a small group of believers at Rock Island, Ill., under the leadership of Gustaf Palmquist, organized the first Swedish Baptist Church in America. Swedish Baptist churches flourished in the upper Midwest and Northeast, and by 1879, when the first annual meeting was held in Village Creek, Iowa, 65 churches had been organized, stretching from Maine to the Dakotas and south to Kansas and Missouri.

By 1871, John Alexis Edgren, an immigrant sea captain and pastor in Chicago, had begun the first publication and a theological seminary. The Conference grew to 324 churches and nearly 26,000 members by 1902. There were 40,000 members in 1945 and 135,000 in 1993.

Many churches began as Sunday schools. The seminary evolved into Bethel, a four-year liberal arts college with 1,800 students, and theological seminaries in Arden Hills, Minn. and San Diego, Calif. Missions and the planting of churches have been main objectives both in America and overseas. Today churches have been established in the United States, Canada and Mexico, as well as twenty countries overseas. In 1985 the churches of Canada founded an autonomous denomination, The Baptist General Conference of Canada.

The Baptist General Conference is a member of the Baptist World Alliance, the Baptist Joint Committee on Public Affairs and the National Association of Evangelicals. It is characterized by the balancing of a conservative doctrine with an irenic and cooperative spirit. Its basic objective is to seek the fulfillment of the Great Commission and the Great Commandment.

### Headquarters

2002 S. Arlington Heights Rd., Arlington Heights, IL 60005, Tel. (847)228-0200 Fax (847)228-5376

Email: gmarsh@baptistgeneral.org

Website: www.bgcworld.org

### Officers

Pres. & Chief Exec. Officer, Dr. Gerald Sheveland, 2002 S. Arlington Hts. Rd., Arlington Heights, IL 60005, Tel. (847)228-0200 Fax (847)228-5376, Email: jsheveland@baptistgeneral.org

Exec, Vice Pres., Ray Swatkowski, (address/ph/fax same as above), Email: rswatkowski@baptistgeneral.org

Director of Mission Advance, Dr. Lou Petrie, (address/ph/fax same as above), Email: lpetrie@baptistgeneral.org

Director of Finance, Stephen R. Schultz, (address/ph/fax same as above), Email: sschultz@baptistgeneral.org

Director of National Ministries, Rev. Paul Johnson, (address/ph/fax same as above), Email: pauljchp@aol.com

Director of International Ministries: Dr. Ronald Larson, (address/ph/fax same as above), Email: rlarson@aol.com

### OTHER ORGANIZATIONS

Bd. of Trustees, Bethel College & Seminary, Pres., Dr. George K. Brushaber, 3900 Bethel Dr., St. Paul, MN 55112

### Periodicals

*BGC World*

## Baptist Missionary Association of America

A group of regular Baptist churches organized in associational capacity in May, 1950, in Little Rock, Ark., as the North American Baptist Association. The name changed in 1969 to Baptist Missionary Association of America. There are several state and numerous local associations of cooperating churches. In theology, these churches are evangelical, missionary, fundamental and for the most part premillennial.

### Headquarters

9219 Sibly Hole Rd., Little Rock, AR Tel. (501) 455-4977 Fax (501)455-3636

Mailing Address, P.O. Box 193920, Little Rock, AR 72219-3920

Media Contact, Dir. of Baptist News Service, Kenneth W. Vanderslice, P.O. Box 97, Jacksonville, TX 75766, Tel. (903)586-2501 Fax (903)586-0378

Email: bmaam@bmaam.com

Website: www.bmaam.com

### Officers

Pres., David Watkins, 318 E. Main St., Magnolia, AR 71753-0456, Tel. (870)234-4292

Vice Pres., Dr. Philip Attebery, 3030 Meadowlark Ln., Tyler, TX 75701-6042, Tel. (903) 586-2500; Dr. Roy L. McLaughlin, 3114 Derby Ln., Swartz Creek, MI 48473-7984, Tel. (810) 635-9568

Rec. Sec., Don J. Brown, P.O. Box 8181, Laurel, MS 39441-8000; Tel. (601)425-1258, Greg Medenwald, 310 Quail Hollow Pl., Hattlesburg, MS 39402-8974; Tel. (601)264-8087; James Ray Raines, 5609 N. Locust, N. Little Rock, AR 72116, Tel. (501)945-2640

### DEPARTMENTS

Missions, Gen. Sec., Rev. Grady L. Higgs, P.O. Box 193920, Little Rock, AR 72219-3920

Publications, Ed.-in-Chief, Rev. James L. Silvey, 311 Main St., P.O. Box 7270, Texarkana, TX 75505

Christian Education, Bapt. Missionary Assoc. Theological Sem., Pres., Dr. Charley Holmes, Seminary Heights, 1530 E. Pine St., Jacksonville, TX 75766

Baptist News Service, Dir., Bobby L. Hudgens, P.O. Box 7270, Texarkana, TX 75505-7270, Tel. (870)772-4550

Life Word Broadcast Ministries, Dir., Rev. George Reddin, P.O. Box 6, Conway, AR 72032

Armed Forces Chaplaincy, Exec. Dir., Bobby C. Thornton, P.O. Box 240, Flint, TX 75762

BMAA Dept. of Church Ministries, Donny Parish, P.O. Box 10356, Conway, AR 72033

Daniel Springs Encampment, James Speer, P.O. Box 310, Gary, TX 75643

Ministers Resource Services, Craig Branham, 4001 Jefferson St., Texarkana, TX 75501

### OTHER ORGANIZATIONS

Baptist Missionary Assoc. Brotherhood, Pres., Matt Hudson, 264 Columbia 25, Magnolia, AR 71753-9141, Tel. (870)234-4893

National Women's Missionary Auxiliary, Pres., Janet Widger, 7409 Rupert Ave., Richmond Height, MO 63117, Tel. (314)644-5009

## Beachy Amish Mennonite Churches

The Beachy Amish Mennonite Church was established in 1927 in Somerset County, Pa. following a division in the Amish Mennonite Church in that area. As congregations in other locations joined the movement, they were identified by the same name. There are currently 97 churches in the United States, 9 in Canada and 34 in other

countries. Membership in the United States is 7,059, according to the 1996 *Mennonite Yearbook.*

Beachy churches believe in one God eternally existent in three persons (Father, Son and Holy Spirit); that Jesus Christ is the one and only way to salvation; that the Bible is God's infallible Word to us, by which all will be judged; that heaven is the eternal abode of the redeemed in Christ; and that the wicked and unbelieving will endure hell eternally.

Evangelical mission boards sponsor missions in Central and South America, Belgium, Ireland, and in Kenya, Africa.

The Mission Interests Committee, founded in 1953 for evangelism and other Christian services, sponsors homes for handicapped youth and elderly people, mission outreaches among the North American Indians in Canada and a mission outreach in Europe.

### Headquarters

Media Contact, Paul L. Miller, 7809 S. Herren Rd. Partridge, KS 67566, Tel. (620)567-2286

### Officers

Amish Mennonite Aid, Sec.-Treas., Ivan Beachy, 8916 Mission Home Rd., Free Union, VA 22940, Tel. (434)985-4954

Mission Interests Committee, Sec.-Treas., Melvin Gingerich, 42555 900W, Topeka, IN 46571, Tel. (219)593-9090

Choice Books of Northern Virginia, Supervisor, Simon Schrock, 4614 Holly Ave., Fairfax, VA 22030, Tel. (703)830-2800

Calvary Bible School, HC 61, Box 202, Calico Rock, AR 72519, Tel. (501)297-8658; Sec.-Treas., Elmer Gingerich, HC 74, Box 282, Mountain View, AR 72560, Tel. (501)296-8764

Penn Valley Christian Retreat, Bd. Chmn., Wayne Schrock, RR 2, Box 165, McVeytown, PA 17015, Tel. (717)529-2935

### Periodicals

*The Calvary Messenger*

## Berean Fellowship of Churches

Founded 1932 in North Platte, Neb., this body emphasizes conservative Protestant doctrines.

### Headquarters

5 Camelot Way, Box 1264, Kearney, NE 68845 Tel. (308)234-5373 Fax (308)234-5373

Media Contact, Pres., Pastor Doug Shada

Email: BereanChurches@aol.com

Website: www.bereanfellowship.org

### Officers

Pres., Doug Shada

Vice Pres., Richard Crocker, 419 Lafayette Blvd., Cheyenne, WY 82009, Tel. (307)635-5914

Sec., Frank Van Campen, 513 Education Dr., Malcolm, NE 68402

Treas., Virgil Wiebe, 125 Split Rock Cir., Hollister, MO 65672

## The Bible Church of Christ, Inc.

The Bible Church of Christ was founded on March 1, 1961 by Bishop Roy Bryant, Sr. Since that time, the Church has grown to include congregations in the United States, Africa, and India. The church is Trinitarian and accepts the Bible as the divinely inspired Word of God. Its doctrine includes miracles of healing, deliverance, and the baptism of the Holy Ghost.

### Headquarters

1358 Morris Ave., Bronx, NY 10456, Tel. (718)588-1288 Fax (718)992-5597
Media Contact, Pres., Bishop Roy Bryant, Sr
Email: bccbookstore@earthlink.net
Website: www.thebiblechurchofchrist.org

### Officers

Pres., Bishop Roy Bryant, Sr.
Vice Pres., Bishop Darue Bryant
Sec., Mother Sissieretta Bryant
Treas., Elder Artie Burney

### EXECUTIVE TRUSTEE BOARD

Chpsn., Bishop Christopher Powell, 1069 Morris Ave., Bronx, NY 10456, Tel. (718)992-4653

### OTHER ORGANIZATIONS

Christian Bookstore, Mgr., Deacon Kenneth Anderson, Tel. (718)293-1928
Foreign Missions, Pres., Sr. Autholene Smith, Tel. (914)664-4602
Home Missions: Pres., Evangelist Mary Jackson, Tel. (718)992-4653
Minister of Education: Minister Abraham Jones, Tel. (718)588-2284
Ministers of Music, Ray Crenshaw, Tyrone Sumter, Ann Dunston
Prison Ministry Team, Evangelist Marvin Smith
Public Relations, Minister Abraham Jones
Sunday Schools, Gen. Supt., Elder A. M. Jones
Alan Bryant Memorial Institute, Principal, Moses Tolborh, Chocolate City, Monrobia, Liberia
Theological Institute, Pres., Dr. Roy Bryant, Sr.; Dean, Elder A. M. Jones
Vessels Unto Honor Deliverance Ministries, Pres., Elder Antoinette Cannaday
Youth, Pres., Deacon Tommy Robinson
Bishops: Bishop Roy Bryant, Sr., Bishop Eddie Citronnelli, Bishop Christopher Powell
Presiding Elders: Delaware: Elder Edward Cannon, RR Box 70-B5, Daimond Acre, Dagsboro, DE 19939, Tel. (302)732-3351; Mount Vernon: Elder Artie Burney, 100 W. 2nd St., Mount Vernon, NY 10550, Tel. (914)664-4602; Bronx, Elder Anita Robinson, 1358 Morris Ave., Bronx, NY 10456, Tel. (718)588-2284; Annex, Elder Reginald Gullette, 1069 Morris Ave., Bronx, NY 10456, Tel. (718)992-4653; Schenectady, New York: Elder Monica Hope, 1132 Congress St., Schenectady, New York 12303, Tel. (518)382-

5625; North Carolina: Elder Darue Bryant, 512 W. Vernon Ave., Kingston, NC 28502, Tel. (252)527-7739; India, Dr. B. Veeraswamy, 46-7-34, Danavaya Peta, Rajahmunry, India, 533103

### Periodicals

*The Gospel Light; The Challenge*

## Bible Fellowship Church

The Bible Fellowship Church grew out of divisions in the Mennonite community in Pennsylvania in the 1850s. Traditional church leadership resisted the freedom of expression and prayer meetings initiated by several preachers and church leaders. These evangelical Mennonites formed the Evangelical Mennonite Society. Over the next two decades various like-minded groups in Canada, Ohio, and Pennsylvania joined the Society.

In 1959 the Conference became the Bible Fellowship Church and new articles of faith were ratified. They now hold a unique combination of Reformed doctrines with insistence on "Believer Baptism" and Premillennialism.

### Headquarters

Bible Fellowship Church, 25 Lemon St., Lititz, PA 17543
Media Contact, David J. Watkins, 416 Cedar Crest Ct., Quakertown, PA 18950, Tel. (215) 529-7453, Email: watkins58@verizon.net
Email: bfc@bfc.org
Website: www.bfc.org

### Officers

Chmn., Randall A. Grossman, 23 Anglin Dr. Newark, DE. 19713
Vice Chmn., Clifford B. Booke, 1256 Clearview Cr, Allentown, PA
Sec., David A. Thomann, 745 Village Rd., Lancaster, PA 17602
Asst. Sec., Robert W. Smock, 38 W. Sunset Ave., Ephrata, PA 17522

### BOARDS AND COMMITTEES

Bd. of Dir., Bible Fellowship Church
Bd. of Christian Education
Board of Extension
Bible Fellowship Church Homes, Inc.
Board of Pensions
Board of Pinebrook Bible Conference
Board of Missions
Committee on Credentials
Board of Publication and Printing
Bd. of Victory Valley Camp
Board of Higher Education
Board of Youth & Adults
Committee on Ministerial Candidates
Strategic Planning Committee
Ministerial Relations Committee
Conference Judicatory

### Periodicals

*Fellowship News*

## Bible Holiness Church

This church came into being about 1890 as the result of definite preaching on the doctrine of holiness in some Methodist churches in southeastern Kansas. It became known as The Southeast Kansas Fire Baptized Holiness Association. The name was changed in 1945 to The Fire Baptized Holiness Church and in 1995 to Bible Holiness Church. It is entirely Wesleyan in doctrine, episcopal in church organization and intensive in evangelistic zeal.

### Headquarters

304 Camp Dr., Independence, KS 67301, Tel. (620)331-3049

Media Contact, Gen. Supt., Leroy Newport

### Officers

Gen. Supt., Leroy Newport

Gen. Sec., Michael Schaper, 944 Linns Mill Rd., Troy, MO 63379

Gen. Treas., Philip Davolt, 10624 Bluestem, Wichita, KS 67207

### Periodicals

*The Flaming Sword; John Three Sixteen*

## Bible Way Church of Our Lord Jesus Christ World Wide, Inc.

This body was organized in 1957 in the Pentecostal tradition for the purpose of accelerating evangelistic and foreign missionary commitment and to effect a greater degree of collective leadership than leaders found in the body in which they had previously participated.

The doctrine is the same as that of the Church of Our Lord Jesus Christ of the Apostolic Faith, Inc., of which some of the churches and clergy were formerly members.

This organization has churches and missions in Africa, England, Guyana, Trinidad, and Jamaica, and churches in 25 states in America. The Bible Way Church is involved in humanitarian as well as evangelical outreach with concerns for urban housing, education and economic development.

### Headquarters

4949 Two-Notch Rd., Columbia, SC 29204, Tel. (800)432-5612 Fax (803)691-0583

Media Contact, Chief Apostle, Presiding Bishop Huie Rogers

Email: mr.ed5strings@worldnet.att.net

Website: www.biblewaychurch.org

### Officers

Presiding Bishop, Bishop Huie Rogers, 4949 Two Notch Rd., Columbia, SC 29204, Tel. (800)432-5612 Fax (803)691-0583

## Brethren in Christ Church

The Brethren in Christ Church was founded in Lancaster County, Pa. in about the year 1778 and was an outgrowth of the religious awakening which occurred in that area during the latter part of the eighteenth century. This group became known as "River Brethren" because of their original location near the Susquehanna River. The name "Brethren in Christ" was officially adopted in 1863. In theology they have accents of the Pietist, Anabaptist, Wesleyan and Evangelical movements.

### Headquarters

General Church Office, P.O. Box A, Grantham, PA 17027, Tel. (717)697-2634 Fax (717) 697-7714

Media Contact, Dr. Warren L. Hoffman, Mod., Tel. (717)697-2634 Fax (717)697-7714

Email: dwinger@messiah.edu

Website: www.bic-church.org

### Officers

Dr. Warren L. Hoffman, Mod. & Gen. Church Office Contact info.

Darrell S. Winger, Gen. Sec. & Gen. Church Office Contact info.

Elizabeth Brown, Treas. & Gen. Church Office Contact info.

### OTHER ORGANIZATIONS

General Conference Board, Chpsn., Dr. Mark Garis, 504 Swartley Rd., Hatfield, PA 19440

Bd. for World Missions, Dr. Grace Holland, Chair, 21A Junction Rd., Dillsburg, PA. 17019-9469; Exec. Dir., Rev. John Brubaker, P.O. Box 390, Grantham, PA 17027-0390

Bd. for Stewardship Services, Terry Hoke; Chair; Box A, Grantham, PA 17027; Pension Fund Trustees, Eric Mann, Chair

Brethren in Christ Foundation, Elvin H. Peifer, CEO, P.O. Box 290, Grantham, PA, 17027-0290

## Brethren Church (Ashland, Ohio)

The Brethren Church (Ashland, Ohio) was organized by progressive-minded German Baptist Brethren in 1883. They reaffirmed the teaching of the original founder of the Brethren movement, Alexander Mack, and returned to limited congregational government.

### Headquarters

524 College Ave., Ashland, OH 44805, Tel. (419) 289-1708 Fax (419)281-0450

Media Contact, Rev. Ken Hunn Official Position: Executive Director Tel; (419)289-1708 Fax (419) 281-0450, Email: Ken@brethrenchurch.org

Email: brethren@brethrenchurch.org

Website: www.brethrenchurch.org

### Officers

Executive Dir., Rev. Ken Hunn

Dir. Of Pastoral Ministries, Rev. David Cooksey

Dir. Of Administrative Services, Mr. Stanley Gentle

### Periodicals

*The Brethren Evangelist*

## Calvary Chapel

Calvary Chapel is a non-denominational

Christian church which began in 1965 in Costa Mesa, Calif. Calvary Chapel's pastor, Chuck Smith, became a leading figure in what has become known as the "Jesus Movement."

It has been estimated that in a two-year period in the mid '70s, Calvary Chapel of Costa Mesa had performed well over eight thousand baptisms. During that same period, we were instrumental in 20,000 conversions to the Christian faith. Our decadal growth rate had been calculated by church growth experts to be near the ten thousand percent level. Calvary Chapel also ministers over the airwaves, and this must account for many of those who travel long distances to fellowship here. A Nielsen survey indicated that our Sunday morning Calvary Chapel service is the most listened-to program in the area during the entire week. As of 1987, Calvary's outreach has included numerous radio programs, television broadcasts, and the production and distribution of tapes and records. The missions outreach is considerable. Calvary Chapel not only supports Wycliffe Bible Translators, Campus Crusade, Missionary Aviation Fellowship, and other groups, but we donate to third world needs. We built a radio station in San Salvador and gave it to the local pastors there. We also gave money to Open Doors to purchase the ship that, in tandem with a barge, delivered one million Bibles to mainland China. Our financial commitment to missions exceeds the local expense budget by over 50%.

Today, Calvary Chapel of Costa Mesa, the church which only had twenty-five members, has established more than five hundred affiliate Calvary Chapels across the world and is among the world's largest churches, with more than thirty-five thousand calling it their home church. It is one of the ten largest Protestant churches in the United States.

### Headquarters

Calvary Chapel of Costa Mesa (Main Office), 3800 S. Fairview Street, Santa Ana, CA 92704-7014, Tel. (714)979-4422

## The Catholic Church

The largest single body of Christians in the United States, the Catholic Church is under the spiritual leadership of His Holiness the Pope. Its establishment in America dates back to the priests who accompanied Columbus on his second voyage to the New World. A settlement, later discontinued, was made in 1565 at St. Augustine, Fla. The continuous history of this Church in the Colonies began at St. Mary's in Maryland, in 1634.

### INTERNATIONAL ORGANIZATION

His Holiness the Pope, Bishop of Rome, Vicar of Jesus Christ, Supreme Pontiff of the Catholic Church.

Pope Benedict XVI, Joseph Ratzinger (born April 16, 1927; installed April 24, 2005)

### APOSTOLIC NUNCIO TO THE UNITED STATES

Archbishop Gabriel Montalvo, 3339 Massachusetts Ave., N.W., Washington, DC 20008, Tel. (202) 333-7121 Fax (202)337-4036

### U.S. ORGANIZATION

United States Conference of Catholic Bishops, 3211 Fourth St NE, Washington, DC 20017-1194. Tel. (202)541-3000

The United States Conference of Catholic Bishops (USCCB) is an assembly of the hierarchy of the United States and the U.S. Virgin Islands who jointly exercise certain pastoral functions on behalf of the Christian faithful of the United States. The purpose of the Conference is to promote the greater good which the Church offers humankind, especially through forms and programs of the apostolate fittingly adapted to the circumstances of time and place. This purpose is drawn from the universal law of the Church and applies to the episcopal conferences which are established all over the world for the same purpose.

The bishops themselves constitute the membership of the Conference and are served by a staff of over 350 people, priests and religious located at the Conference headquarters in Washington, D.C. There is also a small Office of Film and Broadcasting in New York City and a branch office of Migration and Refugee Services in Miami.

The Conference is organized as a corporation in the District of Columbia. Its purposes under civil law are, "To unify, coordinate, encourage, promote and carry on Catholic activities in the United States; to organize and conduct religious, charitable and social welfare work at home and abroad; to aid in education; to care for immigrants; and generally to enter into and promote by education, publication and direction the objects of its being."

On July 1, 2001 the NCCB and the USCC were combined to form the United States Conference of Catholic Bishops (USCCB). The USCCB continues all of the work formerly done by the NCCB and the USCC with the same staff. The bishops themselves form approximately 50 committees, each with its own particular responsibility.

Email: commdept@usccb.org

Website: www.usccb.org

### UNITED STATES CONFERENCE OF CATHOLIC BISHOPS (USCCB)

### GENERAL SECRETARIAT

General Sec., Msgr. David Malloy

Assoc. Gen. Sec., Mr. Bruce E. Egnew, two other associate positions vacant at time of printing

### Officers

Pres., Bishop William S. Skylstad

Vice Pres., Cardinal Francis George, OMI

Treas., Bishop Dennis M. Schnurr

Sec., Archbishop Michael J. Sheehan

### ADMINISTRATIVE COMMITTEE—
### USCCB

Administrative Committee, Chmn., Bishop William S. Skylstad

Executive Committee, Chmn., Bishop William S. Skylstad

Committee on Budget and Finance, Chmn., Bishop Dennis M. Schnurr

Committee on Personnel, Cardinal Francis George, OMI

Committee on Priorities and Plans, Chmn., Archbishop Michael J. Sheehan

African American Catholics, Chmn., Bishop Joseph N. Perry

Canonical Affairs, Chmn., Archbishop John J. Myers

Church in Latin America, Chmn., Bishop John R. Manz; Chmn.-elect Bishop Jaime Soto

Consecrated Life, Chmn., Archbishop Jerome G. Hanus, OSB; Chm.-elect, Bishop J. Terry Steib, SVD

Communications Chmn. Bishop Gerald F. Kicanas; Chmn.-elect, Bishop George H. Niederauer

Diaconate, Chmn., Bishop Frederick F. Campbell

Doctrine, Chmn.,Bishop Arthur J. Serratelli; Chmn.-elect, Bishop William E. Lori

Education, Chmn. Bishop Robert J. McManus

Ecumenical and Interreligious Affairs, Chmn., Bishop Richard J. Sklba

Evangelization, Chmn., Bishop Samuel G. Jacobs

Hispanic Affairs, Chmn., Bishop Placido Rodriguez, CMF

Home Missions, Chmn., Bishop J. Peter Sartain; Chmn.-elect, Bishop Michael W. Warfel

Laity, Chmn., Bishop David A. Zubik

Liturgy, Chmn., Bishop Donald W. Trautman

Marriage and Family Life, Chmn., Bishop Joseph E. Kurtz

Migration, Chmn., Bishop Gerald Barnes

Pastoral Practices, Chmn., Bishop Jerome E. Listecki

Priestly Formation, Chmn., Bishop Thomas J. Olmsted

Priestly Life and Ministry, Chmn., Archbishop Timothy M. Dolan; Chmn.-elect, Bishop Robert J. Carlson

Pro-Life Activities, Chmn., Cardinal William Keeler; Cardinal Justin Rigali

Protection of Young People, Chmn. Bishop Gregory M. Aymond

Relationship Between Eastern and Latin Catholic Churches, Chmn., Archbishop Stefan Soroka

Science and Human Values, Chmn., Bishop John C. Dunne

Vocations, Chmn., Bishop Blase Cupich

Woman in Society and in the Church, Chmn., Bishop Joseph A. Pepe

World Mission, Chmn., Bishop Daniel Walsh

For information on related organizations and individual dioceses, consult the *Official Catholic Directory* (published annually by P.J. Kenedy and Sons) and the USCCB Website (www.usccb.org).

### Periodicals

*Catholic News Service, L'Osservatore Romano, The Living Light, Origins, Lay Ministry Update, Bishops Committee on the Liturgy Newsletter, life Insight, SEIA Newsletter on the Eastern Churches and Ecumenism, Law Briefs, Catholic Trends*

## Christ Catholic Church

The church is a catholic communion established in 1968 to minister to the growing number of people who seek an experiential relationship with God and who desire to make a total commitment of their lives to God. The church is catholic in faith and tradition. Participating cathedrals, churches and missions are located in several states.

### Headquarters

405 Kentling Rd., Highlandville, MO 65669, Tel. (417)443-3951

Media Contact, Archbishop, Most Rev. Karl Pruter

Email: bishopkarl@juno.com

Website: christcatholicchurch.freeyellow.com

### Officers

Archbishop, Most Rev. Karl Pruter, P.O. Box 63, Highlandville, MO 65669, Tel. (417)823-9902

### Periodicals

*St. Willibrord Journal*

## Christ Community Church (Evangelical-Protestant)

This church was founded by the Rev. John Alexander Dowie on Feb. 22, 1896 at Chicago, Ill. In 1901 the church founded the city of Zion, Ill. and moved their headquarters there. Theologically, the church is rooted in evangelical orthodoxy. The Scriptures are accepted as the rule of faith and practice. Other doctrines call for belief in the necessity of repentance for sin and personal trust in Christ for salvation.

The Christ Community Church is a denominational member of The National Association of Evangelicals. It has work in six other nations in addition to the United States. Branch ministries are found in Tonalea, Ariz.

### Headquarters

2500 Dowie Memorial Dr., Zion, IL 60099, Tel. (847)746-1411 Fax (847)746-1452

### Officers

Senior Pastor, Ken Langley

## Christadelphians

The Christadelphians are a body of people

83

who believe the Bible to be the divinely inspired word of God, written by "Holy men who spoke as they were moved by the Holy Spirit" (2 Peter ch. 1 v. 21). They believe that the Old Testament presents God's plan to establish His Kingdom on earth in accord with the promises He made to Abraham and David; and that the New Testament declares how that plan works out in Jesus Christ, who died a sacrificial death to redeem sinners. They believe in the personal return of Jesus Christ as King, to establish "all that God spoke by the mouth of his holy prophets from of old" (Acts ch.3 v.21). They believe that at Christ's return many of the dead will be raised by the power of God to be judged. Those whom God deems worthy will be welcomed into eternal life in the Kingdom on earth. Christadelphians believe in the mortality of man; in spiritual rebirth requiring belief and immersion in the name of Jesus; and in a godly walk in this life. They have no ordained clergy, and are organized in a loose confederation of 2500 autonomous congregations (ecclesias) in approximately 150 countries. They are conscientiously opposed to participation in war. They endeavor to be enthusiastic in work, loyal in marriage, generous in giving, dedicated in preaching, and cheerful in living.

The denomination was organized in 1844 by a medical doctor, John Thomas, who came to the United States from England in 1832, having survived a near shipwreck in a violent storm. This experience affected him profoundly, and he vowed to devote his life to a search for the truth of God and a future hope from the Bible.

### Headquarters

Media Contact, Trustee, Norman D. Zilmer, Christadelphian Action Society, 904 Woodview Ct, Mahomet, IL 61853-3623, Tel. (217)590-4108 Fax (847)888-3334
Email: nzilmer@aol.com
Website: www.christadelphia.org

### LEADERS

(Co-Ministers) Norman Fadelle, 815 Chippewa Dr., Elgin, IL 60120; Norman D. Zilmer, 904 Woodview Ct, Mahomet, IL 61853-3623, Email:nzilmer@aol.com/NFADELLE@juno.com

### Periodicals

*Christadelphian Tidings; Christadelphian Advocate*
Websites: www.Tidings.org; www.Christadelphia.org; www.wcfoundation.org

## Christian Brethren (also known as Plymouth Brethren)

Christian Brethren churches are bound together by common beliefs and practices but not by central organization. They are committed to the inerrancy of Scripture, to Trinitarian doctrine, and to the evangelical message of salvation by faith apart from works or sacrament. Their most recognizable feature is the weekly observance of the Lord's Supper as the focus of a full length service of worship, not prearranged and not clergy-led.

Originating in England and Ireland in the late 1820s, the Brethren were influenced by the counsel of Anthony Norris Groves, an English dentist, and the teaching of John Nelson Darby, an Irish clergyman. They recovered aspects of church practice and simplicity that had been obscured in the course of the centuries, such as an unwillingness to establish denominational governing structures and a reluctance to accept sectarian names. The nickname Plymouth Brethren arose spontaneously when a large Plymouth congregation was evangelizing throughout the English countryside. In recent years the term Christian Brethren has replaced Plymouth Brethren for the open branch of the movement in Canada and the British Commonwealth and to some extent in the United States. Neither name has legal status, except where required by national governments. There are no central offices and no corporate property in the U.S.A. or Canada.

In the late 1840s the movement divided. The so-called open assemblies, led initially by George Mueller of orphanage fame, stressed evangelism and foreign missions. It has grown to be the larger of the two branches. The autonomy of local congregations permits variations in practice and generally avoids wide-ranging division.

The other branch focused more on doctrinal and ecclesiastical issues. From it came notable Bible teachers like Darby, William Kelly, C.H. Mackintosh (CHM), and F. W. Grant. Their books have had a wide influence, especially among premillennialists. These assemblies stress the interdependency of congregations. Local church decisions on doctrine and discipline are generally held to be binding on all assemblies. At times, when actions were debatable, division spread throughout the group. By 1900, there were seven or eight main groups. Since 1925, some divisions have been healed, reducing that number to three or four.

### CORRESPONDENT

James A. Stahr, 327 W. Prairie Ave., Wheaton, Il 60187-3408, Tel. (630)665-3757

### RELATED ORGANIZATIONS

Believers' Bookshelf, P.O. Box 261 Sunbury, PA 17801

Believers' Stewardship Services, 2250 Chaney Rd., Dubuque, IA 50201 Tel. (563)582-4818

ECS Ministries, 2250 Chaney Rd., Dubuque, IA 50201 Tel. (563)585-2070

Emmaus Bible College, 2570 Asbury Rd., Dubuque, IA 52001-3044 Tel. (563)588-8000

Christian Missions in Many Lands, P.O. Box 13, Spring Lake, NJ 07762-0013 Tel. (732)449-8880

Interest Ministries, 2060 Stonington Ave., Suite 101, Hoffman Estates, IL 60195 Tel. (847) 519-1495

Stewards Foundation, 14285 Midway Rd., Ste. 330, Addison, TX 75001-3622 Tel. (972)726-6550

Stewards Ministries, 18-3 E. Dundee Rd., Ste. 100, Barrington, IL 60010 Tel. (847)842-0227

Walterick Publishing Ministries, 6549 State Ave., Kansas City, KS 66102 Tel. (913)334-0100

## Christian Church (Disciples of Christ) in the United States and Canada*

Born on the American frontier in the early 1800s as a movement to unify Christians, this body drew its major inspiration from Thomas and Alexander Campbell in western Pennsylvania and Barton W. Stone in Kentucky. Developing separately, the "Disciples, under Alexander Campbell, and the "Christians," led by Stone, united in 1832 in Lexington, Ky.

The Christian Church (Disciples of Christ) is marked by informality, openness, individualism, and diversity. The Disciples claim no official doctrine or dogma. Membership is granted after a simple statement of belief in Jesus Christ and baptism by immersion—although most congregations accept transfers baptized by other forms in other denominations. The Lord's Supper—generally called Communion—is open to Christians of all persuasions. The practice is weekly Com-munion, although no church law insists upon it.

Thoroughly ecumenical, the Disciples helped organize the National and World Councils of Churches. The church is a member of the Churches Uniting in Christ. The Disciples and the United Church of Christ have declared themselves to be in "full communion" through the General Assembly and General Synod of the two churches. Official theological conversations have been going on since 1967 directly with the Roman Catholic Church.

Disciples have vigorously supported world and national programs of education, agricultural assistance, urban reconciliation, care of persons with retardation, family planning, and aid to victims of war and calamity. Operating ecumenically, Disciples' personnel or funds work in more than 100 countries outside North America.

Three manifestations or expressions of the church (general, regional and congregational) operate as equals, with strong but voluntary covenantal ties to one another. Entities in each manifestation manage their own finances, own their own property, and conduct their own programs. A General Assembly meets every two years and has voting representation from each congregation.

### Headquarters

Disciples Center, 130 E. Washington St., P.O. Box 1986, Indianapolis, IN 46206-1986, Tel. (317)635-3100 Fax (317)635-3700

Media Contact, Communication Ministries, Executive Director, Wanda Bryant Wills Email: cmiller@cm.disciples.org

### Officers

Gen. Minister & Pres., Rev. Dr. Sharon E. Watkins, Tel. (317)635-3100 Fax (317)713-2417, Email: swatkins@ogmp.disciples.org

Mod., Bill Lee, 730 Loudon Ave. NW, Roanoke, VA 24016, Tel. (540)314-3265, Email: billyb307 @aol.com

1st Vice Mod., Charles Gaines, 5804 Emerson Ct. Arlington, TX 76016, Tel. (817)496-0591, Email: ccgaines3@comcast.net

2nd Vice Mod., Carolyn Ho, 4533 35th Ave S, Seattle, WA 98118, Tel. (206)685-2187, Email: ho@hotmail.com

### GENERAL OFFICERS

Gen. Minister & Pres., Rev. Dr. Sharon R. Watkins, Tel. (317)635-3100 Fax (317)713-2417, Email: swatkins@ogmp.disciples.org

Assoc. Gen. Minister & Vice Pres., Vacancy

Assoc. Gen Min. & Admin. Sec. of the National Convocation, Timothy M. James, Email: tjames@ogmp.disciples.org

### ADMINISTRATIVE UNITS

Board of Church Extension, Pres., James L. Powell, 130 E. Washington St., P.O. Box 7030, Indianapolis, IN 46207-7030, Tel. (317) 635-6500 Fax (317) 635-6534, Email: bce @churchextension.org

Christian Board of Publication (Chalice Press), Pres., Cyrus N. White, 1221 Locust St., Suite 1200, P.O. Box 179, St. Louis, MO 63166-0179, Tel. (314)231-8500 or (800)366-3383 Fax (314)231-8524, Email: customerservice @cbp21.com

Christian Church Foundation, Inc., Pres., Gary W. Kidwell, Tel. (317)635-3100 or (800)366-8016 Fax (317)635-1991, Email: jcullumb@ ccf.disciples.org

Church Finance Council, Inc., Pres., Lois Artis, Email: jedmundson@cfc.disciples.org

Council on Christian Unity, Inc., Pres., Robert K. Welsh, Tel. (317)713-2586 Fax(317)713-2588, Email: rozanne@ccu.disciples.org

Disciples of Christ Historical Society, Pres., Glen T. Carson, 1101 19th Ave. S., Nashville, TN 37212-2196, Tel. (615)327-1444 Fax (615) 327-1445, Email: mail@dishistsoc.org

Higher Education and Leadership Ministries (HELM), Pres., Dennis L. Landon, 11477 Olde Cabin Rd., Ste. 310, St. Louis, MO 63141-7130, Tel. (314)991-3000 Fax (314) 991-2957, Email: dhe@dhedisciples.org

Division of Homeland Ministries, dba Disciples Home Missions, Pres., Arnold C. Nelson, Jr. Tel. (317)635-3100 or (888)346-2631 Fax (317)635-4426, Email: homelandministries@ dhm.disciples.org

Division of Overseas Ministries, Pres., David A. Vargas, Fax (317)635-4323, Email: dom@ disciples.org

National Benevolent Association, Pres., Dennis Hagemann, 149 Weldon Parkway, Suite 115, Maryland Heights, MO 63043-3103, Tel. (314) 993-9000 Fax (314)993-9018, Email: nba@nbacares.org

Pension Fund, Pres., James P. Hamlett, 130 E. Washington St., Indianapolis, IN 46204-3645, Tel. (317)634-4504 Fax (317)634-4071, Email: pfcc1@pension.disciples.org

## REGIONAL UNITS OF THE CHURCH

Alabama-Northwest Florida, Regional Minister, John P. Mobley, 861 Highway 52, Helena, AL 35080, Tel. (205)425-5245 Fax (205)425-5246, Email: alnwfl@aol.com

Arizona, Regional Minister, Dennis L. Williams, 4423 N. 24th St., Ste 700, Phoenix, AZ 85016-5544, Tel. (602)468-3815 Fax (602)468-3816, Email: region@arizonadisciples.com

California, Northern-Nevada, Regional Min. and Pres., Ben Bohren, 9260 Alcosta Blvd., C-18, San Ramon, CA 94583-4143, Tel. (925)556-9900 Fax (925)556-9904, Email: info@ccncn. org

Canada, Regional Minister, Catherine Hubbard, P.O. Box 23030, 417 Wellington St., St. Thomas, ON N5R 6A3, Tel. (519)633-9083 Fax (519)637-6407, Email: ccic@bellnet.ca

Capital Area, Regional Minister, Lari R. Grubbs, 11501 Georgia Ave., Ste. 400, Wheaton, MD 20902-1955, Tel. (301)942-8266 Fax (301)942-8366, Email: lgrubbs@cccadisciples.org

Central Rocky Mountain Region, Exec. Regional Minister, Ronald L. Parker, 2950 Tennyson #300, Denver, CO 80212-3029, Tel. (303)561-1790 Fax (303)561-1795, Email: jrowe@crmrdoc.org

Florida, Regional Minister, William C. Morrison, Jr., 924 N. Magnolia Ave., Ste. 200, Orlando, FL 32803-3845, Tel. (407)843-4652 Fax (407)843-0272, Email: RegionalOffice@floridadisciples.org

Georgia, Regional Minister, Ray Miles, 2370 Vineville Ave., Macon, GA 31204-3163, Tel. (478)743-8649 or (800)755-0485 Fax (478)741-1508, Email: ccinga@bellsouth.net

Great River Region, Executive Regional Minister, Barbara E. Jones, 9302 Geyer Springs Rd, P.O. Box 192058, Little Rock, AR 72219-2058, Tel. (501)562-6053 & (888)241-5531 Fax (501)562-7089

Idaho, South, Regional Minister, Larry Crist, 6465 Sunrise Ave., Nampa, ID 83686-9461, Tel. (208)468-8976 Fax (208)468-8973, Email: ccsi1@mindspring.com

Illinois and Wisconsin, Regional Minister and Pres., Herbert L. Knudsen, 1011 N. Main St., Bloomington, IL 61701-1753, Tel. (309)828-6293 Fax (309)829-4612, Email: herb@cciwdiciples.org

Indiana, Regional Minister, Richard L. Spleth, 1100 W. 42nd St., Indianapolis, IN 46208-3375, Tel. (317)926-6051 Fax (317)931-2034, Email: cci@ccindiana.org

Kansas, Interim Regional Minister/Pres., Steven Cranford, 2914 S.W. MacVicar Ave., Topeka, KS 66611-1787, Tel. (785)266-2914 Fax (785) 266-0174, Email: ccks@ksmessenger.org

Kansas City, Greater, Regional Min./Pres., Paul J. Diehl, Jr., 5700 Broadmoor, Ste. 702, Mission, KS 66202-2405, Tel. (913)432-1414 Fax (913)432-3598, Email: KCDisciple@aol.com

Kentucky, General Minister, J. Gregory Alexander, 1125 Red Mile Rd., Lexington, KY 40504-2660, Tel. (859)233-1391 Fax (859)233-2079, Email: cck@ccinky.net

Michigan, Regional Minister, Jon Lacey, 2820 Covington Ct., Lansing, MI 48912-4830, Tel. (517)372-3220 Fax (517)372-2705, Email: ccmr@michigandisciples.org

Mid-America Region, Regional Minister, Danny Stewart, 3328 Bennett Ln., P.O. Box 104298 , Jefferson City, MO 65110-4298, Tel. (573) 636-8149 Fax (573)636-2889, Email: ccma@socket.net

Montana, Regional Minister, Ruth A, Fletcher, 1019 Central Ave., Great Falls, MT 59401-3784, Tel. (406)452-7404 Fax (406)452-7404, Email: ccm@imt.net

Nebraska, Regional Ministers, Kenneth W. Moore, 1268 S. 20th St., Lincoln, NE 68502-1612, Tel. (402)476-0359 or (800)580-8851 Fax (402)476-0350, Email: ccnebraska@alltel

North Carolina, Regional Minister, John M. Richardson, 509 N.E. Lee St., P.O. Box 1568, Wilson, NC 27894-1568, Tel. (252)291-4047 Fax (252)291-3338, Email: ccnc@ncdisciples.org

Northeastern Region, Co-Regional Ministers, Lonnie F. Oates, Rafael Rivera-Rosa, 475 Riverside Dr., Rm. 1950, New York, NY 10115-1999, Tel. (212)870-2734 Fax (870) 2735, Email: n.christian.church@worldnet.att.net

Northwest Region, Regional Minister and Pres., Jack Sullivan, Jr., 6558-35th Ave. SW, Seattle, WA 98126-2899, Tel. (206)938-1008 Fax (206)933-1163, Email: nwrcc@disciplesnw.org

Ohio, Regional Pastor and Pres., William H. Edwards, 355 E. Campus View Blvd, Suite 110, Columbus, OH 43235, Tel. (614)433-0343 Fax (614)433-7285, Email: ccio@christianchurchinohio.org

Oklahoma, Regional Pastor, Thomas R. Jewell, 301 N.W. 36th St., Oklahoma City, OK 73118-8661, Tel. (405)528-3577 Fax (405)528-3584, Email: tjewell@okdisciples.org

Oregon, Co-Regional Ministers, Douglas Wirt & Cathy Myers-Wirt, 0245 S.W. Bancroft St., Ste. F, Portland, OR 97239-4267, Tel. (503) 226-7648 Fax (503)226-0598, Email: odmail@oregondisciples.org

Pacific Southwest Region, Regional Minister-Pres., Don W. Shelton, 2401 N. Lake Ave., Altadena, CA 91001-2418, Tel. (626)296-0385 Fax (626)296-1280, Email: pswr@discipleswr

Pennsylvania, Regional Minister, W. Darwin Collins, 105 Water St., Suite #7, New Stanton, PA 15672, Tel. (724)925-1350 Fax (724)925-1358, Email: wdar@padisciples.org

South Carolina, Regional Minister, Sotello V. Long, 1293 Orange Grove Rd., Charleston, SC 29407-3947, Tel. (843)852-4537 Fax (843)744-5787, Email: rcccsc@aol.com

Southwest Region, Regional MinisterDani Loving Cartwright, 3209 S. University Dr., Fort Worth, TX 76109-2239, Tel. (817)926-4687 Fax (817)926-5121, Email: ccsw@ccsw.org

Tennessee, Regional Minister and Pres., Glen J. Stewart, 50 Vantage Way, Ste. 251, Nashville, TN 37228-1523, Tel. (615)251-3400 Fax (615)251-3415, Email: ccdctn@yahoo.com

Upper Midwest Region, Regional Minister and Pres., Richard L. Guentert, 3300 University Ave., P.O. Box 41217, Des Moines, IA 50311-0504, Tel. (515)255-3168 Fax (515)255-2625, Email: rg@uppermidwestcc.org

Virginia, Regional Minister, George Lee Parker, 518 Brevard St., Lynchburg, VA 24501-3547, Tel. (434)846-3400 Fax (434)528-4919, Email: ccinva@adelphia.net

West Virginia, Regional Minister, William B. Allen, 1400 Washington Ave., P.O. Box 264, Parkersburg, WV 26102-0264, Tel. (304)428-1681 Fax (304)428-1684, Email: linda@ccwv.org

### Periodicals

*DiscipleWorld; Call To Unity*

## Christian Church of North America, General Council

Originally known as the Italian Christian Church, its first General Council was held in 1927 at Niagara Falls, N.Y. This body was incorporated in 1948 at Pittsburgh, Pa., and is described as Pentecostal but does not engage in the "the excesses tolerated or practiced among some churches using the same name."

The movement recognizes two ordinances-baptism and the Lord's Supper. Its moral code is conservative and its teaching is orthodox. Members are exhorted to pursue a life of personal holiness, setting an example to others. A conservative position is held in regard to marriage and divorce. The governmental form is, by and large, congregational. District and National officiaries, however, are referred to as Presbyteries led by Overseers.

The group functions in cooperative fellowship with the Italian Pentecostal Church of Canada and the Evangelical Christian Churches-Assemblies of God in Italy. It is an affiliate member of the Pentecostal Fellowship of North America and of the National Association of Evangelicals.

### Headquarters

1294 Rutledge Rd., Transfer, PA 16154-2299, Tel. (724)962-3501 Fax (724)962-1766

Exec. Sec., Christine Marini; Asst., Candace Tarr Email: cnna@nauticom.net

Website: www.ccna.org

### Officers

Executive Bd., Gen. Overseer, Rev. Dennis G. Karaman, 1294 Rutledge Road, Transfer, PA. 16154

Exec. Vice Pres., Rev. Joseph Shipley, 44-19 Francis Lewis Blvd., Bayside, NY 11361

Asst. Gen. Overseers, Rev. Joseph Shipley 44-19 Francis Lewis Blvd., Bayside, NY 11361; Rev. Trevor Cobarn, 3325 Dry Brook Rd., Falconer, NY 14733; Rev. Patrick Bossio, Sr., 667 Capitol, Lincoln Park, MI 48146;

Rev. Thomas Geyser, 2 Cynthia Circle, Medway, MA 02062, Rev. Douglas Bedgood, Sr., 442 Trinidad Ln., Teakwood Village, Largo, FL 33770

### Departments

Benevolence, Rev. Eugene De Marco, 136 Dana Dr., New Brighton PA 15066

Home Missions, Rev. Richard George, 3395 Waterside Dr., Akron, OH 44319

Faith, Order & Credentials, Rev. Rev. Joseph Shipley, 44-19 Francis Lewis Blvd, Bayside, NY 11361

Missions, Rev. Mark Charles, 703 Somcenter Rd., Mayfield Hts., OH 44143

Publications Relations, Rev. John Tedesco, 1188 Heron Rd., Cherry Hill, NJ 08003

Lay Ministries, Rev. Carmine Zottoli, 27D Shear Hill Rd., Mahopac, NY 10541

Education, Rev. Lucian Gandolfo, 3141 Highland Dr. Easton, PA. 18045

### Periodicals

*Vista*

## Christian Churches and Churches of Christ

The fellowship, whose churches were always strictly congregational in polity, has its origin in the American movement to "restore the New Testament church in doctrine, ordinances and life" initiated by Thomas and Alexander Campbell, Walter Scott and Barton W. Stone in the early nineteenth century.

### Headquarters

Media Contact, No. American Christian Convention Dir., Rod Huron, 4210 Bridgetown Rd., Box 11326, Cincinnati, OH 45211, Tel. (513)598-6222 Fax (513)598-6471

Email: Jowston@cwv.edu

Website: www.cctoday.com; www.nacctheconnecting place.org

### CONVENTIONS

North American Christian Convention, Dir., Rod Huron, 4210 Bridgetown Rd., Box 11326, Cincinnati, OH 45211, Tel. (513)598-6222; NACC Mailing Address, Box 39456, Cincinnati, OH 45239

National Missionary Convention, Coord., Walter

Birney, Box 11, Copeland, KS 67837, Tel. (316)668-5250

Eastern Christian Convention, Kenneth Meade, 5300 Norbeck Rd., Rockville, MD 20853, Tel. (301)460-3550

**Periodicals**

*Christian Standard; Restoration Herald; Horizons; The Lookout*

## The Christian Congregation, Inc.

The Christian Congregation is a denominational evangelistic association that originated in 1787 and was active on the frontier in areas adjacent to the Ohio River. The church was an unincorporated organization until 1887. At that time a group of ministers who desired closer cooperation formally constituted the church. The charter was revised in 1898 and again in 1970.

Governmental polity basically is congregational. Local units are semi-autonomous. Doctrinal positions, strongly biblical, are essentially universalist in the sense that ethical principles, which motivate us to creative activism, transcend national boundaries and racial barriers. A central tenet, John 13 v. 34-35, translates to such respect for sanctity of life that abortions on demand, capital punishment and all warfare are vigorously opposed. All wars are considered unjust and obsolete as a means of resolving disputes.

Early leaders were John Chapman, John L. Puckett and Isaac V. Smith. Bishop O. J. Read was chief administrative and ecclesiastic officer for 40 years until 1961. Rev. Dr. Ora Wilbert Eads has been general Superintendent since 1961. Ministerial affiliation for independent clergymen is provided.

**Headquarters**

812 W. Hemlock St., LaFollette, TN 37766

Media Contact, Gen. Supt., Rev. Ora W. Eads, D.D., Tel. (423)562-5809

Email: Revalnas@aol.com

Website: netministries.org/see/churches.exe/ch10619

**Officers**

Gen. Supt., Rev. Ora W. Eads, D.D., 812 W. Hemlock St. LaFollette, TN 37766

## Christian Methodist Episcopal Church*

The Christian Methodist Episcopal Church (CME) is a historically African-American denomination that was established in Jackson, Tenn. in 1870 when a group of former slaves, representing eight annual conferences of the Methodist Episcopal Church South organized the Colored Methodist Episcopal Church in America. In 1954 at its General Conference in Memphis, Tenn. it was overwhelmingly voted to change the term "Colored" to "Christian." On January 3, 1956 the official name became Christian

Methodist Episcopal Church. Its boundaries reach from the continental United States, Alaska, Haiti, Jamaica, and the West African countries of Nigeria, Ghana, and Liberia. One of its most significant witnessing arenas has been the education of African Americans. Today the CME Church supports Paine College, Augusta, Ga.; Lane College, Jackson, Tenn.; Miles College, Birmingham, Ala.; Texas College, Tyler, Texas; and the Phillips School of Theology in Atlanta, Ga.

**Headquarters**

First Memphis Plaza, 4466 Elvis Presley Blvd., Memphis, TN 38116

Media Contact, Exec. Sec., Attorney Juanita Bryant, 3675 Runnymede Blvd., Cleveland Hts., OH 44121, Tel. (216)382-3559 Fax (216) 382-3516, Email: juanbr4law@aol.com

Email: juanbr4law@aol.com

Website: www.c-m-e.org

**Officers**

Exec. Sec., Attorney Juanita Bryant, 3675 Runnymede Blvd., Cleveland Hts., OH 44121, Tel. (216)382-3559 Fax (216)382-3516, Email: juanbr4law@aol.com

Sec. Gen. Conf., Vacant

**OTHER ORGANIZATIONS**

Christian Education, Gen. Sec., Dr. Carmichael Crutchfield, 4466 Elvis Presley Blvd., Ste. 214, Box 193, Memphis, TN 38116-7100, Tel. (901)345-0580 Fax (901)345-4118

Lay Ministry, Gen. Sec., Dr. Victor Taylor, 9560 Drake Ave., Evanston, IL 60203, Tel. (800)782-4335 x 6029 Fax (312)345-6056, Email: victav@idt.net

Evangelism & Missions, Gen. Sec., Dr. Willie C. Champion, 102 Pearly Top Dr., Glen Heights, TX 75154, Tel. (214)372-9505, Email: champ_dr@msn.com

Finance, Sec., Dr. Joseph C. Neal, Jr., P.O. Box 75085, Los Angeles, CA 90075, Tel. (323) 233-5050

Editor, *The Christian Index*, Dr. Kenneth E. Jones, P.O. Box 431, Fairfield, AL 35064, Tel. (205)929-1640 Fax (205)791-1910, Email: Goodoc@aol.com

Publication Services, Gen. Sec., Rev. William George, 4466 Elvis Presley Blvd., Memphis, TN 38116, Tel. (901)345-0580 Fax (901)767-8514, Email: WEG38@aol.com

Personnel Services, Gen. Sec., Rev. Tyrone T. Davis, P.O. Box 74, Memphis, TN 38101-0074, Tel. (901)261-3228, Email: cmegbps@myexcel.com

Women's Missionary Council, Pres., Dr. Elnora P. Hamb, 11321 S. Aberdeen St., Chicago, IL 60643, Tel. (773)264-2273, Email: hamb@sbcglobal.net Ministry to Men, Gen. Sec., Mr. Leo Pinkett, 2850 Shoreland Dr. S.W., Atlanta, GA 30331, Email: lpinkettace@yahoo.com

## BISHOPS

First District, Bishop William H. Graves, Sr., 4466 Elvis Presley Blvd., Ste. 222, Memphis, TN 38116, Tel. (901)345-0580

Second District, Bishop E. Lynn Brown, 7030 Reading Rd., Suite 244, Cincinnati, OH 45237, Tel. (513)772-8622

Third District, Bishop Paul A. G. Stewart, Sr., 5925 W. Florissant Ave., St. Louis, MO 63136, Tel. (314)381-3111

Fourth District, Bishop Thomas L. Brown Sr., 700 M.L. King Dr. SW, Atlanta, GA 30314, Tel. (404)527-7768 Fax (404)527-7774

Fifth District, Bishop Lawerence L. Reddick III, 310 18th St., N, Ste. 400D, Birmingham, AL 35203, Tel. (205)655-0346

Sixth District, Bishop Othal H. Lakey, 1776 Peachtree Rd. NW, Suite 210, South Tower, Atlanta, GA 30309, Tel. (404)745-9689

Seventh District, Bishop Thomas L. Hoyt, Jr., 6524 16th St. N.W., Washington, DC, Tel. (318)820-9512 & (318)780-8467

Eighth District, Bishop Ronald M. Cunningham., 1616 E. Illinois, Dallas, TX 75216, Tel. (214) 372-9073

Ninth District, Bishop Henry M. Williamson, 3844 W. Slauson Ave., Ste. 1, Los Angeles, CA 90043, Tel. (213)294-3830, Email: hwillia 531@aol.com

Tenth District, Bishop Kenneth Wayne Carter, 2202 Emerald Oaks Ct., Arlington, TX 76017, Tel. (817)468-1397, Email: KWCarter@hotmail.com

Retired, Bishop Nathaniel L. Linsey, Canterbury Subdivision, 190 Squire Lane, Fayettsville, GA 30214, Tel. (770)460-6897, Email: linseyn @bellsouth.net; Bishop Dotcy I. Isom, 4326 Richwood Place, Memphis, TN 36125, Tel. (901)753-8123; Bishop Marshall Gilmore, 683 Beacon-tree Court, Concord, NC 28027, Tel. (704)786-3226; Bishop Charles L. Helton, 5937 Ruth Dr. Charlotte, NC 28215, Tel. (704) 536-8067

### Periodicals

*The Christian Index; The Missionary Messenger*

## The Christian and Missionary Alliance

The Christian and Missionary Alliance was formed in 1897 by the merger of two organizations begun in 1887 by Dr. Albert B. Simpson, The Christian Alliance and the Evangelical Missionary Alliance. The Christian and Missionary Alliance is an evangelical church that stresses the sufficiency of Jesus as Savior, Sanctifier, Healer, and Coming King and has earned a worldwide reputation for its missionary accomplishments. The Canadian districts became autonomous in 1981 and formed The Christian and Missionary Alliance in Canada.

### NATIONAL OFFICE

P.O. Box 35000, Colorado Springs, CO 80935-3500, Tel. (719)599-5999 Fax (719)593-8234

Media Contact, Peter Burgo, Assistant Vice President for Advancement

Email: info@cmalliance.org

Website: www.cmalliance.org

### Officers

Pres., Rev. Gary M. Benedict D.D.

Corp. Vice Pres., Rev. John P. Stumbo

Corp. Sec., Rev. David L. Goodin

Vice Pres., for Advancement, vacant

Vice Pres. for International Ministries, Rev. Robert L. Fetherlin, D. Min.

Vice Pres. for National Church Ministries, vacant

Vice Pres. for Operations/Treasurer, Mr. Kenneth E. Baldes, MBA

### BOARD OF DIRECTORS

Chpsn., Rev. Ronald J. Morrison

Vice-Chpsn., Rev. Douglas L. Grogan

### DISTRICTS

Cambodian, Rev. Nareth May, 1616 S. Palmetto Ave., Ontario, CA 91762, Tel. (909)988-9434

Central, Rev. Gordon F. Meier, D.Min., 1218 High St., Wadsworth, OH 44281, Tel. (330) 336-2911

Central Pacific, Rev. R. Douglas Swinburne, J. R., 715 Lincoln Ave., Woodland, CA 95695, Tel. (530)662-2500

E. Pennsylvania, Rev. J. Wayne Spriggs, 1200 Spring Garden Dr., Middletown, PA 17057, Tel. (717)985-9240

Great Lakes, Rev. Jeffrey P. Brown, 2250 Huron Parkway, Ann Arbor, MI 48104, Tel. (734) 677-8555

Haitian, Rev. Emaneuelle Seide, 14 Glen Road, W. Hempstead, NY 11552, Tel. (516)594-1046

Haitian South, Rev. Joe Kong (Interim Director), P.O. Box 35000 Colorado Springs, CO 80935, Tel. (719)265-2052

Hmong, Rev. Timothy T. Vang, 12287 Pennsylvania St., Thornton, CO 80241, Tel. (303)252-1793

Korean, Rev. Hyung J. Moon, 550 Durie Avenue, #201, Closter, NJ 07640, Tel. (201)750-6750

Metropolitan, Rev. John F. Soper, P.O. Box 7060, 275 Sussex Ave., Ste. B, Newark, NJ 07107, Tel. (973)412-7025

MidAmerica, Rev. Randall S. Burg, 1301 S. 119th St., Omaha, NE 68144, Tel. (402)330-1888

Mid-Atlantic, Rev. Randall B. Corbin, D.Min., Jr., 292 Montevue Lane, Frederick, MD 21702, Tel. (301)620-9934

Midwest, Rev. M. Fred Polding, D. Miss., 260 Glen Ellyn Road, Bloomingdale, IL 60108, Tel. (630)893-1355

Native American, Rev. Craig S. Smith, 19019 N. 74th Dr., Glendale, AZ 85308, Tel. (623)561-8134

New England, Rev. Richard E. Bush, D.Min., P.O. Box 288, South Easton, MA 02375, Tel. (508)238-3820

Northeastern, Rev. David J. Phillips, 6275

Pillmore Dr., Rome, NY 13440, Tel. (315)336-4720

Northwestern, Rev. Craig L. Strawser, 6425 CTYRD 30 #, 740 St. Bonifacius, MN 55375, Tel. (952)446-9318

Ohio Valley, Rev. P. David Klinsing, D.Min., 4050 Executive Park Dr., Ste.402, Cincinnati, OH 45241, Tel. (513)733-4833

Pacific NW, Rev. Kelvin J. Gardiner, P.O. Box 1030, Canby, OR 97013, Tel. (503)266-2238

Puerto Rico, Rev. Luis F. Felipa, P.O. Box 191794, San Juan, PR 00919, Tel. (787)281-0101

Rocky Mountain, Rev. Timothy P. Owen, D.Min., 2545 St. Johns Ave., Billings, MT 59102, Tel. (406)656-4233

South Atlantic, Rev. L. Ferrell Towns, 10801 Johnston Rd., Ste. 125, Charlotte, NC 28226, Tel. (704)543-0470

South Pacific, Rev. Donald M. Brust, 4130 Adams St., Ste. A, Riverside, CA 92504, Tel. (909)351-0111

Southeastern, Rev. Mark T. O' Farrell, D.D., P.O. Box 720430, Orlando, FL 32872-0430, Tel. (407)823-9662

Southern, Rev. Fred G. King, 5998 Deerfoot Parkway, Trussville, AL 35173, Tel. (205)661-9585

Southwestern, Rev. Daniel R. Wetzel, 5600 E. Loop 820 South, Ste. 100, Fort Worth, TX 76119, Tel. (817)561-0879

Spanish Central, Rev. C. José Bruno, P.O. Box 5477 McAllen, TX 78504, Tel. (956)565-1600

Spanish Eastern, Rev. Marcelo Realpe, P.O. Box 865, Union City, NJ 07087, Tel. (201)866-7202

Vietnamese, Dr. Tai Anh Nguyen, Th.D., 2275 W. Lincoln Ave., Anaheim, CA 92801, Tel. (714)491-8007

W. Great Lakes, Rev. Gary E. Russell, W6107 Aerotech Dr., Appleton, WI 54914, Tel. (920)734-1123

W. Pennsylvania, Rev. Jeffrey A. Norris, P.O. Box 600, Punxsutawney, PA 15767, Tel. (814)938-6920

## NATIONAL ETHNIC ASSOCIATIONS

African-American President, Rev. Terrence L. Nichols, 120 Lancaster Way, Vallejo, CA 94591, Tel. (707) 310-3926

Exec. Sec., Rev. Gus H. Brown, 688 Diagonal Rd., Akron, OH 44320, Tel. (330)376-4654

Chinese, President, Rev. Abraham H. Poon, D.Min., 2360 McLaughlin Ave., San Jose, CA 95122-3560, Tel. (408)280-1021

Dega, President, Rev. Ha Giao Cilpam, 3119 Westerwood Dr., Charlotte, NC 28214 Tel. (704)393-7159

Filipino, President, Exec. Dir., Rev. Abednego Ferrer, 20143 Royal Ave., Hayward, CA 94541, Tel. (510)887-6261

Haitian, President, Rev. Emmanuel Seide, 14 Glen Rd., West Hempstead, NY. 11552, Tel. (516)594-1046

## ETHNIC/CULTURAL MINISTRIES

Arab & South Asian, Rev. Joseph S. Kong, P.O. Box 35000, Colorado Springs, CO 80935, Tel. (719)599-5999 x 2052

Alliance Jewish Ministries, Rev. Abraham Sandler, 9820 Woodfern Rd., Philadelphia, PA 19115, Tel. (215)676-5122

### Periodicals

*Alliance Life*

# Christian Reformed Church in North America

The Christian Reformed Church represents the historic faith of Protestantism. Founded in the United States in 1857 and active in Canada since 1905, it asserts its belief in the Bible as the inspired Word of God, and is creedally united in the Belgic Confession (1561), the Heidelberg Catechism (1563), and the Canons of Dort (1618-19).

### Headquarters

2850 Kalamazoo Ave., SE, Grand Rapids, MI 49560, Tel. (616)224-0832 Fax (616)224-5895

Media Contact, Exec. Dir., Rev. Gerard Dykstra

Email: dykstraj@crcna.org

Website: www.crcna.org

### Officers

Exec. Dir. of Ministries, Rev. Gerard Dykstra

Dir. of Canadian Ministries, Rev. Bruce Adema, 3475 Mainway, P.O. Box 5070 STN LCR 1, Burlington, ON L7R 3Y8

Director of Finance and Administration, Mr. John Bolt

### OTHER ORGANIZATIONS

The Back to God Hour, Dir. Dr. Robert C. Heerspink, International Headquarters, 6555 W. College Dr., Palos Heights, IL 60463

Christian Reformed Home Missions, Dir., Rev. John A. Rozeboom

Christian Reformed World Missions, U.S., Dir. Dr. Gary Bekker

Christian Ref. World Missions, Canada, Dir., Albert Karsten, 3475 Mainway, P.O. Box 5070 STN LCR 1, Burlington, ON L7R 3Y8

Christian Reformed World Relief, U.S., Dir., Andrew Ryskamp

Christian Reformed World Relief, Canada, Dir., Ms. Ida Kaastra Mutoigo, 3475 Mainway, P.O. Box 5070 STN LCR 1, Burlington, ON L7R 3Y8

CRC Publications, Dir., Gary Mulder

Ministers' Pension Fund, Admn., Marjorie Csomor

### Periodicals

*The Banner*

## Christian Union

Organized in 1864 in Columbus, Ohio, the Christian Union stresses the oneness of the Church with Christ as its only head. The Bible is the only rule of faith and practice and good fruits the only condition of fellowship. Each local church governs itself.

### Headquarters

6711 South Calhoun, Fort Wayne, IN 46807, Tel. (260)745-1942
Media Contact, Pres., Rev. Phil Harris
Email: pharris316@juno.com
Website: www.christianunion.com

### Officers

Pres., Rev. Phil Harris, 6711 South Calhoun, Fort Wayne, IN 46807, Tel. (260)745-1942
Vice Pres., Rev. Marion Hunerdosse, 10619 N. Marsh Ave., Kansas City, MO 64057, Tel. (816)781-5044
Sec., Joseph Cunningham, 1005 N. 5th St., Greenfield, OH 45123, Tel. (937)981-3476
Asst. Sec., Jim Eschenbrenner, 308 North Waugh Road., Hedrick, IA 52563, Tel. (641)653-4785
Treas., Rev. Neal Skiles, 80 Licking View Dr., Heath, OH 43056-1530, Tel. (740)522-4845 Fax (740)522-6076, Email: skiles@roadrunner.com

### Periodicals

*The Christian Union Witness*

## Church of the Brethren*

Eight German Pietists/Anabaptists, including their leader, Alexander Mack, founded the Brethren movement in 1708 in Schwarzenau, Germany. Begun in reaction to spiritual stagnation in state churches, the Brethren formed their own movement, modeled on the first-century church. They practice church discipline, believer baptism, anointing, and the love feast. They have no other creed than the New Testament, hold to principles of nonviolence, no force in religion, Christian service, and simplicity. They migrated to the colonies beginning in 1710 and settled at Germantown, Pa., moving westward and southward over the next 200 years. Emphasis on religion in daily life led to the formation of Brethren Volunteer Service in 1948, which continues today.

### Headquarters

Church of the Brethren General Offices, 1451 Dundee Ave., Elgin, IL 60120, Tel. (847)742-5100 x 206 Fax (847)753-6103, Email: cobweb @brethren.org
Brethren Service Center, 500 Main Street, P.O. Box 188, New Windsor, MD 21776-0188, Tel. (410)635-8710 Fax (410)635-8789, Email: bsc_gb@brethren.org
Washington Office, 337 North Carolina Ave. SE, Washington, DC 20003, Tel. (202)546-3202 Fax (202)544-5852, Email: washington_office_gb@brethren.org

Media Contact, Cheryl Brumbaugh-Cayford, Director of News Services, 1451 Dundee Ave., Elgin, IL 60120, Tel. (847)742-5100 x 260 Fax 847-742-1407, Email: cbrumbaugh-cayford_gb@brethren.org
Email: cobweb@brethren.org; jclements_gb@brethren.org
Website: www.brethren.org

### Officers

Moderator, Belita D. Mitchell, 219 Hummel Street., Harrisburg, PA 17104, Tel. (717)234-0415, Email: moderator@brethren.org
Moderator-elect, James M. Beckwith, P.O. Box 237, Annville, PA 17003, Tel. (717)867-2972, Email: paji@annvillecob.org
Secretary, Fred W. Swartz, 102 W. Rainbow Drive, Bridgewater, VA 22812, Tel. (540)828-4871, Email: acsecretary@brethren.org

### GENERAL BOARD STAFF

General Secretary, Stanley J. Noffsinger, 1451 Dundee Ave., Elgin, IL 60120-1694, Tel. (847)742-5100 x 201, Email: snoffsinger_gb@brethren.org
Manager of Office Operations, Jon Kobel, 1451 Dundee Ave., Elgin, IL 60120-1694, Tel. (847)742-5100 x 202, Email: jkobel_gb@brethren.org
Director, Human Resources, Karin Krog, 1451 Dundee Ave., Elgin, IL 60120-1694, Tel. (847)742-5100 x 258, Email: kkrog_gb@brethren.org

### LEADERSHIP TEAM

General Secretary, Stanley J. Noffsinger, 1451 Dundee Ave., Elgin, IL 60120-1694, Tel. (847)742-5100 x 201, Email: snoffsinger_gb@brethren.org
Executive Director, Centralized Resources and Chief Financial Officer/Treasurer, Judy E. Keyser, 1451 Dundee Ave., Elgin, IL 60120-1694, Tel. (847)742-5100 x 270, Email: jkeyser_gb@brethren.org
Executive Director and Publisher, Brethren Press, Wendy McFadden, 1451 Dundee Ave., Elgin, IL 60120-1694, Tel. (847)742-5100 x 278, Email: wmcfadden_gb@brethren.org
Executive Director of Congregational Life Ministries, Del L. Keeney, 1451 Dundee Ave., Elgin, IL 60120-1694, Tel. (847)742-5100 x 282, Email: dkeeney_gb@brethren.org
Executive Director of Global Mission Partnerships, Mervin B. Keeney, 1451 Dundee Ave., Elgin, IL 60120-1694, Tel. (847)742-5100 x 226, Email: mission_gb@brethren.org
Executive Director, Brethren Service Center, Roy Winter, P.O. Box 188, New Windsor, MD 21776-0188, Tel. (410)635-8748, Email: rwinter_gb@brethren.org
Executive Director of Ministry, Mary Jo Flory-Steury 1451 Dundee Ave., Elgin, IL 60120, Tel. (847)742-5100 x 466, Email: mjflorysteury_gb@brethren.org

**Periodicals**
*Messenger*

## Church of Christ

Joseph Smith and five others organized the Church of Christ on April 6, 1830 at Fayette, N. Y.. In 1864 this body was directed by revelation through Granville Hedrick to return in 1867 to Independence, Mo. to the "consecrated land" dedicated by Joseph Smith. They did so and purchased the temple lot dedicated in 1831.

### Headquarters

Temple Lot, 200 S. River St., P.O. Box 472, Independence, MO 64051, Tel. (816)833-3995
Media Contact, Gen. Church Rep., William A. Sheldon, P.O. Box 472, Independence, MO 64051, Tel. (816)833-3995
Website: www.church-of-christ.com

### Officers

Council of Apostles, Secy., Apostle Smith N. Brickhouse, P.O. Box 472, Independence, MO 64051
Gen. Bus. Mgr., Bishop Alvin Harris, P.O. Box 472, Independence, MO 64051

### Periodicals
*Zion's Advocate*

## The Church of Christ (Holiness) U.S.A.

The Church of Christ (Holiness) U.S.A. has a divine commission to propagate the gospel throughout the world, to seek the conversion of sinners, to reclaim backsliders, to encourage the sanctification of believers, to support divine healing, and to advance the truth for the return of our Lord and Savior Jesus Christ. This must be done through proper organization.

The fundamental principles of Christ's church have remained the same. The laws founded upon these principles are to remain unchanged. The Church of Christ (Holiness) U.S.A. is representative in form of government; therefore, the final authority in defining the organizational responsibilities rests with the national convention. The bishops of the church are delegated special powers to act in behalf of or speak for the church. The pastors are ordained ministers, who under the call of God and His people, have divine oversight of local churches. However, the representative form of government gives ministry and laity equal authority in all deliberate bodies. With the leadership of the Holy Spirit, respect, loyalty and love will greatly increase.

### Headquarters

329 East Monument Street, P.O. Box 3622, Jackson, MS 39207 Tel. (601)353-0222 Fax (601)353-4002

Media Contact, Maurice D. Bingham, Ed.D., Senior Bishop Emeritus
Email: Everything@cochusa.com
Website: www.cochusa.com

### BOARD OF BISHOPS

Senior Bishop Emeritus, Maurice D. Bingham, Ed.D., P.O. Box 6182, Jackson, MS 39308, Tel. (601)353-0222, Email: Pminis3659@aol. com
Eastern Diocese, Bishop Lindsay E. Jones, 1033 Winchester Way, Chesapeake, VA 23320, Tel. (757)547-1653, Email: Ljones5@aol.com
North Central Diocese, Bishop Bennett Wolfe, 14315 River Oak Court, Florissant, MO 63034 Tel. (314)741-4590, Email: Ned6@Hotmail.com
Northern Diocese, Bishop Emery Lindsay, 62 West 111th Place, Chicago, IL 60628 Tel. (773)821-0088, Email: Bpelind@aol.com
Pacific Northwest Diocese, Bishop Robert Winn, 1376 Oakwood Ave, Vallejo, CA 94591 Tel. (707)554-2493, Email: Awinner323@aol.com
South Central Diocese, Bishop Joseph Campbell, Jr., P.O. Box 3663, Jackson, MS 39207, Tel. (601)373-6223, Email: Bisjcsd@Bellsouth.net
Southeastern Diocese, Bishop Victor P. Smith, 3783 Treebark Trail, Decatur, GA 30034, Tel. (404)288-4885, Email: Victor@hotmail.com
Southwestern Diocese, President Bishop Vernon Kennebrew, 13900 Edgemond Drive, Little Rock, AR 72212, Tel. (501)954-7676
Western Diocese, Bishop Robert Winn, 1376 Oakwood Ave, Vallejo, CA 94591 Tel. (707)554-2493, Email: Awinner323@aol.com
Board Member, Bishop James K. Mitchell, 1580 Waite St., Gary, IN 46404 Tel. (219)944-0051, Email: Jasmitch9@aol.com

### Periodicals
*Truth*

## Church of Christ, Scientist

The Church of Christ, Scientist, was founded in 1879 by Mary Baker Eddy "to commemorate the word and works of our Master [Christ Jesus], which should reinstate primitive Christianity and its lost element of healing" (Church Manual, p. 17). Central to the Church's mission is making available worldwide Mrs. Eddy's definitive work on health and Bible-based Christian healing, *Science and Health With Key to the Scriptures*, as well as its publications, Internet sites, and broadcast programs, all of which respond to humanity's search for spiritual answers to today's pressing needs.

The Church also maintains an international speakers' bureau to introduce the public to Christian Science and Mrs. Eddy. Christian Science practitioners, living in hundreds of communities worldwide are available full-time to pray with anyone seeking comfort and healing.

Christian Science teachers hold yearly classes for those interested in a more specific understanding of how to practice the Christian Science system of healing.

The worldwide activities and business of the Church are transacted by a five-member Board of Directors in Boston. About 2000 congregations, each democratically organized and governed, are located in approximately 80 countries. The church has no clergy. Worship services are conducted by lay persons elected to serve as Readers. Each church maintains a Reading Room—a bookstore open to the community for spiritual inquiry and research—and a Sunday school where young people discuss the contemporary relevance of ideas from the Bible and *Science and Health*.

### Headquarters
The First Church of Christ, Scientist, 175 Huntington Ave., A-13, Boston, MA 02115
Media Contact, Mgr., Committees on Publication, Phil Davis, Tel. (617)450-3300 Fax (617) 450-7397
Website: spirituality.com and churchofchristscientist.org

### Officers
Bd. of Directors: J. Thomas Black; Walter D. Jones; M. Victor Westberg; Mary Metzner Trammell; Nathan Talbot
President, Marian English
Treas., Edward Odegaard
Clk., Nathan Talbot
First Reader, Lyle Young
Second Reader, Christiane Little

### Periodicals
*The Christian Science Monitor* (Website: www.csmonitor.com); *The Christian Science Journal; Christian Science Sentinel; The Herald of Christian Science* (13 languages); *Christian Science* (Quarterly Bible Lessons in 16 languages and English Braille).

## Church Communities International
Church Communities International is a movement of Christian Church Communities originating in Germany in 1920. Driven to England by Nazi persecution in 1937, Church Community members migrated to Paraguay in 1942 with the help of the Mennonite Church. In 1954 the first Church Community in the United States was founded in Rifton, New York, where it continues to flourish. Today, a dozen Church Communities are located in New York and Pennsylvania as well as others in Australia, England, Germany and Thailand. Within each Church Community, residents practice their faith in the manner and spirit of the first-century Christians and the Reformation of the early 1500s, sharing everything in common and caring for each other and their neighbors. Members are baptized as adults on confession of the Apostolic Creed, making a voluntary lifetime commitment to living out the teachings of Jesus.

### Headquarters
2032 Route 213, Rifton, NY 12471 Tel. (845) 658-8351
Media Contact: Johann Huleatt, Tel. (845)658-7766
Email: johannh@rifton.com

### Officers
Pedo Cavanna, Secretary Treasurer, 10 Hellbrook Lane, Ulster Park, NY 12487
The Bruderhof Foundation

## Church of God (Anderson, Indiana)
The Church of God (Anderson, Indiana) began in 1881 when Daniel S. Warner and several associates felt constrained to forsake all denominational hierarchies as formal creeds, trusting solely in the Holy Spirit as their overseer and the Bible as their statement of belief.

These people saw themselves at the forefront of a movement to restore unity and holiness to the church, not to establish another denomination, but to promote primary allegiance to Jesus Christ so as to transcend denominational loyalties.

Deeply influenced by Wesleyan theology and Pietism, the Church of God has emphasized conversion, holiness and attention to the Bible. Worship services tend to be informal, accentuating expository preaching and robust singing. There is no formal membership. Persons are assumed to be members on the basis of witness to a conversion experience and evidence that supports such witness. The absence of formal membership is also consistent with the church's understanding of how Christian unity is to be achieved—that is, by preferring the label Christian before all others. The Church of God is congregational in its government. Each local congregation is autonomous and may call any recognized Church of God minister to be its pastor and may retain him or her as long as is mutually pleasing. Ministers are ordained and disciplined by state or provincial assemblies made up predominantly of ministers. National program agencies serve the church through coordinated ministries and resource materials. There are Church of God congregations in 89 foreign countries, most of which are resourced by one or more missionaries. There are slightly more Church of God adherents overseas than in North America.

### GENERAL OFFICES
### CHURCH OF GOD MINISTRIES, INC.
General Director (President): Dr. Ronald V. Duncan; (1201 E. Fifth St.) P.O. Box 2420, Anderson, IN 46018-2420, Tel. (765)642-0256 Fax (765)642-5652
Website: www.chog.org
Includes Congregational Ministries, Outreach Ministries, and Resource & Linking Ministries.

Media Contact: Stephen Lewis, Communications Coordinator, Email: slewis@chog.org

## OTHER CHURCH OF GOD ORGANIZATIONS

Board of Pensions, President: Jeffery A. Jenness, Box 2299, Anderson IN 46018

Warner Press, Inc., President: Eric King, Box 2499, Anderson IN 46018

Anderson University, President: James L. Edwards, 1100 E 5th St., Anderson IN 46012

Mid-America Christian University, President: John Fozard, 3500 SW 119th St., Oklahoma City OK 73170

Warner Pacific College, President: Jay A. Barber, Jr., 2219 SE 68th Ave, Portland OR 97215

Warner Southern College, President: Gregory V. Hall, 13895 Hwy 27, Lake Wales, FL 33859

Women of the Church of God, Executive Director: Linda J. Mason, Box 2328, Anderson, IN 46018

Email: RDUNCAN@chog.org

Website: www.chog.org

### Periodicals

*Missions Magazine; Pathways to God; Communion; People to People; YMI Update; One Voice*

## The Church of God in Christ

The Church of God in Christ was founded in 1897 in Lexington, Miss. by Bishop Charles Harrison Mason, a former Baptist minister, and organized as a Pentecostal Church during the early stages of the holiness movement and, more specifically, as an outgrowth of the Azusa Street Revival of Los Angeles, Calif., in 1906–9.

Initial growth of the church was attributable to the organization of four departments between 1910-1916, the Women's Department, the Sunday School, Young People's Willing Workers and Home and Foreign Missions.

The Church is Trinitarian and teaches the infallibility of Holy Scripture, the need for regeneration and baptism of the Holy Ghost evidenced by speaking in tongues. It emphasizes holiness as God's standard for Christian conduct and recognizes as ordinances Holy Communion, Water Baptism and Feet Washing.

Its governmental structure is basically episcopal and consists of three branches. The General Board represents the Executive Branch, the General Assembly is the Legislative Branch, and the Judiciary Board represents the Judicial Branch.

### Headquarters

Mason Temple Church of God in Christ, 938 Mason St., Memphis, TN 38126, Tel. (901) 947-9300

Mailing Address, P.O. Box 320, Memphis, TN 38101

Email: EJOHNCOGIC@aol.com

Website: www.cogic.org

### THE PRESIDIUM

Presiding Bishop, Bishop G.E. Patterson, 938 Mason St., Memphis, TN 38126, Tel. (901) 947-9340

1st Assistant, Bishop C.E. Blake, Sr., 3045 S. Crenshaw Blvd., Los Angeles, CA 90016, Tel. (323)733-8300

2nd Assistant, Bishop J.N. Haynes, 1267 Whispering Oaks Dr., Desoto, TX 75115, Tel. (214)375-4105

Secretary, Bishop W.W. Hamilton, 14570 Mountain Quail Rd., Salinas, CA 93908, Tel. (831)395-2774

Asst. Secretary, Bishop R.L.H. Winbush, 235 Diamond Dr., Lafayette, LA 70501, Tel. (318)232-6958

Member, Bishop C.D. Owens, 406 Roswell St., Marietta, GA 30060, Tel. (770)590-8510

Member, Bishop P.A. Brooks, 30945 Wendbrook Ln., Beverly Hills, MI 48025, Tel. (313)835-5329

Member, Bishop L.R. Anderson, 1023 E. Brook Hollow Dr., Phoenix, AZ 85022, Tel. (602)993-4906

Member, Bishop G.D. McKinney, 5825 Imperial Ave., San Diego, CA 92114, Tel. (619)262-2671

Member, Bishop S.L. Green, Jr., 41 St. Johns Dr., Hampton, VA 23666, Tel. (757)380-6118

Member, Bishop N.W. Wells, 717 Bridgeview Bay, Muskegon, MI 49441, Tel. (231)722-3219

Member, Bishop J.W. Macklin, 1027 W. Tennyson Road, Haywood, CA 94544, Tel. (510)783-9377

### GENERAL OFFICERS

General Secretary, Elder A.Z. Hall, Jr., P.O. Box 320, Memphis, TN 38101, Tel. (901)947-9356

General Treasurer, Bishop S.L. Lowe, Tel. 938 Mason St., Memphis, TN 38126, Tel. (901)947-9319

Financial Secretary, Bishop F.O. White, 312 Grand Ave., Freeport, NY 11520, Tel. (516) 623-7513

### ELECTED OFFICERS, DEPARTMENTAL HEADS AND AUXILLIARY LEADERS

Chairman—General Assembly: Bishop J.O. Patterson, Jr., 229 Danny Thomas, Memphis, TN 38126

Chairman—Judiciary Board: Bishop T.L. Westbrook, 1623 S. 11th St., Tacoma, WA 98405

Chairman—Board of Bishops: Bishop J. Sheard, 19511 Afton Rd., Detroit, MI 48203

Chairman—Board of Trustees: Bishop C.M. Ford, 4525 S. Wabash, Chicago, IL 60653, Tel. (773)538-4526

94

Chief of Staff: Bishop J.L. Maynard, 930 Mason St., Memphis, TN 38126, Tel. (901)947-9338
Chief Accountant: Minister A. Perpener, P.O. Box 320, Memphis, TN 38126, Tel. (901)947-9361
National Properties: Elder D.L.S. Wells, 938 Mason St., Memphis, TN 38126, Tel. (901) 947-9332
Chairman—Pastors/Elders: Elder D. Hutchins
Adjutant General: Bishop Matthew Williams, 1516 Dumont Dr., Valrico, FL 33594
President—Women's Dept.: Mother W.M. Rivers, P.O. Box 1052, Memphis, TN 38101
President—Missions Dept.: Bishop C.L. Moody, P.O. Box 320, Memphis, TN 38101, Tel. (901) 947-9316
President—Evangelism: Bishop R. White, 4121 Thurman Dr., Conley, GA 30288, Tel. (404) 361-7020
President—Youth Dept.: Elder Michael Hill, 23746 Riverside Dr., Lathrup, MI 48076
President—Sunday School: Elder Alton Gatlin, 229 Diamond Dr., Lafayette, LA 70501
President—Music Dept.: Professor I. Stevenson
President—Men's Conference: Bishop D. Hines, 8605 W. Goodhope Rd., Milwaukee, WI 53224
President—Sunshine Band: Dr. R.L. Howard
President—Purity: Missionary T. Cotton
Executive Director—Fine Arts: Mrs. S.J. Powell
CEO—Publishing House: Dr. D.A. Hall, Sr., 930 Mason St., Memphis, TN 38126
Chairman—Board of Pub.: Bishop R.L.H. Winbush, 235 Diamond Dr., Lafayette, LA 70501
Manager—COGIC Bookstore: Mrs. G. Miller, 285 S. Main, Memphis, TN 38101, Tel. (901) 947-9304

**EDUCATIONAL INSTITUTIONS**

Charles Harrison Mason Theological Seminary, 671 Beckwith St. SW, Atlanta, GA 30314 Attn: Dean O.L. Haney
C.H. Mason System of Bible Colleges, 930 Mason St., Memphis, TN 38126 Attn: Dr. M.L. Johnson
All Saints Bible College, 930 Mason St., Memphis, TN 38126 Attn: Dr. P. Little
Saints Academy, C.H. Mason Highway, Lexington, MS Attn: Elder L. Weems

**Periodicals**

*The Whole Truth Magazine, The Voice of Missions, The McBrayer Report*

## Church of God in Christ, International

The Church of God in Christ, International was organized in 1969 in Kansas City, Mo., by 14 bishops of the Church of God in Christ of Memphis, Tenn. The doctrine is the same, but the separation came because of disagreement over polity and governmental authority. The church is Wesleyan in theology (two works of grace) but stresses the experience of full baptism of the Holy Ghost with the initial evidence of speaking with other tongues as the Spirit gives utterance.

**Headquarters**

170 Adelphi St., Brooklyn, NY 11205, Tel. (718) 625-9175
Media Contact, Natl. Sec., Rev. Sis. Sharon R. Dunn
Email: laity@cogic.org
Website: www.cogic.org/main

**Officers**

Presiding Bishop, Most Rev. Carl Williams, Jr.
Vice Presiding Bishop, Rt. Rev. J. C. White
Exec. Admn., Horace K. Williams, Word of God Center, Newark, NJ
Women's Dept., Natl. Supervisor, Evangelist Elvonia Williams
Youth Dept., Pres., Dr. Joyce Taylor, 137-17 135th Ave., S., Ozone Park, NY 11420
Music Dept., Pres., Isaiah Heyward
Bd. of Bishops, Chpsn., Bishop J. C. White, 360 Colorado Ave., Bridgeport, CT 06605

## Church of God in Christ, Mennonite

The Church of God in Christ, Mennonite was organized by the evangelist-reformer John Holdeman in Ohio. The church unites with the faith of the Waldensians, Anabaptists and other such groups throughout history. Emphasis is placed on obedience to the teachings of the Bible, including the doctrine of the new birth and spiritual life, noninvolvement in government or the military, head-coverings for the women, beards for the men and separation from the world shown by simplicity in clothing, homes, possessions and lifestyle. The church has a worldwide membership of about 20,150, largely concentrated in the United States and Canada.

**Headquarters**

P.O. Box 313, 420 N. Wedel Ave., Moundridge, KS 67107, Tel. (620)345-2532 Fax (620)345-2582
Media Contact, Dale Koehn, P.O. Box 230, Moundridge, KS 67107, Tel. (620)345-2532 Fax (620)345-2582, Email: dalekoehn.gp@cogicm.org

**Periodicals**

*Messenger of Truth*

## Church of God (Cleveland, Tennessee)

It is one of America's oldest Pentecostal churches founded in 1886 as an outgrowth of the holiness revival under the name Christian Union. In 1907 the church adopted the organizational name Church of God. It has its foundation upon the principles of Christ as revealed in the Bible. The Church of God is Christian, Protestant, foun-

95

dational in its doctrine, evangelical in practice and distinctively Pentecostal. It maintains a centralized form of government and a commitment to world evangelization. The first church of Canada was established in 1919 in Scotland Farm, Manitoba. Paul H. Walker became the first overseer of Canada in 1931.

### Headquarters

Intl. Offices, 2490 Keith St., NW, Cleveland, TN 37320, Tel. (423)472-3361 Fax (423)478-7066
Media Contact, Dir. of Communications, T. Scot Carter, P.O. Box 2430, Cleveland, TN 37320-2430, Tel. (423)478-7112 Fax (423)478-7066
Website: www.churchofgod.cc/default_nav40.asp

### EXECUTIVES

Gen. Overseer, G. Dennis McGuire
Asst. Gen. Overseers, Raymond F. Culpepper; Orville Hagan; and Timothy M. Hill
Sec.-Gen., Paul L. Walker
Canada-Eastern, Rev. George S. Pears, P.O. Box 2036, Brampton, ON L6T 3TO, Tel. (905)793-2213 Fax (905)793-9173
Canada-Western, Rev. Stephen P. Darnell, Box 54055, 2640 52 St. NE, Calgary, AB T1Y 6S6, Tel. (403)293-8817 Fax (403)293-3466
Canada-Quebec-Maritimes, Rev. Jaques Houle, 19 Orly, Granby, QC J2H 1Y4, Tel. (450)378-4442 Fax (450)378-8646
Canada-National, Rev. Ralph R. Glagau, P.O. Box 333, Stn B, Etobicoke, ON M9W 5L3, Tel. (416)741-9222 Fax (416)741-3717

### DEPARTMENTS

Benefits Board—CEO, Arthur D. Rhodes
Business & Records—Exec. Dir., Julian B. Robinson
Care Ministries—Dir., Donnie W. Smith
Chaplains Commission—Dir., Robert D. Crick
Communications, Media Ministries—Dir., T. Scot Carter
Division of Education—Chancellor, Donald S. Aultman
Education—European Bible Seminary, Dir., Paul Schmidgall
Education—U.S.A. Hispanic Educational Ministries Dir., Rudy Giron
Education—International Bible College, Pres., James Dill
Education—Lee University, Pres., Charles Paul Conn
Education—Patten University, Pres., Gary Moncher
Education—Puerto Rico Bible School, Pres., Ildefonso Caraballo
Education—Theological Seminary, President, Steven J. Land
Evangelism & Home Missions—Dir., Wallace J. Sibley
Evangelism—Black Ministries, Dir., Jimmy Campbell
Evangelism—Multi-Cultural Min., Dir., Harvey L. Turner, Sr.

Evangelism—Hispanic Ministries, Dir., Fidenaio Burgueno
Evangelism—Native American Ministries, Dir., Douglas M. Cline
Family Ministries—Coordinator, John K. Vining
Lay Ministries—Dir., Leonard Albert
Legal Services—Dir., Dennis W. Watkins
Men/Women of Action—Dir., L. Hugh Carver
Ministerial Care—Dir., Bill Leonard
Ministerial Development—Dir., Donald S. Aultman
Ministry to Israel—Dir., J. Michael Utterback
Ministry to the Military—Dir., Robert A. Moore
Music Ministries—Dir., Delton L. Alford
Pentecostal Resource Center—Director, Donald D. Smeeton
Pentecostal Research Center—Dir., David G. Roebuck
Publications—Dir., Joseph A. Mirkovich
SpiritCare—Dir., Gene D. Rice
Stewardship—Dir., Kenneth R. Davis
Women's Ministries—Coordinator, Mary Ruth Stone
World Missions—Dir., Roland E. Vaughan
Youth & Christian Education—Dir., Mark S. Abbott
Romanian Ministries—Dir., Thomas A. George

### Periodicals

*Church of God Evangel; Church of God Editorial Evangelica; Save Our World; Ministry Now Profiles*

## Church of God by Faith, Inc.

Founded 1914, in Jacksonville Heights, Fla., by Elder John Bright, this church believes the word of God as interpreted by Jesus Christ to be the only hope of salvation and Jesus Christ the only mediator for people.

### Headquarters

1315 Lane Ave. S., Suite 6, Jacksonville, FL 32205, Tel. (904)783-8500 Fax (904)783-9911
Media Contact, Ofc. Mgr., Sarah E. Lundy
Email: natl-hq@cogbf.org
Website: www.cogbf.org

### Officers

Presiding Bishop, James E. McKnight, P.O. Box 121, Gainesville, FL 32601
Treas., Elder John Robinson, 300 Essex Dr., Ft. Pierce, FL 34946
Exec. Sec., David C. Rourk, 207 Chestnut Hill Drive, Rochester, NY 14617
Ruling Elder, James E. McKnight, Jr., P.O. Box 101, Starke, FL 32091

## The Church of God of the Firstborn

The Church of God of the Firstborn was founded by Pentecostal evangelist Adolph Gustav Etterman in 1936. Headquarters are located in Newton, Kans.,where annual summer conferences are held. In 2002, the denomination consisted of 26 congregations, located primarily in the south central United States and in Mexico. In recent years, the number of Caucasian churches has declined and Hispanic membership has surged. James Etterman, the son of the founder, became president of the denomination in 1986.

### Headquarters
P.O. Box 1041, 720 S. Kansas Ave., Newton, KS 671114-1041
Media Contact, Pres., Rev. James Etterman

### Officers
Pres., Rev. James Etterman

### Periodicals
*The True Messenger*

## Church of God General Conference (Oregon, IL and Morrow, GA)

This church is the outgrowth of several independent local groups of similar faith. Some were in existence as early as 1800, and others date their beginnings to the arrival of British immigrants around 1847. Many local churches carried the name Church of God of the Abrahamic Faith. State and district conferences of these groups were formed as an expression of mutual cooperation. A national organization was instituted at Philadelphia in 1888. Because of strong convictions on the questions of congregational rights and authority, however, it ceased to function until 1921, when the present General Conference was formed at Waterloo, Iowa.

The Bible is accepted as the supreme standard of faith. Adventist in viewpoint, the second (premillenial) coming of Christ is strongly emphasized. The church teaches that the kingdom of God will be literal, beginning in Jerusalem at the time of the return of Christ and extending to all nations. Emphasis is placed on the oneness of God and the Sonship of Christ, that Jesus did not pre-exist prior to his birth in Bethlehem and that the Holy Spirit is the power and influence of God. Membership is dependent on faith, repentance and baptism by immersion.

The work of the General Conference is carried on under the direction of the board of directors. With a congregational church government, the General Conference exists primarily as a means of mutual cooperation and for the development of yearly projects and enterprises.

The headquarters and Bible College were moved to Morrow, Ga. in 1991.

### Headquarters
P.O. Box 100,000, Morrow, GA 30260, Tel. (404)362-0052 Fax (404)362-9307
Media Contact, Tim Jones
Email: info@abc-coggc.org
Website: www.abc-coggc.org

### Officers
Chief Administrative Officer, Mr. Tim Jones, Box 100,000, Morrow, GA 30260, Tel. (404)362-9307, Email: tjones@abc-coggc.org
Chpsn., Pastor Michael Hoffman, 740 W. Oregon Trail, Oregon, IL 61061, Tel. (815)732-6847, Email: hoffon@aol.com
Vice-Chpsn., Pastor Dale Bliss, 2696 Wynterpointe Ct., Kokomo IN 46901, Tel. (765) 455-9866, Email: dale_bliss@hotmail. com
Sec., Andrea Anders, 301 North Ellis St., Salisbury, NC 28144, Tel. (803)461-2150, Email: aanders@suggskelly.com,
Treas. Mr. Joe James, 100 Buck Drive, Piedmont, SC 29673, Tel. (864)845-5808, Email: jjoecarol@aol.com

### OTHER ORGANIZATIONS
Bus. Admn., Operations Manager, Mr. Gary Burnham, Box 100,000, Morrow, GA 30260, Tel. (404)362-0052 Fax (404)362-9307, Email: gburnham@abc-coggc.org
Atlanta Bible College, President, Mr. Tim Jones, Box 100,000, Morrow, GA 30260, Tel. (404) 362-9307, Email: tjones@ abc-coggc.org

### Periodicals
*The Restitution Herald and Progress Journal; A Journal From the Radical Reformation; Church of God*

## Church of God, Mountain Assembly, Inc.

The church was formed in 1895 and organized in 1906 by J. H. Parks, S. N. Bryant, Tom D. Moses and William Douglas.

### Headquarters
256 N. Florence Ave., P.O. Box 157, Jellico, TN 37762, Tel. (423)784-8260 Fax (423)784-3258
Media Contact, Gen. Sec.-Treas., Rev. James Kilgore
Email: cgmahdq@jellico.com
Website: www.cgmahdq.org

### Officers
Gen. Overseer, Rev. Fred R. Cornelius
Asst. Gen. Overseer, World Missions Dir., Rev. Jay Walden
Gen. Sec.-Treas., Rev. James Kilgore
Youth Ministries & Camp Dir., Rev. Nick Hill

### Periodicals
*The Gospel Herald*

## Church of God of Prophecy

The Church of God of Prophecy is one of the churches that grew out of the work of A. J. Tomlinson in the first half of the twentieth century. Historically it shares a common heritage with the Church of God (Cleveland, Tennessee) and is in the mainstream of the classical Pentecostal-Holiness tradition.

At the death of A.J. Tomlinson in 1943, M.A. Tomlinson was named General Overseer and served until his retirement in 1990. He emphasized unity and fellowship unlimited by racial, social, or political differences. The next General Overseer, Billy D. Murray, Sr., who served from 1990 until his retirement in 2000, emphasized a commitment to the promotion of Christian unity and world evangelization. In July 2000, Fred S. Fisher, Sr. was duly selected to serve as the fourth General Overseer of the Church of God of Prophecy.

From its beginnings, the church has based its beliefs on "the whole Bible, rightly divided," and has accepted the Bible as God's Holy Word, inspired, inerrant and infallible. The church is firm in its commitment to orthodox Christian belief. The church affirms that there is one God, eternally existing in three persons, Father, Son and Holy Spirit. It believes in the deity of Christ, His virgin birth, His sinless life, the physical miracles He performed, His atoning death on the cross, His bodily resurrection, His ascension to the right hand of the Father, and his second coming. The church professes that salvation results from grace alone through faith in Christ, that regeneration by the Holy Spirit is essential for the salvation of sinful men, and that sanctification by the blood of Christ makes possible personal holiness. It affirms the present ministry of the Holy Spirit by Whose indwelling believers are able to live godly lives and have power for service. The church believes in, and promotes, the ultimate unity of believers as prayed for by Christ in John 17. The church stresses the sanctity of human life and is committed to the sanctity of the marriage bond and the importance of strong, loving Christian families. Other official teachings include Holy Spirit baptism with tongues as initial evidence; manifestation of the spiritual gifts; divine healing; premillenial second coming of Christ; total abstinence from the use of tobacco, alcohol and narcotics; water baptism by immersion; the Lord's supper and washing of the saints' feet; and a concern for moderation and holiness in all dimensions of lifestyle.

The church is racially integrated on all levels, including top leadership. Women play a prominent role in church affairs, serving in pastoral roles and other leadership positions. The church presbytery has recently adopted plurality of leadership in the selection of a General Oversight Group. This group consists of eight bishops located around the world who, along with the General Overseer, are responsible for inspirational leadership and vision casting for the church body.

The church has local congregations in all 50 states and more than 100 nations worldwide. Organizationally there is a strong emphasis on international missions, evangelism, youth and children's ministries, women's and men's ministries, stewardship, communications, publishing, leadership development, and discipleship.

## CHURCH OF GOD OF PROPHECY INTERNATIONAL OFFICES

P.O. Box 2910, Cleveland, TN 37320-2910
Media Contact, National Overseer, Levi Clarke, 5145 Tomken Rd, Mississauga, ON L4 W1P1, Tel. (905)625-1278 Fax (905)625-1316.
Email: betty@cogop.org
Website: www.cogop.org

### Officers

Gen. Overseer, Bishop Fred S. Fisher, Sr.; General Presbyters, Sherman Allen, Sam Clements, Daniel Corbett, Clayton Endecott, Miguel Mojica, Felix Santiago, Brice Thompson
International Offices Ministries Dirs., Finance, Communications, and Publishing, Perry Gillum; Global Outreach and Administrative Asst. to the General Presbyters, Randy Howard; Leadership Development and Discipleship Ministries, Larry Duncan.

### Periodicals

*White Wing Messenger* (Eng), *Victory* (Youth Magazine/Sunday School Curriculum); *The Happy Harvester, White Wing Messenger* (Spanish).

## The Church of God (Seventh Day), Denver, Colorado

The Church of God (Seventh Day) began in southwestern Michigan in 1858, when a group of Sabbath-keepers led by Gilbert Cranmer refused to give endorsement to the visions and writings of Ellen G. White, a principal in the formation of the Seventh-Day Adventist Church. Another branch of Sabbath-keepers, which developed near Cedar Rapids, Iowa, in 1860, joined the Michigan church in 1863 to publish a paper called *The Hope of Israel*, the predecessor to the *Bible Advocate*, the church's present publication. As membership grew and spread into Missouri and Nebraska, it organized the General Conference of the Church of God in 1884. The words "Seventh Day" were added to its name in 1923. The headquarters of the church was in Stanberry, Mo., from 1888 until 1950, when it moved to Denver.

The church teaches salvation is a gift of God's grace, and is available solely by faith in Jesus Christ, the Savior; that saving faith is more than mental assent, it involves active trust and repentance from sin. Out of gratitude, Christians will give evidence of saving faith by a lifestyle that conforms to God's commandments, including the seventh-day Sabbath, which members observe as a tangible expression of their faith and rest in God as their Creator and Redeemer. The church believes in the imminent, personal, and visible return of Christ; that the dead are in an unconscious state awaiting to be resurrected, the wicked to be destroyed, and the righteous to be rewarded to eternal life in the presence of God on a restored earth. The church observes two ordinances, baptism by immersion and an annual Communion service accompanied by foot-washing.

## Headquarters

330 W. 152nd Ave., P.O. Box 33677, Denver, CO 80233, Tel. (303)452-7973 Fax (303)452-0657
Media Contact, Pres., Whaid Rose
Email: whaidrose@cog7.org
Website: www.cog7.org

### MINISTRIES

Missions Ministries, Dir., William Hicks, Church Planting Dir., Mike Vlad; Home Missions Dir., Mike Vlad; Missions Abroad, Dir., William Hicks

Publications/Bible Advocate Press, Dir., Eddie Villalba

Ministerial Training System, Chairman, Harvey Fischer

Young Adult Ministry, Dir., Kristy Lang

Youth Ministry, Dirs., Kurt & Kristi Lang

Women's Ministry, Dir., Mary Ling

### Periodicals

*The Bible Advocate* (English & Spanish); *Pulse* (English & Spanish)

## The Church of Illumination

The Church of Illumination was organized in 1908 for the express purpose of establishing congregations at large, offering a spiritual, esoteric, philosophic interpretation of the vital biblical teachings, thereby satisfying the inner spiritual needs of those seeking spiritual truth, yet permitting them to remain in, or return to, their former church membership.

### Headquarters

Beverly Hall, 5966 Clymer Rd., Quakertown, PA 18951, Tel. (800)779-3796

Media Contact, Dir. General, Gerald E. Poesnecker, P.O. Box 220, Quakertown, PA 18951, Tel. (215)536-7048 Fax (215)536-7058

Email: bevhall@comcat.com

Website: www.soul.org

### Officers

Dir.-General, Gerald E. Poesnecker, P.O. Box 220, Quakertown, PA 18951

## The Church of Jesus Christ (Bickertonites)

This church was organized in 1862 at Green Oak, Pa., by William Bickerton, who obeyed the Restored Gospel under Sidney Rigdon's following in 1845.

### Headquarters

Sixth & Lincoln Sts., Monongahela, PA 15063, Tel. (412)258-3066

Media Contact, Exec. Sec., John Manes, 2007 Cutter Dr., McKees Rocks, PA 15136, Tel. (412)771-4513

### Officers

Pres., Dominic Thomas, 6010 Barrie, Dearborn, MI 48126

First Counselor, Paul Palmieri, 319 Pine Dr., Aliquippa, PA 15001, Tel. (412)378-4264

Second Counselor, Robert Watson, Star Rt. 5, Box 36, Gallup, NM 87301

Exec. Sec., John Manes, 2007 Cutter Dr., McKees Rocks, PA 15136, Tel. (412)771-4513

## The Church of Jesus Christ of Latter-day Saints

This church was organized April 6, 1830, at Fayette, N.Y., by Joseph Smith. Members believe Joseph Smith was divinely directed to restore the gospel to the earth, and that through him the keys to the Aaronic and Melchizedek priesthoods and temple work also were restored. Members believe that both the Bible and the Book of Mormon (a record of the Lord's dealings with His people on the American continent 600 B.C.–421 A.D.) are Scripture. Membership is over 12 million.

In addition to the First Presidency, the governing bodies of the church include the Quorum of the Twelve Apostles, the Presidency of the Seventy, the Quorums of the Seventy and the Presiding Bishopric.

### Headquarters

47 East South Temple St., Salt Lake City, UT 84150, Tel. (801)240-1000 Fax (801)240-1167

Media Contact, Dir., Media Relations, Michael Otterson, Tel. (801)240-1111 Fax (801)240-1167

Website: www.lds.org

### Officers

Pres., Gordon B. Hinckley

1st Counselor, Thomas S. Monson

2nd Counselor, James E. Faust

Quorum of the Twelve Apostles, Pres., Boyd K. Packer; L. Tom Perry; Russell M. Nelson; Dallin H. Oaks; M. Russell Ballard; Joseph B. Wirthlin; Richard G. Scott; Robert D. Hales; Jeffrey R. Holland; Henry B. Eyring; Dieter F. Uchtdorf; David A. Bednar

### AUXILIARY ORGANIZATIONS

Sunday Schools, Gen. Pres., A. Roger Merrill

Relief Society, Gen. Pres., Bonnie D. Parkin

Young Women, Gen. Pres., Susan W. Tanner

Young Men, Gen. Pres., Charles W. Dahlquist II

Primary, Gen. Pres., Cheryl C. Lant

### Periodicals

*The Ensign; Liahona; New Era; Friend Magazine*

## Church of the Living God (Motto, Christian Workers for Fellowship)

The Church of the Living God was founded by William Christian in April 1889 at Caine Creek, Ark. It was the first black church in America without Anglo-Saxon roots and not founded by white missionaries.

Chief Christian, as he is now referred, was

born a slave in Mississippi on Nov. 10, 1856 and grew up uneducated. In 1875, he united with the Missionary Baptist Church and began to preach. In 1888, he left the Baptist Church and began what was known as Christian Friendship Work. Believing himself to have been inspired by the Spirit of God through divine revelation and close study of the Scriptures, he was led to the truth that the Bible refers to the church as The Church of the Living God (I Timothy. ch.3 v.15). In 1889, he established the Church of the Living God organization.

The organization is nondenominational, non-sectarian and Trinitarian and believer in the infallibility of the Scriptures. It emphasizes believer's baptism by immersion, the use of water and unleavened bread element in the Lord's Supper and the washing of feet that is required only when one unites with the church.

The local organizations are known as "Temple" rather than as "Churches" and are subject to the authority of the general assembly. The presiding officer is styled as "chief bishop." The ministry includes bishops, overseers, evangelists, pastors, missionaries and local preachers. The Executive Board is in charge of the operation of the entire organization, in the absence of the Annual Assembly. Synod, Annual, General Assembly meets quadrennially.

The Church of the Living God, now headquartered in Cincinnati, Ohio, has been in existence for more than 114 years. It is represented by approximately 10,000 members throughout 25 states within the U.S. The presiding officer, Chief Bishop W. E. Crumes, has led the organization for more than 30 years.

### Headquarters

430 Forest Ave., Cincinnati, OH 45229, Tel. (513)569-5660 Fax (513)569-5661; Media Contact: Chief Bishop, W. E. Crumes

### EXECUTIVE BOARD

Chief Bishop, W. E. Crumes, 430 Forest Ave., Cincinnati, OH 45229

Vice Chief Bishop, Robert D. Tyler, 3802 Bedford, Omaha, NE 68110

Exec. Sec., Bishop C. A. Lewis, 1360 N. Boston, Tulsa, OK 73111

Gen. Sec., Elder Raymond Powell, Sr., 2159 E. 95th St., Chicago, IL 60617

Gen. Treas., Elder Harry Hendricks, 11935 Cimarron Ave., Hawthorne, CA 90250

Bishop E. L. Bowie, 2037 N.E. 18th St., Oklahoma City, OK 73111

Bishop Leroy Smith, Jr., 1418 Faraday, Peoria, IL 61605

Bishop Jeff Ruffin, 302 E. Monte Way, Phoenix, AZ 85040

Bishop S. E. Shannon, 1034 S. King Hwy., St. Louis, MO 63110

Bishop, Elbert Jones, 4522 Melwood, Memphis, TN 38109

Bishop, Harold Edwards, P.O. Box 411489,

Dallas, TX 75249

NATIONAL DEPARTMENTS
Convention Planning Committee
Young People's Progressive Union
Christian Education Dept.
Sunday School Dept.
Natl. Evangelist Bd.
Natl. Nurses Guild
Natl. Women's Work Dept.
Natl. Music Dept.
Natl. Usher Board
Natl. Sec. Office

### Periodicals

*The Gospel Truth*

## Church of the Lutheran Brethren of America

The Church of the Lutheran Brethren of America was organized in December 1900. Five independent Lutheran congregations met together in Milwaukee, Wisc., and adopted a constitution patterned very closely on that of the Lutheran Free Church of Norway.

The spiritual awakening in the Midwest during the 1890s crystallized into convictions that led to the formation of a new church body. Chief among the concerns were church membership practices, observance of Holy Communion, confirmation practices and local church government.

The Church of the Lutheran Brethren practices a simple order of worship with the sermon as the primary part of the worship service. It believes that personal profession of faith is the primary criterion for membership in the congregation. The Communion service is reserved for those who profess faith in Christ as savior. Each congregation is autonomous and the synod serves the congregations in advisory and cooperative capacities.

The synod supports a world mission program in Cameroon, Chad, Japan, and Taiwan. Approximately 40 percent of the synodical budget is earmarked for world missions. A growing home mission ministry is planting new congregations in the United States and Canada. Affiliate organizations operate several retirement, nursing homes, conference, and retreat centers.

### Headquarters

1020 Alcott Ave., W., Box 655, Fergus Falls, MN 56538, Tel. (218)739-3336 Fax (218)739-5514
Media Contact, Pres., Rev. Joel Egge
Email: clba@clba.org
Website: www.clba.org

### Officers

Pres., Rev. Joel Egge
Vice Pres., Rev. David Rinden
Sec., Rev. Richard Vettrus, 707 Crestview Dr., West Union, IA 52175
Exec. Dir. of Finance, Bradley Martinson
Lutheran Brethren Schools Representative, Dr. Eugene Boe

World Missions, Exec. Dir., Rev. Matthew Rogness
Home Missions, Exec. Dir., Rev. Armin Jahr
Church Services, Exec. Dir., Rev. Brent Juliot
Youth Ministries, Exec. Dir., Nathan Lee

### Periodicals
*Faith & Fellowship*

## Church of the Lutheran Confession

The Church of the Lutheran Confession held its constituting convention in Watertown, S.D., in August of 1960. The Church of the Lutheran Confession was begun by people and congregations who withdrew from church bodies that made up what was then known as the Synodical Conference over the issue of unionism. Following passages such as I Corinthians ch. 1 v.10 and Romans ch. 16 v.17-18, the Church of the Lutheran Confession holds the conviction that mutual agreement with the doctrines of Scripture is essential and necessary before exercise of church fellowship is appropriate.

Members of the Church of the Lutheran Confession uncompromisingly believe the Holy Scriptures to be divinely inspired and therefore inerrant. They subscribe to the historic Lutheran Confessions as found in the Book of Concord of 1580 because they are a correct exposition of Scripture.

The Church of the Lutheran Confession exists to proclaim, preserve and spread the saving truth of the gospel of Jesus Christ, so that the redeemed of God may learn to know Jesus Christ as their Lord and Savior and follow him through this life to the life to come.

### Headquarters
501 Grover Rd., Eau Claire, WI 54701, Tel. (715) 836-6622
Media Contact, Pres., Daniel Fleischer Tel. (361) 241-5147
Email: JohnHLau@juno.com
Website: www.clclutheran.org

### Officers
Pres., Rev. John Schierenbeck, 3015 Ave. K NW, Winter Haven, FL 33881
Mod., Prof. Ronald Roehl, 515 Ingram Dr. W., Eau Claire, WI 54701
Vice Pres., Rev. Mark Bernthal, 3232 West Point Rd., Middleton, WI 53562, Tel. (608)233-2244
Sec., Rev. James Albrecht, 102 Market St., P.O. Box 98 Okebena, MN 55432-2408
Treas., Dr. James Sydow, 500 Grover Rd., Eau Claire, WI 54701
Archivist, Prof. David Lau, 507 Ingram Dr., Eau Claire, WI 54701
Statistician, Dr. James Sydow, 500 Grover Rd., Eau Claire, WI 54701

### Periodicals
*The Lutheran Spokesman; Journal of Theology*

## Church of the Nazarene

The Church of the Nazarene resulted from the merger of three independent holiness groups. The Association of Pentecostal Churches in America, located principally in New York and New England, joined at Chicago in 1907 with a largely West Coast body called the Church of the Nazarene and formed the Pentecostal Church of the Nazarene. A southern group, the Holiness Church of Christ, united with the Pentecostal Church of the Nazarene at Pilot Point, Texas, in 1908. In 1919 the word "Pentecostal" was dropped from the name. Principal leaders in the organization were Phineas Bresee, William Howard Hoople, H. F. Reynolds and C. B. Jernigan. The first congregation in Canada was organized in November 1902 by Dr. H. F. Reynolds in Oxford, Nova Scotia.

The Church of the Nazarene emphasizes the doctrine of entire sanctification or Christian Holiness. It stresses the importance of a devout and holy life and a positive witness before the world by the power of the Holy Spirit. Nazarenes express their faith through evangelism, compassionate ministries, and education. Nazarene government is representative, a studied compromise between episcopacy and congregationalism. Quadrennially, the various districts elect delegates to a general assembly at which six general superintendents are elected.

The international denomination has 11 liberal arts colleges, two graduate seminaries, 41 Bible colleges, two schools of nursing, and a junior college. The church maintains over 600 (739) missionaries in 119 (148) world areas. World services include medical, educational, and religious ministries. Books, periodicals and other Christian literature are published at the Nazarene Publishing House.

The church is a member of the Christian Holiness Partnership, National Association of Evangelicals and the World Methodist Council.

### Headquarters
6401 The Paseo, Kansas City, MO 64131, Tel. (816)333-7000 Fax (816)822-9071
Media Contact, Gen. Sec./Headquarters Operations Officer (HOO), Dr. Jack Stone, Tel. (816)333-7000 x 2366 Fax(816)362-4983 or (816)822-9071, Email: jstone@nazarene. org
Email: ssm@nazarene.org
Website: www.nazarene.org

### Officers
Gen. Supts., Dr. James H. Diehl; Dr. Paul G. Cunningham; Dr. Jerry D. Porter; Dr. Nina Gunter; Dr. J.K. Warrick; Dr. Jesse C. Middendorf; 6401 The Paseo, Kansas City, MO 64131, Tel. (816)333-7000

Gen. Sec./Headquarters Operation Officer (HOO), Dr. Jack Stone Tel. (816)333-7000 Fax (816)822-9071, Email: jstone@nazarene.org

Gen. Treas./Headquarters Financial Officer (HFO), Dr. Marilyn McCool, Tel. (816)333-7000 Fax (816)361-6216, Email: mmccool @nazarene.org

Sunday school Ministries Director, Dr. David Graves, 6401 The Paseo, Kansas City, MO 64131, Tel. (816)333-7000 Fax (816)363-7092, Email:dgraves@nazarene.org

U.S.A./Canada Mission/Evangelism Director, Dr. Tom Nees, 6401 The Paseo, Kansas City, MO 64131, Tel. 816-333-7000 Fax 816-361-5202, Email: tnees@nazarene.org

Education Commissioner, Dr. Jerry Lambert, 6401 The Paseo, Kansas City, MO 64131, Tel. 816-333-7000 Fax 816-333-2891, Email: jlambert@nazarene.org

Nazarene Youth International Ministries Director., Rev. Gary Hartke, 6401 The Paseo, Kansas City, MO 64131, Tel. 816-333-7000 Fax 816-333-4315, Email: ghartke@nazarene.org

World Mission Director., Dr. Louie Bustle, 6401 The Paseo, Kansas City, MO 64131, Tel. 816-333-7000 Fax 816-363-8216, Email: lbustle @nazarene.org

### Periodicals

*Holiness Today; Preacher's Magazine; Grow Magazine*

## The Church of God

The Church of God was established in about 28 A.D. by Jesus Christ on Mt. Kurn Hattin (Mark ch. 3 v. 13-15). It was endowed with power on the Day of Pentecost, but was in operation prior to this point in time.

The true Church plunged into the Dark Ages on June 14, 325 A.D. with the signing of the "Nicene Creed" and remained in darkness for 1,578 years. From 325 A.D. to 1903, God was not asleep! He began revealing the truth to men once again: Martin Luther—justification by faith; John Wesley—sanctification; Dr. Albert Simpson —divine healing; (though some received the Holy Ghost prior to 1903, it is generally regarded the Pentecostal Movement began with a Holy Ghost revival in California in 1906—Dr. Seymour).

On June 13, 1903 The Church arose from darkness (as prophesied by Isaiah 60:1-5) in North Carolina. In 1923 a disruption caused a split in the Church, resulting in two groups both calling themselves the Church of God. In 1933 God gave the banner (Psalms 60:3, 4), the Church flag, to His Church; to those who feared Him too much to be led astray from the truth. (August 31, 2001 the Holy Ghost gave a new design for the banner of truth.)

On May 2, 1952 "of Prophecy" was added to the name Church of God. In 1990, the Church of God of Prophecy departed from theocratic government. Through the Holy Ghost, God called for a Solemn Assembly to be held July 23-25, 1993. On July 24, the Holy Ghost gave direction to separate ourselves from the apostasy of the past three years, and to continue truly as The Church of God, clearly designating Robert J. Pruitt as the General Overseer. The Church of God thus returned to the true theocracy.

This constituted not a new organization, but the reorganization of The Church of God as the true theocracy of God, the exclusive Body of Christ:

1. Which was set in order by Christ and functioned in theocratic order until A.D. 325;

2. Which arose from the Dark Ages on June 13, 1903;

3. Which continued true to God in "faith and practice, government and discipline" following the 1923 disruption;

4. Which is doing likewise since the similar disruption in 1993.

Details of the future are, of course, unknown; but the prophecies of God are clear concerning His Church. The hour is late, but the brightness of the "Arise, Shine" lies just ahead. Without a doubt, perfection will be attained, for it has already been declared of the Church that Christ will "present it unto himself a glorious church, not having spot, or wrinkle, or any such thing; but that it should be holy and without blemish." (Ephesians 5:27; see also Revelations 19:6-9).

### Headquarters

P.O. Box 450, Charleston, TN 37310, U.S.A., Tel. (423)339-8264

### Officers

General Overseer, Stephen Smith, 197 Tillie Road, Cleveland, TN

Field Sec., Ray D. Dupre

Field Sec., Robert F. Strong

Field Sec., Donaldo Acosta

General Tre./Ass. Editor—*The Evening Light*, Kevin D. Werkheiser

World Mission Coordinator/Bible Training Institute Dir., Herman D. Ard

Mission Representative (Africa, Asia & Europe), Robert J. Hawkins, Jr.

Assembly Band Movement Coordinator, Donald W. Branscum

Evangelism Coordinator, Lanny W. Carter

Church of Prophecy Marker Association Coordinator, Melvin Byers, Jr.

Sunday School Coordinator, Maudie E. Wood

Victory Leaders Band Coordinator, Sharon Griffin

Women's Missionary Band Coordinator, Betty Bishop

### STATES

Alabama, James C. Anders

Alaska, Michael A. Grant

Arizona/Colorado/New Mexico/Texas (W), James R. Horne

Arkansas/Kansas/Missouri/Oklahoma/Texas (E), Dewayne Smith

Idaho (S)/California/Nevada/Utah, Serafin Pimentel

Idaho (N)/Montana (W)/Oregon/Washington, Ray D. Adams

Florida/Georgia, Melvin F. Kramer

Indiana/Illinois (S)/Kentucky/Ohio, Paul S. Jernigan

Louisiana/Mississippi, A. T. Dewberry

North Carolina, Melvin Byers, Jr.

South Carolina, Carl J. Neal

Pennsylvania/Delaware/Maryland/Massachusetts, James T. Smith

Virginia/ West Virginia, Clive Jared

N. Dakota/S. Dakota/Minnesota/Montana (E)/ Nebraska/Wyoming, Delbert G. Bock

Tennessee, Ray D. Dupre

Wisconsin/Illinois (N)/Iowa/Michigan, E. Roger Ammons

### COUNTRIES

Argentina/Brazil/Paraguay/Uruguay, David Coronel

Bahamas/Cayman/Turks & Caicos Islands, George C. Forbes

Belize/Honduras/El Salvador/Spain, Donaldo Acosta

Bolivia/Ecuador, Benito Ramos Quispe

Canada East, E. Roger Ammons

Canada West, Ray Adams

Cameroon/Democratic Republic of Congo/ Republic of Congo, Patrice T. Kalamba

Chile, Javier Diaz

England, Robert J. Hawkins Jr.

Guatemala, Manuel S. Castro

Haiti, Louis E. Gaddis

India (South), Isaac Thomas Adimavunkal

India (North), Ch. Paul Sudhaker

Indonesia, Kalmen E. Nainggolan

Kenya/Ethiopia/Tanzania/Zimbabwe, Renison Mbogo Ngurukiri

Mexico, José G. Bañuelos

Nepal, Herman D. Ard

Nicaragua/Costa Rica/Panama, Caleb Hernández Ramírez

Nigeria, Matthew Ogunmola

Peru, Leonardo Luna

Philippines, Danilo M. Orcino

Puerto Rico/Dominican Republic/St. Vincent/ Netherlands Antilles, Juan Pimentel

Uganda/Burundi/Rwanda, Makohá F. Agati

Zambia, Alfred Nsofwa

### Periodicals
*The Evening Light*

## Church of Our Lord Jesus Christ of the Apostolic Faith, Inc.

This church body was founded by Bishop R.C. Lawson in Columbus, Ohio, and moved to New York City in 1919. It is founded upon the teach-ings of the apostles and prophets, Jesus Christ being its chief cornerstone.

### Headquarters
2081 Adam Clayton Powell Jr. Blvd., New York, NY 10027, Tel. (212)866-1700

Media Contact, Exec. Sec., Bishop T. E. Woolfolk, P.O. Box 119, Oxford, NC 27565, Tel. (919)693-9449 Fax (919)693-6115

Email: tewmsw@earthlink.net

Website: www.apostolic-faith.org

### Officers
Board of Apostles

Bishop William L. Bonner; Chief Apostle

Bishop James I. Clark Jr., Presiding Apostle

Bishop Mathew A. Norwood, Vice-Presider

Bishop Robert L. Sanders, Vice-Presider

Bishop Gentle L. Groover;

Bishop Fred Rubin

Bishop James A. Maye

Bishop Henry A. Moultrie, II

Bishop Wesley M. Taylor

Bishop Samuel R. Peters, Sr.

Bishop Walter L. Jackson

Bishop Bradford Berry

Bd. of Bishops, Chmn., Bishop Herbert Edwards

Bd. of Presbyters, Chairman, Elder Mark E. Jones, Interim

Exec. Sec., Bishop Thomas E. Woolfolk

Natl. Rec. Sec., Bishop Raymond J. Keith, Jr.

Natl. Fin. Sec., Bishop Clarence Groover

Natl. Corr. Sec., Bishop Steven F. Parrott

Natl Treas., Elder Jonathan K. Jefferson

### Periodicals
*Contender For The Faith; Minute Book*

## Church of the United Brethren in Christ, U.S.A.

The Church of the United Brethren in Christ had its beginning with Philip William Otterbein and Martin Boehm, who were leaders in the revival movement in Pennsylvania and Maryland from the late 1760s into the early 1800s.

On Sept. 25, 1800, they and others associated with them formed a society under the name of United Brethren in Christ. Subsequent confer-ences adopted a Confession of Faith in 1815 and a constitution in 1841. The Church of the United Brethren in Christ adheres to the original consti-tution as amended in 1957, 1961 and 1977.

### Headquarters
302 Lake St., Huntington, IN 46750, Tel. (260) 356-2312 Fax (260)356-4730 x 210

Media Contact, Communications Dir., Steve Dennie

Email: sdennie@ub.org

Website: www.ub.org

### Officers
Bishop, Rev. Ron Ramsey

Finance Director, Marci Hammel

Director of Higher Education, Dr. G. Blair Dowden
Global Ministries Director, Rev. Gary Dilley
Director of Healthy Church Ministries, Rev. Patrick Jones
Communications Director, Mr. Steve Dennie

## Churches of Christ

Churches of Christ are autonomous congregations whose members appeal to the Bible alone to determine matters of faith and practice. There are no central offices or officers. Publications and institutions related to the churches are either under local congregational control or are independent of any congregation. Churches of Christ shared a common fellowship in the 19th century with the Christian Churches/Churches of Christ and the Christian Church (Disciples of Christ). This fellowship ended in the decades following the American Civil War due to erosion of confidence in Scripture among many of those who would go on to form these other groups. This shift in belief embraced theistic evolution, doubted the complete truth of Scripture, and permitted unscriptural practices into the work and worship of the church. Chief among the changes in practice were the use of instrumental music in worship, permitting women to officiate in worship services, and conducting the work of the church through centralized agencies. Churches of Christ, following this division, remained strongly united in their belief in the inerrancy and sufficiency of Scripture. From this standpoint they affirm faith in one God who subsists in three persons: Father, Son, and Holy Spirit; they teach that salvation is through the sacrificial death of Christ and is available to all who come to God through repentance and faith, initially expressed through confession of faith and baptism by immersion. Churches of Christ follow the New Testament pattern to direct every facet of the teaching and work of the church.

### Headquarters
Media Contact, Ed., *Gospel Advocate*, Mr. Neil Anderson, 1006 Elm Hill Pike, Nashville, TN 37102, Tel. (800)251-8446 Fax (615)254-7411

### Periodicals
*Action; Christian Woman; Christian Bible Teacher; The Christian Chronicle; Firm Foundation; Gospel Advocate; Guardian of Truth; Restoration Quarterly; 21st Century Christian; Rocky Mountain Christian; The Spiritual Sword; Word and Work*

## Churches of Christ in Christian Union

Organized in 1909 at Washington Court House, Ohio, as the Churches of Christ in Christian Union, this body believes in the new birth and the baptism of the Holy Spirit for believers. It is Wesleyan, with an evangelistic and missionary emphasis.

The Reformed Methodist Church merged with the Churches of Christ in Christian Union in 1952.

### Headquarters
1426 Lancaster Pike, Box 10, Circleville, OH 43113, Tel. (740)474-8856 Fax (740)477-7766
Media Contact, Dir. of Comm., Rev. Ralph Hux

### Officers
Gen. Supt., Dr. Tom Hermiz
Asst. Gen. Supt., Rev. Dan Harrison
Gen. Treas., Rev. Bruce Crabtree
Gen. Bd. of Trustees, Chpsn., Dr. Tom Hermiz; Vice-Chpsn., Rev. Dan Harrison
District Superintendents, West Central District, Rev. Ron Reese; South Central District, Rev. Don Spurgeon; Northeast District, Rev. Brad Dixon; West Indies District, David Chandler

### Periodicals
*The Evangelical Advocate*

## Churches of God, General Conference

The Churches of God, General Conference (CGGC) had its beginnings in Harrisburg, Pa., in 1825. John Winebrenner, recognized founder of the Church of God movement, was an ordained minister of the German Reformed Church. His experience-centered form of Christianity, particularly the "new measures" he used to promote it, his close connection with the local Methodists, his "experience and conference meetings" in the church and his "social prayer meetings" in parishioners' homes resulted in differences of opinion and the establishment of new congregations. Extensive revivals, camp meetings and mission endeavors led to the organization of additional congregations across central Pennsyl-vania and westward through Ohio, Indiana, Illinois and Iowa.

In 1830 the first system of cooperation between local churches was initiated as an "eldership" in eastern Pennsylvania. The organization of other elderships followed. General Eldership was organized in 1845, and in 1974 the official name of the denomination was changed from General Eldership of the Churches of God in North America to its present name.

The Churches of God, General Conference, is composed of 7 conferences in the United States and 1 conference in Haiti. The polity of the church is presbyterial in form. The church has mission ministries in the southwest among native Americans and is extensively involved in church planting and whole life ministries in Bangladesh, Brazil, Haiti and India.

The General Conference convenes in business session triennially. An Administrative Council composed of 16 regional representatives is responsible for the administration and ministries of the church between sessions of the General Conference.

### Headquarters
Legal Headquarters, United Church Center, Rm.

213, 900 S. Arlington Ave., Harrisburg, PA
17109, Tel. (717)652-0255
Administrative Offices, General Conf. Exec.
Dir., Pastor Wayne W. Boyer, 700 E. Melrose
Ave., P.O. Box 926, Findlay, OH 45839, Tel.
(419)424-1961 Fax (419)424-3343, Email:
director@cggc.org
Media Contact, Editor, Rachel L. Foreman, P.O.
Box 926, Findlay, OH 45839, Tel. (419) 424-
1961 Fax (419)424-3343, Email: communica-
tions@cggc.org
Email: director@cggc.org
Website: www.cggc.org

## Officers

Pres., Pastor Earl E. Mills, 242 Audubon Ct.,
Chambersburg, PA 17201, Tel. (717)263-9523
Fax (717)263-6219 Email: pastormills@earth-
link.net
Sec., Pastor E. David Green, 700 E. Melrose
Ave., P.O. Box 1132, Findlay, OH 45839, Tel.
(419)423-7694 Fax(419)423-9092, Email:
GLCdirector@cggc.org
Treas., Robert E. Stephenson, 700 E. Melrose
Ave., P.O. Box 926, Findlay, OH 45839, Tel.
(419)424-1961 Fax(419) 424-3433, Email:
treasurer@cggc.org

## DEPARTMENTS

Cross-Cultural Ministries, Pastor Don Dennison
Pensions, Mr. James P. Thomas
Denominational Communications, Rachel L.
Foreman
Church Development, Dr. Charles A. Hirschy
Youth & Family Ministries, Pastor J. Lance Finley
Children's Ministries, Miss. Charlene Bunch
CGWM—Churches of God Women's Ministries

## Periodicals

*The Church Advocate; The Gem; The Missionary
Signal*

## Community of Christ

Community of Christ's mission is to proclaim
Jesus Christ and promote communities of joy,
hope, love, and peace. Founded on April 6, 1830,
this Christian denomination is present in nearly
50 nations with approximately 250,000 members
worldwide. The church's Temple, located in the
international headquarters complex, is dedicated
to peace, reconciliation, and healing of the Spirit.
Priesthood includes both men and women.

## Headquarters

International Headquarters, 1001 W. Walnut,
Independence, MO 64050-3562, Tel. (816)
833-1000 Fax (816)521-3096
Media Contact; Kendra Friend, Email: kfriend
@cofchrist.org; or Jennifer Killpack, Email:
jkillpack@ cofchrist.org
Email: blindgren@cofchrist.org
Website: www.cofChrist.org

## Officers

(Mailing address for all officers is 1001 W. Walnut,
Independence, MO 64050, Tel. (816) 833-1000)
**First Presidency**
President, Stephen M. Veazey, Email: sveazey
@cofchrist.org
Counselor, Kenneth N. Robinson, Email: krobinson
@cofchrist.org
Counselor, David D. Schaal, Email: dschaal
@cofchrist.org
**Council of Twelve Apostles**
President, James E. Slauter, Email: jslauter@cof
christ.org
**Presiding Bishopric**
Presiding Bishop, Larry R. Norris, Email: lnorris
@cofchrist.org
Counselor, R. Paul Davis, Email: pdavis
@cofchrist.org
Counselor, Stephen M. Jones, Email: sjones
@cofchrist.org
**Presiding Evangelist**
Danny A. Belrose, Email: dbelrose
@cofchrist.org
**World Church Secretary**
A. Bruce Lindgren, Email: blindgren
@cofchrist.org
Public Relations, Fax (816)521-3043
Kendra Friend, Email: kfriend@cofchrist.org
Jennifer Killpack, Email: jkillpack
@cofchrist.org

## Periodicals

*Herald*

## Congregational Holiness Church

This body was organized in 1921 and embraces
the doctrine of Holiness and Pentecost. It carries
on mission work in Mexico, Honduras, Costa
Rica, Cuba, Brazil, Guatemala, India, Nicaragua,
El Salvador, Venezuela, Panama, Chile, Argentina,
Belize, Zimbabwe, Haiti, and Peru.

## Headquarters

3888 Fayetteville Hwy., Griffin, GA 30223, Tel.
(404)228-4833 Fax (404)228-1177
Media Contact, Gen. Supt., Bishop Ronald
Wilson
Email: chchurch@bellsouth.net
Website: www.chchurch.com

## EXECUTIVE BOARD

Gen. Supt., Bishop Ronald Smith
1st Asst. Gen. Supt., Rev. William L. Lewis
2nd Asst. Gen. Supt., Rev. Wayne Hicks
Gen. Sec., Rev. Leslee Bailey
Gen. Treas., Rev. Stephen Phillips
World Missions Supt., Rev. Billy Anderson

## Periodicals

*The Gospel Messenger*

## Conservative Baptist Association of America (CBAmerica)

The Conservative Baptist Association of

105

America (now known as CBAmerica) was organized May 17, 1947 at Atlantic City, N.J. The Old and New Testaments are regarded as the divinely inspired Word of God and are therefore infallible and of supreme authority. Each local church is independent, autonomous and free from ecclesiastical or political authority.

CBAmerica provides wide-ranging support to its affiliate churches and individuals through nine regional associations. CBA offers personnel to assist churches in areas such as growth and health, conflict resolution and financial analysis. The association supports its clergy with retirement planning, referrals for new places of ministry and spiritual counseling. The Conservative Baptist Women's Ministries assist women in the church to be effective in their personal growth and leadership.

Each June or July there is a National Conference giving members an opportunity for fellowship, inspiration, and motivation.

### Headquarters
1501 W. Mineral Ave., Suite B, Littleton, CO 80120-5612, Tel. (888)627-1995 or (720)283-3030 Fax (720)283-3333

Media Contact, Executive Dir., Dr. Dennis L. Gorton

Email: cba@cbamerica.org

Website: www.cbamerica.org

### OTHER ORGANIZATIONS
CBInternational, Exec. Dir., Dr. Hans Finzel, 1501 W. Mineral Ave., Littleton, CO 80120-5612

Mission to the Americas, Exec. Dir., Rev. Rick Miller, Box 828, Wheaton, IL 60189

Conservative Baptist Higher Ed. Council, Dr. Bert Downs, Western Seminary, 5511 S. E. Hawthorne Blvd., Portland, OR 97215

### Periodicals
*Front Line Turnings*

## Conservative Congregational Christian Conference

In the 1930s, evangelicals within the Congregational Christian Churches felt a definite need for fellowship and service. By 1945, this loose association crystallized into the Conservative Congregational Christian Fellowship, committed to maintaining a faithful, biblical witness.

In 1948 in Chicago, the Conservative Congregational Christian Conference was established to provide a continuing fellowship for evangelical churches and ministers on the national level. In recent years, many churches have joined the Conference from backgrounds other than Congregational. These churches include Community or Bible Churches and churches from the Evangelical and Reformed background that are truly congregational in polity and thoroughly evangelical in conviction. The CCCC welcomes all evangelical churches that are, in fact, congregational. The CCCC believes in the necessity of a regenerate membership, the authority of the Holy Scriptures, the Lordship of Jesus Christ, the autonomy of the local church and the universal fellowship of all Christians.

The Conservative Congregational Christian Conference is a member of the World Evangelical Congregational Fellowship (formed in 1986 in London, England) and the National Association of Evangelicals.

### Headquarters
8941 Highway 5, Lake Elmo, MN 55042, Tel. (651)739-1474 Fax (651)739-0750

Media Contact, Conf. Min., Diane Johnson

Email: CCCC4@juno.com

Website: www.ccccusa.com

### Officers
Pres., Rev. Nicholas G. Granitsas, 68 Eustis Rd, Revere, MA 02151

Vice Pres., Rev. Dr. John Kimball, 3657 Carolina Rd., Suffolk, VA 23434

Conf. Min., Rev. Dr. Stephen A. Gammon, 7583 Currell Blvd. #108, St. Paul, MN 55125

Controller, Mr. Leslie Pierce, 5220 E 105th St S, Tulsa, OK 74137

Treas., Rev. Tay Kersey, 8450 Eastwood Rd., Moundsview, MN 55112

Sec., Rev. Peter Murdy, 4 Plympton St., Middleboro, MA 02346

Editor, Dr. Richard and Mrs. Shirley Leonard, P.O. Box 250, Kirkland, IL 60146

Historian, Rev. Alwyn York, 709 N. Cheyenne Ave., Hardin MT 59034

### Periodicals
*Foresee*

## Conservative Lutheran Association

The Conservative Lutheran Association (CLA) was originally named Lutheran's Alert National (LAN) when it was founded in 1965 by 10 conservative Lutheran pastors and laymen meeting in Cedar Rapids, Iowa. Its purpose was to help preserve from erosion the basic doctrines of Christian theology, including the inerrancy of Holy Scripture. The group grew to a worldwide constituency, similarly concerned with maintaining the doctrinal integrity of the Bible and the Lutheran Confessions.

### Headquarters
Trinity Lutheran Church, 4101 E. Nohl Ranch Rd., Anaheim, CA 92807, Tel. (714)637-8370

Media Contact, Pres., Rev. P. J. Moore

Email: PastorPJ@ix.netcom.com

Website: www.tlcanaheim.com/CLA

### Officers
Pres., Rev. P. J. Moore, 4101 E. Nohl Ranch Rd., Anaheim, CA 92807, Tel. (714)637-8370

Vice Pres., Rev. Dr. R. H. Redal, 409 Tacoma Ave. N., Tacoma, WA 98403, Tel. (206)383-5528

Faith Seminary, Dean, Rev. Dr. Michael J.

Adams, 3504 N. Pearl St., P.O. Box 7186, Tacoma, WA 98407, Tel. (888)777-7675 Fax (206)759-1790

## Coptic Orthodox Church*

This body is part of the ancient Coptic orthodox Church of Alexandria, Egypt, which is currently headed by His Holiness Pope Shenouda III, 116th Successor to St. Mark the Apostle. Egyptian immigrants have organized many parishes in the United States. Copts exist outside Egypt in Africa, Europe, Asia, Australia, Canada and the United States. The total world Coptic community is estimated at 27 million. The church is in full communion with the other members of the Oriental Orthodox Church Family, the Syrian Orthodox Church, Armenian Orthodox Church, Ethiopian Orthodox Church, the Indian Orthodox Church and the Eritrean Orthodox Church.

### Headquarters
427 West Side Ave., Jersey City, NJ 07304
Email: Webmaster@coptic.org
Website: www.coptic.org

### Officers
Bishop of Los Angeles, Bishop Serapion, 3803 3803 W. Mission Blvd., Pomona, CA 91766, Tel. (909)865-8378 Fax (909)865-8348, Email: bishopserapion@lacopts.org

### Periodicals
*Agape Magazine, El Keraza*

## Cumberland Presbyterian Church

The Cumberland Presbyterian Church was organized in Dickson County, Tenn., on Feb. 4, 1810. It was an outgrowth of the Great Revival of 1800 on the Kentucky and Tennessee frontier. The founders were Finis Ewing, Samuel King and Samuel McAdow, ministers in the Presbyterian Church who rejected the doctrine of election and reprobation as taught in the Westminster Confession of Faith.

By 1813, the Cumberland Presbytery had grown to encompass three presbyteries, which constituted a synod. This synod met at the Beech Church in Sumner County, Tenn., and formulated a "Brief Statement" which set forth the points in which Cumberland Presbyterians dissented from the Westminster Confession. These points are:

1. That there are no eternal reprobates;
2. That Christ died not for some, but for all people;
3. That all those dying in infancy are saved through Christ and the sanctification of the Spirit;
4. That the Spirit of God operates on the world, or as coextensively as Christ has made atonement, in such a manner as to leave everyone inexcusable.

From its birth in 1810, the Cumberland Presbyterian Church grew to a membership of 200,000 at the turn of the century. In 1906 the church voted to merge with the then-Presbyterian Church. Those who dissented from the merger became the nucleus of the continuing Cumberland Presbyterian Church.

### Headquarters
1978 Union Ave., Memphis, TN 38104, Tel. (901)276-4572 Fax (901)272-3913
Media Contact, Stated Clk., Rev. Robert D. Rush, Fax (901)276-4578
Email: assembly@cumberland.org
Website: www.cumberland.org

### Officers
Mod., The Rev. Donald P. Hubbard, 2128 Campbell Station Road, Knoxville, TN 37932, Email: djhubbard@mindspring.com
Stated Clk., The Rev. Robert D. Rush, Tel. (901)276-4572 x 225 Fax (901)276-4578, Email: rdr@cumberland.org
General Assembly Council, Exec. Dir., Davis Gray, Tel.(901)276-4572 x 216 Fax(901) 272-3913, Email: dg@cumberland.org

### INSTITUTIONS
Cumberland Presbyterian Children's Home, Exec. Dir., Mr. Randy Spencer, Drawer G, Denton, TX 76202, Tel. (940)382-5112 Fax (940)387-0821, Email: cpch@cpch.org
Cumberland Presbyterian Center, Tel.(901)276-4572 Fax (901)272-3913 or (901)276-4578
Memphis Theological Seminary, 168 E. Parkway S., Memphis, TN 38104, Tel. (901)458-8232 Fax (901)452-4051, Website: www.memphis seminary.edu, Pres., Dr. Jay Earheart-Brown
Bethel College, Pres., Dr. Robert Prosser, 325 Cherry St., McKenzie, TN 38201, Tel. (901) 352-4004 Fax (901)352-4069, Email: rprosser @bethel-college.edu
Historical Foundation, Archivist, Susan K. Gore, 1978 Union Avenue, Memphis, TN 38104, Tel. (901)276-8602 Fax (901)272-3913, Email: skg@cumberland.org

### BOARDS
Bd. of Christian Education, Exec. Dir., Claudette Pickle, 1978 Union Ave., Memphis, TN 38104, Tel. (901)276-4572, x 223 Fax(901) 272-3913, Email: chp@cumberland.org
Bd. of Missions, Exec. Dir., Rev. Michael Sharpe, 1978 Union Ave., Memphis, TN 38104, Tel. (901)276-9988 Fax(901)272-3913, Email: mgs@cumberland.org
Bd. of Stewardship, Exec. Sec., Rev. Richard Magrill,1978 Union Ave., Memphis, TN 38104, Tel. (901)276-4572 x 207, Email: jrm@ cumberland.org
Bd. Of the Cumberland Presbyterian, Editor, Patricia White, P.O. Box 935, Antioch, TN 37011, Tel. (615)731-5556, Email: cpmag @comcast.net
Commission on the Ministry, 1978 Union Ave., Memphis, TN 38104, Tel. (901)276-4572 x 235 Fax (901)272-3913, Exec. Dir., The Rev. Stephanie S. Brown

**Periodicals**
*The Cumberland Presbyterian; The Missionary Messenger*

## Cumberland Presbyterian Church in America

This church, originally known as the Colored Cumberland Presbyterian Church, was formed in May 1874. In May 1869, at the General Assembly meeting in Murfreesboro, Tenn., Moses Weir of the Black delegation sucessfully appealed for help in organizing a separate African church so that Blacks could learn self-reliance and independence; they could have more financial assistance; they could minister more effectively among Blacks; and they could worship close to the altar, not in the balconies. He requested that the Cumberland Presbyterian Church organize Blacks into presbyteries and synods, develop schools to train Black clergy, grant loans to assist Blacks to secure hymnbooks, Bibles and church buildings and establish a separate General Assembly.

In 1874 the first General Assembly of the Colored Cumberland Presbyterian Church met in Nashville. The moderator was Rev. P. Price and the stated clerk was Elder John Humphrey.

The denomination's General Assembly, the national governing body, is organized around its three program boards and agencies: Finance, Publication and Christian Education, and Missions and Evangelism. Other agencies of the General Assembly are under these three program boards.

The church has four synods (Alabama, Kentucky, Tennessee and Texas), 15 presbyteries and 153 congregations. The CPC extends as far north as Cleveland, Ohio, and Chicago, as far west as Marshalltown, Iowa, and Dallas, Tx., and as far south as Selma, Ala.

**Headquarters**
Media Contact, Stated Clk., Rev. Dr. Robert. Stanley Wood, 226 Church St., Huntsville, AL 35801 Tel. (205)536-7481 Fax (205)536-7482
Email: mleslie598@aol.com
Website: www.cumberland.org/cpca

**Officers**
Mod., Rev. Endia Scruggs, 1627 Carroll Rd., Harvest, AL 35749
Stated Clk., Rev. Dr. Rorbert. Stanley Wood, 226 Church St., Huntsville, AL 35801 Tel. (205) 536-7481

**SYNODS**
Alabama, Stated Clk., Arthur Hinton, 511 10th Ave. N.W., Aliceville, AL 35442
Kentucky, Stated Clk., Mary Martha Daniels, 8548 Rhodes Ave., Chicago, IL 60619
Tennessee, Stated Clk., Elder Clarence Norman, 145 Jones St., Huntington, TN 38334
Texas, Stated Clk., Arthur King, 2435 Kristen, Dallas, TX 75216

Disciples of Christ—please see Christian Church (Disciples of Christ) in the United States and Canada.

## Elim Fellowship

The Elim Fellowship, a Pentecostal Body established in 1947, is an outgrowth of the Elim Missionary Assemblies formed in 1933.

It is an association of churches, ministers and missionaries seeking to serve the whole Body of Christ. It is of Pentecostal conviction and charismatic orientation, providing ministerial credentials and counsel and encouraging fellowship among local churches. Elim Fellowship sponsors leadership seminars at home and abroad and serves as a transdenominational agency sending long-term, short-term and tent-making missionaries to work with national movements.

**Headquarters**
1703 Dalton Rd., Lima, NY 14485 Tel. (585) 582-2790 Fax (585)624-1229
Media Contact, Gen. Sec., Rev. Chris Ball
Email: executive@elimfellowship.org
Website: www.ElimFellowship.org

**Officers**
Pres., Rev. Dr. Ronald V. Burgio
Gen. Treas., Stephanie Zeller

**Periodicals**
*Elim Herald*

## Episcopal Church*

The Episcopal Church entered the colonies with the earliest settlers at Jamestown, Va., in 1607 as the Church of England. After the American Revolution, it became autonomous in 1789 as The Protestant Episcopal Church in the United States of America. (The Episcopal Church became the official alternate name in 1967.) Samuel Seabury of Connecticut was elected the first bishop and consecrated in Aberdeen by bishops of the Scottish Episcopal Church in 1784.

In organizing as an independent body, the Episcopal Church created a bicameral legislature, the General Convention, modeled after the new U.S. Congress. It comprises a House of Bishops and a House of Deputies and meets every three years. A 38-member Executive Council, which meets three times a year, is the interim governing body. An elected presiding bishop serves as Primate and Chief Pastor.

After severe setbacks in the years immediately following the Revolution, because of its association with the British Crown and the fact that a number of its clergy and members were Loyalists, the church soon established its own identity and sense of mission. It sent missionaries into the newly settled territories of the United States, establishing dioceses from coast to coast, and also undertook substantial missionary work in Africa, Latin America and the Far East. Today, the overseas dioceses are developing into inde-

108

pendent provinces of the Anglican Communion, the worldwide fellowship of 38 churches in communion with the Church of England and the Archbishop of Canterbury.

The beliefs and practices of The Episcopal Church, like those of other Anglican churches, are both Catholic and Reformed, with bishops in the apostolic succession and the historic creeds of Christendom regarded as essential elements of faith and order, along with the primary authority of Holy Scripture and the two chief sacraments of Baptism and Eucharist.

## EPISCOPAL CHURCH CENTER

815 Second Ave., New York, NY 10017, Tel. (212) 716-6240 or (800)334-7626 Fax (212) 867-0395 or (212)490-3298

Media Contact, Dir. of News Service, Robert Williams, Tel. (212)922-5385

Email: cepting@episcopalchurch.org

Website: www.ecusa.anglican.org

### Officers

Presiding Bishop & Primate, Most Rev. Katherine Jeffers-Schori

Vice Pres. & Assist. to the Presiding Bishop for Administration, Patricia C. Mordecai

Assistant to the Presiding Bishop for Communication, Barbara L. Braver

Treas., Kurt Barnes

Canon to the Primate and Presiding Bishop, The Rev. Canon Carlson Gerdau

House of Deputies, Pres., Bonnie Anderson

Exec. Officer and Sec. of the General Convention, Sec. of the House of Deputies, Sec. of the Domestic and Foreign Missionary Society, and Sec. of the Executive Council, The Rev. Gregory Straub

### OFFICE OF THE PRESIDING BISHOP

Presiding Bishop, Most Rev. Katherine Jeffers-Schori, Tel. (212)716-6276

Chief Operating Officer, Patricia Mordecai, Tel. (212)922-5313

Canon to the Presiding Bishop, Rev. Canon Carl Gerdau, Tel. (212)922-5282

Exec. Dir., Church Deployment Office, Rev. Rebecca McClain, Tel. (212)922-5251

Asst. Dir., Church Deployment Office, Pamela Ramsden, Tel. (212)716-6063

Coordinator for Ministry Development, The Rev. Dr. Melford E. Holland, Jr., Tel. (212)922-5246

Exec. Dir., Office of Pastoral Dev., Rt. Rev. Clayton Matthews, Tel. (212)716-6163

Exec. Sec., General Board of Examining Chaplains, The Rev. Dr. Richard F. Tombaugh, Tel. (860)233-2271

Chaplaincies, Suffragan Bishop, Rt. Rev. George Packard, Tel. (212)716-6202

Convocation of American Churches in Europe, Bishop-in-Charge, Rt. Rev. Pierre Whalon, Tel. 011-33-1-472-01792

Deputy, Ecumenical and Interfaith Relations, The Rt. Rev. C. Christopher Epting, Tel. (212) 716-6220

### ADMINISTRATION AND FINANCE

Treasurer of the Domestic and Foreign Missionary Society and Chief Financial Officer, Kurt Barnes, Tel. (212)922-5296

Interim Controller, Alpha Contech, Tel. (212) 922-5366

Archivist, Mark Duffy, Tel. (512)472-6816

Director, Human Resources Management, John Colon, Tel. (212)716-6331

### SERVICE, EDUCATION AND WITNESS

Director of Mission, The Very Rev. James Lemler, Tel. (212)922-5198

Dir., Anglican and Global Relations, Margaret Larom, Tel. (212)716-6224

Editor, *Episcopal Life*, Jerrold Hames, Tel. (212) 716-6009

Dir., Communication, Robert Williams, Tel. (212)922-5385

Dir., News Service, Robert Williams, Tel. (212) 922-5385

Dir., Migration Ministries, Richard Parkins, Tel. (212)716-6252

Dir., Peace & Justice Ministries, The Rev. Canon Brian Grieves, Tel. (212)922-5207

Dir., Ministries with Young People, Thomas Chu, Tel. (212)922-5267

President, Episcopal Relief and Development, Robert Radtke, Tel. (212)716-6020

### BISHOPS IN THE U.S.A.

Presiding Bishop & Primate, Most Rev. Katherine Jeffers-Schori, 815 Second Ave, New York, NY 10017, Tel. (212)716-6276;

Pastoral Dev., The Rt. Rev. F. Clayton Matthews, 815 Second Ave, New York, NY 10017, Tel. (212)716-6163

Alabama, Henry N. Parsley, Jr., 521 N. 20th St., Birmingham, AL 35203, Tel. (205)715-2066

Alaska, Mark MacDonald, 1205 Denali Way, Fairbanks, AK 99701-4137, Tel. (907)452-3040

Albany, Daniel W. Herzog, 68 S. Swan St., Albany, NY 12210-2301, Tel. (518)465-4737

Arizona, Kirk Stevan Smith, 114 W. Roosevelt, Phoenix, AZ 85003-1406, Tel. (602)254-0976

Arkansas, Larry E. Maze, P.O. Box 164668, Little Rock, AR 72216, Tel. (501)372-2168

Atlanta, John Neil Alexander, 2744 Peachtree Rd. N.W., Atlanta, GA 30305, Tel. (404)365-1010

Bethlehem, Paul Marshall, 333 Wyandotte St., Bethlehem, PA 18015, Tel. (610)691-5655

California, Marc Handly Andrus, 1055 Taylor St., San Francisco, CA 94115, Tel. (415)673-5015

Central Ecuador, Glauco Soares de Lima, Apartado Aereo 17-03-353-A, Quito, Ecuador, Ecuador

Central Florida, John W. Howe, 1017 E. Robinson St., Orlando, FL 32801, Tel. (407) 423-3567

109

Central Gulf Coast, Philip M. Duncan II, P.O. Box 13330, Pensacola, FL 32591-3330, Tel. (850)434-7337

Central New York, Gladstone B. Adams III, 310 Montgomery St., Ste. 200, Syracuse, NY 13202, Tel. (315)474-6596

Central Pennsylvania, Michael W. Creighton, P.O. Box 11937, Harrisburg, PA 17108, Tel. (717)236-5959

Chicago, William D. Persell, 65 E. Huron St., Chicago, IL 60611, Tel. (312)751-4200

Colombia, Francisco Duque, Cra. 6 No. 49-85, Bogota, Colombia, Tel. 011-57-1-288-3167

Colorado, Robert J. O'Neill, 1300 Washington St., Denver, CO 80203, Tel. (303)837-1173

Connecticut, Andrew D. Smith, 1335 Asylum Ave., Hartford, CT 06105-2295, Tel. (860) 233-4481

Dallas, James M. Stanton, 1630 Garrett Ave., Dallas, TX 75206, Tel. (214)826-8310

Delaware, Wayne P. Wright, 2020 N. Tatnall St., Wilmington, DE 19802, Tel. (302)656-5441

Dominican Republic, Cesar Holguin, DMG 13602, 7990 15th ST E, Sarasota, FL 34243

East Carolina, Clifton Daniel III, P.O. Box 1336, Kinston, NC 28503, Tel. (252)522-0885

East Tennessee, Charles vonRosenberg, 814 Episcopal School Way, Knoxville, TN 37932, Tel. (865)966-2110

Eastern Michigan, Edwin M. Leidel Jr., 924 N. Niagara St., Saginaw, MI 48602, Tel. (989) 752-6020

Eastern Oregon, William O. Gregg, P.O. Box 1548, The Dalles, OR 97058, Tel. (541)298-4477

Easton, James J. Shand, P.O. Box 1027, Easton, MD 21601, Tel. (410)822-1919

Eau Claire, Keith B. Whitmore, 510 S. Farwell St., Eau Claire, WI 54701, Tel. (715)835-3331

El Camino Real, Assisting, Sylvestre Romero-Palma, 1092 Noche Buena ST, Seaside, CA 93955, Tel. (831)394-4465

Europe, American Ches in-Jurisdiction, Pierre W. Whalon, Bishop in-charge, The American Cathedral, 23 Avenue Georges V, 75008, Paris, France, Tel. 011-33-1-53-23-84-04

Florida, S. Johnson Howard, 325 Market St., Jacksonville, FL 32202, Tel. (904)356-1328

Fond du Lac, Russell E. Jacobus, P.O. Box 149, Fond du Lac, WI 54936-0149, Tel. (920)921-8866

Fort Worth, Jack L. Iker, 2900 Alemeda Street, Fort Worth, TX 76116, Tel. (817)244-2885

Georgia, Henry Louttit, Jr., 611 East Bay St., Savannah, GA 31401, Tel. (912)236-4279

Haiti, Jean Zache Duracin, c/o Lynx Air P.O. Box 407139, Ft Lauderdale, FL 33340, Tel. 011-509-257-1624

Hawaii, Richard S.O. Chang, 229 Queen Emma Square, Honolulu, HI 96813, Tel. (808)536-7776

Honduras, Lloyd Emmanuel Allen, IMC-SAP, Dept 215, P.O. Box 52-3900, Miami, FL 33152-3900, Tel. (504)556-6155

Idaho, Harry B. Bainbridge III, P.O. Box 936, Boise, ID 83701, Tel. (208)345-4440

Indianapolis, Catherine M. Waynick, 1100 W. 42nd St., Indianapolis, IN 46208, Tel. (317) 926-5454

Iowa, Alan Scarfe, 225 37th St., Des Moines, IA 50312-4305, Tel. (515)277-6165

Kansas, Dean E. Wolfe, 835 S.W. Polk St., Topeka, KS 66612-1688, Tel. (785)235-9255

Kentucky, Edwin F. Gulick Jr., 425 S. 2nd Street, Ste. 200, Louisville, KY 40202, Tel. (502)584-7148

Lexington, Stacy F. Sauls, P.O. Box 610, Lexington, KY 40586-0610, Tel. (606)252-6527

Long Island, Orris G. Walker, Jr., 36 Cathedral Ave., Garden City, NY 11530, Tel. (516)248-4800

Los Angeles, J. Jon Bruno; Chester Talton, (S), P.O. Box 512164, Los Angeles, CA 90051-0164, Tel. (213)482-2040

Louisiana, Charles E. Jenkins, III, 1623 7th St., New Orleans, LA 70115-4411, Tel. (504)895-6634

Maine, Chilton R. Knudsen, 143 State St., Portland, ME 04101-3799, Tel. (207)772-1953

Maryland, Robert W. Ihloff, 4 University Pkwy, Baltimore, MD 21218, Tel. (410)467-1399

Massachusetts, M. Thomas Shaw, III, SSJE, 138 Tremont St., Boston, MA 02111-1356, Tel. (617)482-5800

Michigan, Wendell N. Gibbs, Jr., 4800 Woodward Ave., Detroit, MI 48201, Tel. (313)832-4400

Milwaukee, Steven A. Miller, 804 E. Juneau Ave., Milwaukee, WI 53202, Tel. (414)272-3028

Minnesota, James L. Jelinek; 1730 Clifton Place, #201, Minneapolis, MN 55403, Tel. (612)871-5311

Mississippi, Duncan Montgomery Gray, III, P.O. Box 23107, Jackson, MS 39225-3107, Tel. (601)948-5954

Missouri, G. Wayne Smith, 1210 Locust St., St. Louis, MO 63103, Tel. (314)231-1220

Montana, C. Franklin Brookhart, 515 North Park Ave., Helena, MT 59601, Tel. (406)442-2230

Navajoland Area Mission, Rustin Kimsey, inter-im, BOX 720, Farmington, NM 87499-0720, Tel. (505)327-7549

Nebraska, Joe G. Burnett, 109 N. 18th Street, Omaha, NE 68102, Tel. (402)341-5373

Nevada, Katherine Jeffers-Schori, 6135 S. Harrison Drive, Ste. 1, Las Vegas, NV 89120, Tel. (702)737-9190

New Hampshire, V. Gene Robinson, 63 Green St., Concord, NH 03301, Tel. (603)224-1914

New Jersey, George E. Councell, 808 W. State St., Trenton, NJ 08618-5326, Tel. (609)394-5281

New York, Mark Sisk, 1047 Amsterdam Ave., New York, NY 10025, Tel. (212)316-7400

Newark, Jack P. Croneberger; 31 Mulberry St., Newark, NJ 07102, Tel. (973)622-4306

110

North Carolina, Michael B. Curry, 200 W. Morgan ST, Ste 300, Raleigh, NC 27601-1338, Tel. (919)787-6313

North Dakota, Michael Gene Smith, 3600 25 St. SW, Fargo, ND 58104-6861, Tel. (701)235-6688

Northern California, Barry Beisher, P.O. Box 161268, Sacramento, CA 95816, Tel. (916) 442-6918

Northern Indiana, Edward S. Little III, 117 N. Lafayette Blvd., South Bend, IN 46601, Tel. (574)233-6489

Northern Michigan, James A. Kelsey, 131 E. Ridge St., Marquette, MI 49855, Tel. (906) 228-7160

Northwest Texas, C. Wallis Ohl, Jr., 1802 Broadway, Lubbock, TX 79401-3016, Tel. (806)763-1370

Northwestern Pennsylvania, Robert D. Rowley, Jr., 145 W. 6th St., Erie, PA 16501, Tel. (814) 456-4203

Ohio, Mark Hollingsworth, Jr., 2230 Euclid Ave., Cleveland, OH 44115, Tel. (216)771-4815

Oklahoma, Robert M. Moody, 924 N. Robinson, Oklahoma City, OK 73102-2499, Tel. (405) 232-4820

Olympia, Vincent W. Warner, P.O. Box 12126, Seattle, WA 98102, Tel. (206)325-4200

Oregon, Johncy Itty, 11800 SW Military Lane, Portland, OR 97219-8436, Tel. (503)636-5613

Pennsylvania, Charles E. Bennison, Jr., 240 S. 4th St., Philadelphia, PA 19106, Tel. (215)627-6434

Pittsburgh, Robert W. Duncan, Jr., 535 Smithfield Street, Pittsburgh, PA 15222, Tel. (412)281-6131

Puerto Rico, David Alvarez, Centro Diocesano San Justo, P.O. Box 902, St Just Station, St Just, PR 00978, Tel. (787)761-9800

Quincy, Keith L. Ackerman, 3601 N. North St., Peoria, IL 61604-1599, Tel. (309)688-8221

Rhode Island, Geralyn Wolf, 275 N. Main St., Providence, RI 02903-1298,Tel. (401)274-4500

Rio Grande, Jeffrey Steenson, 4304 Carlisle Blvd. NE, Albuquerque, NM 87107, Tel. (505) 881-0636

Rochester, Jack M. McKelvey, 935 East Ave., Rochester, NY 14607, Tel. (585)473-2977

San Diego, James R. Mathes, 2728 6th Ave., San Diego, CA 92103, Tel. (619)291-5947

San Joaquin, John-David Schofield, 4159 East Dakota Ave., Fresno, CA 93726, Tel. (559) 244-4828

South Carolina, Edward L. Salmon, Jr., P.O. Box 20127, Charleston, SC 29413-0127, Tel. (843) 722-4075

South Dakota, Creighton L. Robertson, 500 S. Main Ave., Sioux Falls, SD 57104-6814, Tel. (605)338-9751

Southeast Florida, Leopold Frade, 525 NE 15th St., Miami, FL 33132, Tel. (305)373-0881

Southern Ohio, Herbert Thompson, Jr.; 412 Sycamore St., Cincinnati, OH 45202, Tel. (513)421-0311

Southern Virginia, David C. Bane, Jr., 600 Talbot Hall Rd., Norfolk, VA 23505, Tel. (757)423-8287

Southwest Florida, John B. Lipscomb, 7313 Merchant Court, Sarasota, FL 34240, Tel. (941)556-0315

Southwestern Virginia, F. Neff Powell, P.O. Box 2279, Roanoke, VA 24009, Tel. (540)342-6797

Spokane, James E. Waggoner, Jr., 245 E. 13th Ave., Spokane, WA 99202, Tel. (509)624-3191

Springfield, Peter H. Beckwith, 821 S. 2nd St., Springfield, IL 62704, Tel. (217)525-1876

Tennessee, Bertram N. Herlong, 50 Vantage Way, Suite 107, Nashville, TN 37228, Tel. (615) 251-3322

Texas, Don A. Wimberly, 3203 W. Alabama St., Houston, TX 77098, Tel. (713)520-6444

Upper South Carolina, Dorsey F. Henderson, Jr., 1115 Marion Street, Columbia, SC 29201, Tel. (803)771-7800

Utah, Carolyn T. Irish, Box 3090, Salt Lake City, UT 84110-3090, Tel. (801)322-4131

Vermont, Thomas C. Ely, 5 Rock Point Road, Burlington, VT 05401, Tel. (802)863-3431

Virgin Islands, Ambrose Gumbs, P.O. Box 7488, Charlotte, Amalie, St Thomas, VI 00801

Virginia, Peter J. Lee, 110 W. Franklin St., Richmond, VA 23220, Tel. (804)643-8451

Washington, John Bryson Chane, Episc. Church House, Mt. St. Alban, Washington, DC 20016-5094, Tel. (202)537-6555

West Missouri, Barry R. Howe, P.O. Box 413227, Kansas City, MO 64141-3227, Tel. (816)471-6161

West Tennessee, Don E. Johnson, 692 Poplar Ave., Memphis, TN 38105, Tel. (901)526-0023

West Texas, Gary R. Lillibridge, P.O. Box 6885, San Antonio, TX 78209, Tel. (210)824-5387

West Virginia, W. Michie Klusmeyer, P.O. Box 5400, Charleston, WV 25361-0400, Tel. (304) 344-3597

Western Kansas, James Marshall Adams, P.O. Box 2507, Salina, KS 67402-2507, Tel. (785) 825-1626

Western Louisiana, D. Bruce MacPherson, P.O. Box 2031, Alexandria, LA 71309, Tel. (318) 442-1304

Western Massachusetts, Gordon P. Scruton, 37 Chestnut St., Springfield, MA 01103, Tel. (413)737-4786

Western Michigan, Robert Ronald Gepert, 2600 Vincent Ave., Portage, MI 49024, Tel. (269) 381-2710

Western New York, J. Michael Garrison, 1114 Delaware Ave., Buffalo, NY 14209, Tel. (716)881-0660

Western North Carolina, G. Porter Taylor, 900-B Centre Park Dr., Asheville, NC 28805, Tel. (828)225-6656

Wyoming, Bruce Caldwell, 104 S. 4th St., Laramie, WY 82070, Tel. (307)742-6606

**Periodicals**

*Episcopal Life*

## The Episcopal Orthodox Church

This body was incorporated in 1964 as a self-governing Orthodox Anglican church. The church is committed to the Biblical world view contained in the Holy Scriptures, confessed in the three ancient creeds of the Catholic Church (the Apostles', Nicene, and Athanasian Creeds), experienced in the sacraments, and practiced through the use of orthodox editions of the *Book of Common Prayer*. The Church is the United States member of the Orthodox Anglican Communion, the creation of which it authorized in 1967. The Orthodox Anglican Communion is a fellowship of churches around the world that adhere to orthodox theology. In 1971 the church opened its own theological educational institution: clergy in the United States are trained at the denomination's school, St. Andrew's Theological College and Seminary.

**Headquarters**

464 County Home Road, Lexington, NC 27292, Tel. (336)236-9565 Fax (336)236-4822
Email: eoc@orthodoxanglican.net
Website: www.orthodoxanglican.net

**Officers**

Presiding Bishop, The Most Rev. Scott McLaughlin, The Chancery of the Archdiocese, 464 County Home Road, Lexington, NC 27292 Tel. (336) 236-9565 Fax (336)236-4822, Email: abpmclaughlin@orthodoxanglican. net

**Periodicals**

*The Episcopal Orthodox Encounter*

## The Estonian Evangelical Lutheran Church

For information on the Estonian Evangelical Lutheran Church (EELC), please see the listing in Chapter 4, "Religious Bodies in Canada."

**Headquarters**

383 Jarvis St., Toronto, ON M5B 2C7
Email: konsistoorium@eelk.ee
Website: www.eelk.ee

## The Evangelical Church

The Evangelical Church was born June 4, 1968 in Portland, Oregon, when 46 congregations and about 80 ministers, under the leadership of V. A. Ballantyne and George Millen, met in an organizing session. Within two weeks a group of about 20 churches and 30 ministers from the Evangelical United Brethren and Methodist churches in Montana and North Dakota became a part of the new church. Richard Kienitz and Robert Strutz were the superintendents.

Under the leadership of Superintendent Robert Trosen, the former Holiness Methodist Church became a part of the Evangelical Church in 1969, bringing its membership and a flourishing mission field in Bolivia. The Wesleyan Covenant Church joined in 1977, with its missionary work in Mexico, in Brownsville, Texas, and among the Navajos in New Mexico.

The Evangelical Church in Canada, where T. J. Jesske was superintendent, became an autonomous organization on June 5, 1970. In 1982, after years of discussions with the Evangelical Church of North America, a founding General Convention was held at Billings, Mont., where the two churches united. In 1993 the Canadian conference merged with the Canadian portion of the Missionary Church to form the Evangelical Missionary Church. The new group maintains close ties with their American counterparts. Currently there are nearly 150 U.S. congregations of the Evangelical Church. The headquarters is located in Minneapolis, Minnisota.

The following guide the life, program and devotion of this church: faithful, biblical and sensible preaching and teaching of those truths proclaimed by scholars of the Wesleyan-Arminian viewpoint; an itinerant system which reckons with the rights of individuals and the desires of the congregation; local ownership of all church properties and assets.

The church is officially affiliated with the Christian Holiness Partnership, the National Association of Evangelicals, Wycliffe Bible Translators, World Gospel Mission and OMS International. The denomination has nearly 150 missionaries.

**Headquarters**

Denominational Office, 9421 West River Rd., Minneapolis, MN 55444, Tel. (763)421-2589 Fax (763)424-9230, Email: ecm@usfamily.net
Media Contact, Gen. Supt., Dr. William Vermillion Email: jsditzel@juno.com
Website: quakertownecna.com/conferences

**Officers**

Gen. Supt., Dr. William Vermillion, 9421 West River Rd., Minneapolis, MN 55444
Denominational Secretary, Dr. Bruce Moyer, P.O. Box 29, University Park, IA 52595, Tel. (641)673-8391
Exectuive Director, Evangelical Church Mission, Rev. Duane Erickson, 9421 West River Rd., Minneapolis, MN 55444

**Periodicals**

*HeartBeat; The Evangelical Challenge*

## The Evangelical Church Alliance

What is known today as the Evangelical Church Alliance began in 1887 under the name World's Faith Missionary Association. Years later, on March 28, 1928, a nonprofit organization was incorporated in the state of Missouri under the same name. In October, 1931, the name Fundamental Ministerial Association was chosen to reflect the organization's basis of unity.

On July 21, 1958, during the annual convention at Trinity Seminary and Bible College in Chicago, Ill., a more comprehensive constitution was created and the name was changed to The Evangelical Church Alliance.

The ECA licenses and ordains ministers who are qualified providing them with credentials from a recognized ecclesiastical body; provides training courses through the Bible Extension Institute for those who have not had the opportunity to attend seminary or Bible school; provides Associate Membership for churches and Christian organizations giving opportunity for fellowship and networking with other evangelical ministers and organizations who share the same goals and mission, while remaining autonomous; provides endorsement for military, prison, hospital & other institutional chaplains; provides regional conferences and an annual international conference where members can find fellowship, encouragement and training; cooperates with churches in finding new pastors when they have openings.

ECA is an international, nonsectarian, Evangelical organization.

### Headquarters

205 W. Broadway St., P.O. Box 9, Bradley, IL 60915, Tel. (815)937-0720 Fax (815)937-0001
Media Contact, Pres./CEO, Dr. Samuel Goebel
Email: info@ecainternational.org
Website: www.ecainternational.org

### Officers

Pres./CEO, Dr. Samuel Goebel Chairman, Dr. George L. Miller First Vice Chairman, Dr. Rene Moreno Vice Pres., Dr. Henry A. Roso

### Periodicals

*The Evangel*

**Evangelical Churches—please see Fellowship of Evangelical Churches**

## The Evangelical Congregational Church

This denomination had its beginning in the movement known as the Evangelical Association, organized by Jacob Albright in 1796. A division which occurred in 1891 in the Evangelical Association resulted in the organization of the United Evangelical Church in 1894. An attempt to heal this division was made in 1922, but a portion of the United Evangelical Church was not satisfied with the plan of merger and remained apart, taking the above name in 1928. This denomination is Wesleyan-Arminian in doctrine, evangelistic in spirit and Methodist in church government, with congregational ownership of local church property.

Congregations are located from New Jersey to Illinois. A denominational center, two retirement villages and a seminary are located in Myerstown, Pa. Three summer youth camps and four camp meetings continue evangelistic outreach. A worldwide missions movement includes conferences in North East India, Liberia, Mexico, Costa Rica, and Japan. The denomination is a member of National Association of Evangelicals.

### Headquarters

Evangelical Congregational Church Center, 100 W. Park Ave., Myerstown, PA 17067, Tel. (800)866-7581 Fax (717)866-7383
Media Contact, Bishop, Rev. Michael W. Sigman, Tel. (717)866-7581
Email: eccenter@eccenter.com
Website: www.eccenter.com/church

### Officers

Presiding Bishop, Rev. Michael W. Sigman
1st Vice Chpsn., Rev. Gary Brown
Sec., Rev. Kirk Marks
Conference Attorney, David Roland, Esquire
Treas., Patricia Hartman, Annville, Pa.
E.C.C. Retirement Village, Exec. Dir., Steven J. Reiter, Fax (717)866-6448
Evangelical School of Theology, Pres., Dr. Dennis Hollinger, Fax (717)866-4667

### OTHER ORGANIZATIONS

Evangelism & Discipleship Commission, Chpsn., Bishop Michael Sigman
Leadership Commission, Chpsn., Bishop Michael Sigman
Church Health Commission, Chpsn., Rev. Fred Moury
Church Planting Commission, Chpsn,, Rev. Keith Miller
Church Services Commission, Chpsn., Rev. Keith Miller
Global Ministries Commission, Chpsn., Rev. John Ragsdale
Bd. of Pensions, Pres., William Kautz, New Cumberland, Pa.; Controller, Douglas White, Myerstown, Pa.

### Periodicals

*Window on the World* (Global Ministries Commission)

## The Evangelical Covenant Church

The Evangelical Covenant Church has its roots in historic Christianity as it emerged during the Protestant Reformation, in the biblical instruction of the Lutheran State Church of Sweden and in the great spiritual awakenings of the 19th century.

The Covenant Church adheres to the affirmations of the Protestant Reformation regarding the Holy Scriptures, believing that the Old and the New Testament are the Word of God and the only perfect rule for faith, doctrine and conduct. It has traditionally valued the historic confessions of the Christian church, particularly the Apostles' and the Nicene Creed, while at the same time emphasizing the sovereignty of the Word over all

113

creedal interpretations. It has especially cherished the pietistic restatement of the doctrine of justification by faith as basic to its dual task of evangelism and Christian nurture. It recognizes the New Testament emphasis upon personal faith in Jesus Christ as Savior and Lord, the reality of a fellowship of believers which acknowledges but transcends theological differences, and the belief in baptism and the Lord's Supper as divinely ordained sacraments of the church.

While the denomination has traditionally practiced the baptism of infants, in conformity with its principle of freedom it has also recognized the practice of believer baptism. The principle of personal freedom, so highly esteemed by the Covenant, is to be distinguished from the individualism that disregards the centrality of the Word of God and the mutual responsibilities and disciplines of the spiritual community.

### Headquarters

5101 N. Francisco Ave., Chicago, IL 60625, Tel. (773)784-3000 Fax (773)784-4366

Media Contact, Donald L. Meyer, Email: don. meyer@covchurch.org

Email: Elliott.johnson@covchurch.org

Website: www.covchurch.org

### Officers

Pres., Dr. Glenn R. Palmberg

Exec. Vice Pres., Rev. Donn Engebretson

Vice Pres. Finance, Dr. Dean A. Lundgren

### ADMINISTRATIVE BOARDS

Executive Board, Rev. D. Darrell Griffes, Chair

Bd. of Women Ministries, Exec. Minister, Rev. Ruth Y. Hill

Bd. Of Nominations, Advisory Member, (vacant)

Bd. of the Ordered Ministry, Exec. Minister, Rev. Dr. David Kersten

Bd. of Pensions & Benefits, Dir. of Pensions, Dean A. Lundgren

Bd. of Benevolence, Pres. of Covenant Ministries of Benevolence, David A. Dwight, 5145 N. California Ave., Chicago, IL 60625

North Park University, Pres., Dr. David l. Parkyn, 3225 W. Foster Ave., Chicago, IL 60625; North Park Theological Seminary, Pres. And Dean, Dr. John E. Phelan Jr.

### SERVICE ORGANIZATIONS

National Covenant Properties, Pres., David W. Johnson, 5101 N. Francisco, Chicago, IL 60625, Tel. (773)784-3000

Covenant Trust Company, Pres., Charles A. Walles, 5215 Old Orchard Rd., Ste 725, Skokie, IL 60077 Tel. (847)583-3200, (800)483-2177

### REGIONAL CONFERENCES

Central Conference, Supt., Rev. Jerome O. Nelson, 3319 W. Foster Ave., Chicago, IL 60625, Tel. (773)267-3060

East Coast Conference, Supt., Rev. Howard K. Burgoyne, 52 Missionary Rd., Cromwell, CT 06416, Tel. (860)635-2691

Great Lakes Conference, Supt., Rev. Richard Lucco, 42219 Ann Arbor Road. E., Plymouth, MI 48170, Tel. (734)451-4670

Midwest Conference, Supt., Rev. Kenneth P. Carlson, 13304 W. Center Rd. #223, Omaha, NE 68144, Tel. (402)334-3060

North Pacific Conference, Supt., Rev. Mark A. Novak, 9311 SE 36th St., Ste 120, Mercer Island, WA 98040, Tel. (206)275-3903

Northwest Conference, Supt., Rev. James A. Fretheim, 3106 47th Avenue S., Minneapolis, MN 55406, Tel. (612)721-4893

Pacific Southwest Conference, Supt., Rev. Evelyn M. R. Johnson, 1333 Willow Pass Rd., Ste 212, Concord, CA 94502, Tel. (925)677-2140

Southeast Conference, Supt., Rev. Kurt A. Miericke, 1759 W. Broadway St., #7, Oviedo, FL 32765, Tel. (407)977-8009

Canada Conference, Supt., Rev. Jeffrey Anderson, P.O. Box 34025 RPO, Fort Richmond, Winnipeg, MB R3T, Tel. (204)269-3437

Midsouth Conference, Supt., Rev. Garth T Bolinder, 6119 E. 91st Street, Ste. 2000, Tulsa, OK 74137, Tel. (918)481-9097

E.C.C. of Alaska, Field Dir., Rev. Rodney J. Sawyer, P.O. Box 770749, Eagle River, AK 99577, Tel. (907)694-6348

The Paul Carlson Partnership (affiliated) Pres., Rev. Cartis D. Peterson Exec. Dir., Rev. James V. Sundholm, 5101 N. Francisco Ave., Chicago, IL, 60625 Tel. (773)907-3302

### Periodicals

*Covenant Companion; Covenant Quarterly; Covenant Home Altar*

## The Evangelical Free Church of America

In October 1884, 27 representatives from Swedish churches met in Boone, Iowa, to establish the Swedish Evangelical Free Church. In the fall of that same year, two Norwegian-Danish groups began worship and fellowship (in Boston and in Tacoma) and by 1912 had established the Norwegian-Danish Evangelical Free Church Association. These two denominations, representing 275 congregations, came together at a merger conference in 1950.

The Evangelical Free Church of America is an association of local, autonomous churches across the United States and Canada, blended together by common principles, policies and practices. A 12-point statement addresses the major doctrines but also provides for differences of understanding on minor issues of faith and practice.

Overseas outreach includes 500 missionaries serving in 31 countries.

### Headquarters

901 East 78th St., Minneapolis, MN 55420-1300, Tel. (952)854-1300 Fax (952)853-8488

Media Contact, Exec. Dir. of International Mission, Timothy Addington

Email: president@efca.org

Website: www.efca.org

## Officers

Pres., Dr. William J. Hamel

Exec. Dir. International Mission, Timothy Addington

Exec. Dir. National Ministries, Rev. Steven Hudson

C.F.O., John R. Torvik, CPA

Chair, Brian Cole, 2404 Park Dr., West Des Moines, IA 60265

Sec., Rev. William Culbertson, 958 5th Ave. S., Bloomington, MN 55420

Moderator, Dr. Roland Peterson, 235 Craigbrook Way NE, Fridley, MN 55432

Vice Moderator, Dr. Louis Diaz, 520 E. Roosevelt Rd., Wheaton, IL 60187

### Periodicals

*EFCA Today*

# Evangelical Friends International—North American Region

The organization restructured from Evangelical Friends Alliance in 1990 to become internationalized for the benefit of its worldwide contacts. The North America Region continues to function within the United States as EFA formerly did. The organization represents one corporate step of denominational unity, brought about as a result of several movements of spiritual renewal within the Society of Friends. These movements are, (1) the general evangelical renewal within Christianity, (2) the new scholarly recognition of the evangelical nature of 17th-century Quakerism, and (3) EFA, which was formed in 1965.

The EFA is conservative in theology and makes use of local pastors. Sunday morning worship includes singing, Scripture reading, a period of open worship and a sermon by the pastor.

### Headquarters

5350 Broadmoor Cir. NW, Canton, OH 44709, Tel. (330)493-1660 Fax (330)493-0852

Media Contact, Gen. Supt., Dr. John P. Williams, Jr.

Email: efcer@aol.com

Website: www.evangelical-friends.org

### YEARLY MEETINGS

Evangelical Friends Church, Eastern Region, Wayne Ickes, 5350 Broadmoor Cir., N.W., Canton, OH 44709, Tel. (330)493-1660 Fax (330)493-0852

Rocky Mountain YM, John Brawner, 3350 Reed St., Wheatridge, CO 80033, Tel. (303)238-5200 Fax (303)238-5200

Mid-America YM, Duane Hansen, 2018 Maple, Wichita, KS 67213, Tel. (316)267-0391 Fax (316)267-0681

Northwest YM, Mark Ankeny, 200 N. Meridian St., Newberg, OR 97132, Tel. (503)538-9419 Fax (503)538-9410

Alaska YM, Sam Williams, P.O. Box 687, Kotzebue, AK 99752, Tel. (907)442-3906

Evangelical Friends Church Southwest, YM, Linda Coop, P.O. Box 1607, Whittier, CA 90609-1607, Tel. (562)947-2883 Fax (562)947-9385

### Periodicals

*The Friends Voice*

# Evangelical Lutheran Church in America*

The Evangelical Lutheran Church in America (ELCA) was organized April 30-May 3, 1987, in Columbus, Ohio, bringing together the 2.25-million-member American Lutheran Church, the 2.85-million-member Lutheran Church in America, and the 100,000-member Association of Evangelical Lutheran Churches.

The ELCA is, through its predecessors, the oldest of the major U.S. Lutheran churches. In the mid-17th century, a Dutch Lutheran congregation was formed in New Amsterdam (now New York). Other early congregations were begun by German and Scandinavian immigrants to Delaware, Pennsylvania, New York, and the Carolinas.

The first Lutheran association of congregations, the Pennsylvania Ministerium, was organized in 1748 under Henry Melchior Muhlenberg. Numerous Lutheran organizations were formed as immigration continued and the United States grew.

In 1960, The American Lutheran Church (ALC) was created through a merger of an earlier American Lutheran Church, formed in 1930, the Evangelical Lutheran Church, begun in 1917, and the United Evangelical Lutheran Church started in 1896. In 1963 the Lutheran Free Church, formed in 1897, merged with the ALC.

In 1962, the Lutheran Church in America (LCA) was formed by a merger of the United Lutheran Church in America, formed in 1918, with the Augustana Evangelical Lutheran Church, begun in 1860, the American Evangelical Lutheran Church, founded in 1872, and the Finnish Evangelical Lutheran Church or Suomi Synod, founded in 1891.

The Association of Evangelical Lutheran Churches arose in 1976 from a doctrinal split within the Lutheran Church-Missouri Synod.

The ELCA, through its predecessor church bodies, was a founding member of the Lutheran World Federation, the World Council of Churches, and the National Council of the Churches of Christ in the U.S.A..

The church is divided into 65 geographical areas called synods. These 65 synods are grouped into nine regions for mission, joint programs and service.

### Headquarters

8765 W. Higgins Rd., Chicago, IL 60631, Tel. (773)380-2700 Fax (773)380-1465

Media Contact, Dir. for News, John Brooks, Tel. (773)380-2958 Fax (773)380-2406

Email: info@elca.org

Website: www.elca.org

## Officers

Presiding Bishop, Rev. Mark S. Hanson
Sec., Rev. Dr. Lowell G. Almen
Treas., Ms. Christina L. Jackson-Skelton
Vice Pres., Mr. Carlos E. Pena
Exec. for Admn., Rev. Charles S. Miller
Office of the Presiding Bishop, Exec. Asst to the Presiding Bishop for Federal Chaplaincies, Rev. Darrell D. Morton; Exec. Asst. to the Presiding Bishop, Ms. Myrna J. Sheie

### PROGRAM UNITS

Vocation and Education, Exec. Dir., Rev. Stanley Nolson, Chpsn., Dr. Kathryn L. Johnson
Global Mission, Exec. Dir., Rev. Rafael Malpica Padilla, Bd. Chpsn., Rev. Virginia Anderson-Larson
Evangelical Outreach and Congregational Mission, Exec. Dir., Rev. Dr. Richard A. Magnus, Jr.; Chpsn., Mr. Francis R Ramos-Scharron
Church in Society, Exec. Dir., Rev. Rebecca S. Larson; Chpsn., Ms. Kristin Anderson-Ostrom
ELCA Publishing House, Exec. Dir., Ms. Beth A. Lewis; Bd. Chpsn.,MS. Annette Citzler
Women of the ELCA, Exec. Dir., Ms. Linda Post Bushkofsky; President., Ms. Carmen K. Richards

### COMMISSIONS

Multicultural Ministries, Exec. Dir., Rev. Sherman Hicks; Chpsn., Mr. Aureo F. Andino

### CHURCHWIDE UNITS

Conference of Bishops, Church Periodical, Editor, Mr. Daniel J. Lehmann; Chpsn. Rev. Karen Bockelman; Rev. E. Roy Riley
Development Services, Exec. Dir., Rev. Donald M. Hallberg, Stat. Ms. Tonia I. Lindquist
ELCA Bd. of Pensions, Exec. Dir., Mr. John G. Kapanke; Bd. Chpsn, Ms. Mary S. Ranum

### SECTIONS

Communication Services, Dir., Ms. Kristi Bangert
Ecumenical and Inter-Religious Relations, Dir., Rev. Randall R. Lee
Human Resources, Dir., Ms. Else B Thompson
Research & Evaluation, Dir., Dr. Kenneth W. Inskeep
Synodical Relations, Executive for Synodical Relations, Rev. Kathie Bender-Schwich
Worship and Liturgical Resources, Dir., Rev. Michael L. Burk

### SYNODICAL BISHOPS

**Region 1**

Alaska, Rev. Michael F. Keys, 1847 W. Northern Lights Blvd., #2, Anchorage, AK 99517-3343, Tel. (907)272-8899 Fax (907)274-3141
Northwest Washington, Rev. Wm. Chris Boerger, 5519 Pinney Ave. N, Seattle, WA 98103-5899, Tel. (206)783-9292 Fax (206)783-9833
Southwestern Washington; Rev. Robert D. Hofstad, 420 121st St., S., Tacoma, WA 98444-5218, Tel. (253)535-8300 Fax (253)535-8315
Eastern Washington-Idaho, Rev. Martin D. Wells, 314 South Spruce St., Ste. A, Spokane, WA 99204-1098, Tel. (509)838-9871 Fax (509)838-0941
Oregon, Rev. Paul R. Swanson, 2800 N. Vancouver Ave., Ste. 101, Portland, OR 97227-1643, Tel. (503)413-4191 Fax (503)413-2407
Montana, Rev. Dr. Richard R. Omland, 2415 13th Ave. S., Great Falls, MT 59405-5199, Tel. (406)453-1461 Fax (406)761-4632
Regional Coord., Mr. Steven H. Lansing, Region 1, 766-B John St., Seattle, WA 98109-5186, Tel. (206)624-0093 Fax (206)626-0987

**Region 2**

Sierra Pacific, Rev. David G. Mullen, 401 Roland Way, #215, Oakland, CA 94621-2011, Tel. (510)430-0500 Fax (510)430-8730
Southwest California, Rev. Dean W. Nelson, 1300 E. Colorado St., Glendale, CA 91205-1406, Tel. (818)507-9591 Fax (818)507-9627
Pacifica, Rev. Murray D. Finck, 23655 Via Del Rio, Ste. B, Yorba Linda, CA 92887-2738, Tel. (714)692-2791 Fax (714)692-9317
Grand Canyon, Rev. Stephen S. Talmage, Interchurch Center 4423 N. 24th St., Ste. 400, Phoenix, AZ 85016-5544, Tel. (602)957-3223 Fax (602)956-8104
Rocky Mountain, Rev. Allan C. Bjornberg, 455 Sherman St., Ste. 160, Denver, CO 80203, Tel. (303)777-6700 Fax (303)733-0750
Region 2, Ms. Margaret Schmitt Ajer, Region 2, 3755 Avocado Blvd., PMB 411, La Mesa, CA 91941 Tel. (619)460-9312 Fax (619)460-9314

**Region 3**

Western North Dakota, Rev. Duane C. Danielson, 1614 Capitol Way, P.O. Box 370, Bismarck, ND 58502-0370, Tel. (701)223-5312 Fax (701)223-1435
Eastern North Dakota, Rev. Richard J. Foss, 1703 32nd Ave., S., Fargo, ND 58103-5936, Tel. (701)232-3381 Fax (701)232-3180
South Dakota, Rev. Andrea F. DeGroot-Nesdahl, Augustana College, 29th & S. Summit, Sioux Falls, SD 57197-0001, Tel. (605)247-4011 Fax (605)274-4028
Northwestern Minnesota, Rev. Rolf P. Wangberg, Concordia College, 901 8th St. S., Moorhead, MN 56562-0001, Tel. (218)299-3019 Fax (218)299-3363
Northeastern Minnesota, Rev. E. Peter Strommen, 1105 E. Superior St., Upper Suite, Duluth, MN 55802-2085, Tel. (218)724-4424 Fax (218)724-4393
Southwestern Minnesota, Rev. Jon V. Anderson 175 E. Bridge St., P.O. Box 499, Redwood Falls, MN 56283-0499, Tel. (507)637-3904 Fax (507)637-2809

116

Minneapolis Area, Rev. Craig E. Johnson, 122 W. Franklin Ave., Ste. 600, Minneapolis, MN 55404-2474, Tel. (612)870-3610 Fax (612) 870-0170

Saint Paul Area, Rev. Peter Rogness, 105 W. University Ave., St. Paul, MN 55103-2094, Tel. (651)224-4313 Fax (651)224-5646

Southeastern Minnesota, Rev. Harold L. Usgaard, Assisi Heights, 1001 14th St. NW, Ste. 300, Rochester, MN 55901-2511, Tel. (507)280-9457 Fax (507)280-8824

Regional Coord., Rev. Craig A. Boehlke, Region 3, Luther Seminary, 2481 Como Ave., St. Paul, MN 55108-1445, Tel. (651)649-0454 x 232, Fax (651)649-0468

## Region 4

Nebraska, Rev. David L. deFreese, 4980 S. 118th St., Ste. D, Omaha, NE 68137-2220, Tel. (402)896-5311 Fax (402)896-5354

Central States, Rev. Dr. Gerald L. Mansholt, 3210 Michigan Ave., 4th Fl., Kansas City, MO 64109, Tel. (816)861-6584 Fax (816)861-4753

Arkansas-Oklahoma, Rev. Floyd M. Schoenhals, 693 S. 66th E. Ave., Ste. 310, Tulsa, OK 74133-1760, Tel. (918)492-4288 Fax (918) 491-6275

Northern Texas-Northern Louisiana, Rev. Kevin S. Kanouse, 1230 Riverbend Dr., Ste. 105, P.O. Box 560587, Dallas, TX 75356-0587, Tel. (214)637-6865 Fax (214)637-4805

Southwestern Texas, Rev. Ray Tiemann, 1090 Oestreich Dr., Seguin, TX 78155, Tel. (830) 379-9900, Fax (830)379-9990

Texas-Louisiana Gulf Coast, Rev. Paul J. Blom, 12707 North Fwy, #580, Houston, TX 77060-1239, Tel. (281)873-5665 Fax (281)875-4716

Acting Regional Coord., Rev. Donald R. Just, 7016 Ameranth Ln, Austin, TX, 78723, Tel.(512)585-4809 Fax (512)272-9699

## Region 5

Metropolitan Chicago, Rev. Paul R. Landahl, 1420 West Dickens Ave., Chicago, IL 60614-3004, Tel. (773)248-0021 Fax (773)248-8455

Northern Illinois, Rev. Gary M. Wollersheim, 103 W. State St., Rockford, IL 61101-1105, Tel. (815) 964-9934 Fax (815)964-2295

Central-Southern Illinois, Rev. Warren D. Freiheit, 524 S. Fifth St., Springfield, IL 62701-1822, Tel. (217)753-7915 Fax (217) 753-7976

Southeastern Iowa, Rev. Philip L. Hougen, 2635 Northgate Dr., P.O. Box 3167, Iowa City, IA 52244-3167, Tel. (319)338-1273 Fax (319) 351-8677

Western Iowa, Rev. Michael A. Last, 318 E. Fifth St., P.O. Box 577, Storm Lake, IA 50588-0577, Tel. (712)732-4968 Fax (712)732-6540

Northeastern Iowa, Rev. Steven L. Ullestad, 201-20th St. SW, P.O. Box 804, Waverly, IA 50677-0804, Tel. (319)352-1414 Fax (319)

352-1416

Northern Great Lakes, Rev. Thomas A. Skrenes, 1029 N. Third St., Marquette, MI 49855-3588, Tel. (906)228-2300 Fax (906)228-2527

Northwest Synod of Wisconsin, Rev. Robert D. Berg, 12 W. Marshall St., P.O. Box 730, Rice Lake, WI 54868-0730, Tel. (715)234-3373 Fax (715)234-4183

East-Central Synod of Wisconsin, Rev. James A. Justman, 16 Tri-Park Way, Appleton, WI 54914-1658, Tel. (920)734-5381 Fax (920) 734-5074

Greater Milwaukee, Rev. Paul W. Stumme-Diers, 1212 S. Layton Blvd., Milwaukee, WI 53215-1653, Tel. (414)671-1212 Fax (414)671-1756

South-Central Synod of Wisconsin, Rev. George G. Carlson, 2909 Landmark Pl., Ste. 202, Madison, WI 53713-4237, Tel. (608)270-0201 Fax (608)270-0202

La Crosse Area, Rev. April Culring Larson, 3462 Losey Blvd. S., La Crosse, WI 54601-7217, Tel. (608)788-5000 Fax (608)788-4916

Regional Coord., Rev. Carl R. Evenson, Region 5, 675 Deerwood Dr., Ste. 4., Neenah, WI 54956-1629, Tel. (920)720-9880 Fax (920) 720-9881

## Region 6

Southeast Michigan, Rev. John H. Schreiber, 218 Fisher Bldg., 3011 W. Grand Ave., Detroit, MI 48202-3011, Tel. (313)875-1881 Fax (313) 875-1889

Northwest Lower Michigan, Rev. Gary L. Hansen, 801 S. Waverly Rd., Ste. 201, Lansing, MI 48917-4254, Tel. (517)321-5066 Fax (517)321-2612

Indiana-Kentucky, Rev. James R. Stuck, 911 E. 86th St., Ste. 200, Indianapolis, IN 46240-1840, Tel. (317)253-3522 Fax (317)254-5666

Northwestern Ohio, Rev. Marcus C. Lohrmann, 621 Bright Rd., Findlay, OH 45840-6987, Tel. (419)423-3664 Fax (419)423-8801

Northeastern Ohio, Rev. Lee M. Miller, Interim Bishop, 1890 Bailey Rd., Cuyahoga Falls, OH 44221-5259, Tel. (330)929-9022 Fax (330) 929-9018

Southern Ohio, Rev. Dr. Callon W. Holloway, Jr., 300 S. 2nd St., Columbus, OH 43215-5001, Tel. (614)464-3532 Fax (614)464-3422

Regional Coord., Marilyn McCann Smith, Region 6, P.O. Box 91, 119 1/2 N. Main St. Bluffton, OH 45817, Tel. (419)369-4006 Fax (419)369-4007

## Region 7

New Jersey, Rev. E. Roy Riley, Jr., 1930 State Highway. 33, Hamilton Square, Trenton, NJ 08690-1799, Tel. (609)586-6800 Fax (609) 586-1597

New England, Rev. Margaret G. Payne, 20 Upland St., Worcester, MA 01607-1624, Tel. (508)791-1530 Fax (508)797-9295

117

Metropolitan New York, Rev. Stephen P. Bouman, Interchurch Center, 475 Riverside Dr., Ste.1620, New York, NY 10115, Tel. (212)665-0732 Fax (212)665-8640

Upstate New York, Rev. Marie C. Jerge, 890 E. Brighton Ave., Syracuse, NY 13205, Tel. (315) 446-2502 Fax (315)446-4642

Northeastern Pennsylvania, Rev. Dr. David R. Strobel, 4865 Hamilton Blvd., Wescosville, PA 18106-9705, Tel. (610)395-6891 Fax (610)398-7083

Southeastern Pennsylvania, Rev. Claire S. Burkat, 506 Haws Ave., Norristown, PA 19401-4543, Tel. (610)278-7342 Fax (610) 696-2782

Slovak Zion, Rev. Wilma S. Kucharek, 124 Barbero Dr., Torrington, CT 06790, P.O. Box 1003 (06790-1003), Tel. (860)482-6100, Fax (860)482-7463

Regional Coord., Rev. Peggy M. Wvertele Tel. (215)248-6319 Fax (215)248-7377

**Region 8**

Northwestern Pennsylvania, Rev. Ralph E. Jones, 308 Seneca St., 5th Fl., Oil City, PA 16301, Tel. (814)677-5706 Fax (814)676-8591

Southwestern Pennsylvania, Rev. Donald J. McCoid, 9625 Perry Hwy., Pittsburgh, PA 15237-5590, Tel. (412)367-8222 Fax (412) 369-8840

Allegheny, Rev. Gregory R. Pile, 701 Quail Ave., Altoona, PA 16602-3010, Tel. (814)942-1042 Fax (814)941-9259

Lower Susquehanna, Rev. Carol S. Hendrix, 900 S. Arlington Ave., Ste. 208, Harrisburg, PA 17109-5031, Tel. (717)652-1852 Fax (717) 652-2504

Upper Susquehanna, Rev. Dr. A. Donald Main, Rt. 192 & Reitz Blvd., P.O. Box 36, Lewisburg, PA 17837-0036, Tel. (570)524-9778 Fax (570)524-9757

Delaware-Maryland, Rev. Dr. H. Gerard Knoche, 700 Light St., Baltimore, MD 21230-3850, Tel. (410)230-2860 Fax (410)230-2871

Metropolitan Washington, DC, Rev. Theodore F. Schneider, 1030-15th St., NW, Ste. 1010, Washington, DC 20005-1503, Tel. (202)408-8110 Fax (202)408-8114

West Virginia-Western Maryland, Rev. Ralph W. Dunkin, The Atrium, 503 Morgantown Avenue, Ste. 100, Fairmont, WV 26554-4374, Tel. (304)363-4030 Fax (304)366-9846

Regional Coord., Rev. Judith Cobb, Lutheran Theological Sem. at Gettysburg, 61 Seminary Ridge, Gettysburg, PA 17325-1795, Tel. (717)338-3033 x 2133 Fax(717)334-3469

**Region 9**

Virginia, Rev. James F. Mauney, Roanoke College, 221 College Ln., Bittle Hall, P.O. Drawer 70, Salem, VA 24153-0070, Tel. (540) 389-1000 Fax (540)389-5962

North Carolina, Rev. Leonard H. Bolick, 1988 Lutheran Synod Dr., Salisbury, NC 28144-4480, Tel. (704)633-4861 Fax (704)638-0508

South Carolina, Rev. David A. Donges, 1003 Richland St., P.O. Box 43, Columbia, SC 29202-0043, Tel. (803)765-0590 Fax (803) 252-5558

Southeastern, Rev. Ronald B. Warren, 100 Edgewood Ave., NE, Ste. 1600, Atlanta, GA 30303, Tel. (404)589-1977 Fax (404)521-1980

Florida-Bahamas, Rev. Edward R. Benoway, 3838 W. Cypress St., Tampa, FL 33607-4897, Tel. (813)876-7660 Fax (813)870-0826

Caribbean, Rev. Margarita Martinez, PMB Num 359 Ste. 1, 425 CARR 693, Ste. 1, Dorado, PR 00646-4802, Tel. (787)273-8311 Fax (787) 796-3365

Regional Coord., Rev. Harvey L. Huntley Jr., Region 9, Lutheran Theological Southern Seminary, 4201 N. Main St., Columbia, SC 29203, Tel. (803)461-3263 Fax(803)461-3380

**Periodicals**

*The Lutheran; Lutheran Partners; Lutheran Woman Today; Seeds for the Parish*

## Evangelical Lutheran Synod

The Evangelical Lutheran Synod had its beginning among the Norwegian settlers who brought with them their Lutheran heritage. The synod was organized in 1853. It was reorganized in 1918 by those who desired to adhere to the synod's principles not only in word but also in deed.

The synod owns and operates Bethany Lutheran College and Bethany Lutheran Theological Seminary. It has congregations in 20 states and maintains foreign missions in Peru, Chile, the Czech Republic, Latvia, and Ukraine. It operates a seminary in Lima, Peru and in Ternopil, Ukraine.

**Headquarters**

6 Browns Court, Mankato, MN 56001, Tel. (507) 344-7356 Fax (507)344-7426

Media Contact, Pres., John A. Moldstad

Email: gorvick@blc.edu

Website: www.EvLuthSyn.org

**Officers**

Pres., Rev. John A. Moldstad, 6 Browns Ct., Mankato, MN 56001

Sec., Rev. Craig Ferkenstad, 37777 State Hwy 22, St. Peter, MN 56082

Vice Pres., Rev. Glenn Obengerger, 12309 Pacific Ave., Tacoma, WA 98444

**OTHER ORGANIZATIONS**

Lutheran Synod Book Co., Bethany Lutheran College, 700 Luther Dr., Mankato, MN 56001

Bethany Lutheran Theological Seminary, 6 Browns Court, Mankato, MN 56001

**Periodicals**

*Lutheran Sentinel; Lutheran Synod Quarterly; Young Branches; Oak Leaves; Mission News*

Evangelical Mennonite Church—please see
Fellowship of Evangelical Churches

## Evangelical Methodist Church

The Evangelical Methodist Church was organized in 1946 at Memphis, Tenn., largely as a movement of people who opposed modern liberalism and wished for a return to the historic Wesleyan position. In 1960, it merged with the Evangel Church (formerly Evangelistic Taber-nacles) and with the People's Methodist Church in 1962.

### Headquarters

P.O. Box 17070, Indianapolis, IN 46217, Tel. (317)780-8017 Fax (317)780-8078
Media Contact, Gen. Conf. Sec.-Treas., Rev. James A. Coulston
Email: headquarters@emchurch.org
Website: www.emchurch.org

### Officers

Gen. Supt., Dr. Edward W. Williamson
Gen. Conf. Sec.-Treas., Rev. James A. Coulston

### Periodicals

*The Connection*

## Evangelical Presbyterian Church

The Evangelical Presbyterian Church (EPC), established in March 1981, is a conservative denomination of 8 geographic presbyteries. From its inception with 12 churches, the EPC has grown to 182 churches with a membership of over 74,000.

Planted firmly within the historic Reformed tradition, evangelical in spirit, the EPC places high priority on church planting and development along with world missions. Eighty missionaries serve the church's mission.

Based on the truth of Scripture and adhering to the Westminster Confession of Faith plus its Book of Order, the denomination is committed to the "essentials of the faith." The historic motto "In essentials, unity; in nonessentials, liberty; in all things charity" catches the irenic spirit of the EPC, along with the Ephesians theme, "truth in love."

The Evangelical Presbyterian Church is a member of the World Alliance of Reformed Churches, National Association of Evangelicals, World Evangelical Fellowship and the Evangelical Council for Financial Accountability.

### Headquarters

Office of the General Assembly, 17197 N. Laurel Park Dr., Suite 567, Livonia, MI 48152, Tel. (734)742-2020 Fax (734)742-2033
Media Contact, Stated Clerk, Dr. Jeffrey Jeremiah
Email: EPCHURCH@epc.org
Website: www.epc.org

### Officers

Administration Committee, Chmn., Rev. William Meyer, 2020 Shangrila Dr. # 205, Clearwater, FL 33763

Board of Benefits, Chmn., Rev. Ron Horgan, c/o EPC, 17197 N. Laurel Park Dr. Suite 567, Livonia, MI 48152
Committee on Fraternal Relations, Chmn., Rev. Craig Vaniber, 4700 Victory Dr., Marshall, TX 75670
Committee on National Outreach, Chmn., Rev. Rodger Woodworth, New Hope EPC, 2710 Shadeland Ave., Pittsburgh, PA 15212
Committee on Presbytery Review, Chmn., Mr.Jay Curtis, 3018 Forest Club Drive, Plant City, FL 33566
Committee on World Outreach, Chmn., Dr. Bern Draper, 8103 Saguaro Ridge Road, Parker, CA 80138
Committee on Ministerial Vocation, Chmn., Mr. Jerry Kidd, 624 Reasor Dr., Virginia Beach, VA 23464
Comm. on Christian Educ. & Publ., Chmn., Mr. Dan Tidwell, 3310 Oyster Cove Dr., Missouri City, TX 77459
Committee on Women's Ministries, Chmn., Jeane Mobley, 100 Turtle Cay-Unit 6, Wilmington NC 28412
Committee on Theology, Chmn., Dr. Jeffrey Jeremiah, First Evangelical Presbyterian Church, 19800 108th Avenue SE, Renton, WA 98055
Committee on Student and Young Adult Ministries, Chmn., Rev. George Boomer, Knox Presbyterian Church, 25700 Crocker Blvd, Harrison Township, MI 48045
College Ministries Committee, Chmn., Rev. Rick Stauffer, Tabernacle EPC, 2432 S. Raccoon Rd., Youngstown, OH 44515

### PRESBYTERIES

Central South, Stated Clk., Rev. Dennis Flach, New Covenant Evangelical Presbyterian Church, P.O. Box 842, Natchez, MS 39121
East, Stated Clk., Rev. Ron Meyer, Fourth Presbyterian Church, 5500 River Road, Bethesda, MD 20816
Florida, Stated Clk., Rev. Robert Garment, Hope EPC, 4680 Thomasville Rd., Tallahassee, FL 32309
Mid-America, Stated Clk., Mr. Dexter Kuhlman, 1926 Prospector Ridge, Ballwin, MO 63011
Mid-Atlantic, Stated Clk., Dr. Howard Shockley, P.O. Box 10, Moore, SC 29369
Midwest, Stated Clk., Mr. John C. Manon, P.O. Box 6047, Auburn, IN 46706-6047
Southeast, Stated Clk., Rev. Bill Sharp, 1222 Village Green Dr., Chattanooga, TN 39343
West, Stated Clk., Rev. Marc Huebl, Interim, 1250 S. Buckely Rd., Suite # 146, Aurora, CO 80017

## Fellowship of Evangelical Bible Churches

Formerly known as Evangelical Mennonite Brethren, this body emanates from the Russian immigration of Mennonites into the United

119

States, 1873-74. Established with the emphasis on true repentance, conversion and a committed life to Jesus as Savior and Lord, the conference was founded in 1889 under the leadership of Isaac Peters and Aaron Wall. The founding churches were located in Mountain Lake, Minn., and in Henderson and Jansen, Neb. The conference has since grown to a fellowship of 42 churches with approximately 4,500 members in Canada, Paraguay and the United States.

Foreign missions have been a vital ingredient of the total ministry. Today one missionary is serving for every 35 members in the home churches. The fellowship does not develop and administer foreign mission fields of its own, but actively participates with existing evangelical "faith" mission agencies. The fellowship has missionaries serving under approximately 40 different agencies around the world.

The church is holding fast to the inerrancy of Scripture, the deity of Christ and the need for spiritual regeneration of man from his sinful natural state by faith in the death, burial and resurrection of Jesus Christ as payment for sin. Members look forward to the imminent return of Jesus Christ and retain a sense of urgency to share the gospel with those who have never heard of God's redeeming love.

### Headquarters

3339 N 109th Plz., Omaha, NE 68164, Tel. (402) 965-3860 Fax (402)965-3871

Admn., Paul Boeker, 3339 N 109th Plz., Omaha, NE 68164, Tel. (402)965-3860 Fax (402)965-3871

Email: info@febcministries.org

Website: www.febcministries.org

### Officers

Pres., Mr. Gerald Epp, P.O. Box 86, Waldheim, SK S0K 4R0, Tel. (306)945-2023, Email: president@febcministries.org

Vice President, Rev. Charles Tschetter, 9001 Q St., Omaha, NE 68127-3548, Email: vicepres @febcministries.org

Admn., Paul Boeker, 3339 N 109th Plz., Omaha, NE 68164, Tel. (402)965-3860 Fax (402)965-3871, Email: info@febcministries.org

Ministries Coordinator, Harvey Schultz, 3011 3rd Ave. East, P.O. Box 8, Waldheim, SK S0K 4R0, Tel. (306)945-2220 Fax (306)945-2088, Email: ministries@febcministries.org

### Periodicals

*Fellowship Focus*

## Fellowship of Evangelical Churches

The Evangelical Mennonite Church is an American denomination in the European free church tradition, tracing its heritage to the Reformation period of the 16th century. The Swiss Brethren of that time believed that salvation could come only by repentance for sins and faith in Jesus Christ; that baptism was only for believers; and that the church should be separate from controls of the state. Their enemies called them Anabaptists, since they insisted on rebaptizing believers who had been baptized as infants. As the Anabaptist movement spread to other countries, Menno Simons became its principal leader. In time his followers were called Mennonites.

In 1693 a Mennonite minister, Jacob Amman, insisted that the church should adopt a more conservative position on dress and style of living and should more rigidly enforce the "ban"—the church's method of disciplining disobedient members. Amman's insistence finally resulted in a division within the South German Mennonite groups; his followers became known as the Amish.

Migrations to America, involving both Mennonites and Amish, took place in the 1700s and 1800s, for both religious and economic reasons.

The Evangelical Mennonite Church was formed in 1866 out of a spiritual awakening among the Amish in Indiana. It was first known as the Egly Amish, after its founder Bishop Henry Egly. Bishop Egly emphasized regeneration, separation and nonconformity to the world. His willingness to rebaptize anyone who had been baptized without repentance created a split in his church, prompting him to gather a new congregation in 1866. The conference, which has met annually since 1895, united a number of other congregations of like mind. This group became The Defenseless Mennonite Church in 1898 and has been known as the Evangelical Mennonite Church since 1948. At the 2003 convention the delegates voted to change the name to Fellowship of Evangelical Churches.

### Resource Center

1420 Kerrway Ct., Fort Wayne, IN 46805, Tel. (260)423-3649 Fax (260)420-1905

Media Contact, Admn. Asst., Lynette Augsburger

Email: FECministries@aol.com

Website: www.fecministries.org

### Officers

Pres., Mr. Ronald J. Habegger

Chpsn., Rev. Roger Andrews, 12509 Chapel Cove, Fort Wayne, IN 46845

Vice Chpsn., Rev. Steve Shaffer, 3115 W. Forsythe Rd., Peoria, IL 61614

Sec., Mark Wyse, 7183 SR 66, Archbold, OH 43502

Treas., Alan Rupp, 7304 Brackenwood Ct., Fort Wayne, IN 46825

### Periodicals

*FEConnections*

## Fellowship of Fundamental Bible Churches

The churches in this body represent the 1939

separation from the Methodist Protestant Church, when some 50 delegates and pastors (approximately one-third of the Eastern Conference) withdrew to protest the union of the Methodist Protestant Church with the Methodist Episcopal Church and the Methodist Episcopal Church South, and what they considered the liberal tendencies of those churches. These churches subsequently changed their name to the Bible Protestant Church. In 1985, this group again changed its name to the Fellowship of Fundamental Bible Churches to more accurately define their position.

As fundamentalists, this group strongly adheres to the historic fundamentals of the faith, including the doctrine of separation. This group accepts a literal view of the Bible and, consequently, accepts premillennial theology and a pre-tribulational rapture.

The churches are currently located in New Jersey, New York, Pennsylvania, Virginia, Michigan, and California. It is a fellowship of independent Bible and Baptist churches. Baptism, by immersion, and the Lord's Supper, as a memorial, are recognized as ordinances. There are currently 22 churches representing 1200 members. This constituent body is a member of the American Council of Christian Churches.

The Fellowship of Fundamental Bible Churches owns and operates Tri-State Bible Camp and Conference Center in Montague, New Jersey, oversees a mission board called Fundamental Bible Missions, and conducts a Bible Institute called Fundamental Bible Institute.

## Headquarters

P.O. Box 206, Penns Grove, NJ 08069
Media Contact, Sec., Rev. Edmund G. Cotton, 80 Hudson St., Port Jervis, NY 12771, Tel. (845) 856-7695
Email: FFBC-U.S.A.@juno.com
Website: www.churches-ffbc.org

## Officers

Pres., Rev. Mark Franklin, 284 Whig Lane, Monroeville, NJ 08343, Tel. (609)881-0057
Vice Pres., Rev. Joe Roof, 17 Thoroughbred Lane, Albany, NY 12205, Tel. (518)459-2717
Sec., Rev. Ron Whitehead, 30 Elmwood Ave., Carneys Point, NJ 08069, Tel. (856)299-3307
Treas., Ken Thompson, 501 N. Main Street, Elmer, NJ 08318, Tel. (865)358-0515

## Fellowship of Grace Brethren Churches

A division occurred in the Church of the Brethren in 1882 on the question of the legislative authority of the annual meeting. It resulted in the establishment of the Brethren Church under a legal charter requiring congregational government. This body divided in 1939 with the Grace Brethren establishing headquarters at Winona Lake, Ind., and the Brethren Church at Ashland, Ohio.

## Headquarters

Media Contact, Fellowship Coord., Rev. Thomas Avey, P.O. Box 386, Winona Lake, IN 46590, Tel. (219)269-1269 Fax (219)269-4066
Email: fgbc@fgbc.org
Website: www.fgbc.org

## Officers

Mod., Dr. Galen Wiley, 22713 Ellsworth Ave., Minerva, OH 44657
1st Mod.-Elect, Dr. James Custer, 2515 Carriage Rd., Powell, OH 43065
2nd Mod.-Elect, Dr. Ron Manahan, 2316 E. Kemo Ave., Warsaw, IN 46580
Fellowship Coord., Rev. Thomas Avey, P.O. Box 386, Winona Lake, IN 46590, Tel. (219)269-1269 Fax (219)269-4066
Sec., Fellowship Coord., Rev. Thomas Avey, P.O. Box 386, Winona Lake, IN 46590
Treas., Thomas Staller, 2311 S. Cost-a-Plenty Drive, Warsaw, IN 46580

## OTHER BOARDS

Grace Brethren International Missions, Exec. Dir., Rev. Tom Julien, P.O. Box 588, Winona Lake, IN 46590
Grace Brethren Home Missions, Exec. Dir., Larry Chamberlain, P.O. Box 587, Winona Lake, IN 46590
Grace College & Seminary, Pres., Ronald E. Manahan, 200 Seminary Dr., Winona Lake, IN 46590, Tel. (210)372-5100
Brethren Missionary Herald Co., Pub. & Gen. Mgr., James Bustram, P.O. Box 544, Winona Lake, IN 46590
CE National, Exec. Dir., Rev. Ed Lewis, P.O. Box 365, Winona Lake, IN 46590
Grace Brethren Navajo Ministries, Dir., Steve Galegor, Counselor, NM 87018
Grace Village Retirement Community, Admn., Jeff Carroll, P.O. Box 337, Winona Lake, IN 46590
Natl. Fellowship of Grace Brethren Ministries, Pres., Dr. Steve Taylor, 132 Summerall Ct., Aiken, SC 29801 Women's Missionary Council, Pres., Janet Minnix, 3314 Kenwick Tr., S.W., Roanoke, VA, 24015
Grace Brethren Men International, Pres., Morgan Burgess, 163 N. Franklin St., Delaware, OH 43015

## Free Christian Zion Church of Christ

This church was organized in 1905 at Redemption, Ark., by a company of African-American ministers associated with various denominations. Its polity is in general accord with that of Methodist bodies.

## Headquarters

1315 S. Hutchinson St., Nashville, AR 71852
Media Contact, Gen. Sec., Shirlie Cheatham

**Officers**
Chief Pastor, Willie Benson, Jr.

## Free Methodist Church of North America

The Free Methodist Church was organized in 1860 in Western New York by ministers and laymen who had called the Methodist Episcopal Church to return to what they considered the original doctrines and lifestyle of Methodism. The issues included human freedom (anti-slavery), freedom and simplicity in worship, free seats so that the poor would not be discriminated against and freedom from secret oaths (societies) so the truth might be spoken freely at all times. The founders emphasized the teaching of the entire sanctification of life by means of grace through faith.

The denomination continues to be true to its founding principles. It communicates the gospel and its power to all people without discrimination through strong missionary, evangelistic and educational programs. Six colleges, a Bible college and numerous overseas schools train the youth of the church to serve in lay and ministerial roles.

Its members covenant to maintain simplicity in life, worship, daily devotion to Christ, responsible stewardship of time, talent and finance.

**Headquarters**
World Ministries Center, 770 N. High School Rd., Indianapolis, IN 46214, Tel. (317)244-3660 Fax (317)244-1247
Mailing Address, P.O. Box 535002, Indianapolis, IN 46253, Tel. (800)342-5531
Media Contact, Yearbook Ed., P.O. Box 535002, Indianapolis, IN 46253
Email: info@fmcna.org
Website: www.freemethodistchurch.org

**Officers**
Bishops, Bishop Roger W. Haskins, Jr.; Bishop Joseph F. James; Bishop David W. Kendall; Bishop Richard D. Snyder
General Conference Secretary, Miss Carol Bartlett
Dir. of Administraion and Finance, Mr. Gary Kilgore
Free Methodist Communications, Gerald Coates
Free Methodist World Missions, Dr. Arthur Brown
Men's Ministries International, Director, Rev. Jeffrey Johnson
Women's Ministries International, President, Alice Matthewson

**Periodicals**
*Light and Life Magazine*

## Friends General Conference

Friends General Conference (FGC) is an association of fourteen yearly meetings open to all Friends meetings that wish to be actively associated with FGC's programs and services. Friends General Conference includes Baltimore, Canadian, Illinois, Lake Erie, New England, New York, Northern, Ohio Valley, Philadelphia, South Central, and Southeastern Yearly Meetings; Alaska Friends Conference, Southern Appa-lachian Yearly Meeting and Association, and Piedmont Friends Fellowship; plus seven independently affiliated monthly meetings. Friends General Conference is primarily a service organization with the stated purpose of nurturing the spiritual life within its constituency of predominantly unprogrammed Friends. FGC offers services to all Friends, but has no authority over constituent meetings. A Central Com-mittee, to which constituent Yearly Meetings name appointees (in proportion to membership), and its Executive Committee, are responsible for the direction of FGC's programs and services which include a bookstore, conferences, and traveling ministries program. The 1995 Central Committee approved the following Minute of Purpose:

"Friends General Conference is a Quaker organization in the unprogrammed tradition of the Religious Society of Friends which primarily serves affiliated yearly and monthly meetings. It is our experience that,
\*\*Faith is based on direct experience of God.
\*\*Our lives witness this experience individually and corporately.
\*\*By answering that of God in everyone, we build and sustain inclusive community.
Friends General Conference provides resources and opportunities that educate and invite members and attenders to experience, individually and corporately, God's living presence, and to discern and follow God's leadings. Friends General Conference reaches out to seekers and to other religious bodies inside and outside the Religious Society of Friends."

**Headquarters**
1216 Arch St., 2B, Philadelphia, PA 19107, Tel. (215)561-1700 Fax (215)561-0759
Media Contact, Gen. Sec., Bruce Birchard
Email: friends@fgcquaker.org
Website: www.fgcquaker.org

**Officers**
Gen. Sec., Bruce Birchard, 1216 Arch St., 2B Philadelphia, PA 19107
Presiding Clerk, Marian Beane, 7125 Cardigan Ave, Charlotte, NC 28215
Treas., Byron Sandford, 515 E Capitol St. SE, Washington DC 20003-1142

**YEARLY MEETINGS**
Alaska Friends Conference, Clerk, Bill Schoder-Ehri, 480 Grubstake Ave., Homer, AK, 99603-7639, Tel. (907)479-5257, Email: lovenest @ptialaska.net
\*Baltimore, Clerk, Lauri Perman; Staff, Robert H. Robinson, 17100 Quaker Ln., Sandy Spring, MD 20860, Tel. (301)774-7663, Email: rileyrobinson@bym-rsf.org

*Canadian, Clerk, Beverley Shepard; Staff, Kerry McAdam, 91A Fourth Ave., Ottawa, ON K1S 2L1, Tel. (613)235-8553, Email: cym-office@quaker.ca

Illinois, Clerk, Susanna Davison; Staff, Sharon Haworth, 608 W. Illinois St. Urbana, Il. 61801, Tel. (217)384-9591, Email: shaworth@sbc-global.net

Lake Erie, Clerk, Shirley Bechil, 185 Pineviews Dr. Alma, MI 48801-2156, Tel. (989)463-4539, Email: bechill@alma.edu

*New England, Clerk, Christopher McCandless; Staff, Katharine Clark, 901 Pleasant St., Worcester, MA 01602-1908, Tel. (508)754-6760, Email: adminsec@neym.org

*New York, Clerk, Linda Chidsey; Staff, Helen Garay Toppins, 15 Rutherford Pl., New York, NY 10003, Tel. (212)673-5750, Email: office @ nyym.org

Northern, Clerk, Doug Kirk, 1602 Wicklowway Madison, WI 53711, Tel. (608)442-1642, Email: quirks@tds.net

Ohio Valley, Clerk, Virginia Wood; Staff, Krystin Schmidt, P.O. Box 1333, Richmond, IN 47374, Email: vwovym@donet.com

Philadelphia, Clerk, Thomas Swain, 1515 Cherry St., Philadelphia, PA 19102, Tel. (215)241-7210, Email: tswain@ccil.org

Piedmont Friends Fellowship, Clerk, Virginia Driscoll, 504 Willowbrook Dr., Greensboro, NC 27403, Tel. (336)855-5233, Email: dachel-mama@yahoo.com

South Central, Clerk, John Coffin, 7106 Shamrock, Little Rock, AR 72205, Tel. (501) 663-1439, Email: joticof@aol.com

*Southeastern, Clerk, Susan Taylor; Staff, Lyn Cope-Robinson P.O. Box 510975, Melbourne Beach, FL 32951; Tel. (321)724-1162, Email: admin@seym.org

Southern Appalachian, Clerk, Kristi Estes, Email: adminasst@sayma.org

*also affiliated with Friends United Meeting

### Periodicals

*Newsletter, FGConnections, Friends Journal*

Friends International—please see Evangelical Friends International—North American Region

## Friends United Meeting*

Friends United Meeting was organized in 1902 (the name was changed in 1963 from the Five Years Meeting of Friends) as a confederation of North American yearly meetings to facilitate a united Quaker witness in missions, peace work Christian education and outreach.

Today Friends United Meeting is comprised of 26-full-member and 3-association-member yearly meetings representing about half the Friends in the world. FUM's current work includes programs of mission and service, leadership development and outreach. FUM publishes Christian education cur-riculum, books of Quaker history and religious thought and a magazine, *Quaker Life*.

### Headquarters

101 Quaker Hill Dr., Richmond, IN 47374-1980, Tel. (765)962-7573 Fax (765)966-1293

Media Contact, Interim General Secretary, Sylvia Graves

Email: info@fum.org

Website: www.fum.org

### Officers

Presiding Clk., Brent McKinney

Treas., Don Garner

Interim Gen. Sec., Sylvia Graves

### DEPARTMENTS

Quaker Hill Bookstore, Mgr., Paul Smith

*Quaker Life*, Ed., Trish Edwards-Konic

Friends United Press, Ed., Trish Edwards-Konic

### YEARLY MEETINGS

Baltimore Yearly Meeting, 17100 Quaker Ln., Sandy Spring, MD 20860-1296, Tel. (301)774-7663 (800)962-4766 Fax (301)774-7087, Website: www.bymrsf@igc.org, Lamar Matthew, clerk; Frank Massey, Gen. Sec.

Bware Yearly Meeting, P.O. Box 179, Suna, Kenya; Samuel Kaguni, Gen. Sect., Epainitus Adego, Gen Supt., Jonathan M. Sande, Presiding Clerk

Canadian Yearly Meeting, 91-A Fourth Ave., Ottawa ON K1S 2L1, Canada, Tel. (613)235-8553 Fax (613)235-1753; George McClure, clerk, Email: cym@web.net

Central Yearly Meeting, P.O. Box 1510, Kakamega, Kenya, E. Africa, Evans Nyenzo, Gen. Supt.

Chavakali Yearly Meeting, P.O. Box 102, Chavakali, Kenya, East Africa; Andrew Mukulu, Gen. Sec., Wilson Andenya, Clerk

Cuba Yearly Meeting, Calle 20 #118 Esquina Paz, Reparto Vista, Alegre 80300, Hoguin, Cuba; Maria Renya Yi, President

East Africa Yearly Meeting of Friends, (Kaimosi) P.O. Box 35, Tiriki, Kenya, East Africa; Matthew Tsimbaki, Presiding Clerk, Ephraim Konsolo, Gen. Sec., Erastus Kesohole, Gen Supt.

East Africa Yearly Meeting of Friends (North), P.O. Box 544, Kitale, Kenya, East Africa; Geoffrey M. Wukwanja, Gen. Sec., Titus Adira, Gen. Supt., H. M Mukwanja. Presiding Clerk

VIHIGA Yearly Meeting of Friends, P.O. Box 160, Vihiga, Kenya, East Africa; Joseph Kisia, Presiding Clerk; Lam Kisanya Osodo, Gen. Sec., Gilbert Akenga Oyando, Gen. Supt.

Elgon East Yearly Meeting, P.O. Box 2322, Kitale, Kenya, East Africa; Maurice Simiyu, Gen. Supt, Philip Musungu, Gen. Sec., John Kitui, Presiding Clerk.

Elgon Religious Society of Friends, (West) P.O. Box 4, Lugulu Via Webuye, Kenya, East Africa, Tom Isiye, General Sec., John Ngoya, Gen. Supt., Charles Mbachi, Presiding Clerk

Evangelical Friends Church Uganda, P.O. Box 129, Mbale, Uganda, East Africa; Simon Tsapwe, Gen. Supt., Peter Kutosi, Gen. Sec.

Great Plains Yearly Meeting, 1262 Richland Rd., Lacon, IL 61540, Tel. (309)246-8397, Email: mesnerret@cconline.net, Neil Mesner, Clerk

Indiana Yearly Meeting, 4715 N. Wheeling Ave., Muncie, IN 47304-1222, Tel. (765)284-6900 Fax (765)284-8925, Email: iyminfo@iym.org; Susan Kirkpatrick, Clerk; Alan Weinacht, Gen. Supt.

Iowa Yearly Meeting, P.O. Box 657, Oskaloosa, IA 52577-0657, Tel. (641)673-9717 Fax (641) 673-9718, Email: wpdc9717@wmpenn.edu; Margaret Stoltzfus, Clerk, Ron Bryan, Gen. Super-intendent

Jamaica Yearly Meeting, 4 Worthington Ave., Kingston 5, Jamaica WI, Tel. (876)926-7371

Kakamega Yearly Meeting, P.O. Box 465, Kakamega, Kenya, East Africa; Jonathan Shisanya, Gen. Sec., Blastus Wawire, Presiding Clerk, Meschack Musindi, Gen. Supt.

Lugari Yearly Meeting, P.O. Box 483, Turbo, Kenya, East Africa; David A. Mulama, Gen. Sec., Joshuah Lilande Presiding Clerk, Japheth Vidolo, Gen. Supt.

Malava Yearly Meeting, P.O. Box 26, Malava, Kenya, East Africa; Andrew Namasaka Mulongo, Gen. Sec., Samson Marani, Presiding Clerk, Enoch Shinachi, Gen. Supt.

Nairobi Yearly Meeting, P.O. Box 8321, Nairobi, Kenya, East Africa; Benson Simiyu, Gen. Supt., Zablon Isaac Malenge, Gen. Sec., Nilson Shivachi, Vice-Presiding

New England Yearly Meeting, 901 Pleasant St., Worcester, MA 01602-1908, Tel. (508)754-6760, Email: neym@neym.org; Deana Chase, Clerk; Jonathan Vogel-Borne, Field Secretary

New York Yearly Meeting, 15 Rutherford Pl., New York, NY 10003, Tel. (212)673-5750, Email: office@nyym.org; Linda Chidsey, Clerk; Helen Garay Toppins, Admin. Sec.

North Carolina Yearly Meeting, 5506 W. Friendly Ave., Greensboro, NC 27410, Tel. (336)292-6957, Email: ncfriends@juno.com; Michael Fulp, Clerk; John Porter, Gen. Superintendent

Southeastern Yearly Meeting, P.O. Box 510795, Melbourne Beach, FL 32951-0795, Tel. 321-724-1162; Lyn Cope-Robinson, Adm. Sec., Email: seym@bv.net

Tanzania Yearly Meeting, P.O. Box 151, Mugumu, Serengeti, Tanzania; Joseph Lavuna Oguma, Gen. Supt. & Clerk

Tuloi Yearly Meeting, P.O. Box 102, Kapsabet, Kenya, East Africa; Joseph Anyonge Mulama, Presiding clk., Solomon Mwanzi, Gen. Supt., Frederick Inyangu, Gen. Sec.

Uganda Yearly Meeting, P.O. Box 2384, Mbale, Uganda, East Africa; Francis Wamala, Gen. Supt., Andrew H.S. Kurima, Gen. Sec., Sylvester Khasufa, Clerk

Vokoli Yearly Meetings, P.O. Box 266, Wodanga, Kenya, East Africa; Javan Chondo, Gen. Sec.,

Hannington Mbato, Presiding Clerk, Thomas Kivuya, Gen Supt.

Western Yearly Meeting, P.O. Box 70, Plainfield, IN 46168, Tel. (317)839-2789 and (317)839-2849 Fax (317)839-2616; Steve and Marlene Pediso, Co-Superintendents, Wayne Carter, Clerk

Wilmington Yearly Meeting, Pyle Center Box 1194, Wilmington, OH 45177, Tel. (937)382-2491 Fax (937)382-7077, Email: phackney@wilmington.edu, Gary Farlow, Clerk; Marvin Hall, Ex. Sec.

### Periodicals

*Quaker Life*

# Full Gospel Assemblies International

The Full Gospel Assemblies International was founded in 1962 under the leadership of Dr. Charles Elwood Strauser. The roots of Full Gospel Assemblies may be traced to 1947 with the beginning of the Full Gospel Church of Coatesville, Pa. As an Assemblies of God Pentecostal church, the Full Gospel Church of Coatesville was active in evangelization and educational ministries to the community. In service to the ministers and students of the Full Gospel Church ministries, the Full Gospel Trinity Ministerial Fellowship was formed in 1962, later changing its name to Full Gospel Assemblies International.

Retaining its original doctrine and faith, Full Gospel Assemblies is Trinitarian, believing that the Bible is God's infallible Word to mankind, baptism in the Holy Spirit according to Acts 2, divine healing is made possible by the sufferings of our Lord Jesus Christ, and in the imminent return of Christ for those who love him.

The body of Full Gospel Assemblies is an evangelical missionary fellowship sponsoring ministry at home and abroad, composed of self-governing ministries and churches. Congregations, affiliate ministries, and clerical body are located throughout the United States and over 15 countries of the world.

### Headquarters

International Headquarters: 3018 Lincoln Hwy, Parkesburg, PA

Mailing Address, P.O. Box 1230, Coatesville, PA 19320, Tel. (610)857-2357 Fax(610)857-3109

Media Contact, Simeon Strauser

### Officers

Gen. Supt., Dr. AnnaMae Strauser

Exec. Dir. of Ministry, J. Victor Fisk

Exec. Dir of Admn., Simeon Strauser

Exec. Dir. of Communications, Archie Neale

Exec. Sec., Betty Stewart

Exec. Trustee, Edward Popovich

National Ministers Council and Trustees

Chpsn. Simeon Strauser, Sadsburyville, Pa.

James Capets, Trafford, Pa.

Donald Schiemant, Marilla, NY
Michael Mathews, Eau Claire, Wisc.
Bette Elgin, Zenia, Calif.
John Tortoriello, Fort Lauderdale, Fla.
Raymond Favicha, Spring Hill, Fla.
Carol Strauser, Parkesburg, Pa.

**Periodicals**

*Full Gospel Ministries Outreach Report*

# Full Gospel Fellowship of Churches and Ministers International

In the early 1960s a conviction grew in the hearts of many ministers that there should be closer fellowship between the people of God who believed in the apostolic ministry. At the same time, many independent churches were experiencing serious difficulties in receiving authority from the IRS to give governmentally accepted tax-exempt receipts for donations.

In September 1962 a group of ministers met in Dallas, Texas, to form a fellowship to give expression to the essential unity of the Body of Christ under the leadership of the Holy Spirit— a unity that goes beyond individuals, churches or organizations. This was not a movement to build another denomination, but rather an effort to join ministers, churches and ministry organizations of like mind across denominational lines.

To provide opportunities for fellowship and to support the objectives and goals of local and national ministries regional conventions and an annual international convention are held.

**Headquarters**

1000 N. Belt Line Rd., Irving, TX 75061, Tel. (214)492-1254
Media Contact & Convention Planner, Sec., Dr. Harry Schmidt, 400 E. Gregory, Mt. Prospect, IL 60056
Email: TheFellowship@fgfcmi.org
Website: www.fgfcmi.org

**Officers**

Pres., Dr. Don Arnold, P.O. Box 324, Gadsden, AL 35901
1st Vice Pres., Dr. Harry Schmidt, 400 E. Gregory, Mt. Prospect, IL 60056
Sec., Rev. Deloris Kendrick, 10201 Beacon Ave. S., Seattle, WA 98178
Treas., Rev. Gene Evans P.O. Box 813 Douglasville, GA 30133
CFO, Dr. S.K. Biffle, 1000 N. Belt Line Rd., Irving, TX 75061
Ofc. Sec., Anita Sullivan & Voni Lassiter Receptionist, Nita Biffle
Vice Pres. at Large, Rev. Maurice Hart, P.O. Box 4316, Omaha, NE 68104; Rev. Don Westbrook, 3518 Rose of Sharon Rd., Durham, NC 27705
Chmn. of Evangelism, David Ellis
Chmn. of Mission, Rev. David Robinson, 1121 Shuler St., Elgin. IL 60123

Chmn. of Youth, Rev. Steven K. Biffle, 3833 Westerville Rd., Columbus, OH 43224
Past Pres., Dr. James Helton

**REGIONAL VICE PRESIDENTS**

Southeast, Rev. Steve Holder, 103 Hawkins Dr., Pikeville, NC 27863
South Central, Rev. Billy Gibson, 4249 Winding Brook Dr., Plano, TX 75093
Southwest, Dr. R.G. Dunbar, 121 N. 32nd Street, Colorado Springs, CO 80904
Northeast, Rev. David Ellis, 3636 Winchester Rd., Allertown, PA 18104
North Central, Rev. David Robinson, 1121 Shuler Street, Elgin, IL 60123
Northwest, Rev. Jon R. Engstrom, 19605 12th Ave. W, Lynnwood, WA 98036

**Periodicals**

*Fellowship Tidings*

# Fundamental Methodist Church, Inc.

This group traces its origin through the Methodist Protestant Church. It withdrew from the Methodist Church and organized on August 27, 1942.

**Headquarters**

1034 N. Broadway, Springfield, MO 65802
Media Contact, Betty Nicholson, Rt. 2, Box 397, Ash Grove, MO 65604, Tel. (417)672-2268

**Officers**

Treas., and Sec., Betty Nicholson, Rt. 2, Box 397, Ash Grove, MO 65604, Tel. (417)672-2268

# General Association of General Baptists

Similar in doctrine to those General Baptists organized in England in the 17th century, the first General Baptist churches were organized on the Midwest frontier following the Second Great Awakening. The first church was established by the Rev. Benoni Stinson in 1823 at Evansville, Ind.

Stinson's major theological emphasis was general atonement—Christ tasted death for every man. The group also allows for the possibility of apostasy. It practices open Communion and believer's baptism by immersion.

Called "liberal" Baptists because of their emphasis on the freedom of man, General Baptists organized a General Association in 1870 and invited other "liberal" Baptists (e.g., "Free Will" and Separate Baptists) to participate.

The policy-setting body is composed of delegates from local General Baptist churches and associations. Each local church is autonomous but belongs to an association. The group currently consists of more than 60 associations in 16 states, as well as associations in the Philippines, Guam, Saipan, Jamaica, Honduras, and India.

125

Ministers and deacons are ordained by a presbytery.

The denomination operates Oakland City University in Oakland City, In., and Nursing Homes in Illinois and Missouri. General Baptists belong to the Baptist World Alliance, the North American Baptist Fellowship and the National Association of Evangelicals.

### Headquarters
100 Stinson Dr., Poplar Bluff, MO 63901, Tel. (573)785-7746 Fax (573)785-0564
Media Contact, Exec. Dir., Dr. Ron Black

### Officers
Mod., Dr. James Julian
Clk., Rev. James Schremp
Exec. Dir., Dr. Ron Black

### OTHER ORGANIZATIONS
International Missions, Dir., Rev. Jack Eberhardt
National Missions, Dir., Rev. Stephen Gray
Women's Ministries, Dir., Barbara Wigger
Oakland City University, Dr. James Murray, Chancellor/President, 143 North Lucretia St., Oakland City, IN 47660
Congregational Ministries, Dir., Dr. Franklin Dumond, 100 Stinson Dr., Poplar Bluff, MO 63901
Pastoral Ministries, Dir., Dr. Franklin Dumond, 100 Stinson Dr., Poplar Bluff, MO 63901
Admin., Financial Services, Financial Officer, Linda McDonough, 100 Stinson Dr., Poplar Bluff, MO 63901
Stinson Press, Inc., Pres., Rev. Dale Bates, 400 Stinson Dr., Poplar Bluff, MO 63901
Nursing Home Board, CEO Rev. Jack Cole, Rt. #3, Box 650, Campbell, MO 63933
Compassionate Care Adoption Agency, Dir., Dr. John Clanton, Rt. 3, Box 12B, Oakland City, IN 47660 Stewardship/General Baptist Investment Fund Dir., Rev. Stephen Gray, 100 Stinson Dr., Poplar Bluff, MO 63901

## General Association of Regular Baptist Churches

This association was founded in May, 1932, in Chicago by a group of churches which had withdrawn from the Northern Baptist Convention (now the American Baptist Churches in the U.S.A.) because of doctrinal differences. Its Confession of Faith, which it requires all churches to subscribe to, is essentially the old, historic New Hampshire Confession of Faith with a premillennial ending applied to the last article.

The churches of the General Association of Regular Baptist Churches voluntarily join together to accomplish four goals. (1) Champion Biblical truth—committed to communicating the whole counsel of God in its timeless relevance. (2) Impact the world for Christ—obeying the Lord's Great Commission to take the life-changing gospel to the entire world. (3) Perpetuate its Baptist heritage—faithfully promoting its Scriptural legacy and identity. (4) Advancing GARBC churches—strengthening existing churches and planting new churches for the purposes of evangelism and edification.

### Headquarters
1300 N. Meacham Rd., Schaumburg, IL 60173, Tel. (847)843-1600 Fax (847)843-3757
Media Contact, Natl. Rep., Dr. John Greening
Email: garbc@garbc.org
Website: www.garbc.org

### Officers
Chpsn., Rev. Braaley Quick
Vice Chpsn., David Warren
Treas., Michael Nolan
Sec., John Hastag, III
Natl. Rep., Dr. John Greening

### Periodicals
*Baptist Bulletin; Synergy Newsletter; E-Info Newsletter*

## General Church of the New Jerusalem

The General Church of the New Jerusalem, also called the New Church, was founded in 1897. It is based on the teachings of the 18th Century scientist Emanuel Swedenborg, and stresses the oneness of God, who is the Lord Jesus Christ, a life of faith and love in service to others, in true married love, and in life after death.

### Headquarters
1100 Cathedral Rd, P.O. Box 743, Bryn Athyn, PA 19009, Tel. (267)502-2682
Media Contact, Ed., Church Journal, Rev. Kurt H. Asplundh, Box 26, Bryn Athyn, PA 19009, Tel. (267)502-2682 Fax (267)502-4929
Email: svsimpso@newchurch.edu
Website: www.newchurch.org

### Officers
Presiding Bishop, Rt. Rev. Thomas L. Kline
Sec., Susan V. Simpson
Treas., David Frazier

### Periodicals
*New Church Life*

## General Conference of Mennonite Brethren Churches

A small group, requesting that closer attention be given to prayer, Bible study and a consistent lifestyle, withdrew from the larger Mennonite Church in the Ukraine in 1860. Anabaptist in origin, the group was influenced by Lutheran pietists and Baptist teachings and adopted a quasi-congregational form of church government. In 1874 and years following, small groups of these German-speaking Mennonites left Russia, settled in Kansas and then spread to the Midwest west of the Mississippi and into Canada. Some years later the movement spread to California and the West Coast. In 1960, the

Krimmer Mennonite Brethren Conference merged with this body.

Today the General Conference of Mennonite Brethren Churches conducts services in many European languages as well as in Vietnamese, Mandarin, and Hindi. It works with other denominations in missionary and development projects in 25 countries outside North America.

### Headquarters
4812 E. Butler Ave., Fresno, CA 93727, Tel. (209)452-1713 Fax (209)452-1752
Media Contact, Exec. Sec., Marvin Hein

### Officers
Mod., Ed Boschman, 12630 N. 103rd Ave., Suite 215, Sun City, AZ 85351
Asst. Mod., Herb Kopp, 200 McIvor Ave., Winnipeg, NB R20 028
Sec., Valerie Rempel
Exec. Sec., Marvin Hein

### Periodicals
*Christian Leader*

## Grace Gospel Fellowship

The Grace Gospel Fellowship was organized in 1944 by a group of pastors who held to a dispensational interpretation of Scripture. Most had ministries in the Midwest. Two prominent leaders were J. C. O'Hair of Chicago and Charles Baker of Milwaukee. Subsequent to 1945, a Bible Institute was founded (now Grace Bible College of Grand Rapids, Mich.), and a previously organized foreign mission (now Grace Ministries International of Grand Rapids) was affiliated with the group. Churches have now been established in most sections of the country.

The body has remained a fellowship, each church being autonomous in polity. All support for its college, mission and headquarters is on a contributory basis.

The binding force of the Fellowship has been the members' doctrinal position. They believe in the Deity and Saviorship of Jesus Christ and subscribe to the inerrant authority of Scripture. Their method of biblical interpretation is dispensational, with emphasis on the distinctive revelation to, and the ministry of, the apostle Paul.

### Headquarters
Media Contact, Pres., Frosty Hansen, 2125 Martindale SW, P.O. Box 9432, Grand Rapids, MI 49509, Tel. (616)245-0100 Fax (616)241-2542
Email: ggfinc@aol.com
Website: www.ggfusa.org

### Officers
Pres., Traynor ("Frosty") Hansen, Jr.

### OTHER ORGANIZATIONS
Grace Bible College, Pres., Rev. Ken Kemper, 1011 Aldon St. SW, Grand Rapids, MI 49509
Grace Ministries Intl., Exec. Dir., Dr. Samuel Vinton, 2125 Martindale Ave. SW, Grand Rapids, MI 49509

Prison Mission Association, Gen. Dir., Donald Sommer, P.O. Box 1587, Port Orchard, WA 98366-0140
Grace Publications Inc., Exec. Dir., Wayne Schoonover, 2125 Martindale Ave. SW, Grand Rapids, MI 49509
Bible Doctrines to Live By, Exec. Dir., Lee Homoki, P.O. Box 2351, Grand Rapids, MI 49501

### Periodicals
*Truth*

## Greek Orthodox Archdiocese of America*

THE ORTHODOX CHURCH

The Orthodox Church today, numbering over 250 million worldwide, is a communion of self-governing churches, each administratively independent of the other, but united by a common faith and spirituality. Their underlying unity is based on identity of doctrines, sacramental life and worship, which distinguishes Orthodox Christianity. All recognize the spiritual preeminence of the Ecumenical Patriarch of Constantinople, who is acknowledged as *primus inter pares*, first among equals. All share full communion with one another. The living tradition of the church and the principles of concord and harmony are expressed through the common mind of the universal episcopate as the need arises. In all other matters, the internal life of each independent church is administered by the bishops of that particular church. Following the ancient principle of the one people of God in each place and the universal priesthood of all believers, the laity share equally in the responsibility for the preservation and propagation of the Christian faith and church.

THE GREEK ORTHODOX ARCHDIOCESE OF AMERICA

Before the establishment of an Archdiocese in the Western Hemisphere there were numerous communities of Greek Orthodox Christians. The first Greek Orthodox community in the Americas was founded in New Orleans, La. by a small colony of Greek merchants. History also records that on June 26, 1768 the first Greek colonists landed at St. Augustine, Fla., the oldest city in America. The first permanent community was founded in New York City in 1892, today's Archdiocesan Cathedral of the Holy Trinity and the See of the Archbishop of America. The Greek Orthodox Archdiocese of North and South America was incorporated in 1921 and officially recognized by the State of New York in 1922.

The Greek Orthodox Archdiocese of America is composed of the Direct Archdiocesan District —New York and eight Metropolises: Chicago, Pittsburgh, Boston, Denver, Atlanta, Detroit, San Francisco, and New Jersey. It is governed by the Archbishop and the Synod of Bishops. The Synod of Bishops is headed by the Archbishop and comprised of the Metropolitans who are in charge of a metropolis. It has all the authority and responsibility which the church canons provide for a provincial synod.

## Headquarters

8-10 E. 79th St., New York, NY 10021, Tel. (212) 570-3500 Fax (212)570-3569

Media Contact, Nikki Stephanopoulos, Director, News and Information/Public Affairs, Tel. (212)570-3530 Fax (212)774-0215, Email: nikki@goarch.org

Email: archdiocese@goarch.org

Website: www.goarch.org

## HOLY EPARCHIAL SYNOD OF BISHOPS

His Eminence Archbishop Demetrios, Primate of the Greek Orthodox Archdiocese of America, Exarch of the Atlantic and Pacific Oceans, Chairman of the Holy Synod of Bishops, Greek Orthodox Church in America, 8-10 East 79th Street, New York, NY 10021, Tel. (212)570-3500 Fax (212)570-3592

## METROPOLIS

His Eminence Metropolitan Iakovos of Chicago, Metropolis of Chicago,40 East Burton Place, Chicago, IL 60610, Tel. (312)337-4130 Fax (312)337-9391

His Eminence Metropolitan Maximos of Pittsburgh, Metropolis of Pittsburgh, 5201 Ellsworth Avenue, Pittsburgh, PA 15232, Tel. (412)621-5529 Fax(412)621-1522

His Eminence Metropolitan Methodios of Boston, Metropolis of Boston, 162 Goddard Avenue, Brookline, MA 02146, Tel. (617)277-4742 Fax(617)739-9229

His Eminence Metropolitan Isaiah of Denver, Metropolis of Denver, 4610 East Alameda Ave., Suite D1, Denver, CO 80222, Tel. (303)333-7794 Fax(303)333-7796

His Eminence Metropolitan Alexios of Atlanta, Metropolis of Atlanta, 2480 Clairmont Road NE, Atlanta, GA 30329, Tel. (404)634-9345 Fax (404)634-2471

His Eminence Metropltian Nicholas of Detroit, Metropolis of Detroit, 19405 Renfrew Road, Detroit, MI 48221, Tel. (313)664-5433 Fax (313) 864-5543

His Eminence Metropolitan Gerasimos of San Francisco, Metropolis of San Francisco, 372 Santa Clara Avenue, San Francisco, CA 94127, Tel. (415)753-3075 Fax(415) 753-1165

His Eminence Metropolitan Evangelos of New Jersey, Metropolis of New Jersey 629 Springfield Road, Kenilworth, NJ 07033, Tel. (908) 686-0003 Fax(908)686-0046

## AUXILIARY BISHOPS

His Grace Bishop Dimitrios of Xanthos, His Grace Bishop Savas of Troas, His Grace Bishop Andonios of Phasiane

## CLERGY-LAITY CONGRESS

The Clergy-Laity Congress, the highest legislative body of the Archdiocese, is convened biennially and presided over by the Archbishop. It is concerned with all matters, other than doctrinal or canonical, affecting the life, growth and unity of the church, the institutions, finances, administration, educational and philanthropic concerns and its increasing growing role in the life of the nations of the Western Hemisphere. The delegates are the pastors and elected lay representatives.

There are 510 parishes, 810 priests and approximately 1.5 million faithful in the Greek Orthodox Archdiocese of America

## THE ARCHDIOCESAN COUNCIL

The Archdiocesan Council is the deliberative body of the Greek Orthodox Archdiocese which meets in the interim period between Clergy-Laity Congresses, held every two years.

Executive Committee, His Eminence Archbishop Demetrios Chairman

### The Holy Synod of Bishops

Vice Chairman, Michael Jaharis; Nicholas Bouras, treasurer; Catherine Bouffides-Walsh, secretary, George Behrakis, Dr. John Collis, John Pappajohn, John Payiavlas, Anthony Stefanis; Emanuel G. Demos, General Counsel to the Archdiocese.

## INSTITUTIONS

Archdiocesan Cathedral of the Holy Trinity

The Rev. Dr. Robert G. Stephanopoulos, Dean, 319-337 East 74th Street, New York, NY 10021, Tel. (212)288-3215 Fax (212)288-5876

Website: www.thecathedral.goarch.org

Hellenic College/Holy Cross School of Theology, The Rev. Nicholas Triantafilou, President, 50 Goddard Avenue, Brookline, MA 02445, Tel. (617)731-3500 Fax (617) 850-1460, Email: admission@hchc.edu

Saint Basil Academy, The Rev. Constantine L. Sitaras, Director, 79 Saint Basil Road Garrison, NY 10524, Tel. (845)424-3500 Fax (845)424-4172, Email: stbasil@bestweb.net, Website: www.stbasil.goarch.org

St. Michael's Home, His Grace Bishop Andonios of Phasiane, Director, 3 Lehman Terrace, Yonkers, NY 10705, Tel. (914)476-3374 Fax (914)476-1744, Email: Stmichaelshome@ msn.com, Website: stmichael.goarch.org

## ARCHDIOCESE OF NEW YORK

Office of the Archbishop, Alice Keurian; Director; Office of the Chancellor, His Grace Bishop Savas of Troas, Chancellor; Office of Administration, Jerry Dimitriou, Executive Director.

## ARCHDIOCESAN DEPARTMENTS

Registry, Finance, Stewardship & LOGOS, Religious Education, Greek Education, Communications, Internet Ministries, Information Technologies, Youth and Young Adults, Camping Ministry, Ionian Village Ecumenical,

Interfaith/Interchurch Marriages, Archives, Benefits

**Related Organizations, Auxiliaries**

Ladies Philoptochos Society, Presbyters Council, Sisterhood of Presvyteres, Retired Clergy of America, National Forum of Greek Orthodox Musicians, Hellenic Cultural Center, Archons of the Ecumenical Patriarchate, Archbishop Iakovos Leadership 100 Endowment Fund, St. Photios National Shrine, International Orthodox Christian Charities (IOCC), Orthodox Christian Mission Center, Trinity Children & Family Services.

**OTHER JURISDICTIONS OF THE ECUMENICAL PATRIARCHATE IN THE U.S.A.**

Albanian Orthodox Diocese in America; Belarusian Council of Orthodox Churches in North America; American Carpatho-Russian Orthodox Greek Catholic Diocese of the U.S.A.; Ukrainian Orthodox Church of the U.S.A.

**Periodicals**

*The Orthodox Observer*

TELEVISION MINISTRY: Greek Orthodox Telecommunications (GOTelecom)

# The Holy Eastern Orthodox Catholic and Apostolic Church in North America, Inc.

Canonically established by the Russian Orthodox Synod of Bishops in North America on Feb. 2, 1927 this church was incorporated on Feb. 1, 1928 by Archbishop Aftimios Ofiesh, the first Archbishop-president. Archbishop Aftimios continued as head of this church until he reposed in July 1966. The name and logo are registered service marks of this church. We are a western rite church but some of our clergy do celebrate the Eastern Liturgy.

The first Synod included Archbishop Aftimios and Bishops Sophronios and Zuk. Over the years many have claimed to be this church, its successor, this church under a different name or having our lines. These are members of the independent movement who claim to have lines of apostolic succession that are traced back to us but not recognized by this or any canonical church since they were not administered in accordance to the Rudder (Canons) of the Orthodox Church.

**Headquarters**

Monastery: St. Pachomius Monastery, P.O. Box 8122, Columbus, OH 43201, Tel. (614)297-8055

Primate, Metropolitan Victor

Email: tmetropolitan@theocacna.org

Website: www.theocacna.org

**Officers**

Archbishop Peter Mar Kepa—Archdiocese of the East

Metropolitan Victor—Archdiocese of the West

Bishop Christopher—Diocese of Houston, Tx.

Bishop Cassian—Diocese of Columbus, Oh.

Bishop Arthur—Diocese of Michigan

**SYNOD ADVISORS**

Archbishop James

Bishop Donald

Society: The Society of Clerks Secular of St. Basil, est. 1931

# Holy Synod for the American Diaspora

The Christian Church was established by the Lord Jesus Christ and His Holy Apostles in Jerusalem in 33 A.D. From Jerusalem, the Church spread to other centers of the known world, including Constantinople (founded in 37 A.D.) and Kiev (45 A.D.), founded by St. Andrew the First-Called Holy Apostle. In 864 A.D., missionary of the Church of Constantinople further extended the Orthodox Christian Faith in present-day Russia. In 988 A.D., Rus' Prince Vladimir converted and declared Orthodoxy the state religion, while hundreds of thousands were baptized in the Dnieper River at Kiev. The resulting Russian Orthodox Church became the greatest safeguard and body of Orthodox Christians in the world.

The history of Apostolic Orthodox Catholic Christianity began in 1794 when Russian Orthodox Church missionaries established the first Orthodox mission on North American soil at present-day Kodiak, Alaska. Their missionary efforts continued down the Pacific coast in 1824, then across the whole continent. Being the canonical founder of Orthodox Christianity in North America, the Russian Orthodox Church maintained and presided over all Orthodox missions, churches, and Christians throughout North America without question or challenge for over 100 years. However, the 1917 Bolshevik Revolution which resulted in severe persecution and imprisonment of the Russian Orthodox Mother Church also resulted in the unrestrained rise of old-country nationalism and great ethnic turbulence between Orthodox Catholic Christians and their churches in North America. They separated and divided, often violently, along ethnic and nationalist lines with each creating its own old-world ethnic administrations. The once long-held unity and single Orthodox Church canonical administration in North America was destroyed.

The Apostolic Orthodox Catholic Church (AOCC) is canonically independent and indigenous to North America and comprised of bishops, clergy and faithful possessing unbroken Apostolic Succession since the time of Jesus Christ's appointment of His Twelve Holy Apostles to the present day through American Orthodoxy's Luminary and Defender, Russian Orthodox Prelate-Archbishop Aftimios Ofiesh of Blessed Memory.

The AOCC maintains unquestionable, canonical Apostolic Succession passed on to its bishops through its Russian Orthodox Mother Church by Archbishop Aftimios Ofiesh, his succeeding Bishops Sophronios Beshara and Christopher Contogeorge, their legal successors and through consecrating support of such memorable Orthodox leaders as Russian Patriarchal Exarch of North America Metropolitan Benjamin Fedchenkov and and Albanian Orthodox Church Metropolitan Theophan Noli. In 1945, the Apostolic Succession and Canonicity of these bishops "and their successors" were declared in binding agreement to be unquestionable, valid, authentic and independent by the Orthodox Church Ecumenical Patriarchate of Constantinople, and recognition was furthermore attested to in 1951. English-speaking and non-ethnic-restrictive, the AOCC's further validity is evidenced by its life, mind, discourse and teaching all being governed and directed in accordance with the Sacred Canons of the Most Ancient Holy Orthodox Catholic Church. The AOCC embraces the ideals and theology of Orthodoxy and freedom which Archbishop Aftimios Ofiesh stood for, taught and passed on by selfless devotion and love for Christ and His Church, and by his personal example.

### Headquarters

Holy Synod for the American Diaspora, P.O. Box 346, Seward, NE 68434, Tel. (503)375-6175

Media Contact, Most Rev. Aftimios (L. Sinclair), Vice Presiding Archbishop, 4696 Horseshoe Court SE, Salem, OR 97301, Tel. (575)375-6175

Email: synod@oldorthodox.org

### Officers

Archbishop, Most Rev. Mar Melchizedek

The Secretary of the Synod, Most. Rev. Bishop Aftimios

Synod of Bishops, Most Rev. Bishop Spyridon, Most Rev. Bishop Valerian, Most Rev. Bishop Maximus

### SEMINARY

St Elias School of Orthodox Theology, P.O. Box 346, Seward, NE 68434, Tel. (402)643-9365

## Holy Ukrainian Autocephalic Orthodox Church in Exile

This church was organized in a parish in New York in 1951 by Ukrainian laymen and clergy who settled in the Western Hemisphere after World War II. In 1954 two bishops, immigrants from Europe, met with clergy and laymen and formally organized the religious body.

### Headquarters

103 Evergreen St., W. Babylon, NY 11704

### Officers

Admn., Rt. Rev. Serhij K. Pastukhiv

## House of God, Which is the Church of the Living God, the Pillar and Ground of the Truth, Inc.

This body, founded by Mary L. Tate in 1919, is episcopally organized.

### Headquarters

1301 N. 58th St., Philadelphia, PA 19131

Media Contact, Sec., Rose Canon, 515 S. 57th St., Philadelphia, PA 19143, Tel. (215)474-8913

### Officers

Bishop, Raymond W. White, 6107 Cobbs Creek Pkwy., Philadelphia, PA 19143, Tel. (215)748-6338

## Hungarian Reformed Church in America*

A Hungarian Reformed Church was organized in New York in 1904 in connection with the Reformed Church of Hungary. In 1922, the Church in Hungary transferred most of its congregations in the United States to the Reformed Church in the U.S. Some, however, preferred to continue as an autonomous, self-supporting American denomination, and these formed the Free Magyar Reformed Church in America. This group changed its name in 1958 to Hungarian Reformed Church in America.

This church is a member of the World Alliance of Reformed Churches, Presbyterian and Congregational, the World Council of Churches and the National Council of Churches of Christ.

### Headquarters

Bishop's Office, 13 Grove St., Poughkeepsie, NY 12601, Tel. (914)454-5735

### Officers

Bishop, Rt. Rev. Alexander Forro

Chief Lay-Curator, Prof. Stephen Szabo, 464 Forest Ave., Paramus, NJ 07652

Gen. Sec. (Clergy), Rt. Rev. Stefan M. Torok, 331 Kirkland Pl., Perth Amboy, NJ 08861, Tel. (908)442-7799

Gen Sec. (Lay), Zoltan Ambrus, 3358 Maple Dr., Melvindale, MI 48122

Eastern Classes, Dean (Senior of the Deans, Chair in Bishop's absence), Very Rev. Imre Bertalan, 10401 Grosvenor Pl., #1521, Rockville, MD 20852, Tel. (301)493-5036 Fax (301)571-5111; Lay-Curator, Balint Balogh, 519 N. Muhlenberg St., Allentown, PA 18104

New York Classes, Supervisor, Rt. Rev. Alexander Forro; Lay-Curator, Laszlo B. Vanyi, 229 E. 82nd St., New York, NY 10028

Western Classes, Dean, V. Rev. Andor Demeter, 3921 W. Christy Dr., Phoenix, AZ 85029; Lay-Curator, Zolton Kun, 2604 Saybrook Dr., Pittsburgh, PA 15235

### Periodicals

*Magyar Egyhaz*

## Hutterian Brethren

Small groups of Hutterites derive their names

from Jacob Hutter, a 16th-century Anabaptist who taught true discipleship after accepting Jesus as Saviour, advocated communal ownership of property and was burned as a heretic in Austria in 1536.

Many believers are of German descent and still use their native tongue at home and in church. Much of the denominational literature is produced in German and English. "Colonies" share property, practice non-resistance, dress plainly, do not participate in politics, and operate their own schools. There are 428 colonies with 42,000 members in North America. Each congregation conducts its own youth work through Sunday school. Until age 15, children attend German and English school, which is operated by each colony. All youth ages 15 to 20 attend Sunday school. They are baptized as adults upon confession of faith, around age 20.

### Headquarters
Media Contact, Philip J. Gross, 3610 N. Wood Rd., Reardon, WA 99029, Tel. (509)299-5400 Fax (509)299-3099
Email: philsjg@juno.com

### Officers
Smiedleut Chmn., No. 1, Jacob Waldner—Blumengard Colony, Box 13 Plum Coulee, MB R0G 1R0, Tel. (204)829-3527
Smiedleut Chmn., No. 2, Jacob Wipf, Spring Creek Colony, 36562 102 Street, Forbes, ND 58439, Tel. (701)358-8621
Dariusleut, Chmn., No. 1, Martin Walter, Springpoint Colony, Box 249, Pincher Creek, AB T0K 1W0 Phone (403)553-4368
Lehrerleut, Chmn., Rev. John Wipf, Rosetown Colony, Box 1509, Rosetown, SK S0L 2V0, Tel. (306)882-3344

## IFCA International, Inc.

This group of churches was organized in 1930 at Cicero, Ill., by representatives of the American Council of Undenominational Churches and representatives of various independent churches. The founding churches and members had separated themselves from various denominational affiliations. Founders included J. Oliver Buswell of Wheaton College, Billy McCarrell of Cicero Bible Church and Moody Bible Institute, and M. R. DeHaan of Grand Rapids, Mich. and Radio Bible Class. Members have included J. Vernon McGee, Charles Ryrie, John Walvoord, and John MacArthur.

The IFCA provides a way for independent churches and ministers to unite in close fellowship and cooperation, in defense of the fundamental teachings of Scripture and in the proclamation of the gospel of God's grace.

Today it consists of 1000 associated churches and 1200 individual members (pastors, professors, missionaries, chaplains, and other Christian workers.)

### Headquarters
3520 Fairlanes, Grandville, MI 49418, Tel. (616) 531-1840 Fax (616)531-1814
Mailing Address, P.O. Box 810, Grandville, MI 49468-0810
Media Contact, Exec. Dir., Rev. Les Lofquist
Email: office@ifca.org
Website: www.ifca.org

### Officers
Exec. Dir., Rev. Les Lofquist
Pres., Dr. Roy Sprague, Lakewood, WA

### Periodicals
*The Voice*

## International Church of the Foursquare Gospel

Founded by Aimee Semple McPherson in 1927, the International Church of the Foursquare Gospel proclaims the message of Jesus Christ the Savior, Healer, Baptizer with the Holy Spirit and Soon-coming King. Headquartered in Los Angeles, this evangelistic missionary body of believers consists of nearly 1,900 churches in the United States and Canada. The International Church of the Foursquare Gospel is incorporated in the state of California and governed by a Board of Directors who direct its corporate affairs. A Foursquare Cabinet, consisting of the Corporate Officers, Board of Directors and District Supervisors of the various districts of the Foursquare Church in the United States and other elected or appointed members, serves in an advisory capacity to the President and the Board of Directors. Each local Foursquare Church is a subordinate unit of the International Church of the Foursquare Gospel. The pastor of the church is appointed by the Board of Directors and is responsible for the spiritual and physical welfare of the church. To assist and advise the pastor, a church council is elected by the local church members. Foursquare churches seek to build strong believers through Christian education, Christian day schools, youth camping and ministry, Foursquare Women International who support and encourage Foursquare missionaries abroad, local radio and television ministries, the *Foursquare World ADVANCE Magazine* and over 550 Bible colleges worldwide. Worldwide missions remains the focus of the Foursquare Gospel Church with 38,217 churches and meeting places, 49,287 national pastors, leaders and 4,113,981 members with a combined constituency nearing 5 million in over 140 countries of the world. The church is affiliated with the Pentecostal/Charismatic Churches of North America, the National Association of Evangelicals and the Pentecostal World Conference.

### Headquarters
1910 W. Sunset Blvd., Ste. 200, P.O. Box 26902, Los Angeles, CA 90026-0176, Tel. (213)989-4234 Fax (213)989-4590

Media Contact, Editor, Dr. Ron Williams
Email: comm@foursquare.org
Website: www.foursquare.org

### Officers
President, Dr. Paul C. Risser
Vice President, Dr. Jared D. Roth
General Supervisor, Rev. Glenn C. Burris, Jr.
Director of Missions, Rev. Michael Larkin
Corporate Secretary, Rev. Arthur J. Gray, II
Treasurer, Mr. Brent R. Morgan

### BOARD OF DIRECTORS
Corporate Officers listed above; Robert Bankhead; Greg Campbell; George Cline; Robert Flores; Jeff Hamilton; Dan Hicks; Ken Johnson; Mike McGovern; Carlos Santiago; Steve Schell; Oscar Shepherd; Mark Simon; Devi Titus; Roger Wheeler;

### FOURSQUARE CABINET
Corporate Offices (listed above); Board of Directors (listed above);
John Honold; Teri Orewiler; Kim Pitner; Sharon Snow; Richard Trees; Ken Authier; Robby Booth; Daniel Brown; Richard Casteel; David Coffey; Dennis Estill; Ken Hart; Jim Hayford; Marty Jenkins; Ron Pinkston; Michael Posey; Scott Reece; Dwight Saunders;

### SUPPORT MINISTRIES
National Department of Youth: Walter R. Hoefflin, Director; Department of Christian Education: Rod Light, Director; Foursquare Women International, Kimberly Dirmann, Director.

All of the above can be reached through the corporate address: International Church of the Foursquare Gospel, P. O. Box 26902, Los Angeles, CA 90026, Tel. (888)635-4234 Fax (213)989-4590

### Periodicals
*Foursquare World ADVANCE magazine*

## International Council of Community Churches*
This body is a fellowship of locally autonomous, ecumenically minded, congregationally governed, non-creedal Churches. The Council came into being in 1950 as the union of two former councils of community churches, one formed of black churches known as the Biennial Council of Community Churches in the United States and Elsewhere and the other of white churches known as the National Council of Community Churches.

### Headquarters
21116 Washington Pky., Frankfort, IL 60423-3112, Tel. (815)464-5690 Fax (815)464-5692
Media Contact, Exec. Dir., Rev. Michael E. Livingston
Email: iccc60423@sbcglobal.net

### Officers
Pres., Rev. Herbert Freitag
Vice Pres., Saundra Nelson
Vice Pres., Rev. Leroy McCreary
Sec., Rev. Gary Batey
Treas., Rev. Martin Singley, III

### OTHER ORGANIZATIONS
Commission on Laity and Church Relations, J Philip Smith
Commission on Ecumenical and Inter-faith Relations, Rev. Herman Harmelink, III
Commission on Clergy Relations, Virginia Leopold
Commission on Faith, Justice & Mission, Rev. Dr. Richard Griffith
Women's Christian Fellowship, Pres., Caroline Burke
Samaritans (Men's Fellowship), Pres., Nicholas Brame
Young Adult Fellowship, Pres., Daniel Nelson
Youth Fellowship, Pres., Ta Queena Paulding

### Periodicals
*The Christian Community; The Inclusive Pulpit; Key Lay Notes; Clergy comminique*

## The International Pentecostal Church of Christ
At a General Conference held at London, Ohio, Aug. 10, 1976, the International Pentecostal Assemblies and the Pentecostal Church of Christ consolidated into one body, taking the name International Pentecostal Church of Christ.

The International Pentecostal Assemblies was the successor of the Association of Pentecostal Assemblies and the International Pentecostal Missionary Union. The Pentecostal Church of Christ was founded by John Stroup of Flatwoods, Ky., on May 10, 1917 and was incorporated at Portsmouth, Ohio, in 1927. The International Pentecostal Church of Christ is an active member of the Pentecostal/Charismatic Churches of North America, as well as a member of the National Association of Evangelicals.

The priorities of the International Pentecostal Church of Christ are to be an agency of God for evangelizing the world, to be a corporate body in which people may worship God and to be a channel of God's purpose to build a body of saints being perfected in the image of His Son.

The Annual Conference is held each year during the first full week of August in London, Ohio.

### Headquarters
2245 St. Rt. 42 SW, P.O. Box 439, London, OH 43140, Tel. (740)852-4722 Fax (740)852-0348
Media Contact, Gen. Overseer, Clyde M. Hughes
Email: hqipcc@aol.com
Website: members.aol.com/hqipcc

### EXECUTIVE COMMITTEE
Gen. Overseer, Clyde M. Hughes, P.O. Box 439,

London, OH 43140, Tel. (740)852-4722 Fax (740)852-0348

Asst. Gen. Overseer, B.G. Turner, RR5, Box 1286, Harpers Ferry, WV 25425, Tel. (304) 535-221 Fax (304)535-1357

Gen. Sec., Asa Lowe, 513 Johnstown Rd., Chesapeake, VA 23322, Tel. (757)547-4329

Gen. Treas., Ervin Hargrave, P.O. Box 439, London, OH 43140, Tel. (740)852-4722 Fax (740)852-0348

Dir. of Global Missions, Dr. James B. Keiller, P.O. Box 18145, Atlanta, GA 30316, Tel. (404) 627-2681 Fax (404)627-0702

### DISTRICT OVERSEERS

Central District, Lindsey Hayes, 609 Lansing Rd., Akron, OH 44312, Tel. (330)784-3453

Mid-Eastern District, H. Gene Boyce, 705 W. Grubb St., Hertford, NC 27944, Tel. (252)426-5403

Mountain District, Terry Lykins, P.O. Box 131, Staffordsville, KY 41256, Tel. (606)297-3282

New River District, Calvin Weikel, RR. 2, Box 300, Ronceverte, WV 24970, Tel. (304)647-4301

North Central District, Edgar Kent, P.O. Box 275, Hartford, MI 49057, Tel. (616)621-3326

North Eastern District, Wayne Taylor, 806 8th St., Shenandoah, VA 22849 Tel. (540) 652-8090

South Eastern District, Frank Angie, 2507 Old Peachtree Rd., Duluth, GA 30097, Tel. (770) 476-5196

Tri-State District, Cline McCallister, 5210 Wilson St., Portsmouth, OH 45662, Tel. & fax (740)776-6357

Portugese District, Pedro Messias, 34 Woodside Ave., Danbury, CT 06810, Tel. (203)790-9628

### OTHER ORGANIZATIONS

Beulah Heights Bible College, Pres., Samuel R. Chand, P.O. Box 18145, Atlanta, GA 30316, Tel. (404)627-2681 Fax (404)627-0702

Women's Ministries, Gen. Pres., Janice Boyce, 121 W. Hunters Tr., Elizabeth City, NC 27909, Tel. & fax (252)338-3003

Pentecostal Ambassadors, Dustin Hughes, National Youth Dir., P.O Box 439, London, OH 43140, Tel. (740)852-0448 Fax (740)852-0348

National Christian Education Dept., Dir., Dustin Hughes, P.O. Box 439, London, OH 43140, Tel. (740)852-0448 Fax (740)852-0348

### Periodicals

*The Bridegroom's Messenger; The Pentecostal Leader*

## International Pentecostal Holiness Church

This body grew out of the National Holiness Association movement of the nineteenth century, with roots in Methodism. Beginning in the South and Midwest, the church represents the merger of the Fire-Baptized Holiness Church founded by B. H. Irwin in Iowa in 1895; the Pentecostal Holiness Church founded by A. B. Crumpler in Goldsboro, North Carolina, in 1898; and the Tabernacle Pentecostal Church founded by N. J. Holmes in 1898.

All three bodies joined the ranks of the pentecostal movement as a result of the Azusa Street revival in Los Angeles in 1906 and a 1907 pentecostal revival in Dunn, N.C., conducted by G. B. Cashwell, who had visited Azusa Street. In 1911, the Fire-Baptized and Pentecostal Holiness bodies merged in Falcon, N.C., to form the present church; the Tabernacle Pentecostal Church was added in 1915 in Canon, Ga.

The church stresses the new birth, the Wesleyan experience of sanctification, the pentecostal baptism in the Holy Spirit, evidenced by speaking in tongues, divine healing and the premillennial second coming of Christ.

### Headquarters

P.O. Box 12609, Oklahoma City, OK 73157-2609, Tel. (405)787-7110 Fax (405)789-3957
Email: jdl@iphc.org
Website: www.iphc.org

### Officers

Gen. Supt., Bishop James D. Leggett, Email: jdl@iphc.org

Vice Chpsn. Executive Director of Evangelism U.S.A., Dr. Ronald Carpenter, Sr.

Exec. Dir. of World Missions Ministries, Dr. A.D. Beacham Jr. Executive Director of Church Education Ministries, Rev. Talmadge Gardner

Executive Director of Stewardship Ministries/ General Secretary-Treasurer, Rev. Edward W. Wood

### OTHER ORGANIZATIONS

The Publishing House (LifeSprings Resources), CEO, Greg Hearn, Franklin Springs, GA 30639 Women's Ministries, Exec. Dir., Jewelle Stewart Men's Ministries, Exec. Dir., Rev. Bill Terry, P.O. Box 12609, Oklahoma City, OK 73157

### Periodicals

*IPHC Experience*

## Jehovah's Witnesses

Modern-day Jehovah's Witnesses began in the early 1870s when Charles Taze Russell was the leader of a Bible study group in Allegheny City, Pa. In July 1879, the first issue of *Zion's Watch Tower* and *Herald of Christ's Presence* (now called *The Watchtower* which is published in more than 150 languages with a circulation of upwards of 27 million) appeared. In 1884 Zion's Watch Tower Tract Society was incorporated, later changed to Watch Tower Bible and Tract Society. Congregations spread into other states and countries, and followers witnessed from house to house.

By 1913, printed sermons were in four languages in 3,000 newspapers in the United States, Canada and Europe. Hundreds of millions of

133

books, booklets, and tracts were distributed. Publication of the magazine now known as *Awake!* Began in 1919. Today, it is published in more than 80 languages and has a circulation of upwards of 32,000,000. In 1931 the name Jehovah's Witnesses, based on Isaiah ch. 43 v.10-12, was adopted.

During the 1930s and 1940s, and as recently as 2002, Jehovah's Witnesses fought many court cases in the interest of preserving freedom of speech, press, assembly, and worship. They have won a total of 48 cases before the United States Supreme Court. A missionary training school was established in 1943, and it has been a major factor in the international expansion of the Witnesses. There are now 6.6 million Witnesses in 235 lands.

Jehovah's Witnesses believe in one almighty God, Jehovah, who is the Creator of all things. They believe in Jesus Christ as God's Son, the first of His creations. While Jesus is now an immortal spirit in heaven, ruling as King of God's Kingdom, he is still subject to his heavenly Father, Jehovah God. Christ's human life was sacrificed as a ransom to open up for obedient mankind the opportunity of eternal life. With Christ in heaven, 144,000 individuals chosen from among mankind will rule in righteousness over an unnumbered great crowd who will survive the destruction of wickedness and receive salvation into an earth cleansed of evil. (Rev. ch. 7 v.9, 10; ch.14 v. 1-5). These, along with the resurrected dead, will transform the earth into a global earthly paradise and will have the prospect of living forever on it.

### Headquarters
25 Columbia Heights, Brooklyn, NY 11201-2483, Tel. (718)560-5000

Media Contact, Office of Public Information, J. R. Brown

Editorial Contact, Writing Department, James N. Pellechia

Website: www.watchtower.org

### Officers
Pres. Watch Tower Bible and Tract Society of Pennsylvania, Don Adams

### Periodicals
*Awake!, The Watchtower*

## Korean Presbyterian Church in America, General Assembly of the*

This body came into official existence in the United States in 1976 and is currently an ethnic church, using the Korean and English language.

### Headquarters
General Assembly of the Korean Presbyterian Church in America
17200 Clark Ave., Bellflower, CA 90706
Tel. (714)816-1100 Fax (714)816-1120

### Officers
General Secretary, Rev. Jacob Se Jang, 5848 Pimlico Road, Baltimore, MD 21209, Tel. (410)542-6952

**Latter-day Saints—please see The Church of Jesus Christ of Latter-day Saints**

## The Latvian Evangelical Lutheran Church in America

This body was organized into a denomination on Aug. 22, 1975 after having existed as the Federation of Latvian Evangelical Lutheran Churches in America since 1955. This church is a regional constituent part of the Lutheran Church of Latvia Abroad, a member of the Lutheran World Federation and the World Council of Churches.

The Latvian Evangelical Lutheran Church in America works to foster religious life, traditions and customs in its congregations in harmony with the Holy Scriptures, the Apostles', Nicean and Athanasian Creeds, the unaltered Augsburg Confession, Martin Luther's Small and Large Catechisms and other documents of the Book of Concord.

The LELCA is ordered by its Synod (General Assembly), executive board, auditing committee and district conferences.

### Headquarters
7225 Oak Highlands Dr., Kalamazoo, MI 49009 Tel. (269)375-0389, Email: kaugars@earthlink.net

Media Contact, Juris Pulins, 9531 Knoll Top Rd., Union, IL 60180, Tel. (815)923-5919, Email: pulins@earthlink.net

### Officers
Pres., Dean Lauma Zusevics, Tel. (414)421-3934, Email: izunpz@wi.rr.com

Vice Pres., Rev. Anita Varsberga-Paza, Email: macavp@yahoo.com

Sec., Girts Kaugars, 7225 Oak Highlands Dr., Kalamazoo, MI 49009, Tel. (269)375-0389, Email: kaugars@earthlink.net

Treas., Vilmars Beinikis, 17 John Dr., Old Bethpage, NY 11804, Tel. (516)293-8432

### Periodicals
*Cela Biedrs; Lelba Zinas*

## Liberal Catholic Church (International)

Founded as a reorganization of the Dutch Old Catholic Church in 1915-16. In 1941 a controversy broke out in the church regarding whether or not certain teachings of theosophy (reincarnation, etc.) were to become official teachings of the church. This was resolved by a court decision holding we (the non-Theosophist party) were the legal Liberal Catholic Church.

## Headquarters

741 Cerro Gordo Avenue, San Diego, CA 92102, Tel. & fax (619)239-0637

## Officers

The Most Rev. James P. Roberts, Jr., President and Regionary Bishop, 39 Claire Ave., New Rochelle, NY 10804, Tel. (914)636-7917, Email: Bppal32@aol.com

The Most Rev. Charles W. Finn, Vice President and Presiding Bishop, 741 Cerro Gordo Ave., San Diego, CA 92102, Tel. & fax (619)239-0637, Email: abpchas@msn.com

The Most Rev. Dean Bekken, Secretary-Treasurer, P.O. Box 26044, San Diego, CA 92196-0044, Tel. & fax (858)689-8610, Email: bekken@sbcglobal.net

St. Alban Theological Seminary, P.O. Box 1125, Morongo Valley, CA 92256, Tel. (760)363-6260, Email: liberalcatholic@aol.com

St. Alban Press, 741 Cerro Gordo Ave., San Diego, CA 92102, Tel. & fax (858)689-8610, Email: info@stalbanpress.com

## Periodicals

*Community*

## The Liberal Catholic Church— Province of the United States of America

The Liberal Catholic Church was founded Feb. 13, 1916 as a reorganization of the Old Catholic Church in Great Britain with the Rt. Rev. James I. Wedgwood as the first Presiding Bishop. The first ordination of a priest in the United States was Fr. Charles Hampton, later a Bishop. The first Regionary Bishop for the American Province was the Rt. Rev. Irving S. Cooper (1919-1935).

## Headquarters

Pres., The Rt. Rev. William S.H. Downey, 1206 Ayers Ave., Ojai, CA 93023, Tel. (805)646-2573 Fax (805)646-2575

Media Contact, Regionary Bishop, The Rt. Rev. William S.H. Downey

Email: W. Downey@sbcglobal.net

Website: www.thelcc.org

## Officers

Pres. & Regionary Bishop, The Rt. Rev. William S.H. Downey

Vice Pres., Rev. L. Marshall Heminway, P.O. Box 19957 Hampden Sta., Baltimore, MD 21211-0957

Sec. (Provincial), Rev. Lloyd Worley, 1232 24th Avenue Ct., Greeley, CO 80631, Tel. (303) 356-3002

Provost, Rev. Lloyd Worley

Treas., Rev. Milton Shaw

## BISHOPS

Regionary Bishop for the American Province, The Rt. Rev. William S.H. Downey

Aux. Bishops of the American Province, Rt. Rev. Dr. Robert S. McGinnis, Jr., 3612 N. Labarre Rd., Metaire, LA 70002; Rt. Rev. Joseph L. Tisch, P.O. Box 1117, Melbourne, FL 32901; Rt. Rev. Dr. Hein VanBeusekom, 12 Krotona Hill, Ojai, CA 93023; Rt. Rev. Ruben Cabigting, P.O. Box 270, Wheaton, IL 60189; The Rt. Rev. Lawrence Smith 9740 S. Avers Ave., Evergreen Park, IL.

## Periodicals

*Ubique*

Lutheran Association, Conservative—please see Conservative Lutheran Association

Lutheran Church—please see American Association of Lutheran Churches

Lutheran Church in America—please see Evangelical Lutheran Church in America

Lutheran Church of America—please see Apostolic Lutheran Church of America

## The Lutheran Church—Missouri Synod (LCMS)

The Lutheran Church—Missouri Synod, which was founded in 1847, has more than 6,000 congregations in the United States and works in 78 other countries. It has 2.5 million members and is the second-largest Lutheran denomination in North America.

Christian education is offered for all ages. The North American congregations operate the largest elementary and secondary school systems of any Protestant denomination in the nation, and 18,216 students are enrolled in 12 LCMS institutions of higher learning.

Traditional beliefs concerning the authority and interpretation of Scripture are important. The synod is known for mass-media outreach through *The Lutheran Hour* on radio, *This Is The Life* dramas on television, and the products of Concordia Publishing House, the third-largest Protestant publisher, whose Arch Books children's series has sold more than 60 million copies.

An extensive network of more than 1,000 volunteers in 60 work centers produces Braille, large-type, and audiocassette materials for the blind and visually impaired. Most of the eighty-five or so deaf congregations affiliated with U.S. Lutheran denominations are LCMS; and many denominations use the Bible lessons prepared for developmentally disabled persons. Also, there are 30 centers in the U. S. sponsored by LCMS Blind Missions where blind people are trained for Christian outreach.

The involvement of women is high, although they do not occupy clergy positions. Serving as teachers, deaconesses and social workers, women comprise approximately half of total professional workers.

135

The members' responsibility for congregational leadership is a distinctive characteristic of the synod. Power is vested in voters' assemblies, generally comprised of adults of voting age. Synod decision making is given to the delegates at triennial national and district conventions, where the franchise is equally divided between lay and pastoral representatives.

### Headquarters

The Lutheran Church—Missouri Synod, International Center, 1333 S. Kirkwood Rd., St. Louis, MO 63122-7295

Media Contact, Manager, Public Affairs & Media Relations, Ms. Vicki Biggs, Tel. (314)996-1236

Managing Editor, Reporter, Mr. Joe Isenhower, Tel. (314)996-1231 Fax(314)996-1126

Email: infocenter@lcms.org

Website: www.lcms.org

### Officers

Pres., Dr. Gerald B. Kieschnick

1st Vice Pres., Dr. William R. Diekelman

2nd Vice Pres., Dr. Paul L. Maier, Kalamazoo, MI

3rd Vice Pres., Dr. Dean L. Nadasdy, Woodbury, MN

4th Vice Pres., Dr. Robert L. King, Jefferson City, MO

5th Vice Pres., Dr. David D. Buegler, Avon, OH

Sec., Dr. Raymond L. Hartwigm, St. Louis, MO, Tel. (314)995-9000

Treas., Mr. Thomas Kuchta, St. Louis, MO, Tel. (314)995-9000

Chief Admn. Officer, Ronald Schultz, St. Louis, MO, Tel. (314)995-9000

Legal Counselor, Sherri Strand, Thompson Coburn, LLP, 1 US Bank Plaza, St. Louis, MO, Tel. (314)995-9000

### BOARD OF DIRECTORS

Rev. Edward Balfour, Cape Elizabeth, Me.; Rev. Victor T. Belton, Decatur, Ga.; Dr. Betty Duda, Cocoa Beach, Fla.; Rev. James E. Fandrey, Elgin, Ill.; Elizabeth Fluegel, Alexandria, Va.; Dr. Jean Garton, Benton, Ark.; Dr. Rev. Raymond L. Hartwig, St. Louis, Mo.; David Hawk, Ft. Wayne, Ind.; Dr. Robert T. Kuhn, Oviedo, Fla.; Christan A. Preus, Plymouth, Minn.; Walter F. Tesch, Milwaukee, Wisc.; Dr. Edwin A. Trapp, Jr., Dallas, Texas

### BOARDS AND COMMISSIONS

Black Ministry Services, Exec. Dir., Dr. Phillip Campbell Communication Services, Exec. Dir., David Strand

Ministerial Growth and Support, Exec. Dir., Rev. David Meunch Pastoral Education, Exec. Dir., Dr. L. Dean Hempelmann Mission Services, Exec. Dir., Rev. Robert Roegner

University Education, Exec. Dir., Dr. Kurt Kreuger

World Relief & Human Care Ministries, Exec. Dir., Rev. Matthew Harrison

District and Congregational Services, Exec. Dir., Dr. Jeffery Schubert

Worship, Exec. Dir., Dr. Paul Grime

Theology and Church Relations, Exec. Dir., Dr. Samuel Nafzger

### RELATED ORGANIZATIONS

Concordia Plan Services, Pres. Paul W. Middeke

Lutheran Church—Missouri Synod Foundation, Pres., Rev. Thomas Ries

Lutheran Church Extension Fund, Pres., Dr. Merle Freitag

Concordia Publishing House, Interim Pres., Rev. Paul McCain, 3558 S. Jefferson Ave., St. Louis, MO 63118-3968, Tel. (314)268-1000

Concordia Historical Institute, Dir., Dr. Martin Noland, 801 DeMun Ave., St. Louis, MO 63105, Tel. (314)505-7900

Lutheran Hour Ministries, Exec. Dir., Greg E. Lewis, 660 Mason Ridge Ctr. Dr., St. Louis, MO, 63141, Tel. (314)317-4291

Intl. Lutheran Women's Missionary League, Pres., Linda Reiser, 3558 S. Jefferson Ave., St. Louis, MO 63118-3910, Tel. (314)268-1532

KFUO Radio, Dir., Rev. Dennis Stortz, One Founders Lane, Clayton, MO 63105, Tel, (314)725-3030

### Periodicals

*The Lutheran Witness* (Magazine), Web: www.lcms.org/witness; *Reporter* (Newspaper), Website: www.reporter.lcms.org

## Malankara Orthodox Syrian Church, Diocese of America*

Malankara (Indian) Orthodox Church is an ancient Church of India, and it traces its origin to as far back as A. D. 52 when St. Thomas one of the Disciples of Jesus Christ came to India and established Christianity in the southwestern parts of the subcontinent.

The St. Thomas Christians or the Syrian Christians exist at present in different churches and denominations. But a major section of the parent body of St. Thomas Christians which has maintained its independent nature constitute the Orthodox Church under the Catholicos of the East and Malankara Metropolitan, whose seat is at Devalokam, Kottayam, Kerala, India. The church has dioceses and churches in most parts of India as well as in the United States, Canada, United Kingdom, Western Europe, Persian Gulf nations, South Africa, Malaysia, Singapore, Australia, and New Zealand. The official title of the head of the Church is the "Catholicos of the East, Catholicos of the Apostolic throne of St. Thomas and the Malankara Metropolitan". The present Catholicos of the East and Malankara Metropolitan is H.H. Mar Baselios Mar Thoma Didymos I.

The church, though modern in its vision and outlook, keeps the traditional Orthodox faith and liturgy. It accepts the first three Ecumenical Synods. The liturgy now in use is the translation of the liturgy adopted from the Antiochian church in the 17th century. However, the liturgical rites are uniquely Indian. Today the church uses liturgy in Malayalam, Syriac, Hindi, and English.

The Indian Orthodox community inherited many aspects of Indian civilization and they are as any other member of any other community in India, in their customs, manners, and lifestyle. The church has a theological seminary at Kottayam, Kerala, which was established in A.D. 1815. Another seminary is situated in Nagpur, Maharashtra. The latter was established fairly recently in the later part of the 20th century.

### Headquarters
Indian Orthodox Church Center, 80-34 Commonwealth Boulevard, Bellerose, NY 11426, Tel. (718)470-9844 Fax (718)470-9219
Media Contact, His Grace Mathews Mar Barnabas, Diocesan Metropolitan
Email: Malankara@malankara.org
Website: www.malankara.org/american

### Officers
Diocesan Metropolitan, His Grace Mathews Mar Barnabas
Assistant Metropolitan: His Grace Zachariah Mar Nicholovos
Diocesan Sec., The Rev. Fr. K.G. Philipose
Orthodox Center Manager: The Rev. Dr. P.C. Thomas
Public Relations Director: The Very Rev. Dr. P. S. Samuel Cor Episcopos

### Periodicals
*Diocesan Voice: A quarterly publication of the Diocese; Family and Youth Conference Souvenir:* (An annual publication of the F & Y Conference of the Diocese)

## Mar Thoma Syrian Church of India*
According to tradition, the Mar Thoma Church was established as a result of the apostolic mission of St. Thomas, the apostle in 52 A.D. Church history attests to the continuity of the community of faithful, throughout the long centuries in India. The liturgy and faith practices of the church were based on the relationship between the church in Kerala, India, which St. Thomas founded, with the East-Syrian and Persian Churches. This started in the 3rd century and continued up to the 16th century. In the 17th century, the Malabar Church of St. Thomas (as the church in Kerala was known) renewed her relationship with the Orthodox Patriarchate of Antioch as part of the resistance to forced Latinization by the Portuguese. This process also led to the development of the Kerala Episcopacy, whereby the first Indian Bishop Mar Thoma I was consecrated in Kerala.

The Mar Thoma Church retains her Eastern Orthodoxy. She follows an Orthodox worship form and liturgy, believes in the catholicity of grace, is missionary and evangelistic in approach. She derives Episcopal succession from the Syrian Orthodox Church of Antioch and follows Eastern Reformed Theology. She is independent, autonomous, and indigenous, constitutionally combining democratic values and Episcopal authority. She has been in full communion with the Anglican Church since 1954.

The Mar Thoma Church has been dynamically involved in the socio-cultural settings of North America and Europe for the past 30 years. Fundamentally an immigrant church, she has contextualized her ministry in her new life situation without compromising the rich ethos and tradition received from her motherland of Kerala, India. Currently, under the rubric of the Diocese, there are 51 parishes and 20 congregations. In order to cater to the ministerial needs of the Diocese, there are 48 clergy as well as functioning organizations for children, youth, women, and evangelistic work. The diocese is presided over by the Diocesan Bishop, The Rt. Rev. Dr. Euyakim Mar Coorilos, Episcopa.

The history of the Mar Thoma Church in the North American and European continent represents the dreams and aspirations of the faithful members of the Church. Commencing as a small prayer group in Queens, New York, in 1972, the first approved parish was recognized in New York in 1976. The churches in North America and United Kingdom have become constituents of the newly formed "Diocese of North America and United Kingdom." The Headquarters has subsequently moved to its current location at 2320 South Merrick Avenue, Merrick, N.Y.

### Headquarters
Sinai Mar Thoma Center, 2320 S. Merrick Avenue, Merrick, New York 11566, Tel. (516) 377-3311 Fax (516)377-3322
Email: webmaster@marthomachurch.org
Website: www.marthomanae.org

### Officers
Diocesan Bishop, The Rt. Rev. Dr. Euyakim Mar Coorilos
Diocesan Bishop's Sec., Rev. Joseph Oommen
Diocesan Treasurer, Dr. T.A. Mathew

### Periodicals
*Mar Thoma Messenger*

**Mennonite Brethren Churches—please see General Conference of Mennonite Brethren Churches**

**Mennonite Church of God in Christ—please see Church of God in Christ, Mennonite**

## Mennonite Church U.S.A.
Mennonite Church U.S.A., with 109,000 members, is one of several denominations that trace their beginnings to the Protestant Reformation in the early 1500s. Mennonites hold common core beliefs with other Christian denominations, but they live out God's call in

some ways that make them distinct. Mennonites believe in giving ultimate loyalty to God rather than to the nations in which they live. They believe that Jesus revealed a way for people to live peacefully and nonviolently, and they seek to be peacemakers in everyday life.

Mennonite Church U.S.A. is committed to sharing its faith and passion for Jesus with others and is open to anyone who confesses Jesus Christ as Lord and Savior and wants to live as Jesus taught.

The vision statement of Mennonite Church U.S.A. reads, "God calls us to be followers of Jesus Christ and, by the power of the Holy Spirit, to grow as communities of grace, joy, and peace, so that God's healing and hope flow through us to the world."

Mennonite Church U.S.A.—its congregations, area conferences, executive board, ministry offices and churchwide agencies—focuses on four priorities as it seeks to nurture missional congregations that join in God's activity in the world:

1. In our holistic witness we practice and proclaim the gospel of Jesus Christ through a seamless web of evangelism, justice, and peacebuilding.

2. We create a culture of call by calling, training anf nurturing new leaders.

3. We honor the dignity and value of all people, regardless of their race or ethnicity and denounce racist behavior.

4. We build global connections by fostering and developing partnerships with the broader body of Christ around the world. Mennonite Church U.S.A. lists as its strengths a high level of integrity recognized in both society and the religious community; high church attendance (90% of members attend church regularly); expanded global awareness through exposure to other world cultures; strong commitment to nonviolence and use of conflict resolution skills; above average giving to the work of the church; a natural communitarian impulse demonstrated by an emphasis on congregational relationships and mutual accountabilities; strong support of volunteer efforts, relief and service activities; and a holistic theology that holds word and deed together.

### Headquarters

Great Plains Office: 722 Main St., P.O. Box 347, Newton, KS 67114, Tel. (316)283-5100 Fax (316)283-0454, Email: info@mennoniteusa .org, Website: www.MennoniteUSA.org, toll free phone number for churchwide agencies, Tel. (866)866-2872

Great Lakes Office: 500 S. Main St., P.O. Box 1245, Elkhart, IN 46515-1245, Tel. (574)294-7523 Fax(574)293-1892, Email: info@mennoniteusa.org, Website: www.MennoniteUSA .org, toll free phone number for churchwide agencies, Tel. (866) 866-2872

Media contact, Laura Lee Williard, Communications Director, Tel. (316)283-5100 x 241, Email: lauraleew@mennoniteusa.org

Email: info@MennoniteUSA.org

Website: www.MennoniteChurchUSA.org

### Officers

Moderator, Roy Williams, 22642 Newfield Ct., Land O'Lakes FL 34639, Tel. (813)966-4244, Email: rrrsjw@aol.com

Moderator Elect, Sharon Waltner, 28142 448th Avenue, Parker SD 57053, Tel. (605)648-3224, Email: sharonw@mennoniteusa.org

Executive Director, James M. Schrag, 722 Main St., P.O. Box 347, Newton, KS 67114, Tel. (316)283-5100, Email: jims@mennoniteusa .org

Associate Executive Director, J. Ron Byler, 500 S. Main St., P.O. Box 1245, Elkhart, IN 46515, Tel. (574)523-3040, Email: ronb@mennoniteusa.org

Mennonite Education Agency, Executive Director, Carlos Romero, 63846 County Road, 35 Ste. 1, Goshen, IN 46528-9621, Tel. (574) 642-3164 Fax (574)642-4863, Email: carlosr @mennoniteeducation.org

Mennonite Mission Network, Executive Director, Stanley Green, 500 S Main Box 370, Elkhart, IN 46515-0370, Tel. (574)294-7523, Email: stanleyg@mennonitemission.net

Mennonite Mutual Aid, President, Howard Brenneman, P.O. Box 486, Goshen, IN 46527, Tel. (219)533-9511, Email: howard.brenneman@mma-online.org

Mennonite Publishing Network, Executive Director, Ron Rempel, 616 Walnut Ave., Scottdale, PA 15683, Tel. (724)887-8500, Email: rrempel@mph.org

### Periodicals

*The Mennonite; Leader, Rejoice!; Mennonite Historical Bulletin; Mennonite Quarterly Review; On the Line; Purpose; Story Friends; WITH*

**Methodist Church—please see The United Methodist Church**

**Methodist Church, Evangelical—please see Evangelical Methodist Church**

**Methodist Church, Fundamental—please see Fundamental Methodist Church, Inc.**

## The Missionary Church

The Missionary Church was formed in 1969 through a merger of the United Missionary Church (organized in 1883) and the Missionary Church Association (founded in 1898). It is evangelical and conservative with a strong emphasis on missionary work and church multiplication.

There are three levels of church government with local, district and general conferences. There are 11 church districts in the United States. The general conference meets every two years. The denomination operates one college [Bethel College, Mishawaka, Ind.] in the United States.

## Headquarters

3811 Vanguard Dr., P.O. Box 9127, Ft. Wayne, IN 46899-9127, Tel. (260)747-2027 Fax (260)747-5331

Media Contact, Pres., Rev. William Hossler
Email: ronphipps@mcusa.org
Website: www.mcusa.org

## Officers

Pres., Rev. William Hossler
Vice Pres., Rev. Joel DeSelm
Sec., Rev. Dave Engbrecht
Treas., Darrel Schlabach
Director of U.S. Ministries, Rev. Robert Ransom
Director of World Partners U.S.A., Rev. David Mann
Healthy Church Initiatives Coordinator, Dr. Dan Riemenschneider
Servant Leadership Coordinator, Rev. Greg Getz
Support Ministries Coordinator, Rev. Ron Phipps
Pastoral Leadership Institute Director, Rev. Greg Getz
Director of Development/Communications, Dr. Tom Murphy
Dir. of Ad. Services, Eric Smith
Director of Financial Services, Neil Rinehart
Coordinator of Church Multiplication, Rev. Jeff Getz
Coordinator of Ethnic Ministries, Rev. Jose Manuel Mendez
Missionary Men Liaison, Rev. Ron Phipps
Missionary Women Intl., Pres., Charlotte Beals
Missionary Church Investment Foundation, Mr. Eric Smith

## Periodicals

*Missionary Church Today*

## Moravian Church in America (Unitas Fratrum)*

In 1735 German Moravian missionaries of the pre-Reformation faith of Jan Hus came to Georgia, in 1740 to Pennsylvania, and in 1753 to North Carolina. They established the American Moravian Church, which is broadly evangelical, ecumenical, liturgical, "conferential" in form of government and has an episcopacy as a spiritual office. The Northern and Southern Provinces of the church operate on a semi-autonomous basis.

## Headquarters

Denominational offices or headquarters are called the Provincial Elders' Conference.
See addresses for Northern and Southern Provinces,
Website. www.moravian.org (for Moravian Church, Northern and Southern Provinces)

## NORTHERN PROVINCE HEADQUARTERS

1021 Center St., P.O. Box 1245, Bethlehem, PA 18016-1245, Tel. (610)867-7566 Fax (610) 866-9223
Media Contact, Ms. Deanna Hollenbach

## PROVINCIAL ELDERS' CONFERENCE

Pres., Rev. David L. Wickmann, Email: dave @mcnp.org
Vice Pres./Sec. Rev. Gary Straughan, Email: gary@mcnp.org
Vice Pres. Rev. Lawrence Christianson, Email: christlr@aol.com
Other Members: Nancy Baldwin; Paul DeTilla; Glenn Hertzog; Stephen Gohdes; Carol Messina
Comptroller, Theresa E. Kunda, 1021 Center St., P.O. Box 1245, Bethlehem, PA 18016-1245, Email: theresa@mcnp.org

## NORTHERN PROVINCE

1021 Center St., P.O. Box 1245, Bethlehem, PA 18016-1245, Tel. (610)867-7566 Fax (610) 866-9223
Northern Province Pres., Rev. David L. Wickmann, P.O. Box 1245, Bethlehem, PA 18016-1245, Email: dave@mcnp.org
Eastern District Pres., Rev. Gary Straughan P.O. Box 1245, Bethlehem, PA 18016-1245, Email: gary@mcnp.org
Western District Pres., Rev. Lawrence Christianson, P.O. Box 386, Sun Prairie, WI 53590, Email: christlr @aol.com
Canadian District Pres., Rev. Stephen Gohdes, 600 Arcadia Dr. SE, Calgary, AB T2J 0B8, Email: sgohdes@shaw.ca

## SOUTHERN PROVINCE HEADQUARTERS

459 S. Church St., Winston-Salem, NC 27101 Winston-Salem, NC 27108, Tel. (336)725-5811 Fax (336)723-1029 Email: rsawyer@ mcsp.org

## PROVINCIAL ELDERS' CONFERENCE

Pres., Rt. Rev.Wayne Burkette
Vice President, Betsy Bombick
Sec.—vacant
Treas.,—vacant
Other Members, Ms. Donna Hurt; Rev. Tom Shelton; Rev. Richard Sides
Asst. to Pres., Robert Hunter, Email: rhunter@ mcsp.org

## ALASKA PROVINCE

P.O. Box 545, 361 3rd Ave., Bethel, AK 99559

## PROVINCIAL ELDERS' CONFERENCE

Pres., Rev.Peter Green
Vice Pres., Frank Matthew, Sr.
Sec., Moses Owen
Treas., Arthur Sharp
Dir. of Theological Education, Ray Caldwell
Email: gloria@mcnp.org, wburkette@mcsp.org
Website: www.moravian.org

## Periodicals

*The Moravian*

**Mormons—please see The Church of Jesus Christ of Latter-day Saints**

## National Association of Congregational Christian Churches

This association was organized in 1955 in

Detroit, Mich., by delegates from Congre-gational Christian churches committed to continuing the Congregational way of faith and order in church life. Participation by member churches is voluntary.

### Headquarters

P.O. Box 288, Oak Creek, WI 53154, Tel. (414) 764-1620 Fax (414)764-0319

Media Contact, Assoc. Exec. Sec., Rev. Dr. Donald P. Olsen, 8473 So. Howell Ave., Oak Creek, WI 53154, Tel. (414)764-1620 Fax (414)764-0319

Email: naccc@naccc.org

Website: www.naccc.org

### Officers

Exec. Sec., Rev. Dr. Thomas M. Richard, 8473 South Howell Ave., Oak Creek, WI 53154

Assoc. Exec. Secs., Rev. Phil Jackson and Rev. Dr. Donald P. Olsen

### Periodicals

*The Congregationalist*

## National Association of Free Will Baptists

This evangelical group of Armenian Baptists was organized by Paul Palmer in 1727 at Chowan, N.C. Another movement (teaching the same doctrines of free grace, free salvation and free will) was organized June 30, 1780, in New Durham, N.H., but there was no connection with the southern organization except for a fraternal relationship.

The northern line expanded more rapidly and extended into the West and Southwest. This body merged with the Northern Baptist Convention Oct. 5, 1911, but a remnant of churches reorganized into the Cooperative General Association of Free Will Baptists Dec. 28, 1916, at Pattonsburg, Mo.

Churches in the southern line were organized into various conferences from the beginning and finally united in one General Conference in 1921.

Representatives of the Cooperative General Association and the General Conference joined Nov. 5, 1935 to form the National Association of Free Will Baptists.

### Headquarters

5233 Mt. View Rd., Antioch, TN 37013-2306, Tel. (615)731-6812 Fax (615)731-0771

Mailing Address, P.O. Box 5002, Antioch, TN 37011-5002

Media Contact, Exec. Sec., Keith Burden

Email: webmaster@nafwb.org

Website: www.nafwb.org

### Officers

Exec. Sec.,Keith Burden

Mod., Tim York, 2204 Foster Ave., Nashville, TN 37010

### DENOMINATIONAL AGENCIES

Free Will Baptist Foundation, Exec. Dir., William Evans

Free Will Baptist Bible College, Pres., Mathew Pinson

Foreign Missions Dept., Dir., Rev. James Forlines

Home Missions Dept., Dir., Rev. Larry Powell

Bd. of Retirement, Dir., Rev. D. Ray Lewis

Historical Commission, Chpsn., Dr. Darrell Holley, 3606 West End Avenue, Nashville, TN 37205

Comm. for Theological Integrity, Chpsn., Rev. Leroy Forlines, 3606 West End Avenue, Nashville, TN 37205

Music Commission, Chpsn., Chris Truett, 1936 Banks School Road, Kinston, NC 28504

Media Comm., Chpsn., Rev. Mike Jones, P.O. Box 13266, Florence, SC 29504

Sunday School & Church Training Dept., Dir., Rev. Ron Hunter

Women Nationally Active for Christ, Exec. Sec., Majorie Workman

Master's Men Dept., Dir., Kenneth Akers

### Periodicals

*Co-Laborer*

## National Baptist Convention of America, Inc.*

The National Baptist Convention of America, Inc., was organized in 1880. Its mission is articulated through its history, constitution, articles of incorporation and bylaws. The Convention (corporate churches) has a mission statement with fourteen objectives including fostering unity throughout its membership and the world Christian community by proclaiming the gospel of Jesus Christ; validating and propagating the Baptist doctrine of faith and practice, and its distinctive principles throughout the world; and harnessing and encouraging the scholarly and Christian creative skills of its membership for Christian writing and publications.

### Headquarters

Liaison Officer, Dr. Richard A. Rollins, 777 S. R.L. Thornton Fwy., Ste. 205, Dallas, TX 75203, Tel. (214)946-8913 Fax (214)946-9619

Email: president@nbcamerica.net; djones@nbc america net

Website: www.nbcamerica.net

### Officers

Pres., Rev. Stephen J. Thurston, President, 1327 Pierre Ave., Shreveport, LA 71103, Tel. (773)224-5570 Fax (773)224-8200

Gen. Rec. Sec., Dr. Clarence C. Pennywell, 2016 Russell Rd., Shreveport, LA 71107

Corres. Sec., Rev. E. E. Stafford, 6614 South Western Ave., Los Angeles, CA 90047

Mrs. Donna Jones, Administrative Assistant, Tel. (800)543-4019 x 10 Fax (318)222-7512, Email: djones@nbcamerica.net

### Periodicals

*The Lantern*

# National Baptist Convention, U.S.A., Inc.*

The National Baptist Convention, one of the oldest African American organizations in the nation, traces its history back to 1895. It was formed as a consolidation of the Baptist Foreign Mission Convention (1880), Consolidated American Baptist Convention (1896), and the National Baptist Educational Convention (1882). Rev. W. H. Alpine of Alabama was the first president of the Baptist Foreign Mission Board, which later became the Baptist Foreign Mission Convention, U.S.A.

The constitution of the convention 1895 states: "Whereas, It is the sense of the Colored Baptists of the United States of America, convened in the city of Atlanta, Georgia, September 28, 1895 in the several organizations as "The Baptist Foreign mission Convention of the United States of America," hitherto engaged in mission work on the West Coast of Africa: and the 'National Baptist Convention' which has been engaged in mission work in the United States of America; and the 'National Baptist Educational Conven-tion,' which has sought to look after the educational interest that the interest of the way of the Kingdom of God requires that the several bodies above named should, and do now, unite in one body. Therefore, we do now agree to and adopt the following constitution:

This body shall become known and styled, The National Baptist Convention of the United States of America.

The object of this convention shall be "to do mission work in the United States of America, in Africa, and elsewhere and to foster the cause of education." Dr. L.M. Luke was elected the first Corresponding Secretary of the Foreign Board. In October, 1896 Rev. L.G. Jordan, pastor of the Union Baptist Church of Philadelphia was selected successor of Luke (*The Epoch of Negro Baptists and The Foreign Mission Board, NBC, U.S.A., Inc.* Dr. Edward A. Freeman, The Central Seminary Press 1953.)

In September 1915 at the annual meeting of the convention the constitution was revised with the following changes:

"The particular business and object of this Convention shall be to promote a growth and propagantion of religion, morality, and intelligence among the races of mankind, by engaging in missionary work in the United States of America, and elsewhere, by fostering the cause of education and publishing and circulating literature, and in providing the necessary ways and means for carrying on such work."

## Headquarters

1700 Baptist World Center Dr., Nashville, TN 37207, Tel. (615)228-6292 Fax (615)226-5935

## Officers

Pres., Dr. William J. Shaw, 1700 Baptist World Center Dr., Nashville, TN 37207, Tel. (615) 228-6292 Fax (615)226-5935

Gen. Sec., Dr. Harry Blake, Mt. Canaan Baptist Church, 1666 Alston St., Shreveport, LA 71101, Tel. (318)227-9993

## Periodicals

*Mission Herald*

# National Missionary Baptist Convention of America*

The National Missionary Baptist Convention of America was organized in 1988 as a separate entity from the National Baptist Convention of America, Inc., after a dispute over control of the convention's publishing efforts. The new organization intended to remain committed to the National Baptist Sunday Church School and Baptist Training Union Congress and the National Baptist Publishing Board.

The purpose of the National Missionary Baptist Convention of America is to serve as an agency of Christian education, church extension and missionary efforts. It seeks to maintain and safeguard full religious liberty and engage in social and economic development.

## Headquarters

4269 S. Figueroa St., Los Angeles, CA 90037, Tel. (323)846-1950 Fax (323)846-1964
Media Contact, Dr. Melvin Von Wade, Sr.
Email: gensec@jiacom.net
Website: www.nmbca.com

## Officers

Pres., Dr. C.C. Robertson, President, Dallas, Texas
Vice President-at-Large, Dr. Nehemiah Davis, Fort Worth, Texas
Vice Pres., Ecumenical Affairs, Dr. L.C. Firle Collins, Miss.
Vice Pres., Auxiliaries, Dr. Bernard Black, Phoenix, Ariz.
Vice Pres., Boards, Dr. A. Charles Bowie, Cleveland, Ohio
Vice Pres., Financial Affairs, Dr. Ray W. Williams, Oakland, Calif.
Pres., National Baptist Publishing Bd., Dr. T. B. Boyd, III, 6717 Centennial Blvd., Nashville, TN 37209
Gen. Sec., Dr. A. Wayne Johnson, 106 NE Ivy St., Portland, OR 97212, Tel. (503)281-4925 Fax (503)281-6520, Email: gensec@jiacom. net
Corres. Sec., Dr. Walter Houston, Houston, TX
Treas., Dr. William R. Lott, Chicago, IL
Rec. Sec., Dr. T.L. Brown, Dallas, TX

# National Organization of the New Apostolic Church of North America

The New Apostolic Church of North America claims common origin with the Catholic Apostolic movement in England, which began with the calling of an apostle in 1832. The New Apostolic Church distinguished itself from the parent body in 1863 by recognizing a succession of Apostles.

## Headquarters

3753 N. Troy St., Chicago, IL 60618
Media Contact, Sec. & Treas., Ellen E. Eckhardt,
Tel. (773)539-3652 Fax (773)478-6691
Email: info@nak.org
Website: www.nak.org

## Officers

Pres., Rev. Rev. Richard C. Freund, 404 Glen
Cone Ave., Sea Cliff, NY 11579
Vice Pres., Rev. John W. Fendt, Jr., 2 Willets Ln.,
Plandome, NY 11030-1023
Vice Pres., Rev. Leonard R. Kolb, 5250
Robinhood Ln., Erle, PA 16509-2563
Treas. And Sec., Ellen E. Eckhardt, 6380 N.
Indian Rd., Chicago, IL 60646

## Periodicals

*Our Family*

# National Primitive Baptist Convention, Inc.

Throughout the years of slavery and the Civil
War, the Negro population of the South wor-
shipped with the white population in their various churches. At the time of emancipation, their
white brethren helped them establish their own
churches, granting them letters of fellowship,
ordaining their deacons and ministers and helping them in other ways.

The doctrine and polity of this body are quite
similar to that of white Primitive Baptists, yet
there are local associations and a national convention, organized in 1907.

Each church is independent and receives and
controls its own membership. This body was formerly known as Colored Primitive Baptists.

## Headquarters

6433 Hidden Forest Dr., Charlotte, NC 28213,
Tel. (704)596-1508
Media Contact, Elder T. W. Samuels

## Officers

Natl. Convention, Pres., President—Elder Ernest
Ferrell, Tallahassee, Fla.
Natl. Convention, Vice Pres., Elder Bernard
Yates, Pensacola, Fla.
Natl. Convention, Secretary, Elder W. J.
Williams, Tampa, Fla
Natl. Church School Training Union, Pres., Dr.
Jonathan Yates, Mobile, Ala.
Natl. Ushers Congress, Pres., Dea. Carl Batts,
21213 Garden View Dr., Maple Heights, Oh
44137
Publishing Bd., Chpsn., Elder John R. Cox,
Birmingham, Ala.
Women's Congress, Pres., Mother Ann Cartes,
Dallas, Texas
Natl. Laymen's Council, Pres., Dea. Densimore
Robinson, Huntsville, Ala.
Natl. Youth Congress, Pres., Minister Jacques
Mood, Concord, NC

# National Spiritualist Association of Churches

This organization is made up of believers
that Spiritualism is a science, philosophy, and
religion based upon the demonstrated facts of
communication between this world and the next.

## Headquarters

NSAC General Offices, Rev. Sharon L.
Snowman, Secretary, P.O. Box 217, Lily Dale,
NY 14752-0217
Media Contact, Rev. Lelia Cutler, 7310 Midfield
St. #1, Norfolk, VA 23505-4126
Email: nsac@nsac.org
Website: www.nsac.org

## Officers

Pres., Rev. Lelia Cutler, 7310 Midfield St. #1,
Norfolk, VA 23505-4126
Vice Pres., Rev. Catherine Snell 23 Pleasant St.
Windham, NH 03087
Sec., Rev. Sharon L. Snowman, P.O. Box 217,
Lily Dale, NY 14752, Tel. (716)595-2000 Fax
(716)595-2020
Treas., Peter Berg, 20916 Bellerive Dr., Pflugerville,
TX 78660

## OTHER ORGANIZATIONS

Department of Education, Rev. Barbara Starr,
Director, 4245 Woodmont Road, Great
Cacapon, WV 25422
Department of Lyceums, Rev. Arsenia Williams,
Director, 10913 S. Parnell, Chicago, IL 60628
Department of Missionaries, Rev. E. Ann
Otzelberger, Director, 4332 Woodlynne Lane,
Orlando, FL 32812-7562
Department of Phenomenal Evidence, Revs. Lisa
and Thomas Butler, Directors, 3415 Socrates
Drive, Reno, NV 89512
Department of Public Relations, Mary
Montgomery Clifford, Director, 2426 North
Kimball Street, Chicago, IL 60647
Department of Publications, John Rothamel, Jr.,
Director, 7851 Foxfarm Lane, Glen Burnie,
MD 21061-6324
NSAC Healing Center, Rev. Kathleen Rottino,
President, 74 Scenic Dr., Lebanon, CT 06249
NSAC Minsterial Association, Rev. Barbara Star,
NST, Pres., 4245 Woodmont Road, Great
Cacapon, WV 25422
National Spiritualist Teachers Club, Rev. E. Ann
Otzelberger, NST, Pres., 4332 Woodlynne
Lane, Orlando, FL 32812
Spiritualist Healers League, Rev. E.
Annotzelberger, NST President
Licentiate Ministers & Certified Mediums
Society, Rev. Janet Tisdale, NST, Pres., 1616
N. Alta Mesa Drive #51, Mesa, AZ 85205
The Stow Memorial Foundation, Sec., Rev.
Sharon L. Snowman, P.O. Box 217, Lily Dale,
NY 14752, Tel. (716)595-2000 Fax (716)595-
2020
Spiritualist Benevolent Society, Inc., P.O. Box
217, Lily Dale, NY 14752

**Periodicals**
*The National Spiritualist* (Monthly) *Spotlight—* (children's magazine)

## Netherlands Reformed Congregations

The Netherlands Reformed Congregations organized denominationally in 1907. In the Netherlands, the so-called Churches Under the Cross (established in 1839, after breaking away from the 1834 Secession congregations) and the so-called Ledeboerian churches (established in 1841 under the leadership of the Rev. Ledeboer, who seceded from the Reformed State Church), united in 1907 under the leadership of the then 25-year-old Rev. G. H. Kersten, to form the Netherlands Reformed Congregations. Many of the North American congregations left the Christian Reformed Church to join the Netherlands Reformed Congregations after the Kuyperian presupposed regeneration doctrine began making inroads.

All Netherlands Reformed Congregations, office-bearers and members subscribe to three Reformed Forms of Unity, The Belgic Confession of Faith (by DeBres), the Heidelberg Catechism (by Ursinus and Olevianus) and the Canons of Dort. The Heidelberg Catechism is preached weekly, except on church feast days.

### Headquarters

Media Contact, Rev. A.H.Verhoef, 1142 Lakeshore Rd. W, RR#3, St. Catherines, ON L2R 6P9 CANADA Tel. (905)935-4934

### OTHER ORGANIZATIONS

Netherlands Reformed Book and Publishing, 1233 Leffingwell NE, Grand Rapids, MI 49505

### Periodicals

*The Banner of Truth; Paul* (mission magazine); *Insight Into* (for young people); *Learning and Living* (for school and home)

**New Church—please see General Church of the New Jerusalem**

## North American Baptist Conference

The North American Baptist Conference was begun by immigrants from Germany. The first church was organized by the Rev. Konrad Fleischmann in Philadelphia in 1843. In 1865 delegates of the churches met in Wilmot, Ontario, and organized the North American Baptist Conference. Today only a few churches still use the German language, mostly in a bilingual setting.

The Conference meets in general session once every three years for fellowship, inspiration and to conduct the business of the Conference through elected delegates from the local churches. The General Council, composed of representatives of the various Associations and Conference organizations and departments, meets annually to determine the annual budget and programs for the Conference and its departments and agencies. The General Council also makes recommendations to the Triennial Conference on policies, long-range plans and election of certain personnel, boards and committees.

Approximately 60 missionaries serve in Brazil, Cameroon, Japan, Mexico, Nigeria, Philippines, and Russia.

Eight homes for the aged are affiliated with the Conference and 11 camps are operated on the association level.

### Headquarters

1 S. 210 Summit Ave., Oakbrook Terrace, IL 60181, Tel. (630)495-2000 Fax (630)495-3301
Media Contact, Marlene Minor, Senior Leader/Stewardship and Communications
Email: serve@nabconf.org
Website: www.nabconference.org

### Officers

Exec. Dir., Rev. Ron Berg, 1 So 210 Summit Ave., Oakbrook Terrace, IL 60181, Tel. (630)495-2000 Fax (630)475-3301, Email: RBerg@nabconf.org

### OTHER ORGANIZATIONS

Church Extension Investors Fund, Dir., Les D. Collins

### Periodicals

*NABtoday*

## North American Old Roman Catholic Church (Archdiocese of New York)

This body is identical with the Roman Catholic Church in faith but differs from it in discipline and worship. The Mass is offered with the appropriate rite either in Latin or in the vernacular. All other sacraments are taken from the Roman Pontifical. This jurisdiction allows for married clergy.

### PRIMATIAL HEADQUARTERS

60 ST. Felix St., Brooklyn, NY 11217-1206, Tel. (718)855-0600, Fax (718)522-1231
Media Contact, Primate, Most Rev. Albert J. Berube
Email: info@orccna.org
Website: www.orccna.org

### Officers

Primate, The Most Rev. Albert J. Berube
Diocese of New York, Ordinary, Most Rev. Albert J. Berube
Diocese of Montreal & French Canada, Ordinary, Most Rev. Herve L. Quessy

## The Old Catholic Orthodox Church

The Old Catholic Orthodox Church (formerly, the Apostolic Orthodox Old Catholic Church) was founded in Illinois in the year 1985, originally as a Spanish-speaking community of faith. It has now grown to include English-speaking and other international provinces. We subscribe to the Apostles', Nicene and Athanasian Creeds as matters of faith, along with upholding all sacraments of the One, Holy, Catholic and Apostolic Church.

### Headquarters

The Most Reverend Jorge Rodriguez-Villa, Apostolic Primate (Presiding Bishop), P.O. Box 80193, Rancho Santa Margarita, CA 92688, Tel. (323)806-4045
Website: www.oldcatholicorthodoxchurch.org

### Officers

The Most Reverend Jorge Rodriguez-Villa, Apostolic Primate (Presiding Bishop)
The Most Rev. William Anthony Harrison, Apostolic Vicar General

## Old German Baptist Brethren Church

This group separated from the Church of the Brethren (formerly German Baptist Brethren) in 1881 in order to preserve and maintain historic Brethren Doctrine.

### Headquarters

Vindicator Ofc. Ed., Steven L. Bayer, 6952 N. Montgomery County Line Rd., Englewood, OH 45322-9748, Tel. (937)884-7531

### Periodicals

*The Vindicator*

## Old Order Amish Church

The congregations of this Old Order Amish group have no annual conference. They worship in private homes. They adhere to the older forms of worship and attire. This body has bishops, ministers and deacons.

### Headquarters

Der Neue Amerikanische Calendar, c/o Raber's Book Store, 2467 C R 600, Baltic, OH 43804, LeRoy Beachy, Beachy Amish Mennonite Church, 4324 SR 39, Millerburg, OH 44654, Tel. & fax (330)893-2883

## Old Order (Wisler) Mennonite Church

This body arose from a separation of Mennonites dated 1872, under Jacob Wisler, in opposition to what were thought to be innovations.

The group is in the Eastern United States and Canada. Each state, or district, has its own organization and holds semi-annual conferences.

### Headquarters

Media Contact, Amos B. Hoover, 376 N. Muddy Creek Rd., Denver, PA 17517, Tel. (717)484-4849 Fax (717)484-104

### Periodicals

*Home Messenger, Exchange Messenger*

## Open Bible Standard Churches

Open Bible Standard Churches originated from two revival movements, Bible Standard Conference, founded in Eugene, Ore., under the leadership of Fred L. Hornshuh in 1919, and Open Bible Evangelistic Association, founded in Des Moines, Iowa, under the leadership of John R. Richey in 1932.

Similar in doctrine and government, the two groups amalgamated on July 26, 1935 as "Open Bible Standard Churches, Inc." with headquarters in Des Moines, Iowa.

The original group of 210 ministers has enlarged to incorporate over 2,500 ministers and 1,509 churches in 40 countries. The first missionary left for India in 1926. The church now ministers in Asia, Africa, South America, Europe, Canada, Mexico, Central America, and the Caribbean Islands.

Historical roots of the parent groups reach back to the outpouring of the Holy Spirit in 1906 at Azusa Street Mission in Los Angeles and to the full gospel movement in the Midwest. Both groups were organized under the impetus of pentecostal revival. Simple faith, freedom from fanaticism, emphasis on evangelism and missions and free fellowship with other groups were characteristics of the growing organizations.

The highest governing body of Open Bible Standard Churches meets biennially and is composed of all ministers and one voting delegate per 100 members from each church. A National Board of Directors, elected by the national and regional conferences, conducts the business of the organization. Official Bible College is Eugene Bible College in Oregon.

Open Bible Standard Churches is a charter member of the National Association of Evangelicals and of the Pentecostal/Charismatic Churches of North America. It is a member of the Pentecostal World Conference.

### NATIONAL OFFICE

2020 Bell Ave., Des Moines, IA 50315, Tel. (515)288-6761 Fax (515)288-2510
Media Contact, Exec. Dir., Communications & Resources, Jeff Farmer, Tel. (515)288-6761 Fax (515)288-2510
Email: info@openbible.org
Website: www.openbible.org

### Officers

Pres., Jeffrey E. Farmer, 2020 Bell Ave., Des Moines, IA 50315, Tel. (515)288-6761 Fax (515)288-2510, jeff@openbible.org
Esq.,Sec.-Treas., Teresa A. Beyer, 2020 Bell Ave., Des Moines, IA 50315, Tel. (515)288-6761 Fax (515)288-2510, tbeyer@openbible. org
Dir., of Intl. Min., Paul V. Canfield, 2020 Bell Ave., Des Moines, IA 50315, Tel: 515-288-6761 Fax 515-288-2510, missions@openbible. org

### Periodicals

*Message of the Open Bible*

144

## The (Original) Church of God, Inc.

This body was organized in 1886 as the first church in the United States to take the name "The Church of God." In 1917 a difference of opinion led this particular group to include the word (Original) in its name. It is a holiness body and believes in the whole Bible, rightly divided, using the New Testament as its rule and government.

### Headquarters
P.O. Box 592, Wytheville, VA 24382
Media Contact, Gen. Overseer, Rev. William Dale, Tel. (800)827-9234

### Officers
Gen. Overseer, Rev. William Dale
Asst. Gen. Overseer, Rev. Alton Evans

## The Orthodox Church in America*

The Orthodox Church of America entered Alaska in 1794 before its purchase by the United States in 1867. Its canonical status of independence (autocephaly) was granted by its Mother Church, the Russian Orthodox Church, on April 10, 1970, and it is now known as The Orthodox Church in America.

### Headquarters
P.O. Box 675, Syosset, NY 11791-0675, Tel. (516)922-0550 Fax (516)922-0954
Media Contact, Dir. of Communications, V. Rev. John Matusiak, 1 Wheaton Center, # 912, IL 60187, Tel. (630)668-3071 Fax (708)923-1706
Email: jjm@oca.org
Website: www.oca.org

### HOLY SYNOD OF BISHOPS
### RULING BISHOPS
Primate, Archbishop of Washington & New York, Metropolitan of All America & Canada, His Beatitude, Most Blessed Herman, P.O. Box 675, Syosset, NY 11791
Archbishop of Pittsburgh & Western PA, Most Rev. Kyrill, P.O. Box R, Wexford, PA 15090
Archbishop of Dallas, Archbishop Dimitri, 4112 Throckmorton, Dallas, TX 75219
Archbishop of Detroit, Rt. Rev. Nathaniel, P.O. Box 309, Grass Lake, MI 49240-0309
Archbishop of Chicago, Rt. Rev. Job, 927 N. LaSalle, Chicago, IL 60610
Bishop of San Francisco and Los Angeles, Rt. Rev. Tikhon, 649 North Robinson St., Los Angeles, CA 90026
Bishop of Ottawa and Canada, Rt. Rev. Seraphim, P.O. Box 179, Spencerville, ON K0E 1X0, Tel. (613)925-5226
Bishop of Sitka, Anchorage, and Alaska, Rt. Rev. Nikolai, 513 E. 24 Ave. Ste. #3, Anchorage, AK 99503
Bishop of Boston, Rt. Rev. Nikon, P.O. Box 149, Southbridge, MA 01550, Tel. (508)764-3222
Bishop of Philadelphia and Eastern PA, Rt. Rev. Tikhon, P.O. Box 130, South Canaan, PA 18459

### AUXILIARY BISHOPS
Bishop of Dearborn Heights, Rt. Rev. Irineu, 23300 Davison Ave. West, Detroit, MI 48223
Bishop of Berkeley, Rt. Rev. Benjamin, 701 Park Place, Boulder City, NV 89005
Bishop of Mexico City, Rt. Rev. Alejo, Rio Consulado e Irapuato, Col. Penon de los banos, 15520 Mexico D.F.

### RETIRED BISHOPS
Retired Metropolitan, Most Blessed Theodosius, 156 Rifgon Drive, Canonsburg, PA 15317
Retired Archbishop, Most Rev. Gregory, P.O. Box 94, Jackson, NJ 08527-0094
Retired Archbishop, Most Rev. Lazar, 37323 Hawkins Pickle Rd., Dewdney, BC, Canada V0M 1H0
Retired Bishop, Rt. Rev. Mark, 9511 Sun Pointe Dr., Boynton Beach, FL 33437
Retired Bishop, Rt. Rev. Varlaam, 37323 Hawkins Pickle Rd., Dewdney, BC, Canada V0M 1H0

### OTHER ORGANIZATIONS
Alumni Association of St. Herman Seminary, 414 Mission Rd., Kodiak, AK 99615-9985
Alumni Association of St. Tikhon Seminary, South Canaan, PA 18459
Alumni Association of St. Vladimir Seminary, 575 Scarsdale Rd., Crestwood, NY 10707
Orthodox Peace Fellowship, P.O. Box 390838, Cambridge, MA 02139
Orthodox Theological Society of America, 50 Goddard Ave., Brookline, MA 02445
Association of Romanian Orthodox Ladies' Auxiliaries of America, P.O. Box 309, Grass Lake, MI 49240
Association of Romanian Canadian Orthodox Ladies' Auxiliaries, P.O. Box 4023, Regina, SK, Canada S4P 3R9
Fellowship of Orthodox Christians in America, 10 Downs Drive, Wilkes-Barre, PA 18705
Orthodox Brotherhood U.S.A., P.O. Box 309, Grass Lake, MI 49240
Orthodox Brotherhood of Canada, P.O. Box 4023, Regina, SK, Canada S4P 3R9
American Romanian Orthodox Youth, P.O. Box 309, Grass Lake, MI 49240
Project Mexico, P.O. Box 120028, Chula Vista, CA 91912
Orthodox Christian Adoption Referral Service, P.O. Box 675, Syosset, NY 11791
Fellowship of Orthodox Stewards, P.O. Box 675, Syosset, NY 11791
Orthodox Christian Publications Center, 4653 Memphis Villas South, Brooklyn, OH 44144

## The Orthodox Presbyterian Church

On June 11, 1936, certain ministers, elders and lay members of the Presbyterian Church in the U.S.A. withdrew from that body to form a new denomination. Under the leadership of the late Rev. J. Gresham Machen, noted conservative New Testament scholar, the new church deter-

145

mined to continue to uphold the Westminster Confession of Faith as traditionally understood by Presbyterians and to engage in proclamation of the gospel at home and abroad.

The church has grown modestly over the years and suffered early defections, most notably one in 1937 that resulted in the formation of the Bible Presbyterian Church under the leadership of Dr. Carl McIntire. It now has congregations throughout the states of the continental United States.

The denomination is a member of the North American Presbyterian and Reformed Council and the International Council of Reformed Churches.

### HEADQUARTERS

607 N. Easton Rd., Bldg. E, Box P, Willlow Grove, PA 19090-0920, Tel. (215)830-0900 Fax (215)830-0350

Media Contact, Stated Clerk, Rev. Donald J. Duff

EMail, duff.1@opc.org

Website, www.opc.org

### Officers

Moderator of General Assembly, The Rev. Richard R. Gerber, Box P, Willow Grove, PA 19090

Stated Clk., Rev. Donald J. Duff

### Periodicals

*New Horizons in the Orthodox Presbyterian Church*

## Patriarchal Parishes of the Russian Orthodox Church in the U.S.A.*

This group of parishes is under the direct jurisdiction of the Patriarch of Moscow and All Russia, His Holiness Aleksy II, in the person of a Vicar Bishop, His Grace Mercurius, Bishop of Zaraisk.

### Headquarters

St. Nicholas Cathedral, 15 E. 97th St., New York, NY 10029, Tel. (212)831-6294 Fax (212)427-5003

Media Contact, Sec. to the Bishop, Hieromonk Joseph, Tel. (212)996-6638

Email: bmercurius@ruscon.com

Website: www.russianchurchusa.org

### Officers

Secretary to the Bishop, Hieromonk Joseph; Secretary of the Representation, Rev. Alexander Abramov

## Pentecostal Assemblies of the World, Inc.

This organization is an interracial pentecostal holiness of the Apostolic Faith, believing in repentance, baptism in Jesus's name and being filled with the Holy Ghost, with the evidence of speaking in tongues. It originated in the early part of the century in the Middle West and has spread throughout the country.

### Headquarters

3939 Meadows Dr., Indianapolis, IN 46205, Tel. (317)547-9541 Fax (317)543-0513

Media Contact, Admin., John E. Hampton, Fax (317)543-0512

Website: www.pawinc.org

### Officers

Presiding Bishop, Horace E. Smith

Suff. Bishop, A. Glenn Brady, General Secretary, Youngstown, OH

Bishops, Arthus Brazier; George Brooks; Ramsey Butler; Morris Golder; Francis L. Smith, Francis L.; Brooker T. Jones; C. R. Lee; Robert McMurray; Philip L. Scott; William L. Smith; Samuel A. Layne; Freeman M. Thomas; James E. Tyson; Charles Davis; Willie Burrell; Harry Herman; Jeremiah Reed; Jeron Johnson; Clifton Jones; Robert Wauls; Ronald L. Young; Henry L. Johnson; Leodis Warren; Thomas J. Weeks; Eugene Redd; Thomas W. Weeks, Sr.; Willard Saunders; Davis L. Ellis; Earl Parchia; Vanuel C. Little; Norman Wagner; George Austin; Benjamin A. Pitt; Markose Thopil; John K. Cole; Peter Warkie; Norman Walters; Alphonso Scott; David Dawkins

Gen. Sec, Suffragan Bishop Edward Roberts

Assist. Gen Sec., Suffragan Bishop A. Glenn Brady

Gen. Treas., Suffragan Bishop Mark C. Tolbert

Asst. Treas., Suffragan Bishop Carl A. Turner

## Pentecostal Church of God

Growing out of the pentecostal revival at the turn of the 20th century, the Pentecostal Church of God was organized in Chicago on Dec. 30, 1919, as the Pentecostal Assemblies of the U.S.A. The name was changed to Pentecostal Church of God in 1922; in 1934 it was changed again to The Pentecostal Church of God of America, Inc.; and finally the name became the Pentecostal Church of God (Incorporated.) in 1979.

The International Headquarters was moved from Chicago, Ill. to Ottumwa, Iowa, in 1927, then to Kansas City, Mo., in 1933 and finally to Joplin, Mo., in 1951.

The denomination is evangelical and pentecostal in doctrine and practice. Active membership in the National Association of Evangelicals and the Pentecostal/Charismatic Churches North America is maintained.

The church is Trinitarian in doctrine and teaches the absolute inerrancy of the Scripture from Genesis to Revelation. Among its cardinal beliefs are the doctrines of salvation, which includes regeneration; divine healing, as provided for in the atonement; the baptism in the Holy Ghost, with the initial physical evidence of speaking in tongues; and the premillennial second coming of Christ.

### Headquarters

4901 Pennsylvania, P.O. Box 850, Joplin, MO 64802, Tel. (417)624-7050 Fax (417)624-7102

146

Media Contact, Gen. Sec., Dr. Charles G. Scott
Email: generalsecretary@pcg.org
Website: www.pcg.org

**Officers**

Gen. Bishop., Dr. Charles R. Mosier
Gen. Sec., Dr. Charles G. Scott

**OTHER GENERAL EXECUTIVES**

Dir. of World Missions, Rev. Loyd L. Naten
Dir. of Indian Missions, Dr. C. Don Burke
Dir. of Youth Ministries, Rev. Reggie O. Powers
Dir. of Home Missions, Rev. Harry O. "Pat" Wilson

**ASSISTANT GENERAL
SUPERINTENDENTS/BISHOPS**

Northwestern Division, Rev. Donald Johnson
Southwestern Division, Rev. Jan Lake
North Central Division, Rev. Wayman Ming, Jr.
South Central Division, Rev. Leon A. McDowell
Northeastern Division, Rev. Thomas E. Branham
Southeastern Division, Rev. C.W. Goforth

**OTHER DEPARTMENTAL OFFICERS**

Bus. Mgr., vacant
Director of Women's Ministry, Barbara Mosier
Discipleship Min., Dir., Billie L. Palumbo

**Periodicals**

*The Pentecostal Messenger*

# Pentecostal Fire-Baptized Holiness Church

Organized in 1918, this group consolidated with the Pentecostal Free Will Baptists in 1919. It maintains rigid discipline over members.

**Headquarters**

P.O. Box 261, La Grange, GA 30241-0261, Tel. (706)884-7742
Media Contact, Gen. Mod., Wallace B. Pittman, Jr.

**Officers**

Gen. Treas., Alan Sparkman, 1961 Norjon Circle, Clio, SC 29525, Tel. (843)586-9095
Gen. Sec., Joel Powell, 16841 Springs Mill Rd. Lauringbury, NC 28352, Tel. (901)462-3379
Gen. Mod., Wallace B. Pittman, Jr.
Gen. Supt. Mission Bd., Jerry Powell, Rt. 1, Box 384, Chadourn, NC 28431

# The Pentecostal Free Will Baptist Church, Inc.

The Cape Fear Conference of Free Will Baptists, organized in 1855, merged in 1959 with The Wilmington Conference and The New River Conference of Free Will Baptists and was renamed the Pentecostal Free Will Baptist Church, Inc. The doctrines include regeneration, sanctification, the Pentecostal baptism of the Holy Ghost, the Second Coming of Christ and divine healing.

**Headquarters**

P.O. Box 1568, Dunn, NC 28335, Tel. (910)892-4161 Fax (910)892-6876
Media Contact, Gen. Supt., Preston Heath

Email: pheath@intrstar.net
Website: www.pfwb.org

**Officers**

Gen. Supt., Rev. Preston Heath
Asst. Gen. Supt., Jim Wall
Gen. Sec., Mr. Stephen Garriss
Gen. Treas., Mr. Dewayne Weeks
Christian Ed. Dir., Rev. Randy Barker
World Witness Dir., Rev. Hobbs
Gen. Services Dir., Ms. Cathy Muzingo
Ministerial Council Dir., Rev. Ed Taturn
Ladies' Auxiliary Dir., Dollie Davis
Heritage Bible College, Pres., Dr. Dwarka Ramphal
Crusader Youth Camp, Dir., Rev. Randy Barker

**OTHER ORGANIZATIONS**

Heritage Bible College
Crusader Youth Camp
Blessings Bookstore, 1006 W. Cumberland St., Dunn, NC 28334, Tel. (910)892-2401

**Periodicals**

*The Messenger*

# Philadelphia Yearly Meeting of the Religious Society of Friends*

PYM traces its roots to the yearly meeting of 1681 in Burlington, New Jersey. For more than three centuries, PYM has served Monthly Meetings and Quarterly Meetings throughout eastern Pennsylvania, southern New Jersey, eastern Maryland and Delaware. In general, the activities of PYM are organized under five Standing Committees: Standing Committee on Worship and Care; Standing Committee on Education; Standing Committee on Peace and Concerns; Standing Committee on Support and Outreach; Standing Committee on General Services.

**Headquarters**

Philadelphia Yearly Meeting, 1515 Cherry Street, Philadelphia, PA 19102-1479, Tel. (215)241-7000 Fax (215)241-7045
Website: www.pym.org

**Officers**

Presiding Clerk, Thomas Swain
Clerk of Interim Meeting, Arthur Larrabee
Interim Gen. Sec., Mark Myers
Clerk, Standing Committee on Worship and Care, Alison A. Anderson
Clerk, Standing Committee on Education, Deborah Lyons
Clerk, Standing Committee on Peace and Concerns, Patricia Finley
Clerk, Standing Committee on Support and Outreach, Susan White & Pamela Carter
Clerk, Standing Committee on General Services, Patricia Hunt

**Periodicals**

*PYM News*

# Pillar of Fire

The Pillar of Fire was founded by Alma

Bridwell White in Denver on Dec. 29, 1901 as the Pentecostal Union. In 1917, the name was changed to Pillar of Fire. Alma White was born in Kentucky in 1862 and taught school in Montana, where she met her husband, Kent White, a Methodist minister, who was a university student in Denver.

Because of Alma White's evangelistic endeavors, she was frowned upon by her superiors, which eventually necessitated her withdrawing from Methodist Church supervision. She was ordained as Bishop and her work spread to many states, to England, and since her death to Liberia, West Africa, Malawi, East Africa, Yugoslavia, Spain, India and the Philippines.

The Pillar of Fire organization has a college and two seminaries stressing Biblical studies. It operates eight separate schools for young people. The church continues to keep in mind the founder's goals and purposes.

### Headquarters

P.O. Box 9159, Zarephath, NJ 08890, Tel. (732) 356-0102

Western Headquarters, 1302 Sherman St., Denver, CO 80203, Tel. (303)427-5462

Media Contact, 1st Vice Pres., Robert B. Dallenbach, 3455 W. 83 Ave., Westminster, CO 80031, Tel. (303)427-5462 Fax (303)429-0910

Email: info@zarephath.edu

Website: www.gospelcom.net/pof

### Officers

Pres. & Gen. Supt., Dr. Robert B. Dallenbach

1st Vice Pres. & Asst. Supt., Rev. Joseph Gross

2nd Vice Pres./Sec.-Treas., Lois R. Stewart

Trustees, Kenneth Cope; S. Rea Crawford; Lois Stewart; Dr. Donald J. Wolfram; Robert B. Dallenbach; Rob W. Cruver; Joseph Gross

## Polish National Catholic Church of America*

After a number of attempts to resolve differences regarding the role of the laity in parish administration in the Roman Catholic Church in Scranton, Pa., this church was organized in 1897. With the consecration to the episcopacy of the Most Rev. F. Hodur, this church became a member of the Old Catholic Union of Utrecht in 1907.

### Headquarters

Office of the Prime Bishop, 1006 Pittston Ave., Scranton, PA 18505, Tel. (570)346-9131

Media Contact, Prime Bishop, Most Rev. Robert M. Nemkovich, 1006 Pittston Ave., Scranton, PA 18505, Tel. (570)346-9131 Fax (570)346-2188

Email: PNCCCenter@adelphia.net

Website: www.PNCC.org

### Officers

Prime Bishop, Most Rev. Robert M. Nemkovich, 115 Lake Scranton Rd., Scranton, PA 18505

Central Diocese, Bishop, Sede Vacante

Eastern Diocese, Bishop, Rt. Rev. Thomas J. Gnat, 166 Pearl St., Manchester, NH 03104

Buffalo-Pittsburgh Diocese, Bishop, Rt. Rev. Thaddeus S. Peplowski, 5776 Broadway, Lancaster, NY 14086

Western Diocese, Rt. Rev. Jan Dawidziuk, 920 N. Northwest Hwy., Park Ridge, IL 60068

Canadian Diocese, Bishop, Sede Vacante

Ecumenical Officer, Rev. Dr. Anthony Mikovsky

Savonarola Theological Seminary, 1031 Cedar Avenue, Scranton, PA 18505 Rector: Most Rev. Robert M. Nemkovich Vice-Rector: Rev. Dr. Czeslan Kuliczkowski

### Periodicals

*God's Field; Polka*

**Plymouth Brethren—please see Christian Brethren**

**Presbyterian Church—please see Evangelical Presbyterian Church**

## Presbyterian Church in America

The Presbyterian Church in America is an Evangelical, Reformed covenant community of churches in the United States and Canada committed to a common doctrinal standard (The Westminster Standards), mutual accountability (representative church government), and cooperative ministry. The PCA traces its historical roots to the First General Assembly of the Church of Scotland of 1560, the establishment of the Presbytery of Philadelphia, 1789, and the General Assembly of the Southern Presbyterian Church, Augusta in 1861. Organized in 1973 by conservative churches formerly associated with the Presbyterian Church in the United States, the church was first known as the National Presbyterian Church but changed its name in 1974 to the Presbyterian Church in America. The PCA seeks to be "Faithful to the Scriptures, True to the Reformed Faith, and Obedient to the Great Commission." In 1982 the Reformed Presbyterian Church, Evangelical Synod joined the PCA bringing with it a rich tradition that had antecedents in colonial America.

The PCA holds to the ancient creeds of the Church such as the Apostles' Creed and the Nicene Creed and has a firm commitment to its doctrinal standards, The Westminster Confession of Faith, Larger and Shorter Catechisms, that have been significant in Presbyterianism since 1645, These doctrinal standards reflect the distinctives of the Reformed tradition, Calvinism, and Covenant Theology. Ministers, ruling elders, and deacons are required to subscribe to the Westminster Standards in good faith. Individuals are received by a Session as communing members of the church upon their profession of faith in Jesus Christ as Lord and Saviour, their promise to live a Christian lifestyle, and their commitment to worship and service in the church.

The PCA is a connectional church, led by ruling elders (lay leaders) and teaching elders (ministers). The Session governs a local congregation; the Diaconate carries out mercy ministries. The Presbytery is responsible for regional matters and the General Assembly is responsible for national matters in the U.S.A. and Canada. Cooperative ministry is carried out through over sixty Presbyteries and ten General Assembly Ministries.

The educational institutions of the church are Covenant College of Lookout Mountain, Ga and Covenant Theological Seminary of St. Louis, Mo. The PCA and the Orthodox Presbyterian Church participate in a joint publication venture, Great Commission Publications, for the publication of Christian Education materials.

In its ecumenical relations the PCA is a member of the North American Presbyterian and Reformed Council, the National Association of Evangelicals, and the World Reformed Fellowship.

The General Assembly approved a statement of purpose, "It is the purpose of the PCA to bring glory to God as a worshipping and serving community until the nations in which we live are filled with churches that make Jesus Christ and His word their chief joy, and the nations of the world, hearing the Word, are discipled in obedience to the Great Commission."

The church has grown beyond its origin in the southeastern states to have congregations in forty-nine states in the U.S.A. and in several provinces of Canada. Growth is due to the PCA's ministry in evangelism, discipleship, church planting, church renewal, and campus ministry. Indicative of her concern for cross-cultural ministry, the PCA has the largest international missionary force in Presbyterian Church history.

**Headquarters**

1700 N. Brown Rd., Lawrenceville, GA 30043-8122, Tel. (678)825-1000
Email: ac@pcanet.org
Website: www.pcanet.org

**Officers**

Moderator: Dr. Dominic Aquila, New Geneva Seminary, 3622 East Galley Road, Colorado Springs, CO 80909, Tel. (719)573-5395 Fax (719)573-5398, Email: daquila6@aol.com
Stated Clerk/Coordinator of Administration, Dr. L. Roy Taylor, 1700 N. Brown Rd., Suite 105, Lawrenceville, GA 30043-8122, Tel. (678) 825-1100, Email: ac@pcanet.org
Christian Education & Publications Coordinator, Dr. Charles Dunahoo, 1700 N. Brown Rd., Suite 102, Lawrenceville, GA 30043-8122, Tel. (678)825-1100, Email: cep@pacnet.org
Mission to the World Coordinator, Dr. Paul D. Kooistra, 1600 N. Brown Rd., Lawrenceville, GA 30043-8141, Tel. (678)-823-0004, Email: mtw@mtw.org
Mission to North America Coordinator, Dr. James C. Bland, 1700 N. Brown Rd., Suite

101, Lawrenceville, GA 30043-8122, Tel. (678)825-1200, Email: mna@pcanet.org
Reformed University Ministries Coordinator, Dr. Rod Mays, 1700 N. Brown Rd., Suite 104, Lawrenceville, GA 30043-8122, Tel. (678)825-1070, Email: rum@pcanet.org
PCA Foundation President, Mr. Randel Stair, 1700 N. Brown Rd., Suite 103, Lawrenceville, GA 30043-8122, Tel. (678)825-1040, Email: pcaf@pcanet.org
PCA Retirement and Benefits, Inc., Mr. Randel Stair, 1700 North Brown Road, Suite 103, Lawrenceville, GA 30043-8143, Tel. (678) 825-1260 Fax. (678)825-1261
Ridge Haven Conference Director, Rev. Morse Up De Graff, P.O. Box 969, Rosman, NC 28772, Tel. (828)862-3916 Fax(828)884-6988, Email: ridgehaven@citcom.net
Covenant College President, Dr. Niel Nielson, 14049 Scenic Highway, Lookout Mountain, GA 30750, Tel. (706)820-1560 Fax (706)820-2165, Email: webmaster@ covenant.edu
Covenant Theological Seminary President, Dr. Bryan Chapell, 12330 Conway Rd., St. Louis, MO 63141, Tel. (314)434-4044 Fax (314)434-4819, Email: president@covenant seminary.edu

**Periodicals**

*Equip, Covenant, Mission Report, The View, Network, byFaith,* www.byfaithonline.com

## Presbyterian Church (U.S.A.)*

The Presbyterian Church (U.S.A.) was organized June 10, 1983, when the Presbyterian Church in the United States and the United Presbyterian Church in the United States of America united in Atlanta. The union healed a major division which began with the Civil War when Presbyterians in the South withdrew from the Presbyterian Church in the United States of America to form the Presbyterian Church in the Confederate States.

The United Presbyterian Church in the United States of America had been created by the 1958 union of the Presbyterian Church in the United States of America and the United Presbyterian Church of North America. Of those two uniting bodies, the Presbyterian Church in the U.S.A. dated from the first Presbytery organized in Philadelphia, about 1706. The United Presbyter-ian Church of North America was formed in 1858, when the Associate Reformed Presbyterian Church and the Associate Presbyterian Church united.

Strongly ecumenical in outlook, the Presbyterian Church (U.S.A.) is the result of at least 10 different denominational mergers over the last 250 years. A restructure, adopted by the General Assembly meeting in June 1993, has been implemented. The Presbyterian Church (U.S.A.) dedicated its new national offices in Louisville, Ken. in 1988.

**Headquarters**

100 Witherspoon St., Louisville, KY 40202, Tel.

(888)728-7228 Fax (502)569-5018
Media Contact, Assoc. Dir. for Communications, Barry Creech, Tel. (502)569-5515 Fax (502) 569-8073
Email: presytel@pcusa.org
Website: www.pcusa.org

### Officers

Mod., Joan Gray, 100 Witherspoon St, Louisville KY 40202, Tel. (888)728-7228
Vice-Mod., Robert Wilson, 100 Witherspoon St, Louisville KY 40202, Tel. (888)728-7228
Stated Clk., Clifton Kirkpatrick, 100 Witherspoon St, Louisville KY 40202, Tel. (888)728-7228

### THE OFFICE OF THE GENERAL ASSEMBLY

100 Witherspoon St, Louisville KY 40202-1396, Tel. (888)728-7228 x 5424 Fax (502)569-8005
Stated Clk., Rev. Clifton Kirkpatrick
Strategic Operations, Dir., Rev. Gradye Parsons
Middle Governing Body Relations, Coord., Rev. Gary Torrens
Dept. of the Stated Clerk, Dir., Loyda Aja
Dept. of Constitutional Services, Dir., Rev. Mark Tammen
Ecumenical & Agency Relations, Dir., Rev. Robina Winbush
Dept. of Communication & Technology, Dir., Rev. Kerry Clements
Dept. of Hist., Philadelphia, 425 Lombard St., Philadelphia, PA 19147, Tel. (215)627-1852 Fax (215)627-0509; Dir., Frederick J. Heuser, Jr.; Deputy Dir., Margery Sly

### GENERAL ASSEMBLY COUNCIL

Exec. Dir., Linda Valentine
Deputy Exec. Dir., Rev. Helen Locklear
Worldwide Ministries Division, Dir., Rev. Marian McClure
Congregational Ministries Division, Dir., Donald G. Campbell
National Ministries Division, Dir., Rev. Curtis A. Kearns, Jr.
Mission Support Services Dir., Joey Bailey

### BOARD OF PENSIONS

200 Market St., Philadelphia, PA 19103-3298, Tel. (800)773-7752 Fax (215)587-6215
Chpsn. of the Bd., Earldean V. S. Robbins
Pres., & CEO, Robert W. Maggs, Jr.

### FOUNDATION

200 E. Twelfth St., Jeffersonville, IN 47130, Tel. (812)288-8841 Fax (502)569-5980
Chpsn. of the Bd., James Henderson
Pres. & CEO, Robert E. Leech

### INVESTMENT & LOAN PROGRAM, INC.

Tel. (800)903-7457 Fax (502)569-8868
Chpsn. of the Board, Ben McAnally
Pres. & CEO, James L. Hudson

### PRESBYTERIAN PUBLISHING CORPORATION

Chpsn. of the Bd., Robert Bohl
Pres. & CEO, Davis Perkins

### SYNOD EXECUTIVES

Alaska-Northwest, Rev. Doug Kelly, 217 6th Ave. N., Seattle, WA 98109, Tel. (206)448-6403
Boriquen in Puerto Rico, Rev. Harry Fred Del Valle, Ave. Hostos Edificio 740, Cond. Medical Center Plaza, Ste. 216, Mayaguez, PR 00680, Tel. (787)832-8375
Covenant, Rev. Richard D. Brownlee and Rev. Marie T. Cross, 1911 Indian Wood Cir #B Tel. (419)754-4050
Lakes & Prairies, Rev. Philip Brown, 8012 Cedar Ave. S., Bloomington, MN 55425-1210, Tel. (612)854-0144
Lincoln Trails, Rev. Carol McDonald and Rev. David Crittenden, 1100 W. 42nd St., Indianapolis, IN 46208-3381, Tel. (317)923-3681
Living Waters, Rev. Terry Newland, 318 Seaboard Ln, Ste. 205, Franklin, TN 37067, Tel. (615)261-4008
Mid-America, Rev. John Williams, 6400 Glenwood, Ste. 111, Overland Park, KS 66202-4072, Tel. (913)384-3020
Mid-Atlantic, Rev. Roger C. Harp, P.O. Box 27026, Richmond, VA 23261-7026, Tel. (804) 342-0016
Northeast, Rev. Clinton McCoy, Int., 5811 Heritage Landing Dr., East Syracuse, NY 13057-9360, Tel. (315)446-5990
Pacific, Rev. Robert Brinks, 8 Fourth St., Petaluma, CA 94952-3004, Tel. (707)765-1772
Rocky Mountains, Rev. Zane Buxton, 3025 West 37th Ave., Ste. 206, Denver, CO 80211-2799, Tel. (303)477-9070
South Atlantic, Rev. Reginald Parsons, 118 E. Monroe St., Ste. 3, Jacksonville, FL 32202, Tel. (904)356-6070
Southern California & Hawaii, Rev. Edith Gause, 1501 Wilshire Blvd., Los Angeles, CA 90017-2293, Tel. (213)483-3840
Southwest, Rev. Janet DeVries, 401 E. 4th St. #A, Tucson, AZ 85705, Tel. (520)791-9600
The Sun, Rev. Judy R. Fletcher, 1925 E. Belt Line Rd. #220, Carrollton, TX 75006, Tel. (214)390-1894
The Trinity, Rev. Bruce G. Stevens and Thomas E. Robinson, 3040 Market St., Camp Hill, PA 17011-4599, Tel. (717)737-0421

### Periodicals

*American Presbyterians, Journal of Presbyterian History; Presbyterian News Service "News Briefs"; Church & Society Magazine; Horizons; Presbyterians Today; Interpretation; Presbyterian Outlook*

## Primitive Advent Christian Church

This body split from the Advent Christian Church. All its churches are in West Virginia.

The Primitive Advent Christian Church believes that the Bible is the only rule of faith and practice and that Christian character is the only test of fellowship and communion. The church agrees with Christian fidelity and meekness; exercises mutual watch and care; counsels, admonishes, or reproves as duty may require and receives the same from each other as becomes the household of faith. Primitive Advent Christians do not believe in taking up arms.

The church believes that three ordinances are set forth by the Bible to be observed by the Christian church, (1) baptism by immersion; (2) the Lord's Supper, by partaking of unleavened bread and wine; (3) feet washing, to be observed by the saints' washing of one another's feet.

### Headquarters
Media Contact, Sec.-Treas., Roger Wines, 1971 Grapevine Rd., Sissonville, WV 25320, Tel. (304)988-2668

### Officers
Pres., Herbert Newhouse, 7632 Hughart Dr., Sissonville, WV 25320, Tel. (304)984-9277

Vice Pres., Roger Hammons, 273 Frame Rd., Elkview, WV 25071, Tel. (304)965-6247

Sec. & Treas., Roger Wines, 1971 Grapevine Rd., Sissonville, WV 25320, Tel. (304)988-2668

## Primitive Baptists
This group of Baptists has churches in the United States, the Philippines, India, and Africa. While they oppose centralization and modern mission boards, they believe in the circulation of the gospel. They preach salvation by grace alone.

### Headquarters
P.O. Box 38, Thornton, AR 71766, Tel. (501)352-3694

Media Contact, Elder W. Hartsel Cayce

### Officers
Elder W. Hartsel Cayce

Elder Lasserre Bradley, Jr., Box 17037, Cincinnati, OH 45217, Tel. (513)821-7289

Elder S. T. Tolley, P.O. Box 68, Atwood, TN 38220, Tel. (901)662-7417

### Periodicals
*Baptist Witness*

## Primitive Methodist Church in the U.S.A.
Hugh Bourne and William Clowes, local preachers in the Wesleyan Church in England, organized a daylong meeting at Mow Cop in Staffordshire on May 31, 1807, after Lorenzo Dow, an evangelist from America, told them of American camp meetings. Thousands attended and many were converted, but the Methodist church, founded by the open-air preacher John Wesley, refused to accept the converts and reprimanded the preachers.

After waiting for two years for a favorable

action by the Wesleyan Society, Bourne and Clowes established The Society of the Primitive Methodists. This was not a schism, Bourne said, for "we did not take one from them ... it now appeared to be the will of God that we ... should form classes and take upon us the care of churches in the fear of God." Primitive Methodist missionaries were sent to New York in 1829. An American conference was established in 1840.

Missionary efforts reach into Guatemala, Spain, and other countries. The denomination joins in federation with the Evangelical Congregational Church, the United Brethren in Christ Church and the Southern Methodist Church and is a member of the National Association of Evangelicals.

The church believes the Bible is the only true rule of faith and practice, the inspired Word of God. It believes in one Triune God, the Deity of Jesus Christ, the Deity and personality of the Holy Spirit, the innocence of Adam and Eve, the Fall of the human race, the necessity of repentance, justification by faith of all who believe, regeneration witnessed by the Holy Spirit, sanctification by the Holy Spirit, the second coming of the Lord Jesus Christ, the resurrection of the dead and conscious future existence of all people and future judgments with eternal rewards and punishments.

### Headquarters
Media Contact, Pres., Rev. Kerry Ritts, 723 Preston Ln., Hatboro, PA 19040, Tel. (215) 675-2639/(215)672-1576

Email: pmconf@juno.com

Website: www.primitivemethodistchurch.org

### Officers
Pres., Rev. Kerry R. Ritts, 723 Preston Ln., Hatboro, PA 19040-2321, Tel.(215)672-1576

Vice Pres., Rev. Reginald H. Thomas, 110 Pittston Blvd., Wilkes-Barre, PA. 18702-9620, Tel. (570)823-3425

Recording Secretary, Rev. John Stange, 55 Cherry St., Plymouth, PA. 18651-2336, Tel. (570)779-1332

General. Secretary., Rev. David Allen, Jr., 1199 Lawrence St., Lowell, MA 01852-5526, Tel. (978) 453-2052

Email: pahson@earthlink.net

Treas., Mr. Raymond C. Baldwin, 18409 Mill Run Ct., Leesburg, VA 20176-4583, Email: Rbaldwin32@aol.com

## Progressive National Baptist Convention, Inc.*
This body held its organizational meeting in Cincinnati in November, 1961. Subsequent regional sessions were followed by the first annual session in Philadelphia in 1962.

### Headquarters
601 50th Street, N.E., Washington, DC 20019, Tel. (202)396-0558 Fax (202)398-4998

Media Contact, Gen. Sec., Dr. Tyrone S. Pitts

Website: www.pnbc.org

151

## CONVENTION OFFICERS

Dr. Major L. Jemison, President, St. John Missionary Baptist Church, 5700 North Kelley Avenue Oklahoma City, OK 73111
Dr. T. DeWitt Smith, 1st Vice President
Dr. Carroll A. Baltimore, 2nd Vice President
Dr. Tyrone S. Pitts, General Secretary

## REGIONAL VICE PRESIDENTS

Dr. Frank Blackshear, Eastern Region
Dr. Lawrence Foster, Midwest Region
Dr. Willie Davis, Southwest Region
Dr. Michael Harris, Southern Region
Dr. Timothy Stewart, International Region
Dr. Terry Streeter, Congress of Christian Education
Mrs. Brenda Tribett, Executive Director, Christian Education
Dr. Robert Dennis, President, Mission Ministry
Dr. Earl Trent, Interim Executive Director, Mission Ministry
Mrs. Arlene Tyler, Women's Department, 8220 Cheyenne St., Detroit, MI 48228
Mr. Wilmer Jones, Laymen's Department
The Rev. Samuel Nixon, Seminarian Development
The Rev. Calvin Hailstock, Young Adult Men
Ms Regina Lenoir, Young Adult Women
Mrs. Shirley Hayes, Principal, Nannie Helen Burroughs School, Tel. (202)398-5266

## Protestant Reformed Churches in America

The Protestant Reformed Churches (PRC) have their roots in the sixteenth century Reformation of Martin Luther and John Calvin, as it developed in the Dutch Reformed churches. The denomination originated as a result of a controversy in the Christian Reformed Church in 1924 involving the adoption of the "Three Points of Common Grace." Three ministers in the Christian Reformed Church, the Reverends Herman Hoeksema, George Ophoff, and Henry Danhof, and their consistories (Eastern Avenue, Hope, and Kalamazoo, respectively) rejected the doctrine. Eventually these men were deposed, and their consistories were either deposed or set outside the Christian Reformed Church. The denomination was formed in 1926 with three congregations. Today the denomination is comprised of some twenty-eight churches (more than 7,000 members) in the U.S.A. and Canada. The presbyterian form of church government as determined by the Church Order of Dordt is followed by the PRC. The doctrinal standards of the PRC are the Reformed confessions: the Heidelberg Catechism, Belgic Confession of Faith, and Canons of Dordrecht. The doctrine of the covenant is a cornerstone of their teaching. They maintain an unconditional, particular covenant of grace that God establishes with His elect.

### Headquarters

16511 South Park Ave., South Holland, IL 60473, Tel. (708)333-1314
Media Contact, Stated Clerk, Don Doezema, 4949 Ivanrest Ave., Grandville, MI 49418, Tel. (616)531-1490
Email: doezema@prca.org
Website: www.prca.org

### Officers

Stat. Clk., Don Doezema, 4949 Ivanrest Ave., Grandville, MI 49418, Tel. (616)531-1490, Fax (616)531-3033, Email: doezema@prca.org

### Periodicals

*The Standard Bearer*

Quakers—please see Friends General Conference

Quakers, Philadelphia—please see Philadelphia Yearly meeting of the Religious Society of Friends

Quakers, Conservative—please see Religious Society of Friends (conservative)

Quakers, International—please see Evangelical Friends International—North American Region

Quakers, Unaffiliated Meetings—please see Religious Society of Friends (Unaffiliated Meetings)

## Reformed Catholic Church

The Reformed Catholic Church is a rapidly growing faith community with parishes and missions in many parts of the world. The Reformed Catholic Church is a community created to shepherd those who have felt excluded, unwanted or disenfranchised and to become a home for all those without a spiritual home. We retain basic Catholic beliefs of love, faith, spirituality, prayer and sacramentality. Although a newly formed rite, we remain in, and honor, the traditions of the Orthodox Catholic Churches and the Old Catholic, Church of Utrecht, Netherlands. We are a truly Catholic church, with ordained clergy tracing succession back to Peter in 38 A.D. While the liturgical celebrations are similar to that of Roman Catholicism, there are theological differences. Most prominently: the role of women in the church, social justice and human sexuality, we are an inclusive, affirming and accepting church. We accept all people and hold no bounds or limits to those seeking the love of God. We encourage women to prepare for and assume leadership roles, including the fullness of the priesthood.

### Headquarters

St. Sebastian Reformed Catholic Church, P.O. Box 2, Worthington, OH 43085-9998, Tel. (866)769-0075
Media Contact, Fr. Marcis Heckman, RSJ, P.O. Box 4907, Toledo, OH 43610, Tel. (419)517-6762, Email: PaxPressRCC@aol.com
Email: Presiding bishop@reformedcatholic-church.org
Website: www.reformedcatholicchurch.org

### Officers

Metropolitan Archbishop Phillip Zimmmerman, RSJ

## Reformed Church in America*

The Reformed Church in America was established in 1628 by the earliest settlers of New York. It is the oldest Protestant denomination with a continuous ministry in North America. Until 1867 it was known as the Reformed Protestant Dutch Church.

The first ordained minister, Domine Jonas Michaelius, arrived in New Amsterdam from the Netherlands in 1628. Throughout the colonial period, the Reformed Church lived under the authority of the Classis of Amsterdam. Its churches were clustered in New York and New Jersey. Under the leadership of Rev. John Livingston, it became a denomination independent of the authority of the Classis of Amsterdam in 1776. Its geographical base was broadened in the 19th century by the immigration of Reformed Dutch and German settlers in the midwestern United States. The Reformed Church now spans the United States and Canada.

The Reformed Church in America accepts as its standards of faith the Heidelberg Catechism, Belgic Confession and Canons of Dort. It has a rich heritage of world mission activity. It claims to be loyal to reformed tradition which emphasizes obedience to God in all aspects of life.

Although the Reformed Church in America has worked in close cooperation with other churches, it has never entered into merger with any other denomination. It is a member of the World Alliance of Reformed Churches, the World Council of Churches and the National Council of the Churches of Christ in the United States of America. In 1998 it also entered into a relationship of full communion with the Evangelical Lutheran Church in America, Presbyterian Church (U.S.A.), and the United Church of Christ by way of the Formula of Agreement.

### Headquarters

475 Riverside Dr., New York, NY 10115, Tel. (212)870-3243 Fax (212)870-2499

Media Contact, Communication Officer, Paul Boice, 4500 60th St. SE, Grand Rapids, MI 49512, Tel. (616)698-7071 Fax (616)698-6606

Email: dmorris@rca.org

Website: www.rca.org

#### OFFICERS AND STAFF OF GENERAL SYNOD

President, The Rev. Bradley Lewis, 18th Floor, New York, NY 10115

General Synod Council; Moderator, The Rev. Steven VanderMolen 475 Riverside Drive., 18th Floor, NY, NY 10115

General Secretary, The Rev. Wesley Granberg-Michaelson, 475 Riverside Dr., 18th Floor, New York, NY 10115; 4500 69th St. SE, Grand Rapids, MI 49512

Operations and Support, Director, The Rev. Kenneth Bradsell, 475 Riverside Drive, 18th Floor, New York, NY 10115

Leadership/Revitalization, Director, The Rev. Kenneth Eriks

Church Multiplication/Discipleship, Director, The Rev. Richard Welscott

Finance Services, Treasurer, Ms. Susan Converse

Global Mission, Director, The Rev. Bruce Menning

African-American Council, Executive Director, The Rev. Dr. Glen Missick

Council for Hispanic Ministries, Executive Secretary, The Rev. Brigido Cabrera

Native American Indian Ministries Council, Vacant

Council for Pacific/Asian-American Ministries, Executive Secretary, Ms. Ella Campbell

#### OTHER ORGANIZATIONS

Board of Benefits Services, Director, Mr. L. Wood Bedell, 475 Riverside Drive, 18th Floor, New York, NJ 10115; President, The Rev. Thomas Bos; Secretary, The Rev. Kenneth Bradsell

RCA Building and Extension Fund, Fund Executive, Mr. Paul Karssen, 612 8th St. SE, Orange City, IA 51014

#### Periodicals

*Perspectives; The Church Herald*

# Reformed Church in the United States

Lacking pastors, early German Reformed immigrants to the American colonies were led in worship by "readers." One reader, schoolmaster John Philip Boehm, organized the first congregations near Philadelphia in 1725. A Swiss pastor, Michael Schlatter, was sent by the Dutch Reformed Church in 1746. Strong ties with the Netherlands existed until the formation of the Synod of the German Reformed Church in 1793.

The Eureka Classis, organized in North and South Dakota in 1910 and strongly influenced by the writings of H. Kohlbruegge, P. Geyser and J. Stark, refused to become part of the 1934 merger of the Reformed Church with the Evangelical Synod of North America, holding that it sacrificed the Reformed heritage. (The merged Evangelical and Reformed Church became part of the United Church of Christ in 1957.) Under the leadership of pastors W. Grossmann and W. J. Krieger, the Eureka Classis in 1942 incorporated as the continuing Reformed Church in the United States.

The growing Eureka Classis dissolved in 1986 to form a Synod with four regional classes. An heir to the Reformation theology of Zwingli and Calvin, the Heidelberg Catechism, the Belgic Confession and the Canons of Dort are used as the confessional standards of the church. The Bible is strictly held to be the inerrant, infallible Word of God.

The RCUS supports Dordt College, Mid-America Reformed Seminary, New Geneva Theological Seminary, West Minster Theological Seminary in California, and Hope Haven. The RCUS is the official sponsor to the Reformed Confessing Church of Zaire.

### Headquarters

Media Contact, Rev. Frank Walker Th.M., 6121

Pine Vista Way, Elk Grove City, CA 95758-4205, Tel. (661)827-9885
Email: TriWheeler@aol.com
Website: www.rcus.org

### Officers

Pres., Rev. Vernon Pollema, 235 James Street, Shafter, CA 93263, Tel. (661)746-6907
Vice Pres., Rev. Robert Grossmann, Th.M., 1905 200th St., Garner, IA 50438, Tel. (515)923-3060
Stated Clk., Rev. Frank Walker Th.M., 5601 Spring Blossom St., Bakersfield, CA 93313-6025, Tel. (661)827-9885
Treas., Clayton Greiman, 2115 Hwy. 69, Garner, IA 50438, Tel. (515)923-2950

## Reformed Episcopal Church

The Reformed Episcopal Church was founded December 2, 1873 in New York City by Bishop George D. Cummins, an assistant bishop in the Protestant Episcopal Church from 1866 until 1873. Cummins and other evangelical Episcopalians were concerned about the exclusiveness propagated by what they perceived to be an excessive ritualism then sweeping the church. Throughout the late 1860s evangelicals and ritualists clashed over ceremonies, vestments, open or closed communion, the Articles of Religion, interpretation of the meaning of the sacraments, and the understanding of Apostolic Succession.

In October, 1873, other bishops of the Episcopal Church publicly attacked Cummins in major newspapers for participating in an ecumenical communion service sponsored by the Evangelical Alliance. Cummins resigned from the Episcopal Church and drafted a call to organize a new Episcopal Church for the "purpose of restoring the old paths of their fathers." On December 2, 1873, a Declaration of Principles which expressed the evangelical understanding of the Articles of Religion was adopted. Dr. Charles Edward Cheney of Chicago was elected as bishop to serve with Bishop Cummins. The Second General Council, meeting in May 1874 in New York City, approved a Constitution and Canons and adopted the 1785 Proposed Book of Common Prayer for use in the new Church.

In recent years the Reformed Episcopal Church has revised the Prayer Book to conform to the 1662 and 1928 Books of Common Prayer. The Church still embraces the Thirty Nine Articles of Religion, and has approved the Chicago-Lambeth Quadrilateral of 1886-1888.

Since 1993, the Reformed Episcopal Church has been in official dialogue with the Episcopal Church U.S.A. with occasional meetings at the demoninational level.

There are presently five geographic diocese in the United States and Canada, as well as various missionary jurisdictions including India, Liberia, the West Indies, and others.

The Reformed Episcopal Church is a member of the National Association of Evangelicals.

### Headquarters

826 2nd Ave, Blue Bell, PA 19422-1257, Tel. (215)483-1196 Fax (215)483-5235
Media Contact, Rt. Rev. Leonard Riches
Media Contact, Rt. Rev. Royal U. Grote, Jr., Church Growth Office, 211 Byrne Ave., Houston, TX 77009, Tel. (713)862-4929
Email: wycliffe@jps.net
Website: recus.org

### Officers

Pres. & Presiding Bishop, Rt. Rev. Leonard W. Riches
Vice Pres., Rt. Rev. Royal U. Grote, Jr.
Sec., Rev. Walter Banek
Treas., Ven. Jon W. Abboud

### OTHER ORGANIZATIONS

Bd. of Foreign Missions, Pres., Dr. Barbara J. West, 316 Hunters Rd., Swedesboro, NJ 08085, Tel. (609)467-1641
Bd. of Natl. Church Extension, Pres., Rt. Rev. Royal U. Grote, Jr., 211 Byrne Ave., Houston, TX 77009, Tel. (713)862-4929
Publication Society, Pres., Rt. Rev. Royal U. Grote; 211 Byrne Ave., Houston, TX 77009, Tel. (713)862-4929, 7372 Henry Ave., Philadelphia, PA 19128, Tel: 215-956-0655
The Reapers, Pres., Susan Higham, 472 Leedom St., Jenkintown, PA 19046
Committee on Women's Work, Pres., Joan Workowski, 1162 Beverly Rd., Rydal, PA 19046
Committee on Constitutions and Canons, Rev. Canon James T. Payne, P.O. Box 973, Missouri City TX 77495

### BISHOPS

Leonard W. Riches, Sr., 85 Smithtown Rd., Pipersville, PA 18947, Tel. (215)483-1196 Fax (215)294-8009
Royal U. Grote, Jr., 211 Byrne Ave., Houston, TX 77009
James C. West, Sr., 408 Red Fox Run, Summerville, SC 29485
Robert H. Booth, 1611 Park Ave., #212, Quakertown, PA 18951
Gregory K. Hotchkiss, 318 E. Main St., Somerville, NJ 08876
George B. Fincke, 155 Woodstock Circle, Vacaville, CA 95687-3381
Daniel R. Morse, 11259 Wexford Dr., Eads, TN 38025
Michael Fedechko, Box 2532, New Liskeard, ON P0J 1P0
Charles W. Dorrington, 626 Blanshard St., Victoria, BC V8W 3G6
Ray R. Sutton, 17405 Muirfield Dr., Dallas TX 75287, Tel. (972)248-6505

### Periodicals

*Reformed Episcopalians*

## Reformed Mennonite Church

This is a small group of believers in Pennsylvania, Ohio, Michigan, Illinois, and Ontario, Canada who believe in non-resistance of evil, and non-conformity to the world and who practice separation from unfaithful worship. They believe that Christian unity is the effect of brotherly love and are of one mind and spirit. Their church was established in 1812 by John Herr who agreed with the teachings of Menno Simon as well as those of Jesus Christ.

### Headquarters
Lancaster County only, Reformed Mennonite Church, 602 Strasburg Pike, Lancaster, PA 17602

Media Contact, Bishop, Glenn M. Gross, Tel. (717)795-8695

Website: www.reformedmennonitechurch.org

### Officers
Bishop Glenn M. Gross, 906 W. Grantham Rd., Mechanicsburg, PA 17055

## Reformed Methodist Union Episcopal Church

The Reformed Methodist Union Episcopal church was formed after a group of ministers withdrew from the African Methodist Episcopal Church following a dispute over the election of ministerial delegates to the General Conference.

These ministers organized the Reformed Methodist Union church during a four-day meeting beginning on January 22, 1885 at Hills Chapel (now known as Mt. Hermon RMUE church), in Charleston, S.C.. The Rev. William E. Johnson was elected president of the new church. Following the death of Rev. Johnson in 1896, it was decided that the church would conform to regular American Methodism (the Episcopacy). The first Bishop, Edward Russell Middleton, was elected, and "Episcopal" was added to the name of the church. Bishop Middleton was consecrated on Dec. 5, 1896, by Bishop P. F. Stephens of the Reformed Episcopal Church.

### Headquarters
1136 Brody Ave., Charleston, SC 29407

Media Contact, Gen. Secretary, Brother Willie B. Oliver, P.O. Box 1995, Orangeburg, SC 29116, Tel. (803)536-3293

### Officers
Bishop, Rt. Rev. Leroy Gethers, Tel. (803)766-3534

Asst. Bishop, Rt. Rev. Jerry M. DeVoe, Jr.

Gen. Sec., Brother Willie B. Oliver

Treas., Rev. Daniel Green

Sec. of Education, Rev. William Polite

Sec. of Books Concerns, Sister Ann Blanding

Sec. of Pension Fund, Rev. Joseph Powell

Sec. of Church Extension, Brother William Parker

Sec. of Sunday School Union, Sister Wine

Sec. of Mission, Rev. Warren Hatcher

## Reformed Presbyterian Church of North America

Also known as the Church of the Covenanters, this church's origin dates back to the Reformation days of Scotland when the Covenanters signed their Covenants in resistance to the king and Roman Church in the enforcement of state church practices. The church in America has signed two Covenants in particular, those of 1871 and 1954. The Westminster Confession of Faith and the Larger and Shorter Catechism are among the subordinant standards of the denomination.

### Headquarters
Media Contact, Stated Clk., James K. McFarland, 7408 Penn Ave., Pittsburgh, PA 15208, Tel. (412)731-1177 Fax (412)731-8861

Email: RPTrustees@aol.com

Website: www.reformedpresbyterian.org

### Officers
Mod., The Rev. Dr. Jonathan Watt, 2907 Fifth Ave., Beaver Falls, PA , 15010, Tel. (724)846-5430

Clk., J. Bruce Martin, 310 Main St., Ridgefield Park, NJ 07660, Tel. (201)440-5993

Asst. Clk., Raymond E. Morton, 411 N. Vine St., Sparta, IL 62286, Tel. (618)443-3419

Stated Clk., James K. McFarland, 7408 Penn Ave., Pittsburgh, PA 15208, Tel. (412)731-1177

Geneva College, 3200 College Ave, Beaver Falls, PA 15010, Tel. (724)846-5100 Pres., Kenneth A. Smith, Ph.D.

Reformed Presbyterian Theological Seminary, 7418 Penn Ave., Pittsburgh, PA 15208, Tel. (412)731-8690, Pres., The Rev. Jerry F. O' Neill, D.D.

Reformed Presbyterian Home, 2344 Perrysville Ave., Pittsburgh, PA 15214, Tel. (412)321-4139 Director, Margaret Hemphill

Crown and Covenant Publications, 7408 Penn Ave., Pittsburgh, PA 15208, Tel. (412)241-0436 Drew and Lynne Gordon, Managing Editors.

### Periodicals
*The Witness, The Reformed Presbyterian Witness*

## Reformed Zion Union Apostolic Church

This group was organized in 1869 at Boydton, Va., by Elder James R. Howell of New York, a minister of the A.M.E. Zion Church, with doctrines of the Methodist Episcopal Church.

### Headquarters
Rt. 1, Box 64D, Dundas, VA 23938, Tel. (804)676-8509

Media Contact, Bishop G. W. Studivant

### Officers
Exec. Brd., Chair, Rev. Hilman Wright, Tel. (804)447-3988

Sec., Joseph Russell, Tel. (804)634-4520

## Religious Society of Friends (Conservative)

These Friends mark their present identity from separations occurring by regions at different times from 1845 to 1904. They hold to a minimum of organizational structure. Their meetings for worship, which are unprogrammed and based on silent, expectant waiting upon the Lord, demonstrate the belief that all individuals may commune directly with God and may share equally in vocal ministry.

They continue to stress the importance of the Living Christ and the experience of the Holy Spirit working with power in the lives of individuals who obey it.

### YEARLY MEETINGS

North Carolina YM, Sidney Lee Kitchens, P.O. Box 4591, Greensboro, NC 27404, Tel. (252)587-2571

Iowa YM, Deborah Frisch, Clerk, 3400 King Dian Blvd, Des Moines, Iowa 50311

Ohio YM, Seth Hinshaw, Clerk, 61830 Sandy Ridge Road, Barnesville, OH 43713

## Religious Society of Friends (Unaffiliated Meetings)

Though all groups of Friends acknowledge the same historical roots, 19th-century divisions in theology and experience led to some of the current organizational groupings. Many newer yearly meetings, have chosen not to identify with past divisions by affiliating in traditional ways with the larger organizations within the Society.

### YEARLY MEETINGS

Central Yearly Meeting [Friends Evangel] (I), Supt., Jonathan Edwards, 5597 West County Rd., 700 N., Ridgeville, IN 47380, Tel. (765) 857-2347 Fax(765)857-2347

Intermountain Yearly Meeting (I), Clerk, Rebecca Henderson, Website: www.imym.org

North Pacific Yearly Meeting (I), Email: npym-06@npym.org

Pacific Yearly Meeting (I), Clerk, Jim Anderson, 25 Gideon Lane, Chico, CA 95973

Website: www.pacificyearlymeeting.org

Email: margaretf@fwccamericas.org

Website: www.centralyearlymeetingoffriends.org

Central Yearly Meeting, 255 Members
Intermountain Yearly Meeting, 1008 Members
North Pacific Yearly Meeting, 921 Members
Pacific Yearly Meeting, 1,527 Members

### Periodicals

*Friends Bulletin* (for Intermountain, Pacific & North Pacific Yearly Meetings) and *Friends Evangel*

## The Romanian Orthodox Church in America

The Romanian Orthodox Church in America is an autonomous Archdiocese chartered under the name of "Romanian Orthodox Archdiocese in America." The diocese was founded in 1929 and approved by the Holy Synod of the Romanian Orthodox Church in Romania in 1934. The Holy Synod of the Romanian Orthodox Church granted ecclesiastical autonomy in American Diocese on July 12, 1950. The Diocese continues to hold dogmatic and canonical ties with the Holy Synod and the Romanian Orthodox Patriarchate of Romania.

In 1951, approximately 40 parishes with their clergy from the United States and Canada separated from this church. In 1960, they joined the Russian Orthodox Greek Catholic Metropolia, now called the Orthodox Church in America, which reordained for these parishes a bishop with the title "Bishop of Detroit and Michigan."

On June 11, 1973 the Holy Synod of the Romanian Orthodox church elevated the Bishop of Romanian Orthodox Missionary Episcopate in America to the rank of Archbishop.

### Headquarters

P.O. Box 27, Skokie, IL 60076-0027, Tel. (847)674-3900, Fax (847)674-4110, Email: ArchNicolae@aol.com, Website: www.romarch.org

Media Contact, Archdiocesan Secretary, V. Rev. Fr. Nicholas Apostola, 44 Midland St., Worcester, MA 01602-4217, Tel. (508)845-0088 Fax (508)845-8850, Email: Nicholas.Apostola@verizon.net

Email: ArchNicolae@aol.com

Website: www.romarch.org

### Officers

Archbishop, His Eminence Dr. Nicolae Condrea, P.O. Box 27, Skokie, IL 60076-0027, Tel. (847)674-3900 Fax (847)674-4110, Email: ArchNicolae@aol.com

Vicar, V. Rev. Fr. Ioan Ionita, 17601 Wentworth Avenue, Lansing, IL 60438-2074, Tel. & fax (708)474-0340, Email: Tintari@aol.com

Inter-Church Relations, Dir., V. Rev. Fr. Nicholas Apostola, 44 Midland St., Worcester, MA 01602-4217, Tel. (508)845-0088 Fax (508)845-8850, Email: Nicholas.Apostola@ verizon.net

### Periodicals

*Credinta-The Faith*

**Reorganized Church of Jesus Christ of Latter-day Saints—please see Community of Christ**

## The Romanian Orthodox Episcopate of America

This body of Eastern Orthodox Christians of Romanian descent is part of the Autocephalous Orthodox Church in America.

### Headquarters

2535 Grey Tower Rd., Jackson, MI 49201, Tel. (517)522-4800

Media Contact, Ed. Sec., Rev. Archdeacon David Oancea, P.O. Box 185, Grass Lake, MI 49240-0185 Tel. (517)522-3656
Email: roeasolia@aol.com
Website: www.roea.org

**Officers**

Ruling Hierarch, Most Rev. Archbishop Nathaniel Popp
P.O. Box 309, Grass Lake, MI 49240-0309

**Periodicals**

*Solia—The Herald; Good News—Buna Vestire* (in Canada only)

**Russian Orthodox Church—please see Patriarchal Parishes of the Russian Orthodox Church in the U.S.A.**

## The Russian Orthodox Church Outside of Russia

This group was organized in 1920 to unite in one body of dioceses the missions and parishes of the Russian Orthodox Church outside of Russia. The governing body, set up in Constantinople, was sponsored by the Ecumenical Patriarchate. In November 1950, it came to the United States. The Russian Orthodox Church Outside of Russia emphasizes being true to the old traditions of the Russian Church. It is presently discussing the re-establishment of communion with the Moscow Patriarchate.

**Headquarters**

75 E. 93rd St., New York, NY 10128, Tel. (212)534-1601 Fax (212)426-1086
Media Contact, Dep. Sec., Nicholas A. Ohotin, Tel. (212)534-1610 x 37
Email: nohotin@synod.com

**SYNOD OF BISHOPS**

Pres., His Eminence Metropolitan Laurus
Vice Pres., His Eminence Archbishop Hilarion, Tel. (212)534-1601

**Periodicals**

*Living Orthodoxy; Orthodox Family; Orthodox Russia; Pravoslavnaya Rus; Pravoslavnaya Zhisn; Orthodox America*

## The Salvation Army

The Salvation Army, founded in 1865 by William Booth (1829-1912) in London, England, and introduced into America in 1880, is an international religious and charitable movement organized and operated on a paramilitary pattern and is a branch of the Christian church. To carry out its purposes, the Salvation Army has established a widely diversified program of religious and social welfare services which are designed to meet the needs of children, youth and adults in all age groups.

**Headquarters**

615 Slaters Ln., Alexandria, VA 22313, Tel. (703)684-5500 Fax (703)684-5538

Media Contact: National Community Rel. & Dev. Secretary, Major George Hood, Tel. (703)684-5526 Fax (703)684-5538, Email: george_hood@usn.salvationarmy.org
Website: www.salvationarmyusa.org

**Officers**

Natl. Commander, Commissioner W. Todd Bassett
Natl. Chief Sec., Lt. Colonel Larry Bosh
Natl. Community Relations and Development Secretary, Dir., Major George Hood

**TERRITORIAL ORGANIZATIONS**

Central Territory, 10 W. Algonquin Rd., Des Plaines, IL 60016, Tel. (847)294-2000 Fax (847)294-2299; Territorial Commander, Commissioner Kenneth Baillie
Eastern Territory, 440 W. Nyack Rd., P.O. Box C-635, West Nyack, NY 10994, Tel. (914)620-7200 Fax (914)620-7766; Territorial Commander, Commissioner Lawrence Moretz
Southern Territory, 1424 Northeast Expressway, Atlanta, GA 30329, Tel. (404)728-1300 Fax (404)728-1331; Territorial Commander, Commissioner Philip Needham
Western Territory, 180 E. Ocean Blvd., Long Beach, CA, Tel. (562)436-7000 Fax (562)491-8792; Territorial Commander, Commissioner Philip Swyers

**Periodicals**

*The War Cry*

## The Schwenkfelder Church

The Schwenkfelders are the spiritual descendants of the Silesian nobleman Caspar Schwenkfeld von Ossig (1489–1561), a scholar, reformer, preacher and prolific writer who endeavored to aid in the cause of the Protestant Reformation. A contemporary of Martin Luther, John Calvin, Ulrich Zwingli and Phillip Melanchthon, Schwenkfeld sought no following, formulated no creed and did not attempt to organize a church based on his beliefs. He labored for liberty of religious belief, for a fellowship of all believers and for one united Christian church.

He and his cobelievers supported a movement known as the Reformation by the Middle Way. Persecuted by state churches, ultimately 217 Schwenkfelders exiled from Silesia emigrated to Pennsylvania in six migrations, 1731–1734. The largest migration, about 180, landed at Philadelphia Sept. 22, 1734. In 1782, the Society of Schwenkfelders, the forerunner of the present Schwenkfelder Church, was formed. The church was incorporated in 1909.

The Schwenkfelder Church is a voluntary association of six Schwenkfelder Churches at Palm, Worcester, Lansdale, and Norristown and two in Philadelphia, Pennsylvania.

They practice adult baptism, dedication and baptism of children, and observe the Lord's Supper regularly with open Communion. In theology, they are Christo-centric; in polity, congregational;

157

in missions, world-minded; in ecclesiastical organization, ecumenical.

The ministry is recruited from graduates of accredited theological seminaries. The churches take leadership in ecumenical concerns through ministerial associations, community service and action groups, councils of Christian education, and other agencies.

### Headquarters
105 Seminary St., Pennsburg, PA 18073, Tel. (215)679-3103
Media Contact, David W. Luz
Email: info@schwenkfelder.com

### Officers
Mod., David W. Luz, Pennsburg, PA
Sec., Linda Anders, Souderton, PA
Treas., Pat McGinnis, Central Schwenkfelder Church, Worcester, PA 19490

### Periodicals
*The Schwenkfeldian*

## Separate Baptists in Christ

The Separate Baptists in Christ are a group of Baptists found in Indiana, Ohio, Kentucky, Tennessee, Virginia, West Virginia, Florida, and North Carolina dating back to an association formed in 1758 in North Carolina and Virginia.

Today this group consists of approximately 100 churches. They believe in the infallibility of the Bible, the divine ordinances of the Lord's Supper, feet-washing, baptism and that those who endureth to the end shall be saved.

The Separate Baptists are Arminian in doctrine, rejecting both the doctrines of predestination and eternal security of the believer.

At the 1991 General Association, an additional article of doctrine was adopted. "We believe that at Christ's return in the clouds of heaven all Christians will meet the Lord in the air, and time shall be no more," thus leaving no time for a literal one-thousand-year reign. Seven associations comprise the General Association of Separate Baptists.

### Headquarters
Media Contact, Clk., Greg Erdman, 10102 N. Hickory Ln., Columbus, IN 47203, Tel. (812)526-2540
Email: mail@separatebaptist.org
Website: www.separatebaptist.org

### Officers
Mod., Rev. Jim Goff, 1020 Gagel Ave., Louisville, KY 40216
Asst. Mod., Rev. Jimmy Polston, 785 Kitchen Rd., Mooresville, IN 46158, Tel. (317)831-6745
Clk., Greg Erdman, 10102 N. Hickory Ln., Columbus, IN 47203, Tel. (812)526-2540
Asst. Clk., Rev. Mattew Cowan, 174 Oak Hill School Rd., Lot 30, Smiths Grove, KY 42171, Tel. (270)678-5599

## Serbian Orthodox Church in the U.S.A. and Canada*

The Serbian Orthodox Church is an organic part of the Christian Orthodox Church. As a local church it received its autocephaly from Constantinople in 1219 A.D.

In 1921, a Serbian Orthodox Diocese in the United States of America and Canada was organized. In 1963, it was reorganized into three dioceses, and in 1983 a fourth diocese was created for the Canadian part of the church. The Serbian Orthodox Church in the U.S.A. and Canada received its administrative autonomy in 1928. However, it remains canonically an integral part of the Serbian Orthodox Patriarchate with its see in Belgrade. The Serbian Orthodox Church is in absolute doctrinal unity with all other local Orthodox Churches.

### Headquarters
St. Sava Monastery, P.O. Box 519, Libertyville, IL 60048, Tel. (847)367-0698
Email: oea@oea.serbian-church.net
Website: oea.serbian-church.net

### BISHOPS
Metropolitan of Midwestern America, Most Rev. Metropolitan Christopher
Bishop of Canada, Georgije, 5A Stockbridge Ave., Toronto, ON M8Z 4M6, Tel. (416)231-4009
Bishop of Eastern America, Rt. Rev. Bishop Mitrophan, 138 Carriage Hill Dr., Mars, PA 16046, Tel. (724)772-8866
Diocese of Western America, Bishop Maxim, 2541 Crestline Terr., Alhambra, CA 91803, Tel. (818)264-6825

### OTHER ORGANIZATIONS
Brotherhood of Serbian Orth. Clergy in U.S.A. & Canada, Pres., V. Rev. Dennis Pavichevich
Federation of Circles of Serbian Sisters
Serbian Singing Federation

### Periodicals
*The Path of Orthodoxy*

## Seventh-day Adventist Church

The Seventh-day Adventist Church grew out of a worldwide religious revival in the mid-19th century. People of many religious persuasions believed Bible prophecies indicated that the second coming or advent of Christ was imminent.

When Christ did not come in the 1840s, a group of these disappointed Adventists in the United States continued their Bible studies and concluded that they had misinterpreted prophetic events and that the second coming of Christ was still in the future. This same group of Adventists later accepted the teaching of the seventh-day Sabbath and became known as Seventh-day Adventists. The denomination organized formally in 1863.

The church was largely confined to North America until 1874, when its first missionary was sent to Europe. Today, over 57,850 congregations meet in 204 countries. Membership exceeds 14 million and increases between four and five percent each year.

In addition to a mission program, the church has the largest worldwide Protestant parochial school system, with approximately 6,471 schools with more than 1,294,000 students on elementary through college and university levels.

The Adventist Development and Relief Agency (ADRA) helps victims of war and natural disasters, and many local congregations have community service facilities to help those in need close to home.

The church also has a worldwide publishing ministry with 57 printing facilities producing magazines and other publications in over 350 languages and dialects. In the United States and Canada, the church sponsors a variety of radio and television programs, including *Christian Lifestyle Magazine, It Is Written, Breath of Life, Ayer, Hoy, y Mañana, Voice of Prophecy*, and *La Voz de la Esperanza*.

The North American Division of Seventh-day Adventist includes 58 Conferences which are grouped together into nine organized Union Conferences. The various Conferences work under the general direction of these Union Conferences.

### Headquarters
12501 Old Columbia Pike, Silver Spring, MD 20904-6600, Tel. (301)680-6000
Media Contact, Dir., Communication, Rajmund Dabrowski
Email: kjones@gc.adventist.org
Website: www.adventist.org

### WORLDWIDE OFFICERS
Pres., Jan Paulsen
Sec., Matthew A. Bediako
Treas., Robert E. Lemon

### WORLDWIDE DEPARTMENTS
Adventist Chaplaincy Ministries, Dir., Martin W. Feldbush
Children's Ministries, Dir., Linda Koh
Education, Dir.,C. Garland Dulan
Communication, Dir., Rajmund Dabrowski
Family Ministries, Dir., Ronald M. Flowers
Health Ministries, Dir., Allan R. Handysides
Ministerial Assoc., Dir., James A. Cress
Public Affairs & Religious Liberty, Dir., John Graz
Publishing, Dir., Howard F. Faigao
Sabbath School & Personal Ministries, Jonathan Kuntaraf
Stewardship, Dir., Erika Puni
Trust Services, Jeffrey K. Wilson
Women's Ministries, Heather-Dawn Small
Youth, Baraka G. Muganda

### NORTH AMERICAN OFFICERS
Pres., Don C. Schneider
Vice Pres., Debra Brill; Gerald Kovalski; Alvin M. Kibble; R. Ernest Castillo
Sec., Roscoe J. Howard III
Treas., Juan R. Prestol

Assoc. Treas., Michael Park; Del L. Johnson; Kenneth W. Osborn

### NORTH AMERICAN ORGANIZATIONS
Atlantic Union Conf., P.O. Box 1189, South Lancaster, MA 01561-1189; Pres., Donald G. King
Canada, Seventh-day Adventist Church in Canada (see Ch. 4)
Columbia Union Conf., 5427 Twin Knolls Rd., Columbia, MD 21045; Pres., David Weigley
Lake Union Conf., P.O. Box C, Berrien Springs, MI 49103; Pres., Walter L. Wright
Mid-America Union Conf., P.O. Box 6128, Lincoln, NE 68506; Pres., Dennis N. Carlson
North Pacific Union Conf., Pres., Jere D. Patzer, P.O. Box 871150, Vancouver, WA 98687
Pacific Union Conf., P.O. Box 5005, Westlake Village, CA 91359; Pres., Thomas J. Mostert, Jr.
Southern Union Conf., P.O. Box 849, Decatur, GA 30031; Pres., Gordon L. Retzer
Southwestern Union Conf., P.O. Box 4000, Burleson, TX 76097; Pres., Max A. Trevino

### Periodicals
*ADRA Works; The Adventist Chaplain; Adventist Review; ASI Magazine; Children's Friend; Christian Record; College and University Dialogue; Collegiate Quarterly; Cornerstone Youth Resource Magazine; Cornerstone Connections; Elder's Digest; Encounter; For God and Country; Geoscience Reports; Guide; It is Written Channels; The Journal of Adventist Education; Kid's Ministry Ideas; Liberty; Lifeglow; Listen; Literature Evangelist; Message; Ministry; Mission—children, youth, adult; Origins; Our Little Friend; Primary Treasure; Publishing Mirror; Sabbath School Teaching Aids; Sabbath School Program Helps; Sabbath School Leadership; Shabbat Shalom; Shepherdess International Journal; Signs of the Times; Transmissions; Vibrant Life; Voice of Prophecy News; Winner; Women of Spirit; Young and Alive; Youth Ministry ACCENT*

## Seventh Day Baptist General Conference, U.S.A. and Canada

Seventh Day Baptists emerged during the English Reformation, organizing their first churches in the mid-1600s. The first Seventh Day Baptists of record in America were Stephen and Ann Mumford, who emigrated from England in 1664. Beginning in 1665 several members of the First Baptist Church at Newport, R.I. began observing the seventh-day Sabbath, or Saturday. In 1671, five members, together with the Mumfords, formed the first Seventh Day Baptist Church in America at Newport.

Beginning about 1700, other Seventh Day Baptist churches were established in New Jersey and Pennsylvania. From these three centers, the denomination grew and expanded westward. They founded the Seventh Day Baptist General Conference in 1802.

The organization of the denomination reflects an interest in home and foreign missions, publications and education. Women have been encouraged to participate. From the earliest years religious freedom has been championed for all and the separation of church and state, advocated.

Seventh Day Baptists are members of the Baptist World Alliance and Baptist Joint Committee. The Seventh Day Baptist World Federation has 17 member conferences on six continents.

### Headquarters

Seventh Day Baptist Center, 3120 Kennedy Rd., P.O. Box 1678, Janesville, WI 53547-1678, Tel. (608)752-5055 Fax (608)752-7711, Media Contact, Ex. Dir., Robert Appel Financial Dir., Morgan D. Shepard
Email: sdbgen@inwave.com
Website: www.seventhdaybaptist.org

### OTHER ORGANIZATIONS

Seventh Day Baptist Missionary Society, Exec. Dir., Kirk Looper, 119 Main St., Westerly, RI 02891

Seventh Day Bapt. Bd. of Christian Ed., Exec. Dir., Rev. Andrew Camenga, Box 115, Alfred Station, NY 14803

Women's Soc. of the Gen. Conference, Pres., Marjorie Jacob, P.O. Box 122, Pomona Park, FL 32181-0122

American Sabbath Tract & Comm. Council, Dir. of Communications, Rev. Kevin J. Butler, 3120 Kennedy Rd., P.O. Box 1678, Janesville, WI 53547

Seventh Day Baptist Historical Society, Historian, Nicholas Kersten, 3120 Kennedy Rd., P.O. Box 1678, Janesville, WI 53547

Seventh Day Baptist Center on Ministry, Dir. of Pastoral Services, Rev. Gordon Lawton, 3120 Kennedy Rd., P.O. Box 1678, Janesville, WI 53547

### Periodicals

*Sabbath Recorder*

## Southern Baptist Convention

The Southern Baptist Convention was organized on May 10, 1845, in Augusta, Ga. Cooperating Baptist churches are located in all 50 states, the District of Columbia, Puerto Rico, American Samoa and the Virgin Islands. The members of the churches work together through 1,182 district associations and 42 state conventions or fellowships. The Southern Baptist Convention has an Executive Committee and 12 national agencies, four boards, six seminaries, one commission, and one auxiliary organization.

The purpose of the Southern Baptist Convention is "to provide a general organization for Baptists in the United States and its territories for the promotion of Christian missions at home and abroad and any other objects such as Christian education, benevolent enterprises, and social services which it may deem proper and advisable

for the furtherance of the Kingdom of God". (Constitution, Article II)

The Convention exists in order to help the churches lead people to God through Jesus Christ.

From the beginning, there has been a mission desire to share the gospel with the peoples of the world. The Cooperative Program is the basic channel of mission support. In addition, the Lottie Moon Christmas Offering for Foreign Missions and the Annie Armstrong Easter Offering for Home Missions support Southern Baptists' world mission programs.

In 2005, there were approximately 5,100 foreign missionaries serving in foreign countries and more than 5,300 home missionaries serving in North America.

### Headquarters

901 Commerce St., Nashville, TN 37203, Tel. (615)244-2355

Media Contact, Vice Pres. for Convention Relations, Kenyn M. Cureton, Tel. (615)244-2355 Fax (615)782-8684
Email: bmerrell@sbc.net
Website: www.sbc.net

### Officers

Pres., Frank Page, 200 West Main St., Taylors, SC 29687

Recording Sec., John Yeats, 1250 MacArthur Dr., Alexandria, LA 71303

Executive Committee, Pres., Morris H. Chapman; Vice Pres., Business & Finance, Jack Wilkerson; Vice Pres., Convention News, Will Hall; Vice Pres., Convention Relations, Kenyn M. Cureton; Vice Pres., Convention Policy, Augie Boto; Vice Pres., Cooperative Program, Bob Rodgers

### GENERAL BOARDS AND COMMISSION

International Mission Board, Pres., Jerry A. Rankin, 3806 Monument Ave, Richmond, VA 23230, Tel. (804)353-6655 x 1207

North American Mission Board, Pres., Vacant, 4200 No. Point Pkwy., Alpharetta, GA 30022-4176, Tel. (770)410-6519

Pres., O. S. Hawkins, 2401 Cedar Springs Rd, Dallas, TX 75201, Tel. (214)720-4700

LifeWay Christian Resources, Pres., Thom S Rainer, One Lifeway Plaza, Nashville, TN 37234, Tel. (615)251-2605

Ethics and Religious Liberty Commission, Pres., Richard D. Land, 901 Commerce St., Suite 550, Nashville, TN 37203, Tel. (615)782-8404

### STATE CONVENTIONS

Alabama, Rick Lance, 2001 E. South Blvd., Montgomery, AL 36116, Tel. (334)288-2460

Alaska, David N. Baldwin, 1750 O'Malley Rd., Anchorage, AK 99516, Tel. (907)344-9627

Arizona, Steve Bass, 2240 N. Hayden Rd., Ste. 100 Scottsdale, AZ 85257 Tel. (480)945-0880

Arkansas, Emil Turner, 525 West Capitol, Little Rock, AR 72203, Tel. (501)376-4791 x 5102

California, Fermin A. Whittaker, 678 E. Shaw Ave., Fresno, CA 93710, Tel. (559)229-9533 x 230

Canadian Convention of Southern Baptists, Gerry Taillon, Postal Bag 300, Cochrane, Alberta T0L 0W0, Tel. (403)932-5688

Colorado, Mark Edlund, 7393 So. Alton Way, Centennial, CO 80112, Tel. (303)771-2480

Dakota Baptist Comvention, Jim Hamilton, P.O. Box 2616, Bismarck, ND 58502, Tel. (701)255-3765

District of Columbia, Rev. Jeffrey Haggray, 1628 16th St. NW, Washington, DC 20009, Tel. (202)265-1526

Florida, John Sullivan, 1230 Hendricks Ave., Jacksonville, FL 32207, Tel. (904)396-2351 x 8101

Georgia, J. Robert White, 6405 Sugarloaf Pkwy., Duluth, GA 30097, Tel. (770)455-0404

Hawaii, Veryl F. Henderson, 2042 Vancouver Dr., Honolulu, HI 96822, Tel. (808)946-9581 x 229

Illinois, Nate Adams, Exec. Dir, 3085 Stevenson Dr, Springfield, IL 62794, Tel. (217)786-2600

Indiana, Stephen P. Davis, 900 N. High School Rd., Indianapolis, IN 46214, Tel. (317)241-9317

Iowa, Jimmy L. Barrentine, Suite #27, 2400 86th St., Des Moines, IA 50322, Tel. (515)278-4369

Kansas-Nebraska, R. Rex Lindsay, 5410 SW. Seventh St., Topeka, KS 66606, Tel. (785)273-4880

Kentucky, Bill F. Mackey, 13420 Eastpoint Centre Dr., Louisville, KY 40223, Tel. (502)489-3370

Louisiana, David E. Hankins, 1250 MacArthur Dr., Alexandria, LA 71303, Tel. (318)448-3402

Maryland-Delaware, David H. Lee, 10255 Old Columbia Rd., Columbia, MD 21046, Tel. (410)290-5290

Michigan, Michael R. Collins, 8420 Runyan Lake Rd., Fenton, MI 48430, Tel. (810)714-1907

Minnesota-Wisconsin, Leo Endel, Exec. Dir., 519 16th St. SE, Rochester, MN 55904, Tel. (507)282-3636

Mississippi, James R. Futral, 515 Mississippi St., Jackson, MS 39201, Tel. (601)968-3800

Missouri, David Clippard, Exec. Dir., 400 E. High Street, Jefferson City, MO 65101, Tel. (573)635-7931 x 200

Montana, Jeffery A. Clark, P.O. Box 99, Billings, MT 59103-0099, Tel. (406)252-7537

Nevada, Thane E. Barnes, Exec. Dir., 406 California Ave., Reno, NV 89509, Tel. (775) 786-0406

New England, James Wideman, 87 Lincoln St., Northborough, MA 01532, Tel. (508)393-6013 x 224

New Mexico, Joseph L. Bruce, 5325 Wyoming, NE, Albuquerque, NM 87109, Tel. (505)924-2300 x 11

New York, Terry M. Robertson, 6538 Baptist Way, East Syracuse, NY 13057, Tel. (315)433-1001

North Carolina, Milton Hollifield, 205 Convention Dr., Cary, NC 27511, Tel. (919)467-5100 x 102

Northwest, Gus Suarez, 3200 NE 109th Ave., Vancouver, WA 98682, Tel. (360)882-2100 x 121

Ohio, Exec. Dir., Jack P. Kwok, 1680 E. Broad, Columbus, OH 43203, Tel. (614)827-1777

Oklahoma, Anthony L. Jordan, 3800 N. May Ave., Oklahoma City, OK 73112, Tel. (405) 942-3800

Pennsylvania-South Jersey, David C. Waltz, 4620 Fritchey St., Harrisburg, PA 17109, Tel. (717)652-5856

South Carolina, B. Carlisle Driggers, 190 Stoneridge Dr., Columbia, SC 29210, Tel. (803)765-0030 x 1200

Tennessee, James M. Porch, 5001 Maryland Way, Brentwood, TN 37027, Tel. (615)371-2090

Texas, (BGCT) Baptist General Convention of Texas, Charles R. Wade, 333 N. Washington, Dallas, TX 75246, Tel. (214)828-5301

Texas, (SBTC) Southern Baptists of Texas, James W. Richards, 4500 State Hwy. 360, Grapevine, TX 76051, Tel. (817)552-2500

Utah-Idaho, Tim Clark, 12401 South 450 East #G-1, Draper, UT 84020, Tel. (801)572-5350

Virginia, (BGAV) Baptist General Association of Virginia, John V. Upton Jr., 2828 Emerywood Pkwy, Richmond, VA 23226, Tel. (804)915-2430 x 223

Virginia, (SBCV) Southern Baptist Conservatives of Virginia, H. Doyle Chauncey, 4101 Cox Rd., Suite 100, Glen Allen, VA 23060, Tel. (804)270-1848

West Virginia, Terry L. Harper, Number One Missions Way, Scott Depot, WV 25560, Tel. (304)757-0944

Wyoming, Lynn Nikkel, 3925 Casper Mountain Rd., Casper, WY 82601, Tel. (307)472-4087

**Periodicals**

*The Commission; SBC Life; On Mission*

## Southern Methodist Church

Organized in 1939, this body is composed of congregations desirous of continuing in true Biblical Methodism and preserving the fundamental doctrines and beliefs of the Methodist Episcopal Church, South. These congregations declined to be a party to the merger of the Methodist Episcopal Church, The Methodist Episcopal Church, South and the Methodist Protestant Church into The Methodist Church.

**Headquarters**

P.O. Box 39, Orangeburg, SC 29116-0039, Tel. (803)536-1378 Fax (803)535-3881

Media Contact, Pres., Rev. John T. Hucks, Jr.

Email: smchq@juno.com, smpresid@bellsouth.net

Pres., Rev. John T. Hucks, Jr.
Dir. Of Admin. & Finance, Rev. Cecil Clark
Director of Foreign Missions, Rev. Bedford Landers, P.O. Box 39, Orangeburg, SC 29116-0039
Southern Methodist College Pres., Rev. Gary Briden, P.O. Box 1027, Orangeburg, SC 29116-1027
The Eastern Conf., Vice Pres., Rev. Ellison Evans, 7980 Forge Rd., Turbeville, SC 29162
Alabama-Florida-Georgia Conf., Vice Pres., Rev. Bob Waites, 220 South Trace Lane, Hoover, AL 35244
Mid-South Conf., Vice Pres., Rev. Joseph Hallman, 11483 Centerhill Martin Rd., Collinsville, MS 39325
South-Western Conf., Vice Pres., Rev. Ira Schilling, 106 Albert Drive, Haughton, LA 71037
Gen. Conf., Treas., Rev. Cecil Clark, P.O. Box 39, Orangeburg, SC 29116-0039

**Periodicals**
*The Southern Methodist*

## Sovereign Grace Believers

The Sovereign Grace Believers are a contemporary movement which began its stirrings in the mid-1950s, when some pastors in traditional Baptist churches returned to a Calvinist-theological perspective.

The first "Sovereign Grace" conference was held in Ashland, Ky., in 1954 and since then, conferences of this sort have been sponsored by various local churches on the West Coast, Southern and Northern states and Canada. This movement is a spontaneous phenomenon concerning reformation at the local church level. Consequently, there is no interest in establishing a Sovereign Grace Baptist "Convention" or "Denomination." Each local church is to administer the keys to the kingdom.

Most Sovereign Grace Believers formally or informally relate to the "First London" (1646), "Second London" (1689) or "Philadelphia" (1742) Confessions.

There is a wide variety of local church government in this movement. Many Calvinist Baptists have a plurality of elders in each assembly. Other Sovereign Grace Believers, however, prefer to function with one pastor and several deacons.

Membership procedures vary from church to church but all require a credible profession of faith in Christ, and proper baptism as a basis for membership.

Calvinistic Baptists financially support gospel efforts (missionaries, pastors of small churches at home and abroad, literature publication and distribution, radio programs, etc.) in various parts of the world.

**Headquarters**
Media Contact, Corres., Jon Zens, P.O. Box 548,
St. Croix Falls, WI 54024, Tel. (651)465-6516
Fax (651)465-5101
Email: jon@searchingtogether.org
Website: www.searchingtogether.org

**Periodicals**
*Searching Together, Sound of Grace*

## The Swedenborgian Church*

Founded in North America in 1792 as the Church of the New Jerusalem, the Swedenborgian Church was organized as a national body in 1817 and incorporated in Illinois in 1861. Its biblically-based theology is derived from the spiritual, or mystical, experiences and exhaustive biblical studies of the Swedish scientist and philosopher Emanuel Swedenborg (1688–1772).

The church centers its worship and teachings on the historical life and the risen and glorified present reality of the Lord Jesus Christ. It looks with an ecumenical vision toward the establishment of the kingdom of God in the form of a universal Church, active in the lives of all people of good will who desire and strive for freedom, peace and justice for all. It is a member of the NCCC and active in many local councils of churches.

With churches and groups throughout the United States and Canada, the denomination's central administrative offices and its seminary, "Swedenborg House of Studies" are located in Newton, Mass. and Berkeley, Calif. Affiliated churches are found in Africa, Asia, Australia, Canada, Europe, the United Kingdom, Japan, South Korea, and South America. Many philosophers and writers have acknowledged their appreciation of Swedenborg's teachings.

**Headquarters**
11 Highland Ave., Newtonville, MA 02460, Tel. (617)969-4240 Fax (617)964-3258
Media Contact, Central Ofc. Mgr., Martha Bauer
Email: manager@swedenborg.org
Website: www.swedenborg.org

**Officers**
Pres., Rev. Christine Laitner, 10 Hannah Court, Midland, MI 48642
Vice Pres., James Erickson, 1340 Snelling Ave, N., St. Paul, MN 55108
Rec. Sec., Susan Wood, 552 Fifth Court, Palm Beach Gardens, FL 33410-5105
Treas., Lawrence Conant, 290 Berlin St., Apt. 89, Clinton, MA 01510, Tel. (978) 368-6269
Ofc. Mgr., Martha Bauer, Tel., (617) 969-4240 Email: manager@swedenborg.org

**Periodicals**
*The Messenger; Our Daily Bread*

## Syrian (Syriac) Orthodox Church of Antioch*

The Syrian Orthodox Church of Antioch traces its origin to the Patriarchate established in Antioch by St. Peter the Apostle. It is under the supreme ecclesiastical jurisdiction of His Holiness the Syrian Orthodox Patriarch of Antioch and All the East, now residing in Damascus, Syria. The Syrian Orthodox Church—composed of several archdioceses, numerous parishes, schools and seminaries—professes the faith of the first three Ecumenical Councils of Nicaea, Constantinople and Ephesus, and numbers faithful in the Middle East, India, the Americas, Europe, Australia and New Zealand.

The first Syrian Orthodox faithful came to North America during the late 1800s, and by 1907 the first Syrian Orthodox priest was ordained to tend to the community's spiritual needs. In 1949, His Eminence Archbishop Mor Athanasius Y. Samuel came to America and was appointed Patriarchal Vicar in 1952. The Archdiocese was officially established in 1957. In 1995, the Archdiocese of North America was divided into three separate Patriarchal Vicariates (Eastern United States, Western United States, and Canada), each under a hierarch of the Church.

There are 28 official archdiocesan parishes in the United States, located in Arizona, California, District of Columbia, Florida, Georgia, Indiana, Illinois, Massachusetts, Michigan, New Jersey, New York, Oregon, Rhode Island, and Texas. In Canada, there are six official parishes—three in the Province of Ontario, two in the Province of Quebec, and one in the Province of Alberta.

### Headquarters

Archdiocese of the Eastern U.S., 260 Elm Avenue, Teaneck, NJ 07666, Tel. (201)801-0660 Fax (201)801-0603

Archdiocese of the Western U.S., 417 E. Fairmount Rd., Burbank, CA 91501, Tel. (818) 953-7170 Fax (818)953-7203

Media Contact, Archdiocesan Gen. Sec., Very Rev. Chorepiscopus John Meno, 260 Elm Ave., Teaneck, NJ 07666, Tel. (201)907-0122 Fax (201)907-0551

Email: hasio@syrianorthodoxchurch.org

Website: www.syrianorthodoxchurch.org

### Officers

Archdiocese for Eastern U.S., Archbishop, Mor Cyril Aphrem Karim

Archdiocese of Los Angeles and Environs, Archbishop, Mor Clemis Eugene Kaplan

## Syro-Russian Orthodox Catholic Church

The Syro-Russian Orthodox Catholic Church was established in May of 1892 as the American Orthodox Catholic Archdiocese of America, and was canonized by His Holiness Ignatius Peter III, Patriarch of Antioch. It was this same Patriarch that issued the Bull for the consecration of its first Archbishop Metropolitan, Timotheos Vilathi, as named by Patriarch Ignatius. The Syro-Russian Orthodox Catholic Church is an Eastern Rite jurisdiction but also has a few Western Rite parishes.

The Synod of Bishops is referred to as the "Syro-Russian Synod of Bishops." This jurisdiction is the Byzantine Rite continuation of what Archbishop Timotheos established in the United States. First parishes of this jurisdiction were established in Wisconsin among Belgians, Italians, Slavs, and other ethnic groups. After Archbishop Timotheos' consecration, parishes were later formed in Ohio, Illinois, and New York, and some missionary work begun in Canada.

After much disagreement with the Patriarchate concerning administration and the Council of Chalcedon, Archbishop Timotheos separated from the Patriarchate. A Consistory was convened on January 1, 1910 concerning the future of the Archdiocese of America. The Bishops agreed upon and decided that, "Our reality as a branch, a part of the true Catholic and Orthodox Church of God, is not dependent upon the recognition of any ecclesiastical authority outside the Councils of our own American Ecclesiastical Consistory and National Synod of Bishops and Clergy." Archbishop Timotheos believed strongly in the truths of the Council of Chalcedon and all the Ecumenical Councils, and the right of the American Church to name its own bishops, and from then on the church was autocephalous and severed from the Patriarchate of Antioch. However, after this time several schisms occurred that gave way to some heretical newly established "churches" that caused the Church to eventually be renamed "Syro-Russian Orthodox Catholic." In the 1970's, after the retirement for health reasons of Archbishop John, Archbishop Joseph of Blessed Memory became the newly enthroned Metropolitan Hierarch of the Church. He possessed Apostolic Succession from both the Syrian and Russian Orthodox Churches later giving the Synod the name of Syro-Russian Orthodox Catholic Church. In 1987, before his death, a meeting was held at St. Paul's Monastery in LaPorte, Indiana and Very Right Reverend Archimandrite Stephen (Thomas) was duly elected Metropolitan Hierarch. He was consecrated Bishop on October 18th, 1987, by Archbishop Joseph assisted by Archbishop George and Bishop Norman at St. Mary's Chapel, LaPorte, Ind., and the following year enthroned as metropolitan Archbishop Hierarch. Archbishop Stephen has caused the church to grow throughout the world. From 1994-96, he endured many sufferings as the result of some clergy who went astray and were since deposed of their faculties and offices. Since that time, the church has experienced peace, growth, and new viability. The Divine Liturgy of St. John Chrysostom is the official liturgy of the Church. In addition, as with all other Orthodox Churches, the Liturgy of Saint Basil is used ten times a year, and the Presanctified Liturgy as prescribed. The Traditions of Holy Orthodoxy are observed in the administration of the Holy Mysteries (Sacraments) and, as is practice in the Russian Orthodox

163

Church, Holy Myron (Chrism) is consecrated by the Metropolitan Hierarch on Holy Thursday and distributed to the clergy of the church.

Some western customs exist within the church. Hyperveneration is given to icons that memorialize the saints and events in the life of Jesus Christ and the Holy Theotokos Mary. It follows the Gregorian Calendar and the Orthodox date of Pascha (Easter), and the Julian Calendar is allowed. The Syro-Russian Orthodox Catholic Church, strongly believes in the separation of church and state, and healing by licensed practitioners is allowed but only by the clergy is the Mystery of Holy Unction administered. The Synodal Metropolinate has received official recognition from the Hellenic (Greek) Orthodox Church of Athens, and is in full communion with the Ukrainian Orthodox Church in Exile. It maintains dialogue with other Julian Calendar Churches and seeks communion with them. It also has dialogue with True Orthodox Church of Greece, The Macedonian Orthodox Church, and several other jurisdictions. There is one monastic order, The Monastic Community of Saint Basil, which is open to men and women that is headquartered in England. The Synod of Bishops is composed of the following: Archbishop Stephen (United States), Bishop Benjamin (Bangladesh), Bishop George (United Kingdom), Bishop John (India), Chorbishop Joseph (Belgium), Bishop-elect Ricardo (Cuba), Bishop-elect Steven (Nigeria), and retired Chorbishop John (United States). The Vicariate of Pakistan is currently served by a Vicar General, Very Reverend Father John Asir, as the result of an episcopal vacancy there. Vicars serve the mission territories of Belgium, Nicaragua, Kenya, The Congo, and Tanzania. The Church of Bangladesh recently united with the Syro-Russian Orthodox Catholic Church. Clergy are trained for the church through St. Mark's (RBC) Seminary of Fairfax Virginia; St. Basil's Seminary of Havana, Cuba; Holy Trinity Seminary (Lahore Pakistan) or Holy Apostles School and College (Dar es Salaam Tanzania). A distance education program for mature candidates is offered by the Archdiocese through St Mark / Romano Byzantine College (Virginia). The national headquarters at this time is located at St. Mary the Theotokos Pro-Cathedral in Duluth, Minn.

### Headquarters

St. Mary the Theotokos Pro-Cathedral, 5907 Grand Ave, Duluth, MN 55087, Tel. (218)624-0202 Fax (218)590-8435
Email: rbsocc@juno.com

### Officers

Primate: Most Reverend Archbishop Stephen, St Mary Pro-Cathedral, 5907 Grand Avenue, Duluth Minnesota 55807, Tel. (218)624-0202, Email: rbsocc@juno.com
Vicar General: Fr. Archimandrite Timothy Kjera, St Nicholas Center, 1318 Baxter Avenue, Superior, WI 54880, Tel. (218)590-8435, Email: fr_timothy_kjera@hotmail.com

Archdiocesan Chaplain: V.R. Father Patrick Lemming, 304 Grace Avenue, Sevierville TN 37862, Tel. (865)429-3641
Chivalric Order of Christ the Pantocrator: Father Demetrios E Wruck DC—(Interim Chaplain and Moderator)
Commission on Religious Counseling and Healing: Mod., Fr Archimandrite Timothy Kjera; Pres., Father Haralambos Winger; Rec., Father Mark K Mwaga; Can. Liaison, Dr Peter Smyth
Monastic Community of St. Basil and Sisters of the Community of St. Basil: Abbot, Bishop George, Superior—St. Mary Mother of God Convent in the Congo, Africa, Mother Helena

### Periodicals

*Orthodox Christian Herald*

# Triumph the Church and Kingdom of God in Christ Inc. (International)

This church was given through the wisdom and knowledge of God to the Late Apostle Elias Dempsey Smith on Oct. 20, 1897, in Issaquena County, Miss., while he was pastor of a Methodist church.

The Triumph Church, as this body is more commonly known, was founded in 1902. Its doors opened in 1904 and it was confirmed in Birmingham, Alabama, with 225 members in 1915. It was incorporated in Washington, D.C. in 1918 and currently operates in 31 states and overseas. The General Church is divided into 13 districts, including the Africa District.

Triumphant doctrine and philosophy are based on the principles of life, truth and knowledge; the understanding that God is in man and expressed through man; the belief in manifested wisdom and the hope for constant new revelations. Its concepts and methods of teaching the second coming of Christ are based on these and all other attributes of goodness.

Triumphians emphasize that God is the God of the living, not the God of the dead.

### Headquarters

213 Farrington Ave. S.E., Atlanta, GA 30315
Media Contact, Bishop Zephaniah Swindle, 7114 Idlewild, Pittsburg, PA 15208, Tel. (412)731-2286

### Officers

Chief Bishop, Bishop Zephaniah Swindle, Rt. 1, Box 1927, Shelbyville, TX 75973, Tel. (936) 598-3082
Gen. Bd of Trustees, Chmn., Rev. Oprah Francis
Gen. Rec. Sec., Bishop R.D. Clarke
Gen. Treas., Bishop W.R. Matt Malcolm

# True Orthodox Church of Greece (Synod of Metropolitan Cyprian), American Exarchate

The American Exarchate of the True (Old

Calendar) Orthodox Church of Greece adheres to the tenets of the Eastern Orthodox Church, which considers itself the legitimate heir of the historical Apostolic Church.

When the Orthodox Church of Greece adopted the New, or Gregorian, Calendar in 1924, many felt that this breach with tradition compromised the Church's festal calendar, based on the Old, or Julian, Calendar, and its unity with world Orthodoxy. In 1935, three State Church Bishops returned to the Old Calendar and established a Synod in Resistance, the True Orthodox Church of Greece. When the last of these Bishops died, the Russian Orthodox Church Abroad consecrated a new Hierarchy for the Greek Old Calendarists and, in 1969, declared them a Sister Church.

In the face of persecution by the State Church, some Old Calendarists denied the validity of the Mother Church of Greece and formed two synods, now under the direction of Archbishop Chrysostomos of Athens and Archbishop Andreas of Athens. A moderate faction under Metropolitan Cyprian of Oropos and Fili does not maintain communion with the Mother Church of Greece, but recognizes its validity and seeks a restoration of unity by a return to the Julian Calendar and traditional ecclesiastical polity by the State Church. About 1.5 million Orthodox Greeks belong to the Old Calendar Church.

The first Old Calendarist communities in the United States were formed in the 1930s. The Exarchate under Metropolitan Cyprian was established in 1986. Placing emphasis on clergy education, youth programs, and recognition of the Old Calendarist minority in American Orthodoxy, the Exarchate has encouraged the establishment of monastic communities and missions. Cordial contacts with the New Calendarist and other Orthodox communities are encouraged. A center for theological training and Patristic studies has been established at the Exarchate headquarters in Etna, Calif.

In July 1994, the True Orthodox Church of Greece (Synod of Metropolitan Cyprian), the True Orthodox Church of Romania, the True Orthodox Church of Bulgaria, and the Russian Orthodox Church Abroad entered into liturgical union, forming a coalition of traditionalist Orthodox bodies several million strong.

### Headquarters
St. Gregory Palamas Monastery, P.O. Box 398, Etna, CA 96027-0398, Tel. (530)467-3228 Fax (530) 467-5828
Media Contact, Exarch in America, His Eminence Archbishop Chrysostomos

### Officers
Acting Synodal Exarch in America, His Grace Bishop Auxentios
Chancellor of the Exarchate, The Very Rev. Raphael Abraham, 3635 Cottage Grove Ave. S.E., Cedar Rapids, IA 52403-1612

### Periodicals
*Orthodox Tradition* (quarterly theological journal)

## Ukrainian Orthodox Church of the U.S.A.*

The Ukrainian Orthodox Church of the U.S.A. has its origin in the ancient lands of Rus-Ukraine (present day Ukraine). It was to the inhabitants of these lands that the Apostle Andrew first preached the gospel. Christianization began early in the history of Rus-Ukraine by missionaries from the Orthodox Christian See of Constantinople. In 988 A.D., the Saintly Prince Volodymyr, crowned a process of Christian Evangelization begun in the 4th century, by personally accepting Orthodox Christianity and inspiring his subjects to do the same. The baptism of Volodymyr, his household and the inhabitants of Kyiv, altered the face of Kyivan Rus-Ukraine and Slavic history for all time. Kyiv became the spiritual heart of Orthodox Christians in Rus-Ukraine. It was from this See that missionaries were sent into every corner of St. Volodymyr's realm. Through their efforts the gospel was preached and new communities were established. The Mother Church of Kyiv and its See of Saint Sophia, modeled after Constantinople's See of the same name, gave birth to many Orthodox Christian centers and communities in the west, east and north of the Dnipro river, among them the Orthodox Christian See of Moscow, Russia (Rosia).

The Ukrainian Orthodox Church of U.S.A. ministers to the needs of the faithful whose ancestral roots are in Ukraine. The church found haven in America in the early 1920s. Its first bishop, Metropolitan Ioan (John) Teodorovych, arrived from Ukraine in 1924 and shepherded the Church as Metropolitan until his death in 1971. His successor, Archbishop Mstyslav, arrived in the U.S.A. in 1950, and shepherded the Church as Metropolitan from 1971 until his death in 1993. It was Metropolitan Mstyslav who, as a consequence of Ukraine's independence, was named Patriarch of Kyiv and All Ukraine, in 1990. Previous to 1996 there were two Ukrainian Orthodox jurisdictions in the U.S.A. Formal unification of the Ukrainian Orthodox Church of the U.S.A., shepherded by His Beatitude Metropolitan Constantine, and the Ukrainian Orthodox Church of America, shepherded by His Grace Bishop Vsevolod, was concluded in November 1996.

### Headquarters
Saint Andrew the Firstcalled Apostle Ukrainian Orthodox Church Center, P.O. Box 495, South Bound Brook, NJ 08880, Tel. (732)356-0090 Fax (732)356-5556
Media Contact, His Eminence Antony, Archbishop of New York, Consistory President
Email: consistory@uocofusa.org
Website: www.uocofusa.org

165

**Officers**

Metropolitan, His Beatitude Constantine, 1803 Sidney Street, Pittsburgh, PA 15203

**CENTRAL EPARCHY**

Eparchial Bishop, Metropolitan Constantine

Eparchial See, St. Volodymyr Cathedral, 5913 State Rd., Parma, OH 44134, Tel. (440)885-1509

Eparchial Territory: Florida, Georgia, Ohio, Western Pennsylvania

**EASTERN EPARCHY**

Eparchial Bishop, Archbishop Antony.

Eparchial Seat, St. Volodymyr Cathedral, 160 West 82nd St. New York, NY 10024, Tel. (212)873-8550

Eparchial Territory: Connecticut, Deleware, Massachusetts, Maryland, New Jersey, New York, Pennsylvania, Rhode Island

**WESTERN EPARCHY**

Eparchial Bishop, Archbishop Vsevolod

Eparchial Seat, St. Volodymyr Cathedral, 2230-50 West Cortez St. Chicago, IL 60622, Tel. (312)278 2827

Eparchial Territory: Arizona, California, Colorado, Illinois, Indiana, Michigan, Minnesota, North Dakota, Nebraska, Oregon, Washington, Wisconsin, Ontario Province

**COUNCIL OF BISHOPS**

Metropolitan Constantine—Chair

Achbishop Antony—Secretary

Achbishop Vsevolod—Member

**METROPOLITAN COUNCIL MEMBERS**

Archimandrite Andriy—Vice-chairman

Protopresbyter William Diakiw

Protopresbyter Frank Estocin, JCB

Protopriest John Nakonachny

Protopriest Michael Kochis

Protopriest Eugene Meschisen

Protopriest Bazyl Zawierucha

Dr. Gayle Woloschak—English Language Secretary

Mr. Emil Skocypec

Dr. Paul Micevych

Dr. George Krywolap—Ukrainian Language Secretary

Dr. Anatol Lysyj

Mrs. Helen Greenleaf

Mr. Michael Kapeluck

Daria Pishko, Ukrainian Orthodox League President

Mrs. Nadia Mirchuk, United Ukrainian Orthodox Sisterhoods President

Mr. Michael Heretz, Saint Andrew Society, President

**CONSISTORY**

Consistory President, His Eminence Antony, Archbishop of New York, P.O. Box 495, South Bound Brook, NJ 08880, Tel. (732)356-0090 Fax (732)356-5556, Email: uocofusa@aol.com

Vice Pres., Protopresbyter Willam Diakiw

Sec., Protopriest Frank Estocin

Treas., Mr. Emil Skocypec

Member, Protopriest John Nakonachny

Member, Protopriest Bazyl Zawierucha

Member, Dr. George Krywolap

**Periodicals**

*Ukrainian Orthodox Word; Vira*

## Unitarian Universalist Association of Congregations

History: The Unitarian Universalist Association (UUA), created in 1961 through a consolidation of the Universalist Church of America with the American Unitarian Association, combines two liberal religious traditions. The religion traces its roots back to Europe where in 1569, the Transylvanian king, John Sigismund (1540-1571), issued an edict of religious freedom. The religious philosophy led to the organization of the Universalists in this country in 1793, and the Unitarians (organized here in 1825).

Beliefs: Founders of Universalism believed in universal salvation of all humans by God, while founders of Unitrarianism believed in the unity of God (as opposed to the Trinity). Unitarian Universalism is a liberal, creedless religion with Judeo-Christian roots. It draws also from Eastern, humanist, and other religious traditions, and encourages its members to seek religious truth out of their own reflection and experience. The denomination teaches tolerance and respect for other religious viewpoints, and affirms the worth and dignity of every person.

Organization and Government: The Unitarian Universalist Association consists of over 1,010 congregations in the United States and Canada, with over 220,000 members, and is served by more than 1,100 ministers. The Association is the fastest-growing liberal religion in North America, and this year completed its twenty-first consecutive year of growth, at an average annual rate of nearly 2 percent. Each member congregation within the UUA is governed independently. In North America, the Association is made up of 20 Districts (served by a District Executive who is a member of the UUA staff), with each congregation having district affiliation. The Association is governed by an elected Board of Trustees, chaired by an elected Moderator. An elected President, three vice presidents, and directors of five departments form the Executive Staff that administers the daily activities of the Association.

The General Assembly, held each June in a different UUA District, serves as the Association's annual business meeting. The UUA includes Departments of Ministry and Professional Leadership; Lifespan Faith Development; Congregational Services; Identity Based Ministries; District Services; Advocacy and Witness; Financial Development; and Communications. "The World", published bi-monthly, is the denominational journal. Beacon Press, an internationally honored publishing house, is wholly owned by the Unitarian Universalist Association.

### Headquarters
25 Beacon Street, Boston, MA 02108, Tel. (617) 742-2100 Fax (617)367-3237
Media Contact, John Hurley, Director of Information, Tel. (617)742-2100 x 131
Email: jhurley@uua.org
Website: www.uua.org

### Officers
President, The Rev. William Sinkford
Moderator, Gini Courter
Executive Vice President, Kathleen C. Montgomery

### Periodicals
*UU World; InterConnections*

## The United Catholic Church, Inc.
History: In 1996, a group of independent Catholic bishops, meeting in synod, asked then Bishop Robert M. Bowman to draw up guide-lines for "inclusivity." Under these guidelines a fellowship of independent Catholic churches and clergy was born under the leadership of now Archbishop Robert M. Bowman. This fellowship was Incorporated in the State of Florida as a not-for-profit corporation in August of 1996 for the purposes of educating and ordaining clergy, organizing dioceses, parishes and ministries, conducting religious services, entering into vari-ous affiliations with other Christian churches, and educating the public on religious, moral and social issues. In June 2006, Bishop Rose Tressel became Presiding Bishop.

### Headquarters
Media Contact: Bishop Rose Tressel, Presiding Bishop, 51 Hilltop Rd., Bethany, CT 06524, Tel. (203)393-3260, Email: unitedcatholic @snet.net
Email: catholic@rmbowman.com
Website: www.united-catholic-church.org

### Officers
Archbishop Robert M. Bowman, Primate, 5017 Bellflower Ct, Melbourne, FL 32940, Tel. (321)752-5955, Email: catholic@rmbowman. com
Bishop Rose Tressel, Presiding Bishop, 51 Hilltop Rd., Bethany, CT 06524, Tel. (203) 393-3260, Email: unitedcatholic@snet.net
Monsignor William Menter, Vicar General; member, Board of Directors, 271 Dickinson St NE, Palm Bay, FL 32907, Tel. (321)956-6792, Cell: (321)223-1179, Email: menterwm@ earthlink.net
Bishop Hollis Dodge, Vicar for Military Chaplaincy, 802 Donaghue St., Staunton, VA

24401, Tel. (540)448-4623, Email: Christchurch staunton@msn.com
Deacon Margaret E. Bowman, Director of Music and Liturgy, 5017 Bellflower Ct, Melbourne, FL 32940, Tel. (321)752-5955, Cell: (321) 759-5726, Email: maggie@rmbowman.com
Bishop Bernardo Morales, Docesan Bishop, 6315 Bass Highway, P.O. Box 702192, St. Cloud, FL 34771, Tel. (407)498-0333, Email: bmorales3@cfl.rr.com
Bishop Hollis Dodge, Diocesan Bishop, 802 Donaghue St., Staunton, VA 24401, Tel. (540) 448-4623, Email: Christchurchstaunton @msn. com
Bishop William Christen, Associate Church Bishop, 3060 W. Belle Ave, Queen Creek, AZ 85242, Cell: (480)857-4070, Email: frbill2002 @yahoo.com

### Periodicals
*The United Catholic Quarterly*

## United Christian Church
The United Christian Church originated about 1864. There were some ministers and laymen in the United Brethren in Christ Church who dis-agreed with the position and practice of the church on infant baptism, voluntary bearing of arms and belonging to oath-bound secret combi-nations. This group developed into United Christian Church, organized at a conference held in Campbelltown, Pa., on May 9, 1877. The prin-cipal founders of the denomination were George Hoffman, John Stamn and Thomas Lesher. Before they were organized, they were called Hoffmanites.

The United Christian Church has district con-ferences, a yearly general conference, a general board of trustees, a mission board, a board of directors of the United Christian Church Home, a camp meeting board, a young peoples' board and local organized congregations.

It believes in the Holy Trinity and the inspired Holy Scriptures with the doctrines they teach. The church practices the ordinances of Baptism, Holy Communion and Foot-Washing.

It welcomes all into its fold who are born again, believe in Jesus Christ as Savior and Lord and have received the Holy Spirit.

### Headquarters
Media Contact, Presiding Elder, John W. Graybill, 35 Oakwood Dr. Palmyra, PA. 17078, Tel. (717)838-4798, Email: graybilly@aol.com

### Officers
Presiding Elder, Elder John W. Graybill
Conf. Sec., Mr. Lee Wenger, 1625 Thompson Ave., Annville, PA 17003
Conf. Moderator, Elder Gerald Brinser, 2360 Horseshoe Pike, Annville, PA 17003

### OTHER ORGANIZATIONS
Mission Board, Pres., Elder John Graybill, 35 Oakwood Drive, Palmyra, PA 17078 Email:

167

graybilly@aol.com; Sec., Elder David Heagy, 4129 Oak St., Lebanon, PA 17042; Treas., Mr. Robert Morgan, 1413 Harding Ave., Hershey, PA 17033

## United Church of Christ*

The United Church of Christ was constituted on June 25, 1957 by representatives of the Congregational Christian Churches and of the Evangelical and Reformed Church, in Cleveland, Ohio.

The Preamble to the Constitution states, "The United Church of Christ acknowledges as its sole head, Jesus Christ ... It acknowledges as kindred in Christ all who share in this confession. It looks to the Word of God in the Scriptures, and to the presence and power of the Holy Spirit ... It claims ... the faith of the historic Church expressed in the ancient creeds and reclaimed in the basic insights of the Protestant Reformers. It affirms the responsibility of the Church in each generation to make this faith its own in ... worship, in honesty of thought and expression, and in purity of heart before God. ... it recognizes two sacraments, Baptism and the Lord's Supper."

The creation of the United Church of Christ brought together four unique traditions-

(1) Groundwork for the Congregational Way was laid by Calvinist Puritans and Separatists during the late 16th-early 17th centuries, then achieved prominence among English Protestants during the civil war of the 1640s. Opposition to state control prompted followers to emigrate to the United States, where they helped colonize New England in the 17th century. Congregationalists have been self-consciously a denomination from the mid-19th century.

(2) The Christian Churches, an 18th-century American restorationist movement emphasized Christ as the only head of the church, the New Testament as their only rule of faith, and "Christian" as their sole name. This loosely organized denomination found in the Congregational Churches a like disposition. In 1931, the two bodies formally united as the Congregational Christian Churches.

(3) The German Reformed Church comprised an irenic aspect of the Protestant Reformation, as a second generation of Reformers drew on the insights of Zwingli, Luther and Calvin to formulate the Heidelberg Catechism of 1563. People of the German Reformed Church began immigrating to the New World early in the 18th century, the heaviest concentration in Pennsylvania. Formal organization of the American denomination was completed in 1793. The church spread across the country. In the Mercersburg Movement, a strong emphasis on evangelical catholicity and Christian unity was developed.

(4) In 19th-century Germany, Enlightenment criticism and Pietist inwardness decreased longstanding conflicts between religious groups. In Prussia, a royal proclamation merged Lutheran and Reformed people into one United Evangelical Church (1817). Members of this new church way migrated to America. The Evangelicals settled in large numbers in Missouri and Illinois, emphasizing pietistic devotion and unionism; in 1840 they formed the German Evangelical Church Society in the West. After union with other Evangelical church associations, in 1877 it took the name of the German Evangelical Synod of North America.

On June 25, 1934, this Synod and the Reformed Church in the U.S. (formerly the German Reformed Church) united to form the Evangelical and Reformed Church. They blended the Reformed tradition's passion for the unity of the church and the evangelical tradition's commitment to the liberty of conscience inherent in the gospel.

### Headquarters

700 Prospect Avenue, Cleveland, OH 44115, Tel. (216)736-2100 Fax (216)736-2103 Toll-free (866)822-8224 (866-UCC-UCC4)

Media Contact, Rev. J. Bennett Guess, 700 Prospect Ave., Cleveland, OH 44115, Tel. (216)736-2177 Fax (216)736-2223

Email: kellys@ucc.org

Website: www.ucc.org

### Officers

Gen. Minister and Pres., Rev. John H. Thomas

Assoc. Gen. Minister, Ms. Edith A. Guffey

Exec. Minister, Wider Church Ministries, Rev. Cally Rogers-Witte

Exec. Minister, Justice and Witness Ministries, Rev. M. Linda Jaramillo

Exec. Minister, Local Church Ministries, Rev. José A. Malayang

Chair, Executive Council, Rev. Sharom MacArthur

Vice Chair, Executive Council, Mr. Aaron Gould

Mod., General Synod, Mr. Merlyn Lawrence

Asst. Mod., General Synod, Rev. Elizabeth King

Asst. Mod., General Synod, Mr. Kevin Manz

### ORGANIZATIONS

Office of General Ministries, National Office, 700 Prospect Avenue, Cleveland, Ohio 44115. Tel. (216)736-2100 Fax (216)736-2103, General Minister and President, Rev. John H. Thomas; Associate General Minister, Ms. Edith A. Guffey

Justice and Witness Ministries, National Offices (as above), Tel. (216)736-3700 Fax (216)736-3703, Franklinton Center at Bricks, P.O. Box 220, Whitakers, NC 27891 Tel. (252)437-1723 Fax (252)437-1278, Washington Office, 100 Maryland Avenue North East, Suite 330, Washington, DC. 20002 Tel. (202)543-1517 Fax (202)543-5994, Executive Minister, Rev. M. Linda Jaramillo Local Church Ministries, National Offices, Tel. (216)736-3800 Fax (216)736-3803 Executive Minister, Rev. José A. Malayang

Wider Church Ministries, National Offices (as

above), Tel. (216)736-3200 Fax (216)736-3203, Disciples of Christ Division of Overseas Ministries, P.O. Box 1986, Indianapolis, IN 46206, Tel. (317)635-3100 Fax (317)635-4323, Executive Minister, Rev. Cally Rogers-Witte

Pension Boards, Main Office, 475 Riverside Drive, New York, NY 10115, Tel. (212)729-2700 Fax (212)729-2701; National Office, 475 Riverside Drive, New York, NY 10115, Tel. (216)736-2271 Fax (216)736-2274, Executive Vice President, Mr. Michael A. Downs

United Church Foundation, Inc., 475 Riverside Drive, New York, NY 10115, Tel. (212)729-2600 Fax (212)729-2601, President/Chief Executive Officer, Mr. Donald G. Hart, Council for American Indian Ministry, 1200E. Highland Acres Rd., Bismarck, ND 58501, Tel. (701)255-2035, Executive Director, Vacant

Council for Health and Human Services Ministries, National Office (as above), Tel. (216)736-2250 Fax (216)736-2251, President and Chief Executive Officer, Rev. Bryan W. Sickbert

## CONFERENCES
### Western Region
California, Nevada, Northern, Rev. Mary Susan Gast, 21425 Birch Street, Hayward, CA 94541-2131

California, Southern, Rev. Daniel F. Romero and Rev. Jane E. Heckles, 2401 N. Lake Ave., Altadena, CA 91001

Central Pacific, Rev. Héctor E. López and Eugene Ross, 0245 SW Bancroft St. Ste. E, Portland, OR 97239

Hawaii, Rev. Charles Buck, 15 Craigside Pl., Honolulu, HI 96817

Montana-Northern Wyoming, Rev. Randall Hyvonen, 2016 Alderson Ave., Billings, MT 59102

Pacific Northwest, Rev. Mark Miller, 6218 Beacon Ave. So., Seattle, WA 98108

Rocky Mountain, Rev. Tom Rehling, 1140 W. 5th Ave., Denver, CO 80204

Southwest, Rev. Cally Rogers-Witte, 4423 N. 24th St., Ste. 600, Phoenix, AZ 85016

### West Central Region
Iowa, Rev. Lark J. Hapke, 600 42nd St., Des Moines, IA 50312

Kansas-Oklahoma, Rev. David Hansen, 1245 Fabrique, Wichita, KS 67218

Minnesota, Rev. David McMahill, 122 W. Franklin Ave., Rm. 323, Minneapolis, MN 55404

Missouri, Mid-South, Rev. A. Gayle Engel, 461 E. Lockwood Ave., St. Louis, MO 63119

Nebraska, Rev. Roddy Dunkerson, 825 M St. #201, Lincoln, NE 68508

Northern Plains, Rev. Wade Schemmel, 1200 E. Highland Acres Rd., Bismarck, ND 58501

South Dakota, Rev. Gene E. Miller, 3500 S. Phillips Ave., #241, Sioux Falls, SD 57105-6864

### Great Lakes Region
Illinois, Rev. Jane Fisler Hoffman, 1840 Westchester Blvd. #200, Westchester, IL 60154

Illinois South, Rev. Gene Kraus, P.O. Box 325, 1312 Broadway, Highland, IL 62249

Indiana-Kentucky, Rev. Stephen C. Gray, 1100 W. 42nd St. #350, Indianapolis, IN 46208

Michigan, Rev. Kent J. Ulery, P.O. Box 1006, 5945 Park Lake Rd., East Lansing, MI 48826

Ohio, Rev. Jack Seville, 6161 Busch Blvd., #95, Columbus, OH 43229

Wisconsin, Rev. David Moyer, 4459 Gray Rd., P.O. Box 435, De Forest, WI 53532-0495

### Southern Region
Florida, Rev. Jack Richards, 924 Magnolia Ave. #250, Orlando, FL 32803

South Central, Rev. Bill Royster, 6633 E. Hwy. 290, #200, Austin, TX 78723-1157

Southeast, Rev. Timothy C. Downs, 756 W. Peachtree St., NW, Atlanta, GA 30308

Southern, Rev. Steve Camp, 216 S. Antioch Ave., Box 215, Elon, NC 27244

### Middle Atlantic Region
Central Atlantic, Rev. John R. Deckenback, 916 S. Rolling Rd., Baltimore, MD 21228

New York, Rev. Geoffrey A. Black, 5800 Heritage Landing Drive, Suite 2D, East Syracuse, NY 13057

Penn Central, Rev. Marja Coons-Torn, 900 S. Arlington Ave. #112, Harrisburg, PA 17109

Penn Northeast, Rev. Alan C. Miller, 431 Delaware Ave., Palmerton, PA 18071

Pennsylvania Southeast, Rev. F. Russell Mittman, 505 S. Second Ave., P.O. Box 26400, Collegeville, PA 19426-0400

Penn West, Rev. Alan McLarty, 320 South Maple Ave., Greensburg, PA 15601

Puerto Rico, Rev. Luis Rosario, P.O. Box 8609, Caguas, PR 00762

### New England Region
Connecticut, Rev. Davida Foy Crabtree, 125 Sherman St., Hartford, CT 06105

Maine, Rev. David R. Gaewski, 28 Yarmouth Crossing Dr., P.O. Box 966, Yarmouth, ME 04096

Massachusetts, Rev. Jim Antal, 1 Badger Rd., Framingham, MA 01702

New Hampshire, Rev. Gary Schulte, 140 Sheep Davis Rd, Pembroke, NH 03275

Rhode Island, Rev. Charles Barnes, 56 Walcott St., Pawtucket, RI 02860

Vermont, Rev. Susan Henderson, INT, 36 N. Main St., Randolph, VT 05060

### Nongeographic
Calvin Synod, Rev. Koloman K. Ludwig, 7319 Tapper Ave., Hammond, IN 46324

### Periodicals
*United Church News; Common Lot*

## United Holy Church of America, Inc.
The United Holy Church of America, Inc. is an outgrowth of the great revival that began with the

169

outpouring of the Holy Ghost on the Day of Pentecost. The church is built upon the foundation of the Apostles and Prophets, Jesus Christ being the cornerstone.

During a revival of repentence, regeneration and holiness of heart and life that swept through the South and West, the United Holy Church was born. The founding fathers had no desire to establish a denomination but were pushed out of organized churches because of this experience of holiness and testimony of the Spirit-filled life.

On the first Sunday in May 1886, in Method, North Carolina, what is today known as the United Holy Church of America, Inc. was born. The church was incorporated on Sept. 25, 1918.

Baptism by immersion, the Lord's Supper and feet washing are observed. The premillennial teaching of the Second Coming of Christ, Divine healing, justification by faith, sanctification as a second work of grace and Spirit baptism are accepted.

### Headquarters

5104 Dunstan Rd., Greensboro, NC 27405, Tel. (336)621-0669

Media Contact, Gen. Statistician, Ms. Jacquelyn B. McCain, 1210 N. Euclid Ave., Apt. A, St. Louis, MO 63113-2012, Tel. (314)367-8351 Fax (314)367-1835

Email: books@mohistory.org

### GENERAL ADMINISTRATION

Gen. Pres., The Rt. Rev. Odell McCollum, 707 Woodmark Run, Gahanna, OH 43230, Tel. (614)475-4713 Fax (614)475-4713

Gen. Vice Pres., Bishop Elijah Williams, 901 Briarwood St., Reidsville, NC 27320, Tel. (919)349-7275

Gen. 2nd Vice Pres., The Rt. Rev. Kenneth O. Robinson, Sr., 33 Springbrook Road, Nanuet, NY 10954-4423, Tel. (914)425-8311 Fax (914)352-2686

Gen. Rec. Sec., Rev. Mrs. Elsie Harris, 2304 Eighth Street, Portsmouth, VA 23704, Tel. (757)399-0926

Asst. Rec. Sec., Cassandra Jones, 3869 JoAnn Drive, Cleveland, OH 44122, Tel. (216)921-0097

Gen. Fin. Sec., Vera Perkins-Hughes, P.O. Box 6194, Cleveland, OH Tel. (216)851-7448

Asst. Fin. Sec., Bertha Williams, 4749 Shaw Dr., Wilmington, NC 28405, Tel. (919)395-4462

Gen. Corres. Sec., Ms. Gwendolyn Lane, 3069 Hudson Street, Columbus, OH 43219

Gen. Treas., Louis Bagley, 8779 Wales Dr., Cincinnati, OH 45249, Tel. (513)247-0588

### GENERAL OFFICERS

Gen. Pres. Missionary Dept., Rev. Ardelia M. Corbett, 519 Madera Dr., Youngstown, OH 44504, Tel. (216)744-3284

Gen. Evangelism & Extension Dept., Pres., Elder Clifford R. Pitts, 3563 North 14th St., Milwaukee, WI 53206, Tel. (414)244-1319

Gen. Bible Church School Dept., Superintendent, Robert L. Rollins, 1628 Avondale Ave.,

Toledo, OH 43607, Tel. (419)246-4046

Gen. Y.P.H.A., Pres., Elder James W. Brooks, Rt. 3 Box 105, Pittsboro, NC 27312, Tel. (919) 542-5357

Gen. Ushers Department, Pres., Ms. Sherly M. Hughes, 1491 East 191st Street, #H-604, Euclid, OH 44117, Tel. (216)383-0038

Gen. Educ. Dept., Elder Roosevelt Alston, 168 Willow Creek Run, Henderson, NC 27636, Tel. (919)438-5854

Gen. Music Dept., Chair, Rosie Johnson, 2009 Forest Dale Dr., Silver Spring, MD 20932

Gen. Historian, Dr. Chester Gregory, Sr., 1302 Lincoln Woods Dr., Baltimore, MD 21228, Tel. (410)788-5144

Gen. Counsel, Mr. Joe L. Webster, Esquire, Attorney-At-Law, P.O. Box 2301, Chapel Hill, NC 27515-2301, Tel. (919)542-5150

UHCA Academy, Dir., Ms. Stephanie Davis, The United Holy Church of America, Inc., 5104 Dunstan Road, Greensboro, NC 27405, Tel. (336)621-0069

Gen. Statistician, Ms. Jacquelyn B. McCain, 1210 N. Euclid Ave., Apt. A, St. Louis, MO 63113-2012, Tel. (314)367-8351 Fax (314) 367-1835

### PRESIDENTS OF CONVOCATIONAL DISTRICTS

Barbados District; The Rt. Rev. Jestina Gentles, 5 West Ridge St., Britton's Hill, St. Michael, BH2 Barbados, West Indies, Tel. (246)427-7185

Bermuda Dist., The Rt. Rev. Calvin Armstrong, P.O. Box 234, Paget, Bermuda, Tel. (441)296-0828 or (441)292-8383

Central Western Dist., Bishop Bose Bradford, 6279 Natural Bridge, Pine Lawn, MO 63121, Tel. (314)355-1598

Ghana, West Africa Dist., The Rt. Rev. Robert Blount, 231 Arlington Av., Jersey City, NJ 07035, Tel. (201)433-5672

New England Dist., The Rt. Rev. Lowell Edney, 85 Woodhaven St., Mattapan, MA 02126, Tel. (617)296-5366

Northern Dist., The Rt. Rev. Kenneth O. Robinson, Sr., 33 Springbrook Rd., Nanuet, NY 10954, Tel. (914)425-8311

Northwestern Dist., The Rt. Rev. M. Daniel Borden, 8655 North Melody Lane, Macedonia, OH 44056, Tel. (330)468-0270

Pacific Coast Dist., The Rt. Rev. Irvin Evans, 235 Harvard Rd., Linden, NJ 07036, Tel. (908)925-6138

Southeastern Dist., The Rt. Rev. James C. Bellamy, 1825 Rockland Dr., SE, Atlanta, GA 30316, Tel. (404)241-1821

Southern Dist., Goldsboro, The Rt. Rev. Ralph E. Love, Sr., 200 Barrington Rd., Greenville, NC 27834, Tel. (252)353-0495

Southern Dist.- Henderson, The Rt. Rev. Jesse Jones, 608 Cecil Street, Durham, NC 27707, Tel. (919)682-8249

St. Lucia Dist., The Rt. Rev. Carlisle Collymore, P.O. Box 51, Castries, St. Lucia, West Indies, Tel. (758)452-5835

Virginia Dist., The Rt. Rev. Albert Augson, 1406 Melton Ave., Richmond, VA 23223, Tel. (804)222-0463

West Virginia Dist., The Rt. Rev. Alvester McConnell, Route 3, Box 263, Bluefield, WV 24701, Tel. (304)248-8046

Western North Carolina Dist., The Rt. Rev. Elijah Williams, 901 Briarwood St., Reidsville, NC 27320-7020, Tel. (336)349-7275

## United House of Prayer

The United House of Prayer was founded and organized as a hierarchical church in the 1920s by the late Bishop C. M. Grace, who had built the first House of Prayer in 1919 in West Wareham, Mass., with his own hands. The purpose of the organization is to establish, maintain and perpetuate the doctrine of Christianity and the Apostolic Faith throughout the world among all people; to erect and maintain houses of prayer and worship where all people may gather for prayer and to worship the almighty God in spirit and in truth, irrespective of denomination or creed, and to maintain the Apostolic faith of the Lord and Savior, Jesus Christ.

### Headquarters

628 M St. NW, Washington, DC 20001, Tel. (202)289-9890 Fax (202)289-3690
Media Contact, Apostle S. Green
Email: apostlegreen@hotmail.com

### Officers

CEO, Bishop S. C. Madison, 1665 N. Portal Dr. NW, Washington, DC 20012, Tel. (202)882-3956 Fax (202)829-4717

#### NATIONAL PROGRAM STAFF

The General Assembly, Presiding Officer, Bishop S. C. Madison, 1665 N. Portal Dr. NW, Washington, DC 20012, Tel. (202)882-3956 Fax (202)829-4717

General Council Ecclesiastical Court, Clerk, Apostle R. Price, 1665 N. Portal Dr. NW, Washington, DC 20012, Tel. (202)882-3956 Fax (202)829-4717

Nationwide Building Program, General Builder, Bishop S. C. Madison, 1665 N. Portal Dr. NW, Washington, DC 20012, Tel. (202)882-3956 Fax (202)829-4717

Special Projects, Dir., Apostle S. Green

Annual Truth & Facts Publication, Exec. Editor, Bishop S. C. Madison, 1665 N. Portal Dr. NW, Washington, DC 20012, Tel. (202)882-3956 Fax (202)829-4717

## The United Methodist Church*

The United Methodist Church was formed April 23, 1968, in Dallas by the union of The Methodist Church and The Evangelical United Brethren Church. The two churches shared a common historical and spiritual heritage. The Methodist Church resulted in 1939 from the unification of three branches of Methodism—the Methodist Episcopal Church, the Methodist Episcopal Church, South, and the Methodist Protestant Church.

The Methodist movement began in 18th-century England under the preaching of John Wesley, but the Christmas Conference of 1784 in Baltimore is regarded as the date on which the organized Methodist Church was founded as an ecclesiastical organization. It was there that Francis Asbury was elected the first bishop in this country.

The Evangelical United Brethren Church was formed in 1946 with the merger of the Evangelical Church and the Church of the United Brethren in Christ, both of which had their beginnings in Pennsylvania in the evangelistic movement of the 18th and early 19th centuries. Philip William Otterbein and Jacob Albright were early leaders of this movement among the German-speaking settlers of the Middle Colonies.

### Headquarters

Media Contact, Executive Director, Public Information, Diane Denton, Tel. (615)742-5406, Email: ddenton@umcomm.org

General Information, Director, InfoServ, Vicki Wallace, Tel. (800)251-8140 Fax (615)742-5423
Email: infoserv@umcom.umc.org
Website: www.umc.org

### Officers

General Conference, Sec., Rev. L. "Gere" Fitzgerald Reist II, 2420 Nottingham Rd, Williamsport, PA 17701-4057

Council of Bishops, Pres., Bishop Peter D. Weaver, (276 Essex St., 5th Fl, 01840-1516), P.O. Box 249, Lawrence, MA 01842-0449, Tel. (978)682-7555 Fax (978)682-9555, Email: bishopsoffice@neumc.org; Sec., Bishop Ernest S. Lyght, United Methodist Center, 900 Washington St. E., Ste. 300, Charleston, WV 25301-1710, Tel. (304)344-8330 Fax (304) 344-8330, Email: WVareaumc@aol.com

#### JURISDICTIONAL BISHOPS
**North Central Jurisdiction:**

Chicago Episcopal Area, Bishop Hee-Soo Jung, 77 W. Washington St., Ste. 1820, Chicago, IL 60602-3181, Tel. (312)346-9766 x 102 Fax (312)214-9031, Email: hsjung@umcnic.org

Dakotas Episcopal Area, Bishop Deborah L. Kiesey, 3910 25th St. S., Fargo, ND 58104-6880, Tel. (701)232-2241 Fax(701)232-2615, Email: debkiesey@juno.com

Illinois Episcopal Area, Bishop Sharon Brown Christopher, (5900 S 2nd St., 62711), P.O. Box 19215, Springfield, IL 62794-9215, Tel. (217) 529-3820 Fax (217)529-4190, Email: bishopsabc@aol.com

Indiana Episcopal Area, Bishop Michael J. Coyner, 1100 W. 42nd St., Ste. 210, Indianapolis, IN 46208-3382, Tel. (317)924-1321 Fax (317)924-1380, Email: Bishopcoyner@inareaumc.org

Iowa Episcopal Area, Bishop Gregory V. Palmer, 2301 Rittenhouse St., Des Moines, IA 50321-3101, Tel. (515)974-8902 Fax(515)974-8952, Email: bishop.palmer@iaumc.org

Michigan Episcopal Area, Bishop Jonathan D. Keaton (2164 University Park Dr., Ste. 250, Okemos, MI 48864), P.O. Box 25068, Lansing MI 48909-5068, Tel. (517)347-4030 Fax (517) 347-4003, Email: bishopsoffice@miareaumc.org

Minnesota Episcopal Area, Bishop Sally Dyck, 122 W. Franklin Ave., Ste. 200, Minneapolis, MN 55404-2472, Tel. (612)870-4007 Fax (612)870-3587, Email: bishop.dyck@mnumc.org

Ohio East Episcopal Area, Bishop John L. Hopkins (8800 Cleveland Ave. NW), P.O. Box 2800, North Canton, OH 44720-0800, Tel. (330)499-3972 x 112 Fax (330)497-4911, Email: bishop@eocumc.com

Ohio West Episcopal Area, Bishop Bruce R. Ough, 32 Wesley Blvd., Worthington, OH 43085-3585, Tel. (614)844-6200 x 215 Fax (614)781-2625, Email: Bishop@wocumc.org

Wisconsin Episcopal Area, Bishop Linda Lee, 750 Windsor St., Ste. 303, Sun Prairie, WI 53590-2149, Tel. (608)837-8526 Fax (608) 837-0281, Email: bishoplee@WisconsinUMC.org

**North Eastern Jurisdiction:**

Albany Episcopal Area, Bishop Susan M. Morrison, 215 Lancaster St., Albany, NY 12210-1131, Tel. (518)426-0386 Fax (518) 426-0347, Email: AlbEpisArea@Worldnet.att.net

Boston Episcopal Area, Bishop Peter D. Weaver (276 Essex St. 5th Fl., 01840), P.O. Box 249, Lawrence, MA 01842-0449, Tel. (978)682-7555 x 250 Fax (978)682-9555, Email: bishopsoffice@neumc.org

Harrisburg Episcopal Area, Bishop Jane Allen Middleton, 303 Mulberry Dr., Ste. 100, Mechanicsburg, PA 17050-3141, Tel. (717) 766-7871 x 3100 Fax (717)766-3210, Email: bishop@cpcumc.org

New Jersey Episcopal Area, Bishop Sudarshana Devadhar, 1001 Wickapecko Dr., Ocean, NJ 07712-4733, Tel. (732)359-1010 Fax (732) 359-1019, Email: Bishop@gnjumc.org

New York Episcopal Area, Bishop Jeremiah J. Park, 20 Soundview Ave., White Plains, NY 10606-3302, Tel. (914)615-2221 Fax (914) 615-2246, Email: Bishop@NYAC.com

New York West Episcopal Area, Bishop Violet L. Fisher, 1010 East Ave, Rochester, NY 14607-2220, Tel. (585)271-3400 Fax (585)271-3404, Email: nywaumc@frontiernet.net

Philadelphia Episcopal Area, Bishop Marcus Matthews (980 Madison Ave, Norristown, 19403), P.O. Box 820, Valley Forge, PA 19482-0820, Tel. (610)666-9090 x 233 Fax (610)666-9181, Email: marcus.matthews@epaumc.org

Pittsburgh Episcopal Area, Bishop Thomas J. Bickerton (1204 Freedom Rd.), P.O. Box 5002, Cranberry Township, PA 16066-1902, Tel. (724)776-1499/1599 Fax (724)776-1683, Email: umbishop@wpaumc.org

Washington Episcopal Area (DC), Bishop John R. Schol, 100 Maryland Ave,. NE Ste. 510, Washington, DC 20002-5625, Tel. (202)546-3110 Fax (202)546-3186, Email: bishopsoffice@bwcumc.org

West Virginia Episcopal Area, Bishop Ernest S. Lyght, United Methodist Center, 900 Washington St. E., Ste. 300, Charleston, WV 25301-1710, Tel. (304)344-8330 Fax (304) 344-8330, Email: WVareaumc@aol.com

**South Central Jurisdiction:**

Arkansas Episcopal Area, Bishop Charles N. Crutchfield, 2 Trudie Kibbe Reed Dr., Little Rock, AR 72202-3770, Tel. (501)324-8019 Fax(501)324-8021, Email: bishopcnc@arumc.org

Dallas Episcopal Area, Bishop Rhymes H. Moncure, Jr. 16475 Dallas Parkway, Ste. 680, Addison, TX 75001, Tel. (214)522-6741 Fax (214)528-4435, Email: ntcbishop@sbcglobal.net

Fort Worth Episcopal Area, Bishop Ben R. Chamness, 464 Bailey Ave., Fort Worth, TX 76107-2153, Tel. (817)877-5222 Fax (817) 332-4609, Email: bishop@ctcumc.org

Houston Episcopal Area, Bishop Janice Riggle Huie, 5215 Main St., Houston, TX 77002-9792, Tel. (713)528-6881 Fax(713)529-7736, Email: ijarratt@methodists.net

Kansas Episcopal Area, Bishop Scott J. Jones 9440 E. Boston, Ste. 160, Wichita, KS 67207-3600, Tel. (316)686-0600, Fax (316)684-0044, Email: kansasbishop@kswestumc.org

Louisiana Episcopal Area, Bishop William W. Hutchinson, 527 North Blvd., Baton Rouge, LA 70802-5700, Tel. (225)346-1646 x 212 Fax (225)387-3662, Email: lcumc@bellsouth.net

Missouri Episcopal Area, Bishop Robert C. Schnase, 4800 Santana Cir., Ste. 100, Columbia, MO 65203-7138, Tel. (573)441-1770 Fax (573)441-0765, Email: rschnase@moumethodist.org

Nebraska Episcopal Area, Bishop Ann Brookshire Sherer, 2641 N. 49th St., Lincoln, NE 68504-2802, Tel. (402)466-4955 Fax (402)466-7931, Email: bishopsherer@umc-neb.org

Northwest Texas-New Mexico Episcopal Area, Bishop D. Max Whitfield, 7920 Mountain Rd. NE, Albuquerque, NM 87110-7805, Tel.

(505)255-8786 Fax (505)255-8738, Email: whitmax@nmconfum.com

Oklahoma Episcopal Area, Bishop Robert E. Hayes, Jr. (1501 NW 24th St, 73106), P.O. Box 60467, Oklahoma City, OK 73146-0467, Tel. (405)530-2025 Fax(405)530-2040, Email: cnoble@okumc.org

San Antonio Episcopal Area, Bishop Joel N. Martinez (16400 Huebner Rd, 78248), P.O. Box 781688, San Antonio, TX 78278-1688, Tel. (210)408-4500 Fax (210)408-4501, Email: bishop@umcswtx.org

**South Eastern Jurisdiction:**

Alabama-West Florida Episcopal Area, Bishop Larry M. Goodpaster, 312 Interstate Park Dr., Montgomery, AL 36109-5408, Tel. (334)277-1787 Fax(334)277-0109, Email: bishop.awf@knology.net

Birmingham Episcopal Area, Bishop William H. Willimon, 898 Arkadelphia Rd., Birmingham, AL 35204-5011, Tel. (205)226-7992 Fax (205) 322-8938, Email: wwillimon@northalabama umc .org

Charlotte Episcopal Area, Bishop J. Lawrence McCleskey (3400 Shamrock Dr., 28215), P.O. Box 18750, Charlotte, NC 28218-0750, Tel. (704)535-2260 Fax (704)535-9160, Email: bishop@wnccumc.org

Columbia Episcopal Area, Bishop Mary Virginia Taylor, 4908 Colonial Dr., Ste. 121, Columbia, SC 29203-6080, Tel. (803)786-9486 Fax (803)754-9327, Email: bishop@umcsc.org

Florida Episcopal Area, Bishop Timothy Whitaker (1122 E. McDonald St., 33801), P.O. Box 1747, Lakeland, FL 33802-1747, Tel. (863)688-4427 Fax(863)687-0568, Email: bishop@flumc.org

Holston Episcopal Area, Bishop James E. Swanson, Sr. (9915 Kingston Pike, Ste. C, 37922), P.O. Box 32939, Knoxville, TN 37930-2939, Tel. (865)690-4080 Fax (865)690-7112, Email: bishop@holston.org

Louisville Episcopal Area, Bishop James R. King, Jr., 7400 Floydsburg Rd., Crestwood, KY 40014-8202, Tel. (502)425-4240 Fax (502)425-9232, Email: jking@kyumc.org

Mississippi Episcopal Area, Bishop Hope Morgan Ward (321 Mississippi St., 39201), P.O. Box 931, Jackson, MS 39205-0931, Tel. (601)948-4561 Fax (601)948-5981, Email: bishop@mississippi-umc.org

Nashville Episcopal Area, Bishop Richard J. Wills, Jr., 520 Commerce St., Ste. 201, Nashville, TN 37203-3714, Tel. (615)742-8834 Fax (615)742-3726, Email: bishop@nasharea.org

North Georgia Episcopal Area, Bishop G. Lindsey Davis 4511 Jones Bridge Cir. NW, Norcross, GA 30092-1406, Tel. (678)533-1360 Fax (678)533-1361, Email: bishop@ngumc.org

Raleigh Episcopal Area, Bishop Alfred W. Gwinn, Jr. (1307 Glenwood Ave., Rm. 203), P.O. Box 10955, Raleigh, NC 27605-0955, Tel. (919)832-9560 x 243 Fax (919)832-4721, Email: bishopgwinn@nccumc.org

Richmond Episcopal Area, Bishop Charlene Payne Kammerer (10330 Staples Mill Rd.), P.O. Box 1719, Glen Allen, VA 23060-0659, Tel. (804)521-1100 Fax (804)521-1171, Email: bishopk@vaumc.org

South Georgia Episcopal Area, Bishop B. Michael Watson (3370 Vineville Ave., Ste. 101, 31204), P.O. Box 13616, Macon, GA 31208-3616, Tel. (478)475-9286 Fax (478) 475-9248, Email: bishopsga@aol.com

**Western Jurisdiction:**

Denver Episcopal Area, Bishop Warner H. Brown, Jr., 2200 S. University Blvd., Denver, CO 80210-4708, Tel. (303)733-3736 x 601 Fax (303)733-5047, Email: bishop@bishopbrown.org

Los Angeles Episcopal Area, Bishop Mary Ann Swenson (110 S. Euclid Ave., 91101), P.O. Box 6006, Pasadena, CA 91102-6006, Tel. (626)568-7312 Fax (626)568-7377, Email: calpacbishop@earthlink.net

Phoenix Episcopal Area, Bishop Minerva G. Carcaño, 1550 E. Meadowbrook Ave., Phoenix, AZ 85014-4040, Tel. (602)266-6956 x 209 Fax (602)279-1355, Email: Bishopmc@desertsw.org

Portland Episcopal Area, Bishop Robert T. Hoshibata, 1505 SW 18th Ave., Portland, OR 97201-2599, Tel. (503)226-1530 Fax (503) 228-3189, Email: bishop@umoi.net

San Francisco Episcopal Area, Bishop Beverly J. Shamana (1276 Halyard Dr., 95691), P.O. Box 980250, West Sacramento, CA 95798-0250, Tel. (916)374-1510 Fax (916)372-9062, Email: bishop@calnevumc.org

Seattle Episcopal Area, Bishop Edward W. Paup, 2112 3rd Ave., Ste. 301, Seattle, WA 98121-2333, Tel. (206)728-7674 Fax (206)728-8442, Email: bishop@pnwumc.org

### Periodicals

*Mature Years; El Intérprete; New World Outlook; Newscope; Interpreter; Methodist History; Christian Social Action; Pockets; Response; Social Questions Bulletin; United Methodist Reporter; Quarterly Review; Alive Now; Circuit Rider; El Aposento Alto; Weavings—A Journal of the Christian Spiritual Life; The Upper Room*

## United Pentecostal Church International

The United Pentecostal Church International came into being through the merger of two one-ness Pentecostal organizations—the Pentecostal Church, Inc., and the Pentecostal Assemblies of Jesus Christ. The first of these was known as the Pentecostal Ministerial Alliance from its inception in 1925 until 1932. The second was formed in 1931 by a merger of the Apostolic Church of Jesus Christ with the Pentecostal Assemblies of the World.

The church contends that the Bible teaches that there is one God who manifested himself as the Father in creation, in the Son in redemption, and as the Holy Spirit in regeneration; that Jesus is the name of this absolute deity and that water baptism should be administered in his name, not in the titles Father, Son and Holy Ghost (Acts ch. 2 v. 38, ch. 8 v. 16, and ch.19 v. 6).

The Fundamental Doctrine of the United Pentecostal Church International, as stated in its Articles of Faith, is "the Bible standard of full salvation, which is repentance, baptism in water by immersion in the name of the Lord Jesus Christ for the remission of sins, and the baptism of the Holy Ghost with the initial sign of speaking with other tongues as the Spirit gives utterance."

Further doctrinal teachings concern a life of holiness and separation, the operation of the gifts of the Spirit within the church, the second coming of the Lord, and the church's obligation to take the gospel to the whole world.

### Headquarters
8855 Dunn Rd., Hazelwood, MO 63042, Tel. (314)837-7300 Fax (314)837-4503
Media Contact, Gen. Sec.-Treas., Rev. Jerry Jones
Email: rfuller@upci.org

### Officers
Gen. Supt., Rev. Kenneth F. Haney
Asst. Gen. Supts., Rev. Paul. Mooney and Rev. Randy Keyes
Gen. Sec.-Treas., Rev. Jerry Jones
Dir. of Foreign Missions, Rev. Bruce Howell
Gen. Dir. of Home Missions, Rev. Carlton Coon
Editor-in-Chief, Rev. Robert H. Fuller
Gen. Sunday School Dir., Rev. Gary Erickson
Youth Pres., Rev. Todd Gaddy

### OTHER ORGANIZATIONS
Pentecostal Publishing House, Mgr., Rev. Robert H. Fuller
Ladies Ministries, Pres., Gwyn Oakes
Stewardship Dept., Dir., Rev., Stephen Drury
Division of Education, Supt., Rev. Don Batchelor
Word Aflame Publications, Editor, Rev. Richard Davis Media Missions Asst. Dir., Rev. Morman R. Paslay II Media Missions Announcer, Rev. J. Hugh Rose
Public Relations, Contact church administration
Historical Society & Archives
Urshan Graduate School of Theology

### Periodicals
*The Pentecostal Herald; World Harvest Today; The North American Challenge; Conqueror; Reflections; Forward; Apostolic Man*

## The United Pentecostal Churches of Christ
In a time when the Church of Jesus Christ is challenged to send the "Evening Light Message" to the uppermost part of the Earth, a group of men and women came together on May 29, 1992 at the Pentecostal Church of Christ in Cleveland, Ohio to form what is now called The United Pentecostal Churches of Christ.

Organized and established by Bishop Jesse Delano Ellis, II, the United Pentecostal Churches of Christ is about the business of preparing people to see the Lord of Glory. The traditional barriers of yesteryear must not keep saints of like faith apart ever again and this fellowship of Pentecostal, Apostolic Independent Churches have discovered the truth of Our Lord's Prayer in the seventeenth chapter of Saint John, "that they may all be One."

The United Pentecostal Churches of Christ is a fellowship of holiness assemblies which has membership in the universal Body of Christ. As such, we preserve the message of Christ's redeeming love through His atonement and declare holiness of life to be His requirement for all men who would enter into the Kingdom of God. We preach repentence from sin, baptism in the Name of Jesus Christ, a personal indwelling of the Holy Spirit, a daily walk with the Lord and life after death. Coupled with the cardinal truths of the church are the age old customs of ceremony and celebration.

### Headquarters
10515 Chester Ave., (at University Circle), Cleveland, OH 44106, Tel. (216)721-5935 Fax (216)721-6938
Contact Person, Public Relations., Rev. W. Michelle James Williams

### REGIONAL OFFICE
493-5 Monroe St., Brooklyn, New York 11221, Tel. (718)574-4100 Fax (718)574-8504
Contact Person, Secretary General., Rev. Rodney McNeil Johnson

### Officers
Presiding Bishop and Gen. Overseer, Bishop J. Delano Ellis, II, Cleveland, Ohio
Asst. Presiding Bishop, Bishop Carl Halloway Montgomery, II, Baltimore, Md.
Secretary General, Bishop James R. Chambers, Brookyn, N.Y.
Pres. Of Pentacostal Youth Congress, Overseer Darryl D. Woodson, Memphis, Tenn.

### Periodicals
*The Pentecostal Flame*

## United Zion Church
A branch of the Brethren in Christ which settled in Lancaster County, Pa., the United Zion Church was organized under the leadership of Matthias Brinser in 1855.

### Headquarters
United Zion Retirement Community, 722 Furnace Hills Pk., Lititz, PA 17543

Media Contact, Bishop Charles Brown, 4041 Shanamantown Rd., Annville, PA 17003, Tel. (717)867-1133

**Officers**

Gen. Conf. Mod., Bishop Charles Brown, 4041 Shanamantown Rd., Annville, PA 17003, Tel. (717)867-1133
Asst. Mod., Rev. Leon Eberly
Gen. Conf. Sec., Rev. Clyde Martin
Gen. Conf. Treas., Kenneth Kleinfelter, 919 Sycamore Lane, Lebanon, PA 17042

## Unity of the Brethren

Czech and Moravian immigrants in Texas (beginning about 1855) established congregations which grew into an Evangelical Union in 1903, and with the accession of other Brethren in Texas, into the Evangelical Unity of the Czech-Moravian Brethren in North America. In 1959, it shortened the name to the original name used in 1457, the Unity of the Brethren (Unitas Fratrum, or Jednota Bratrska).

**Headquarters**

4009 Hunter Creek, College Station, TX 77845
Media Contact, Sec. of Exec. Committee, Ginger McKay, 148 N. Burnett, Baytown, TX 77520
Email: lkoslovsky@teleshare.net
Website: www.unityofthebrethren.org

**Officers**

Pres., Kent Laza, 4009 Hunter Creek, College Station, TX 77845
1st Vice Pres., Rev. Michael Groseclose, 902 Church St., Belleville, TX 77418, Tel. (512)365-6890
Sec. of Exec. Committee, Ginger McKay, 148 N. Burnett, Baytown, TX 77520
Fin. Sec., Rev. Joseph Polasek, 4241 Blue Heron, Bryan, TX 77807
Treas., Arranna Jakubik, P.O. Box 408, Snook, TX 77878

**OTHER ORGANIZATIONS**

Bd. of Christian Educ., Dr., Donald Ketcham, 900 N. Harrison, West, TX 76691
Brethren Youth Fellowship, Pres., Jamie Brooke Bryan, 1231 Four Corners, West, TX 76691
Friends of the Hus Encampment, Jim Baletka, 727 San Benito, College Station, TX 77845
Christian Sisters Union, Pres., Janet Pomykal, P.O. Box 560, Brenham, TX 77834
Sunday School Union, Pres., Dorothy Kocian, 107 S. Barbara Dr., Waco, TX 76705
Youth Director, Kimberly Stewart, 1500 Lawnmont Dr., Apt. 208, Round Rock, TX 78664

**Periodicals**

*Brethren Journal*

## Universal Fellowship of Metropolitan Community Churches

The Universal Fellowship of Metropolitan Community Churches was founded Oct. 6, 1968 by the Rev. Troy D. Perry in Los Angeles, with a particular but not exclusive outreach to the gay community. Since that time, the Fellowship has grown to include congregations throughout the world.

The group is Trinitarian and accepts the Bible as the divinely inspired Word of God. The Fellowship has two sacraments, baptism and holy communion, as well as a number of traditionally recognized rites such as ordination.

This Fellowship acknowledges "the Holy Scriptures interpreted by the Holy Spirit in conscience and faith, as its guide in faith, discipline, and government." The government of this Fellowship is vested in its General Council (consisting of Elders and District Coordinators), clergy and church delegates, who exert the right of control in all of its affairs, subject to the provisions of its Articles of Incorporation and By-Laws.

**Headquarters**

8704 Santa Monica Blvd. 2nd Floor, West Hollywood, CA 90069-4548, Tel. (310)360-8640 x 226 Fax (310)360-8680
Media Contact, Dir. of Communications, Jim Birkett
Email: CindiLove@MCCchurch.org
Website: www.mcchurch.org

**Officers**

Mod., Rev. Elder Troy D. Perry
Vice Mod., Rev. Elder Nancy L. Wilson
Treas., Rev. Elder Donald Eastman
Clk., Rev. Elder Darlene Garner
Elder Mel Johnson, PMB #63, 2261 Market St., San Francisco, CA 94114-1600
Rev. Elder Nori Rost, 214 S. Prospect St., Colorado Springs, CO 80903
Rev. Elder Hong Kia Tan, 72 Fleet Rd., Hampstead, London, NW3 2QT England
Deputy Chief Executive Officer, Jane Wagner, 8704 Santa Monica Blvd., 2nd Floor, West Holywood, CA 90069-4548
Dir., Communications, Jim Birkett, 8704 Santa Monica Blvd., 2nd Floor, West Hollywood, CA 90069-4548

**OTHER COMMISSIONS & COMMITTEES**

Min. of Global Outreach, Field Dir., Rev. Judy Dahl
Commission on the Laity, Chpsn., Stan Kimer
Clergy Credentials & Concerns, Admn., Rev. Justin Tanis
UFMCC AIDS Ministry, AIDS Liaison., Rev. Robert Griffin
Chief Financial Officer, Margaret Mahlman, 8704 Santa Monica Blvd., 2nd Floor, West Hollywood, CA 90069-4548

**Periodicals**

*Keeping in Touch; UFMCC Email: News Service* (FREE)

## Volunteers of America

Volunteers of America is a national, nonprofit, spiritually based organization that provides local human service programs and opportunities for individual and community involvement through 39 local affiliate offices and the National Services Housing and Health Care Division. Founded in 1896 by Christian social reformers Ballington and Maud Booth, Volunteers of America provides over 100 different types of programs and services in more than 400 communities nationwide. Programs include services for abused and neglected children, youth at risk, the elderly, people with disabilities, homeless individuals and families, and many others. Volunteers of America is one of the nation's largest providers of affordable housing for seniors and low-income families and individuals. It also provides a national prison aftercare program that engages local congregations of all denominations as mentors to newly released prisoners. It employs 14,000 individuals whose work is assisted by over 70,000 committed volunteers.

### Headquarters

1660 Duke St., Alexandria, VA 22314-3427, Tel. (800)899-0089
Email: voa@voa.org
Website: www.voa.org

### Officers

Chpsn., David Kikumoto
Pres., Charles W. Gould, 1660 Duke St., Alexandria, VA. 22314, Tel. (703)341-5000
Dir., of Ecclesiastical Services, Harry V. Quiett, 1660 Duke St., Alexandria, VA. 22314, Tel. (703)341-5054, Fax (703)341-7000
Email: hquiett@voa.org
Website: www.voa.org

### Periodicals

*Spirit Magazine, Gazette Publications: No Limits To Caring, Era of The Founders* and *Ministry Of Service*

## The Wesleyan Church

The Wesleyan Church was formed on June 26, 1968, through the union of the Wesleyan Methodist Church of America (1843) and the Pilgrim Holiness Church (1897). The headquarters was established at Marion, Ind., and relocated to Indianapolis in 1987, and relocated again in Fishers, Indiana in 2004.

The Wesleyan movement centers around the beliefs, based on Scripture, that the atonement in Christ provides for the regeneration of sinners and the entire sanctification of believers. John Wesley led a revival of these beliefs in the 18th century.

When a group of New England Methodist ministers led by Orange Scott began to crusade for the abolition of slavery, the bishops and others sought to silence them. This led to a series of withdrawals from the Methodist Episcopal Church. In 1843, the Wesleyan Methodist

Connection of America was organized and led by Scott, Jotham Horton, LaRoy Sunderland, Luther Lee and Lucius C. Matlack.

During the holiness revival in the last half of the 19th century, holiness replaced social reform as the major tenet of the Connection. In 1947 the name was changed from Connection to Church and a central supervisory authority was set up.

The Pilgrim Holiness Church was one of many independent holiness churches which came into existence as a result of the holiness revival. Led by Martin Wells Knapp and Seth C. Rees, the International Holiness Union and Prayer League was inaugurated in 1897 in Cincinnati. Its purpose was to promote worldwide holiness evangelism and the Union had a strong missionary emphasis from the beginning. It developed into a church by 1913.

The Wesleyan Church is now spread across most of the United States and Canada and in over 80 other countries. The International Conference of The Wesleyan Church, originally named Wesleyan World Fellowship, was organized in 1972 to unite Wesleyan mission bodies developing into mature churches. The Wesleyan Church is a member of the Christian Holiness Partnership, the National Association of Evangelicals and the World Methodist Council.

### Headquarters

P.O. Box 50434, Indianapolis, IN 46250, Tel. (317)774-7900
Media Contact, Gen. Sec., Dr. Ronald D. Kelly, Tel. (317)744-3922 Fax (317)744-3924, P.O. Box 50434, Indianapolis, IN 46250, Email: kellyr@wesleyan.org
Email: generalsecretary@wesleyan.org
Website: www.wesleyan.org

### Officers

**General Superintendents:**
Dr. Earle L. Wilson, Tel. (317)774-3932 Fax (317)774-3931, Email: wilsone@wesleyan.org
Dr. Thomas E. Armiger, Tel. (317)774-3933 Fax (317)774-3931, Email: armigert@wesleyan.org
Dr. Jerry G. Pence, Tel. (317)774-3934 Fax (317)774-3931, Email: pencej@wesleyan.org

**General Officers:**
Gen. Sec., Dr. Ronald D. Kelly, Tel. (317)774-3922 Fax (317)744-3924, Email: kellyr@wesleyan.org
Gen. Treas., Donald M. Frase, Tel. (317)774-3941 Fax (317)744-3948, Email: frased@wesleyan.org
Gen. Publisher, Mr. Donald D. Cady, Tel. (317)774-3853 Fax (317)774-3860, Email: cadyd@wesleyan.org
Gen. Director of Communications, Dr. Norman G. Wilson, Tel. (317)774-7907 Fax (317)774-7913, Email: wilsonn@wesleyan.org

Gen. Dir. of Spiritual Formation, Dr. James A. Dunn, Tel. (317)744-3888 Fax (317)774-3880, Email: dunnj@jwesleyan.org

Gen. Dir. of Evangelism & Church Growth, Rev. Philip T. Stevenson, Tel. (317)744-3900 Fax (317)774-3899, Email: stevensonp@wesleyan.org

Gen. Dir. of Education & the Ministry, Rev. Kerry D. Kind, Tel. (317)774-3911 Fax (317)774-3915, Email: kindk@wesleyan.org

Gen. Dir. of World Missions, Dr. Donald L. Bray, Tel. (317)774-7950 Fax (317)774-7948, Email: brayd@wesleyan.org

**Auxiliaries/Subsidiary Agencies:**

Estate & Gift Planning, Gen. Dir., Rev. Larry J. Moore, Tel. (317)774-7338 Fax (317)774-7341, Email: moorej@wesleyan.org

Wesleyan Investment Foundation, Gen. Dir., Dr. Craig A. Dunn, Tel. (317)774-7300 Fax (317)774-7321, Email: wif@wesleyan.org

Wesleyan Pension Fund, Gen. Dir., Dr. Craig A. Dunn, Tel. (317)774-7300 Fax (317)774-7321, Email: dunnc@wesleyan.org

Wesleyan Women, Martha Blackburn, Tel. (317)774-7974 Fax (317)774-7975, Email: blackburnm@wesleyan.org

Wesleyan Kids for Mission, Peggy Ann Camp, Tel. (704)892-3744 Fax (317)570-5254, Email: camppeg@aol.com

Wesleyan Men, Dr. James A. Dunn, Tel. (317) 774-3888 Fax (317)774-3880, Email: dunnj@wesleyan.org

Address Service, Tel. (317)744-7900

Archives & Historical Library, Tel. (317)774-7996

Computer Information Services, Tel. (317)774-7922

Wesleyan Publishing House, Tel. (317)774-3954

**Periodicals**
*Wesleyan Life; Wesleyan World*

## Wesleyan Holiness Association of Churches

This body was founded Aug. 4, 1959 near Muncie, Ind. by a group of ministers and laymen who were drawn together for the purpose of spreading and conserving sweet, radical, scriptural holiness. These men came from various church bodies. This group is Wesleyan in doctrine and standards.

**Headquarters**
1141 North US Hwy 27, Fountain City, IN 47341-9757, Tel. (765)584-3199       •

Media Contact, Gen. Sec.-Treas., Rev. Robert W. Wilson, P.O. Box 218, Selinsgrove, PA 17870

**Officers**
Gen. Supt., Rev. John Brewer

Asst. Gen. Supt., Rev. Armen O. Rhoads, 7812 Portland Ave., Tacoma, WA 98404

Gen. Sec.-Treas., Rev. Robert W. Wilson, P.O. Box 218, Selinsgrove, PA 17870, Tel. (570) 539-9821

Gen. Youth Pres., Rev. Nathan Shockley, 504 W. Tyrell St., St. Louis, MI 48880, Tel. (517)681-2591

**Periodicals**
*Eleventh Hour Messenger*

## Wisconsin Evangelical Lutheran Synod

Organized in 1850 at Milwaukee, Wisc., by three pastors sent to America by a German mission society, the Wisconsin Evangelical Lutheran Synod still reflects its origins, although it now has congregations in 50 states and three Canadian provinces. It supports missions in 26 countries.

The Wisconsin Synod federated with the Michigan and Minnesota Synods in 1892 in order to more effectively carry on education and mission enterprises. A merger of these three Synods followed in 1917 to give the Wisconsin Evangelical Lutheran Synod its present form.

Although at its organization in 1850 WELS turned away from conservative Lutheran theology, today it is ranked as one of the most conservative Lutheran bodies in the United States. WELS confesses that the Bible is the verbally inspired, infallible Word of God and subscribes without reservation to the confessional writings of the Lutheran Church. Its interchurch relations are determined by a firm commitment to the principle that unity of doctrine and practice are the prerequisites of pulpit and altar fellowship and ecclesiastical cooperation. It is a founding member of the Confessional Evangelical Lutheran Conference, a federation of 21 like-minded bodies worldwide.

**Headquarters**
2929 N. Mayfair Rd., Milwaukee, WI 53222, Tel. (414)256-3888 Fax (414)256-3899

MCG Director, Rev. J.D. Liggett

Email: webbin@sab.wels.net

Website: www.wels.net

**Officers**
Pres., Rev. Karl R. Gurgel, 2929 N Mayfair Rd., Milwaukee, WI 53222,

1st Vice Pres., Rev. Wayne D. Mueller, 2929 N Mayfair Rd., Milwaukee, WI 53222, Tel. (414)256-3888 Fax (414)256-3899

2nd Vice Pres., Rev. Thomas F. Zarling, 6 Wiltshire C T E, Sterling, VA 20165

Sec., Rev. Robert Pasbrig, 876 Fairview Dr., Hartford, WI 53027

**OTHER ORGANIZATIONS**

Bd. for Ministerial Education, Admn., Rev. Peter Kruschel

Bd. for Parish Services, Admn., Rev. Bruce Becker

Bd. for Home Missions, Admn., Rev. Harold J. Hagedorn

177

Bd. for World Missions, Admn., Rev. Daniel
  Koelpin

**Periodicals**

*Forward in Christ; Wisconsin Lutheran
Quarterly; The Lutheran Educator; Lutheran
Leader; Mission Connection*

# Religious Bodies in the United States Arranged by Families

The following list of religious bodies appearing in the Directory Section of the *Yearbook* shows the "families," or related clusters into which American religious bodies can be grouped. For example, there are many communions that can be grouped under the heading "Baptist" for historical and theological reasons. It should not be assumed, however, that all denominations under one family heading are necessarily consistent in belief or practice. The family clusters tend to represent historical factors more often than theological or practical ones. These family categories provide one of the major pitfalls when compiling church statistics because there is often a tendency to combine the statistics by "families" for analytical and comparative purposes. Such combined totals are deeply flawed, even though they are often used as variables for sociological analysis. The arrangement by families offered here is intended only as a general guide for conceptual organization when viewing the broad sweep of American religious culture.

Religious bodies that cannot be categorized under family headings appear alphabetically and are not indented in the following list.

## Adventist Bodies

*Advent Christian Church*
*Church of God General Conference (Oregon,
    IL and Morrow, GA)*
*Primitive Advent Christian Church*
*Seventh-day Adventist Church*

**American Evangelical Christian Churches**
**American Rescue Workers**

## Anglican Bodies

*Episcopal Church*
*The Episcopal Orthodox Church*
*Reformed Episcopal Church*

**Apostolic Christian Church (Nazarene)**
**Apostolic Christian Churches of America**
**Apostolic Episcopal Church**

## Baptist Bodies

*The Alliance of Baptists*
*The American Baptist Association*
*American Baptist Churches in the U.S.A.*
*Baptist Bible Fellowship International*
*Baptist General Conference*
*Baptist Missionary Association of America*
*Conservative Baptist Association of America*
*General Association of General Baptists*
*General Association of Regular Baptist Churches*
*National Association of Free Will Baptists*
*National Baptist Convention of America, Inc.*
*National Baptist Convention, U.S.A., Inc.*
*National Missionary Baptist Convention of
    America*
*National Primitive Baptist Convention, Inc.*
*North American Baptist Conference*
*Primitive Baptists*
*Progressive National Baptist Convention, Inc.*
*Separate Baptists in Christ*
*Seventh Day Baptist General Conference,
    U.S.A. and Canada*

*Southern Baptist Convention*
*Sovereign Grace Believers*

**Berean Fellowship of Churches**

## Brethren (German Baptists)

*Brethren Church (Ashland, Ohio)*
*Church of the Brethren*
*Fellowship of Grace Brethren Churches*
*Old German Baptist Brethren Church*

## Brethren, River

*Brethren in Christ Church*
*United Zion Church*

**The Catholic Church**
**Christ Community Church (Evangelical-
    Protestant)**
**Christadelphians**
**Christian Brethren (also known as Plymouth
    Brethren)**
**The Christian Congregation, Inc.**
**The Christian and Missionary Alliance**
**Christian Union**
**The Church of Christ (Holiness) U.S.A.**
**Church of Christ, Scientist**
**Church Communities International**
**The Church of Illumination**
**Church of the Living God**
**Church of the Nazarene**

## Churches of Christ—Christian Churches

*Christian Church (Disciples of Christ) in the
    United States and Canada*
*Christian Churches and Churches of Christ*
*Churches of Christ*

**Churches of Christ in Christian Union**

## Churches of God

*Church of God (Anderson, Indiana)*
*The Church of God (Seventh Day), Denver,*
*Colorado*
*Churches of God, General Conference*

## Churches of the New Jerusalem

*General Church of the New Jerusalem*
*The Swedenborgian Church*

**Conservative Congregational Christian
Conference**

## Eastern Orthodox Churches

*Albanian Orthodox Diocese of America*
*The American Carpatho-Russian Orthodox
Greek Catholic Church*
*The Antiochian Orthodox Christian
Archdiocese of North America*
*Apostolic Catholic Assyrian Church of the
East, North American Dioceses*
*Apostolic Orthodox Catholic Church of North
America*
*Greek Orthodox Archdiocese of America*
*The Holy Eastern Orthodox Catholic and
Apostolic Church in North America, Inc.*
*Holy Ukrainian Autocephalic Orthodox
Church in Exile*
*The Orthodox Church in America*
*Patriarchal Parishes of the Russian Orthodox
Church in the U.S.A.*
*The Romanian Orthodox Church in America*
*The Romanian Orthodox Episcopate of
America*
*The Russian Orthodox Church Outside of
Russia*
*Serbian Orthodox Church in the U.S.A. and
Canada*
*The Syro-Russian Orthodox Catholic Church*
*True Orthodox Church of Greece (Synod of
Metropolitan Cyprian), American
Exarchate*
*Ukrainian Orthodox Church of the U.S.A.*

**The Evangelical Church**
**The Evangelical Church Alliance**
**The Evangelical Congregational Church**
**The Evangelical Covenant Church**
**The Evangelical Free Church of America**
**Fellowship of Fundamental Bible Churches**
**Free Christian Zion Church of Christ**

## Friends

*Evangelical Friends International—North
American Region*
*Friends General Conference*
*Friends United Meeting*
*Philadelphia Yearly Meeting of the Religious
Society of Friends*
*Religious Society of Friends (Conservative)*
*Religious Society of Friends (Unaffiliated
Meetings)*

**Grace Gospel Fellowship**
**IFCA International, Inc.**
**International Council of Community
Churches**
**Jehovah's Witnesses**

## Latter-day Saints (Mormons)

*Church of Christ*
*The Church of Jesus Christ (Bickertonites)*
*The Church of Jesus Christ of Latter-day
Saints*
*Community of Christ*

**The Liberal Catholic Church—Province of
the United States of America**

## Lutheran Bodies

*The American Association of Lutheran
Churches*
*Apostolic Lutheran Church of America*
*The Association of Free Lutheran
Congregations*
*The Association of Independent Evangelical
Lutheran Churches*
*Church of the Lutheran Brethren of America*
*Church of the Lutheran Confession*
*Conservative Lutheran Association*
*The Estonian Evangelical Lutheran Church*
*Evangelical Lutheran Church in America*
*Evangelical Lutheran Synod*
*The Latvian Evangelical Lutheran Church in
America*
*The Lutheran Church—Missouri Synod*
*Wisconsin Evangelical Lutheran Synod*

## Mennonite Bodies

*Beachy Amish Mennonite Churches*
*Bible Fellowship Church*
*Church of God in Christ, Mennonite*
*Fellowship of Evangelical Bible Churches*
*Fellowship of Evangelical Churches*
*General Conference of Mennonite Brethren
Churches*
*Hutterian Brethren*
*Mennonite Church, U.S.A.*
*Old Order Amish Church*
*Old Order (Wisler) Mennonite Church*
*Reformed Mennonite Church*

## Methodist Bodies

*African Methodist Episcopal Church*
*The African Methodist Episcopal Zion
Church*
*Allegheny Wesleyan Methodist Connection
(Original Allegheny Conference)*
*Bible Holiness Church*
*Christian Methodist Episcopal Church*
*Evangelical Methodist Church*
*Free Methodist Church of North America*
*Fundamental Methodist Church, Inc.*
*Primitive Methodist Church in the U.S.A.*

Reformed Methodist Union Episcopal Church
Reformed Zion Union Apostolic Church
Southern Methodist Church
The United Methodist Church
The Wesleyan Church

**The Missionary Church**

## Moravian Bodies

Moravian Church in America (Unitas Fratrum)
Unity of the Brethren

**National Association of Congregational Christian Churches**
**National Organization of the New Apostolic Church of North America**
**National Spiritualist Association of Churches**
**North American Old Roman Catholic Church (Archdiocese of New York)**

## Old Catholic Churches

Apostolic Catholic Orthodox Church
Christ Catholic Church
Liberal Catholic Church (International)
The Old Catholic Orthodox Church (formerly
   the Apostolic Orthodox Old Catholic Church)
The United Catholic Church, Inc.

## Oriental Orthodox Churches

Armenian Apostolic Church of America
Armenian Apostolic Church, Diocese of
   America
Coptic Orthodox Church
Malankara Orthodox Syrian Church, Diocese
   of America
Syrian (Syriac) Orthodox Church of Antioch

## Pentecostal Bodies

Apostolic Faith Mission Church of God
Apostolic Faith Mission of Portland, Oregon
Assemblies of God
Assemblies of God International Fellowship
   (Independent/Not affiliated)
Association of Vineyard Churches
The Bible Church of Christ, Inc.
Bible Way Church of Our Lord Jesus Christ
   World Wide, Inc.
Calvary Chapel
Christian Church of North America, General
   Council
The Church of God
The Church of God In Christ
Church of God in Christ, International
Church of God (Cleveland, Tennessee)
The Church of God of the Firstborn
Church of God by Faith, Inc.
Church of God, Mountain Assembly, Inc.
Church of God of Prophecy
Church of Our Lord Jesus Christ of the
   Apostolic Faith, Inc.
Congregational Holiness Church
Elim Fellowship
Full Gospel Assemblies International

Full Gospel Fellowship of Churches and
   Ministers International
House of God, Which is the Church of the
   Living God, the Pillar and Ground of the
   Truth
International Church of the Foursquare Gospel
The International Pentecostal Church of Christ
International Pentecostal Holiness Church
Open Bible Standard Churches
The (Original) Church of God, Inc.
Pentecostal Assemblies of the World, Inc.
Pentecostal Church of God
Pentecostal Fire-Baptized Holiness Church
The Pentecostal Free Will Baptist Church, Inc.
United Holy Church of America, Inc.
United House of Prayer
United Pentecostal Church International
The United Pentecostal Churches of Christ

**Pillar of Fire**
**Polish National Catholic Church of America**

## Reformed Bodies

Associate Reformed Presbyterian Church
   (General Synod)
Christian Reformed Church in North America
Cumberland Presbyterian Church
Cumberland Presbyterian Church in America
Evangelical Presbyterian Church
Hungarian Reformed Church in America
Korean Presbyterian Church in America,
   General Assembly of the
Netherlands Reformed Congregations
The Orthodox Presbyterian Church
Presbyterian Church in America
Presbyterian Church (U.S.A.)
Protestant Reformed Churches in America
Reformed Church in America
Reformed Church in the United States
Reformed Presbyterian Church of North
   America
United Church of Christ

**Reformed Catholic Church**
**The Salvation Army**
**The Schwenkfelder Church**

## Thomist Churches

Mar Thoma Syrian Church of India

**Triumph the Church and Kingdom of God in Christ Inc. (International)**
**Unitarian Universalist Association of Congregations**

## United Brethren Bodies

Church of the United Brethren in Christ
United Christian Church

**Universal Fellowship of Metropolitan Community Churches**
**Volunteers of America**
**Wesleyan Holiness Association of Churches**

# 4. Religious Bodies in Canada

A large number of Canadian religious bodies were organized by immigrants from Europe and elsewhere, and a smaller number sprang up originally on Canadian soil. In the case of Canada, moreover, many denominations that transcend the U.S.-Canada border have headquarters in the United States.

A final section in this directory lists churches according to denominational families. This can be a helpful tool in finding a particular church if you don't know the official name. Complete statistics for Canadian churches are found in the statistical section in Chapter 3. Table 1 contains membership figures, and Table 4 contains giving figures. Addresses for periodicals are found in the directory entitled, "Religious Periodicals in Canada."

## The Anglican Church of Canada

Anglicanism came to Canada with the early explorers such as Martin Frobisher and Henry Hudson. Continuous services began in Newfoundland about 1700 and in Nova Scotia in 1710. The first Bishop, Charles Inglis, was appointed to Nova Scotia in 1787 The Anglican Church of Canada includes a large number of the original inhabitants of Canada (Indians, Inuit and Metis) and has been a strong advocate of their rights.

The Anglican Church of Canada has enjoyed self-government for over a century since 1893 and is an autonomous member of the worldwide Anglican Communion. The Church also has a strong international role in development and disaster relief through the Primate's World Relief and Development Fund (PWRDF). The General Synod, which normally meets triennially (next meeting 2010), consists of the Archbishops, Bishops and elected clerical and lay representatives of the 30 dioceses. Each of the Ecclesiastical Provinces—Canada, Ontario, Rupert's Land and British Columbia—is organized under a Metropolitan and has its own Provincial Synod and Executive Council. Each diocese has its own Diocesan Synod.

### Headquarters
Church House, 80 Hayden St., Toronto, ON M4Y 3G2 Tel. (416)924-9192 (Switchboard) (416)924-9199 (Voice mail) Fax (416)968-7983, Website: www.anglican.ca
Media Contact, Mr. Vianney (Sam) Carriere
General E-mail: info@national.anglican.ca

### GENERAL SYNOD OFFICERS
Primate of the Anglican Church of Canada, The Most Rev. Andrew S. Hutchison
Prolocutor, The Very Rev. Peter G. Elliott
Gen. Sec., The Ven. Michael F. Pollesel
Treas., Gen. Synod, Mr. Peter Blachford

### DEPARTMENTS AND DIVISIONS
Faith, Worship & Ministry, Dir., Rev. Canon Alyson Barnett-Cowan
Financial Management and Dev., Dir., Mr. Peter Blachford
Inform. Resources Dir., Mr. Vianney (Sam) Carriere
Partnerships, Dir., Dr. Eleanor Johnson

Pensions, Dir., Ms. Judith Robinson
Primate's World Relief and Dev. Fund, Dir., Ms. Cheryl Curtis

### METROPOLITANS (ARCHBISHOPS)
British Columbia, The Rt. Rev. Terrence O. Buckle, Metropolitan, Box 31136, Whitehorse YT Y1A 5P7, Tel. (867)667-7746 Fax (867) 667-6125, Email: synodoffice@klondiker. com
Ecclesiastical Province of, Canada, The Most Rev. A. Bruce Stavert, 31 rue des Jardins, Quebec, QC G1R 4L6, Tel. (418)692-3858 Fax (418)692-3876 Email: synodoffice@quebec.anglican.ca
Ontario, The Most Rev. Caleb J. Lawrence, Box 841, Schumacher, ON P0N 1G0, Tel. (705) 360-1129 Fax (705) 360-1120, Email: dmoose @domaa.ca
Rupert's Land, The Most Rev. John R. Clarke, Box 6868, Peace River, AB T8S 1S6, Tel. (780) 624-2767 Fax (780)624-2365, Email: bpath@ telusplanet.net

### DIOCESAN BISHOPS
Algoma, The Rt. Rev. Ronald Ferris, Box 1168, Sault Ste. Marie, ON P6A 5N7, Tel. (705)256-5061 Fax (705)946-1860, Email: dioceseofalgoma@on.aibn.com
Arctic, The Rt. Rev. Andrew P. Atagotaalnuk, 4910 51st St., Box 190, Yellowknife, NT X1A 2N2, Tel. (867)873-5432 Fax (867)873-8478, Email: diocese@arcticnet.org
Athabasca, The Most Rev. John R. Clarke, Box 6868, Peace River, AB T8S 1S6, Tel. (780) 624-2767 Fax (780)624-2365, Email: bpath@ telusplanet.net
Brandon, Rt. Rev. James D. Njegovan, Box 21009 WEPO, Brandon, MB R7B 3W8, Tel. (204)727-7550 Fax (204)727-4135, Email: bishopbdn@mts.net
British Columbia, The Rt. Rev. A.J. Cowan, 900 Vancouver St., Victoria, BC V8V 3V7, Tel. (250)386-7781 Fax (250)386-4013, Email: synod@bc.anglican.ca
Caledonia, The Rt. Rev. William J. Anderson, Box 278, Prince Rupert, BC V8J 3P6, Tel. (250)624-6013 Fax (250)624-4299, Email: synodofc@citytel.net
Calgary, Bishop, The Rt. Rev. Derek B.E. Hoskin, #560, 1207 11th Ave., SW, Salgary, AB T3C

0M5, Tel. (403)243-3673 Fax (403)243-2182, Email: synod@calgary.anglican.ca

Central Interior, Anglican Parishes (APCI) The Rt. Rev. Gordon Light, Box 1979, 100 Mile House, BC V0K 2E0, Tel. (250)395-1222 Fax (250)395-1252, Email: apci-office@telus.net

Central Newfoundland, The Rt. Rev. F. David Torraville, 34 Fraser Rd., Gander, NF A1V 2E8, Tel. (709)256-2372 Fax (709)256-2396, Email: bishopcentral@nfld.net

Eastern Newfoundland and Labrador, The Rt. Rev. Cyrus C.J. Pitman, 19 King's Bridge Rd., St. John's, NF A1C 3K4, Tel. (709)576-6697 Fax (709)576-7122, Email: cpitman@anglicanenl. nf.net

Edmonton, The Rt. Rev. Victoria Matthews, 10035 - 103 St., Edmonton, AB T5J 0X5, Tel. (780)439-7344 Fax (780)439-6549, Email: bishopv@telusplanet.net

Fredericton, The Rt. Rev. Claude E.W. Miller, 115 Church St., Fredericton, NB E3B 4C8, Tel. (506)459-1801 Fax (506)459-8475, Email: bishfton@nbnet.nb.ca

Huron, The Rt. Rev. Bruce H. W. Howe, 190 Queens Ave., London, ON N6A 6H7, Tel. (519)434-6893 Fax (519)673-4151, Email: bishops@huron.anglican.ca

Keewatin, Rt. David N. Ashdown, 915 Ottawa St., Keewatin, ON P0X 1C0, Tel. (807)547-3353 Fax (807)547-3356, Email: dioceseof-keewatin@gokenora.com

Kootenay, Archbishop, The Rt. Rev. John E. Privett, 1876 Richter St., Kelowna, BC V1Y 2M9, Tel. (250)762-3306 Fax (250)762-4150, Email: diocese_of_kootenay@telus.net

Montreal, The Rt. Rev. Barry B. Clarke, 1444 Union Ave., Montreal, QC H3A 2B8 Tel. (514)843-6577 Fax (514)843-3221, Email: bishops.office@montreal.anglican.ca

Moosonee, TheMost Rev. Caleb J. Lawrence, Box 841, Schumacher, ON P0N 1G0, Tel. (705)360-1129 Fax (705)360-1120, Email: dmoose@domaa.ca

New Westminster, The Rt. Rev. Michael C. Ingham, 580-401 W. Georgia St., Vancouver, BC V6B 5A1, Tel. (604)684-6306 Fax (604) 684-7017, Email: bishop@vancouver.anglican. ca

Niagara, The Rt. Rev. Ralph Spence, 252 James St. N., Hamilton, ON L8R 2L3, Tel. (905)527-1278 Fax (905)527-1281, Email: bishop@niagara. anglican.ca

Nova Scotia and Prince Edward Is., The Rt. Rev. Frederick J. Hiltz, 5732 College St., Halifax, NS B3H 1X3, Tel. (902)420-0717 Fax (902) 425-0717, Email: office@nspeidiocese.ca

Ontario, The Rt. Rev. George L. R. Bruce, 90 Johnson St., Kingston, ON K7L 1X7, Tel. (613)544-4774 Fax (613)547-3745, Email: synod@ontario.anglican.ca

Ottawa, The Rt. Rev. Peter R. Coffin, 71 Bronson Ave., Ottawa, ON K1R 6G6, Tel. (613)232-7124 Fax (613)232-7088, Email: dayadmin@ottawa.anglican.ca

Qu'Appelle, The Rt. Rev. Gregory K. Kerr-Wilson, 1501 College Ave., Regina, SK S4P 1B8, Tel. (306)522-1608 Fax (306)352-6808, Email: quappelle@ca sasktel.net

Quebec, The Most Rev. A. Bruce Stavert, 31 rue des Jardins, Quebec, QC G1R 4L6, Tel. (418)692-3858 Fax (418)692-3876, Email: synodoffice@quebec.anglican.ca

Rupert's Land, The Rt. Rev. Donald D. Phillips, 935 Nesbitt Bay, Winnipeg, MB R3T 1W6, Tel. (204)922-4200 Fax (204)922-4219, Email: general@rupertsland.ca

Saskatchewan, The Rt. Rev. Anthony Burton, 1308 5th Ave. East, Prince Albert, SK S6V 2H7, Tel. (306)763-2455 Fax (306)764-5172, Email: synod@sasktel.net

Saskatoon, The Rt. Rev. Rodney Andrews, Box 1965, Saskatoon, SK S7K 3S5, Tel. (306)244-5651 Fax (306)933-4606, Email: anglican-bishop@sasktel.net

Toronto, The Rt. Rev. Colin R. Johnson, 135 Adelaide St. East, Toronto, ON M5C 1L8, Tel. (416)363-6021 Fax (416)363-3683, Email: cjohnson@toronto.anglican.ca

Western Newfoundland, The Rt. Rev. Percy D. Coffin, 25 Main St., Corner Brook, NF A2H 1C2, Tel. (709)639-8712 Fax (709)639-1636, Email: dsownc@nf.aibn.com

Yukon, The Rt. Rev. Terry Buckle, Box 4247, Whitehorse, YT Y1A 3T3, Tel. (867)667-7746 Fax (867)667-6125, Email: synodoffice@ klondiker.com

### Periodicals
*Anglican Journal* (National Newspaper); *Ministry Matters*

## The Antiochian Orthodox Christian Archdiocese of North America

The approximately 100,000 members of the Antiochian Orthodox community in Canada are under the jurisdiction of the Antiochian Orthodox Christian Archdiocese of North America with headquarters in Englewood, N.J. There are churches in Edmonton, Winnipeg, Halifax, London, Ottawa, Toronto, Windsor, Montreal, Saskatoon, Hamilton, Vancouver, Charlottestown, PEI, Calgary, and Mississauga.

### Headquarters
Metropolitan Philip Saliba, 358 Mountain Rd., Englewood, NJ 07631 Tel. (201)871-1355 Fax (201)871-7954

Media Contact, Rev. Fr. Thomas Zain, 355 State Street, Brooklyn, NY 11217 Tel. (718)855-6225 Fax (718)855-3608 Email: abouna@aol.com

Website: www.antiochian.org

### Periodicals
*The Word; Again; Handmaiden*

## Apostolic Christian Church (Nazarene)

This church was formed in Canada as a result of immigration from various European countries.

183

The body began as a movement originated by the Rev. S. H. Froehlich, a Swiss pastor, whose followers are still found in Switzerland and Central Europe.

### Headquarters

Apostolic Christian Church Foundation, 1135 Sholey Rd., Richmond, VA 23231 Tel. (804) 222-1943

Media Contact, James Hodges

### Officers

Exec. Dir., James Hodges

## The Apostolic Church in Canada

The Apostolic Church in Canada is affiliated with the worldwide organization of the Apostolic Church with headquarters in Great Britain (www.apostolicworld.net). A product of the Welsh Revival (1904 to 1908), its Canadian beginnings originated in Nova Scotia in 1927. Today its main centers are in Nova Scotia, Ontario and Quebec. This church is evangelical, fundamental and Pentecostal, with special emphasis on the ministry gifts listed in Ephesians 4:11-12.

### Headquarters

27 Castlefield Ave., Toronto, ON M4R 1G3

Media Contact, Pres., Rev. D. Karl Thomas, 220 Adelaide St. London, ON N6B-3H4, Tel. (519)438-7036 Fax (705)742-2948

Email: nlcrevival@goldon.net

Website, www.apostolic.ca

### Officers

Pres., Rev. D. Karl Thomas, 220 Adelaide St., London, ON N6B 344, Tel. (519)438-7036 Fax (519)438-5800, Email: nlcrevival@ goldon.net

Natl. Sec., Rev. James Hackner, R.R. #1 Uxbridge, ON L9P-1R1, Tel. (905)852-3563

### Periodicals

*Canadian News Up-Date; The News Magazine of the Apostolic Church in Canada*

## Apostolic Church of Pentecost of Canada Inc.

The Apostolic Church of Pentecost, Incorporated, was founded in 1921 at Winnipeg, Manitoba, by Pastor Frank Small and is a network of ministers and churches providing fellowship, encouragement and accountability in the proclamation of the Gospel of Jesus Christ by the power of the Holy Spirit.

### Headquarters

#119-2340 Pegasus Way NE, Calgary, AB T2E 8M5

Media Contact, Moderator, Rev. Wes Mills, Tel. (403)273-5777 Fax (403)273-8102

Email: acop@acop.ca

Website: www.acop.ca

### Officers

Mod., Rev. Wes Mills

Mission Director, Rev. Brian Cooper

### Periodicals

*Fellowship Focus; Apostolic Women's Ministry (AWM) Newsletter*

## Armenian Evangelical Church

Founded in 1960 by immigrant Armenian evangelical families from the Middle East, this body is conservative doctrinally, with an evangelical, biblical emphasis. The polity of churches within the group differ, with congregationalism being dominant, but there are presbyterian Armenian Evangelical churches as well. Most of the local churches have joined main-line denominations. All of the remaining Armenian Evangelical (congregational or presbyterian) local churches in the United States and Canada have joined with the Armenian Evangelical Union of North America.

### Headquarters

Armenian Evangelical Church of Toronto, 2851 John St., P.O. Box 42015, Markham, ON L3R 5R0, Tel. (905)305-8144

Media Contact, Chief Editor, Rev. Yessayi Sarmazian

A.E.U.N.A. OFFICERS

Min. to the Union, Rev. Karl Avakian, 1789 E. Frederick Ave., Fresno, CA 93720

Mod., Rev. Bernard Geulsgeugian

Min., Rev. Yessayi Sarmazian

### Periodicals

*Armenian Evangelical Church*

## Armenian Holy Apostolic Church— Canadian Diocese

The Canadian branch of the ancient Church of Armenia founded in A.D. 301 by St. Gregory the Illuminator was established in Canada at St. Catharines, Ontario, in 1930. The diocesan organization is under the jurisdiction of the Holy See of Etchmiadzin, Armenia. The Diocese has churches in St. Catharines, Hamilton, Toronto, Ottawa, Vancouver, Mississauga, Montreal, Laval, Windsor, Halifax, Winnipeg, Edmonton, and Calgary.

### Headquarters

Diocesan Offices, Primate, Canadian Diocese, Archbishop Hovnan Derderian, 615 Stuart Ave., Outremont, QC H2V 3H2, Tel. (514) 276-9479 Fax (514)276-9960

Media Contact, Exec. Dir. Deacon Hagop Arslanian; Silva Mangassarian, Secretary

Email: adiocese @aol.com,

Website: www.canarmdiocese.org

### Officers

Sec., Silva Mangassarian

Webmaster, Albert Yeglikian

## Associated Gospel Churches

The Associated Gospel Churches (AGC) traces its historical roots to the 1890s. To counteract the growth of liberal theology evident in many established denominations at this time, individuals and whole congregations seeking to uphold the final authority of the Scriptures in all matters of faith and conduct withdrew from those denominations and established churches with an evangelical ministry. These churches defended the belief that "all Scripture is given by inspiration of God" and also declared that the Holy Spirit gave the identical word of sacred writings of holy men of old, chosen by Him to be the channel of His revelation to man.

At first this growing group of independent churches was known as the Christian Workers' Churches of Canada, and by 1922 there was desire for forming an association for fellowship, counsel and cooperation. Several churches in southern Ontario banded together under the leadership of Dr. P. W. Philpott of Hamilton and Rev. H. E. Irwin, K. C. of Toronto.

When a new Dominion Charter was obtained on March 18, 1925, the name was changed to Associated Gospel Churches. Since that time the AGC has steadily grown, spreading across Canada by invitation to other independent churches of like faith and by actively beginning new churches.

### Headquarters
1500 Kerns Rd., Burlington, ON L7P 3A7, Tel. (905)634-8184 Fax (905)634-6283
Administrative Assistant, Donna Leung, 1500 Kerns Rd., Burlington, ON L7P 3A7, Tel. (905)634-8184 Fax (905)634-6283 Email: donna@agcofcanada.com
Email: admin@agcofcanada.com
Website: www.agcofcanada.com

### Officers
Pres., Rev. A.F. (Bud) Penner, 1500 Kerns Rd., Burlington, ON L7P 3A7, Tel. (905)634-8184 Fax (905)634-6283
Mod., Rev. David Collins, 1500 Kerns Rd, Burlington, L7P3A7, Tel. (905)634-8184 Fax (905)634-6283
Sec.-Treas., Mr. Charles Lyle, 1245 Stephenson Dr., Burlington, ON L7S 2L9, Tel. (905)633-8960

### Periodicals
*Insidedge*

## Association of Regular Baptist Churches (Canada)

The Association of Regular Baptist Churches was organized in 1957 by a group of churches for the purpose of mutual cooperation in missionary activities. The Association believes the Bible to be God's word, stands for historic Baptist principles, and opposes modern ecumenism.

### Headquarters
17 Laverock St., Tottenham, ON L0G 1W0, Tel. (905)936-3786

### Officers
Chmn., Rev. S. Kring, 67 Sovereen St., Delhi, ON N4B 1L7

## Baptist Convention of Ontario and Quebec

The Baptist Convention of Ontario and Quebec is a family of 365 churches in Ontario and Quebec, united for mutual support and encouragement and united in missions in Canada and the world.

The Convention was formally organized in 1888. Its one educational institution—McMaster Divinity College—was founded in 1887. The Convention works through the all-Canada missionary agency, Canadian Baptist Ministries. The churches also support the Sharing Way, the relief and development arm of Canadian Baptist Ministries.

### Headquarters
195 The West Mall, Ste. 414, Etobicoke, ON M9C 5K1 Tel. (416)622-8600 Fax (416)622-2308
Media Contact, Exec. Min., Dr. Ken Bellous, Website: www.Baptist.ca

### Officers
Past Pres., Rev. John Torrance
President, Mr. Evan Whitehead
1st Vice-Pres., Mrs. Marie Toompuu
2nd Vice Pres., Mr. Don Hallman
Treas.-Bus. Admn., Nancy Bell
Exec. Min., Dr. Ken Bellous

### Periodicals
*The Canadian Baptist*

## Baptist General Conference of Canada

The Baptist General Conference was founded in Canada by missionaries from the United States. Originally a Swedish body, BGC Canada now includes people of many nationalities and is conservative and evangelical in doctrine and practice.

### Headquarters
#205 15824 131 Avenue Edmonton, AB T5V 1J4 Tel. (780)438-9127 Fax (780)435-2478
Media Contact, Exec. Dir., Jamey S. McDonald

### Officers
Exec. Dir., Jamey S. McDonald, #205 15824 131 Avenue Edmonton, AB T5V 1J4, Tel. (780) 438-9127 Fax (780)435-2478
Exec. Dir., Gordon H. Sorensen, BGC Stewardship Foundation, #205 15824 131 Avenue Edmonton, AB T5V 1J4, Tel. (780)438-9127 Fax (780)435-2478

## DISTRICTS

Baptist Gen. Conf.—Central Canada, Exec. Min., Lorne Meisner, 877 Wilkes Avenue, Winnipeg, MB R3P 1B8, Tel. (204)772-6742 Fax (204) 269-5505

Baptist General Conference in Alberta, Exec. Min., Cal Netterfield, 11525 23 Ave., Edmonton, AB T6J 4T3, Tel. (780)438-9126 Fax (780)438-5258

British Columbia Baptist Conference, Exec. Min., Walter W. Wieser, 7600 Glover Rd., Langley, BC V2Y 1Y1, Tel. (604)888-2246 Fax (604)888-0046

Baptist General Conf. in Saskatchewan, Exec. Min., Abe Funk

## Baptist Union of Western Canada

### Headquarters

302,902-11 Ave., SW, Calgary, AB T2R 0E7

Media Contact, Exec. Min., Dr. Gerald Fisher

### Officers

Pres., Mr. Bill Mains, 4576 Rainer Crescent, Prince George, BC V2K 1X4

Exec. Minister, Dr. Gerald Fisher, 302, 902-11 Ave SW, Calgary, AB T2R 0E7

Alberta Area Minister, Rev. Ed Dyck, 302, 902-11 Ave SW, Calgary, AB T2R 0E7

BC Area Minister, Dr. Paul Pearce, 201, 20349-88th Ave., Langely, BC V1M 2K5

SK-MB Area Minister, Dr. Robert Krahn, 414 Cowley Place, Saskatoon, SK S7N 3X2

Carey Theological College, Principal, Dr. Brian Stelck, 5920 Iona Dr., Vancouver, BC V6T 1J6

Baptist Resources Centre, 302, 902-11 Ave SW, Calgary, AB T2R 0E7

## The Bible Holiness Movement

The Bible Holiness Movement, organized in 1949 as an outgrowth of the city mission work of the late Pastor William James Elijah Wakefield, an early-day Salvation Army officer, has been headed since its inception by his son, Evangelist Wesley H. Wakefield, its Bishop-General.

It derives its emphasis on the original Methodist faith of salvation and scriptural holiness from the late Bishop R. C. Horner. It adheres to the common evangelical faith in the Bible, the deity and the atonement of Christ. It stresses a personal experience of salvation for the repentant sinner, of being wholly sanctified for the believer and of the fullness of the Holy Spirit for effective witness.

Membership involves a life of Christian love and evangelistic and social activism. Members are required to totally abstain from liquor and tobacco. They may not attend popular amusements or join secret societies. Divorce and remarriage are forbidden. Similar to Wesley's Methodism, members are, under some circumstances, allowed to retain membership in other evangelical church fellowships. Interchurch affiliations are maintained

with a number of Wesleyan-Arminian Holiness denominations.

Year-round evangelistic outreach is maintained through open-air meetings, visitation, literature and other media. Noninstitutional welfare work, including addiction counseling, is conducted among minorities. There is direct overseas famine relief, civil rights action, environment protection, and antinuclearism. The movement sponsors a permanent committee on religious freedom and an active promotion of Christian racial equality.

The movement has a world outreach with branches in the United States, India, Nigeria, Philippines, Ghana, Liberia, Cameroon, Kenya, Zambia, South Korea, Mulawi, and Tanzania. It also ministers to 89 countries in 42 languages through literature, radio, and audiocassettes.

### Headquarters

Box 223, Postal Stn. A, Vancouver, BC V6C 2M3, Tel. (250)492-3376

Media Contact, Bishop-General, Evangelist Wesley H. Wakefield, P.O. Box 223, Postal Station A, Vancouver, BC V6C 2M3, Tel. (250) 492-3376

Website: www.bible-holiness-movement.com

### DIRECTORS

Bishop-General, Evangelist Wesley H. Wakefield, (Intl. Leader)

Evangelist M. J. Wakefield, Penticton, BC

Pastor Vincente & Mirasal Hernando, Phillipines

Pastor & Mrs. Daniel Stinnett, 1425 Mountain View W., Phoenix, AZ 85021

Pastor Monday S. Attai, Abak, Akwalbom, Nigeria, West Africa

Pastor Choe Chong Dee, Iksun City, S. Korea

Pastor T. Chandra, Sekhor Rao, India

Pastor and Mrs. Daniel Vandee, Ghana, W. Africa

Pastor L.W. Hutchings, Protem, Vancouver, B.C., Canada

Pastor Victor Freeman Holmquist, Vancouver, B.C., Canada

Bro. Aaron Louis Birch, Vancouver, B.C., Evangelist, Mrs. Stephen Richards, Uyo, Akwa Ibom State, Nigeria, West Africa

### Periodicals

*Hallelujah!*

## Brethren in Christ Church, Canadian Conference

The Brethren in Christ, formerly known as Tunkers in Canada, arose out of a religious awakening in Lancaster County, Pa. late in the 18th century. Representatives of the new denomination reached Ontario in 1788 and established the church in the southern part of the present province. Presently the conference has congregations in Ontario, Alberta, Quebec, and Saskatchewan. In theology they have accents of the Pietist, Anabaptist, Wesleyan and Evangelical movements.

## Headquarters

Brethren in Christ Church, Gen. Ofc., P.O. Box A, Grantham, PA 17027-0901, Tel. (717)697-2634 Fax (717)697-7714

Canadian Headquarters, Bishop's Ofc., 416 North Service Rd. E., Suite 1, Oakville, ON L6H 5R2, Tel. (905)339-2335

Media Contact, Mod., Dr. Warren L. Hoffman, Brethren in Christ Church Gen. Ofc.

## Officers

Mod., Bishop Brian Bell, 416 North Service Road, Suite 1, Oakville, ON L6H 5R2, Tel. (905)339-2335 Fax (905)337-2120

Sec., Betty Albrecht, RR 2, Petersburg, ON N0B 2H0

Sec., Carole Phillips, 416 North Service Rd. E., Suite 1, Oakville, ON L6H 5R2

## Periodicals

*Evangelical Visitor; "Yes," Shalom*

## British Methodist Episcopal Church of Canada

The British Methodist Episcopal Church was organized in 1856 in Chatham, Ontario and incorporated in 1913. It has congregations across the province of Ontario.

## Headquarters

430 Grey Street, London, ON N6B 1H3

Media Contact, Gen. Sec., Rev. Jacqueline Collins, 47 Connolly St., Toronto, ON M6N 4Y5, Tel. (416)653-6339

## Officers

Gen. Supt., Rt. Rev. Dr. Douglas Birse, R.R. #5, Thamesville, ON N0P 2K0, Tel. (519)692-3628

Asst. Gen. Supt., Maurice M. Hicks, 3 Boxdene Ave., Scarborough, ON M1V 3C9, Tel. (416) 298-5715

Gen. Sec., Rev. Jacqueline Collins, 47 Connolly St., Toronto, ON M6N 4Y5, Tel. (416)653-6339

Gen. Treas., Ms. Hazel Small, 7 Wood Fernway, North York, ON M2J 4P6, Tel. (416)491-0313

## Periodicals

*B.M.E. Church Newsletter*

## Canadian and American Reformed Churches

The Canadian and American Reformed Churches accept the Bible as the infallible Word of God, as summarized in The Belgic Confession of Faith (1561), The Heidelberg Cathechism (1563) and The Canons of Dort (1618-1619). The federation was founded in Canada in 1950 and in the United States in 1955.

## Headquarters

Synod, 607 Dynes Rd., Burlington, ON L7N 2V4

Canadian Reformed Churches, Ebenezer Canadian Reformed Church, 607 Dynes Rd., Burlington, ON L7N 2V4

Theological College, Dr. N. H. Gootjes, 110 W. 27th St., Hamilton, ON L9C 5A1, Tel. (905)575-3688 Fax (905)575-0799

Media Contact, Rev. Dr. G. Nederveen, 3089 Woodward Ave., Burlington, ON L7N 2M3, Tel. (905)681-7055 Fax (905)681-7055

## Periodicals

*Reformed Perspective, A Magazine for the Christian Family; Evangel, The Good News of Jesus Christ; Clarion, The Canadian Reformed Magazine; Diakonia—A Magazine of Office-Bearers; Book of Praise; Koinonia, A periodical of the Ministers of the CanRC; Horizon, (A quarterly magazine published by the League of CanRC Women Societies); A Gift from Heaven, A Reformed Bible course.*

## Canadian Assemblies of God (formerly The Italian Pentecostal Churches of Canada)

This body had its beginnings in Hamilton, Ont., in 1912 when a few people of an Italian Presbyterian Church banded themselves together for prayer and received a pentecostal experience of the baptism in the Holy Spirit. Since 1912, there has been a close association with the teachings and practices of the Pentecostal Assemblies of Canada.

The work spread to Toronto, then to Montreal, where it also flourished. In 1959, the church was incorporated in the province of Quebec. The early leaders of this body were the Rev. Luigi Ippolito and the Rev. Ferdinand Zaffuto. The churches carry on their ministry in both the English and Italian languages.

## Headquarters

6724 Fabre St., Montreal, QC H2G 2Z6, Tel. (514)279-1100 Fax (514)279-1131

Media Contact, Gen. Sec., Rev. John DellaForesta, 12216 Pierre Baillargeon, Montreal, QC H1E 6R7, Tel. (514)494-6969 Fax (514)279-1131

## Officers

Gen. Supt., Rev. David Mortelliti, 6724 Fabre St., Montreal, QC H2G 2Z6, Tel. (514)279-1100 Fax (514)279-1131

Gen. Sec., Rev. John DellaForesta, 12216 Pierre Baillargeon, Montreal, QC H1E 6R7, Tel. (514)494-6969

Gen. Treas., Rev. David Quackenbush, 686 Ossington, Toronto ON M6G 3T7, Tel. (416)532-3951 Fax (416)532-0267

Overseer, Rev. David DiStaulo, 5811 Maurice Duplessis, Montreal QC H1G 1Y2, Tel. (514)328-3131

## Periodicals

*Voce Evangelica-Evangel Voice*

187

## Canadian Baptist Ministries

The Canadian Baptist Ministries has four federated member bodies, (1) Baptist Convention of Ontario and Quebec, (2) Baptist Union of Western Canada, (3) the United Baptist Convention of the Atlantic Provinces, (4) Union d'Églises Baptistes Françaises au Canada (French Baptist Union). Its main purpose is to act as a coordinating agency for the four groups for mission in all five continents.

### Headquarters

7185 Millcreek Dr., Mississauga, ON L5N 5R4, Tel. (905)821-3533 Fax (905)826-3441
Media Contact, Communications, David Rogelstad
Email: daver@cbmin.org
Website: www.cbmin.org

### Officers

Pres., Doug Coomas
Gen. Sec., Rev. Gart Nelson
Email, NelsonG@cbmin.org

## Canadian Conference of Mennonite Brethren Churches

The conference was incorporated November 22, 1945.

### Headquarters

1310 Taylor Ave., Winnipeg, MB R3M 3Z6, Tel. (204)669-6575 Fax (204)654-1865 Toll Free (888)669-6575
Media Contact, Exec. Dir., Dave Wiebe
Website: www.mbconf.ca

### Periodicals

*Mennonite Brethren Herald; Mennonitische Rundschau; IdeaBank; Le Lien; Expression; Chinese Herald; Mennonite Historian*

## Canadian Convention of Southern Baptists

The Canadian Convention of Southern Baptists was formed at the Annual Meeting, May 7-9, 1985, in Kelowna, B.C. It was formerly known as the Canadian Baptist Conference, founded in Kamloops, British Columbia, in 1959 by pastors of existing churches.

### Headquarters

100 Convention Way, Cochrane, AB T4C 2G2, Tel. (403)932-5688 Fax (403)932-4937
Email: office@ccsb.ca
Media Contact, Exec. Dir.-Treas., Rev.Gerald Taillon

### Officers

Exec. Dir.-Treas., Gerald Taillon, 17 Riverview Close, Cochrane, AB T4C 1K7
Pres., Robert Blackaby, 9920 Fairmount Drive SE, Calgary, AB T2J 0S4

### Periodicals

*The Baptist Horizon*

## Canadian District of the Moravian Church in America, Northern Province

The work in Canada is under the general oversight and rules of the Moravian Church, Northern Province, general offices for which are located in Bethlehem, Pennsylvania. For complete information, see "Religious Bodies in the United States" section of the Yearbook.

### Headquarters

1021 Center St., P.O. Box 1245, Bethlehem, PA 18016-1245
Media Contact, Ms. Deanna Hollenbach

### Officers

Pres.,Rev. Stephen Gohoes, 600 Acadia Dr. SE Calgary, AB T2J OB8, Email: sgohdes@shaw.ca

### Periodicals

*The Moravian*

## Canadian Evangelical Christian Churches

The Canadian Evangelical Christian Church is an international, full-gospel new apostolic denomination, emphasizing the New Testament apostolic paradigm pattern which recognizes the ministry gifts beyond the apostle, prophet, evangelist, pastor and teacher to spread the gospel, according to Ephesians 4:11,12. The congregations are associated through full-gospel doctrine that is in combination with Calvinistic and Arminian beliefs. Each and every congregation is connected with CECC as congregational and ordination is supervised by National Office.

### Headquarters

General Superintendent, Rev. David P. Lavigne, 410-125 Lincoln Rd., Waterloo, ON N2J 2N9, Tel. (519)880-9110, Toll free (888)981-8881
Email: cecc@rogers.com
Website: www.cecconline.com

### Officers

Gen. Supt., Rev. David P. Lavigne, 410-125 Lincoln Rd., Waterloo, ON N2J 2N9, Tel. (519)725-5578, Toll free (888)981-8881, Email: cecc@rogers.com
Gen. Sec., Rev. Bill St. Pierre, Box 7, Ontario, ON N3P 1B9, Tel. (888)297-5551

## Canadian Yearly Meeting of the Religious Society of Friends

Canadian Yearly Meeting of the Religious Society of Friends was founded in Canada as an offshoot of the Quaker movement in Great Britain and colonial America. Genesee Yearly Meeting, founded 1834, Canada Yearly Meeting (Orthodox), founded in 1867, and Canada Yearly Meeting, founded in 1881, united in 1955 to form the Canadian Yearly Meeting. Canadian Yearly Meeting is affiliated with Friends United Meeting and Friends General Conference. It is also a member of Friends World Committee for Consultation.

### Headquarters
91A Fourth Ave., Ottawa, ON K1S 2L1 Tel. (613)235-8553 or (888)296-3222 Fax (613) 235-1753
Email: cym-office@quaker.ca

### Officers
Clerk, Dale Dewar
Archivist, Jane Zavitz Bond
Archives, Arthur G. Dorland, Pickering College, 389 Bayview St., Newmarket, ON L3Y 4X2, Tel. (416)895-1700

### Periodicals
*The Canadian Friend; Quaker Concern*

**Catholic church—please see Roman Catholic Church**

## Christ Catholic Church International

Christ Catholic Church International now has churches and/or missions in 14 countries spread over four continents. They are located in the United States, Canada, Poland, Bahamas, Ukraine, Trinidad-Tobago, Colombia, Australia, Slovakia, Belarus, Kenya, and the Phillipines. Some countries have active churches and missions; some just missions and/or prayer groups.

CCCI is an Orthodox-Catholic Communion tracing apostolic succession through the Old Catholic and Orthodox Catholic Churches.

The church ministers to a growing number of people seeking an experiential relationship with their Lord and Savior Jesus Christ in a sacramental and Scripture based church.

### Headquarters
4695 St. Lawrence Ave., Niagara Falls, ON L2G 1Y4
Media Contact, The Rt. Rev. John W. Brown, 1504-75 Queen St., Hamilton, ON L8R 3J3, Tel. (905)527-9089 Fax (905)522-6240, Email: bishopjohn@primus.ca
Email: dioceseofniagara@cogeco.net
Website: www3.sympatico.ca/dwmullan

### PRESIDING ARCHBISHOP
The Most Rev. Donald Wm. Mullan, 6190 Barker St., Niagara Falls, ON L2G 1Y4, Tel. (905)354-2329, Fax (905)357-9934, Email: dmullan1@cogeco.net

### ARCHBISHOPS
The Most Rev. Jose Ruben Garcia Matiz, Calle 52 Sur #24A-35-Bq. #1, Ap. 301, Santa Fe de Bogota, D.C., Colombia, South America, Tel. 57-714-47-87, Email: jorugama@col1.telecom.com.co

### BISHOPS
The Rt. Rev. John Wm. Brown, 1504-75 Queen St., N. Hamilton, ON L8R 3J3, Tel. (905)522-6240, Email: bishopjohn@primus.ca
The Rt. Rev. Luis Fernando Hoyos Maldonado, A. A. 24378 Santa Fe de Bogota, D.C., Colombia, South America, Tel. 57-276-68-16, Email: jourgama@col1.telecom.com.co
The Rt. Rev. Jose Moises Moncada Quevedo, A.A. 24378 Santa Fe de Bogota, D.C., Colombia, South America, Tel. 57-276-68-16, Email: jourgama@col1.telecom.com.co
The Rt. Rev. Jerome Robben, Vicar General, P.O. Box 566, Chesterfield, MO 63006-0566, Tel. (314)205-8422, Email: abbajn17@aol.com
The Rt. Rev. Andrzej J. Sarwa, ul. Krucza 16 27-600 Sandomierz, Poland, Tel. & fax 084-(0-15) 833-21-41, Email: andrzej-san@poczta.wp.pl
The Rt. Rev. Robert Smith, 824 Royal Oak Dr., Orlando, FL 32809, Tel. (407)240-7833, Email: yshwa@webtv.net
The Rt. Rev. Ted Lorah Jr., 430 Wawassan Drive, P.O. Box 208, Honey Brook, PA 19344, Tel. (610)273-7209, Email: tlorah@temple.edu
The Rt. Rev. John Gilbert-Cougar, Box 7305, D. L. Atkinson Station, Pasadena, TX 77508-7305

### Periodicals
*St. Luke Magazine*

## Christian Brethren (also known as Plymouth Brethren)

The Christian Brethren are a loose grouping of autonomous local churches, often called "assemblies." They are firmly committed to the inerrancy of Scripture and to the evangelical doctrine of salvation by faith alone apart from works or sacrament. Characteristics are a weekly Breaking of Bread and freedom of ministry without a requirement of ordination. For their history, see "Religious Bodies in the United States" in the Directories section of this *Yearbook*.

### CORRESPONDENT
James A. Stahr, 327 W. Prairie Ave., Wheaton, IL 60187, U.S.A., Tel.(630)665-3757

### RELATED ORGANIZATIONS
Christian Brethren Churches in Quebec, P.O. Box 1054, Sherbrooke, QC J1H 5L3, Tel. (819)820-1693 Fax (819)821-9287
Kawartha Lakes Bible College, Box 1101, Peterborough, ON K9J 7H4, Tel. (705)742-2437
Mount Carmel Bible School, 4725 106th Ave., Edmonton, AB T6A 1E7, Tel. (780)465-3015
MSC Canada, 509-3950 14th Ave., Markham, ON L3R 0A9, Tel. (905)947-0468 Fax (905)947-0352
Vision Ministries Canada, 145 Lincoln Road, Waterloo, ON N2J 2N8, Tel. (519)725-1212 Fax (519)725-9421

### Periodicals
*News of Quebec*

189

## Christian Church (Disciples of Christ) in Canada

Disciples have been in Canada since 1810, and were organized nationally in 1922. This church served the Canadian context as a region of the whole Christian Church (Disciples of Christ) in the United States and Canada.

### Headquarters

Christian Church in Canada, P.O. Box 23030, 417 Wellington St., St. Thomas, ON N5R 6A3, Tel. (519)633-9083 Fax (519)637-6407, Email: ccic@netrover.com
Media Contact, Reg. Min., F. Thomas Rutherford

### Officers

Mod., Peter Fountain, P.O. Box 344, Milton, NS B0T 1P0, Tel. (902)354-5988, Email: pjfountain@auracom.com
Reg. Min., F. Thomas Rutherford, P.O. Box 23030, 417 Wellington St., St. Thomas, ON N5R 6A3, Tel. (519)633-9083 Fax (519)637-6407, Email: ccic@netrover.com

## Christian Churches/Churches of Christ

First congregation organized: Cross Roads Christian Church, Cross Roads, Prince Edward Island, Canada, 1810, by "Scotch Baptists" influenced by James and Robert Haldane of Edinburgh. Since the 1820s when the writings of Thomas and Alexander Campbell were widely circulated and reprinted in periodicals, these congregations have identified with the 19th-century "Restoration Movement" (also known as, "Stone-Campbell Movement") which came to be known as "Disciples of Christ." In late 19th-century Ontario, some congregations separated over the use of musical instruments into a group known as the *a capella* Churches of Christ. From the 1880s to the 1930s, Disciples of Christ migrating from Ontario and emigrating from the United States organized congregations in Manitoba, Saskatchewan, Alberta, and British Columbia. From about 1948, when the Disciples of Christ in Canada first moved toward and then declared a formal denominational structure in 1968, 65-70 congregations across Canada did not identify with this structure preferring to remain free, congregationally governed fellowships. While especially in western Canada these congregations cooperate and fellowship with congregations identified with the Disciples of Christ in Canada, *a capella* Churches of Christ, and people and congregations of several other traditions, they generally tend to identify with the interpretation of the Restoration or Stone-Campbell Movement as exemplified by U.S. Christian Churches and Churches of Christ in affinity with the North American Christian Convention, an annual, non-delegated, preaching and teaching convention. (See "The Movement in Canada," *Encyclopedia of the Stone-Campbell Movement*. Grand Rapids, Mich.: Eerdmans, 2004, pp. 151-163).

### Headquarters

Media Contact: Russell E. Kuykendall, 25 Grenville Street, 1507, Toronto, ON M4Y 2X5, Tel. (416)895-1098, Email: kuykendall@canada.com

### Other Institutions

All of the following are free-standing, para-church institutions. Mortgage financing for congregations and para-church institutions: Church of Christ Development Company, Edmonton, Alberta. Church-planting associations: Partners in Atlantic Canada Evangelism, Impact Ontario, and Alberta Church Planting Association. Degree-granting colleges: Maritime Christian College, Charlottetown, PEI, and Alberta Bible College, Calgary, AB. Cross-cultural missions: Church of Christ Mission Jamaica; Church of Christ Mission India; Global Missionary Ministries (Central Europe); Frontier Labourers for Christ Canada (Thailand, Laos, and Myanmar); Graceland Ministries (Poland); Terri Scruggs, Partners with Nationals, Wycliffe Bible Translators; Benevolent Social Services of India; and others. Christian camps: Canoe Cove (PEI), Ontario Christian Assembly, Camp Christian (Pine Lake, AB), Pine Ridge Christian (Grande Prairie, AB), and Double VM (Lumby, BC). Annual fellowship meetings: Maritime Christian Fellowship, Ontario Christian Missionary Conference, Western Canada Christian Convention (with Disciples of Christ and *a capella* Churches of Christ), and the North American Christian Convention.

## Christian and Missionary Alliance in Canada

A Canadian movement, dedicated to the teaching of Jesus Christ the Saviour, Sanctifier, Healer and Coming King, commenced in Toronto in 1887 under the leadership of the Rev. John Salmon. Two years later, the movement united with The Christian Alliance of New York, founded by Rev. A. B. Simpson, becoming the Dominion Auxiliary of the Christian Alliance, Toronto, under the presidency of the Hon. William H. Howland. Its four founding branches were Toronto, Hamilton, Montreal, and Quebec. The movement focused on the deeper life and missions. In 1980, the Christian and Missionary Alliance in Canada became autonomous. Its General Assembly is held every two years.

### NATIONAL OFFICE

30 Carrier Dr, Suite 100, Toronto, ON M9W 5T7, Tel. (416)674-7878 Fax (416)674-0808
Email: info@cmacan.org
Media Contact, Director of Communications, Barrie Doyle

### Officers

Pres., Dr. Franklin Pyles, Email: pylesf@cmacan.org

Vice Pres.—Global Ministries, Dr. Ray Downey, Email: downeyr@cmacan.org
Vice Pres.—Fin., Paul D. Lorimer, Email: lorimerp @cmacan.org
Vice Pres.—Canadian Ministries, Rev. C. Stuart Lightbody, Email: lightbodys@cmacan.org
Vice Pres.—Advancement, Rev. David Freeman, Email: freemand@cmacan.org
Chairman of the Board, Dr. T. V. Thomas
Secretary of the Board, Connie Driedger

### Periodicals
*Alliance Life*

## Christian Reformed Church in North America

Canadian congregations of the Christian Reformed Church in North America have been formed since 1905. For detailed information about this denomination, please refer to the listing for the Christian Reformed Church in North America in Chapter 3, "Religious Bodies in the United States."

### Headquarters
United States Office, 2850 Kalamazoo Ave., S.E., Grand Rapids, MI 49560, Tel. (616)224-0832 Fax (616)224-5895
Canadian Office, 3475 Mainway, P.O. Box 5070 STN LCR 1, Burlington, ON L7R 3Y8, Tel. (905)336-2920 Fax (905)336-8344
Media Contact, Exec. Dir., Dr. Peter Borgdorff, U.S. Office; Director of Communication, Mr. Henry Hess, Canadian Office
Website: www.crcna.org

### Officers
Executive Director: Rev. Gerard Dykstra
Director of Finance & Administration: Mr. John Bolt, U.S. Office
Director of Denominational Ministries: Rev. Gerard L. Dykstra

### Periodicals
*The Banner*

## Church of God (Anderson, Ind.)

This body is one of the largest of the groups which have taken the name "Church of God." Its headquarters are at Anderson, Indiana. It originated about 1880 and emphasizes Christian unity.

### Headquarters
Western Canada Assembly, Chpsn., Hilda Nauenburg, 4717- 56th St., Camrose, AB T4V 2C4, Tel. (780)672-0772 Fax (780)672-6888
Eastern Canada Assembly, Chpsn., Jim Wiebe, 38 James St., Dundas, ON L9H 2J6
Media Contact for Western Canada, Executive Dir. Of Ministry Services, John D. Campbell, 4717 56th St., Camrose, AB T4V 2C4, Tel. (780)672-0772 Fax (780)672-6888
Email: admincoo@cable-lynx.net; baughman@cable-lynx.net

Website: www.chog.ca

### Periodicals
*The Gospel Contact; The Messenger*

## Church of God in Christ (Mennonite)

The Church of God in Christ, Mennonite was organized by the evangelist-reformer John Holdeman in Ohio. The church unites with the faith of the Waldenses, Anabaptists and other such groups throughout history. Emphasis is placed on obedience to the teachings of the Bible, including the doctrine of the new birth and spiritual life, noninvolvement in government or the military, a head-covering for women, beards for men and separation from the world shown by simplicity in clothing, homes, possessions and lifestyle. The church has a worldwide membership of about 20,150, largely concentrated in the United States and Canada.

### Headquarters
P.O. Box 313, 420 N. Wedel Ave., Moundridge, KS 67107, Tel. (620)345-2532 Fax (620)345-2582
Media Contact, Dale Koehn, P.O. Box 230, Moundridge, KS 67107, Tel. (620)345-2532 Fax (620)345-2582

### Periodicals
*Messenger of Truth*

## Church of God (Cleveland, Tenn.)

It is one of America's oldest Pentecostal churches founded in 1886 as an outgrowth of the holiness revival under the name Christian Union. In 1907 the church adopted the organizational name Church of God. It has its foundation upon the principles of Christ as revealed in the Bible. The Church of God is Christian, Protestant, foundational in its doctrine, evangelical in practice and distinctively Pentecostal. It maintains a centralized form of government and a commitment to world evangelization.

The first church in Canada was established in 1919 in Scotland Farm, Manitoba. Paul H. Walker became the first overseer of Canada in 1931.

### Headquarters
Intl. Offices, 2490 Keith St., NW, Cleveland, TN 37320, Tel. (423)472-3361 Fax (423)478-7066
Media Contact, Dir. of Communications, Michael L. Baker, P.O. Box 2430, Cleveland, TN 37320-2430, Tel. (423)478-7112 Fax (423) 478-7066

### EXECUTIVES
Gen. Overseer, G. Dennis McGuire
Asst. Gen. Overseers, Raymond F. Culpepper; Orville Hagan; and Paul L. Walker
Sec.-Gen., Timothy M. Hill

191

Canada—Eastern, Rev. Andrew Binda, P.O.Box 2036, Brampton, ON L6T 3TO, Tel. (905) 793-2213 Fax (905)793-9173

Canada—Western, Rev. Stephen P. Darnell, Box 54055, 2640 52 St. NE, Calgary, AB T1Y 6S6, Tel. (403)293-8817 Fax (403)293-3466

Canada-Quebec-Maritimes, Rev. Jaques Houle, 19 Orly, Granby, QC J2H 1Y4, Tel. (450)378-4442 Fax (450)378-8646

Canada-National, Rev. Ralph R. Glagau, P.O. Box 333, Stn B, Etobicoke, ON M9W 5L3, Tel. (416)741-9222 Fax (416)741-3717

### DEPARTMENTS

Benefits Board—CEO, Arthur D. Rhodes

Business & Records—Exec. Dir., Julian B. Robinson

Care Ministries—Dir., John D. Nichols

Chaplains Commission—Dir., Robert D. Crick

Communications, Media Ministries—Dir., T. Scot Carter

Division of Education—Chancellor, R. Lamar Vest

Education—European Bible Seminary, Dir., Paul Schmidgall

Education—Hispanic Institute of Ministry, Dir., Jose D. Montanez

Education—International Bible College, Pres., Cheryl Busse

Education—Lee University, Pres., Charles Paul Conn

Education—Patten University, Pres., Gary Moncher

Education—Puerto Rico Bible School, Pres., Ildefonso Caraballo

Education—School of Ministry, Dir., Donald S. Aultman

Education—Theological Seminary, President, Steven J. Land

Evangelism & Home Missions—Dir., Larry J. Timmerman

Evangelism—Black Ministries, Dir., Asbury R. Sellers

Evangelism—Multi-Cultural Min., Dir., Wallace J. Sibley

Evangelism—Hispanic Ministries, Dir., Esdras Betancourt

Evangelism—Native American Ministries, Dir., Douglas M. Cline

Family Ministries—Coordinator, John K. Vining

Lay Ministries—Dir., Leonard Albert

Legal Services—Dir., Dennis W. Watkins

Men/Women of Action—Dir., L. Hugh Carver

Ministerial Care—Dir., Bill Leonard

Ministerial Development—Dir., Larry G. Hess

Ministry to Israel—Dir., J. Michael Utterback

Ministry to the Military—Dir., Robert A. Moore

Music Ministries—Dir., Delton L. Alford

Pentecostal Resource Center—Director, Donald D. Smeeton

Pentecostal Research Center—Dir., David G. Roebuck

Publications—Dir., M. Thomas Propes

SpiritCare—Dir., Gene D. Rice

Stewardship—Dir., Kenneth R. Davis

Women's Ministries—Coordinator, Mary Ruth Stone

World Missions—Dir., Roland E. Vaughan

Youth & Christian Education—Dir., Mark S. Abbott

Romanian Ministries—Dir., Thomas A. George

### Periodicals

*Church of God Evangel, Editorial Evangelica, Save Our World,; Ministry Now Profiles, Ministries Now Profiles*

## The Church of God of Prophecy Canada East

The Church of God of Prophecy is one of the churches that grew out of the work of A. J. Tomlinson in the first half of the twentieth century. Historically it shares a common heritage with the Church of God (Cleveland, Tennessee) and is in the mainstream of the classical Pentecostal-holiness tradition.

At the death of A.J. Tomlinson in 1943, M.A. Tomlinson was named General Overseer and served until his retirement in 1990. He emphasized unity and fellowship unlimited by racial, social, or political differences. The next General Overseer, Billy D. Murray, Sr., who served from 1990 until his retirement in 2000, emphasized a commitment to the promotion of Christian unity and world evangelization. In July 2000, Fred S. Fisher, Sr. Was duly selected to serve as the fourth General Overseer of the Church of God of Prophecy.

From its beginnings, the Church has based its beliefs on "the whole Bible, rightly divided," and has accepted the Bible as God's Holy Word, inspired, inerrant and infallible. The church is firm in its commitment to orthodox Christian belief. The church affirms that there is one God, eternally existing in three persons, Father, Son and Holy Spirit. It believes in the deity of Christ, His virgin birth, His sinless life, the physical miracles He performed, His atoning death on the cross, His bodily resurrection, His ascension to the right hand of the Father and his second coming. The church professes that salvation results from grace alone through faith in Christ, that regeneration by the Holy Spirit is essential for the salvation of sinful men, and that sanctification by the blood of Christ makes possible personal holiness. It affirms the present ministry of the Holy Spirit by whose indwelling believers are able to live godly lives and have power for service. The church believes in, and promotes, the ultimate unity of believers as prayed for by Christ in John 17. The church stresses the sanctity of human life and is committed to the sanctity of the marriage bond and the importance of strong, loving Christian families. Other official teachings include Holy Spirit baptism with tongues as initial evidence; manifestation of the spiritual gifts; divine healing; premillenial second coming of Christ; total abstinence from the use of tobacco, alcohol and narcotics; water baptism by immersion; the Lord's supper and washing of the saints' feet; and a concern for moderation and holiness in all dimensions of lifestyle.

The church is racially integrated on all levels, including top leadership. Women play a prominent role in church affairs, serving in pastoral roles and other leadership positions. The church presbytery has recently adopted plurality of leadership in the selection of a General Oversight Group. This group consists of eight bishops located around the world who, along with the General Overseer, are responsible for inspirational leadership and vision casting for the church body.

The Church has local congregations in all 50 states and more than 100 nations worldwide. Organizationally there is a strong emphasis on international missions, evangelism, youth and children's ministries, women's and men's ministries, stewardship, communications, publishing, leadership development, and discipleship.

### CHURCH OF GOD OF PROPHECY INTERNATIONAL OFFICES

P.O. Box 2910, Cleveland, TN 37320-2910
Media Contact, National Overseer, Levi Clarke, 5145 Tomken Rd, Mississauga, ON L4 W1P1, Tel. (905)625-1278 Fax (905)625-1316
Website: www.cogop.ca

#### Officers

Gen. Overseer, Bishop Fred S. Fisher, Sr.; General Presbyters, Sherman Allen, Sam Clements, Daniel Corbett, Clayton Endecott, Miguel Mojica, José Reyes, Sr., Felix Santiago, Brice Thompson
International Offices Ministries Dirs., Finance, Communications, and Publishing, Perry Gillum; Global Outreach and Administrative Asst. to the General Presbyters, Randy Howard; Leadership Development and Discipleship Ministries, Larry Duncan

#### Periodicals

*White Wing Messenger* (Eng), *Victory (Youth Magazine/Sunday School Curriculum); The Happy Harvester, White Wing Messenger* (Spanish).

## The Church of Jesus Christ of Latter-day Saints in Canada

The Church has had a presence in Canada since the early 1830s. Joseph Smith and Brigham Young both came to Eastern Canada as missionaries. There are now 157,000 members in Canada in more than 400 congregations.

Leading the Church in Canada are the presidents of over 40 stakes (equivalent to a diocese). World headquarters is in Salt Lake City, Utah (See U.S. Religious Bodies chapter of the Directories section of this *Yearbook*).

#### Headquarters

50 East North Temple St., Salt Lake City, UT 84150

Media Contact, Public Affairs Dir., Bruce Smith, 1185 Eglinton Ave., Box 116, North York, ON M3C 3C6, Tel. (416)431-7891 Fax (416)438-2723

## Church of the Lutheran Brethren

The Church of the Lutheran Brethren of America was organized in December 1900. Five independent Lutheran congregations met together in Milwaukee, Wis., and adopted a constitution patterned very closely to that of the Lutheran Free Church of Norway.

The spiritual awakening in the Midwest during the 1890s crystallized into convictions that led to the formation of a new church body. Chief among the concerns were church membership practices, observance of Holy Communion, confirmation practices and local church government.

The Church of the Lutheran Brethren practices a simple order of worship with the sermon as the primary part of the worship service. It believes that personal profession of faith is the primary criterion for membership in the congregation. The Communion service is reserved for those who profess faith in Christ as savior. Each congregation is autonomous and the synod serves the congregations in advisory and cooperative capacities.

The synod supports a world mission program in Cameroon, Chad, Japan, and Taiwan. Approximately 40 percent of the synodical budget is earmarked for world missions. A growing home mission ministry is planting new congregations in the United States and Canada. Affiliate organizations operate several retirement-nursing homes, conference, and retreat centers.

#### Headquarters

1020 Alcott Ave., W., P.O. Box 655, Fergus Falls, MN 56538, Tel. (218)739-3336 Fax (218)739-5514
Media Contact, Rev. Brent Juliot
Email: rmo@clba.org
Website: www.clba.org

#### Officers

Pres., Rev. Arthur Berge, 72 Midridge Close SE, Calgary, AB T2X 1G1
Vice Pres., Rev. Luther Stenberg, P.O. Box 75, Hagen, SK S0J 1B0
Sec., Mr. Alvin Herman, 3105 Taylor Street E., Saskatoon, SK S7H 1H5
Treas., Edwin Rundbraaten, Box 739, Birch Hills, SK S0J 0G0
Youth Coord., Rev. Harold Rust, 2617 Preston Ave. S., Saskatoon, SK S7J 2G3

#### Periodicals

*Faith and Fellowship*

## Church of the Nazarene in Canada

The first Church of the Nazarene in Canada was organized in November, 1902, by Dr. H. F. Reynolds. It was in Oxford, Nova Scotia. The Church of the Nazarene is Wesleyan Arminian in

193

theology, representative in church government and warmly evangelistic.

### Headquarters

20 Regan Rd., Unit 9, Brampton, ON L7A 1C3, Tel. (905)846-4220 Fax (905)846-1775

Media Contact, Gen. Sec., Dr. Jack Stone, 6401 The Paseo, Kansas City, MO 64131, Tel. (816)333-7000 Fax (816)822-9071

Email: national@nazarene.ca

Website: www.nazarene.ca

### Officers

Natl. Dir., The Rev. Clare MacMillan, 20 Regan Rd. Unit 9, Brampton, ON L7A 1C3, Tel. (905)846-4220 Fax (905)846-1775, Email: cmacmillan@nazarene.ca

Exec. Asst., John T. Martin, 20 Regan Rd. Unit 9, Brampton, ON L7A 1C3, Tel. (905)846-4220 Fax (905)846-1775, Email: national@nazarene.ca

## Churches of Christ in Canada

Churches of Christ are autonomous congregations, whose members appeal to the Bible alone to determine matters of faith and practice. There are no central offices or officers. Publications and institutions related to the churches are either under local congregational control or independent of any one congregation.

Churches of Christ shared a common fellowship in the 19th century with the Christian Churches—Churches of Christ and the Christian Church (Disciples of Christ). Fellowship was broken after the introduction of instrumental music in worship and centralization of churchwide activities through a missionary society. Churches of Christ began in Canada soon after 1800, largely in the middle-eastern provinces. The few pioneer congregations were greatly strengthened in the mid-1800s, growing in size and number.

Members of Churches of Christ believe in the inspiration of the Scriptures, the divinity of Jesus Christ, and immersion into Christ for the remission of sins. The New Testament pattern is followed in worship and church organization.

### Headquarters

Media Contact, Man. Ed., *Gospel Herald*, Max Craddock, 5 Lankin Blvd., ON M4J 4W7, Tel. (416)461-7406 Fax (416)424-1850

Email: maxc@strathmorecofc.ca

### Periodicals

*Gospel Herald*

## Community of Christ

Founded April 6, 1830, by Joseph Smith, Jr., the church was reorganized under the leadership of the founder's son, Joseph Smith III, in 1860. The Church is established in 38 countries including the United States and Canada, with nearly a quarter of a million members. A biennial world conference is held in Independence, Mo. The current president is W. Grant McMurray.

### Headquarters

World Headquarters Complex, 1001 W. Walnut, Independence, MO 64050, Tel. (816)833-1000 Fax (816)521-3095

Ontario Regional Ofc., 390 Speedvale Ave. E., Guelph, ON N1E 1N5

Media Contact, Public Relations Coordinator, Susan Naylor

### Officers

Canada East Mission Centre

Ken Barrows, Mission Centre President, 390 Speedvale Ave E., Guelph, ON N1E 1N5, Tel. (519)822-4150, Email: ken@communityof christ.ca

Jim Poirier, Mission Centre Financial Officer, 390 Speedvale Ave. E., Guelph, ON N1E 1N5, Tel. (519)822-4150, Email: jim@communityof christ.ca

Canada West Mission Centre

Darrell Belrose, Mission Centre President, 194 Tuscarora Circle NW, Calgary AB T3L 2B8, Tel. (403)241-9616, Email: darrellcswm@ shaw.ca

Bob Hodgson, Mission Centre Financial Officer, 181 Hamptons Square NW, Calgary AB T3A 5C3, Tel. (403)241-8221, Email: bobwcmc @shaw.ca

### Periodicals

*Saints Herald*

## Congregational Christian Churches in Canada

This body originated in the early 18th century, when devout Christians within several denominations in the northern and eastern United States, dissatisfied with sectarian controversy, broke away from their own denominations and took the simple title "Christians." First organized in 1821 at Keswick, Ont., the Congregational Christian Churches in Canada was incorporated on Dec. 4, 1989, as a national organization. In doctrine the body is evangelical, being governed by the Bible as the final authority in faith and practice. It believes that Christian character must be expressed in daily living; it aims at the unity of all true believers in Christ that others may believe in Him and be saved. In church polity, the body is democratic and autonomous. It is also a member of The World Evangelical Congregational Fellowship.

### Headquarters

241 Dunsdon St. Ste. 405, Brantford, ON N3R 7C3, Tel. (519)751-0606 Fax (519)751-0852

Media Contact, Rev. David Schrader, 241 Dunsdon St. Ste. 405, Brantford, ON N3R 7C3, Tel. (519)751-0606 Fax (519)751-0852

### Officers

Pres., Rev. Jim Potter

Exec. Dir., Rev. David Schrader

Sec., Rev. Ron Holden

## Convention of Atlantic Baptist Churches

The Convention of Atlantic Baptist Churches is the largest Baptist Convention in Canada. Through the Canadian Baptist Ministries, it is a member of the Baptist World Alliance.

In 1763 two Baptist churches were organized in Atlantic Canada, one in Sackville, New Brunswick and the other in Wolfville, Nova Scotia. Although both these churches experienced crises and lost continuity, they recovered and stand today as the beginning of organized Baptist work in Canada.

Nine Baptist churches met in Lower Granville, Nova Scotia in 1800 and formed the first Baptist Association in Canada. By 1846 the Maritime Baptist Convention was organized, consisting of 169 churches. Two streams of Baptist life merged in 1905 to form the United Baptist Convention. This is how the term "United Baptist" was derived. Today there are 554 churches within 21 associations across the Convention.

The Convention has two educational institutions, Atlantic Baptist University in Moncton, New Brunswick, a Christian Liberal Arts University, and Acadia Divinity College in Wolfville, Nova Scotia, a Graduate School of Theology. The Convention engages in world mission through Canadian Baptist Ministries, the all-Canada mission agency. In addition to an active program of home mission, evangelism, training, social action and stewardship, the Convention operates ten senior citizen complexes and a Christian bookstore.

### Headquarters

1655 Manawagonish Rd., Saint John, NB E2M 3Y2, Tel. (506)635-1922 Fax (506)635-0366
Media Contact, Executive Minister, Dr. Harry G. Gardner
Email: cabc@baptist.atlantic.ca
Website: www.baptist.atlantic.ca

### Officers

Pres. (2004-2005), Mr. George H. Powell, 3 Elton Place, St. John's, WL A1A 5B8, Tel. (709)722-5007
Vice Pres. (2004-2005), Dr. Ralph Richardson, 129 Athabaska Ave., Riverview, NB E1B 2T2, Tel. (506)863-8456
Exec. Min., Dr. Harry G. Gardner, 1655 Manawagonish Rd., Saint John, NB E2M 3Y2, Tel. (506)635-1922 Fax (506)635-0366, Email: harry.gardner@baptist-atlantic.ca
Dir. of Operations., Daryl MacKenzie, 1655 Manawagonish Rd., Saint John, NB E2M 3Y2, Tel. (506)635-1922 Fax (506)635-0366, Email: daryl.mackenzie@baptist-atlantic.ca
Dir. of Atlantic Baptist Mission, Dr. Malcolm Beckett, 1655 Manawagonish Rd., Saint John, NB E2M 3Y2, Tel. (506)635-1922 Fax (506) 635-0366, Email: malcolm.beckett@baptist-atlantic.ca

Dir. of Youth and Family, Rev. Bruce Fawcett, 1655 Manawagonish Rd., Saint John, NB E2M 3Y2, Tel. (506)635-1922 Fax (506)635-0366, Email: bruce.fawcett@baptist-atlantic. ca
Dir. Of Development, Rev. Greg Jones, 1655 Manawagonish Rd., Saint John, NB E2M 3Y2, Tel. (506)635-1922 Fax (506)635-0366, Email: greg.jones@baptist-atlantic.ca
Part-time Dir. Of Public Witness and Social Concern, Dr. Lois P. Mitchell c/o 1655 Manawagonish Rd., Saint John, NB E2M 3Y2, Tel. (506)635-1922, Fax (506)635-0366, Email: lois.mitchell@baptist-atlantic.ca

## The Coptic Orthodox Church in Canada

The Coptic Orthodox Church in North America was begun in Canada in 1964 and was registered in the province of Ontario in 1965. The Coptic Orthodox Church has spread rapidly since then. The total number of local churches in both Canada and the U.S.A. exceeded one hundred twenty. Two dioceses, two monasteries with monks and novices, and two theological seminaries were established in the U.S.A.

The Coptic Orthodox Church is the church of Alexandria founded in Egypt by St. Mark the Apostle in the first century A.D. She is a hierarchical church and the administrative governing body of each local church is an elected Board of Deacons approved by the Bishop. The current patriarch of the church is H. H. Pope Shenouda III, Pope of Alexandria and Patriach of the see of St. Mark. The Coptic Orthodox Church is a member of the Canadian Council of Churches.

### Headquarters

St. Mark's Coptic Orthodox Church, 41 Glendinning Ave., Toronto, ON M1W 3E2, Tel. (416)494-4449 Fax (416)494-2631
Media Contact, Fr. Ammonius Guirguis, Tel. (416)494-4449 Fax (416)494-2631, Email: frammonius@coptorthodox.ca
Email: mail@coptorthodox.ca
Website: www.stmark.toronto.on.coptorthodox.ca

**Disciples of Christ—please see Christian Church (Disciples of Christ) in Canada**

**Doukhobors—please see Union of Spiritual Communities in Christ**

## Elim Fellowship of Evangelical Churches and Ministers

The Elim Fellowship of Evangelical Churches and Ministers, a Pentecostal body, was established in 1984 as a sister organization of Elim Fellowship in the United States.

This is an association of churches, ministers and missionaries seeking to serve the whole body of Christ. It is Pentecostal and has a charismatic orientation.

## Headquarters

379 Golf Road, RR#6, Brantford, ON N3T 5L8, Tel. (519)753-7266 Fax (519)753-5887, Ofc. Mgr., Larry Jones
Email: elim@bfree.on.ca
Website: Bfree.ON.ca/comdir/churchs/elim

## Officers

Pres., Howard Ellis, 102 Ripley Crescent., Kitchener, ON N2N 1V4
Vice Pres., Rev. Errol Alchin, 1694 Autumn Crescent, Pickering, ON L1V 6X5
Sec./Treas., Larry Jones, 107 Hillside Ave., Paris ON K2G 4N1

### COUNCIL OF ELDERS

Rev. Bud Crawford, Brampton, Ont.
Rev. Howard Ellis, Kitchener, Ont.
Rev. Bernard Evans, Lima, N.Y.
Rev. Claude Favreau, Drummondville, Que.
Rev. Aubrey Phillips, Blairsville, Ga.

## The Estonian Evangelical Lutheran Church Abroad

The Estonian Evangelical Lutheran Church (EELC) was founded in 1917 in Estonia and reorganized in Sweden in 1944. The teachings of the EELC are based on the Old and New Testaments, explained through the Apostolic, Nicean and Athanasian confessions, the unaltered Confession of Augsburg and other teachings found in the Book of Concord.

## Headquarters

383 Jarvis St., Toronto, ON M5B 2C7, Tel. (416)925-5465 Fax (416)925-5688
Media Contact, Archbishop, Rev. Udo Petersoo
Email: udo.petersoo@eelk.ee
Website: www.eelk.ee/~e.e.l.k./

## Officers

Archbishop, The Rev. Udo Petersoo
Gen. Sec., Mr. Ivar Nippak
Sec./Clerk, Mrs. Eerika Lage

### Periodicals

*Eesti Kirik*

## The Evangelical Covenant Church of Canada

A Canadian denomination organized in Canada at Winnipeg in 1904, which is affiliated with the Evangelical Covenant Church of America and with the International Federation of Free Evangelical Churches, which includes 31 federations in 26 countries.

This body believes in the one triune God as confessed in the Apostles' Creed, that salvation is received through faith in Christ as Saviour, that the Bible is the authoritative guide in all matters of faith and practice. Christian Baptism and the Lord's Supper are accepted as divinely ordained sacraments of the church. As descendants of the 19th-century northern European pietistic awakening, the group believes in the need of a per-sonal experience of commitment to Christ, the development of a virtuous life and the urgency of spreading the gospel to the "ends of the world."

Four Core Values: to be a Missional Church; to be a Biblical Church; to be a Devotional Church; and to be a Connnectional Church.

Four Ministry Priorities: Leadership Development; Church Planting & Mission; Church Renewal/ Transition; and Christian Services.

### Headquarters

P.O. Box 34025, RPO Fort Richmond, Winnipeg, MB R3T 5T5
Media Contact, Supt., Jeff Anderson

### Officers

Pres./Supt., Rev. Jeff Anderson, P.O. Box 34025, RPO Fort Richmond, Winnipeg, MB R3T 5T5
Chpsn., Rod Johnson, Box 217, Norquay, SK S0A 2V0
Sec., Judy Nelson, Box 194, Norquay, SK S0A 2V0
Treas., Ingrid Wildman, Box 93, Norquay, SK S0A 2V0

### Periodicals

*The Covenant Messenger*

## Evangelical Free Church of Canada

The Evangelical Free Church of Canada traces its beginning back to 1917 when the church in Enchant, Alberta opened its doors. Today the denomination has 140 churches from the West Coast to Quebec. Approximately 80 missionaries are sponsored by the EFCC in 17 countries. The Evangelical Free Church is the founding denomination of Trinity Western University in Langley, British Columbia. Church membership is 8,441, average attendance is 18,455

### Headquarters

Mailing Address, P.O. Box 850 LCD1, Langley, BC V3A 8S6, Tel. (604)888-8668 Fax (604) 888-3108
Location, 7600 Glover Rd., Langley, BC
Media Contact, Executive Assistant Maureen Wilson, P.O. Box 850 LCD1, Langley, BC V3A 8S6, Tel. (604)888-8668 Fax (604)888-3108
Email: efcc@twu.ca
Website: www.efcc.ca

### Officers

President, Dr. Ron Unruh, P.O. Box 850 LCD 1, Langley, BC, Canada V3A 8S6, Tel.(604)888-8668 Fax (604) 888-3108, Email: efcc@twu.ca

### Periodicals

*The Pulse*

## Evangelical Lutheran Church in Canada

The Evangelical Lutheran Church in Canada

was organized in 1985 through a merger of The Evangelical Lutheran Church of Canada (ELCC) and the Lutheran Church in America—Canada Section.

The merger is a result of an invitation issued in 1972 by the ELCC to the Lutheran Church in America—Canada Section and the Lutheran Church—Canada. Three-way merger discussions took place until 1978 when it was decided that only a two-way merger was possible. The ELCC was the Canada District of the ALC until autonomy in 1967.

The Lutheran Church in Canada traces its history back more than 200 years. Congregations were organized by German Lutherans in Halifax and Lunenburg County in Nova Scotia in 1749. German Lutherans, including many United Empire Loyalists, also settled in large numbers along the St. Lawrence and in Upper Canada. In the late 19th century, immigrants arrived from Scandinavia, Germany, and central European countries, many via the United States. The Lutheran synods in the United States have provided the pastoral support and help for the Canadian church.

### Headquarters
302-393 Portage Avenue, Winnipeg, MB R3B 3H6, Tel. (204)984-9150 Fax (204)984-9185
Media Contact, Bishop, Rev. Raymond L. Schultz

### Officers
Evangelical Lutheran Women Inc., ELCIC Group Services Inc.

### Periodicals
*Canada Lutheran; Esprit*

## Evangelical Mennonite Conference

The Evangelical Mennonite Conference is a modern church of historic Christian convictions, tracing its indebtedness to the Radical Reformation, which, in turn, is rooted in the Protestant Reformation of the 16th century. The Centre of faith, and of Scripture, is found in Jesus Christ as Saviour and Lord.

The church's name was chosen in 1959. Its original name, Kleine Gemeinde, which means "small church," reflected its origins as a renewal movement among Mennonites in southern Russia. Klaas Reimer, a minister, was concerned about a decline of spiritual life and discipline in the church, and inappropriate involvement in the Napoleanic War. About 1812, Reimer and others began separate worship services, and two years later were organized as a small group.

Facing increasing government pressure, particularly about military service, the group migrated to North America in 1874 to 1875. Fifty families settled in Manitoba and 36 in Nebraska. Ties between the groups weakened and eventually the U.S. group gave up its KG identity. The KG survived several schisms and migrations, dating from its years in Russia through the 1940s.

As an evangelical church, The Evangelical Mennonite Conference holds that Scripture has final authority in faith and practice, a belief in Christ's finished work, and that assurance of salvation is possible. As Mennonite, the denomination has a commitment to discipleship, baptism upon confession of faith, community, social concern, non-violence and the Great Commission. As a conference, it seeks to encourage local churches, to work together on evangelism and matters of social concern, and relates increasingly well to other denominations.

In the year 2000 its membership surpassed 7,270, with many more people as treasured adherents and a wider circle of ministry influence. Membership is for people baptized on confession of faith (usually in adolescence or older). Children are considered safe in Christ until they reach an age where they are accountable for their own spiritual decision and opt out; they are considered part of the church, while full inclusion occurs upon personal choice.

The Conference has 57 churches from British Columbia to Ontario (35 in Manitoba) and roughly 149 mission workers in 25 countries. The cultural makeup of the Conference is increasingly diverse, though its Dutch-German background remains dominant nationally. Fourteen churches have pastors or leaders who are of non-Dutch-German background.

Some churches have a multiple leadership pattern (ministers and deacons can be selected from within the congregation); others have new patterns. Most churches support their leading minister full time. Its church governance moved from a bishop system to greater local congregational autonomy. It currently functions as a conference of churches with national boards, a conference council, and a moderator.

Women can serve on most national boards, as conference council delegates, as missionaries, and within a wide range of local church activities; while they can be selected locally, they cannot currently serve as nationally recognized or commissioned ministers.

It is a supporting member of Mennonite Central Committee and the Evangelical Fellowship of Canada. About 80 percent of its national budget goes toward mission work in Canada and other countries.

### Headquarters
440 Main St., Steinbach, MB R5G 1Z5, Tel. (204)326-6401 Fax (204)326-1613
Email: emconf@mts.net
Media Contact: Conf. Pastor, David Thiessen

### Officers
Conf. Mod., Ron Penner
General Sec., Len Barkman
Conference Pastor, Bd. of Leadership and Outreach, David Thiessen
Bd. of Missions, Exec. Sec., Len Barkman
Bd. of Missions, Foreign Sec., Ken Zacharias

197

Bd. of Church Ministries, Exec. Sec.-Editor, Terry M. Smith

Bd. Of Trustees, Exec. Sec. Larry Eidse

Canadian Church Planting Coordinator, Exec. Sec., Ward Parkinson

Conference Youth Minister, Gerald Reimer

### Periodicals

*The Messenger*

## Evangelical Mennonite Mission Conference

This group was founded in 1936 as the Rudnerweider Mennonite Church in Southern Manitoba and organized as the Evangelical Mennonite Mission Conference in 1959. It was incorporated in 1962. The annual conference meeting is held in July.

### Headquarters

Box 52059, Niakwa P.O., Winnipeg, MB R2M 5P9, Tel. (204)253-7929 Fax (204)256-7384, Email: emmc@mb.sympatico.ca

Media Contact, Lil Goertzen

Email: lil@emmc.ca

### Officers

Mod., David Penner, 906-300 Sherk St., Leamington, ON N8H 4N7

Vice Mod., Carl Zacharias, R.R. 1, Box 205, Winkler, MB R6W 4A1

Sec., Darrell Dyck, R.R. 1, Box 186, Winkler, MB R6W 4A1

Dir. of Conference Ministries, Jack Heppner

Dir. of Missions, Rev. Leonard Sawatzky

Business Admin., Henry Thiessen

### OTHER ORGANIZATIONS

*The Gospel Message*, Box 1622, Saskatoon, SK S7K 3R8, Tel. (306)242-5001 Fax (306)242-6115; 210-401-33rd St. W., Saskatoon, SK S7L 0V5, Tel. (306)242-5001

Radio Pastor, Rev. Ed Martens

### Periodicals

*EMMC Recorder*

## The Evangelical Missionary Church of Canada

This denomination was formed in 1993 with the merger of The Evangelical Church of Canada and The Missionary Church of Canada. The Evangelical Missionary Church of Canada maintains fraternal relations with the worldwide body of the Missionary Church, Inc. and with the Evangelical Church of North America. The Evangelical Church of Canada was among those North American Evangelical United Brethern Conferences which did not join the EUB in merging with the Methodist Church in 1968. The Missionary Church of Canada is Anabaptist in heritage. Its practices and theology were shaped by the Holiness Revivals of the late 1800s. The Evangelical Missionary Church consists of 135 churches in two conferences in Canada.

### Headquarters

4031 Brentwood Rd., NW, Calgary, AB T2L 1L1, Tel. (403)250-2759 Fax (403)291-4720

Media Contact, Exec. Dir., Missions and Administration, G. Keith Elliott

Email: info@emcc.ca

### Officers

Pres. and Canada East District, Dist. Supt., Rev. Phil Delsaut, 130 Fergus Ave., Kitchener, ON N2A 2H2, Tel. (519)894-9800, Email: pdelsaut @emcced.ca

Canada West District, Acting Dist. Supt., Rev. Don Adolf, 4031 Brentwood Rd., NW, Calgary, AB T2L 1L1, Tel. (403)291-5525 Fax (403)291-4720, Email: don@emcwest.ca

## The Fellowship of Evangelical Baptist Churches in Canada

The Fellowship is a family of 500 Evangelical Baptist Churches across Canada, holding worship services in 13 different languages.

### Headquarters

P.O. Box 457, Guelph ON, Canada, N1H 6K9 Tel. (519)821-4830 Fax (519)821-9829

### Periodicals

*B.C. Fellowship Baptist; The Evangelical Baptist Magazine; Intercom*

## Foursquare Gospel Church of Canada

The Western Canada District was formed in 1964 with the Rev. Roy Hicks as supervisor. Prior to 1964 it had been a part of the Northwest District of the International Church of the Foursquare Gospel with headquarters in Los Angeles, Calif.

A Provincial Society, the Church of the Foursquare Gospel of Western Canada, was formed in 1976; a federal corporation, the Foursquare Gospel Church of Canada, was incorporated in 1981 and a national church formed. The provincial society was closed in 1994.

### Headquarters

#100 8459 160th St., Surrey, BC V3S 3T9

Email: fgcc@canada.com

Media Contact, Pres., Timothy J. Peterson, #100-8459 160th St., Surrey, BC V3S 3T9, Tel. (604)543-8414 Fax (604)543-8417

### Officers

Pres., Timothy J. Peterson

### Periodicals

*VIP Communique*

## Free Methodist Church in Canada

The Free Methodist Church was founded in New York in 1860 and expanded in 1880. It is Methodist in doctrine, evangelical in ministry and emphasizes the teaching of holiness of life through faith in Jesus Christ.

The Free Methodist Church in Canada was incorporated in 1927 after the establishment of a Canadian Executive Board. In 1959 the Holiness Movement Church merged with the Free Methodist Church. Full autonomy for the Canadian church was realized in 1990 with the formation of a Canadian General Conference. Mississauga, Ont., continues to be the location of the Canadian headquarters.

The Free Methodist Church ministers in 70 countries through its World Ministries Center in Indianapolis, Ind.

### Headquarters
4315 Village Centre Ct., Mississauga, ON L4Z 1S2, Tel. (905)848-2600 Fax (905)848-2603
Media Contact, Dan Sheffield
Email: ministrycentre@fmc-canada.org
Website: www.fmc-canada.org

### Officers
Bishop, Rev. Keith Elford
Dir. of Admn. Ser., Norman Bull
Dir. Of Global and Intercultural Ministries, Rev. Dan Sheffield
Supt., Personnel, Rev. Alan Retzman
Supt., Growth Ministries, in transition

### Periodicals
*Mosaic*

## Free Will Baptists
As revival fires burned throughout New England in the mid- and late 1700s, Benjamin Randall proclaimed his doctrine of Free Will to large crowds of seekers. In due time, a number of Randall's converts moved to Nova Scotia. One such believer was Asa McGray, who was to become instrumental in the establishment of several Free Baptist churches. Local congregations were organized in New Brunswick. After several years of numerical and geographic gains, disagreements surfaced over the question of music, Sunday school, church offerings, salaried clergy and other issues. Adherents of the more progressive element decided to form their own fellowship. Led by George Orser, they became known as Free Christian Baptists.

The new group faithfully adhered to the truths and doctrines which embodied the theological basis of Free Will Baptists. Largely through Archibald Hatfield, contact was made with Free Will Baptists in the United States in the 1960s. The association was officially welcomed into the Free Will Baptist family in July 1981, by the National Association.

### Headquarters
5233 Mt. View Rd., Antioch, TN 37013-2306, Tel. (615)731-6812 Fax (615)731-0771
Media Contact, Mod., Dwayne Broad, RR 3, Bath, NB E0J 1E0 Tel. (506)278-3771

### Officers
Mod., Dwayne Broad
Promotional Officer, Dwayne Broad

## General Church of the New Jerusalem
The Church of the New Jerusalem, also called The New Church, is a Christian Church founded on the Bible and the Writings of Emanuel Swedenborg (1688-1772). These Writings were first brought to Ontario in 1835 by Christian Enslin.

### Headquarters
c/o Olivet Church, 279 Burnhamthorpe Rd., Etobicoke, ON M9B 1Z6, Tel. (416)239-3054 Fax (416)239-4935
Media Contact, Exec. Vice Pres., Rev. Michael D. Gladish
Email: olivetchurch@on.aibn.com
Website: www.newchurch.org

### Officers
Pres., Rt. Rev. T. Kline, Bryn Athyn, PA 19009
Exec. Vice Pres., Rev. Michael D. Gladish
Sec., Carolyn Bellinger, 110 Chapel Hill Dr., Kitchener, ON N2G 3W5

## Greek Orthodox Metropolis of Toronto (Canada)
Greek Orthodox Christians in Canada are under the jurisdiction of the Ecumenical Patriarchate of Constantinople (Istanbul).

### Headquarters
86 Overlea Blvd., Toronto, ON M4H 1C6, Tel. (416)429-5757 Fax (416)429-4588
Email: greekomt@on.aibn.com
Media Contact, Orthodox Way Committee

### Officers
Metropolitan Archbishop of the Metropolis of Toronto (Canada), His Eminence Metropolitan Archbishop Sotirios

### Periodicals
*Orthodox Way*

## Independent Assemblies of God International (Canada)
This fellowship of churches has been operating in Canada for over 58 years. It is a branch of the Pentecostal Church in Sweden. Each church within the fellowship is completely independent.

### Headquarters
1211 Lancaster St., London, ON N5V 2L4, Tel. (519)451-1751 Fax (519)453-3258
Media Contact, Gen. Sec., Rev. Harry Wuerch
Email: h.wuerch@rogers.com

### Officers
Gen. Sec., Rev. Paul McPhail, Box 653 Chatham, ON, N7M 5K8, Tel. (519)352-1743
Treas., Rev. David Ellyatt, 1795 Parkhurst Ave., London, ON N5V 2C4, Email: david.ellyatt@odyssey.on.ca

### Periodicals
*The Mantle* (published in March, July & October)

## Independent Holiness Church

The former Holiness Movement of Canada merged with the Free Methodist Church in 1958. Some churches remained independent of this merger and they formed the Independent Holiness Church in 1960, in Kingston, Ont. The doctrines are Methodist and Wesleyan. The General Conference is every three years.

### Headquarters

Rev. R. E. Votary, 1564 John Quinn Rd., R.R.1, Greely, ON K4P 1J9, Tel. (613)821-2237

Media Contact, Gen. Sec., Dwayne Reaney, 5025 River Rd. R.R. #1, Manotick, ON K4M 1B2, Tel. (613)692-3237

### Officers

Gen. Supt., Rev. R. E. Votary, 1564 John Quinn Rd., Greeley, ON K4P 1J9

Gen. Sec., Dwayne Reaney

Additional Officers, E. Brown, 104-610 Pesehudoff Cresc., Saskatoon, SK S7N 4H5; D. Wallace, 1456 John Quinn Rd., R#1, Greely, ON K4P 1J9

### Periodicals

*Gospel Tidings*

## Jehovah's Witnesses

For a description of Jehovah's Witnesses see "Religious Bodies in United States" in this edition of the *Yearbook*.

### Headquarters

25 Columbia Heights, Brooklyn, NY 11201-2483, Tel. (718)560-5600 Fax (718)560-8850

Canadian Branch Office, Box 4100, Halton Hills, ON L7G 4Y4, Tel. (888)301-4259

Media Contact, Office of Public Information, J. Richard Brown

Media Contact, Office of Public Information in Canada, Mark Ruge

Editorial Contact, Writing Department, James N. Pellechia

**Latter-day Saints—please see Church of Jesus Christ of Latter-day Saints in Canada**

**Lutheran—pleasee see Evangelical Lutheran Church in Canada**

## Lutheran Church—Canada

Lutheran Church—Canada was established in 1959 at Edmonton, Alberta, as a federation of Canadian districts of the Lutheran Church—Missouri Synod; it was constituted in 1988 at Winnipeg, Man., as an autonomous church.

The church confesses the Bible as both inspired and infallible, the only source and norm of doctrine and life and subscribes without reservation to the Lutheran Confessions as contained in the Book of Concord of 1580.

### Headquarters

3074 Portage Ave., Winnipeg, MB R3K 0Y2, Tel. (204)895-3433 Fax (204)832-3018, Email: info@lutheranchurch.ca

Media Contact, Dir. of Comm., Ian Adnams

Email: communications@lutheranchurch.ca

### Officers

Pres., The Rev. Dr. Ralph Mayan, 3074 Portage Ave., Winnipeg, MB R3K 0Y2, Tel. (204)895-3433 Fax (204)897-4319, Email: president@lutheranchurch.ca

Pres. Emeritus, Rev. Dr. Edwin Lehman, 686 Lee Ridge Road, Edmonton AB T6K 0P2, Tel. (780)462-9608 Fax (780)468-2172, Email: dwinlehman@shaw.ca

Vice Pres., Rev. Daryl Solie, P.O.Box 500, Church Bridge, SK SOA OMD (2008), Tel. (306)896-2566 Fax (306)896-2617, Email: lutheran.trinity@sasktel.net

Vice Pres., Rev. Robert C. Krestrick, 78 John St., W. Waterloo, ON N2L 1B8, Tel. (519)745-5027 Fax (519)745-7165, Email: rekrestick @sympatico.ca

Vice Pres., Rev. Nolan D. Astley, 2925-57A Lloydminster, AB T9V 1W5, Tel. (780)875-9797 Fax (780)875-9799, Email: luthfrst@telusplanet.net

Treas., Mr. Dwayne Cleave, 3074 Portage Avenue, Winnipeg, MB R3K 0Y2, Tel. (204)895-3433 Fax (204) 897-4319, Email: treasurer@lutheranchurch.ca

### DISTRICT OFFICES

Alberta-British Columbia, Pres., Rev. D. Schiemann, 7100 Ada Blvd., Edmonton, AB T5B 4E4, Tel. (780)474-0063 Fax (780)477-9829, Email: info@lccabc.ca

Central, Pres., Rev. T. Prachar, 1927 Grant Dr., Regina, SK S4S 4V6, Tel. (306)586-4434 Fax (306)586-0656, Email: tprachar@access-comm.ca

East, Pres., Rev. A. Maleske, 275 Lawrence Ave., Kitchener, ON N2M 1Y3, Tel. (519)578-6500 Fax (519)578-3369, Email: amaleske@lcceast district.ca

### Periodicals

*The Canadian Lutheran*

**Mennonite—see also Canadian Conference of Mennonite Brethren Churches, Evangelical Mennonite Mission Conference, or Reinland Mennonite Church**

## Mennonite Church Canada

Mennonite Church Canada (formerly Conference of Mennonites in Canada) was founded in 1903 by 15 prairie congregations. In the late 1990s it merged with the Mennonite Church to become Mennonite Church Canada.

The first Mennonites came to Canada in 1786, moving from Pennsylvania in Conestoga wagons. Over the next 150 years, more arrived by ship from Europe, in at least four successive waves.

Its members hold to traditional Christian

beliefs, believer's baptism and congregational polity. They emphasize practical Christianity, opposition to war, service to others and personal ethics.

Some people who have joined the Canadian Mennonite body in recent years have arrived from Asia, Africa, or Latin and South America. Native brothers and sisters, whose people were here long before the first Conastoga wagons arrived, have added their voices to the mix.

Meanwhile, French-speaking and English-speaking Canadians from the wider community have enriched the Mennonite people. Together we are Christian believers moving into the future under the umbrella of the Mennonite Church Canada.

Mennonite Church Canada is affiliated with Mennonite Church U.S.A. whose offices are at Newton, Kan. and Elkhart, Ind. (See, Mennonite Church U.S.A. description in the section "Religious Bodies in the United States")

The first annual sessions were held in July, 1903. Further immigration from Russia in the 1920s and 1940s increased the group which is now located in all provinces from New Brunswick to British Columbia. In recent years a variety of other ethnic groups, including native Canadians, have joined the conference. This conference is affiliated with Mennonite Church U.S.A. whose offices are at Newton, Kansas. (See, Mennonite Church U.S.A. description in the section "Religious Bodies in the United States")

### Headquarters
600 Shaftesbury Blvd., Winnipeg, MB R3P 0M4
Tel. (204)888-6781 Fax (204)831-5675
Media Contact, Dan Dyck
Email: ddyck@mennonitechurch.ca
Website: www.mennonitechurch.ca

### Officers
Chpsn., Henry Krause
Gen. Sec., Robert J. Suderman

### Periodicals
*Canadian Mennonite, Der Bote, Intotemak*

**Moravian Church—please see Canadian District of the Moravian Church in America, Northern Province**

**Mormons—please see Church of Jesus Christ of Latter-day Saints in Canada**

## North American Baptist Conference
Churches belonging to this conference emanated from German Baptist immigrants of more than a century ago. Although scattered across Canada and the U.S., they are bound together by a common heritage, a strong spiritual unity, a Bible-centered faith and a deep interest in missions.

Note, The details of general organization, officers, and periodicals of this body will be found in the North American Baptist Conference directory in the "Religious Bodies in the United States" section of this *Yearbook*.

### Headquarters
1 S. 210 Summit Ave., Oakbrook Terrace, IL 60181, Tel. (630)495-2000 Fax (630)495-3301
Media Contact, Marilyn Schaer

### Officers
Exec. Dir., Dr. Philip Yntema

### Periodicals
*N.A.B. Today*

## The Old Catholic Church of Canada
The church was founded in 1948 in Hamilton, Ontario. The first bishop was the Rt. Rev. George Davis. The Old Catholic Church of Canada accepts all the doctrines of the Eastern Orthodox Churches and, therefore, not papal infallibility or the immaculate conception. The ritual is Western (Latin Rite) and is in the vernacular language. Celibacy is optional.

### Headquarters
2185 Sheridan Park Drive, Apt. 105, Mississauga, ON L5K 1C7, Tel. (905)855-3643
Media Contact, Bishop, The Right Rev. Pat Davies, Vicar General

### Officers
Vicar General and Auxiliary Bishop, The Rt. Rev. A.C. Keating, PhD., 5066 Forest Grove Crest, Burlington, ON L7L GG6, Tel. (905)681-9983

## Old Order Amish Church
This is the most conservative branch of the Mennonite Church and direct descendants of Swiss Brethren (Anabaptists) who emerged from the Reformation in Switzerland in 1525. The Amish, followers of Bishop Jacob Ammann, became a distinct group in 1693. They began migrating to North America about 1736; all of them still reside in the United States or Canada. They first migrated to Ontario in 1823 directly from Bavaria, Germany and later from Pennsylvania and Alsace-Lorraine. Since 1953 more Amish have migrated to Ontario from Ohio, Indiana and Iowa.

In 2004 there were 27 congregations in Ontario, each being autonomous. No membership figures are kept by this group, and there is no central headquarters. Each congregation is served by a bishop, two ministers and a deacon, all of whom are chosen from among the male members by lot for life.

### Correspondent
Pathway Publishers, David Luthy, Rt. 4, Aylmer,

ON N5H 2R3

**Periodicals**
Blackboard Bulletin; Herold der Wahreit; The Budget; The Diary; Die Botschaft; Family Life; Young Companion, Plain Interests.

## Open Bible Faith Fellowship of Canada

This is an Evangelical, Full Gospel Fellowship of Churches and Ministries emphasizing evangelism, missions and the local church for success in the present harvest of souls. OBFF was chartered January 7, 1982.

**Headquarters**
Niagara Celebration Church, P.O. Box 31020, St. Catharines, ON L2N 7S5, Tel. (905)646-0970

**Officers**
President, David Youngren
Vice President, Lindsey Burt
Sec./Treasurer, George Woodward
Director, Jim Buslon
Director, Lindsey Burt
Director, Mike Welch
Director, Christer Ihreborg

## Orthodox Church in America (Archdiocese of Canada)

The Archdiocese of Canada of the Orthodox Church in America was established in 1916. First organized by St. Tikhon, martyr Patriarch of Moscow, previously Archbishop of North America, it is part of the Russian Metropolia and its successor, the autocephalous Orthodox Church in America.

The Archdiocesan Council meets twice yearly, the General Assembly of the Archdiocese takes place every three years. The Archdiocese is also known as "Orthodox Church in Canada."

**Headquarters**
P.O. Box 179, Spencerville, ON K0E 1XO, Tel. (613)925-5226, Email: zoe@ripnet.com

**Officers**
Bishop of Ottawa & Canada, The Rt. Rev. Seraphim; Chancellor, V. Rev. Dennis Pihach, 15992-107A Ave, Edmonton, AB T5P 0Z2
Treas., Nikita Lopoukhine, P.O. Box 179, Spencervillt, ON K0E 1X0
Sec., Archpriest Cyprian Hutcheon, P.O. Box 179, Spencerville, ON K0E 1X0

**ARCHDIOCESAN COUNCIL**
Clergy Members, Rev. Lawrence Farley; Rev. R.S. Kennaugh; Rev. Larry Reinheimer; Igumen Irenee Rochon; Rev. John Jillions, Rev. Ovest Olekshy
Lay Members, David Grier, John Hadjinicolaou, Mother Sophia (Zion), David Rystephanuk, Rod Tkachuk, Sandra Ellis, Alexei Vassiouchkine
Ex Officio, Chancellor; Treas.; Sec.

**Periodicals**
Canadian Orthodox Messenger

## Patriarchal Parishes of the Russian Orthodox Church in Canada

This is the diocese of Canada of the former Exarchate of North and South America of the Russian Orthodox Church. It was originally founded in 1897 by the Russian Orthodox Archdiocese in North America.

**Headquarters**
St. Barbara's Russian Orthodox Cathedral, 10105 96th St., Edmonton, AB T5H 2G3
Media Contact, Roman Lopushinsky, 11620 134 Ave., Edmonton, AB T5E 1K9, Tel. & fax (780)455-6314

**Officers**
Admn., Bishop of Kashira, Most Rev. Iov, 10812-108 St., Edmonton, AB T5H 3A6, Tel. (780)420-9945

## The Pentecostal Assemblies of Canada

This body is incorporated under the Dominion Charter of 1919 and is also recognized in the Province of Quebec as an ecclesiastical corporation. Its beginnings are to be found in the revivals at the turn of the century, and most of the first Canadian Pentecostal leaders came from a religious background rooted in the Holiness movements.

The original incorporation of 1919 was implemented among churches of eastern Canada only. In the same year, a conference was called in Moose Jaw, Saskatchewan, to which the late Rev. J. M. Welch, general superintendent of the then-organized Assemblies of God in the U.S., was invited. The churches of Manitoba and Saskatchewan were organized as the Western District Council of the Assemblies of God. They were joined later by Alberta and British Columbia. In 1921, a conference was held in Montreal, to which the general chairman of the Assemblies of God was invited. Eastern Canada also became a district of the Assemblies of God, joining Eastern and Western Canada as two districts in a single organizational union.

In 1920, at Kitchener, Ontario, eastern and western churches agreed to dissolve the Canadian District of the Assemblies of God and unite under the name The Pentecostal Assemblies of Canada.

Today the Pentecostal Assemblies of Canada operates throughout the nation and in about 30 countries around the world. Religious services are conducted in more than 25 different languages in the 1,100 local churches in Canada. Members and adherents number about 230,000. The number of local churches includes approximately 100 native congregations.

**Headquarters**
2450 Milltower Court, Mississauga, ON L5N

5Z6, Tel. (905)542-7400 Fax (905)542-7313

## Officers

Gen. Supt., Rev. William D. Morrow

Asst. Supt., for Ministerial Services, Rev. David E. Hazzard

Asst. Supt. for Financial Resources, Rev. David Ball

### DISTRICT SUPERINTENDENTS

British Columbia, Rev. D.R. Wells, 20411 Douglas Crescent, Langley, BC V3S 4B6, Tel. (604)533-2232 Fax (604)533-5405

Alberta, Rev. Lorne D. McAlister, 10585-111 St., #101, Edmonton, AB T5H 3E8, Tel. (403)426-0084 Fax (403)420-1318

Saskatchewan, Rev. J.I. Guskjolen, 3488 Fairlight Dr., Saskatoon, SK S7M 3Z4, Tel. (306)683-4646 Fax (306)683-3699

Manitoba, Rev. R.W. Pierce, 187 Henlow Bay, Winnipeg, MB R3Y 1G4, Tel. (204)940-1000 Fax (204)940-1009

Western Ontario, Rev. D.A Shepherd, 3214 S. Service Rd., Burlington, ON L7N 3J2, Tel. (905)637-5566 Fax (905)637-7558

Eastern Ontario and Quebec, Rev. R. T. Hilsden, Box 337, Cobury, ON K9A 4K8, Tel. (905)373-7374 Fax (905)373-1911

Quebec, Rev. G.C. Connors, 911, Boul Roland-Therrien, Longueuil, QC JAJ 4L3, Tel. (405)442-2732 Fax (405)442-3818

Maritime Provinces, Rev. Douglas Moore, Box 1184, Truro, NS B2N 5H1, Tel. (902)895-4212 Fax (902)897-0705

### BRANCH CONFERENCES

Slavic Conferences, Eastern District, Rev. A. Muravski, 445 Stevenson Rd., Oshawa, ON L1J 5N8, Tel. (905)576-3584; Western District, Rev. Michael Brandebura, 4108-134 Ave., Edmonton, AB T5A 3M2, Tel. (780)743-2410 Fax (780) 473-2410

Finnish Conference, Rev. E. Ahonen, 1920 Argyle Dr., Vancouver, BC V5P 2A8, Tel. (604)321-0555 Fax (604)321-0555

### Periodicals

*Testimony* (The official magazine of The Pentecostal Assemblies of Canada); *Enrich* (National Leadership Magazine); *Contact* (Magazine for those 50 years +); *HonorBound* (Magazine for Men)

## The Pentecostal Assemblies of Newfoundland

This body began in 1911 and held its first meetings at Bethesda Mission at St. John's. It was incorporated in 1925 as The Bethesda Pentecostal Assemblies of Newfoundland and changed its name in 1930 to The Pentecostal Assemblies of Newfoundland.

### Headquarters

57 Thorburn Rd., Box 8895, Stn. "A", St. John's, NF A1B 3T2, Tel. (709)753-6314 Fax (709) 753-4945

Email: paon@paon.nf.ca

Media Contact, Gen. Sup't., H. Paul Foster, 57 Thorburn Rd., Box 8895, Stn. "A", St. John's, NF A1B 3T2

### GENERAL EXECUTIVE OFFICERS

Gen. Sup't.: H. Paul Foster, 57 Thorburn Rd., Box 8895, Stn. "A", St. John's, NF A1B 3T2

Gen. Sec.-Treas.: Clarence Buckle, 57 Thorburn Rd., Box 8895, Stn. "A", St. John's, NF A1B 3T2

Ex. Dir. of Home Missions: Andrew R. Anstey, 57 Thorburn Rd., Box 8895, Stn. "A", St. John's, NF A1B 3T2

Ex. Dir. of Ch. Ministries: Robert H. Dewling, 57 Thorburn Rd., Box 8895, Stn. "A", St. John's, NF A1B 3T2

### PROVINCIAL DIRECTORS

Sunday School & Children's Ministries: Kelly L. Brenton, 42 Franks Road, Conception Bay South, NL A1X 6W8

Women's Ministries: Catherine J. Snow, 14 Jeddores Lane, Deer Lake, NL A8A 1P4

Men's Ministries: Wilfred S. Buckle, 52 Premier Dr., Corner Brook, NL A2H 1S4

Youth Ministries: B. Dean Brenton, Box 21100, St. John's, NF A1B 3L5

Mature Adult Ministries: Barry D. Pelley, Box 1715, Lewisporte, NL A0G 3A0

Family Ministries: Sharmaine R. Reid, Box 2, Hant's Harbour, NL A0B 1Y0

### AUXILIARY SERVICES

Chaplain of Institutions: Robert G. Parsons, 29 Caster's Drive, Mount Pearl, NL A1N 4X3

Pentecostal Senior Citizens Home Administrator: Beverley Bellefleur, Box 130, Clarke's Beach, NF A0A 1W0

Evergreen Manor, Summerford, NF A0G 4E0

Chaplain: Memorial University of Newfoundland, Gregory R. Dewling, Memorial University of Newfoundland, Box 102, St. John's, NF A1C 5S7

Emmanuel Convention Centre Administrator: Sterling E. Warr, P.O. Box 1409, Lewisporte, NL A0G 3A0

Managing Editor, Good Tidings: Burton K. Janes, 57 Thornburn Rd., Box 8895, Stn. "A," St. John's, NF A1B 3T2

### Periodicals

*Good Tidings*

**Plymouth Brethren—please see Christian Brethren**

## Presbyterian Church in America (Canadian Section)

Canadian congregations of the Reformed Presbyterian Church, Evangelical Synod, became a part of the Presbyterian Church in America when the RPCES joined PCA in June 1982. Some of the churches were in predecessor

203

bodies of the RPCES, which was the product of a 1965 merger of the Reformed Presbyterian Church in North America, General Synod and the Evangelical Presbyterian Church. Others came into existence later as a part of the home missions work of RPCES. Congregations are located in seven provinces, and the PCA is continuing church extension work in Canada. The denomination is committed to world evangelization and to a continuation of historic Presbyterianism. Its officers are required to subscribe to the Reformed faith as set forth in the Westminster Confession of Faith and Catechisms.

### Headquarters
Media Contact, Dr. Dominic Aquila, Editor Byfaithonline Newletter, New Geneva Seminary, 3622 East Galley Rd., Colorado Springs, CO 80909, Tel. (719)573-5395 Fax (719)573-5398, Email: daquila6@aol.com

### Periodicals
*Equip for Ministry; Multiply; Network; byFaith*

## Presbyterian Church in Canada
This is the nonconcurring portion of the Presbyterian Church in Canada that did not become a part of The United Church of Canada in 1925.

### Headquarters
50 Wynford Dr., Toronto, ON M3C 1J7, Tel. (416)441-1111 Fax (416)441-2825
Media Contact, Principal Clk., Rev. Stephen Kendall or Associate Secretary for Resource Production & Communication, Mr. Keith Knight
Website: www.presbyterian.ca

### Officers
Principal Clk., Rev. Stephen Kendall

### Periodicals
*Channels; The Presbyterian Message; Presbyterian Record; Glad Tidings; La Vie Chrétienne*

## Reformed Church in Canada
The Canadian region of the Reformed Church in America was organized under the General Synod of the Reformed Church in America. The RCA in Canada has 40 churches which includes three classes (lower assemblies). The Reformed churches in Canada are member congregations of the Reformed Church in America and the Regional Synod of Canada (one of eight RCA regional synods established by its General Synod) and three classes, Ontario, Canadian Prairies and British Columbia.

The first ordained minister, Domine Jonas Micahelius, arrived in New Amsterdam from the Netherlands in 1628. Throughout the colonial period, the Reformed Church lived under the authority of the Classis of Amsterdam. Its churches were clustered in New York and New

Jersey. Under the leadership of Rev. John Livingston, it became a denomination independent of the authority of the Classis of Amsterdam in 1776. Its geographical base was broadened in the 19th century by the immigration of Reformed Dutch and German settlers in the midwestern United States. The Reformed Church now spans the United States and Canada. The Reformed Church in America accepts as its standards of faith the Heidelberg Catechism, Belgic Confession and Canons of Dort. It has a rich heritage of world mission activity. It claims to be loyal to Reformed tradition which emphasizes obedience to God in all aspects of life.

Although the Reformed Church in America has worked in close cooperation with other churches, it has never entered into merger with any other denomination. It is a member of the World Alliance of Reformed Churches, the World Council of Churches and the National Council of the Churches of Christ in the United States of America. In 1998 it also entered into a relationship of full communion with the Evangelical Lutheran Church in America, Presbyterian Church (U.S.A.), and the United Church of Christ by way of the Formula of Agreement.

### Headquarters
475 Riverside Dr., 18th Floor, New York, NY 10115, Tel. (212)870-3243 Fax (212)870-2499
Media Contact, Communications Officer, Paul Boice, 4500 60th St., SE, Grand Rapids, MI 49512, Tel. (616)698-7071 Fax (616)698-6606
Website: www.rca.org

### OFFICERS AND STAFF OF GENERAL SYNOD
Regional Synod of Canada, Synod Executive, Mr. Fred Algera, 1985 Beke Rd. R.R.#4, Cambridge, ON N1R 5S5
President, The Rev. Bradley Lewis, 475 Riverside Dr., 18th Floor, New York, NY 10115
General Synod Council; Moderator, The Rev. Steven Vander Molen, 475 Riverside Dr., 18th Floor, New York, NY 10115
General Secretary, The Rev. Wesley Granberg-Michaelson, 475 Riverside Dr., 18th Floor, New York, NY 10115; 4500 60th St. S.E., Grand Rapids, MI 49512
Operations and Support, Director & Assistant Secretary, The Rev. Kenneth Bradsell
Global Mission, Director, The Rev. Bruce Menning
Leadership/Revitalization, Director, The Rev. Kenneth Eriks
Church Multiplication/Discipleship, Director, The Rev. Richard Welscott
Finance Services, Treasurer, Ms. Susan Converse

## The Reformed Episcopal Church of Canada
The Reformed Episcopal Church is a separate

entity. It was established in Canada by an act of Parliament given royal assent on June 2, 1886. It maintains the founding principles of episcopacy (in historic succession from the Apostles), Anglican liturgy and Reformed doctrine and evangelical zeal. In practice it continues to recognize the validity of certain nonepiscopal orders of evangelical ministry. The Church has reunited with the Reformed Episcopal Church and is now composed of two Dioceses in this body—the Diocese of Central and Eastern Canada and the Diocese of Western Canada and Alaska.

## Headquarters
Box 2532, New Liskeard, ON P0J 1P0, Tel. (705) 647-4565 Fax (705)647-1340
Media Contact, Pres., The Rt. Rev. Michael Fedechko, M. Div., D.D.
Email: fed@nt.net
Website: www.recus.org

## Officers
Pres., The Rt. Rev. Michael Fedechko, 320 Armstrong St., Temiskaming Shores, ON P0J 1P0
Vice Pres., Jeff Shanlin, Hamilton, ON
Sec., Sharlene Graham, New Liskeard, ON P0J 1P0

## BISHOPS
Diocese of Central & Eastern Canada, The Rt. Rev. Michael Fedechko, 320 Armstrong St., Temiskaming Shores, ON P0J 1P0, Tel. (705) 647-4565 Fax (705)647-1340
Diocese of Western Canada & Alaska, Rt. Rev. Charles W. Dorrington, 54 Blanchard St., Victoria, BC V8X 4R1, Tel. (604)744-5014 Fax (604)388-5891

## Periodicals
*The Messenger*

## Reinland Mennonite Church
This group was founded in 1958 when 10 ministers and approximately 600 members separated from the Sommerfelder Mennonite Church. In 1968, four ministers and about 200 members migrated to Bolivia. The church has work in five communities in Manitoba and one in Ontario

## Headquarters
Bishop William H. Friesen, P.O. Box 96, Rosenfeld, MB R0G 1X0, Tel. (204)324-6339
Media Contact, Deacon, Henry Wiebe, Box 2587, Winkler, MB R6W 4C3, Tel. (204)325-8487

## Reorganized Church of Jesus Christ of Latter-day Saints—please see Community of Christ

## The Roman Catholic Church in Canada
The largest single body of Christians in Canada, the Roman Catholic Church is under the spiritual leadership of His Holiness the Pope. Catholicism in Canada dates back to 1534, when the first Mass was celebrated on the Gaspé Peninsula on July 7, by a priest accompanying Jacques Cartier. Catholicism had been implanted earlier by fishermen and sailors from Europe. Priests came to Acadia as early as 1604. Traces of a regular colony go back to 1608 when Champlain settled in Quebec City. The Récollets (1615), followed by the Jesuits (1625) and the Sulpicians (1657), began the missions among the native population. The first official Roman document relative to the Canadian missions dates from March 20, 1618. Bishop François de Montmorency-Laval, the first bishop, arrived in Quebec in 1659. The church developed in the East, but not until 1818 did systematic missionary work begin in western Canada.

In the latter 1700s, English-speaking Roman Catholics, mainly from Ireland and Scotland, began to arrive in Canada's Atlantic provinces. After 1815 Irish Catholics settled in large numbers in what is now Ontario. The Irish potato famine of 1847 greatly increased that population in all parts of eastern Canada.

By the 1850s the Catholic Church in both English- and French-speaking Canada had begun to erect new dioceses and found many religious communities. These communities did educational, medical and charitable work among their own people as well as among Canada's native peoples. By the 1890s large numbers of non-English and non-French-speaking Catholics had settled in Canada, especially in the Western provinces. In the 20th century the pastoral horizons have continued to expand to meet the needs of what has now become a very multicultural church.

The Canadian Conference of Catholic Bishops is the national association of the Latin and Eastern Catholic Bishops of Canada. Its main offices are in Ottawa, Ont.

## CANADIAN ORGANIZATION
Conférence des évêques catholiques du Canada—Canadian Conference of Catholic Bishops, 2500 Don Reid Drive, Ottawa, ON K1H 2J2, Tel. (613)241-9461 Fax (613)241-9048
Email: cecc@cccb.ca
Website: www.cccb.ca

## Headquarters
Media Contact, M. Sylvain Salvas, Tel. (613) 241-7538 or (800)769-1147, Email: salvas@cecc.ca; cecc@cccb.ca

## Officers
General Secretariat of the Canadian Conference of Catholic Bishops
General Secretary: Msgr. Mario Paquette, P.H.
Associate General Secretaries: M. Benoît Bariteau (French Sector); Mr. Bede Hubbard (English Sector)

## EXECUTIVE COMMITTEE
Pres., Most Rev. Andre Gaumond; Vice Pres.,

Most Rev. V. James Weisgerber; Co-Treas., Most Rev. Pierre Morissette and Most Rev. V. James M. Wingle

### EPISCOPAL COMMISSIONS—NATIONAL LEVEL

Social Affairs: Most Rev. Roger Ebacher
Canon Law: Most Rev. Robert Harris
Relations with Assoc. of Clergy, Consecrated Life & Laity: Most Rev. Fred Colli
Evangelization of Peoples: Most Rev. Vincent Cadieux, O.M.I.
Christian Unity, Religious Relations with the Jews, and Interfaith Dialogue: Most Rev. John Boissonneau
Theology: Most Rev. Luc Bouchard

### EPISCOPAL COMMISSIONS—SECTOR LEVEL

Communications sociales: Most Rev. Louis Dicaire
Social Communication: Most Rev. J. Keron Fougere
Christian Education; Most Rev. Richard Smith
Liturgie: Most Rev. Dorylas Moreau
Liturgy: Most Rev. Gerald Wiesner, O.M.I.

### OFFICES

Justice, Paix et Missions—Justice Peace and Missions, Mr. Benoit Bariteau, Dir.
Communications: M. Sylvain Salvas, Dir.
Droit canonique—inter-rites-Canon Law—Inter-rite: Msgr. Mario Paquette, P.H. Secr.
Éditions-Publications, Dr. Vicki Bennett, Dir.
Liturgie-Liturgy: M. Gaëtan Baillargeon, Dir. (French Sector); Rev. Camille Jacques, O.S.M., Dir. (English Sector)
National Office of Religious Education: Ms. Joanne Chafe, Dir.
Relations ecclésiales et doctrine—Ecclesial Relations and Doctrine: Mr. Beck Hubbard
Tribunal d'appel du Canada—The Canadian Appeal Tribunal: Msgr. Alan McCormack, P.H., Vicaire judiciaire-Judicial Vicar

### REGIONAL EPISCOPAL ASSEMBLIES

Atlantic Episcopal Assembly—Assemblée des évêques de l'Atlantique: Pres., Most Rev. Raymond I Lahey; Vice Pres., Most Rev. Terrence Prendergast, S.J. and Most Francois Thibodeau, C.J.M.; Secretary-Treasurer, Fr. Léo Grégoire, I.V. Dei, Tel. (506)735-5578, Fax (506)735-4271
Assemblée des évêques Catholiques du Québec: Pres., Most Rev. Gilles Cazabon, O.M.I.; Vice Prés., Most Rev. Martin Veillette, O.M.I.; Secrétaire général, M. Pierre Gaudette, Tel. (514)274-4323, Fax (514)274-4383 Ontario Conference of Catholic Bishops—Conférence des évêques catholiques de l'Ontario: Pres., Most Rev. Richard Smith, Vice Pres., Most Rev. Richard Grecco; Secretary-Treasurer, Mr. Alphonse Ainsworth, Tel. (416)923-1423 Fax (416)923-1509
Assembly of Western Catholic Bishops Assembliee ches e veques catholique de l'ouest

Pres., Most Rev. Gerald Weisner, O.M.I.; Vice Pres., Most Rev. Raymond Roussin, S.M.; Sec.-Treasurer, Rt. Rev. Peter Novecosky, O.S.B.; Tel. (306)682-1788, Fax (306)682-1766

### MILITARY ORDINARIATE-ORDINARIAT MILITAIRE

Bishop, Most Rev. Donald J. Theriault, Military Ordinariate of Canada, Canadian Forces Support Unit (Ottawa), Uplands Site Building 469, Ottawa, ON K1A 0K2, Tel. (613)990-7824, Fax (613)991-1056
Canadian Religious Conference, Sec. Gen., Sr. Margaret Toner, SCIC. 4135, rue de Rouen, Montréal, Québec H1V 1G5, Tel. (514)259-0856, Fax (514)259-0857
Organisme catholique pour la vie et la famille/ Catholic Organization for Life and Family, co-directors: Ms. Michèle Boulva (French Sector) Tel. (613)241-9461, Fax (613)241-9048, Email: ocvfcolf@cccb.ca

#### Periodicals

*Foi et Culture* (Bulletin natl. de liturgie)

## Romanian Orthodox Church in America (Canadian Parishes)

The first Romanian Orthodox immigrants in Canada called for Orthodox priests from their native country of Romania. Between 1902 and 1914, they organized the first Romanian parish communities and built Orthodox churches in different cities and farming regions of western Canada (Alberta, Saskatchewan, Manitoba) as well as in the eastern part (Ontario and Quebec).

In 1929, the Romanian Orthodox parishes from Canada joined with those of the United States in a Congress held in Detroit, Mich., and asked the Holy Synod of the Romanian Orthodox Church of Romania to establish a Romanian Orthodox Missionary Episcopate in America. The first Bishop, Policarp (Morushca), was elected and consecrated by the Holy Synod of the Romanian Orthodox Church and came to the United States in 1935. He established his headquarters in Detroit with jurisdiction over all the Romanian Orthodox parishes in the United States and Canada.

In 1950, the Romanian Orthodox Church in America (i.e. the Romanian Orthodox Missionary Episcopate in America) was granted administrative autonomy by the Holy Synod of the Romanian Orthodox Church of Romania, and only doctrinal and canonical ties remain with this latter body.

In 1974 the Holy Synod of the Romanian Orthodox Church of Romania recognized and approved the elevation of the Episcopate to the rank of the Romanian Orthodox Archdiocese in America and Canada and completed the administrative autonomy.

#### Headquarters

Romanian Orthodox Archdiocese in America and Canada, 5410 N. Newland Ave., Chicago, IL 60656

Archbishop, Most Rev. Nicolae Condrea, 5410 N. Newland Ave., Chicago, IL 60656, Tel. (773)774-1677 Fax (773)774-1805, Email: archnicolee@aol.com

Vicar, V. Rev. Fr. Ioan Ionita, 17527 Wentworth Ave., Lansing, IL 60438, Tel. (708)889-9768

Secretary, V. Rev. Fr. Nicholas Apostola, 44 Midland St. Worchester, MA 01602-4217, Tel. (508)845-0088, Fax (508)752-8180

**Periodicals**
*Credinte—The Faith*

## The Romanian Orthodox Episcopate of America (Jackson, MI)

This body of Eastern Orthodox Christians of Romanian descent is part of the Autocephalous Orthodox Church in America. For complete description and listing of officers, please see Chapter 3, "Religious Bodies in the United States."

**Headquarters**
2535 Grey Tower Rd., Jackson, MI 49201, Tel. (517)522-4800

Mailing Address, P.O. Box 309, Grass Lake, MI 49240-0309

Media Contact, Ed.-Sec., Rev. Archdeacon David Oancea, P.O. Box 185, Grass Lake, MI 49240-0185, Tel. (517)522-3656

Email: chancery@roea.org
Website: www.roea.org

**Officers**
Ruling Hierarch, Most. Rev. Archbishop Nathaniel Popp

Dean of All Canada, Very Rev. Daniel Nenson, 2855 Helmsing St., Regina, SK S4V 0W7, Tel. (306)761-2379

**Periodicals**
*Solia—The Herald; Good News- Buna Vestire* (in Canada only)

**Russian Orthodox Church—please see Patriarchal Parishes of the Russian Orthodox Church in America**

## The Salvation Army in Canada

The Salvation Army, an evangelical branch of the Christian Church, is an international movement founded in 1865 in London, England. The ministry of Salvationists, consisting of clergy (officers) and laity, comes from a commitment to Jesus Christ and is revealed in practical service, regardless of race, color, creed, sex, or age.

The goals of The Salvation Army are to preach the gospel, disseminate Christian truths, instill Christian values, enrich family life and improve the quality of all life.

To attain these goals, the Salvation Army operates local congregations, provides counseling, supplies basic human needs and undertakes spir-

itual and moral rehabilitation of any needy people who come within its influence.

A quasi-military system of government was set up in 1878, by General William Booth, founder (1829-1912). Converts from England started Salvation Army work in London, Ont., in 1882. Two years later, Canada was recognized as a Territorial Command, and since 1933 it has included Bermuda. An act to incorporate the Governing Council of the Salvation Army in Canada received royal assent on May 19, 1909.

**Headquarters**
2 Overlea Blvd., Toronto, ON M4H 1P4, Tel. (416)425-2111

Media Contact, Major Len Miller, Tel. (416)425-6153 Fax (416)425-6157

Email: len-miller@can.salvationarmy.org
Website: www.salvationarmy.ca

**Officers**
Territorial Commander, Commissioner Bill Luttrell

Territorial Pres., Women's Organizations, Commissioner Gwen Luttrell

Chief Sec., Col. Bob Redhead

Sec. for Personnel, Lt. Col. Wayne Pritchett

Bus. Adm. Sec., Lt. Col. Susan McMillan

Fin. Sec., Major Paul Goodyear

Program Sec., Lt. Col. David Luginbuhl

Public Rel., Major Len Millar

Property Sec., Major Neil Watt

**Periodicals**
*The War Cry; Faith & Friends; En Avant!; The Edge; Horizons*

## Serbian Orthodox Church in the U.S.A. and Canada, Diocese of Canada

The Serbian Orthodox Church is an organic part of the Eastern Orthodox Church. As a local church it received its autocephaly from Constantinople in A.D. 1219. The Patriarchal seat of the church today is in Belgrade, Yugoslavia. In 1921, a Serbian Orthodox Diocese in the United States of America and Canada was organized. In 1963, it was reorganized into three dioceses, and in 1983 a fourth diocese was created for the Canadian part of the church. The Serbian Orthodox Church is in absolute doctrinal unity with all other local Orthodox Churches.

**Headquarters**
7470 McNiven Rd., RR 3, Campbellville, ON L0P 1B0, Tel. (905)878-0043 Fax (905)878-1909

Media Contact, Rt. Rev. Georgije
Email: vladika@istocnik.com
Website: www. istocnik.com

**Officers**
Serbian Orthodox Bishop of Canada, Rt. Rev. Georgije

Dean of Western Deanery, V. Rev. Mirko Malinovic, 924 12th Ave., Regina, SK S4N

0K7, Tel. (306)352-2917
Dean of Eastern Deanery, V. Rev. Zivorad
Subotic, 351 Mellville Ave., Westmount, QC
H3Z 2Y7, Tel. & Fax (514)931-6664

### Periodicals
*Istocnik, Herald of the Serbian Orthodox
Church—Canadian Diocese*

## Seventh-day Adventist Church in Canada

The Seventh-day Adventist Church in Canada
is part of the worldwide Seventh-day Adventist
Church with headquarters in Silver Spring, Md.
(See "Religious Bodies in the United States" section of this *Yearbook* for a fuller description.)
The Seventh-day Adventist Church in Canada
was organized in 1901 and reorganized in 1932.

### Headquarters
1148 King Street East, Oshawa, ON L1H 1H8,
Tel. (905)433-0011 Fax (905)433-0982
Media Contact, Nilton D. Amorim

### Officers
Pres., Daniel R. Jackson
Sec., Nilton D. Amorim
Treas., John Ramsay

### DEPARTMENTS
Asst. Treas., Joyce Jones
Education, Mike Lekic
Family Ministries, Celest Corkum, Ken Corkum
Sabbath School and Personal Ministries, Gary
Hodder
Trust Services, Barry W. Bussey
ADRA Canada, Oliver Lofton-Brook

### Periodicals
*Canadian Adventist Messenger*

**Southern Baptists—please see Canadian
Convention of Southern Baptists**

## Syriac Orthodox Church of Antioch

The Syriac Orthodox Church professes the
faith of the first three ecumenical councils of
Nicaea, Constantinople and Ephesus and num-
bers faithful in the Middle East, India, the
Americas, Europe and Australia. It traces its ori-
gin to the Patriarchate established in Antioch by
St. Peter the Apostle and is under the supreme
ecclesiastical jurisdiction of His Holiness the
Syrian Orthodox Patriarch of Antioch and All the
East, now residing in Damascus, Syria.

The Archdiocese of the Syrian Orthodox
Church in the U.S. and Canada was formally
established in 1957. In 1995, the Archdiocese of
North America was divided into three separate
Patriarchal Vicariates, including one for Canada.
The first Syrian Orthodox faithful came to
Canada in the 1890s and formed the first
Canadian parish in Sherbrooke, Quebec. Today

five official parishes of the Archdiocese exist in
Canada—two in Quebec and three in Ontario.
There is also an official mission congregation in
Calgary, Alberta and Ottawa, Ontario.

### Headquarters
Archdiocese of Canada, The New Archdiocesan
Centre, 4375 Henri-Bourassa Ouest, St.-
Laurent, Quebec H4L 1A5, Tel. (514)334-
6993 Fax (514)334-8233

### Officers
Archbishop Mor Timotheos Aphrem Aboodi

## Ukrainian Orthodox Church of Canada

Toward the end of the 19th century many
Ukrainian immigrants settled in Canada. In 1918,
a group of these pioneers established the
Ukrainian Orthodox Church of Canada (UOCC),
today the largest Ukrainian Orthodox Church
beyond the borders of Ukraine. In 1990, the
UOCC entered into a eucharistic union with the
Ecumenical Patriarchate at Constantinople
(Istanbul).

### Headquarters
Ukrainian Orthodox Church of Canada, Office of
the Consistory, 9 St. Johns Ave., Winnipeg,
MB R2W 1G8, Tel. (204)586-3093 Fax
(204)582-5241
Media Contacts, Rev. Fr. Andrew Jarmus, 9 St.
Johns Ave., Winnipeg, MB R2W 1G8, Tel.
(204)586-3093 Fax (204)582-5241; Ms. M.
Zurek, 9 St. Johns Ave., Winnipeg, MB R2W
1G8, Tel. (204)586-3093 Fax (204)582-5241
Email: consistory@uocc.ca
Website: www. uocc.ca

### Officers
Primate, Most Rev. Metropolitan Wasyly Fedak,
9 St. Johns Ave., Winnipeg, MB R2W 1G8,
Tel. (204)586-3093 Fax (204)582-5241
Chancellor, Rt. Rev. Fr. William Makarenko

### Periodicals
*Visnyk-The Herald-Le Messager* (newspaper),
*Ridna Nyva* (almanac-annual)

## Union d'Eglises Baptistes Françaises au Canada

Baptist churches in French Canada first came
into being through the labors of two missionaries
from Switzerland, Rev. Louis Roussy and Mme.
Henriette Feller, who arrived in Canada in 1835.
The earliest church was organized in Grande
Ligne (now St. Blaise), Quebec in 1838.

By 1900 there were 7 churches in the province
of Quebec and 13 French-language Baptist
churches in the New England states. The leadership was totally French Canadian.

By 1960, the process of Americanization had
caused the disappearance of the French Baptist
churches in the New England states. During the
1960s, Quebec as a society, began rapidly chang-

ing in all its facets, education, politics, social values and structures. Mission, evangelism, and church growth once again flourished. In 1969, in response to the new conditions, the Grande Ligne Mission passed control of its work to the newly formed Union of French Baptist Churches in Canada, which then included 8 churches. By 2005 the French Canadian Baptist movement had grown to include 34 congregations present in three provinces: Quebec, New Brunswick, and Ontario.

The Union d'Églises Baptistes Françaises au Canada is a member body of the Canadian Baptist Ministries and thus is affiliated with the Baptist World Alliance.

### Headquarters

2285 Avenue Papineau, Montreal, QC H2K 4J5, Tel. (514)526-6643 Fax (514)526-9269

Media Contact, Gen. Sec., Rev. Roland Grimard

### Officers

Sec. Gen., Rev. Roland Grimard

### Periodicals

*www.UnionBaptiste.com (Internet)*

## Union of Spiritual Communities of Christ (Orthodox Doukhobors in Canada)

The Doukhobors are Canadians of Russian origin living primarily in the western provinces of Canada, but their beginnings in Russia are unknown. The name "Doukhobors," or "Spirit Wrestlers," was given them in derision by the Russian Orthodox clergy in Russia as far back as 1785. The Doukhobors were persecuted by the church for rejecting Orthodoxy, and following the counsel of their leader, Peter V. Verigin, earned the wrath of the Tsarist government by destroying all of their weapons and adopting pacifism in 1895. In 1899 the Tsarist government allowed 8,000 Doukhobors to leave Russia in response to an international uproar over their persecution by the church and state. They made their way to Canada with the assistance of Count Leo Tolstoy, who saw in these people the living embodiment of his philosophy, the Religious Society of Friends, commonly known as Quakers and other people of good will. Originally settled in Saskatchewan, by 1911 the majority followed Verigin to Bristish Columbia because of government efforts to assismilate them.

The teaching of the Doukhobors is penetrated with the gospel spirit of love. Worshiping God in the spirit, they affirm that the outward church and all that is performed in it and concerns it has no importance for them; the church is where two or three are gathered together, united in the name of Christ. They do not believe in icon worship or in intermediaries between themselves and God. Their spiritual teachings are founded on ancient tradition, which they call the "Book of Life," because it lives in their memory and hearts. In this book are psalms composed by their elders and leaders, partly formed out of the contents of the Bible partly out of their historical experience. These are committed to memory by each succeeding generation. Doukhobors observe complete pacifism and non-violence, are lacto-vegetarians, and attempt to maintain a communal lifestyle.

The majority of Canadian Doukhobors were reorganized in 1938 by Peter P. Verigin, son of P.V. Verigin, shortly before his death, into the Union of Spiritual Communities of Christ to distinguish themselves from a radical offshoot who call themselves Sons of Freedom, and whose embrace of nudity and depradations has been sensationalized by the media and has stigmatized all Doukhobors. Today the USCC is governed by Trustees elected from member communities and administered by an elected Executive Committee headed by Honourary Chairman, John J. Verigin, CM OBC. The USCC executes the will and protects the interests of its member communities and its members living beyond south central British Columbia where the USCC is headquartered. The USCC is the largest organization of Doukhobors and maintains relations with other Doukhobor groups across Canada, in the U.S.A., the Russian Federation, the Ukraine, and Georgia. The USCC also cooperates with other non governmental organizations working non violently to promote peace and justice, and respect for human dignity and ecological integrity.

### Headquarters

USCC Central Office, Box 760, Grand Forks, BC V0H 1H0, Tel. (250)442-8252 Fax (250) 442-3433

Media Contact, John J. Verigin, Sr.

### Officers

Hon. Chmn. of the Exec. Comm., John J. Verigin, Sr.

Chpsn., Fred Bojey

### Periodicals

*ISKRA*

## United Brethren Church in Canada

Founded in 1767 in Lancaster County, Pa., missionaries came to Canada about 1850. The first class was held in Kitchener in 1855, and the first building was erected in Port Elgin in 1867.

The Church of the United Brethren in Christ had its beginning with Philip William Otterbein and Martin Boehm, who were leaders in the revivalistic movement in Pennsylvania and Maryland during the late 1760s.

### Headquarters

302 Lake St., Huntington, IN 46750, Tel. (219) 356-2312 Fax (219)356-4730

209

## GENERAL OFFICERS

Pres., Rev. Brian Magnus, 120 Fife Rd., Guelph, ON N1H 6Y2, Tel. (519)836-0180

Treas., Brian Winger, 2233 Hurontario St., Apt. 916, Mississauga, ON L5A 2E9, Tel. (905) 275-8140

## The United Church of Canada

The United Church of Canada was formed on June 10, 1925, through the union of the Methodist Church, Canada, the Congregational Union of Canada, the Council of Local Union Churches and 70 percent of the Presbyterian Church in Canada. The union culminated years of negotiation between the churches, all of which had integral associations with the development and history of the nation.

In fulfillment of its mandate to be a uniting as well as a United Church, the denomination has been enriched by other unions during its history. The Wesleyan Methodist Church of Bermuda joined in 1930. On January 1, 1968, the Canada Conference of the Evangelical United Brethren became part of The United Church of Canada. At various times, congregations of other Christian communions have also become congregations of the United Church.

The United Church of Canada is a full member of the World Methodist Council, the World Alliance of Reformed Churches (Presbyterian and Congregational), and the Canadian and World Councils of Churches. The United Church is the largest Protestant denomination in Canada.

### NATIONAL OFFICES

General Council Office, 3250 Bloor St. W., Ste. 300, Toronto, ON M8X 2Y4, Tel. (416)231-5931 Fax (416)231-3103

Media Contact, Communications Officer, Mary Frances Denis

Email: info@united-church.ca

Website: www.united-church.ca

### GENERAL COUNCIL

Mod., Rt. Rev. Peter B. Short

Gen. Sec., Rev. James H. Sinclair

### GENERAL COUNCIL MINISTERS

Planning Processes, Janet McDonald

Programs for Mission & Ministry, Rev. Bruce Gregersen

Racial Justice, Kim Uyeded-Kai

Regional Relations, Rev. Carol L. Hancock

Resources for Mission & Ministry, Ian S. Fraser

Archivist, Sharon Larade, 73 Queen's Park Cr. E., Toronto, ON M5C 1K7, Tel. (416)585-4563 Fax (416)585-4584

Email: uccvu.archives@utoronto.ca

Website: www.united-church.ca/archives

### ADMINISTRATIVE UNITS
### (Executive Ministers)

Ethnic Ministries, Exec. Min., Rev. Richard C. Choe

Faith Formation and Education, Exec. Min., Rev. Steven Chambers

Financial Services, Exec. Officer, Ron Olsen

Financial Stewardship, Exec. Min., Rev. William Steadman

Information Technology Services, Exec. Officer, vacant

Justice, Global & Ecumenical Relations, Exec. Min., Rev. Omega C. Bula

Ministries in French, Exec. Min., Rev. Pierre Goldberger

Ministry & Employment Policies & Services, Exec. Min., Michael Burke

Resource Production and Distribution, Exec. Min., vacant

Support to Local Ministries, Exec. Min., Rev. Harry Oussoren

### CONFERENCE EXECUTIVE
### SECRETARIES

Alberta and Northwest, Rev. Lynn I. Maki, 9911-48 Ave., NW, Edmonton, AB T6E 5V6, Tel. (780)435-3995 Fax (780)438-3317, Email: coffice@anwconf.com

All Native Circle, Speaker, Cheryl Jourdain, 367 Selkirk Ave., Winnipeg, MB R2W 2M3, Tel. (204)582-5518 Fax (204)582-6649, Email: allnative@mts.net

Bay of Quinte, Rev. Wendy Bulloch, P.O. Box 700, 67 Mill St., Frankford, ON K0K 2C0, Tel. (613)398-1051 Fax (613)398-8894, Email: bayq.conference@sympatico.ca

British Columbia, Rev. Douglas Goodwin, 4383 Rumble St., Burnaby, BC V5J 2A2, Tel. (604)431-0434 Fax (604)431-0439, Email: bcconf@bc.united-church.ca

Hamilton, Rev. Fred Monteith, Box 100, Carlisle, ON L0R 1H0, Tel. (905)659-3343 Fax (905)659-7766, Email: office@hamconf.org

London, W. Peter Scott, 747 Hyde Park Rd., Ste. 116, London, ON N6H 3S3, Tel. (519)672-1930 Fax (519)439-2800, Email: lonconf@execulink.com

Manitoba and Northwestern Ontario, Rev. Bruce Faurschou, 170 Saint Mary's Rd., Winnipeg, MB R2H 1H9, Tel. (204)233-8911 Fax (204) 233-3289, Email: office@confmnwo.mb.ca

Manitou, Rev. Rev. William Kunder, 319 McKenzie Ave., North Bay, ON P1B 7E3, Tel. (705)474-3350 Fax (705)497-3597, Email: office@manitouconference.ca

Maritime, Rev. Catherine H. Gaw, 32 York St., Sackville, NB E4L 4R4, Tel. (506)536-1334 Fax (506)536-2900, Email: info@marconf.ca

Montreal and Ottawa, Rev. Rosemary Lambie, 225-50 Ave., Lachine, QC H8T 2T7, Tel. (514) 634-7015 Fax (514)634-2489, Email: lachine@istar.ca

Newfoundland and Labrador, Rev. William G. Bartlett, 320 Elizabeth Ave., St. John's, NL A1B 1T9, Tel. (709)754-0386 Fax (709)754-8336, Email: unitedchurch@ nfld.net

Saskatchewan, Rev. G. Robert Campbell, 418 A. McDonald St., Regina, SK S4N 6E1, Tel. (306)721-3311 Fax (306)721-3171, Email: ucskco@sasktel.net

Toronto, Rev. David W. Allen, 65 Mayall Ave., Downsview, ON M3L 1E7, Tel. (416)241-2677 Fax (416)241-2689, Email: torontoconference@bellnet.ca

### Periodicals
*United Church Observer; Mandate; Aujourd'hui Credo*

## United Pentecostal Church in Canada

This body, which is affiliated with the United Pentecostal Church, International, with headquarters in Hazelwood, Mo., accepts the Bible standard of full salvation, which is repentance, baptism by immersion in the name of the Lord Jesus Christ for the remission of sins and the baptism of the Holy Ghost, with the initial signs of speaking in tongues as the Spirit gives utterance. Other tenets of faith include the Oneness of God in Christ, holiness, divine healing and the second coming of Jesus Christ.

### Headquarters
United Pentecostal Church Intl., 8855 Dunn Rd., Hazelwood, MO 63042, Tel. (314)837-7300 Fax (314)837-4503

Media Contact, Gen. Sec.-Treas., Rev. C. M. Becton

### DISTRICT SUPERINTENDENTS
Atlantic, Rev. Harry Lewis, P.O. Box 1046, Perth Andover, NB E0J 1V0

British Columbia, Rev. Paul V. Reynolds, 13447-112th Ave., Surrey, BC V3R 2E7

Canadian Plains, Rev. Johnny King, 615 Northmount Dr., NW, Calgary, AB T2K 3J6

Central Canadian, Rev. Clifford Heaslip, 4215 Roblin Blvd., Winnipeg, MB R3R 0E8

Newfoundland, Jack Cunningham

Nova Scotia, Superintendent, Rev. John D. Mean, P.O. Box 2183, D.E.P.S., Dartmouth, NS B2W 3Y2

Ontario, Rev. Carl H. Stephenson, 63 Castlegrove Blvd., Don Mills, ON M3A 1L3

## Universal Fellowship of Metropolitan Community Churches

The Universal Fellowship of Metropolitan Community Churches is a Christian church which directs a special ministry within, and on behalf of, the gay and lesbian community. Involvement, however, is not exclusively limited to gays and lesbians; U.F.M.C.C. tries to stress its openness to all people and does not call itself a "gay church."

Founded in 1968 in Los Angeles by the Rev. Troy Perry, the U.F.M.C.C. has over 300 member congregations worldwide. Congregations are in Vancouver, Edmonton, Windsor, London, Toronto, Ottawa (2), Guelph, Fredericton, Winnipeg, Halifax, Barrie, and Belleville.

Theologically, the Metropolitan Community Churches stand within the mainstream of Christian doctrine, being "ecumenical" or "inter-denominational" in stance (albeit a "denomination" in their own right).

The Metropolitan Community Churches are characterized by their belief that the love of God is a gift, freely offered to all people, regardless of sexual orientation and that no incompatibility exists between human sexuality and the Christian faith.

The Metropolitan Community Churches in Canada were founded in Toronto in 1973 by the Rev. Robert Wolfe.

### Headquarters
Media Contact: The Rev. Cheryl Meyer, 135 Simpson Ave., Toronto, ON M4K 1A4

## The Wesleyan Church of Canada

This group is the Canadian portion of the Wesleyan Church, which consists of the Atlantic and Central Canada districts. The Central Canada District of the former Wesleyan Methodist Church of America was organized at Winchester, Ontario, in 1889 and the Atlantic District was founded in 1888 as the Alliance of the Reformed Baptist Church, which merged with the Wesleyan Methodist Church in July, 1966.

The Wesleyan Methodist Church and the Pilgrim Holiness Church merged in June, 1968, to become The Wesleyan Church. The doctrine is evangelical and Wesleyan Arminian and stresses holiness beliefs. For more details, consult the U.S. listing under the Wesleyan Church.

### Headquarters
The Wesleyan Church Intl. Center, P.O. Box 50434, Indianapolis, IN 46250-0434

Media Contact, Dist. Supt., Central Canada, Rev. Donald E. Hodgins, 17 Saint Paul St., Belleview, ON K8N 1A4, Tel. (613)966-7527 Fax (613)968-6190

### DISTRICT SUPERINTENDENTS
Central Canada, Rev. Donald E. Hodgins, 17 Saint Paul St., Belleview, ON K8N 1A4, Email: ccd@on.aibn.com

Atlantic, Rev. Dr. H. C. Wilson, 1600 Main St., Ste. 216, Moncton, NB E1E 1G5, Email: ncwilson@nbnet.nb.ca

### Periodicals
*Central Canada; The Clarion*

# Religious Bodies in Canada
# Arranged by Families

The following list of religious bodies appearing in the Directory Section of the *Yearbook* shows the "families," or related clusters into which Canadian religious bodies can be grouped. For example, there are many communions that can be grouped under the heading "Baptist" for historical and theological reasons. It should not be assumed, however, that all denominations under one family heading are necessarily consistent in belief or practice. The family clusters tend to represent historical factors more often than theological or practical ones. These family categories provide one of the major pitfalls when compiling church statistics because there is often a tendency to combine the statistics by "families" for analytical and comparative purposes. Such combined totals are deeply flawed, even though they are often used as variables for sociological analysis. The arrangement by families offered here is intended only as a general guide for conceptual organization when viewing the broad sweep of Canadian religious culture.

Religious bodies that cannot be categorized under family headings appear alphabetically and are not indented in the following list.

The Anglican Church of Canada
Apostolic Christian Church (Nazarene)
Armenian Evangelical Church
Associated Gospel Churches

## Baptist Bodies
*Association of Regular Baptist Churches (Canada)*
*Baptist Convention of Ontario and Quebec*
*Baptist General Conference of Canada*
*Baptist Union of Western Canada*
*Canadian Baptist Ministries*
*Canadian Convention of Southern Baptists*
*Convention of Atlantic Baptist Churches*
*The Fellowship of Evangelical Baptist Churches in Canada*
*Free Will Baptists*
*North American Baptist Conference*
*Union d'Eglises Baptistes Françaises au Canada*

Brethren in Christ Church, Canadian Conference
Canadian District of the Moravian Church in America, Northern Province
Canadian Evangelical Christian Churches
Canadian Yearly Meeting of the Religious Society of Friends
Christ Catholic Church International
Christian Brethren (also known as Plymouth Brethren)
Christian and Missionary Alliance in Canada
Church of God (Anderson, Ind.)
Church of the Nazarene in Canada

## Churches of Christ—Christian Churches
*Christian Church (Disciples of Christ) in Canada*
*Christian Churches/Churches of Christ*
*Churches of Christ in Canada*

Congregational Christian Churches in Canada

## Eastern Orthodox Churches
*The Antiochian Orthodox Christian Archdiocese of North America*
*Greek Orthodox Metropolis of Toronto (Canada)*
*Orthodox Church in America (Canada Section)*
*Patriarchal Parishes of the Russian Orthodox Church in Canada*
*Romanian Orthodox Church in America (Canadian Parishes)*
*The Romanian Orthodox Episcopate of America (Jackson, MI)*
*Serbian Orthodox Church in the U.S.A. and Canada, Diocese of Canada*
*Ukrainian Orthodox Church of Canada*

The Evangelical Covenant Church of Canada
Evangelical Free Church of Canada
The Evangelical Missionary Church of Canada
General Church of the New Jerusalem
Jehovah's Witnesses

## Latter-day Saints (Mormons)
*The Church of Jesus Christ of Latter-day Saints in Canada*
*Community of Christ*

## Lutheran Bodies
*Church of the Lutheran Brethren*
*The Estonian Evangelical Lutheran Church*
*Evangelical Lutheran Church in Canada*
*Lutheran Church—Canada*

## Mennonite Bodies
*Canadian Conference of Mennonite Brethren Churches*
*Church of God in Christ (Mennonite)*
*The Evangelical Mennonite Conference*

*Evangelical Mennonite Mission Conference*
*Mennonite Church Canada*
*Old Order Amish Church*
*Reinland Mennonite Church*

## Methodist Bodies
*British Methodist Episcopal Church of Canada*
*Free Methodist Church in Canada*
*Independent Holiness Church*
*The Wesleyan Church of Canada*

**The Old Catholic Church of Canada**
**Open Bible Faith Fellowship of Canada**

## Oriental Orthodox Churches
*Armenian Holy Apostolic Church—Canadian Diocese*
*The Coptic Orthodox Church in Canada*
*Syriac Orthodox Church of Antioch*

## Pentecostal Bodies
*The Apostolic Church in Canada*
*Apostolic Church of Pentecost of Canada Inc.*
*The Bible Holiness Movement*
*Canadian Assemblies of God (formerly the Italian Pentecostal Church of Canada)*
*Church of God (Cleveland, Tenn.)*
*The Church of God of Prophecy in Canada*
*Elim Fellowship of Evangelical Churches and Ministers*
*Foursquare Gospel Church of Canada*
*Independent Assemblies of God International (Canada)*
*The Pentecostal Assemblies of Canada*
*Pentecostal Assemblies of Newfoundland*
*United Pentecostal Church in Canada*

## Reformed Bodies
*Canadian and American Reformed Churches*
*Christian Reformed Church in North America*
*Presbyterian Church in America (Canadian Section)*
*Presbyterian Church in Canada*
*Reformed Church in Canada*

**The Reformed Episcopal Church of Canada**
**The Roman Catholic Church in Canada**
**The Salvation Army in Canada**
**Seventh-day Adventist Church in Canada**
**Union of Spiritual Communities of Christ (Orthodox Doukhobors in Canada)**
**United Brethren Church in Canada**
**The United Church of Canada**
**Universal Fellowship of Metropolitan Community Churches**

213

# 5. Sources of Religion-Related Research
## I. Directory of Selected Research Organizations

The editorial office of the *Yearbook of American & Canadian Churches* receives innumerable requests for data about churches, religious organizations, attendance patterns, and comparative religion concerns. Sometimes we are able to furnish the requested data, but more often we refer the inquirer to other research colleagues in the field. We are always interested in and aided by such requests, and we find ourselves informed by each question.

In response to such inquiries, the "Sources in Religion-Related Research" directory was initiated in the 1999 edition of the *Yearbook* In addition to asking each organization to provide a brief overall description, each was also asked to indicate any special research foci (i.e. denominational, congregational, interfaith, gender, etc.). Further, each organization is asked to identify the sociological, methodological, or theological approaches that serve to guide their research, and to describe any current or recent research projects. Lastly, we asked for a list of recurrent publications. Below the organizations' responses to these questions are reported as clearly and completely as is possible. Contact information appears just beneath the title of each organization. In most cases, the organization's website provides very detailed information about current research projects.

Numerous other research centers in the area of American religious life, each with specific areas of concern, conduct timely and significant research. We hope that readers will find utility in this directory and we invite them to identify additional sources by email: yearbook@ncccusa.org or by Fax: (212) 870-2817.

## American Academy of Religion (AAR)

AAR Executive Office
825 Houston Mill Rd., Ste. 300
Atlanta, GA 30329
Tel. (404)727-7920
Fax (404)727-7959
Email: aar@aarweb.org
Website: www.aarweb.org
President, Dr. Diana Eck
Exec. Dir., Dr. John Fitzmier

The AAR is the major learned society and professional association for scholars whose object of study is religion. Its mission—in a world where religion plays so central a role in social, political and economic events, as well as in the lives of communities and individuals—is to meet a critical need for ongoing reflection upon and understanding of religious traditions, issues, questions, and values. As a learned society and professional association of teachers and research scholars, the American Academy of Religion has over 8,500 members who teach in some 1,500 colleges, universities, seminaries, and schools in North America and abroad. The Academy is dedicated to furthering knowledge of religion and religious institutions in all their forms and manifestations. This is accomplished through Academy-wide and regional conferences and meetings, publications, programs, and membership services. Within a context of free inquiry and critical examination, the Academy welcomes all disciplined reflection on religion—both from within and outside of communities of belief and practice—and seeks to enhance its broad public understanding.

The AAR's annual meeting, over 8,000 scholars gather to share research and collaborate on scholarly projects. The annual meeting sessions are grouped into over 70 program units, each representing an ongoing community of scholars who are collectively engaged in pursuing knowledge about a specific religious tradition or a specific aspect of religion. In addition, the AAR's ten regional organizations sponsor smaller annual meetings that are similar in structure to the Academy-wide meeting. All of the world's major religious traditions, as well as indigenous and historical religions, are explored in the work of AAR members.

### Current or Recent Research

Currently, for example, the AAR offers teaching workshops for both junior and senior scholars. It is organizing efforts to gather data on the field to facilitate departmental planning and funding. A full explanation of the many current research projects is available on the AAR website, which is listed above.

### Periodicals

*The Journal of the American Academy of Religion* is the scholarly periodical of the AAR. In addition, the AAR publishes a quarterly newsletter, *Religious Studies News, AAR Edition.*

## Association of Religion Data Archives (ARDA)

Department of Sociology
The Pennsylvania State University
211 Oswald Tower
University Park, PA 16802-6207
Tel. (814)865-6258
Fax (814)863-7216
Email: arda@pop.psu.edu
Website: www.TheARDA.com
Director, Dr. Roger Finke

The ARDA allows you to interactively explore the highest quality data on American and international religion using online features for generating national profiles, maps, church membership overviews, denominational heritage trees, tables, charts, and other summary reports. Nearly 400 data files are available for online preview and most can be downloaded for additional review. The ARDA (www.TheARDA.com) is supported by the Lilly Endowment and the John Templeton Foundation and is housed in the Social Science Research Institute at the Pennsylvania State University. All services are provided free of charge.

## Association of Theological Schools (ATS)

10 Summit Park Dr.
Pittsburgh, PA 15275-1103
Tel. (412)788-6505
Fax (412)788-6510
Email: ats@ats.edu
Website: www.ats.edu
Exec. Dir., Daniel O. Aleshire
Dir. of Communications and Membership Services, Nancy Merrill

The mission of the Association of Theological Schools in the United States and Canada (ATS) is to promote the improvement and enhancement of theological schools to the benefit of communities of faith and the broader public. The Association seeks to fulfill this mission by engaging in four core areas of work, (1) accreditation, (2) leadership education for administrative officers and faculty, (3) development of theological education, which involves the study of critical issues in theological education, and (4) communications and membership.

The Association is a membership organization of approximately 250 graduate schools of theology, including Protestant, Roman Catholic, and Orthodox schools, both freestanding seminaries and university-related divinity schools. A full list of members is available on the above website.

Targeted areas of the Association's work currently include Theological Schools and the Church, the Character and Assessment of Learning for Religious Vocation, Race and Ethnicity in Theological Education, Women in Leadership in Theological Education, and Technology and Educational Practices.

### Current or Recent Research

The ATS project on Theological Schools and the church has three goals that, together, will provide a perspective about theological schools' relationships with ecclesial bodies and prescriptions for strengthening them. The goals are (1) to cultivate a broad-based conversation about the institutional relationships between theological schools and church bodies, (2) to define the current patterns of relationship between seminaries and their respective communities of faith, and (3) to develop proposals for strengthening and renewing institutional relationships that benefit both the church and theological schools.

A project on Technology and Educational Practices is identifying best practices in the use of educational technology in theological education, conducting educational events that provide information about and skill development in the use of educational technology, and creating resources about education and technology for use by theological schools.

### Periodicals

*Fact Book on Theological Education* is published annually and provides statistical data on the member institutions. The Association publishes a journal, *Theological Education,* bi-annually, a bi-monthly newsletter entitled *Colloquy,* and the formal institutional documents of the Association entitled *Bulletin,* part 2 of which is the ATS membership list.

## Auburn Theological Seminary

3041 Broadway
New York, NY 10027
Tel. (212)662-4315
Fax (212)663-5214

SOURCES

Email: cste@auburnsem.org; krh@auburnsem.org; slm@auburnsem.org
Website: www.auburnsem.org
President, Dr. Barbara G. Wheeler
Executive Vice President, Rev. Katharine R. Henderson

Auburn Theological Seminary's mission is to strengthen religious leadership. It carries out its mission through programs of non-degree theological education for clergy and laity; through programs for Presbyterian students enrolled at its partner institution, Union Seminary in New York City; and by conducting research on theological education at its Center for the Study of Theological Education. Auburn was founded in 1818 in Auburn, New York; it is currently located on Union Seminary's campus.

Auburn Seminary is related by covenant agreement with Presbyterian Church (U.S.A.), but most of its programs are ecumenical, and many have a multi-faith focus. The Center for the Study of Theological Education includes rabbinical schools and Protestant and Roman Catholic seminaries and divinity schools in its studies.

Research is conducted using a variety of methods, including survey and ethnographic research, structured interview and documentary research, research reports on surveys and case studies. Reports of findings are frequently published with accompanying information on the history of the issue being studied and with theological commentaries written from a variety of perspectives.

### Current or Recent Research

The Center is undertaking a systematic study of U.S. and Canadian M.A.-level graduates from across the religious spectrum in order to find out how graduates have used their theological training, how many are in ministry five and ten years after graduation, and how they look back and assess their seminary experience. A second study underway is on seminary institutional advancement. Through analysis of available data, site visits, surveys and interviews, the researchers will examine the techniques, costs, best practices and barriers to effective fundraising in theological schools.

### Periodicals

*Auburn Studies,* an occasional bulletin in which the Center publishes its research results. Research reports are also available on Auburn's website (listed above).

## The Barna Group, Ltd.

1957 Eastman Ave.
Ventura, CA 93003
Tel. (805)658-8885
Fax (805)658-7298
Email: barna@barna.org
Website: www.barna.org
President, George Barna
Vice President, David Kinnaman

The Barna Group conducts primary research related to cultural change, people's lifestyles, values, attitudes, beliefs, and religious practices.

Its vision is to provide current accurate and reliable information, in bite-sized pieces and at reasonable costs, to its clients to facilitate strategic decisions. Barna also produces many research-based books, reports, and ministry tools to help churches understand the national context of ministry. The organization works with churches from all Christian denominations.

It conducts projects based upon existing needs in the church at-large, or for its clients specifically. Methodologically, The Barna Group uses both qualitative approaches (focus groups, depth interviews) and quantitative approaches (cross-sectional surveys, longitudinal studies, panel research).

Data collection methods include telephone surveys, mail surveys, in-person interviews, on-line surveys, self-administered surveys, focus groups.

### Current or Recent Research

The Barna Group conducts more than 50 studies each year, covering a broad range of topics. Some of the recent non-proprietary studies completed are focused on understanding the state of the church; the habits of highly effective churches; worship efficacy; the unchurched; strategies and techniques for developing lay leaders; understanding effective discipleship processes; pastoral profiles; beliefs, behaviors and core attitudes of ministry donors; Biblical knowledge, and many others.

### Periodicals

The Barna Group offers a free bi-weekly report—*The Barna Update*—on current information related to faith matters from its national non-proprietary research. This information is free to those who register for it at the website (listed above).

216

## Center for the Study of Religion and American Culture

Indiana University
Purdue University at Indianapolis
425 University Blvd, Room 341
Indianapolis, IN 46202-5140
Tel. (317)274-8409
Fax (317)278-3354
Email: pgoff@iupui.edu
Website: www.iupui.edu/~raac
Director, Dr. Phillip Goff
Program Coordinator, Rebecca Vasko

The Center for the Study of Religion and American Culture is a research and public outreach institute devoted to the promotion of the understanding of the relation between religion and other features of American culture. Research methods are both inter-disciplinary and multi-disciplinary. Established in 1989, the Center is based in the School of Liberal Arts and Indiana University-Purdue University at Indianapolis. Center activities include national conferences and symposia, commissioned books, essays, bibliographies, and research projects, fellowships for younger scholars, data-based communication about developments in the field of American religion, a newsletter devoted to the promotion of Center activities, and the semi-annual scholarly periodical, *Religion and American Culture, A Journal of Interpretation.*

### Current or Recent Research

The Center is presently overseeing two intiatives. The "Young Scholars in American Religion Program" is a multi-year project to assist early-career scholars in developing their teaching skills and research agendas. The "Centers and Institutes Project," meanwhile, brings together those organizations dedicated to the academic study of religion in the U.S. in order to discuss common problems and solutions, as well as to identify areas for cooperative efforts. The work of these various centers and institutes will be highlighted in future issues of the "Newsletter from the Center for the Study of Religion and American Culture" and the Center's reception at the annual meeting of the American Academy of Religion.

We continue to explore other areas of potential research in the relation between religion and other aspects of American culture. As these projects materialize, they will be announced on this website and in the "Newsletter."

### Periodicals

*Religion and American Culture, A Journal of Interpretation.* Center books include the series, "The Public Expressions of Religion in America."

## empty tomb, inc.

301 North Fourth Street
P.O. Box 2404
Champaign, IL 61825-2404
Tel. (217)356-9519
Fax (217)356-2344
Email: research@emptytomb.org
Website: www.emptytomb.org
CEO, John L. Ronsvalle
Exec.Vice Pres., Sylvia Ronsvalle

empty tomb, inc. is a Christian research and service organization. On a local level, it coordinates direct services to people in need in cooperation with area congregations. On a national level, it studies church member giving patterns of historically Christian churches, including Roman Catholic, mainline and evangelical Protestant, Anabaptist, Pentecostal, Orthodox, and fundamentalist communions. empty tomb publishes the annual *State of Church Giving* series. Also, empty tomb offers a mission-funding incentive program, Mission Match, in an effort to help reverse the negative giving trends indicated by national data.

### Current or Recent Research

Current research monitors and analyzes church member giving patterns, and is published in *The State of Church Giving* series produced by empty tomb, inc.

### Periodicals

*The State of Church Giving* series is an annual publication. It considers denominational giving data, analysis of giving and membership trends, and other estimates of charitable giving. Each edition has featured a special- focus chapter, which discusses giving issues relevant to church giving patterns. Past *State of Church Giving* special focus chapters are posted on the www.emptytomb.org website.

## The Hartford Institute for Religion Research of Hartford Seminary

Hartford Seminary
77 Sherman Street
Hartford, CT 06105
Tel. (860)509-9543
Fax (860)509-9551
Email: hirr@hartsem.edu
Website: www.hirr.hartsem.edu
Director of Research, Dr. David A. Roozen
Administrative Assistant, Mary Jane Ross

The Hartford Institute for Religion Research of Hartford Seminary was established in 1981, formalizing a research program initiated by the Seminary in 1974. Until recently it was known as The Center for Social and Religious Research. The Institute's work is guided by a disciplined understanding of the interrelationship between (a) the inner life and resources of American religious institutions and (b) the possibilities and limits placed on those institutions by the social and cultural context into which God has called them.

Its twenty-one-year record of rigorous, policy-relevant research, anticipation of emerging issues, commitment to the creative dissemination of learning, and strong connections to both theological education and the church has earned the Institute an international reputation as an important bridge between the scholarly community and the practice of ministry.

### Current or Recent Research

Some of the titles of current projects at the Institute are, "Organizing Religious Work for the 21st Century, Exploring 'Denominationalism';" "Cooperative Congregational Studies Project"; "Congregational Consulting Services"; "New England Religion Discussion Society (NERDS)"; "Congregational Studies Team." Descriptions of these programs are available on the Institute's website, listed above.

### Periodicals

*Praxis* is Hartford Seminary's magazine, which focuses on the activities and faculty of the Seminary.

## Institute for Ecumenical & Cultural Research

14027 Fruit Farm Road
P.O. Box 2000
Collegeville, MN 56321-2000
Tel. (320)363-3366
Fax (320)363-3313
Email: iecr@iecr.org; mbanken@iecr.org
Website: www.iecr.org
Exec. Dir., Dr. Don B. Ottenhoff
Administrative Assistant, Mary Beth Banken, OSB

The Institute for Ecumenical and Cultural Research brings together well-trained, creative, articulate men and women for careful thought and dialogue in a place of inquiry and prayer. The Resident Scholars Program welcomes researchers and their families for either individual semesters or for an entire academic year. Resident scholars work on their own projects but meet once a week for seminars, and have other occasions for conversation. Each scholar presents a public lecture. Ecumenism happens at the Institute as people come to know one another in community. The Institute is an independent corporation, but shares in the Benedictine and academic life of Saint John's Abbey and University, and of nearby Saint Benedict's Monastery and the College of Saint Benedict. In the summer the Institute uses its facilities for invitational consultations on subjects considered by the Board of Directors to be of special ecumenical interest.

In the Resident Scholars Program, the subjects of research are determined by the interests of the applicants who are invited to come by the admissions committee. While most of the work tends to be in traditional theological areas, we encourage people in all fields to consider applying, both because ecumenism is of concern across the spectrum of disciplines, and because the term "cultural" in our title extends our reach beyond theology and religious studies. In particular cases, work done here may have a denominational, congregational, or interfaith focus, but the Institute does not prescribe or delimit, in any narrow way, what is appropriate.

### Current or Recent Research

Recent summer consultations have had the following titles, "Ecumenical Formation: The Heart of the Matter" and "Igniting Biblical Imagination." Among subjects dealt with in earlier years are "Prayer in the Ecumenical Movement"; "Virtues for an Ecumenical Heart"; "The Price of Disunity"; "Living Faithfully in North America Today"; "Orthodoxy at Home in North America"; "Transmitting Tradition to Children and Young People"; "The Nature of Christian Hope"; "Women and the Church"; Jewish and Christian Relatedness to Scripture"; "Confessing Christian Faith in a Pluralistic Society."

### Periodicals
*Ecumenical People, Programs, Papers* is a bi-annual newsletter containing brief sketches of resident scholars, reports on Institute programs, and, in nearly every issue, an "An Occasional Paper" on a subject of ecumenical interest. The newsletter is free.

## Institute for the Study of American Evangelicals (ISAE)

Wheaton College
Wheaton, IL 60187
Tel. (630)752-5437
Fax (630)752-5516
Email: isae@wheaton.edu
Website: www.wheaton.edu/isae
Director, Dr. Edith Blumhofer
Reserch and Resource Assistant, Katria Delac

Founded in 1982, the Institute for the Study of American Evangelicals is a center for research and functions as a program of Wheaton College. The purpose of the ISAE is to encourage and support research on evangelical Christianity in the United States and Canada. The institute seeks to help evangelicals develop a mature understanding of their own heritage and to inform others about evangelicals' historical significance and contemporary role. For the most part, the ISAE focuses on historical research, with occasional sociological or economic researchers participating in the projects.

### Current or Recent Research
One recently completed project entitled "Hymnody in American Protestantism" was a research project focusing on the history of hymnology in American religious life. We have published two books from this project: *Singing the Lord's Song in a Strange Land* by University of Alabama Press and *Wonderful Words of Life: Hymns in American Protestant History and Theology* published by William B. Eerdmans.

Two new projects include "Confessional Traditions and American Christianity," a grant from the Lilly Endowment, Inc., and "The Changing Face of American Evangelicalism," a grant from the Henry Luce Foundation.

### Periodicals
*Evangelical Studies Bulletin (ESB)* is designed to aid both the scholar and the layman in his or her education and research of evangelicalism. Issued quarterly, the bulletin contains articles, book reviews, notices, a calendar of events, and bibliographic information on the latest dissertations, articles and books related to the study of evangelicals.

## Institute for the Study of American Religion

P.O. Box 90709
Santa Barbara, CA 93190-0709
Tel. (805)967-7721
Email: jgordon@linkline.com
Website: www.americanreligion.org
Director, Dr. J. Gordon Melton
Associate Director, Dr. James Beverley

The Institute for the Study of American Religion was founded in 1968 in Evanston, Ill. as a religious studies research facility with a particular focus upon the smaller religions of the United States. Those groups that it has concentrated upon have been known under a variety of labels including sect, cult, minority religion, alternative religion, non-conventional religion, spiritual movement, and new religious movement.

In the 1970's the Institute extended its attention to Canada and in the 1990s developed an even more global focus. In 1985, the institute moved to its present location in Santa Barbara, Calif. Over the years the institute built a large collection of both primary and secondary materials on the religious groups and movements it studied. In 1985 this collection of more than 40,000 volumes and thousands of periodicals and archival materials was deposited with the Davidson Library at the University of California in Santa Barbara. The reference material exists today as the American Religions Collection and is open to scholars and the interested public. The institute continues to support the collection with donations of additional materials.

**Current or Recent Research**

Today the institute has two main foci. It monitors all of the religious denominations, organizations, and movements functioning in North America and regularly publishes reports drawing from that activity in a series of reference books. The most important of these reference books is the *Encyclopedia of American Religions* (Detroit, Gale Group, 7th edition, 2002).

Among the most called-for information is factual data on the many new and more controversial religious movements, which are popularly labeled as "cults." The institute's second focus developed out of its more recent refocusing on the international scene, provoked by the international life of most of the religious groups which it has studied in previous decades.

## J.M. Dawson Institute of Church-State Studies at Baylor University

P.O. Box 97308
Waco, TX 76798-7308
Tel. (254)710-1510
Fax (254)710-1571
Email: derek_davis@baylor.edu
Website: www.baylor.edu/~Church_State
Director, Dr. Derek Davis
Administrative Assistant, Wanda Gilbert

Baylor University established the J.M. Dawson Institute of Church-State Studies in 1957, so named in honor of an outstanding alumnus, an ardent advocate of religious liberty, and a distinguished author of publications on church and state. The Institute is the oldest and most well-established facility of its kind located in a university setting. It is exclusively devoted to research in the broad field of church and state and the advancement of religious liberty around the world.

From its inception in 1957, the stated purpose of the Institute has been to stimulate academic interest and encourage research and publication in the broad area of church-state relations. In carrying out its statement of purpose, the Institute has sought to honor a threefold commitment, to be interfaith, interdisciplinary, and international.

**Current or Recent Research**

Some current research includes, Government persecution of minority religions in Europe; original intent of Founding Fathers regarding religion and public life; Christian Right views on political activism; conservative versus moderate Baptist views on church-state relations; role of civil religion in America; international treaties and religious liberty.

**Periodicals**

*Journal of Church and State* is the only scholarly journal expressly devoted to church-state relations.

## The Louisville Institute

1044 Alta Vista Road
Louisville, KY 40205-1798
Tel. (502) 992-9341
Fax (502) 894-2286
Email: jlewis@louisville-institute.org
Website: www.louisville-institute.org
Exec. Dir., Dr. James W. Lewis

The Louisville Institute is a Lilly Endowment program for the study of American religion based at the Louisville Presbyterian Seminary. As a program of Lilly Endowment, the Louisville Institute builds upon the Endowment's long-standing support of both leadership education and scholarly research on American religion. The distinctive mission of the Louisville Institute is to enrich the religious life of American Christians and to encourage the revitalization of their institutions by bringing together those who lead religious institutions with those who study them, so that the work of each might stimulate and inform the other. The Louisville Institute seeks to fulfill its mission through a coordinated strategy of grantmaking and convening within a programmatic focus on three issues. The first, Christian faith and life, concerns the character and role of the theology and spirituality that are effectively at work in the lives of American Christians. The second, religious institutions, asks how America's religious institutions might respond most constructively in the midst of the bewildering institutional reconfiguration occurring in American society.

The third, pastoral leadership, explores various strategies for improving the quality of religious leadership in North America. The several grant programs of the Louisville Institute offer financial support to a broad range of projects that seek to address both the mission of the Louisville Institute to bring pastors and academics together and the Institute's focus on Christian faith and life, religious institutions, and pastoral leadership. Although many of these grants support research projects, an increasing number of them support other types of projects that contribute to the work of the Louisville Institute.

220

**Current or Recent Research**

Please see the Louisville Institute website (listed above) for lists of recent grants made by the Louisville Institute.

**Periodicals**

*Intersections* newsletter

## The Pluralism Project

Harvard University
1531 Cambridge St.
Cambridge, MA 02139
Tel. (617)496-2481
Fax (617)496-2428
Email: staff@pluralism.org
Website: www.pluralsm.org
Director, Dr. Diana L. Eck
Managing Director, Grove Harris

The Pluralism Project was developed by Dr. Diana L. Eck at Harvard University to study and document the growing religious diversity of the United States, with a special view to its new immigrant religious communities. The religious landscape of the U.S. has radically changed in the past 30 years; in light of these changes, how Americans of all faiths begin to engage with one another in shaping a positive pluralism is one of the most important questions American society faces in the years ahead. In addressing these phenomena, the Project has three goals, 1) To document some further changes taking place in America's cities and towns by beginning to map their new religious demography with old and new mosques and Islamic centers, Sikh gurdwaras, Hindu and Jain temples, Buddhist temples and meditation centers, Zoroastrian and Taoist religious centers. 2) To begin to study how these religious traditions are changing as they take root in American soil and develop in a new context. How are they beginning to recreate their community life, religious institutions, rites and rituals, and forms of transmission in the cultural environment of the United States? 3) To explore how the United States is changing as we begin to appropriate this new religious diversity in our public life and institutions, and in emerging forms of interfaith relationships.

The Pluralism Project has the most comprehensive archive anywhere of the print materials of America's new immigrant religious communities, newsletters, serial publications, anniversary programs, handbooks, prayer books, calendars, and educational materials. The Project files also include research papers as well as a variety of materials donated directly by centers.

The Pluralism Project On-Line Directory maintains an extensive directory of religious centers in the United States. At present, this directory exists in a sortable database, with listings of over 6,000 centers across the U.S.

**Current or Recent Research**

The Pluralism Project produced a CD-ROM, *On Common Ground—World Religions in America*, to present some of the wide range of work that had emerged from three years of research. Further grants from the Ford Foundation and the Rockefeller Foundation have enabled the Project to extend its research on the American religious landscape. Numerous affiliate research reports from a wide network of university professors and students are available on their website. *Religious Diversity News* summarizes news stories on pressing issues in the United States including most minority faiths, with a companion *International News*; both of these resources are available online in searchable databases. A new video release, *Acting on Faith: Women and the New Religious Activism,*" is available from the Project, and one can subscribe to their electronic newsletter online.

# II. Directory of Selected Faith Communities in America

Compiling a directory of faith communities is an arduous but rewarding task in religiously plural America. In part, because the very self-understanding and definition of community varies so greatly from tradition to tradition. In order to present a reasonably parallel and well-balanced listing of organizations for each faith, care must be taken not to impose categories or terms from one's own universe of understanding upon other contexts. The very terms, "church," "membership," "denomination," "hierarchy" which are essential constructs of certain Christian universes of understanding, are rendered meaningless when applied to other faith groups.

Further, it is important to remember that many religious communities lack a centralized organization that speaks for the whole. Often, this lack of centralization reflects the existence of several distinct forms or branches of the religion. In some instances, different ethnic groups immigrating to the U.S., bring with them a distinctive form of their religion, which is particular to their culture of origin. In other cases, plural forms of a faith exist resulting from theological, political, or economic differences. Still other faith groups may be more tightly organized, but the religious center that provides guidance in matters of faith and, perhaps, even organizational discipline may not be in the United States. Hence, the organizations before us are not necessarily religious hierarchical organizations, but are often groups assembled for other purposes that are associated with a particular faith group, or subdivision of that faith group. Caution is advised in regarding these entries as one might regard a "church headquarters."

The compilation of any directory relies upon the existence of some common organizational structure within all the entities listed. Yet, when compiling a directory of faith groups, it cannot be assumed such organizational parallels exist. Oblique ways must be found to adequately represent individual faith groups. The many religious communities in the United States are associated with myriad organizations of all different types. Some of these are primarily places of worship; others are organizations seeking to represent either the religious community as a whole or some particular constituency within it. Others are community centers; some are educational groups; some are organizations particularly for women or youths; and some are political action groups. Still others are peace organizations or relief organizations. That said, a directory of this sort cannot include an exhaustive list of organizations for each faith group nationwide. The omission of any particular organization or branch of any of the major faith groups listed does not reflect a deliberate attempt to homogenize the rich pluralities that exist within faith groups. Instead, the listings that follow are intended to provide the interested reader with a few initial contacts within each religious community, in alphabetical order within the tradition.

Despite the above cautions, this directory provides a rich resource for readers and researchers who wish to learn more about other faith groups. The agencies listed here consist of organizations of importance within the communities they represent, and serve as excellent introductory points of contact with those communities.

In some cases, these religious communities are in a state of flux; the Internet is an excellent way to keep contact with changing religious organizations. There is a plethora of information available about nearly all religious traditions online, but sites vary widely in their accuracy and reliability. Nearly any Internet search engine will provide extensive links to information about specific religious traditions.

For directory information about national Interfaith organizations in the United States, please see Directory 1, "U.S. Cooperative Organizations." For directory information on local Interfaith organizations, please see Directory 7, "U.S. Regional and Local Ecumenical Bodies."

# BAHÁ'Í FAITH

The Bahá'í Faith arose in 19th-century Persia, and refers to followers of Mirza Hussein Ali Nuri, whom they call Bahá'u'lláh (Arabic for *Glory of God*). In 1863, Bahá'u'lláh proclaimed himself to be the Manifestation of God for the present age. His coming had been heralded in 1844 by Mirza Ali Muhammad, also known as the Báb (*the Door*) whom Bahá'ís consider a Manifestation of God as well. Shortly afterward there was a severe persecution. The Báb was executed in 1850; Bahá'u'lláh died in exile, under house arrest in Acre, Palestine, in 1892. Bahá'ís believe in Progressive Revelation. Thus, as the manifestation of God for the present age, Bahá'u'lláh is considered to be the most recent in a lineage of messengers which includes Abraham, Krishna, the Buddha, Zarathustra, Jesus, and Muhammad. The oneness of God, the oneness of religion, and the oneness of humanity (with stress on racial and gender equality) are key principles of the Bahá'í Faith. Bahá'u'lláh's son Abd-al-Baha organized the religion's sacred texts, and established its system of representative governance through consensus, collaboration, and consultation. This includes the Universal House of Justice (the supreme administrative body, which meets in Haifa, Israel), National Spiritual Assemblies, and Local Spiritual Assemblies.

**The Bahá'í National Center of the U.S.A.**
**and, The National Spiritual Assembly of the Bahá'ís of the United States**

1233 Central Street
Evanston, IL 60201
Tel. (847)869-9039 Fax (847)733-3578
Website: www.us.bahai.org

The home of the National Spiritual Assembly of the Bahá'ís of the United States, the center is an official source of information about the Bahá'í faith, resources on many issues (such as peace, justice, economic development, racial unity, and education), and networking with Bahá'í spiritual assemblies throughout the world, of which there are more than 1700 in the U.S.A.

# BUDDHISM

Buddhism is a Western term for the many and varied expressions of practices based on the teachings of Siddhartha Gautama, who lived in northern India c. 563-483 B.C.E. Called the Buddha (the Enlightened One) by his followers, Siddhartha proposed a Middle Way between self-indulgence and extreme Hindu asceticism. Central to Buddhist teaching are the Four Noble Truths: that life inevitably involves suffering; that the origin of suffering is desire; that suffering can be eradicated by extinguishing desire; and that the way to accomplish this is to follow the Noble Eightfold Path of morality, concentration, and wisdom. Buddhists "take refuge" in the Triple Gem: the Buddha, the *dhamma* (his teachings), and the *sangha* (the community). Buddhism has two major branches. Theravada (Way of the Elders) which defines the sangha primarily as the community of ascetics. Mahayana (Great Vehicle) defines the *sangha* as all Buddhists, and includes the many schools such as Pure Land, Zen (Ch'an), and Tibetan Buddhism. Vajrayana (Diamond Vehicle) is a rigorous form of Mahayana associated frequently (but not exclusively) with Tibetan practice. Distinctive Western eclectic forms have emerged in recent decades. While there is much variation, Buddhist practice is characterized by meditation, chanting, and emphasis on compassion. Although most practice-groups and temples function autonomously and some are affiliated with a particular teacher or movement, there are continuing local or regional attempts to bridge philosophical differences.

## American Buddhist Association

4524 N. Richmond Street
Chicago, IL 60625
Tel. (773)583-5794
Contact person, Richard Brandon (Zenyo)
Email: brightdawn_1@juno.org
Website: www.awakenedone.org

Founded in 1955 for the study and propagation of Buddhism and to encourage the understanding and application of Buddhist principles in the general American public, this organization's roots are in Japanese Buddhism (Jodo Shinshu and Zen), but is now independent and nonsectarian. It publishes books, pamphlets, and audio-visual materials, sponsors seminars, and acts as a resource center.

## American Buddhist Congress

3835 E. Thousand Oaks Blvd., Ste. 450
Westlake Village, CA 91362
Tel. (877)7BUDDHA, (877)728-3342
Email: BuddhistCongress@adelphia.net
Website: www.americanbuddhistcongress.org

Founded in 1987 to bring together individuals and organizations of various Buddhist traditions, denominations, and ethnic backgrounds, this organization is dedicated to developing an "American" Buddhism which, while paying respect and acknowledging its debt to Buddhist traditions of other cultures, seeks to synthesize American values and traditions with the basic Buddhism of the *tripitaka* (scripture) without the linguistic and cultural aspects which are not understood or confusing to most Americans.

## Buddhist Churches of America

1710 Octavia St.
San Francisco, CA 94109
Tel. (415)776-5600
Fax (415)771-6293
Email: bcahq@pacbell.net
Website: buddhistchurchesofamerica.org

Founded in 1899, this is a national headquarters and resource center for temples in the Japanese Shin (Pure Land) tradition. It also serves as a regional center of the World Fellowship of Buddhists.

## Buddhist Council of the Midwest

1812 Washington Street
Evanston, IL 60202
Tel. (847)869-5806
Website: www.buddhapia.com/hmu/bcm/front.htm

Incorporated as a nonprofit religious organization in 1987, the Buddhist Council of the Midwest includes 95 Buddhist groups in Chicago and the Midwest area. Its purpose is to foster the learning and practice of Buddhism; to represent the Midwest Buddhist community in matters affecting its membership; and to pool resources and coordinate efforts by its membership to create an atmosphere of fellowship and cooperation.

## Buddhist Council of the Northwest

1530 184th Ave. NE
Bellevue, WA 98008
Tel. (425)442-0986
Fax (425)643-2490
Email: info@buddhistcouncilnw.org
Website: www.buddhistcouncilnw.org

    Founded in 2002, the Buddhist Council of the Northwest is a nonprofit organization formed to pool resources and coordinate efforts by its membership. It serves as a consultant to and advocate for Buddhist temples, study groups, and individuals on matters of cultural, legal, and government concern related to the preservation and promotion of the Buddha Dhamma (teaching) in the Pacific Northwest, with special focus on the Asian-American Buddhist temples and communities, and realizing and respecting the diversity of Buddhist traditions within the Pacific Northwest. It initiates and supports religious, cultural or social welfare project which will help to disseminate the spirit of the Buddha Dhamma, and works ecumenically with over religious groups.

## The Buddhist Peace Fellowship

P.O. Box 3470
Berkeley, CA 94703
Tel. (510)655-6169
Fax (510)655-1369
Website: www.bpf.org

    Founded in 1978, the Buddhist Peace Fellowship's purpose is to serve as a catalyst for socially engaged Buddhism, striving for peace where there is conflict, promoting communication and cooperation among Buddhist *sanghas*, and seeking to alleviate suffering wherever possible. BPF's programs, publications, and practice groups link Buddhist teachings of wisdom and compassion with progressive social change.

## Insight Meditation Society

1230 Pleasant St.
Barre, MA 01005
Tel. (978)355-4378
Email: RC@dharma.org
Website: www.dharma.org

    Dedicated to *Vipassana* (insight meditation), a practice associated with Theravada Buddhism, this is a loosely associated network of groups, including major centers in New York, Washington D.C., Seattle, San Francisco, Los Angeles, and Boston, and smaller centers and practice groups in many other cities and towns.

## New York Buddhist Council

c/o Staten Island Buddhist Vihara
115 John Street
Staten Island, NY 10302
Tel. (718)556-2051

    An umbrella organization bringing together the leaders of New York City's Buddhist organizations across traditions and ethnicities.

## Soka Gakkai International-U.S.A.

National Headquarters
606 Wilshire Blvd.
Santa Monica, CA 90401
Tel. (310)260-8900
Fax (310)260-8917
Website: www.sgi-usa.org

    An American Buddhist association that promotes world peace and individual happiness based on the teachings of the Nichiren school of Mahayana Buddhism. Its members reflect a cross section of our diverse American society, representing a broad range of ethnic and social backgrounds.

## Texas Buddhist Council

8727 Radio Rd.
Houston, TX 77075
Tel. (281)467-7277

A regional coordinating body and advocacy agency for Buddhists of all traditions, it seeks to unify Buddhist practitioners across Texas by increasing communication between temples, study groups, and individuals from various schools and by providing opportunities for mutually beneficial interaction. It also strives to bring Buddhist teachings into the Texas mainstream through education and opportunities for social service.

### Unified Buddhist Church, Inc.

c/o Green Mountain Dharma Center
Ayers Lane, P.O. Box 182
Hartland-Four-Corners, Vermont 05049, U.S.A.
Tel. (802)436-1103
Fax (802)436-1101
Email: MF-Office@plumvillage.org
Website: www.plumvillage.org

This organization of Thich Nhat Hanh and his Sangha (network of practitioners and practice-groups) in the United States of America is also known as the Community of Mindful Living.

### Won Buddhism of America Headquarters

143-42 Cherry Avenue
Flushing, NY 11355
Tel. (718)762-4103
Email: info@wonbuddhism.info

Won Buddhism is a Korean reform movement with many non-Korean adherents and an abiding commitment to promoting interreligious understanding. While this is the seat of the U.S. branch of the Won movement, English-speakers may find it easier to contact the Manhattan temple, 431 East 57th Street, New York, NY 10022, Tel. (212)750-2774.

# HINDUISM

Hinduism is a western term for *Sanatana Dharma* (Eternal Law), the various streams of practice, ancient texts, and theological traditions associated with the Indian subcontinent. Hindus worship Brahman (Ultimate Reality) which is both the formless Absolute and the divine-as-personal. Hindus fall into schools of devotion to particular forms of the ultimate-as-personal: *Vaishnavites* (devotees of Vishnu, known also through his *avatars* [manifestations] such as Rama and Krishna), *Shaivites* (devotees of Shiva), and devotees of the Parashakti, the Divine Feminine (embodied variously as Durga, Parvati, Kali, and more). Other deities may be regarded as subordinate to, or as personifications of various functions of, the ultimate-as-personal. In the U.S.A., an ecumenical Hindu theology which sees all deities as pointers to the one Brahman, and emphasizes the non-duality of all things is also prevalent. Hindus agree for the most part on notions of *karma* and reincarnation, but fall into various philosophical schools of thought regarding the nature of the divine-human relationship. Yoga can take the form of intellectual or physical discipline, selfless service, or devotional practices. Most Hindus acknowledge the authority of the Vedas, but some pay more attention to the Bhaghavad-Gita, the Yoga Sutras of Patanjali, or the writings of the founding guru of their movement. Most North American *mandirs* (temples) are autonomous, but some are affiliated with a national or international movement.

### American Hindus Against Defamation

8914 Rotherdam Ave.
San Diego, CA 92129
Tel. (858)484-4564
Email: ajay@hindunet.org
Website: www.hindunet.org/ahad
Director, Mr. Ajay Shah

An organization devoted to defending Hindus from stereotyping and discriminatory or defamatory acts or speech.

### Bochasanwasi Shri Akshar Purushottam Swaminarayan Sanstha (B.A.P.S.)

BAPS Swaminarayan Sanstha
81 Suttons Lane
Piscattaway, NJ 08854-5723
Tel. (732)777-1414
Fax (732)777-1616

B.A.P.S. is a reform movement within the Vaishnava Visishtadvaita tradition. This North American headquarters serves about 50 temples in U.S. and Canada.

## Council of Hindu Temples of North America

Sri Siva Vishnu Temple
Lanham, MD
Tel. (301) 552-3335
Email: info@councilofhindutemples.org
Website: www.councilofhindutemples.org
President, Dr. Siva Subramanian

> The council is an independent association of autonomous temples and Hindu religious organizations which promotes the establishment of Hindu temples, encourages interfaith dialogue, and aids in instruction in Indian languages and culture.

## The International Society for Krishna Consciousness (ISKCON)

26 Second Avenue, 10003
(mail: P. O. Box 2509)
New York, NY 10009
Tel. (212)420-1130
Email: dayananda@msn.com

> A modern expression of Vaishnavite belief and practice established by A. C. Bhaktivedanta Swami (called Prabhubapa by devotees), ISKCON is one of many Indian spiritual movements planted in North America during the 20th century. The Second Avenue temple, which dates from 1966, was the movement's first in the U.S.

## Vedanta Society of New York

34 West 71st Street
New York, NY 10023
Tel. (212)877-9197, (212)873-7439
Email: Vedantasoc@aol.com
Website: www.vedanta-newyork.org
National Directory: www.vedantasociety.net/centers.asp

> Founded in 1894, Vedanta Society of New York is the first Vedanta Center in the West, and has been joined by many other such centers. The various centers of the Vedanta Society are affiliates of the worldwide network of the Ramakrishna Order, headquartered in Belur Math, India. Adherents follow the teachings and example of Sri Ramakrishna (1836-1886), his wife and spiritual companion, Holy Mother Sri Sarada Devi (1853-1920), and Ramakrishna's chief disciple, Swami Vivekananda.

# ISLAM

Islam dates to 7th-century Arabia and the Prophet Muhammad's receipt of the Qur'an. The word *islam* means submission, and is related linguistically to *salaam*, the Arabic word for peace. A Muslim is one who practices Islam by following the Qur'an and the Prophet's *sunna* (example). Muslims consider the Qur'an (in its original Arabic) to be God's speech. They place great emphasis on *tawhid* (God's absolute oneness and its implications). They use the Arabic word Allah for God, stressing that it refers to God as worshiped by Jews and Christians as well. Muslims are to maintain Five Pillars of practice. The first of these is *iman*, the profession of faith called the *shahadah*, which states "There is no God but God, and Muhammad is his prophet." The second, *salah*, is the ritual prayer, done five times a day, facing Mecca. Third is *zakah*, the returning of a portion of one's wealth to the community annually. Fourth is *swam*, the fasting from dawn to dusk during the holy month of Ramadan. Fifth is *Hajj*, the pilgrimage to Mecca once in one's lifetime (health and means permitting). Early in its history, Islam split into two branches, Sunni and Shi'ah (and several subgroups of the latter) which differ on some matters of belief and practice, and notions of transmission of authority.

## The Islamic Society of North America (ISNA)

P.O. Box 38
Plainfield, IN 46168
Tel. (317)839-8157
Fax (317)839-1840
Website: www.isna.net
Sec. Gen., Dr. Munner Fareed

> The Islamic Society of North America grew out of the Muslim Students Association and is one of the oldest national Muslim organizations in the United States. It has a varied program primarily serving the Muslim community, but also seeks to promote relations between Muslims and non-Muslims. It has a speakers' bureau, film loans, library assistance program, and several other services. It has

226

also has a number of publications. Its annual convention during Labor Day weekend usually in Chicago attracts over 35,000 participants.

## Council for American-Islamic Relations (CAIR)

453 New Jersey Ave. SE
Washington DC 20003-4034
Tel. (202)488-8787
Fax (202)488-0833
Email: info@cair.com
Website: www.cair.com
    CAIR's mission is to enhance understanding of Islam, encourage dialogue, protect civil liberties, empower American Muslims, and build coalitions that promote justice and mutual understanding.

## Islamic Circle of North America (ICNA)

166-26 89th Avenue
Jamaica, NY 11432
Tel. (718)658-1199
Fax (718)658-1255
Website: www.icna.org
    A non-ethnic, non-sectarian grassroots organization with a varied program of education and support for Muslims. Its subsidiary, ICNA Relief, provides humanitarian aid wherever it is needed.

## The Mosque Cares (Ministry of Imam W. Deen Mohammed)

P.O. Box 1061
Calumet City, IL 60409
Tel. (708)798-6750
Fax (708)798-6827
Email: WdMinistry@aol.com
Website: www.themosquecares.com
    Also known as the American Society of Muslims, this is the headquarters of the community in association with the leadership of W. D. Mohammed.

## Muslim American Society

P.O. Box 1896
Falls Church, VA 22041
Tel. (703)998-6525
Fax (703)998-6526
Email for General Information: mas@masnet.org
Email for Inquiries by non-Muslims: sg@masnet.org
Website: www.masnet.org
    Founded in 1992, this is a charitable, religious, social, cultural, and educational, not-for-profit organization. It is a pioneering Islamic organization, an Islamic revival, and reform movement that uplifts the individual, family, and society. This organization is not to be confused with the ministry of W. D. Mohammad, which once used this name.

## Muslim Peace Fellowship

P.O. Box 271
Nyack, New York 10960
Tel. (845)358-4601
Fax (845)358-4924
Email: mpf@mpfweb.org
Website: www.mpfweb.org
    The Muslim Peace Fellowship (*Ansar as-Salam*) is a network of peace and justice-oriented Muslims of all backgrounds who are dedicated to making the beauty of Islam evident in the world.

## Muslim Public Affairs Council (MPAC)

3010 Wilshire Blvd. Ste. 217
Los Angeles, CA 90010
Tel. (213)383-3443
Fax (213)383-9674
Email: inf@mpac.org
Website: www.mpac.org
Exec. Dir, Salam Al-Marayati

SOURCES

227

MPAC seeks to establish a vibrant American Muslim community that will enrich American society through promoting the Islamic values of mercy, justice, peace, human dignity, freedom, and equality for all.

# JAINISM

Jainism is an ancient Indian religion based on the notion that, periodically, humanity is blessed with a series of twenty-four *tirthankaras* (crossing-makers)—great spiritual leaders who attain infinite knowledge; revive a way of life that is based on the principles of non-harming, non-attachment, and open-mindedness, and directed by right knowledge, right faith, and right conduct; establish an order of renunciates; and assist in the liberation of countless other human beings from the cycle of reincarnation. Vardhamana (599–527 B.C.E.), a contemporary of the Buddha, was the twenty-fourth and last *tirthankara* for the current eon, and is known as Mahavira (Great Hero). His sermons provide the core of Jain scriptures, the Agam Sutras, but Jainism's two main branches differ over the exact contents. Jainism stresses asceticism. Digambara (sky-clad) monks renounce all clothing; Svetambara (white-clad) monks and nuns wear simple, white robes. Both branches may use *murtis* (images) of *tirthankaras* in devotional practice, but Digambara *murtis* will be plainer. The doctrine of *ahimsa* (non-harming) leads to strict vegetarianism, avoidance of animal products of any kind, and avoidance of interpersonal conflicts. Mahatma Gandhi was influenced greatly by Jain teachings.

## JAINA: Federation of Jain Associations in North America

P.O. Box 700
Getzville, NY 14068
Tel. (716)636-5342
Email: jainahq@jaina.org
Website: www.jaina.org

An umbrella organization linking local U.S. and Canadian Jain associations. It seeks to promote Jain principles and better understanding of Jainism. It also engages in humanitarian work.

## Siddhachalam International Mahavira Jain Mission

65 Mud Pond Road
Blairstown, NJ 07825
Tel. (908)362-9793
Fax (908)362-9649
Email: info@siddhachalan.org
Website: www.siddhachalan.org

Founded by Acharya Shri Shushil Kumarji in 1983, this resident community for monks, nuns, laymen, and laywomen is described as the first Jain pilgrimage site outside India. It promotes *ahimsa* for world peace, vegetarianism, and nonviolence to animals; and is headquarters for the International Jain Mission, the World Fellowship of Religions, and the World Jain Congress.

# JUDAISM

Judaism is one of the world's oldest religions, encompassing a rich and complex tradition that has evolved over centuries and has given rise to, or influenced, other major world traditions. Numerous expressions of Judaism have always coexisted with one another, as they do today. The central concern shared by all is to live in relation to God and to follow God's will. Jews understand themselves to be in covenant with God, who is the one transcendent God, Creator of the Universe. God revealed the Torah to the people of Israel as his way of life. History brought the Jewish people into contact with many cultures and civilizations, contacts that continuously transformed the nature of their worship, the understanding of God's law, and even their conceptualization of peoplehood. At the time of the second Diaspora, or great migration of Jews throughout the Middle East, North Africa, and Europe at the beginning of the common era, was the rise of the Rabbinical Tradition, with its emphasis on the study of scripture. Today's Judaism has grown out of these roots. In the 19th century, Reform Judaism arose in Europe and the United States as one Jewish response to modernity. Conservative Judaism and Reconstructionism are branches of Jewish practice that first developed in America. Orthodox Judaism also has a number of modern forms.

## ALEPH Administrative Office

7000 Lincoln Drive #B2
Philadelphia, PA 19119-3046
Email: alephajr@aol.com
Website: www.aleph.org
CEO, Ms. Susan Saxe

A core institution of the Jewish Renewal movement dedicated to the Jewish people's sacred purpose of partnership with the Divine in the inseparable tasks of healing the world and healing our hearts.

## The American Jewish Committee

P.O. Box 705
New York, NY 10150
Fax (212)891-1492
Email: pr@ajc.org
Website: www.ajc.org
Exec. Dir., David A. Harris

Founded in 1906, The AJC protects the rights and freedoms of Jews worldwide; combats bigotry and anti-Semitism, and promotes democracy and human rights for all. It is an independent community-relations organization, with strong interest in interreligious relations and public-policy advocacy. The AJC publishes the *American Jewish Yearbook*, and *Commentary* magazine.

## The Anti-Defamation League of B'nai B'rith

823 United Nations Plaza
New York, NY 10017
Tel. (212)885-7707
Fax (212)867-0779
Website: www.adl.org
National Dir., Abraham H. Foxman

Since 1913, the Anti-Defamation League has been involved in combating and documenting anti-Semitism. It also works to secure fair treatment for all citizens through law, education and community relations.

## Jewish Council for Public Affairs

443 Park Ave. S., 11th Floor
New York, NY 10016
Tel. (212)684-6950
Fax (212)686-1353
Email: contactus@thejcpa.org
Website: www.jewishpublicaffairs.org

This national coordinating body for the field of Jewish community relations comprises 13 national and 122 local Jewish communal agencies. Through the Council's work, and in its collaboration with other religious groups, its constituent agencies work on public policy issues, both international and domestic.

## Jewish Reconstructionist Federation

Beit Derora, 1010 Greenwood Avenue
Jenkintown, PA 19046
Tel. (212)782-8500
Fax (215) 782-8805
Email: info@jrf.org
Website: www.jrf.org

Fosters the establishment and ongoing life of Reconstructionist congregations and fellowship groups. Publishes *The Reconstructionist* and other materials. Rabbis who relate to this branch of Judaism are often members of the Reconstructionist Rabbinical Association.

## Religious Action Center of Reform Judaism

2027 Massachusetts Ave. NW
Washington, DC 20036
Tel. (202)387-2800
Fax (202)667-9070
Email: rac@urj.org
Website: www.rac.org
Exec. Dir., Rabbi David Saperstein

The Religious Action Center pursues social justice and religious liberty by mobilizing the American Jewish community and serving as its advocate in the capitol of the United States.

SOURCES

## The Union of Orthodox Jewish Congregations of America

11 Broadway
New York, NY 10004-1003
Tel. (212)613-8124
Fax (212)564-9058
Website: www.ou.org
Exec. Vice Pres., Rabbi Tzvi Hersh Weinreb

The national central body of Orthodox synagogues since 1898, providing *kashrut* supervision, women's and youth organizations, and a variety of educational, religious, and public policy programs and activities. Publishers of *Jewish Action* magazine and other materials. The Rabbinical Council of America is the related organization for Orthodox Rabbis.

## Union of Reform Judaism

633 Third Ave.
New York, NY 10017
Tel. (212)650-4000
Fax (212)650-4169
Website: www.urj.org
Pres., Rabbi Eric H. Yoffie

The central congregational body of Reform Judaism, founded in 1873. It serves approx. 875 affiliated temples and its members through religious, educational, cultural, and administrative programs. Women's Men's and Youth organizations. *Reform Judaism* is one of its publications. The Central Conference of American Rabbis is the affiliated rabbinical body.

## The United Synagogue of Conservative Judaism

155 Fifth Ave.
New York, NY 10010-6802
Tel. (212)533-7800
Fax (212)353-9439
Website: www.uscj.org
Exec. Vice Pres., Rabbi Jerome M. Epstein

The International organization of 800 congregations, founded in 1913. Provides religious, educational, youth, community and administrative programming. Publishes *United Synagogue Review* and other materials. The Rabbinical Assembly is the association of Conservative Rabbis.

# NATIVE AMERICAN TRADITIONAL SPIRITUALITY

Native American spirituality is difficult to define or categorize because it varies so greatly across the continent. Further, it is deeply entwined with elements of nature which are associated with different geographical regions. For example, while Plains Indians possess a spiritual relationship with the buffalo, Indigenous Peoples from the Northwest share a similar relationship with salmon. Hence, the character of Native American spirituality is dependent, to some extent, on the surrounding geography and its incumbent ecosystems. Despite this great variety, there are some similarities which allow us to consider the many Native American forms of spirituality together: Contrary to popular belief, Native American peoples are monotheistic; they do not worship the sun or buffalo or salmon, but rather understand that these elements of nature are gifts from the "Great Mystery," and are parts of it. Today, while still working toward religious freedom in the United States, Native Americans are also struggling to protect sacred sites, which they consider to be comparable to "churches." But since these sites are actually part of the land, not man-made structures, many are constantly under attack for the natural resources they contain. Such exploitation of these resources is an offense to the Native American sense of spirituality, which views resources like timber, oil, and gold, as gifts from the Great Mystery. The struggle to protect and respect these sacred sites is a universal and essential part of Native American spirituality.

## National Congress of American Indians (NCAI)

1301 Connecticut Ave. NW, Ste. 200
Washington, DC 20036
Tel. (202)466-7767
Fax (202)466-7797
Email: ncia@ncia.org
Website: www.ncai.org
Exec. Dir., Jacqueline Johnson

The National Congress of American Indians (NCAI), founded in 1944, is the oldest, largest and most representative national Indian organization serving the needs of a broad membership of American Indian and Alaska Native governments. NCAI stresses the need for unity and cooperation among tribal governments and people for the security and protection of treaty and sovereign rights. As the preeminent national Indian organization, NCAI is organized as a representative congress aiming for consensus on national priority issues.

The NCAI website contains links for a directory of Indian nations in the continental U.S. and Alaska as well as a directory of tribal governments. There are also links to other Native American websites.

## Native American Rights Fund (NARF)

1506 Broadway
Boulder, CO 80302
Tel. (303)447-8760
Fax (303)433-7776
Email: pereira@narf.org
Website: www.narf.org
Exec. Dir., John Echohawk

The Native American Rights Fund is the nonprofit legal organization devoted to defending and promoting the legal rights of the Indian people. NARF attorneys, most of whom are Native Americans, defend tribes who otherwise cannot bear the financial burden of obtaining justice in the courts of the United States. The NARF mission statement outlines five areas of concentration: 1) preservation of tribal existence; 2) protection of tribal natural resources; 3) promotion of human rights; 4) accountability of government; 5) development of Indian law.

# SIKHISM

Sikhism was founded by Guru Nanak during the 15th and 16th centuries in the state of Punjab in northwestern India. Nanak was greatly influenced by the teachings of Kabir, a Muslim who became deeply inspired by Hindu philosophies. Kabir's poems called for a synthesis between Islam and Hinduism. In the footsteps of Kabir's wisdom, Nanak drew upon elements of Bhakti Hinduism and Sufi Islam: He stressed the existence of a universal, single God, who transcends religious distinctions. Union with God is accomplished through meditation and surrender to the divine will. Nanak also called for the belief in reincarnation, karma, and also the cyclical destruction and recreation of the universe. However, he rejected the caste system, the devotion to divine incarnations, priesthood, idol worship, all of which were elements of the Hindu tradition. Nanak was the first of ten *gurus*, or teachers. The fourth guru, built the Golden Temple in Amritsar, the Sikh religious center. The fifth guru compiled the *Adi Granth*, a sort of hymn-book of spiritual authority. All male sikhs are initiated into the religious brotherhood called the *Khalsa*. Members of this order vow never to cut their beard or hair, to wear special pants, to wear an iron bangle as an amulet against evil, to carry a steel dagger, and a comb.

## Sikh American Heritage Organization (SAHO)

P.O. Box 63
Wayne, IL 60184-0063
Tel. (630)377-5893
Fax (630)377-5893
Email: SikhAmerican@aol.com
Website: www.sikhamerican.org

Promotes and fosters fellowship with the American mainstream and minority communities while maintaining Sikh values, heritage, and identity; participates in Asian American events, interfaith programs, community affairs, social services, and other civic activities.

## Sikh American Legal Defense and Education Fund (SALDEF)

1413 K Street
5th Floor
Washington, DC 20005
Tel. (202)393-2700
Fax (202)318-4433
Website: www.saldef.org

Formerly Sikh Mediawatch and Research Task Force (SMART), SALDEF is a national civil rights and educational organization which provides legal assistance, educational outreach, legislative advocacy, and media relations.

## Sikh Coalition

396 Broadway, Suite 701
New York, N.Y. 10013
Email: info@sikhcoalition.org
Website: www.sikhcoalition.org

Founded in response to bias attacks following the September 11, 2001, Sikh Coalition defends civil rights and liberties, educates the broader community about Sikhs and diversity, promotes local community empowerment, and fosters civic engagement amongst Sikh Americans.

## Sikh Foundation

580 College Avenue
Palo Alto, CA 94306
Tel. (650)494-7454
Fax (650)494-3316
Email: info@sikhfoundation.org
Website: www.sikhfoundation.org

Founded in 1967 to promote the heritage and future of Sikhism, the Sikh Foundation's sponsors academic courses, conferences and chairs of Sikh studies at leading universities in the West; promotes Sikh art exhibitions and the establishing permanent Sikh art galleries at major museums worldwide; and works to provide the community with highest quality of educational products on Sikhism.

## Sikh Research Institute

P.O. Box 690504
San Antonio, TX 78269-0504
Tel. (210)582-3371
Fax (210)582-3002
Email: info@sikhri-org
Website: www.sikhri.org

The goals of this organization are leadership enhancement, community revival, and facilitation of connections between various Sikh organizations. It is active in interfaith work and education of Americans about Sikhism.

## World Sikh Council—America Region

P.O. Box 3635,
Columbus, Ohio 43210
Tel. (614)210-0591
Fax (419)535-6794
Email: contact@worldsikhcouncil.org
Website: www.worldsikhcouncil.org
Secretary General, Dr. Manmohan Singh

A national unit of the World Sikh Council, WSC-AR is a representative and elected body of Sikh Gurudwaras and institutions in the U.S. Its members include 31 Gurudwaras (Sikh places of worship) and 6 other Sikh institutions across the nation. Its mission is to promote Sikh interests at the national and international level focusing on issues of advocacy, education, and well-being of humankind

# ZOROASTRIANISM

The western name for "The Good Religion" based on the teachings of the Prophet Zarathustra, who lived sometime between 1200 and 550 B.C.E., in what is now Iran. Zoroastrians from India are often called Parsis (Parsees). Zoroastrians worship Ahura Mazda (Wise Lord): the one God, the uncreated, immanent and transcendent source of all that is good, true, and beautiful, for whom the only appropriate symbol is fire. Zoroastrians fall into two streams: traditionalists, for whom all ancient Zoroastrian texts are scripture; and progressives, for whom only the Gathas (the oldest texts) have authority. The two streams differ sharply in beliefs and practices. There are also informal denominations according to which of several Zoroastrian calendars one prefers.

## Federation of Zoroastrian Associations of North America (FEZANA)

6464 Pumpkin Seed Circle, # 108
Boca Raton, FL 33433
Website: www.fezana.org
Secretary, Ms. Rita Engineer

A coordinating organization for Zoroastrian Associations of North America.

# 6. United States Regional and Local Ecumenical Bodies

One of the many ways Christians and Christian churches relate to one another locally and regionally is through ecumenical bodies. The membership in these ecumenical organizations is diverse. Historically, councils of churches were formed primarily by Protestants, but many local and regional organizations now include Orthodox and Roman Catholics. Many are made up of congregations or judicatory units of churches. Some have a membership base of individuals. Others foster cooperation between ministerial groups, community ministries, coalitions, or church agencies. While "council of churches" is a term still commonly used to describe this form of cooperation, other terms such as "conference of churches," "ecumenical councils," "churches united," "metropolitan ministries," are coming into use. Ecumenical organizations that are national in scope are listed in Directory 1, "United States Cooperative Organizations."

An increasing number of ecumenical bodies have been exploring ways to strengthen the interreligious aspect of life in the context of religious pluralism in the U.S. today. Some organizations in this listing are fully interfaith agencies primarily through the inclusion of Jewish congregations in their membership. Other organizations nurture partnerships with a broader base of religious groups in their communities, especially in the areas of public policy and interreligious dialogue.

This list does not include all local and regional ecumenical and interfaith organizations in existence today. The terms regional and local are relative, making identification somewhat ambiguous. Regional councils may cover sections of large states or cross state borders. Local councils may be made up of several counties, towns, or clusters of congregations. State councils or state-level ecumenical contacts exist in 45 of the 50 states. These state-level or multi-state organizations are marked with a "*". The organizations are listed alphabetically by state.

## ALABAMA

### Greater Birmingham Ministries
2304 12th Ave. N, Birmingham, AL 35234-3111, Tel. (205)326-6821 Fax (205)252-8458
Email: robert@gbm.org
Website: www.gbm.org
Media Contact, Robert Montgomery
Exec. Dir., Scott Douglas
Economic Justice, Co-Chpsn., Helen Holdefer, Betty Likis
Direct Services, Chpsn., Patty Warren
Faith in Community, Chpsn., Patricia Ross
Finance & Fund-Raising, Chpsn., Richard Ambrose
Pres., Tom Forsee
Treas., Helen Tibbs Wilson
Major Activities: Direct Service Ministries (Food, Utilities, Rent and Nutrition Education, Shelter); Alabama Arise (Statewide legislative network focusing on low income issues); Economic Justice Issues (Low Income Housing and Advocacy, Health Care, Community Development, Jobs Creation, Public Transportation); Faith in Community Ministries (Interchurch Forum, Interpreting and Organizing, Bible Study)

### Interfaith Mission Service
701 Andrew Jackson Way NE, Huntsville, AL 35801-3504, Tel. (256)536-2401 Fax (256) 536-2284
Email: ims@hiwaay.net

Exec. Dir., Susan J. Smith
Pres., Richard C. Titus
Major Activities: Foodline & Food Pantry; Local FEMA Committee; Ministry Development; Clergy Luncheon; Workshops; Response to Community Needs; Information and Referral; Interfaith Understanding; Christian Unity; Homeless Needs; School Readiness Screenings

## ALASKA

### Alaska Christian Conference
Episcopal Diocese of Alaska, 1205 Denali Way, Fairbanks, AK 99701-4178, Tel. (907)452-3040
Email: mmcdonald@gci.net
Media Contact, Rt. Rev. Mark MacDonald
Pres., The Rt. Rev. Mark MacDonald
Vice Pres., The Rev. David I. Blanchett, 1100 Pullman Drive, Wasilla, AK 99654, Tel. (907)352-2517
Treas., Carolyn M. Winters, 2133 Bridgewater Drive, Fairbanks, AK 99709-4101, Tel. (907) 456-8555
Major Activities: Legislative & Social Concerns; Resources and Continuing Education; New Ecumenical Ministries; Communication; Alcoholism (Education & Prevention); Family Violence (Education & Prevention); Native Issues; Ecumenical-Theological Dialogue; HIV-AIDS Education and Ministry; Criminal Justice

233

## ARIZONA

### Arizona Ecumenical Council*

4423 N. 24th St., Ste. 750, Phoenix, AZ 85016, Tel. (602)468-3818 Fax (602)468-3311
Email: aec@aecunity.org
Website: www.aecunity.org
Media Contact, Exec. Dir., Rev. Jan Olav Flaaten, Tel. (602)468-3818, Fax (602)468-3311, Cell (602)670-1594
Pres., Bishop Michael Neils
Major Activities: Facilitating collaboration among the 20 judicatories for Theological Dialogue, Services of Prayer, Public Policy and Social Justice, Church Leadership School (called Survival School), Local Ecumenism (encouraging and being a resource for local ecumenical groupings), Earth Care Commission (presents annual "Caring for Creation" conference), Arizonans for the Protection of Exploited Children and Adults (APECA), Disaster Relief, Non-Violence Education for Youth, Souper-Bowl

## ARKANSAS

### Arkansas Interfaith Conference*

P.O. Box 151, Scott, AR 72142, Tel. (501)961-2626 Fax
Email: aicark@aol.com
Media Contact, Conf. Exec., Mimi Dortch
Conf. Exec., Mimi Dortch
Pres., Rev. Steve Copley, 6701 JFK Blvd., N. Little Rock, AR. 72116 (Methodist)
Sec., Imam John Hasan, P.O. Box 1607, Little Rock, AR 72203. (Muslim)
Treas., Jim Davis, Box 7239, Little Rock, AR 72217 (Catholic)
Major Activities: Institutional Ministry; Interfaith Executives' Advisory Council; Interfaith Relations; Church Women United; Our House-Shelter; Legislative Liaison; Ecumenical Choir Camp; Tornado Disaster Relief; Camp for Jonesboro School Children Massacre; Welfare Reform Work; Med Center Chaplaincy; Peace Service

## CALIFORNIA

### California Council of Churches-California Church Impact*

2715 K Street, Suite D, Sacramento, CA 95816, Tel. (916)442-5447 Fax (916)442-3036
Email: cccinfo@calchurches.org
Website: www.calchurches.org
Media Contact, Exec. Dir., The Rev. Rick Schlosser
Exec. Dir., The Rev. Rick Schlosser
Major Activities: Monitoring State Legislation; California IMPACT Network; Legislative Principles; Food Policy Advocacy; Family Welfare Issues; Health; Church-State Issues; Violence Prevention; Child Care Program-Capacity Coordinator to Increase Quality Child Care within California for the Working Poor; Building Bridges of Understanding: An Interfaith Response to Septerber 11.

### The Council of Churches of Santa Clara County

1710 Moorpark Avenue, San Jose, CA 95128, Tel. (408)297-2660 Fax (408)297-2661
Email: councilofchurches@sbcglobal.net
Website: www.councilofchurches-scc.org
Media Contact, Co-executive Directors: Rev. Margo Tenold, Rev. Diana Gibson
Co-executive Directors: Rev. Margo Tenold, Rev. Diana Gibson
Major Activities: Social Education-Action; Ecumenical and Interfaith Witness; Affordable Housing; Environmental Ministry; Family-Children; Convalescent Hospital Ministries; Gay Ministry; Strengthening Congregations for Ministry

### The Ecumenical Council of Pasadena Area Churches

P.O. Box 41125, 444 E. Washington Blvd., Pasadena, CA 91114-8125, Tel. (626)797-2402 Fax (626)797-735
Email: ecpac@prodigy.net
Media Contact, Rev. Frank B. Clark
Exec. Dir., Rev. Frank B. Clark
Major Activities: Christian Education; Community Worship; Community Concerns; Christian Unity; Ethnic Ministries; Hunger; Peace; Food, Clothing Assistance for the Poor; Emergency Shelter

### Ecumenical Council of San Diego County

1880 Third Ave., #13, San Diego, CA 92101, Tel. Fax
Email: nrankin@ecsd.org
Website: www.ecsd.org
Media Contact, Nancy Rankin
Exec. Dir. (interim), Nancy Rankin
Pres. Jane Barry
Treas., Rev. Robert Ard
Major Activities: Interfaith Shelter Network-Rational Shelter and El Nido Transitional Living Program; Emerging Issues; Faith Order & Witness; Worship & Celebration; Ecumenical Tribute Dinner; Advent Prayer Breakfast; Seminars and Workshops; Called to Dance Assn.; Children's Sabbath Workshops and events; Edgemoor Chaplaincy; Stand for Children events; Continuing Education for clergy and laypersons; Inter-Religious Council; Sacred Spaces church tour

### Fresno Metro Ministry

1055 N. Van Ness, Ste. H, Fresno, CA 93728, Tel. (559)485-1416 Fax (559)485-9109
Email: metromin@fresnometmin.org
Website: www.fresnometmin.org

Media Contact, Exec. Dir., Rev. Walter P. Parry
Exec. Dir., Rev. Walter P. Parry
Pres., Tony Gonzalez
Major Activities: Hunger Relief & Nutrition Advocacy; Cultural Diversity and Anti-Racism; Health Care Advocacy; Environmental Health and Quality; Access and Public Health; Public Education Concerns; Children's Needs; Air Quality; Ecumenical & Interfaith Celebrations & Cooperation; Youth Needs; Community Network Building; Human Services Facilitation; Anti-Poverty Efforts; Low-Income and Immigrant Leadership Development related to public policies

## Interfaith Council of Contra Costa County

1543 Sunnyvale Ave., Walnut Creek, CA 94596, Tel. (925)933-6030 Fax (925)952-4554
Media Contact, Rev. Steve Harms
Chaplains, The Rev. Charles Tinsley; The Rev. Duane Woida; The Rev. Harold Wright; Laurie Maxwell
Pres., Rev. Steve Harms
Treas., Robert Bender
Major Activities: Institutional Chaplaincies, Community Education, Interfaith Cooperation; Social Justice

## Interfaith Service Bureau

2212 K. St., Sacramento, CA 95816-4923, Tel. (916)456-3815 Fax (916)456-3816
Email: isbdexter@aol.com
Media Contact, Exec. Dir., Dexter McNamara
Executive Dir., Dexter McNamara
Pres., Richard Montgomery
Vice-Pres., Lloyd Hanson
Major Activities: Religious and Racial Cooperation and Understanding; Welfare Reform Concerns; Refugee Resettlement & Support; Religious Cable Television; Violence Prevention; Graffiti Abatement

## Marin Interfaith Council

1510 5th Avenue, San Rafael, CA 94901-1807, Tel. (415)456-9657 Fax (415)456-6959
Email: admin@marinifc.org
Website: marininterfaithcouncil.org
Media Contact, Exec. Dir., Rev. Carol Hovis
Exec. Dir., Rev. Carol Hovis
Major Activities: Interfaith Dialogue; Education; Advocacy; Convening; Interfaith Worship Services & Commemorations

## Northern California Interreligious Conference

534 22nd St., Oakland, CA 94612, Tel. (510)433-0822 Fax (510)433-0813
Email: NCIC@igc.org
Website: ncic.home.igc.org
Media Contact, Pres., Rev. Phil Lawson

Exec. Dir., Catherine Coleman
Pres., Rev. Phil Lawson
Vice-Pres., Esther Ho
Sec., Robert Forsberg
Major Activities: Peace with Justice Commission; Interreligious Relationships Commission; Public Policy Advocacy; Welfare Reform, founding member of California Council of Churches and of California Interfaith Power and Light; Soul of Justice, a spiritual and leadership concepts interactive performance troupe of teens and young adults; death penalty moratorium; video produced for sale for congregations; organizations to study legal, theological and social implications of marriage and same-gender marriage, widening our circle of religious groups participating; a cooperating circle of URL.

## Pomona Inland Valley Council of Churches

1753 N. Park Ave., Pomona, CA 91768, Tel. (909)622-3806 Fax (909)622-0484
Media Contact, Dir. of Dev., Mary Kashmar
Pres., The Rev. Henry Rush
Acting Exec. Dir., The Rev. La Quetta Bush-Simmons
Sec., Ken Coates
Treas., Anne Ashford
Major Activities: Advocacy and Education for Social Justice; Ecumenical Celebrations; Hunger Advocacy; Emergency Food and Shelter Assistance; Farmer's Market; Affordable Housing; Transitional Housing

## San Fernando Valley Interfaith Council

10824 Topanga Canyon Blvd., No. 7, Chatsworth, CA 91311, Tel. (818)718-6460 Fax (818)718-0734
Email: info@vic-LA.org
Website: www.vic-LA.org
Media Contact, Comm. Coord., Eileen Killoren, ext. 3002
Pres., Barry Smedberg; Ext. 3011
Chair, Board of Dir., Earl Fagin, Esq.
Major Activities: Seniors Multi-Purpose Centers; Nutrition & Services; Meals to Homebound; Meals on Wheels; Interfaith Reporter; Interfaith Relations; Social Adult Day Care; Hunger-Homelessness; Volunteer Care-Givers; Clergy Gatherings; Food Pantries and Outreach; Social Concerns; Aging; Hunger; Human Relations; Immigration Services; Self-Sufficiency Program for Section 8 Families

## South Coast Interfaith Council

759 Linden Ave., Long Beach, CA 90813, Tel. (562)983-1665 Fax (562)983-8812
Email: scic@charterinternet.com
Website: www.SCInterfaith.org

235

Media Contact, Exec. Dir., Rev. Ginny Wagener
Exec. Dir., Rev. Ginny Wagener
President, John Ishuaradas Abdallah
Farmers' Markets, Rev. Dale Whitney
Centro Shalom, Amelia Nieto
Good Samaritan Counseling Center, Dr. William Scar
Major Activities: Farmers' Markets; CROP Hunger Walks; Church Athletic Leagues; Community Action; Easter Sunrise Worships; Interreligious Dialogue; Justice Advocacy; Martin Luther King, Jr. Celebration; Violence Prevention; Long Beach Interfaith Clergy; Publishing Area Religious Directories, Crop Hunger, Walks, Counseling services

## Southern California Ecumenical Council
195 So. Hill Ave., Pasadena, CA 91106, Tel. (626) 578-6371 Fax (626)578-6358
Email: scec1@scec1.net
Website: www.scec1.net
Media Contact, Exec. Dir., Rev. Albert G. Cohen
Exec. Dir., The Rev. Albert G. Cohen
Pres., The Rev. Dr. Paul Lance
Treas., The Rev. Larry Hixon
Sec., Ms. Lucy Guernsey
Vice Pres. The Rev. Dr. Gwynne Guibord
Second Vice Pres., Carol Kostura
Members at Large, The Rev. Frank Brougker, Rev. Sara Armstrong, Fr. Alexei Smith
Faith and Order Chair, The Rev. Dr. Rod Parrott
Past Pres., Fr. Arshag Khatchadorian
Major Activities: Consultation with the regional religious sector concerning the well-being and spiritual vitality of this most diverse and challenging area

## Westside Interfaith Council
P.O. Box 1402, Santa Monica, CA 90406, Tel. (310)394-1518 Fax (310)576-1895
Media Contact, Rev. Janet A. Bregar
Exec. Dir., Rev. Janet A. Bregar
Major Activities: Meals on Wheels; Community Religious Services; Convalescent Hospital Chaplaincy; Homeless Partnership; Hunger & Shelter Coalition

## COLORADO

## Colorado Council of Churches*
3690 Cherry Creek S. Dr., Denver, CO 80209, Tel. (303)825-4910 Fax (303)744-8605
Email: jrryan7@qwest.net
Website: www.coloradocouncilofchurches.org
Media Contact, Council Exec., Rev. Dr. James R. Ryan
Pres., Rev. Janet Schlenker
Staff Assoc, Dori Wilson
Major Activities: Addressing issues of Christian Unity, Justice, and Environment

## Interfaith Council of Boulder
3700 Baseline Rd., Boulder, CO 80303, Tel. (303)494-8094
Media Contact, Pres., Stan Grotegut, 810 Kalma Ave., Boulder, CO 80304, Tel. (303)443-2291
Pres., Stan Grotegut
Major Activities: Interfaith Dialogue and Programs; Thanksgiving Worship Services; Food for the Hungry; Share-A-Gift; Monthly Newsletter

## CONNECTICUT

## Association of Religious Communities
325 Main St., Danbury, CT 06810, Tel. (203)792-9450 Fax (203)792-9452
Email: arc325@aol.com
Media Contact, Exec. Dir., Rev. Phyllis J. Leopold
Exec. Dir., Rev. Phyllis J. Leopold
Pres., The Rev. Mark Lingle
Major Activities: Refugee Resettlement; Family Counseling; Family Violence Prevention; Affordable Housing, Inter-Faith Dialogue, Racial Justice

## The Capitol Region Conference of Churches
60 Lorrain St., Hartford, CT 06105, Tel. (860)236-1295 Fax (860)236-8071
Email: crcc@conferenceofchurches.org
Website: www.conferenceofchurches.org
Media Contact, Exec. Dir., Rev. Shelley Copeland
Exec. Dir., The Rev. Shelley Copeland
Pastoral Care & Training, Dir., The Rev. Kathleen Davis
Aging Project, Dir., Barbara Malcolm
Community Organizer, Joseph Wasserman
Broadcast Ministry Consultant, Ivor T. Hugh
Pres., Mr. David O. White
Major Activities: Organizing for Peace and Justice; Aging; Legislative Action; Cooperative Broadcast Ministry; Ecumenical Cooperation; Interfaith Reconciliation; Chaplaincies; Low-Income Senior Empowerment; Anti-Racism Education

## Center City Churches
40 Pratt Street, Ste. 210, Hartford, CT 06103-1601, Tel. (860)728-3201 Fax (860)549-8550
Email: info@centercitychurches.org
Website: www.centercitychurches.org
Media Contact, Exec. Dir., Paul C. Christie
Exec. Dir., Paul C. Christie
Pres., Jeannette L. Brown
Treas., Rusty Spears
Major Activities: Senior Services; Family Resource Center; Food Pantry; Assistance & Advocacy; After-School Tutoring and Arts Enrichment; Summer Day Camp; Housing for persons with AIDS; Community Soup Kitchen

236

## Christian Community Action

168 Davenport Ave., New Haven, CT 06519, Tel. (203)777-7848 Fax (203)777-7848
Email: cca@ccahelping.org
Website: www.ccahelping.org
Media Contact, Exec. Dir., The Rev. Bonita Grubbs
Exec. Dir., The Rev. Bonita Grubbs
Major Activities: Emergency Food Program; Used Furniture & Clothing; Security and Fuel; Emergency Housing for Families; Advocacy; Transitional Housing for Families

## Christian Conference of Connecticut*

60 Lorraine St., Hartford, CT 06105, Tel. (860) 236-4281 Fax (860)236-9977
Email: ssidorak@aol.com
Website: www.christconn.org
Media Contact, Exec. Dir., Rev. Dr. Stephen J. Sidorak, Jr.
Exec. Dir., The Rev. Dr. Stephen J. Sidorak, Jr.
Pres., The Rt. Rev. Andrew D. Smith
Vice Pres., The Rev. Dr. Robert C. Dvorak
Sec., The Rev. Samuel N. Slie
Treas., Mr. Minot B. Nettleton
Major Activities: Communications; Institutional Ministries; Connecticut Ecumenical Small Church Project; Ecumenical Forum; Faith & Order; Social Concerns; Public Policy; Peace and Justice Convocation; Restorative Justice & Death Penalty; Interreligious Dialogue; AntiNuclear Activities; Problem Gambling; Jewish-Christian Dialogue

## Council of Churches of Greater Bridgeport, Inc.

180 Fairfield Ave., Bridgeport, CT 06604, Tel. (203)334-1121 Fax (203)367-8113
Email: ccgb@ccgb.org
Website: www.ccgb.org
Media Contact, Exec. Dir., Rev. Dr. Brian R. Schofield-Bodt
Exec. Dir., Rev. Dr. Brian R. Schofield-Bodt
Pres. Bonnie McWain
Vice Pres., Rev. Hopeton Scott
Sec., Valerie Peterkin
Treas., Roger Perry
Major Activities: Youth in Crisis; Youth in Crisis Hotline, Responses & Safe Places; Host Home Shelter Care; Criminal Justice Services for Ex-offenders; Jail Ministry; Hunger Outreach and Networking; Ecumenical & Interreligious Relations, Prayer and Celebration; Covenantal Ministries; Homework Help; Summer Programs; Race Relations-Bridge Building

## Council of Churches and Synagogues of Southwestern Connecticut

461 Glenbrook Rd, Stamford, CT 06901, Tel. (203)348-2800 Fax (203)358-0627
Email: council@flvax.ferg.lib.ct.us
Website: www.interfaithcouncil.org
Media Contact, Comm. Ofc., Lois Alcosser
Exec. Dir., Jack Penfield, Interim Director
Major Activities: Partnership Against Hunger; The Food Bank of Lower Fairfield County; Friendly Visitors and Friendly Shoppers; Senior Neighborhood Support Services; Christmas in April; Interfaith Programming; Prison Visitation; Friendship House; Help a Neighbor; Operation Fuel; Teaching Place

## Greater Waterbury Interfaith Ministries, Inc.

16 Church St, Waterbury, CT 06702, Tel. (203) 756-7831 Fax (203)419-0024
Media Contact, Exec. Dir., Carroll E. Brown
Exec. Dir., Carroll E. Brown
Pres., The Rev. Dr. James G. Bradley
Major Activities: Emergency Food Program; Emergency Fuel Program; Soup Kitchen; Ecumenical Worship; Christmas Toy Sale; Annual Hunger Walk

## Manchester Area Conference of Churches

P.O. Box 3804, Manchester, CT 06045-3804, Tel. (860)647-8003
Media Contact, Exec. Dir., Denise Cabana
Exec. Dir., Denise Cabana
Dir. of Community Ministries, Joseph Piescik
Dept. of Ministry Development, Dir., Karen Bergin
Pres., Rev. Charles Ericson
Vice Pres., Theresa Ghabrial
Sec., Jean Richert
Treas., Clive Perrin
Major Activities: Provision of Basic Needs (Food, Fuel, Clothing, Furniture); Emergency Aid Assistance; Emergency Shelter; Soup Kitchen; Reentry Assistance to Sex Offenders; Pastoral Care in Local Institutions; Interfaith Day Camp; Advocacy for the Poor; Ecumenical Education and Worship

## New Britain Area Conference of Churches (NEWBRACC)

830 Corbin Ave., New Britain, CT 06052, Tel. (860)229-3751 Fax (860)223-3445
Media Contact, Acting Exec. Dir., Rev. Teresa A. Hughes
Acting Exec. Dir., The Rev. Teresa A. Hughes
Pastoral Care-Chaplaincy, The Rev. Ron Smith; The Rev. Will Baumgartner
Pres., The Rev. Charles Tillet
Treas., Dierdre Elloian
Major Activities: Worship; Social Concerns; Emergency Food Bank Support; Communications-Mass Media; Hospital; Elderly Programming; Homelessness and Hunger Programs; Telephone Ministry

## DELAWARE

### The Christian Council of Delaware and Maryland's Eastern Shore*

2020 N. Tatnall Street, Wilmington, DE 19802, Tel. (302)-656-5441 Fax

Website: www.DeMdSynod.org

Media Contact, Pres., Bishop Wayne P. Wright, Diocese of Delaware, 2020 N. Tatnall Street, Wilmington, DE 19802

Pres., Bishop Wayne P. Wright, Diocese of Delaware, 2020 N. Tatnall Street, Wilmington, DE 19802

Major Activities: Exploring Common Theological, Ecclesiastical and Community Concerns; Racism; Prisons

## DISTRICT OF COLUMBIA

### The Council of Churches of Greater Washington

5 Thomas Circle N.W., Washington, DC 20005, Tel. (202)722-9240 Fax (202)722-9240

Media Contact, Exec. Dir., The Rev. Rodger Hall Reed, Sr.

Pres., The Rev. Lewis Anthony

Exec. Dir., The Rev. Rodger Hall Reed, Sr.

Program Officer, Daniel M. Thompson

Major Activities: Promotion of Christian Unity-Ecumenical Prayer & Worship; Coordination of Community Ministries; Summer Youth Employment; Summer Camping-Inner City Youth; Supports wide variety of social justice concerns

### InterFaith Conference of Metropolitan Washington

1426 Ninth St., NW, Washington, DC 20001-3344, Tel. (202)234-6300 Fax (202)234-6303

Email: ifc@ifcmw.org

Website: www.ifcmw.org

Media Contact, Exec. Dir., Rev. Dr. Clark Lobenstine

Exec. Dir., Rev. Dr. Clark Lobenstine

Admn. Sec., Judy Bond

Pres., Mrs. Carole Miller

1st Vice Pres., Siva Subramanian, M.D.

Chpsn., Rev. Dr. Robert Maddo

Sec., Mrs. Iris Lav

Treas., Sheikh Bassam Estwani

Major Activities: Helps end hunger, homelessness, and racism. Strengthens families and youth and deepens understanding by bringing together 10 world religions to build a just, compassionate community in metropolitan Washington D.C.

## FLORIDA

### Christian Service Center for Central Florida, Inc.

808 W. Central Blvd., Orlando, FL 32805-1809, Tel. (407)425-2523 Fax (407)425-9513

Website: www.christianservicecenter.org

Media Contact, Exec. Dir., Robert F. Stuart

Exec. Dir., Robert F. Stuart

Family Emergency Services, Dir., Rev. Haggeo Gautier

Fresh Start, Dir., Rev. Haggeo Gautier

Pres., Dr. Bryan Fulwider

Treas., Peter Reinert

Sec., Terry Bitner

Major Activities: Provision of Basic Needs (food, clothing, shelter); Emergency Assistance; Noon-time Meals; Collection and Distribution of Used Clothing; Shelter & Training for Homeless; Children After-School and Summer Programs

### Florida Council of Churches*

5025 Southampton Circle, Tampa, FL 33647, Tel. (813)910-1532 Fax (813)435-3239

Email: rmeyer@floridachurches.org

Website: www.floridachurches.org

Media Contact, Exec. Dir., Rev. Russell L. Meyer

Exec. Dir., The Rev. Russell L. Meyer

Major Activities: Justice and Peace; Disaster Response; Legislation & Public Policy; Local Ecumenism; Farmworker Ministry; Cherishing the Creation (Environmental Stewardship)

## GEORGIA

### Georgia Christian Council*

P.O. Box 7193 (2370 Vineville Ave. ), Macon, GA 31209-7193, Tel. (478)743-2085 Fax (478)743-2085

Email: GAChristiancouncil@alltel.net

Media Contact, Exec. Dir., Rev. Leland C. Collins

Exec. Dir., Rev. Leland C. Collins

Pres., Bishop B. Michael Watson, 3370 Vineville, Ave., Suite 101, Macon, GA 31204

Sec., Dr. Willis Moore, 5312 W. Mountain St., Suite 200, Stone Mountain, GA 30083-2073

Major Activities: Local Ecumenical Support and Resourcing; Legislation; Rural Development; Racial Justice; Networking for Migrant Coalition; Aging Coalition; Ga. To Ga. With Love; Medical Care; Prison Chaplaincy; Training for Church Development; Souper Bowl; Disaster Relief; Clustering; Development of Local Ecumenism; Prison Ministry; Hunger Advocacy; Family Advocacy; Developing Discipleship

### The Regional Council of Churches of Atlanta

2195 Defoor Hills Rd., Suite L, Atlanta, GA 30318, Tel. (404)389-0590 Fax (404)389-0594

Email: info@rccatl.org

Website: www.rccatl.org

Pres., Dr. Robert Franklin

Vice Pres., Mr. Steve Brown

Vice Pres., Dr. R. Alan Culpepper
Vice Pres., Rev. Tim McDonald
Sec., Dr. C.P. Huang
Treas., Ms. Dorothy James
Exec. Dir., Roy Craft
Assoc. Dir., Ethel Ware Carter
Major Activities: Forums of ecumenical interests; promotional collaboration and communication across denominational lines; and across geographical areas of Atlanta, interfaith work, coalition building.

## IDAHO

### The Regional Council for Christian Ministry, Inc.

237 N. Water, Idaho Falls, ID 83403, Tel. (208) 524-9935 Fax
Email: rccm@onewest.net
Media Contact, Daniel Sene
Exec. Sec., Daniel Sene
Major Activities: Island Park Ministry; Community Food Bank; Community Observances; F.I.S.H.

## ILLINOIS

### Churches United of the Quad City Area

630 9th St., Rock Island, IL 61201, Tel. (309) 786-6494 Fax (309)786-5916
Email: mjones@churchesunited.net
Website: www.churchesunited.net
Media Contact, Exec. Dir., Rev. Ronald Quay
Exec. Dir., Ronald Quay
Program Manager, Anne E. Wachal
Shelter Manager, Kit Miller
Financial Manager, Melanie Jones
Major Activities: Jail Ministry; Hunger Projects; Minority Enablement; Criminal Justice; Radio-TV; Peace; Local Church Development; Living Wage; Women's Shelter

### Community Renewal Society

332 South Michigan Ave. Suite 500, Chicago, IL 60604, Tel. (312)673-3835 Fax (312)427-6130
Email: bborst@crs-ucc.org
Website: www.crs-ucc.org
Media Contact, Exec. Dir., Dr. Calvin S. Morris

### Contact Ministries of Springfield

1100 E. Adams, Springfield, IL 62703, Tel. (217) 753-3939 Fax (217)753-8643
Email: rtarrcm@springnetl.com
Media Contact, Exec. Dir., Rita Tarr
Exec. Dir., Rita Tarr
Major Activities: Information; Referral and Advocacy; Ecumenical Coordination; Low Income Housing Referral; Food Pantry Coordination; Prescription & Travel Emergency; Low-Income Budget Counseling; 24 hours on call; Emergency Shelter On-site Women with Children

### Evanston Ecumenical Action Council

P.O. Box 1414, Evanston, IL 60204, Tel. (847) 475-1150 Fax (847)475-2526
Website: members.aol.com/eeachome/eeac.html
Media Contact, Comm. Chpsn., Ken Wylie
Dir. Hospitality Cntr. for the Homeless, Sue Murphy
Co-Pres., The Rev. Ted Miller; The Rev. Hardist Lane
Treas., Caroline Frowe
Major Activities: Interchurch Communication and Education; Peace and Justice Ministries; Coordinated Social Action; Soup Kitchens; Multi-Purpose Hospitality Center for the Homeless; Worship and Renewal, Racial Reconciliation, Youthwork

### Greater Chicago Broadcast Ministries

112 E. Chestnut St., Chicago, IL 60611-2014, Tel. (312)988-9001 Fax (312)988-9004
Email: gcbm@ameritech.net
Website: gcbm.org
Media Contact, Exec. Dir., Lydia Talbot
Pres., Bd. of Dir., Rev. Phil Blackwell
Exec. Dir., Lydia Talbot
Major Activities: Television, Inter-faith-Ecumenical Development; Social-Justice Concerns

### The Hyde Park & Kenwood Interfaith Council

5745 S. Blackstone Ave., Chicago, IL 60637, Tel. (773)752-1911 Fax (773)752-2676
Media Contact, Exec. Dir., Lesley M. Radius
Exec. Dir., Lesley M. Radius
Pres., The Rev. David Grainger
Sec., Barbara Krell
Major Activities: Interfaith Work; Hunger Projects; Community Development

### Illinois Conference of Churches*

522 East Monroe, Ste. 208, Springfield, IL 62701, Tel. (217)522-7099 Fax (217)522-7105
Email: adminstaff@ilconfchurches.org
Website: ilconfchurches.org
Media Contact, Exec. Dir., Rev. David A. Anderson, Email davidanderson@ilconf churches.org
Exec. Dir., Rev. David A. Anderson
Assoc. Dir., vacant
Pres., Rev. Donald E. Mason
Major Activities: Ecumenical Education and Dialogue, Public Policy Education and Advocacy.

### Oak Park-River Forest Community of Congregations

P.O. Box 3365, Oak Park, IL 60303-3365, Tel. (708)386-8802 Fax (708)386-1399

239

Website: http://lgrossman.comcomcong.htm
Media Contact, The Rev. Marguerite Rourke
Pres., The Rev. Marguerite Rourke
Treas., The Rev. Dwight Bailey
Major Activities: Community Affairs; Ecumenical-Interfaith Affairs; Youth Education; Food Pantry; Senior Citizens Worship Services; Interfaith Thanksgiving Services; Good Friday Services; Literacy Training; CROP-CWS Hunger Walkathon; Work with Homeless Through PADS (Public Action to Deliver Shelter; Diversity Education; Walk-in Ministry

## Peoria Friendship House of Christian Service

800 N.E. Madison Ave., Peoria, IL 61603, Tel. (309)671-5200 Fax (309)671-5206
Media Contact, Exec. Dir., Beverly Isom
Pres. of Bd., David Dadds
Major Activities: Children's After-School; Teen Programs; Recreational Leagues; Senior Citizens Activities; Emergency Food-Clothing Distribution; Emergency Payments for Prescriptions, Rent, Utilities; Community Outreach; Economic Development; Neighborhood Empowerment; GED Classes; Family Literacy; Mother's Group; Welfare to Work Programs

## INDIANA

## The Associated Churches of Fort Wayne & Allen County, Inc.

602 E. Wayne St., Fort Wayne, IN 46802, Tel. (260)422-3528 Fax (260)422-6721
Email: Vernchurch@aol.com
Website: www.associatedchurches.org
Media Contact, Exec. Dir., Rev. Vernon R. Graham
Exec. Dir., Rev. Vernon R. Graham
Administrative Assistant, Elaine Williamson
Foodbank—Director, Ellen Graham; John Kaiser; Isaac Nickleson; Gordon Matoon
Dir. of Prog. Development & Mission Outreach, Ellen Graham
Dir. Of Weekday Religious Education, Kathy Rolf
Pres., Charles Hutton, 10211 Greenmoor Drive, New Haven, Indiana 46774
Treas., The Rev. Alycia Smith, 3223 Hobson Rd., Ft. Wayne, IN 46805
Major Activities: Weekday Religious Ed.; Church Clusters; Overcoming Racism; A Baby's Closet;; Hunger Walk; Campus Ministry; Feeding the Babies; Food Bank System; Peace & Justice Commission; Welfare Reform; Endowment Development; Child Care Advocacy; Advocates Inc.; Ecumenical Dialogue; Children Feeding Children; Vincent House (Homeless); A Learning Journey (Literacy); Reaching Out in Love; The Jail Ministry; The Samaritan Counseling Center; Habitat for Humanity.

## Christian Ministries of Delaware County

401 E. Main St., Muncie, IN 47305, Tel. (317) 288-0601 Fax (317)282-4522
Email: christianministries@netzero.net
Website: www.christianministries.ws
Media Contact, Exec. Dir., Marie Evans
Exec. Dir., Marie Evans
Pres., Dr. J. B. Black, Jr.
Treas., Joan McKee
Major Activities: Baby Care Program; Youth Ministry at Detention Center; Community Church Festivals; Food Pantry; Emergency Assistance; CROP Walk; Social Justice; Family Life Education; Homeless Shelter (sleeping room only); Clothing and household items available free; workshops for low-income clients; homeless apartments available—short stays only at no cost; provide programs and workshops for pastors and churches in community; work with schools sponsoring programs.

## Church Community Services

629 S. 3rd Street, Elkhart, IN 46516-3241, Tel. (574)295-3673 Fax (574)295-5593
Email: ccs6293rd@aol.com
Website: www.soupofsuccess.com
Media Contact, Dean Preheim-Bartel
Exec. Director, Dean Preheim-Bartel
Major Activities: Financial Assistance for Emergencies; Food Pantry; Information and Referral; Clothing Referral; Rent Assistance; Utility Assistance; Medication Vouchers; Transportation Vouchers; Job and Life Skills Training Program for Women

## The Church Federation of Greater Indianapolis, Inc.

1100 W. 42nd St., Ste. 345, Indianapolis, IN 46208, Tel. (317)926-5371 Fax (317)926-5373
Email: churches@churchfederationindy.org
Website: www.churchfederationindy.org
Media Contact, Comm. Consultant, Julie Foster
Exec. Dir., Rev. Dr. Angelique Walker-Smith
Pres., Father John Beitans
Treas., Hugh Moore
Major Activities: "Preserving Christian Diversity & Impacting Our Society Through Unity in Christ": Organizing, Energizing, Mobilizing Since 1912 (John 17:20-23), Benevolence Ministry-C.R.O.P. (Church World Service; Celebration of Hope Partnership (Racial Reconciliation); Clergy ID Badge Program; Faith and Fathers; Family Congregation and Mentoring Program (FCMP); Hispanic-Latino Forum; Loving Our Children/Children's Sabbath; Greater Indianapolis Prayer Network to Stop the Violence; Ecumenical Project for Reconciliation and Healing; TV Broadcasts; Loaves and Fishes Advocacy Network

## Evansville Area Community of Churches, Inc.

713 N. 2nd Ave., Evansville, IN 47710, Tel. (812) 425-3524 Fax (812)425-3525
Email: eacc@evansville.net
Media Contact, EACC Administrator and Weekday Director, Janet Battram
Weekday Dir., Janet Battram
Pres., The Rev. G. Philip Hoy
Vice. Pres., Evelyn Cave
Sec., The Rev. C. E. Erickson
Treas., Paul Farmer
Major Activities: Food Pantry System; Jail Ministry; Weekday Christian Ed.; Ecumenical and Community Service & Activities

## Indiana Partners for Christian Unity and Mission

P.O. Box 88790, Indianapolis, IN 46208-0790, Tel. (800)746-2310 Fax (315)292-5990
Email: INDUnity@aol.com
Website: www.ipcum.org
Media Contact, Rev. Janet Wanner
Pres., The Rev. Janet Wanner
Treas., Mrs. Marilyn Moffett
Major Activities: Initiating dialogue on issues of social concern by organizing conferences on the death penalty, racism, welfare reform and violence; facilitating communication through an electronic newsletter and website; promoting the National Day of Prayer and the Week of Prayer for Christian Unity; and advancing Churches Uniting in Christ.

## Interfaith Community Council, Inc.

702 E. Market St., New Albany, IN 47150, Tel. (812)948-9248 Fax (812)948-9249
Email: icc@digicove.com
Website: www.interfaithinc.org
Media Contact, Exec. Dir., Houston Thompson
Exec. Dir., Houston Thompson
Programs - Emergency Assistance
RSVP, Dir., Ceil Sperzel
Major Activities: Emergency Assistance; Retired Senior Volunteer Program; New Clothing and Toy Drives; Emergency Food Distribution; Homeless Prevention; Kids' Café; Youth Development Services

**Kentuckiana Interfaith Community (see listing under Kentucky)**

## Lafayette Urban Ministry

525 N. 4th St., Lafayette, IN 47901, Tel. (317) 423-2691 Fax (317)423-2693
Media Contact, Exec. Dir., Joseph Micon
Exec. Dir., Joseph Micon
Advocate Coord., Rebecca Smith
Public Policy Coord., Harry Brown
Pres., John Wilson
Major Activities: Social Justice Ministries with and among the Poor

## United Religious Community of St. Joseph County

2015 Western Ave., Suite 336, South Bend, IN 46629, Tel. (574)282-2397 Fax (574)282-8014
Email: urc@urcsjc.org
Website: www.urcsjc.org
Media Contact, Exec. Dir., Carol Thon
Exec. Dir., Carol Thon
Pres.,Tom Callahan
Refugee Program Director, Carol McDonnell
Victim Impact Panel Director, Marchell Wesaw
Advocacy Centers Director, Marchell Wesaw
Major Activities: Religious Understanding; Interfaith-Ecumenical Education; Interfaith Newsletter "Torch"; CROP Walk; On-site Prayer Ministry; Peacemaker Awards; Hunger Education; Housing and Homelessness Issues; Clergy Education and Support; Refugee Resettlement; Victim Assistance; Advocacy for the Needy; Family Justice Center (Partner addressing chaplaincy), Housing Project for Grandparents raising Grandchildren

## Wellspring Interfaith Social Services, Inc. (previously West Central Neighborhood Ministry, Inc.)

1316 Broadway, Fort Wayne, IN 46802-3304, Tel. (219)422-6618 Fax (219)422-9319
Email: fzirille@wellspringinterfaith.org
Media Contact, Exec. Dir., Francis M. Zirille
Exec. Dir., Francis M. Zirille
Ofc. Mgr., J. R. Stopperich
Neighborhood Services Dir., Carol Salge
Senior Citizens Dir., Gayle Mann
Youth Director, Lois Ehinger
Major Activities: After-school Programs; Teen Drop-In Center; Summer Day Camp; Summer Overnight Camp; Information and Referral Services; Food Pantry; Nutrition Program for Senior Citizens; Senior Citizens Activities; Tutoring; Developmental Services for Families & Senior Citizens; Parent Club

## IOWA

## Churches United, Inc.

1035 3rd Ave., Suite 202, Cedar Rapids, IA 52403-2463, Tel. (319)366-7163 Fax (319)366-7163
Email: churchesunited@yahoo.com
Website: www.churchesunitedcr.org
Media Contact, Exec. Dir., Darci Morin
Exec. Dir., Darci Morin
Pres., Rev. David Loy
Treas., Ellen Bruckner
Major Activities: Communication-resource center for member churches; Community Information and Referral; Ecumenical Citywide Celebrations; Restorative Justice programs

## Des Moines Area Religious Council

3816 36th St., Ste. 202, Des Moines, IA 50310, Tel. (515)277-6969 Fax (515)274-8389

241

Email: info@dmreligious.org
Website: dmreligious.org
Media Contact, Exec. Dir., Forrest Harms
Exec. Dir., Forrest Harms
Pres., James Swanstrom
Pres. Elect, Faith Ferre
Treas., Leonara Waller
Major Activities: Education; Social Initiatives Advocacy; Mission; Emergency Food Pantry; Ministry to Widowed; Child Care Assistance, Compassion in Action; Cross-cultural

## Ecumenical Ministries of Iowa (EMI)*
P.O. Box 41487, Des Moines, IA 50311, Tel. (515)274-2278 Fax (515)274-2278
Email: emofiowa@aol.com
Website: www.iowachurches.org
Media Contact, Comm. Coord., Mary Swalla Holmes
Exec. Dir., Rev. Sarai Schnucker Beck
Major Activities: Facilitating the denominations' cooperative agenda of resourcing local expression of the church; assess needs & develop responses through Justice and Unity Commissions

## Iowa Religious Media Services*
3816 36th Street, Suite 100, Des Moines, IA 50310-4710, Tel. (515)277-2920 Fax (515) 277-0842
Email: questions@irms.org
Website: www.irms.org
Media Contact, Exec. Dir., Sharon E. Strohmaier
Exec. Dir., Sharon E. Strohmaier
Major Activities: Media Library for Churches in seven Denominations in the Midwest; Provide Video Production Services for Churches, Nonprofit & Educational organizations; will rent media to churches in the continental U.S. (details on the website)

### KANSAS

## Cross-Lines Cooperative Council
736 Shawnee Ave., Kansas City, KS 66105, Tel. (913)281-3388 Fax (913)281-2344
Email: theresa@cross-lines.org
Website: www.cross-lines.org
Media Contact, Dir. of Dev., Theresa Swartwood
Exec. Dir., Rick Caplan
Dir. of Programs, Lora McDonald
Major Activities: Emergency Assistance; Family Support Advocacy; Thrift Store; Workcamp Experiences; School Supplies; Christmas Store; Hunger Relief

## Inter-Faith Ministries—Wichita
829 N. Market, Wichita, KS 67214-3519, Tel. (316)264-9303 Fax (316)264-2233
Email: smuyskens@ifmnet.org
Website: www.ifmnet.org

Media Contact, Exec. Dir., Sam Muyskens
Exec. Dir., Rev. Sam Muyskens
Adm. Asst., Kathy Freed
ASAP Haiti, Dir. Bonnie Chadick
Homeless and Housing Services, Dir., Sandy Swank
Special Projects, Dir., Ashley Davis
Development, Dir., Karen Dobbin
Campaign to End Childhood Hunger, Karole Bradford Community Ministry/Restorative Justice/Family Group Conferencing/Racial Justice, Coord., Jeannine Little
Faith in Action, Coord., Richard Hanley
GoZones! Dir., Johanna Wilson
Major Activities: Communications; Urban Education; Interreligious Understanding; Community Needs and Issues; Theology and Worship; Hunger; Family Life; Multi-Cultural Concerns

## Kansas Ecumenical Ministries*
5833 SW 29th St., Topeka, KS 66614-2499, Tel. (785)272-9531 Fax
Email: kemstaff@ecunet.org
Media Contact, Interim Dir., Rev. Linda Kemp
Pres., Rev. Marvin Zehr
Vice Pres., Rev. Nancy Gammill
Sec., Tom McGraw
Exec. Dir., Dr. Joe M. Hendrixson
Pres.,Winnie Crapson
Vice Pres., Marvin Zehr
Sec., The Rev. Art Jaggard
Major Activities: State Council of Churches; Legislative Activities; Program Facilitation and Coordination; Education; Mother-to-Mother Program; Rural Concerns; Hate group monitoring; Children & Families; Faith and Order

### KENTUCKY

## Eastern Area Community Ministries
P.O. Box 43049, Louisville, KY 40253-0049, Tel. (502)244-6141 Fax (502)254-5141
Email: easternacm@cs.com
Media Contact, Acting Exec. Dir., Sharon Eckler
Acting Exec. Dir., Sharon Eckler
Board Pres., Rev. Elwood Sturtevant
Board Sec., Mary Stephens
Board Treas., Homer Lacy, Jr.
Youth and Family Services, Rachael Elrod
Older Adult Services, Associate Program Dir., Joni Snyder
Neighborhood Visitor Program, Acting Prog. Dir., Jane Parker
Major Activities: Emergency Assistance; Clothes Closet; Meals on Wheels; Community Worship Services; Good Start for Kids; Juvenile Court Diversion; Community Development; Transient Fund; Ministerial Association; Juvenile Court Diversion

## Fern Creek-Highview United Ministries

7502 Tangelo Dr., Louisvlle, KY 40228, Tel. (502)239-7407 Fax (502)239-7454
Email: FernCreek.Ministries@crnky.org
Media Contact, Exec. Dir., Kay Sanders, 7502 Tangelo Dr., Louisville, KY 40228, Tel. (502)239-7407
Exec. Dir., Kay Sanders
Pres., David Pooler
Major Activities: Ecumenically supported social service agency providing services to the community, including Emergency Financial Assistance, Food-Clothing, Health Aid Equipment Loans, Information-Referral, Advocacy, Checks; Holiday Programs, Life Skills Training; Mentoring; Case Management; Adult Day-Care Program

## Hazard-Perry County Community Ministries, Inc.

P.O. Box 1506, Hazard, KY 41702-1506, Tel. (606)436-0051 Fax (606)436-0071
Media Contact, Gerry Feamster-Roll
Exec. Dir., Gerry Feamster-Roll
Chpsn., Sarah Hughes
V. Chpsn., Susan Duff
Sec., Virginia Campbell
Treas., Margaret Adams
Major Activities: Food Pantry-Crisis Aid Program; Day Care; Summer Day Camp; After-school Program; Christmas Tree; Family Support Center; Adult Day Care; Transitional Housing

## Highlands Community Ministries

1140 Cherokee Rd., Louisville, KY 40204, Tel. (502)451-3695 Fax (502)451-3609
Email: hcmexecu@hotmail.com
Website: www.hcmlou.org
Media Contact, Exec. Dir., Stan Esterle
Exec. Dir., Stan Esterle
Major Activities: Welfare Assistance; Children Day Care; Adult DayHealth Care; Social Services for Elderly; Housing for Elderly and Handicapped; Ecumenical Programs; Interfaith Programs; Community Classes; Activities for Children; Neighborhood and Business organization

## Kentuckiana Interfaith Community

P.O. Box 7128, Louisville, KY 40257, Tel. (502) 587-6265 Fax (502)451-9827
Email: churchoffice@salemucc.com
Website: www.neighborhoodlink.com/org/kic
Media Contact, Exec. Dir., Rev. Douglas Fowler
Pres., Ron Gaddie
Vice Pres., Laura Metzger
Treas., Charles Hawkins
Major Activities: Christian-Jewish, Islamic, Bahai Ministries in Ky., Southern Ind.; Consensus Advocacy; Interfaith Dialogue; Community Hunger Walk; Racial Justice Forums; Network for Neighborhood-based Ministries; Hunger & Racial Justice Commission; Faith Channel—Cable TV Station, Horizon News Paper; Police-Comm. Relations Task Force; Ecumenical Strategic Planning; Networking with Seminaries & Religious-Affiliated Institutions

## Kentucky Council of Churches*

1500 Leestown Rd., Suite 108, Lexington, KY 40511, Tel. (859)269-7715 Fax (859)269-1240
Email: kcc@kycouncilofchurches.org
Website: www.kycouncilofchurches.org
Media Contact, Exec. Dir., Nancy Jo Kemper
Exec. Dir., The Rev. Dr. Nancy Jo Kemper
Pres., The Rev. Ron Gaddie
Kentucky Interchurch Disaster Recovery Program Coodinator., Mr. Harper Davis
Director Associate for Local Ecumenism, The Rev. W. Chris Benham Skidmore
Major Activities: Christian Unity; Public Policy; Justice; Disaster Response; Peace Issues; Anti-Racism; Health Care Issues; Local Ecumenism; Rural Land-Farm Issues; Gambling; Capital Punishment

## Ministries United South Central Louisville (M.U.S.C.L., Inc.)

1207 Hart Avenue, Louisville, KY 42013, Tel. (502)363-9087 Fax (502)363-9087
Media Contact, Exec. Dir., Rev. Antonio (Tony) Aja, M.Div., Tel. (502)363-2383, Email Tony_ Aja@pcusa.org
Ex. Dir., Rev. Antonio (Tony) Aja, M.Div.
Airport Relocation Ombudsman, Rev. Phillip Garrett, M.Div., Tel. (502)361-2706; E-mail, philombud@aol.com
Senior Adults Programs, Dir., Mrs. Jeannine Blakeman, BSSW
Emergency Assistance, Dir., Mr. Michael Hundley
Low-Income Coord., Ms. Wanda Irvio
Youth Services, Dir., The Rev. Bill Sanders, M.Div.
Volunteers Coord., Mrs. Carol Stemmle

## Northern Kentucky Interfaith Commission, Inc.

901 York St., P.O. Box 72296, Newport, KY 41072-0296, Tel. (859)581-2237 Fax (859) 261-6041
Website: www.nkyinterfaith.com
Media Contact, Exec. Dir., Rev. James A. Bishop
Pres., Mr. Paul Whalen
Sec., Ms.Cordelia Koplow
Treas., Mr. John Wilgus
Admin. Asst., Pat McDermott
Major Activities: Understanding Faiths; Meeting Spiritual and Human Needs; Enabling Churches to Greater Ministry

243

## Paducah Cooperative Ministry

1359 S. 6th St., Paducah, KY 42003, Tel. (270) 442-6795 Fax (270)442-6812
Email: pcministry@hotmail.com
Media Contact, Dir., Heidi Suhrheinrich
Dir., Heidi Suhrheinrich
Chpsn., Rev. Larry McBride
Vice Chpsn., Tommy Tucker
Major Activities: Programs for Hungry, Elderly, Poor, Homeless, Handicapped, Undereducated

## St. Matthew's Area Ministries

201 Biltmore Rd., Louisville, KY 40207, Tel. (502)893-0205 Fax (502)893-0206
Media Contact, Exec. Dir., Dan G. Lane
Exec. Dir., Dan G. Lane
Child Care, Dir., Janet Hennessey
Dir. Assoc., Eileen Bartlett
Major Activities: Child Care; Emergency Assistance; Youth Services; Interchurch Worship and Education; Housing Development; Counseling; Information & Referral; Mentor Program; Developmentally Disabled

## South East Associated Ministries (SEAM)

6500 Six Mile Ln., Ste.A, Louisville, KY 40218, Tel. (502)499-9350 Fax
Media Contact, Mary Beth Helton
Exec. Dir., Mary Beth Helton
Life Skills Center, Dir., Robert Davis
Youth Services, Dir., Bill Jewel
Pres., David Ehresman
Treas., Bill Trusty
Major Activities: Emergency Food, Clothing and Financial Assistance; Life Skills Center (Programs of Prevention and Case Management and Self-Sufficiency Through Education, Empowerment, Support Groups, etc.); Bloodmobile; Ecumenical Education and Worship; Juvenile Court Diversion; TEEN Court; Teen Crime & the Community

## South Louisville Community Ministries

Peterson Social Services Center, 4803 Southside Dr., Louisville, KY 40214, Tel. (502)367-6445 Fax (502)361-4668
Email: slcm@slcm.org
Website: www.slcm.org
Media Contact, Exec. Dir., J. Michael Jupin
Bd. Chair., Ray Whitener
Bd. Vice Chair., Jim Woodward
Bd. Treas., Greg Greenwood
Exec. Dir., Rev. J. Michael Jupin
Major Activities: Food, Clothing & Financial Assistance; Home Delivered Meals; Ecumenical Worship; Affordable Housing; Adult Day Care; Truancy Prevention; Dare to Care Kids Café

## Greater Baton Rouge Federation of Churches and Synagogues

3112 Convention St., Baton Rouge, LA 70806, Tel. (225)267-5600 Fax (225)267-5100
Website: gbrfed.org
Media Contact, Exec. Dir., Rev. Jeff Day
Exec. Dir., Rev. Jeff Day
Admn. Asst., Ashley Griffin
Pres., Rev. Amy Mercer
Pres.-Elect, Joyce Robinson
Treas., Melvin Davis
Major Activities: Combating Hunger; Interfaith Relations; Interfaith Concert; Race Relations; Interfaith Caregivers (Faith in Action)

## Greater New Orleans Federation of Churches

4640 S. Carrollton Ave, Suite 2B, New Orleans, LA 70119-6077, Tel. (504)488-8788 Fax (504)488-8823
Media Contact, The Rev. J. Richard Randels
Exec. Dir., The Rev. J. Richard Randels
Major Activities: Information and Referral; Food Distribution (FEMA); Forward Together TV Program; Sponsors seminars for pastors (e.g. church growth, clergy taxes, etc.); Police Chaplaincy; Fire Chaplaincy

## Louisiana Interchurch Conference*

527 North Boulevard, Fourth Floor, Baton Rouge, LA 70802, Tel. (225)924-0213 Fax (225)927-7860
Email: lainterchurch@aol.com
Website: www.lainterchurch.org
Media Contact, Exec. Dir., Rev. C. Dana Krutz
Exec. Dir., Rev. C. Dana Krutz
Pres., Bishop C. Garnett Henning
Major Activities: Ministries to Aging; Prison Reform; Liaison with State Agencies; Ecumenical Dialogue; Institutional Chaplains; Racism; Environmental; Public Policy Advocacy

## Maine Council of Churches*

19 Pleasant Ave., Portland, ME 04103, Tel. (207) 772-1918 Fax (207)772-2947
Email: info@mainecouncilofchurches.org
Website: www.mainecouncilofchurches.org
Media Contact, Comm. Dir., Karen Caouette
Exec. Dir., Rev. Jill Saxby
Assoc. Dir., Douglas Cruger
Admin. Asst., Sandra Buzzell
Pres., Br. Francis Blouin
Treas., Rev. Richard Swan
Major Activities: Criminal Justice Reform/ Restorative Justice; Economic Justice; Environmental Justice; Peace Issues; Civil Rights

244

## MARYLAND

### Central Maryland Ecumenical Council*

Cathedral House, 4 E. University Pkwy., Baltimore, MD 21218, Tel. (410)467-6194 Fax (410)554-6387
Email: cmec@bcpl.net
Media Contact, Exec. Dir., Martha Young
Pres., The Rev. Iris Farabee-Lewis
Major Activities: Interchurch Communications and Collaboration; Information Systems; Ecumenical Relations; Urban Mission and Advocacy; Staff for Judicatory Leadership Council; Commission on Dialogue; Commission on Church & Society; Commission on Admin. & Dev.; Ecumenical Choral Concerts; Ecumenical Worship Services

**The Christian Council of Delaware and Maryland's Eastern Shore (see listing under Delaware)**

### Community Ministries of Rockville

114 West Montgomery Ave., Rockville, MD 20850, Tel. (301)762-8682 Fax (301)762-2939
Email: asaenz@cmrocks.org
Media Contact, Managing Dir., Agnes Saenz
Exec. Dir. & Comm. Min., Mansfield M. Kaseman
Managing Dir., Agnes Saenz
Major Activities: Shelter Care; Emergency Assistance; Elderly Home Care; Affordable Housing; Political Advocacy; Community Education; Education to Recent Immigrants

### Community Ministry of Montgomery County

114 West Montgomery Ave., Rockville, MD 20850, Tel. (301)762-8682 Fax (301)762-2939
Media Contact, Exec. Dir., Rebecca Wagner
Exec. Dir., Rebecca Wagner
Major Activities: Interfaith Clothing Center; Emergency Assistance Coalition; The Advocacy Function; Information and Referral Services; Friends in Action; The Thanksgiving Hunger Drive; Thanksgiving in February; Community-Based Shelter

## MASSACHUSETTS

### Attleboro Area Council of Churches, Inc.

7 North Main St., Ste. 200, Attleboro, MA 02703, Tel. (508)222-2933 Fax (508)222-2008
Email: aacc@naisp.net
Media Contact, Pres., Bd. of Dir., Rev. Ruth Shaver
Exec. Adm., Kathleen Trowbridge
Staff Asst., Food 'n Friends Program Dir., Dorothy Embree
Hosp. Chplns., Rev. Dr. William B. Udall, Rev. Lynn MacLagan

Pres., Rev. Ruth Shaver, Minister of Christian Ed. And Family Life, Second Congregational Ch., 50 Pk. St., Attleboro, MA 02703
Treas., Mr. Richard Shaw, 70 Stanson Dr., N. Attleboro, MA 02760
Major Activities: Hospital Chaplaincy; personal Growth-Skill Workshops; Ecumenical Worship; Interfaith Worship; Media Resource Center; Referral Center; Communications-Publications; Community Social Action; Food 'n Friends Kitchens; Nursing Home Volunteer Visitation Program; Clergy Fellowship-Learning Events

### The Cape Cod Council of Churches, Inc.

P.O. Box 758, Hyannis, MA 02601, Tel. (508) 775-5073 Fax
Email: cccounchur@capecod.net
Media Contact, Exec. Dir., Diane Casey-Lee
Exec. Dir., Diane Casey-Lee
Chaplain, Rev. Sandra Junier
Chaplain, Rehabilitation Hospital of the Cape and Islands, Rev. Stanley Knull
Hand of Hope Outreach Center, P.O. Box 125, Dennisport, MA 02639, Tel. (508)394-6361
Major Activities: Social Concerns; Religious Education; Emergency Distribution of Food, Clothing, Furniture; Referral and Information; Church World Service; Interfaith Relations; Media Presence; Hospital & Jail Chaplaincy; Arts & Religion

### Cooperative Metropolitan Ministries

474 Centre St., Newton, MA 02158, Tel. (617) 244-3650 Fax (617)630-9172
Email: coopmet@aol.com
Website: www.coopment.org
Media Contact, Exec. Dir., Claire Kashuck
Exec. Dir., Claire Kashuck
Bd. Pres., Robert Stephens
Treas., Ricardo Neal
Clk., The Rev. John Odams
Major Activities: Low-Income; Suburban-Urban Bridges; Racial and Economic Justice

### Council of Churches of Greater Springfield

39 Oakland St., Springfield, MA 01108, Tel. (413)733-2149 Fax (413)733-9817
Media Contact, Asst. to Dir., Andrea Skeene
Exec. Dir., Rev. Dr. David F. Hunter
Community Min., Dir. Don A. Washington
Pres., The Rev. Dr. David Hunter
Treas., John Pearson, Esq.
Major Activities: Advocacy; Emergency Fuel Fund; Peace and Justice Division; Community Ministry; Hospital and Jail Chaplaincies; Pastoral Service; Crisis Counseling; Christian Social Relations; Relief Collections; Ecumenical and Interfaith Relations; Church-

Community Projects and Community Dialogues; Publication, *Knowing My Neighbor—Religious Beliefs and Traditions at Times of Death*

## Greater Lawrence Council of Churches

95 E. Haverhill Street, Lawrence, MA 01841, Tel. 978-686-4012 Fax 978-689-2006
Email: davidedwards@conversent.net
Website: greater-lawrence-churches.org
Media Contact, Exec. Dir., David Edwards
Exec. Dir., David Edwards
Pres., Jane Barlow
Vice-Pres., Rev. Dr. Richard Haley
Admn. Asst., Barbara Payson
Major Activities: Ecumenical Worship; Radio Ministry; Hospital and Nursing Home Chaplaincy; After-school Children's Program; Vacation Bible School, Interfaith care givers of Greater Lawrence

## Inter-Church Council of Greater New Bedford

412 County St., New Bedford, MA 02740-5096, Tel. (508)993-6242 Fax (508)991-3158
Email: administration@inter-churchcouncil.org
Website: www.inter-churchcouncil.org
Media Contact, Min., Rev. Edward R. Dufresne, Ph.D.
Exec. Min., Rev. Edward R. Dufresne, Ph.D.
Pres., The Rev. David Lima
Treas., George Mock
Major Activities: Counseling; Spiritual Direction; Chaplaincy; Housing for Elderly and Disabled; Urban Affairs; Community Spiritual Leadership; Parish Nurse Ministry; Accounting and Spiritual Care for the Developmentally Challenged; Ecumenical and Interfaith Ministries; Advocacy for the Homeless; Support for Urban School District; Opposition to Expanded Gambling

## Massachusetts Commission on Christian Unity

82 Luce St, Lowell, MA 01852, Tel. (978)453-5423 Fax (978)453-5423
Email: kgordonwhite@msn.com
Media Contact, Exec. Dir., Rev. K. Gordon White
Exec. Sec., Rev. K. Gordon White
Pres., Rev. Fr. Edward O'Flaherty, Ecumenical Officer, Roman Catholic Archdiocese of Boston
Major Activities: Faith and Order Dialogue with Church Judicatories; Guidelines & Pastoral Directives for Inter-Church Marriages; Guidelines for Celebrating Baptism in an Ecumenical Context

## Massachusetts Council of Churches*

14 Beacon St., Suite 416, Boston, MA 02108, Tel. (617)523-2771 Fax (617)523-1486
Email: www.council@masscouncilofchurches.org
Website: www.masscouncilofchurches.org
Media Contact, Dir., Rev. Dr. Diane C. Kessler
Exec. Dir., The Rev. Dr. Diane C. Kessler
Adjunct Assoc. Dir., The Rev. Dr. Carol Flett
Pres., The Rev. John Stendahl
Vice-Pres., Fr. John Maheras
Sec., The Rev. Sara Irwin
Treas., The Rev. Kenneth G. Y. Grant
Major Activities: Christian Unity; Education and Evangelism; Social Justice & Individual Rights; Ecumenical Worship; Services and Resources for Individuals and Churches

## Worcester County Ecumenical Council

128 Providence Street, Worcester, MA 01604-5432, Tel. (508)757-8385 Fax (508)795-7704
Email: wcec@verizon.net
Media Contact, Exec. Dir., Rev. Allyson D. Platt
The Rev. Allyson D. Platt, Email: wcec.Allyson@verizon.net
Pres.,Mrs. Fran Langille
Major Activities: Ecumenical worship and dialogue networking congregations together in partnerships of mission, education and spiritual renewal. Clusters of Churches; Ecumenical Worship and Dialogue; Interfaith Activities; Resource Connection for Churches; Group Purchasing Consortium

## MICHIGAN

## Bay Area Ecumenical Forum

103 E. Midland St., Bay City, MI 48706, Tel. (517)686-1360 Fax
Media Contact, Rev. Karen Banaszak
Major Activities: Ecumenical Worship; Community Issues; Christian Unity; Education; CROP Walk

## Berrien County Association of Churches

275 Pipestone, Benton Harbor, MI 49022, Tel. (616)926-0030 Fax (616)926-2159*51
Website: berrienchurches.org
Media Contact, Sec., Mary Ann Hinz
Pres., Rev. George Lawton
Dir., Street Ministry, The Rev. Yvonne Hester
Major Activities: Street Ministry; CROP Walk; Community Issues; Fellowship; Christian Unity; Hospital Chaplaincy Program; Publish Annual County Church Directory and Monthly Newsletter; Resource Guide for Helping Needy; Distribution of Worship Opportunity— Brochure for Tourists

## Grand Rapids Area Center for Ecumenism (GRACE)

207 East Fulton, Grand Rapids, MI 49503-3210, Tel. (616)774-2042 Fax (616)774-2883
Email: dbaak@graceoffice.org
Website: www.graceoffice.org

Media Contact, Rev. David P. Baak
Leadership Team: Rev. David P. Baak; Lisa H. Mitchell; Rev. David G. May
Major Activities: AIDS Care Network; Volunteer Transportation; Hunger Walk; Education; Christian Unity Worship (Ecumenical Lecture, Christian Unity Worship Events, Interfaith Dialogue Conference); (Affiliate, FISH for My People-transportation); Racial Justice Institute; West Michigan Call to Renewal (Response to Poverty Advocacy); Publications (Grace In~Site); Faith In Motion (Mass Transit and Land Use); Restorative Justice Coalition

## Greater Flint Council of Churches

310 E. Third St., Suite 600, Flint, MI 48502, Tel. (810)238-3691 Fax (810)238-4463
Email: gfcc1929@aol.com
Media Contact, Coord., Mrs. Constance D. Neely
Barbara Spaulding Westcott, Publicity Chairperson
President, Overseer Bernadel L. Jefferson
Major Activities: Christian Education; Christian Unity; Christian Missions; Nursing Home Visitor; Church in Society; American Bible Society Materials; Interfaith Dialogue; Church Teacher Exchange Sunday; Directory of Area Faiths and Clergy; Thanksgiving & Easter Sunrise Services; CROP Walks

## The Jackson County Interfaith Council

425 Oakwood, P.O. Box 156, Clarklake, MI 49234-0156, Tel. (517)529-9721
Media Contact, Exec. Dir., vacant
Exec. Dir., vacant
Major Activities: Chaplaincy at Institutions and Senior Citizens Residences; Martin L. King, Jr. Day Celebrations; Ecumenical Council Representation; Radio and TV Programs; Food Pantry; Interreligious Events; Clergy Directory

## The Metropolitan Christian Council: Detroit-Windsor

28 W. Adams, Suite 320, Detroit, MI 48226, Tel. (313)962-0340 Fax (313)962-9044
Email: councilweb@aol.com
Website: users.aol.com/councilweb
Media Contact, Rev. Richard Singleton
Exec. Dir., Rev. Richard Singleton
Meals for Shut-ins, Prog. Dir., John Simpson; Admin. Asst., Mrs. Elaine Kisner
Web Calendar Supervisor, Mr. Gerald Morgan
Major Activities: Theological and Social Concerns; Ecumenical Worship; Educational Services; Electronic Media; Print Media; Meals for Shut-Ins; Summer Feeding Program

## Muskegon County Cooperating Churches

1095 Third St., Suite 10, Muskegon, MI 49441-1976, Tel. (231)727-6000 Fax (231)727-0841

Media Contact, Prog. Coord., Delphine Hogston
Co-Presidents, Judy Clark-Ochs and Rev. Donna Smith-Snyder
Major Activities: Local Faith Community Information Source, Racial Reconciliation, Dialogue, & Healing; Multiracial Family Support; Responsible Fathers Empower-ment; Ecumenical Worship; Faith News TV Ministry; CROP Walk Against Hunger; Jewish-Christian Dialogue; Environmental Issues, Social Justice Issues, Pastoral Support, Homeless Sheltering, Second Harvest Gleaners Food Trucks

### SUBSIDIARY ORGANIZATION

**Muskegon Responsible Fathers' Initiative**
Tel. 231-725-7268, Fax 231-728-4558
Media Contact: Christopher Sandford, Program Coordinator
Major Activities: Responsible Fathers Empowerment; Providing education, job skills & support for fathers to connect and support their children financially, emotionally, & spiritually; Fatherhood skills for incarcerated fathers; Teen Pregnancy Prevention, Prisoner Re-Entry.

**Community Uniting for Peace**
Media Contact: Delphine Hogston, Secretary
Major Activities: Advocacy to remove the effects of Racism; Community Civil Rights Health Assessment Survey; Responsible Consumer Spending Initiative

**Interfaith Hospitality Network in Muskegon**
Media Contact: Delphine Hogston
Major Activities: Helping congregations shelter homeless families

**Community Connects Choir**
Media Contact: Darlene Collett
Major Activities: Winter Holiday Concert. Intentionally interracial, intergenerational, ecumenical singing blending gospel and traditional music. Supports other diverse music opportunities for the community.

**In the City for Good—Muskegon**
Media Contact: Kryssis Bjork
Major Activities: Bringing together residents, churches, schools, and businesses for hands-on activities to promote cultural diversity and community good. Back-to-school fairs including health screenings, summer work projects, and quarterly gatherings. Interfaith worship events and education. Focus is on urban areas of Muskegon County.

## MINNESOTA

## Arrowhead Interfaith Council*

102 W. 2nd St., Duluth, MN 55802, Tel. (218) 722-7166 Fax
Email: president@arrowheadinterfaith.org
Website: www.arrowheadinterfaith.org
Media Contact, Pres., Doug Bowen-Bailey
Pres., Doug Bowen-Bailey
Sec., Sister Lois Eckes
Treas., David Carlson

Major Activities: InterFaith Dialogue; Joint Religious Legislative Coalition; Corrections Chaplaincy; Human Justice and Community Concerns; Community Seminars; Children's Concerns

## Community Emergency Assistance Program (CEAP)

6840 78th Ave N, Brooklyn Park, MN 55445, Tel. (763)566-9600 Fax (763)566-9604
Email: smklein@isd.net
Website: www.ceap.homestead.com
Media Contact, Exec. Dir., Stephen Klein
Exec. Dir., Stephen Klein
Major Activities: Provision of Basic Needs (Food, Clothing); Emergency Financial Assistance for Shelter; Home-Delivered Meals; Chore Services and Homemaking Assistance; Family Loan Program; Volunteer Services

## Greater Minneapolis Council of Churches

1001 E. Lake St., P.O. Box 7509, Minneapolis, MN 55407-0509, Tel. (612)721-8687 Fax (612)722-8669
Email: info@gmcc.org
Website: www.gmcc.org
Media Contact, Dir. of Communications, Darcy Hanzlik
President and CEO, The Rev. Dr. Gary B. Reierson, Email: reierson@gmcc.org
Chair, Kent Eklund
Treas., Mervin Winston
Division Indian Work, Senior Vice President & Exec. Dir., Noya Woodrich;
Finance & Administration, Vice President and CFO, Peter Lee
Program Development, Exec. Dir., Bruce Bjork
Minnesota FoodShare, Dir., Barbara Thell
Handyworks, Dir., Megan Nolan-Elliasen
Correctional Chaplains, Rev. Susan Allers Hatlie; Rev. Thomas Van Leer; Rev. Paula Nordhem; Rev. Cheryl Powers Williams
Div. of Indian Work, Dir., Youth Leadership Development Program, Louise Matson;
Div. Of Indian Work Adult Services, Dir., Suzanne Simerson;
Div. Of Indian Work Horizons Unlimited, Food Shelf Mgr., Todd Jourdain
Div. Of Indian Work Teen Indian Parents, Dir., Carol Ladd;
Div. Of Indian Work Healing Spirit Program, Dir., Kirk Crowshoe;
Div. Of Indian Work American Indian Community Wellness Project, Proj. Mgr., Cheryl Secola
Advancement, Sr. Vice President., Don R. Riggs
Urban Immersion Service Retreats,. Dir., Gennae Falconer
Metro Paint-A-Thon, Dir., Deidre Pope
Discover Support Groups, Coord. Sandra Vaugh-Kelley

Community Justice Project, Co-Dirs., Brian Herron, Hillary Freeman
Minnesota Churches Anti-Racism Initiative, Co-Dirs., James Addington and Carmen Valenzuela
Church and Community Initiatives/Compassion Capital Fund, Coord., Bridget Ryan
Major Activities: Indian Work (Emergency Assistance, Youth Leadership, self-sufficiency, Teen Indian Parents Program, Healing Spirit Program (Foster Care), supportive housing, American Indian Community Wellness Project, and Family Violence Program); Minnesota FoodShare; Metro Paint-A-Thon; Correctional Chaplaincy Program; Handy-Works; Anti-racism Initiative; Social Justice Advocacy; Supportive Housing; Urban Immersion Service Retreats; Welfare Reform; Economic Self-Sufficiency; Discover Support Groups; Church and Community Initiatives/ Compassion Capital Fund; Immigrant and Refugee Services; Community Health Promotion; Correctional Aftercare; Restorative Justice

## The Joint Religious Legislative Coalition

122 W. Franklin Ave., Ste 315, Minneapolis, MN 55404, Tel. (612)870-3670 Fax (612)870-3671
Email: info@jrlc.org
Website: www.jrlc.org
Media Contact, Exec. Dir., Brian A. Rusche
Exec. Dir., Brian A. Rusche
Research Dir., Dr. James Casebolt
Network Organizer, Jody McCardle
Major Activities: Lobbying at State Legislature; Researching Social Justice Issues and Preparing Position Statements; Organizing Grassroots Citizen's Lobby, Social Justice Advocacy.

## Metropolitan Interfaith Council on Affordable Housing (MICAH)

122 W. Franklin Ave., #310, Minneapolis, MN 55404, Tel. (612)871-8980 Fax (612)813-4501
Email: info@micah.org
Website: www.micah.org
Media Contact, Exec. Dir., Joy Sorensen Navarre
Ex. Dir., Joy Sorensen Navarre
Assoc. Dir., José Trejo
Congregational Organizer, Jodi Nelson, Jean Pearson, The Rev. John Buzza, The Rev. John Buzza
Sec., Sue Watlov Phillips
Pres., The Rev. Paul Robinson
Vice Pres., Nancy L. Anderson
Treas., Joseph Holmberg
Past Pres. Kristine Reynolds
Major Activities: The Metropolitan Interfaith Council on Affordable Housing, MICAH, seeks to live out the prophetic vision that calls us "to do justice, to love mercy and to walk humbly with God." (Micah 6:8). We envision a

metropolitan area where everyone without exception has a safe, decent and affordable home. MICAH will realize this vision through organizing congregations of faith and community partners to change the political climate and public policies so that all communities preserve and build affordable housing. MICAH's faith-based organizing creates power that produces results. During the past five years MICAH: Mobilized congregations to build community support for 1,348 affordable homes for families with very low incomes. Prevented the demolition and gentrification of 1,919 structurally sound apartments. Half of the tenants were people of color or people with disabilities. Earned HUD's 1999 National Best Practices Award and the Headwaters Fund Social Justice Award in 2001.

## Minnesota Council of Churches*

122 W. Franklin Ave., Rm. 100, Minneapolis, MN 55404, Tel. (612)870-3600 Fax (612)870-3622
Email: mcc@mnchurches.org
Website: www.mnchurches.org
Media Contact, Exec. Dir., Rev. Peg Chemberlin, Email chemberlinp@mnchurches.org
**Officers and Staff**
Exec. Dir., Rev. Peg Chemberlin, chemberlinp@mnchurches.org
Director of Programs, Rev. Christopher Morton, mortonc@mnchurches.org
Refugee Services, Dir., Joel Luedtke, luedtkej@mnchurches.org
Communications, Dir., Christopher Dart, dartc@mnchurches.org
Finance & Facilities, Dir., Douglas Swanson, swansond@mnchurches.org
Tri-Council Coordinating Commission, Co-Dirs., James Addington, Carmen Valenzuela
Joint Religious Legislative Coalition, Research Dir. & Admn. Asst., James Casebolt
Joint Religious Legislative Coalition, Exec., Brian A. Rusche
Pres. Bishop James Jelinek
Major Activities: Minnesota Church Center, Rural Life-Ag Crisis; Racial Reconciliation; Indian Ministry; Legislative Advocacy; Refugee Services; Service to Newly Legalized-Undocumented persons; Unity & Relationships, Sexual Exploitation within the Religious Community; Jewish-Christian Relations; Muslim-Christian Relations; Tri-Council Coordinating Commission (Minnesota Churches Anti-Racism Initiative); Hindu-Christian Relations; Peace Works; Minnesota Foodshare

## Saint Paul Area Council of Churches

1671 Summit Ave, St. Paul, MN, 55105, Tel. (651) 646-8805 Fax (651)646-6866
Email: info@spacc.org
Website: www.spacc.org
Media Contact, Mary Kane

Exec. Dir., The Rev. Grant Abbott
Dir. of Development, Kristi Anderson
Congregations in Community, Julie Quello
Congregations Concerned for Children, Peg Wangensteen
Project Spirit, Darcel Hill
Project Home, Sara Liegl
Dept. of Indian Work, Sheila WhiteEagle
Pres. of the Board, Art Sidner
Treas., David F. Taylor
Sec., Stella Lundquist
Major Activities: Education and Advocacy Regarding Children and Poverty; Assistance to Churches Developing Children's Parenting Care Services; Ecumenical Encounters and Activities; Indian Ministries; Leadership in Forming Cooperative Ministries for Children and Youth; After-School Tutoring; Assistance to Congregations; Training Programs in Anti-racism; Shelters for homeless

## Tri-Council Coordinating Commission

122 W. Franklin, Rm. 100, Minneapolis, MN 55404, Tel. (612)871-0229 Fax (612)870-3622
Email: naja@gmcc.org
Website: www.gmcc.org/tcc.html
Media Contact, Co.-Dir., R. James Addington, Assoc. Rev. Carmen Valenzuela
Exec. Cmte.: The Rev. Peg Chemberlin, The Rev. Gary Reierson and The Rev. Thomas Duke
Major Activities: Anti-Racism training and organizational consultation; Institutional anti-racism team development and coaching; training and coaching of anti-racism trainers and organizers (in cooperation with cross roads ministry)

### MISSISSIPPI

## Mississippi Religious Leadership Conference*

P.O. Box 68123, Jackson, MS 39286-8123, Tel. (601)924-7430 Fax (601)924-7430
Email: mrlc@netdoor.com
Media Contact, Exec. Dir., Rev. Paul Griffin Jones, II, Th.D., PhD.
Exec. Dir., The Rev. Paul Griffin Jones, II, Th.D., PhD.
Chair, Bishop Duncan Gray, III
Treas., The Rev. Jim White
Major Activities: Cooperation among Religious Leaders; Lay-Clergy Retreats; Social Concerns Seminars; Disaster Task Force; Advocacy for Disadvantaged

### MISSOURI

## Council of Churches of the Ozarks

P.O. Box 3947, Springfield, MO 65808-3947, Tel. (417)862-3586 Fax (417)862-2129
Email: ccozarks@ccozarks.org
Website: www.ccozarks.org
Media Contact, Comm. Dir., Susan Jackson

249

Exec. Dir., Dr. David W. Hockensmith, Jr.

Chief Operating Officer, Julie Guillebeau

Major Activities: Ministerial Alliance; Child Care Food Program-FDA Food Program; Child Care Resource & Referral; Connections Handyman Service; Crosslines-Food and Clothing Pantry; Daybreak Adult Day Care Center; Long-Term Care Ombudsman Programs; Ozarks Food Harvest; Retired and Senior Volunteer Program; Sigma House-Treatment Center for Alcohol and Drug Abuse; Therapeutic Riding of the Ozarks

## Ecumenical Ministries

829 Jefferson St., Fulton, MO 65251, Tel. (573) 642-6065 Fax (573)592-0247

Email: emfulton@coin.org

Website: www.callaway.county.missouri.org/em

Media Contact, Admin. Asst., Karen Luebbert

Chair, Bd. Of Dir.; Rev. Raymond Dunlap

Major Activities: Kingdom Respite Care and Hospice; CROP Hunger Walk; Little Brother and Sister; Unity Service; Senior Center Bible Study; County Jail Ministry; Fulton High School Baccalaureate Service, HAVEN House; Missouri Youth Treatment Center Ministry, Parish Nurses of Callaway

## Interfaith Community Services

200 Cherokee St., P.O. Box 4038, St. Joseph, MO 64504-0038, Tel. (816)238-4511 Fax (816)238-3274

Email: DaveB@PonyExpress.net

Website: www.inter-serv.org

Media Contact, Exec. Dir., David G. Berger

Exec. Dir., David G. Berger

Major Activities: Child Development; Neighborhood Family Services; Group Home for Girls; Retired Senior Volunteer Program; Nutrition Program; Mobile Meals; Southside Youth Program; Church and Community; Housing Development; Homemaker Services to Elderly; Emergency Food, Rent, Utilities; AIDS Assistance; Family Respite; Family and Individual Casework

## Interfaith Partnership of Metropolitan St. Louis

4144 Lindell Blvd Ste 221, St Louis, MO 63108, Tel. (314)531-4784 Fax (314)531-4785

Email: okimbrough@interfaithpartnership.org

Website: http://www.interfaithpartnership.org/

Media Contact, R. Irene Randall, Program Manager, Membership & Events

Cabinet Chair, The Rev. Anthony Witherspoon

President, Ghazala Hayat, M.D.

Executive Director, Orvin Kimbrough

Major Activities: Speaking out with concerted faith voice on public issues

Celebrating our diversity, encouraging respect for our faith traditions through interfaith dialogue, music events, dinner programs, and public forums. Projects that promote bridge building across racial, religious, and cultural divides, and health promotion through congregational health initiatives. Projects responding to hunger, natural disasters, environmental restoration, improving impoverished neighborhood

## MONTANA

## Montana Association of Churches*

25 South Ewing, Ste 408, Helena, MT 59601, Tel. (406)449-6010 Fax (406)449-6657

Email: montanachurches@earthlink.net

Website: www.montana-churches.org

Media Contact, Exec. Dir.: The Rev. Dr. Brady J. Vardemann

Exe. Dir.: The Rev. Dr. Brady J. Vardemann

Pres., Fr. Jay Peterson, Box 1399, Great Falls, MT 59403

President Elect: Dr. Walter Gulick, 2018 12th Street West, Billings, MT 59102

Treas., The Rev. Barbara Archer, 2210 Pryor Lane, Billings, MT 59102

Sec., The Rev. Kama Morton, P.O. Box 115, Choteau, MT 59422

Major Activities: Christian Unity; Lay Ministries Institute; Junior Citizen Camp; Montana Christian Advocates Network; Renewing the Public Church; Partnership For Rural Life; Health Ministries.

## NEBRASKA

## Interchurch Ministries of Nebraska*

215 Centennial Mall S., Suite 300, Lincoln, NE 68508-1888, Tel. (402)476-3391 Fax (402) 202-2005

Email: im50427@alltel.net

Website: www.interchurchministries.org

Media Contact, Exec., Mrs. Marilyn P. Mecham

Pres., Rev. Roddy Dunkerson

Treas., Ms. Susan Gillies

Exec., Mrs. Marilyn Mecham

Adm. Asst., Sharon K. Kalcik

Domestic Violence Program Coordinator, Patricia L. Brown

Disaster Response Program: Caroline Walles, Harry Walles

Major Activities: Planning and Development; Indian Ministry; Rural Church Strategy; United Ministries in Higher Education; Disaster Response; Rural Response Hotline; Health Ministry; Community Organizing Initiative Planning; Peace with Justice; Angel Connection; Domestic Violence Program; Social Ministries; Nurturing & Enhancing the Spiritual Tapestry

## Lincoln Interfaith Council

140 S. 27th St., Ste. B, Lincoln, NE 68510-1301, Tel. (402)474-3017 Fax (402)475-3262

Email: mail@lincolninterfaith.org

Website: www.lincolninterfaith.org

Media Contact, Doug Boyd

250

Interim Coordinator, Kim Beyer Nelson
Pres., Sue Howe
Vice Pres., Gene Crump
Sec., Stephanie Dohner
Treas.,Terri Lee
Major Activities: M.L.K., Jr. Observance; Week of Prayer Christian Unity; Festival of Faith & Culture; Holocaust Memorial Observance; Citizens Against Racism & Discrimination; Community organization; Multi-Faith & Multi-Cultural Training; New Clergy Orientation; Directory of Clergy, Congregations & Religious Resources; Multi-Faith Planning Calendar Publication

## NEW HAMPSHIRE

## New Hampshire Council of Churches*
140 Sheep Davis Road, Ste. 1, Pembroke, NH 03275, Tel. (603)224-1352 Fax (603)224-9161
Email: churches@nhchurches.org
Website: www.nhchurches.org
Media Contact, Exec. Dir., David Lamarre-Vincent, PO Box 1087, Concord, NH 03302-1087, Tel. (603)224-1352 Fax (603)224-9161, Email david@nhchurches.org
Pres., The Rev. David Yasenka, Triumphant Cross ELCA, 171 Zion's Hill Rd, Salem, NH 03079
Treas., Mr. Alvah Chisholm
Major Activities: Statewide Ecumenical Work For Christian Unity, Interfaith Understanding, and Social Justice

## NEW JERSEY

## Bergen County Council of Churches
58 James Street, Bergenfield, NJ 07621, Tel. (201)384-7505 Fax (201)384-2585
Email: bergenccc@hotmail.com
Website: www.bergenccc.org
Media Contact, Pres., Rev. Dr. Stephen T. Giordano, Clinton Avenue Reformed Church, Clinton Ave. & James St., Bergenfield, NJ 07621, Tel. (201)384-2454 Fax (201)384-2585
Exec. Sec. Anne Annunziato
Major Activities: Ecumenical and Religious Institute; Brotherhood-Sisterhood Breakfast; Center for Food Action; Homeless Aid; Operation Santa Claus; Aging Services; Boy & Girl Scouts; Easter Dawn Services; Music; Youth; Ecumenical Representation; Support of Chaplains in Jails & Hospitals; Faith & Values Online project www.njfaithandvalues.org; Welfare into Workplace

## Ecclesia
700 West State St., Trenton, NJ 08618, Tel. (609) 394-9229 Fax
Media Contact, Sec., Mrs. Tina Swan
Pres., Rev. Joseph P. Ravenell
Campus Chaplains, Rev. Nancy Schulter; Rev. Robert Wittin, Rev. Richard Kocses

Major Activities: Racial Justice; Children & Youth Ministries; Advocacy; CROP Walk; Ecumenical Worship; Hospital Chaplaincy; Church Women United; Campus Chaplaincy; Congregational Empowerment; Prison Chaplaincy; Substance Abuse Ministry Training

## Metropolitan Ecumenical Ministry
525 Orange St., Newark, NJ 07107, Tel. (973) 485-8100 Fax (973)485-1165
Media Contact, Consultant, Rev. M. L. Emory
Exec. Dir., C. Stephen Jones
Major Activities: Community Advocacy (education, housing, environment); Church Mission Assistance; Community and Clergy Leadership Development; Economic Development; Affordable Housing

## Metropolitan Ecumenical Ministry Community Development Corp.
525 Orange St., Newark, NJ 07107, Tel. (973) 481-3100 Fax (201)481-7883
Email: memcdc@juno.com
Media Contact, Jacqueline Jones
Exec. Dir., Jacqueline Jones
Major Activities: Housing Development; Neighborhood Revitalization; Commercial-Small Business Development; Economic Development; Community Development; Credit Union; Home Ownership Counseling; Credit Repair; Mortgage Approval; Technical Assitance To Congregations

## New Jersey Council of Churches*
176 W. State St., Trenton, NJ 08608, Tel. (609) 396-9546 Fax (609)396-7646
Media Contact, Public Policy Dir., Joan Diefenbach, Esq.
Pres., Rev. Jack Johnson
Sec., Beverly McNally
Treas., Marge Christie
Major Activities: Racial Justice; Children's Issues; Theological Unity; Ethics Public Forums; Advocacy; Economic Justice

## NEW MEXICO

## Faith Community Assistance Center
P.O. Box 15517, Santa Fe, NM 87592, Tel. (505) 438-4782 Fax (505)473-5637
Media Contact, Barbara A. Robinson
Major Activities: Faith Community Assistance Center; providing emergency assistance to the poor; Interfaith Dialogues-Celebrations-Visitations; Peace Projects; Understanding Hispanic Heritage; Newsletter

## New Mexico Conference of Churches*
720 Vassar Dr NE, Albuquerque, NM 87106-2724, Tel. (505)255-1509 Fax (505)256-0071
Email: nmcc@nmchurches.org
Website: www.nmchurches.org

251

Media Contact, Exec. Dir.., Rev. Barbara E. Dua
Pres., Mr. Jim Gleason
Treas., Robert Sandoval
Exec. Dir., Rev. Dr. Barbara E. Dua
Major Activities: Affordable Housing; Social Justice Coalitions; Spiritual Life & Ministries

## NEW YORK

## Brooklyn Council of Churches

125 Ft. Greene Place, Brooklyn, NY 11217, Tel. (718)625-5851 Fax (718)522-1231
Media Contact, Dir., Charles Henze
Program Dir., Charles Henze (Deacon)
Pres., The Rev. James H. Eggleston
Treas., The Rev. Charles H. Straut, Jr.
Major Activities: Education Workshops; Food Pantries; Hospital and Nursing Home Chaplaincy; Church Women United; Legislative Concerns; Directory of Churches; Ecumenical Dialogue

## Broome County Council of Churches, Inc.

William H. Stanton Center, 3 Otseningo St., Binghamton, NY 13903, Tel. (607)724-9130 Fax (607)724-9148
Email: mfrick@broomecouncil.ort
Website: www.broomecouncil.net
Media Contact, Rev. Dr. Murray Frick
Exec. Dir., Rev. Dr. Murray Frick
Exec. Asst., Brigitte Stella
Hospital Chaplains, Betty Pomeroy; Rev. David Rockwell
Jail Chaplain, Rev. Cris Mogenson
Aging Ministry Coord., Linda McColgin
CHOW Prog. Coord., Wendy Primavera
Pres., Dr. Thomas Kelly
Treas., Rey Hull
Caregiver Program Coord., Joanne Kays
Community and Donor Relations, Dir., Dr. Murray Frick
Major Activities: Hospital and Jail Chaplains; Youth and Aging Ministries; Broome Bounty (Food Rescue Program); Emergency Hunger & Advocacy Program; Faith & Family Values; Ecumenical Worship and Fellowship; Media; Community Affairs; Peace with Justice; Day by Day Marriage Prep Program; Interfaith Coalition; Interfaith Volunteer Caregiver Program

## Capital Area Council of Churches, Inc.

646 State St., Albany, NY 12203-1217, Tel. (518) 462-5450 Fax (518)462-5450
Email: capareacc@aol.com
Website: www.capareacc.org
Media Contact, Admin. Director, Kitt Jackson
Exec. Dir., Rev. John U. Miller
Admn. Dir., Kitt Jackson
Pres., Rev. Vernon Victorson
Treas., William Hedberg

Major Activities: CROP Walk; Jail and Nursing Home Ministries; Martin Luther King Memorial Service and Scholarship Fund; Emergency Shelter for the Homeless; Campus Ministry; Ecumenical Dialogue; Forums on Social Concerns; Peace and Justice Education; Inter-Faith Programs; Legislative Concerns; Comm. Thanksgiving Day and Good Friday Services; Annual Ecumenical Musical Celebration

## Capital Region Ecumenical Organization (CREO)

812 N. Church St., Schenectady, NY 12305, Tel. (518)382-7505 Fax (518)382-7505
Email: mishamarvel@juno.com
Media Contact, Coord., Misha Marvel
Rev. Donna Elia, President (PCUSA)
Rev. John U. Miller, Vice President (UCC)
Rev. Dr. Charles Lindholm, Treasurer (ELCA)
Ms. Kitt Jackson, Secretary (RCA)
Misha Marvel, Coord.,
Major Activities: Promote Cooperation-Coordination Among Member Judicatories and Ecumenical Organizations in the Capital Region in Urban Ministries, Social Action

## Chautaugua County Rural Ministry

127 Central Ave., P.O. Box 362, Dunkirk, NY 14048, Tel. (716)366-1787 Fax (716)366-1787
Email: ccrm@netsync.net
Website: www.ccrm.netsync.net
Media Contact,
Exec. Dir., Kathleen Peterson
Major Activities: Chautaugua County Food Bank; Collection-Distribution of Furniture, Clothing, & Appliances; Homeless Services; Advocacy for the Poor; Soup Kitchen; Emergency Food Pantry; Thrift Store

## Concerned Ecumenical Ministry to the Upper West Side

286 Lafayette Ave., Buffalo, NY 14213, Tel. (716)882-2442 Fax (716)882-2477
Email: information@cembuffalo.org
Website: www.cembuffalo.org
Media Contact, Exec. Dir., The Rev. Catherine Rieley-Goddard
Pres., Mr. Peter Hogan
Major Activities: Community Center Serving Youth, Families, Seniors and the Hungry

## Cortland County Council of Churches, Inc.

7 Calvert St., Cortland, NY 13045, Tel. (607)753-1002 Fax
Media Contact, Office Mgr., Joy Niswender
Exec. Dir., The Rev. Donald M. Wilcox
Major Activities: College Campus Ministry; Hospital Chaplaincy; Nursing Home Ministry;

Newspaper Column; Interfaith Relationships; Hunger Relief; CWS; Crop Walk; Leadership Education; Community Issues; Mental Health Chaplaincy; Grief Support; Jail Ministry

## Council of Churches of Chemung County, Inc.

330 W. Church St., Elmira, NY 14901, Tel. (607)734-2294 Fax
Email: ecumenic2000@yahoo.com
Media Contact, Exec. Dir., Joan Geldmacher, Tel. (607)734-7622
Exec. Dir., Joan Geldmacher
Pres., Rev. Ann Taylor, 115 Dewitt, Elmira, NY 14901
Major Activities: CWS Collection; CROP Walk; UNICEF; Institutional Chaplaincies; Radio, Easter Dawn Service; Communications Network; Produce & Distribute Complete Church Directories; Representation on Community Boards and Agencies; Ecumenical Services; Interfaith Coalition; Taskforce on Children & Families; Compeer; Interfaith Hospitality Center

## Council of Churches of the City of New York

475 Riverside Dr., Rm. 727, New York, NY 10115, Tel. (212)870-1020 Fax (212)870-1025
Email: JEHiemstra@aol.com
Media Contact, Exec. Dir., Dr. John E. Hiemstra
Exec. Dir., Dr. John E. Hiemstra
Pres., The Rev. Calvin O. Butts
Prog. Dir., The Rev. Jimmy Lim
1st Vice Pres., Friend Carol Holmes
2nd Vice Pres., The Rev. Carolyn Holloway
3rd Vice Pres., The Venerable Michael Kendall
4th Vice Pres., Morris Gurley
Sec., The Rev. N. J. L'Heureux
Treas., The Rev. Jon Norton
Major Activities: Radio & TV; Pastoral Care; Christ for the World Chapel, Kennedy International Airport; Coordination and Strategic Planning; Interfaith Coordinator, Religious Conferences; Interfaith Commission of Religious Leaders; Referral & Advocacy; Youth Development; Directory of Churches and Database Available

## Dutchess County Interfaith Council, Inc.

9 Vassar St., Poughkeepsie, NY 12601, Tel. (845)471-7333 Fax (845)471-5253
Email: dic@bestweb.net
Website: www.dutchessinterfaithcouncil.org
Media Contact, Exec. Dir., The Rev. Philip Carr-Harris
Exec. Dir., The Rev. Philip Carr-Harris
Pres., Rabbi Paul Golumb
Treas., Amy Harding King
Major Activities: CROP Hunger Walk; Interfaith Music Festival; Public Worship Events; Interfaith Story Circles; Oil Purchase Group; Tour Of Houses Of Worship; Weekly Radio Program; Racial Unity Work; Poverty Forums

## Genesee County Churches United, Inc.

P.O. Box 547, Batavia, NY 14021, Tel. (716)343-6763 Fax
Media Contact, Pres., Captain Leonard Boynton, Salvation Army, 529 East Main St., Batavia, NY 14020, Tel. (716)343-6284
Pres., James Woodruff
Exec. Sec., Cheryl Talone
Chaplain, The Rev. Peter Miller
Major Activities: Jail Ministry; Food Pantries; Serve Needy Families; Radio Ministry; Pulpit Exchange; Community Thanksgiving; Ecumenical Services at County Fair

## Genesee-Orleans Ministry of Concern

Arnold Gregory Memorial Complex, Suite 271 243 South Main St., Albion, NY 14411, Tel. (585)589-9210 Fax (585)589-9617
Email: gomoc1@rochester.rr.com
Media Contact, Exec. Dir., Malika Hill
Exec. Dir., Malika Hill
Pres., John W. Cebula, Esq.
Vice Pres., Rev. Joseph Fifagrowicz
Sec., Jane Balbick
Treas., Mary Grace Demarse
Major Activities: Advocacy Services for the Disadvantaged, Homeless, Ill, Incarcerated and Victims of Family Violence; Emergency Food, Shelter, Utilities, Medicines, Just Friends (a mentoring program for children), Parenting Program, Furniture Program.

## Greater Rochester Community of Churches

2 Riverside St., Rochester, NY 14613-1222, Tel. (585)254-2570 Fax (585)254-6551
Email: grcc1@frontiernet.net
Website: www.grcc.org
Media Contact, Administrator., Elder Marie E. Gibson
Rev. Richard N. Myers, President
Sue Murray, VP for Program and Discipleship
Elder Jack Wheeler, VP for Organization
Deacon Marvin Mich, VP for Social Justice Ministry
Sister Patricia Switzer, Secretary
Kenneth Anderson, Treasurer
Rev. Gordon V. Webster, Interfaith Liaison
Rev. Roy Hedman, Officer-at-Large
Major Activities: Ecumenical Worship; Christian Unity; Interfaith Health Care Coalition; Interfaith Dialogue; Annual Faith in Action Celebration; Rochester's Religious Community Directory; Religious Information-Resources; Justice Issues; Children's Emergency Fund

## InterReligious Council of Central New York

3049 E. Genesee St., Syracuse, NY 13224, Tel. (315)449-3552 Fax (315)449-3103
Email: mbowles@irccny.org
Website: www.irccny.org
Media Contact, Dir. of Dev., Renée McCaffrey
Executive Dir., Dr. James B. Wiggins
Pres., The Rev. Dr. Thomas V. Wolfe
Bus. Mgr., Laura J. Haley
Director for Resource Development, Renée McCaffrey
Spiritual Care Program Director, The Rev. Tanya Atwood-Adams
Center for New Americans, Dir. Hope Wallis
Senior Companion Prog., Dir., Karen O'Hara
Long Term Ombudsman Prog., Dir., Linda Kashdin
Covenant Housing Prog., Dir., Kimberlee Dupcak
Community Wide Dialogue on Racism, Race Relations and Racial Healing, Beth Broadway
InterReligious Council News, Ed., Renée McCaffrey
Major Activities: Pastoral Ministries; Community Ministries; Interrreligious and Ecumenical Relations; Diversity Education; Worship; Community Advocacy and Planning

## The Long Island Council of Churches

1644 Denton Green, Hempstead, NY 11550, Tel. (516)565-0290 Fax (516)565-0291
Email: licchemp@aol.com
Website: www.ncccusa.org/ecmin/licc
Media Contact, Exec. Dir., Thomas W. Goodhue
Exec. Dir., Rev. Thomas W. Goodhue
Pastoral Care, Dir., Rev. Richard Lehman
Community Resources Dir., Alric Kennedy, Tel. (516)565-0390 ext. 204
Nassau County Ofc., Social Services Sec., Yolanda Murray
Suffolk County Ofc., Food Program & Family Support, Carolyn Gumbs, Tel: (631)727-2210
Major Activities: Pastoral Care in Jails; Emergency Food; Family Support & Advocacy; Advocacy for Peace & Justice; Church World Service; Multifaith Education; Clergy-Laity Training; Newsletter; Church Directory; AIDS Interfaith of Long Island

## Network of Religious Communities

1272 Delaware Ave., Buffalo, NY 14209-2496, Tel. (716)882-4793 Fax (716)882-3797
Email: nrc@religiousnet.org
Website: ReligiousNet.org
Media Contact, Co-Exec. Dir., Rev. Dr. G. Stanford Bratton
Co-Exec. Dir. & COO, The Rev. Dr. G. Stanford Bratton
Co-Exec. Dir., The Rev. Francis X. Mazur (Ecumenical Officer, Diocese of Buffalo-Roman Catholic)
Co-Presidents, Marlene Clickman (Judaism); Rev. Frances Manly (Unitarian Universalist Church of WNY)
Immediate Past President, Imam Fajri Ansari (Masjid Nu"Man)
Vice Pres. for Program, Deacon James Anderson, National Baptist
Vice Pres. for Administration, Dr. ViJay Chakravarthy (Hindu Cultural Society)
Secretary, Rev. Mary Masters (Unitarian Church of Practical Christitanity)
Treasurer, Ms Eula Hooker, Christian Methodist Episcopal
Chpsn., Interreligious Concerns, Rabbi Charles Shalman (Buffalo Board of Rabbis) and Dr. Othman Shibly (Islamic Society of the Niagara Frontier)
Chpsn., Personnel, The Rev. James Croglio (Diocese of Buffalo- Roman Catholic)
Chpsn., Membership, The Rev. Jeff Carter (Pentecostal)
Chpsn., Christian Concerns, The Rev. Robert Grimm (United Church of Christ)
Chpsn., Riefler Enablement Fund, Rev. Charles Bang (Evangelical Lutheran Church in America)
Chpsn., Public Issues, The Rev. Merle Showers (United Methodist Church)
Chpsn., Religious Leaders Forum, The Rev. Paul Litwin (Chancelor, Diocese of Buffalo—Roman Catholic)
Chpsn., Church Women United, Ms. Norma Roscover (Presbytery WNY)
Financial/office administrator, Ms. Bonnie Jehle
Church Women United Coordinator, Ms. Sally Giordano
Food For All, Coordinator, Ms. Kelly Kowalski
Medicaid Coordinator, Mr. Bruce Davidson
Major Activities: Regionwide Interreligious Conversation, Hunger Advocacy, Food Distribution, Roll Call Against Racism, Buffalo Coalition for Common Ground, Ecumenical and Interreligious Relations and Celebrations, Radio-TV Broadcast and Production, Church Women United, Lay-Religious Leaders Education, Community Development, Chaplaincy, Yom Hashoah Commemoration Service, AIDS Memorial Service, Police-Community Relations, CROP Walks, Interfaith Thanksgiving Service. Spirituality and Health Initiative. Community-wide interreligious education. U.S.-Canadian Border Policy and enforcement issues.

## New York State Council of Churches, Inc.*

18 Computer Dr. West, Suite 107, Albany, NY 12205, Tel. (518)436-9319 Fax (518)427-6705
Email: nyscoc@nycap.rr.com
Website: www.nyscoc.org
Media Contact, Ms. Mary Lu Bowen
Executive Dir., Ms. Mary Lu Bowen

Pres., The Rev. Geoffrey A. Black
Vice Pres., The Rev. Clint McCoy
Vice Pres., Bishop Marie C. Jerge
Corp. Sec., The Rev. Dr. Jon Norton
Treas., The Rev. Dr. John Hiemstra
Convener of Collegium, Vacant
Coordinator of Chaplaincy Services, Ms. Damaris McGuire
Public Policy Consultant, The Rev. Daniel Hahn
Communications Consultant, The Rev. Daniel Hahn
Admin. Asst., Sylvenia F. Cochran
Major Activities: State Chaplaincy; Public Policy Advocacy in the following areas: Anti-Racism; Campaign Reform; Criminal Justice System Reform; Disability; Ecomomic-Social Justice; Environmental; Health care; Homelessness-Shelter; Hunger-Food; Immigrant Issues; Public Education; Rural Issues; Substance Abuse; Violence; Women's Issues; Peace

## The Niagara Council of Churches Inc.

St. Paul UMC, 723 Seventh St., Niagara Falls, NY 14301, Tel. (716)285-7505 Fax
Media Contact, Pres., Nessie S. Bloomquist, 7120 Laur Rd., Niagara Falls, NY 14304, Tel. (716)297-0698 Fax (716)298-1193
Exec. Dir., Ruby Babb
Pres., Nessie S. Bloomquist
Treas., Shirley Bathurst
Trustees Chpsn., The Rev. Vincent Mattoni, 834 19th St., Niagara Falls, NY 14304
Major Activities: Ecumenical Worship; Bible Study; Christian Ed. & Social Concerns; Church Women United; Evangelism & Mission; Institutional Min. Youth Activities; Hymn Festival; Week of Prayer for Christian Unity; CWS Projects; Audio-Visual Library; UNICEF; Food Pantries and Kitchens; Community Missions, Inc.; Political Refugees; Eco-Justice Task Force; Migrant-Rural Ministries; Interfaith Coalition on Energy

## Queens Federation of Churches

86-17 105th St., Richmond Hill, NY 11418-1597, Tel. (718)847-6764 Fax (718)847-7392
Email: qfc@queenschurches.org
Website: www.queenschurches.org
Media Contact, The Rev. N. J. L'Heureux, Jr.
Exec. Dir., The Rev. N. J. L'Heureux, Jr.
York College Chaplain, The Rev. Dr. Henrietta Fullard
Pres., Shirley K. Ford
Treas., Annie Lee Phillips
Major Activities: Queens Interfaith Hunger Network—Emergency Food Service; York College Campus Ministry; Scouting & Youth Ministry; Christian Education Workshops; Planning and Strategy; Church Women United; Community Consultations; Seminars

for Church Leaders; Online Directory of Congregations; Christian Relations (Prot-RC); Chaplaincies; Public Policy Issues; N.Y.S. Interfaith Commission on Landmarking of Religious Property; *The Nexus of Queens* (online, weekly newspaper)

## Rural Migrant Ministry

P.O. Box 4757, Poughkeepsie, NY 12602, Tel. (845)485-8627 Fax (845)485-1963
Email: rmmhope3@aol.com
Website: ruralmigrantministry.org
Media Contact, Exec. Dir., Rev. Richard Witt
Exec. Dir., The Rev. Richard Witt
Pres., Melinda Trotti
Major Activities: Serving the Rural Poor and Migrants Through a Ministry of Advocacy & Empowerment; Youth Program; Latino Committee; Organization and Advocacy with and for Rural Poor and Migrant Farm Workers

## Schenectady Inner City Ministry

930 Albany St., Schenectady, NY 12307-1514, Tel. (518)374-2683 Fax (518)382-1871
Email: INFORMATION@SICM.US
Website: www. Timesunion.com/community/sicm
Media Contact, Patricia Rush
Urban Agent, Rev. Phillip N. Grigsby
Business Manager, Barbara Bieniek
Emergency Food, Gail Van Vallenburgh
Pres., Helga Sutroeter
Damien Center, Ujuana Anderson
Jobs, Etc, Annalene Antonio
Summer Food, Crystal Hameliml
Housing Task Force, Rev. Phil Grigsby
Major Activities: Food Security; Advocacy; Housing; Neighborhood and Economic Issues; Ecumenical Worship and Fellowship; Community Research; Education in Congregations on Faith Responses to Social Concerns; Legislative Advocacy; CROP Walk; HIV-AIDS Ministry; Job Training and Placement Center; Summer Lunch for Youth; Study Circles Initiative on Embracing Diversity; Community Crisis Nework; Housing Services and Advocacy; Youth Initiative; After-School Program; Committee for Social Justice; Theological Center; Computer for Kids

## Southeast Ecumenical Ministry

25 Westminster Rd., Rochester, NY 14607, Tel. (585)271-5350 Fax (585)271-8526
Email: sem@frontiernet.net
Media Contact, Laurie Jenkins
Dir., Laurie Jenkins
Pres., Ronald K. Fox
Major Activities: Transportation of Elderly & Disabled; Emergency Food Cupboard for Case Managers to access for their clients;

255

Supplemental Nutrition Program for seniors; Community Health and Pharmacy Partnership ( CHAPP).

## Staten Island Council of Churches

2187 Victory Blvd., Staten Island, NY 10314, Tel. (718)761-6782 Fax
Email: sicoc@verizon.net
Media Contact, Pres., Rev. Virginia Kaada, 2187 Victory Blvd., Staten Island, NY 10314, Tel. (718)761-6782
Pres., The Rev. Virginia Kaada
Exec. Sec., Rebekah A. Ellis
Major Activities: Congregational Support & Outreach; Education & Pastoral Care; Ecumenical & Interfaith Witness; Social Witness

## Troy Area United Ministries

392 Second St., Troy, NY 12180, Tel. (518)274-5920 Fax (518)271-1909
Email: info@TAUM.org
Website: www.taum.org
Media Contact, Exec. Dir., Rev. Donna Elia
Pres., Laura M. Rogers
Chaplain, R.P.I. And Russel Sage, Rev. Beth Illingworth
Damien Center, Dir., Glenn Read
Furniture Program, Dir., Michael Barrett
Major Activities: College Ministry; Nursing Home Ministry; CROP Walk; Homeless and Housing Concerns; Weekend Meals Program at Homeless Shelter; Community Worship Celebrations; Racial Relations; Furniture Program; Damien Center of Troy Hospitality for persons with HIV-AIDS; Computer Ministries; Youth Ministry

## Wainwright House

260 Stuyvesant Ave., Rye, NY 10580, Tel. (914) 967-6080 Fax (914)967-6114
Email: frandavies@wainwright.org
Website: www.wainwright.org
Media Contact, Exec. Dir., Fran Davies
Exec. Dir., Fran Davies
Pres., Robert Laughlin
Vice-Pres., Michael Standen
Major Activities: Educational Programs, Retreat and Conference Center; Intellectual, Psychological, Physical and Spiritual Growth; Healing and Health

## NORTH CAROLINA

## Asheville-Buncombe Community Christian Ministry (ABCCM)

30 Cumberland Ave., Asheville, NC 28801, Tel. (828)259-5300 Fax (828)259-5923
Email: srogers@abccm.org
Website: www.abccm.org
Media Contact, Exec. Dir., Rev. Scott Rogers, Fax (828)259-5323
Exec. Dir., The Rev. Scott Rogers

Pres., Stephen Williamson
Major Activities: Crisis Ministry; Jail-Prison Ministry; Shelter Ministry; Medical Ministry

## Greensboro Urban Ministry

305 West Lee St., Greensboro, NC 27406, Tel. (910)271-5959 Fax (910)271-5920
Email: Guministry@aol.com
Website: www.greensboro.com/gum
Media Contact, Exec. Dir., Rev. Mike Aiken
Exec. Dir., The Rev. Mike Aiken
Major Activities: Emergency Financial Assistance; Emergency Housing; Hunger Relief; Inter-Faith and Interracial Understanding; Justice Ministry; Chaplaincy with the Poor

## North Carolina Council of Churches*

Methodist Bldg., 1307 Glenwood Ave., Suite 156, Raleigh, NC 27605-3256, Tel. (919)828-6501 Fax (919)828-9697
Email: nccofc@nccouncilofchurches.org
Website: www.nccouncilofchurches.org
Media Contact, Comm. Assoc., Aleta Payne
Exec. Dir., The Rev. J. George Reed
Program Associate, Steve Smith
Program Associate, Denise Long
Program Associate, Barbara Zelter
Communications Associate, Aleta Payne
Health Program Associate, Dr. Gordon DeFriese
Pres., The Rev. Michael Cogsdale, 806 College Ave., Lenoir, NC 28645
Treas., Dr. James W. Ferree, 168 Brook Landing Drive Winston-Salem, NC 27106
Climate Connection Associate, Alice Boyd
Program Associates, Jason Jenkins, Rollin Russell
Major Activities: Health Care Justice; Christian Unity; Legislative Program; Farmworker Ministry; Rural Crisis; Racial and Ethnic Justice; Climate Change; Public Education; Economic Justice; Peace

## NORTH DAKOTA

## North Dakota Conference of Churches*

9195 70th Avenue, SE, Ashley, ND 58413-9600, Tel. (701)647-2063 Fax
Email: ndconchu@drtel.net
Website: ndconference.org
Media Contact, Exec. Sec., Renee Gopal
Pres., Bishop Paul Zipfel
Vice Pres. I, Dr. Wade Schemmel
Vice Pres. II, Grace Wisthoff
Treas., The Rev. Michael Hicken
Secretary, Bishop Duane Danielson
Major Activities: Rural Life Ministry; Faith and Order; North Dakota 101; Victims & Offenders Ministry; Rural Life Convocation; Restorative Justice

256

## OHIO

## Akron Area Association of Churches

800 East Market Street, Akron, OH 44305-2424, Tel. (330)535-3112 Fax (330)374-5041
Email: akronchurches@earthlink.net
Website: www.triple-ac.org
Media Contact, Exec. Dir., Chloe Ann Kriska
Bd. of Trustees, Pres., Rev. Dr. J. Wayman Butts
Vice Pres., The Rev. Mark Frey
Sec., Dale Kline
Treas., Ms. Sherrie Petrochuk
Major Activities: Messiah Sing; Interfaith Council; Newsletters; Resource Center; Community Worship; Training of Local Church Leadership; Radio Programs; Clergy and Lay Fellowship Luncheons; Neighborhood Development; Community Outreach; Church Interracial Partnerships; Pastor Peer Group Program; Advocacy, Social Justice

## Alliance of Churches

470 E. Broadway, Alliance, OH 44601, Tel. (330) 821-6648 Fax
Media Contact, Dir., Lisa A. Oyster
Dir., Lisa A. Oyster
Pres., Rev. Bud Hoffman
Treas., Betty Rush
Major Activities: Christian Education; Community Relations & Service; Ecumenical Worship; Community Ministry; Peacemaking; Medical Transportation for Anyone Needing It; Emergency Financial Assistance

## Churchpeople for Change and Reconciliation

Box 488, Lima, OH 45802-0488, Tel. (419)224-2086 Fax (419)224-2086
Media Contact, Exec. Dir., The Rev. Darwin Ralston
Exec. Dir., The Rev. Darwin Ralston
Major Activities: Developing Agencies for Minorities, Poor, Alienated and Despairing; especially Our Daily Bread Soup Kitchen

## Council of Christian Communions of Greater Cincinnati

7030 Reading Road
Suite 642, Cincinnati, OH 45237, Tel. (513)-351-6789 Fax 513-458-2252
Email: joellengrady@zoomtown.com
Website: www.cccgc.org
Media Contact, Exec. Dir., Joellen W. Grady
Exec. Dir., Joellen W. Grady
Justice Chaplaincy, Assoc. Dir., Rev. Jack Marsh
Educ., Assoc., Lillie D. Bibb
Pres., Rev. Damon Lynch III
Major Activities: Christian Unity & Interfaith Cooperation; Justice Chaplaincies; Police-Clergy Team; Adult and Juvenile Jail Chaplains; Religious Education

## Greater Dayton Christian Connections

601 W. Riverview Ave., Dayton, OH 45406, Tel. (937)227-9485 Fax (937)227-9407
Email: gdcc@Christianconnections.org
Website: www.christianconnections.org
Media Contact, Exec. Dir., Rev. Darryl Fairchild
Exec. Dir., Rev. Darryl Fairchild
Major Activities: Ecumenical and Interfaith Dialogue; Peace Making; Environmental Justice; Racial Reconciliation; Pastoral Leadership Resources; Ministry Recruitment and Placement; Communication

## Mahoning Valley Association of Churches

30 W. Front St., Youngstown, OH 44503, Tel. (330)744-8946 Fax (330)774-0018
Email: mvac@onecom.com
Media Contact, Exec. Dir., Elsie L. Dursi
Exec. Dir., Elsie L. Dursi
Pres., Rev. Joyce Lawson
Treas., Carol Williams
Major Activities: Communications; Christian Education; Ecumenism; Social Action; Advocacy

## Metropolitan Area Church Council

760 E. Broad St., Columbus, OH 43205, Tel. (614)461-7103 Fax (614)280-0352
Email: church_council@yahoo.com
Media Contact, Exec. Dir., Alvin Hadley
President: The Rev. Melvin Richardson
Vice-Pres.: The Rev. Frank Ball
Secretary: Ms. Ariene Reynolds
Treasurer: Ms. Marilyn Shreffler
Exec. Dir.: Alvin Hadley
Major Activities: Newspaper; Published nine times annually; Annual Living Faith Awards; Quarterly Racial Unity Services; Clergy Hospital Indentification Badges; Community Computer Center; Social Concerns relating to human needs in our community; Older Adult ministries; Collaborations to facilitate unity among religious denominations.

## Metropolitan Area Religious Coalition of Cincinnati

617 Vine St., Suite 1035, Cincinnati, OH 45202-2423, Tel. (513)721-4843 Fax (513)721-4891
Email: marcc@fuse.net
Media Contact, Dir., Rev. Duane Holm
Pres., Mr. William K. Woods
Dir., Rev. Duane Holm
Major Activities: Local social policy decisions chosen annually. 2005, Affordable Housing & Youth & Violence

## Ohio Council of Churches*

6230 Busch Blvd., Ste 430, Columbus, OH 43229-1879, Tel. (614)885-9590 Fax (614) 885-6097
Email: mail@ohcouncilchs.org

257

Website: www.ohcouncilchs.org
Exec. Dir., The Rev. Rebecca J. Tollefson
Public Policy, Dir., Tom Smith
Major Activities: Economic & Social Justice; Ecumenical Relations; Health Care Reform; Theological Dialogue; Racial Relations; Education-Funding; Childcare-Children Issues; Poverty-Welfare; Environment, Gambling, Global Warming

## Pike County Outreach Council
107-9 West Second Street, Waverly, OH 45690, Tel. (740)941-4348 Fax
Email: bridgehaven@intelliwave.com
Website: http://www.pcoutreach.org/
Dir., Judy Dixon
Major Activities: Emergency Service Program; Self Help Groups; Homeless Shelter, Food Pantry

## Toledo Ecumenical Area Ministries
444 Floyd St., Toledo, OH 43620, Tel. (419)242-7401 Fax (419)242-7404
Media Contact, Admin., Nancy Lee Atkins
Metro-Toledo Churches United, Admn., Nancy Lee Atkins
Toledo Metropolitan Mission, Exec. Dir., Nancy Lee Atkins
Major Activities: Ecumenical Relations; Interfaith Relations; Food Program; Housing Program; Social Action-Public Education; Health Care; Urban Ministry; Employment; Welfare Rights; Housing; Mental Retardation; Voter Registration-Education; Substance Abuse Treatment; Youth Leadership; Children At-risk; Elimination of Discrimination

## Tuscarawas County Council for Church and Community
1458 5th St. NW, New Philadelphia, OH 44663, Tel. (330)343-6012 Fax (330)343-9845
Email: mooredj3@adelphia.net
Media Contact, Donna J. Moore
Exec. Dir., Donna J. Moore
Pres., Lillian Devlin 1767 Hillandale Rd. NE, New Philadelphia, OH 44663
Treas., James Barnhouse, 120 N. Broadway, New Philadelphia, OH 44663
Major Activities: Human Services; Legislative Concerns; Home Improvements; Character Counts; Abstinence Education; Youth Boosters; Emergency Assistance

## West Side Ecumenical Ministry
5209 Detroit Ave, Cleveland, OH 44102, Tel. (216)651-2037 Fax (216)651-4145
Email: Eotero@wsem.org
Website: www.wsem.org
Media Contact, Dir. of Marketing and Public Relations, Kami L. Marquardt
Pres., & CEO, Judith Peters

Chief Operation Officer, Adam Roth
Major Activities: WSEM is dedicated to serving urban low-income families by providing programs that encourage self-sufficiency. Three food pantries and outreach centers, a job-training program, early childhood, preschool, and schol-age child care, crisis intervention, counseling, youth services, a theatre education program and a senior nutrition program are among the services available. WSEM serves more than 56,000 children, families, and individuals annually with a staffing of more than 300 employees and 3,200 volunteers.

## OKLAHOMA

## Oklahoma Conference of Churches*
301 Northwest 36th St., Oklahoma City, OK 73118, Tel. (405)525-2928 Fax (405)525-2636
Email: okchurches@okchurches.org
Website: www.okchurches.org
Media Contact, Deborah Canary-Marshall
Exec. Dir., The Rev. Don Vaught
Pres., Rev. George Young
Major Activities: Christian Unity Issues; Community Building Among Members; Rural Community Care; Children's Advocacy; Day at the Legislature; Impact; Criminal Justice; Hunger & Poverty; Legislative Advocacy; Aging; Women's Issues; Interfaith Coalition and Activities

## Tulsa Metropolitan Ministry
221 S. Nogales, Tulsa, OK 74127, Tel. (918)582-3147 Fax (918)582-3159
Email: tummtulsa@aol.com
Website: www.TUMM.org
Media Contact, Exec. Dir., Stephen Cranford
Exec. Dir., The Rev. Dr. Stephen V. Cranford
Pres., The Rev. Sara Jo Waggoner
Vice-Pres., Martin Belsky
Treas., Robert Dormont
Major Activities: Religious Understanding; Legislative Issues; Christian Unity Issues; Justice Issues; Against Racism; Disability Awareness; Directory of Metro; Religious Community; Airport Interfaith Chapel; Caring Companions; Native American Issues.

## OREGON

## Ecumenical Ministries of Oregon*
0245 S.W. Bancroft St., Ste. B, Portland, OR 97239, Tel. (503)221-1054 Fax (503)223-7007
Email: emo@emoregon.org
Website: www.emoregon.org
Media Contact, Bob Baker, Dir. Of Development & Communications
Exec. Dir., David A. Leslie
Finance and Administrative Services, Dir., Gary B. Logsdon

Development & Communications, Bob Baker
Sponsors Organized to Assist Refugees, Vesna Vila
Russian Oregon Social Services, Yelena Sergeva
Portland International Community School, Skip Adams
Public Policy Dir., Phillip Kennedy-Wong
Interfaith Network for Earth Concerns, Jenny Holmes
Parent Mentor Program, Patti Clothier
HIV Day Center, Lowen Berman
Shared Housing, Barbara Stone
Oregon Recovery Homes, Mike Morgester
Northeast Emergency Food Program, John Elizade
President, The Rev. Mark Knutson
Major Activities: Ecumenical Ministries of Oregon is a statewide association of seventeen Christian denominations including Protestant, Roman Catholic, and Orthodox bodies working together to improve the lives of Oregonians through theological education and dialogue, public policy advocacy, environmental ministry and community ministry programs.

## PENNSYLVANIA

### Allegheny Valley Association of Churches

1913 Freeport Rd., Natrona Heights, PA 15065, Tel. (724)226-0606 Fax (724)226-3197
Email: avac@avaoc.org
Website: www.avaoc.org
Media Contact, Exec. Dir., Karen Snair
Exec. Dir., Karen Snair
Pres., The Rev. Dr. W. James Legge, 232 Tarentum-Culmerville Rd., Tarentum, PA 15084
Treas., Libby Grimm, 312 Butternut Ln., Tarentum, PA 15084
Major Activities: Ecumenical Services; Dial-a-Devotion; Walk for Hunger; Food Bank; Emergency Aid; Cross-on-the-Hill; AVAC Hospitality Network for Homeless Families; Senior Citizen Housing-Pine Ridge Heights Senior Complex, AVAC Chaplaincy Program; Summer Camp for Children, Case Management, Faith-in-Action

### Christian Associates of Southwest Pennsylvania

204 37th St., Suite 201, Pittsburgh, PA 15201, Tel. (412)688-9070 Fax (412)688-9091
Email: info@casp.org
Website: www.casp.org
Media Contact, Dir. of Television Ministry, Monica Kao
Exec., Dir., Rev. Dr. Donald B. Green
Chair of Council, Bishop Robert W. Duncan
Pres., Board of Delegates, Rev. Deane Lavender
Executive Administrative Asst., Tracy Ritchie
Director of Television Ministry, Monica Kao
Television Studio Director, Frank Cindrich

Director of Jail Chaplaincy Services, Chaplain Lynn Yeso
Protestant Chaplain, Shuman Youth Detention Center, Rev. Floyd Palmer
Protestant Chaplains, Rev. Dallas Brown and Rev. Shawn Drummond
Catholic Chaplain, Fr. Malcolm McDonald
Jail Administrative Assistant, Karen Mack
Major Activities: Jail Chaplaincy; Youth-Incarceration Chaplaincies; Theological Dialogue-Religious Education; Religious Leadership Forum; Christian Associates Television (CATV); The Call...Newsletter; Media Ministries Internet ministry; Indigent Burial program; Interfaith Dialogue

### Christian Churches United of the Tri-County Area

413 South 19th St.
P.O. Box 60750, Harrisburg, PA 17106-0750, Tel. (717)230-9550 Fax (717)230-9554
Email: ccuhbg@aol.com
Website: christianchurchesunited.com
Media Contact, Exec. Dir., Jacqueline P. Rucker
Exec. Dir., Jacqueline P. Rucker
Pres., John Carroll
Treas., Henry Greenawald
Vice Pres., Rev. Paul Baranek
Sec., Patricia Greenawald
HELP & LaCasa Ministries, John Scarpato, Program Director, P.O. Box 60750, Harrisburg, PA 17106-0750, Tel. (717)238-2851 Fax (717) 238-1916
Major Activities: Volunteer Ministries to Prisons; HELP (Housing, Rent, Food, Medication, Transportation, Home Heating, Clothing); La Casa de Amistad (The House of Friendship) Social Services; AIDS Outreach; Prison Chaplaincy;

### Christians United in Beaver County

1098 Third St., Beaver, PA 15009, Tel. (724)774-1446 Fax (724)774-1446
Email: cubc@access995.com
Media Contact, Exec. Sec., Lois L. Smith
Exec. Sec., Lois L. Smith
Chaplains, The Rev. Dennis Ugoletti; The Rev. Anthony Massey; The Rev. Arthur Peters; John Pusateri, Rev. Bertha Lay
Pres., Mrs. Delores Tisdale, 1021-5th Street, New Brighton, PA. 15066
Treas., Mr. Richard Puryear, 2 McCabe Street, Sewickley, PA. 15143
Major Activities: Christian Education; Evangelism; Social Action; Church Women United; United Church Men; Ecumenism; Hospital, Detention Home and Jail Ministry, Behavioral Health Clinic.

### East End Cooperative Ministry

250 N. Highland Ave., Pittsburgh, PA 15206, Tel. (412)361-5549 Fax (412)361-0151

259

Email: eecm@eecm.org
Website: www.eecm.org
Media Contact, Exec. Dir., Myrna Zelenitz
Exec. Dir., Myrna Zelenitz
Ass. Dir., Rev. Darnell Leonard
Major Activities: Food Pantry; Soup Kitchen; Men's Emergency Shelter; Drop-In Shelter for Homeless; Meals on Wheels; Information and Referral; Programs for Children and Youth; Bridge Housing Program for Men and PennFree Housing for Women in Recovery

## Ecumenical Conference of Greater Altoona
P.O. Box 771, Altoona, PA 16693, Tel. (814)942-0512 Fax (814)942-0512
Email: ecumenaltoona@charter.net
Media Contact, Exec. Dir., Susanna M. Tomlinson
Exec. Dir., Susanna M. Tomlinson
Major Activities: Religious Education; Workshops; Ecumenical Activities; Religious Christmas Parade; Campus Ministry; Community Concerns; Peace Forum; Religious Education for Mentally Challenged, and Interfaith Committee

## Greater Bethlehem Area Council of Churches
1021 Center St., P.O. Box 1245, Bethlehem, PA 18016-1245, Tel. (610)867-8671 Fax (610)866-9223
Email: gbacc@enter.net
Media Contact, The Rev. Patricia Dwyer MacMillan
Exec. Dir., The Rev. Patricia Dwyer MacMillan
Pres., William L. Cauller
Treas., Mr. David G. Boltz, 1831 Levering Place, Bethlem, PA. 18017
Major Activities: World-local hunger projects; Ecumenical Worship-Cooperation; Prison Ministry Programs; Support for Homeless and Welfare to Work Programs; Emergency Food Pantry; Support for Hospice and Share Care Programs; Regional Grave Bank; Support Summer Youth Camps and Church Sports League

## Hanover Area Council of Churches
136 Carlisle St., Hanover, PA 17331-2406, Tel. (717)633-6353 Fax (717)633-1992
Email: opsmanhacc@netrax.net
Website: www.hanoverareacouncilofchurches.org
Operations Manager, Carol Hinkle
Major Activities: Meals on Wheels, Provide a Lunch Program, Fresh Air Program, Clothing Bank, Hospital Chaplaincy Services; Congregational & Interfaith Relations, Public Ecumenical Programs and Services, State Park Chaplaincy Services & Children's Program; Compeer; Faith at Work; CROP Walk; Stolte

Scholarship Fund; Community Needs; Cold Weather Shelter; AA

## Inter-Church Ministries of Erie County
2216 Peach St., Erie, PA 16502, Tel. (814)454-2411
Email: icm@icmeriecounty.com
Website: www.icmeriecounty.com
Pres., The Rev. Dr. Andrew Harvey
Treas., Mary C. Stewart
Major Activities: Local Ecumenism; Social Ministry; Continuing Education; North West Pennsylvania Conference of Bishops and Judicatory Execs.; Theological Dialogue; Coats for Kids; Voucher Program for Emergency Assistance; Worship; Advocacy

## Lancaster County Council of Churches
344 N. Marshall St., Lancaster, PA 17602, Tel. (717)291-2261 Fax (717)291-6403
Email: office@lccouncilofchurches.org
Website: www.lccouncilofchurches.org
Media Contact, Interim Exec. Dir., Kenneth Trauger
Pres.: Steve Mentzer
Service Ministry Interim Director: Doug Hopwood
Major Activities: Social Ministries

## Lebanon County Christian Ministries
250 S. 7th St., P.O. Box 654, Lebanon, PA 17042, Tel. (717)274-2601
Email: lccm@lmf
Media Contact, Exec. Dir., Lillian Morales
Exec. Dir., Lillian Morales
Noon Meals Coord., Wenda Dinatale
Major Activities: H.O.P.E. (Helping Our People in Emergencies); Food & Clothing Bank; Free Meal Program; Commodity Distribution Program; Ecumenical Events

## Lehigh County Conference of Churches
534 Chew St., Allentown, PA 18102, Tel. (610)433-6421 Fax (610)439-8039
Email: lccc@lcconfchurch.org
Website: www.lcconfchurch.org
Media Contact, Dir. of Dev., Ira Faro
Exec. Dir., The Rev. Dr. Christine L. Nelson
Pres., Ms. Joanne Gantz-Jalowiecki
1st Vice Pres.,The Rev. Thomas Thomas
Sec., Mrs. Eunice Schermerhorn
Treas., Mr. Nelson Rabenold
Major Activities: Social Concerns and Action; Clergy Dialogues; Daybreak Drop-In-Center for Mental Health Adults; Soup Kitchen; Housing Advocacy Program; Pathways (Referral to Social Services); Street Ministry

260

via Linkage; Homelessness Prevention; Pharmaceutical Assistance; Campbell Christian-Unity lecture; Clothing Distribution; Aspires Mentoring Program; Ecumenical & Interfaith Services; Homeless Supportive Services; CROP Walk

## Lewisburg Council of Churches
5. S. Asper Place, Lewisburg, PA 17837, Tel. (570)524-2834
Media Contact, Guy Temple, 139 Iron Cave Lane, Lewisburg, PA 17837, Tel. (570)524-4877
President, Mrs. Gail Pepper, First Baptist Church, 51 S. 3rd St, Lewisburg, PA 17837, Tel. (570)524-7438
Treasurer, Mrs. Jan Temple, 139 Iron Cave Lane, Lewisburg, PA 17837, Tel. (570)524-4877
Major Activities: Supplementary and Emergency Food Pantries; Clothing Bank; CROP Walk; Week of Prayer for Christian Unity; Soup & Scripture Lenten Series; Three-hour Good Friday Service; Human Services Directory; Transient-Homeless Aid

## Metropolitan Christian Council of Philadelphia
1501 Cherry St., Philadelphia, PA 19102-1429, Tel. (215)563-7854 Fax (215)563-6849
Email: geiger@mccp.org
Website: www.mccp.org
Media Contact, Assoc. Communications, Nancy L. Nolde
Exec. Dir., Rev. C. Edward Geiger
Assoc. Communications, Nancy L. Nolde
Office Mgr., Joan G. Shipman
Pres., Rev. Steven B. Laurence
First Vice Pres., Rev. G. Daniel Jones
Treas., A. Louis Denton, Esq.
Major Activities: Congregational Clusters; Public Policy Advocacy; Communication; Theological Dialogue (Christian & Interfaith); Women's Issues

## North Hills Youth Ministry Counseling Center
802 McKnight Park Dr., Pittsburgh, PA 15237, Tel. (412)366-1300
Email: NHYM@nhymcc.org
Website: www.nhymcc.org
Media Contact, Exec. Dir., Rev. Ronald B. Barnes
Exec. Dir., Ronald B. Barnes
Major Activities: Elementary, Junior and Senior High School Individual and Family Counseling; Elementary Age Youth Early Intervention Counseling; Educational Programming for Churches and Schools; Youth Advocacy; Parent Education; Marital Counseling; Tutoring for Elementary, Junior and Senior High Students; Healthy Communities-Healthy Youth Training and workshops based on Search Institutes; 40 Assets

## Northside Common Ministries
P.O. Box 99861, Pittsburgh, PA 15233, Tel. (412)323-1163 Fax (412)323-1749
Email: NCM@city-net.com
Media Contact, Exec. Dir., Janet E. Holtz
Exec. Dir., Janet E. Holtz
Major Activities: Pleasant Valley Shelter for Homeless Men; Advocacy around Hunger, Housing, Poverty, and Racial Issues; Community Food Pantry and Service Center; Supportive Housing

## Northwest Interfaith Movement
6757 Greene St., Philadelphia, PA 19119, Tel. (215)843-5600 Fax (215)843-2755
Email: jejohnson@nim-phila.org
Website: www.nim-phila.org
Media Contact, Exec. Dir., Rabbi George M. Stern
Exec. Dir., Rabbi George M. Stern
Chpsn., Judy Weinstein
Long Term Care Program, Dir., Donald Carlin
Neighborhood Child Care Resource Prog., Dir., Leslie S. Eslinger
Major Activities: Resources amd Technical Assistance for Child Care Programs; Conflict Mediation and Support for Nursing and Boarding Home Residents

## Pennsylvania Conference on Interchurch Cooperation*
P.O. Box 2835, 223 North St., Harrisburg, PA 17105, Tel. (717)238-9613 Fax (717)238-1473
Email: staff@pacatholic.org
Website: www.pacatholic.org/ecumenism
Media Contact, Carolyn Astfalk
Co-Staff, Dr. Robert J. O'Hara, Jr., Rev. Gary Harke
Co-Chpsns., Bishop Joseph Martino; Bishop Donald Main.
Major Activities: Theological Consultation; Social Concerns; Public Policy; Conferences and Seminars

## The Pennsylvania Council of Churches*
900 S. Arlington Ave., Ste. 100, Harrisburg, PA 17109-5089, Tel. (717)545-4761 Fax (717) 545-4765
Email: pcc@pachurches.org
Website: www.pachurches.org
Media Contact, Exec. Dir., The Rev. Gary L. Harke
Exec. Dir., The Rev. Gary L. Harke
Dir. of Public Advocacy, The Rev. Sandra L. Strauss
Dir. Of Finance & Facilities, Janet A. Gulick
Coord. for Contract Chaplaincy, vacant

261

Coord. for Leisure Ministries, Dr. Paul L. Herring
Pres., Rev. Bishop A. Donald Main
Vice-Pres., Ms. Barbara Adams-Smelter
Sec., The Rev. Dr. Warren M. Eshbach
Treas., Ms. Zedna M. Haverstock
Major Activities: Inter-church dialogue; trade association activities; faith and order; seasonal farmworker ministry; trucker-traveler ministry; public policy advocacy and education; leisure ministry; conferences and continuing education events; disaster response

## Project of Easton, Inc.
330 Ferry St., Easton, PA 18042, Tel. (215)258-4361
Pres., Dr. John H. Updegrove
Vice Pres. Public Relations, Rev. Charles E. Staples
Vice Pres. Operations, Don Follett
Sec., Rosemary Reese
Treas., Steve Barsony
Exec. Dir., Maryellen Shuman
Major Activities: Food Bank; Adult Literacy Program; English as a Second Language; Children's Programs; Parents as Student Support; CROP Walk; Interfaith Council; Family Literacy; Emergency Assistance; Even Start Family Literacy

## Reading Berks Conference of Churches
519 Elm St., P.O.Box 957, Reading, PA 19603, Tel. (610)375-6108 Fax (610)375-6205
Email: rdgbrkscc@comcast.net
Website: www.readingberksconferenceofchurches.com
Media Contact, Exec. Dir., Rev. Calvin Kurtz
Admin Asst., Donna Boyajcan
Exec. Dir., Rev. Calvin Kurtz
Pres., John Roland
Treas., William Maslo
Major Activities: Institutional Ministry; Social Action; CROP Walk for Hunger; Emergency Assistance; Prison Chaplaincy; Hospital Chaplaincy; Interchurch-Intercultural Services; Children & Youth Ministry; Healthy Family & Marriage Initiatives; Lazarus Project

## South Hills Interfaith Ministries
1900 Sleepy Hollow Rd., South Park, PA 15129, Tel. (412)854-9120 Fax (412)854-9123
Website: www.shimcenters.org
Media Contact, Exec. Dir., Jerry Ellis
Prog. Dir., Director of Youth Programs, Sarah Henkel
Psychological Services, Don Zandier
Family Assistance Coordinator, Harry Dietz
Business Mgr., Amy Puglisi
Volunteer Coordinator, Barbara Houston
Major Activities: Basic Human Needs; Community Organization and Development; Inter-Faith Cooperation; Personal Growth; At-Risk Youth Development; Women in Transition; Elderly Support; After School Homework Club; Early Childhood Program (Pre-School); Interfaith Educational Programs & Observances

## United Churches of Lycoming County
202 E. Third St., Williamsport, PA 17701, Tel. (570)322-1110 Fax (570)326-4572
Email: uclc@sunlink.net
Website: www.uclc.org
Media Contact, Exec. Dir., Rev. Gwen Nelson Bernstine
Exec. Dir., Rev. Gwen Nelson Bernstine
Ofc. Sec., Linda Winter
Pres., Rev. Glenn McCreary, 526 South Main Street, Muncy PA17756
Treas., Mrs. Madeline Bird, 407 South Market Street, Muncy PA17756
Shepherd of the Streets, Rev. J. Morris Smith, 669 Center Street., Williamsport, PA 17701
Ecumenism, Dir., Rev. Leo McKernan, 800 Mulberry Street, Montoursville PA 17754
Educ. Ministries, Dir., Rev. Ted Corcelius, 148 South Main Street, Hughesville PA 17737
Institutional Ministry, Dir., Rev. Dr. James Behrens, 1971 Lycoming Creek Rd., Williamsport, PA 17701
Radio-TV, Dir., Rev. Judy Stanley, 102 East Third St., Williamsport, PA 17701
Prison Ministry, Dir., Mrs. Evadna Cline, 3336 West Fourth St., Williamsport, PA 17701
Christian Social Concerns, Dir., Rev. Dr. J. Jeffrey Zetto, 369 Broad St., Montoursville, PA 17754
Major Activities: Ecumenism; Educational Ministries; Church Women United; Church World Service and CROP; Prison Ministry; Radio-TV; Nursing Homes; Fuel Bank; Food Pantry; Family Life; Shepherd of the Streets Urban Ministry; Peace Concerns; Housing Initiative; Interfaith Dialogue, Youth Ministry, Campus Ministry

## Wilkinsburg Community Ministry
710 Mulberry St., Pittsburgh, PA 15221, Tel. (412)241-8072 Fax (412)241-8315
Email: wcm15221@juno.com
Website: trfn.clpgh.org/wcm
Media Contact, Dir., Rev. Vivian Lovingood
Acting Dir., Elizabeth Mulvaney, MSW, LSW
Pres. Of Bd., Glenna Wilson, MSW, LSW
Major Activities: Hunger Ministry; Summer Reading Camp; Teen-Moms Infant Care; Meals on Wheels; Church Camp Scholarships; Utility Assistance; Clothing-Furniture Assistance; Case Management for Elderly Homebound Persons and Families, Soup Kitchen

## Wyoming Valley Council of Churches

70 Lockhart St., Wilkes-Barre, PA 18702, Tel. (570)825-8543
Media Contact, Exec. Dir., Beth Titus
Exec. Dir., Beth Titus
Ofc. Sec., Sandra Karrott
Pres., Very Rev. Joseph Martin
Treas., Rev. Dr. Robert Zanicky
Major Activities: Nursing Home Chaplaincy; Hospital Referral Service; CROP Hunger Walk; Pastoral Care Ministries; Clergy Retreats and Seminars; Meals on Wheels Fuel Service; Citizen's Voice articles

## York County Council of Churches

P.O. Box 1865, York, PA 17405-1865, Tel. (717)854-9504 Fax (717)843-5295
Email: ycccoffice@yccchurches.org
Website: www.yccchurches.org
Media Contact, Ryan Sattler, Chariman of P.R. Comm.
Pres., Mrs. Jody Appell
Vice Pres., Rev. William Snyder
Exec. Dir., in hiring process
Major Activities: Educational Development; Spiritual Growth and Renewal; Worship and Witness; Congregational Resourcing; Outreach and Mission

### RHODE ISLAND

## The Rhode Island State Council of Churches*

225 Chapman Street, Ste. 303, Providence, RI 02905, Tel. (401)461-5558 Fax (401)461-5233
Email: pmacnie@councilofchurchesri.org
Website: www.councilofchurchesri.org
Media Contact, Exec. Minister, Vacant
Exec. Min., Vacant
Admn. Asst., Peggy Macnie
Pres., Marie Bouvier-Newman
Treas., George Weavill
Major Activities: Urban Ministries; Institutional Chaplaincy; Advocacy-Justice & Service, Legislative Liaison; Faith & Order; Community Network; Campus Ministries; Prison Ministry

### SOUTH CAROLINA

## South Carolina Christian Action Council, Inc.*

P.O. Drawer 3248, Columbia, SC 29230, Tel. (803)786-7116 Fax (803)786-7116
Email: sccouncil@sccouncil.net
Website: www.sccouncil.net
Media Contact, Exec. Minister, Rev. Brenda Kneece
Exec. Minister, The Rev. Brenda Kneece
Pres., Debbie Dantzler,
Major Activities: Advocacy and Ecumenism;

Continuing Education; Interfaith Dialogue; Citizenship and Public Affairs; Publications; Race Relations; Child Advocacy; Faith and Health; Environmental Stewardship

## United Ministries

606 Pendleton St., Greenville, SC 29601, Tel. (864)232-6463 Fax (864)370-3518
Email: info@united-ministries.org
Website: www.united-ministries.org
Media Contact, Exec. Dir., Rev. Beth Templeton
Exec. Dir., The Rev. Beth Templeton
Pres., Nancy Orders Smith
Vice Pres., Anne Ellefson
Sec., Becky Bouton
Treas., Lan Nix
Major Activities: Assistance with rent, utilities, prescriptions, food, heat; Place of Hope (A day shelter for people who are homeless); Assistance with getting and keeping jobs; A GED program for adults; Case Management as part of all activities, College assistance with books and scholarships.

### SOUTH DAKOTA

## Association of Christian Churches of South Dakota*

100 S. Spring Ave., Suite 106, Sioux Falls, SD 57104-3626, Tel. (605)334-1980
Email: office@accsd.org
Website: www.accsd.org
Media Contact, Gary Nesdahl, 100 S. Spring Ave., Sioux Falls, SD 57104, Tel. (605)334-1980
Pres., Bd. Of Directors, Dr. Gail Arnold
Major Activities: Ecumenical Forums; Continuing Education for Clergy; Legislative Information; Resourcing Local Ecumenism; Native American Issues; Ecumenical Fields Ministries; Rural Economic Development; Children at Risk

## Metropolitan Inter Faith Association (MIFA)

P.O. Box 3130, Memphis, TN 38173-0130, Tel. (901)527-0208 Fax (901)527-3202
Media Contact, Dir., Media Relations, Caroline Vonicessler
Exec. Dir., Margaret Craddock
Major Activities: Emergency Services (Rent, Utility, Food, Clothing Assistance); Home-Delivered Meals and Senior Support Services; Youth Services; Homeless Programs

### TENNESSEE

## Tennessee Association of Churches*

103 Oak St., Ashland City, TN 37015, Tel. (615) 792-4631
Ecumenical Admn., vacant
Pres., Rev. Steve Mosley

263

Treas., Paul Milliken

Major Activities: Faith and Order; Christian Unity; Social Concern Ministries; Governmental Concerns; Governor's Prayer Breakfast

## Volunteer Ministry Center

103 South Gay St., Knoxville, TN 37902, Tel. (423)524-3926 Fax (423)524-7065
Media Contact, Exec. Dir., Angelia Moon
Exec. Dir., Angelia Moon
Pres., David Leech
Vice Pres., John Moxham
Treas., Doug Thompson
Major Activities: Homeless Program; Food Line; Crisis Referral Program; Subsidized Apartment Program; Counselling Program; Parenting Education for Single Parents

## TEXAS

## Austin Area Interreligious Ministries

701 Tillery St., Ste. 8, Austin, TX 78705, Tel. (512)386-9145 Fax (512)385-1430
Email: aaim@ammaustin.org
Website: www.ammaustin.org
Media Contact, Exec. Dir., Susan Wills, LPC
Exec. Dir., Susan Wills
Pres., Rev. Mel Waxler
Treas., Anita Maxwell
Major Activities: Youth at Risk Mentoring; Housing Rehabilitation; Broadcast Ministry; Interfaith Dialogues; Family Issues; Homeless Issues; Hunger Issues; Racial Reconciliation, ESL

## Border Association for Refugees from Central America (BARCA), Inc.

P.O. Box 1725, Edinburg, TX 78540, Tel. (956)631-7447 Fax (956)687-9266
Email: barcainc@aol.com
Media Contact, Exec. Dir., Ninfa Ochoa-Krueger
Exec. Dir, Ninfa Ochoa-Krueger
Outreach Services, Dir., Juanita Ledesma
Major Activities: Food, Shelter, Clothing to Newly Arrived Indigent Immigrants & Refugees; Medical and Other Emergency Aid; Special Services to Children; Speakers on Refugee and Immigrant Concerns for Church Groups; Orientation, Advocacy and Legal Services for Immigrants and Refugees

## Corpus Christi Metro Ministries

1919 Leopard St., P.O. Box 4899, Corpus Christi, TX 78469-4899, Tel. (361)887-0151 Fax (361)887-7900
Email: edseeger@ccmetrominstries.com
Website: www.ccmetroministries.com
Media Contact, Exec. Dir., The Reverend Robert G. Trache

Exec. Dir., The Reverend Robert G. Trache, Email; btrache@ccmetroministries.com
Admn. Dir., Ginger Flewelling-Leeds
Volunteer Dir., Ann Cox
Fin. Coord., Sue McCown
Loaves & Fishes Dir., Ray Gomez
Emergency Services Mgr., Ann Cox
Employment Dir., Larry Curtis
Health and Human Services, Dir., Ann Cox
Major Activities: Clothing Distribution, Employment Assistance, Healthcare, Homelessness/Shelter, and Hunger/Food Programs.

## East Dallas Cooperative Parish

P.O. Box 720305, Dallas, TX 75372-0305, Tel. (214)823-9149 Fax (214)823-2015
Email: edcp@swbell.net
Media Contact, Exec. Dir., Nancy Jellinek
Pres., Debbie Thorpe
Major Activities: Emergency Food, Clothing, Job Bank; Medical Clinic; Legal Clinic; Tutorial Education; Home Companion Service; Pre-School Education; Hispanic Ministry; Activity Center for Low Income Older Adults; Pastoral Counseling; English Language Ministry, Pre-GED program

## Greater Dallas Community of Churches

624 N. Good-Latimer #100, Dallas, TX 75204-5818, Tel. (214)824-8680 Fax (214)824-8726
Email: gdcc@churchcommunity.org
Media Contact, Exec. Dir., Rev. Elzie Odom
Exec. Dir., Rev. Elzie Odom
AmeriCorps-Building Blocks Dir., Venita Allen-Kent
Development Vice Pres., Charlotte Coyle
Pres., Richard Selby
Treas., John Rutzler
Major Activities: Interdenominational, Interfaith and Interracial Understanding and Joint Work; AmeriCorps-Building Blocks (Direct Service to Develop Inner City Children, Youth & Families); Summer Food & Reading; Hunger; Peacemaking; Public Policy; Social Justice; Faith & Life; Children's Health Outreach; Child Advocacy; Dismanteling Racism

## Interfaith Ministries for Greater Houston

3217 Montrose Blvd., Houston, TX 77006, Tel. (713)522-3955 Fax (713)520-4663
Media Contact, Exec. Dir., Betty P. Taylor
Exec. Dir., Betty P. Taylor
Pres., Charles R. Erickson
Development, Dir., Sharon Ervine
Assoc. Exec. Dir., Larry Norton
Treas., Fort D. Flowers, Jr.
Sec., Darlene Alexander
Major Activities: Community Concerns, Hunger; Older Adults; Families; Youth; Child Abuse;

Refugee Services; Congregational Relations and Development; Social Service Programs, Refugee Services; Hunger Coalition; Youth Victim Witness; Family Connection; Meals on Wheels; Senior Health; RSVP; Foster Grandparents

## North Dallas Shared Ministries

2530 Glenda Ln., #500, Dallas, TX 75229, Tel. (214)620-8696 Fax (214)620-0433
Media Contact, Exec. Dir., J. Dwayne Martin
Exec. Dir., J. Dwayne Martin
Pres., vacant
Major Activities: Emergency Assistance; Job Counseling; ESL

## Northside Inter-Church Agency (NICA)

1600 Circle Park Blvd., Fort Worth, TX 76106-8943, Tel. (817)626-1102 Fax (817)626-9043
Email: nicaagency@sbcglobal.net
Website: www.nicaagency.org
Media Contact, Exec. Dir., Connie Nahoolewa
Exec. Dir., Connie Nahoolewa
Major Activities: Food; Clothing; Counseling; Information and Referral; Furniture and Household Items; Nutrition Education; Employment Services; Thanksgiving Basket Program; "Last Resort" Christmas Program; Community Networking; Ecumenical Worship Services; Volunteer Training; Newsletter; Senior Home Repairs; School Clothing Program; Advocacy; GED Preparation; Literacy; Computer Training; English as a Second Language

## San Antonio Community of Churches

1101 W. Woodlawn, San Antonio, TX 78201, Tel. (210)733-9159 Fax (210)733-5780
Email: SACC@juno.com
Media Contact, Exec. Dir., Dr. Kenneth Thompson
Exec. Dir., Dr. Kenneth Thompson
Pres., Rev. Thomas Robinson
Major Activities: Christian Education; Missions; Infant Formula and Medical Prescriptions for Children of Indigent Families; Continuing Education For Clergy and Laity; Media Resource Center; Social Issues; Aging Concerns; Youth Concerns; Family Concerns; Sponsor annual CROP Walk for Hunger; Peace and Anti-Violence Initiatives

## San Antonio Urban Ministries

535 Bandera Rd., San Antonio, TX 78228
Media Contact, Sue Kelly
Exec. Dir., Sue Kelly
Pres., Rev. Leslie Ellison
Major Activities: Homes for Discharged Mental Patients; After-School Care for Latch Key Children; Christian-Based Community Ministry

## Southeast Area Churches (SEARCH)

P.O. Box 51256, Fort Worth, TX 76105, Tel. (817)531-2211
Exec. Dir., Dorothy Anderson-Develrow
Major Activities: Emergency Assistance; Advocacy; Information and Referral; Community Worship; School Supplies; Direct Aid to Low Income and Elderly

## Tarrant Area Community of Churches

P.O. Box 11471, Fort Worth, TX 76110-0471, Tel. (817)534-1790 Fax (817)534-1995
Email: revkm@flash.net
Media Contact, Regina Taylor
Pres., Regina Taylor
Treas., Don Hoak
Exec. Dir., Dr. Kenneth W. McIntosh
Major Activities: Eldercare Program; Children's Sabbath Sponsorship; Week of Prayer for Christian Unity; CROP Walk for Hunger Relief; Community Issues Forums; Family Pathfinders

## Texas Conference of Churches*

1033 La Posada, Ste. 125, Austin, TX 78752, Tel. (512)451-0991 Fax (512)451-5348
Email: tcc@txconfchurches.org
Website: www.txconfchurches.org
Media Contact, Comm. and Web Services, Caryn Wontor
Exec. Dir., Rev. Dr. George P. Bithos
Dir. Of Business Administration, Caryn Wontor
Pres., Rev. Dr. T. Randall Smith
Major Activities: Faith & Order; Related Ecumenism; Christian-Jewish Relations; Church and Society Issues

## United Board of Missions

1701 Bluebonnet Ave., P.O. Box 3856, Port Arthur, TX 77643-3856, Tel. (409)982-9412 Fax (409)985-3668
Media Contact, Admin. Asst., Carolyn Schwarr
Exec. Dir., Clark Moore
Pres., Glenda McCoy
Major Activities: Emergency Assistance (Food and Clothing, Rent and Utility, Medical, Dental, Transportation); Share a Toy at Christmas; Counseling; Back to School Clothing Assistance; Information and Referral; Hearing Aid Bank; Meals on Wheels; Super Pantry; Energy Conservation Programs; Job Bank Assistance to Local Residents Only

## VERMONT

## Vermont Ecumenical Council and Bible Society*

P.O. Box 728, Richmond, VT 05477, Tel. (802) 434 -7307 Fax (802) 434-7306

Email: info@vecbs.org
Website: www.vecbs.org
Media Contact, Admin. Asst., Betsy Wackernagel
Exec. Officer, vacant
Pres., The Rev. Robert Lowenthal
Vice Pres., The Rev. Robert Atlas
Treas., Mr. Christopher McCandless
Major Activities: Christian Unity; Bible
Distribution; Social Justice; Committee on
Faith and Order; Committee on Peace, Justice
and the Integrity of Creation; Committee on
Prayer and Worship

## VIRGINIA

## Virginia Council of Churches, Inc.*

1214 W. Graham Rd., Richmond, VA 23220-
1409, Tel. (804)321-3300 Fax (804)329-5066
Email: Barton@vcc-net.org
Website: www.vcc-net.org
Media Contact, Gen. Min., Rev. Jonathan Barton
Gen. Min., The Rev. Jonathan Barton
Migrant Head Start, Dir., Richard D. Cagan
Refugee Resettlement, Dir., The Rev. Richard D.
Cline
Weekday Rel. Educ., Coord., vacant, 2699
Lanier Lane, McGaheysville, VA 22840
Campus Ministry Forum, Coord., The Rev. Steve
Darr, c/o Community College Ministries, 305
Washington St., N.W., Blacksburg, VA 24060-
4745
Major Activities: Faith and Order; Network
Building & Coordination; Ecumenical Com-
munications; Justice and Legislative
Concerns; Educational Development; Rural
Concerns; Refugee Resettlement; Migrant
Ministries and Migrant Head Start; Disaster
Coordination; Infant Mortality Prevention

## WASHINGTON

## Associated Ministries of Tacoma-Pierce County

1224 South I St., Tacoma, WA 98405-5021, Tel.
(253)383-3056 Fax (253)383-2672
Email: info@associatedministries.org
Website: www. associatedministries.org
Media Contact, Exec. Dir., Rev. David T. Alger
Dir. Of Communications, Judy Jones
Pres., Rev. Arne Bergland
Vice Pres., Danna Clancy
Sec., Connie Robey
Treas., Jeff Cunningham
Exec. Dir., The Rev. David T. Alger
Deputy Dir., Diane Powers
Dir. of Mental Health Chaplaincy, Terry Mattock
Dir. of Project Interdependence, Valorie Crout
Dir. of Paint Tacoma-Pierce Beautiful, Sallie
Shawl
Dir. Of Development, Stephanie Paige Barnett
Dir. of Hilltop Action Coalition, Jeanie Peterson

Director of Communication and Education, Judy
Jones
Program Manager of Pierce County Asset
Building Coalition, Barbara Gorzinski
Major Activities: County-wide Hunger Walk;
Hunger Awareness; Economic Justice;
Religious Education; Social Service Program
Advocacy; Communication and Networking
of Churches; Housing; Paint Tacoma-Pierce
Beautiful; Mental Health Chaplaincy;
Theological Dialogue; Welfare to Work
Mentoring; Hilltop Action Coalition;
Compeer; Homelessness; Youth Ministry;
Ecumenical Formation; Interfaith Roundtable,
Domestic Violence Chaplain, Asset Building
Coalition; Family Emergency Fund

## Church Council of Greater Seattle

4 Nickerson Street, Seattle, WA 98109-1699, Tel.
(206)525-1213 Fax (206)525-1218
Email: info@thechurchcouncil.org
Website: www.thechurchcouncil.org
Media Contact, Exec. Dir., The Rev. Dr. Sanford
Brown
Executive Dir., The Rev. Dr. Sanford Brown
Emergency Feeding Prog., Dir., Arthur Lee
Friend to Friend, Dir., Marilyn Soderquist
Youth Chaplaincy Program, Dir., Chaplain Rev.
Benny Wright
The Sharehouse, Dir., Michal Nortness
The Homelessness Project, Dir., Nancy Dorman
Mission for Music & Healing, Dir., Susan
Gallaher & Esther "Little Dove" John
Sound Youth-AmeriCorps, Dir., Cat Koehn
Academy of Religious Broadcasting, Dir., Rev. J.
Graley Taylor
Board Chair, Verlene Jones
Board Treas., The Rev. Jeb Parr
Board Secretary, Susan Segall
Editor, The Source, Tricia Schug
Seattle Youth Garden Works, Dir., Conner Sharpe
SW King County Mental Health Ministry, Dir.,
The Rev. Stephen Jones
JOY Initiative, Prog. Dir., Rick Jump
St. Petersburg—Seattle Sister Churches Program
Chair, Nigel Taber-Hamilton
Asia Pacific Task Force, Contact Person, Akio
Yanagihara
Self-Managed Housing Programs, Dir., Misti
Uptain
Cuba Friendshipment Committee, Chair, Monica
Zapeda
Palestinian Concerns Task Force, Chair,
Constance Trowbridge
Interfaith Network of Concern for the People of
Iraq, Chair, The Rev. Rich Gamble & Andrew
Fung
Major Activities: Children; Youth & Families;
Hunger Relief; Global Peace and Justice;
Housing and Homelessness; Pastoral Care;
Services for the Aging; Public Witness; Interfaith
and Ecumenical Relations; Publisher of the The
Source, monthly ecumenical newspaper

266

## FaithTrust Institute

2400 N. 45th St, Suite 10, Seattle, WA 98103, Tel. (206)634-1903 Fax (206)634-0115
Email: info@faithtrustinstitute.org
Website: www.faithtrustinstitute.org
Media Contact, Ko-Eun Kim
Executive Director, Rev. Kathryn J. Johnson, kjohnson@faithtrustinstitute.org
Founder & Senior Analyst, Rev. Dr. Marie M. Fortune, mfortune@faithtrustinstitute.org
Director of Training & Education, Rev. Thelma Burgonio-Watson, burgonio@faithtrustinstitute.org
Director of the Jewish Program, Rabbi Cindy Enger, cenger@faithtrustinstitute.org
Clearinghouse Coordinator, Dinah Hall, dhall@faithtrustinstitute.org
Finance Director, Marion J. Ward
Major Activities: Training - Domestic Violence, Healthy teen relationships, Child Abuse, Sexual Abuse by Clergy and Religious Leaders, Sexual Violence
Consultation - Expertise to develop policies to address and prevent sexual abuse by clergy, guidance on integrating issues of sexual and domestic violence into religious education
Educational Materials - multicultural and multifaith educational materials, extensive resource catalog includes videos, books and curricula

## The Interfaith Association of Snohomish County

2301 Hoyt, P.O. Box 12824, Everett, WA 98206, Tel. (206)252-6672
Email: admin@.tiasccom
Website: www.tiasc.com
Media Contact, Exec. Dir., Janet Pope
Exec. Dir., Janet Pope
Pres., William Comfort
Major Activities: Housing and Shelter; Economic Justice; Hunger; Interfaith Worship and Collaboration

## Interfaith Council

1620 N. Monroe, Spokane, WA 99205, Tel. (509) 329-1410 Fax (509)329-1409
Email: info@interfaithnw.org
Website: www.interfaithnw.org
Media Contact, Dir.,Kateri Caron
Director: Kateri Caron
Board President: Stephen Rorie
Vice President: Elliot Fabric
Sec., Rev. Dr. Richard Erhardt
Major Activities: Camp PEACE; Multi-Cultural Human Relations; High School Youth Camp; Eastern Washington Legislative Conference; CROP Walk; Interfaith Thanksgiving Worship; Easter Sunrise Service; Dir. Of Churches & Community Agencies; Circle of Caring (for Women in Domestic Violence); Guatemala Dialogues

## Interfaith Works

P.O. Box 1221, Olympia, WA 98507, Tel. (360) 357-7224
Email: interfaithworks@aol.com
Website: www.interfaith-works.org
Media Contact, Exec. Dir., Kathy Erlandson
Exec. Dir., Kathy Erlandson
Pres., Jim Fulton
Treas., Paddy Mackin
Major Activities: Interfaith Relations; Social and Health Concerns; Community Action; Social Justice

### Northwest Harvest-E. M. M.

P.O. Box 12272, Seattle, WA 98102, Tel. (206) 625-0755 Fax (206)625-7518
Email: nharvest@blarg.net
Website: www. northwestharvest.org
Media Contact, Comm. Affairs Dir., Ellen Hansen
Exec. Dir., Ruth M. Velozo
Chpsn., Patricia Barcott
Major Activities: Northwest Harvest (Statewide Hunger Response); Cherry Street Food Bank (Community Hunger Response); Northwest Infants Corner (Special Nutritional Products for Infants and Babies)

## Washington Association of Churches*

419 Occidental Ave. S., Ste. 201, Seattle, WA 98104-2886, Tel. (206)625-9790 Fax (206) 625-9791
Email: wac@thewac.org
Website: www.thewac.org
Director for Operations, Bette Schneider, schneider@thewac.org
Major Activities: Faith and Order; Ecumenical Dialogue; Justice Advocacy; Confronting Poverty; Hunger Action; Legislation; Denominational Ecumenical Coordination; Theological Formation; Leadership Development; Immigrant Rights Advocacy; Racial Justice Advocacy; International Solidarity; Environmental Justice Advocacy; Tax Justice Advocacy; Congregation Public Policy Organizing

### WEST VIRGINIA

## Greater Fairmont Council of Churches

P.O. Box 108, Fairmont, WV 26554, Tel. (304) 367-0962
Media Contact, Pres., Rev. Jeremiah Jasper
President, Rev. Jeremiah Jasper
Major Activities: Community Ecumenical Services; Youth and Adult Sports Leagues; CROP Walk Sponsor; Weekly Radio Broadcasts

## West Virginia Council of Churches*

2207 Washington St. E., Charleston, WV 25311-2218, Tel. (304)344-3141 Fax (304)342-1506
Email: wvcc@wvcc.org
Website: www.wvcc.org
Media Contact, Exec. Dir., The Rev. Dennis D. Sparks, Email: dsparks@wvcc.org
Office Manager, Bob Rosier, Email: bob@wvcc.org
Pres., Bishop Ralph Dunkin (ELCA)
1st Vice Pres., The Rt. Rev. W. Michie Klusmeyer (ECUSA)
2nd Vice Pres., Ms. Ernestine Casson (AME)
Sec., Rev. Dr. William B. Allen (DOC)
Treas., The Very Rev. Frederick P. Annie (RC)
Major Activities: Disaster Response; Faith and Order; Family Concerns; Inter-Faith Relations; Peace and Justice; Government Concerns; Support Services Network

## WISCONSIN

### Christian Youth Council

1715-52nd St., Kenosha, WI 53140, Tel. (262)654-6200 x120 Fax (414)652-4461
Media Contact, Exec. Dir., Steven L. Nelson
Exec. Dir., Steven L. Nelson
Sports Dir., Jerry Tappen
Outreach Dir., Linda Osborne
Accountant, Debbie Cutts
Class Director, Jill Cox
Pres. & Chmn. of Board, Lon Knoedler
Gang Prevention Dir., Sam Sauceda
Major Activities: Leisure Time Ministry; Institutional Ministries; Ecumenical Committee; Social Concerns; Outreach Sports (with a Christian Philosophy)

### Interfaith Conference of Greater Milwaukee

1442 N. Farwell Ave., Ste. 200, Milwaukee, WI 53202, Tel. (414)276-9050 Fax (414)276-8442
Email: IFCGM@aol.com
Media Contact, Exec. Dir., Marcus White
Chpsn., Rev. Velma Smith
First Vice Chair, Archbishop Rembert G. Weakland
Second Vice Chair, Rev. Charles Graves
Sec., Paula Simon
Treas., The Rev. Mary Ann Neevel
Exec. Dir., Marcus White
Consultant in Communications, Rev. Robert P. Seater
Major Activities: Economic Issues; Racism; CROP Walk; Public Policy; Suburban and Urban Partnerships; TV Programming; Peace and International Issues Committee; Annual Membership Luncheon; Religion Diversity; Restorative Justice

### Madison-area Urban Ministry

2300 S. Park St., Madison, WI 53713, Tel. (608) 256-0906 Fax (608)256-4387

Email: mum@emum.org
Website: www.emun.org
Media Contact, Office Mgr., Jackie Austin
Exec. Dir., Mary K. Baum
Program Mgr., vacant
Major Activities: Community Projects; Dialogue-Forums

### Wisconsin Council of Churches*

750 Windsor St. Ste. 301, Sun Prairie, WI 53590-2149, Tel. (608)837-3108 Fax (608)837-3038
Email: sanderson@wichurches.org
Website: www.wichurches.org
Exec. Dir., Exec. Dir., Scott D. Anderson
Public Policy Coordinator, Dr. Peter Bakker
Coordinator for Local Ecumenism, The Rev. Kenneth Pennings
Pres., The Rt. Rev. Russell E. Jacobus
Treas., Dr. Robert Bock
Accountant, Rick Fluechtling
Coordinator for Program Support Services, Mr. Christopher Marceil
Major Activities: Social Witness; Migrant Ministry; Peace and Justice; Faith and Order; Anti-Hunger Campaign; American Indian Ministries Council; Park Ministry; Wisconsin Housing Partnership; Nonviolence, Affordable Housing; Economic Justice; Corporate Responsibility

## WYOMING

### Wyoming Association of Churches*

1131 13th St., Suite 210, Cody, WY 82414, Tel. (307)635-4251 Fax (307)637-4737
Email: wychurches@wyoming.com
Website: www.wyomingassociationofchurches.org
Media Contact, The Rev. Warren Murphy, Director
Dir., Rev. Warren Murphy
Chair, The Rev. Tim Trippel
Treasurer, Don Kesselheim
Office Manager, Pam Noesner
Major Activities: Alternatives to Violence; Beyond Tolerance; Malicious Harrasment; Domestic Violence; Empowering the Poor and Oppressed; Peace and Justice; Public Health Issues; Welfare Reform; Anti-Death Penalty, Community Networking Facilitation

# Index of Select Programs for U.S. Regional and Local Ecumenical Bodies

For many years the *Yearbook of American & Canadian Churches* has published the previous chapter, The Directory of U.S. Regional and Local Ecumenical Bodies. Each entry of that directory contains a brief description of the diverse programs offered by each agency. However, researchers, pastors, service organizations and theological seminaries often inquire about specific programs and which agencies carry out such programs. In response we have created this chapter, which indexes the various regional and local ecumenical agencies by twenty-five different program areas. These program areas are the twenty-five that have been the most frequent subjects of inquiry in our office. We have collected this program information directly from these organizations by means of a simple response form. There is an enormous diversity of ministries and missions conducted by these diverse organizations. Most organizations pursue several kinds of programs at once. However, some of these may focus their efforts most especially on only one of their programs; their other programs may be less well developed than their specialty. Consequently, the extent to which any of these ministries is a priority for any particular organization cannot be inferred from this list. For detailed information about the nature and extent of any particular ministry, the reader is urged to contact the organization directly using the directory of "U.S. Regional and Local Ecumenical Bodies," which is found in the pages just prior to this index.

## AIDS/HIV Programs

Arizona Ecumenical Council—Phoenix, AZ
Center City Churches—Hartford, CT
Christian Churches United of the Tri-County Area—Harrisburg, PA
The Council of Churches of Santa Clara County—San Jose, CA
East Dallas Cooperative Parish—Dallas, TX
Ecumenical Ministries of Oregon—Portland, OR
Grand Rapids Area Center for Ecumenism (GRACE)—Grand Rapids, MI
Greater Baton Rouge Federation of Churches and Synagogues—Baton Rouge, LA
Greater Chicago Broadcast Ministries—Chicago, IL
Interfaith Community Services—St. Joseph, MO
Lehigh County Conference of Churches—Allentown, PA
Metropolitan Ecumenical Ministry—Newark, NJ
Network of Religious Communities—Buffalo, NY
The Regional Council of Churches of Atlanta—Atlanta, GA
Schenectady Inner City Ministry—Schenectady, NY
South Carolina Christian Action Council, Inc.—Columbia, SC
Southeast Ecumenical Ministry—Rochester, NY
Troy Area United Ministries—Troy, NY
Wyoming Valley Council of Churches—Wilkes-Barre, PA
York County Council of Churches—York, PA

## Anti-Gambling Programs

The Associated Churches of Fort Wayne & Allen County, Inc.—Fort Wayne, IN

Associated Ministries of Tacoma-Pierce County—Tacoma, WA
Ecumenical Ministries of Iowa (EMI)—Des Moines, IA
Genesee County Churches United, Inc.—Batavia, NY
Greater Chicago Broadcast Ministries—Chicago, IL
Greater Lawrence Council of Churches—Lawrence, MA
The Joint Religious Legislative Coalition—Minneapolis, MN
Kentuckiana Interfaith Community—Louisville, KY
Kentucky Council of Churches—Lexington, KY
Lehigh County Conference of Churches—Allentown, PA
Mahoning Valley Association of Churches—Youngstown, OH
Massachusetts Council of Churches—Boston, MA
Mississippi Religious Leadership Conference—Jackson, MS
Montana Association of Churches—Helena, MT
Network of Religious Communities—Buffalo, NY
New Mexico Conference of Churches—Albuquerque, NM
The Pennsylvania Council of Churches—Harrisburg, PA
The Rhode Island State Council of Churches—Providence, RI
South Carolina Christian Action Council, Inc.—Columbia, SC
Texas Conference of Churches—Austin, TX
United Churches of Lycoming County—Williamsport, PA
Washington Association of Churches—Seattle, WA

West Virginia Council of Churches—Charleston, WV

Wisconsin Council of Churches—Sun Prairie, WI

Worcester County Ecumenical Council—Worcester, MA

## Anti-Racism Programs

Akron Area Association of Churches—Akron, OH

Arizona Ecumenical Council—Phoenix, AZ

The Associated Churches of Fort Wayne & Allen County, Inc.—Fort Wayne, IN

Associated Ministries of Tacoma-Pierce County—Tacoma, WA

Association of Religious Communities—Danbury, CT

Austin Area Interreligious Ministries—Austin, TX

Broome County Council of Churches, Inc.—Binghamton, NY

The Cape Cod Council of Churches, Inc.—Hyannis, MA

Capital Region Ecumenical Organization (CREO)—Schenectady, NY

The Capitol Region Conference of Churches—Hartford, CT

Christian Ministries of Delaware County—Muncie, IN

The Church Federation of Greater Indianapolis, Inc.—Indianapolis, IN

Colorado Council of Churches—Denver, CO

Community Emergency Assistance Program (CEAP)—Brooklyn Park, MN

Cooperative Metropolitan Ministries—Newton, MA

Council of Churches of the City of New York—New York, NY

Council of Churches of Greater Bridgeport, Inc.—Bridgeport, CT

The Council of Churches of Santa Clara County—San Jose, CA

Council of Churches and Synagogues of Southwestern Connecticut—Stamford, CT

Dutchess County Interfaith Council, Inc.—Poughkeepsie, NY

East Dallas Cooperative Parish—Dallas, TX

Ecclesia—Trenton, NJ

Ecumenical Conference of Greater Altoona—Altoona, PA

Ecumenical Ministries of Oregon—Portland, OR

Evanston Ecumenical Action Council—Evanston, IL

Faith Community Assistance Center—Santa Fe, NM

FaithTrust Institute—Seattle, WA

Fresno Metro Ministry—Fresno, CA

Georgia Christian Council—Macon, GA

Grand Rapids Area Center for Ecumenism (GRACE)—Grand Rapids, MI

Greater Baton Rouge Federation of Churches and Synagogues—Baton Rouge, LA

Greater Birmingham Ministries—Birmingham, AL

Greater Chicago Broadcast Ministries—Chicago, IL

Greater Dallas Community of Churches—Dallas, TX

Greater Dayton Christian Connections—Dayton, OH

Greater Minneapolis Council of Churches—Minneapolis, MN

Greater Rochester Community of Churches—Rochester, NY

Greensboro Urban Ministry—Greensboro, NC

Illinois Conference of Churches—Springfield, IL

Indiana Partners for Christian Unity and Mission—Indianapolis, IN

Inter-Church Council of Greater New Bedford—New Bedford, MA

Interfaith Conference of Greater Milwaukee—Milwaukee, WI

InterFaith Conference of Metropolitan Washington—Washington, DC

Interfaith Council—Spokane, WA

Interfaith Council of Contra Costa County—Walnut Creek, CA

Inter-Faith Ministries-Wichita—Wichita, KS

Interfaith Mission Service—Huntsville, AL

Interfaith Service Bureau—Sacramento, CA

InterReligious Council of Central New York—Syracuse, NY

The Joint Religious Legislative Coalition—Minneapolis, MN

Kansas Ecumenical Ministries—Topeka, KS

Kentuckiana Interfaith Community—Louisville, KY

Kentucky Council of Churches—Lexington, KY

Lincoln Interfaith Council—Lincoln, NE

The Long Island Council of Churches—Hempstead, NY

Louisiana Interchurch Conference—Baton Rouge, LA

Mahoning Valley Association of Churches—Youngstown, OH

Massachusetts Council of Churches—Boston, MA

The Metropolitan Christian Council: Detroit-Windsor—Detroit, MI

Metropolitan Christian Council of Philadelphia—Philadelphia, PA

Metropolitan Ecumenical Ministry—Newark, NJ

Metropolitan Interfaith Council on Affordable Housing (MICAH)—Minneapolis, MN

Minnesota Council of Churches—Minneapolis, MN

Mississippi Religious Leadership Conference—Jackson, MS

Montana Association of Churches—Helena, MT

Muskegon County Cooperating Churches—Muskegon, MI

Network of Religious Communities—Buffalo, NY

New Britain Area Conference of Churches (NEWBRACC)—New Britain, CT

New Hampshire Council of Churches—Pembroke, NH

New Mexico Conference of Churches—Albuquerque, NM

North Carolina Council of Churches—Raleigh, NC

Northern California Interreligious Conference—Oakland, CA

Northside Common Ministries—Pittsburgh, PA

The Pennsylvania Council of Churches—Harrisburg, PA

The Regional Council of Churches of Atlanta—Atlanta, GA

The Rhode Island State Council of Churches—Providence, RI

Saint. Paul Area Council of Churches—St. Paul, MN

South Carolina Christian Action Council, Inc.—Columbia, SC

South Coast Interfaith Council—Long Beach, CA

South Hills Interfaith Ministries—South Park, PA

Tarrant Area Community of Churches—Fort Worth, TX

Texas Conference of Churches—Austin, TX

Tri-Council Coordinating Commission—Minneapolis, MN

Troy Area United Ministries—Troy, NY

Tulsa Metropolitan Ministry—Tulsa, OK

United Churches of Lycoming County—Williamsport, PA

Virginia Council of Churches, Inc.—Richmond, VA

Wainwright House—Rye, NY

Washington Association of Churches—Seattle, WA

West Virginia Council of Churches—Charleston, WV

Wisconsin Council of Churches—Sun Prairie, WI

Wyoming Association of Churches—Cody, WY

## Christian Education Programs

Akron Area Association of Churches—Akron, OH

Arizona Ecumenical Council—Phoenix, AZ

Arkansas Interfaith Conference—Scott, AR

The Associated Churches of Fort Wayne & Allen County, Inc.—Fort Wayne, IN

Associated Ministries of Tacoma-Pierce County—Tacoma, WA

Attleboro Area Council of Churches, Inc.—Attleboro, MA

Berrien County Association of Churches—Benton Harbor, MI

Border Association for Refugees from Central America (BARCA), Inc.—Edinburg, TX

Brooklyn Council of Churches—Brooklyn, NY

The Cape Cod Council of Churches, Inc.—Hyannis, MA

Christian Ministries of Delaware County—Muncie, IN

Christians United in Beaver County—Beaver, PA

Churches United of the Quad City Area—Rock Island, IL

Council of Christian Communions of Greater Cincinnati—Cincinnati, OH

The Council of Churches of Santa Clara County—San Jose, CA

Council of Churches and Synagogues of Southwestern Connecticut—Stamford, CT

East Dallas Cooperative Parish—Dallas, TX

Ecclesia—Trenton, NJ

Ecumenical Conference of Greater Altoona—Altoona, PA

Ecumenical Ministries of Oregon—Portland, OR

Evansville Area Community of Churches, Inc.—Evansville, IN

FaithTrust Institute—Seattle, WA

Georgia Christian Council—Macon, GA

Grand Rapids Area Center for Ecumenism (GRACE)—Grand Rapids, MI

Greater Bethlehem Area Council of Churches—Bethlehem, PA

Greater Chicago Broadcast Ministries—Chicago, IL

Greater Dayton Christian Connections—Dayton, OH

Greater Fairmont Council of Churches—Fairmont, WV

Greater Flint Council of Churches—Flint, MI

Greater Lawrence Council of Churches—Lawrence, MA

Greater New Orleans Federation of Churches—New Orleans, LA

Greensboro Urban Ministry—Greensboro, NC

Inter-Church Council of Greater New Bedford—New Bedford, MA

InterReligious Council of Central New York—Syracuse, NY

Iowa Religious Media Services—Des Moines, IA

Massachusetts Council of Churches—Boston, MA

The Metropolitan Christian Council: Detroit-Windsor—Detroit, MI

Metropolitan Christian Council of Philadelphia—Philadelphia, PA

Metropolitan Ecumenical Ministry—Newark, NJ

Montana Association of Churches—Helena, MT

New Britain Area Conference of Churches (NEWBRACC)—New Britain, CT

New Hampshire Council of Churches—Pembroke, NH

New Mexico Conference of Churches—Albuquerque, NM

Northern Kentucky Interfaith Commission, Inc.—Newport, KY

271

Oklahoma Conference of Churches—Oklahoma City, OK

Peoria Friendship House of Christian Service—Peoria, IL

Reading Berks Conference of Churches—Reading, PA

The Regional Council of Churches of Atlanta—Atlanta, GA

San Antonio Community of Churches—San Antonio, TX

Schenectady Inner City Ministry—Schenectady, NY

South Carolina Christian Action Council, Inc.—Columbia, SC

South Coast Interfaith Council—Long Beach, CA

Staten Island Council of Churches—Staten Island, NY

Tarrant Area Community of Churches—Fort Worth, TX

Texas Conference of Churches—Austin, TX

Troy Area United Ministries—Troy, NY

United Churches of Lycoming County—Williamsport, PA

Wainwright House—Rye, NY

Wyoming Association of Churches—Cody, WY

Wyoming Valley Council of Churches—Wilkes-Barre, PA

## Clothing Distribution Programs

Asheville-Buncombe Community Christian Ministry (ABCCM)—Asheville, NC

Associated Ministries of Tacoma-Pierce County—Tacoma, WA

Attleboro Area Council of Churches, Inc.—Attleboro, MA

The Cape Cod Council of Churches, Inc.—Hyannis, MA

Chautauqua County Rural Ministry—Dunkirk, NY

Christian Ministries of Delaware County—Muncie, IN

Christian Service Center for Central Florida, Inc.—Orlando, FL

Community Emergency Assistance Program (CEAP)—Brooklyn Park, MN

Community Ministry of Montgomery County—Rockville, MD

Contact Ministries of Springfield—Springfield, IL

Cooperative Metropolitan Ministries—Newton, MA

Corpus Christi Metro Ministries—Corpus Christi, TX

Council of Churches of the Ozarks—Springfield, MO

Cross-Lines Cooperative Council—Kansas City, KS

East Dallas Cooperative Parish—Dallas, TX

Eastern Area Community Ministries—Louisville, KY

The Ecumenical Council of Pasadena Area Churches—Pasadena, CA

Evanston Ecumenical Action Council—Evanston, IL

Fern Creek-Highview United Ministries—Louisvlle, KY

Greater Birmingham Ministries—Birmingham, AL

Greater Fairmont Council of Churches—Fairmont, WV

Greater Lawrence Council of Churches—Lawrence, MA

Greater Minneapolis Council of Churches—Minneapolis, MN

Greensboro Urban Ministry—Greensboro, NC

Hanover Area Council of Churches—Hanover, PA

Highlands Community Ministries—Louisville, KY

Inter-Church Ministries of Erie County—Erie, PA

Interfaith Community Services—St. Joseph, MO

Lancaster County Council of Churches—Lancaster, PA

Lebanon County Christian Ministries—Lebanon, PA

Lehigh County Conference of Churches—Allentown, PA

Lewisburg Council of Churches—Lewisburg, PA

Metropolitan Ecumenical Ministry—Newark, NJ

New Mexico Conference of Churches—Albuquerque, NM

Northside Inter-Church Agency (NICA)—Fort Worth, TX

Peoria Friendship House of Christian Service—Peoria, IL

Reading Berks Conference of Churches—Reading, PA

Saint. Paul Area Council of Churches—St. Paul, MN

South East Associated Ministries (SEAM)—Louisville, KY

South Hills Interfaith Ministries—South Park, PA

Tuscarawas County Council for Church and Community—New Philadelphia, OH

West Side Ecumenical Ministry—Cleveland, OH

Wilkinsburg Community Ministry—Pittsburgh, PA

## CROP Walks

Akron Area Association of Churches—Akron, OH

Asheville-Buncombe Community Christian Ministry (ABCCM)—Asheville, NC

Associated Ministries of Tacoma-Pierce County—Tacoma, WA

Attleboro Area Council of Churches, Inc.—Attleboro, MA

Austin Area Interreligious Ministries—Austin, TX

Berrien County Association of Churches—Benton Harbor, MI

Broome County Council of Churches, Inc.—Binghamton, NY

Capital Area Council of Churches, Inc.—Albany, NY

Chautaugua County Rural Ministry—Dunkirk, NY

Christian Churches United of the Tri-County Area—Harrisburg, PA

Christian Ministries of Delaware County—Muncie, IN

Christian Service Center for Central Florida, Inc.—Orlando, FL

Church Community Services—Elkhart, IN

The Church Federation of Greater Indianapolis, Inc.—Indianapolis, IN

Churches United, Inc.—Cedar Rapids, IA

Churches United of the Quad City Area—Rock Island, IL

Community Emergency Assistance Program (CEAP)—Brooklyn Park, MN

Council of Churches of Chemung County, Inc.—Elmira, NY

Council of Churches of Greater Bridgeport, Inc.—Bridgeport, CT

Council of Churches of Greater Springfield—Springfield, MA

The Council of Churches of Santa Clara County—San Jose, CA

Dutchess County Interfaith Council, Inc.—Poughkeepsie, NY

East Dallas Cooperative Parish—Dallas, TX

East End Cooperative Ministry—Pittsburgh, PA

Ecclesia—Trenton, NJ

The Ecumenical Council of Pasadena Area Churches—Pasadena, CA

Ecumenical Ministries—Fulton, MO

Evanston Ecumenical Action Council—Evanston, IL

Evansville Area Community of Churches, Inc.—Evansville, IN

Greater Bethlehem Area Council of Churches—Bethlehem, PA

Greater Dayton Christian Connections—Dayton, OH

Greater Fairmont Council of Churches—Fairmont, WV

Greater Flint Council of Churches—Flint, MI

Greater Waterbury Interfaith Ministries, Inc.—Waterbury, CT

Greensboro Urban Ministry—Greensboro, NC

Hanover Area Council of Churches—Hanover, PA

Inter-Church Ministries of Erie County—Erie, PA

Interfaith Conference of Greater Milwaukee—Milwaukee, WI

Interfaith Council—Spokane, WA

Inter-Faith Ministries—Wichita—Wichita, KS

Interfaith Works—Olympia, WA

Lancaster County Council of Churches—Lancaster, PA

Lebanon County Christian Ministries—Lebanon, PA

Lehigh County Conference of Churches—Allentown, PA

Lewisburg Council of Churches—Lewisburg, PA

The Long Island Council of Churches—Hempstead, NY

Mahoning Valley Association of Churches—Youngstown, OH

The Metropolitan Christian Council: Detroit-Windsor—Detroit, MI

Metropolitan Ecumenical Ministry—Newark, NJ

Muskegon County Cooperating Churches—Muskegon, MI

Network of Religious Communities—Buffalo, NY

New Mexico Conference of Churches—Albuquerque, NM

Northside Inter-Church Agency (NICA)—Fort Worth, TX

Oak Park-River Forest Community of Congregations—Oak Park, IL

Peoria Friendship House of Christian Service—Peoria, IL

Pike County Outreach Council—Waverly, OH

Reading Berks Conference of Churches—Reading, PA

Saint. Paul Area Council of Churches—St. Paul, MN

San Antonio Community of Churches—San Antonio, TX

San Fernando Valley Interfaith Council—Chatsworth, CA

Schenectady Inner City Ministry—Schenectady, NY

South Coast Interfaith Council—Long Beach, CA

Staten Island Council of Churches—Staten Island, NY

Tarrant Area Community of Churches—Fort Worth, TX

Troy Area United Ministries—Troy, NY

Tuscarawas County Council for Church and Community—New Philadelphia, OH

United Churches of Lycoming County—Williamsport, PA

United Religious Community of St. Joseph County—South Bend, IN

Wilkinsburg Community Ministry—Pittsburgh, PA

Worcester County Ecumenical Council—Worcester, MA

Wyoming Valley Council of Churches—Wilkes-Barre, PA

York County Council of Churches—York, PA

## Domestic Violence

Arizona Ecumenical Council—Phoenix, AZ

Asheville-Buncombe Community Christian Ministry (ABCCM)—Asheville, NC

Associated Ministries of Tacoma-Pierce County—Tacoma, WA

Association of Religious Communities—Danbury, CT

Chautaugua County Rural Ministry—Dunkirk, NY

Churches United of the Quad City Area—Rock Island, IL

Colorado Council of Churches—Denver, CO

Contact Ministries of Springfield—Springfield, IL

The Council of Churches of Santa Clara County—San Jose, CA

Dutchess County Interfaith Council, Inc.—Poughkeepsie, NY

The Ecumenical Council of Pasadena Area Churches—Pasadena, CA

Ecumenical Council of San Diego County—San Diego, CA

Ecumenical Ministries of Oregon—Portland, OR

FaithTrust Institute—Seattle, WA

Genesee-Orleans Ministry of Concern—Albion, NY

Greater Chicago Broadcast Ministries—Chicago, IL

Greater Minneapolis Council of Churches—Minneapolis, MN

Indiana Partners for Christian Unity and Mission—Indianapolis, IN

Inter-Church Council of Greater New Bedford—New Bedford, MA

Interchurch Ministries of Nebraska—Lincoln, NE

Interfaith Council—Spokane, WA

Interfaith Service Bureau—Sacramento, CA

The Long Island Council of Churches—Hempstead, NY

The Metropolitan Christian Council: Detroit-Windsor—Detroit, MI

Metropolitan Ecumenical Ministry—Newark, NJ

Mississippi Religious Leadership Conference—Jackson, MS

Network of Religious Communities—Buffalo, NY

New Hampshire Council of Churches—Pembroke, NH

New Mexico Conference of Churches—Albuquerque, NM

North Hills Youth Ministry Counseling Center—Pittsburgh, PA

Peoria Friendship House of Christian Service—Peoria, IL

The Rhode Island State Council of Churches—Providence, RI

Saint. Paul Area Council of Churches—St. Paul, MN

San Antonio Community of Churches—San Antonio, TX

South Carolina Christian Action Council, Inc.—Columbia, SC

Southeast Ecumenical Ministry—Rochester, NY

Troy Area United Ministries—Troy, NY

Tulsa Metropolitan Ministry—Tulsa, OK

United Religious Community of St. Joseph County—South Bend, IN

Vermont Ecumenical Council and Bible Society—Richmond, VT

West Side Ecumenical Ministry—Cleveland, OH

Wyoming Association of Churches—Cody, WY

## Economic/Social Justice Programs

Arizona Ecumenical Council—Phoenix, AZ

Arkansas Interfaith Conference—Scott, AR

Asheville-Buncombe Community Christian Ministry (ABCCM)—Asheville, NC

The Associated Churches of Fort Wayne & Allen County, Inc.—Fort Wayne, IN

Associated Ministries of Tacoma-Pierce County—Tacoma, WA

Association of Christian Churches of South Dakota—Sioux Falls, SD

Austin Area Interreligious Ministries—Austin, TX

Brooklyn Council of Churches—Brooklyn, NY

Broome County Council of Churches, Inc.—Binghamton, NY

California Council of Churches-California Church Impact—Sacramento, CA

The Cape Cod Council of Churches, Inc.—Hyannis, MA

Capital Area Council of Churches, Inc.—Albany, NY

Capital Region Ecumenical Organization (CREO)—Schenectady, NY

The Capitol Region Conference of Churches—Hartford, CT

Chautauqua County Rural Ministry—Dunkirk, NY

Christian Associates of Southwest Pennsylvania—Pittsburgh, PA

Christian Churches United of the Tri-County Area—Harrisburg, PA

Christian Ministries of Delaware County—Muncie, IN

Christian Service Center for Central Florida, Inc.—Orlando, FL

Church Council of Greater Seattle—Seattle, WA

Churches United, Inc.—Cedar Rapids, IA

Colorado Council of Churches—Denver, CO

Community Emergency Assistance Program (CEAP)—Brooklyn Park, MN

Community Ministry of Montgomery County—Rockville, MD

Community Renewal Society—Chicago, IL

Contact Ministries of Springfield—Springfield, IL

Cooperative Metropolitan Ministries—Newton, MA

Council of Churches of the City of New York—New York, NY

Council of Churches of Greater Bridgeport, Inc.—Bridgeport, CT

Council of Churches of Greater Springfield—Springfield, MA

The Council of Churches of Santa Clara County—San Jose, CA

Eastern Area Community Ministries—Louisville, KY

Ecclesia—Trenton, NJ

Ecumenical Conference of Greater Altoona—Altoona, PA

The Ecumenical Council of Pasadena Area Churches—Pasadena, CA

Ecumenical Ministries of Oregon—Portland, OR

Evanston Ecumenical Action Council—Evanston, IL

Faith Community Assistance Center—Santa Fe, NM

Florida Council of Churches—Tampa, FL

Fresno Metro Ministry—Fresno, CA

Grand Rapids Area Center for Ecumenism (GRACE)—Grand Rapids, MI

Greater Birmingham Ministries—Birmingham, AL

Greater Chicago Broadcast Ministries—Chicago, IL

Greater Dallas Community of Churches—Dallas, TX

Greater Dayton Christian Connections—Dayton, OH

Greater Minneapolis Council of Churches—Minneapolis, MN

Greater Rochester Community of Churches—Rochester, NY

Highlands Community Ministries—Louisville, KY

Illinois Conference of Churches—Springfield, IL

Inter-Church Council of Greater New Bedford—New Bedford, MA

Inter-Church Ministries of Erie County—Erie, PA

Interchurch Ministries of Nebraska—Lincoln, NE

Interfaith Community Council, Inc.—New Albany, IN

Interfaith Conference of Greater Milwaukee—Milwaukee, WI

InterFaith Conference of Metropolitan Washington—Washington, DC

Interfaith Council—Spokane, WA

Interfaith Council of Contra Costa County—Walnut Creek, CA

Inter-Faith Ministries-Wichita—Wichita, KS

Interfaith Mission Service—Huntsville, AL

Interfaith Service Bureau—Sacramento, CA

InterReligious Council of Central New York—Syracuse, NY

The Joint Religious Legislative Coalition—Minneapolis, MN

Kansas Ecumenical Ministries—Topeka, KS

Kentuckiana Interfaith Community—Louisville, KY

Kentucky Council of Churches—Lexington, KY

Lancaster County Council of Churches—Lancaster, PA

Lehigh County Conference of Churches—Allentown, PA

Lincoln Interfaith Council—Lincoln, NE

Louisiana Interchurch Conference—Baton Rouge, LA

Madison-area Urban Ministry—Madison, WI

Mahoning Valley Association of Churches—Youngstown, OH

Maine Council of Churches—Portland, ME

Marin Interfaith Council—San Rafael, CA

Massachusetts Council of Churches—Boston, MA

The Metropolitan Christian Council: Detroit-Windsor—Detroit, MI

Metropolitan Christian Council of Philadelphia—Philadelphia, PA

Metropolitan Ecumenical Ministry—Newark, NJ

Metropolitan Inter-Faith Association (MIFA)—Memphis, TN

Metropolitan Interfaith Council on Affordable Housing (MICAH)—Minneapolis, MN

Minnesota Council of Churches—Minneapolis, MN

Mississippi Religious Leadership Conference—Jackson, MS

Montana Association of Churches—Helena, MT

Muskegon County Cooperating Churches—Muskegon, MI

New Britain Area Conference of Churches (NEWBRACC)—New Britain, CT

New Hampshire Council of Churches—Pembroke, NH

New Mexico Conference of Churches—Albuquerque, NM

North Carolina Council of Churches—Raleigh, NC

North Dakota Conference of Churches—Ashley, ND

Northern California Interreligious Conference—Oakland, CA

Northside Inter-Church Agency (NICA)—Fort Worth, TX

Northwest Interfaith Movement—Philadelphia, PA

Oak Park-River Forest Community of Congregations—Oak Park, IL

Oklahoma Conference of Churches—Oklahoma City, OK

Pennsylvania Conference on Interchurch Cooperation—Harrisburg, PA

The Pennsylvania Council of Churches—Harrisburg, PA

Peoria Friendship House of Christian Service—Peoria, IL

Queens Federation of Churches—Richmond Hill, NY

The Regional Council of Churches of Atlanta—Atlanta, GA

The Rhode Island State Council of Churches—Providence, RI

Rural Migrant Ministry—Poughkeepsie, NY

Saint. Paul Area Council of Churches—St. Paul, MN

275

San Antonio Community of Churches—San Antonio, TX

San Fernando Valley Interfaith Council—Chatsworth, CA

Schenectady Inner City Ministry—Schenectady, NY

South Carolina Christian Action Council, Inc.—Columbia, SC

South Coast Interfaith Council—Long Beach, CA

South East Associated Ministries (SEAM)—Louisville, KY

South Louisville Community Ministries—Louisville, KY

Southern California Ecumenical Council—Pasadena, CA

Tarrant Area Community of Churches—Fort Worth, TX

Texas Conference of Churches—Austin, TX

Troy Area United Ministries—Troy, NY

Tulsa Metropolitan Ministry—Tulsa, OK

United Churches of Lycoming County—Williamsport, PA

United Religious Community of St. Joseph County—South Bend, IN

Vermont Ecumenical Council and Bible Society—Richmond, VT

Virginia Council of Churches, Inc.—Richmond, VA

Wainwright House—Rye, NY

Washington Association of Churches—Seattle, WA

West Virginia Council of Churches—Charleston, WV

Wilkinsburg Community Ministry—Pittsburgh, PA

Wisconsin Council of Churches—Sun Prairie, WI

Wyoming Association of Churches—Cody, WY

## Employment Assistance Programs

Asheville-Buncombe Community Christian Ministry (ABCCM)—Asheville, NC

The Associated Churches of Fort Wayne & Allen County, Inc.—Fort Wayne, IN

Chautauqua County Rural Ministry—Dunkirk, NY

Christian Community Action—New Haven, CT

Community Emergency Assistance Program (CEAP)—Brooklyn Park, MN

Contact Ministries of Springfield—Springfield, IL

Corpus Christi Metro Ministries—Corpus Christi, TX

Council of Churches of Greater Bridgeport, Inc.—Bridgeport, CT

East Dallas Cooperative Parish—Dallas, TX

East End Cooperative Ministry—Pittsburgh, PA

Eastern Area Community Ministries—Louisville, KY

Evanston Ecumenical Action Council—Evanston, IL

Fern Creek-Highview United Ministries—Louisvlle, KY

Genesee-Orleans Ministry of Concern—Albion, NY

Greater Chicago Broadcast Ministries—Chicago, IL

Greater Dallas Community of Churches—Dallas, TX

Greater Minneapolis Council of Churches—Minneapolis, MN

Greensboro Urban Ministry—Greensboro, NC

Kentuckiana Interfaith Community—Louisville, KY

Lehigh County Conference of Churches—Allentown, PA

Metropolitan Ecumenical Ministry—Newark, NJ

Muskegon County Cooperating Churches—Muskegon, MI

Network of Religious Communities—Buffalo, NY

Northside Inter-Church Agency (NICA)—Fort Worth, TX

Peoria Friendship House of Christian Service—Peoria, IL

Schenectady Inner City Ministry—Schenectady, NY

South East Associated Ministries (SEAM)—Louisville, KY

Southeast Ecumenical Ministry—Rochester, NY

United Ministries—Greenville, SC

Virginia Council of Churches, Inc.—Richmond, VA

West Side Ecumenical Ministry—Cleveland, OH

## Environmental Programs

Akron Area Association of Churches—Akron, OH

Arizona Ecumenical Council—Phoenix, AZ

California Council of Churches-California Church Impact—Sacramento, CA

The Capitol Region Conference of Churches—Hartford, CT

Christian Associates of Southwest Pennsylvania—Pittsburgh, PA

Colorado Council of Churches—Denver, CO

The Council of Churches of Santa Clara County—San Jose, CA

Ecumenical Ministries of Iowa (EMI)—Des Moines, IA

Ecumenical Ministries of Oregon—Portland, OR

Florida Council of Churches—Tampa, FL

Fresno Metro Ministry—Fresno, CA

Georgia Christian Council—Macon, GA

Greater Chicago Broadcast Ministries—Chicago, IL

Greater Dayton Christian Connections—Dayton, OH

Inter-Church Council of Greater New Bedford—New Bedford, MA

Interfaith Conference of Greater Milwaukee—Milwaukee, WI

InterFaith Conference of Metropolitan Washington—Washington, DC

Interfaith Mission Service—Huntsville, AL

Kentucky Council of Churches—Lexington, KY

Louisiana Interchurch Conference—Baton Rouge, LA

Maine Council of Churches—Portland, ME

Marin Interfaith Council—San Rafael, CA

Massachusetts Council of Churches—Boston, MA

The Metropolitan Christian Council: Detroit-Windsor—Detroit, MI

Metropolitan Christian Council of Philadelphia—Philadelphia, PA

Metropolitan Ecumenical Ministry—Newark, NJ

Mississippi Religious Leadership Conference—Jackson, MS

Montana Association of Churches—Helena, MT

Muskegon County Cooperating Churches—Muskegon, MI

Network of Religious Communities—Buffalo, NY

New Hampshire Council of Churches—Pembroke, NH

New Mexico Conference of Churches—Albuquerque, NM

North Carolina Council of Churches—Raleigh, NC

Northern California Interreligious Conference—Oakland, CA

Oklahoma Conference of Churches—Oklahoma City, OK

The Pennsylvania Council of Churches—Harrisburg, PA

The Regional Council of Churches of Atlanta—Atlanta, GA

South Carolina Christian Action Council, Inc.—Columbia, SC

South Coast Interfaith Council—Long Beach, CA

Southern California Ecumenical Council—Pasadena, CA

United Churches of Lycoming County—Williamsport, PA

Vermont Ecumenical Council and Bible Society—Richmond, VT

Washington Association of Churches—Seattle, WA

West Virginia Council of Churches—Charleston, WV

## Faith and Order Programs

Akron Area Association of Churches—Akron, OH

Arizona Ecumenical Council—Phoenix, AZ

Associated Ministries of Tacoma-Pierce County—Tacoma, WA

Association of Christian Churches of South Dakota—Sioux Falls, SD

The Cape Cod Council of Churches, Inc.—Hyannis, MA

Capital Area Council of Churches, Inc.—Albany, NY

Capital Region Ecumenical Organization (CREO)—Schenectady, NY

Christian Associates of Southwest Pennsylvania—Pittsburgh, PA

Church Council of Greater Seattle—Seattle, WA

Churches United, Inc.—Cedar Rapids, IA

Colorado Council of Churches—Denver, CO

Council of Churches of the City of New York—New York, NY

Council of Churches of Greater Bridgeport, Inc.—Bridgeport, CT

Council of Churches of Greater Springfield—Springfield, MA

The Council of Churches of Santa Clara County—San Jose, CA

Council of Churches and Synagogues of Southwestern Connecticut—Stamford, CT

East Dallas Cooperative Parish—Dallas, TX

Ecclesia—Trenton, NJ

Ecumenical Council of San Diego County—San Diego, CA

Ecumenical Ministries of Iowa (EMI)—Des Moines, IA

Ecumenical Ministries of Oregon—Portland, OR

Evansville Area Community of Churches, Inc.—Evansville, IN

Florida Council of Churches—Tampa, FL

Georgia Christian Council—Macon, GA

Greater Chicago Broadcast Ministries—Chicago, IL

Greater Dallas Community of Churches—Dallas, TX

Greater Dayton Christian Connections—Dayton, OH

Greater Lawrence Council of Churches—Lawrence, MA

Greater New Orleans Federation of Churches—New Orleans, LA

Greater Rochester Community of Churches—Rochester, NY

Greater Waterbury Interfaith Ministries, Inc.—Waterbury, CT

Illinois Conference of Churches—Springfield, IL

Inter-Church Council of Greater New Bedford—New Bedford, MA

Interchurch Ministries of Nebraska—Lincoln, NE

InterFaith Conference of Metropolitan Washington—Washington, DC

Interfaith Council of Contra Costa County—Walnut Creek, CA

InterReligious Council of Central New York—Syracuse, NY

277

Kansas Ecumenical Ministries—Topeka, KS

Kentuckiana Interfaith Community—Louisville, KY

Kentucky Council of Churches—Lexington, KY

Lehigh County Conference of Churches—Allentown, PA

Louisiana Interchurch Conference—Baton Rouge, LA

Mahoning Valley Association of Churches—Youngstown, OH

The Metropolitan Christian Council: Detroit-Windsor—Detroit, MI

Metropolitan Christian Council of Philadelphia—Philadelphia, PA

Metropolitan Ecumenical Ministry—Newark, NJ

Minnesota Council of Churches—Minneapolis, MN

Montana Association of Churches—Helena, MT

Network of Religious Communities—Buffalo, NY

New Britain Area Conference of Churches (NEWBRACC)—New Britain, CT

New Hampshire Council of Churches—Pembroke, NH

New Mexico Conference of Churches—Albuquerque, NM

North Carolina Council of Churches—Raleigh, NC

North Dakota Conference of Churches—Ashley, ND

Northern California Interreligious Conference—Oakland, CA

Northern Kentucky Interfaith Commission, Inc.—Newport, KY

Ohio Council of Churches—Columbus, OH

Oklahoma Conference of Churches—Oklahoma City, OK

The Pennsylvania Council of Churches—Harrisburg, PA

Queens Federation of Churches—Richmond Hill, NY

The Rhode Island State Council of Churches—Providence, RI

Schenectady Inner City Ministry—Schenectady, NY

South Carolina Christian Action Council, Inc.—Columbia, SC

South Coast Interfaith Council—Long Beach, CA

Southern California Ecumenical Council—Pasadena, CA

Texas Conference of Churches—Austin, TX

Troy Area United Ministries—Troy, NY

Tulsa Metropolitan Ministry—Tulsa, OK

United Religious Community of St. Joseph County—South Bend, IN

Vermont Ecumenical Council and Bible Society—Richmond, VT

Virginia Council of Churches, Inc.—Richmond, VA

Wainwright House—Rye, NY

Washington Association of Churches—Seattle, WA

West Virginia Council of Churches—Charleston, WV

Wisconsin Council of Churches—Sun Prairie, WI

Wyoming Valley Council of Churches—Wilkes-Barre, PA

## Health Care Issues

Asheville-Buncombe Community Christian Ministry (ABCCM)—Asheville, NC

California Council of Churches-California Church Impact—Sacramento, CA

Churchpeople for Change and Reconciliation—Lima, OH

Community Ministries of Rockville—Rockville, MD

Community Renewal Society—Chicago, IL

Corpus Christi Metro Ministries—Corpus Christi, TX

Council of Churches of the City of New York—New York, NY

The Council of Churches of Santa Clara County—San Jose, CA

East Dallas Cooperative Parish—Dallas, TX

Eastern Area Community Ministries—Louisville, KY

Ecumenical Ministries of Iowa (EMI)—Des Moines, IA

Fresno Metro Ministry—Fresno, CA

Greater Baton Rouge Federation of Churches and Synagogues—Baton Rouge, LA

Greater Chicago Broadcast Ministries—Chicago, IL

Greater Rochester Community of Churches—Rochester, NY

Greensboro Urban Ministry—Greensboro, NC

Highlands Community Ministries—Louisville, KY

Inter-Church Council of Greater New Bedford—New Bedford, MA

Interfaith Conference of Greater Milwaukee—Milwaukee, WI

Lehigh County Conference of Churches—Allentown, PA

Louisiana Interchurch Conference—Baton Rouge, LA

Marin Interfaith Council—San Rafael, CA

The Metropolitan Christian Council: Detroit-Windsor—Detroit, MI

Metropolitan Ecumenical Ministry—Newark, NJ

Metropolitan Ecumenical Ministry Community Development Corp.—Newark, NJ

Mississippi Religious Leadership Conference—Jackson, MS

Montana Association of Churches—Helena, MT

Network of Religious Communities—Buffalo, NY

New Hampshire Council of Churches—Pembroke, NH

New Mexico Conference of Churches—Albuquerque, NM

North Carolina Council of Churches—Raleigh, NC

Oklahoma Conference of Churches—Oklahoma City, OK

The Pennsylvania Council of Churches—Harrisburg, PA

Peoria Friendship House of Christian Service—Peoria, IL

Pike County Outreach Council—Waverly, OH

The Regional Council of Churches of Atlanta—Atlanta, GA

Schenectady Inner City Ministry—Schenectady, NY

Southeast Ecumenical Ministry—Rochester, NY

Tarrant Area Community of Churches—Fort Worth, TX

Tuscarawas County Council for Church and Community—New Philadelphia, OH

United Religious Community of St. Joseph County—South Bend, IN

Washington Association of Churches—Seattle, WA

West Virginia Council of Churches—Charleston, WV

## Homelessness/Shelter Programs

Allegheny Valley Association of Churches—Natrona Heights, PA

Arkansas Interfaith Conference—Scott, AR

Asheville-Buncombe Community Christian Ministry (ABCCM)—Asheville, NC

The Associated Churches of Fort Wayne & Allen County, Inc.—Fort Wayne, IN

Associated Ministries of Tacoma-Pierce County—Tacoma, WA

Attleboro Area Council of Churches, Inc.—Attleboro, MA

Austin Area Interreligious Ministries—Austin, TX

The Cape Cod Council of Churches, Inc.—Hyannis, MA

Capital Area Council of Churches, Inc.—Albany, NY

The Capitol Region Conference of Churches—Hartford, CT

Center City Churches—Hartford, CT

Chautauqua County Rural Ministry—Dunkirk, NY

Christian Churches United of the Tri-County Area—Harrisburg, PA

Christian Community Action—New Haven, CT

Christian Ministries of Delaware County—Muncie, IN

Christian Service Center for Central Florida, Inc.—Orlando, FL

Church Council of Greater Seattle—Seattle, WA

Churches United, Inc.—Cedar Rapids, IA

Churches United of the Quad City Area—Rock Island, IL

Colorado Council of Churches—Denver, CO

Community Emergency Assistance Program (CEAP)—Brooklyn Park, MN

Community Ministries of Rockville—Rockville, MD

Community Ministry of Montgomery County—Rockville, MD

Community Renewal Society—Chicago, IL

Contact Ministries of Springfield—Springfield, IL

Cooperative Metropolitan Ministries—Newton, MA

Corpus Christi Metro Ministries—Corpus Christi, TX

Council of Churches of the City of New York—New York, NY

Council of Churches of Greater Bridgeport, Inc.—Bridgeport, CT

Council of Churches of Greater Springfield—Springfield, MA

The Council of Churches of Santa Clara County—San Jose, CA

East End Cooperative Ministry—Pittsburgh, PA

The Ecumenical Council of Pasadena Area Churches—Pasadena, CA

Ecumenical Council of San Diego County—San Diego, CA

Ecumenical Ministries—Fulton, MO

Ecumenical Ministries of Oregon—Portland, OR

Evanston Ecumenical Action Council—Evanston, IL

Faith Community Assistance Center—Santa Fe, NM

Genesee-Orleans Ministry of Concern—Albion, NY

Grand Rapids Area Center for Ecumenism (GRACE)—Grand Rapids, MI

Greater Bethlehem Area Council of Churches—Bethlehem, PA

Greater Chicago Broadcast Ministries—Chicago, IL

Greater Minneapolis Council of Churches—Minneapolis, MN

Greensboro Urban Ministry—Greensboro, NC

Hanover Area Council of Churches—Hanover, PA

Highlands Community Ministries—Louisville, KY

Inter-Church Ministries of Erie County—Erie, PA

Interfaith Community Council, Inc.—New Albany, IN

Interfaith Community Services—St. Joseph, MO

Interfaith Conference of Greater Milwaukee—Milwaukee, WI

InterFaith Conference of Metropolitan Washington—Washington, DC

279

Inter-Faith Ministries-Wichita—Wichita, KS

Interfaith Mission Service—Huntsville, AL

Interfaith Works—Olympia, WA

InterReligious Council of Central New York—Syracuse, NY

Lehigh County Conference of Churches—Allentown, PA

Lewisburg Council of Churches—Lewisburg, PA

The Long Island Council of Churches—Hempstead, NY

Maine Council of Churches—Portland, ME

Marin Interfaith Council—San Rafael, CA

Metropolitan Ecumenical Ministry—Newark, NJ

Metropolitan Inter Faith Association (MIFA)—Memphis, TN

Metropolitan Interfaith Council on Affordable Housing (MICAH)—Minneapolis, MN

Mississippi Religious Leadership Conference—Jackson, MS

Montana Association of Churches—Helena, MT

Muskegon County Cooperating Churches—Muskegon, MI

New Britain Area Conference of Churches (NEWBRACC)—New Britain, CT

New Hampshire Council of Churches—Pembroke, NH

New Mexico Conference of Churches—Albuquerque, NM

North Carolina Council of Churches—Raleigh, NC

Northside Common Ministries—Pittsburgh, PA

Northside Inter-Church Agency (NICA)—Fort Worth, TX

Paducah Cooperative Ministry—Paducah, KY

Peoria Friendship House of Christian Service—Peoria, IL

Pike County Outreach Council—Waverly, OH

Reading Berks Conference of Churches—Reading, PA

The Regional Council of Churches of Atlanta—Atlanta, GA

The Rhode Island State Council of Churches—Providence, RI

Saint. Paul Area Council of Churches—St. Paul, MN

San Antonio Community of Churches—San Antonio, TX

Schenectady Inner City Ministry—Schenectady, NY

South Carolina Christian Action Council, Inc.—Columbia, SC

South Coast Interfaith Council—Long Beach, CA

South Louisville Community Ministries—Louisville, KY

Tarrant Area Community of Churches—Fort Worth, TX

Troy Area United Ministries—Troy, NY

Tulsa Metropolitan Ministry—Tulsa, OK

Tuscarawas County Council for Church and Community—New Philadelphia, OH

United Ministries—Greenville, SC

United Religious Community of St. Joseph County—South Bend, IN

Wyoming Valley Council of Churches—Wilkes-Barre, PA

## Hunger/Food Programs

Allegheny Valley Association of Churches—Natrona Heights, PA

Arkansas Interfaith Conference—Scott, AR

Asheville-Buncombe Community Christian Ministry (ABCCM)—Asheville, NC

The Associated Churches of Fort Wayne & Allen County, Inc.—Fort Wayne, IN

Associated Ministries of Tacoma-Pierce County—Tacoma, WA

Attleboro Area Council of Churches, Inc.—Attleboro, MA

Austin Area Interreligious Ministries—Austin, TX

Brooklyn Council of Churches—Brooklyn, NY

Broome County Council of Churches, Inc.—Binghamton, NY

California Council of Churches-California Church Impact—Sacramento, CA

The Cape Cod Council of Churches, Inc.—Hyannis, MA

Capital Area Council of Churches, Inc.—Albany, NY

Center City Churches—Hartford, CT

Chautauqua County Rural Ministry—Dunkirk, NY

Christian Churches United of the Tri-County Area—Harrisburg, PA

Christian Community Action—New Haven, CT

Christian Ministries of Delaware County—Muncie, IN

Christian Service Center for Central Florida, Inc.—Orlando, FL

Church Community Services—Elkhart, IN

Church Council of Greater Seattle—Seattle, WA

The Church Federation of Greater Indianapolis, Inc.—Indianapolis, IN

Churches United of the Quad City Area—Rock Island, IL

Community Emergency Assistance Program (CEAP)—Brooklyn Park, MN

Community Ministry of Montgomery County—Rockville, MD

Concerned Ecumenical Ministry to the Upper West Side—Buffalo, NY

Contact Ministries of Springfield—Springfield, IL

Corpus Christi Metro Ministries—Corpus Christi, TX

Council of Churches of the City of New York—New York, NY

Council of Churches of Greater Bridgeport, Inc.—Bridgeport, CT

Council of Churches of the Ozarks—Springfield, MO

The Council of Churches of Santa Clara County—San Jose, CA

Council of Churches and Synagogues of Southwestern Connecticut—Stamford, CT

Cross-Lines Cooperative Council—Kansas City, KS

Des Moines Area Religious Council—Des Moines, IA

Dutchess County Interfaith Council, Inc.—Poughkeepsie, NY

East Dallas Cooperative Parish—Dallas, TX

East End Cooperative Ministry—Pittsburgh, PA

Eastern Area Community Ministries—Louisville, KY

Ecclesia—Trenton, NJ

The Ecumenical Council of Pasadena Area Churches—Pasadena, CA

Ecumenical Ministries of Oregon—Portland, OR

Evanston Ecumenical Action Council—Evanston, IL

Evansville Area Community of Churches, Inc.—Evansville, IN

Faith Community Assistance Center—Santa Fe, NM

Fern Creek-Highview United Ministries—Louisvlle, KY

Fresno Metro Ministry—Fresno, CA

Genesee County Churches United, Inc.—Batavia, NY

Genesee-Orleans Ministry of Concern—Albion, NY

Grand Rapids Area Center for Ecumenism (GRACE)—Grand Rapids, MI

Greater Baton Rouge Federation of Churches and Synagogues—Baton Rouge, LA

Greater Bethlehem Area Council of Churches—Bethlehem, PA

Greater Birmingham Ministries—Birmingham, AL

Greater Chicago Broadcast Ministries—Chicago, IL

Greater Dallas Community of Churches—Dallas, TX

Greater Minneapolis Council of Churches—Minneapolis, MN

Greater New Orleans Federation of Churches—New Orleans, LA

Greater Waterbury Interfaith Ministries, Inc.—Waterbury, CT

Greensboro Urban Ministry—Greensboro, NC

Hanover Area Council of Churches—Hanover, PA

Highlands Community Ministries—Louisville, KY

Inter-Church Ministries of Erie County—Erie, PA

Interfaith Community Council, Inc.—New Albany, IN

Interfaith Community Services—St. Joseph, MO

InterFaith Conference of Metropolitan Washington—Washington, DC

Inter-Faith Ministries-Wichita—Wichita, KS

Interfaith Mission Service—Huntsville, AL

InterReligious Council of Central New York—Syracuse, NY

Kentuckiana Interfaith Community—Louisville, KY

Lancaster County Council of Churches—Lancaster, PA

Lebanon County Christian Ministries—Lebanon, PA

Lehigh County Conference of Churches—Allentown, PA

Lewisburg Council of Churches—Lewisburg, PA

The Long Island Council of Churches—Hempstead, NY

The Metropolitan Christian Council: Detroit-Windsor—Detroit, MI

Metropolitan Ecumenical Ministry—Newark, NJ

Minnesota Council of Churches—Minneapolis, MN

Mississippi Religious Leadership Conference—Jackson, MS

Montana Association of Churches—Helena, MT

Muskegon County Cooperating Churches—Muskegon, MI

Network of Religious Communities—Buffalo, NY

New Britain Area Conference of Churches (NEWBRACC)—New Britain, CT

New Hampshire Council of Churches—Pembroke, NH

New Mexico Conference of Churches—Albuquerque, NM

Northside Common Ministries—Pittsburgh, PA

Northside Inter-Church Agency (NICA)—Fort Worth, TX

Northwest Harvest-E. M. M.—Seattle, WA

Oak Park-River Forest Community of Congregations—Oak Park, IL

Paducah Cooperative Ministry—Paducah, KY

Peoria Friendship House of Christian Service—Peoria, IL

Pike County Outreach Council—Waverly, OH

Queens Federation of Churches—Richmond Hill, NY

Reading Berks Conference of Churches—Reading, PA

The Regional Council for Christian Ministry, Inc.—Idaho Falls, ID

The Regional Council of Churches of Atlanta—Atlanta, GA

The Rhode Island State Council of Churches—Providence, RI

Saint. Paul Area Council of Churches—St. Paul, MN

281

San Antonio Community of Churches—San Antonio, TX

San Fernando Valley Interfaith Council—Chatsworth, CA

Schenectady Inner City Ministry—Schenectady, NY

South Carolina Christian Action Council, Inc.—Columbia, SC

South Coast Interfaith Council—Long Beach, CA

South East Associated Ministries (SEAM)—Louisville, KY

South Hills Interfaith Ministries—South Park, PA

South Louisville Community Ministries—Louisville, KY

Southeast Ecumenical Ministry—Rochester, NY

Staten Island Council of Churches—Staten Island, NY

Tulsa Metropolitan Ministry—Tulsa, OK

Tuscarawas County Council for Church and Community—New Philadelphia, OH

United Churches of Lycoming County—Williamsport, PA

United Ministries—Greenville, SC

United Religious Community of St. Joseph County—South Bend, IN

Washington Association of Churches—Seattle, WA

Wellspring Interfaith Social Services, Inc. (previously West Central Neighborhood Ministry, Inc.)—Fort Wayne, IN

West Side Ecumenical Ministry—Cleveland, OH

Wilkinsburg Community Ministry—Pittsburgh, PA

Wyoming Valley Council of Churches—Wilkes-Barre, PA

York County Council of Churches—York, PA

## Immigration Issues

Arkansas Interfaith Conference—Scott, AR

Association of Religious Communities—Danbury, CT

Austin Area Interreligious Ministries—Austin, TX

Border Association for Refugees from Central America (BARCA), Inc.—Edinburg, TX

Chautauqua County Rural Ministry—Dunkirk, NY

Community Emergency Assistance Program (CEAP)—Brooklyn Park, MN

Community Ministries of Rockville—Rockville, MD

Concerned Ecumenical Ministry to the Upper West Side—Buffalo, NY

Council of Churches of the City of New York—New York, NY

East Dallas Cooperative Parish—Dallas, TX

Eastern Area Community Ministries—Louisville, KY

The Ecumenical Council of Pasadena Area Churches—Pasadena, CA

Ecumenical Ministries of Oregon—Portland, OR

Florida Council of Churches—Tampa, FL

Fresno Metro Ministry—Fresno, CA

Greater Minneapolis Council of Churches—Minneapolis, MN

Interfaith Community Services—St. Joseph, MO

InterReligious Council of Central New York—Syracuse, NY

Lincoln Interfaith Council—Lincoln, NE

Marin Interfaith Council—San Rafael, CA

Minnesota Council of Churches—Minneapolis, MN

Mississippi Religious Leadership Conference—Jackson, MS

New York State Council of Churches, Inc.—Albany, NY

Northside Inter-Church Agency (NICA)—Fort Worth, TX

Peoria Friendship House of Christian Service—Peoria, IL

Reading Berks Conference of Churches—Reading, PA

San Antonio Community of Churches—San Antonio, TX

San Fernando Valley Interfaith Council—Chatsworth, CA

South Coast Interfaith Council—Long Beach, CA

Tulsa Metropolitan Ministry—Tulsa, OK

United Religious Community of St. Joseph County—South Bend, IN

Virginia Council of Churches, Inc.—Richmond, VA

## Interfaith Dialogue/Relationships

Akron Area Association of Churches—Akron, OH

Arizona Ecumenical Council—Phoenix, AZ

Arkansas Interfaith Conference—Scott, AR

The Associated Churches of Fort Wayne & Allen County, Inc.—Fort Wayne, IN

Associated Ministries of Tacoma-Pierce County—Tacoma, WA

Association of Religious Communities—Danbury, CT

Attleboro Area Council of Churches, Inc.—Attleboro, MA

Austin Area Interreligious Ministries—Austin, TX

Brooklyn Council of Churches—Brooklyn, NY

Broome County Council of Churches, Inc.—Binghamton, NY

California Council of Churches-California Church Impact—Sacramento, CA

The Cape Cod Council of Churches, Inc.—Hyannis, MA

Capital Area Council of Churches, Inc.—Albany, NY

The Capitol Region Conference of Churches—Hartford, CT

Christian Associates of Southwest Pennsylvania—Pittsburgh, PA

Christian Churches United of the Tri-County Area—Harrisburg, PA

Christian Ministries of Delaware County—Muncie, IN

Churches United, Inc.—Cedar Rapids, IA

Churches United of the Quad City Area—Rock Island, IL

Colorado Council of Churches—Denver, CO

Community Emergency Assistance Program (CEAP)—Brooklyn Park, MN

Community Ministries of Rockville—Rockville, MD

Community Ministry of Montgomery County—Rockville, MD

Community Renewal Society—Chicago, IL

Cooperative Metropolitan Ministries—Newton, MA

Council of Churches of Chemung County, Inc.—Elmira, NY

Council of Churches of the City of New York—New York, NY

Council of Churches of Greater Bridgeport, Inc.—Bridgeport, CT

Council of Churches of Greater Springfield—Springfield, MA

The Council of Churches of Santa Clara County—San Jose, CA

Council of Churches and Synagogues of Southwestern Connecticut—Stamford, CT

Des Moines Area Religious Council—Des Moines, IA

Dutchess County Interfaith Council, Inc.—Poughkeepsie, NY

East Dallas Cooperative Parish—Dallas, TX

Eastern Area Community Ministries—Louisville, KY

Ecclesia—Trenton, NJ

Ecumenical Conference of Greater Altoona—Altoona, PA

The Ecumenical Council of Pasadena Area Churches—Pasadena, CA

Ecumenical Council of San Diego County—San Diego, CA

Ecumenical Ministries of Iowa (EMI)—Des Moines, IA

Ecumenical Ministries of Oregon—Portland, OR

Evanston Ecumenical Action Council—Evanston, IL

Faith Community Assistance Center—Santa Fe, NM

FaithTrust Institute—Seattle, WA

Florida Council of Churches—Tampa, FL

Fresno Metro Ministry—Fresno, CA

Georgia Christian Council—Macon, GA

Grand Rapids Area Center for Ecumenism (GRACE)—Grand Rapids, MI

Greater Baton Rouge Federation of Churches and Synagogues—Baton Rouge, LA

Greater Bethlehem Area Council of Churches—Bethlehem, PA

Greater Birmingham Ministries—Birmingham, AL

Greater Chicago Broadcast Ministries—Chicago, IL

Greater Dallas Community of Churches—Dallas, TX

Greater Dayton Christian Connections—Dayton, OH

Greater Flint Council of Churches—Flint, MI

Greater Lawrence Council of Churches—Lawrence, MA

Greater New Orleans Federation of Churches—New Orleans, LA

Greater Rochester Community of Churches—Rochester, NY

Greater Waterbury Interfaith Ministries, Inc.—Waterbury, CT

Greensboro Urban Ministry—Greensboro, NC

Highlands Community Ministries—Louisville, KY

Inter-Church Council of Greater New Bedford—New Bedford, MA

Inter-Church Ministries of Erie County—Erie, PA

Interchurch Ministries of Nebraska—Lincoln, NE

Interfaith Community Services—St. Joseph, MO

Interfaith Conference of Greater Milwaukee—Milwaukee, WI

InterFaith Conference of Metropolitan Washington—Washington, DC

Interfaith Council—Spokane, WA

Interfaith Council of Contra Costa County—Walnut Creek, CA

Inter-Faith Ministries-Wichita—Wichita, KS

Interfaith Mission Service—Huntsville, AL

Interfaith Service Bureau—Sacramento, CA

Interfaith Works—Olympia, WA

InterReligious Council of Central New York—Syracuse, NY

The Joint Religious Legislative Coalition—Minneapolis, MN

Kentuckiana Interfaith Community—Louisville, KY

Lancaster County Council of Churches—Lancaster, PA

Lehigh County Conference of Churches—Allentown, PA

Lewisburg Council of Churches—Lewisburg, PA

Lincoln Interfaith Council—Lincoln, NE

The Long Island Council of Churches—Hempstead, NY

Louisiana Interchurch Conference—Baton Rouge, LA

Mahoning Valley Association of Churches—Youngstown, OH

Maine Council of Churches—Portland, ME

Marin Interfaith Council—San Rafael, CA

Massachusetts Council of Churches—Boston, MA

283

The Metropolitan Christian Council: Detroit-Windsor—Detroit, MI

Metropolitan Christian Council of Philadelphia—Philadelphia, PA

Metropolitan Ecumenical Ministry—Newark, NJ

Metropolitan Interfaith Council on Affordable Housing (MICAH)—Minneapolis, MN

Minnesota Council of Churches—Minneapolis, MN

Mississippi Religious Leadership Conference—Jackson, MS

Montana Association of Churches—Helena, MT

Muskegon County Cooperating Churches—Muskegon, MI

Network of Religious Communities—Buffalo, NY

New Britain Area Conference of Churches (NEWBRACC)—New Britain, CT

New Hampshire Council of Churches—Pembroke, NH

New Mexico Conference of Churches—Albuquerque, NM

North Dakota Conference of Churches—Ashley, ND

Northern California Interreligious Conference—Oakland, CA

Northern Kentucky Interfaith Commission, Inc.—Newport, KY

Northwest Interfaith Movement—Philadelphia, PA

Oak Park-River Forest Community of Congregations—Oak Park, IL

Oklahoma Conference of Churches—Oklahoma City, OK

Paducah Cooperative Ministry—Paducah, KY

Pennsylvania Conference on Interchurch Cooperation—Harrisburg, PA

Peoria Friendship House of Christian Service—Peoria, IL

Reading Berks Conference of Churches—Reading, PA

The Regional Council of Churches of Atlanta—Atlanta, GA

The Rhode Island State Council of Churches—Providence, RI

Saint. Paul Area Council of Churches—St. Paul, MN

San Antonio Community of Churches—San Antonio, TX

San Fernando Valley Interfaith Council—Chatsworth, CA

South Carolina Christian Action Council, Inc.—Columbia, SC

South Coast Interfaith Council—Long Beach, CA

South Hills Interfaith Ministries—South Park, PA

Staten Island Council of Churches—Staten Island, NY

Texas Conference of Churches—Austin, TX

Troy Area United Ministries—Troy, NY

Tulsa Metropolitan Ministry—Tulsa, OK

Tuscarawas County Council for Church and Community—New Philadelphia, OH

United Churches of Lycoming County—Williamsport, PA

United Religious Community of St. Joseph County—South Bend, IN

Vermont Ecumenical Council and Bible Society—Richmond, VT

Virginia Council of Churches, Inc.—Richmond, VA

Wainwright House—Rye, NY

Washington Association of Churches—Seattle, WA

West Side Ecumenical Ministry—Cleveland, OH

West Virginia Council of Churches—Charleston, WV

Wisconsin Council of Churches—Sun Prairie, WI

Worcester County Ecumenical Council—Worcester, MA

Wyoming Association of Churches—Cody, WY

Wyoming Valley Council of Churches—Wilkes-Barre, PA

## Peace Advocacy

Arkansas Interfaith Conference—Scott, AR

The Associated Churches of Fort Wayne & Allen County, Inc.—Fort Wayne, IN

Associated Ministries of Tacoma-Pierce County—Tacoma, WA

Association of Christian Churches of South Dakota—Sioux Falls, SD

Capital Area Council of Churches, Inc.—Albany, NY

Church Council of Greater Seattle—Seattle, WA

Churches United of the Quad City Area—Rock Island, IL

Community Renewal Society—Chicago, IL

Council of Churches of the City of New York—New York, NY

Council of Churches of Greater Springfield—Springfield, MA

The Council of Churches of Santa Clara County—San Jose, CA

Ecumenical Conference of Greater Altoona—Altoona, PA

Ecumenical Ministries of Iowa (EMI)—Des Moines, IA

Ecumenical Ministries of Oregon—Portland, OR

Greater Chicago Broadcast Ministries—Chicago, IL

Greater Dallas Community of Churches—Dallas, TX

Greater Rochester Community of Churches—Rochester, NY

Interchurch Ministries of Nebraska—Lincoln, NE

Interfaith Works—Olympia, WA

Kentuckiana Interfaith Community—Louisville, KY

Lancaster County Council of Churches—Lancaster, PA

Lincoln Interfaith Council—Lincoln, NE

Massachusetts Council of Churches—Boston, MA

Minnesota Council of Churches—Minneapolis, MN

Montana Association of Churches—Helena, MT

Network of Religious Communities—Buffalo, NY

New Mexico Conference of Churches—Albuquerque, NM

North Carolina Council of Churches—Raleigh, NC

Ohio Council of Churches—Columbus, OH

Oklahoma Conference of Churches—Oklahoma City, OK

The Pennsylvania Council of Churches—Harrisburg, PA

The Regional Council of Churches of Atlanta—Atlanta, GA

The Rhode Island State Council of Churches—Providence, RI

San Fernando Valley Interfaith Council—Chatsworth, CA

South Carolina Christian Action Council, Inc.—Columbia, SC

South Coast Interfaith Council—Long Beach, CA

Southern California Ecumenical Council—Pasadena, CA

Staten Island Council of Churches—Staten Island, NY

Texas Conference of Churches—Austin, TX

United Churches of Lycoming County—Williamsport, PA

United Religious Community of St. Joseph County—South Bend, IN

Vermont Ecumenical Council and Bible Society—Richmond, VT

Washington Association of Churches—Seattle, WA

West Virginia Council of Churches—Charleston, WV

Worcester County Ecumenical Council—Worcester, MA

## Prison Chaplaincy

Akron Area Association of Churches—Akron, OH

Asheville-Buncombe Community Christian Ministry (ABCCM)—Asheville, NC

Berrien County Association of Churches—Benton Harbor, MI

Broome County Council of Churches, Inc.—Binghamton, NY

The Cape Cod Council of Churches, Inc.—Hyannis, MA

Capital Area Council of Churches, Inc.—Albany, NY

Christian Associates of Southwest Pennsylvania—Pittsburgh, PA

Christian Churches United of the Tri-County Area—Harrisburg, PA

Christians United in Beaver County—Beaver, PA

Church Council of Greater Seattle—Seattle, WA

The Church Federation of Greater Indianapolis, Inc.—Indianapolis, IN

Churches United of the Quad City Area—Rock Island, IL

Churchpeople for Change and Reconciliation—Lima, OH

Community Renewal Society—Chicago, IL

Council of Christian Communions of Greater Cincinnati—Cincinnati, OH

Council of Churches of the City of New York—New York, NY

Council of Churches of Greater Bridgeport, Inc.—Bridgeport, CT

Council of Churches of Greater Springfield—Springfield, MA

The Council of Churches of Santa Clara County—San Jose, CA

Ecclesia—Trenton, NJ

Ecumenical Ministries—Fulton, MO

Evansville Area Community of Churches, Inc.—Evansville, IN

Genesee County Churches United, Inc.—Batavia, NY

Greater Bethlehem Area Council of Churches—Bethlehem, PA

Greater Chicago Broadcast Ministries—Chicago, IL

Greater Minneapolis Council of Churches—Minneapolis, MN

Greater Rochester Community of Churches—Rochester, NY

Inter-Church Ministries of Erie County—Erie, PA

Interfaith Council of Contra Costa County—Walnut Creek, CA

InterReligious Council of Central New York—Syracuse, NY

The Long Island Council of Churches—Hempstead, NY

Louisiana Interchurch Conference—Baton Rouge, LA

Maine Council of Churches—Portland, ME

Montana Association of Churches—Helena, MT

New Hampshire Council of Churches—Pembroke, NH

New Mexico Conference of Churches—Albuquerque, NM

Reading Berks Conference of Churches—Reading, PA

The Rhode Island State Council of Churches—Providence, RI

San Antonio Community of Churches—San Antonio, TX

285

United Churches of Lycoming County—Williamsport, PA

United Religious Community of St. Joseph County—South Bend, IN

West Virginia Council of Churches—Charleston, WV

Wyoming Association of Churches—Cody, WY

York County Council of Churches—York, PA

## Programs with/for Persons with Disabilities

Associated Ministries of Tacoma-Pierce County—Tacoma, WA

Christian Ministries of Delaware County—Muncie, IN

Ecumenical Ministries of Oregon—Portland, OR

Greater Chicago Broadcast Ministries—Chicago, IL

Inter-Church Council of Greater New Bedford—New Bedford, MA

Inter-Faith Ministries—Wichita—Wichita, KS

InterReligious Council of Central New York—Syracuse, NY

Lehigh County Conference of Churches—Allentown, PA

Massachusetts Council of Churches—Boston, MA

Metropolitan Ecumenical Ministry—Newark, NJ

New Hampshire Council of Churches—Pembroke, NH

Reading Berks Conference of Churches—Reading, PA

The Rhode Island State Council of Churches—Providence, RI

Southeast Ecumenical Ministry—Rochester, NY

Tulsa Metropolitan Ministry—Tulsa, OK

## Public Education Advocacy

Akron Area Association of Churches—Akron, OH

Arizona Ecumenical Council—Phoenix, AZ

The Associated Churches of Fort Wayne & Allen County, Inc.—Fort Wayne, IN

Associated Ministries of Tacoma-Pierce County—Tacoma, WA

Austin Area Interreligious Ministries—Austin, TX

California Council of Churches-California Church Impact—Sacramento, CA

Center City Churches—Hartford, CT

Christian Ministries of Delaware County—Muncie, IN

Churches United of the Quad City Area—Rock Island, IL

Colorado Council of Churches—Denver, CO

Community Emergency Assistance Program (CEAP)—Brooklyn Park, MN

Community Ministries of Rockville—Rockville, MD

Community Ministry of Montgomery County—Rockville, MD

Community Renewal Society—Chicago, IL

Concerned Ecumenical Ministry to the Upper West Side—Buffalo, NY

Contact Ministries of Springfield—Springfield, IL

Council of Churches of the City of New York—New York, NY

Council of Churches of Greater Springfield—Springfield, MA

Evanston Ecumenical Action Council—Evanston, IL

Fresno Metro Ministry—Fresno, CA

Greater Baton Rouge Federation of Churches and Synagogues—Baton Rouge, LA

Greater Bethlehem Area Council of Churches—Bethlehem, PA

Greater Birmingham Ministries—Birmingham, AL

Greater Chicago Broadcast Ministries—Chicago, IL

Greater Fairmont Council of Churches—Fairmont, WV

Greater Minneapolis Council of Churches—Minneapolis, MN

Greater Rochester Community of Churches—Rochester, NY

Greater Waterbury Interfaith Ministries, Inc.—Waterbury, CT

Inter-Church Council of Greater New Bedford—New Bedford, MA

Interfaith Conference of Greater Milwaukee—Milwaukee, WI

InterFaith Conference of Metropolitan Washington—Washington, DC

Interfaith Council—Spokane, WA

The Joint Religious Legislative Coalition—Minneapolis, MN

Lehigh County Conference of Churches—Allentown, PA

Louisiana Interchurch Conference—Baton Rouge, LA

Maine Council of Churches—Portland, ME

Metropolitan Christian Council of Philadelphia—Philadelphia, PA

Metropolitan Ecumenical Ministry—Newark, NJ

Metropolitan Inter Faith Association (MIFA)—Memphis, TN

Metropolitan Interfaith Council on Affordable Housing (MICAH)—Minneapolis, MN

Mississippi Religious Leadership Conference—Jackson, MS

Network of Religious Communities—Buffalo, NY

New Hampshire Council of Churches—Pembroke, NH

New Mexico Conference of Churches—Albuquerque, NM

North Carolina Council of Churches—Raleigh, NC

Oak Park-River Forest Community of Congregations—Oak Park, IL

Oklahoma Conference of Churches—Oklahoma City, OK

The Pennsylvania Council of Churches—Harrisburg, PA

Peoria Friendship House of Christian Service—Peoria, IL

San Antonio Community of Churches—San Antonio, TX

South Carolina Christian Action Council, Inc.—Columbia, SC

Tarrant Area Community of Churches—Fort Worth, TX

Tulsa Metropolitan Ministry—Tulsa, OK

Tuscarawas County Council for Church and Community—New Philadelphia, OH

United Churches of Lycoming County—Williamsport, PA

United Religious Community of St. Joseph County—South Bend, IN

Washington Association of Churches—Seattle, WA

West Virginia Council of Churches—Charleston, WV

Wisconsin Council of Churches—Sun Prairie, WI

## Refugee Assistance Programs

Association of Religious Communities—Danbury, CT

Austin Area Interreligious Ministries—Austin, TX

The Capitol Region Conference of Churches—Hartford, CT

Community Emergency Assistance Program (CEAP)—Brooklyn Park, MN

Ecumenical Ministries of Oregon—Portland, OR

Fresno Metro Ministry—Fresno, CA

Greater Chicago Broadcast Ministries—Chicago, IL

Interfaith Service Bureau—Sacramento, CA

InterReligious Council of Central New York—Syracuse, NY

Kentuckiana Interfaith Community—Louisville, KY

Metropolitan Ecumenical Ministry—Newark, NJ

Minnesota Council of Churches—Minneapolis, MN

Network of Religious Communities—Buffalo, NY

The Regional Council of Churches of Atlanta—Atlanta, GA

United Religious Community of St. Joseph County—South Bend, IN

Virginia Council of Churches, Inc.—Richmond, VA

## Rural Issues

Alaska Christian Conference—Fairbanks, AK

Association of Christian Churches of South Dakota—Sioux Falls, SD

Berrien County Association of Churches—Benton Harbor, MI

Chautaugua County Rural Ministry—Dunkirk, NY

Christian Associates of Southwest Pennsylvania—Pittsburgh, PA

Ecumenical Ministries of Iowa (EMI)—Des Moines, IA

Ecumenical Ministries of Oregon—Portland, OR

Fresno Metro Ministry—Fresno, CA

Georgia Christian Council—Macon, GA

Interchurch Ministries of Nebraska—Lincoln, NE

Interfaith Conference of Greater Milwaukee—Milwaukee, WI

Kansas Ecumenical Ministries—Topeka, KS

Kentucky Council of Churches—Lexington, KY

Louisiana Interchurch Conference—Baton Rouge, LA

Minnesota Council of Churches—Minneapolis, MN

Mississippi Religious Leadership Conference—Jackson, MS

Montana Association of Churches—Helena, MT

North Carolina Council of Churches—Raleigh, NC

North Dakota Conference of Churches—Ashley, ND

Oklahoma Conference of Churches—Oklahoma City, OK

Pike County Outreach Council—Waverly, OH

Reading Berks Conference of Churches—Reading, PA

United Religious Community of St. Joseph County—South Bend, IN

Virginia Council of Churches, Inc.—Richmond, VA

West Virginia Council of Churches—Charleston, WV

## Senior Citizen Programs

Allegheny Valley Association of Churches—Natrona Heights, PA

Associated Ministries of Tacoma-Pierce County—Tacoma, WA

Attleboro Area Council of Churches, Inc.—Attleboro, MA

The Capitol Region Conference of Churches—Hartford, CT

Center City Churches—Hartford, CT

Christian Ministries of Delaware County—Muncie, IN

Church Council of Greater Seattle—Seattle, WA

Community Emergency Assistance Program (CEAP)—Brooklyn Park, MN

287

Community Ministries of Rockville—Rockville, MD

Community Renewal Society—Chicago, IL

Concerned Ecumenical Ministry to the Upper West Side—Buffalo, NY

Council of Churches of Greater Springfield—Springfield, MA

Council of Churches of the Ozarks—Springfield, MO

Council of Churches and Synagogues of Southwestern Connecticut—Stamford, CT

Cross-Lines Cooperative Council—Kansas City, KS

East Dallas Cooperative Parish—Dallas, TX

East End Cooperative Ministry—Pittsburgh, PA

Eastern Area Community Ministries—Louisville, KY

Ecumenical Ministries—Fulton, MO

Ecumenical Ministries of Oregon—Portland, OR

Fern Creek-Highview United Ministries—Louisvlle, KY

Florida Council of Churches—Tampa, FL

Georgia Christian Council—Macon, GA

Greater Baton Rouge Federation of Churches and Synagogues—Baton Rouge, LA

Greater Chicago Broadcast Ministries—Chicago, IL

Greater Lawrence Council of Churches—Lawrence, MA

Greater Minneapolis Council of Churches—Minneapolis, MN

Highlands Community Ministries—Louisville, KY

Inter-Church Council of Greater New Bedford—New Bedford, MA

Interfaith Community Council, Inc.—New Albany, IN

Interfaith Community Services—St. Joseph, MO

Interfaith Council of Contra Costa County—Walnut Creek, CA

Inter-Faith Ministries-Wichita—Wichita, KS

InterReligious Council of Central New York—Syracuse, NY

The Long Island Council of Churches—Hempstead, NY

Louisiana Interchurch Conference—Baton Rouge, LA

Metropolitan Ecumenical Ministry—Newark, NJ

Metropolitan Inter Faith Association (MIFA)—Memphis, TN

Mississippi Religious Leadership Conference—Jackson, MS

Montana Association of Churches—Helena, MT

New Hampshire Council of Churches—Pembroke, NH

New Mexico Conference of Churches—Albuquerque, NM

Northside Inter-Church Agency (NICA)—Fort Worth, TX

Northwest Interfaith Movement—Philadelphia, PA

Oklahoma Conference of Churches—Oklahoma City, OK

Paducah Cooperative Ministry—Paducah, KY

Peoria Friendship House of Christian Service—Peoria, IL

San Antonio Community of Churches—San Antonio, TX

San Fernando Valley Interfaith Council—Chatsworth, CA

Schenectady Inner City Ministry—Schenectady, NY

South Hills Interfaith Ministries—South Park, PA

South Louisville Community Ministries—Louisville, KY

Southeast Ecumenical Ministry—Rochester, NY

Tarrant Area Community of Churches—Fort Worth, TX

Troy Area United Ministries—Troy, NY

Tulsa Metropolitan Ministry—Tulsa, OK

Tuscarawas County Council for Church and Community—New Philadelphia, OH

United Churches of Lycoming County—Williamsport, PA

United Religious Community of St. Joseph County—South Bend, IN

Wainwright House—Rye, NY

Wellspring Interfaith Social Services, Inc. (previously West Central Neighborhood Ministry, Inc.)—Fort Wayne, IN

West Side Ecumenical Ministry—Cleveland, OH

Wilkinsburg Community Ministry—Pittsburgh, PA

## Substance Abuse Programs

Community Ministries of Rockville—Rockville, MD

Corpus Christi Metro Ministries—Corpus Christi, TX

Council of Churches of Greater Bridgeport, Inc.—Bridgeport, CT

Council of Churches of the Ozarks—Springfield, MO

East End Cooperative Ministry—Pittsburgh, PA

Ecumenical Ministries of Iowa (EMI)—Des Moines, IA

Ecumenical Ministries of Oregon—Portland, OR

Evanston Ecumenical Action Council—Evanston, IL

Greater Chicago Broadcast Ministries—Chicago, IL

Greensboro Urban Ministry—Greensboro, NC

Hanover Area Council of Churches—Hanover, PA

The Metropolitan Christian Council: Detroit-Windsor—Detroit, MI

Metropolitan Ecumenical Ministry—Newark, NJ

Metropolitan Ecumenical Ministry Community Development Corp.—Newark, NJ

Mississippi Religious Leadership Conference—Jackson, MS

Montana Association of Churches—Helena, MT

Muskegon County Cooperating Churches—Muskegon, MI

New Hampshire Council of Churches—Pembroke, NH

North Hills Youth Ministry Counseling Center—Pittsburgh, PA

Pike County Outreach Council—Waverly, OH

San Antonio Community of Churches—San Antonio, TX

Southeast Ecumenical Ministry—Rochester, NY

Tulsa Metropolitan Ministry—Tulsa, OK

United Religious Community of St. Joseph County—South Bend, IN

Vermont Ecumenical Council and Bible Society—Richmond, VT

West Side Ecumenical Ministry—Cleveland, OH

## Theology and Worship Programs

Akron Area Association of Churches—Akron, OH

Allegheny Valley Association of Churches—Natrona Heights, PA

Arizona Ecumenical Council—Phoenix, AZ

Arkansas Interfaith Conference—Scott, AR

The Associated Churches of Fort Wayne & Allen County, Inc.—Fort Wayne, IN

Associated Ministries of Tacoma-Pierce County—Tacoma, WA

Association of Christian Churches of South Dakota—Sioux Falls, SD

Attleboro Area Council of Churches, Inc.—Attleboro, MA

Border Association for Refugees from Central America (BARCA), Inc.—Edinburg, TX

Brooklyn Council of Churches—Brooklyn, NY

Broome County Council of Churches, Inc.—Binghamton, NY

The Cape Cod Council of Churches, Inc.—Hyannis, MA

Capital Area Council of Churches, Inc.—Albany, NY

Christian Associates of Southwest Pennsylvania—Pittsburgh, PA

Christian Churches United of the Tri-County Area—Harrisburg, PA

Christians United in Beaver County—Beaver, PA

Church Council of Greater Seattle—Seattle, WA

Churches United of the Quad City Area—Rock Island, IL

Colorado Council of Churches—Denver, CO

Council of Churches of the City of New York—New York, NY

The Council of Churches of Santa Clara County—San Jose, CA

Council of Churches and Synagogues of Southwestern Connecticut—Stamford, CT

Dutchess County Interfaith Council, Inc.—Poughkeepsie, NY

East Dallas Cooperative Parish—Dallas, TX

The Ecumenical Council of Pasadena Area Churches—Pasadena, CA

Ecumenical Ministries—Fulton, MO

Ecumenical Ministries of Iowa (EMI)—Des Moines, IA

Ecumenical Ministries of Oregon—Portland, OR

FaithTrust Institute—Seattle, WA

Florida Council of Churches—Tampa, FL

Georgia Christian Council—Macon, GA

Grand Rapids Area Center for Ecumenism (GRACE)—Grand Rapids, MI

Greater Bethlehem Area Council of Churches—Bethlehem, PA

Greater Chicago Broadcast Ministries—Chicago, IL

Greater Dallas Community of Churches—Dallas, TX

Greater Dayton Christian Connections—Dayton, OH

Greater Fairmont Council of Churches—Fairmont, WV

Greater Lawrence Council of Churches—Lawrence, MA

Greater New Orleans Federation of Churches—New Orleans, LA

Greater Rochester Community of Churches—Rochester, NY

Greensboro Urban Ministry—Greensboro, NC

Illinois Conference of Churches—Springfield, IL

Inter-Church Council of Greater New Bedford—New Bedford, MA

Inter-Church Ministries of Erie County—Erie, PA

Interchurch Ministries of Nebraska—Lincoln, NE

Interfaith Council—Spokane, WA

Interfaith Mission Service—Huntsville, AL

InterReligious Council of Central New York—Syracuse, NY

Kentuckiana Interfaith Community—Louisville, KY

Lehigh County Conference of Churches—Allentown, PA

The Long Island Council of Churches—Hempstead, NY

Mahoning Valley Association of Churches—Youngstown, OH

Marin Interfaith Council—San Rafael, CA

289

The Metropolitan Christian Council: Detroit-Windsor—Detroit, MI

Metropolitan Christian Council of Philadelphia—Philadelphia, PA

Metropolitan Ecumenical Ministry—Newark, NJ

Montana Association of Churches—Helena, MT

Muskegon County Cooperating Churches—Muskegon, MI

New Britain Area Conference of Churches (NEWBRACC)—New Britain, CT

New Hampshire Council of Churches—Pembroke, NH

New Mexico Conference of Churches—Albuquerque, NM

North Carolina Council of Churches—Raleigh, NC

Northern Kentucky Interfaith Commission, Inc.—Newport, KY

Oak Park-River Forest Community of Congregations—Oak Park, IL

Oklahoma Conference of Churches—Oklahoma City, OK

The Pennsylvania Council of Churches—Harrisburg, PA

Reading Berks Conference of Churches—Reading, PA

The Regional Council for Christian Ministry, Inc.—Idaho Falls, ID

The Regional Council of Churches of Atlanta—Atlanta, GA

The Rhode Island State Council of Churches—Providence, RI

San Antonio Community of Churches—San Antonio, TX

Schenectady Inner City Ministry—Schenectady, NY

South Carolina Christian Action Council, Inc.—Columbia, SC

South Coast Interfaith Council—Long Beach, CA

South East Associated Ministries (SEAM)—Louisville, KY

Tarrant Area Community of Churches—Fort Worth, TX

Texas Conference of Churches—Austin, TX

Troy Area United Ministries—Troy, NY

Tulsa Metropolitan Ministry—Tulsa, OK

United Religious Community of St. Joseph County—South Bend, IN

Vermont Ecumenical Council and Bible Society—Richmond, VT

Virginia Council of Churches, Inc.—Richmond, VA

Wainwright House—Rye, NY

Washington Association of Churches—Seattle, WA

West Virginia Council of Churches—Charleston, WV

Worcester County Ecumenical Council—Worcester, MA

Wyoming Association of Churches—Cody, WY

York County Council of Churches—York, PA

## Women Issues

Associated Ministries of Tacoma-Pierce County—Tacoma, WA

California Council of Churches-California Church Impact—Sacramento, CA

Chautauqua County Rural Ministry—Dunkirk, NY

Christian Ministries of Delaware County—Muncie, IN

Church Community Services—Elkhart, IN

Community Ministries of Rockville—Rockville, MD

Council of Churches of the City of New York—New York, NY

The Council of Churches of Santa Clara County—San Jose, CA

East Dallas Cooperative Parish—Dallas, TX

Ecumenical Ministries of Oregon—Portland, OR

FaithTrust Institute—Seattle, WA

Fresno Metro Ministry—Fresno, CA

Genesee-Orleans Ministry of Concern—Albion, NY

Georgia Christian Council—Macon, GA

Greater Birmingham Ministries—Birmingham, AL

Greater Chicago Broadcast Ministries—Chicago, IL

Greater Dallas Community of Churches—Dallas, TX

Inter-Church Council of Greater New Bedford—New Bedford, MA

Interfaith Community Services—St. Joseph, MO

Interfaith Council—Spokane, WA

The Metropolitan Christian Council: Detroit-Windsor—Detroit, MI

Metropolitan Christian Council of Philadelphia—Philadelphia, PA

Metropolitan Ecumenical Ministry—Newark, NJ

Mississippi Religious Leadership Conference—Jackson, MS

Montana Association of Churches—Helena, MT

Network of Religious Communities—Buffalo, NY

New Mexico Conference of Churches—Albuquerque, NM

Oklahoma Conference of Churches—Oklahoma City, OK

Peoria Friendship House of Christian Service—Peoria, IL

The Regional Council of Churches of Atlanta—Atlanta, GA

San Antonio Community of Churches—San Antonio, TX

South Hills Interfaith Ministries—South Park, PA

Tulsa Metropolitan Ministry—Tulsa, OK

Wainwright House—Rye, NY

West Side Ecumenical Ministry—Cleveland, OH

## Youth Activities

Arizona Ecumenical Council—Phoenix, AZ

Associated Ministries of Tacoma-Pierce County —Tacoma, WA

Austin Area Interreligious Ministries—Austin, TX

Center City Churches—Hartford, CT

Christian Ministries of Delaware County—Muncie, IN

The Church Federation of Greater Indianapolis, Inc.—Indianapolis, IN

Community Renewal Society—Chicago, IL

Concerned Ecumenical Ministry to the Upper West Side—Buffalo, NY

Cooperative Metropolitan Ministries—Newton, MA

Council of Churches of the City of New York —New York, NY

Council of Churches of Greater Bridgeport, Inc.—Bridgeport, CT

The Council of Churches of Santa Clara County—San Jose, CA

Dutchess Interfaith Council, Inc.—Poughkeepsie, NY

East Dallas Cooperative Parish—Dallas, TX

East End Cooperative Ministry—Pittsburgh, PA

Eastern Area Community Ministries—Louisville, KY

Ecclesia—Trenton, NJ

Ecumenical Ministries—Fulton, MO

Evanston Ecumenical Action Council—Evanston, IL

FaithTrust Institute—Seattle, WA

Fresno Metro Ministry—Fresno, CA

Genesee-Orleans Ministry of Concern—Albion, NY

Grand Rapids Area Center for Ecumenism (GRACE)—Grand Rapids, MI

Greater Bethlehem Area Council of Churches—Bethlehem, PA

Greater Chicago Broadcast Ministries—Chicago, IL

Greater Dallas Community of Churches—Dallas, TX

Greater Fairmont Council of Churches—Fairmont, WV

Greater Minneapolis Council of Churches—Minneapolis, MN

Highlands Community Ministries—Louisville, KY

Inter-Church Council of Greater New Bedford —New Bedford, MA

Interfaith Community Council, Inc.—New Albany, IN

Interfaith Community Services—St. Joseph, MO

Interfaith Conference of Greater Milwaukee—Milwaukee, WI

InterFaith Conference of Metropolitan Washington—Washington, DC

Interfaith Council—Spokane, WA

Inter-Faith Ministries-Wichita—Wichita, KS

Lehigh County Conference of Churches—Allentown, PA

Lincoln Interfaith Council—Lincoln, NE

Marin Interfaith Council—San Rafael, CA

The Metropolitan Christian Council: Detroit-Windsor—Detroit, MI

Metropolitan Ecumenical Ministry—Newark, NJ

Metropolitan Ecumenical Ministry Community Development Corp.—Newark, NJ

Metropolitan Inter Faith Association (MIFA)—Memphis, TN

Montana Association of Churches—Helena, MT

New Mexico Conference of Churches—Albuquerque, NM

Northern California Interreligious Conference —Oakland, CA

Peoria Friendship House of Christian Service—Peoria, IL

Queens Federation of Churches—Richmond Hill, NY

Reading Berks Conference of Churches—Reading, PA

The Regional Council of Churches of Atlanta—Atlanta, GA

Rural Migrant Ministry—Poughkeepsie, NY

St. Paul Area Council of Churches—St. Paul, MN

San Antonio Community of Churches—San Antonio, TX

Schenectady Inner City Ministry—Schenectady, NY

South East Associated Ministries (SEAM)—Louisville, KY

South Hills Interfaith Ministries—South Park, PA

South Louisville Community Ministries—Louisville, KY

Southeast Ecumenical Ministry—Rochester, NY

Staten Island Council of Churches—Staten Island, NY

Troy Area United Ministries—Troy, NY

Tulsa Metropolitan Ministry—Tulsa, OK

Tuscarawas County Council for Church and Community—New Philadelphia, OH

United Churches of Lycoming County—Williamsport, PA

Vermont Ecumenical Council and Bible Society —Richmond, VT

Wainwright House—Rye, NY

Wellspring Interfaith Social Services, Inc. (previously West Central Neighborhood Ministry, Inc.)—Fort Wayne, IN

West Side Ecumenical Ministry—Cleveland, OH

291

# 7. Canadian Regional and Local Ecumenical Bodies

Most of the organizations listed below are councils of churches in which churches participate officially, whether at the parish or judicatory level. They operate at the city, metropolitan area, or county level. Parish clusters within urban areas are not included.

Canadian local ecumenical bodies operate without paid staff, with the exception of a few which have part-time staff. In most cases, the name and address of the president or chairperson is listed. As these offices change from year to year, some of the information may be out of date by the time the *Yearbook of American & Canadian Churches* is published.

## ALBERTA

**Calgary Council of Churches**
120 17th Ave., Calgary, AB T2S 2T2 Tel. (403) 218-5521

**Calgary Inter-Faith Community Action Association**
2405 Macleod Trail SW, Calgary, AB T2G 2P3, Tel. (403)262-5171
Email: jmcgrath@shawcable.com
Website: www.calgary-interfaith.ab.ca

### BRITISH COLUMBIA

**Greater Victoria Council of Churches**
St. Alban's Church, 1468 Ryan St. at Balmont, Victoria, BC V8R 2X1

**Multifaith Action Society of British Columbia**
305 41st Ave. W, Vancouver, BC V5Y 2S5, Tel. (604)321-1302 Fax (604)321-1370
Email: admin@multifaithaction.org
Website: www.multifaithaction.org

**Vancouver Council of Churches**
700 Kingsway, Vancouver, BC V5V 3C1, Tel. (604)420-0761

## MANITOBA

**Association of Christian Churches in Manitoba**
150 de la Cathedrale Ave., Winnipeg, MB R2H 0H6, Tel. (204)237-9851*

## NEW BRUNSWICK

**Atlantic Ecumenical Council of Churches**
170 Daniel Ave., Saint John, NB E2K 4S7, Tel. (506)538-2491

**First Miramichi Inter-Church Council**
Pres., Ellen Robinson, Doaktown, NB E0C 1G0

**Moncton Area Council of Churches**
135 Mount Royal Blvd., Moncton, NB E1E 2V5, Tel. (506)382-7725

## NEWFOUNDLAND

**St. John's Area Council of Churches**
Rev. Canon Ralph Billard, 31 Hazelwood Cres., St. John's, NF A1E 6B3, Tel. (709)579-0536

## NOVA SCOTIA

**Atlantic Ecumenical Council of Churches**
Rev. John E. Boyd, P.O. Box 637, 90 Victoria St., Amherst, NS B4H 4B4

**Bridgewater Inter-Church Council**
Mr. Wilson Jones, 30 Parkdale Ave., Bridgewater, NS B4V 1L8

**Cornwallis District Inter-Church Council**
Mr. Tom Regan, Centreville, RR 2, Kings County, NS B0T 1J0

**Industrial Cape Breton Council of Churches**
24 Huron Ave., Sydney Mines, NS B1S 1V2

**Kentville Council of Churches**
Rev. Canon S.J.P. Davies, 325-325 Main St., Kentville, NS B4N 1C5

**Lunenburg Queens BA Association**
Mrs. Nilda Chute, 66 Hillside Dr., RR 4, Bridgewater, NS B4V 2W3 Tel. 902-543-3328
Email: n-chute@ns.sympatico.ca

**Mahone Bay Interchurch Council**
RR 1, Blockhouse, NS B0J 1E0

**Pictou Council of Churches**
P.O. Box 70, Pictou, NS B0K 1H0

**Queens County Association of Churches**
Mr. Donald Burns, P.O. Box 537, Liverpool, NS B0T 1K6

## Burlington Inter-Church Council
Mr. Fred Townsend, 425 Breckenwood, Burlington, ON L7L 2J6

## Christian Leadership Council of Downtown Toronto
Mr. Ken Bhagan, 40 Homewood Ave. #509, Toronto, ON M4Y 2K2

## Ecumenical Committee
Rev. William B. Kidd, 76 Eastern Ave., Sault Ste. Marie, ON P6A 4R2

## Glengarry-Prescott-Russell Christian Council
Pres., Rev. G. Labrosse, St. Eugene's, Prescott, ON K0B 1P0

## The Greater Toronto Council of Christian Churches
Fr. Damian MacPherson, 1155 Yonge St., Toronto, ON M4T 1W2, Tel. (416) 934-3400 x 344

## Hamilton & District Christian Churches Association
Rev. John Allsop, 86 Homewood Ave., Hamilton, ON L8P 2M4, Tel. (905)387-2135 Fax (905) 387-5858
Email: allsopjs@hotmail.com

## Ignace Council of Churches
Box 5, 205 Pine St., Ignace, ON P0T 1H0

## Inter Church Council of Burlington
Rev. Moe Anderson, P.O. Box 62120, Burlington Mall R.P.O., Burlington, ON L7R 4K2, Tel. (905)333-0515
Website: www.iccb.ca

## Kitchener-Waterloo Council of Churches
Rev. Clarence Hauser, 53 Allen St. E., Waterloo, ON N2J 1J3

## London Inter-City Faith Team
Mr. David Carouthers, United Church, 711 Colbourne St., London, ON N6A 3Z4

## Massey Inter-Church Council
Rev. Brian Sonneburg, Box 238, Massey, ON P0P 1P0, Tel. (705)865-2202

## Ottowa Christian Council of the Capital Area
1247 Kilborn Ave., Ottowa, ON K1H 6K9

## St. Catharines & District Clergy Fellowship
Rev. Victor Munro, 663 Vince St., St. Catharines, ON L2M 3V8

## Spadina-Bloor Interchurch Council
Rev. Frances Combes, Bathurst St. United Church, 427 Bloor St. W., Toronto, ON M5S 1X7

## Stratford & District Council of Churches
Chair, Rev. Ted Heinze, 202 Erie St., Stratford, ON N5A 2M8

## Thorold Inter-Faith Council
1 Dunn St., St. Catharines, ON L2T 1P3

## Thunder Bay Council of Churches
Rev. Richard Darling, 1800 Moodie St. E., Thunder Bay, ON P7E 4Z2

### PRINCE EDWARD ISLAND

## Atlantic Ecumenical Council
Sec., Rev. Arthur J. Pendergast, Immaculate Conception Church, St. Louis, PEI C0B 1Z0, Tel. (902)963-2202 or (902)882-2610

## Summerside Christian Council
Ms. A. Kathleen Miller, P.O. Box 1551, Summerside, PEI C1N 4K4

### QUEBEC

## Action des Chrétiens pour l'Abolition de la Torture
Raoul Lincourt, 15 rue de Castelnau Ouest, Montréal, QC H2R 2W3, Tel. (514)890-6169

## AGAPÉ Deux-Montagnes
Donald Tremblay, 1002 chemin d'Oka, Deux-Montagnes, QC J7R 1L7, Tel. (450)473-9877

## Canadian Centre for Ecumenism
Dir., Dr. Stuart Brown, 2065 Sherbrooke St. West, Montreal, QC H3H 1G6, Tel. (514) 937-9176
Email: ccocce@oecumenisme.ca

## Centre Emmaüs
Centre de spiritualité des Églisesd'Orient, 3774 chemin Queen-Mary, 3e étage, Montréal, QC H3V 1A6, Tel. (514)276-2144
Website: www.centre-emmaus.qc.ca

## Christian-Jewish Dialogue of Montreal
Rev. Ihor Kutash, c/o Temple Emanu-El-Beth Sholom, 4100 Sherbrooke St. West, Westmount, QC H3Z 1A5, Tel. (514)937-3575 or (514)937-3708

## Comité Québécois du Dialogue musulman-chrétien
RP Bernard Tremblay, 1640 rue St. Hubert, Montréal, QC H2L 3Z2, Tel. (514)849-1167 Fax (514)284-2034
Email: bernard@bcube.com

293

## Direction Chrétienne
Rev. Glenn Smith, 1450 rue City Councillors, bureau 720, Montréal, QC H3A 2E6, Tel. (514)878-3035 Fax (514)878-8048
Email: info@direction.ca
Website: www.direction.ca

## Hemmingford Ecumenical Committee
Catherine Prist, Box 300, Hemmingford, QC J0L 1H0

## Interfaith Council of Montréal
Pres., Mr. Mandit Singh, 2065 Sherbrooke West, Montréal, QC H3H 1G6, Tel. (514)937-9176 Fax (514)937-4986
Email: ccocce@oecumenisme.ca
Website: www.oecumenisme.ca

## Montreal Association for the Blind Foundation
Rev. Dr. John A. Simms, 7000 Sherbrooke St. W., Montréal, QC H4B 1R3, Tel. (514)489-8201 Fax (514)489-3477
Email: info@mab.ca
Website: www.mab.ca

## Radio Ville-Marie
Radio religieuse, 505 avenue de Mont-Cassin, Montréal, QC H3L 1W7, Tel. (514)382-3913 or (877)668-6601 Fax (514)858-0965
Email: cira@radiovm.com
Website: www.radiovm.com

## Réseau Oecuménique Justice et Paix
Mme. Renaude Gregoire, 114 Secc. D., Montréal, QC H3K 3B9, Tel. (514)937-2683 Fax (514)937-2683
Email: info@justicepaix.org
Website: www.justicepaix.org

## Réseau Oecuménique du Québec (Quebec Ecumenical Network)
le Centre canadien d'oecuménisme en assure le secretariat, 2065 rue Sherbrooke ouest, Montréal, QC H3H 1G6, Tel. (514)937-9176 Fax (514)937-4986
Email: ccocce@oecumenisme.ca
Website: www.oecumenisme.ca

## The St. Bruno Ecumenical Group
Holy Trinity Anglican Church, 140 Beaumont St. East, St. Bruno, QC J3V 5L9, Tel. (450)653-4531

## UNITAS
Centre oecuménique de meditation chrétienne et de spiritualité, 1950 rue St. Antoine Ouest, Montréal, QC H3J 1A5, Tel. (514)485-0009
Email: unitas@bellnet.ca
Website: www.unitasmeditation.ca

## SASKATCHEWAN

## Humboldt Clergy Council
Fr. Leo Hinz, OSB, Box 1989, Humboldt, SK S0K 2A0

## Melville Association of Churches
Catherine Gaw, Box 878, Melville, SK S0A 2P0

## Prairie Centre for Ecumenism
Dir., Rev. Dr. Jan Bigland-Pritchard, 600 45th Street W., Saskatoon, SK S7L 5W9, Tel. (306)653-1633 Fax (306)653-1821
Email: pce@ecumenism.net
Website: www.ecumenism.net

## Regina Council of Churches
Joan Galvin, 2660 Albert St, Regina, SK S4P 2V9, Tel. (306)545-3375

# 8. Theological Seminaries and Bible Colleges in the United States

The following list includes theological seminaries, Bible colleges and departments in colleges and universities in which ministerial training is given. Many denominations have additional programs.

Inclusion in or exclusion from this list implies no judgment about the quality or accreditation of any institution. Those schools that are members of the Association of Theological Schools are marked with an asterisk (*). Those schools that are accredited by the Transnational Association of Christian Colleges and Schools are marked with (|). Additional information about enrollment in ATS member schools can be found in the "Trends in Seminary Enrollment" section of Chapter III. Information about TRACS and ATS can be found in the United States Cooperative Organizations section of Chapter II.

Each of the listings include when available: the institution name, denominational sponsor, location, the president or dean of the institution, telephone and fax numbers and email and website addresses.

**Abilene Christian University Graduate School of Theology*** (Churches of Christ), Jack R. Reese, Dean, College of Biblical Studies, ACU Box 29422, 1850 N. Judge Ely Boulevard, CBS Room 297, Abilene, TX 79699-9422, Tel. (325)674-3700 Fax (325)674-6180
Email: thompson@bible.acu.edu
Website: www.acu.edu/GST

**Alaska Bible College** (Nondenominational), Steven J. Hostetter, President, P.O. Box 289, Glennallen, AK 99588, Tel. (907)822-3201 Fax (907)822-5027
Email: info@akbible.edu
Website: www.akbible.edu

**Alliance Theological Seminary*** (Christian and Missionary Alliance), Michael G. Scales, President, 350 N. Highland Ave., Nyack, NY 10960-1416, Tel. (845)353-2020 Fax (845)727-3002
Website: www.alliance.edu

**American Baptist College** (National Baptist Convention U.S.A., Inc.), Dr. Forrest E. Harris, Sr., President, 1800 Baptist World Center Dr., Nashville, TN 37207, Tel. (615)256-1463 Fax (615)226-7855
Email: jwright@abcnash.edu
Website: www.abcnash.edu

**American Baptist Seminary of the West*** (American Baptist Churches in the U.S.A.), Keith A. Russell, President, 2606 Dwight Way, Berkeley, CA 94704-3029, Tel. (510)841-1905 Fax (510)841-2446
Email: krussell@absw.edu
Website: www.absw.edu

**Anderson University School of Theology*** (Church of God [Anderson, Ind.]), James L. Edwards, President, 1100 East Fifth Street, Anderson, IN 46012-3495, Tel. (765)641-4032 Fax (765)641-3851
Website: www.anderson.edu/academics/sot

**Andover Newton Theological School*** (American Baptist Churches in the U.S.A.; United Church of Christ), Nick Carter, President, 210 Herrick Rd., Newton Centre, MA 02459, Tel. (617)964-1100 Fax (617)558-9785
Email: admissions@ants.edu
Website: www.ants.edu

**Apex School of Theology** (Interdenominational), Dr. Joseph E. Perkins, President, 5104 Revere Road, Durham, NC 27713, Tel. (919)572-1625 Fax (919)572-1762
Email: info@apexsot.edu
Website: www.apexsot.edu

**Appalachian Bible College** (Nondenominational), Daniel L. Anderson, President, P.O. Box ABC, Bradley, WV 25818, Tel. (304)877-6428 Fax (304)877-5082
Email: abc@abc.edu
Website: www.abc.edu

**Aquinas Institute of Theology*** (Catholic Church), The Rev. Charles E. Bouchard, O.P., President, 3642 Lindell Blvd., St. Louis, MO 63108-3396, Tel. (314)977-3882 Fax (314)977-7225
Email: aquinas@slu.edu
Website: www.ai.edu

**Arlington Baptist College** (Baptist), David Bryant, President, 3001 W. Division, Arlington, TX 76012-3425, Tel. (817)461-8741 Fax (817)274-1138

**Asbury Theological Seminary*** (Inter/Multi-denominational), Jeffrey E Greenway, President, 204 N. Lexington Ave., Wilmore, KY 40390-1199, Tel. (859)858-3581
Website: www.asburyseminary.edu

**Ashland Theological Seminary*** (Brethren Church (Ashland, Ohio)), John C. Shultz, President, 910 Center St., Ashland, OH 44805,

295

Tel. (419)289-5161 Fax (419)289-5969
Email: ffinks@ashland.edu
Website: www.ashland.edu/seminary

**Assemblies of God Theological Seminary***
(Assemblies of God), Byron D. Klaus,
President, 1435 North Glenstone Avenue,
Springfield, MO 65802-2131, Tel. (417)268-
1000 Fax (417)268-1001
Email: agts@agseminary.edu
Website: www.agts.edu

**Associated Mennonite Biblical Seminary***
(Mennonite Church; General Conference
Mennonite Church), J. Nelson Kraybill,
President, 3003 Benham Ave., Elkhart, IN
46517-1999, Tel. (574)295-3726 Fax (574)
295-0092
Email: nkraybill@ambs.edu
Website: www.ambs.edu

**Athenaeum of Ohio*** (Catholic Church),
Edward P. Smith, President and Rector, 6616
Beechmont Ave., Cincinnati, OH 45230-2091,
Tel. (513)231-2223 Fax (513)231-3254
Email: atheathenaeum.edu
Website: www.athenaeum.edu

**Atlanta Christian College** (Christian Churches
and Churches of Christ), R. Edwin Groover,
President, 2605 Ben Hill Rd., East Point, GA
30344, Tel. (404)761-8861 Fax (404)669-2024
Email: admissions@acc.edu
Website: www.acc.edu

**Austin Presbyterian Theological Seminary***
(Presbyterian Church (U.S.A.)), Theodore J.
Wardlaw, President, 100 E. 27th St., Austin,
TX 78705-5797, Tel. (512)472-6736 Fax
(512)479-0738
Website: www.austinseminary.edu

**Bakke Graduate University of Ministry** (Non-
denominational), Brad Smith, President, 1013
Eighth Ave, Seattle, WA 98104, Tel. (206)
264-9100 Fax (206)624-8828
Email: bgu@bgu.edu
Website: www.bgu.edu

**Bangor Theological Seminary*** (United Church
of Christ), William C. Imes, President, Two
College Circle, P.O. Box 411, Bangor, ME 04402-
0411, Tel. (207)942-6781 Fax (207)942-4914
Email: mhuddy@bts.edu
Website: www.bts.edu

**Baptist Bible College** (Baptist Bible Fellowship
International), Leland Kennedy, President,
628 E. Kearney, Springfield, MO 65803, Tel.
(417)268-6060 Fax (417)268-6694

**Baptist Bible College and Seminary** (Baptist),
Jim Jeffery, President, 538 Venard Rd., Clarks

Summit, PA 18411, Tel. (570)586-2400 Fax
(570)586-1753
Email: bbc@bbc.edu
Website: www.bbc.edu

**Baptist Missionary Association Theological
Seminary*** (Baptist Missionary Association
of America), Charley Holmes, President, 1530
E. Pine St., Jacksonville, TX 75766, Tel.
(903)586-2501 Fax (903)586-0378
Email: bmatsem@bmats.edu
Website: www.bmats.edu

**Baptist Theological Seminary at Richmond***
(Cooperative Baptist Fellowship), Thomas H.
Graves, President, 3400 Brook Rd.,
Richmond, VA 23227, Tel. (804)355-8135 Fax
(804)355-8182
Email: tgraves@btsr.edu
Website: www.btsr.edu

**Barclay College** (Interdenominational), Maurice
G. Chandler, President, 607 N Kingman,
Haviland, KS 67059, Tel. (620)862-5252 Fax
(620)862-5403
Email: carju@barclaycollege.edu
Website: www.barclaycollege.edu

**Barry University Department of Theology
and Philosophy***, Mark E. Wedig, Chair of
the Department of Theology and Philosophy,
11300 Northeast Second Avenue, Miami
Shores, FL 33161-6695, Tel. (305)899-3469
Fax (305)899-3385
Email: theology@mail.barry.edu
Website: www.barry.edu/TheologyPhilosophy/
default

**Bay Ridge Christian College** (Church of God
[Anderson, Ind.]), Dr. Verda Beach, President,
P.O. Box 726, Kendleton, TX 77451, Tel.
(979)532-3982 Fax (979)532-4352
Email: brcccampus@wcnet.net
Website: brcconline.org

**Beacon College & Graduate School** (Non-
denominational), Dr. John Durden, Dean, 6003
Veterans Parkway, Columbus, GA 31909, Tel.
(706)323-5364 Fax (706)323-3236
Email: beacon@beacon.edu
Website: www.beacon.edu

**Beeson Divinity School of Samford University***
(Inter/Multidenominational), Timothy George,
Dean, 800 Lakeshore Dr., Birmingham, AL
35229-2252, Tel. (205)726-2991 Fax (205)
726-2260
Email: JTPrince@samford.edu
Website: www.beesondivinity.com

**Berkeley Divinity School*** (Episcopal Church),
Joseph H. Britton, Dean, 409 Prospect Street,
New Haven, CT 06511, Tel. (203)432-9285-
9290 Fax (203)432-9353

Email: joseph.britton@yale.edu
Website: www.yale.edu/berkeleydivinity

**Bethany Lutheran Theological Seminary** (Evangelical Lutheran Synod), G. R. Schmeling, President, 6 Browns Court, Mankato, MN 56001, Tel. (507)344-7354 Fax (507)344-7426
Email: gschmeli@blc.edu
Website: www.blts.edu

**Bethany Theological Seminary\*** (Church of the Brethren), Eugene F. Roop, President, 615 National Rd. W., Richmond, IN 47374, Tel. (765)983-1800 Fax (765)983-1840
Email: snydesu@bethanyseminary.edu
Website: www.bethanyseminary.edu

**Bethel Seminary of the East\*** (Conservative Baptist Association of America—Baptist General Conference), Douglas W. Fombelle, Dean and Executive Officer, 1605 N. Limekiln Pike, Dresher, PA 19025, Tel. (215)641-4801 Fax (215)641-4804
Email: d-fombelle@bethel.edu
Website: www.seminary.bethel.edu

**Bethel Seminary San Diego\*** (General Bapist Conference), George Brushaber, President, 6116 Arosa Street, San Diego, CA 92115-3902, Tel. (619)582-8188 Fax (619)583-9114
Email: bsem-admit@bethel.edu
Website: seminary.bethel.edu/sandiego

**Bethel Theological Seminary\*** (Baptist General Conference), George K. Brushaber, President, 3949 Bethel Dr., St. Paul, MN 55112, Tel. (651)638-6180 Fax (651)638-6002
Email: c-pfingsten@bethel.edu
Website: www.bethel.edu

**Beulah Heights Bible College** (International Pentecostal Church of Christ), Dr. Benson M. Karanja, Ed.D., President, 892 Berne St. SE, Atlanta, GA 30316, Tel. (404)627-2681 Fax (404)627-0702
Email: Benson.Karanja@beulah.org
Website: www.beulah.org

**Bexley Hall Seminary\*** (Episcopal Church), John R. Kevern, President and Dean, 583 Sheridan Avenue, Columbus, OH 43209-2325, Tel. (614)231-3095 Fax (614)231-3236
Email: bexleyhall@bexley.edu
Website: www.bexley.edu

**Bible Church of Christ Theological Institute** (Nondenominational), Roy Bryant, Sr., President, 1358 Morris Ave., Bronx, NY 10456-1402, Tel. (718)588-2284 Fax (718) 992-5597
Website: www.thebiblechurchofchrist.org

**Biblical Theological Seminary\*** (Inter/Multi-denominational), David G. Dunbar, President, 200 N. Main St., Hatfield, PA 19440, Tel. (215)368-5000 Fax (215)368-2301
Email: president@biblical.edu
Website: www.biblical.edu

**Blessed John XXIII National Seminary\*** (Catholic Church), Francis D. Kelly, Rector, 558 South Avenue, Weston, MA 02493-2699, Tel. (781)899-5500 Fax (781)899-9057
Email: seminary@blessedjohnxxiii.edu
Website: www.blessedjohnxxiii.edu

**Boise Bible College** (Christian Churches and Churches of Christ), Dr. Charles A. Crane, President, 8695 Marigold St., Boise, ID 83714, Tel. (208)376-7731 Fax (208)376-7743
Email: boisebible@boisebible.edu
Website: www.boisebible.edu

**Boston Baptist College** (Baptist), Rev. David Melton, President, 950 Metropolitan Avenue, Boston, MA 02136, Tel. (617)364-3510 Fax (617)364-0723
Email: admin@boston.edu/gsnavely@boston.edu
Website: www.boston.edu

**Boston College Institute of Religious Education and Pastoral Ministry and Department of Theology** (Catholic Church), Thomas H. Groome, Director, 31 Lawrence Ave., Chestnut Hill, MA 02467-3931, Tel. (617)552-8440 Fax (617)552-0811
Website: www.bc.edu/irepm

**Boston University School of Theology\*** (The United Methodist Church), Ray L. Hart, Dean, 745 Commonwealth Ave., Boston, MA 02215, Tel. (617)353-3050 Fax (617)353-3061
Website: www.bu.edu/STH

**Brite Divinity School, Texas Christian University\*** (Christian Church [Disciples of Christ]), Newell Williams, President, TCU Box 298130, Ft. Worth, TX 76129-0002, Tel. (817)257-7575 Fax (817)257-7305
Email: l.s.anderson@tcu.edu
Website: www.brite.tcu.edu

**Byzantine Catholic Seminary of SS. Cyril and Methodius\*** (Byzantine Catholic Archeparchy of Pittsburgh), John G. Petro, Rector, 3605 Perrysville Ave., Pittsburgh, PA 15214, Tel. (412)321-8383 Fax (412)321-9936
Website: www.archeparchy.org/page/seminary

**California Christian College** (Free Will Baptist), Wendell Walley, President, 4881 E. University Avenue, Fresno, CA 93703, Tel. (559)251-4215 Fax (559)251-4231
Email: cccregistrar@sbcglobal.net
Website: www.calchristiancollege.org

297

Calvary Bible College and Calvary Theological Seminary (Independent Fundamental Churches of America, International), Elwood H. Chipchase, D.Min., D.D., President, 15800 Calvary Rd., Kansas City, MO 64147-1341, Tel. (800)326-3960 Fax (816)331-4474
Email: president@calvary.edu
Website: www.calvary.edu

Calvin Theological Seminary* (Christian Reformed Church in North America), The Rev. Dr. Cornelius Plantinga, Jr., President, 3233 Burton St. S.E., Grand Rapids, MI 49546-4387, Tel. (616)957-6036; (616)957-6044 Fax (616)957-8621
Email: sempres@calvinseminary.edu
Website: www.calvinseminary.edu

Campbell University Divinity School* (Baptist State Convention of North Carolina), Michael G. Cogdill, Dean, 116 T. T. Lanier Street, P.O. Drawer 4050, Buies Creek, NC 27506, Tel. (910)893-1830 Fax (910)893-1835
Email: cogdill@campbell.edu
Website: www.campbell.edu/divinity

Candler School of Theology of Emory University* (The United Methodist Church), Jan Love, Dean, 500 Kilgo Circle N.E., Emory Univ., Atlanta, GA 30322, Tel. (404)727-6324 Fax (404)727-3182
Email: candler@emory.edu
Website: www.emory.edu/candler

Capital Bible Seminary* (Nondenominational), Larry A. Mercer, President, 6511 Princess Garden Parkway, Lanham, MD 20706, Tel. (301)552-1400 Fax (301)614-1024
Email: bfox@bible.edu
Website: www.bible.edu

Carolina Evangelical Divinity School* (Religious Society of Friends), Frank P. Scurry, President, P.O. Box 5831, High Point, NC 27265, Tel. (336)882-3370 Fax (336)882-3370
Email: fscurry@ceds.edu
Website: www.ceds.edu

Catholic Theological Union at Chicago* (Catholic Church), Donald Senior, C.P., President, 5401 S. Cornell Ave., Chicago, IL 60615-5664, Tel. (773)324-8000 Fax (773)324-8490
Email: donald@ctu.edu
Website: www.ctu.edu

Catholic University of America* (Catholic Church), Kevin W. Irwin, Dean, 620 Michigan Avenue NE, Washington, DC 20064, Tel. (202)319-5683 Fax (202)319-4967
Email: cua-deansrs@cua.edu
Website: www.religiousstudies.cua.edu

Central Baptist College (Baptist Missionary Association of Arkansas), Terry Kimbrow, President, 1501 College Ave., Conway, AR 72032, Tel. (501)329-6872 Fax (501)329-2941
Email: TKimbrow@cbc.edu
Website: www.cbc.edu

Central Baptist Theological Seminary* (Baptist), The Rev. Dr. Molly T. Marshall, President, 6601 Monticello Road, Shawnee, KS 66226-3513, Tel. (913)371-5313 Fax (913)371-8110
Email: rsandbothe@cbts.edu
Website: www.cbts.edu

Central Baptist Theological Seminary in Indiana (National Baptist Convention U.S.A., Inc.), Dr. Robert Lee, President-Dean, 1535 Dr. A. J. Brown Ave. N., Indianapolis, IN 46202, Tel. (317)636-6622
Email: henriettabrown@webtv.net

Central Bible College (Assemblies of God), In Transition, President, 3000 N. Grant Ave., Springfield, MO 65803, Tel. (417)833-2551 Fax (417)833-5141
Email: info@cbcag.edu
Website: www.cbcag.edu

Central Christian College of the Bible (Christian Churches and Churches of Christ), Ronald L. Oakes, President, 911 E. Urbandale Dr., Moberly, MO 65270-1997, Tel. (660)263-3900 Fax (660)263-3936
Email: develop@cccb.edu
Website: www.cccb.edu

Central Indian Bible College (Assemblies of God), M. George Kallappa, President, P.O. Box 550, Mobridge, SD 57601, Tel. (605)845-7801 Fax (605)845-7744

Chapman School of Religious Studies of Oakland City University* (General Association of General Baptists), James W. Murray, Chancellor and President, 143 Lucretia Street, Oakland City, IN 47660, Tel. (812)749-4781 Fax (812)749-1233
Email: ocuexec@oak.edu, ebenson@oak.edu
Website: www.oak.edu

Chicago Theological Seminary* (United Church of Christ), Susan Brooks Thistlethwaite, President, 5757 South University Ave., Chicago, IL 60637-1507, Tel. (773)752-5757 Fax (773)752-5925
Email: sthistle@ctschicago.edu, lredmond@ctschicago.edu
Website: www.ctschicago.edu

Christ the King Seminary* (Catholic Church), Rev. Richard W. Siepka, President and Rector, 711 Knox Rd., P.O. Box 607, East Aurora, NY

14052-0607, Tel. (716)652-8900 Fax (716) 652-8903
Email: rsiepka@cks.edu
Website: www.cks.edu

**Christ the Savior Seminary** (American Carpatho-Russian Orthodox Greek Catholic Church), Nicholas Smisko, President, 225 Chandler Ave., Johnstown, PA 15906, Tel. (814)539-0116 Fax (814)536-4699
Email: csseminary@atlanticbb.net
Website: www.acrod.org/seminary

**Christian Heritage College** (Southern Baptist), Dr. David Jeremiah, President, 2100 Greenfield Drive, El Cajon, CA 92019, Tel. (619) 441-2200 Fax (619)440-0209
Email: chcadm@christianheritage.edu
Website: www.christianheritage.edu

**Christian Life College** (Nondenominational), Harry Schmidt, President, 400 E. Gregory Street, Mount Prospect, IL 60056, Tel. (847)259-1840 Fax (847)259-3888
Email: admissions@christianlifecollege.edu
Website: www.christianlifecollege.edu

**Christian Theological Seminary\*** (Christian Church [Disciples of Christ]), Dr. Edward L. Wheeler, President, 1000 W. 42nd St., Indianapolis, IN 46208-3301, Tel. (317)924-1331 Fax (317)923-1961
Email: wheeler@cts.edu
Website: www.cts.edu

**Christian Witness Theological Seminary\*** (Nondenominational), Rev. David A. Cheung, Interim President, 1040 Oak Grove Rd., Concord, CA 94518, Tel. (925)676-5002 Fax (925)676-5220
Email: admin@cwts.edu
Website: www.cwts.edu

**Church Divinity School of the Pacific\*** (Episcopal Church), Donn F. Morgan, President, 2451 Ridge Rd., Berkeley, CA 94709-1217, Tel. (510)204-0700 Fax (510)644-0712
Email: jparkin@cdsp.edu
Website: www.cdsp.edu

**Church of God Theological Seminary\*** (Church of God [Cleveland, Tenn.]), Steven J. Land, President, P.O. Box 3330, Cleveland, TN 37320-3330, Tel. (423)478-1131 Fax (423)478-7711
Email: tgilbert@cogts.edu
Website: www.cogts.edu

**Cincinnati Christian University\*** (Christian Churches and Churches of Christ), David M. Faust, President, 2700 Glenway Ave., Cincinnati, OH 45204-3200, Tel. (513)244-8120, (513)244-8100, 800-949-4228 Fax (513)244-8434

Email: judy.pratt@ccuniversity.edu/linda.palmer ccuniversity.edu
Website: www.CCuniversity.edu

**Circleville Bible College** (Churches of Christ in Christian Union), John Conley, President, P.O. Box 458, Circleville, OH 43113, Tel. (740)474-8896 Fax (740)477-7755
Email: stolbert@biblecollege.edu
Website: www.biblecollege.edu

**Claremont School of Theology\*** (The United Methodist Church), Jerry D. Campbell, President, 1325 N. College Ave., Claremont, CA 91711-3199, Tel. (909)447-2500 Fax (909)626-7062
Email: admission@cst.edu
Website: www.cst.edu

**Clear Creek Baptist Bible College** (Southern Baptist Convention), President Bill Whittaker, President, 300 Clear Creek Rd., Pineville, KY 40977, Tel. (606)337-3196 Fax (606)337-2372
Email: ccbbc@ccbbc.edu
Website: www.ccbbc.edu

**Clinton Junior College** (African Methodist Episcopal Zion Church), Dr. Elaine Johnson Copeland, President, 1029 Crawford Road, Rock Hill, SC 29730, Tel. (803)327-7402 Fax (803)327-3261
Email: ecopeland@clintonjrcollege.org
Website: www.clintonjrcollege.org

**Colegio Biblico Pentecostal de Puerto Rico** (Church of God [Cleveland, Tenn.]), Dr. Ildefonso Caraballo, President, P.O. Box 901, Saint Just, PR 00978, Tel. (787)761-0640 Fax (787)748-9228
Email: ildefonso@cbp.edu
Website: www.cbp.edu

**Colgate Rochester Crozer Divinity School\*** (American Baptist Churches in the U.S.A.), Eugene C. Bay, President, 1100 S. Goodman St., Rochester, NY 14620, Tel. (585)271-1320 Fax (585)271-8013
Email: thalbrooks@crcds.edu
Website: www.crcds.edu

**Colorado Christian University** (Nondenominational), Larry R. Donnithorne, President, 180 S. Garrison St., Lakewood, CO 80226, Tel. (303)202-0100 Fax (303)274-7560
Email: dlong@ccu.edu
Website: www.ccu.edu

**Columbia International University Seminary & School of Missions\*** (Multidenominational), George W. Murray, President, P.O. Box 3122, Columbia, SC 29230-3122, Tel. (803)754-4100 Fax (803)786-4209
Email: publicrelations@ciu.edu
Website: www.ciu.edu

Columbia Theological Seminary* (Presbyterian Church [U.S.A.]), Laura S. Mendenhall, President, 701 Columbia Dr., P.O. Box 520, Decatur, GA 30031, Tel. (404)378-8821 Fax (404)377-9696
Email: MendenhallL@CTSnet.edu
Website: www.CTSnet.edu

Concordia Seminary* (The Lutheran Church-Missouri Synod), Dale A. Meyer, President, 801 Seminary Place, St. Louis, MO 63105, Tel. (314)505-7010 Fax (314)505-7002
Email: bartelta@csl.edu
Website: www.csl.edu

Concordia Theological Seminary* (The Lutheran Church-Missouri Synod), Dean O. Wenthe, President, 6600 N. Clinton St., Ft. Wayne, IN 46825-4996, Tel. (260)452-2100 Fax (260)452-2121
Email: wenthedo@mail.ctsfw.edu
Website: www.ctsfw.edu

Covenant Theological Seminary* (Presbyterian Church in America), Dr. Bryan Chapell, President, 12330 Conway Rd., St. Louis, MO 63141-8697, Tel. (314)434-4044 Fax (314)434-4819
Email: admissions@covenantseminary.edu
Website: www.covenantseminary.edu

Cranmer Seminary (Episcopal Orthodox Church; The Anglican Rite Synod in the Americas; The Orthodox Anglican Communion), The Most Rev. Scott E. McLaughlin, D.D., Ph.D., President, 901 English Rd., High Point, NC 27262, Tel. (336)885-6032 Fax (336)885-6021
Email: seminaryinfo@orthodoxanglican.net
Website: orthodoxanglican.net; divinityschool.org

Criswell Center for Biblical Studies (Southern Baptist Convention), President, 4010 Gaston Ave., Dallas, TX 75246, Tel. (214)821-5433 Fax (214)818-1320
Email: jjohnson@criswell.edu
Website: www.criswell.edu

Crossroads College (Christian Churches and Churches of Christ-Nondenominational), Michael Benson, Interim, President, 920 Mayowood Rd. S.W., Rochester, MN 55902, Tel. (507)288-4563 Fax (507)288-9046
Email: academic@crossroadscollege.edu
Website: www.crossroadscollege.edu

Crown College (The Christian and Missionary Alliance), Timothy D. Savaloja, Interim President, 8700 College View Dr., St. Bonifacius, MN 55375-9001, Tel. (952)446-4100 Fax (952)446-4149
Email: crown@crown.edu
Website: www.crown.edu

Cummins Theological Seminary (Reformed Episcopal Church), James C. West, President, 705 S. Main St., Summerville, SC 29483, Tel. (843)873-3451 Fax (843)875-6200
Email: jcw121@aol.com, canon_moock@prodigy.net
Website: www.recus.org

Dallas Christian College (Christian Churches and Churches of Christ), Dustin "Dusty" Rubeck, President, 2700 Christian Pkwy, Dallas, TX 75234, Tel. (972)241-3371 Fax (972)241-8021
Email: dcc@dallas.edu
Website: www.dallas.edu

Dallas Theological Seminary* (Inter/Multi-denominational), Dr. Mark L. Bailey, President, 3909 Swiss Ave., Dallas, TX 75204, Tel. (214)824-3094 Fax (214)841-3625
Email: kgrassmick@dts.edu
Website: www.dts.edu

Davis College (Practical Bible College) (Independent Baptist), Dr. George Miller, President, 400 Riverside Drive, Johnson City, NY 13790, Tel. (607)729-1581 Fax (607)729-2962
Website: www.davisny.edu

Denver Seminary* (Nondenominational), Craig Williford, Ph.D., President, 6399 S. Santa Fe Drive, Littleton, CO 80120, Tel. (303)761-2482 Fax (303)761-8060
Email: info@denverseminary.edu
Website: www.denverseminary.edu

The Disciples Divinity House of the University of Chicago (Christian Church [Disciples of Christ]), Dr. Kristine A. Culp, Dean, 1156 E. 57th St., Chicago, IL 60637-1536, Tel. (773)643-4411 Fax (773)643-4413
Email: ddh.uchicago.admin@attglobal.net
Website: ddh.uchicago.edu

Dominican House of Studies* (Catholic Church), Dwight Reginald Whitt, O.P., President, 487 Michigan Ave. N.E., Washington, DC 20017-1585, Tel. (202)529-5300 Fax (202)636-1700
Email: assistant@dhs.edu
Website: www.dhs.edu

Dominican School of Philosophy and Theology* (Catholic Church), Michael Sweeney, President, 2401 Ridge Rd., Berkeley, CA 94709, Tel. (510)849-2030 Fax (510)849-1372
Email: msweeney@dspt.edu
Website: www.dspt.edu

Dominican Study Center of the Caribbean* (Catholic Church), Rev. Fr. Dr. Félix Struik, O.P., Regent of the Center, Apartado Postal

1968, Bayamon, PR 00960-1968, Tel. (787) 787-1826 Fax (787)798-2712
Email: fstruik@cedocpr.org
Website: www.cedocpr.org

**Drew University Theological School*** (The United Methodist Church), Maxine C. Beach, Vice President and Dean, 36 Madison Ave., Madison, NJ 07940-4010, Tel. (973)408-3258 Fax (973)408-3534
Email: miannuzzi@drew.edu
Website: www.drew.edu/theo

**Duke University Divinity School*** (The United Methodist Church), L. Gregory Jones, Dean, Box 90968, Durham, NC 27708-0968, Tel. (888)462-3853 Fax (919)660-3535
Email: admissions@div.duke.edu
Website: www.divinity.duke.edu

**Earlham School of Religion*** (Interdenominational-Friends), Jay Wade Marshall, Dean, 228 College Ave., Richmond, IN 47374, Tel. (800)432-1377 Fax (765)983-1688
Email: woodna@earlham.edu
Website: www.esr.earlham.edu

**Eastern Mennonite Seminary of Eastern Mennonite University*** (Mennonite Church), Loren Swartzendruber, President, 1200 Park Road, Harrisonburg, VA 22802, Tel. (540)432-4260 Fax (540)432-4598
Email: swartlej@emu.edu
Website: www.emu.edu/seminary

**Ecumenical Theological Seminary*** (Inter/Multidenominational), Marsha Foster Boyd, President, 2930 Woodward Ave., Detroit, MI 48201, Tel. (313)831-5200 Fax (313)831-1353
Website: www.etseminary.edu

**Eden Theological Seminary*** (United Church of Christ), David M. Greenhaw, President, 475 E. Lockwood Ave., St. Louis, MO 63119-3192, Tel. (314)961-3627 Fax (314)918-2626
Email: dgreenhaw@eden.edu
Website: www.eden.edu

**Emmanuel School of Religion*** (Christian Churches and Churches of Christ), C. Robert Wetzel, President, One Walker Dr., Johnson City, TN 37601-9438, Tel. (423)926-1186 Fax (423)926-6198
Email: wetzelr@esr.edu
Website: www.esr.edu

**Emmaus Bible College** (Christian Brethren [also known as Plymouth Brethren]), Kenneth Alan Daughters, President, 2570 Asbury Rd., Dubuque, IA 52001, Tel. (563)588-8000 Fax (563)588-1216
Email: info@emmaus.edu
Website: www.emmaus.edu

**Episcopal Divinity School*** (Episcopal Church), The Rt. Rev. Steven Charleston, President and Dean, 99 Brattle St., Cambridge, MA 02138-3494, Tel. (617)868-3450 Fax (617)864-5385
Email: scharleston@episdivschool.org
Website: www.episdivschool.edu

**Episcopal Theological Seminary of the Southwest*** (Episcopal Church), Titus L. Presler, Dean and President, P.O. Box 2247, Austin, TX 78768-2247, Tel. (512)472-4133 Fax (512)472-3098
Email: salexander@etss.edu
Website: www.etss.edu

**Erskine Theological Seminary*** (Associate Reformed Presbyterian Church [General Synod]), Dr. Randall T. Ruble, President, P.O. Box 668, Due West, SC 29639, Tel. (864)379-8833 Fax (864)379-2171
Email: ruble@erskine.edu
Website: www.erskineseminary.org

**Eugene Bible College** (Open Bible Standard Churches, Inc.), David Cole, President, 2155 Bailey Hill Rd., Eugene, OR 97405, Tel. (541)485-1780 Fax (541)343-5801
Email: davidc@ebc.edu
Website: www.ebc.edu

**Evangelical School of Theology*** (Evangelical Congregational Church), Dennis P. Hollinger, President, 121 S. College St., Myerstown, PA 17067, Tel. (717)866-5775 Fax (717)866-4667
Email: dhollinger@evangelical.edu
Website: www.evangelical.edu

**Evangelical Seminary of Puerto Rico*** (Inter/Multidenominational), Sergio Ojeda-Carcamo, President, Ponce de Leon Avenue 776, San Juan, PR 00925, Tel. (787)763-6700 Fax (787)751-0847
Website: www.seminarioevangelicopr.org

**Faith Baptist Bible College and Theological Seminary** (General Association of Regular Baptist Churches), Richard W. Houg, President, 1900 N.W. 4th St., Ankeny, IA 50021-2152, Tel. (515)964-0601 Fax (515)964-1638
Website: www.faith.edu

**Faith Evangelical Lutheran Seminary** (Conservative Lutheran Association), R. H. Redal, President, 3504 N. Pearl St., Tacoma, WA 98407, Tel. (253)752-2020/(888)777-7675 Fax (206)759-1790
Email: fsinfo@faithseminary.edu
Website: www.faithseminary.edu

**Florida Center for Theological Studies*** (Inter/Multidenominational), Patrick H. O'Neill,

301

President, 111 NE First St., Eighth Floor, Miami, FL 33132, Tel. (305)379-3777 Fax (305)379-1006
Website: www.fcfts.org

**Florida Christian College** (Christian Churches and Churches of Christ), A. Wayne Lowen, President, 1011 Bill Beck Blvd., Kissimmee, FL 34744, Tel. (407)847-8966 Fax (407)847-3925
Email: fcc@fcc.edu
Website: www.fcc.edu

**Franciscan School of Theology*** (Catholic Church), Mario DiCicco, President, 1712 Euclid Ave., Berkeley, CA 94709, Tel. (510) 848-5232 Fax (510)549-9466
Email: wcieslak@fst.edu
Website: www.fst.edu

**Free Will Baptist Bible College** (National Association of Free Will Baptists), J. Matthew Pinson, President, 3606 West End Ave., Nashville, TN 37205, Tel. (615)383-1340 Fax (615)269-6028
Email: president@fwbbc.edu
Website: www.fwbcc.edu

**Fuller Theological Seminary*** (Multidenominational), Richard J. Mouw, President, 135 N. Oakland Ave., Pasadena, CA 91182, Tel. (626)584-5200 Fax (626)795-8767
Email: lguernse@fuller.edu
Website: www.fuller.edu

**Garrett-Evangelical Theological Seminary*** (The United Methodist Church), Philip A. Amerson, President, 2121 Sheridan Rd., Evanston, IL 60201-3298, Tel. (847)866-3900 Fax (847)866-3957
Email: seminary@garrett.edu
Website: www.garrett.edu

**The General Theological Seminary*** (Episcopal Church), Ward B. Ewing, President, 175 Ninth Ave., New York, NY 10011-4977, Tel. (212) 243-5150 Fax (212)647-0294
Email: ewing@gts.edu
Website: www.gts.edu

**George Fox Evangelical Seminary*** (Inter/Multidenominational), Jules Glanzer, Dean, 12753 SW 68th Ave., Portland, OR 97223, Tel. (503)554-6150 Fax (503)554-6155
Email: seminary@georgefox.edu
Website: www.seminary.georgefox.edu

**George Mercer Jr. Memorial School of Theology** (Episcopal Church), The Rev. Canon Juan M.C. Oliver, Director, 65 Fourth St., Garden City, NY 11530, Tel. (516)248-4800 Fax (516)248-4883
Email: rseetahal@dioceseli.org
Website: www.mercerschool.org

**George W. Truett Theological Seminary of Baylor University*** (Baptist General Convention of Texas), Paul W. Powell, Dean, P.O. Box 97126, Waco, TX 76798-7126, Tel. (254)710-3755 Fax (254)710-3753
Email: Nancy_Floyd@Baylor.edu
Website: www.truettseminary.net

**God's Bible School and College** (Nondenominational), Dr. Michael Avery, President, 1810 Young St., Cincinnati, OH 45202, Tel. (513)721-7944 Fax (513)721-3971
Email: president@gbs.edu
Website: www.gbs.edu

**Golden Gate Baptist Theological Seminary*** (Southern Baptist Convention), Jeff Iorg, President, 201 Seminary Dr., Mill Valley, CA 94941-3197, Tel. (415)380-1300 Fax (415)380-1302
Email: seminary@ggbts.edu
Website: www.ggbts.edu

**Gonzaga University Department of Religious Studies*** (Catholic Church), Pat McCormick, Dept. Head, Spokane, WA 99258-0001, Tel. (509)328-6782 Fax (509)323-5718
Email: McCormick@Gonzaga.edu
Website: www.gonzaga.edu

**Gordon-Conwell Theological Seminary*** (Inter/Multidenominational), James Emery White, President, 130 Essex St., South Hamilton, MA 01982, Tel. (978)468-7111 Fax (978)468-6691
Email: info@gcts.edu
Website: www.gordonconwell.edu

**Grace Bible College** (Grace Gospel Fellowship), Kenneth B. Kemper, President, P.O. Box 910, Grand Rapids, MI 49509, Tel. (616)538-2330 Fax (616)538-0599
Email: info@gbcol.edu
Website: www.gbcol.edu

**Grace Theological Seminary*** (Fellowship of Grace Brethren Churches), Ronald E. Manahan, President, 200 Seminary Dr., Winona Lake, IN 46590-1294, Tel. (574)372-5100 Fax (574)372-5139
Email: rmanahan@grace.edu
Website: www.grace.edu

**Grace University** (Interdenominational), Dr. James Eckman, President, 1311 South 9th St., Omaha, NE 68108, Tel. (402)449-2809 Fax (402)341-9587
Email: jofast@graceu.edu
Website: www.graceuniversity.edu

**Graduate Theological Foundation** (Interdenominational/Interfaith), John Morgan, Ph.D., D.Sc., Psy.D., President, 218 West Washington

Street, The Tower Building, Suite 300, South Bend, IN 46601, Tel. (800)423-5983, (574) 287-3642 Fax (574)287-7520
Email: gtfed@sbcglobal.net
Website: www.gtfeducation.org

**Graduate Theological Union\*** (Interdenominational), James A. Donahue, President, 2400 Ridge Rd., Berkeley, CA 94709-1212, Tel. (510)649-2400 Fax (510)649-1417
Email: libref@gtu.edu
Website: www.gtu.edu

**Grand Rapids Theological Seminary of Cornerstone University\*** (Nondenominational), Douglas L. Fagerstrom, 1001 East Beltline NE, Grand Rapids, MI 49525-5897, Tel. (616)222-1422 Fax (616)222-1502
Website: www.grts.cornerstone.edu

**Great Lakes Christian College** (Christian Churches and Churches of Christ), Larry Carter, President, 6211 W. Willow Hwy., Lansing, MI 48917, Tel. (517)321-0242 Fax (517)321-5902
Email: lcarter@glcc.edu
Website: www.glcc.edu

**Greenville College** (Free Methodist Church of North America), President Robert E. Smith, President, 315 E. College Ave., P.O. Box 159, Greenville, IL 62246, Tel. (618)664-2800 Fax (618)664-1748
Email: rsmith@Greenville.edu
Website: www.greenville.edu

**Haggard School of Theology at Azusa Pacific University\*** (Interdenominational), David W. Wright, President, 901 E. Alosta, P.O. Box 7000, Azusa, CA 91702-7000, Tel. (845)969-3434 Fax (845)969-7180
Website: www.apu.edu/theology

**Harding University Graduate School of Religion\*** (Churches of Christ), Evertt W. Huffard, Executive Director, 1000 Cherry Rd., Memphis, TN 38117-5499, Tel. (901)761-1352 Fax (901)761-1358
Email: dean@hugsr.edu
Website: www.hugsr.edu

**Hartford Seminary\*** (Interdenominational), Heidi Hadsell, President, 77 Sherman St., Hartford, CT 06105-2260, Tel. (860)509-9500 Fax (860)509-9509
Email: info@hartsem.edu
Website: www.hartsem.edu

**Harvard University Divinity School\*** (Inter/Multidenominational), Professor William A. Graham, Dean, 45 Francis Ave., Cambridge, MA 02138, Tel. (617)495-5761 Fax (617)496-8026

Email: suzanne_rom@harvard.edu
Website: www.hds.harvard.edu

**Hebrew Union College-Jewish Institute of Religion** (Jewish), Rabbi David Ellenson, President, 3077 University Ave., Los Angeles, CA 90007, Tel. (213)749-3424 Fax (213)747-6128
Email: presoff@huc.edu
Website: www.huc.edu

**Hebrew Union College-Jewish Institute of Religion**, NY (Reform Judaism), Rabbi David Ellenson, Ph.D., President, 1 W. 4th St., New York, NY 10012, Tel. (212)674-5300 Fax (212)533-0129
Email: presoff@huc.edu/jrosensaft@huc.edu
Website: www.huc.edu

**Heritage Bible College** (Pentecostal Free Will Baptist), Dr. Dwarka Ramphal, President, 1747 Bud Hawkins Road, P.O. Box 1628, Dunn, NC 28335, Tel. (910)892-3178 Fax (910)892-1809
Email: generalinfo@heritagebiblecollege.org
Website: www.heritagebiblecollege.org

**Hillsdale Free Will Baptist College** (Free Will Baptist), Carl Cheshier, President, P.O. Box 7208, Moore, OK 73153-1208, Tel. (405)912-9000 Fax (405)912-9050
Email: hillsdale@hc.edu
Website: www.hc.edu

**Hobe Sound Bible College** (Nondenominational), P. Daniel Stetler, President, P.O. Box 1065, Hobe Sound, FL 33475, Tel. (407)546-5534 Fax (407)545-1421

**Holy Cross Greek Orthodox School of Theology\*** (Greek Orthodox Archdiocese of America), Rev. Nicholas C. Triantafilou, President, 50 Goddard Ave., Brookline, MA 02445-7495, Tel. (617)731-3500 Fax (617) 850-1460
Email: admissions@hchc.edu
Website: www.hchc.edu

**Holy Trinity Orthodox Seminary** (Russian Orthodox Church Outside of Russia), Archbishop Laurus Skurla, President, P.O. Box 36, Jordanville, NY 13361, Tel. (315)858-0945 Fax (315)858-0945
Email: seminary@telenet.net

**Hood Theological Seminary\*** (African Methodist Episcopal Zion Church), Albert J.D. Aymer, President, 1810 Lutheran Synod Drive, Salisbury, NC 28144, Tel. (704)636-7611 Fax (704)636-7699
Email: pwells@hoodseminary.edu
Website: www.hoodseminary.edu

**Hope International University** (Christian Churches and Churches of Christ), John Derry, President, 2500 E. Nutwood Ave., Fullerton, CA 92831-3104, Tel. (714)879-3901 Fax (714)681-7451
Email: slcarter@hiu.edu
Website: www.hiu.edu

**Houston Graduate School of Theology*** (Friends), Keith A. Jenkins, President, 2501 Cent-ral Parkway, Suite A-19, Houston, TX 77092, Tel. (713)942-9505 Fax (713)942-9506
Email: hgst@hgst.edu
Website: www.hgst.edu

**Howard University School of Divinity*** (Nondenominational), Bertram Melbourne, Interim Dean, 1400 Shepherd St. N.E., Washington, DC 20017, Tel. (202)806-0500 Fax (202)806-0711
Website: www.howard.edu/schooldivinity

**Huntington University, Graduate School of Christian Ministries** (Church of the United Brethren in Christ), G. Blair Dowden, President, 2303 College Ave., Huntington, IN 46750, Tel. (260)359-4039 Fax (260)359-4126
Email: gscm@huntington.edu
Website: www.huntington.edu/gscm

**Iliff School of Theology*** (The United Methodist Church), David Trickett, President, 2201 S. University Blvd., Denver, CO 80210-4798, Tel. (303)744-1287 Fax (303)777-3387
Email: dgtrickett@iliff.edu
Website: www.iliff.edu

**Immaculate Conception Seminary Seton Hall University*** (Catholic Church), Rev. Msgr. Robert F. Coleman, J. C. D., Rector and Dean, 400 S. Orange Ave., South Orange, NJ 07079, Tel. (973)761-9575 Fax (973)761-9577
Email: theology@shu.edu
Website: www.theology.shu.edu

**Indiana Wesleyan University** (Wesleyan Church), James Barnes, President, 4201 S. Washington, Marion, IN 46953-4974, Tel. (765)674-6901 Fax (765)677-2465
Email: james.barnes@indwes.edu
Website: www.indwes.edu

**Institute for Creation Research Graduate School** (Nondenominational), Dr. John Morris, President, 10946 Woodside Avenue North, Santee, CA 92071, Tel. (619)448-0900 Fax (619)448-3469
Email: kcumming@icr.edu; jkriege@icr.org
Website: www.icr.org

**Inter-American Adventist Theological Seminary*** (Seventh-day Adventist), Jaime Castrejon, President and Dean, P.O. Box 830518, Miami, FL 33283, Tel. (305)403-4700 Fax (305)403-4600
Email: Jaime@interamerica.org
Website: www.interamerica.org

**Interdenominational Theological Center*** (Interdenominational), Dr. Michael A. Battle, President, 700 Martin Luther King, Jr. Dr. S.W., Atlanta, GA 30314-4143, Tel. (404)527-7702 Fax (404)527-7770
Email: info@itc.edu
Website: www.itc.edu

**International Baptist College** (Baptist), Dr. Jerry Tetreau, President, 2150 East Southern Avenue, Tempe, AZ 85282-7504, Tel. (480) 838-7070 Fax (480)505-3299
Email: info@ibconline.edu
Website: www.tri-citybaptist.org

**International College & Graduate School** (Nondenominational), Dr. Rick Stinton, President, 20 Dowsett Avenue, Honolulu, HI 96817, Tel. (808)595-4247 Fax (808)595-4779
Email: icgs@hawaii.rr.com
Website: www.icgshawaii.org

**International Theological Seminary*** (Nondenominational), Joseph Tong, President, 3215-3225 N. Tyler Ave., El Monte, CA 91731, Tel. (626)448-0023 Fax (626)350-6343
Website: www.itsla.edu

**James and Carolyn McAfee School of Theology of Mercer University*** (Cooperative Baptist Fellowship), R. Alan Culpepper, Dean of the School of Theology, 3001 Mercer University Drive, Atlanta, GA 30341-4115, Tel. (678)547-6470 Fax (678)547-6478
Email: culpepper_ra@mercer.edu
Website: theology.mercer.edu

**Jesuit School of Theology at Berkeley*** (Catholic Church), Joseph P. Daoust, President, 1735 LeRoy Ave., Berkeley, CA 94709-1193, Tel. (510)549-5000 Fax (510) 841-8536
Email: cdodson@jstb.edu
Website: www.jstb.edu

**Jewish Theological Seminary of America** (Jewish), Ismar Schorsch, President, 3080 Broadway, New York, NY 10027-4649, Tel. (212)678-8000 Fax (212)678-8947
Email: webmaster@jtsa.edu
Website: www.jtsa.edu

**The John Leland Center for Theological Studies*** (Baptist), K. Randel Everett, President, 1301 N. Hartford St., Arlington, VA 22201, Tel. (703)812-4757 Fax (703)812-4764
Website: www.johnlelandcenter.edu

**John Wesley College** (Interdenominational), Brian C. Donley, President, 2314 N. Centennial St., High Point, NC 27265, Tel. (336)889-2262 Fax (336)889-2261 Email: admissions@johnwesley.edu Website: www.johnwesley.edu

**Johnson Bible College** (Christian Churches and Churches of Christ), David L. Eubanks, President, 7900 Johnson Dr., Knoxville, TN 37998, Tel. (865)573-4517 Fax (865)251-2336 Email: jbc@jbc.edu Website: www.jbc.edu

**Kansas City College and Bible School** (Church of God [Holiness]), Gayle Woods, President, 7401 Metcalf Ave., Overland Park, KS 66204, Tel. (913)722-0272 Fax (913)722-2135

**Kenrick-Glennon Seminary\*** (Catholic Church), Ted L. Wojcicki, President-Rector, 5200 Glennon Dr., St. Louis, MO 63119-4399, Tel. (314)792-6100 Fax (314)792-6500 Website: www.kenrick.edu

**Kentucky Christian University** (Christian Churches and Churches of Christ), Keith P. Keeran, Ph.D., President, 100 Academic Parkway, Grayson, KY 41143, Tel. (606)474-3000 Fax (606)474-3155 Email: TLW@kcu.edu Website: www.kcu.edu

**Kentucky Mountain Bible College** (Inter-denominational), Philip Speas, President, P.O. Box 10, Vancleve, KY 41385, Tel. (606)666-5000 Fax (606)666-7744

**King's College and Seminary** (Nondenominational), Paul G. Chappell, Ph.D., Chief Academic Officer, 14800 Sherman Way, Van Nuys, CA 91405, Tel. (818)779-8040 Fax (818)779-8241 Email: admissions@kingsseminary.edu Website: www.kingsseminary.edu; www.kings college.edu

**Knox Theological Seminary\*** (Presbyterian Church in America), R. Fowler White, Administrator and Dean of the Faculty, 5554 North Federal Highway, Fort Lauderdale, FL 33308, Tel. (954)771-0376 Fax (954)351-3343 Email: knox@crpc.org Website: www.knoxseminary.org

**Kuyper College** (Interdenominational), Nicholas V. Kroeze, President, 3333 East Beltline N.E., Grand Rapids, MI 49525-9749, Tel. (616)222-3000 Fax (616)988-3608 Email: jheyboer@kuyper.edu Website: www.kuyper.edu

**La Sierra University School of Religion\*** (Seventh-day Adventist Church), Lawrence T. Geraty, President, 4500 Riverwalk Parkway, Riverside, CA 92515-8247, Tel. (951)785-2000 Fax (951)785-2901 Email: pr@lasierra.edu Website: www.lasierra.edu

**Lancaster Bible College** (Nondenominational), Peter W. Teague, President, P.O. Box 83403, Lancaster, PA 17601, Tel. (717)560-8278 Fax (717)560-8260 Email: president@lbc.edu Website: www.lbc.edu

**Lancaster Theological Seminary\*** (United Church of Christ), Rev. Dr. Riess W. Potterveld, President, 555 W. James St., Lancaster, PA 17603-2897, Tel. (717)393-0654 Fax (717)393-4254 Email: seminary@lancasterseminary.edu Website: www.lancasterseminary.edu

**Lexington Theological Seminary\*** (Christian Church [Disciples of Christ]), R. Robert Cueni, President, 631 S. Limestone St., Lexington, KY 40508, Tel. (859)252-0361 Fax (859)281-6042 Website: www.lextheo.edu

**Liberty Baptist Theological Seminary** (Independent Baptist), Dr. Ergun Caner, Dean, 1971 University Blvd., Lynchburg, VA 24502-2269, Tel. (804)582-2000 Fax (804)582-2304 Email: ecaner@liberty.edu Website: www.liberty.edu/Academics/Religion/ Seminary

**Liberty University** (Baptist), Dr. John Borek, President, 1971 University Boulevard, Lynchburg, VA 24502, Tel. (434)582-2000 Fax (434)582-2304 Email: admissions@liberty.edu Website: www.liberty.edu

**Life Pacific College** (International Church of the Foursquare Gospel), Dan R. Stewart, President, 1100 Covina Blvd., San Dimas, CA 91773, Tel. (909)599-5433 Fax (909)599-6690 Email: info@lifepacific.edu Website: www.lifepacific.edu

**Lincoln Christian Seminary\*** (Christian Churches and Churches of Christ), Keith H. Ray, President, 100 Campus View Dr., Lincoln, IL 62656, Tel. (217)732-3168 x 2354 Fax (217)732-5718 Email: ttanner@lccs.edu Website: www.lccs.edu

**Lipscomb University College of Bible and Ministry\*** (Churches of Christ), Terry Briley, Dean, 3901 Granny White Pike, Nashville, TN 37204-3951, Tel. (615)279-6051 Fax (615) 279-6052 Website: www.lipscomb.edu

305

**Logos Evangelical Seminary*** (Evangelical Formosan Church), Felix Liu, President, 9358 Telstar Ave., El Monte, CA 91731, Tel. (626) 571-5110 Fax (626)571-5119
Email: logos@les.edu
Website: www.logos-seminary.edu

**Logsdon Seminary of Hardin-Simmons University*** (Baptist General Convention of Texas), Thomas Brisco, Dean, P.O. Box 16235, Abilene, TX 79698-6235, Tel. (325) 670-1287 Fax (325)670-1406
Website: www.hsutx.edu/academics/logsdon

**Louisville Presbyterian Theological Seminary*** (Presbyterian Church [U.S.A.]), Dean K. Thompson, President, 1044 Alta Vista Rd., Louisville, KY 40205, Tel. (502)895-3411 Fax (502)895-1096
Email: dthompson@lpts.edu
Website: www.lpts.edu

**Loyola Marymount University Department of Theological Studies*** (Catholic Church), Jeffrey S. Siker, Chair, One LMU Drive, Los Angeles, CA 90045-2659, Tel. (310)338-7670 Fax (310)338-1947
Email: jsiker@lmu.edu
Website: bellarmine.lmu.edu/theology

**Loyola University Chicago Institute of Pastoral Studies*** (Catholic Church), Robert A. Ludwig, Director, 820 N. Michigan Ave., Chicago, IL 60611, Tel. (312)915-7400 Fax (312)915-7410
Email: rludwig@luc.edu
Website: www.luc.edu/depts/ips

**Luther Rice Bible College & Seminary** (Baptist), Dr. James Flanagan, President, 3038 Evans Mill Road, Lithonia, GA 30038, Tel. (770)484-1204 Fax (770)484-1155
Email: lrs@lrs.edu
Website: www.lrs.edu

**Luther Seminary*** (Evangelical Lutheran Church in America), Richard H. Bliese, President, 2481 Como Ave., St. Paul, MN 55108, Tel. (651)641-3456 Fax (651)641-3425
Email: admissions@luthersem.edu
Website: www.luthersem.edu

**Lutheran Bible Institute in California** (Intersynodical Lutheran), Samuel Giesy, Acting President, 5321 University Dr., Ste. G, Irvine, CA 92612-2942, Tel. (949)262-9222, (800) 261-5242 Fax (949)262-0283
Email: info@lbic.org
Website: www.lbic.org

**Lutheran Brethren Seminary** (Church of the Lutheran Brethren of America), Joel T. Nordtvedt, Ph.D., President, 815 W. Vernon,

Fergus Falls, MN 56537, Tel. (218)739-3375 Fax (218)739-1259
Email: lbs@clba.org
Website: www.lbs.edu

**Lutheran School of Theology at Chicago*** (Evangelical Lutheran Church in America), James Kenneth Echols, President, 1100 E. 55th St., Chicago, IL 60615-5199, Tel. (773) 256-0700 Fax (773)256-0782
Email: jechols@lstc.edu
Website: www.lstc.edu

**Lutheran Theological Seminary at Gettysburg*** (Evangelical Lutheran Church in America), The Rev. Michael L. Cooper-White, President, 61 Seminary Ridge, Gettysburg, PA 17325-1795, Tel. (717)334-6286 Fax (717)334-3469
Email: info@ltsg.edu
Website: www.ltsg.edu

**Lutheran Theological Seminary at Philadelphia*** (Evangelical Lutheran Church in America), Philip D.W. Krey, President, 7301 Germantown Ave., Philadelphia, PA 19119, Tel. (215)248-4616 Fax (215)248-4577
Email: mtairy@ltsp.edu
Website: www.ltsp.edu

**Lutheran Theological Southern Seminary*** (Evangelical Lutheran Church in America), Marcus J. Miller, President, 4201 North Main St., Columbia, SC 29203, Tel. (803)786-5150 Fax (803)786-6499
Email: Mmiller@ltss.edu
Website: www.ltss.edu

**M. Christopher White School of Divinity of Gardner-Webb University*** (Baptist State Convention of North Carolina), Charles B. Bugg, Dean, 110 N. Main Street, Noel Hall, Boiling Springs, NC 28017, Tel. (704)406-4400 Fax (704)406-3935
Email: rcanoy@gardner-webb.edu
Website: www.divinity.gardner-webb.edu

**Magnolia Bible College** (Churches of Christ), Dr. Garvis Semore, President, P.O. Box 1109, Kosciusko, MS 39090, Tel. (662)289-2896 Fax (662)289-1850
Email: gsemore@magnolia.edu
Website: www.magnolia.edu

**Manhattan Christian College** (Christian Churches and Churches of Christ), Jolene Rupe, Secretary, Institutional Advancement, 1415 Anderson Ave., Manhattan, KS 66502, Tel. (785)539-3571 Fax (785)539-0832
Email: jrupe@mccks.edu
Website: www.mccks.edu

**Maple Springs Baptist Bible College and Seminary** (Nondenominational), Dr. Larry W.

306

Jordan, President, 4130 Belt Road, Capital Heights, MD 20743, Tel. (301)736-3631 Fax (301)735-6507
Email: larry.jordan@msbbcs.edu
Website: www.msbbcs.edu

**Mars Hill Graduate School\*** (Nondenominational), Dr. Dan Allander, President, 2525 - 220th Street, Bothell, WA 98021, Tel. (425) 415-0505 Fax (425)806-5599
Email: info@mhgs.edu
Website: www.mhgs.net

**McCormick Theological Seminary\*** (Presbyterian Church [U.S.A.]), Cynthia M. Campbell, President, 5460 S. University Ave., Chicago, IL 60615-5108, Tel. (773)947-6300 Fax (773) 288-2612
Email: ccampbell@mccormick.edu
Website: www.mccormick.edu

**Meadville Lombard Theological School\*** (Unitarian Universalist), Lee Barker, President, 5701 S. Woodlawn Ave., Chicago, IL 60637, Tel. (773)256-3000 Fax (773)753-1323
Email: LBarker@meadville.edu
Website: www.meadville.edu

**Memphis Theological Seminary\*** (Cumberland Presbyterian Church), Daniel J. Earheart-Brown, President, 168 E. Parkway S. at Union, Memphis, TN 38104-4395, Tel. (901)458-8232 Fax (901)452-4051
Email: jebrown@memphisseminary.edu
Website: www.memphisseminary.edu

**Mennonite Brethren Biblical Seminary\*** (General Conference of Mennonite Brethren Churches), Jim Holm, President, 4824 E. Butler Ave. (at Chestnut Ave.), Fresno, CA 93727-5097, Tel. (559)251-8628 Fax (559) 251-7212
Email: fresno@mbseminary.edu
Website: www.mbseminary.edu

**Messenger College** (Pentecostal Church of God), Tiffany Stump, Dir. of Admissions, 300 E. 50th Street, Joplin, MO 64804, Tel. (417) 624-7070 Fax (417)624-5070
Email: info@messengercollege.edu
Website: www.messengercollege.edu

**Methodist Theological School in Ohio\*** (The United Methodist Church), Jay Rundell, President, 3081 Columbus Pike, P.O. Box 8004, Delaware, OH 43015-8004, Tel. (740) 363-1146 Fax (740)362-3135
Email: ndewire@mtso.edu, pres@mtso.edu
Website: www.mtso.edu

**Michigan Theological Seminary\*** (Non-denominational), Bruce W. Fong, President, 41550 E. Ann Arbor Trail, Plymouth, MI 48170-4308, Tel. (734)207-9581 Fax (734) 207-9582
Email: admissions@mts.edu
Website: www.mts.edu

**Mid-America Christian University** (The Church of God - Anderson, IN), Dr. John D. Fozard, President, 3500 S.W. 119th St., Oklahoma City, OK 73170, Tel. (405)691-3800 Fax (405)692-3165
Email: info@macu.edu
Website: www.macu.edu

**Mid-America Reformed Seminary\*** (Inter/ Multidenominational), Cornelius P. Venema, President, 229 Seminary Drive, Dyer, IN 46311, Tel. (219)864-2400 Fax (219)864-2410
Email: info@midamerica.edu
Website: www.midamerica.edu

**Midwest University (Korean language)** (Interdenominational), Dr. James Song, President, 851 Parr Road, Wentzville, MO 63385, Tel. (636)327-4645 Fax (636)327-4715
Email: inf@midwest.edu
Website: www.midwest.edu

**Midwestern Baptist Theological Seminary\*** (Southern Baptist Convention), Dr. R. Philip Roberts, President, 5001 N. Oak Trafficway, Kansas City, MO 64118, Tel. (816)414-3700 Fax (816)414-3799
Email: president@mbts.edu
Website: www.mbts.edu

**Moody Bible Institute** (Interdenominational), Michael J. Easley, President, 820 N. La Salle Blvd., Chicago, IL 60610, Tel. (312)329-4000 Fax (312)329-4109
Email: pr@moody.edu
Website: www.moody.edu

**Moravian Theological Seminary\*** (Moravian Church in America [Unitas Fratrum]), Christopher M. Thomforde, President, 1200 Main St., Bethlehem, PA 18018, Tel. (610)861-1516 Fax (610)861-1569
Email: seminary@moravian.edu
Website: www.moravianseminary.edu

**Moreau Seminary (Congregation of Holy Cross)** (Catholic Church), Rev. Wilson Miscamble, C.S.C., President, Moreau Seminary, University of Notre Dame, Notre Dame, IN 46556, Tel. (574)631-7735 Fax (574)631-9233
Website: www.nd.edu /~mdiv

**Morehouse School of Religion** (Interdenominational Baptist), William T. Perkins, President, 645 Beckwith St. S.W., Atlanta, GA 30314, Tel. (404)527-7777 Fax (404)681-1005

307

**Mount Angel Seminary\*** (Catholic Church), Very Rev. Fr. Richard Paperini, President Rector, St. Benedict, OR 97373, Tel. (503)845-3951 Fax (503)845-3126
Email: tswanson@mtangel.edu
Website: www.mtangel.edu

**Mt. St. Mary's Seminary\*** (Catholic Church), Steven P. Rohlfs, Rector, 16300 Old Emmitsburg Rd., Emmitsburg, MD 21727-7797, Tel. (301)447-5295 Fax (301)447-5636
Email: rhoades@msmary.edu
Website: www.msmary.edu

**Mt. St. Mary's Seminary of the West** (Catholic Church), Gerald R. Haemmerle, President, 6616 Beechmont Ave., Cincinnati, OH 45230, Tel. (513)231-2223 Fax (513)231-3254
Email: jhaemmer@mtsm.org
Website: mtsm.org

**Multnomah Biblical Seminary\*** (Multnomah Biblical Seminary), Dr. Daniel R. Lockwood, President, 8435 N.E. Glisan St., Portland, OR 97220, Tel. (503)255-0332 Fax (503)251-6701
Email: dlockwood@multnomah.edu
Website: www.multnomah.edu

**Mundelein Seminary of the Univ. of St. Mary-of-the-Lake** (Catholic Church), Dennis J. Lyle, Rector-President, 1000 E. Maple, Mundelein, IL 60060-1174, Tel. (847)566-6401 Fax (847)566-7330
Email: dgiovannetti@usml.edu
Website: www.vocations.org

**Nashotah House (Theological Seminary)\*** (Episcopal Church), Robert S. Munday, President and Dean, 2777 Mission Rd., Nashotah, WI 53058-9793, Tel. (262)646-6500 Fax (262)646-6504
Email: smills@nashotah.edu
Website: www.nashotah.edu

**Nazarene Bible College** (Church of the Nazarene), Hiram Sanders, President, 1111 Academy Park Loop, Colorado Springs, CO 80910-3704, Tel. (719)884-5000 Fax (719) 884-5199
Email: info@nbc.edu
Website: www.nbc.edu

**Nazarene Theological Seminary\*** (Church of the Nazarene), Ron Benefiel, President, 1700 E. Meyer Blvd., Kansas City, MO 64131-1246, Tel. (816)333-6254 Fax (816)333-6271
Email: lneely@nts.edu
Website: www.nts.edu

**Nebraska Christian College** (Christian Churches and Churches of Christ), Richard D. Milliken, President, 1800 Syracuse Ave., Norfolk, NE 68701-2458, Tel. (402)379-5000 Fax (402)391-5100

Email: info@nechristian.edu
Website: www.nechristian.edu

**New Brunswick Theological Seminary\*** (Reformed Church in America), Gregg A. Mast, President, 17 Seminary Pl., New Brunswick, NJ 08901-1196, Tel. (732)247-5241 Fax (732)249-5412
Email: egm@nbts.edu
Website: www.nbts.edu

**New Orleans Baptist Theological Seminary\*** (Southern Baptist Convention), Charles S. Kelley, President, 3939 Gentilly Blvd., New Orleans, LA 70126, Tel. (504)282-4455 Fax (504)816-8023
Email: nobts@nobts.edu
Website: www.nobts.edu

**New York Theological Seminary\*** (Inter/ Multidenominational), Dale T. Irvin, President, 475 Riverside Drive, Ste. 500, New York, NY 10115, Tel. (212)870-1250 Fax (212)870-1236
Email: drhgaston@nyts.edu
Website: www.nyts.edu

North American Baptist Seminary\* (North American Baptist Conference), G. Michael Hagan, President, 1525 S. Grange Ave., Sioux Falls, SD 57105-1526, Tel. (605)336-6588 Fax (605)335-9090
Email: admissions@nabs.edu
Website: www.nabs.edu

**North Central Bible College** (Assemblies of God), Gordon L. Anderson, President, 910 Elliot Ave. S., Minneapolis, MN 55404, Tel. (612)332-3491 Fax (612)343-4778
Email: INFO@NCBC.EDU
Website: www.NCBC.EDU

**North Park Theological Seminary\*** (The Evangelical Covenant Church), John E. Phelan Jr., President and Dean, 3225 W. Foster Ave., Chicago, IL 60625, Tel. (773)244-6214 Fax (773)244-6244
Email: jphelan@northpark.edu
Website: www.northpark.edu

**Northeastern Seminary at Roberts Wesleyan College\*** (Nondenominational), John A. Martin, President, 2265 Westside Dr., Rochester, NY 14624-1977, Tel. (585)594-6800 Fax (585)594-6801
Website: www.nes.edu

**Northern Baptist Theological Seminary\*** (American Baptist Churches in the U.S.A.), John Kirn, Interim President, 660 E. Butterfield Rd., Lombard, IL 60148-5698, Tel. (630)620-2100 Fax (630)620-2194
Email: cwmoore@northern.seminary.edu
Website: www.seminary.edu

**Northwest Baptist Seminary** (Baptist), Dr. Mark Wagner, President, 4301 N. Stevens, Tacoma, WA 98407, Tel. (253)759-6104 Fax (253)759-3299
Email: nbs@nbs.edu
Website: www.nbs.edu

**Northwest College** (Assemblies of God), Don H. Argue, Ed.D., President, 5520 108th Ave. N.E., P.O. Box 579, Kirkland, WA 98083-0579, Tel. (425)822-8266 Fax (425)827-0148
Email: receptionist@NorthwestU.edu
Website: www.nwcollege.edu

**Notre Dame Seminary*** (Catholic Church), Patrick J. Williams, M. Div., M.S., President and Rector, 2901 S. Carrollton Ave., New Orleans, LA 70118-4391, Tel. (504)866-7426 Fax (504)866-3119
Email: pjwilliams@nds.edu
Website: www.nds.edu

**Oak Hills Christian College** (Interdenominational), Dr. Daniel Clausen, President, 1600 Oak Hills Rd. S.W., Bemidji, MN 56601, Tel. (218)751-8670 Fax (218)751-8825
Email: dclausen@oakhills.edu
Website: www.oakhills.edu

**Oblate School of Theology*** (Catholic Church), Ronald Rolheiser, President, 285 Oblate Dr., San Antonio, TX 78216-6693, Tel. (210)341-1366 Fax (210)341-4519
Email: oblate@connecti.com
Website: www.ost.edu

**Oral Roberts University School of Theology*** (Inter/Multidenominational), Dr. Thomson K. Mathew, Dean, 7777 S. Lewis Ave., Tulsa, OK 74171, Tel. (918)495-7016 Fax (918)495-6259
Email: jcope@oru.edu
Website: www.oru.edu

**Ozark Christian College** (Christian Churches and Churches of Christ), Matt Proctor, President, 1111 N. Main St., Joplin, MO 64801, Tel. (417)624-2518 Fax (417)624-0090
Email: pres@occ.edu
Website: www.occ.edu

**Pacific Islands Bible College**, The Rev. David L. Owen, President, P.O. Box 22619, GMF, GU 96921, Tel. (671)734-1812 Fax (671)734-1813
Email: GuamCampus@pibc.edu; ChuukCampus @pibc.edu
Website: www.pibc.edu

**Pacific Lutheran Theological Seminary*** (Evangelical Lutheran Church in America), Phyllis Anderson, President, 2770 Marin Ave., Berkeley, CA 94708-1530, Tel. (510)524-5264 Fax (510)524-2408
Email: president@plts.edu
Website: www.plts.edu

**Pacific School of Religion*** (Inter/Multidenominational), William McKinney, President, 1798 Scenic Ave., Berkeley, CA 94709, Tel. (510)848-0528 Fax (510)845-8948
Email: wmckinney@psr.edu
Website: www.psr.edu

**Palmer Theological Seminary*** (American Baptist Churches in the U.S.A.), Wallace C. Smith, President, 6 Lancaster Ave., Wynnewood, PA 19096, Tel. (610)896-5000 Fax (610)649-3834
Email: sempres@eastern.edu
Website: www.ebts.edu

**Payne Theological Seminary*** (African Methodist Episcopal Church), Leah Gaskin Fitchue, Ed.D., President, P.O. Box 474, 1230 Wilberforce-Clifton Rd., Wilberforce, OH 45384-0474, Tel. (937)376-2946 Fax (937)376-3330
Email: LFitchue@payne.edu
Website: www.payne.edu

**Pepperdine University** (Churches of Christ), Dr. Randall Chesnutt, Chair of Religion Division, Religion Division, Malibu, CA 90263-4352, Tel. (310)506-4352 Fax (310)317-7271
Email: randall.chesnutt@pepperdine.edu
Website: pepperdine.edu/religion

**Perkins School of Theology (Southern Methodist University)*** (The United Methodist Church), William B. Lawrence, Dean, P.O. Box 750133, Dallas, TX 75275-0133, Tel. (214)768-2293 Fax (214)768-4245
Email: jpangiar@smu.edu
Website: www.smu.edu/perkins

**Philadelphia Biblical University** (Nondenominational), W. Sherrill Babb, President, 200 Manor Ave., Langhorne, PA 19047-2990, Tel. (215)752-5800 Fax (215)702-4341
Email: president@pbu.edu
Website: www.pbu.edu

**Phillips Theological Seminary*** (Christian Church [Disciples of Christ]), William Tabbernee, President, 901 North Mingo Road, Tulsa, OK 74116, Tel. (918)610-8303 Fax (918)610-8404
Email: Myrna.Jones@ptstulsa.edu
Website: www.ptstulsa.edu

**Phoenix Seminary*** (Nondenominational), Darryl DelHousaye, President, 4222 E. Thomas Road, Phoenix, AZ 85018, Tel. (480)443-1020 Fax (480)443-1120
Email: ddelhousaye@phoenixseminary.edu
Website: www.phoenixseminary.edu

**Piedmont Baptist College** (Baptist [Independent]), Charles W. Petitt, President, 716

Franklin St., Winston-Salem, NC 27101, Tel. (336)725-8344 Fax (336)725-5522
Email: admissions@pbc.edu
Website: www.pbc.edu

**Pittsburgh Theological Seminary\*** (Presbyterian Church [U.S.A.]), William J. Carl III, President, 616 N. Highland Ave., Pittsburgh, PA 15206, Tel. (412)362-5610 Fax (412)363-3260
Email: calian@pts.edu
Website: www.pts.edu

**Pontifical College Josephinum\*** (Catholic Church), Msgr. Paul J. Langsfeld, Rector and President, 7625 N. High St., Columbus, OH 43235, Tel. (614)885-5585 Fax (614)885-2307
Email: plangsfeld@pcj.edu
Website: www.pcj.edu

**Pope John XXIII National Seminary** (Catholic Church), Francis D. Kelly, President, 558 South Ave., Weston, MA 02193, Tel. (617)899-5500 Fax (617)899-9057
Email: seminary@blessedjohnxxiii.edu
Website: www.blessedjohnxxiii.edu

**Princeton Theological Seminary\*** (Presbyterian Church [U.S.A.]), Iain R. Torrance, President, P.O. Box 821, Princeton, NJ 08542-0803, Tel. (609)921-8300 Fax (609)924-2973
Email: comm-pub@ptsem.edu
Website: www.ptsem.edu

**Protestant Episcopal Theological Seminary in Virginia\*** (Episcopal Church), Martha J. Horne, Dean and President, 3737 Seminary Rd., Alexandria, VA 22304, Tel. (703)370-6600 Fax (703)370-6234
Email: mhorne@vts.edu
Website: www.vts.edu

**Puget Sound Christian College** (Christian Churches and Churches of Christ), Randy J. Bridges, Ph.D., President, P.O. Box 13108, Everett, WA 98206-3108, Tel. (425)257-3090 Fax (425)258-1488
Email: president@pscc.edu
Website: www.pscc.edu

**Rabbi Isaac Elchanan Theological Seminary** (Jewish), Dr. Norman Lamm, President, 2540 Amsterdam Ave., New York, NY 10033, Tel. (212)960-5344 Fax (212)960-0061
Email: amlevin@ymail.yu.edu
Website: www.yu.edu/riets

**Reconstructionist Rabbinical College** (Jewish), Dan Ehrenkrantz, President, 1299 Church Rd, Wyncote, PA 19095, Tel. (215)576-0800 Fax (215)576-6143
Email: admissions@rrc.edu
Website: www.rrc.edu

**Reformed Episcopal Seminary\*** (Reformed Episcopal Church), Wayne A. Headman, President, 826 Second Ave., Blue Bell, PA 19422-1257, Tel. (610)292-9852 Fax (610) 292-9853
Email: reseminary.edu
Website: www.reseminary.edu

**Reformed Presbyterian Theological Seminary\*** (Reformed Presbyterian Church of North America), Jerry F. O'Neill, President, 7418 Penn Ave., Pittsburgh, PA 15208-2594, Tel. (412)731-8690 Fax (412)731-4834
Email: info@rpts.edu
Website: www.rpts.edu

**Reformed Theological Seminary\*** (Inter/Multidenominational), Dr. Robert C. Cannada, Jr., President, 5422 Clinton Blvd., Jackson, MS 39209-3099, Tel. (601)923-1600 Fax (601) 923-1654
Email: rts.orlando@rts.edu
Website: www.rts.edu

**Regent University School of Divinity\*\*** (Nondenominational/Evangelical), Michael Palmer, Dean, 1000 Regent University Dr, Virginia Beach, VA 23464-9870 Tel. Fax (757) 226-4597
Email: vinssyn@regent.edu
Website: www.regent.edu/acad/schdiv

**Roanoke Bible College** (Christian Churches and Churches of Christ), William A. Griffin, President, 715 N. Poindexter St, Elizabeth City, NC 27909-4054, Tel. (252)334-2070 Fax (252)334-2071
Email: wag@roanokebible.edu
Website: www.roanokebible.edu

**Sacred Heart Major Seminary\*** (Catholic Church), Very Rev. Steven Boguslawski, OP, President, 2701 Chicago Blvd., Detroit, MI 48206, Tel. (313)883-8501 Fax (313)868-6440
Email: Information@shms.edu
Website: www.shmsonline.org

**Sacred Heart School of Theology\*** (Catholic Church), Thomas P. Cassidy, S.C.J., President-Rector, P.O. Box 429, Hales Corners, WI 53130-0429, Tel. (414)425-8300 Fax (414) 529-6999
Email: rector@shst.edu
Website: www.shst.edu

**St. Bernard's School of Theology and Ministry\*** (Catholic Church), Patricia A. Schoelles,

President, 120 French Road, Rochester, NY 14618, Tel. (585)271-3657 Fax (585)271-2045
Email: pschoelles@sbi.edu
Website: www.stbernards.edu

**St. Charles Borromeo Seminary*** (Catholic Church), Rev. Msgr. Joseph G. Prior, M.Div., M.A., S.S.L., S.T.D., President and Rector, 100 East Wynnewood Rd., Wynnewood, PA 19096-3001, Tel. (610)667-3394 Fax (610)667-0452
Email: developmentscs@adphila.org
Website: www.scs.edu

**St. Francis Seminary*** (Catholic Church), Very Rev. Michael G. Witczak, Rector, 3257 S. Lake Dr., St. Francis, WI 53235, Tel. (414)747-6400 Fax (414)747-6442
Email: mwitczak@sfs.edu
Website: www.sfs.edu

**St. John Vianney Theological Seminary*** (Catholic Church), Michael Glenn, Rector, 1300 S. Steele St., Denver, CO 80210-2599, Tel. (303)282-3427 Fax (303)282-3453

**St. John's Seminary*** (Catholic Church), John Farren, Rector and President, 127 Lake St., Brighton, MA 02135, Tel. (617)254-2610 Fax (617)787-2336
Email: Reverend_John_L_Sullivan@rcab.org
Website: www.sjs.edu

**St. John's Seminary*** (Catholic Church), Monsignor Helmut Hefner, Rector and President, 5012 Seminary Rd., Camarillo, CA 93012-2598, Tel. (805)482-2755 Fax (805)482-0637
Email: helmut@stjohnsem.edu
Website: www.stjohnsem.edu

**St. John's University, School of Theology - Seminary*** (Catholic Church), William J. Cahoy, Dean, Box 7288, Collegeville, MN 56321-7288, Tel. (320)363-2622 Fax (320)363-3145
Email: bduffy@csbsju.edu
Website: www.csbsju.edu/sot

**St. Joseph's Seminary*** (Catholic Church), Peter G. Finn, President, 201 Seminary Ave., Yonkers, NY 10704, Tel. (914)968-6200 Fax (914)968-7912
Email: sjsirs@aol.com
Website: www.ny-archdiocese.org/pastoral/seminary.cfm

**St. Louis Christian College** (Christian Churches and Churches of Christ), Dr. Guthrie Veech, President, 1360 Grandview Dr., Florissant, MO 63033, Tel. (314)837-6777 Fax (314)837-8291
Email: agall@slcconline.edu
Website: www.slcconline.edu

**St. Mary Seminary and Graduate School of Theology*** (Catholic Church), Thomas W. Tifft, President, 28700 Euclid Ave., Wickliffe, OH 44092-2585, Tel. (440)943-7600 Fax (440)943-7577
Website: www.stmarysem.edu

**St. Mary's Seminary*** (Catholic Church), Very Rev. Brendan Cahill, Rector, 9845 Memorial Dr., Houston, TX 77024-3498, Tel. (713)686-4345 Fax (713)681-7550
Email: cahillb@stthom.edu
Website: www.diocese-gal-hou.org/education_stmarysseminary

**St. Mary's Seminary and University*** (Catholic Church), Robert F. Leavitt, President and Rector, 5400 Roland Ave., Baltimore, MD 21210, Tel. (410)864-4000 Fax (410)864-4278
Email: rleavitt@stmarys.edu
Website: www.stmarys.edu

**Saint Meinrad School of Theology*** (Catholic Church), Mark O'Keefe, President, 200 Hill Drive, St. Meinrad, IN 47577, Tel. (812)357-6611 Fax (812)357-6964
Email: theology@saintmeinrad.edu
Website: www.saintmeinrad.edu

**St. Patrick's Seminary and University*** (Catholic Church), Gerald L. Brown, President and Rector, 320 Middlefield Rd., Menlo Park, CA 94025, Tel. (650)325-5621 Fax (650)322-0997
Website: www.stpatricksseminary.org

**Saint Paul School of Theology*** (The United Methodist Church), Myron F. McCoy, President, 5123 Truman Rd., Kansas City, MO 64127-2499, Tel. (816)483-9600 Fax (816)483-9605
Email: spst@spst.edu
Website: www.spst.edu

**St. Paul Seminary School of Divinity of the University of St. Thomas*** (Catholic Church), The Rev. Aloysius R. Callaghan, Rector and Vice President, 2260 Summit Ave., St. Paul, MN 55105, Tel. (651)962-5050 Fax (651)962-5790
Email: jlubel@stthomas.edu
Website: www.stthomas.edu/spssod

**St. Petersburg Theological Seminary** (Inter/Multidenominational), Dr. Myron P. Miller, President, 10830 Navajo Dr., St. Petersburg, FL 33708, Tel. (727)399-0276 Fax (727)399-1324
Email: sptseminary@tampabay.rr.com
Website: www.sptseminary.edu

**St. Tikhon's Orthodox Theological Seminary*** (The Orthodox Church in America),

Metropolitan Herman (Swaiko), President and Very Rev. Michael G. Dahulich, Ph.D., Dean and Bishop Tikhon (Mollard), Rector, President, Box 130, St. Tikhon's Rd., South Canaan, PA 18459-0130, Tel. (570)937-4411 Fax (570)937-3100
Email: info@stots.edu
Website: www.stots.edu

**St. Vincent de Paul Regional Seminary\*** (Catholic Church), Keith Brennan, Rector and President, 10701 South Military Trail, Boynton Beach, FL 33436-4899, Tel. (561) 732-4424 Fax (561)737-2205
Email: Kbrennan@svdp.edu
Website: www.svdp.edu

**St. Vincent Seminary\*** (Catholic Church), Very Rev. Kurt Belsole, O.S.B., Rector, 300 Fraser Purchase Rd., Latrobe, PA 15650-2690, Tel. (724)537-4592 Fax (724)532-5052
Email: kurt.belsole@email.stvincent.edu
Website: benedictine.stvincent.edu/seminary

**St. Vladimir's Orthodox Theological Seminary\*** (Orthodox Church in America), John H. Erickson, Dean, 575 Scarsdale Rd., Crestwood, NY 10707-1699, Tel. (914)961-8313 Fax (914)961-4507
Email: info@svots.edu
Website: www.svots.edu

**SS. Cyril and Methodius Seminary\*** (Catholic Church), Very Rev. Charles G. Kosanke, Rector, 3535 Indian Trail, Orchard Lake, MI 48324-1623, Tel. (248)683-0310 Fax (248)738-6735
Email: sscms.dean@comcast.net
Website: www.orchardlakeseminary.org

**Samuel DeWitt Proctor School of Theology of Virginia Union University\*** (American Baptist Churches in the U.S.A., National Baptist Convention, Progressive National Baptist Convention), Dr. John W. Kinney, Dean, 1500 North Lombardy Street, Richmond, VA 23330, Tel. (804)257-5715 Fax (804)342-3911
Email: JWKinney@vuu.edu
Website: www.vuu.edu

**San Francisco Theological Seminary\*** (Presbyterian Church [U.S.A.]), Rev. Dr. Philip W. Butin, President, 105 Seminary Rd., San Anselmo, CA 94960, Tel. (415)451-2800 Fax (415)451-2811
Email: sftsinfo@sfts.edu
Website: www.sfts.edu

**Savonarola Theological Seminary** (Polish National Catholic Church of America), Most Rev. Robert M. Nemkovich, Prime Bishop, Rector, 1031 Cedar Ave., Scranton, PA 18505, Tel. (570)343-0100 Fax
Email: pncccenter@adelphia.net

**Seabury-Western Theological Seminary\*** (Episcopal Church), Gary Hall, Dean and President, 2122 Sheridan Rd., Evanston, IL 60201-2976, Tel. (847)328-9300 Fax (847) 328-9624
Email: seabury@seabury.edu
Website: www.seabury.edu

**Seattle University School of Theology and Ministry\*** (Catholic Church and Ten Mainline Protestant Denominations and Associations), Mark Lloyd Taylor, Dean, 901 12th Avenue, P.O. Box 222000, Seattle, WA 98122-1090, Tel. (206)296-5330 Fax (206)296-5329
Email: stm@seattleu.edu
Website: www.seattleu.edu/theomin

**Seminario Evangelico de Puerto Rico** (Interdenominational), Samuel Pagán, President, 776 Ponce de León Ave., San Juan, PR 00925, Tel. (787)763-6700 Fax (787)751-0847
Email: drspagan@icepr.com, jvaldes@tld.net
Website: netministries.org/see/charmin/CM01399

**Seminary of the Immaculate Conception\*** (Catholic Church), Msgr. Francis J. Schneider, J.C.D., Rector/President, 440 West Neck Rd., Huntington, NY 11743, Tel. (631)423-0483 Fax (631)423-2346
Email: eluckstone@icseminary.edu
Website: www.icseminary.edu

**Seventh-day Adventist Theological Seminary of Andrews University\*** (Seventh-day Adventist Church), John K. McVay, Dean, Andrews University, Berrien Springs, MI 49104-1500, Tel. (269)471-3537 Fax (269)471-6202
Email: seminary@andrews.edu
Website: www.andrews.edu/sem

**Seventh Day Baptist School of Ministry** (Seventh Day Baptist General Conference U.S.A. and Canada Ltd.), Gordon P. Lawton, Dean of School of Ministry, 3120 Kennedy Rd., P.O. Box 1678, Janesville, WI 53547, Tel. (608)752-5055 Fax (608)752-7711
Email: Com@sdbministry.org,
Website: sdbministry.org

**Sewanee: The University of the South School of Theology\*** (Episcopal Church), The Very Rev. William S. Stafford, Ph.D. D.D, Dean, 335 Tennessee Ave., Sewanee, TN 37383-0001, Tel. (800)722-1974 Fax (931)598-1412
Email: theology@sewanee.edu
Website: www.theology.sewanee.edu

**Shasta Bible College and Graduate School** (Baptist), Dr. David Nicholas, President, 2951 Goodwater Avenue, Redding, CA 96002, Tel. (530)221-4275 Fax (530)221-6929
Email: sbcadm@shasta.edu
Website: www.shasta.edu

312

**Shaw University Divinity School\*** (General Baptist State Convention, N.C.; American Baptist Churches), James T. Roberson, Jr., Dean, P.O. Box 2090, Raleigh, NC 27602, Tel. (919)546-8569 Fax (919)546-8571
Email: JTRob@ShawU.edu
Website: www.shawuniversity.edu

**Simpson College** (The Christian and Missionary Alliance), James M. Grant, President, 2211 College View Dr., Redding, CA 96003, Tel. (916)224-5600 Fax (916)224-5608
Email: rerickson@simpsonuniversity.edu
Website: www.simpsonuniversity.edu

**Southeastern Baptist College** (Baptist Missionary Association of America), Dr. Medrick Savell, Interim President, 4229 Highway 15N, Laurel, MS 39440, Tel. (601)426-6346 Fax (601)426-6347
Email: info@southeasternbaptist.edu
Website: www.southeasternbaptist.edu

**Southeastern Baptist Theological Seminary\*** (Southern Baptist Convention), Daniel L. Akin, President, P.O. Box 1889, Wake Forest, NC 27588-1889, Tel. (919)556-3101 Fax (919)556-8550
Email: president@sebts.edu
Website: www.sebts.edu

**Southeastern Bible College** (Interdenominational), Dr. Don Hawkins, President, 2545 Valleyvale Rd., Birmingham, AL 35244, Tel. (205)408-7073 or (205)970-9200 Fax (205) 970-9207
Email: President@sebc.edu
Website: www.sebc.edu

**Southeastern University** (Assemblies of God), Mark Rutland, President, 1000 Longfellow Blvd., Lakeland, FL 33801, Tel. (863)667-5000 Fax (863)667-5200
Email: info@seuniversity.edu
Website: www.seuniversity.edu

**Southern Baptist Theological Seminary\*** (Southern Baptist Convention), R. Albert Mohler, Jr., President, 2825 Lexington Rd., Louisville, KY 40280-, Tel. (502)897-4011 Fax (502)899-1770
Email: communications@sbts.edu
Website: www.sbts.edu

**Southern California Seminary** (Southern Baptist Convention), Dr. Gary F. Coombs, President, 2075 East Madison Avenue, El Cajon, CA 92019, Tel. (619)442-9841 or (619) 590-2128 Fax (619)442-4510
Email: eherrelko@socalsem.edu
Website: www.socalsem.edu

**Southern Evangelical Seminary\*** (Interdenominational), Dr. Norman Geisler, President, 3000 Tilley Morris Road, Matthews, NC 28104, Tel. (704)847-5600 Fax (704)845-1747
Email: ses@ses.edu
Website: www.ses.edu

**Southern Methodist College** (Southern Methodist Church), The Rev. Gary Briden, President, 541 Broughton Street, P.O. Box 1027, Orangeburg, SC 29116-1027, Tel. (803) 534-7826 Fax (803)534-7827
Email: smcinfo@smcollege.edu
Website: www.smcollege.edu

**Southern Wesleyan University** (Wesleyan Church), President David J. Spittal, President, 907 Wesleyan Dr., P.O. Box 1020, Central, SC 29630-1020, Tel. (864)644-5000 Fax (864) 644-5900
Email: dspittal@swu.edu
Website: www.swu.edu

**Southwestern Assemblies of God University** (Assemblies of God), Kermit S. Bridges, President, 1200 Sycamore St., Waxahachie, TX 75165, Tel. (972)937-4010 Fax (972)923-0488
Email: president@sagu.edu
Website: www.sagu.edu

**Southwestern Baptist Theological Seminary\*** (Southern Baptist Convention), Paige Patterson, President, 2001 W. Seminary Dr., Fort Worth, TX 76115, Tel. (817)923-1921 Fax (817)923-0610
Email: ppatterson@swbts.edu
Website: www.swbts.edu

**Southwestern College** (Conservative Baptist Association of America), Brent D. Garrison, President, 2625 E. Cactus Rd., Phoenix, AZ 85032, Tel. (602)992-6101 Fax (602)404-2159
Email: swc@swcaz.edu
Website: www.southwesterncollege.edu

**Starr King School for the Ministry\*** (Unitarian Universalist Association), Rebecca Parker, President, 2441 LeConte Ave., Berkeley, CA 94709, Tel. (510)845-6232 Fax (510)845-6273
Email: rparker@sksm.edu; starrking@sksm.edu
Website: www.sksm.edu

**Swedenborgian House of Studies at the Pacific School of Religion** (The Swedenborgian Church), Dr. James F. Lawrence, Dean, 1798 Scenic Ave., Berkeley, CA 94709, Tel. (510) 849-8228 Fax (510)849-8296
Email: jlawrence@shs.psr.edu

**Talbot School of Theology of Biola University\*** (Inter/Multidenominational), Clyde Cook, President, 13800 Biola Ave., La Mirada, CA

313

90639-0001, Tel. (562)903-4816 Fax (562) 903-4759
Email: talbot.receptionist@biola.edu
Website: www.talbot.edu

**Temple Baptist Seminary** (Interdenominational), Dr. Barkev Trachian, President, 1815 Union Ave., Chattanooga, TN 37404, Tel. (423)493-4221 Fax (423)493-4471
Email: tbsinfo@templebaptistseminary.edu
Website: www.templebaptistseminary.edu

**Tennessee Temple University**, President, 1815 Union Avenue, Chattanooga, TN 37404, Tel. (423)493-4202 Fax (423)493-4114
Email: ttuinfo@tntemple.edu
Website: www.tntemple.edu

**Theological School of the Protestant Reformed Churches** (Protestant Reformed Churches in America), David J. Engelsma, President, 4949 Ivanrest Ave., Grandville, MI 49418, Tel. (616)531-1490 Fax (616)531-3033
Email: doezema@prca.org
Website: www.prca.org/seminary

**Toccoa Falls College** (Christian and Missionary Alliance), Dr. W. Wayne Gardner, President, P.O. Box 800777, Toccoa Falls, GA 30598, Tel. (706)886-6831 Fax (706)282-6005
Email: president@tfc.edu
Website: www.tfc.edu

**Trevecca Nazarene University** (Church of the Nazarene), Millard Reed, President, 333 Murfreesboro Rd., Nashville, TN 37210-2877, Tel. (615)248-1200 Fax (615)248-7728
Email: mlanden@trevecca.edu
Website: www.trevecca.edu

**Trinity Baptist College** (Baptist), Tom Messer, Pastor, 800 Hammond Boulevard, Jacksonville, FL 32221, Tel. (904)596-2400 Fax (904)596-2531
Email: trinity@tbc.edu
Website: www.tbc.edu

**Trinity Bible College** (Assemblies of God), Dennis D. Niles, President, 50 S. 6th Ave., Ellendale, ND 58436, Tel. (701)349-3621, (800)523-1603 Fax (701)349-5443
Email: president@trinitybiblecollege.edu
Website: www.trinitybiblecollege.edu

**Trinity College of Florida** (Nondenominational), Mark T. O'Farrell, President, 2430 Welbilt Blvd., New Port Richey, FL 34655-4401, Tel. (727)376-6911 Fax (727)376-0781
Email: admissions@trinitycollege.edu
Website: www.trinitycollege.edu

**Trinity Episcopal School for Ministry*** (Episcopal Church), The Very Rev. Dr. Paul

F.M. Zahl, Dean and President, 311 Eleventh St., Ambridge, PA 15003, Tel. (724)266-3838 Fax (724)266-4617
Email: tesm@tesm.edu
Website: www.tesm.edu

**Trinity Evangelical Divinity School of Trinity International University*** (Evangelical Free Church of America), Gregory L. Waybright, President, 2065 Half Day Rd., Deerfield, IL 60015, Tel. (847)945-8800 Fax (847)317-8141
Email: gwaybrig@tiu.edu
Website: www.tiu.edu/divinity

**Trinity Lutheran College** (Interdenominational-Lutheran), John M. Stamm, Ph.D., President, 4221 - 228th Ave., S.E., Issaquah, WA 98029-9299, Tel. (425)392-0400 Fax (425)392-0404
Email: info@tlc.edu, sconner@tlc.edu
Website: www.tlc.edu

**Trinity Lutheran Seminary*** (Evangelical Lutheran Church in America), Mark R. Ramseth, President, 2199 East Main Street, Columbus, OH 43209-2334, Tel. (614)235-4136 Fax (614)238-0263
Email: mramseth@TrinityLutheranSeminary.edu
Website: www.TrinityLutheranSeminary.edu

**Turner School Of Theology of Southern Christian University*** (Churches of Christ), Dr. Rex A. Turner, Jr., President, 1200 Taylor Rd., Montgomery, AL 36117-3553, Tel. (334) 387-3877 Fax (334)387-3878
Email: RexTurner@southernchristian.edu
Website: www.southernchristian.edu

**Union Theological Seminary*** (Inter/Multi-denominational), Joseph C. Hough, Jr., President, 3041 Broadway at 121st Street, New York, NY 10027-0003, Tel. (212)662-7100 Fax (212)280-1440
Email: spak@uts.columbia.edu
Website: www.uts.columbia.edu

**Union Theological Seminary and Presbyterian School of Christian Education (Union-PSCE)*** (Presbyterian Church [U.S.A.]), Louis B. Weeks, President, 3401 Brook Rd., Richmond, VA 23227, Tel. (800)229-2990 Fax (804)355-3919
Email: gbirch@union-psce.edu
Website: www.union-psce.edu

**United Theological Seminary*** (The United Methodist Church), Rev. Dr. G. Edwin Zeiders, President and Chief Exec. Officer, 4501 Denlinger Rd, Dayton, OH 45426, Tel. (937)278-5817 Fax (937)278-1218
Email: utscom@united.edu
Website: www.united.edu

United Theological Seminary of the Twin Cities* (United Church of Christ), Kita McVay, Interim President, 3000 Fifth St. N.W., New Brighton, MN 55112, Tel. (651) 633-4311 Fax (651)633-4315
Email: general@unitedseminary-mn.org
Website: www.unitedseminary-mn.org

University of Chicago Divinity School* (Interdenominational), Richard A. Rosengarten, Dean, 1025 E. 58th St., Chicago, IL 60637, Tel. (773)702-8221 Fax (773)702-6048
Email: raroseng@midway.uchicago.edu
Website: www.uchicago.edu/divinity

University of Dubuque Theological Seminary* (Presbyterian Church [U.S.A.]), Jeffrey Bullock, President, 2000 University Ave., Dubuque, IA 52001-5099, Tel. (563)589-3122 Fax (563)589-3110
Email: udtsadms@dbq.edu
Website: www.UDTSeminary.net

University of Notre Dame Department of Theology* (Catholic Church), John C. Cavadini, Department Chair, 130 Malloy Hall, Notre Dame, IN 46556-5639, Tel. (574)631-6662 Fax (574)631-4291
Email: Cavadini.1@nd.edu
Website: www.nd.edu /~theo

University of St. Mary of the Lake Mundelein Seminary* (Catholic Church), Dennis J. Lyle, Rector and President, 1000 E. Maple Avenue, Mundelein, IL 60060, Tel. (847)566-6401 Fax (847)566-7330
Email: LZubert@usml.edu
Website: www.usml.edu

University of St. Thomas School of Theology at St. Mary's Seminary* (Catholic Church), Sandra Magie, Dean, 9845 Memorial Dr., Houston, TX 77024, Tel. (713)686-4345 Fax (713)683-8673
Email: sms@stthom.edu
Website: www.stthom.edu/stmary

Urshan Graduate School of Theology* (United Pentecostal Church International), David Bernard, President, P.O. Box 40, Hazelwood, MO 63042, Tel. (314)921-9290 Fax (314) 921-9203
Email: info@ugst.org
Website: www.ugst.org

Valley Forge Christian College (Assemblies of God), Don Meyer, President, 1401 Charlestown Rd., Phoenixville, PA 19460, Tel. (610)935-0450 Fax (610)935-9353
Email: admissions@vfcc.edu
Website: www.vfcc.edu

Vanderbilt University Divinity School* (Inter/Multidenominational), James Hudnut-Beumler, Dean, 411 21st Av. So., Nashville, TN 37240, Tel. (615)322-2776 Fax (615)343-9957
Email: james.hudnut-beumler@vanderbilt.edu
Website: divinity.lib.vanderbilt.edu/vds/vds-home

Vennard College (Interdenominational), Dr. Bruce Moyer, President, Box 29, University Park, IA 52595, Tel. (641)673-8391 Fax (641) 673-8365
Email: bruce.moyer@vennard.edu
Website: www.vennard.edu

Virginia Union University (School of Theology) (American Baptist Churches in the U.S.A., National Baptist Convention, U.S.A., Inc., Progressive National Baptist Convention, Inc.), Dr. John W. Kinney, Dean, 1500 N. Lombardy St., Richmond, VA 23220, Tel. (804)257-5715 Fax (804)342-3911
Email: JWKinney@vuu.edu
Website: www.vuu.edu/theology

Wake Forest University Divinity School* (Inter/Multidenominational), Bill J. Leonard, Dean, P.O. Box 7719, Winston-Salem, NC 27109-7719, Tel. (336)758-5121 Fax (336) 758-4316
Website: www.wfu.edu

Walla Walla College (School of Theology) (Seventh-day Adventist Church), Dr. Jon Dybdahl, President, 204 S. College Ave., College Place, WA 99324-1198, Tel. (509)527-2194 Fax (509)527-2253
Email: dybdjo@wwc.edu
Website: www.wwc.edu

Wartburg Theological Seminary* (Evangelical Lutheran Church in America), Duane H. Larson, President, 333 Wartburg Pl., P.O. Box 5004, Dubuque, IA 52004-5004, Tel. (563)589-0200 Fax (563)589-0333
Email: mailbox@wartburgseminary.edu
Website: www.wartburgseminary.edu

Washington Baptist College and Seminary* (Baptist), Jacob S. Shin, President, 4300 Evergreen Lane, Annandale, VA 22003, Tel. (703)333-5904 Fax (703)333-5906
Website: www.wbcs.edu

Washington Theological Consortium (Nondenominational), The Rev. John W. Crossin, O.S.F.S., Executive Director, 487 Michigan Ave. N.E., Washington, DC 20017, Tel. (202) 832-2675 Fax (202)526-0818
Email: wtc@washtheocon.org
Website: www.washtheocon.org

Washington Theological Union* (Catholic Church), Louis Iasiello, President, 6896

315

Laurel St. N.W., Washington, DC 20012-2016, Tel. (202)726-8800 Fax (202)726-1716
Email: welch@wtu.edu
Website: www.wtu.edu

**Wesley Biblical Seminary*** (Interdenominational), Ronald E. Smith, President, P.O. Box 9938, Jackson, MS 39286-0938, Tel. (601)366-8880 Fax (601)366-8832
Email: rsmith@wbs.edu
Website: www.wbs.edu

**Wesley Theological Seminary*** (The United Methodist Church), David F. McAllister-Wilson, President, 4500 Massachusetts Ave. N.W., Washington, DC 20016-5690, Tel. (800)885-8600 or (800)882-4987 Fax (202) 885-8605
Email: caldridge@wesleysem.edu
Website: www.Wesleysem.edu

**Western Seminary*** (Conservative Baptist Association of America), Bert E. Downs, President, 5511 S.E. Hawthorne Blvd., Portland, OR 97215, Tel. (877) 517-1800 or (503) 517-1800 Fax (503)517-1801
Email: admiss@westernseminary.edu
Website: westernseminary.edu

**Western Theological Seminary*** (Reformed Church in America), Dennis N. Voskuil, President, 101 E. 13th St., Holland, MI 49423, Tel. (616)392-8555 Fax (616)392-7717
Email: dennis@westernsem.edu
Website: www.westernsem.edu

**Westminster Theological Seminary*** (various Reformed), Peter A. Lillback, President, Chestnut Hill, P.O. Box 27009, Philadelphia, PA 19118, Tel. (215)887-5511 Fax (215)887-5404
Email: admissions@wts.edu
Website: www.wts.edu

**Westminster Seminary California*** (Nondenominational), W. Robert Godfrey, President, 1725 Bear Valley Pkwy, Escondido, CA 92027-4128, Tel. (760)480-8474 Fax (760) 480-0252
Email: info@wscal.edu
Website: www.wscal.edu

**Weston Jesuit School of Theology*** (Catholic Church), Robert Manning, President, 3 Phillips Place, Cambridge, MA 02138-3495, Tel. (617)492-1960 Fax (617)492-5833
Email: Admissionsinfo@wjst.edu
Website: www.wjst.edu

**William Jessup University** (Christian Churches and Churches of Christ), Bryce L. Jessup, D.D., President, 333 Sunset Blvd., Rocklin, CA 95765, Tel. (916)577-2210 Fax 916-577-2213

Email: bjessup@jessup.edu
Website: www.jessup.edu

**William Tyndale College** (Interdenominational), Robert E. Hagerty, President, 35700 W. Twelve Mile Rd., Farmington Hills, MI 48331, Tel. (248)553-7200 Fax (248)553-5963
Website: www.williamtyndale.edu

**Williamson Christian College** (Nondenominational), Dr. Ken Oosting, President, 200 Seaboard Lane, Franklin, TN 37067, Tel. (615)771-7821 Fax (615)771-7810
Email: info@williamsoncc.edu
Website: www.williamsoncc.edu

**Winebrenner Theological Seminary*** (Churches of God, General Conference), David E. Draper, President, 950 N. Main Street, Findlay, OH 45840, Tel. (419)434 4200 Fax (419)434 4267
Email: wts@winebrenner.edu
Website: www.winebrenner.edu

**Wisconsin Lutheran Seminary** (Wisconsin Evangelical Lutheran Synod), Paul O. Wendland, President, 11831 N. Seminary Dr., 65W, Mequon, WI 53092-1597, Tel. (262)242-8100 Fax (262)242-8110
Email: president@wls.wels.net
Website: www.wls.wels.net

**Word of Life Bible Institute** (Nondenominational), Dr. Joe Jordan, Chancellor, P.O. Box 129, 4200 Glendale Road, Pottersville, NY 12860, Tel. (518)494-4723 Fax (518)494-7474
Email: admissions@wol.org
Website: www.wol.org

**Yale University Divinity School*** (Inter/Multidenominational), Harold W. Attridge, Dean, 409 Prospect Sreet, New Haven, CT 06511-2167, Tel. (203)432-5303 Fax (203) 432-5356
Email: divinity.admissions@yale.edu
Website: www.yale.edu/divinity

# 9. Theological Seminaries and Bible Colleges in Canada

The following list includes theological seminaries and departments in colleges and universities in which ministerial training is provided. Many denominations have additional programs. The list has been developed from direct correspondence with the institutions. Inclusion in or exclusion from this list implies no judgment about the quality or accreditation of any institution. Those schools that are members of the Association of Theological Schools are marked with an asterisk (*). Each of the listings includes: the institution name, denominational sponsor when appropriate, location, the president or dean, telephone and fax numbers when known and email and website addresses when available.

**Acadia Divinity College\*** (Convention of the Atlantic Baptist Church), Lee M. McDonald, Principal and Dean of the Faculty of Theology, 31 Horton Street, Wolfville, NS B4P 2R6, Tel. (866)875-8975, or (902)585-2210 Fax (902) 585-2233
Email: adcinfo@acadiau.ca
Website: adc.acadiau.ca

**Alberta Bible College** (Christian Churches and Churches of Christ in Canada), Ronald A. Fraser, President, 635 Northmount Dr. NW, Calgary, AB T2K 3J6, Tel. (877)542-9492, or (403)282-2994 Fax (403)282-3084
Email: generalinquiries@abc-ca.org
Website: www.abc-ca.org

**Arthur Turner Training School** (Anglican Church of Canada), Roy Bowkett, Principal, Box 378, Pangnirtung, NU X0A 0R0, Tel. (867)473-8375 Fax (867)473-8375
Email: diocese@arcticnet.org

**Associated Canadian Theological Schools of Trinity Western University\*** (Baptist General Conference of Canada, Evangelical Free Church of Canada, Fellowship of Evangelical Baptist Churches in Canada, Christian and Missionary Alliance, Canadian Conference of Mennonite Brethren Churches), Dr. Phil Zylla, Principal, 7600 Glover Rd., Langley, BC V2Y 1Y1, Tel. (888)468-6898, or (604)513-2044 Fax (604)513-2045
Email: acts@twu.ca
Website: www.acts.twu.ca

**Atlantic School of Theology\*** (Interdenominational), The Rev. Canon Eric Beresford, President, 660 Francklyn St., Halifax, NS B3H 3B5, Tel. (902)423-6801 Fax (902)492-4048
Website: www.astheology.ns.ca

**Bethany Bible College-Canada** (The Wesleyan Church), Dr. David S. Medders, President, 26 Western St., Sussex, NB E4E 1E6, Tel. (506) 432-4400 Fax (506)432-4425
Email: meddersd@bethany-ca.edu
Website: www.bethany-ca.edu

**Bethany College** (Canadian Conference of Mennonite Brethren Churches [Saskatchewan and Alberta Conferences]), Rick Schellenberg, President, Box 160, Hepburn, SK S0K 1Z0, Tel. (306)947-2175 Fax (306)947-4229
Email: info@bethany.sk.ca
Website: www.bethany.sk.ca

**Briercrest Seminary\*** (Interdenominational), Dwayne Uglem, Interim President, 510 College Dr., Caronport, SK S0H 0S0, Tel. (800)667-5199 Fax (306)756-5500
Email: seminary@briercrest.ca
Website: www.briercrest.ca

**Canadian Bible College & Canadian Theological Seminary of Alliance University College\*** (Christian and Missionary Alliance in Canada), Dr. George Durance, President, 833-4th Avenue SW #630, Calgary, AB T2P 3T5, Tel. (403)410-2000 Fax (403)571-2556, Email: gdurance@auc-nuc.ca
Email: Info: Info@aun-nuc.ca
Website: www.auc-nuc.ca

**Canadian Lutheran Bible Institute** (Lutheran), Pastor Harold Rust, President, 4837 52A St., Camrose, AB T4V 1W5, Tel. (780)672-4454 Fax (780)672-4455
Email: clbi@clbi.edu
Website: www.clbi.edu

**Canadian Mennonite University** (Mennonite Brethren Churches, Mennonite Church Canada), Gerald Gerbrandt, President, 500 Shaftesbury Blvd, Winnipeg, MB R3P 2N2, Tel. (204)487-3300 Fax (204)487-3858
Email: reception@cmu.ca
Website: www.cmu.ca

**Canadian Nazarene University College** (Church of the Nazarene Canada), Riley Coulter, President, 610, 833 4th Ave. SW, Calgary, AB T2P 3T5, Tel. (403)571-2550 Fax (403)571-2556
Email: reception@auc-nuc.ca
Website: www.auc-nuc.ca

Canadian Southern Baptist Seminary* (Canadian Convention of Southern Baptists), G. Richard Blackaby, President, 200 Seminary View, Cochrane, AB T4C 2G1, Tel. (877)922-2727, or (403)932-6622 Fax (403)932-7049 Email: csbs@compuserve.com Website: www.csbs.edu

Carey Theological College* (Baptist Union of Western Canada), Brian F. Stelck, President, 5920 Iona Drive, Vancouver, BC V6T 1J6, Tel. (604)224-4308 Fax (604)224-5014 Website: www.careytheologicalcollege.ca

Central Pentecostal College, University of Saskatchewan (Pentecostal Assemblies of Canada), D. Munk, Academic Dean, 1303 Jackson Ave., Saskatoon, SK S7H 2M9, Tel. (306)374-6655 Fax (306)373-6968 Email: admissions@cpc-paoc.edu Website: www.cpc-paoc.edu

Centre for Christian Studies (Anglican Church of Canada, United Church of Canada), Caryn Douglas, Principal, 60 Maryland, Winnipeg, MB R3G 1K7, Tel. (204)783-4490 Fax (204)786-3012 Email: info@ccsonline.ca Website: www.ccsonline.ca

College Biblique Québec (Pentecostal Assemblies of Canada), William Raccah, President, 740 Lebourgneuf, Ste. 100, Ancienne Lorette, QC G2J 1E2, Tel. (418)622-7552 Fax (418) 622-1470 Email: mlecompte@ibq-canada.org Website: http://www.ibq-canada.org/

Collège Dominicain de Philosophie et de Théologie (Roman Catholic Church in Canada), Gabor Csepregi, President, 96 Avenue Empress, Ottawa, ON K1R 7G3, Tel. (613)233-5696 Fax (613)233-6064 Email: service.accueil@collegedominicain.ca Website: www.collegedominicain.ca

College of Emmanuel and St. Chad (Anglican Church of Canada), Dr. Walter Deller, Principal, 114 Seminary Crescent, Saskatoon, SK S7N 0X3, Tel. (306)975-3753 Fax (306) 934-2683 Email: emmanuel.stchad@usask.ca Website: www.usask.ca/stu/emmanuel

Columbia Bible College (BC Conference of Mennonite Brethren Churches & Mennonite Church in BC), Dr. Paul Wartman, President, 2940 Clearbrook Rd., Abbotsford, BC V2T 2Z8, Tel. (604)853-3358 Fax (604)853-3063 Email: info@columbiabc.edu Website: www.columbiabc.edu

Concordia Lutheran Seminary* (Lutheran Church-Canada), Edward G. Kettner, President,

7040 Ada Blvd., Edmonton, AB T5B 4E3, Tel. (780)474-1468 Fax (780)479-3067 Email: info@concordiasem.ab.ca Website: www.concordiasem.ab.ca

Concordia Lutheran Theological Seminary* (Lutheran Church—Canada), Harald Tomesch, President, 470 Glenridge Ave., St. Catharines, ON L2T 4C3, Tel. (905)688-2362 Fax (905) 688-9744 Email: concordia@brocku.ca Website: www.brocku.ca/concordiaseminary

Covenant Bible College (Evangelical Covenant Church of Canada), President, 630 Westchester Road, Strathmore, AB T1P 1H8, Tel. (403)934-6200 Fax (403)934-6220 Email: office@covenantbiblecollege.ab.ca; COLORADO: cbc@covbibcolorado.edu Website: www.covenantbiblecollege.ab.ca

Ecole de Theologie Evangelique de Montreal (Canadian Conference of Mennonite Brethren Churches), Eric Wingender, President, 1775, boul Édouard-Laurin, Ville Saint-Laurent, QC H4L 2B9, Tel. (514)331-0878 Fax (514)331-0879 Email: iblinstitute@proxyma.net

Emmanuel Bible College (Evangelical Missionary Church of Canada), Thomas E. Dow, President, 100 Fergus Ave., Kitchener, ON N2A 2H2, Tel. (519)894-8900 Fax (519) 894-5331 Email: dmin@ebcollege.on.ca Website: www.ebcollege.on.ca

Emmanuel College of Victoria University* (United Church of Canada), The Rev. Dr. Peter Wyatt, Principal, 75 Queens Park Crescent East, Toronto, ON M5S 1K7, Tel. (416)585-4539 Fax (416)585-4516 Email: ec.office@utoronto.ca Website: vicu.utoronto.ca

Faculté De Théologie Évangélique (Interdenominational), Amar Djaballah, President, 2285 Avenue Papineau, Montréal, QC H2K 4J5, Tel. (514)526-2003 Fax (514)526-6887 Email: reg@fteacadia.ca Website: www.fteacadia.ca

Faith Alive Bible College (Nondenominational), David Pierce, President, 637 University Dr., Saskatoon, SK S7N 0H8, Tel. (306)652-2230 Fax (306)665-1125 Email: faithalive@dlcwest.com

Full Gospel Bible Institute (Apostolic Church of Pentecost of Canada Inc.), Rev. Lauren E. Miller, President, Box 579, Eston, SK S0L 1A0, Tel. (306)962-3621 Fax (306)962-3810 Email: fgbi@fgbi.sk.ca Website: fgbi.sk.ca

**Gardner College, A Centre for Christian Studies** (Church of God [Anderson, Ind.]), John Alan Howard, President, 4707 56th St., Camrose, AB T4V 2C4, Tel. (780)672-0171 Fax (780)672-2465
Email: gardnercollege@gardnercollege.org
Website: www.gardnercollege.org

**Grand Seminaire de Montréal** (Roman Catholic Church in Canada), Monsg. Lionel Gendron. p.s.s., President, 2065 Sherbrooke Ouest, Montréal, QC H3H 1G6, Tel. (514)935-1169 Fax (514)935-5497
Email: Information Generale, info@gsdm.qc.ca OR Bibliotheque, biblio@gsdm.qc.ca
Website: www.gsdm.qc.ca

**Great Lakes Bible College** (Churches of Christ in Canada), Mr. J. Arthur Ford, President, 470 Glenelm Crescent, Waterloo, ON N2L 5C8, Tel. (519)884-4310 Fax (519)884-4412
Email: learn@glbc.on.ca
Website: www.glbc.on.ca

**Heritage Theological Seminary\*** Marvin R. Brubacher, President, 175 Holiday Inn Dr., Cambridge, ON N3C 3T2, Tel. (519)651-2869, or (800)465-1961 Fax (519)651-2870
Email: recruitment@heritage-theo.edu
Website: www.heritageseminary.net
OR www.heritagecollege.net

**Huron University College Faculty of Theology\*** (Anglican Church of Canada), Dr. Ramona Lumpkin, Principal, 1349 Western Rd., London, ON N6G 1H3, Tel. (519)438-7224 Fax (519)438-9981
Email: huron@uwo.ca
Website: www.huronuc.on.ca

**Institut Biblique Beree** (Pentecostal Assemblies of Canada), André L. Gagnon, President, 1711 Est Boul. Henri-Bourassa, Montréal, QC H2C 1J5, Tel. (514)385-4238 Fax (514)385-4238
Email: mlecompte@ibq-canada.org
Website: http://www.ibq-canada.org

**Institute for Christian Studies** (Nondenominational), Harry Fernhout, President, 229 College St., Suite 200, Toronto, ON M5T 1R4, Tel. (416)979-2331, or (888)326-5347 Fax (416)979-2332
Email: email@icscanada.edu
Website: www.icscanada.edu

**International Bible College** (Church of God [Cleveland, Tenn.]), Cheryl Busse, President, 401 Trinity La., Moose Jaw, SK S6H 0E3, Tel. (306)692-4041 Fax (306)692-7968
Email: ibc@cofg.net
Website: www.ibc.cofg.net

**Key-Way-Tin Bible Institute** (Nondenominational), Dir. Dave Petkau, President, Box 540, Lac La Biche, AB T0A 2C0, Tel. (780)623-4565 Fax (780)623-1788
Email: kbi@telusplanet.net

**Knox College\*** (Presbyterian Church in Canada), J. Dorcas Gordon, Principal, 59 St. George St., Toronto, ON M5S 2E6, Tel. (416) 978-4500 Fax (416)971-2133
Email: knox.college@utoronto.ca
Website: www.utoronto.ca/knox

**Living Faith Bible College** (Fellowship of Christian Assemblies [Canada]), Dan Pope, President, Box 100, Caroline, AB T0M 0M0, Tel. (403)722-2225, or (800)838-2975 Fax (403) 722-2459
Email: office@lfbc.net
Website: www.lfbc.net

**Lutheran Theological Seminary\*** (Evangelical Lutheran Church in Canada), Kevin A. Ogilvie, President, 114 Seminary Crescent, Saskatoon, SK S7N 0X3, Tel. (306)966-7850 Fax (306)966-7852
Email: lutheran.seminary@usask.ca
Website: www.usask.ca/stu/luther

**Maritime Christian College** (Christian Churches and Churches of Christ), Fred C. Osborne, President, 503 University Ave., Charlottetown, PE C1A 7Z4, Tel. (902)628-8887 Fax (902) 892-3959
Email: registrar@maritimechristiancollege.pe.ca
Website: www.maritimechristiancollege.pe.ca

**Master's College and Seminary** (Pentecostal Assemblies of Canada), Dr. Evon G. Horton, President, 3080 Yonge St., Box 70, Suite 3040, Toronto, ON M4N 3N1, Tel. (416)482-2224 Fax (416)482-7004
Email: info@mcs.edu
Website: www.mcs.edu

**McGill University Faculty of Religious Studies\*** (Interdenominational), B. Barry Levy, Dean, 3520 University St., Montréal, QC H3A 2A7, Tel. (514)398-4125 Fax (514)398-6665
Website: www.mcgill.ca/religiousstudies

**McMaster Divinity College\*** (Baptist Convention of Ontario and Quebec [BCOQ]), Stanley E. Porter, Principal/Dean, 1280 Main St. West, Hamilton, ON L8S 4K1, Tel. (905)525-9140 x 24401 Fax (905)577-4782
Email: divinity@mcmaster.ca
Website: www.macdiv.ca

**Millar College of the Bible** (Interdenominational), A. Brian Atmore, President, Box 25, Pambrun, SK S0N 1W0, Tel. (306)582-2033 Fax (306)582-2027

319

**Montreal Diocesan Theological College** (Anglican Church of Canada), Bishop of Montreal, President, 3473 University St., Montreal, QC H3A 2A8, Tel. (514)849-3004 Fax (514)849-4113
Email: diocoll@netrover.com
Website: www.montreal.anglican.org/mdtc

**Montreal School of Theology\*** (Inter/ Multidenominational), Dr. Philip Joudrey, Administrative Officer, 3473 University St., Montréal, QC H3A 2A8, Tel. (514)849-8511 Fax (514)849-4113
Email: pjoudrey@utc.ca
Website: www.mst-etm.ca

**Mount Carmel Bible School** (Transdenominational), Gordon King, President, 4725 106 Ave., Edmonton, AB T6A 1E7, Tel. (780)465-3015, or Toll-free (800)561-6443 Fax (780) 466-2485
Email: mail@mountcarmel.net
Website: www.mountcarmel.net

**National Native Bible College** (Elim Fellowship of Evangelical Churches and Ministers), Michael Hart, College Director, Box 478, Deseronto, ON K0K 1X0, Tel. (613)396-2311

**Newman Theological College\*** (Catholic Church in Canada), Rev. John (Jack) Gallagher, President, 15611 St. Albert Trail, Edmonton, AB T6V 1H3, Tel. (780)447-2993 Fax (780)447-2685
Email: patricia.hauck@newman.edu
Website: www.newman.edu

**Nipawin Bible Institute** (Interdenominational), Mr. Wes Fehr, Acting President, Box 1986, Nipawin, SK S0E 1E0, Tel. (306)862-5095 Fax (306)862-3651
Email: info@nipawin.org
Website: www.nipawin.org

**Northwest Baptist Theological College and Seminary** (Fellowship of Evangelical Baptist Churches of Canada), Dr. Larry Perkins, President, 7600 Glover Rd., Langley, BC V2Y 1Y1, Tel. (604)888-7592 Fax (604) 513-8511
Email: nbs@twu.ca
Website: www.nbseminary.com

**Ontario Christian Seminary** (Christian Churches and Churches of Christ in Canada), James R. Cormode, President, 260 High Park Ave., Toronto, ON M6P 3J9, Tel. (416)769-7115 Fax (416)769-7047

**Pacific Life Bible College** (Foursquare), Rob Buzza, President, 15100 66 A Ave., Surrey, BC V3S 2A6, Tel. (604)597-9082 Fax (604)597-9090

Email: paclife@pacificlife.edu
Website: www.pacificlife.edu

**Parole de Vie Bethel/Word of Life Bethel** (Nondenominational), Mark Strout, Director, 1175, ch. Woodward, Lennoxville, QC J1M 2A2, Tel. (819)823-8435 Fax (819)823-2468
Email: quebec@pdvb.org
Website: www.pdvb.org

**Peace River Bible Institute** (Interdenominational), Rod Masterson, President, Box 99, Sexsmith, AB T0H 3C0, Tel. (780)568-3962 Fax (780)568-4431
Email: prbi@prbi.edu
Website: www.prbi.edu

**Prairie Graduate School** (Interdenominational), Dr. Charlotte Kinvig Bates, Co President, 330 6th Ave., Three Hills, AB T0M 2N0, Tel. (403)443-5511 Fax (403) 443-5540
Email: prairie@prairie.edu
Website: www.pbi.ab.ca

**The Presbyterian College, Montreal\*** (Presbyterian Church in Canada), John Vissers, Principal, 3495 University St., Montreal, QC H3A 2A8, Tel. (514)288-5256 Fax (514)288-8072
Email: info@presbyteriancollege.ca
Website: www.presbyteriancollege.ca

**Providence College and Theological Seminary\*** (Inter/Multidenominational), August H. Konkel, President, General Delivery, Otterburne, MB R0A 1G0, Tel. (204)433-7488 Fax (204)433-7158
Email: info@prov.ca
Website: www.prov.ca

**Queens College Faculty of Theology\*** (Anglican Church of Canada), John Mellis, President, 210 Prince Phillip Dr.. Suite 3000, St. Johns, NF A1B 3R6, Tel. (709)753-0116 Fax (709)753-1214
Email: queens@mun.ca
Website: www.mun.ca/queens

**Queen's Theological College\*** (United Church of Canada), M. Jean Stairs, Principal, Room 212 Theological Hall, Kingston, ON K7L 3N6, Tel. (613)533-2110 Fax (613)533-6879
Email: theology@post.queensu.ca
Website: www.queensu.ca/theology

**Reformed Episcopal Theological College** (Reformed Episcopal Church of Canada), Rt. Rev. Michael Fedechko, President, P.O. Box 2532, Hwy 11 North, New Liskeard, ON P0J 1P0, Tel. (705)647-4565 Fax (705)647-4565
Email: fed@nt.net
Website: www.retcc.com

Reformed Episcopal Theological College (Reformed Episcopal Church of Canada), Rt. Rev. Michael Fedechko, President, 320 Armstrong St., Box 2532, New Liskeard, ON P0J 1P0, Tel. (705)647-4565 Fax (705)647-4565 Email: fed@nt.net
Website: www.retcc.com

Regent College* (Interdenominational), Rod Wilson, Ph.D., President, 5800 University Blvd., Vancouver, BC V6T 2E4, Tel. (800)663-8664, or (604)224-3245 Fax (604)224-3097
Email: administration@regent-college.edu
Website: www.regent-college.edu

Regis College* (Roman Catholic Church in Canada), Joseph G. Schner, S.J, President, 15 St. Mary St., Toronto, ON M4Y 2R5, Tel. (416) 922-5474 Fax (416)922-2898
Email: regis.registrar@utoronto.ca
Website: www.regiscollege.ca

Rocky Mountain College, Centre for Biblical Studies (Evangelical Missionary Church of Canada), Gordon Dirks, President, 4039 Brentwood Rd. NW, Calgary, AB T2L 1L1, Tel. (403)284-5100 Fax (403)220-9567
Email: admissions@rockymountaincollege.ca
Website: www.rockymountaincollege.ca

St. Andrew's College* (United Church of Canada), Laura Balas, Acting Interim President, 1121 College Dr., Saskatoon, SK S7N 0W3, Tel. (306)966-8970, or (877)644-8970 Fax (306) 966-8981
Email: goldiej@duke.usask.ca
Website: www.standrews.ca

St. Augustine's Seminary of Toronto* (Roman Catholic Church in Canada), Rev. Msgr. A. Robert Nusca, President and Rector, 2661 Kingston Rd., Toronto, ON M1M 1M3, Tel. (416)261-7207 Fax (416)261-2529
Email: info@staugustines.on.ca
Website: www.staugustines.on.ca

St. John's College, Univ. of Manitoba, Faculty of Theology (Anglican Church of Canada), Dr. Janet A. Hoskins, Warden & Vice Chancellor, 92 Dysart Rd., Winnipeg, MB R3T 2M5, Tel. (204)474-8531 Fax (204)474-7610
Email: stjohns_college@umanitoba.ca
Website: www.umanitoba.ca/colleges/st_johns

Saint Paul University, Faculty of Theology (Roman Catholic Church), Normand Bonneau, Ph.D., Dean, 223 Main St., Ottawa, ON K1S 1C4, Tel. (613)236-1393 x 2246 Fax (613) 751-4016
Email: fquesnel@ustpaul.uottawa.ca
Website: www.ustpaul.ca

St. Peter's Seminary* (Roman Catholic Church in Canada), William T. McGrattan, Rector, 1040 Waterloo St. North, London, ON N6A 3Y1, Tel. (519)432-1824 Fax (519)432-0964
Website: www.stpetersseminary.ca

St. Stephen's College (United Church of Canada), Dr. Tom Faulkner, President, 8810 112th St., Edmonton, AB T6G 2J6, Tel. (800) 661-4956 Fax (780)433-8875
Email: westema@ualberta.ca
Website: www.ststephenscollege.ca

Salvation Army College for Officer Training (Salvation Army in Canada), Wayne N. Pritchett, Principal, 2130 Bayview Ave., North York, ON M4N 3K6, Tel. (416)481-6131 Fax (416)481-6810, or (416)481-2895 (Library)
Email: sandra_rice@can.salvationarmy.org; ray_harris@can.salvationarmy.org

The Salvation Army William and Catherine Booth College (Salvation Army in Canada), Dr. Jonathan S. Raymond, President, 447 Webb Pl., Winnipeg, MB R3B 2P2, Tel. (204)947-6701 Fax (204)942-3856
Email: wcbc@boothcollege.ca
Website: www.boothcollege.ca

Steinbach Bible College (Mennonite), Abe Bergen, President, 50 PTH 12 N, Steinbach, MB R5G 1T4, Tel. (204)326-6451 Fax (204) 326-6908
Email: info@sbcollege.mb.ca
Website: www.sbcollege.mb.ca

Summit Pacific College (Pentecostal Assemblies of Canada), James G. Richards, President, Box 1700, Abbotsford, BC V2S 7E7, Tel. (604) 853-7491 Fax (604)853-8951
Email: pr@summitpacific.ca
Website: www.summitpacific.ca

Taylor College of Mission and Evangelism (Church Army Canada), Rev. Capt. David Edwards, Principal, 105 Mountain View Drive, Saint John, NB E2J 5B5, Tel. (866)693-8975 Fax (506)657-8217
Email: edwa@nbnet.nb.ca
Website: www.taylorcollege.com or www.churcharmy.com/taylor

Taylor Seminary* (North American Baptist Conference), Dr. Marvin L. Dewey, President, 11525-23 Ave., Edmonton, AB T6J 4T3, Tel. (780)431-5200 Fax (780)436-9416
Email: marvin.dewey@taylor-edu.ca
Website: www.taylor-edu.ca

Theological College of the Canadian Reformed Churches (Canadian and American Reformed Churches), N. H. Gootjes, President,

110 West 27th St., Hamilton, ON L9C 5A1, Tel. (905) 575-3688 Fax (905)575-0799
Email: theocollege@seminary.canrc.org
Website: www.canrc.org/college

**Toronto Baptist Seminary and Bible College** (Baptist), Dr. Glendon G. Thompson, President, 130 Gerrard St., E., Toronto, ON M5A 3T4, Tel. (416)925-3263 Fax (416)925-8305
Email: tbs@tbs.edu
Website: www.tbs.edu

**Toronto School of Theology\*** (Inter/Multi-denominational), Christopher J.L. Lind, Director, 47 Queens Park Crescent E., Toronto, ON M5S 2C3, Tel. (416)978-4039 Fax (416)978-7821
Email: registrar.tst@utoronto.ca
Website: www.tst.edu

**Trinity College Faculty of Divinity\*** (Anglican Church of Canada), David Neelands, Dean, 6 Hoskin Ave., Toronto, ON M5S 1H8, Tel. (416)978-2146 Fax (416)978-4949
Email: divinity@trinity.utoronto.ca
Website: www.trinity.utoronto.ca/divinity

**Tyndale University College & Seminary\*** (Trans-denominational), Dr. Brian C. Stiller, President, 25 Ballyconnor Ct., Toronto, ON M2M 4B3, Tel. (416)226-6380 Fax (416)226-9464
Email: info@tyndale.ca
Website: www.tyndale.ca

**United Theological College/Le Séminaire Uni** (United Church of Canada), Rev. Philip Joudrey, President, 3521 rue Université, Montréal, QC H3A 2A9, Tel. (514)849-2042 Fax (514)849-8634
Email: admin@utc.ca
Website: www.utc.ca

**Université Laval, Faculté de Théologie et de Sciences Religieuses** (Roman Catholic Church in Canada), Jacques Racine, Doyen, Cité Universitaire, Quebec, QC G1K 7P4, Tel. (418)656-3576 Fax (418)656-3273
Email: ftsr@ftsr.ulaval.ca
Website: www.ftsr.ulaval.ca

**Université de Montréal, Faculté de théologie** (Roman Catholic Church in Canada), Jean-Marc Charron, President, C. P. 6128 Succ. Centre Ville, Montréal, QC H3C 3J7, Tel. (514)343-7160 Fax (514)343-5738
Email: theologie@ere.umontreal.ca
Website: www.theo.umontreal.ca

**Université de Sherbrooke, Faculté de theologié, d'éthique et de philosophie** (Roman Catholic Church in Canada), Jean-François Malherbe, President, 1111, rue Saint-Charles Ouest,

Tourquest - Bureau 310, Longueuil, QC J4K 5G4, Tel. (450)670-7157 Fax (450)670-1959
Email: jf.malherbe@sympatico.ca
Website: www.usherb.ca/longueuil

**University of St. Michael's College Faculty of Theology\*** (Roman Catholic Church), Dr. Anne T. Anderson, CSJ, Dean, 81 St. Mary St., Toronto, ON M5S 1J4, Tel. (416)926-7265 Fax (416)926-7294
Website: www.utoronto.ca/stmikes

**The University of Winnipeg Faculty of Theology\*** (Multidenominational and United Church of Canada), Gordon E. MacDermid, Dean, 515 Portage Ave., Winnipeg, MB R3B 2E9, Tel. (204)786-9390 Fax (204)772-2584
Email: theology@uwinnipeg.ca
Website: www.uwinnipeg.ca/academic/theology

**Vancouver School of Theology\*** (Inter/Multi-denominational), Dr. Kenneth G. MacQueen, Principal, 6000 Iona Dr., Vancouver, BC V6T 1L4, Tel. (866)822-9031 Fax (604)822-9212
Email: vstinfo@vst.edu
Website: www.vst.edu

**Vanguard College** (The Pentecostal Assemblies of Canada), Stephen Hertzog, President, 12140 103 St., Edmonton, AB T5G 2J9, Tel. (780)452-0808 Fax (780)452-5803
Email: info@vanguardcollege.com
Website: www.vanguardcollege.com

**Waterloo Lutheran Seminary\*** (Evangelical Lutheran Church in Canada), Richard C. Crossman, President, 75 University Ave. W., Waterloo, ON N2L 3C5, Tel. (519)884-1970 Fax (519)725-2434
Email: seminary@wlu.ca
Website: www.wlu.ca/~wwwsem/index.shtml

**Western Christian College** (Churches of Christ in Canada), John McMillan, President, 100-4400 4th Ave., Regina, SK S4T 0H8, Tel. (306)545-1515 Fax (306)352-2198
Email: president@westernchristian.ca
Website: www.westernchristian.ca

**Wycliffe College\*** (Anglican Church of Canada), Rev. Dr. George R. Sumner, Jr., President, 5 Hoskin Ave., Toronto, ON M5S 1H7, Tel. (416)946-3535 Fax (416)946-3545
Email: wycliffe.college@utoronto.ca
Website: www.utoronto.ca/wycliffe

# 10. Religious Periodicals in the United States

This directory lists publications primarily of the organizations listed in Directory 3, "Religious Bodies in the United States." Some independent publications are also listed. The list does not include all publications prepared by religious bodies, and not all the publications listed here are necessarily the official publication of a particular church. Regional publications and newsletters are not included. A more extensive list of religious periodicals published in the United States can be found in *Gale Directory of Publications and Broadcast Media*, (Gale Research, Inc., P.O. Box 33477, Detroit MI 48232-5477).

Each entry in this directory contains the title of the periodical, frequency of publication, religious affiliation, editor's name, address, telephone and fax number, and e-mail and website addresses when available. The frequency of publication, which appears in parentheses after the name of the publication is represented by a "W." for weekly; "M." for monthly; "Q." for quarterly; "I." for Internet.

**21st Century Christian**, (M.) Churches of Christ, M. Norvel Young and Prentice A. Meador, Jr., P.O. Box 40304, Nashville, TN 37204, Tel. (800)331-5991 Fax (615)385-5915 Email: eric@nafwb.org

**Action**, (6-Y.) Churches of Christ, John D. Reese, P.O. Box 2169, Cedar Park, TX 78630-2169, Tel. (512)345-8191 Fax (512)401-8265 Email: wbsinfo@wbschool.org Website: www.wbschool.org

**Adra Today**, (Q.) Seventh-day Adventist Church, Beth Schaefer, 12501 Old Columbia Pike, Silver Spring, MD 20904-6600, Tel. (301)680-6355 Fax (301)680-6370 Email: 74617.2105@compuserve.com Website: www.adra.org

**The Adult Quarterly**, (Q.) Associate Reformed Presbyterian Church (General Synod), The Rev. William B. Evans, Ph.D., P.O. Box 275, Due West, SC 29639, Tel. (864)379-8896 Email: wbevans@erskine.edu

**Advent Christian News**, (M.) Advent Christian Church, Rev. Keith D. Wheaton, P.O. Box 23152, Charlotte, NC 28227, Tel. (704)545-6161 Fax (704)573-0712 Email: Acpub@Adventchristian.org

**The Adventist Chaplain**, (Q.) Seventh-day Adventist Church, Deena Bartel-Wagner—Editor, Martin W. Feldbush—Executive Editor, Adventist Chaplaincy Ministries General Conference of Seventh-day Adventists, 12501 Old Columbia Pike, Silver Spring, MD 20904-6600, Tel. (301)680-6780 Fax (301) 680-6783 Email: acm@gc.adventist.org Website: www.adventistchaplains.org

**Adventist Review**, (3-M.) Seventh-day Adventist Church, W. G. Johnsson, 12501 Old Columbia Pike, Silver Spring, MD 20904-6600, Tel. (301)680-6560 Fax (301)680-6638

Email: letters@adventistreview.org
Website: www.adventistreview.org

**Adventist World**, (M.) Seventh-day Adventist Church, William G. Johnson, 12501 Old Columbia Pike, Silver Spring, MD 20904-6600, Tel. (301)680-6560 Fax (301)680-6638

**Again Magazine**, (Q.) The Antiochian Orthodox Christian Archdiocese of North America, R. Thomas Zell, P.O. Box 76, Ben Lomond, CA 95005-0076, Tel. (831)336-5118 Fax (831) 336-8882 Email: marketing@conciliarpress.com Website: www.conciliarpress.com

**Agape Magazine**, (bi-M.) Coptic Orthodox Church, Bishop Serapion, P.O. Box 4960, Diamond Bar, CA 91765, Tel. (909)865-8378 Fax (909)865-8348 Email: agape@lacopts.org Website: lacopts.org

**Alive Now**, (bi-M.) The United Methodist Church, JoyAnn Miller (Interim), P.O. Box 340004, Nashville, TN 37203-0004, Tel. (615) 340-7218 Email: alivenow@upperroom.org Website: www.alivenow.org

**The Allegheny Wesleyan Methodist**, (M.) The Allegheny Wesleyan Methodist Connection (Original Allegheny Conference), William Cope, P.O. Box 357, Salem, OH 44460, Tel. (330)337-9376 Fax (330)337-9700 Email: awmc@juno.com

**Alliance Life**, (M.) The Christian and Missionary Alliance, Mark Failing, P.O. Box 35000, Colorado Springs, CO 80935, Tel. (719)599-5999 Fax (719)599-8234 Email: alife@cmalliance.org Website: www.alliancelife.org

**The A.M.E. Christian Recorder**, (bi-W.) African Methodist Episcopal Church, Dr.

Calvin H. Sydnor, III, 500 Eighth Ave. South, Nashville, TN 37203-4181

**American Baptist Quarterly**, (Q.) American Baptist Churches in the U.S.A., Dr. Robert E. Johnson, P.O. Box 851, Valley Forge, PA 19482-0851, Tel. (610)768-2269 Fax (610) 768-2266
Email: dbvanbro@abc-usa.org
Website: www.cbts.edu/rejohnsonweb/AB Quarterly

**American Baptists In Mission**, (Q.) American Baptist Churches in the U.S.A., Richard W. Schramm, P.O. Box 851, Valley Forge, PA 19482-0851, Tel. (610)768-2077 Fax (610) 768-2320
Email: richard.schramm@abc-usa.org
Website: www.abc-usa.org

**American Bible Society Record**, (Q.) Non-denominational, Liz Smith, 1865 Broadway, New York, NY 10023-7505, Tel. (212)408-1367 Fax (212)582-7245
Email: absrecord@americanbible.org
Website: www.americanbible.org

**The Anchor of Faith**, (M.) The Anglican Orthodox Church, The Most Rev. Jerry L. Ogles, Anglican Orthodox Church, P.O. Box 128, Statesville, NC 28687-0128, Tel. (704) 873-8365 Fax (704)873-5359
Email: aocusa@energyunited.net
Website: www.anglicanorthodoxchurch.org

**Annual Catholic Directory, The**, (Y.) The Catholic Church, Michelle Laque Johnson, 222 N. 17th St., Philadelphia, PA 19103, Tel. (215)587-3660 Fax (215)587-3979

**El Aposento Alto**, (bi-M.) The United Methodist Church, Carmen Gaud, P.O. Box 340004, Nashville, TN, 37203-0004, Tel. (615)340-7253 Fax (615)340-7267
Email: ElAposentoAlto@upperroom.org
Website: www.upperroom.org

**The Armenian Church**, (2-Y.) Diocese of the Armenian Church of America, Arpie McQueen, 630 Second Avenue, New York, NY 10016, Tel. (212)686-0710 Fax (212)779-3558
Email: tac@armeniandiocese.org
Website: www.armenianchurch.org

**Around the Fellowship**, (M.) Universal Fellowship of Metropolitan Community Churches, Director of Communications: James N. Birkitt, Jr., 8704 Santa Monica Blvd, 2nd Fl., West Hollywood, CA 90069-4548, Tel. (310)360-8640 Fax (310)360-8680
Email: info@mccchurch.org
Website: www.mccchurch.org

**The Associate Reformed Presbyterian**, (M.) Associate Reformed Presbyterian Church (General Synod), Mrs. Sabrina M. Cooper, One Cleveland St., Greenville, SC 29601, Tel. (864)232-8297 Fax (864)271-3729
Email: arpmaged@arpsynod.org
Website: www.arpmagazine.org

**Attack, A Magazine for Christian Men**, (Q.) National Association of Free Will Baptists, James E. Vallance, P.O. Box 5002, Antioch, TN 37011-5002, Tel. (615)731-4950 Fax (615)731-0771

**Awake!** (M.) Jehovah's Witnesses, Watch Tower Society, 25 Columbia Heights, Brooklyn, NY 11201-2483, Tel. (718)560-5000
Website: watchtower.org

**The Banner**, (M.) Christian Reformed Church in North America, Robert DeMoor, 2850 Kalamazoo Ave., S.E., Grand Rapids, MI 49560, Tel. (616)224-0732 Fax (616)224-0834
Email: editorial@thebanner.org
Website: www.thebanner.org

**The Banner of Truth**, (M.) Netherlands Reformed Congregations, J. den Hoed, 1113 Bridgeview Dr., Lynden, WA 98264, Tel. (360)354-4203 Fax (360)354-7565

**The Baptist Bible Tribune**, (M.) Baptist Bible Fellowship International, Mike Randall, P.O. Box 309, Springfield, MO 65801-0309, Tel. (417)831-3996 Fax (417)831-1470
Email: editors@tribune.org
Website: www.tribune.org

**Baptist Bulletin**, (M.) General Association of Regular Baptist Churches, Sr. Editor: Norman A. Olson, 1300 N. Meacham Rd., Schaumburg, IL 60173-4806, Tel. (847)843-1600 Fax (847) 843-3757
Email: baptistbulletin@garbc.org
Website: www.garbc.org

**Baptist History And Heritage Society**, (3-Y.) Baptist, Pamela R. Durso, P.O. Box 728, Brentwood, TN 37021-0728, Tel. (615)371-7937 Fax (615)371-7939
Email: pdurso@tnbaptist.org
Website: www.baptisthistory.org

**Baptist Peacemaker**, (Q.) Baptist, Katie Cook, 4800 Wedgewood Dr., Charlotte, NC 28210, Tel. (704)521-6051 Fax (704)521-6053
Email: bpfna@bpfna.org
Website: www.bpfna.org

**The Baptist Preacher**, (bi-M.) Baptist Bible Fellowship International, Mike Randall, P.O. Box 309 HSJ, Springfield, MO 65801, Tel. (417)831-3996 Fax (417)831-1470

Email: editors@tribune.org
Website: www.tribune.org

**The Baptist Preacher's Journal**, (Q.) Baptist Bible Fellowship International, Keith Bassham, P.O. Box 309, Springfield, MO 65801, Tel. (417)831-3996 Fax (417)831-1470 Email: editor@tribune.org
Website: tribune.org

**Missions Ministry**, (Q.) Progressive National Baptist Convention, Inc., Justus Y. Reeves, 601 50th St. NE, Washington, DC 20019, Tel. (202)396-0558 Fax (202)398-4998
Email: justusreeves@aol.com
Website: www.PNBC.org

**Baptist Witness**, (M.) Primitive Baptists, Lasserre Bradley, Jr., P.O. Box 17037, Cincinnati, OH 45217, Tel. (513)821-7289 Fax (513)821-7303
Email: bbh45217@aol.com
Website: www.BaptistBibleHour.org

**BGC World**, (8-Y.) Baptist General Conference, Bob Putman, 2002 S. Arlington Heights Rd., Arlington Heights, IL 60005, Tel. (847)228-0200 Fax (847)228-5376
Email: bgcworld@bgcworld.org
Website: www.bgcworld.org

**The Bible Advocate**, (8-Y.) The Church of God (Seventh Day), Denver, Colo., Calvin Burrell, P.O. Box 33677, Denver, CO 80233, Tel. (303)452-7973 Fax (303)452-0657
Email: bibleadvocate@cog7.org
Website: www.cog7.org/BA

**The Brethren Evangelist**, (4-6-Y.), 524 College Ave., Ashland, OH 44805, Tel. (419)289-1708 Fax (419)281-0450
Email: brethren@brethrenchurch.org
Website: www.brethrenchurch.org

**Brethren Journal**, (10-Y.) Unity of the Brethren, Rev. Milton Maly, 6703 FM 2502, Brenham, TX 77833-9803, Tel. (409)830-8762
Website: www.unityofthebrethren.org

**Brethren Life and Thought**, (Q.) Church of the Brethren, Carol Gardner, Managing Editor, Bethany Seminary, 615 National Road West, Richmond, IN 47374-4019, Tel. (765)983-1811 Fax (765)983-1840
Email: gardnca@bethanyseminary.edu
Website: www.bethanyseminary.edu

**The Bridegroom's Messenger**, (bi-M.) The International Pentecostal Church of Christ, Janice Boyce, 121 W. Hunters Trail, Elizabeth City, NC 27909, Tel. (919)338-3003 Fax (919) 338-3003

**The Burning Bush**, (Q.) The Metropolitan Church Association, Inc. (Wesleyan), Rev. Gary Bowell, The Metropolitan Church Assoc., 2425 West Ramsey Ave, Milwaukee, WI 53221-4907, Tel. (414)282-8539
Email: metrochurch assn@wi.rr.com
Website: www.TheMCA.net

**Call to Unity: Resourcing the Church for Ecumenical Ministry**, (bi-M.) Christian Church (Disciples of Christ), Robert K. Welsh, P.O. Box 1986, Indianapolis, IN 46206-1986, Tel. (317)713-2586 Fax (317)713-2588
Email: rwelsh@ccu.disciples.org
Website: www.disciples.org/ccu

**Calvary Messenger**, (M.) Beachy Amish Mennonite Churches, Paul L. Miller, 7809 Soul Herren Road, Partridge, KS 67566, Tel. (620)567-2286 Fax (620)567-2286
Email: paullmiller@mindspring.com

**Ignite Your Faith**, (9-Y.) Nondenominational, Christopher Lutes, 465 Gunderson Dr., Carol Stream, IL 60188, Tel. (630)260-6200 Fax (630)480-2004
Email: iyf@igniteyourfaith.com
Website: www.igniteyourfaith.com

**Caring**, (Q.) Assemblies of God, Owen Wilkie, Gospel Publishing House, 1445 N. Boonville Ave., Springfield, MO 65802, Tel. (417)862-2781 Fax (417)862-0503
Email: benevolences@ag.org
Website: www.benevolences.ag.org

**Cathedral Age**, (Q.) Interdenominational, Craig W. Stapert, Washington National Cathedral, 3101 Wisconsin Ave., NW, Washington, DC 20016-5098, Tel. (202)537-5681 Fax (202) 364-6600
Email: cathedral_age@cathedral.org
Website: www.cathedralage.org

**Catholic Chronicle**, (M.) The Catholic Church, Angela Kessler, P.O. Box 985, Toledo, OH 43697-0985, Tel. (419)244-6711 ext. 133 Fax (419)244-0468
Email: ccnews@toledodiocese.org
Website: www.catholicchronicle.org

**Catholic Digest**, (M.) The Catholic Church, Joop Koopman, 185 Willow St., Mystic, CT 06355, Tel. (800)321-0411 Fax (860)536-5600
Email: jkoopman@bayard-inc.com
Website: www.CatholicDigest.org

**Catholic Herald (Milwaukee)**, (W.) The Catholic Church, Brian T. Olszewski, 3501 S. Lake Dr., St. Francis, WI 53235-0913, Tel. (414)769-3500 Fax (414)769-3468
Email: chnonline@archmil.org
Website: www.chnonline.org

**Catholic Light**, (Every Three Weeks) The Catholic Church, William R. Genello, 300 Wyoming Ave., Scranton, PA 18503, Tel. (570)207-2229 Fax (570)207-2271
Email: william-genello@dioceseofscranton.org
Website: www.dioceseofscranton.org

**The Catholic Peace Voice**, (bi-M.) The Catholic Church, Dave Robinson, 532 W. 8th Street, Erie, PA 16502, Tel. (814)453-4955 Fax (814) 452-4784
Email: info@paxchristiusa.org
Website: www.paxchristiusa.org

**The Catholic Review**, (W.) The Catholic Church, Daniel L. Medinger, Associate Publisher, P.O. Box 777, Baltimore, MD 21203, Tel. (443)524-3150 Fax (443)524-3155
Email: mail@catholicreview.org
Website: www.catholicreview.org

**Catholic Standard and Times**, (W.) The Catholic Church, Michelle Laque Johnson, 222 N. 17th St., Philadelphia, PA 19103, Tel. (215)587-3660 Fax (215)587-3979
Email: standard@adphila.org
Website: www.cst-phl.com

**Catholic Trends**, (bi-W.) The Catholic Church, David E. Gibson, 3211 Fourth St. NE, Washington, DC 20017-1100, Tel. (202)541-3250 Fax (202)541-3255
Email: cns@catholicnews.com
Website: www.catholicnews.com

**The Catholic Worker**, (7-Y.) The Catholic Church, Joanne Kennedy, Tanya Thevialt & Matt Vogel, Managing Editors, 36 E. First St., New York, NY 10003, Tel. (212)777-9617

**Cela Biedrs**, (bi-M.) The Latvian Evangelical Lutheran Church in America, Vieturs Bamban, 7630 S.W. 26th Ave., Portland, OR 97219, Tel. (503)781-6724
Email: celabiedrs@yahoo.com

**Celebration: An Ecumenical Worship Resource**, (M.) Interdenominational, Patrick Marrin, 115 East Armor Blvd., Kansas City, MO 64111, Tel. (816)531-0538 Fax (816)968-2291
Email: patmarrin@aol.com
Website: www.ncrpub.com

**The Challenge**, (Q.) The Bible Church of Christ, Inc., A.M. Jones, 1358 Morris Ave., Bronx, NY 10456, Tel. (718)588-2284 Fax (718)992-5597
Website: www.thebiblechurchofchrist.org

**Charisma**, (M.) Nondenominational, J. Lee Grady, 600 Rinehart Rd., Lake Mary, FL 32746, Tel. (407)333-0600 Fax (407)333-7133

Email: grady@strang.com
Website: www.charismamag.com

**The Children's Friend, (Braille)**, (Q.) Seventh-day Adventist Church, Gaylena Gibson, P.O. Box 6097, Lincoln, NE 68506, Tel. (402)488-0981 Fax (402)488-7582
Email: editorial@christianrecord.org
Website: www.ChristianRecord.org

**Christadelphian Advocate**, (M.) Christadelphians, James I. Millay, 27 Delphian Road, Springfield, VT 05156-9335, Tel. (802) 885.2316 Fax (802)885.2319
Email: jimillay@vermontel.net
Website: www.christadelphian-advocate.org

**Christadelphian Tidings**, (M.) Christadelphians, Donald H. Styles, 42076 Hartford Dr., Canton, MI 48187, Tel. (313)844-2426 Fax (313)844-8304

**The Christian Baptist**, (Q.) Primitive Baptists, Elder S. T. Tolley, P.O. Box 68, Atwood, TN 38220, Tel. (901)662-7417
Email: cbl@aeneas.net

**Christian Bible Teacher**, (Q.) Churches of Christ, Bob Connel, P.O. Box 7385, Ft. Worth, TX 76111, Tel. (817)838-2644 Fax (817)838-2644

**The Christian Century**, (bi-W.) Nondenominational, John Buchanan, 104 South Michigan Ave. Suite 700, Chicago, IL 60603, Tel. (312)263-7510 Fax (312)263-7540
Email: main@christiancentury.org
Website: www.christiancentury.org

**The Christian Chronicle**, (M.) Churches of Christ, Lynn McMillon, P.O. Box 11000, Oklahoma City, OK 73136-1100, Tel. (405) 425-5070 Fax (405)425-5076
Website: www.christianchronicle.org

**The Christian Community**, (8-Y.) International Council of Community Churches, Rev. Michael E. Livingston, 21116 Washington Pkwy., Frankfort, IL 60423, Tel. (815)464-5690 Fax (815)464-5692
Email: ICCC60423@sbcglobal.net
Website: icccusa.com

**The Christian Contender**, (M.) Mennonite Church, James Boll, P.O. Box 3, Highway 172, Crockett, KY 41413, Tel. (606)522-4348 Fax (606)522-4896

**The Christian Index**, (M.) Christian Methodist Episcopal Church, Dr. Kenneth E. Jones, P.O. Box 431, Fairfield, AL 35064, Tel. (205)929-1410 Fax (205)744-0010
Email: goodoc@aol.com
Website: www.c-m-e.org

**Christian Journal**, (Q.) Churches of Christ, J.E. Snelson, P.O. Box 7385, Ft. Worth, TX 76111, Tel. (817)838-2644

**Christian Leader**, (M.) U.S. Conference of Mennonite Brethren Churches, Connie Faber, P.O. Box 220, Hillsboro, KS 67063, Tel. (316)947-5543 Fax (316)947-3266
Email: chleader@southwind.net

**Christian Monthly**, (M.) Apostolic Lutheran Church of America, Linda Mattson, P.O. Box 2126, Battle Ground, WA 98604, Tel. (360) 687-6493 Fax (360)687-6493
Email: christianm@apostolic-lutheran.org
Website: www.Apostolic-Lutheran.org

**Christian Record**, (Braille), (Q.) Seventh-day Adventist Church, Gaylena Gibson, P.O. Box 6097, Lincoln, NE 68506, Tel. (402)488-0981 Fax (402)488-7582
Email: editorial@christianrecord.org
Website: www.ChristianRecord.org

**Christian Record Talking Magazine (Audio)**, (Q.) Seventh-day Adventist Church, Bert Williams, P.O. Box 6097, Lincoln, NE 68506, Tel. (402)488-0981
Email: Bert.Williams@christianrecord.org
Website: http://www.christianrecord.org/services/recorded_magazines/christianrecord.php

**The Christian Science Journal**, (M.) Church of Christ, Scientist, Mary M. Trammell, Editor in Chief; William G. Dawley, Editor, One Norway St., Boston, MA 02115-3195, Tel. (617)450-2000 Fax (617)450-2930
Email: trammellm@csps.com OR dawleyw@csps.com
Website: www.csjournal.com

**The Christian Science Monitor**, (D. & W.) Church of Christ, Scientist, David T. Cook, One Norway St., Boston, MA 02115, Tel. (617)450-2000 Fax (617)450-7575
Website: www.csmonitor.com

**Christian Science Quarterly Weekly Bible Lessons**, (M. & Q.) Church of Christ, Scientist, Carol Humphry, Circulation Marketing Manager, One Norway St., C-40, Boston, MA 02115, Tel. (617)450-2000 Fax (617)450-2930
Email: service@csps.com
Website: www.BibleLesson.com

**Christian Science Sentinel**, (W.) Church of Christ, Scientist, Mary M. Trammell, Editor in Chief; William G. Dawley, Editor, One Norway St., Boston, MA 02115-3195, Tel. (617)450-2000 Fax (617)450-2930
Email: sentinel@csps.com/trammellm@csps.com (the Editor)
Website: www.cssentinel.com

**Christian Social Action**, (bi-M.) The United Methodist Church, vacant, 100 Maryland Ave. NE, Washington, DC 20002, Tel. (202)488-5621 Fax (202)488-1617
Website: www.umc-gbcs.org

**Christian Standard**, (W.) Christian Churches and Churches of Christ, Mark A. Taylor, 8121 Hamilton Ave., Cincinnati, OH 45231, Tel. (513)931-4050 Fax (513)931-0950
Email: christianstd@standardpub.com
Website: www.christianstandard.com

**The Christian Union Witness**, (M. (except Jy-Ag)) Christian Union, Joseph Cunningham, P.O. Box 361, Greenfield, OH 45123, Tel. (937)981-2760 Fax (937)981-2760
Email: ohiocu@bright.net
Website: christianunionbright.net

**Christian Woman**, (bi-M.) Churches of Christ, Sandra Humphrey, P.O. Box 150, Nashville, TN 37202, Tel. (615)254-8781 Fax (615)254-7411

**The Church Advocate**, (Q.) Churches of God, General Conference, Rachel L. Foreman, P.O. Box 926, 700 E. Melrose Ave., Findlay, OH 45839, Tel. (419)424-1961 Fax (419)424-3433
Email: communications@cggc.org
Website: www.cggc.org

**Church of God Evangel**, (M.) Church of God (Cleveland, Tenn.), James E. Cossey, P.O. Box 2250, Cleveland, TN 37320, Tel. (423)478-7592 Fax (423)478-7616
Email: editor@pathwaypress.org
Website: www.pathwaypress.org

**The Church Herald**, (11-Y.) Reformed Church in America, Christina Van Eyl, 4500 60th St. SE, Grand Rapids, MI 49512, Tel. (616)698-7071
Email: herald@rca.org
Website: herald.rca.org

**The Church Herald**, (11-Y.) Reformed Church in America, Christina Van Eyl, 4500 60th St., SE, Grand Rapids, MI 49512, Tel. (616)698-7071 Fax (616)698-6606
Email: herald@rca.org
Website: www.rca.org/herald

**Church History: Studies in Christianity and Culture**, (Q.) Scholarly, John Corrigan, Amanda Porterfield, Florida State Univesity Dept of Religion, M05 Dodd Hall, Tallahassee, FL 32306-1520, Tel. (850)644-9038 Fax (850) 644-7225
Email: church-history@admin.fsu.edu
Website: www.churchhistory.org/churchhistory.html

**The Church Messenger**, (bi-W.) The American Carpatho-Russian Orthodox Greek Catholic

Church, V. Rev. Michael Rosco, 145 Broad St., Perth Amboy, NJ 08861, Tel. (732)826-4442
Email: mrosco2@excite.com
Website: www.acrod.org/news/messenger1.html

**Church School Herald**, (Q.) African Methodist Episcopal Zion Church, Ms. Mary A. Love, P.O. Box 26769, Charlotte, NC 28221-6769, Tel. (704)599-4630 ext. 324 Fax (704)688-2548
Email: MaLove@amezhqtr.org

**Church & Society Magazine**, (bi-M.) Presbyterian Church (U.S.A.), Rev. Dr. Bobbi Wells Hargleroad, 100 Witherspoon St., Louisville, KY 40202-1396, Tel. (502)569-5810 Fax (502)569-8116
Email: c-s@ctr.pcusa.org
Website: www.pcusa.org/churchsociety

**Church Talk**, (Q.) General Association of General Baptists, Mike Warren, 100 Stinson Drive, Poplar Bluff, MO 63901, Tel. (573)785-7746 Fax (573)785-0564
Email: cmdir@generalbaptist.com
Website: generalbaptist.com

**Churchwoman**, (Q.) Interdenominational, Annie Llamoso-Songco, 475 Riverside Dr., Suite 500, New York, NY 10115, Tel. (212)870-3339 Fax (212)870-2338
Email: allamoso@churchwomen.org
Website: www.churchwomen.org

**Circuit Rider**, (bi-M.) The United Methodist Church, Jill S. Reddig, 201 Eighth Ave. S, Nashville, TN 37203, Tel. (615)749-6538 Fax (615)749-6061
Email: jreddig@umpublishing.org
Website: www.circuitrider.com

**Clarion Herald**, (bi-W.) The Catholic Church, Peter P. Finney, Jr., P.O. Box 53247, 1000 Howard Ave. Suite 400, New Orleans, LA 70153, Tel. (504)596-3035 Fax (504)596-3020
Email: clarionherald@clarionherald.org
Website: www.clarionherald.org

**Clergy Comminique**, (2-Y.) International Council of Community Churches, Virginia Leopold, 21116 Washington Pky., Frankfort, IL 60423-3112, Tel. (815)464-5690 Fax (815) 464-5692
Email: iccc60423@aol.com
Website: icccusa.com

**The Clergy Journal**, (9-Y.) Nondenominational, Sharon L. Firle, Managing Editor & Clyde J. Steckel, Executive Editor, 6160 Carmen Avenue E, Inver Grove Heights, MN 55076-4422, Tel. (800)328-0200 Fax (651)457-4617
Email: editor@logostaff.com
Website: www.logosproductions.com

**Club Connection**, (Q.) Assemblies of God, Debby Seler, 1445 Boonville Ave., Springfield, MO 65802-1894, Tel. (417)862-2781 Fax (417)862-0503
Email: clubconnection@ag.org
Website: www.missionettes.ag.org

**CoLaborer**, (bi-M.) National Association of Free Will Baptists, Sarah Fletcher, Women Nationally Active for Christ, P.O. Box 5002, Antioch, TN 37011-5002, Tel. (615)731-6812 Fax (615)731-0771
Email: wnac@nafwb.org

**College and University Dialogue**, (3-Y.) Seventh-day Adventist Church, John M. Fowler, 12501 Old Columbia Pike, Silver Spring, MD 20904-6600, Tel. Fax (301)622-9627
Website: dialogue.adventist.org

**Collegiate Quarterly**, (Q.) Seventh-day Adventist Church, Gary B. Swanson, 12501 Old Columbia Pike, Silver Spring, MD 20904, Tel. (301)680-6160 Fax (301)680-6155

**Columbia**, (M.) The Catholic Church, Tim S. Hickey, One Columbus Plaza, New Haven, CT 06510, Tel. (203)752-4398 Fax (203)752-4109
Email: tim.hickey@kofc-supreme.com
Website: www.kofc.org

**The Commission**, (2-Y.) International Mission Board, Southern Baptist Convention, Michael Chute, P.O. Box 6767, Richmond, VA 23230-0767, Tel. (804)219-1373 Fax (804)219-1410
Email: commission@imb.org
Website: www.tconline.org

**Common Lot**, (Q.) United Church of Christ, Martha J. Hunter, 700 Prospect Ave., Cleveland, OH 44115, Tel. (216)736-2150 Fax (216)736-2156

**Commonweal**, (bi-W.) The Catholic Church, Paul Baumann, 475 Riverside Drive, Rm. 405, New York, NY 10115, Tel. (212)662-4200 Fax (212)662-4183
Email: editors@commonwealmagazine.org
Website: www.commonwealmagazine.org

**Communion**, (bi-M.) Church of God (Anderson, Indiana), Arthur Kelly, P.O. Box 2420, 1201 E. 5th Street, Anderson, IN 46018-2420, Tel. (765)642-0256 Fax (765)652-5652
Email: AKelly@chog.org
Website: chog.org/news/communion.asp

**The Congregationalist**, (5-Y.) National Association Congregational Christian Churches, Rev. James E. Eaton, 87 Broadway, Norwich, CT 06360, Tel. (860)889-1363 Fax (860)887-5715
Email: jeaton@unitedcongregational.org
Website: www.congregationalist.org

**Connections,** (M.) The Alliance of Baptists, Sue Harper Poss, 1328 16th St. N.W., Washington, DC 20036, Tel. (202)745-7609 Fax (202)745-0023
Email: editor@allianceofbaptists.org
Website: www.allianceofbaptists.org

**Conqueror,** (bi-M.) United Pentecostal Church International, John F. Sills, 8855 Dunn Rd., Hazelwood, MO 63042, Tel. (314)837-7300 Fax (314)837-4503
Email: GYouth8855@aol.com

**Context,** (M.) Nondenominational, Martin Marty, 205 W. Monroe St., Chicago, IL 60606-5013, Tel. (312)236-7782 Fax (312)236-8207
Email: editors@uscatholic.org
Website: www.contextonline.org

**Covenant,** (Q.) Presbyterian Church in America, Jackie Fogas, Covenant Theological Seminary, 12330 Conway Road, St. Louis, MO 63141, Tel. (314)434-4044 Fax (314)434-4819
Email: covenantmagazine@covenantseminary.edu
Website: www.convenantseminary.edu

**Cornerstone Connections,** (Q.) Seventh-day Adventist Church, Gary B. Swanson, 12501 Old Columbia Pike, Silver Spring, MD 20904, Tel. (301)680-6160 Fax (301)680-6155

**The Covenant Companion,** (M.) Evangelical Covenant Church, Donald L. Meyer, Editor Jane K. Swanson-Nystrom, Managing Editor, 5101 N. Francisco Ave., Chicago, IL 60625, Tel. (773)906-3328 Fax (773)784-4366
Email: communication@covchurch.org
Website: www.covchurch.org/cov/companion

**Covenant Home Altar,** (Q.) Evangelical Covenant Church, Jane K. Swanson-Nystrom, 5101 N. Francisco Ave., Chicago, IL 60625, Tel. (773)784-3000 Fax (773)784-4366
Email: communication@covchurch.org

**Covenant Quarterly,** (Q.) Evangelical Covenant Church, Paul E. Koptak, 3225 W. Foster Ave., Chicago, IL 60625-4895, Tel. (773)244-6242
Email: pkoptak@northpark.edu

**The Covenanter Witness,** (11-Y.) Reformed Presbyterian Church of North America, Drew Gordon and Lynne Gordon, 7408 Penn Ave., Pittsburgh, PA 15208, Tel. (412)241-0436 Fax (412)731-8861
Email: info@psalms4u.com
Website: www.psalms4u.com

**Credinta—The Faith,** (Q.) The Romanian Orthodox Church in America, V. Rev. Archim. Dr. Vasile Vasilac, 45-03 48th Ave., Woodside, Queens, NY 11377, Tel. (313)893-8390

**The Cumberland Presbyterian,** (11-Y.) Cumberland Presbyterian Church, Patricia P. White, Cumberland Presbyterian Church, 1978 Union Ave., Memphis, TN 38104, Tel. (615)731-5556
Email: cpmag@comcast.net
Website: www.cumberland.org/cpmag/

**Currents in Theology and Mission,** (bi-M.) Evangelical Lutheran Church in America, Ralph W. Klein, 1100 E. 55th St., Chicago, IL 60615, Tel. (773)256-0751 Fax (773)256-0782
Email: currents@lstc.edu
Website: www.lstc.edu/pub_peo/pub/currents.html

**Cutting Edge,** (Q.) Association of Vineyard Churches, Jeff Bailey, 2495 Howard St., Evanston, IL 60202, Tel. (847)328-4544 Fax (847)328-5153
Email: cuttingedge@vineyardusa.org
Website: www.vineyardusa.org/publications/newsletters/cutting_edge

**Decision,** (11-Y.) Nondenominational, Bob Paulson, 1 Billy Graham Parkway, Charlotte, NC 28201-0001, Tel. (704)401-2432 Fax (704)401-3009
Email: decision@bgea.org
Website: www.decisionmag.org

**DisciplesWorld,** (10-Y.) Christian Church (Disciples of Christ) in the United States and Canada, Verity A. Jones, 6325 N. Guilford Ave Suite 213, Indianapolis, IN 46220, Tel. (317) 375-8846 Fax (317)375-8849
Email: info@disciplesworld.com
Website: www.disciplesworld.com

**EcuLink,** (Several-Y.) Interdenominational, Philip E. Jenks, 475 Riverside Drive, 8th Floor, New York, NY 10115-0050, Tel. (212)870-2227 Fax (212)870-2030
Email: pjenks@councilofchurches.org
Website: www.councilofchurches.org

**Ecumenical Trends,** (M.) The Catholic Church, Rev. James Loughran, SA, Graymoor Ecumenical & Interreligious Institute, P.O. Box 300, Garrison, NY 10524-0300, Tel. (845)424-3671 ext. 3323 Fax (845)424-2163
Email: jlgeii@aol.com
Website: www.geii.org

**Eleventh Hour Messenger,** (bi-M.) Wesleyan Holiness Association of Churches, John Brewer, 11411 N US Hwy. 27, Fountain City, IN 47341-9757, Tel. (317)584-3199

**Encounter (Audio),** (Q.) Seventh-day Adventist Church, Bert Williams, P.O. Box 6097, Lincoln, NE 68506, Tel. (402)488-0981

329

Email: Bert.Williams@christianrecord.org
Website: http://www.christianrecord.org/services/recorded_magazines/christianrecord.php

**Enrichment: A Journal for Pentecostal Ministry**, (Q.) Assemblies of God, Gary Allen; Rick Knoth, Managing Editor, 1445 N. Boonville Ave., Springfield, MO 65802, Tel. (417)862-2781 Fax (417)862-0416
Email: rKnoth@ag.org
Website: www.enrichmentjournal.ag.org

**The Ensign**, (M.) The Church of Jesus Christ of Latter-day Saints, Don L. Searle, Managing Editor, 50 E North Temple Street, 24th Fl., Salt Lake City, UT 84150, Tel. (801)240-2950 Fax (801)240-2270
Email: ensign@ldschurch.org
Website: www.magazines.lds.org

**Episcopal Life**, (M.) The Episcopal Church, Jerrold Hames, 815 Second Ave., New York, NY 10017-4503, Tel. (800)334-7626 Fax (212)949-8059
Email: jhames@episcopalchurch.org
Website: www.episcopal-life.org

**Equip**, (bi-M.) Presbyterian Church in America, Dr. Charles Dunahoo, 1700 N. Brown Road Ste. 102, Lawrenceville, GA 30043, Tel. (678) 825-1100 Fax (678)825-1101
Email: cep@pcanet.org
Website: pcanet.org

**The Evangel**, (bi-M.) American Association of Lutheran Churches, The, Rev. Charles D. Eidum, 801 W. 106th St, Suite 203, Minneapolis, MN 55420-5603, Tel. (952)884-7784 Fax (952)884-7894
Email: aa2taalc@aol.com
Website: www.taalc.com

**The Evangel**, (Q.) The Evangelical Church Alliance, Dr. Henry A. (Hank) Roso, 205 W. Broadway, P.O. Box 9, Bradley, IL 60915, Tel. (815)937-0720 Fax (815)937-0001
Email: info@ecainternatinal.org
Website: www.ecainternational.org

**The Evangelical Advocate**, (bi-M.) Churches of Christ in Christian Union, Ralph Hux, P.O. Box 30, Circleville, OH 43113, Tel. (740)474-8856 Fax (740)477-7766
Email: doc@cccuhg.org
Website: www.cccuhq.org

**Evangelical Beacon**, (bi-M.) The Evangelical Free Church of America, Ms. Carol Madison, 901 East 78th St., Minneapolis, MN 55420-1300, Tel. (877)293-5653 Fax (952)853-8488
Email: beacon@efca.org
Website: www.efca.org

**Evangelical Challenge**, (Q.) The Evangelical Church, Shirley Roehl, 9421 West River Road, Minneapolis, MN 55444, Tel. (763)424-2589 Fax (763)424-9230
Email: ecdenom@usfamily.net
Website: www.theevangelicalchurch.org

**The Evangelist**, (W.) The Roman Catholic Church, James Breig, 40 N. Main Ave., Albany, NY 12203, Tel. (518)453-6688 Fax (518)453-8448
Email: james.breig@rcda.org
Website: www.evangelist.org

**Explorations**, (Q.) Nondenominational, Irvin J. Borowsky, 321 Chestnut Street, 4th Floor, Philadelphia, PA 19106-2779, Tel. (215)925-2800 Fax (215)925-3800
Email: aii@interfaith-scholars.org

**Extension**, (M.) The Catholic Church, Bradley Collins, Editor, 150 S. Wacker Drive, 20th Floor, Chicago, IL 60606, Tel. (312)236-7240 Fax (312)236-5276
Email: magazine@catholic-extension.org
Website: www.catholic-extension.org

**Faith & Fellowship**, (M.) Church of the Lutheran Brethren of America, Bruce Stumbo, P.O. Box 655, Fergus Falls, MN 56538, Tel. (218)736-7357 Fax (218)736-2200
Email: ffpress@clba.org
Website: www.faithandfellowship.org

**Faith-Life**, (bi-M.) Lutheran, Pastor Marcus Albrecht, 2107 N. Alexander St., Appleton, WI 54911, Tel. (920)733-1839 Fax (920)733-4834
Email: malbrecht@milwpc.com

**FEConnections**, (Q.) Fellowship of Evangelical Churches, Ron Habegger, 1420 Kerrway Ct., Fort Wayne, IN 46805, Tel. (260)423-3649 Fax (260)420-1905
Email: FECministries@aol.com
Website: www.fecministries.org

**Fellowship**, (bi-M.) Interfaith, Ethan Vesely-Flad, P.O. Box 271, Nyack, NY 10960-0271, Tel. (845)358-4601 Fax (845)358-4924
Email: fellowship@forusa.org
Website: www.forusa.org

**Fellowship Focus**, (bi-M.) Fellowship of Evangelical Bible Churches, Sharon K. Berg, 3339 N 109th Plz, Omaha, NE 68164-2908, Tel. (402)965-3860 Fax (402)965-3871
Email: fellowshipfocus@febcministries.org
Website: www.febcministries.org

**Fellowship News**, (M.) Bible Fellowship Church, Carol Snyder, 3000 Fellowship Drive, Whitehall, PA 18052-3343, Tel. (877)795-1212 Fax (215)536-2120

330

Email: ccsnyder@supernet.com
Website: www.bfc.org

**Fellowship Tidings**, (Q.) Full Gospel Fellowship of Churches and Ministers International, Cynthia Mattox, 1000 N. Beltline Road, Irving, TX 75061, Tel. (214)492-1254 Fax (214)492-1736
Email: FGFCMI@aol.com
Website: www.fgfcmi.org

**FGConnections**, (3-Y.) Friends General Conference, Barbara Hirshkowitz, 1216 Arch Street 2B, Philadelphia, PA 19107, Tel. (215) 561-1700 Fax (215)561-0759
Email: connections@fgcquaker.org
Website: www.fgcquaker.org/connect

**Firm Foundation**, (M.) Churches of Christ, H. A. Dobbs, P.O. Box 690192, Houston, TX 77269-0192, Tel. (713)469-3102 Fax (713)469-7115
Email: HAD@onramp.net

**First Things: A Monthly Journal of Religion & Public Life**, (10-Y.) Interdenominational, Richard J. Neuhaus, 156 Fifth Ave., Ste. 400, New York, NY 10010, Tel. (212)627-1985 Fax (212)627-2184
Email: ft@firstthings.com
Website: www.firstthings.com

**The Flaming Sword**, (M.) Bible Holiness Church, Susan Davolt, 10th St. & College Ave., Independence, KS 67301, Tel. (316)331-2580 Fax (316)331-2580

**For God and Country**, (Q.) Seventh-Day Adventist Church, Deena Bartel-Wagner, Editor; Gary R. Councell, Executive Editor, Adventist Chaplaincy Ministries
General Conference of Seventh-Day Adventists, 12501 Old Columbia Pike, Silver Spring, MD 20904-6600

**Foresee**, (bi-M.) Conservative Congregational Christian Conference, Richard & Shirley Leonard, 8941 Highway 5, Lake Elmo, Lake Elmo, MN 55042, Tel. (651)739-1474 Fax (651)739-0750
Email: dmjohnson@ccccusa.com
Website: www.ccccusa.com

**Forum Letter**, (M.) Independent, Intra-Lutheran (companion publication to the quarterly, **Lutheran Forum**), Pastor Russell E. Saltzman, Ruskin Heights Lutheran Church, 10801 Ruskin Way, Kansas City, MO 64134, Tel. (816)761-6815 Fax (816)761-6523
Email: rhlcpastor@sbcglobal.net
Website: www.alpb.org

**Forward**, (Q.) United Pentecostal Church International, Rev. J. L. Hall, 8855 Dunn Rd.,

Hazelwood, MO 63042, Tel. (314)837-7300 Fax (314)837-4503

**Forward in Christ**, (M.) Wisconsin Evangelical Lutheran Synod, Rev. John A. Braun, 2929 N. Mayfair Rd., Milwaukee, WI 53222, Tel. (414)256-3210 Fax (414)256-3862
Email: fic@sab.wels.net
Website: www.wels.net

**Foursquare World Advance**, (Q. w/ a bonus issue) International Church of the Foursquare Gospel, Dr. Ron Williams, P.O. Box 26902, 1910 W. Sunset Blvd., Ste 400, Los Angeles, CA 90026-0176, Tel. (213)989-4230 Fax (213)989-4544
Email: comm@foursquare.org
Website: www.advancemagazine.org

**Free Will Baptist Gem**, (M.) National Association of Free Will Baptists, Gary Fry, P.O. Box 991, Lebanon, MO 65536, Tel. (417) 532-6537 Fax (417)588-7068
Email: gwfry@webound.com

**Friend Magazine**, (M.) The Church of Jesus Christ of Latter-day Saints, Vivian Paulsen, 50 E South Temple Street, 24th Fl., Salt Lake City, UT 84150, Tel. (801)240-2210 Fax (801) 240-2270

**Friends Bulletin**, (10-Y.) Religious Society of Friends, Anthony Manousos, 3223 Danaha St., Torrance, CA 90505, Tel. (310-325-3581
Email: friendsbul@aol.com
Website: www.westernquaker.net

**Friends Journal**, (M.) Religious Society of Friends, Susan Corson-Finnerty, Publisher & Exec. Editor, 1216 Arch St., 2A, Philadelphia, PA 19107-2835, Tel. (215)563-8629 Fax (215) 568-1377
Email: info@friendsjournal.org
Website: www.friendsjournal.org

**The Friends Voice**, (3-Y.) Evangelical Friends International—North America Region, Dr. Becky Towne, Sr. Editor; Dr. Kathy Roblyer, Assoc. Editor, 2748 E. Pikes Peak Ave, Colorado Springs, CO 80909, Tel. (719)632-5721 (800)351-2973
Email: thevoice@evangelicalfriends.org
Website: evangelicalfriends.org

**Front Line**, (3-Y.) Conservative Baptist Association of America, Al Russell, P.O. Box 58, Long Prairie, MN 56347, Tel. (320)732-8072 Fax (509)356-7112
Email: chaplruss@earthlink.net
Website: www.cbchaplains.net

**Full Gospel Ministries Outreach Report**, (Q.) Full Gospel Assemblies International, Simeon

Strauser, P.O. Box 1230, Coatsville, PA 19320, Tel. (610)857-2357 Fax (610)857-3109

**The Gem**, (W.) Churches of God, General Conference, Rachel Foreman, P.O. Box 926, Findlay, OH 45839, Tel. (419)424-1961 Fax (419)424-3433
Email: communications@cggc.org
Website: www.cggc.org

**God's Field**, (bi-W. (except Dec.)) Polish National Catholic Church of America and Canada, Rev. Anthony Mikovsky (English) and Rt. Rev. Casimir Grotnik (Polish), 1006 Pittston Ave., Scranton, PA 18505-4109, Tel. (570)346-9131 Fax (570)346-2188
Email: GodsField@adelphia.net
Website: www.pncc.org

**Good News - Buna Vestire**, (Q.) The Romanian Orthodox Episcopate of America, The Romanian Orthodox Deanery of Canada, c/o Psa. Alice Nenson, 2855 Helmsing St., Regina, SK S4V 0W7, Tel. (306)761-2379 Fax (306)525-9650
Email: danenson@accesscomm.ca

**Gospel Advocate**, (M.) Churches of Christ, Neil W. Anderson, 1006 Elm Hill Pike, Nashville, TN 37202, Tel. (615)254-8781 Fax (615)254-7411
Email: info@gospeladvocate.com
Website: www.gospeladvocate.com

**The Gospel Herald**, (M.) Church of God, Mountain Assembly, Inc., Scott Isham, P.O. Box 157, Jellico, TN 37762, Tel. (423)784-8260 Fax (423)784-3258
Email: cgmahdq@jellico.com
Website: www.cgmahdq.org

**The Gospel Light**, (2-Y.) The Bible Church of Christ, Inc., Carole Crenshaw, 1358 Morris Ave., Bronx, NY 10456, Tel. (718)588-2284 Fax (718)992-5597
Website: www.thebiblechurchofchrist.org

**The Gospel Messenger**, (M.) Congregational Holiness Church, Inc., Rev. Danny K. Jones, Congregational Holiness Church, 3888 Fayetteville Highway, Griffin, GA 30223, Tel. (770)228-4833 Fax (770)228-1177
Email: messenger@CHChurch.com
Website: www.CHChurch.com

**The Gospel Truth**, (bi-M.) Church of the Living God, C.W.F.F., W.E. Crumes, 430 Forest Avenue, Cincinnati, OH 45229, Tel. (513)569-5660 Fax (513)569-5661
Email: cwff430@aol.com

**Grow Magazine**, (Q.) Church of the Nazarene, Jim Dorsey, 6401 The Paseo, Kansas City, MO 64131, Tel. (816)333-7000 x 2828 Fax (816)523-1872
Email: jdorsey@nazarene.org
Website: www.growmagazine.org

**Guide**, (W.) Seventh-day Adventist Church, Randy Fishell, 55 W. Oak Ridge Dr., Hagerstown, MD 21740, Tel. (301)393-4037 Fax (301)393-4055
Email: guide@rhpa.org
Website: www.guidemagazine.org

**The Handmaiden**, (Q.) The Antiochian Orthodox Christian Archdiocese of North America, Virginia Nieuwsma, P.O. Box 76, Ben Lomond, CA 95005-0076, Tel. (831)336-5118 Fax (831)336-8882
Email: czell@conciliarpress.com
Website: www.conciliarpress.com

**The Happy Harvester**, (M.) Church of God of Prophecy, Diane Pace, P.O. Box 2910, Cleveland, TN 37320-2910, Tel. (423)559-5435 Fax (423)559-5444
Email: JoDiPace@wingnet.net

**Herald**, (M.) Community of Christ, Editorial Board, 1001 W. Walnut, Independence, MO 64050, Tel. (816)833-1000 Fax (816)521-3043
Email: Herald@cofochrist.org
Website: www.heraldhouse.org or www.cofchrist.org

**The Herald of Christian Science**, (M. & Q.) Church of Christ, Scientist, Mary M. Trammell, Editor-in-Chief, The Christian Science Publishing Society, One Norway St., Boston, MA 02115-3195, Tel. (617)450-2000 Fax (617)450-2930
Email: trammellm@csps.com or herald@csps.com
Website: www.csherald.com

**Heritage**, (Y.) Assemblies of God, Darrin Rodgers, 1445 Boonville Ave., Springfield, MO 65802, Tel. (417)862-1447 Ext. 4400 Fax (417)862-6203
Email: drodgers@ag.org
Website: www.agheritage.org

**High Adventure**, (Q.) Assemblies of God, John M. Hicks, Gospel Publishing House, 1445 N. Boonville Ave., Springfield, MO 65802-1894, Tel. (417)862-2781 Fax (417)831-8230
Email: rangers@ag.org
Website: www.royalrangers.ag.org

**Higher Way**, (Q.) Apostolic Faith Mission of Portland, Oregon, Darrel D. Lee, 6615 S.E. 52nd Ave., Portland, OR 97206, Tel. (503)777-1741 Fax (503)777-1743
Email: kbarrett@apostolicfaith.org

U.S. PERIODICALS

332

Website: www.apostolicfaith.org

**Holiness Today**, (bi-M.) Church of the Nazarene, David J. Felter, 6401 The Paseo, Kansas City, MO 64131, Tel. (816)333-7000 Fax (816)333-1748
Email: HolinessToday@nazarene.org
Website: www.holinesstoday.com

**Homiletic and Pastoral Review**, (M.) The Roman Catholic Church, Kenneth Baker, 50 S. Franklin Tpk., P.O. Box 297, Ramsey, NJ 07446, Tel. (201)236-9336

**Horizons**, (M.) Christian Churches and Churches of Christ, Leah Ellison Bradley, Susan Jackson Dowd, 100 Witherspoon St, Louisville, KY 40202-1396, Tel. (505)569-5368 Fax (502) 569-8085
Email: msa@missionservices.org
Website: www.missionservices.org

**Horizons**, (7-Y.) Presbyterian Church (U.S.A.), Leah Ellison Bradley, Susan Jackson Dowd, Presbyterian Women, 100 Witherspoon St., Louisville, KY 40202-1396, Tel. (502)569-5368 Fax (502)569-8085
Email: lbradley@ctr.pcusa.org
Website: www.pcusa.org/horizons

**The Inclusive Pulpit**, (Y.) International Council of Community Churches, Larry and Carolyn Dipboye, 21116 Washington Pky., Frankfort, IL 60423-3112, Tel. (815)464-5690 Fax (815) 464-5692
Email: iccc60423@aol.com
Website: icccusa.com

**Insight Into**, (bi-M.) Netherlands Reformed Congregations, Mr. Schipper, 4732 E. C Avenue, Kalamazoo, MI 49004, Tel. (269)349-9448

**InterLit**, (Q.) Nondenominational magazine on Christian publishing worldwide, Kim A. Pettit, 4050 Lee Vance View Drive, Colorado Springs, CO 80918, Tel. (719)536-0100 Fax (719)536-3266
Email: ccmintl@ccmi.org
Website: www.ccmi.org

**International Bulletin of Missionary Research**, (Q.) Nondenominational, Jonathan J. Bonk, Overseas Ministries Study Center, 490 Prospect St., New Haven, CT 06511-2196, Tel. (203)624-6672 Fax (203)865-2857
Email: ibmr@OMSC.org
Website: www.OMSC.org
www.DACB.org

**Interpretation: A Journal of Bible and Theology**, (Q.) Ecumenical, Co - Editors, James Brashler and Sam Balentine, 3401 Brook Rd., Richmond, VA 23227, Tel. (804)278-4296 Fax (804)278-4208

Email: email@interpretation.org
Website: www.interpretation.org

**el Intérprete**, (bi-M.) The United Methodist Church, Amanda M. Bachus, Director/Editor, Spanish Resources, United Methodist Communications, P.O. Box 320, Nashville, TN 37202-0320, Tel. (615)742-5113 Fax (615) 742-5460
Email: abachus@umcom.org
Website: www.interpretermagazine.org; www.noticias.umc.org

**Interpreter**, (6-Y.) United Methodist Church, Kathy Noble, United Methodist Communications, P.O. Box 320, Nashville, TN 37202-0320, Tel. (615)742-5441 Fax (615)742-5469
Email: knoble@umcom.org
Website: www.interpretermagazine.org

**IPHC Experience**, (bi-M.) International Pentecostal Holiness Church, Shirley Spencer, P.O. Box 12609, Oklahoma City, OK 73157, Tel. (405)787-7110 Fax (405)789-3957
Website: www.iphc.org/wms

**John Three Sixteen**, (Q.) Bible Holiness Church, Mary Cunningham, 10th St. & College Ave., Independence, KS 67301, Tel. (316)331-2580 Fax (316)331-2580

**Journal of Adventist Education**, (5-Y.) Seventh-day Adventist Church, Beverly J. Robinson-Rumble, 12501 Old Columbia Pike, Silver Spring, MD 20904-6600, Tel. (301)680-5075 / (301)680-5069 Fax (301)622-9627
Email: rumbleb@gc.adventist.org or goffc@gc.adventist.org
Website: education.gc.adventist.org/jae

**Journal of the American Academy of Religion**, (Q.) Nondenominational, Charles T. Mathews, Department of Religous Studies, University of Virginia, P.O. Box 400126, Charlottesville, VA 22904-4126
Email: jaar@virginia.edu
Website: www.aarweb.org

**Journal of Christian Education**, (Q.) African Methodist Episcopal Church, Kenneth H. Hill, 500 Eighth Ave., S., Nashville, TN 37203, Tel. (615)242-1420 Fax (615)726-1866
Email: ameced@edge.net
Website: www.ameced.com

**Journal of Ecumenical Studies**, (Q.) Interdenominational/Interfaith, Leonard Swidler, Temple Univ. (022-38), 1114 West Berks St.- Anderson #511, Philadelphia, PA 19122-6090, Tel. (215) 204-7714 Fax (215)204-4569
Email: nkrody@temple.edu
Website: ecumene.org/jes

**The Journal of Pastoral Care & Counseling,** (Q.) Nondenominational, Orlo Strunk, Jr., 1068 Harbor Dr., SW, Calabash, NC 28467, Tel. (910)579-5084 Fax (910)579-5084
Email: jpcp@jpcp.org
Website: www.jpcp.org

**Journal of Presbyterian History,** (bi-Y.) Presbyterian Church (U.S.A.), James H. Moorhead; Frederick J. Heuser, Jr., 425 Lombard St., Philadelphia, PA 19147, Tel. (215)627-1852 Fax (215)627-0509
Email: jph@history.pcusa.org
Website: www.history.pcusa.org

**Journal From the Radical Reformation,** (Q.) Church of God General Conference (Morrow, Ga.), Kent Ross and Anthony Buzzard, Sr. Editors, P.O. Box 100,000, Morrow, GA 30260-7000, Tel. (404)362-0052 Fax (404)362-9307
Email: info@abc-coggc.org
Website: www.abc-coggc.org

**Journal of Theology,** (Q.) Church of the Lutheran Confession, Prof. Steve Sippert, Immanuel Lutheran College, 501 Grover Rd., Eau Claire, WI 54701-7199, Tel. (715)832-9936 Fax (715)836-6634
Email: ilcgreekprof@yahoo.com
Website: www.clcpub/clc/clc.html

**The Joyful Noiseletter,** (10-Y.) Interdenominational, Cal Samra, P.O. Box 895, Portage, MI 49081-0895, Tel. (616)324-0990 Fax (616)324-3984
Email: joyfulnz@aol.com
Website: www.joyfulnoiseletter.com

**Judaism,** (Q.) Jewish (Sponsored by the American Jewish Conference), Rabbi Shammai Engelmayer, 15 E. 84th St., New York, NY 10028, Tel. (212)879-4500 Fax (212)249-3672
Email: judaism@ajcongress.org
Website: humwww.ucsc.edu/judaism/judaism.html

**Key Lay Notes,** (2-Y.) International Council of Community Churches, Phil Smith, 21116 Washington Pky., Frankfort, IL 60423-3112, Tel. (815)464-5690 Fax (815)464-5692
Email: iccc60423@aol.com
Website: icccusa.com

**The Lantern,** (bi-M.) National Baptist Convention of America, Inc., Robert Jeffrey, 1320 Pierre Avenue, Shreveport, LA 71103, Tel. (318)221-3701 Fax (318)222-7512

**Leadership: A Practical Journal for Church Leaders,** (Q.) Nondenominational, Marshall Shelley, 465 Gundersen Dr., Carol Stream, IL 60188, Tel. (630)260-6200 Fax (630)260-0114

Email: LJeditor@leadershipjournal.net
Website: www.Leadershipjournal.net

**Learning and Living,** (Q.) Netherlands Reformed Congregations, David Engelsma, 1000 Ball, Northeast, Grand Rapids, MI 49505, Tel. (616)458-4367 Fax (616)458-8532
Email: engelsma@plymouthchristian.put.k12.mi.us

**Liberty,** (bi-M.) Seventh-day Adventist Church, Clifford R. Goldstein, 12501 Old Columbia Pike, Silver Spring, MD 20904, Tel. (301)680-6691 Fax (301)680-6695

**Lifeglow, Large Print,** (6-Y) Seventh-day Adventist Church, Gaylena Gibson, Christian Record Services, Inc., P.O. Box 6097, Lincoln, NE 68506, Tel. (402)488-0981 Fax (402)488-7582
Email: editorial@christianrecord.org
Website: www.christianrecord.org

**Light and Life Magazine,** (bi-M.) Free Methodist Church, Douglas M. Newton, P.O. Box 535002, Indianapolis, IN 46253-5002, Tel. (317)244-3660
Email: llmeditor@fmcna.org
Website: www.freemethodistchurch.org

**Liguorian,** (10-Y.) The Catholic Church, William J. Parker, C.SS.R., 1 Liguori Dr., Liguori, MO 63057, Tel. (636)464-2500 Fax (636)464-8449
Email: liguorianeditor@liguori.org
Website: www.liguorian.org

**Listen,** (Sep.-May) Seventh-day Adventist Church, Céleste Walker, 55 W. Oak Ridge Dr., Hagerstown, MD 21740, Tel. (301)393-4082 Fax (301)393-4055
Email: listen@healthconnection.org
Website: www.listenmagazine.org

**Living Orthodoxy,** (bi-M.) The Russian Orthodox Church Outside of Russia, Fr. Gregory Williams, 1180 Orthodox Way, Liberty, TN 37095, Tel. (615)536-5239 Fax (615)536-5945
Email: info@sjkp.org
Website: www.sjkp.org

**The Long Island Catholic,** (W.) The Roman Catholic Church, Elizabeth O'Connor, P. O. Box 9000, 200 W. Centennial Ave. Suite 201, Roosevelt, NY 11575, Tel. (516)594-1000 Fax (516)594-1092
Website: www.licatholic.org

**The Lookout,** (W.) Christian Churches and Churches of Christ, Shawn McMullen, 8121 Hamilton Ave., Cincinnati, OH 45231, Tel. (513)931-4050 Fax (513)931-0950

Email: lookout@standardpub.com
Website: www.lookoutmag.com

**Lumicon Digital Productions**, (Internet) Independent, Protestant, Rev. Dr. Tom Boomershine, UMR Communications, P.O. Box 660275, Dallas, TX 75266-0275, Tel. (214)630-6495 Fax (214)630-0079
Email: tboom@umr.org
Website: www.lumicon.org

**The Lutheran**, (M.) Evangelical Lutheran Church in America, Daniel J. Lehmann, 8765 W. Higgins Rd., Chicago, IL 60631-4183, Tel. (773)380-2540 Fax (773)380-2751
Email: lutheran@elca.org
Website: www.thelutheran.org

**The Lutheran Ambassador**, (16-Y.) The Association of Free Lutheran Congregations, Craig Johnson, 575 34th Street, Astoria, OR 97103, Tel. (541)687-8643 Fax (541)683-8496
Email: cjohnson@efn.org

**The Lutheran Educator**, (Q.) Wisconsin Evangelical Lutheran Synod, Prof. Jack N. Minch, Martin Luther College, 1995 Luther Ct., New Ulm, MN 56073, Tel. (507)354-8221 Fax (507)354-8225
Email: lutheraneducator@mlc-wels.edu

**Lutheran Forum**, (Q.) Interdenominational Lutheran, Ronald B. Bagnall, 207 Hillcrest Ave., Trenton, NJ 08618, Tel. (856)696-0417

**The Lutheran Layman**, (bi-M.) The Lutheran Church—Missouri Synod, Gerald Perschbacher, 600 Mason Ridge Center Dr., St. Louis, MO 63142-8557, Tel. (314)317-4100 Fax (314)317-4295

**Lutheran Partners**, (bi-M.) Evangelical Lutheran Church in America, William A. Decker, 8765 W. Higgins Rd., Chicago, IL 60631-4101, Tel. (773)380-2884 Fax (773) 380-2829
Email: lutheran.partners@elca.org
Website: www.elca.org/lutheranpartners

**Lutheran Sentinel**, (M.) Evangelical Lutheran Synod, Theodore Gullixson, 105 Indian Ave., Forest City, IA 50436, Tel. (641)585-1683 Fax (641)585-1683
Email: elsentinel@wctatel.net

**Lutheran Spokesman**, (M.) Church of the Lutheran Confession, Rev. Paul Fleischer, 1741 E. 22nd St., Cheyenne, WY 82001, Tel. (307)638-8006
Email: paulgf@qwest.net
Website: www.lutheranspokeman.org

**Lutheran Synod Quarterly**, (Q.) Evangelical Lutheran Synod, G.R. Schmeling, Bethany Lutheran Theological Semi, 6 Browns Ct., Mankato, MN 56001, Tel. (507)344-7855 Fax (507)344-7426
Email: elsynod@blc.edu
Website: www.blts.edu

**The Lutheran Witness**, (M.) The Lutheran Church—Missouri Synod, Don Folkemer, 1333 S. Kirkwood Road, St. Louis, MO 63122-7295, Tel. (314)965-9000 Fax (314) 966-1126
Email: lutheran.witness@lcms.org
Website: www.lcms.org/witness

**Lutheran Woman Today**, (10-Y.) Evangelical Lutheran Church in America, Kate Sprutta Elliott, Women of the ELCA, 8765 W. Higgins Rd., Chicago, IL 60631-4101, Tel. (773)380-2730 Fax (773)380-2419
Email: lwt@elca.org
Website: www.elca.org/wo/lwthome.html

**Lyceum Spotlight**, (10-Y.) National Spiritualist Association of Churches, Rev. Cosie Allen, 1418 Hall St., Grand Rapids, MI 49506, Tel. (616)241-2761 Fax (616)241-4703
Email: cosie@dnx.net
Website: www.nsac.org/spotlight

**Magyar Egyhaz—Magyar Church**, (Q.) Hungarian Reformed Church in America, Stephen Szabo, 464 Forest Ave., Paramus, NJ 07652, Tel. (201)262-2338 Fax (845)359-5771

**Mar Thoma Messenger**, (Q.) Mar Thoma Syrian Church of India, Eapen Daniel, 2320 S. Merrick Ave., Merrick, NY 11566, Tel. (516) 377-3311 Fax (516)377-3322
Email: marthoma@aol.com

**Maranatha**, (Q.) Advent Christian Church, John Roller, P.O. Box 23152, Charlotte, NC 28227, Tel. (704)545-6161 Fax (704)573-0712
Email: jroller@acgc.us
Website: www.acgc.us

**Marriage Partnership**, (Q.) Nondenominational, Ginger Kolbaba, Managing Editor, 465 Gundersen Dr., Carol Stream, IL 60188, Tel. (630)260-6200 Fax (630)260-0114
Email: mp@marriagepartnership.com
Website: www.marriagepartnership.com

**Mature Years**, (Q.) The United Methodist Church, Marvin W. Cropsey, 201 Eighth Ave. S, Nashville, TN 37202, Tel. (615)749-6292 Fax (615)749-6512
Email: matureyears@umpublishing.org

**The Mennonite**, (24-Y.) Mennonite Church U.S.A., Everett J. Thomas, 1700 S. Main St., Goshen, IN 46526, Tel. (574)535-6051 Fax (574)535-6050

Email: editor@themennonite.org
Website: www.themennonite.org

**Mennonite Historical Bulletin**, (Q.) Mennonite Church U.S.A., Susan Fisher Miller, 1700 South Main St., Goshen, IN 46526, Tel. (574)535-7477 Fax (574)535-7756
Email: archives@goshen.edu
Website: www.MennoniteUSA.org/history

**Mennonite Quarterly Review**, (Q.) Mennonite Church, John D. Roth, 1700 S. Main St., Goshen, IN 46526, Tel. (574)535-7433 Fax (574)535-7438
Email: MQR@goshen.edu
Website: www.goshen.edu/mgr

**Message**, (bi-M.) Seventh-day Adventist Church, Dr. Ron C. Smith, Review and Herald Publishing Association, 55 West Oak Ridge Dr., Hagerstown, MD 21740, Tel. (301)393-4099 Fax (301)393-4103
Email: pharris@rhpa.org or ronsmith@rhpa.org
Website: www.messagemagazine.org

**Message of the Open Bible**, (bi-M.) Open Bible Standard Churches, Inc., Andrea Johnson, 2020 Bell Ave., Des Moines, IA 50315-1096, Tel. (515)288-6761 Fax (515)288-2510
Email: message@openbible.org
Website: www.openbible.org

**The Messenger**, (M.) Pentecostal Free Will Baptist Church, Inc., Patte Levan, P.O. Box 1568, Dunn, NC 28335, Tel. (910)892-4161 Fax (910)892-6876
Email: messengerpwl@ixpres.com

**The Messenger**, (M.) The Swedenborgian Church, Patte LeVan, Central Office, 11 Higland Ave, Newton Ville, Julian, MA 02460, Tel. (760)765-2915
Email: messengerpwl@ixpres.com
Website: www.swedenborg.org

**Messenger**, (11-Y.) Church of the Brethren, Walt Wiltschek, 1451 Dundee Ave., Elgin, IL 60120, Tel. (847)742-5100 Fax (847)742-1407
Email: messenger@brethren.org

**Messenger of Truth**, (bi-W.) Church of God in Christ (Mennonite), Gladwin Koehn, P.O. Box 230, Moundridge, KS 67107, Tel. (620)345-2532 Fax (620)345-2582
Email: gospelpublishers@cogicm.org

**Methodist History**, (Q.) The United Methodist Church, Charles Yrigoyen, Jr., P.O. Box 127, Madison, NJ 07940, Tel. (973)408-3189 Fax (973)408-3909
Email: cyrigoyen@gcah.org
Website: www.gcah.org

**Ministry**, (M.) Seventh-day Adventist Church, Willmore D. Eva, 12501 Old Columbia Pike, Silver Spring, MD 20904, Tel. (301)680-6510 Fax (301)680-6502
Email: 74532.2425@compuserve.com

**Mission, Adult, and Youth Children's Editions**, (Q.) Seventh-day Adventist Church, Charlotte Ishkanian, 12501 Old Columbia Pike, Silver Spring, MD 20904, Tel. (301)680-6167 Fax (301)680-6155
Email: 74532.2435@compuserve.com

**Mission Connection**, (Q.) Wisconsin Evangelical Lutheran Synod, Rev. Gary Baumler, 2929 N. Mayfair Rd., Milwaukee, WI 53222, Tel. (414)256-3210 Fax (414)256-3862
Email: mc@sab.wels.net

**Mission Herald**, (Q.) National Baptist Convention, U.S.A., Inc., Dr. Bruce N. Alick, 701 S. 19th Street, Philadelphia, PA 19146, Tel. (215)735-9853 Fax (215)735-1721

**Missionary Church Today**, (Q.) Missionary Church, Rev. Thomas Murphy, P.O. Box 9127, Ft. Wayne, IN 46899, Tel. (260)747-2027 Fax (260)747-5331
Email: tommurphy@mcusa.org
Website: www.mcusa.org

**The Missionary Messenger**, (bi-M.) Cumberland Presbyterian Church, Michael G. Sharpe, 1978 Union Ave., Memphis, TN 38104, Tel. (901)276-9988 Fax (901)276-4578
Email: messenger@cumberland.org
Website: www.cumberland.org/bom/Communication_and_Publication_Unit/Missionary Messenger. htm

**The Missionary Messenger**, (bi-M.) Christian Methodist Episcopal Church, Doris F. Boyd, 213 Viking Dr., W., Cordova, TN 38018, Tel. (901)757-1103 Fax (901)751-2104
Email: doris.boyd@williams.com

**Missionary Seer**, (bi-M.) African Methodist Episcopal Zion Church, Rev. Kermit J. DeGraffenreidt, 475 Riverside Dr., Rm. 1935, New York, NY 10115, Tel. (212)870-2952 Fax (212)870-2808
Email: domkd5@aol.com

**The Missionary Signal**, (bi-M.) Churches of God, General Conference, Rachel Foreman, P.O. Box 926, Findlay, OH 45839, Tel. (419)424-1961 Fax (419)424-3433
Email: communications@cggc.org
Website: www.cggc.org

**The Moravian**, (10-Y.) Moravian Church in North America (Unitas Fratrum), Deanna L. Hollenbach, Dir. Of Communication, Interprovincial Bd. Of Communication, 1021

Center St., P.O. Box 1245, Bethlehem, PA 18016, Tel. (610)867-0593/800-732-0591 Fax (610)866-9223
Email: pubs@mcnp.org
Website: www.moravian.org

**The Mother Church**, (bi-M.) Western Diocese of the Armenian Church of North America, Archpriest Fr. Sipan Mekhsian, 3325 N. Glenoaks Blvd., Burbank, CA 91504, Tel. (818)558-7474 Fax (818)558-6333
Email: mgizlechyan@armenianchurchwd.com
Website: www.armenianchurchwd.com

**Multiply**, (Q.) Presbyterian Church in America, Fred Marsh, Mission to North America, 1700 North Brown Road, Ste. 101, Lawrenceville, GA 30044, Tel. (678)825-1200 Fax (678)825-1201
Email: mna@pcanet.org
Website: www.pca-mna.org

**NABtoday for you**, (Q.) North American Baptist Conference, Lucinda Armas, 1 So. 210 Summit Ave., Oakbrook Terrace, IL 60181, Tel. (630) 495-2000 Fax (630)495-3301
Email: serve@nabconference.org
Website: www.nabconference.org

**NAE Leadership Alert**, (bi-M.) Interdenominational, Rev. Richard Cizik, 701 G St SW, WASHINGTON, DC 20024, Tel. (202)789-1011 Fax (202)842-0392
Email: rcizike@nae.net

**NAE Washington Insight**, (M.) Interdenominational, Rev. Richard Cizik, 718 Capitol Square Place, SW, Washington, DC 20024, Tel. (202) 789-1011
Email: rcizik@aol.com
Website: www.nae.net

**National Catholic Reporter**, (44-Y.) The Catholic Church, Tom Roberts, P.O. Box 419281, Kansas City, MO 64141, Tel. (816) 531-0538 Fax (816)968-2280
Email: editor@natcath.org
Website: www.NCRonline.org

**The National Spiritualist Summit**, (M.) National Spiritualist Association of Churches, Rev. Sandra Pfortmiller, 3521 W. Topeka Dr., Glendale, AZ 85308-2325, Tel. (623)581-6686 Fax (623)581-5544
Email: G2s2pfort@aol.com
Website: www.nsac.org

**Network**, (Q.) Presbyterian Church in America, Susan Fikse, 1600 North Brown Road, Lawrenceville, GA 30047, Tel. (678)823-0004 Fax (678)823-0027
Website: www.pca.org

**New Church Life**, (M.) General Church of the New Jerusalem, Rev. Donald L. Rose, P.O. Box 277, Bryn Athyn, PA 19009, Tel. (215)947-6225 x 209 Fax (215)938-1871
Email: DonR@BACS-GC.org
Website: www.newchurch.org

**New Horizons in the Orthodox Presbyterian Church**, (11-Y.) The Orthodox Presbyterian Church, Danny E. Olinger, 607 N. Easton Rd., Bldg. E, P.O. Box P, Willow Grove, PA 19090-0920, Tel. (215)830-0900 Fax (215)830-0350
Email: olinger.1@opc.org
Website: www.opc.org

**New Oxford Review**, (11-Y.) The Catholic Church, Dale Vree, 1069 Kains Ave., Berkeley, CA 94706, Tel. (510)526-5374 Fax (510)526-3492
Website: www.newoxfordreview.org

**New World Outlook**, (bi-M.) Mission Magazine of The United Methodist Church, Christie R. House, 475 Riverside Dr., Rm. 1476, New York, NY 10115, Tel. (212)870-3765 Fax (212)870-3654
Email: NWO@gbgm-umc.org
Website: gbgm-umc.org/now

**Newscope**, (W.) The United Methodist Church, Andrew J. Schleicher, P.O. Box 801, Nashville, TN 37202, Tel. (615)749-6320 Fax (615)749-6512
Email: umnewscope@umpublishing.org
Website: www.umph.org

**Newsline**, (Internet; Bi-W.) Church of the Brethren, Cheryl Brumbaugh-Cayford, 1451 Dundee Ave., Elgin, IL 60120-1694, Tel. (847) 742-5100 (800)323-8039 Fax (847)742-6103
Email: cbrumbaugh-cayford_gb@brethren.org
Website: http://www.brethren.org/genbd/news line/index.htm

**The North American Catholic**, (M.) North American Old Roman Catholic Church, Theodore J. Remalt, 4154 W. Berteau Ave, Chicago, IL 60641, Tel. (312)685-0461 Fax (312)485-0461
Email: chapelhall@aol.com

**The North American Challenge**, (M.) Home Missions Division of The United Pentecostal Church International, Joseph Fiorino, 8855 Dunn Rd., Hazelwood, MO 63042-2299, Tel. (314)837-7300 Fax (314)837-5632

**NRB Magazine**, (9-Y.) Nondenominational, Christine Pryor, National Religious Broadcasters, 9510 Technology Drive, Manassas, VA 20110, Tel. (703)330-7000 Fax (703)330-6996
Email: cpryor@nrb.org
Website: www.nrb.org

**On Course**, (bi-M.) Assemblies of God, Kristi Arnold and Amber Weigand-Buckley (Interim co-editors), 1445 N. Boonville Ave., Springfield, MO 65802-1894, Tel. (417)862-2781 Fax (417)862-1693
Email: oncourse@ag.org
Website: oncourse.ag.org

**On the Line**, (M.) Mennonite Church, Mary C. Meyer, 616 Walnut Ave., Scottdale, PA 15683, Tel. (724)887-8500 Fax (724)887-3111
Email: otl@mph.org
Website: www.mph.org/otl

**On Mission**, (Q.) Southern Baptist Convention, Carol Pipes, 4200 North Point Pkwy., Alphretta, GA 30202-4174, Tel. (770)410-6394 Fax (770)410-6105
Website: www.onmission.com

**ONE Magazine**, (bi-M.) National Association of Free Will Baptists, Eric Thomsen, P.O. Box 5002, Antioch, TN 37011-5002, Tel. (615)731-6812 Fax (615)731-0771
Email: eric@nafwb.org
Website: http://www.onemag.org/plymouth_rock.htm

**OnSite**, (Q.) United Pentecostal Church International, Bryan Abernathy, 8855 Dunn Rd., Hazelwood, MO 63042, Tel. (314)837-7300 Fax (314)837-2387
Email: fmmail@upci.org
Website: www.foreignmissions.com

**Orthodox America**, (8-Y.) The Russian Orthodox Church Outside of Russia, Mary Mansur, P.O. Box 383, Richfield Springs, NY 13439-0383, Tel. (315)858-1518
Email: info@orthodoxamerica.org
Website: www.orthodoxamerica.org

**The Orthodox Church**, (M.) The Orthodox Church in America, Very Rev. John Matusiak, Managing Editor; Very Rev. Leonid Kishkovsky, Editor, Editorial Office, One Wheaton Center #912, Wheaton, IL 60187, Tel. (630)668-3071 Fax (630)668-5712
Email: tocmed@hotmail.com
Website: www.oca.org

**Orthodox Family**, (Q.) The Russian Orthodox Church Outside of Russia, George Johnson and Deborah Johnson, P.O. Box 45, Beltsville, MD 20705, Tel. Fax (301)890-3552
Email: 1lew@cais.com
Website: www.roca.org/orthodox

**Orthodox Life**, (bi-M.) The Russian Orthodox Church Outside of Russia, Fr. Luke, Holy Trinity Monastery, P.O Box 36, Jordanville, NY 13361-0036, Tel. (315)858-0940 Fax (315)858-0505
Email: 72204.1465@compuserve.com

**The Orthodox Observer**, (M.) Greek Orthodox Archdiocese of America, Stavros H. Papagermanos, 8 E. 79th St., New York, NY 10021, Tel. (212)570-3555 Fax (212)774-0239
Email: observer@goarch.org
Website: www.observer.goarch.org

**Orthodox Russia (English translation of Pravoslavnaya Rus)**, (24-Y.) The Russian Orthodox Church Outside of Russia, Archbishop Laurus, Holy Trinity Monastery, P.O. Box 36, Jordanville, NY 13361-0036, Tel. (315)858-0940 Fax (315)858-0505
Email: orthrus@telenet.net

**Our Daily Bread**, (M.) The Swedenborgian Church, Lee Woofenden, P.O. Box 396, Bridgewater, MA 02324, Tel. (508)946-1767 Fax (508)946-1757
Email: odb@swedenborg.org
Website: www.swedenborg.org/odb/index.cfm

**Our Little Friend**, (W.) Seventh-day Adventist Church, Aileen Andres Sox, P.O. Box 5353, Nampa, ID 83653-5353, Tel. (208)465-2500 Fax (208)465-2531
Email: ailsox@pacificpress.com
Website: www.pacificpress.com

**Our Sunday Visitor**, (W.) The Catholic Church, Gerald Korson, 200 Noll Plaza, Huntington, IN 46750, Tel. (219)356-8400
Email: oursunvis@osv.com
Website: www.osv.com

**Outreach**, (6-Y.) Armenian Apostolic Church of America, Iris Papazian, 138 E. 39th St., New York, NY 10016, Tel. (212)689-7810 Fax (212)689-7168
Email: info@armenianprelacy.org
Website: www.armenianprelacy.org

**The Path of Orthodoxy (Serbian)**, (M.) Serbian Orthodox Church in the U.S.A. and Canada, V. Rev. Nedeljko Lunich, 300 Striker Ave., Joliet, IL 60436, Tel. (815)741-1023 Fax (815)741-1883
Email: nedlunich300@comcast.net

**Paul**, (Q.) Netherlands Reformed Congregations, J. Spans, 47 Main Street E., Norwich, ON N0J 1PO, Tel. (519)863-3306 Fax (519)863-2793

**Today's Pentecostal Evangel**, (W.) Assemblies of God, Hal Donaldson, Gospel Publishing House, 1445 N. Boonville Ave., Springfield, MO 65802-1894, Tel. (417)862-2781 Fax (417)862-0416
Email: tpe@ag.org
Website: www.tpe.ag.org

**Pentecostal Evangel, Missions World Edition**, (M.) Assemblies of God, Hal Donaldson,

Editor in Chief, Gospel Publishing House, 1445 N. Boonville Ave., Springfield, MO 65802, Tel. (417)862-2781 Fax (417)862-0416
Email: pe@ag.org
Website: www.pe.ag.org

**The Pentecostal Herald**, (M.) United Pentecostal Church International, Rev. J. L. Hall, 8855 Dunn Rd., Hazelwood, MO 63042, Tel. (314)837-7300 Fax (314)837-4503

**Pentecostal Leader**, (bi-M.) The International Pentecostal Church of Christ, Clyde M. Hughes, P.O. Box 439, London, OH 43140, Tel. (740)852-4722 Fax (740)852-0348
Email: hqipcc@aol.com
Website: www.IPCC.CC

**The Pentecostal Messenger**, (M.) Pentecostal Church of God (Joplin, Mo.), John Mallinak, P.O. Box 850, Joplin, MO 64802, Tel. (417) 624-7050 Fax (417)624-7102
Email: johnm@pcg.org
Website: www.pcg.org

**Perspectives**, (10-Y.) Reformed Church in America, James Bratt, David E. Timmer, Scott Hoezee (co-editors), P.O. Box 1196, Holland, MI 49422-1196, Tel. (616)392-8555 x 131 Fax (616)392-7717
Email: perspectives_@rca.org
Website: www.perspectivesjournal.org

**Perspectives on Science and Christian Faith**, (Q.) Nondenominational, Dr. Roman J. Miller, 4956 Singers Glen Rd., Harrisonburg, VA 22802, Tel. (540)432-4412 Fax (540)432-4488
Email: millerrj@rica.net
Website: www.asa3.org

**The Pilot—America's Oldest Catholic Newspaper**, (49-Y.) The Catholic Archdiocese of Boston, Antonio Enrique, 2121 Commonwealth Ave., Brighton, MA 02135, Tel. (617)746-5889 Fax (617)783-2684
Email: editorial@bostonpilot.org
Website: www.rcab.org

**Pockets**, (11-Y.) The United Methodist Church, Lynn W. Gilliam, P.O. Box 340004, Nashville, TN 37203-0004, Tel. (615)340-7333 Fax (615)340-7267
Email: pockets@upperroom.org
Website: www.pockets.org

**Polka**, (Q.) Polish National Catholic Church of America, Cecelia Lallo, 1127 Frieda St., Dickson City, PA 18519-1304, Tel. (570)489-4364 Fax (570)346-2188

**Pravoslavnaya Rus (Russian)**, (24-Y.) The Russian Orthodox Church Outside of Russia, Archbishop Laurus, Holy Trinity Monastery,

P.O. Box 36, Jordanville, NY 13361-0036, Tel. (315)858-0940 Fax (315)858-0505
Email: orthrus@telenet.net

**Pravoslavnaya Zhisn (Monthly Supplement to Pravoslavnaya Rus)**, (M.) The Russian Orthodox Church Outside of Russia, Archbishop Laurus, Holy Trinity Monastery, P.O. Box 36, Jordanville, NY 13361-0036, Tel. (315)858-0940 Fax (315)858-0505
Email: Orthrus@telenet.net

**Preacher's Magazine**, (3-Y.) Church of the Nazarene, Jeren Rowell and David Busic, 6401 Paseo Blvd, Kansas City, MO 64131-1213
Website: www.nph.com/nphweb/html/pmol/index.htm

**Presbyterian News Service "The News"**, (bi-M.) Presbyterian Church (U.S.A.), Jerry L. VanMarter, 100 Witherspoon St., Rm. 5418, Louisville, KY 40202, Tel. (502)569-5493 Fax (502)569-8073
Email: JVanMart@ctr.pcusa.org
Website: www.pcusa.org/pcnews

**Presbyterian Outlook**, (43-Y.) Presbyterian Church (U.S.A.), Robert H. Bullock, Jr., P.O. Box 85623, Richmond, VA 23285-5623, Tel. (804)359-8442 Fax (804)353-6369
Email: rbullock@pres-outlook.com
Website: www.pres-outlook.com

**Presbyterians Today**, (10-Y.) Presbyterian Church (U.S.A.), Eva Stimson, 100 Witherspoon St., Louisville, KY 40202-1396, Tel. (502)569-5637 Fax (502)569-8632
Email: today@pcusa.org
Website: www.pcusa.org/today

**Primary Source**, (Q.) American Baptist Historical Society, Deborah Van Broekhoven, P.O. Box 851, Valley Forge, PA 19482-0851, Tel. Fax (610)768-2266
Email: dbvanbro@abc-usa.org
Website: www.abc-usa.org/abhs

**Primary Treasure**, (W.) Seventh-day Adventist Church, Aileen Andres Sox, P.O. Box 5353, Nampa, ID 83653-5353, Tel. (208)465-2500 Fax (208)465-2531
Email: ailsox@pacificpress.com
Website: www.pacificpress.com

**Priority**, (M.) Missionary Church, Dr. Thomas Murphy, P.O. Box 9127, Ft. Wayne, IN 46899, Tel. (260)747-2027 Fax (260)747-5331
Email: mcdenomusa@aol.com
Website: mcusa.org

**Pulse**, (M.) The Church of God (Seventh Day), Denver, Colo., Jamie Stroupe, P.O. Box

33677, 330 W. 152nd Ave., Denver, CO 80233, Tel. (303)452-7973 Fax (303)452-0657
Email: offices@cog7.org
Website: cog7.org

**Purpose**, (M. in weekly parts) Mennonite Church Canada and Mennonite Church U.S.A., James E. Horsch, 616 Walnut Ave., Scottdale, PA 15683, Tel. (724)887-8500 Fax (724)887-3111
Email: horsch@mph.org
Website: www.mph.org

**PYM News**, (5-Y.) Philadelphia Yearly Meeting of the Religious Society of Friends, Allen R. Reeder, 1515 Cherry St., Philadelphia, PA 19102-1479, Tel. (215)241-7000 Fax (215) 241-7045
Email: news@pym.org
Website: www.pym.org

**Quaker Life**, (6-Y.) Friends United Meeting, Patricia Edwards-Konic, 101 Quaker Hill Dr., Richmond, IN 47374-1980, Tel. (765)962-7573 Fax (765)966-1293
Email: QuakerLife@fum.org
Website: www.fum.org

**Quarterly Review**, A.M.E. Zion, (Q.) African Methodist Episcopal Zion Church, Rev. James D. Armstrong, P.O. Box 33247, Charlotte, NC 28233, Tel. (704)599-4630 Fax (704)688-2544
Email: jaarmstrong@amezhqtr.org

**Reflections**, (bi-M.) United Pentecostal Church International, Melissa Anderson, 8855 Dunn Rd., Hazelwood, MO 63042, Tel. (918)371-2659 Fax (918)371-6320
Email: manderson@tums.org
Website: www.upci.org/ladies

**Reformed Worship**, (Q.) Christian Reformed Chuch in North America, Rev. Joyce Borger, 2850 Kalamazoo Ave. SE, Grand Rapids, MI 49560-0001, Tel. (800)777-7270 Fax (616) 224-0834
Email: info@reformedworship.org
Website: www.reformedworship.org

**Rejoice!**, (Q.) Mennonite Church, Byron Rempel-Burkholder, 600 Shaftesbury Blvd., Winnipeg, MB R3P 0M4, Tel. (204)888-6781 Fax (204)831-5675
Email: byronrb@mph.org
Website: www.mph.org/rejoice

**Report From The Capital**, (10-Y.) Baptist Joint Committee, Jeff Huett, 200 Maryland Ave. NE, Washington, DC 20002-5797, Tel. (202) 544-4226 Fax (202)544-2094
Email: jhuett@bjconline.org
Website: www.bjconline.org

**Reporter**, (M.) The Lutheran Church—Missouri Synod, Joe Isenhower Jr., Managing Editor, 1333 S. Kirkwood Rd., St. Louis, MO 63122-7295, Tel. (314)996-9000 Fax (314)966-1126
Email: vicki.biggs@lcms.org
Website: vicki.biggs@lcms.org

**Reporter Interactive**, (D.) Independent, Protestant, Cynthia B. Astle, UMR Communications, P.O. Box 660275, Dallas, TX 75266-0275, Tel. (214)630-6495 Fax (214)630-0079
Email: news@umr.org
Website: www.lumicon.org

**The Rescue Herald**, (3-Y.) American Rescue Workers, Rev. Col. Robert N. Coles, National Field Office, 1209 Hamilton Blvd., Hagerstown, MD 21742, Tel. (301)797-0061 Fax (301)797-1480
Email: chiefcoles@aol.com
Website: www.arwus.com

**Response**, (M.) The United Methodist Church, Dana Jones, 475 Riverside Dr., Room 1356, New York, NY 10115, Tel. (212)870-3755 Fax (212)870-3940

**The Restitution Herald and Church of God Progress Journal**, (bi-M.) Church of God General Conference (Oregon, Ill. & Morrow Ga.), Tim Jones, P.O. Box 100,000, Morrow, GA 30260, Tel. (504)362-0052 Fax (404)362-9307
Email: info@abc-coggc.org
Website: www.abc-coggc.org

**Restoration Herald**, (M.) Christian Churches and Churches of Christ, H. Lee Mason, 7133 Central Parks Blvd., Mason, OH 45040, Tel. (513)229-8000 Fax (513)229-8003
Email: thecra@aol.com
Website: www.thecra.org

**Restoration Quarterly**, (Q.) Churches of Christ, James W. Thompson, P.O. Box 28227, Abilene, TX 79699-8227, Tel. (915)674-3781 Fax (915)674-3776
Email: rq@bible.acu.edu
Website: www.rq.acu.edu

**Review for Religious**, (Q.) The Catholic Church, David L. Fleming, S.J., 3601 Lindell Blvd., St. Louis, MO 63108, Tel. (314)663-4160 Fax (314)633-4611
Email: review@slu.edu
Website: www.reviewforreligious.org

**Review of Religious Research**, (Q.) Nondenominational, Patricia Wittberg, Sociology Department, Indiana University Purdue University, Indianapolis, IN 46202, Tel. (317)274-4478 Fax (317)278-3654
Email: pwittber@iupui.edu
Website: www.rra.hartsem.edu

340

**Road to Emmaus**, (Q.) Orthodox Christian, Nun Nectaria, 1516 N. Delaware, Indianapolis, IN 46202, Tel. (317)631-1344 Fax (317)637-1897 Email: csb@indy.net
Website: www.roadtoemmaus.net

**Rocky Mountain Christian**, (M.) Churches of Christ, Ron L. Carter, P.O. Box 26620, Colorado Springs, CO 80936, Tel. (719)598-4197 Fax (719)528-1549
Email: 76102.2461@compuserve.com

**Sabbath Recorder**, (M.) Seventh Day Baptist General Conference, U.S.A. and Canada, Rev. Kevin J. Butler, 3120 Kennedy Rd., P.O. Box 1678, Janesville, WI 53547, Tel. (608)752-5055 Fax (608)752-7711
Email: sdbmedia@charter.net
Website: www.seventhdaybaptist.org

**Sabbath School Leadership**, (M.) Seventh-day Adventist Church, Faith Crumbly, Review and Herald Publishing Assoc., 55 W. Oak Ridge Dr., Hagerstown, MD 21740, Tel. (301)393-4090 Fax (301)393-4055
Email: sabbathschoolleadership@rhpa.org
Website: www.rhpa.org

**Saint Anthony Messenger**, (M.) The Catholic Church, Fr. Pat McCloskey, O.F.M., St. Anthony Messenger Editorial, Dept., 28 W. Liberty St., Cincinnati, OH 45202, Tel. (513) 241-5615 Fax (513)241-0399
Email: StAnthony@AmericanCatholic.org
Website: www.AmericanCatholic.org

**Saint Willibrord Journal**, (Q.) Christ Catholic Church, The Rev. Monsignor Charles E. Harrison, P.O. Box 217151, Houston, TX 77277-1751, Tel. (713)515-8206 Fax (713)622-5311
Website: www.christcatholic.org

**Saints Herald**, (M.) Community of Christ, Linda Booth, The Herald Publishing House, P.O. Box 390, Independence, MO 64051-0390, Tel. (816)521-3015 Fax (816)521-3066
Email: Herald@CofChrist.org
Website: www.heraldhouse.org

**SBC Life**, (10-Y.) Southern Baptist Convention, John Revell, Executive Editor; Kenyn Cureton, V.P. for Convention Relations, 901 Commerce St., Nashville, TN 37203, Tel. (615)244-2355 Fax (615)782-8684
Email: jrevell@sbc.net
Website: sbc.net

**The Schwenkfeldian**, (3-Y.) The Schwenkfelder Church, Gerald Heebner, 105 Seminary Street, Pennsburg, PA 18073, Tel. (215)679-3103 Fax (215)679-8175
Email: info@schwenfelder.com
Website: www.schwenkfelder.com

**Searching Together**, (Q.) Sovereign Grace Believers, Jon Zens, P.O. Box 548, St. Croix Falls, WI 54024, Tel. (651)465-6516 Fax (651)465-5101
Email: jzens@searchingtogether.org
Website: www.searchingtogether.org

**The Secret Place**, (Q.) American Baptist Churches U.S.A., Kathleen Hayes, Senior Editor, P.O. Box 851, Valley Forge, PA 19482-0851, Tel. (610)768-2434 Fax (610)768-2441
Email: thesecretplace@abc-usa.org
Website: www.judsonpress.com

**Seeds for the Parish**, (bi-M.) Evangelical Lutheran Church in America, Janice Rizzo, 8765 W. Higgins Rd., Chicago, IL 60631, Tel. (773)380-2949 Fax (773)380-2406
Email: Janice.Rizzo@elca.org
Website: www.elca.org/seeds

**Shalom!**, (Q.) Brethren in Christ Church, Harriet Bicksler, P.O. Box A, Grantham, PA 17027, Tel. (717)697-2634
Email: bickhouse@aol.com
Website: bic-church.org/shalom

**Shiloh's Messenger of Wisdom**, (M.) Israelite House of David, William Robertson, P.O. Box 1067, Benton Harbor, MI 49023

**The Shofar**, Apostolic Catholic Church, Myra Calahan, 7813 N. Nebraska Ave., Tampa, FL 33604, Tel. (813)238-6060
Email: Bishop-Chuck@apostoliccatholicchurch.com
Website: www.ApostolicCatholicChurch.com

**Signs of the Times**, (M.) Seventh-day Adventist Church, Marvin Moore, P.O. Box 5353, Nampa, ID 83653-5353, Tel. (208)465-2577 Fax (208)465-2531
Website: www.signstimes.com

**The Silver Lining**, (M.) Apostolic Christian Churches of America, Bruce Leman, R.R. 2, P.O. Box 50, Roanoke, IL 61561-9625, Tel. (309)923-7777 Fax (309)923-7359

**Social Questions Bulletin**, (bi-M.) The United Methodist Church, Rev. Kathryn J. Johnson, 212 East Capitol St., NE, Washington, DC 20003, Tel. (202)546-8806 Fax (202)546-6811
Email: mfsa@mfsaweb.org
Website: www.mfsaweb.org

**Sojourners**, (M.) Ecumenical, Jim Wallis, 3333 14th Street NW, Suite 200, Washington, DC 20010, Tel. (202)328-8842 Fax (202)328-8757
Email: sojourners@sojo.net
Website: www.sojo.net

**Solia Calendar**, (Y.) The Romanian Orthodox Episcopate of America, The Department of

Publications of the Romanian Orthodox Episcopate of America, P.O. Box 185, Grass Lake, MI 49240-0185, Tel. (517)522-4800 Fax (517)522-5907
Email: solia@roea.org
Website: www.roea.org

**Solia—The Herald**, (M.) The Romanian Orthodox Episcopate of America, Rev. Archdeacon David Oancea, P.O. Box 185, Grass Lake, MI 49240-0185, Tel. (517)522-3656 Fax (517)522-5907
Email: solia@roea.org
Website: www.roea.org

**Sound of Grace**, (Q.) Sovereign Grace Believers, 5317 Wye Creek Dr, Frederick, MD 21703-6938

**The Southern Methodist**, (bi-M.) Southern Methodist Church, Thomas M. Owens, Sr., P.O. Box 39, Orangeburg, SC 29116-0039, Tel. (803)534-9853 Fax (803)535-3881
Email: foundry@bellsouth.net

**Spirit**, (Q.) Volunteers of America, Arthur Smith and Denis N. Baker, 1809 Carrollton Ave, New Orleans, LA 70118-2829, Tel. (504)897-1731

**The Spiritual Sword**, (Q.) Churches of Christ, Alan E. Highers, 1511 Getwell Rd., Memphis, TN 38111, Tel. (901)743-0464 Fax (901)743-2197
Email: getwellcc@aol.com
Website: www.getwellchurchofchrist.org

**The Standard Bearer**, (21-Y.) Protestant Reformed Churches in America, Russell J. Dykstra, 4949 Ivanrest Ave. SW, Grandville, MI 49418, Tel. (616)531-1490 Fax (616)531-3033
Email: dykstra@prca.org
Website: www.rfpa.org/sb.asp

**The Star of Zion**, (bi-W.) African Methodist Episcopal Zion Church, Mr. Mike Lisby, P.O. Box 26770, Charlotte, NC 28221-6770, Tel. (704)599-4630 x 318 Fax (704)688-2546
Email: service@starofzion.org
Website: www.starofzion.org

**Story Friends**, (24-Y.) Mennonite Church, Rose Mary Stutzman, 616 Walnut Ave., Scottdale, PA 15683, Tel. (574)887-8500 Fax (574)887-3111
Email: editor@themennonite.org
Website: www.themennonite.org

**The Student (Braille & Cassette)**, (M.) Seventh-day Adventist Church, Bert Williams, P.O. Box 6097, Lincoln, NE 68506-0097, Tel. (402)488-0981 Fax (402)488-7582

Email: info@christianrecord.org
Website: www.ChristianRecord.org

**Sunday**, (Q.) Interdenominational, Timothy A. Norton, 2930 Flowers Rd., S., Atlanta, GA 30341-5532, Tel. (770)936-5376 Fax (770)936-5385
Email: tnorton@ldausa.org
Website: www.sundayonline.org

**The Tablet**, (W.) The Catholic Church, Ed Wilkinson, 310 Prospect Park West, Brooklyn, NY 11215, Tel. (718)965-7333 Fax (718)965-7337
Email: TheTablet@aol.com
Website: http://www.dioceseofbrooklyn.org/tablet/contact/index.html

**Theology Digest**, (Q.) The Catholic Church, Bernhard Asen, Rosemary Jermann (co-editors), 3800 Lindell Blvd., St. Louis, MO 63108, Tel. (314)977-3410 Fax (314)977-3704
Email: thdigest@slu.edu

**Theology Today**, (Q.) Nondenominational, James F. Kay, Reviews Editor: Gordon S. Mikoski, P.O. Box 821, Princeton, NJ 08542-0803, Tel. (609)497-7714 Fax (609)497-1826
Email: theology.today@ptsem.edu
Website: theologytoday.ptsem.edu

**These Days**, (Q.) Interdenominational, Vince Patton, 100 Witherspoon St., Louisville, KY 40202-1396, Tel. (502)569-5080 Fax (502)569-5113
Website: www.ppcpub.com

**The Three-Fold Vision**, (M.) Apostolic Faith Mission Church of God, Alice Walker, 156 Walker Street, Munford, AL 36268, Tel. (256)358-9763
Email: alicemtwalker@aol.com

**Timbrel: The Publication for Mennonite Women The**, (bi-M.) Mennonite Church Canada and U.S.A., Laurie Oswald Robinson, 420 SE Richland Ave., Corvallis, Newton, OR 97333, Tel. (316)283-5100
Email: timbrel@mennonitewomenUSA.org
Website: www.mennonitewomenusa.org

**Today's Christian**, (bi-M.) Nondenominational, Ed Gilbreath, 465 Gundersen Dr., Carol Stream, IL 60188, Tel. (630)260-6200 Fax (630)480-2004
Email: tceditor@todays-christian.com
Website: www.todays-christian.com

**Today's Christian Woman**, (bi-M.) Nondenominational, Jane Johnson Struck, 465 Gundersen Dr., Carol Stream, IL 60188, Tel. (630)260-6200 Fax (630)260-0114
Email: TCWedit@christianitytoday.com
Website: www.todayschristianwoman.com

**Tomorrow Magazine**, (Q.) American Baptist Churches in the U.S.A., Sara E. Hopkins, 475 Riverside Dr., Room 1700, New York, NY 10115-0049, Tel. (800)986-6222 Fax (800) 986-6782

**The Tover of St. Cassian**, (bi-M.) Apostolic Episcopal Church, Rev. Stacy C. Douglas M.A., M.Th., Society of St. Cassian; c/o S.C. Douglas, P.O.Box 5016, Athens, GA 30604, Tel. (917)373-4036
Email: apostolic.episcopal@gmail.com
Website: www.apostolic-episcopal.org

**Truth**, (Q.) Grace Gospel Fellowship, Phil Cereghino, 2125 Martindale SW, Grand Rapids, MI 49509, Tel. (616)247-1999 Fax (616)241-2542
Email: ggfinc@aol.com
Website: www.ggfusa.org

**Truth Magazine**, (bi-W.) Churches of Christ, Mike Willis, P.O. Box 9670, Bowling Green, KY 42102, Tel. (800)428-0121
Website: truthmagazine.com

**Turnings**, (bi-M.) Conservative Baptist Association of America (CBAmerica), Dr. Dennis L. Gorton, 1501 W. Mineral Ave., Suite B, Littleton, CO 80120, Tel. (720)283-3030 ext. 1830 Fax (720)283-3333
Email: CBA@CBAmerica.org
Website: www.CBAmerica.org

**Ubique**, (Q.) The Liberal Catholic Church—Province of the United States, Mrs. Erin S.W. Satterlee, 2033 22nd Ave. #302, Greeley, CO 80631
Email: ubiquetlcc@fastmail.fm
Website: www.TheLCC.org

**Ukrainian Orthodox Herald**, Ukrainian Orthodox Church of America (Ecumenical Patriarchate), Rev. Dr. Anthony Ugolnik, P.O. Box 774, Allentown, PA 18105

**Ukrainian Orthodox Word**, (M.) Ukrainian Orthodox Church of the U.S.A., Heiromonk Daniel (Zelinskyy), P.O. Box 495, South Bound Brook, NJ 08880, Tel. (732)356-0090 Fax (732)356-5556
Email: FatherVZ@aol.com
Website: www.uocofusa.org

**UMR Communications, Inc.**, (D., W., Bi-W.) Independent, Protestant organization which publishes The United Methodist Reporter (w); The United Methodist Reporter (bi-w); The National Christian Reporter (w); Lumicon Digital Productions (worship resources); Reporter Interactive (daily Internet), Cynthia B. Astle, P.O. Box 660275, Dallas, TX 75266-0275, Tel. (214)630-6495 Fax (214)630-0079

Email: info@umr.org
Websites: www.umr.org
www.reporterinteractive.org (news site)
www.lumicon.org

**United Church News**, (10-Y.) United Church of Christ, W. Evan Golder, 700 Prospect Ave., Cleveland, OH 44115, Tel. (216)736-2218 Fax (216)736-2223
Email: goldere@ucc.org
Website: www.ucc.org

**The United Methodist Reporter**, (W.) Independent, Protestant, Cynthia B. Astle, UMR Communications, P.O. Box 660275, Dallas, TX 75266-0275, Tel. (214)630-6495 Fax (214)630-0079
Email: news@umr.org
Website: www.umr.org

**United Methodists in Service (Korean)**, (b-M.) United Methodist Church (Korean), Keihwan Ryoo, UMCom, P.O. Box 320, Nashville, TN 37202-0320, Tel. (615)742-5400 Fax (615) 742-5469
Email: kumc@umcom.org
Website: http://www.koreanumc.org/

**UOL Bulletin (Ukrainian Orthodox League Bulletin)**, (7-Y.) Ukrainian Orthodox Church of the U.S.A., Dr. Stephen Sivulich, 206 Christopher Circle, Pittsburgh, PA 15205, Tel. (412)276-1140
Email: ssivulich1@juno.com
Website: www.uocofusa.org

**The Upper Room**, (bi-M.) The United Methodist Church, Steven D. Bryant, P. O. Box 340004, Nashville, TN 37203-0004, Tel. (877)899-2780 Fax (615)340-7289
Email: sbryant@upperroom.org
Website: www.upperroom.org

**U.S. Catholic**, (M.) The Catholic Church, Rev. John Molyneux, 205 W. Monroe St., Chicago, IL 60606, Tel. (312)236-7782 Fax (312)236-8207
Email: editors@uscatholic.org
Website: www.uscatholic.org

**UU World**, (Q.) Unitarian Universalist Association of Congregations, Christopher L. Walton, Executive Editor, 25 Beacon St., Boston, MA 02108-2803, Tel. (617)948-6518 Fax (617)742-7025
Email: world@uua.org
Website: www.uuworld.org

**Vibrant Life**, (bi-M.) Seventh-day Adventist Church, Charles Mills, 55 W. Oak Ridge Dr., Hagerstown, MD 21740, Tel. (301)393-4019 Fax (301)393-4055
Email: vibrantlife@rhpa.org
Website: www.vibrantlife.com

**Victory (Youth Sunday School/Bible Study Curriculum)**, (Q.) Church of God of Prophecy, David Bryan, P.O. Box 2910, Cleveland, TN 37320-2910, Tel. (423)559-5321 Fax (423)559-5461
Email: david@cogop.org
Website: www.cogop.org

**The Vindicator**, (M.) Old German Baptist Brethren Church, Steven L. Bayer, 6952 N. Montgomery Co. Line Rd., Englewood, OH 45322-9748, Tel. (937)884-7531 Fax (937) 884-7531

**Vira/Faith**, (Q.) Ukrainian Orthodox Church of the U.S.A., Hieromonk Daniel (Zelinskyy), P.O. Box 495, South Bound Brook, NJ 08880, Tel. (732)356-0090 Fax (732)356-5556
Email: virafaith@aol.com
Website: uocofusa.org

**Vista**, (Q.) Christian Church of North America, General Council, Wallace Smith, 1294 Rutledge Rd., Transfer, PA 16154, Tel. (412) 962-3501 Fax (412)962-1766
Email: ccnahq@adelphia.net
Website: www.ccna.org

**The Voice**, (bi-M.) IFCA International, Inc., Les Lofquist, P.O. Box 810, Grandville, MI 49468-0810, Tel. (616)531-1840 Fax (616) 531-1814
Email: Voice@ifca.org

**The Voice**, (Q.) The Bible Church of Christ, Inc., Montrose Bushrod, 1358 Morris Ave., Bronx, NY 10456, Tel. (718)588-2284 Fax (718)992-5597
Website: www.thebiblechurchofchrist.org

**Voice of Mission**, (Q.) African Methodist Episcopal Church, Dr. John W.P. Collier, 1587 Savannah Highway, Ste. A, Charleston, SC 29407, Tel. (843)852-2645 Fax (843)852-2648
Email: gwmame@bellsouth.net
Website: www.amegobalmissions.com

**The War Cry**, (bi-M.) The Salvation Army, Ed Forster, Editor in Chief; Jeff McDonald, Managing Editor, 615 Slaters Lane, Alexandria, VA 22314, Tel. (703)684-5500 Fax (703)684-5539
Email: war_cry@usn.salvationarmy.org

**Watchtower**, (bi-W.) Jehovah's Witnesses, Watch Tower Society, 25 Columbia Heights, Brooklyn, NY 11201-2483, Tel. (718)560-5000 Fax (718)560-8850
Website: www.watchtower.org

**Weavings: A Journal of the Christian Spiritual Life**, (bi-M.) The United Methodist Church, John S. Mogabgab, 1908 Grand Avenue,

Nashville, TN 37212, Tel. (615)340-7254 Fax (615)340-7267
Email: weavings@upperroom.org
Website: www.upperroom.org/weavings

**Wesleyan Life**, (Q.) The Wesleyan Church, Norman G. Wilson, P.O. Box 50434, Indianapolis, IN 46250-0434, Tel. (317)774-7909 Fax (317)774-7913
Email: wilsonn@wesleyan.org
Website: www.wesleyan.org

**Wesleyan World**, (Q.) The Wesleyan Church, Joy Bray, P.O. Box 50434, Indianapolis, IN 46250, Tel. (317)774-7950 Fax (317)774-7958
Email: ghpm@wesleyan.org
Website: www.praygivego.com

**The White Wing Messenger**, (bi-W.) Church of God of Prophecy, Virginia E. Chatham, P.O. Box 3000, Cleveland, TN 37320-3000, Tel. (423)559-5413 Fax (423)559-5444
Website: www.cogop.org

**Window on the World**, (4-Y.) The Evangelical Congregational Church, Patricia Strain, 100 W. Park Ave, Myerstown, PA 17067, Tel. (717) 866-7584 Fax (717)866-7383
Email: ecglobalministries@eccenter.com
Website: www.eccenter.com

**Wineskins**, (bi-M.) Churches of Christ, Mike Cope and Rubel Shelly, P.O. Box 41028, Nashville, TN 37024-1028, Tel. (615)373-5004 Fax (615)373-5006
Email: wineskinsmagazine@msn.com
Website: www.wineskins.org

**The Winner**, (9-Y.) Nondenominational, Anita Jacobs, The Health Connection, P.O. Box 859, Hagerstown, MD 21741, Tel. (301)393-4082 Fax (301)393-4055
Email: winner@healthconnection.org
Website: www.winnermagazine.org

**Wisconsin Lutheran Quarterly**, (Q.) Wisconsin Evangelical Lutheran Synod, John F. Brug, 11831 N. Seminary Dr., Mequon, WI 53092, Tel. (262)242-8139 Fax (262)242-8110
Email: brugj@wls.wels.net
Website: www.wls.wels.net

**With: The Magazine for Radical Christian Youth**, (bi-M.) Mennonite Church U.S.A., Carol Duerksen, P.O. Box 347, 722 Main Street, Newton, KS 67114, Tel. (620)367-8432 Fax (620)367-8218
Email: carold@mennoniteusa.org
Website: www.withonline.org

**The Witness**, (10-Y.) Nondenominational, Julie A. Wortman, 7000 Michigan Ave., Detroit, MI 48210, Tel. (313)841-1967 Fax (313)841-1956

Email: office@thewitness.org
Website: www.thewitness.org

**Woman to Woman**, (M.) General Association of General Baptists, Barbara Wigger, 100 Stinson Dr., Poplar Bluff, MO 63901, Tel. (573)785-7746 Fax (573)785-0564
Email: wmofc@generalbaptist.com
Website: www.generalbaptist.com

**The Woman's Pulpit**, (Q.) Nondenominational, LaVonne Althouse, 14 St. Mark Avenue, Lititz, PA 17543, Tel. (717)626-0463
Email: revla32@hotmail.com
Website: www.womenministers.org

**Woman's Touch**, (bi-M.) Assemblies of God, Arlene Allen, 1445 N. Boonville Ave., Springfield, MO 65802-1894, Tel. (417)862-2781 Fax (417)862-0503
Email: womanstouch@ag.org
Website: www.womanstouch.ag.org

**Women's Missionary Magazine**, (9-Y.) African Methodist Episcopal Church, Dr. Bettye J. Allen, 17129 Bennett Dr, South Holland, IL 60473, Tel. (708)339-5997 Fax (708)339-5987
Email: bettye1901@aol.com

**The Word**, (10-Y.) The Antiochian Orthodox Christian Archdiocese of North America, V. Rev. John Abdalah, 635 Miranda Dr., Pittsburgh, PA 15241-2041, Tel. (412)681-2988 Fax (412)831-5554
Email: frjpa@aol.com
Website: www.antiochian.org

**Word and Work**, (11-Y.) Churches of Christ, Alex V. Wilson, 2518 Portland Ave., Louisville, KY 40212, Tel. (502)897-2831

**The Worker**, (Q.) Progressive National Baptist Convention, Inc., Mattie A Robinson, 601 50th St. NE, Washington, DC 20019, Tel. (202)398-5343 Fax (202)398-4998
Email: info@pnbc.org
Website: www.pnbc.org

**World Parish: International Organ of the World Methodist Council**, (M.) Inter-denominational Methodist (Christian World Communion of Methodist and WMC-Related Churches), Dr. George Freeman, P.O. Box 518, Lake Junaluska, NC 28745, Tel. (828) 456-9432 Fax (828)456-9433
Email: georgefreeman@charter.net
Website: www.worldmethodistcouncil.org

**Worldorama**, (M.) Pentecostal Holiness Church, International, Donald Duncan, P.O. Box 12609, Oklahoma City, OK 73157, Tel. (405) 787-7110 Fax (405)787-7729
Email: donald@iphc.org

**Worship**, (bi-M.) The Catholic Church, R. Kevin Seasoltz, St. John's Abbey, Collegeville, MN 56321, Tel. (320)363-3883 Fax (320)363-3145
Email: kseasoltz@csbsju.edu
Website: www.sja.org/worship

**Worship Arts**, (bi-M.) United Methodist Church, David A. Wiltse, P.O. Box 6247, Grand Rapids, MI 49516-6247, Tel. (616)459-4503 Fax (616)459-0191
Email: graphics@iserv.net
Website: www.fummwa.org

**Youth Ministry Accent**, (Q.) Seventh-day Adventist Church, Vacant, 12501 Old Columbia Pike, Silver Spring, MD 20904-6600, Tel. (301)680-6180 Fax (301)680-6155
Email: 74532.1426@compuserve.com

**YPD Newsletter**, (3-M.) African Methodist Episcopal Church, Adrienne A. Morris and Andrea Smith, 327 Washington Avenue, Wyoming, OH 45215, Tel. (513)821-1481 Fax (513)821-3073
Email: amconndri@cs.com
Website: ameypd.org

**Zion's Advocate**, (M.) Church of Christ, Gordon McCann, P.O. Box 472, Independence, MO 64051-0472, Tel. (816)796-6255

# 11. Religious Periodicals in Canada

The religious periodicals below constitute a basic core of important journals and periodicals circulated in Canada. The list does not include all publications prepared by religious bodies, and not all the publications listed here are necessarily the official publication of a particular church. Each entry gives the title of the periodical, frequency of publication, religious affiliation, editor's name, address, telephone and fax number and email and website addresses when available. The frequency of publication, which appears in parenthesis after the name of the publication, is represented by a "W." for weekly; "M." for monthly; "Q." for quarterly.

**Again**, (Q.) The Antiochian Orthodox Christian Archdiocese of North America, R. Thomas Zell, Conciliar Press, P.O. Box 76, Ben Lomond, CA 95005-0076, Tel. (800)967-7377 Fax (831)336-8882
Email: tzell@conciliarpress.com
Website: www.conciliarpress.com

**The Anglican**, (10-Y.) The Anglican Church of Canada, Stuart Mann, 135 Adelaide St. E., Toronto, ON M5C 1L8, Tel. (416)363-6021 Fax (416)363-7678
Email: smann@toronto.anglican.ca
Website: www.toronto.anglican.ca

**Anglican Journal**, (10-Y.) The Anglican Church of Canada, Leanne Larmondin, 80 Hayden St., Toronto, ON M4Y 3G2, Tel. (416)924-9199 x 306 Fax (416)921-4452
Email: editor@national.anglican.ca
Website: www.anglicanjournal.com

**Armenian Evangelical Church Newsletter**, (bi-M.) Armenian Evangelical Church, Rev. Samuel Albarian, 2600 14th Avenue, Markham, ON L3R 3X1, Tel. (905)305-8144 Fax (905)305-8125
Email: aectoronto@yahoo.com

**Aujourd'hui Credo**, (10-Y.) The United Church of Canada, David Fines, 1332 Victoria, Longueuil, QC J4V 1L8, Tel. (450)446-7733 Fax (450)466-2664
Email: davidfines@egliseunce.org
Website: www.united-church/credo

**The Baptist Horizon**, (M.) Canadian Convention of Southern Baptists, Nancy McGough, 100 Convention Way, Cochrane, AB T4C 2G2, Tel. (403)932-5688 Fax (403) 932-4937
Email: office@ccsb.ca

**B.C. Fellowship Baptist**, (Q.) The Fellowship of Evangelical Baptist Churches in BC and Yukon, Bruce Christensen, #201-26620-56th Ave, Langley, BC V4W 3X5, Tel. (604)607-1192 Fax (604)607-1193
Email: fellowship@shaw.ca

**Blackboard Bulletin**, (10-Y.) Old Order Amish Church, Old Order Amish Church, Rt. 4, Aylmer, ON N5H 2R3

**Die Botschaft**, (W.) Old Order Amish Church, James Weaver, Brookshire Publishing, Inc., 200 Hazel St., Lancaster, PA 17603, Tel. (717) 392-1321 Fax (717)392-2078

**The Budget**, (W.) Old Order Amish Church, Fannie Erb-Miller, P.O. Box 249, Sugarcreek, OH 44681, Tel. (330)852-4634 Fax (330)852-4421
Email: budgetnews@aol.com

**Cahiers de Spiritualite Ignatienne**, (3-Y.) The Roman Catholic Church in Canada, Gaetane Guillemette, Gaetane Guillemette, 2370 Rue Nicolas-Pinel, Ste-Foy, QC G1V 4L6, Tel. (418)653-6353 Fax (418)653-1208
Email: cahiersi@centremanrese.org
Website: www.centremanrese.org

**Canada Lutheran**, (8-Y.) Evangelical Lutheran Church in Canada, Ida Reichardt Backman, Interim Editor; Trina Gallop, Manager of Communications; Kristen Guy, Graphic Designer, 302-393 Portage Avenue, Winnipeg, MB R3B 3H6, Tel. (204)984-9150 Toll Free: (888) 786-6707 Fax (204)984-9185
Email: canaluth@elcic.ca
Website: www.elcic.ca/clweb

**Canada Update**, (Q.) The Church of God of Prophecy in Canada, Editor, 5145 Tomkin Road, Mississaugh, ON L4W 1P1, Tel. (905) 625-1278 Fax (905)843-3990

**Canadian Adventist Messenger**, (12-Y.) Seventh-day Adventist Church in Canada, Carolyn Willis, 1148 King St. E., Oshawa, ON L1H 1H8, Tel. (905)433-0011 Fax (905) 433-0982
Email: cwillis@sdacc.org
Website: www.sdacc.org

**The Canadian Baptist**, (10-Y.) Baptist Convention of Ontario and Quebec, Larry Matthews, 195 The West Mall, Ste.414, Etobicoke, ON M9C 5K1, Tel. (416)622-8600 Fax (416)622-0780
Email: thecb@baptist.ca

**The Canadian Friend**, (bi-M.) Canadian Yearly Meeting of the Religious Society of Friends,

Anne Marie Zilliacus, 218 Third Ave., Ottawa, ON K1S 2K3, Tel. (613)567-8628 Fax (613) 567-1078
Email: zilli@cyberus.ca

**The Canadian Lutheran**, (9-Y.) Lutheran Church—Canada, Ida Backman, Interim Editor, 3074 Portage Ave., Winnipeg, MB R3K 0Y2, Tel. (204)895-3433 x 24 Fax (204) 897-4319
Website: www.lutheranchurch.ca

**Canadian Mennonite**, (bi-W.) Mennonite Church Canada, Tom Miller Dyck, Suite C5, 490 Dutton Dr., Waterloo, ON N2L 6H7, Tel. (519)884-3810 Fax (519)884-3331
Email: editor@canadianmennonite.org
Website: www.canadianmennonite.org

**Canadian Orthodox Messenger**, (Q.) Orthodox Church in America (Canada Section), Nun Sophia (Zion), P.O. Box 179, Spencerville, ON K0E 1X0, Tel. (613)925-0645 Fax (613) 925-1521
Email: sophia@ripnet.com

**The Catalyst**, (6-Y.) Nondenominational, Murray MacAdam, Citizens for Public Justice, 229 College St. #311, Toronto, ON M5T 1R4, Tel. (416)979-2443 Fax (416)979-2458
Email: cpj@cpj.ca
Website: www.cpj.ca

**The Catholic Register**, (W.) The Roman Catholic Church in Canada, Joseph Sinasac, 1155 Yonge St., Ste. 401, Toronto, ON M4Y 1W2, Tel. (416)934-3410 Fax (416)934-3409
Email: editor@catholicregister.org
Website: www.catholicregister.org

**The Catholic Times (Montreal)**, (10-Y.) The Roman Catholic Church in Canada, Eric Durocher, 2005 St. Marc St., Montreal, QC H3H 2G8, Tel. (514)937-2301 Fax (514)937-3051

**Channels**, (3-Y.) Presbyterian Church in Canada, Calvin Brown, Managing Editor; Dal Schindell, Renewal Fellowship, 3819 Bloor St W, Etobicoke, ON M9B 1K7, Tel. (416)233-6581 Fax (416)233-1743
Email: cbbrown@rogers.com
Website: www.presbycan.ca/rfpc

**Chinese Herald**, (bi-M.) Canadian Conference of Mennonite Brethren Churches, Joseph Kwan, 8143 Burnlake Drive, Burnaby, BC V5A 3R6, Tel. (604)421-4100 Fax (604)421-4100
Email: chineseherald@mbconf.ca

**Church of God Beacon**, (Q.) Church of God (Cleveland, Tenn.), Andrew Binda, P.O. Box 2036, Brampton Commercial Service Center,

Brampton, ON L6T 3T0, Tel. (905)793-2213 Fax (905)793-9173
Email: afinda@cogontario.com

**Clarion—The Canadian Reformed Magazine**, (bi-W.) Canadian and American Reformed Churches, J. Visscher, One Beghin Ave., Winnipeg, MB R2J 3X5, Tel. (204)663-9000 Fax (204)663-9202
Email: clarion@premier.mb.ca
Website: www.premier.mb.ca/clarion.html

**CLBI-Cross Roads**, (6-Y.) Lutheran, Dean J. Rostand, 4837-52A St., Camrose, AB T4V 1W5, Tel. (780)672-4454 Fax (780)672-4455
Email: communications@clbi.edu
Website: www.clbi.edu

**The Communicator**, (3-Y.) The Roman Catholic Church in Canada, Box 2400, London, ON N6A 4G3, Tel. (519)439-7514 Fax (519)439-0207
Email: info@arccc.ca
Website: www.arccc.ca/news.htm

**Connexions**, (4-Y.) Interdenominational, Ulli Diemer, 489 College St., Ste. 305, Toronto, ON M6G 1A5, Tel. (416)964-1511
Website: www.connexions.org

**The Covenant Messenger**, (Q.) The Evangelical Covenant Church of Canada, Doug Wildman, Box 93, Norquay, SK S0A 2V0, Tel. (204)269-3437 Fax (204)269-3584
Email: messengr@escape.ca
Website: www.canadacovenantchurch.org

**Crux**, (Q.) Nondenominational, Donald Lewis, Regent College, 5800 University Blvd., Vancouver, BC V6T 2E4, Tel. (604)224-3245 Fax (604)224-3097
Email: crux@regent.college.edu
Website: www.cruxonline.net

**Diakonia—A Magazine of Office-Bearers**, (4-Y.) Canadian and American Reformed Churches, J. Visscher, Brookside Publishing, 3911 Mt. Lehman Rd., Abbotsford, BC V4X 2M9, Tel. (604)856-4127 Fax (604)856-6724

**The Diary**, (M.) Old Order Amish Church, Don Carpenter, P.O. Box 98, Gordonville, PA 17529, Tel. (717)529-3938 Fax (717)529-3292

**Ecumenism-Oecumenisme**, (Q.) Interdenominational, Dr. Stuart E. Brown, 2065 Sherbrooke St. W, Montreal, QC H3H 1G6, Tel. (514) 937-9176 Fax (514)937-4986
Email: ccocce@oecumenisme.ca
Website: www.oecumenisme.ca

**The Edge (Christian Youth Magazine)**, (10-Y.) The Salvation Army in Canada, John McAlister, 2 Overlea Blvd., Toronto, ON

M4H 1P4, Tel. (416)422-6116 Fax (416)422-6120
Email: edge@can.salvationarmy.org
Website: www.salvationarmy.ca

**Eesti Kirik,** (Q.) The Estonian Evangelical Lutheran Church Abroad, Rev. U. Petersoo, 383 Jarvis St., Toronto, ON M5B 2C7, Tel. (416)925-5465 Fax (416)925-5688

**EMMC Recorder,** (M.) Evangelical Mennonite Mission Conference, Lil Goertzen, Box 52059 Niakwa P.O., Winnipeg, MB R2M 5P9, Tel. (204)253-7929 Fax (204)256-7384
Email: info@emmc.ca
Website: www.emmc.ca

**En Avant!,** (11-Y.) The Salvation Army in Canada, Marie-Michèle Roy, 2050 Rue Stanley, bureau 400, Montreal, QB H3A 3G3, Tel. (514)288-2848 x 2236 Fax (514)288-4657
Email: enavant@can.salvationarmy.org

**Esprit,** (Q.) Evangelical Lutheran Church in Canada (Evangelical Lutheran Women), Catehrine Pate, 302-393 Portage Avenue, Winnipeg, MB R3B 3H6, Tel. (204)984-9160 Fax (204)984-9162
Email: esprit@elcic.ca
Website: www.elw.ca

**Evangel—The Good News of Jesus Christ,** (4-Y.) Canadian and American Reformed Churches, D. Moes, 21804 52nd Ave., Langley, BC V2Y 1L3, Tel. (604)576-2124 Fax (604)576-2101
Email: canrc@uniserve.com or jvisscher@telus.ca

**Evangel Voice-Voce Evangelica,** (Q.) Canadian Assemblies of God, Rev. Daniel Costanza, 140 Woodbridge Ave., Suite 400, Woodbridge, ON L4L 4K9, Tel. (905)850-1578 Fax (905)850-1578
Email: bethel@idirect.com
Website: www.the-ipcc.org

**The Evangelical Baptist,** (5-Y.) The Fellowship of Evangelical Baptist Churches in Canada, Terry D. Cuthbert, 679 Southgate Dr., Suite 100, Guelph, ON N1G 4S2, Tel. (519)821-4830 Fax (519)821-9829
Email: president@fellowship.ca
Website: www.fellowship.ca

**Faith & Friends,** (M.) The Salvation Army in Canada, Geoff Moulton, 2 Overlea Blvd., Toronto, ON M4H 1P4, Tel. (416)422-6110 Fax (416)422-6120
Website: www.faithandfriends.sallynet.org

**Faith Today,** (bi-M.) Evangelical Fellowship of Canada (a cooperative organization of more than 40 Protestant denominations), Gail Reid, M.I.P. Box 3745, Markham, ON L3R 0Y4, Tel. (905)479-5885 Fax (905)479-4742
Email: ft@efc-canada.com
Website: www.faithtoday.ca

**Family Life,** (11-Y.) Old Order Amish Church, Joseph Stoll and David Luthy, Old Order Amish Church, Rt. 4, Aylmer, ON N5H 2R3

**Family Life Network Newsline,** (3-Y.) Canadian Conference of Mennonite Brethren Churches, Dorothy Siebert, 225 Riverton Ave., Winnipeg, MB R2L 0N1, Tel. (204)667-9576 Fax (204)669-9920
Email: info@fln.ca
Website: www.fln.ca

**Fellowship Magazine,** (4-Y.) The United Church of Canada, Rev. Diane Walker, Bob McC, Box 237, Barrie, ON L4M 4T2, Tel. (705)737-0114 or (800)678-2607 Fax (705) 737-1086
Email: felmag@csolve.net
Website: www.fellowshipmagazine.org

**Foi & Vie,** (12-Y.) The Salvation Army in Canada, Marie-Michele Roy, 2050 Rue Stanley, Bureau 400, Montreal, QC H3A 3G3, Tel. (514)288-2848 x 2236 Fax (514)288-4657
Email: foivie@can.salvationarmy.org

**Glad Tidings,** (6-Y.) Presbyterian Church in Canada, Holly Wilson, Women's Missionary Society, 50 Wynford Dr., Toronto, ON M3C 1J7, Tel. (800)619-7301/(416)441-1111 Fax (416)441-2825
Email: hwilson@presbyterian.ca
Website: www.presbyterian.ca/wms

**Good Tidings,** (10-Y.) The Pentecostal Assemblies of Newfoundland and Labrador, H. Paul Foster, 57 Thorburn Rd., P.O. Box 8895, Sta. A, St. John's, NL A1B 3T2, Tel. (709)753-6314 Fax (709)753-4945
Email: paon@paon.nf.ca

**The Gospel Contact,** (4-Y.) Church of God (Anderson, Ind.), Editorial Committee, 4717 56th St., Camrose, AB T4V 2C4, Tel. (780) 672-0772 Fax (780)672-6888
Email: winscho@chog.ca
Website: www.chog.ca

**Gospel Herald,** (M.) Churches of Christ in Canada, Wayne Turner and Max E. Craddock, 4904 King St., Beamsville, ON L0R 1B6, Tel. (905)563-7503 Fax (905)563-7503
Email: editorial@gospelherald.org
Website: www.gospelherald.org

348

**The Gospel Standard**, (M.) Nondenominational, Perry F. Rockwood, Box 1660, Halifax, NS B3J 3A1, Tel. (902)423-5540 Fax (902)423-0820

**Gospel Tidings**, (M.) Independent Holiness Church, Marilyn E. Votary, 1564 John Quinn Rd., Greely, ON K4P 1J9, Tel. (613)821-2237 Fax (613)821-4663
Email: marilynv@hotmail.com
Website: www.holiness.ca

**The Grape Vine**, (12-Y.) Reformed Episcopal Church in Canada, Ingrid Andreller, 626 Blanshard Street, Victoria, BC V8W 3G6, Tel. (250)383-8915 Fax (250)383-8916
Email: office@churchofourlord.org
Website: www.churchofourlord.org

**Hallelujah!**, (bi-M.) The Bible Holiness Movement, Wesley H. Wakefield, Box 223, Postal Stn. A, Vancouver, BC V6C 2M3, Tel. (250) 492-3376

**Herold der Wahrheit**, (M.) Old Order Amish Church, Cephas Kauffman, 1827 110th St., Kalona, IA 52247

**Horizons**, (bi-M.) The Salvation Army in Canada, 2 Overlea Blvd., Toronto, ON M4H 1P4, Tel. (416)425-6118 Fax (416)422-6120

**Insight\*Insound\*In Touch**, (6-Y. (Insight); 6-Y. (In Sound); 4-Y. (In Touch)) Interdenominational. Insight (large print newspaper); In Sound (audio magazine); In Touch (Braille newspaper), Rebekah Chevalier, Graham Down, John Milton Society for the Blind in Canada, 40 St. Clair Ave. E., Ste. 202, Toronto, ON M4T 1M9, Tel. (416)960-3953 Fax (416)960-3570
Email: admin@jmsblind.ca
Website: www.jmsblind.ca

**Intercom**, (Q.) The Fellowship of Evangelical Baptist Churches in Canada, Terry D. Cuthbert, 679 Southgate Dr., Suite 100, Guelph, ON N1G 4S2, Tel. (519)821-4830 Fax (519)821-9829
Email: president@fellowship.ca
Website: www.fellowship.ca

**ISKRA**, (20-Y.) Union of Spiritual Communities of Christ (Orthodox Doukhobors in Canada), Dmitri E. (Jim) Popoff, Box 760, Grand Forks, BC V0H 1H0, Tel. (604)442-8252 Fax (604) 442-3433
Email: iskra@sunshinecable.com

**Istocnik**, (4-Y.) Serbian Orthodox Church in the U.S.A. and Canada, Diocese of Canada, Very Rev. VasilijeTomic, 7470 McNiven Rd., RR 3, Campbellville, ON L0P 1B0, Tel. (905)878-0043 Fax (905)878-1909

Email: vladika@istocnik.com
Website: www.istocnik.com

**Leader**, (Q.) Mennonite Church U.S.A. and Mennonite Church Canada, Sr Editor: Richard A. Kaufman, Managing Editor: Byron Rempel-Burkholder, 600 Shaftesbury Blvd., Winnipeg, MB R3P 0M4, Tel. (204)888-6781 Fax (204)831-2454
Email: byronrb@mph.org
Website: www.leaderonline.org

**Leader: Equipping the Missional Congregation**, (Q.) Mennonite Church, Byron Rempel-Burkholder, Faith & Life Resources/ Mennonite Publishing Network, 600 Shaftesbury Blvd, Winnipeg, Manitoba R3P 0M4, Tel. (204) 888-6781 x 179 Fax (204)831-5675
Email: byronrb@mph.org

**Le Lien**, (11-Y.) Canadian Conference of Mennonite Brethren Churches, Annie Brosseau, 1775 Edouard-Laurin, St. Laurent, QC H4L 2B9, Tel. (514)331-0878 Fax (514) 331-0879
Email: LeLien@total.net
Website: www.mbconf.ca/comm/lelien

**Liturgie, Foi et Culture** (Bulletin Natl. de Liturgie), (4-Y.) The Roman Catholic Church in Canada, Service des Editions de la CECC, Office national de liturgie, 3530 rue Adam, Montreal, QC H1W 1Y8, Tel. (514)522-4930 Fax (514)522-1557
Email: onl.cecc@ccb.ca
Website: www.cccb.ca

**Mandate**, (4-Y.) The United Church of Canada, Rebekah Chevalier, 3250 Bloor St W., Ste. 300, Etobicoke Toronto, ON M8X 2Y4, Tel. (416)231-5931 Fax (416)231-3103
Email: rchevali@united-church.ca
Website: www.united-church.ca/mandate

**The Mantle**, (M.) Independent Assemblies of God International (Canada), Philip Rassmussen, P.O. Box 2130, Laguna Hills, CA 92654-9901, Tel. (514)522-4930 Fax (514)522-1557

**Mennonite Brethren Herald**, (3-W.) Canadian Conference of Mennonite Brethren Churches, Laura Kalmar, 1310 Taylor Ave., Winnipeg, MB R3M 3Z6, Tel. (204)654-5760 Fax (204) 654-1865
Email: mbherald@mbconf.ca
Website: www.mbherald.com

**Mennonite Historian**, (Q.) Canadian Conference of Mennonite Brethren Churches, Mennonite Church Canada, Abe Dueck and Alf Redekopp, Ctr. for Menn. Brethren Studies, 169 Riverton Ave., Winnipeg, MB R2L 2E5, Tel. (204)669-6575 Fax (204)654-1865

Email: adueck@mbconf.ca
Website: www.mbconf.ca/mbstudies

**Die Mennonitische Post**, (bi-M.) Mennonite Central Committee Canada, Kennert Giesbrecht, 383 Main St., Steinbach, MB R5G 1S1, Tel. (204)326-6790 Fax (204)326-6302
Email: mennpost@mts.net

**Mennonitische Rundschau**, (M.) Canadian Conference of Mennonite Brethren Churches, Brigitte Penner; Marianne Dulder, 3-169 Riverton Ave., Winnipeg, MB R2L 2E5, Tel. (204)669-6575 Fax (204)654-1865
Email: MR@mbconf.ca
Website: www.mbconf.ca

**The Messenger**, (Q.) The Reformed Episcopal Church of Canada, Rt. Rev. Michael Fedechko, 320 Armstrong St., New Liskeard, ON P0J 1P0, Tel. (705)647-4565 Fax (705)647-4565
Email: fed@nt.net
Website: www.forministry.com/REC-Canada

**The Messenger**, (22-Y.) The Evangelical Mennonite Conference, Terry Smith, Editor; Becky Buhler, Assistant Editor, 440 Main Street, Steinbach, MB R5G 1Z5, Tel. (204) 326-6401 Fax (204)326-1613
Email: emcmessenger@mts.net
Website: www.emconf.ca/Messenger

**The Messenger**, (bi-M.) Church of God (in Eastern Canada), Rosemary Krashel, 20625 Winston Churchill Blvd., Alton, ON L0N 1A0, Tel. (514)938-9994 Fax
Email: rosemarykrushel@sympatico.ca

**MinistryMatters**, (3-Y.) The Anglican Church of Canada, Vianney (Sam) Carriere, 80 Hayden St., Toronto, ON M4Y 3G2, Tel. (905) 833-6200 Fax (905)833-2116
Email: matters@national.anglican.ca
Website: www.ministrymatters.ca

**Missions Today**, (bi-M.) Roman Catholic, Patricia McKinnon, Society for the Propagation of the Faith, 3329 Danforth Ave., Scarborough, ON M1L 4T3, Tel. (416)699-7077 or 800-897-8865 Fax (416)699-9019
Email: missions@eda.net
Website: www.eda.net/~missions

**Mosaic**, (Q.) Canadian Baptist Ministries, Jennifer Lau, 7185 Millcreek Dr., Mississauga, ON L5N 5R4, Tel. (905)821-3533 Fax (905) 826-3441
Email: mosaic@cbmin.org
Website: www.cbmin.org

**The New Freeman**, (W.) The Roman Catholic Church in Canada, Margie Traftan, One Bayard Dr., Saint John, NB E2L 3L5, Tel. (506)653-6806 Fax (506)653-6818
Email: tnf@nbnet.nb.ca

**News of Québec**, (3-Y.) Christian Brethren (also known as Plymouth Brethren), Richard E. Strout, P.O. Box 1054, Sherbrooke, QC J1H 5L3, Tel. (819)820-1693 Fax (819)821-9287

**Orthodox Way**, (M.) Greek Orthodox Metropolis of Toronto (Canada), Orthodox Way Committee, 86 Overlea Blvd., 4th Floor, Toronto, ON M4H 1C6, Tel. (416)429-5757 Fax (416)429-4588
Email: greekomt@on.aibn.com
Website: www.gocanada.org

**Passport**, (3-Y.) Interdenominational, Briercrest Family of Schools, 510 College Dr., Caronport, SK S0H 0S0, Tel. (306)756-3200 Fax (306)756-3366
Email: info@briercrest.ca
Website: www.briercrest.ca

**Pourastan**, (bi-M.) Armenian Holy Apostolic Church—St. Gregory the Illuminator Armenian Cathedral of Montreal, 615 Stuart Ave., Outremont, QC H2V 3H2, Tel. (514)279-3066 Fax (514)279-8008
Email: sourpkrikor@qc.aibn.com
Website: www.sourpkrikor.org

**Prairie Messenger**, (W.) The Roman Catholic Church in Canada, Peter Novecosky, O.S.B., Box 190, 11 College Drive, Muenster, SK S0K 2Y0, Tel. (306)682-1772 Fax (306)682-5285
Email: pm.editor@stpeters.sk.ca
Website: www.stpeters.sk.ca/prairie_messenger

**The Presbyterian Message**, (10-Y.) Presbyterian Church in Canada, Janice Carter, 563 Tweedie Brook Rd, Kouchibouguac, NB E4X 1M2, Tel. (506)876-4379 Fax
Email: mjcarter@nb.sympatico.ca

**Presbyterian Record**, (11-Y.) The Presbyterian Church in Canada, Rev. David Harris, 50 Wynford Dr., Toronto, ON M3C 1J7, Tel. (416)441-1111 Fax (416)441-2825
Email: pcrecord@presbyterian.ca
Website: www.presbyterian.ca/record

**Presence**, (8-Y.) The Roman Catholic Church in Canada, Jean-Claude Breton, Presence Magazine Inc., 2715 chemin de la Cote Ste-Catherine, Montreal, QC H3T 1B6, Tel. (514) 739-9797 Fax (514)739-1664
Email: presence@presencemag.qc.ca

**The Pulse**, (4-Y.) Evangelical Free Church of Canada, Dr. Ron Unruh, Editor-in-Chief; Tracy Morris, Managing Editor, Box 850, LCDI, Langley, BC V3A 8S6, Tel. (604)888-8668 Fax (604)888-3108

Email: efcc@twu.ca
Website: www.efcc.ca

**Quaker Concern**, (3-Y) Canadian Yearly Meeting of the Religious Society of Friends, Jane Orion Smith, 60 Lowther Ave., Toronto, ON M5R 1C7, Tel. (416)920-5213 Fax (416) 920-5214
Email: cfsc-office@quaker.ca
Website: www.cfsc.quaker.ca

**Reformed Perspective—A Magazine for the Christian Family**, (M.) Canadian and American Reformed Churches and United Reformed Churches in North America, Jon Dykstra, 13820-106 A Avenue, Edmonton, AB T5N 1C9, Tel. (780)452-3978 Fax
Email: editor@reformedperspective.ca
Website: www.reformedperspective.ca

**Relations**, (8-Y.) The Roman Catholic Church in Canada, Jean-Marc Biron, 25 Jarry Ouest, Montreal, QC H2P 1S6, Tel. (514)387-2541 Fax (514)387-0206
Email: relations@cjf.qc.ca
Website: www.cjf.qc.ca

**RESCUE**, (bi-M.) Association of Gospel Rescue Missions, Philip Rydman, 1045 Swift, N. Kansas City, MO 64116, Tel. (816)471-8020 Fax (816)471-3718
Email: pwydman@agrm.org
Website: www.agrm.org

**Revival News**, (Q.) Interdenominational, Harold Lutzer & Neill K. Foster, Canadian Revival Fellowship, Box 584, Regina, SK S4P 3A3, Tel. (306)522-3685 Fax (306)522-3686
Email: crfellowship@accesscomm.ca
Website: www.revivalfellowship.com

**Rupert's Land News**, (10-Y.) The Anglican Church of Canada, Irvin J. Kroeker, Anglican Centre, 935 Nesbitt Bay, Winnipeg, MB R3T 1W6, Tel. (204)992-4205 Fax (204)992-4219
Email: rlnews@rupertsland.ca

**St. Luke Magazine**, (M.) Christ Catholic Church International, Donald W. Mullan, 4695 St. Lawrence Ave, Niagara Falls, ON L2E 6S8, Tel. (905)354-2329 Fax (905)354-9934
Email: dmullan1@cogeco.ca

**Scarboro Missions**, (7-Y.) The Roman Catholic Church in Canada, Cathy Van Loon, 2685 Kingston Rd., Scarborough, ON M1M 1M4, Tel. (416)261-7135 or 800-260-4815 (In Canada) Fax (416)261-0820
Email: editor@scarboromissions.ca
Website: www.scarboromissions.ca

**The Shantyman**, (6-Y.) Nondenominational, Ken Godevenos, Editor in Chief; Phil Hood,

Managing Editor, 1885 Clements Rd., Unite 226, Pickering, ON L1W 3V4, Tel. (905)686-2030 Fax (905)427-0334
Email: shanty@pathcom.com
Website: www.shantymen.org

**Sister Triangle**, (Q.) Churches of Christ, Marilyn Muller, P.O. 948, Dauphin, MB R7N 3J5, Tel. (204)638-9812 Fax (204)638-6231
Email: dmmuller@mb.sympatico.ca

**SR—Studies in Religion—Sciences religieuses**, (Q.) Nondenominational, Dr. Aaron Hughes, Dept. of Religion & Culture, Wilfrid Laurier University, Waterloo, ON N2L 3C5, Tel. (519)884-0710 x 3329 Fax (519)884-9387
Email: hugesa@ucalgaray.ca
Website: info.wlu.ca/~wwwpress/jrls/sr

**Testimony**, (M.) The Pentecostal Assemblies of Canada, Richard P. Hiebert, 2450 Milltower Ct., Mississauga, ON L5N 5Z6, Tel. (905)542-7400 Fax (905)542-7313
Email: testimony@PAOC.org

**Topic**, (10-Y.) The Anglican Church of Canada, Neale Adams, 580-401 W. Georgia St., Vancouver, BC V6B 5A1, Tel. (604)684-6306 x 223 Fax (604)684-7017
Email: nadams@vancouver.anglican.ca
Website: www.vancouver.anglican.ca

**United Church Observer**, (M.) The United Church of Canada, Muriel Duncan, 478 Huron St., Toronto, ON M5R 2R3, Tel. (416)960-8500 Fax (416)960-8477
Email: general@ucobserver.org
Website: www.ucobserver.org

**La Vie Chretienne** (French), (M.) Presbyterian Church in Canada, Jean Porret, P.O. Box 272, Suzz. Rosemont, Montreal, QC H1X 3B8, Tel. (514)737-4168

**La Vie des Communautes religieuses**, (5-Y.) The Roman Catholic Church in Canada, Religious Communities (Consortium), 251 St-Jean-Baptiste, Nicolet, QC J3T 1X9, Tel. (819) 293-8736 Fax (819)293-2419
Email: viecr@sogetel.net

**Vie Liturgique**, (6-Y.) The Roman Catholic Church in Canada, Novalis, 4475, rue Frontenac, Montreal, QC H2H 2S2, Tel. (800) 668-2547 Fax (514)278-3030
Email: info@novalis-inc.com
Website: www.novalis.ca

**VIP Communique**, Foursquare Gospel Church of Canada, Timothy Peterson, 8459-160th St., Ste. 100, Surrey, BC V3S 3T9, Tel. (604)543-8414 Fax (604)543-8417

Email: foursquare@foursquare.ca
Website: www.foursquare.ca

**Visnyk—The Herald**, (2-M.) Ukrainian Orthodox Church of Canada, Rt. Rev. Fr. William Makarenko, 9 St. John's Ave., Winnipeg, MB R2W 1G8, Tel. (204)586-3093 Fax (204)582-5241
Email: visnky@uocc.ca
Website: www.uocc.ca

**The War Cry**, (M.) The Salvation Army in Canada and Bermuda, Major Kenneth Smith, Associate Editor, 2 Overlea Blvd., Toronto, ON M4H 1P4, Tel. (416)425-2111 Fax (416) 422-6120
Email: warcry@can.salvationarmy.org
Website: www.salvationarmy.ca

**Word Alive**, (Q.) Nondenominational, Dwayne Janke and Dave Crough, Wycliffe Bible Translators of Canada Inc., 4316 10 St. NE, Calgary, AB T2E 6K3, Tel. (403)250-5411 Fax (403)250-2623
Email: editors_wam@wycliffe.ca
Website: www.wycliffe.ca

**Young Companion**, (11-Y.) Old Order Amish Church, Joseph Stoll and Christian Stoll, Old Order Amish Church, Rt. 4, Aylmer, ON N5H 2R3

# 12. Church Archives and Historical Records Collections

American and Canadian history is interwoven with the social and cultural experience of religious life and thought. Most repositories of primary research materials in North America will include some documentation on religion and church communities. This directory is not intended to replace standard bibliographic guides to those resources. The intent is to give a new researcher entry to major archival holdings of religious collections and to programs of national scope. In the interest of space, no attempt has been made to list the specific contents of the archives or to include the numerous specialized research libraries of North America. The repositories listed herein are able to re-direct inquirers to significant regional and local church archives, and specialized collections such as those of religious orders, educational and charitable organizations, and personal papers.

Repositories marked with an asterisk (*) are designated by their denomination as the official archives. The reference departments at these archives will assist researchers in locating primary material of geographic or subject focus.

## UNITED STATES

### Adventist

Aurora University, Aurora University, Charles B. Phillips Library, 347 S. Gladstone, Aurora, IL 60506, Volunteer Curator, David T. Arthur, Tel. (630)844-5437 Fax (630)844-3848, Email: jhuggins@aurora.edu

Adventual archival materials on the Millerite/Early Adventist movement (1830-1860); also denominational archives relating to Advent Christian Church, Life and Advent Union, and to a lesser extent, Evangelical Adventists and Age-to-Come Adventists.

Ellen G. White Estate Branch Office, Loma Linda University Library, Department of Archives and Special Collections, Loma Linda, CA 92350, Interim Chairman/Director, Michael Campbell, Tel. (909)558-4942 Fax (909)558-0381, Email: whiteestate@llu.edu, Website: www.llu.edu/llu/library/heritage

Photographs, sound and video recordings, personal papers, and library pertaining to the Seventh-day Adventist Church.

Ellen G. White Estate, Inc., 12501 Old Columbia Pike, Silver Spring, MD 20904, Archivist, Tim Poirier, Tel. (301)680-6540 Fax (301)680-6559, Website: www.whiteestate.org

Records include letters and manuscripts (1840s to 1915), pamphlets and publications, and the White papers.

*General Conference of Seventh-day Adventists: Archives and Statistics, 12501 Old Columbia Pike, Silver Spring, MD 20904-6600, Director: Bert Haloviak, Tel. (301)680-5020 Fax (301)680-5038, Email: haloviakb@gc. adventist.org, Website: www.ast.gc.adventist.org

Repository of the records created at the world administrative center of the Seventh-day Adventist Church and includes the period from the 1860s to the present.

Center for Adventist Research, James White Library, Andrews University, Berrien Springs, MI 49103-1440, Director, Dr. Merlin D. Burt, Tel. (269)471-3209 Fax (269)471-2646, Email: car@andrews.edu, Website: www. andrews.edu/library/car

Large collection of Seventh-day Adventist material.

### Assemblies of God

*Flower Pentecostal Heritage Center, 1445 Boonville Ave., Springfield, MO 65802, Director, Darrin Rodgers, Tel. (417)862-1447 x 4400 Fax (417)862-6203, Email: archives@ag.org, Website: www.agheritage.org

Official repository for materials related to the Assemblies of God, as well as materials related to the early Pentecostal movement in general.

### Baptist

*Seventh-day Baptist Historical Society, 3120 Kennedy Rd., P.O. Box 1678, Janesville, WI 53547, Historian, Don A. Sanford, Tel. (608)752-5055 Fax (608)752-7711, Email: sdbhist@inwave.com, Website: www.home.inwave.com/sdbhist

Serves as a depository for records of Seventh-day Baptists, Sabbath and Sabbath-keeping Baptists since the mid-seventeenth century.

*Southern Baptists Historical Library & Archives, 901 Commerce St., Suite 400, Nashville, TN 37203-3630, Director and Archivist, Bill Sumners, Tel. (615)244-0344 Fax (615)782-4821, Email: bill@sbhla.org, Website: www.sbhla.org

Central depository of the Southern Baptist

Convention. Materials include official records of denominational agencies; personal papers of denominational leaders; records of related Baptist organizations; and annual proceedings of national and regional bodies.

Primitive Baptist Library of Carthage, Ill., 416 Main St., Carthage, IL 62321, Director of Library, Elder Robert Webb, Tel. (217)357-3723 Fax (217)357-3723, Email: bwebb9@juno.com, Website: www.carthage. lib.il.us/community/churches/primbap/pbl.html

Collects the records of congregations and associations.

American Baptist-Samuel Colgate Historical Library, 1106 S. Goodman St., Rochester, NY 14620-2532, Director, Stuart W. Campbell, Tel. (716)473-1740 Fax (716)473-1740, Email: abhs@crcds.edu, Website: www.crds.edu/abhs

Manuscript holdings include collections of Baptist ministers, missionaries, and scholars, and some records of Baptist churches, associations, and national and international bodies.

*American Baptist Archives Center, P.O. Box 851, Valley Forge, PA 19482-0851, Archivist, Betty Layton, Tel. (610)768-2374 Fax (610) 768-2266, Website: www.abc-usa.org/ abhs

Repository for the non-current records of the national boards and administrative organizations of American Baptist churches in the U.S.A. Collections include mission files, publications, correspondence, official minutes and annual reports.

## Baptist and United Church of Christ

Andover Newton Theological School, Andover Newton Theological School, Franklin Trask Library, 210 Herrick Rd., Newton Centre, MA 02459, Associate Director for Special Collections, Diana Yount, Tel. (617)964-1100 x 252 Fax (617)965-9756, Email: dyount @ants.edu, Website: www.ants.edu/ftlibrary

The collections document Baptist, Congregational and United Church history, including personal papers relating to national denominational work and foreign missions, with emphasis on New England Church history.

## Brethren in Christ

*Brethren in Christ Historical Library and Archives, One College Avenue, P.O. Box 3002, Grantham, PA 17027, Director, Dori I. Steckbeck, Tel. (717)691-6048 Fax (717)691-6042, Email: archives@messiah.edu

Records of general church boards and agencies, regional conferences, congregations and organizations; also includes library, manuscripts, and oral history collection.

## Church of the Brethren

*Brethren Historical Library and Archives, 1451 Dundee Ave., Elgin, IL 60120, Librarian/Archivist, Kenneth M. Shaffer, Jr., Tel. (847) 742-5100 x 294 Fax (847)742-6103, Email: kshaffer_gb@brethren.org, Website: www. brethren.org/genbd/bhla

Archival materials dating from 1800-present relating to the cultural, socio-economic, theological, genealogical, and institutional history of the Church of the Brethren.

## Churches of Christ

Center for Restoration Studies, Abilene Christian University, 760 Library Court, P.O. Box 29208, Abilene, TX 79699, Archivist, Erma Jean Loveland, Tel. (915)674-2538 Fax (915) 674-2202, Email: lovelande@acu.edu, Website: www.bible.acu.edu/crs

Archival materials connected with the Stone-Campbell Movement. The chief focus is on the Church of Christ in the twentieth century.

Emmanuel School of Religion Library, One Walker Drive, Johnson City, TN 37601-9438, Director, Thomas E. Stokes, Tel. (423)926-1186 Fax (423)926-6198, Email: library@esr.edu, Website: www.library.esr.edu

Materials related to the Stone-Campbell/Restoration Movement tradition. Collection includes items from the Christian Church and Churches of Christ, the a cappella Churches of Christ, and the Christian Church (Disciples of Christ).

## Churches of God General Conference

*Winebrenner Theological Seminary Library, Winebrenner Theological Seminary, 950 N. Main St., Findlay, OH 45840, Director of Library Services, Margaret Hirschy, Tel. (419) 434-4260 Fax (419)434-4267, Email: library @winebrenner.edu, Website: www.winebrenner. edu/Library

Archival materials of the Churches of God, General Conference including local conference journals.

## Disciples of Christ

Christian Theological Seminary Library, Christian Theological Seminary Library, 1000 W. 42nd St., P.O. Box 88267, Indianapolis, IN 46208, Archives Manager, Don Haymes, Tel. (317)931-2368 Fax (317)931-2363, Email: don.haymes@cts.edu, Website: www.cts.edu/Library

Archival materials dealing with the Disciples of Christ and related movements.

*Disciples of Christ Historical Society, 1101 19th Ave. S, Nashville, TN 37212, Director of Library and Archives, Sara Harwell, Tel. (615)327-1444 Fax (615)327-1445, Email:

harwellsj@dishistsoc.org, Website: www.dishist-soc. org

Collects documents of the Stone-Campbell Movement.

## Episcopal

*Archives of the Episcopal Church, P.O. Box 2247, Austin, TX 78768-2247, Canonical Archivist and Director, Mark J. Duffy, Tel. (512)472-6816 Fax (512)480-0437, Email: research@episcopalarchives.org, Website: www.episcopalarchives.org

Repository for the official records of the national church, its corporate bodies and affiliated agencies, personal papers, and some diocesan archives. Contact the Archives for reference to diocesan and parochial church records.

## Evangelical and Reformed

*Evangelical and Reformed Historical Society, Lancaster Theological Seminary, 555 W. James St., Lancaster, PA 17603, Archivist, Richard R. Berg, Tel. (717)290-8704 Fax (717) 393-4254, Email: erhs@lancasterseminary. edu, Website: www.erhs.info

Manuscripts and transcriptions of early German Reformed Church (U.S.) 1725-1863; Reformed Church in the United States 1863-1934, and Evangelical and Reformed Church 1934-1957 records of coetus, synods, and classes, pastoral records, and personal papers.

## Evangelical Congregational Church

*Archives of the Evangelical Congregational Church, Evangelical School of Theology, Rostad Library, 121 S. College St., Myerstown, PA 17067, Archivist, Terry M. Heisey, Tel. (717) 866-5775 Fax (717)866-4667, Email: theisey @evangelical.edu, Website: www.evangelical. edu

Repository of records of the administrative units of the denomination, affiliated organizations, and closed churches. Also collected are records of local congregations and materials related to the United Evangelical Church and the Evangelical Association.

## Friends

*Historical Library of Swarthmore, Swarthmore College, 500 College Ave., Swarthmore, PA 19081-1399, Curator, Christopher Densmore, Tel. (610)328-8497 Fax (610)328-7329, Email: friends@swarthmore.edu, Website: www.swarthmore.edu/library/friends

Official depository for the records of the Philadelphia, Baltimore, and New York Yearly Meetings. Comprehensive collection of originals and copies of other Quaker meeting archives.

Special Collections-Quaker Collection, Haverford College, 370 Lancaster Ave., Haverford, PA 19041-1392, Quaker Bibliographer, Emma Jones Lapsansky, Tel. (610)896-1161 Fax (610)896-1102, Email: elapsansky@haverford. edu, Website: www.haverford.edu/library/special

Repository for material relating to the Society of Friends (Quakers), especially to the segment known from 1827 to the mid-20th century as "Orthodox" in the Delaware Valley.

## Interdenominational

American Bible Society Library and Archives, 1865 Broadway, New York, NY 10023-9980, Curator, Liana Lupas, Tel. (212)408-1204 Fax (212)408-1526, Email: llupas@american-bible.org, Website: www.americanbible.org/ BiblicalHeritage/library.dsp

Core of collections includes founders' documents, minutes, and correspondence related to the worldwide mission of the ABS.

Billy Graham Center Archives, Wheaton College, 500 College Ave., 3rd Floor, Wheaton, IL 60187-5593, Director of Archives, Paul Erickson, Tel. (630)752-5910 Fax (630)752-5916, Email: bgcarc@wheaton. edu, Website: www.wheaton.edu/bgc/archives/ archhp1.html

Graduate Theological Union Archives, 2400 Ridge Road, Berkeley, CA 94709, Archivist, Lucinda Glenn Rand, Tel. (510)649-2507 Fax (510)649-2508, Email: lglenn@gtu.edu, Website: www.gtu.edu/library/archives

Holy Spirit Research Center, Oral Roberts University, LRC 5E 02, 7777 S. Lewis Ave., Tulsa, OK 74171, Director, Mark E. Roberts, Tel. (918)495-6391 Fax (918)495-6662, Email: mroberts@oru.edu, Website: www.oru. edu/university/library/holyspirit

Pentecostal and Charismatic records, with emphasis on divine healing.

National Council of Churches of Christ Archives, Presbyterian Church (U.S.A.), Dept. of History & Records Management Services, 425 Lombard St., Philadelphia, PA 19147-1516, Manager, Margery N. Sly, Tel. (215) 627-1852 Fax (215)627-0509, Email: preshist @shrsys.hslc.org, Website: www.libertynet. org/pacscl/phs

Schomburg Center for Research in Black Culture, 515 Malcolm X Blvd., New York, NY 10037, Manuscripts, Archives, and Rare Books Division, Curator, Diana Lachatanere, Tel. (212)491-2200 Fax (212)491-6067, Email: scmarbref@nypl.org, Website: www. schomburgcenter.org

Union Theological Seminary, Union Theological Seminary, Burke Library, 3041 Broadway,

New York, NY 10027, Archivist and Head of Special Collections, Michael Boddy, Tel. (212)280-1501 Fax (212)280-1456, Email: mboddy@uts.columbia.edu, Website: www.columbia.edu/cu/lweb/indiv/burke

The largest theological library in the western hemisphere, with extensive rare and antique holdings.

University of Chicago, University of Chicago, Regenstein Library, 1100 E 57th St., Chicago, IL 60537-1502, Acting Bibliographer for Religion, David Larsen, Tel. (773)702-8626, Email: d-larsen@uchicago.edu, Website: www.lib.uchicago.edu/e/su/rel

Yale Divinity School Library, 409 Prospect St., New Haven, CT 06511, Research Services Librarian, Martha Smalley, Tel. (203)432-5290 Fax (203)432-3906, Email: divinity.library@yale.edu, Website: www.library.yale.edu/div

## Jewish

American Jewish Historical Society (NY Location), Center for Jewish History, 15 W. 16th St., New York, NY 10011, Director of Research, Michael Feldberg, Tel. (212)294-6160 Fax (212)294-6161, Email: info@ajhs.org, Website: www.ajhs.org

Archival repositories of the Jewish people in America, including significant religious contributions to American life.

American Jewish Historical Society (Mass. location), Friedman Memorial Library, 160 Herrick Rd., Newton Centre, MA 02459, Director of Research, Michael Feldberg, Tel. (617)559-8880 Fax (617)559-8881, Email: info@ajhs.org, Website: www.ajhs.org

Archival repositories of the Jewish people in America, including significant religious contributions to American life.

Jacob Rader Marcus Center of the American Jewish Archives, Hebrew Union College, 3101 Clifton Ave., Cincinnati, OH 45220, Senior Archivist, Kevin Proffitt, Tel. (513)221-1875 Fax (513)221-7812, Email: aja@huc.edu, Website: www.huc.edu/aja

Materials documenting the Jewish experience in the Western Hemisphere with emphasis on the Reform movement. Included in the collection are congregational and organizational records, personal papers of rabbis and secular leaders, and genealogical materials.

## Latter-day Saints

*Archives, Church of Jesus Christ of Latter-day Saints, 50 E. North Temple, Salt Lake City, UT 84150-3800, Director, Steven R. Sorensen, Tel. (801)240-2273 Fax (801)240-6134

Repository of official records of church departments, missions, congregations, and associated organizations. Includes personal papers of church leaders and members.

Family History Library, 35 North West Temple, Salt Lake City, UT 84150-3400, Tel. (801)240-2331 Fax (801)240-5551, Email: fhl@ldschurch.org

Primarily microfilmed vital, church, probate, land, census, and military records including local church registers.

## Lutheran

Lutheran History Center of the West, 1712 Greentree Dr., Concord, CA, Editor, Duane A. Peterson, Tel. (925)825-2109, Email: duanep@astound.net

*Archives of the Evangelical Lutheran Church in America, 321 Bonnie Lane, Elk Grove Village, IL 60007, Chief Archivist for Management, Reference Services, and Technology, Joel Thoreson, Tel. (847)690-9410 Fax (847)690-9502, Email: archives@elca.org, Website: www.elca.org/archives

Official repository for the churchwide offices of the ELCA and its predecessors. For further information on synod and regional archives, contact the Chicago archives or check the ELCA World Wide Web site. For ELCA college and seminary archives, contact those institutions directly, or consult the ELCA Archives.

*Concordia Historical Institute, Concordia Seminary, 804 Seminary Place, St. Louis, MO 63105, Director, Martin R. Noland, Tel. (314)505-7900 Fax (314)505-7901, Email: chi@chi.lcms.org, Website: www.chi.lcms.org

Official repository of The Lutheran Church-Missouri Synod. Collects synodical and congregational records, personal papers and records of Lutheran agencies.

## Mennonite

*Mennonite Church U.S.A. Archives-Goshen, 1700 South Main, Goshen, IN 46526, Interim Director, Rich Preheim, Tel. (574)535-7477 Fax (574)535-7756, Email: archives@goshen.edu, Website: www.MennoniteUSA.org/History

Repository of the official organizational records of the Mennonite Church and personal papers of leaders and members.

Center for Mennonite Brethren Studies, 1717 S. Chestnut, Fresno, CA 93702, Archivist, Kevin Enns-Rempel, Tel. (559)453-2225 Fax (559)453-2124, Email: kennsrem@fresno.edu, Website: www.fresno.edu/dept/library/cmbs

Official repository for the General Conference of Mennonite Brethren Churches.

*Mennonite Church U.S.A. Archives-North Newton, Bethel College, 300 E. 27th St.,

North Newton, KS 67117-0531, Archivist, John Thiesen, Tel. (316)284-5304 Fax (316) 284-5843, Email: mla@bethelks.edu, Website: www.bethelks.edu/services/mla

An official repository for the General Conference Mennonite Church and several other organizations related to the General Conference.

## Methodist

B.L. Fisher Library, Asbury Theological Seminary, 204 N. Lexington Ave., Wilmore, KY 40390, Archivist and Special Collections Librarian, Grace Yoder, Tel. (859)858-2352 Fax (859)858-2350, Email: grace_yoder@asburyseminary.edu, Website: www.asburyseminary.edu

Documents the Holiness Movement and evangelical currents in the United Methodist Church. Holdings include records of related associations, camp meetings, personal papers, and periodicals.

*Heritage Hall at Livingstone College, 701 W. Monroe St., Salisbury, NC 28144, Director, Phyllis H. Galloway, Tel. (704)216-6094 Fax (704)216-6280, Email: pgallow@livingstone.edu, Website: www.livingstone.edu/heritage_hall.htm

Records of the African Methodist Episcopal Zion Church.

*Office of the Historiographer of the African Methodist Episcopal Church, P.O. Box 301, Williamstown, MA 02167, Historiographer, Dennis C. Dickerson, Tel. (413)597-2484 Fax (413)597-3673, Email: dennis.c.dickerson@williams.edu

General and annual conference minutes; reports of various departments such as missions and publications; and congregational histories and other local materials. The materials are housed in the office of the historiographer and other designated locations.

*General Commission on Archives and History, The United Methodist Church, P.O. Box 127, Madison, NJ 07940, Archivist/Records Administrator, L. Dale Patterson, Tel. (973) 408-3189 Fax (973)408-3909, Email: research@gcah.org, Website: www.gcah.org

Collects administrative and episcopal records, and personal papers of missionaries and leaders. Holds limited genealogical information on ordained ministers. Will direct researchers to local and regional collections of congregational records and information on United Methodism and its predecessors.

Center for Evangelical United Brethren Heritage, United Theological Seminary, 1810 Harvard Blvd., Dayton, OH 45406-4599, Interim Director, Sarah D. Brooks Blair, Tel.

(937)278-5817 x 2218 Fax (937)275-5701, Email: sblair@united.edu, Website: www.united.edu/eubcenter

Documents predecessor and cognate church bodies of the United Methodist Church including the Evangelical Association, United Brethren in Christ, United Evangelical, Evangelical, Evangelical United Brethren, Evangelical Congregational, and Evangelical of North America.

## Moravian

Moravian Archives—Southern Province, 457 S. Church St., Winston-Salem, NC 27101, Archivist, C. Daniel Crews, Tel. (336)722-1742 Fax (336)725-4514, Email: moravianarchives@mcsp.org, Website: www.moravianarchives.org

Repository of the records of the Moravian Church, Southern Province, its congregations, and its members.

Moravian Archives—Northern Province, 41 W. Locust St., Bethlehem, PA 18018-2757, Archivist, Vernon H. Nelson, Tel. (610)866-3255 Fax (610)866-9210, Email: morarchbeth@enter.net, Website: www.moravianchurcharchives.org

Records of the Northern Province of the Moravian Church in America, including affiliated provinces in the Eastern West Indies, Nicaragua, Honduras, Labrador, and Alaska.

## Nazarene

*Nazarene Archives, Church of the Nazarene, 6401 The Paseo, Kansas City, MO 64131, Archives Manager, Stan Ingersol, Tel. (816)333-7000 x 2437 Fax (816)361-4983, Email: singersol@nazarene.org, Website: www.nazarene.org/archives

Focus is on general and district materials, including those of leaders, agencies, and study commissions. The Archives also collects materials on congregations, church colleges and seminaries world-wide, and social ministries.

## Pentecostal

David du Plessis Archives, Fuller Theological Seminary, 135 North Oakland Ave., Pasadena, CA 81182, Archivist, Roger Robins, Tel. (626)584-5311 Fax (626)584-5644, Email: archive@fuller.edu, Website: www.fuller.edu/archive

Collects material related to the Pentecostal and Charismatic movements; also includes material related to Charles Fuller and the Old Fashioned Revival Hour broadcast, Fuller Theological Seminary, and neo-evangelicalism.

*Hal Bernard Dixon Jr. Pentecostal Research Center, 260 11th St. NE, Cleveland, TN 37311, Director, David G. Roebuck, Tel.

357

(423)614-8576 Fax (423)614-8555, Email: dixon_research@leeuniversity.edu, Website: www.faculty.leeu.edu/~drc
Official repository of the Church of God (Cleveland, Tenn.). Also collects other Pentecostal and Charismatic materials.

*International Pentecostal Holiness Church Archives and Research Center, P.O. Box 12609, Oklahoma City, OK 73157, Director, Harold D. Hunter, Tel. (405)787-7110 x 3132 Fax (405)789-3957, Email: archives@iphc.org, Website: www.pctii.org/arc/archives.html
Official repository for records and publications produced by the international headquarters, conferences, and influential leaders.

Center for the Study of Oneness Pentecostalism, 700 Howdershell Road,Florissant, MO 63031, Chair, Historical Committee, J. L. Hall, Tel. (314)838-8858 x 2107 Fax (314) 838-8848, Email: Rjohnston@lupci.org, Website: www.upci.org
Collects a variety of Pentecostal archives, primarily the United Pentecostal (Oneness) Branch.

## Polish National Catholic

*Polish National Catholic Church Commission on History and Archives, 1031 Cedar Ave., Scranton, PA 18505, Chair, Joseph Wieczerzak, Tel. (717)343-0100
Documents pertaining to the church's national office, parishes, Prime Bishop, leaders, and organizations.

## Presbyterian

*Presbyterian Historical Society Headquarters, 425 Lombard St., Philadelphia, PA 19147-1516, Deputy Director, Margery N. Sly, Tel. (215)627-1852 Fax (215)627-0509, Email: refdesk@history.pcusa.org, Website: www.history. pcusa.org
Collects the official records of the church's national offices and agencies, synods, presbyteries, and some congregations. The Society also houses records of the church's predecessor denominations, personal papers of prominent Presbyterians, and records of ecumenical organizations. In addition, the Southern Regional Office in Montreat, N.C. holds local and regional records for the fourteen southern states.

*Presbyterian Church in America Historical Center, 12330 Conway Rd., St. Louis, MO 63141, Director, Wayne Sparkman, Tel. (314)469-9077 Fax (314)469-9077, Email: wsparkman@pcanet.org, Website: www.pcahistory.org
Center serves as the official archive of the Presbyterian Church in America. The Center also holds the records of five other Presbytrerian denominations and the manuscript collections of over one hundred individuals connected with these church bodies.

*Presbyterian Historical Society Southern Regional Office, P.O. Box 849, Montreat, NC 28757, Acting Deputy Director, Bill Bynum, Tel. (828)669-7061 Fax (828)669-5369, Email: refdesk@history.pcusa.org, Website: www.history.pcusa.org
Collects the official records of the church's national offices and agencies, synods, presbyteries, and some congregations. The Society also houses records of the church's predecessor denominations, personal papers of prominent Presbyterians, and records of ecumenical organizations. In addition, the Southern Regional Office in Montreat, N.C. holds local and regional records for the fourteen southern states.

*Historical Foundation of the Cumberland Presbyterian Church and the Cumberland Presbyterian Church in America, 1978 Union Ave., Memphis, TN 38104, Director and Archivist, Susan Knight Gore, Tel. (901)276-8602 Fax (901)272-3913, Email: archives@cumberland.org, Website: www.cumberland.org/hfcpc

Princeton Theological Seminary Libraries, Library Place and Mercer Street, P.O. Box 111, Princeton, NJ 08542-0803, Director of Special Collections, Robert Benedetto, Tel. (609)497-7953 Fax (609)497-1826, Email: special.collections@ptsem.edu, Website: www.library.ptsem.edu/collections
The strengths of the collection are its documentation of the history of the Seminary; American Presbyterianism; English and American Puritanism; Presbyterian missions; hymnology; works by and about Reformed theologians Karl Barth and Abraham Kuyper; and the history of Presbyterians in Korea.

## Reformed

*Heritage Hall, Calvin College, 1855 Knollcrest Circle SE, Grand Rapids, MI 49546, Curator of Archives, Richard H. Harms, Tel. (616)957-6313 Fax (616)957-6470, Email: crcarchives@calvin.edu, Website: www.calvin.edu/hh
Repository of the official records of the Christian Reformed Church in North America, including classes, congregations, and denominational agencies and committees.

*Reformed Church Archives, 21 Seminary Place, New Brunswick, NJ 08901-1159, Archivist, Russell Gasero, Tel. (732)246-1779 Fax (732)249-5412, Email: rgasero@rca.org, Website: www.rca.org/aboutus/archives
Official repository for denominational records including congregations, classes, synods, missions, and national offices.

## Roman Catholic

American Catholic History Research Center and University Archives, Catholic University of America, 101 Life Cycle Institute, Washington, DC 20064, Archivist, Timothy Meagher, Tel. (202)319-5065 Fax (202)319-6554, Email: meagher@cua.edu, Website: www.libraries .cua. edu/achrcua

Department of Special Collections and Archives, Marquette University, P.O. Box 3141, Milwaukee, WI 53233-3141, Department Head and Archivist, Matt Blessing, Tel. (414) 288-7256 Fax (414)288-6709, Email: matt. blessing@marquette.edu, Website: www. marquette.edu/library/collections/archives

Collection strengths are in the areas of Catholic social action, American missions and missionaries, and other work with Native Americans and African Americans.

United States Catholic Historical Society, 201 Seminary Ave., Yonkers, NY 10704, Tel. (914)337-8381 Fax (914)337-6379, Website: www.uschs.com

University of Notre Dame Archives, 607 Hesburgh Library, Notre Dame, IN 46556, Archivist and Curator of Manuscripts, William Kevin Cawley, Tel. (574)631-6448 Fax (574)631-7980, Email: archives@nd.edu, Website: www.archives.nd.edu

Papers of bishops and prominent Catholics and records of Catholic organizations. Includes parish histories, but few parish records.

## Salvation Army

*Salvation Army Archives and Research Center, 615 Slaters Lane, Alexandria, VA 22313, Archivist, Susan Mitchem, Tel. (703)684-5500 Fax (703)299-5552, Email: archives@ usa.salvationarmy.org, Website: www.salvationarmy.org

Holds the documents of Salvation Army history, personalities, and events in the United States from 1880.

## Swedenborgian

*Swedenborg Library, Bryn Athyn College of the New Church, 2875 College Drive, P.O. Box 740, Bryn Athyn, PA 19009-0740, Director, Carroll C. Odhner, Tel. (215)938-2547 Fax (215)938-2637, Email: carroll.odhner@brynathyn.edu, Website: www.newchurch.edu/college/facilities/library

## Unitarian Universalist

*Andover-Harvard Theological Library, Andover-Harvard Theological Library, Harvard Divinity School, 45 Francis Ave., Cambridge, MA 02138, Curator, Frances O'Donnell, Tel. (617)496-5153 Fax (617) 496-4111, Email: frances_odonnell@harvard.edu, Website: www.hds.harvard.edu/ library

Institutional archives of the Unitarian Universalist Association including the Unitarian Universalist Service Committee; also houses records of many congregations; personal papers of ministers and other individuals.

Meadville-Lombard Theological School Library, Meadville/Lombard Theological School Library, 5701 S. Woodlawn Ave., Chicago, IL 60637, Director, Neil W. Gerdes, Tel. (773) 256-3000 x 225 Fax (773)256-3008, Email: ngerdes@meadville.edu, Website: www. meadville.edu/library.html

Repository for materials relating to Unitarian Universalism in particular and liberal religion in general. Includes personal papers of several noted UU ministers, and church records from many UU churches in the Midwestern U.S.A.

## United Church of Christ

Elon University Library, Elon University Library, 2550 Campus Box, Elon, NC 27244, Archivist/Technical Services Librarian, Connie L. Keller, Tel. (336)278-6599 Fax (336)278-6639, Email: keller@elon.edu, Website: www.elon.edu/library

Collection of membership records and other archival material on the predecessor churches of the UCC: Christian Church and the Southern Conference of the Christian Church; also maintains records of churches that no longer exist.

*United Church of Christ Archives, 700 Prospect Ave, Cleveland, OH 44115, Archivist, Bridgette Kelly, Tel. (216)736-2106, Email: kellyb@ucc. org, Website: www.ucc.org/about us archives

Records created in the national setting of the church since its founding in 1957, including the General Synod, Executive Council, officers, instrumentalities, and bodies created by and/or related to the General Synod.

Congregational Library, Congregational Library, 14 Beacon St., Boston, MA 02108, Archivist, Jessica Steytler, Tel. (617)523-0470 Fax (617)523-0491, Email: jsteytler@14beacon. org, Website: www.congregationallibrary.org

Documentation on the Congregational, Congregational Christian, Christian, and United Church of Christ throughout the world, including local church records, associations, charitable organizations, and papers of clergy, missionaries and others.

Archives of the Evangelical Synod, Eden Theological Seminary, Luhr Library, 475 E. Lockwood Ave., St. Louis, MO 63119-3192,

Sr. Research Consultant, Lowell Zuck, Tel. (314)252-3140, Email: lzuck@eden.edu, Website: www.eden.edu/Archives/edenarch. html

Archival records include organization records, personal papers and immigration records.

## Anglican

*General Synod Archives, 80 Hayden St., Toronto, ON M4Y 3G2, Archivist, Nancy Hurn, Tel. (416)924-9199 x 279 Fax (416) 968-7983, Email: nhurn@national.anglican.ca, Website: www.anglican.ca

Collects the permanent records of the General Synod, its committees, and its employees. The Archives has a national scope, and provides referral services on local church records.

## Baptist

*Atlantic Baptist Historical Collection of the Acadia University Archives, Vaughan Memorial Library, P.O. Box 4, Wolfville, NS B4P 2R6, Archives and Special Collections Services Assistant, Winnie Bodden, Tel. (902)585-1011 Fax (902)585-1748, Email: archives@acadiau.ca, Website: www.library .acadiau.ca/archives

Records of associations and churches of the United Baptist Convention of the Atlantic Provinces; also personal papers of pastors and missionaries.

Canadian Baptist Archives, McMaster Divinity College, 1280 Main St. W, Hamilton, ON L8S 4K1, Director, Dr. Gordon Heath, Tel. (905)525-9140 x 23511 Fax (905)577-4782, Email: gheath@mcmaster.ca, Website: www .divinity.mcmaster.ca/academics/resources/ba ptistArchives

## Friends

Canadian Yearly Meeting Archives, Pickering College, 16945 Bayview Ave., New Market, ON L3Y 4X2, Yearly Meeting Archivist, Jane Zavitz-Bond, Tel. (905)895-1700 x 247 Fax (905)895-9076, Email: cym-archivist @quak-er.ca, Website: www.quaker.ca/archives. html

Holds the extant records for Quakers in Canada beginning with Adolphus in 1798 to the present, including the records of the Canadian Friends Service Committee.

## Interdenominational

Canadian Council of Churches Archives, National Archives of Canada, 395 Wellington, Ottawa, ON K1A 0N3, Tel. (613)992-3884 Fax (613)995-6274, Email: reference@ archives.ca, Website: www.archives.ca

Genealogical assistance: (613) 996-7458

National Archives of Canada, 395 Wellington, Ottawa, ON K1A 0N3, Director, Ian E. Wilson, Tel. (613)992-3884 Fax (613)995-6274, Email: reference@archives.ca, Website: www.archives.ca

Records of interdenominational and ecumenical organizations, missionary societies, denominational churches, parish registers, and papers of prominent clergy.

## Jewish

Canadian Jewish Congress National Archives, 1590 Avenue Docteur Penfield, Montreal, QC H3G 1C5, Director of Archives, Janice Rosen, Tel. (514)931-7531 x 2 Fax (514)931-0548, Email: archives@cjc.ca, Website: www.cjc.ca

Collects documentation on all aspects of social, political, and cultural history of the Jewish presence in Quebec and Canada.

## Lutheran

*Archives of the Evangelical Lutheran Church in Canada, 302-393 Portage Ave., Winnipeg, MB R3B 3H6, National Secretary/Archivist, Robert H. Granke, Tel. (204)984-9150 Fax (204)984-9185, Email: rhgranke@elcic.ca, Website: www.elcic.ca

Official repository for the ELCIC and its predecessor bodies, the Evangelical Lutheran Church of Canada and the Evangelical Lutheran Church of America-Canada Section.

Lutheran Historical Institute, 7100 Ada Blvd., Edmonton, AB T5B 4E4, Archivist, Karen Baron, Tel. (780)474-8156 Fax (780)477-9829, Email: abclcc@connect.ab.ca, Website: www.lccarchives.ca

## Mennonite

*Centre for Mennonite Brethren Studies, 169 Riverton Ave., Winnipeg, MB R2L 2E5, Archivist, Conrad Stoesz, Tel. (204)669-6575 Fax (204)654-1865, Email: cstoesz@mbconf. ca, Website: www.mbconf.ca/mbstudies

Institutional records of the boards and agencies of the Mennonite Brethren Church in Canada with some holdings pertaining to other parts of North America; also personal papers of leaders.

*Mennonite Heritage Centre, Canadian Mennonite University, 600 Shaftesbury Blvd., Winnipeg, MB R3P OM4, Director, Alf Redekopp, Tel. (204)888-6781 Fax (204)831-5675, Email: aredekopp@mennonitechurch. ca, Website: www.mennonitechurch.ca/pro-grams/archives

Institutional records and personal papers of leaders within the Mennonite Community. Holdings include the records of the Conference and related agencies

## Pentecostal

*Pentecostal Assemblies of Canada, 2450 Milltower Court, Mississauga, ON L5N 5Z6, Director of Archives, James D. Craig, Tel. (905)542-7400 Fax (905)542-7313, Email: archives@paoc.org, Website: www.paoc.org/administration/archives.html

Repository of archival records created by the Pentecostal Assemblies of Canada.

## Presbyterian

*Presbyterian Church in Canada Archives and Records, 50 Wynford Dr., Toronto, ON M3C 1J7, Archivist/Records Administrator, Kim M. Arnold, Tel. (416)441-1111 x 310 Fax (416) 441-2825, Email: karnold@presbyterian.ca, Website: www.presbyterian.ca/archives

Records of the Presbyterian Church in Canada, its officials, ministers, congregations and organizations.

## Roman Catholic

Research Centre for the Religious History of Canada, St. Paul University, 223 Main St., Ottawa, ON K1S 1C4, Director, Pierre Hurtubise, Tel. (613)236-1393 x 2270 Fax (613)782-3001, Email: crh-rc-rhc@ustpaul.uottowa.ca, Website: www.ustpaul.ca

Holds 900 linear feet of documents, mainly records on deposit from other institutions; and also guides to many Canadian Catholic archives.

## Salvation Army

George Scott Railton Heritage Centre, 2130 Bayview Ave., North York, ON M4N 3K6, Director, Ira Barrow, Tel. (416)481-4441 Fax (416)481-6096, Email: Ira.Barrow@sallynet.org

Records include publications; also financial, personnel, social welfare, and immigration records.

## United Church of Canada

*United Church of Canada Central Archives, Victoria University, 73 Queens Park Crescent E., Toronto, ON M5S 1K7, Chief Archivist, Sharon Larade, Tel. (416)585-4563 Fax (416)585-4584, Email: info@unitedchurcharchives.ca, Website: www.vicu.utoronto.ca/ archives/archives.htm

Records of the United Church and its antecedent denominations and local and regional records of the church in Ontario. Call or view the web page for information on other regional archives.

# III

## STATISTICAL SECTION

## Guide to Statistical Tables

Since questions regarding religious affiliation are no longer a part of the United States Census, the *Yearbook of American & Canadian Churches* is as near an "official" record of denominational statistics as is available.

Because these data represent the most complete annual compilation of church statistics, there is a temptation to expect more than is reasonable. These tables provide the answers to very simple and straightforward questions. Officials in church bodies were asked: "How many members does your organization have?" "How many clergy?" and "How much money does your organization spend?" Each respondent interprets the questions according to the policies of the organization.

Caution should, therefore, be exercised when comparing statistics across denominational lines, comparing statistics from one year to another and adding together statistics from different denominations.

Some particular methodological issues and therefore cautions in interpretation include the following considerations:

1. Definitions of membership, clergy, and other important characteristics differ from religious body to religious body. In this section, full or confirmed membership refers to those with full communicant status. Inclusive membership refers to those who are full communicants or confirmed members plus other members baptized, non-confirmed or non-communicant. Each church determines the age at which a young person is considered a member. Churches also vary in their approaches to statistics. For some, very careful counts are made of members. Other groups only make estimates.

2. Each year the data are collected with the same questions. While most denominations have consistent reporting practices from one year to the next, some change in practices does occur. We endeavor to note such changes when we are made aware of them. Church mergers and schisms can also influence the statistics when they are compared over a number of years. Churches have different reporting schedules and some do not report on a regular basis.

3. The two problems listed above make adding figures from different denominations problematic. However, an additional complication is that individuals who attend two different churches may be included more than once. For example, a person who attends the Church of God in Christ Wednesday evening and an AME service on Sunday morning will likely be included in both counts.

# Table 1. Membership Statistics in Canada

| Religious Body | Year Reporting | Number of Churches Reporting | Full Communicant or Confirmed Members | Inclusive Membership | Number of Pastors Serving Parishes | Total Number of Clergy | Number of Sunday or Sabbath Schools | Total Enrollment |
|---|---|---|---|---|---|---|---|---|
| The Anglican Church of Canada | 2001 | 2,884 | 641,845 | 641,845 | 1,930 | 3,591 | 1,633 | 54,345 |
| The Antiochian Orthodox Christian Archdiocese of North America | 2003 | 16 | 105,000 | 150,000 | 30 | 31 | 16 | 1,300 |
| Apostolic Christian Church (Nazarene) | 1985 | 14 | | 830 | 49 | 49 | | |
| The Apostolic Church in Canada | 2002 | 20 | 1,450 | 1,740 | 22 | 28 | 17 | 687 |
| Apostolic Church of Pentecost of Canada, Inc. | 2005 | 154 | 26,000 | 26,000 | 342 | 452 | | |
| Armenian Holy Apostolic Church—Canadian Diocese | 2002 | 15 | 85,000 | 85,000 | 10 | 49 | 5 | 424 |
| Associated Gospel Churches | 2005 | 137 | 10,758 | 10,758 | 130 | 263 | | |
| Baptist Convention of Ontario and Quebec | 2004 | 363 | 43,513 | 57,852 | 309 | 621 | | |
| Baptist General Conference of Canada | 1999 | 103 | 7,500 | 14,000 | 150 | 240 | | |
| Baptist Union of Western Canada | 2000 | 155 | 20,427 | 20,427 | 279 | 530 | | |
| The Bible Holiness Movement | 2004 | 26 | 521 | 1,146 | 14 | 16 | 25 | |
| Brethren in Christ Church, Canadian Conference | 2003 | | 3,287 | 3,287 | 81 | 81 | | |

Table 1. Membership Statistics in Canada (*continued*)

| Religious Body | Year Reporting | Number of Churches | Full Communicant or Confirmed Reporting | Inclusive Membership Members | Number of Pastors Serving | Total Number of Clergy Parishes | Number of Sunday or Sabbath Schools | Total Enrollment |
|---|---|---|---|---|---|---|---|---|
| Canadian and American Reformed Churches | 2005 | 53 | 9,202 | 16,165 | 46 | 69 | | |
| Canadian Conference of Mennonite Brethren Churches | 2003 | 246 | 36,028 | 36,028 | | | | |
| Canadian Convention of Southern Baptists | 2005 | 245 | 11,578 | 11,578 | 250 | 250 | 124 | 4,907 |
| Canadian District of the Moravian Church in America, Northern Province | 2005 | 9 | 1,008 | 1,476 | 8 | 11 | 9 | 369 |
| Canadian Evangelical Christian Churches | 2004 | 25 | 600 | 2,000 | 53 | 100 | 40 | 4,000 |
| Canadian Yearly Meeting of the Religious Society of Friends | 2005 | 24 | 1,175 | 1,232 | | | 24 | 101 |
| Christian Brethren (also known as Plymouth Brethren) | 2005 | 580 | | 47,000 | | 250 | 500 | |
| Christian Church (Disciples of Christ) in Canada | 2002 | 25 | 1,599 | 2,631 | 24 | 32 | 23 | 390 |
| Christian Churches/Churches of Christ | 2004 | 65 | 5,500 | 9,500 | 75 | 105 | 60 | 3,300 |
| Christian and Missionary Alliance in Canada | 2005 | 428 | 44,852 | 131,031 | 1,037 | 1,381 | 353 | 37,681 |
| Christian Reformed Church in North America | 2005 | 248 | 51,754 | 81,577 | 214 | 358 | | |

Table 1. Membership Statistics in Canada (*continued*)

| Religious Body | Year Reporting | Number of Churches Reporting | Full Communicant or Confirmed Members | Inclusive Membership | Number of Pastors Serving Parishes | Total Number of Clergy | Number of Sunday or Sabbath Schools | Total Enrollment |
|---|---|---|---|---|---|---|---|---|
| Church of God (Anderson, Ind.) | 2002 | 48 | 3,711 | 3,711 | 41 | 88 | 37 | 1,794 |
| Church of God (Cleveland, Tenn.) | 2005 | 150 | 13,504 | 13,504 | 90 | 212 | 121 | 4,626 |
| Church of God in Christ (Mennonite) | 2005 | 52 | 4,664 | 4,664 | 172 | 174 | 52 | |
| Church of God of Prophecy Canada East | 2003 | 26 | 3,830 | 3,830 | 64 | 78 | 29 | 1,357 |
| The Church of Jesus Christ of Latter-day Saints in Canada | 2005 | 479 | 159,386 | 172,433 | 1,437 | 1,614 | 479 | 123,708 |
| Church of the Lutheran Brethren | 2004 | 8 | 425 | 676 | 10 | 13 | 7 | 336 |
| Church of the Nazarene in Canada | 2005 | 165 | 12,873 | 12,874 | 126 | 245 | 133 | 18,374 |
| Churches of Christ in Canada | 2005 | 149 | 6,857 | 6,857 | 122 | 122 | | |
| Community of Christ | 2003 | 75 | 11,536 | 11,536 | 1,100 | 1,100 | | |
| Congregational Christian Churches in Canada | | 95 | | 7,500 | 174 | 235 | | |
| Convention of Atlantic Baptist Churches | 2003 | 539 | 62,766 | 62,766 | 282 | 619 | 314 | |
| The Coptic Orthodox Church in Canada | 2005 | 24 | 55,000 | 55,000 | 33 | 33 | | |
| The Estonian Evangelical Lutheran Church Abroad | 2004 | 11 | 4,996 | 4,996 | 7 | 10 | 4 | 55 |

Table 1. Membership Statistics in Canada (*continued*)

| Religious Body | Year Reporting | Number of Churches Reporting | Full Communicant or Confirmed Members | Inclusive Membership | Number of Pastors Serving Parishes | Total Number of Clergy | Number of Sunday or Sabbath Schools | Total Enrollment |
|---|---|---|---|---|---|---|---|---|
| The Evangelical Covenant Church of Canada | 2002 | 21 | 1,384 | 1,384 | 6 | 25 | | 1,763 |
| Evangelical Free Church of Canada | 2004 | 140 | 8,441 | 8,441 | 199 | 199 | | |
| Evangelical Lutheran Church in Canada | 2002 | 623 | 142,865 | 199,236 | 485 | 866 | 447 | 17,926 |
| The Evangelical Mennonite Conference | 2005 | 57 | 7,250 | 7,250 | | | 55 | |
| Evangelical Mennonite Mission Conference | 1997 | 44 | 4,633 | 4,633 | 75 | 201 | | |
| The Evangelical Missionary Church of Canada | 2003 | 130 | 10,390 | 10,390 | 218 | 309 | | |
| The Fellowship of Evangelical Baptist Churches in Canada | 2004 | 499 | 71,073 | | 318 | 348 | | |
| Foursquare Gospel Church of Canada | 2004 | 55 | 3,031 | 3,031 | 117 | 141 | | 860 |
| Free Methodist Church in Canada | 2003 | 149 | 7,603 | 7,603 | 123 | 223 | | 5,955 |
| Free Will Baptists | 1998 | 10 | 347 | | 3 | 4 | 8 | |
| General Church of the New Jerusalem | 2005 | 3 | 281 | 791 | 5 | 5 | 2 | 57 |
| Greek Orthodox Metropolis of Toronto (Canada) | 2004 | 76 | 350,000 | 350,000 | 62 | 73 | 76 | |

# Table 1. Membership Statistics in Canada (continued)

| Religious Body | Year Reporting | Number of Churches Reporting | Full Communicant or Confirmed Members | Inclusive Membership | Number of Pastors Serving Parishes | Total Number of Clergy | Number of Sunday or Sabbath Schools | Total Enrollment |
|---|---|---|---|---|---|---|---|---|
| Independent Holiness Church | 1994 | 5 | | 150 | 4 | 10 | 4 | 118 |
| Jehovah's Witnesses | 2003 | 1,325 | 110,221 | 110,221 | | | | |
| Lutheran Church—Canada | 2005 | 329 | 54,955 | 75,616 | 233 | 369 | 1,381 | 6,183 |
| Mennonite Church—Canada | 2005 | 232 | 34,124 | 34,124 | | | | |
| North American Baptist Conference | 2005 | 130 | 16,316 | 16,316 | 120 | 189 | 130 | |
| The Old Catholic Church of Canada | 2000 | 4 | 30 | 100 | 4 | 5 | | |
| Open Bible Faith Fellowship of Canada | 2003 | 75 | 2,500 | 9,000 | 164 | 256 | 77 | 3,900 |
| Orthodox Church in America (Archdiocese of Canada) | 2004 | 68 | 2,000 | 10,000 | 59 | 73 | 20 | 450 |
| Patriarchal Parishes of the Russian Orthodox Church in Canada | 2005 | 24 | 1,200 | 1,200 | 5 | 6 | 4 | 108 |
| The Pentecostal Assemblies of Canada | 2003 | 1,111 | 77,736 | 236,579 | | 2,112 | 731 | 36,623 |
| The Pentecostal Assemblies of Newfoundland | 2004 | 128 | 8,864 | 26,432 | 212 | 308 | 95 | 5,770 |
| Presbyterian Church in America (Canadian Section) | 2004 | 19 | 756 | 1,104 | | | | 447 |
| Presbyterian Church in Canada | 2005 | 961 | 122,786 | 190,600 | | 1,318 | 961 | |

# Table 1. Membership Statistics in Canada (continued)

| Religious Body | Year Reporting | Number of Churches Reporting | Full Communicant or Confirmed Members | Inclusive Membership | Number of Pastors Serving Parishes | Total Number of Clergy | Number of Sunday or Sabbath Schools | Total Enrollment |
|---|---|---|---|---|---|---|---|---|
| Reformed Church in Canada | 2004 | 40 | 3,753 | 5,642 | 38 | 67 | | |
| The Reformed Episcopal Church of Canada | 2004 | 11 | 780 | 900 | 10 | 14 | 3 | 35 |
| Reinland Mennonite Church | 1995 | 6 | 877 | 1,816 | 10 | 13 | 5 | 347 |
| The Roman Catholic Church in Canada | 2003 | 5,391 | 12,987,637 | 12,987,637 | | 8,641 | | |
| The Romanian Orthodox Church in America (Canadian Parishes) | 2004 | 24 | 3,300 | 7,300 | 23 | 23 | 21 | 347 |
| The Romanian Orthodox Episcopate of America (Jackson, MI) | 2005 | 25 | 1,294 | 2,067 | 21 | 3 | 12 | |
| The Salvation Army in Canada | 2005 | 356 | 21,645 | 75,732 | 567 | 1,923 | | |
| Serbian Orthodox Church in the U.S.A. and Canada, Diocese of Canada | 2004 | 23 | 8,500 | 230,000 | 26 | 31 | 14 | 2,068 |
| Seventh-day Adventist Church in Canada | 2005 | 334 | 55,431 | 55,431 | 197 | 332 | 400 | 21,630 |
| Syriac Orthodox Church of Antioch | 1995 | 5 | 2,500 | 2,500 | 3 | 4 | | |
| Ukrainian Orthodox Church of Canada | 1988 | 258 | | 120,000 | 75 | 91 | | |
| Union d'Églises Baptistes Françaises au Canada | 2004 | 34 | 1,868 | 1,868 | 29 | 40 | 62 | 629 |

369

# Table 1. Membership Statistics in Canada (continued)

| Religious Body | Year Reporting | Number of Churches Reporting | Full Communicant or Confirmed Members | Inclusive Membership | Number of Pastors Serving Parishes | Total Number of Clergy | Number of Sunday or Sabbath Schools | Total Enrollment |
|---|---|---|---|---|---|---|---|---|
| United Brethren Church in Canada | 1992 | 9 | 835 | 835 | 5 | 12 | 9 | 447 |
| The United Church of Canada | 2004 | 3,527 | 593,600 | 1,441,000 | 1,902 | 4,129 | 2,686 | 51,960 |
| Universal Fellowship of Metropolitan Community Churches | 1992 | 12 | 50 | 1,500 | 8 | 9 | 1 | 36 |
| The Wesleyan Church of Canada | 2002 | 89 | 5,977 | 6,481 | 131 | 201 | 80 | 5,306 |
| **Totals** | | **25,151** | **16,304,033** | **18,158,835** | **14,168** | **35,623** | **11,289** | **420,719** |

# Table 2. Membership Statistics in the United States

| Religious Body | Year Reporting | Number of Churches Reporting | Full Communicant or Confirmed Members | Inclusive Membership | Number of Pastors Serving Parishes | Total Number of Clergy | Number of Sunday or Sabbath Schools | Total Enrollment |
|---|---|---|---|---|---|---|---|---|
| Advent Christian Church | 2004 | 304 | 24,182 | 24,182 | 290 | 493 | 281 | 13,002 |
| African Methodist Episcopal Church* | 1999 | 4,174 | 1,857,186 | 2,500,000 | 7,741 | 14,428 | 6,128 | 303,199 |
| African Methodist Episcopal Zion Church* | 2005 | 3,260 | 1,215,508 | 1,440,405 | 3,507 | 4,063 | 2,715 | 74,853 |
| Albanian Orthodox Diocese of America | 2004 | 2 | 2,407 | 2,407 | 3 | 3 | 2 | 60 |
| The Allegheny Wesleyan Methodist Connection (Original Allegheny Conference) | 2005 | 109 | 1,516 | 1,636 | 70 | 165 | 108 | 4,804 |
| The Alliance of Baptists* | 2005 | 117 | 62,460 | 62,460 | 274 | 399 | | |
| The American Association of Lutheran Churches | 2004 | 84 | 11,771 | 25,908 | 55 | 187 | 88 | 3,920 |
| The American Baptist Association | 2000 | 1,760 | 275,000 | 275,000 | 1,740 | 1,760 | | |
| American Baptist Churches in the U.S.A.* | 2005 | 5,740 | 1,396,700 | 1,396,700 | 4,267 | 7,524 | | 100,121 |
| The American Carpatho-Russian Orthodox Greek Catholic Church | 2005 | 78 | 14,210 | 14,210 | 72 | 104 | 78 | |
| American Evangelical Christian Churches | 2003 | 180 | 15,470 | 18,412 | 192 | 268 | 180 | 14,935 |
| American Rescue Workers | 2004 | 15 | 3,500 | 3,500 | 35 | 35 | 8 | 300 |
| The Antiochian Orthodox Christian Archdiocese of North America | 2005 | 245 | 400,000 | 400,000 | 425 | 485 | 245 | 21,000 |
| Apostolic Catholic Church | 2005 | 6 | 1,888 | 2,608 | 10 | 16 | 5 | 621 |
| Apostolic Catholic Orthodox Church | 2004 | 10 | 10,000 | 25,000 | 12 | 21 | 4 | |

371

Table 2. Membership Statistics in the United States (continued)

| Religious Body | Year Reporting | Number of Churches Reporting | Full Communicant or Confirmed Members | Inclusive Membership | Number of Pastors Serving Parishes | Total Number of Clergy | Number of Sunday or Sabbath Schools | Total Enrollment |
|---|---|---|---|---|---|---|---|---|
| Apostolic Christian Church (Nazarene) | 2005 | 57 | 3,629 | 3,629 | 201 | 201 | 53 | 1,548 |
| Apostolic Christian Churches of America | 2005 | 87 | 12,744 | 12,744 | 319 | 420 | 84 | 6,413 |
| Apostolic Episcopal Church | 2005 | 200 | 6,200 | 12,000 | 250 | 255 | | 800 |
| Apostolic Faith Mission Church of God | 2004 | 23 | 8,240 | 10,340 | 46 | 99 | 23 | 3,935 |
| Apostolic Faith Mission of Portland, Oregon | 1994 | 54 | 4,500 | 4,500 | 60 | 85 | 54 | |
| Armenian Apostolic Church of America | 2005 | 35 | 360,000 | 360,000 | 29 | 48 | 24 | 1,700 |
| Armenian Apostolic Church, Diocese of America* | 1991 | 72 | 14,000 | 414,000 | 49 | 70 | | |
| Assemblies of God | 2005 | 12,298 | 1,612,336 | 2,830,861 | 19,663 | 33,553 | 11,331 | 1,418,607 |
| Associate Reformed Presbyterian Church (General Synod) | 2004 | 256 | 35,211 | 41,019 | 229 | 401 | 208 | 16,374 |
| The Association of Free Lutheran Congregations | 2003 | 257 | 29,200 | 39,409 | 138 | 217 | 211 | 11,576 |
| The Association of Independent Evangelical Lutheran Churches | 2004 | 25 | 5,000 | 5,500 | 25 | 35 | 15 | 320 |
| Association of Vineyard Churches | 2004 | 600 | 140,000 | 140,000 | 700 | 1,205 | | 54,000 |
| Baptist Bible Fellowship International | 2004 | 4,500 | 1,200,000 | 1,200,000 | | | | |
| Baptist General Conference | 2002 | 902 | 145,148 | 145,148 | | | | 65,735 |
| Baptist Missionary Association of America | 2004 | 1,270 | 232,350 | 232,350 | 1,300 | 1,500 | 1,205 | 81,593 |
| Beachy Amish Mennonite Churches | 2005 | 207 | 11,487 | 11,487 | 559 | 594 | 207 | |

# Table 2. Membership Statistics in the United States *(continued)*

| Religious Body | Year Reporting | Number of Churches Reporting | Full Communicant or Confirmed Members | Inclusive Membership | Number of Pastors Serving Parishes | Total Number of Clergy | Number of Sunday or Sabbath Schools | Total Enrollment |
|---|---|---|---|---|---|---|---|---|
| Berean Fellowship of Churches | 2005 | 56 | 12,000 | 12,000 | | | | |
| The Bible Church of Christ, Inc. | 1993 | 6 | 4,150 | 6,850 | 11 | 52 | 6 | |
| Bible Fellowship Church | 2005 | 61 | 7,470 | 7,470 | 61 | 130 | 52 | 5,526 |
| Brethren in Christ Church | 2001 | 232 | 20,739 | 20,739 | 151 | 295 | | 12,404 |
| Brethren Church (Ashland, Ohio) | 2004 | 115 | 10,240 | 10,240 | 89 | 202 | 105 | |
| The Catholic Church | 2005 | 18,992 | 69,135,254 | 69,135,254 | 28,538 | 42,271 | | |
| Christ Catholic Church | 2003 | 6 | 1,797 | 2,887 | 7 | 7 | 1 | 23 |
| Christ Community Church (Evangelical-Protestant) | 2005 | 3 | 1,149 | 1,819 | 3 | 7 | 1 | 265 |
| Christian Brethren (also known as Plymouth Brethren) | 2005 | 1,150 | | 86,000 | | 600 | 1,000 | |
| Christian Church (Disciples of Christ) in the United States and Canada* | 2005 | 3,777 | 462,510 | 722,823 | 4,112 | 7,197 | 3,200 | 180,010 |
| Christian Church of North America, General Council | 2003 | 90 | 363 | 363 | 100 | 162 | 90 | |
| Christian Churches and Churches of Christ | 1988 | 5,579 | 1,071,616 | 1,071,616 | 5,525 | | | |
| The Christian Congregation, Inc. | 2004 | 1,496 | 122,181 | 122,181 | 1,574 | 1,575 | 1,347 | 41,891 |
| Christian Methodist Episcopal Church* | 2005 | 3,320 | 850,000 | 850,000 | 3,006 | 3,424 | 2,485 | 68,155 |
| The Christian and Missionary Alliance | 2005 | 2,004 | 201,009 | 429,760 | 2,429 | 3,019 | | |
| Christian Reformed Church in North America | 2005 | 776 | 187,060 | 272,130 | 679 | 1,340 | | |

Table 2. Membership Statistics in the United States (continued)

| Religious Body | Year Reporting | Number of Churches Reporting | Full Communicant or Confirmed Members | Inclusive Membership | Number of Pastors Serving Parishes | Total Number of Clergy | Number of Sunday or Sabbath Schools | Total Enrollment |
|---|---|---|---|---|---|---|---|---|
| Christian Union | 2005 | | 5,129 | 6,034 | | | | 2,407 |
| Church of the Brethren* | 2005 | 1,068 | 128,820 | 128,820 | 760 | 1,838 | 761 | 33,031 |
| The Church of Christ (Holiness) U.S.A. | 2003 | 154 | 10,460 | 10,460 | 192 | 214 | 148 | 7,489 |
| Church of God (Anderson, Indiana) | 2004 | 2,240 | 252,419 | 252,419 | 5,124 | 6,064 | 2,287 | 123,194 |
| The Church of God in Christ | 1991 | 15,300 | 5,499,875 | 5,499,875 | 28,988 | 33,593 | | |
| Church of God in Christ, Mennonite | 2005 | 130 | 13,822 | 13,822 | 490 | 503 | 130 | |
| Church of God (Cleveland, Tennessee) | 2005 | 6,587 | 1,013,488 | 1,013,488 | 4,764 | 10,458 | 5,570 | 340,842 |
| Church of God, Mountain Assembly, Inc. | 2005 | 120 | 7,200 | 7,200 | 140 | | 120 | 11,040 |
| Church of God of Prophecy | 2004 | 1,901 | 86,476 | 114,476 | 3,100 | | 1,901 | 119,500 |
| The Church of God (Seventh Day), Denver, Colorado | 2001 | 200 | 9,000 | 11,000 | 90 | 130 | 200 | |
| The Church of Illumination | 2000 | 4 | 1,200 | 1,200 | | 16 | 1 | 216 |
| The Church of Jesus Christ (Bickertonites) | 1989 | 63 | 2,707 | 2,707 | 183 | 262 | | |
| The Church of Jesus Christ of Latter-day Saints | 2005 | 12,753 | 5,095,959 | 5,690,672 | 38,259 | 42,786 | 12,753 | 4,370,613 |
| Church of the Living God (Motto, Christian Workers for Fellowship) | 2002 | 120 | 20,000 | 20,000 | 105 | 214 | 65 | |
| Church of the Lutheran Brethren of America | 2005 | 107 | 8,736 | 14,223 | 136 | 219 | 105 | 11,218 |

# Table 2. Membership Statistics in the United States (continued)

| Religious Body | Year Reporting | Number of Churches Reporting | Full Communicant or Confirmed Members | Inclusive Membership | Number of Pastors Serving Parishes | Total Number of Clergy | Number of Sunday or Sabbath Schools | Total Enrollment |
|---|---|---|---|---|---|---|---|---|
| Church of the Lutheran Confession | 2003 | 77 | 6,365 | 8,390 | 64 | 90 | 67 | 943 |
| Church of the Nazarene | 2005 | 5,225 | 630,150 | 636,296 | 5,484 | 9,355 | 4,699 | 839,054 |
| Church of the United Brethren in Christ | 2004 | 215 | 23,000 | 23,000 | 160 | 210 | | |
| Churches of Christ | 2005 | 15,000 | 1,265,844 | 1,639,495 | 14,500 | 16,350 | 12,500 | 1,999 |
| Churches of Christ in Christian Union | 2005 | 231 | 10,645 | 10,645 | 153 | 341 | | 12,948 |
| Churches of God, General Conference | 2005 | 324 | 32,855 | 32,855 | 244 | 387 | 324 | 13,629 |
| Community of Christ | 2005 | 1,236 | 180,339 | 180,339 | | 20,420 | | |
| Congregational Holiness Church | 2005 | 225 | 25,000 | 25,000 | 225 | 225 | | |
| Conservative Baptist Association of America (CBAmerica) | 2002 | 1,200 | 200,000 | 200,000 | 1,800 | 2,100 | | |
| Conservative Congregational Christian Conference | 2005 | 275 | 42,838 | 42,838 | 300 | 566 | 241 | 12,798 |
| Conservative Lutheran Association | 2002 | 3 | 852 | 1,267 | 8 | 29 | 3 | 120 |
| Coptic Orthodox Church* | 2000 | 100 | 250,000 | 300,000 | 140 | 145 | 100 | 5,500 |
| Cumberland Presbyterian Church | 2005 | 759 | 81,464 | 81,464 | 600 | 858 | 650 | 31,505 |
| Cumberland Presbyterian Church in America | 1996 | 152 | 15,142 | 15,142 | 141 | 156 | 152 | 9,465 |
| Episcopal Church* | 2004 | 7,200 | 1,834,530 | 2,247,819 | 5,719 | 15,870 | 6,333 | 275,087 |
| The Estonian Evangelical Lutheran Church | 2001 | 21 | 3,508 | 3,508 | 10 | 12 | | |

# Table 2. Membership Statistics in the United States (continued)

| Religious Body | Year Reporting | Number of Churches Reporting | Full Communicant or Confirmed Members | Inclusive Membership | Number of Pastors Serving Parishes | Total Number of Clergy | Number of Sunday or Sabbath Schools | Total Enrollment |
|---|---|---|---|---|---|---|---|---|
| The Evangelical Church | 2000 | 133 | 12,475 | 12,475 | 164 | 255 | 125 | 8,000 |
| The Evangelical Church Alliance | 2005 | | 293,375 | 293,375 | 2,347 | 2,347 | | |
| The Evangelical Congregational Church | 2003 | 146 | 20,743 | 20,743 | 169 | 252 | | |
| The Evangelical Covenant Church | 2005 | 775 | 117,962 | 117,962 | 1,157 | 1,512 | | 101,182 |
| The Evangelical Free Church of America | 2003 | 1,420 | 130,000 | 350,000 | 2,025 | 2,733 | | |
| Evangelical Friends International—North American Region | 2005 | 285 | 27,360 | 27,360 | | | | |
| Evangelical Lutheran Church in America* | 2005 | 10,549 | 3,636,948 | 4,850,776 | 9,185 | 17,665 | 7,858 | 641,364 |
| Evangelical Lutheran Synod | 2005 | 138 | 15,917 | 20,429 | 114 | 173 | 115 | 2,523 |
| Evangelical Methodist Church | 2005 | 108 | 7,348 | 7,348 | 101 | 202 | 102 | 4,920 |
| Evangelical Presbyterian Church | 2005 | 182 | 65,924 | 73,019 | 295 | 498 | 155 | 32,840 |
| Fellowship of Evangelical Bible Churches | 2005 | 19 | 2,250 | 2,250 | 17 | 47 | 19 | 966 |
| Fellowship of Evangelical Churches | 2005 | 42 | 12,906 | 12,906 | 99 | 180 | 42 | 5,003 |
| Fellowship of Fundamental Bible Churches | 2004 | 22 | 821 | 1,208 | 33 | 48 | 19 | 872 |
| Fellowship of Grace Brethren Churches | 1997 | 260 | 30,371 | 30,371 | | 564 | | |
| Free Methodist Church of North America | 2005 | 1,032 | 65,816 | 75,885 | | 1,913 | | 38,570 |

Note: *Changing census methodologies

# Table 2. Membership Statistics in the United States (continued)

| Religious Body | Year Reporting | Number of Churches Reporting | Full Communicant or Confirmed Members | Inclusive Membership | Number of Pastors Serving Parishes | Total Number of Clergy | Number of Sunday or Sabbath Schools | Total Enrollment |
|---|---|---|---|---|---|---|---|---|
| Friends General Conference | 2002 | 832 | 32,000 | 32,000 | | | 400 | |
| Friends United Meeting* | 2005 | 427 | 37,595 | 42,680 | 306 | 355 | 273 | |
| Full Gospel Assemblies International | 2002 | 41 | 3,075 | 3,075 | 224 | | 41 | |
| Full Gospel Fellowship of Churches and Ministers International | 2004 | 902 | 412,000 | 414,100 | 2,248 | 2,887 | | |
| Fundamental Methodist Church, Inc. | 1993 | 12 | 682 | 787 | 17 | 22 | 12 | 454 |
| General Association of General Baptists | 2004 | 842 | 78,863 | 78,863 | 1,281 | 1,281 | 1,092 | 20,792 |
| General Association of Regular Baptist Churches | 2005 | 1,383 | 132,900 | 132,900 | | | | |
| General Church of the New Jerusalem | 2005 | 37 | 3,469 | 6,701 | 27 | 67 | | |
| General Conference of Mennonite Brethren Churches | 1996 | 368 | 50,915 | 82,130 | 590 | | | 34,668 |
| Grace Gospel Fellowship | 1992 | 128 | 60,000 | 60,000 | 160 | 196 | 128 | |
| Greek Orthodox Archdiocese of America* | 2005 | 566 | 1,500,000 | 1,500,000 | 553 | 840 | 550 | |
| The Holy Eastern Orthodox Catholic and Apostolic Church in North America, Inc. | 2001 | 17 | 4,138 | 4,138 | 9 | | 17 | |
| Holy Synod of the American Diaspora | 2005 | 25 | 15,900 | 15,900 | 40 | 49 | | |
| Hungarian Reformed Church in America* | 2001 | 27 | 6,000 | 6,000 | 27 | 30 | | |
| Hutterian Brethren | 2000 | 444 | 36,800 | 43,000 | 600 | 600 | | |

377

Table 2. Membership Statistics in the United States *(continued)*

| Religious Body | Year Reporting | Number of Churches Reporting | Full Communicant or Confirmed Members | Inclusive Membership | Number of Pastors Serving Parishes | Total Number of Clergy | Number of Sunday or Sabbath Schools | Total Enrollment |
|---|---|---|---|---|---|---|---|---|
| IFCA International, Inc. | 1998 | 659 | 61,655 | 61,655 | | | 659 | 57,768 |
| International Church of the Foursquare Gospel | 2003 | 1,888 | 251,614 | 326,614 | 5,506 | 7,254 | 1,450 | 61,000 |
| International Council of Community Churches* | 2005 | 150 | 108,806 | 108,806 | 283 | 374 | | |
| The International Pentecostal Church of Christ | 2003 | 67 | 2,004 | 4,961 | 51 | 157 | 48 | 1,918 |
| International Pentecostal Holiness Church | 2005 | 1,990 | 244,184 | 303,277 | 2,942 | 3,949 | | |
| Jehovah's Witnesses | 2005 | 12,384 | 1,046,006 | 1,046,006 | | | | |
| Korean Presbyterian Church in America, General Assembly of the* | 2003 | 302 | 38,500 | 55,000 | 465 | 583 | | 17,760 |
| The Latvian Evangelical Lutheran Church in America | 2005 | 60 | 10,800 | 12,100 | 40 | 63 | 16 | |
| Liberal Catholic Church (International) | 2005 | 11 | 1,200 | 6,500 | 22 | 26 | 3 | |
| The Liberal Catholic Church—Province of the United States of America | 2003 | 21 | 5,800 | 5,800 | 50 | 53 | | |
| The Lutheran Church—Missouri Synod (LCMS) | 2005 | 6,144 | 1,870,659 | 2,440,864 | 5,270 | 8,502 | 5,106 | 423,958 |
| Malankara Orthodox Syrian Church, Diocese of America* | 2005 | 80 | 30,000 | 30,000 | 90 | 100 | 77 | 3,780 |

Table 2. Membership Statistics in the United States (*continued*)

| Religious Body | Year Reporting | Number of Churches Reporting | Full Communicant or Confirmed Members | Inclusive Membership | Number of Pastors Serving Parishes | Total Number of Clergy | Number of Sunday or Sabbath Schools | Total Enrollment |
|---|---|---|---|---|---|---|---|---|
| Mar Thoma Syrian Church of India* | 2005 | 74 | 25,000 | 40,000 | 46 | 46 | 60 | 4,500 |
| Mennonite Church U.S.A. | 2005 | 913 | 109,315 | 109,315 | | 2,561 | | |
| The Missionary Church | 2005 | 426 | 35,528 | 35,528 | 699 | 1,055 | | 25,500 |
| Moravian Church in America (Unitas Fratrum)* | 2004 | 92 | 18,529 | 23,377 | 87 | 170 | 88 | 5,223 |
| National Association of Congregational Christian Churches | 2001 | 432 | 65,392 | 65,392 | 507 | 650 | | |
| National Association of Free Will Baptists | 2005 | 2,425 | 198,924 | 198,924 | | 3,959 | | 116,520 |
| National Baptist Convention of America, Inc.* | 2000 | | 3,500,000 | 3,500,000 | | | 9,000 | |
| National Baptist Convention, U.S.A., Inc.* | 2004 | 9,000 | 5,000,000 | 5,000,000 | | | 9,000 | |
| National Missionary Baptist Convention of America* | 1992 | | 2,500,000 | 2,500,000 | | | | |
| National Organization of the New Apostolic Church of North America | 2005 | 388 | 38,060 | 38,060 | 1,741 | 1,741 | 335 | 3,788 |
| National Primitive Baptist Convention, Inc. | 2002 | 1,565 | 600,000 | 600,000 | | | | |
| Netherlands Reformed Congregations | 2003 | 27 | 4,523 | 9,524 | 9 | 10 | | |
| North American Baptist Conference | 2005 | 268 | 47,657 | 46,657 | 280 | 405 | 268 | |

Table 2. Membership Statistics in the United States *(continued)*

| Religious Body | Year Reporting | Number of Churches Reporting | Full Communicant or Confirmed Members | Inclusive Membership | Number of Pastors Serving Parishes | Total Number of Clergy | Number of Sunday or Sabbath Schools | Total Enrollment |
|---|---|---|---|---|---|---|---|---|
| North American Old Roman Catholic Church (Archdiocese of New York) | 2005 | 6 | 575 | 590 | | 7 | 3 | 16 |
| The Old Catholic Orthodox Church | | 11 | 11,000 | 11,470 | 29 | 29 | | |
| Old German Baptist Brethren Church | 2005 | 55 | 6,429 | 6,429 | 273 | 273 | | |
| Old Order Amish Church | 2001 | 898 | 80,820 | 80,820 | 3,592 | 3,617 | 55 | |
| Old Order (Wisler) Mennonite Church | 2004 | 47 | 7,100 | 7,100 | 135 | 135 | | |
| Open Bible Standard Churches | 2005 | 326 | 33,000 | 39,000 | 405 | 1,050 | | |
| The Orthodox Church in America* | 2004 | 737 | 970,000 | 1,064,000 | 824 | 905 | 517 | |
| The Orthodox Presbyterian Church | 2005 | 255 | 19,965 | 27,540 | | 449 | | |
| Patriarchal Parishes of the Russian Orthodox Church in the U.S.A.* | | 31 | 7,000 | 17,000 | 37 | 63 | | |
| Pentecostal Assemblies of the World, Inc. | 1998 | 1,750 | 1,500,000 | 1,500,000 | 4,500 | 4,500 | | |
| Pentecostal Church of God | 2005 | 1,170 | 40,000 | 117,000 | | 2,870 | 1,000 | |
| Pentecostal Fire-Baptized Holiness Church | 1996 | 27 | 223 | 223 | | 28 | 25 | 400 |
| Philadelphia Yearly Meeting of the Religious Society of Friends* | 2005 | 104 | 11,746 | 11,746 | | | 80 | |
| Polish National Catholic Church of America* | 2004 | 126 | 60,000 | 60,000 | 112 | 137 | | |

Table 2. Membership Statistics in the United States *(continued)*

| Religious Body | Year Reporting | Number of Churches Reporting | Full Communicant or Confirmed Members | Inclusive Membership | Number of Pastors Serving Parishes | Total Number of Clergy | Number of Sunday or Sabbath Schools | Total Enrollment |
|---|---|---|---|---|---|---|---|---|
| Presbyterian Church in America | 2003 | 1,534 | 260,919 | 325,791 | 3,287 | 3,287 | | 120,468 |
| Presbyterian Church (U.S.A.)* | 2005 | 10,960 | 2,313,662 | 3,098,842 | 8,752 | 21,312 | 8,703 | 1,081,084 |
| Primitive Advent Christian Church | 1993 | 10 | 345 | 345 | 11 | 11 | 10 | 292 |
| Primitive Methodist Church in the U.S.A. | 2005 | 76 | 3,965 | 4,290 | 57 | 97 | 61 | 2,232 |
| Progressive National Baptist Convention, Inc.* | 1995 | 2,000 | 2,500,000 | 2,500,000 | | | | |
| Protestant Reformed Churches in America | 2005 | 28 | 4,212 | 7,328 | 25 | 41 | 23 | |
| Reformed Catholic Church | 1997 | 100 | 25,000 | 25,000 | 80 | 100 | | |
| Reformed Church in America* | 2005 | 894 | 164,697 | 269,815 | 827 | 1,838 | | |
| Reformed Church in the United States | 2002 | 48 | 3,258 | 4,369 | 42 | 50 | 48 | 951 |
| Reformed Episcopal Church | 2003 | 142 | 8,631 | 11,281 | 185 | 211 | | |
| Reformed Mennonite Church | 2005 | 8 | 151 | 161 | 38 | | | |
| Reformed Presbyterian Church of North America | 2004 | 80 | 4,542 | 6,347 | 77 | 147 | | |
| Religious Society of Friends (Conservative) | 1994 | 1,200 | 104,000 | 104,000 | | | | |
| The Romanian Orthodox Episcopate of America | 2002 | 22 | 1,000 | 1,500 | 16 | 19 | 12 | |

# Table 2. Membership Statistics in the United States (continued)

| Religious Body | Year Reporting | Number of Churches Reporting | Full Communicant or Confirmed Members | Inclusive Membership | Number of Pastors Serving Parishes | Total Number of Clergy | Number of Sunday or Sabbath Schools | Total Enrollment |
|---|---|---|---|---|---|---|---|---|
| The Russian Orthodox Church Outside of Russia | 2003 | 190 | 480,000 | 480,000 | 210 | 258 | 32 | 2,120 |
| The Salvation Army | 2005 | 1,316 | 101,654 | 422,543 | 2,632 | 5,526 | 1,316 | 101,711 |
| The Schwenkfelder Church | 2003 | 6 | 2,500 | 2,500 | 9 | 11 | 6 | 700 |
| Separate Baptists in Christ | 1992 | 100 | 8,000 | 8,000 | 95 | 140 | 100 | |
| Serbian Orthodox Church in the U.S.A. and Canada* | 1986 | 68 | 67,000 | 67,000 | 60 | 82 | | |
| Seventh-day Adventist Church | 2005 | 4,750 | 964,811 | 964,811 | 2,580 | 5,210 | 5,545 | 262,842 |
| Seventh Day Baptist General Conference, U.S.A. and Canada | 2004 | 97 | 5,000 | 5,900 | 55 | 74 | | |
| Southern Baptist Convention | 2005 | 43,669 | 16,270,315 | 16,270,315 | 99,062 | 117,072 | 38,965 | 8,068,780 |
| Southern Methodist Church | 2005 | 104 | 6,300 | 6,300 | 109 | 158 | 105 | 3,774 |
| Sovereign Grace Believers | 2002 | 350 | 4,000 | 4,000 | 450 | 450 | 350 | |
| The Swedenborgian Church* | 2004 | 39 | 1,410 | 1,802 | 21 | 60 | | |
| Syrian (Syriac) Orthodox Church of Antioch* | 2005 | 31 | 32,500 | 32,500 | 28 | 31 | 22 | 1,585 |
| Syro-Russian Orthodox Catholic Church | 2004 | 125 | 21,500 | 23,000 | 110 | 125 | 35 | 1,250 |
| True Orthodox Church of Greece (Synod of Metropolitan Cyprian), American Exarchate | 1999 | 9 | 1,095 | 1,095 | 18 | 19 | | |
| Ukrainian Orthodox Church of the U.S.A.* | 2000 | 115 | 8,000 | 13,000 | 103 | 124 | 65 | 500 |

Table 2. Membership Statistics in the United States (continued)

| Religious Body | Year Reporting | Number of Churches Reporting | Full Communicant or Confirmed Members | Inclusive Membership | Number of Pastors Serving Parishes | Total Number of Clergy | Number of Sunday or Sabbath Schools | Total Enrollment |
|---|---|---|---|---|---|---|---|---|
| Unitarian Universalist Association of Congregations | 2002 | 1,010 | 214,738 | 214,738 | 1,267 | 171 | 1,010 | 1,819 |
| The United Catholic Church, Inc. | 2005 | 36 | 2,160 | 2,640 | 50 | 57 | | |
| United Christian Church | 2005 | 9 | 280 | 280 | 9 | 15 | 7 | 577 |
| United Church of Christ* | 2005 | 5,567 | 1,224,297 | 1,224,297 | 4,293 | 10,231 | 4,762 | 257,170 |
| The United Methodist Church* | 2004 | 34,660 | 8,075,010 | 8,075,010 | 24,380 | 45,149 | 31,790 | 3,528,760 |
| The United Pentecostal Church International | 2005 | 4,358 | | 646,304 | 9,085 | 9,085 | | |
| The United Pentecostal Churches of Christ | 2000 | 62 | 7,059 | 7,059 | 466 | 483 | 62 | 2,289 |
| United Zion Church | 2005 | 12 | 615 | 615 | 13 | 22 | 11 | 600 |
| Unity of the Brethren | 1998 | 27 | 2,548 | 3,218 | 25 | 39 | 24 | 1,442 |
| Universal Fellowship of Metropolitan Community Churches | 1998 | 300 | 44,000 | 44,000 | 324 | 372 | | |
| The Wesleyan Church | 2005 | 1,626 | 116,151 | 128,385 | 2,182 | 3,341 | 1,626 | 441,495 |
| Wisconsin Evangelical Lutheran Synod | 2005 | 1,263 | 313,553 | 398,282 | 1,281 | 1,844 | 1,186 | 38,618 |
| **Totals** | | **330,742** | **156,702,658** | **165,878,323** | **412,532** | **600,025** | **215,268** | **24,269,132** |

*National Council of Churches U.S.A. member communion

Table 3. Membership Statistics for the National Council of the Churches of Christ in the U.S.A.

| Religious Body | Year Reporting | Number of Churches Reporting | Inclusive Membership | Number of Pastors Serving Parishes |
|---|---|---|---|---|
| African Methodist Episcopal Church | 1999 | 4,174 | 2,500,000 | 7,741 |
| The African Methodist Episcopal Zion Church | 2005 | 3,260 | 1,440,405 | 3,507 |
| The Alliance of Baptists | 2005 | 117 | 62,460 | 274 |
| American Baptist Churches in the U.S.A. | 2005 | 5,740 | 1,396,700 | 4,267 |
| Armenian Apostolic Church, Diocese of America | 1991 | 72 | 414,000 | 49 |
| Christian Church (Disciples of Christ) in the United States and Canada | 2005 | 3,777 | 722,823 | 4,112 |
| Christian Methodist Episcopal Church | 2005 | 3,320 | 850,000 | 3,006 |
| Church of the Brethren | 2005 | 1,068 | 128,820 | 760 |
| Coptic Orthodox Church | 2000 | 100 | 300,000 | 140 |
| Episcopal Church | 2004 | 7,200 | 2,247,819 | 5,719 |
| Evangelical Lutheran Church in America | 2005 | 10,549 | 4,850,776 | 9,185 |
| Friends United Meeting | 2005 | 427 | 42,680 | 306 |
| Greek Orthodox Archdiocese of America | 2005 | 566 | 1,500,000 | 553 |
| Hungarian Reformed Church in America | 2001 | 27 | 6,000 | 27 |
| International Council of Community Churches | 2005 | 150 | 108,806 | 283 |
| Korean Presbyterian Church in America, General Assembly of the | 2003 | 302 | 55,000 | 465 |
| Malankara Orthodox Syrian Church, Diocese of America | 2005 | 80 | 30,000 | 90 |
| Mar Thoma Syrian Church of India | 2005 | 74 | 40,000 | 46 |

# Table 3. Membership Statistics for the National Council of the Churches of Christ in the U.S.A. (continued)

| Religious Body | Year Reporting | Number of Churches Reporting | Inclusive Membership | Number of Pastors Serving Parishes |
|---|---|---|---|---|
| Moravian Church in America (Unitas Fratrum) | 2004 | 92 | 23,377 | 87 |
| National Baptist Convention of America, Inc. | 2000 | | 3,500,000 | |
| National Baptist Convention, U.S.A., Inc. | 2004 | 9,000 | 5,000,000 | |
| National Missionary Baptist Convention of America | 2004 | | 2,500,000 | |
| The Orthodox Church in America | 2004 | 737 | 1,064,000 | 824 |
| Patriarchal Parishes of the Russian Orthodox Church in the U.S.A. | | 31 | 17,000 | 37 |
| Philadelphia Yearly Meeting of the Religious Society of Friends | 2005 | 104 | 11,746 | |
| Polish National Catholic Church of America | 2004 | 126 | 60,000 | 112 |
| Presbyterian Church (U.S.A.) | 2005 | 10,960 | 3,098,842 | 8,752 |
| Progressive National Baptist Convention, Inc. | 1995 | 2,000 | 2,500,000 | |
| Reformed Church in America | 2005 | 894 | 269,815 | 827 |
| Serbian Orthodox Church in the U.S.A. and Canada | 2005 | 68 | 67,000 | 60 |
| The Swedenborgian Church | 2004 | 39 | 1,802 | 21 |
| Syrian (Syriac) Orthodox Church of Antioch | 2005 | 31 | 32,500 | 28 |
| Ukrainian Orthodox Church of the U.S.A. | 2000 | 115 | 13,000 | 103 |
| United Church of Christ | 2005 | 5,567 | 1,224,297 | 4,293 |
| The United Methodist Church | 2004 | 34,660 | 8,075,010 | 24,380 |
| **Totals** | | **105,427** | **44,154,678** | **80,054** |

# Table 4. Selected Statistics of Churc

| Religious Body | Year | Full or Confirmed Members | Inclusive Members | TOTAL CONTRIBUTIONS | | |
|---|---|---|---|---|---|---|
| | | | | Total Contributions | Per Capita Full or Confirmed Members | Per Cap Inclusiv Member |
| The Apostolic Church in Canada | 2002 | 1,450 | 1,740 | $1,705,737 | $1,176.37 | $980.3 |
| Armenian Holy Apostolic Church—Canadian Diocese | 2000 | 85,000 | 85,000 | $855,000 | $10.06 | $10.06 |
| Baptist Convention of Ontario and Quebec | 2004 | 43,513 | 57,852 | $42,120,960 | $968.01 | $728.0 |
| Baptist Union of Western Canada | 1999 | 20,427 | 20,427 | $5,107,654 | $250.04 | $250.0 |
| The Bible Holiness Movement | 2004 | 521 | 1,146 | $274,493 | $526.86 | 239.52 |
| Canadian District of the Moravian Church in America, Northern Province | 2005 | 1,008 | 1,476 | $1,474,127 | $1,462,43 | $998.7 |
| Canadian Evangelical Christian Churches | 2004 | 600 | 2,000 | $56,000 | $93.33 | $28.00 |
| Christian Church (Disciples of Christ) in Canada | 2002 | 1,599 | 2,631 | $1,449,009 | $906.20 | $550.7 |
| Christian and Missionary Alliance in Canada | 2005 | 44,852 | 131,031 | $136,297,640 | $3,038.83 | $1,040.1 |
| Church of the Lutheran Brethren | 2004 | 425 | 676 | $755,605 | $1,777.89 | $1,117. |
| Church of the Nazarene in Canada | 2005 | 12,873 | 12,874 | $14,359,388 | $1,115.47 | $1,115.3 |
| Convention of the Atlantic Baptist Churches | 2003 | 62,766 | 62,766 | $36,457,660.00 | $580.85 | $580.8 |
| Evangelical Lutheran Church in Canada | 2002 | 142,865 | 199,236 | $61,270,705 | $428.87 | $307.5 |
| Foursquare Gospel Church of Canada | 1996 | 3,031 | 3,031 | $4,376,923 | $1,444.05 | $1,444. |
| The Latvian Evangelical Lutheran Church in America | 1995 | 4,162 | 4,647 | $1,201,332 | $288.64 | $258.5 |
| North American Baptist Conference | 2005 | 16,316 | 16,316 | $30,134,437 | $1,846.93 | $1,846.9 |
| The Pentecostal Assemblies of Newfoundland | 2004 | 8,864 | 26,432 | $5,624,770 | $634.56 | $212.8 |
| Presbyterian Church in America (Canadian Section) | 2004 | 756 | 1,104 | $1,459,707 | $1,930.83 | $1,322.2 |
| Reformed Church in Canada | 2005 | 3,753 | 5,642 | $4,909,664 | $1,308.20 | $870.2 |
| The Reformed Episcopal Church of Canada | 2004 | 780 | 900 | $222,600 | $285.38 | $247.3 |
| Seventh-day Adventist Church in Canada | 2005 | 55,431 | 55,431 | $79,419,927 | $1,432.77 | $1,432.7 |
| Union d'Eglises Baptistes Françaises au Canada | 2004 | 1,868 | 1,868 | $888,230 | $475.50 | $475.5 |
| The United Church of Canada | 2004 | 593,600 | 1,441,000 | $345,976,000 | $582.84 | $240.0 |
| **Totals** | | **1,106,460** | **2,135,226** | **$776,397,568** | **$701.70** | |

Table 3: ATS member schools offer a variety of degree programs. Table 3 displays enrollment by categories degree programs. The Master of Divinity (M.Div.) degree is the normative degree to prepare persons for dained ministry and for pastoral and religious leadership responsibilities in congregations. Over the past five ars, from fall 2001 to fall 2005, the M.Div. experienced an 11% increase in the *number* of students enrolled. those students enrolled in full degree programs in fall 2005 (eliminating the category "Other"), 49% of stunts were enrolled in the Master of Divinity degree, 16% in Basic Ministerial Leadership (Non-M.Div.), 14% General Theological Studies, 13% in Advanced Ministerial Leadership, and 8% in Advanced Theological search.

ble 3  Head Count Enrollment by Degree Categories 1995 to 2005

| Year | Basic Ministerial Leadership (M.Div.) | (Non-M.Div.) | General Theological Studies | Advanced Ministerial Leadership | Advanced Theological Research | Other |
|------|------|------|------|------|------|------|
| 1995 | 27,497 | 6,964 | 7,211 | 8,233 | 5,302 | 9,273 |
| 1996 | 28,035 | 7,474 | 7,157 | 8,315 | 5,499 | 8,157 |
| 1997 | 28,283 | 7,463 | 7,048 | 8,195 | 5,391 | 8,981 |
| 1998 | 29,263 | 8,066 | 7,602 | 8,641 | 5,712 | 9,591 |
| 1999 | 29,842 | 8,361 | 7,862 | 8,743 | 5,396 | 10,228 |
| 2000 | 30,427 | 9,098 | 8,436 | 8,758 | 5,692 | 10,317 |
| 2001 | 31,128 | 8,652 | 8,503 | 8,790 | 5,756 | 11,096 |
| 2002 | 32,005 | 9,493 | 8,626 | 9,209 | 5,653 | 11,544 |
| 2003 | 33,287 | 10,343 | 8,708 | 9,213 | 5,804 | 11,354 |
| 2004 | 34,096 | 10,417 | 9,257 | 9,435 | 5.541 | 11,394 |
| 2005 | 34,505 | 11,018 | 9,831 | 9,330 | 5,790 | 10,828 |

Table 4: In fall 2005, women constituted 36% of the total enrollment in all ATS schools and 31% of the enroll-ent in the M.Div. degree program. When ATS first began gathering enrollment data by gender in 1972, women resented 10% of the total enrollment and 5% of the M.Div. enrollment. Only once in the past 34 years has the mber of women students decreased from one year to the next, that being in 1993, with a 0.65% decrease.

ble 4 Women Student Head Count Enrollment 1995 to 2005

| Year | Number of Students | % Annual Increase | % of Total Enrollment |
|------|------|------|------|
| 1995 | 20,795 | 1.12 | 32.25% |
| 1996 | 21,523 | 3.50 | 32.76% |
| 1997 | 21,652 | 0.60 | 33.10% |
| 1998 | 23,176 | 7.04 | 33.65% |
| 1999 | 24,057 | 3.73 | 34.16% |
| 2000 | 25,391 | 5.55 | 34.91% |
| 2001 | 25,999 | 2.39 | 35.17% |
| 2002 | 27,328 | 5.06 | 35.70% |
| 2003 | 27,920 | 2.2 | 35.50% |
| 2004 | 28,875 | 3.4 | 36.03% |
| 2005 | 29,257 | 1.3 | 35.98% |

395

Tables 5, 6, 7: Enrollment of North American racial/ethnic students in ATS schools has grown from 6% total head count enrollment in 1977 to 23% in 2005. African Americans were 12.1% of the total enrollment fall 2005; Hispanic students, 3.9%, and Pacific/Asian American students, 7.0%.

Table 5 African American Student Head Count Enrollment 1995 to 2005

| Year | Number of Students | % Annual Increase | % of Total Enrollment |
|------|--------------------|--------------------|------------------------|
| 1995 | 5,698 | 3.11 | 8.84% |
| 1996 | 5,550 | -2.60 | 8.45% |
| 1997 | 5,802 | 4.54 | 8.87% |
| 1998 | 6,328 | 9.07 | 9.19% |
| 1999 | 6,854 | 8.31 | 9.42% |
| 2000 | 7,161 | 4.48 | 9.85% |
| 2001 | 7,462 | 4.20 | 10.09% |
| 2002 | 8,192 | 9.78 | 10.71% |
| 2003 | 8,144 | -0.6 | 10.30% |
| 2004 | 8,393 | 3.06 | 10.47% |
| 2005 | 8,946 | 6.59 | 12.10% |

Table 6 Hispanic Student Head Count Enrollment 1995 to 2005

| Year | Number of Students | % Annual Increase | % of Total Enrollment |
|------|--------------------|--------------------|------------------------|
| 1995 | 1,817 | 1.00 | 2.82% |
| 1996 | 1,785 | -1.76 | 2.72% |
| 1997 | 1,915 | 7.28 | 2.93% |
| 1998 | 2,175 | 13.58 | 3.16% |
| 1999 | 2,256 | 3.72 | 3.10% |
| 2000 | 2,685 | 19.02 | 3.69% |
| 2001 | 2,756 | 2.64 | 3.72% |
| 2002 | 2,449 | -11.14 | 3.20% |
| 2003 | 2,863 | 16.9 | 3.60% |
| 2004 | 2,842 | -0.73 | 3.54% |
| 2005 | 2,899 | 2.00 | 3.90% |

Table 7 Pacific/Asian American Student Head Count Enrollment 1995 to 2005

| Year | Number of Students | % Annual Increase | % of Total Enrollment |
|------|--------------------|--------------------|------------------------|
| 1995 | 4,245 | 9.52 | 6.58% |
| 1996 | 4,492 | 5.82 | 6.84% |
| 1997 | 4,545 | 1.18 | 6.95% |
| 1998 | 4,992 | 8.95 | 7.25% |
| 1999 | 4,932 | -1.20 | 6.78% |
| 2000 | 5,003 | 1.44 | 6.88% |
| 2001 | 5,021 | 0.36 | 6.79% |
| 2002 | 5,005 | -0.32 | 6.54% |
| 2003 | 5,499 | 9.90 | 7.00% |
| 2004 | 5,226 | -4.96 | 6.52% |
| 2005 | 5,189 | -7.08 | 7.00% |

# IV

## A CALENDAR FOR CHURCH USE

## 2007–2010

This Calendar presents the major days of religious observances for Christians, Jews, Bahá'ís, and Muslims; and, within the Christian community, major dates observed by Catholic, Eastern, and Oriental Orthodox, Episcopal, and Lutheran churches. Within each of these traditions many other observances, such as saints' days, exist, but only those generally regarded as the most important are listed. Dates of interest to many Protestant communions are also included.

In the Orthodox dates, immovable observances are listed in accordance with the Gregorian calendar. Movable dates (those depending on the date of Easter) will often differ from Western observance, since the date of Easter (*Pascha*) in the Orthodox communions does not always correlate with the date for Easter of the Western churches. For Orthodox churches that use the old Julian calendar, observances are held thirteen days later than listed here.

Jewish and Muslim holidays begin after sunset the day previous to the date listed in this Calendar. For Jews and Muslims, who follow differing lunar calendars, the dates of major observances are translated into Gregorian dates. Since the actual beginning of a new month in the Islamic calendar is determined by the appearance of the new moon, the corresponding dates given here on the Gregorian calendar may vary by geographic location and practice. Following the lunar calendar, Muslim dates fall roughly eleven days earlier each year on the Gregorian calendar. Practice concerning transliteration of the titles of holidays varies widely as well.

(Note: This listing reflects the first full day of holidays extending over two or more days. "C" stands for Catholic, "O" for Orthodox, "E" for Episcopal, "L" for Lutheran, "ECU" for Ecumenical.)

| Event | 2007 | 2008 | 2009 | 2010 |
|---|---|---|---|---|
| New Year's Day (C-Solemnity of Mary; O-Circumcision of Jesus Christ; E-Feast of Holy Name; L-Naming of Jesus), (RC, O, E, L) | Jan 01 | Jan 01 | Jan 01 | Jan 01 |
| Epiphany (RC, O, E, L) | Jan 06 | Jan 06 | Jan 06 | Jan 06 |
| Epiphany Sunday (RC) | Jan 07 | Jan 06 | Jan 04 | Jan 03 |
| Armenian Christmas, (O) | Jan 06 | Jan 06 | Jan 06 | Jan 06 |
| Waqf al Arafah (Eve of 'Id al-Adha) (Muslim) | Dec 19 | Dec 07 | Nov 26 | Nov 15 |
| First Sunday After Epiphany (Feast of the Baptism of Our Lord), (Christian) | Jan 14 | Jan 13 | Jan 11 | Jan 10 |
| 'Id al-Adha (Festival of Sacrifice at time of Pilgrimage to Mecca), (Muslim) | Dec 20 | Dec 08 | Nov 27 | Nov 16 |
| Feast Day of St. John the Baptist, (Armenian O) | Jan 13 | Jan 13 | Jan 13 | Jan 13 |
| Ecumenical Sunday, (ECU) | Jan 21 | Jan 20 | Jan 18 | Jan 17 |
| Week of Prayer for Christian Unity, Canada (ECU) | Jan 22 | Jan 21 | Jan 19 | Jan 18 |
| Week of Prayer for Christian Unity, (ECU) | Jan 18 | Jan 18 | Jan 18 | Jan 18 |
| Theophany, (Oriental O) | Jan 19 | Jan 19 | Jan 19 | Jan 19 |
| Muharram Begins (First Day of the Month of Muharram; Muslim New Year), (Muslim) | Jan 20 | Jan 10 | Dec 18 | Dec 07 |
| Presentation of Jesus in the Temple (Candlemas; Purification of the Virgin Mary; O-The Meeting of Our Lord and Savior Jesus Christ), (Christian) | Feb 02 | Feb 02 | Feb 02 | Feb 02 |
| Ashura' (Martyrdom of Imam Hussein), (Muslim [Shi'a]) | Jan 29 | Jan 19 | Jan 07 | Dec 16 |
| Tu B'Shevat (Jewish) | Feb 03 | Jan 22 | Feb 09 | Jan 30 |

397

| Event | 2007 | 2008 | 2009 | 2010 |
|---|---|---|---|---|
| Brotherhood Week, (Interfaith) | Feb 18 | Feb 17 | Feb 15 | Feb 21 |
| Ash Wednesday, (Western Churches) | Feb 21 | Feb 06 | Feb 25 | Feb 17 |
| Bahá'í Fasting Season begins (19 days), (Bahá'í) | Mar 02 | Mar 02 | Mar 02 | Mar 02 |
| World Day of Prayer, (ECU) | Mar 02 | Mar 07 | Mar 06 | Mar 05 |
| Great Lent (First Day of Lent), (O) | Feb 19 | Feb 06 | Mar 01 | Feb 21 |
| Purim, (Jewish) | Mar 04 | Mar 21 | Mar 10 | Feb 28 |
| Joseph, Husband of Mary, (RC, E, L) | Mar 19 | Mar 19 | Mar 19 | Mar 19 |
| Feast of Naw-Ruz (Bahá'í New Year), (Bahá'í) | Mar 21 | Mar 21 | Mar 21 | Mar 21 |
| The Annunciation, (Christian) | Mar 25 | Mar 25 | Mar 25 | Mar 25 |
| Holy Week (Western Churches) | Apr 01 | Mar 16 | Apr 05 | Mar 28 |
| Mawlid al-Nabi (Anniversary of the Prophet Muhammed's Birthday), (Muslim) | Mar 31 | Mar 20 | Mar 09 | Feb 26 |
| Passover (Pesach) (8 days), (Jewish) | Apr 03 | Apr 20 | Apr 09 | Mar 30 |
| Holy Thursday, (Western Churches) | Apr 05 | Mar 20 | Apr 09 | Apr 01 |
| Good Friday (Friday of the Passion of Our Lord) (Western Churches) | Apr 06 | Mar 21 | Apr 10 | Apr 02 |
| Palm Sunday (O) | Apr 01 | Apr 20 | Apr 12 | Mar 28 |
| Holy Week (O) | Apr 01 | Apr 20 | Apr 12 | Mar 28 |
| Easter (Western Churches) | Apr 08 | Mar 23 | Apr 12 | Apr 04 |
| Holy Thursday (O) | Apr 05 | Apr 24 | Apr 16 | Apr 01 |
| Feast of Ridvan (Declaration of Bahá'u'llah) (12 days), (Bahá'í) | Apr 21 | Apr 21 | Apr 21 | Apr 21 |
| Holy Friday (Good Friday; Burial of Jesus Christ), (O) | Apr 06 | Apr 25 | Apr 17 | Apr 02 |
| Pascha (Orthodox Easter), (O) | Apr 08 | Apr 27 | Apr 19 | Apr 04 |
| Yom Hashoah, (Jewish) | Apr 15 | May 02 | Apr 21 | Apr 11 |
| Yom Haatzma'ut, (Jewish) | Apr 23 | May 10 | Apr 29 | Apr 19 |
| National Day of Prayer, (ECU) | May 03 | May 02 | May 07 | May 06 |
| May Friendship Day, (ECU) | May 04 | May 03 | May 08 | May 07 |
| Rural Life Sunday, (ECU) | May 13 | May 12 | May 10 | May 09 |
| Lag B'Omer, (Jewish) | May 06 | May 23 | May 12 | May 02 |
| Declaration of the Bab, (Bahá'í) | May 23 | May 23 | May 23 | May 23 |
| Ascension Thursday (Western Churches) | May 17 | May 01 | May 21 | May 13 |
| Ascension of Baha'u'll ah, (Bahá'í) | May 29 | May 29 | May 29 | May 29 |
| Visitation of the Blessed Virgin Mary, (RC, E, L) | May 31 | May 31 | May 31 | May 31 |
| Shavuout (Pentecost) (2 days), (Jewish) | May 23 | Jun 09 | May 29 | May 19 |
| Pentecost (Whitsunday), (Western Churches) | May 27 | May 11 | May 31 | May 23 |
| Martyrdom of the Bab, (Bahá'í) | Jun 09 | Jun 09 | Jun 09 | Jun 09 |
| Pentecost (O) | May 27 | Jun 15 | Jun 07 | May 23 |
| Ascension Day (O) | Jun 11 | May 17 | Jun 05 | May 28 |
| Holy Trinity, (RC, E, L) | Jun 03 | May 18 | Jun 07 | May 30 |
| Corpus Christi, (RC) | Jun 10 | May 25 | Jun 14 | Jun 06 |
| Sacred Heart of Jesus, (RC) | Jun 15 | May 30 | Jun 19 | Jun 11 |
| Nativity of St. John the Baptist, (RC, E, L) | Jun 24 | Jun 24 | Jun 24 | Jun 24 |
| Saint Peter and Saint Paul, Apostles of Christ, (O) | Jun 29 | Jun 29 | Jun 29 | Jun 29 |
| Feast Day of the Twelve Apostles of Christ, (O) | Jun 30 | Jun 30 | Jun 30 | Jun 30 |
| Tish'a B'Av, (Jewish) | Jul 24 | Aug 10 | Jul 30 | Jul 20 |
| Transfiguration of the Lord, (RC, O, E) | Aug 06 | Aug 06 | Aug 06 | Aug 06 |
| Assumption of the Blessed Virgin Mary (E-Feast of the Blessed Virgin Mary; O-Falling Asleep (Domition) of the Blessed Virgin), (RC, O, E) | Aug 15 | Aug 15 | Aug 15 | Aug 15 |
| Laylat al-Miraj (Ascension of the Prophet, (Muslim) | Aug 11 | Jul 31 | July 20 | July 09 |
| The Birth of the Blessed Virgin, (RC, O) | Sep 08 | Sep 08 | Sep 08 | Sep 08 |
| Laylat-ul-Bara'h (Night of Forgiveness), (Muslim) | Aug 29 | Aug 16 | Aug 06 | July 27 |
| Holy Cross Day (RC-Triumph of the Cross; O-Adoration of the Holy Cross), (Christian) | Sep 14 | Sep 14 | Sep 14 | Sep 14 |
| Rosh Hashanah (New Year) (2 days), (Jewish) | Sep 13 | Sep 30 | Sep 19 | Sep 09 |
| Ramadan Begins (First day of the month of Ramadan), (Muslim) | Sep 13 | Sep 01 | Aug 22 | Aug 11 |

398

| Event | 2007 | 2008 | 2009 | 2010 |
|---|---|---|---|---|
| Michaelmas (St. Michael and All Angels), (Christian) | Sep 29 | Sep 29 | Sep 29 | Sep 29 |
| World Communion Sunday, (ECU) | Oct 07 | Oct 05 | Oct 04 | Oct 03 |
| Yom Kippur (Day of Atonement), (Jewish) | Sep 22 | Oct 09 | Sep 28 | Sep 18 |
| Sukkot (Tabernacles) (7 days), (Jewish) | Sep 27 | Oct 14 | Oct 09 | Sep 23 |
| Laity Sunday, (ECU) | Oct 14 | Oct 12 | Oct 11 | Oct 10 |
| Thanksgiving Day (Canada), (National) | Oct 08 | Oct 13 | Oct 12 | Oct 11 |
| Shimchat Torah (Rejoicing of the Law), (Jewish) | Oct 05 | Oct 22 | Oct 11 | Oct 01 |
| Shmini Atzeret (Solemn Assembly), (Jewish) | Oct 04 | Oct 21 | Oct 10 | Sep 30 |
| Laylat al-Qadr (Night of Destiny, Revelation of the Holy Qur'an), (Muslim) | Oct 09 | Sep 27 | Sep 17 | Sep 06 |
| Birth of the Bab. (Bahá'í) | Oct 20 | Oct 20 | Oct 20 | Oct 20 |
| 'Id al-Fitr (Festival of the End of Ramadan; First day of the month of Shawwal), (Muslim) | Oct 13 | Aug 01 | Sep 20 | Sep 10 |
| Reformation Sunday, (L) | Oct 28 | Oct 26 | Oct 25 | Oct 31 |
| Reformation Day, (L) | Oct 31 | Oct 31 | Oct 31 | Oct 31 |
| All Saints Day, (RC, E, L) | Nov 01 | Nov 01 | Nov 01 | Nov 01 |
| World Community Day, (ECU) | Nov 01 | Nov 06 | Nov 05 | Nov 04 |
| Birth of Bahá'u'lláh, (Baha'í) | Nov 12 | Nov 12 | Nov 12 | Nov 12 |
| Thanksgiving Sunday (U.S.), (Christian) | Nov 18 | Nov 23 | Nov 22 | Nov 21 |
| Bible Sunday, (ECU) | Nov 18 | Nov 23 | Nov 15 | Nov 21 |
| National Bible Week, (ECU) | Nov 18 | Nov 23 | Nov 15 | Nov 21 |
| Presentation of the Blessed Virgin Mary in the Temple (Presentation of the Theotokos), (O) | Nov 21 | Nov 21 | Nov 21 | Nov 21 |
| Thanksgiving Day (U.S.), (National) | Nov 22 | Nov 27 | Nov 26 | Nov 25 |
| Last Sunday After Pentecost (L-Feast of Christ the King), (RC, L) | Nov 25 | Nov 23 | Nov 22 | Nov 21 |
| The Day of the Covenant, (Bahá'í) | Nov 26 | Nov 26 | Nov 26 | Nov 26 |
| Ascension of 'Abdu'l-Baha, (Bahá'í) | Nov 28 | Nov 28 | Nov 28 | Nov 28 |
| Feast Day of St. Andrew the Apostle, (RC, O, E, L) | Nov 30 | Nov 30 | Nov 30 | Nov 30 |
| First Sunday of Advent (Advent Sunday), (Christian) | Dec 02 | Nov 30 | Nov 29 | Nov 28 |
| Immaculate Conception of the Blessed Virgin May, (RC) | Dec 08 | Dec 08 | Dec 08 | Dec 08 |
| Hanukkah (Chanukah, Festival of Lights) (8 days), (Jewish) | Dec 05 | Dec 22 | Dec 11 | Dec 01 |
| Fourth Sunday of Advent (Christmas Sunday), (Christian) | Dec 23 | Dec 21 | Dec 20 | Dec 19 |
| Christmas, (Christian, Except Armenian) | Dec 25 | Dec 25 | Dec 25 | Dec 25 |

# V
# INDEXES
## Organizations

AAR (American Academy of Religion) . . . . . . .214
ABCCM (Asheville-Buncombe Community
  Christian Ministry) . . . . . . . . . . . . . . . . . . . . .256
Action des Chrétiens pour l'Abolition de la
  Torture (ACAT) . . . . . . . . . . . . . . . . . . . . . . .293
Advent Christian Church . . . . . . . . . . . . . . . . . .60
ADRIS (Association for the Development of
  Religious Information Services) . . . . . . . . . . .25
African Methodist Episcopal Church . . .11, 13, 60,
  371, 384
African Methodist Episcopal Zion Church, The
  11, 13, 61, 371, 384
AGAPÉ Deux-Montagnes . . . . . . . . . . . . . . . . .293
Akron Area Association of Churches . . . . . . . .257
Alaska Christian Conference . . . . . . . . . . . . . . .233
Alban Institute, Inc., The . . . . . . . . . . . . . . . . . .21
Albanian Orthodox Archdiocese in America . . . .64
Albanian Orthodox Diocese of America . . .64, 371,
  388
Alcohol and Drug Concerns Inc. . . . . . . . . . . . . .52
ALEPH Administrative Office . . . . . . . . . . . . .228
Allegheny Valley Association of Churches . . . .259
Allegheny Wesleyan Methodist Connection (Original
  Allegheny Conference), The . . . . . . .64, 371, 388
Alliance of Baptists, The . . . . . . . . . . . .64, 371, 384
Alliance of Churches . . . . . . . . . . . . . . . . . . . . .257
AMERC (Appalachian Ministries Educational
  Resource Center) . . . . . . . . . . . . . . . . . . . . . . .23
American Academy of Religion (AAR) . . . . . . .214
American Association of Lutheran Churches, The
  65, 371
American Baptist Association, The . . . . . . . .65, 371
American Baptist Churches in the U.S.A. . . .11, 12,
  13, 66, 371, 384, 388
American Bible Society . . . . . . . . . . . . . . . . . . . .21
American Buddhist Association . . . . . . . . . . . .223
American Buddhist Congress . . . . . . . . . . . . . .223
American Carpatho-Russian Orthodox Greek
  Catholic Church, The . . . . . . . . . . . . . . . .67, 371
American Council of Christian Churches . . . . . .22
American Evangelical Christian Churches . . . . .67,
  371, 388
American Friends Service Committee . . . . . . . .22
American Hindus Against Defamation . . . . . . .225
American Jewish Committee . . . . . . . . . . . . . .229
American Orthodox Catholic Church. See Apostolic
  Orthodox Catholic Church of North America
American Rescue Workers . . . . . . . . . . . . .68, 371
American Theological Library Association, The .22

American Tract Society . . . . . . . . . . . . . . . . . . . .23
American Waldensian Society, The . . . . . . . . . . .23
Amish. See Old Order Amish Church
Anglican Church of Canada, The . . . . . . . .182, 364
Anglican Orthodox Church. See Episcopal
  Orthodox Church, The
Anti-Defamation League of B'nai B'rith, The . .229
Antiochian Orthodox Christian Archdiocese of
  North America, The . . . . .68, 183, 364, 371, 388
Apostolic Catholic Assyrian Church of the East,
  North American Dioceses . . . . . . . . . . . . . . . .69
Apostolic Catholic Church . . . . . . . . . . . . . . . . .70
Apostolic Catholic Orthodox Church . . . . . .70, 371
Apostolic Christian Church (Nazarene) . . . .71, 183,
  364, 372
Apostolic Christian Churches of America . .71, 372
Apostolic Church in Canada, The . . .184, 364, 386
Apostolic Church of Pentecost of Canada, Inc.
  184, 364
Apostolic Episcopal Church . . . . . . . . . . . . .71, 372
Apostolic Faith Mission Church of God . . .72, 372,
  388
Apostolic Faith Mission of Portland, Oregon
  72, 372
Apostolic Lutheran Church of America . . . . . . . .73
Appalachian Ministries Educational Resource
  Center (AMERC) . . . . . . . . . . . . . . . . . . . . . . .23
ARDA Association of Religion . . . . . . . . . . . . .215
  Data Archives
Arizona Ecumenical Council . . . . . . . . . . . . . . .234
Arkansas Interfaith Conference . . . . . . . . . . . . .234
Armenian Apostolic Church of America . . . . . . .73
Armenian Apostolic Church, Diocese of America
  73, 372, 384
Armenian Evangelical Church . . . . . . . . . . . . . .184
Armenian Holy Apostolic Church—Canadian
  Diocese . . . . . . . . . . . . . . . . . . . . . .184, 364, 386
Arrowhead Interfaith Council . . . . . . . . . . . . . .247
Asheville-Buncombe Community Christian
  Ministry (ABCCM) . . . . . . . . . . . . . . . . . . . .256
Assemblies of God . . . . . . . . . .11, 12, 13, 74, 372
Assemblies of God International Fellowship
  (Independent/Not Affiliated) . . . . . . . . . . . . . .75
Associate Reformed Presbyterian Church (General
  Synod) . . . . . . . . . . . . . . . . . . . . . . .75, 372, 388
Associated Church Press, The . . . . . . . . . . . . . . .24
Associated Churches of Fort Wayne & Allen
  County, Inc., The . . . . . . . . . . . . . . . . . . . . . .240
Associated Gospel Churches . . . . . . . . . . .185, 364

Associated Gospel Churches, The . . . . . . . . . . . . .24
Associated Ministries of Tacoma-Pierce County  266
Association for the Development of Religious
    Information Services . . . . . . . . . . . . . . . . . . . . .25
Association of Catholic Diocesan Archivists . . . .24
Association of Christian Churches in Manitoba .292
Association of Christian Churches of South Dakota
    263
Association of Free Lutheran Congregations, The
    76, 372
Association of Gospel Rescue Missions . . . . . . .25
Association of Independent Evangelical Lutheran
    Churches . . . . . . . . . . . . . . . . . . . . . . . . . .76, 372
Association of Regular Baptist Churches (Canada)
    185
Association of Religion Data Archives . . . . . . .215
    (ARDA)
Association of Religious Communities . . . . . .236
Association of Statisticians of American Religious
    Bodies . . . . . . . . . . . . . . . . . . . . . . . . . . . . . . . .25
Association of Theological Schools in the United
    States and Canada, The (ATS) . . . . . . . .26, 215
Association of Vineyard Churches . . . . . . .77, 372
Atlantic Ecumenical Council . . . . . . . . . . . . . . .293
Atlantic Ecumenical Council of Churches . . . . .292
ATS (Association of Theological Schools) .26, 215
Attleboro Area Council of Churches, Inc. . . . . .245
Auburn Theological Seminary . . . . . . . . . . . . .215
Austin Area Interreligious Ministries . . . . . . . .264

Baha'i National Center of the U.S.A., The . . . . .222
B.A.P.S. (Bochasanwasi Shri Akshar Purushottam
    Swaminarayan Sanstha) . . . . . . . . . . . . . . . . .225
Baptist Bible Fellowship International . .11, 77, 372
Baptist Convention of Ontario and Quebec . . .185,
    364, 386
Baptist General Conference . . . . . . . . . . . . .78, 372
Baptist General Conference of Canada . . .185, 368
Baptist Missionary Association of America . . . .78,
    374, 390
Baptist Union of Western Canada . . .186, 364, 386
BARCA (Border Association for Refugees from
    Central America, Inc.) . . . . . . . . . . . . . . . . . .264
Barna Group, Ltd., The . . . . . . . . . . . . . . . . . . .216
Bay Area Ecumenical Forum . . . . . . . . . . . . . .246
Beachy Amish Mennonite Churches . . . . . .79, 372
Berean Fellowship of Churches . . . . . .79, 373, 388
Bergen County Council of Churches . . . . . . . . .251
Berrien County Association of Churches . . . . . .246
Bible Church of Christ, Inc., The . . . . . . . . .80, 373
Bible Fellowship Church . . . . . . . . . . .80, 373, 388
Bible Holiness Church . . . . . . . . . . . . . . . . . . . . .81
Bible Holiness Movement, The . . . . .186, 364, 384
Bible Way Church of Our Lord Jesus Christ World
    Wide, Inc. . . . . . . . . . . . . . . . . . . . . . . . . . . . . .81
Blanton-Peale Institute . . . . . . . . . . . . . . . . . . . .26
Bochasanwasi Shri Akshar Purushottam
    Swaminarayan Sanstha (B.A.P.S.) . . . . . . . . .225
Border Association for Refugees from Central
    America (BARCA), Inc. . . . . . . . . . . . . . . . . .264
Bread for the World . . . . . . . . . . . . . . . . . . . . . . .26
Brethren Church (Ashland, Ohio) . . . . . . . .81, 373
Brethren in Christ Church . . . . . . . . . .81, 373, 388

Brethren in Christ Church, Canadian Conference
    186, 364
Bridgewater Inter-Church Council . . . . . . . . . .292
British Methodist Episcopal Church of Canada .187
Brooklyn Council of Churches . . . . . . . . . . . . .252
Broome County Council of Churches, Inc. . . . .252
Bruderhof Communities . . . . . . . . . . . . . . . . . . .81
Buddhist Churches of America . . . . . . . . . . . . .223
Buddhist Council of the Midwest . . . . . . . . . . .223
Buddhist Council of the Northwest . . . . . . . . . .224
Buddhist Peace Fellowship, The . . . . . . . . . . . .224
Burlington Inter-Church Council . . . . . . . . . . .293

CAIR (Council for American-Islamic Relations)227
Calgary Council of Churches . . . . . . . . . . . . . .292
Calgary Inter-Faith Community Action Association
    292
California Council of Churches—California Church
    Impact . . . . . . . . . . . . . . . . . . . . . . . . . . . . . .234
Calvary Chapel . . . . . . . . . . . . . . . . . . . . . . . . . .81
Campus Crusade for Christ International . . . . . .26
Canadian and American Reformed Churches
    187, 358, 365
Canadian Assemblies of God (formerly The Italian
    Pentecostal Churches of Canada) . . . . . . . . .187
Canadian Baptist Ministries . . . . . . . . . . . .188, 365
Canadian Bible Society . . . . . . . . . . . . . . . . . . . .52
Canadian Centre for Ecumenism . . . . . . . .52, 293
Canadian Conference of Mennonite Brethren
    Churches . . . . . . . . . . . . . . . . . . . . . . . . .188, 365
Canadian Convention of Southern Baptists 188, 365
Canadian Council of Churches, The . . . . . . . . . .53
Canadian District of the Moravian Church in America,
    Northern Province . . . . . . . . . . . . . . . .188, 365, 386
Canadian Evangelical Christian Churches . . . . .188,
    365, 386
Canadian Evangelical Theological Association . .53
Canadian Society of Biblical Studies-Société
    Canadienne des Études Bibliques . . . . . . . . . .54
Canadian Tract Society . . . . . . . . . . . . . . . . . . . .54
Canadian Yearly Meeting of the Religious Society
    of Friends . . . . . . . . . . . . . . . . . . . . . . . .188, 367
Cape Cod Council of Churches, Inc., The . . . . .245
Capital Area Council of Churches, Inc. . . . . . .252
Capital Region Conference of Churches, The . .236
Capital Region Ecumenical Organization (CREO)
    252
CARA (Center for Applied Research in the
    Apostolate) . . . . . . . . . . . . . . . . . . . . . . . . . . . .26
Catholic Church, The . . . . . . . . .11, 12, 13, 82, 373
Catholic Church in Canada, The. See Roman
    Catholic Church in Canada, The
CB America (Conservative Baptist Association of
    America) . . . . . . . . . . . . . . . . . . . . . . . . .105, 375
CEAP (Community Emergency Assistance
    Program) . . . . . . . . . . . . . . . . . . . . . . . . . . . .248
Center City Churches . . . . . . . . . . . . . . . . . . . .236
Center for Applied Research in the Apostolate
    (CARA) . . . . . . . . . . . . . . . . . . . . . . . . . . . . . .26
Center for Parish Development . . . . . . . . . . . . . .27
Center for the Study of Religion and American
    Culture . . . . . . . . . . . . . . . . . . . . . . . . . . . . .217
Center on Conscience & War (NISBCO) . . . . . .27

Central Maryland Ecumenical Council . . . . . . . .245
Centre Emmaüs . . . . . . . . . . . . . . . . . . . . . . . . . .293
Chaplaincy of Full Gospel Churches . . . . . . . . .27
Chautauqua County Rural Ministry . . . . . . . . .252
Christ Catholic Church . . . . . . . . . . . . . . . .83, 373
Christ Catholic Church International . . . . . . . . .189
Christ Community Church (Evangelical-Protestant)
83, 373, 388
Christadelphians . . . . . . . . . . . . . . . . . . . . . . . . . .83
Christian and Missionary Alliance, The . . . . . . .89,
373, 388
Christian and Missionary Alliance in Canada . .190,
365, 386
Christian Associates of Southwest Pennsylvania 259
Christian Brethren (also known as Plymouth
Brethren) . . . . . . . . . . . . . . . . .84, 189, 365, 373
Christian Church (Disciples of Christ) in Canada
190, 365, 386
Christian Church (Disciples of Christ) in the United
States and Canada . . . . . . . . . .84, 373, 384, 388
Christian Church of North America, General
Council . . . . . . . . . . . . . . . . . . . . . . . . . . .87, 373
Christian Churches and Churches of Christ . . . . .11,
87, 373
Christian Churches / Churches of Christ . .190, 365
Christian Churches Together in the U.S.A. . . . . .28
Christian Churches United of the Tri-County Area
259
Christian Community Action . . . . . . . . . . . . . . .237
Christian Conference of Connecticut . . . . . . . . .237
Christian Congregation, Inc., The . . . . . . . . .88, 373
Christian Council of Delaware and Maryland's
Eastern Shore, The . . . . . . . . . . . . . . . . . . . . .238
Christian Council on Persons with Disabilities . .28
Christian Endeavor International . . . . . . . . . . . . .28
Christian-Jewish Dialogue of Montreal . . . . . .293
Christian Leadership Council of Downtown
Toronto . . . . . . . . . . . . . . . . . . . . . . . . . . . . . .293
Christian Management Association . . . . . . . . . . .29
Christian Methodist Episcopal Church .88, 373, 384
Christian Ministries of Delaware County . . . . .240
Christian Ministry in the National Parks, A . . . . .29
Christian Reformed Church in North America . .90,
191, 365, 373
Christian Service Center for Central Florida, Inc. 238
Christian Union . . . . . . . . . . . . . . . . . . . . . .91, 388
Christian Youth Council . . . . . . . . . . . . . . . . . . .268
Christians United in Beaver County . . . . . . . . .259
Church Army in Canada, The . . . . . . . . . . . . . . .54
Church Community Services . . . . . . . . . . . . . . .240
Church Communities International . . . . . . . . . . .93
Church Council of Greater Seattle . . . . . . . . . .266
Church Federation of Greater Indianapolis, . . . .240
Inc., The
Church Growth Center—Home of Church . . . . . .29
Doctor Ministries
Church of Christ . . . . . . . . . . . . . . . . . . . . . . . . . .92
Church of Christ (Holiness) U.S.A., The . . . . . . .92,
374, 388
Church of Christ, Scientist . . . . . . . . . . . . . . . . .92
Church of God, The . . . . . . . . . . . . . . . . . . . . . .102
Church of God (Anderson, Indiana) . . . . . .93, 191,
366, 374

Church of God (Cleveland, Tennessee) . . . .95, 191,
366, 374
Church of God, Mountain Assembly, Inc. . .97, 374
Church of God, The (Seventh Day), Denver,
Colorado . . . . . . . . . . . . . . . . . . . . . . . . . .98, 374
Church of God by Faith, Inc. . . . . . . . . . . . . . . . .96
Church of God in Christ, International . . . . . . . . .95
Church of God in Christ, Mennonite . . . . . .95, 191,
366, 374
Church of God in Christ, The . . . . . .11, 13, 94, 374
Church of God General Conference (Oregon, IL
and Morrow, GA) . . . . . . . . . . . . . . . . . . . . . . .97
Church of God of Prophecy . . . . . . . . . . . .97, 374
Church of God of Prophecy Canada East, The . .192,
366
Church of God of the Firstborn . . . . . . . . . . . . . .96
Church of Illumination, The . . . . . . . . . . . . .99, 374
Church of Jesus Christ, The (Bickertonites) .99, 374
Church of Jesus Christ of Latter-day Saints,
The . . . . . . . . . . . . . . . . . . . . . . . .11, 12, 13, 99, 374
Church of Jesus Christ of Latter-day Saints in
Canada, The . . . . . . . . . . . . . . . . . . . . . . . .193, 366
Church of the Brethren . . . . . . . . .91, 374, 384, 388
Church of the Living God (Motto, Christian
Workers for Fellowship) . . . . . . . . . . . . . .99, 374
Church of the Lutheran Brethren . . . .193, 366, 386
Church of the Lutheran Brethren of America . .100,
374, 388
Church of the Lutheran Confession . .101, 374, 388
Church of the Nazarene . . . . . . . . . . .101, 375, 388
Church of the Nazarene in Canada . . .193, 366, 386
Church of Our Lord Jesus Christ of the Apostolic
Faith, Inc. . . . . . . . . . . . . . . . . . . . . . . . . . . . .103
Church of the United Brethren in Christ, USA
103, 375
Church Women United in the U.S.A. . . . . . . . . .30
Churches' Council on Theological Education in
Canada, An Ecumenical Foundation, The . . . .54
Churches of Christ . . . . . . . . . . . . .11, 104, 375, 388
Churches of Christ in Canada . . . . . . . . . . .194, 366
Churches of Christ in Christian Union . . . .104, 375
Churches of God, General . . . . . . . . .104, 375, 388
Conference
Churches United, Inc. . . . . . . . . . . . . . . . . . . . .241
Churches United of the Quad City Area . . . . . .239
Churches Uniting in Christ . . . . . . . . . . . . . . . . .30
Churchpeople for Change and Reconciliation . .257
Colorado Council of Churches . . . . . . . . . . . . .236
Comité Québécois du Dialogue . . . . . . . . . . . .293
musulman-chrétien
Community Emergency Assistance . . . . . . . . . .248
Program (CEAP)
Community Ministries of Rockville . . . . . . . . .245
Community Ministry of Montgomery County . .245
Community of Christ . . . . .105, 194, 366, 375, 388
Community Renewal Society . . . . . . . . . . . . . .239
Concerned Ecumenical Ministry to the . . . . . .252
Upper West Side
Congregational Christian Churches . . . . . . .194, 366
in Canada
Congregational Holiness Church . . . . . . . .105, 375
Conservative Baptist Association of . . . . .105, 375
America (CB America)

Conservative Congregational .......106, 375, 388
  Christian Conference
Conservative Lutheran Association ......106, 375
Consultation on Church Union .............30
Contact Ministries of Springfield ...........239
Convention of Atlantic Baptist Churches .....195,
  366, 386
Cooperative Metropolitan Ministries .........245
Coptic Orthodox Church ...........107, 375, 384
Coptic Orthodox Church in Canada, The ..195, 366
Cornwallis District Inter-Church Council .....292
Corpus Christi Metro Ministries .............264
Cortland County Council of Churches, Inc. ....252
Council for American-Islamic ...............27
  Relations (CAIR)
Council of Christian Communions of Greater
  Cincinnati ...........................257
Council of Churches and Synagogues of
  Southwestern Connecticut ...............237
Council of Churches of Chemung County, Inc. ..253
Council of Churches of Greater Bridgeport, Inc. .237
Council of Churches of Greater Springfield ....245
Council of Churches of Greater Washington, The
  238
Council of Churches of Santa Clara County, The
  234
Council of Churches of the City of New York ..253
Council of Churches of the Ozarks ..........249
Council of Hindu Temples of North America ..226
CREO (Capital Region Ecumenical Organization)
  252
Cross-Lines Cooperative Council ............242
Cumberland Presbyterian Church ....107, 375, 390
Cumberland Presbyterian Church ...108, 375, 390
  in America

Day 1/Episcopal Media Center ..............31
Des Moines Area Religious Council .........241
Direction Chrétienne .....................294
Disciples of Christ. See Christian Church (Disciples
  of Christ) in Canada or Christian Church
  (Disciples of Christ) in the United States and
  Canada
Doukhobors. See Union of Spiritual Communities
  in Christ (Orthodox Doukhobors in Canada)
Dutchess County Interfaith Council, Inc. ......253

East Dallas Cooperative Parish .............264
East End Cooperative Ministry .............259
Eastern Area Community Ministries .........242
Ecclesia ...............................251
Ecumenical Committee ....................293
Ecumenical Conference of Greater Altoona ....260
Ecumenical Council of Pasadena Area Churches,
  The ................................234
Ecumenical Council of San Diego County .....234
Ecumenical Ministries ....................250
Ecumenical Ministries of Iowa (EMI) ........242
Ecumenical Ministries of Oregon ...........258
Elim Fellowship .........................108
Elim Fellowship of Evangelical Churches and
  Ministers ............................195
EMI (Ecumenical Ministries of Iowa) ........242

empty tomb, inc. ........................217
Episcopal Church ......11, 13, 108, 375, 384, 390
Episcopal Orthodox Church, The ............112
Estonian Evangelical Lutheran Church, The 112, 375
Estonian Evangelical Lutheran Church ...196, 366
  Abroad, The
Evangelical Church, The ...........112, 376, 390
Evangelical Church Alliance, The ............112
Evangelical Churches. See Fellowship of
  Evangelical Churches
Evangelical Congregational Church, The .....113,
  378, 392
Evangelical Council for Financial Accountability 31
Evangelical Covenant Church, The ..113, 376, 390
Evangelical Covenant Church of Canada, .196, 367
  The
Evangelical Fellowship of Canada ...........55
Evangelical Free Church of America, The .114, 376
Evangelical Free Church of Canada .....196, 367
Evangelical Friends International—North American
  Region ............................115, 376
Evangelical Lutheran Church in America ...11, 12,
  13, 115, 376, 384, 390
Evangelical Lutheran Church in Canada ......196
  367, 386
Evangelical Lutheran Synod ........118, 376, 390
Evangelical Mennonite Church. See Fellowship of
  Evangelical Churches
Evangelical Mennonite Conference, The ..197, 367
Evangelical Mennonite Mission Conference ...198,
  367
Evangelical Methodist Church .........118, 376
Evangelical Missionary Church of Canada, The
  198, 367
Evangelical Presbyterian Church ........119, 376
Evangelical Press Association ...............31
Evanston Ecumenical Action Council ........239
Evansville Area Community of Churches, Inc. .241

Faith & Values Media .....................32
Faith Community Assistance Center .........251
FaithTrust Institute ......................267
Federation of Christian Ministries ...........32
Federation of Jain Associations in North America228
Federation of Zoroastrian Associations of North
  America (FEZANA) ....................232
Fellowship of Evangelical Baptist Churches in
  Canada, The .......................198, 367
Fellowship of Evangelical Bible Churches ....119,
  376, 390
Fellowship of Evangelical Churches .120, 376, 390
Fellowship of Fundamental Bible Churches ...120,
  376
Fellowship of Grace Brethren Churches ..121, 376
Fern Creek-Highview United Ministries .....243
FEZANA (Federation of Zorastrian Associations
  of North America) ....................232
First Miramichi Inter-Church Council .......292
Florida Council of Churches ...............238
Foundation for a Conference on Faith and Order
  in North America .....................32
Foursquare Gospel Church of Canada 198, 367, 386
Free Christian Zion Church of Christ .........121

Free Methodist Church in Canada ...198, 367, 386
Free Methodist Church of .........122, 376, 390
  North America
Free Will Baptists ....................199, 367
Fresno Metro Ministry ....................234
Friends General Conference ............122, 377
Friends International. *See* Evangelical Friends
  International—North American Region
Friends United Meeting ..........123, 377, 384
Friends World Committee for Consultation .....33
  (Section of the Americas)
Full Gospel Assemblies International .....124, 377
Full Gospel Fellowship of Churches and Ministers
  International ......................125, 377
Fundamental Methodist Church, Inc. .....125, 377
Fund for Theological Education, Inc., The ......33

GEII (Graymoor Ecumenical & Interreligious ...33
  Institute)
General Association of General Baptists ..125, 377,
  390
General Association of Regular Baptist Churches
  126, 377
General Church of the New Jerusalem .......126,
  199, 367, 377
General Conference of Mennonite Brethren
  Churches ....................126, 377, 392
Genesee County Churches United, Inc. .......253
Genesee-Orleans Ministry of Concern .......253
Georgia Christian Council ..................238
Glengarry-Prescott-Russell Christian Council ..293
Glenmary Research Center ..................33
GRACE (Grand Rapids Area Center for ......246
  Ecumenism)
Grace Gospel Fellowship ..............127, 377
Grand Rapids Area Center for Ecumenism
  (GRACE) ..............................246
Graymoor Ecumenical & Interreligious Institute
  (GEII) .................................33
Greater Baton Rouge Federation of Churches and
  Synagogues ...........................244
Greater Bethlehem Area Council of Churches ..260
Greater Birmingham Ministries .............233
Greater Chicago Broadcast Ministries .......239
Greater Dallas Community of Churches .......264
Greater Dayton Christian Connections .......257
Greater Fairmont Council of Churches .......267
Greater Flint Council of Churches ..........247
Greater Lawrence Council of Churches ......246
Greater Minneapolis Council of Churches .....248
Greater New Orleans Federation of Churches ..244
Greater Rochester Community of Churches ....253
Greater Toronto Council of Christian Churches,
  The ..................................293
Greater Victoria Council of Churches ........292
Greater Waterbury Interfaith Ministries, Inc. ...237
Greek Orthodox Archdiocese of America ...11, 13,
  127, 377, 384
Greek Orthodox Metropolis of Toronto (Canada)
  199, 367
Greensboro Urban Ministry ................256

Hamilton & District Christian Churches Association
  293

Hanover Area Council of Churches ..........260
Hartford Institute for Religion Research of Hartford
  Seminary, The ...........................218
Hazard-Perry County Community Ministries, Inc.
  243
Hemmingford Ecumenical Committee .......294
Highlands Community Ministries ...........243
Holy Eastern Orthodox Catholic and Apostolic
  Church in North America, Inc., The ....129, 377
Holy Synod of the American Diaspora ........129
Holy Ukrainian Autocephalic Orthodox Church
  in Exile ...............................130
House of God, Which is the Church of the Living
  God, the Pillar and Ground of the Truth, Inc. .130
Humboldt Clergy Council ..................294
Hungarian Reformed Church in America .....130,
  377, 384
Hutterian Brethren ....................130, 378
Hyde Park & Kenwood Interfaith Council, The .239

ICNA (Islamic Circle of North America) .....227
IFCA International, Inc.................131, 378
IFCO (Interreligious Foundation for Community
  Organization) ...........................36
Ignace Council of Churches ...............293
Illinois Conference of Churches ............239
Independent Assemblies of God International
  (Canada) ..............................199
Independent Holiness Church ..........200, 368
Indiana Partners for Christian Unity and Mission 241
Industrial Cape Breton Council of Churches ...292
Insight Meditation Society ..................224
Institute for Ecumenical and Cultural Research .218
Institute for the Study of American Evangelicals
  (ISAE) ................................219
Institute for the Study of American Religion ...219
Inter Church Council of Burlington .........293
InterChurch Council of Greater New Bedford .246
InterChurch Ministries of Erie County .......260
Interchurch Communications ...............55
Interchurch Ministries of Nebraska ..........250
Interfaith Association of Snohomish County, The 268
Interfaith Community Council, Inc. ..........241
Interfaith Community Services .............250
Interfaith Conference of Greater Milwaukee ...268
InterFaith Conference of Metropolitan Washington
  238
Interfaith Council ........................267
Interfaith Council of Boulder ..............236
Interfaith Council of Contra Costa County .....235
Interfaith Council of Montréal .............294
Interfaith Impact for Justice and Peace .........34
Interfaith Ministries for Greater Houston .....264
Inter-Faith Ministries—Wichita ............242
Interfaith Mission Service .................233
Interfaith Partnership of Metropolitan St. Louis 250
Interfaith Service Bureau .................235
Interfaith Worker Justice ...................35
Interfaith Works ........................267
International Church of the Foursquare Gospel .131,
  378, 390
International Council of Community Churches 132,
  378, 384

International Pentecostal Church of Christ, The .132, 378, 390

International Pentecostal Holiness Church .133, 378

International Society for Krishna Consciousness (ISKCON), The .........................226

InterReligious Council of Central New York ...254

Interreligious Foundation for Community Organization (IFCO) ....................36

InterVarsity Christian Fellowship of Canada ....55

InterVarsity Christian Fellowship of the U.S.A. ..34

Iowa Religious Media Services ..............242

ISAE (Institute for the Study of American Evangelicals) .........................217

ISKCON (The International Society for Krishna Consciousness).......................226

Islamic Circle of North America (ICNA) .....227

Islamic Society of North America (ISNA), The ..................................226

ISNA (The Islamic Society of North America) 226

Jackson County Interfaith Council, The ......247

JAINA: Federation of Jain Associations in North America ...........................228

Jehovah's Witnesses ....11, 13, 133, 200, 368, 378

Jewish Council for Public Affairs ...........229

Jewish Reconstructionist Federation ........229

J. M. Dawson Institute of Church-State Studies at Baylor University ....................220

John Howard Society of Ontario .............56

Joint Religious Legislative Coalition, The .....248

Kairos Institute, Inc., The ..................36

Kansas Ecumenical Ministries .............242

Kentuckiana Interfaith Community ..........243

Kentucky Council of Churches .............243

Kentville Council of Churches .............292

Kitchener-Waterloo Council of Churches .....293

Korean Presbyterian Church in America, General Assembly of the ...............134, 378, 384

Lafayette Urban Ministry ..................241

Lancaster County Council of Churches ......260

Latter-day Saints. See Church of Jesus Christ of Latter-day Saints, The or Church of Jesus Christ of Latter-day Saints in Canada, The

Latvian Evangelical Lutheran Church in America, The .....................134, 378, 386, 390

LCMS (Lutheran Church—Missouri Synod, The) 11, 12, 135, 378, 390

Lebanon County Christian Ministries ........260

Lehigh County Conference of Churches .....260

Lewisburg Council of Churches .............261

Liberal Catholic Church (International) ...134, 378

Liberal Catholic Church, The—Province of the United States of America ...........135, 378

Lincoln Interfaith Council ..................250

Liturgical Conference, The .................36

Lombard Mennonite Peace Center ...........36

London Inter-City Faith Team ..............293

Long Island Council of Churches, The ........254

Lord's Day Alliance of the United States, The ...37

Louisiana Interchurch Conference ..........244

Louisville Institute, The ...................220

Lunenburg Queens BA Association .........292

Lutheran Association, Conservative. See Conservative Lutheran Association

Lutheran Church. See American Association of Lutheran Churches, The

Lutheran Church. See Evangelical Lutheran Church in Canada

Lutheran Church—Canada ............200, 368

Lutheran Church, The—Missouri Synod (LCMS) 11, 12, 135, 378, 390

Lutheran Church in America. See Evangelical Lutheran Church in America

Lutheran Church of America. See Apostolic Lutheran Church of America

Lutheran Council in Canada ................56

Lutheran Synod. See Evangelical Lutheran Synod

Lutheran World Relief .....................37

Madison-area Urban Ministry ..............268

Mahone Bay Interchurch Council ...........292

Mahoning Valley Association of Churches .....257

Maine Council of Churches ................244

Malankara Orthodox Syrian Church, Diocese of America .........................136, 384

Manchester Area Conference of Churches .....237

Marin Interfaith Council ...................235

Mar Thoma Syrian Church of India .....137, 379, 384, 390

Massachusetts Commission on Christian Unity .246

Massachusetts Council of Churches .........246

Massey Inter-Church Council ...............293

MCCC (Mennonite Central Committee .......56 Canada)

Melville Association of Churches ...........294

Mennonite. See also Canadian Conference of Mennonite Brethren Churches or Mennonite Brethren Churches. See General Conference of Mennonite Brethren Churches

Mennonite Central Committee ..............56 Canada (MCCC)

Mennonite Central Committee, The ..........37

Mennonite Church—Canada ...........200, 368

Mennonite Church of God in Christ. See Church of God in Christ, Mennonite

Mennonite Church USA ..............137, 379

Mennonite Mission Conference or Reinland Mennonite Church

Methodist Church. See United Methodist Church, The

Methodist Church, Evangelical. See Evangelical Methodist Church

Methodist Church, Fundamental. See Fundamental Methodist Church, Inc.

Metropolitan Area Church Council ..........257

Metropolitan Area Religious Coalition of Cincinnati 257

Metropolitan Christian Council: Detroit-Windsor, The .................................247

Metropolitan Christian Council of Philadelphia .261

Metropolitan Ecumenical Ministry ..........251

Metropolitan Ecumenical Ministry Community Development Corp. .....................251

Metropolitan Inter Faith Association (MIFA) . . .264
Metropolitan Interfaith Council on Affordable
  Housing (MICAH) . . . . . . . . . . . . . . . . . . . . .248
MICAH (Metropolitan Interfaith Council on
  Affordable Housing) . . . . . . . . . . . . . . . . . . .248
MIFA (Metropolitan Inter Faith Association) . . .264
Ministries United South Central Louisville
  (M.U.S.C.L., Inc.) . . . . . . . . . . . . . . . . . . . . .243
Minnesota Council of Churches . . . . . . . . . . . .249
Missionary Church, The . . . . . . . . . . .138, 379, 390
Mississippi Religious Leadership Conference . .249
Moncton Area Council of Churches . . . . . . . . .292
Montana Association of Churches . . . . . . . . . .250
Montreal Association for the Blind Foundation .294
Moravian Church. See Canadian District of the
  Moravian Church in America, Northern Province
Moravian Church in America (Northern Province)
  379, 390
Moravian Church in America (Unitas Fratrum)
  139
Mormons. See Church of Jesus Christ of Latter-day
  Saints, The or Church of Jesus Christ of Latter-
  day Saints in Canada, The
Mosque Cares (Ministry of Imam W. Deen
  Mohammed), The . . . . . . . . . . . . . . . . . . . . . .227
MPAC (Muslim Public Affairs Council) . . . . .227
Multifaith Action Society of British Columbia .292
M.U.S.C.L., Inc. (Ministries United South Central
  Louisville) . . . . . . . . . . . . . . . . . . . . . . . . . . .243
Muskegon County Cooperating Churches . . . . .247
Muslim American Society . . . . . . . . . . . . . . . .227
Muslim Peace Fellowship . . . . . . . . . . . . . . . .227
Muslim Public Affairs Council (MPAC) . . . . .227

NARF (Native American Rights Fund) . . . . . . .231
National Association of Congregational Christian
  Churches . . . . . . . . . . . . . . . . . . . . . . . . .139, 379
National Association of Ecumenical and
  Interreligious Staff . . . . . . . . . . . . . . . . . . . . .38
National Association of Evangelicals, The . . . . .38
National Association of Free Will Baptists . . . .140,
  379, 390
National Baptist Convention of America, Inc. . . .11,
  140, 378, 385
National Baptist Convention, U.S.A., Inc. . . .11, 13,
  141, 379, 385
National Bible Association . . . . . . . . . . . . . . . .39
National Conference for Community and Justice,
  The . . . . . . . . . . . . . . . . . . . . . . . . . . . . . . . . .39
National Conference on Ministry to the Armed
  Forces . . . . . . . . . . . . . . . . . . . . . . . . . . . . . . .39
National Congress of American Indians (NCAI) 230
National Council of the Churches of Christ in the
  U.S.A. . . . . . . . . . . . . . . . . . . . . . . . . . . . . . . .40
National Institute of Business and Industrial
  Chaplains . . . . . . . . . . . . . . . . . . . . . . . . . . . .41
National Interfaith Cable Coalition, Inc. (NICC) .42
National Interfaith Coalition on Aging . . . . . . . .42
National Missionary Baptist Convention of
  America . . . . . . . . . . . . . . . . . . . .11, 13, 141, 379
National Organization of the New Apostolic Church
  of North America . . . . . . . . . . . . . . . . . .141, 379

National Primitive Baptist Convention, Inc. . . .142,
  379
National Religious Broadcasters . . . . . . . . . . . .42
National Spiritual Assembly of the Baha'is of the
  United States, The . . . . . . . . . . . . . . . . . . . . .222
National Spiritualist Association of Churches . .142
National Woman's Christian Temperance Union .42
Native American Rights Fund (NARF) . . . . . . .231
NCAI (National Congress of American Indians) 230
Netherlands Reformed Congregations . . . .142, 379
Network of Religious Communities . . . . . . . . .254
NEWBRACC (New Britain Area Conference of
  Churches) . . . . . . . . . . . . . . . . . . . . . . . . . . . .237
New Britain Area Conference of Churches
  (NEWBRACC) . . . . . . . . . . . . . . . . . . . . . . .237
New Church. See General Church of the New
  Jerusalem
New Hampshire Council of Churches . . . . . . .251
New Jersey Council of Churches . . . . . . . . . . .251
New Mexico Conference of Churches . . . . . . .251
New York Buddhist Council . . . . . . . . . . . . . . .224
New York State Council of Churches, Inc. . . . .254
Niagara Council of Churches Inc., The . . . . . .255
NICA (Northside Inter-Church Agency) . . . . . .265
NICC (National Interfaith Cable Coalition, Inc.)
  32, 42
NISBCO (Center on Conscience & War) . . . . . .27
North American Baptist Conference .143, 201, 368,
  379, 386, 390
North American Baptist Fellowship . . . . . . . . . .43
North American Old Roman Catholic Church
  (Archdiocese of New York) . . . . . . . . .143, 380
North Carolina Council of Churches . . . . . . . .256
North Dakota Conference of Churches . . . . . . .256
North Dallas Shared Ministries . . . . . . . . . . . .265
North Hills Youth Ministry Counseling Center .261
Northern California Interreligious Conference . .235
Northern Kentucky Interfaith Commission, Inc. 243
Northside Common Ministries . . . . . . . . . . . . .261
Northside Inter-Church Agency (NICA) . . . . . .265
Northwest Harvest—E.M.M. . . . . . . . . . . . . . .267
Northwest Interfaith Movement . . . . . . . . . . . .261

Oak Park-River Forest Community of
  Congregations . . . . . . . . . . . . . . . . . . . . . . . .239
Ohio Council of Churches . . . . . . . . . . . . . . . .257
Oikocredit-Ecumenical Development Cooperative
  Society . . . . . . . . . . . . . . . . . . . . . . . . . . . . . . .43
Oklahoma Conference of Churches . . . . . . . . .258
Old Catholic Church of Canada, The . . . . .201, 368
Old Catholic Orthodox Church, The . . . . .143, 380
Old German Baptist Brethren Church . . . .144, 380
Old Order Amish Church . . . . . . . . . .144, 201, 380
Old Order (Wisler) Mennonite Church . . . . . . .144
Open Bible Faith Fellowship of Canada .202, 368
Open Bible Standard Churches . . . . . . . . . .144, 380
(Original) Church of God, Inc., The . . . . . . . . .145
Orthodox Church in America (Archdiocese of
  Canada) . . . . . . . . . . . . . . . . . . . . . . . . .202, 368
Orthodox Church in America, The . . . .11, 13, 144,
  380, 385
Orthodox Presbyterian Church, The . .145, 380, 390
Ottawa Christian Council of the Capital Area . .293

Paducah Cooperative Ministry . . . . . . . . . . . . .244
Parish Resource Center, Inc. . . . . . . . . . . . . . . . .43
Patriarchal Parishes of the Russian Orthodox
  Church in Canada . . . . . . . . . . . . . . . . . .202, 368
Patriarchal Parishes of the Russian Orthodox
  Church in the U.S.A. . . . . . . . . . . . .146, 380, 385
Pennsylvania Conference on Interchurch
  Cooperation . . . . . . . . . . . . . . . . . . . . . . . . . .261
Pennsylvania Council of Churches, The . . . . . . .261
Pentecostal Assemblies of Canada, The . . .202, 368
Pentecostal Assemblies of Newfoundland, The 203,
  368, 386
Pentecostal Assemblies of the World, Inc. . . .11, 13,
  146, 380
Pentecostal-Charismatic Churches of North
  America . . . . . . . . . . . . . . . . . . . . . . . . . . . . . .44
Pentecostal Church of God . . . . . . . . . . . .146, 380
Pentecostal Fire-Baptized Holiness Church 147, 380
Pentecostal Free Will Baptist Church, Inc., The 147
Peoria Friendship House of Christian Service . .240
Philadelphia Yearly Meeting of the Religious
  Society of Friends . . . . . . . . . . . . . .147, 380, 385
Pictou Council of Churches . . . . . . . . . . . . . . . .292
Pike Country Outreach Council . . . . . . . . . . . .258
Pillar of Fire . . . . . . . . . . . . . . . . . . . . . . . . . . .147
Pluralism Project, The . . . . . . . . . . . . . . . . . . . .221
Plymouth Brethren. *See* Christian Brethren (also
  known as Plymouth Brethren)
Polish National Catholic Church of America . .148,
  385
Pomona Inland Valley Council of Churches . . . .235
Prairie Centre for Ecumenism . . . . . . . . . . . . . .294
Presbyterian Church. *See* Evangelical Presbyterian
  Church
Presbyterian Church in America . . . . .148, 380, 390
Presbyterian Church in America (Canadian Section)
  203, 368, 386
Presbyterian Church in Canada . . . . . . . . .204, 368
Presbyterian Church (U.S.A.) .11, 12, 13, 149, 381,
  385, 390
Primitive Advent Christian Church . . . . . . .150, 381
Primitive Baptists . . . . . . . . . . . . . . . . . . . . . . . .151
Primitive Methodist Church in the U.S.A. . . . .151,
  381, 390
Progressive National Baptist Convention, Inc. . .11,
  13, 151, 381, 385
Project Equality, Inc. . . . . . . . . . . . . . . . . . . . . . .44
Project of Easton, Inc. . . . . . . . . . . . . . . . . . . . .262
Project Ploughshares . . . . . . . . . . . . . . . . . . . . . .56
Protestant Reformed Churches in America 152, 381

Quakers. *See* Friends General Conference
Quakers, Conservative. *See* Religious Society of
  Friends (Conservative)
Quakers, International. *See* Evangelical Friends
  International—North American Region
Quakers, Philadelphia. *See* Philadelphia Yearly
  Meeting of the Religious Society of Friends
Quakers, Unaffiliated Meetings. *See* Religious
  Society of Friends (Unaffiliated Meetings)
Quebec Ecumenical Network (Réseau Oecuménique
  du Québec) . . . . . . . . . . . . . . . . . . . . . . . . . . .294
Queens County Association of Churches . . . . . .292

Queens Federation of Churches . . . . . . . . . . . .255

Radio Ville-Marie . . . . . . . . . . . . . . . . . . . . . . .294
Reading Berks Conference of Churches . . . . . .262
Reformed Catholic Church . . . . . . . . . . . . .152, 381
Reformed Church in America . .152, 381, 385, 392
Reformed Church in Canada . . . . . . .204, 369, 386
Reformed Church in the United States 153, 381, 392
Reformed Episcopal Church . . . . . . . . . . .154, 381
Reformed Episcopal Church of Canada, The . .204,
  369, 386
Reformed Mennonite Church . . . . . . . . . .154, 381
Reformed Methodist Union Episcopal Church .155
Reformed Presbyterian Church of North America
  155, 381, 392
Reformed Zion Union Apostolic Church . . . . . .155
Regina Council of Churches . . . . . . . . . . . . . . .294
Regional Council for Christian Ministry, Inc., The
  239
Regional Council of Churches of Atlanta, The . .238
Reinland Mennonite Church . . . . . . . . . . .205, 369
Religion Communicators Council, Inc., The . . . .45
Religion In American Life, Inc. . . . . . . . . . . . . .45
Religion News Service . . . . . . . . . . . . . . . . . . . .46
Religion Newswriters Association and . . . . . . . .46
  Foundation
Religions for Peace-USA, Inc. . . . . . . . . . . . . . .46
Religious Action Center of Reform Judaism . . .229
Religious Conference Management Association,
  Inc. . . . . . . . . . . . . . . . . . . . . . . . . . . . . . . . . . .46
Religious Society of Friends (Conservative) . . .156,
  381
Religious Society of Friends (Unaffiliated Meetings)
  156
Religious Television Associates . . . . . . . . . . . . .57
Reorganized Church of Jesus Christ of Latter-day
  Saints. *See* Community of Christ
Réseau Oecuménique du Québec (Quebec
  Ecumenical Network) . . . . . . . . . . . . . . . . . .294
Réseau Oecuménique Justice et Paix . . . . . . . .294
Rhode Island State Council of Churches, The . .263
Roman Catholic Church in Canada, The . .205, 369
Romanian Orthodox Church in America (Canadian
  Parishes) . . . . . . . . . . . . . . . . . . . . . . . . . .206, 368
Romanian Orthodox Church in America, The . .156
Romanian Orthodox Episcopate of America, The
  156, 381
Romanian Orthodox Episcopate of America, The
  (Jackson, MI) . . . . . . . . . . . . . . . . . . . . .207, 369
Rural Migrant Ministry . . . . . . . . . . . . . . . . . . .255
Russian Orthodox Church. *See* Patriarchal Parishes
  of the Russian Orthodox Church in Canada *or*
Patriarchal Parishes of the Russian Orthodox Church
  in the U.S.A.
Russian Orthodox Church Outside of Russia, The
  157, 381

SAHO (Sikh American Heritage Organization) .231
SALDEF (Sikh American Legal Defense and
  Education Fund) . . . . . . . . . . . . . . . . . . . . . . . .231
Salvation Army, The . . . . . . . . . . . . . . . . .157, 382
Salvation Army in Canada, The . . . . . . . . .207, 369
San Antonio Community of Churches . . . . . . . .265

INDEX

San Antonio Urban Ministries . . . . . . . . . . . . . .265
San Fernando Valley Interfaith Council . . . . . .235
Schenectady Inner City Ministry . . . . . . . . . . . .255
Schwenkfelder Church, The . . . . . . . .157, 382, 392
Scripture Union . . . . . . . . . . . . . . . . . . . . . . . . . .57
SCUPE (Seminary Consortium for Urban Pastoral
    Education, The) . . . . . . . . . . . . . . . . . . . . . . . .47
SEAM (South East Associated Ministries) . . . . .244
SEARCH (Southeast Area Churches) . . . . . . . . .265
Seminary Consortium for Urban Pastoral Education,
    The (SCUPE) . . . . . . . . . . . . . . . . . . . . . . . . .47
Separate Baptists in Christ . . . . . . . . . . . .158, 382
Serbian Orthodox Church in the U.S.A. and Canada
    158, 382, 385
Serbian Orthodox Church in the U.S.A. and Canada,
    Diocese of Canada . . . . . . . . . . . . . . . . .207, 369
Seventh-day Adventist Church . . . . . .158, 382, 392
Seventh-day Adventist Church in Canada . . . . .208,
    369, 386
Seventh Day Baptist General Conference, USA and
    Canada . . . . . . . . . . . . . . . . . . . . . . . . . .159, 382
Siddhachalam International Mahavira Jain Mission
    228
Sikh American Heritage Organization (SAHO) .231
Sikh American Legal Defense and Education Fund
    (SALDEF) . . . . . . . . . . . . . . . . . . . . . . . . . . .231
Sikh Coalition . . . . . . . . . . . . . . . . . . . . . . . . . . .231
Sikh Foundation . . . . . . . . . . . . . . . . . . . . . . . . .232
Sikh Research Institute . . . . . . . . . . . . . . . . . . .232
Soka Gakkai International—USA . . . . . . . . . . .224
South Carolina Christian Action Council, Inc. . .263
South Coast Interfaith Council . . . . . . . . . . . . .235
Southeast Area Churches (SEARCH) . . . . . . . .265
South East Associated Ministries (SEAM) . . . . .244
Southeast Ecumenical Ministry . . . . . . . . . . . . .255
South Hills Interfaith Ministries . . . . . . . . . . . .262
South Louisville Community Ministries . . . . . .244
Southern Baptist Convention . . . .9, 11, 12, 13, 160,
    382, 392
Southern Baptists. See Canadian Convention of
    Southern Baptists
Southern California Ecumenical Council . . . . .236
Southern Methodist Church . . . . . . . . . . . .161, 382
Sovereign Grace Believers . . . . . . . . . . . .162, 382
Spadina-Bloor Interchurch Council . . . . . . . . .293
Staten Island Council of Churches . . . . . . . . . .256
St. Bruno Ecumenical Group, The . . . . . . . . . .294
St. Catharines & District Clergy Fellowship . . .293
St. John's Area Council of Churches . . . . . . . .292
St. Matthews Area Ministries . . . . . . . . . . . . . .244
St. Paul Area Council of Churches . . . . . . . . . .249
Stratford & District Council of Churches . . . . .293
Student Christian Movement of Canada . . . . . . .57
Summerside Christian Council . . . . . . . . . . . . .293
Swedenborgian Church, The . . . . . . . .162, 382, 385
Syriac Orthodox Church of Antioch . . . . . .208, 369
Syrian (Syriac) Orthodox Church of Antioch . .163,
    382, 385
Syro-Russian Orthodox Catholic Church . . . . .163,
    382, 392

Tarrant Area Community of Churches . . . . . . . .265
Tennessee Association of Churches . . . . . . . . .263

Texas Buddhist Council . . . . . . . . . . . . . . . . . . .224
Texas Conference of Churches . . . . . . . . . . . . .265
Thorold Inter-Faith Council . . . . . . . . . . . . . . . .293
Thunder Bay Council of Churches . . . . . . . . . .293
Toledo Ecumenical Area Ministries . . . . . . . . .258
Transnational Association of Christian Colleges
    and Schools . . . . . . . . . . . . . . . . . . . . . . . . . . .47
Tri-Council Coordinating Commission . . . . . .249
Triumph the Church and Kingdom of God in Christ
    Inc. (International) . . . . . . . . . . . . . . . . . . . . .164
Troy Area United Ministries . . . . . . . . . . . . . . .256
True Orthodox Church of Greece (Synod of
    Metropolitan Cyprian), . . . . . . . . . . . . . .164, 382
    American Exarchate . . . . . . . . . . . . . . . . . . . . .
Tulsa Metropolitan Ministry . . . . . . . . . . . . . . .258
Tuscarawas County Council for Church and
    Community . . . . . . . . . . . . . . . . . . . . . . . . . . .258

Ukrainian Orthodox Church of Canada . . .208, 369
Ukrainian Orthodox Church of the U.S.A. . . . .165,
    383, 385
Unified Buddhist Church, Inc. . . . . . . . . . . . . .225
Union d'Eglises Baptistes Françaises au Canada
    208, 369, 386
Union of Orthodox Jewish Congregations of
    America, The . . . . . . . . . . . . . . . . . . . . . . . . .230
Union of Reform Judaism . . . . . . . . . . . . . . . . .230
Union of Spiritual Communities of Christ (Orthodox
    Doukhobors in Canada) . . . . . . . . . . . . . . . . .209
Unitarian Universalist Association of Congregations
    166, 383
UNITAS . . . . . . . . . . . . . . . . . . . . . . . . . . . . . . .294
United Board of Missions . . . . . . . . . . . . . . . . .265
United Brethren Church in Canada . . . . . .209, 371
United Catholic Church, Inc., The . . . . . . .167, 383
United Christian Church . . . . . . . . . . . . . .167, 383
United Church of Canada, The . . . . . .210, 370, 386
United Church of Christ .11, 13, 168, 383, 385, 392
United Churches of Lycoming County . . . . . . .262
United Holy Church of America, Inc. . . . . . . . .169
United House of Prayer . . . . . . . . . . . . . . . . . . .171
United Methodist Church, The . .9, 11, 12, 13, 171,
    383, 385, 392
United Ministries . . . . . . . . . . . . . . . . . . . . . . . .263
United Ministries in Higher Education . . . . . . . .47
United Pentecostal Church in Canada . . . . . . . .211
United Pentecostal Church International . . . . . .173
United Pentecostal Churches of Christ, The174, 383
United Religions Initiative . . . . . . . . . . . . . . . . . .48
United Religious Community of St. Joseph County
    241
United Synagogue of Conservative Judaism, The
    230
United Zion Church . . . . . . . . . . . . . . . . . .174, 383
Unity of the Brethren . . . . . . . . . . . . . .175, 383, 392
Universal Fellowship of Metropolitan Community
    Churches . . . . . . . . . . . . .175, 211, 370, 383, 392

Vancouver Council of Churches . . . . . . . . . . . .292
Vedanta Society of New York . . . . . . . . . . . . . .226
Vellore Christian Medical College Board (USA),
    Inc. . . . . . . . . . . . . . . . . . . . . . . . . . . . . . . . . . .49
Vermont Ecumenical Council and Bible Society .265

INDEX

409

Virginia Council of Churches, Inc. . . . . . . . . . . .266
Volunteer Ministry Center . . . . . . . . . . . . . . . . .264
Volunteers of America . . . . . . . . . . . . . . . . . . . .175

Wainwright House . . . . . . . . . . . . . . . . . . . . . . .256
Washington Association of Churches . . . . . . . . .267
Wellspring Interfaith Social Services, Inc. . . . . .241
Wesleyan Church, The . . . . . . . . . . . .176, 384, 392
Wesleyan Church of Canada, The . . . . . . .211, 370
Wesleyan Holiness Association of Churches . . .177
West Central Neighborhood Ministry, Inc. *See*
   Wellspring Interfaith Social Services, Inc.
West Side Ecumenical Ministry . . . . . . . . . . . .258
Westside Interfaith Council . . . . . . . . . . . . . . . .236
West Virginia Council of Churches . . . . . . . . . .268
Wilkinsburg Community Ministry . . . . . . . . . . .262
Wisconsin Council of Churches . . . . . . . . . . . . .268
Wisconsin Evangelical Lutheran Synod . . . . . .177,
   383, 392
Women's Inter-Church Council of Canada . . . . . .57

Won Buddhism of American Headquarters . . . .225
Worcester County Ecumenical Council . . . . . .246
World Council of Churches, United States Office 49
World Day of Prayer International Committee . . .49
World Methodist Council-North American . . . . . .49
   Section 49
World Sikh Council—American Region . . . . . .232
World Vision . . . . . . . . . . . . . . . . . . . . . . . . . . . .50
World Vision Canada . . . . . . . . . . . . . . . . . . . . . .58
Wyoming Association of Churches . . . . . . . . . .268
Wyoming Valley Council of Churches . . . . . . .263

YMCA of the USA . . . . . . . . . . . . . . . . . . . . . . .50
York County Council of Churches . . . . . . . . . .263
Young Men's Christian Association in Canada . .58
Young Women's Christian Association of-du
   Canada . . . . . . . . . . . . . . . . . . . . . . . . . . . . . . .58
Youth for Christ—Canada . . . . . . . . . . . . . . . . .59
Youth for Christ–USA . . . . . . . . . . . . . . . . . . . . .51
YWCA of the U.S.A. . . . . . . . . . . . . . . . . . . . . . .50

INDEX

410

# Individuals

Abare, Brad..........................132
Abbott, Grant ......................249
Abbott, Mark S. ...........96, 192
Abbott, Z. Allen ....................67
Abboud, Jon W.....................153
Abdalah, John .....................345
Abdallah, John Ishuaradas..236
  Abdallah
Abernathy, Bryan ................338
Abraham, Raphael ..............165
Abramov, Alexanfer............146
Ackerman, Keith L..............111
Acosta, Donaldo ........102, 103
Acuña, Adolfo .......................77
Adams, Don .......................134
Adams, Dorothy....................64
Adams, Gladstone B., III ....110
Adams, James Marshall ......111
Adams, Margaret..................243
Adams, Michael J. ..............106
Adams, Nate........................161
Adams, Neale......................351
Adams, Ray D.....................160
Adams, Skip.........................259
Adams-Smelter, Barbara .....262
Addington, James................249
Addington, Timothy............114
Addland, Thomas V. .............65
Adego, Epainitus.................123
Adema, Bruce ......................89
Adenya, Wilson...................123
Adimavunkal, Isaac ...........103
  Thomas
Adira, Titus .........................123
Adnams, Ian .......................200
Adolf, Don .........................198
Aftimios (Archbishop).........203
Ahonen, E. ..........................203
Aiken, David A., Sr..............63
Aiken, Mike ........................256
Aja, Antonio (Tony)............243
Aja, Loyda ..........................150
Ajer, Margaret Schmitt........116
Akers, Kenneth ..................140
Akin, Daniel L.....................313
Alagiah, Sabapath .................48
Albarian, Samuel ................346
Albert, Leonard............96, 192
Albrecht, Betty....................187
Albrecht, James...................101
Albrecht, Marcus ................330
Alchin, Errol ......................196
Alcosser, Lois ....................237
Aldred, Ray..........................55
Alejo (Bishop)....................145
Aleshire, Daniel O. ............ 215

Alexander, Darlene .............264
Alexander, J. Gregory ...........86
Alexander, John Neil ..........109
Alexios (Metropolitan) .......128
Alford, Delton L. ..........96, 192
Alger, David T.....................266
Algera, Fred .......................204
Alick, Bruce N. ...................336
Allander, Dan .....................307
Allen, Arlene ......................345
Allen, Bettye J. ...................345
Allen, Cosie .......................335
Allen, David W. ..................211
Allen, David, Jr. ..................151
Allen, Gary..........................330
Allen, John ...........................26
Allen, Lloyd Emmanuel......109
Allen, Sherman ............98, 193
Allen, William B...........87, 268
Allen-Kent, Venita ..............265
Allinson, Pat.........................58
Allsop, John .......................295
Al-Marayati, Salam.............227
Almen, Lowell G. ...............116
Alston, Roosevelt................170
Alston, Wallace M., Jr..........33
Alterbarmakian, Varouj.........74
Althouse, LaVonne..............345
Alvarez, David ...................111
Alvis, Rick ...........................25
Ambrose, Richard ..............233
Ambrus, Zoltan ...................127
Amerson, Philip A. ............302
Amjad-Ali, Charles.............35
Ammerman, E. H. Jim .........28
Ammons, E. Roger ............103
Amorim, Nilton D...............207
Anders, Andrea ....................97
Anders, James ....................102
Anders, Linda......................158
Anderson, Alison A............147
Anderson, Anne T. .............322
Anderson, Billy ..................105
Anderson, Bonnie ..............109
Anderson, Daniel L.............295
Anderson, David A. ............239
Anderson, E. Byron .............36
Anderson, Gordon L. .........308
Anderson, James ................254
Anderson, Jeff ....................196
Anderson, Jeffrey ...............114
Anderson, Jim ....................156
Anderson, Jon V. ................116
Anderson, Kenneth .............80
Anderson, Kristi..................249
Anderson, Leith ...................38

Anderson, L. R.....................94
Anderson, Melissa ..............340
Anderson, Moe....................295
Anderson, Nancy L. ............248
Anderson, Neil...........104, 332
Anderson, Phyllis................309
Anderson, Scott D...............268
Anderson, Ujuana ..............256
Anderson, Vinton .................33
Anderson, William J. ..........182
Anderson-Develrow, ..........265
  Dorothy
Anderson-Larson, Virginia..116
Anderson-Ostrom, Kristin...116
Andonios (Bishop)..............128
Andreller, Ingrid .................349
Andres, Oseas ......................68
Andrews, Roger ..................120
Andrews, Ruth .....................55
Andriy (Archimandrite) ......166
Andrus, Marc Handly .........109
Angeline, Peter.....................56
Angie, Frank .......................133
Ankeny, Mark......................115
Annie, Frederick P. .............268
Annunziato, Anne ..............251
Ansari, Fajri ........................254
Ansell, Fred A. .....................66
Antal, Jim............................169
Anstey, Andrew R. ..............203
Anthony, Lewis ...................238
Antonio, Annalene ..............255
Antony (Archbishop) ..........165
Apostola, Nicholas......156, 207
Appel, Robert......................160
Appell, Jody.........................263
Aquila, Dominic ........149, 203
Archer, Barbara...................250
Ard, Herman D ..........102, 103
Ard, Robert ........................234
Archim, Rev........................329
Ardis, Randy .......................22
Argue, Don H......................309
Armas, Lucinda...................337
Armiger, Thomas E.............176
Armstrong, Calvin ..............170
Armstrong, George ..............49
Armstrong, James D. ....62, 340
Armstrong, Ken ...................78
Armstrong, Sara .................236
Arnold, Don .......................125
Arnold, Gail .......................263
Arnold, Kim M. ..................361
Arnold, Kristi .....................338
Arslanian, Hagop .................18
Arthur (Bishop)...................129

411

Arthur, David T. .................353
Artis, Lois .............................85
Ascough, Richard.................54
Asen, Bernhard .................342
Ashdown, David N. ...........183
Ashford, Anne ....................235
Asplundh, Kurt H...............126
Astfalk, Carolyn.................262
Astin, Claude S., Jr. .............68
Astin, Dawn R. ....................68
Astin, Sam (Claude S., III) ...68
Astle, Cynthia B. ........340, 343
Astley, Nolan D. ................200
Atagotaalnuk, Andrew P. ....182
Atkins, Nancy Lee .............258
Atlas, Robert .....................266
Atmore, A. Brian.................319
Attai, Monday S..................186
Atteberry, Philip..................79
Attridge, Harold W..............316
Atwood-Adams, Tanya .......254
Augsburger, Donald (Rick)...41
Augsburger, Lynette...........120
Augson, Albert ...................171
Aultman, Donald S. ......96, 191
Austin, George ..................146
Austin, Jackie.....................268
Authier, Ken.......................131
Auxentios (Bishop) .............165
Avakian, Karl .....................184
Avera, Alan ..........................76
Avery, Michael...................302
Avey, Thomas.....................121
Aykazian, Vicken ................40
Ayloush, Hussam .................35
Aymer, Albert J. D. .............303
Aymond, Gregory M............83

Baak, David P.....................247
Babb, Ruby ........................255
Babb, W. Sherrill.................309
Bachus, Amanda .................333
Backman, Ida .............346, 347
Bagley, Louis .....................170
Bagnall, Ronald B...............335
Bahruth, Dick......................29
Bailey, Dwight ...................240
Bailey, Jeff ........................329
Bailey, Joey .......................150
Bailey, Mark L. ..................300
Baillargeon, Gaëtan.............206
Baillie, Kenneth ..................158
Bainbridge, Harry B., III.....110
Baird, Bob ...........................78
Baker, Bob ..................258, 259
Baker, Denis N. ...................342
Baker, Kenneth ..................333
Baker, Marsha......................24
Baker, Michael L. ...............191
Bakker, Peter.......................268
Balanian, Nayira ..................73
Balas, Laura .......................321
Balbick, Jane......................254

Baldes, Kenneth E ...............89
Baldwin, David N. ..............160
Baldwin, Nancy .................139
Baldwin, Raymond C.........152
Balentine, Sam ...................333
Baletka, Jim ......................175
Balfour, Edward.................133
Balian, Hrair........................73
Ball, Chris ..........................108
Ball, David .........................203
Ball, Frank .........................258
Ballard, M. Russell .............99
Balogh, Balint ....................129
Baltimore, Carroll A. ..........150
Bamban, Vieturs.................326
Banaszak, Karen .................246
Bancroft, Timothy...............42
Bane, David C., Jr. .............111
Banek, Walter.....................153
Banken, Mary Beth...........218
Bang, Charles.....................254
Bangert, Kristi ...................116
Bankhead, Robert...............132
Bankord, Mark A. ................29
Bañuelos, José G.................103
Baranek, Paul .....................260
Baranowski, Bernice...........53
Barber, Jay A.......................94
Barbour, Johnny, Jr. .............61
Barcott, Patricia .................267
Bariteau, Benoît .................205
Barker, Lee.........................307
Barker, Randy ....................147
Barlow, Jane.......................246
Barkman, Len......................197
Barna, George ....................216
Barnabas, Mathews Mar.....137
Barnes, Charles...................169
Barnes, Gerald .....................83
Barnes, James....................304
Barnes, Kurt ......................109
Barnes, Ronald B. ...............261
Barnes, Thane ....................161
Barnett, Paige.....................266
Barnett-Cowan, Alyson.......182
Barnhouse, James.................258
Baron, Karen......................360
Barrentine, Jimmy L. ..........161
Barrett, Michael .................256
Barrow, Ira ........................361
Barrows, Ken .....................194
Barry, Jane .........................234
Barsamian, Khajag..........45, 74
Barsony, Steve ...................262
Bartell-Wagner, Deena...323, 331
Bartlett, Carol.....................122
Bartlett, Eileen ....................244
Bartlett, William G..............210
Barton, Jonathan ...............266
Bass, Deborah .......................41
Bass, Steve .........................160

Bassett, W. Todd ................157
Bassham, Keith ..................325
Batchelor, Don ...................174
Bates, Charlotte Kinvig .....320
Bates, Dale .........................125
Batey, Gary .......................132
Bathurst, Shirley ................255
Battle, George Edward, Jr. ..61, 62
Battle, Michael A. ..............304
Battler, Jack........................56
Battram, Janet ....................241
Batts, Carl .........................142
Bauer, Martha ....................162
Baugham, Billy ....................24
Baugham, Eva......................24
Baum, Mary K. ...................268
Baumann, Paul ...................328
Baumgartner, Will..............237
Baumler, Gary.....................336
Bawai, Mar...........................70
Baxter, Rosa ........................61
Bay, Eugene C ...................299
Bayer, Steven L...........144, 344
Bayiha, Suzie, II ..................49
Beach, Maxine C. ...............301
Beach, Verda ......................296
Beacham, A. D., Jr. .............133
Beachy, Ivan........................79
Beachy, LeRoy....................144
Beals, Charlotte...................139
Beane, Marian....................122
Beard, C. Ronald..................76
Beaupe, Richard...................56
Bechil, Shirley ...................123
Beck, Sarai Schnucker .......242
Becker, Bruce.....................177
Becker, Susan.......................30
Beckett, Malcolm................194
Beckmann, David.................26
Beckwith, James .................91
Beckwith, Peter H. .............111
Becton, C. M.......................210
Bedell, L. Wood .................153
Bediako, Matthew A. ..........159
Bednar, David A. ..................99
Behrakis, George.................128
Behr, Ken .............................31
Behrens, James...................262
Beinikis, Vilmars................134
Beisher, Barry.....................111
Beitans, John ......................240
Beizer, Lance .......................71
Bekken, Dean .....................135
Bekker, Gary .......................90
Bell, Nancy .......................185
Bellamy, James C................170
Bellefleur, Beverley ...........203
Bellinger, Gale .....................71
Bellous, Ken ..............43, 185
Belrose, Darrell...................194
Belsky, Martin....................259
Belsole, Kurt .....................312

Belton, Victor T. ..................136
Bender, Robert ..................235
Bendyna, Mary E. ................27
Benedetto, Robert ............358
Benedict, Gary M. ...............89
Benefiel, Ron ....................308
Benjamin (Bishop) .............145
Benjamin, Waveney .............49
Bennett, Robertson H. .........45
Bennett, Vicki ...................206
Bennison, Charles E., Jr. .....111
Benoway, Edward R. ...........118
Benson, Michael ................300
Benson, Willie, Jr. ..............122
Beresford, Eric ..................317
Berg, Peter ........................142
Berg, Richard R. ................355
Berg, Robert D. ..................117
Berg, Ron ..........................143
Berg, Sharon K. ..................330
Berge, Arthur .....................193
Bergen, Abe .......................321
Berger, David G. ................250
Bergin, Karen .....................237
Bergland, Arne ...................266
Berlamino, Cheryl ................22
Berman, Lowen ...................259
Bernard, David ...................315
Bernstine, Gwen Nelson .....262
Bernthal, Mark ...................101
Berry, Bradford ..................103
Bertalan, Imre ....................129
Berube, Albert J. ................143
Betancourt, Esdras .............191
Betzer, Dan .........................75
Bevens, Stephen B. ..............27
Beverley, James ..................219
Beyer, Teresa A. .................144
Bhagan, Ken .......................293
Bibb, Lillie D. .....................257
Bickerton, Thomas J. ..........171
Bicksler, Harriet .................341
Bieniek, Barbara .................256
Biffle, S. K. ........................125
Biffle, Steven K. .................125
Bigland-Pritchard, Jan. .......294
Biggs, Vicki .......................136
Billard, Ralph .....................292
Binda, Andrew ...........192, 347
Bingham, Maurice D. ...........92
Birch, Aaron Louis ..............186
Birchard, Bruce ...................122
Bird, Madeline ....................262
Birkitt, James N., Jr. ...........324
Birkett, Jim ........................175
Birney, Walter .....................88
Birse, Douglas ....................187
Bishop, Betty .....................102
Bishop, Cecil .......................62
Bishop, James A. .................243
Bithos, George P. ................265
Bitner, Terry ......................238
Bjork, Bruce ......................248

Bjork, Kryssis ....................247
Bjornberg, Allan C. .............116
Blachford, Peter .................182
Black, Bernard ...................141
Black, Geoffrey A. ......169, 255
Black, J. B., Jr. ...................240
Black, J. Thomas ..................93
Black, Ron .........................125
Blackaby, Robert ................188
Blackburn, Martha ..............177
Blackburn, Richard G. ..........37
Blackshear, Frank ...............152
Blackwell, George L. ............63
Blackwell, Phil ...................239
Blair, Sarah D. Brooks ........357
Blake, C. E., Sr. ....................94
Blake, Harry .......................141
Blakeman, Jeannine ............243
Blanchett, David I. ..............233
Bland, James C. ..................149
Blanding, Ann ....................155
Blessing, Matt ....................359
Bliese, Richard H ................306
Bliss, Dale ...........................97
Blom, Paul J. ......................117
Bloom, Peter ........................54
Bloomquist, Nessie S. .........255
Blouin, Francis ...................244
Blount, Robert ...................170
Blowers, David ....................64
Blumhofer, Edith .................219
Blythe, David ......................67
Bobo, Kim ...........................36
Bock, Robert ......................268
Bockelman, Karen ..............116
Bodden, Winnie .................360
Boddy, Michael ..................356
Boe, Eugene .......................100
Boehlke, Craig A. ................117
Boehm, John Philip .............153
Boeker, Paul .......................120
Boerger, Wm Chris .............116
Boguslawski, Steven ...........310
Bohl, Robert .......................150
Bohren, Ben .........................85
Boice, Paul .................153, 204
Boissoneau, John ...............206
Bojey, Fred ........................209
Bolick, Leonard H. ..............118
Bolinder, Garth T. ...............114
Boll, James ........................326
Bolt, John ....................90, 191
Boltz, David G. ...................260
Bombick, Betsy ..................139
Bond, Jane Zavitz ..............189
Bond, Judy ........................238
Bonk, Jonathan J. ...............333
Bonneau, Normand ............321
Bonner, Harrison .................31
Bonner, Margie J. .................63
Bonner, William L. ..............103
Book, Clifford B. .................80
Boomer, George ..................119

Boomershine, Tom ..............335
Boone, Martha Moody .........30
Boonstra, John .....................35
Booth, Linda L. ...................341
Booth, Robby .....................131
Booth, Robert H. .................154
Borden, M. Daniel ..............170
Borden, Paul D. ....................67
Borek, John ........................305
Borgdorff, Peter .................191
Borger, Joyce .....................340
Borowsky, Irvin J. ................33
Bos, Thomas ......................153
Bosh, Larry ........................157
Boto, Augie ........................160
Bott, Richard .......................42
Bottorff, Dan .......................36
Bouchard, Charles E. ..........295
Bouchard, Luc ....................206
Bouffides-Walsh, ................128
  Catherine
Boulva, Michèle ..................206
Bouman, Stephen P. ............118
Bouras, Nicholas ................128
Bourne, Hugh .....................151
Bouton, Becky ....................263
Bouvier-Newman, Marie ....263
Bouvter, Barry .....................51
Bowell, Gary ......................325
Bowen, Mary Lu .................254
Bowen-Bailey, Doug ...........247
Bowie, A. Charles ...............141
Bowie, E. L. ........................100
Bowman, Margaret E. .........167
Bowman, Robert M. ...........167
Boyajcan, Donna ................262
Boyce, H. Gene ...................133
Boyce, Janice .............133, 325
Boyd, Alice ........................256
Boyd, Doris F. ....................336
Boyd, Douglas ....................250
Boyd, John E. .....................292
Boyd, Marsha Foster ..........301
Boyd, T. B., III ...................141
Boyer, Wayne W. ...............105
Boyles, Lemuel ....................39
Bradford, Bose ...................170
Bradford, Karole .................242
Bradley, James G. ...............237
Bradley, Lasserre, Jr. ....151, 325
Bradley, Leah Ellison ..........333
Bradsell, Kenneth .......153, 204
Brady, A. Glenn ..................146
Brame, Nicholas .................132
Brandebura, Michael ...........203
Brandon (Zenyo), ...............223
  Richard
Branham, Craig ....................79
Branham, Thomas E. ...........147
Branscum, Donald W. .........102
Brashler, James ...................333
Bratt, James .......................339
Bratton, G. Stanford ...........254

Braun, John A .....................331
Braver, Barbara L................109
Bravo-Guzman, Pedro ..........77
Brawner, John ....................115
Bray, Donald L....................177
Bray, Imam Mahdi ...............35
Bray, Joy .............................344
Brazier, Arthus ...................146
Bregar, Janet A....................236
Breig, James........................330
Brennan, Keith ...................312
Brennan, Peter P..............72, 77
Brenton, B. Dean ................203
Brenton, Kelly L. ................203
Breton, Jean-Claude...........350
Brewer, John .......................329
Brice, James T......................76
Brickhouse, Smith N............92
Briden, Gary ..............162, 313
Bridges, James E.................75
Bridges, Kermit S. ..............313
Bridges, Randy J.................310
Briggs, Robert L. ................21
Briley, Terry .......................305
Brill, Debra .........................159
Brinks, Robert.....................150
Brinser, Gerald ...................168
Brisco, Thomas ...................306
Briscoe, John A. ...................40
Britton, Joseph H. ..............296
Broad, Dwayne ...................199
Broadway, Beth...................254
Brodeur, Adèle .....................52
Brooke, Jamie .....................175
Brookhart, C. Franklin ........110
Brooks, George ...................146
Brooks, James W.................170
Brooks, John .......................115
Brooks, Thomas ....................72
Brosseau, Annie ..................349
Brougker, Frank ..................236
Brower, E. Alex .....................63
Brown, Arthur .....................122
Brown, Carroll E.................237
Brown, Charles ...................175
Brown, Cynthia Vasil............64
Brown, Daniel.....................131
Brown, Don J. ......................79
Brown, Donice ......................72
Brown, E. ............................200
Brown, Elizabeth ..................81
Brown, Gary........................113
Brown, Gerald L. ................311
Brown, Gus H. ......................90
Brown, Harry ......................241
Brown, J. R. ........................134
Brown, James R. ...................68
Brown, Jeannett L................236
Brown, Jeffrey P....................89
Brown, John W.....................189
Brown, Lynn. ........................89
Brown, Patricia L.................250

Brown, Philip ......................150
Brown, Sanford ...................266
Brown, Stephanie S. ...........107
Brown, Steve........................238
Brown, Stuart E. ...53, 293, 347
Brown, Thomas.....................89
Brown, T.L ..........................141
Brown, Vivian W....................63
Brown, Warner H., Jr. .........173
Brown, Warren M. ....61, 62, 63
Brown, W. Wayne .................66
Brownlee, Richard D. .........150
Brubacher, Marvin R. .........319
Brubaker, John ......................81
Bruce, George L. R. ............183
Bruce, Joseph L ..................161
Bruckner, Ellen ...................241
Bruehl, J. Roger ....................26
Brug, John F. .......................344
Brumbaugh-Cayford, ...91, 337
   Cheryl
Bruno, C. José......................90
Bruno, J. Jon ......................110
Brushaber, George K. ...78, 297
Brust, Donald M. ..................90
Bryan, David .......................344
Bryan, Ron .........................124
Bryant, Darue .......................80
Bryant, David ......................295
Bryant, John Richard ............61
Bryant, Juanita ....................88
Bryant, Roy, Sr..............80, 297
Bryant, Sissieretta ................80
Bryant, Steven D.................343
Buchanan, John ...................326
Buck, Charles......................169
Buckle, Clarence .................203
Buckle, Terrence ..........182, 183
Buckle, Wilfred S.................203
Buegler, David D. ...............136
Bueno, John ........................75
Buhler, Becky .....................350
Bula, Omega C....................210
Bull, Norman ......................199
Bulloch, Wendy...................210
Bullock, Jeffrey...................315
Bullock, Marsha....................46
Bullock, Robert H., Jr. .........339
Bullock, Warren ...................75
Bunch, Charlene..................105
Burden, Keith......................140
Burg, Randall S. ...................89
Burger, Delores ....................25
Burger, Elizabeth ..................67
Burger, Stephen E. ...............25
Burgess, Morgan .................121
Burgio, Ron.........................108
Burgonio-Watson, .............267
   Thelma
Burgoyne, Howard K ..........114
Burgueno, Fidenaio..............96
Burkat, Claire S..................118
Burke, Caroline...................132

Burke, C. Don .....................147
Burke, Michael....................210
Burke, Michael L ................116
Burkette, Spencer ...............139
Burkhardt, Patricia ...............30
Burleigh, Elizabeth F. ..........71
Burnett, Joe G. ...................110
Burney, Artie ........................80
Burnham, Gary......................97
Burns, C ...............................95
Burns, Donald .....................292
Burns, Patricia......................54
Burns, Robert J. ...................54
Burrell, Calvin ....................325
Burrell, Willie .....................146
Burris, Glenn C., Jr. ............132
Burt, Lindsey ...............201, 202
Burt, Merlin D. ....................353
Burton, Anthony..................183
Busby, Dan............................31
Bush, Richard E. ...................89
Bushkofsky, Linda Post ......115
Bushrod, Montrose..............344
Bush-Simmons, ..................235
   La Quetta
Busic, David.........................339
Buslon, Jim .........................201
Busse, Cheryl..............191, 319
Bussey, Barry W..................208
Bustle, Louie .......................102
Butimore, David, Sr. ............66
Butin, Philip W....................312
Butler, Kevin J. ...................341
Butler, Lisa..........................142
Butler, Ramsey....................146
Butler, Thomas....................142
Butts, Calvin O. ..................253
Butts, J. Wayman ...............257
Buxton, Zane.......................150
Buzza, John ........................248
Buzza, Rob..........................320
Buzzard, Anthony, Sr. .........334
Buzzell, Sandra ...................244
Byers, Melvin Jr .........102, 103
Byler, J. Ron .......................138
Bynum, Bill.........................358

Cabana, Denise ...................237
Cabigting, Ruben ...............135
Cabrera, Brigido..................153
Cackler-Veazey, ..................44
   Cathleen D.
Cadieux, Vincent................206
Cady, Donald D. .................176
Cagan, Richard D................266
Cahill, Brendan ...................313
Cahoy, William J.................311
Caldwell, Bruce..................112
Caldwell, Ray......................139
Caldwell, William ...............251
Calahan, Myra.....................341
Callaghan, Aloysius R.........311
Callahan, Tom .....................241

Calvin, Elizabeth..................49
Camenga, Andrew..............160
Camp, Peggy Ann ..............177
Camp, Richard P., Jr..............29
Camp, Steve ......................169
Campbell, Cynthia M.........307
Campbell, Donald G. ..........150
Campbell, Ella ...................153
Campbell, Frederick F.........83
Campbell, Greg..................132
Campbell, G. Robert ..........211
Campbell, Jerry D ..............299
Campbell, Jimmy ................96
Campbell, John D. ..............191
Campbell, Joseph ................92
Campbell, Michael............353
Campbell, Phillip ..............136
Campbell, Scott..................55
Campbell, Stuart W.............353
Campbell, Virginia .............243
Canary-Marshall, ..............258
    Deborah
Caner, Ergun ......................305
Canfield, Paul V. ................144
Cannada, Robert C., Jr. .....310
Cannaday, Antoinette ...........80
Cannon, Edward..................80
Cano-Landivar, Jeannette .....77
Caouette, Karen ..................244
Capets, James.....................124
Caplan, Rick......................242
Caraballo, Ildefonso......96, 299
Carcaño, Minerva G............173
Carr-Harris, Philip..............253
Carl, William J III ..............310
Carlin, Donald....................261
Carlsen, William A...............66
Carlson, David ...................247
Carlson, Dennis N..............160
Carlson, George G..............117
Carlson, Kenneth P.............114
Carlson, Robert J. ................83
Carmi, Laila........................49
Carmichael, Cassandra.........40
Caron, Kateri......................267
Carouthers, David ..............295
Carpenter, Don ..................347
Carpenter, Ron ...................44
Carpenter, Ronald, Sr.........133
Carr, Clarence ...............61, 62
Carriere, Vianney ........182, 359
    (Sam)
Carroll, Jeff .......................121
Carroll, John......................259
Carroll, Leon ......................24
Carson, Glen T. ...................85
Carson, John L.....................76
Carson, Kathy .....................46
Carter, Ethel Ware..............239
Carter, Janice.....................350
Carter, Jeff ........................254
Carter, Kenneth Wayne .........89
Carter, Lanny W..................102

Carter, Larry ......................303
Carter, Nick ......................295
Carter, Ron L. .....................341
Carter, T. Scott ..............96, 192
Carter, Wayne.....................124
Cartes, Ann........................142
Cartwright, Dani Loving.......87
Carver, L. Hugh ...........96, 191
Casebolt, James...................248
Casey, Daniel E....................50
Casey-Lee, Diane...............245
Cassian (Bishop).................129
Cassidy, Thomas P. .............310
Casson, Ernestine................268
Casteel, Richard .................131
Castillo, R. Ernest ..............159
Castrejon, Jaime..................304
Castro, Manuel S ................103
Cauller, William L. .............260
Cavadini, John C.................315
Cavalero, Robert .................39
Cavanaugh, Donald...............22
Cavanna, Pedro ...................93
Cave, Evelyn ......................241
Cawley, William Kevin.......359
Cayce, W. Hartsel ...............151
Cazabon, Gilles...................206
Cebula, John W. ..................253
Cereghino, Phil ..................343
Chadden, Shane ...................57
Chadick, Bonnie..................242
Chafe, Joanne.....................206
Chakravarthy, ViJay............254
Chamberlain, Larry.............121
Chambers, James R..............174
Chambers, Steven ...............210
Chambers-Young, Thelma ....40
Chamness, Ben R................172
Champion, Willie C. ............88
Chand, Samuel R..................133
Chandler, David ..................104
Chandler, Maurice G...........296
Chandra, T..........................186
Chane, John Bryson ............111
Chang, Richard S. O. ..........110
Change, Lamont....................46
Channan, James ...................48
Chapell, Bryan .............149, 300
Chapman, Morris H. ...........160
Chappell, Paul G.................305
Chappelle, Richard .........61, 63
Charles, Mark......................87
Charleston, Steven ..............301
Charron, Jean-Marc ............322
Chase, Deana ......................124
Chatham, Virginia E. ..........344
Chauncey, H. Doyle ............161
Chavez, Silvia ......................24
Chavez-Thompson, Linda.....35
Cheatham, Shirlie...............121
Chemberlin, Peg..................249
Cheney, Charles Edward.....154
Cheshier, Carl ....................303

Chesnutt, Randall...............311
Chetti, Samuel S. .................66
Chevalier, Rebekah .............349
Cheung, David A ................299
Chidsey, Linda ...........123, 124
Chiles, Lois ..........................67
Chipchase, Elwood H. ........298
Chisholm, Alvah .................251
Choe, Richard C...................210
Choloyan, Oshagan..............73
Chondo, Javan.....................122
Chow, Rita K. ......................42
Christen, William L. ...........167
Christensen, Bruce...............346
Christianson, Lawrence ......139
Christie, Marge ...................251
Christie, Paul C...................236
Christopher (Bishop)...........129
Christopher, Sharon ...........171
    Brown
Chrysostomos......................165
    (Archbishop)
Chu, Thomas ......................107
Chute, Michael....................328
Chute, Nilda .......................294
Ciceva-Aleksic, Marija.........49
Cilpam, Ha Giao ...................90
Cindrich, Frank ...................259
Cinson, Victor .....................36
Citronnelli, Eddie.................80
Citzler, Annette ..................116
Cizik, Rich ...........................38
Cizik, Richard .....................337
Clancy, Danna ....................266
Clanton, John .....................126
Clark, Cecil ........................162
Clark, Charles ......................68
Clark, Frank B. ...................234
Clark, James I., Jr...............103
Clark, Jeffery A....................161
Clark, Katharine.................123
Clark, Kathryn (Penny).........36
    Vennard
Clark, Neal ..........................66
Clark, Tim ..........................160
Clarke, Barry B...................183
Clarke, John R. ...................182
Clarke, Levi .......................193
Clark-Oakes, Judy..............247
Clausen, Daniel...................309
Cleave, Dwayne ..................200
Clement, Marilyn .................35
Clements, Kerry ..................150
Clements, Larry ...................66
Clements, Philip J. ...............39
Clements, Sam ..............98, 193
Clickman, Marlene..............254
Clifford, Mary....................142
    Montgomery
Cline, Douglas M..........96, 192
Cline, Evadna .....................263
Cline, George ......................132
Cline, Richard D. ................266

415

Clippard, David................161
Clothier, Patti ....................259
Cloud, Randy .......................66
Cloud, Sanford, Jr. ..............39
Clowes, William..................151
Coates, Gerald....................122
Coates, Ken ........................235
Coats, John W. .....................68
Cobarn, Trevor .....................87
Cobb, Judith .........................18
Cochran, Sylvenia F...........255
Coen, Joseph W ....................24
Coffey, David.....................131
Coffin, John.......................123
Coffin, Percy D. .................183
Coffin, Peter R. ..................183
Cogdill, Michael G. ...........298
Cogsdale, Michael ..............257
Cohen, Albert G. ................236
Colas, Ralph.........................22
Cole, Brian ........................115
Cole, David ........................301
Cole, Jack...........................126
Cole, John K. .....................146
Coleman, Catherine ...........235
Coleman, Robert F. .............303
Coles, Robert N. ..........68, 340
Colli, Fred ..........................206
Collier, John W. P...............344
Colligan, John .....................22
Collins, Arnold....................50
Collins, Bradley .................330
Collins, David ....................185
Collins, Jacqueline .............187
Collins, Leland C. ..............238
Collins, Les D. ...................143
Collins, Michael R. .............161
Collins, W. Darwin ..............87
Collins, Tamara ....................22
Collis, John ........................128
Collymore, Carlisle.............171
Colon, John ........................109
Combes, Frances ................293
Comfort, William ...............267
Compton, Gordon ................29
Conant, Lawrence ...............162
Condrea, Nicolae ........156, 207
Conley, John.......................299
Conn, Charles Paul .......96, 191
Connel, Bob .......................326
Conner, Len..........................25
Connors, G. C. ....................203
Constantine (Metropolitan).166
Converse, Susan..........153, 204
Cook, Clyde .......................313
Cook, David T.....................327
Cook, Katie ........................324
Cooksey, David....................81
Coomas, Doug ....................186
Coombs, Gary F. .................313
Coons-Torn, Marja..............169
Coop, Linda........................115
Cooper, Brian .....................184

Cooper, Irving S..................135
Cooper, Sabrina M........76, 324
Cooper-White, Michael L. ...306
Coorilos, Euyakim Mar ......137
Cope, Mike.........................344
Cope, William ..............64, 323
Copeland, Elaine Johnson...299
Copeland, Shelley ..............236
Cope-Robinson, Lyn ...123, 124
Copley, Steve .....................234
Corbett, Ardelia M. .............170
Corbett, Daniel.............98, 193
Corbin, Randall B. ..............89
Corcelius, Ted ....................262
Corkum, Celest ..................208
Corkum, Ken.......................208
Cormode, James R. .............320
Cornelius, Fred R.................97
Coronel, David...................103
Corrigan, John....................327
Corson-Finnerty, Susan.......331
Cossey, James E..................327
Costanza, Daniel ................348
Cotton, Edmund G. .............121
Cotton, T. ............................95
Coulston, James A...............119
Coulter, Riley......................317
Councell, Gary R. ..............331
Councell, George E.............108
Courter, Gini ......................167
Cousin, Philip Robert, Sr. .....61
Cowan, A.J.........................182
Cowan, Mattew ..................158
Cox, Ann ............................264
Cox, Brian ...........................54
Cox, Jill ..............................268
Cox, John R. .......................142
Coyle, Charlotte .................264
Coyner, Michael J. ..............172
Crabtree, Bruce ..................104
Crabtree, Charles T. ............44,
  74, 75
Crabtree, David Foy............169
Craddock, Margaret ............263
Craddock, Max....................194
Craddock, Max E. ...............348
Craft, Betty Jo ......................37
Craft, Roger L. .....................26
Craft, Roy...........................238
Craig, James D....................361
Crane, Charles A.................297
Cranford, Stephen ..............259
Cranford, Steven ..................86
Crank, Charles ....................75
Crapson, Winnie.................242
Craven, Paul J. .....................37
Crawford, Bud ....................196
Crawford, S. Rea................148
Creech, Barry .....................150
Creighton, Michael W.........109
Creighton, Philip .................57
Crenshaw, Carole ...............332
Crenshaw, Ray ....................80

Cress, James A. ..................159
Crews, C. Daniel.................357
Crick, Robert D.............96, 192
Crist, Larry...........................86
Crittenden, David...............150
Crocker, Richard ..................80
Crockett, Joseph ...................22
Croft, Donna ........................54
Croglio, James ...................254
Croneberger, Jack P............110
Crook, Eleanor Butt .............26
Cropsey, Marvin W. ...........335
Cross, Marie T....................150
Crossin, John W. .................315
Crossman, Richard C. ...54, 324
Crough, Dave .....................352
Crough, Janke .....................352
Crouse, C. E. ........................29
Crout, Valorie.....................266
Crowder, Sandra B..............63
Crowshoe, Kirk ..................248
Cruger, Douglas .................244
Crum, John..........................72
Crumbly, Faith ...................341
Crumes, W. E. ...........100, 332
Crump Gene .......................251
Crutchfield, Carmichael.......88
Crutchfield, Charles N. .......172
Cruver, Rob W. ..................148
Cruz, John ...........................21
Csepregi, Gabor .................318
Csomor, Marjorie .................90
Cudjoe, Dale ........................92
Cueni, R. Robert ................305
Culbertson, William ...........115
Culp, Kristine A. ................300
Culpepper, R. Alan......239, 304
Culpepper, Raymond F. .......96,
  191
Cummins, George D. ...........154
Cunningham, Jack...............211
Cunningham, Jeff................266
Cunningham, Johnny ...........72
Cunningham, Joseph.....91, 327
Cunningham, Mary .............333
Cunningham, Paul G...........101
Cunningham, Ronald M........89
Cunningham, Ronald ...........31
Cupich, Blase .......................83
Cureton, Kenyn...........160, 341
Curry, Michael B. ................111
Curtis, Cheryl.....................182
Curtis, Jay .........................119
Curtis, Larry.......................264
Cushman-Wood, Darren ......35
Custer, James .....................121
Cuthbert, Richard.................68
Cuthbert, Terry D........348, 349
Cutler, Lelia .......................142
Cutts, Debbie .....................268

Dabrowski, Rajmund ..........159
Dadds, David ....................240

Dadourian, Haig...................74
Dahl, Judy...........................176
Dahlquist, Charles W. II.......99
Dahulich, Michael G............312
Dale, Diana C. ................41, 71
Dale, William.....................145
Dallenbach, Robert B..........148
D'Angelo, Mary Rose...........54
Danhof, Henry....................152
Daniel, Hieromonk .....343, 344
   (Zelinsky)
Daniel, Clifton, III ..............107
Daniel, Eapen.....................335
Daniels, David Rwhynica, Jr.61
Daniels, Henrietta ................64
Daniels, Mary Martha.........108
Danielson, Duane................256
Danielson, Duane C. ...........116
Dantzler, Debbie .................263
Daoust, Joseph P. ................304
Darden, Samuel.....................72
Darnell, Stephen P.......967, 191
Darr, Steve .........................266
Dart, Christopher ...............249
Daughters, Kenneth Alan.....301
David, Rebecca .....................32
Davidson, Brian ...................76
Davidson, Bruce..................255
Davies, Fran .......................256
Davies, Pat .........................201
Davies, S. J. P.....................294
Davies, Susan E. ...................33
Davis, Ashley .....................242
Davis, Bessie........................72
Davis, Charles.....................146
Davis, Derek .......................220
Davis, Dollie ......................147
Davis, Earl ...........................40
Davis, G. Lindsey ...............173
Davis, Harper......................243
Davis, James Levert..............61
Davis, Jim ..........................234
Davis, Kathleen...................236
Davis, Kenneth R.........96, 192
Davis, Melvin......................244
Davis, Nehemiah..................141
Davis, Richard ....................174
Davis, Robert......................244
Davis, R. Paul .....................105
Davis, Sarah Frances ............61
Davis, Stephanie .................170
Davis, Stephen P. ................161
Davis, Tyrone T....................88
Davis, Willie ......................152
Davison, Susanna.................123
Davolt, Philip.......................81
Davolt, Susan .....................331
Dawidziuk, Jan....................148
Dawkins, David ..................146
Day, Jeff ............................244
Dean, Amy Jacks ..................65
Deckenback, John R. ..........169
Decker, William A. .............335

Dee, Choe Chong...............186
deFreese, David L. ..............117
DeFriese, Gordon................256
DeGraffenreidt, Kermit........62,
   337
DeGroot-Nesdahl, .............116
   Andrea F.
Delac, Katria ......................219
de Leon, Daniel....................44
DelHousaye, Darryl ............309
De Lima, Glauco Soares.....109
DellaForesta, John ..............187
Deller, Walter......................318
Delmonte, Elisabeth.............49
Delsaut, Phil.......................198
Del Valle, Harry Fred..........150
Demarse, Mary Grace..........253
De Marco, Eugene ...............87
Demeter, Andor...................130
Demetrios (Archbishop) ...... 33
DeMoor, Robert ..................324
Demos, Emanuel G. ............128
Demson, Sandra ...................53
den Hoed, J. ........................324
Denis, Mary Frances...........210
Dennie, Steve...........103, 104
Dennis, Robert ...................152
Dennison, Don ...................105
Densmore, Christopher .......355
Denton, A. Louis.................261
Depot, Scott .......................161
Derderian, Hovnan........74, 184
DeRose, Robert .....................35
Derr, Donna..........................41
Derrenbacker, Robert A .......54
Derry, John .........................304
DeSelm, Joel ......................139
Desgagne, Jean.....................52
DeTilla, Paul .......................139
Devadhar, Sudarshana.........172
DeVeaux, William ................35
DeVeaux, William Phillips....61
Devlin, Lillian.....................258
DeVoe, Jerry M., Jr. ............155
DeVries, Janet ....................150
Dewey, Marvin L. ...............321
Dewar, Dale .......................189
DeWinter, Deborah ..............49
Dewberry, A.T.....................103
Dewling, Gregory R............203
Dewling, Robert H..............203
DeYoung, Terry ...................24
Diakiw, William ..................166
Diaz, Javier ........................103
Diaz, Louis ........................115
Diaz-Montanez, Cristino.......67
Dicaire, Louis......................206
DiCicco, Mario ...................302
Dickerson, Dennis................21
Dickerson, Dennis C.....61, 357
Diefenbach, Joan.................252
Diehl, James H....................101
Diehl, Paul J., Jr....................86

Diekelman, William R. .......136
Diemer, Ulli .......................347
Dietz, Harry .......................262
Dill, James ...........................96
Dilley, Gary........................104
Dimitrios (Bishop).............128
Dimitriou, Jerry...................128
Dinatale, Wenda.................261
Dipboye, Carolyn................333
Dipboye, Larry...................333
Dirks, Gordon ....................321
Dirmann, Kimberly.............131
DiStaulo, David .................187
Dixon, Brad........................104
Dixon, Judy .......................258
Djaballah, Amar..................318
Dimitri (Archbishop) ..........145
Dobbin, Karen....................242
Dobbs, H. A. ......................331
Dobush, Christine ...............77
Dodds, Ed............................25
Dodge, Hollis .....................167
Doezema, Don ...................152
Dohner, Stephanie..............251
Dolan, Timothy M. ...............83
Donahue, James A. .............303
Donald (Bishop).................129
Donaldson, Hal ..................338
Donges, David A.................118
Donley, Brian C. .................305
Donnithorne, Larry R.........299
Dorland, Arthur G..............189
Dorman, Nancy...................266
Dormont, Robert ................259
Dorrington,................154, 205
   Charles W.
Dorsey, Daniel .....................33
Dorsey, Jim ........................332
Dortch, Mimi .....................234
Douglas, Caryn ..................318
Douglas, S.C........................72
Douglas, Scott....................233
Douglas, Stacey C. .............343
Douglass, Steve....................26
Dow, Lorenzo.....................151
Dow, Thomas E...................318
Dowd, Susan Jackson .........333
Dowden, G. Blair........104, 304
Downey, Ray ......................191
Downey, William S. H........135
Downs, Bert...........106, 316
Downs, Michael A ..............169
Downs, Timothy C..............169
Downton, Keelan ..................40
Doyle, Barrie ......................190
Draper, Bern .......................119
Draper, David E. .................316
Dresselhaus, Richard ...........75
Driedger, Connie................191
Driggers, B. Carlisle ...........161
Driscoll, Virginia................123
Drummond, Shawn .............259
Drury, Stephen ...................174

INDEX

417

Dua, Barbara E..................252
Duda, Betty .........................136
Dueck, Abe.........................350
Duerksen, Carol .................345
Duff, Donald J....................146
Duff, Susan ........................243
Duffy, Mark J.............109, 355
Dufresne, Edward R...........246
Dugas, Jacqueline ...............55
Duggins, Dominic................33
Duke, Thomas ....................249
Dulan, C. Garland ..............157
Dulder, Marianne ...............350
Dumond, Franklin ..............126
Dunahoo, Charles .......149, 330
Dunbar, David G.................297
Dunbar, R. G......................125
Duncan, Donald .................345
Duncan, Larry .............98, 193
Duncan, Muriel ..................351
Duncan, Philip M................110
Duncan, Robert W., Jr. .......111,
259
Duncan, Ronald V. ...............93
Dunham, Rosetta J................63
Dunkerson, Roddy ......169, 250
Dunkin, Ralph ....................268
Dunkin, Ralph W................118
Dunlap, Raymond ...............250
Dunn, Craig A. ...................177
Dunn, James A. ...................177
Dunn, John C. ......................83
Dunn, Sharon R. ...................95
Dunston, Ann ......................80
Dupcak, Kimberlee ............254
Dupre, Ray. D .....................03
Duque, Francisco ...............110
Duracin, Jean Zache...........110
Durakis, Thomas ..................22
Durance, George .................317
Durden, John......................296
Durocher, Eric....................347
Dursi, Elsie L. ....................257
Durso, Pamela R. ...............324
Duvall, Charles ....................31
Dvorak, Robert C................237
Dwight, David A. ...............114
Dybdahl, Jon .....................315
Dyck, Dan ..........................201
Dyck, Darrell .....................198
Dyck, Ed ............................186
Dyck, Sally ........................172
Dyck, Tom Miller ...............347
Dykstra, Gerard L. ........90, 191
Dykstra, Jon ......................351
Dykstra, Russell J. .............342

Eads, Ora W. .......................88
Earheart-Brown, Daniel J. ..307
Earheart-Brown, Jay ..........107
Easley, Michael J. ..............307
Eastman, Donald ................175
Eaton, James E....................328

Ebacher, Roger...................206
Eberhardt, Jack...................126
Eberly, Leon ......................174
Echohawk, John .................231
Echols, James Kenneth .......306
Eck, Diana L. ..............214, 221
Eckes, Lois.........................247
Eckhardt, Ellen E. ..............142
Eckler, Sharon ....................242
Eckman, James....................302
Eckstrom, Kevin ...................46
Edgar, Robert W...................40
Edlund, Mark .....................159
Edney, Lowell ....................170
Edwards, David..........246, 321
Edwards, Gregory .................42
Edwards, Harold ................100
Edwards, Herbert ...............103
Edwards, James L. ........94, 295
Edwards, Jonathan .............156
Edwards, William H.............86
Edwards-Konic, Patricia ....123,
340
Egge, Joel ............................99
Eggleston, James H.............252
Egnew, Bruce E. ..................82
Ehinger, Lois......................241
Ehrenkrantz, Dan ...............310
Ehresman, David.................244
Eibl, Shawnda ......................26
Eidse, Larry........................198
Eidson, E. Larry...................37
Eidum, Charles D................330
Ekemam, Samuel .................62
Chuka, Sr.
Ekeroth, George E................75
Ekeroth, M. J.......................75
Eklund, Kent ......................248
Elam, Betty ...................32, 42
Eldred, Timothy ...................29
Elford, Keith ......................199
Elgin, Bette ........................125
Elia, Donna ...............252, 256
Eliason, Leland V. ................26
Elizade, John ......................259
Ellefson, Anne....................263
Ellenson, David...................303
Elliott, G. Keith..................198
Elliott, Kate Sprutta ...........335
Elliott, Peter G. ..................182
Ellis, David ........................125
Ellis, Davis L. ....................146
Ellis, Howard .....................195
Ellis, Jerry .........................262
Ellis, Jesse Delano, II .........174
Ellis, Rebekah A. ...............256
Ellis, Sandra.......................202
Ellis, Wayne ........................72
Ellison, Leslie ....................265
Elloian, Dierdre..................237
Ellyatt, David .....................199
Elmore, Don ........................78
Elrod, Rachael....................242

Ely, Thomas C.....................111
Embree, Dorothy................245
Emory, M. L........................251
Endecott, Clayton ........98, 193
Endel, Leo ..........................161
Engbrecht, Dave.................139
Engebretson, Donn.............114
Engel, A. Gayle..................169
Engelmayer, Shammai ........334
Engelsma, David........314, 334
Engineer, Rita ....................232
English, Marian....................93
Enger, Cindy ......................267
Engstrom, Jon R..................125
Enns-Rempel, Kevin...........356
Enrique, Antonio ................339
Episcopos, P. S. Samuel .....137
Cor
Epp, Gerald ........................120
Epstein, Jerome M. ............230
Epting, C. Christopher ........109
Erb-Miller, Fannie..............346
Erdman, Greg.....................158
Erhardt, Richard.................267
Erickson, C. E.....................240
Erickson, Charles R. ...........265
Erickson, Paul ....................355
Ericson, Charles .................237
Eriks, Kenneth ...................204
Erickson, Duane .................112
Erickson, Gary....................174
Erickson, James .................162
Erickson, John H.................312
Erlandson, Kathy ...............267
Ervine, Sharon ...................265
Eschenbrenner, Jim ............91
Eshbach, Warren M............262
Eslinger, Leslie S. ..............261
Essey, Basil ..........................69
Esterle, Stan .......................243
Estes, Kristi ........................123
Estill, Dennis......................131
Estocin, Frank ....................166
Estwani, Sheikh Bassam .....238
Etterman, James ...................97
Eubanks, David L. ..............305
Eva, Willmore D. ...............336
Evangelos (Metropolitan) ...128
Evans, Alton.......................145
Evans, Bernard J ................196
Evans, Ellison1 ....................62
Evans, Gene .......................125
Evans, Irvin .......................170
Evans, Marie ......................240
Evans, William ...................140
Evans, William B. ........76, 323
Evenson, Carl R. ................117
Everett, K. Randel..............304
Evison, Ian ..........................21
Ewell, Thomas C.................244
Ewing, Ward B...................302
Eyring, Henry B..................99

418

Faber, Connie ......................327
Fabric, Elliot ......................267
Fadelle, Norman..................84
Fagerstrom, Douglas L. ......303
Fagin, Earl.........................235
Fahey, Brian .......................24
Faigao, Howard F...............159
Failing, Mark .....................323
Fairchild, Darryl.................257
Falco, Chris..........................41
Falconer, Gennae ...............248
Fandrey, James E. ..............136
Fareed, Munner...................226
Faris, Robert........................54
Farley, Lawrence................200
Farlow, Gary .....................124
Farmer, Jeffrey E. .........44, 144
Farmer, Paul .....................241
Faro, Ira.............................261
Farren, John......................311
Fast, Ken .............................25
Fast, Rick ............................56
Faulkner, Tom ...................321
Faurschou, Bruce ..............210
Faust, David M. .................299
Favicha, Raymond .............125
Favreau, Claude ................196
Fawcett, Bruce ..................195
Feamster-Roll, Gerry .........243
Fecher, Roger J. ..................32
Fedak, Wasyly...................208
Fedchko, Michael......155, 204
    205, 320, 321, 350
Fehr, Wes...........................320
Feldberg, Michael .............356
Feldbush, Martin W. ...159, 323
Feldman, James...................27
Feliciano, Gloria ................49
Felter, David J....................333
Fendt, John W., Jr...............142
Ferkenstad, Craig ..............118
Ferlino, Jack.........................23
Fernhout, Harry..................319
Ferre, Faith........................242
Ferree, James W. ...............257
Ferrell, Ernest....................142
Ferrer, Abednego.................90
Ferris, Ronald....................182
Fetherlin, Robert L..............89
Field, Ron............................42
Fifagrowicz, Joseph ...........253
Fikse, Susan.......................337
Finch, Dody .......................47
Finck, Murray D. ...............116
Fincke, George B. ..............155
Fines, David ......................346
Finke, Roger......................215
Finley, J. Lance ..................105
Finley, Patricia ..................148
Finn, Charles W. ................135
Finn, Peter G. ....................311
Finney, Peter P., Jr..............328
Finzel, Hans ......................106

Fiorino, Joseph...................337
Firle, L.C............................141
Firle, Sharon L ..................328
Fischer, Harvey ...................99
Fishell, Randy ...................332
Fisher, Fred S., Sr. ........98, 193
Fisher, Gerald.....................186
Fisher, Violet L. .................172
Fisk, J. Victor.....................124
Fitchue, Leah Gaskin ..........309
Fitzgerald, Russell G. ..........47
Fitzmier, John ....................214
Flaaten, Jan Olav ...............234
Flach, Dennis .....................119
Flanagan, James ................306
Fleischer, Daniel ................100
Fleischer, Paul....................335
Fleischmann, Konrad ..........143
Fleming, David L................341
Flesher, Chuck ....................24
Fletcher, Alfred ...................66
Fletcher, James ....................22
Fletcher, Judy R. ................149
Fletcher, Ruth A. ..................86
Fletcher, Sarah ...................328
Flett, Carol.........................246
Flewelling-Leeds, Ginger ...264
Flores, Robert.....................132
Flory-Steury, Mary Jo..........91
Flowers, Fort D., Jr.............264
Flowers, George F................61
Flowers, Ronald M. ............157
Fluechtling, Rick................268
Fluegel, Elizabeth ..............136
Fluit, Charlie ........................58
Fluker, Sharon Watson ..........33
Folkemer, Don ...................335
Follett, Don .......................262
Fombelle, Douglas W..........297
Fogas, Jackie......................329
Fong, Bruce W. ..................307
Forbes, George...................103
Ford, C. Barney....................34
Ford, C. M............................94
Ford, J. Arthur....................319
Ford, Lowell.........................68
Ford, Shirley K. ..................255
Foreman, Rachel L............105,
    327, 332, 336
Forlines, James...................140
Forlines, Leroy...................140
Forro, Alexander ................130
Forsberg, Robert ................235
Forsee, Tom........................233
Forster, Ed..........................344
Fortune, Marie M................267
Foss, Richard J...................116
Foster, H. Paul ...........203, 348
Foster, Julie .......................240
Foster, Lawrence................152
Foster, Neill K....................351
Fougere, J. Keron...............206
Fowler, Doug .....................243

Fowler, John M. .................328
Fox, Ronald K.....................255
Foxman, Abraham H...........229
Fozard, John D.............94, 307
Frade, Leopold ...................111
Francis, Maureen .................39
Francis, Oprah....................165
Franklin, Mark ...................121
Franklin, Robert M. ..............33
Frase, Donald M. ...............176
Fraser, Ian S. ......................210
Fraser, Margaret...................33
Fraser, Ronald A. ...............317
Frazier, David. ...................126
Freed, Kathy.......................242
Freelander, Daniel...........32, 42
Freeman, David...................191
Freeman, Edward A. ...........141
Freeman, George.................345
Freeman, George H...............50
Freeman, Hillary ................248
Freeman, Linda Danby ........47
Freiheit, Warren D..............117
Freitag, Herbert..................131
Freitag, Merle.....................136
French, Juletha N...................64
Frenchak, David....................47
Fretheim, James A...............114
Freund, Richard C...............142
Frew, Don.............................48
Frey, Mark..........................257
Frick, Murray .....................252
Friend, Kendra ...................105
Friesen, William H..............205
Frisch, Deborah..................156
Frowe, Caroline .................239
Fry, Gary ...........................331
Fryling, Robert A. ................34
Fuchs, Lorelei Francis ..........34
Fugh, Clement W. .................61
Fulenweider, Douglas ..........75
Fullard, Henriettaa .............255
Fuller, John .........................42
Fuller, Paula ........................34
Fuller, Robert H .................174
Fullwood, James ..................68
Fulp, Michael.....................124
Fulton, Jim ........................267
Fulwider, Bryan .................238
Fung, Andrew.....................266
Funk, Abe.....................55, 186
Futral, James R. ..................161

Gaboury, David...................32
Gaddie, Ron.......................243
Gaddis, Louis E ..................103
Gaddy, Todd ......................174
Gaewski, David R...............169
Gage, J. Marshall .................39
Gagnon, André L. ...............319
Gaines, Charles ....................85
Galegor, Steve....................120
Gallagher, John (Jack) ........320

Gallaher, Susan ..................266
Galles, Karen...................40
Gallop, Trina .....................346
Galloway, Phyllis H. .....63, 357
Galvin, Joan ......................294
Gamble, Rich .....................266
Gammill, Nancy..................242
Gammon, Stephen A. ..........106
Gandolfo, Lucian .................87
Gangler, Dan ......................46
Gantz-Jalowiecki, Joanne ...260
Garbidakis, Nicholas.............22
Gardiner, Kelvin J. ...............90
Gardner, Carol...................325
Gardner, Harry G. ..............195
Gardner, Joan.....................40
Gardner, Talmadge.............133
Gardner, W. Wayne ...........315
Garis, Mark ........................81
Garment, Robert................119
Garner, Darlene.................175
Garner, Don......................123
Garrett, Phillip ..................243
Garrison, Brent D...............313
Garrison, J. Michael...........111
Garrison, L. Alton ...............75
Garriss, Stephen ................147
Garton, Jean .....................136
Gasero, Russell .................358
Gast, Mary Susan..............169
Gaston, Sandra L. ...............63
Gatlin, Alton......................95
Gaud, Carmen ...................324
Gaudette, Pierre ................206
Gaumond, André ...............205
Gause, Edith......................150
Gautier, Haggeo ................238
Gautier, Mary ....................25
Gaw, Catherine .........208, 294
Geernaert, Donna ...............33
Geiger, C. Edward..............261
Geisler, Norman ................313
Geldmacher, Joan.............253
Gendron, Lionel ................319
Genello, William R. ...........326
Gentle, Stanley..................81
Gentles, Jestina ................170
George, Francis..................82
George, J. Don ...................75
George, Richard ..................87
George, Thomas A. ...96, 192
George, Timothy ................296
George, William ................88
Georgije (Bishop) .......158, 207
Gepert, Robert Ronald ........111
Gerasimos (Metropolitan)...128
Geraty, Lawrence T...........305
Gerber, Richard R .............146
Gerbrandt, Gerald .............317
Gerdau, Carlson ................109
Gerdes, Neil W..................359
Gerendas, Greg .................65
Gethers, Leroy ..................155

Getz, Greg .........................139
Geyser, P. ..........................154
Geyser, Thomas .................87
Ghabrial, Theresa...............237
Ghougassian, Vazken ..........73
Giacoletto, Kenneth P. .........67
Gibbs, Charles P..................48
Gibbs, Wendell N., Jr. ........110
Gibson, Billy .....................125
Gibson, David E.................326
Gibson, Diana ...................234
Gibson, Gaylena .326, 327, 334
Gibson, J. Daniel.................53
Gibson, Marie E.................254
Giesbrecht, Kennert ...........350
Giesy, Samuel ...................306
Gilbert, Jack .......................33
Gilbert, Wanda ..................220
Gilbert-Cougar, John...........189
Gilbertson, Leon C..............56
Gilbreath, Ed .....................342
Gilliam, Lynn W..................339
Gillians, Larry ....................52
Gillies, Susan ..............65, 250
Gillming, Keith ...................78
Gillum, Perry ..............98, 193
Gilmore, Marshall, Sr. .........89
Gingerich, Elmer.................79
Gingerich, Melvin...............79
Giordano, Sally ..................255
Giordano, Stephen T. .........251
Giron, Rudy .......................96
Girton-Mitchell, Brenda...40,41
Gist, Richard .......................43
Gladish, Michael D.............199
Glagau, Ralph R. .........96, 192
Glanzer, Jules ....................302
Gleason, Jim......................252
Glenn, Michael..................311
Gnat, Thomas J. ................148
Goatley, David Emmanuel....43
Godevenos, Ken.................351
Godfrey, W. Robert ............316
Goebel, Samuel .................113
Goertzen, Lil ..............198, 348
Goff, Jim ..........................158
Goff, Phillip ......................217
Goforth, C. W....................147
Gohdes, Stephen ...............139
Gohoes, Stephen ...............188
Goldberger, Pierre ..............210
Golder, Morris ...................146
Golder, W. Evan.................343
Goldstein, Clifford R. .........334
Golumb, Paul ....................253
Gomez, Ray ......................264
Gonzalez, Gerado...............48
Gonzalez, Tony .................235
Goodhue, Thomas W..........254
Goodin, David L...................89
Goodpaster, Larry M..........173
Goodwin, Douglas .............210
Goodyear, Paul..................207

Gootjes, N.H. .....................321
Gopal, Renee.....................257
Gordon, Dennis L ..............106
Gordon, Dorcas...................55
Gordon, Drew ............155, 329
Gordon, J. Dorcas ..............319
Gordon, Lynne ...........155, 329
Gore, Susan K....................107
Gore, Susan Knight............358
Gorton, Dennis L ...............343
Gorzinski, Barbara .............266
Gould, Aaron.....................168
Govier, Gordon ...................34
Grady, J. Lee .....................326
Grady, Joellen W. ...............257
Graham, Ellen ...................240
Graham, Sharlene ...............205
Graham, Vernon R. ............240
Graham, William A. ............303
Grainger, David..................239
Granberg-Michaelson,
  Wesley...............28, 153, 24
Granke, Robert H................360
Granitsas, Nicholas ............106
Grant, James M..................313
Grant, Kenneth G. Y. ..........246
Grant, Michael A. ..............102
Grant, Sumner M. ...............67
Graves, Charles .................268
Graves, David ...................102
Graves, Sylvia....................123
Graves, Thomas H. ............296
Graves, William H., Sr.........89
Gray, Art.............................44
Gray, Arthur J., II...............132
Gray, Davis .......................107
Gray, Duncan, III...............249
Gray, Duncan ....................110
  Montgomery, III
Gray, Joan .........................150
Gray, Melva ........................66
Gray, Stephen....................128
Gray, Stephen C.................169
Graybill, John....................167
Graz, John .........................159
Grecco, Richard .................206
Greco, John ........................22
Green, Daniel ....................155
Green, Donald B. ...............259
Green, E. David .................105
Green, Peter ..............138, 139
Green, S. ...........................171
Green, Samuel ....................61
  Lawrence, Sr.
Green, S. L., Jr.....................94
Greenawald, Henry ............260
Greenawald, Patricia...........260
Greenhaw, David M...........301
Greening, John ..................126
Greenleaf, Helen ...............166
Greenway, Jeffrey E............295
Greenwood, Greg...............244
Gregersen, Bruce ...............210

Gregg, William O. .............110
Grégoire, Léo .....................206
Grégoire, Renaude .............296
Gregory, Chester, Sr. .........170
Greiman, Clayton...............154
Grein, Richard F. .................33
Grier, David ......................202
Grieves, Brian ...................109
Griffes, Darrell D. .............114
Griffin, Arlee, Jr. ................66
Griffin, Ashley ..................244
Griffin, Robert...................176
Griffin, Sharon ..................102
Griffin, William A. .............310
Griffith, Craig ....................22
Griffith, Richard.................132
Grigsby, Phillip N. .............256
Grimard, Roland ...............208
Grime, Paul .......................136
Grimm, Libby ...................259
Grimm, Robert ..................254
Grogan, Douglas L. ..............89
Groome, Thomas H. ...........297
Groover, Gentle L. ..............101
Groover, R. Edwin ..............296
Groseclose, Michael...........175
Gross, Glenn M. .................155
Gross, Joseph ....................148
Grossman, Randall A. ..........80
Grossman, Robert ..............154
Grossman, W. ....................153
Grote, Royal U., Jr. .............154
Grotegut, Stan ...................236
Grotnick, Casimir...............332
Grubbs, Bonita ..................237
Grubbs, Lari R. ...................86
Geulsgugian, Bernard .........184
Guengerich, Larry ...............38
Guentert, Richard L. .............87
Guernsey, Lucy ..................236
Guess, J. Bennett................168
Guffey, Edith A. .................168
Guibord, Gwynne...............236
Guido, Sam .........................72
Guidry, Carolyn Tyler ..........61
Guillebeau, Julie ...............250
Guillemette, Gaetane .........346
Guirguis, Ammonius...........195
Guiterrez, Rosalia ...............48
Gulasekharam, Nesa ...........52
Gulick, Edwin F., Jr. ..........110
Gulick, Janet A. .................261
Gulick, Walter ...................250
Gullette, Reginald ...............80
Gullixson, Theodore ...........335
Gumbs, Ambrose................111
Gumbs, Carolyn .................254
Gunter, Nina......................101
Guretzki, David...................54
Gurgel, Karl R. ...................177
Gurley, Morris....................253
Guskjolen, J. I. ..................203
Guy, Kristen ......................346

Gwinn, Alfred W., Jr. .........173

Haas, Steve.........................50
Habegger, Ron ...................330
Habegger, Ronald J. ...........120
Hackett, Charles.................75
Hadley, Alvin ....................258
Hadsell, Heidi ...................303
Haemmerle, Gerald R. ........308
Hagan, Michael..................308
Hagan, Orville....................191
Hagedorn, Harold J. ...........177
Hagemann, Dennis...............86
Hagerty, Robert E. .............316
Haggray, Jeffrey...........66, 161
Hagop, Deacon...................184
Hahn, Daniel .....................255
Hai, Iftekhar ......................48
Hailstock, Calvin ...............152
Hales, Robert D. .................99
Haley, Laura J. ...................254
Haley, Richard ...................246
Hall, A. Z., Jr. .....................94
Hall, D. A., Sr. .....................95
Hall, Dinah........................267
Hall, Gary..........................312
Hall, J.L .............331, 339, 358
Hall, Marvin ......................124
Hall, Will...........................161
Hallberg, Donald M. ...........116
Hallman, Don.....................185
Hallman, Joseph.................162
Halloway, Carl ...................174
Hallstrand, Sarah.................66
Haloviak, Bert....................353
Hamb, Elnora P. ...................88
Hamel, William J. ...............115
Hamelink, Crystal...............256
Hames, Jerrold .............109, 330
Hamilton, Jeff ...................132
Hamilton, Jim.....................161
Hamilton, Karen..................53
Hamilton, W. W. ..................94
Hamlett, James P. ................86
Hammel, Marci ..................103
Hammock, Cheryl................47
Hammons, Roger .............1451
Hampton, Charles ..............135
Hampton, John E. ...............146
Hancock, Carol L. ...............210
Handysides, Allan R. ..........159
Haney, Kenneth F. ..............174
Haney, O. L. .........................95
Hankins, David E. ...............161
Hanley, Richard .................242
Hanse, Brian W. ...................37
Hansen, David....................169
Hansen, Duane ..................116
Hansen, Ellen ....................267
Hansen, Gary L. .................115
Hanson, Lloyd....................235
Hanson, Mark S. ................116
Hanus, Jerome G.................83

Hanzlik, Darcy ...................248
Hapke, Lark J. ....................169
Hardesty, Jane .....................77
Hardy, Ralph, Jr. ............32, 42
Hargrave, Ervin..................133
Harke, Gary L. ....................261
Harkins, Derrick...................43
Harmelink, Herman, III ......131
Harms, Forrest ...................242
Harms, Richard H. ..............358
Harms, Steve .....................235
Harp, Roger C. ...................150
Harriger, James ...................25
Harris, Alvin........................92
Harris, David......................350
Harris, David A. .................229
Harris, Elsie.......................170
Harris, Forrest E. ................295
Harris, Grove .....................221
Harris, Jerome V. .................61
Harris, Michael ..................152
Harris, Nanci .......................52
Harris, Phil..........................91
Harris, Robert.....................206
Harris, Ron L ......................42
Harrison, Charles E. ............341
Harrison, Dan.....................104
Harrison, David P ...............44
Harrison, Matthew ..............136
Harrison, William
  Anthony .........................144
Hart, Donald G. ..................169
Hart, Ken...........................132
Hart, Maurice .....................125
Hart, Michael .....................320
Hart, Ray L. .......................297
Hartford, Barbara H. .............48
Hartke, Gary.......................102
Hartman, Patricia ...............113
Hartwig, Raymond L. ..........136
Harvey, Andrew .................260
Harvey, Carole (Kate) H. ......67
Harvey, Jane Hull.................34
Harwell, Sara .....................354
Hasan, John .......................234
Haskins, Roger W., Jr. .........122
Hastag, John III...................126
Hastey, Stan ........................65
Hatcher, Warren .................155
Hatlie, Susan Allers .............248
Hauck, Michael...................40
Hauser, Clarence .................295
Haverstock, Zedna M. .........262
Hawk, David ......................136
Hawkins, Charles ...............243
Hawkins, Don ....................313
Hawkins, O. S. ...................160
Hawkins, Robert ........102, 103
  J., Jr
Haworth, Sharon ................123
Hayat, Ghazala...................250
Hayes, Franklin ...................65
Hayes, Kathleen .................341

421

Hayes, Lindsey....................133
Hayes, Robert E., Jr. ...........173
Hayes, Shirley....................152
Hayford, Jim ......................131
Haymes, Don .....................354
Haynes, J. N........................94
Hays, Franklin.....................65
Hazuda, Ronald A................67
Hazzard, David E.................203
Headman, Wayne A. ...........310
Heagy, David .....................168
Hearn, Greg........................133
Heaslip, Clifford..................211
Heath, Gordon....................360
Heath, Preston....................145
Heckles, Jane E...................169
Heckman, Bud .....................46
Hedberg, William................252
Hedman, Roy .....................253
Heebner, Gerald .................343
Heerspink, Robert C ............90
Hefner, Helmut....................311
Heidkamp, Mary .................35
Hein, Marvin..............126, 127
Heinze, Ted ........................295
Heisey, Terry M. ................355
Heleine, Berton G. ..............68
Helena (Mother).................164
Helton, Charles L................89
Helton, James....................125
Helton, Mary Beth ..............244
Heminway, L. Marshall ......135
Hempelmann, L. Dean........136
Hemphill, Margaret.............155
Henderson, Dorsey F., Jr. ....111
Henderson, James ...............150
Henderson, Katharine R......216
Henderson, Rebecca............156
Henderson, Susan................169
Henderson, Veryl F.............161
Hendricks, Harry.................100
Hendrix, Carol S.................118
Hendrixson, Joe M.............242
Hendrickson, Mary Lynn .....24
Henkel, Sarah.....................262
Hennessy, Janet..................244
Henning, Cornal ..........61, 244
    Garnett, Sr.
Henze, Charles ...................252
Heppner, Jack.....................198
Herbrandson, DeWayne ........29
Heretz, Michael...................166
Herlong, Bertram N............111
Herman (Metropolitan).64, 312
Herman, Alvin....................193
Herman, Harry ...................144
Hermiz, Tom ......................104
Hernando, Mirasal ..............186
Hernando, Vincente.............186
Heron, Claire.......................58
Herr, John..........................155
Herring, Paul L. .................262
Herrling, Karen ...................35

Hertzog, Glenn....................139
Hertzog, Stephen.................322
Herzog, Daniel W................109
Hess, Larry G......................190
Hessel, Karen Mcclean ........35
Hester, Yvonne ...................246
Heuser, Frederick J., Jr........150
    334
Heyward, Isaiah ...................95
Hicken, Michael...................257
Hickey, Tim S. ....................328
Hicks, Dan ..........................132
Hicks, John M......................333
Hicks, Maurice M. ..............187
Hicks, Sherman ...................116
Hicks, Wayne ......................105
Hicks, William ......................99
Hiebert, Richard P...............351
Hiemstra, John E.........253, 255
Higgens, Stan .......................29
Higgs, Grady .......................79
Higham, Susan .....................154
Highers, Alan E....................342
Hilarion (Archbishop).........157
Hill, Alec..............................34
Hill, Darcel ..........................249
Hill, Kenneth H....................333
Hill, Malika ..........................254
Hill, Michael ........................95
Hill, Nick ..............................97
Hill, R. Eugene .....................68
Hill, Ruth Y. .........................114
Hill, Timothy M. ..................191
Hilliard, William ...................62
    Alexander
Hilsden, R. T. ......................203
Hiltz, Frederick J. ...............183
Hinkle, Carol.......................260
Hines, D................................95
Hinshaw, Seth ....................156
Hinton, Arthur....................108
Hinz, Mary Ann ..................246
Hirschy, Charles A. .............102
Hirschy, Margaret ..............354
Hirshkowitz, Barbara .........331
Hixon, Larry.......................236
Ho, Carolyn..........................85
Ho, Esther...........................235
Hoak, Don ..........................265
Hobbs (Reverend)...............147
Hockensmith, David .........250
    W., Jr.
Hodder, Gary......................208
Hodges, James .............71, 184
Hodgins, Donald E.............210
Hodgson, Bob ....................194
Hodgson, Robert .................22
Hodur, F. ............................148
Hoefflin, Walter R..............132
Hoeksema, Herman............152
Hoffman, Bud .....................257
Hoffman, Jane Fisler...........169
Hoffman, Michael................97

Hoffman, Warren L.......81, 187
Hoffmeister, Desmond .........67
Hofstad, Robert D. .............116
Hogan, Ed ...........................76
Hogan, Peter.......................252
Hogston, Delphine ..............247
Hoke, Terry ..........................81
Holbrook, Mark G. ...............29
Holdefer, Helen...................233
Holden, Ron .......................194
Holder, Steve......................125
Holguin, Cesar ...................110
Holland, Grace......................81
Holland, Jeffrey R................99
Holland, Melford E., Jr. ......109
Hollenbach, Deanna L. .......139
    188, 336
Holley, Darrell ....................140
Hollifield, Milton ................161
Hollinger, Dennis ...............113
Hollinger, Dennis P.............301
Hollingsworth, Mark, Jr. .....111
Holloway, Callon W., Jr. .....117
Holloway, Carolyn ..............253
Holm, Duane.......................257
Holm, Jim...........................307
Holmberg, Joseph ..............248
Holmes, Carol ....................253
Holmes, Charley ..........79, 296
Holmes, Jenny.....................259
Holmes, Mary Swalla .........242
Holmes, Roy A......................62
Holmquist, Victor ...............186
    Freeman
Holmstrom, Virginia ...........67
Holt, Jeanette .......................65
Holtz, Janet E......................261
Homoki, Lee .......................127
Hood, George......................157
Hood, Phil ..........................351
Hooker, Eula ......................254
Hoolahan, Michae................41
Hoover, Amos B. ................144
Hope, Monica.......................80
Hopkins, Jim ........................65
Hopkins, John L...................172
Hopkins, Sara E. .................343
Hopwood, Doug..................260
Hopyan, Takvor....................74
Horgan, Ron .......................119
Horne, James R ...................103
Horne, Martha J...................310
Hornshuh, Fred L...............144
Horsch, James E..................340
Horton, Evon G...................319
Hoshibata, Robert T............173
Hoskin, Derek B.E..............182
Hoskins, Janet A. ................321
Hossler, William .................139
Hostetter, Steven J. ............295
Hotchkiss, Gregory K..........154
Houg, Richard W. ...............301
Hougen, Philip L..................117

INDEX

422

Hough, Joseph C., Jr. .........314
Houle, Jacques ..............96, 192
House, Alvin ........................68
House, Christie R. ...............337
Houseal, Rich.......................25
Houser, Charles....................22
Houston, Barbara ...............262
Houston, Walter .................141
Hovis, Carol ......................235
Hovsepian, Vatche................74
Howard, John Alan ............319
Howard, Randy ..................193
Howard, R. L.......................95
Howard, Roscoe J., III........159
Howard, S. Johnson ...........110
Howe, Barry R.....................109
Howe, Bruce H. W..............183
Howe, John W.....................109
Howe, Sue...........................251
Howell, Bruce ....................174
Hoy, G. Philip ....................241
Hoyt, Thomas L., Jr. .......40, 89
Huang, C. P. ......................239
Hubbard, Beck ...................206
Hubbard, Catherine..............86
Hubbard, Donald P .............107
Hucks, John T., Jr................161
Hudgens, Bobby L ................79
Hudnut-Beumler, James......315
Hudson, James L..................150
Hudson, Matt .......................79
Hudson, Steven ..................115
Huebl, Marc ......................119
Huett, Jeff.........................340
Huffard, Everett W..............303
Hugh, Ivor T......................236
Hughes, Aaron ...................351
Hughes, Clyde M..44, 132, 339
Hughes, Dustin...................132
Hughes, Sarah ...................243
Hughes, Sherly M. .............170
Hughes, Teresa A. ..............237
Huh, Young Chin ................134
Huie, Janice Riggle ............172
Hukill, Jim ..........................29
Huleatt, Johann ...................93
Hull, Rey ..........................252
Hulteen, Bob .......................35
Hultquist, Timothy A. ..........45
Humphrey, Sandra .............327
Humphry, Carol .................327
Hundley, Michael................243
Hunerdosse, Marion............91
Hunn, Ken............................81
Hunneus, Antonio ...............77
Hunt, Janet E.......................26
Hunt, Patricia ....................147
Hunt, Raymon......................63
Hunter, David ....................245
Hunter, Harold D. ..............358
Hunter, Kent R. ...................30
Hunter, Louis, Sr. ................62
Hunter, Martha J. ...............328

Hunter, Robert....................139
Hunter, Ron........................140
Hunter, Stewart ...................55
Huntley, Harvey .................118
Hurley, John ......................167
Hurn, Nancy......................360
Huron, Rod..........................87
Hurt, Donna .......................139
Hurtubise, Pierre ................361
Hus, Jan.............................139
Hutcheon, Cyprian .............202
Hutchings, L. W. ................186
Hutchins, D..........................95
Hutchinson, Moira ...............57
Hutchinson, William W.......172
Hux, Ralph.................104, 330
Hyvonen, Randall ..............169

Iakovos (Metropolitan) .......128
Iasiello, Louis.....................315
Ickes, Wayne .....................114
Ihloff, Robert W. ................110
Ihreborg, Christer...............202
Iker, Jack L........................110
Ilia (Bishop) ........................64
Illingworth, Beth ................256
Imbens, Annie ......................48
Imes, William C. ................296
Ingersol, Stan.....................357
Ingham, Michael C. ............183
Ingram, Daryl B. ..................61
Ingram, Gerald McKinley.....61
Inskeep, Kenneth W. ...........116
Inyangu, Frederick .............124
Ionita, Ioan ..................156, 207
Iorg, Jeff............................302
Iov (Bishop) .......................202
Irish, Carolyn T. ................111
Irons, B...............................95
Irvin, Dale T.......................308
Irvio, Wanda......................243
Irwin, John ..........................57
Irwin, Kevin ......................298
Irwin, Paul G........................21
Irwin, Sara.........................246
Isaiah (Metropolitan) ..........128
Isenhower, Joe.............136, 340
Isham, Scott ......................332
Ishkanian, Charlotte ...........336
Isiye, Tom .........................123
Isner, Vince .........................40
Isom, Beverly ....................240
Isom, Dotcy I. .....................89
Itty, Johncy .......................111

Jackson, Bernice Powell .......49
Jackson, Daniel R. .............207
Jackson, Elmira....................63
Jackson, Kitt......................252
Jackson, Mary ......................80
Jackson, Phil ......................140
Jackson, Susan ...................249
Jackson, Thomas M. ............47

Jackson, Walter L...............103
Jackson-Skelton, ................116
    Christina L.
Jacob, Marjorie ..................160
Jacobs, Anita .....................344
Jacobs, Samuel G.................83
Jacobus, Russell E. .....110, 268
Jacques, Camille ................206
Jaggard, Art .......................242
Jaharis, Michael .................128
Jahr, Armin........................101
Jakubik, Arranna ...............175
James (Archbishop) ............129
James, Joe ...........................97
James, Joseph F..................122
James, Timothy M. ..............85
Janes, Burton K..................203
Jang, Jacob Se ...................134
Jaramillo, M. Linda............168
Jared, Clive .......................103
Jarmus, Andrew ................208
Jarrett, Nathaniel, Jr. ...........62
Jasper, Jeremiah .................267
Jeffers-Schori, Katherine ....109
    110
Jefferson, Bernadel L. ........247
Jeffery, Jim ........................296
Jefferson, Jonathan K.........101
Jeffrey, Robert....................334
Jehle, Bonnie.....................255
Jelinek, James ...................249
Jelinek, James L. ................110
Jellinek, Nancy...................264
Jemerson, Robert ...............39
Jemison, L.........................152
Jenkins, Charles E., III........108
Jenkins, Jason....................256
Jenkins, Keith A................304
Jenkins, Laurie ..................255
Jenkins, Marty...................131
Jenks, Philip ................40, 329
Jenness, Jeffery A. ..............94
Jennings, Charles................68
Jenson, Robert W. ................33
Jeremiah, David .................299
Jeremiah, Jeffrey ...............119
Jerge, Marie C..........118, 255
Jernigan, Paul S .................103
Jesson, Nicholas................54
Jessup, Bryce L...................316
Jewel, Bill .........................244
Jewell, Thomas R..................86
Jillions, John .....................202
Jobson, Harriett Tumlin.......31
Johanson, Paul ....................65
John, Esther .......................266
    "Little Dove"
Johns, Cheryl Bridges...........33
Johnson, Andrea.................336
Johnson, A. Wayne.............141
Johnson, Ben .......................73
Johnson, Bill .......................66
Johnson, Colin R................183

423

Johnson, Craig E. ........117, 335
Johnson, David W. .............114
Johnson, Deborah...............338
Johnson, Del L. .................159
Johnson, Diane..................106
Johnson, Donald.................147
Johnson, Don E. .................111
Johnson, Eleanor.................182
Johnson, Evelyn M. R........114
Johnson, George.................338
Johnson, Harold C. .............65
Johnson, Henry L...............146
Johnson, Holly ....................26
Johnson, Jack ....................251
Johnson, Jacqueline ...........230
Johnson, Jeffrey .................122
Johnson, Jeron ..................146
Johnson, Joseph ..................62
Johnson, Kathryn J. ....267, 341
Johnson, Kathryn L.............116
Johnson, Ken ....................132
Johnson, Margaret................66
Johnson, Mel.....................175
Johnson, Michelle Laque ..... 95
324, 326
Johnson, Nelson ..................35
Johnson, Paul ......................78
Johnson, Robert E. .............324
Johnson, Rod......................196
Johnson, Rodney McNeil....174
Johnson, Rosie ...................170
Johnson, Thomas S. .............45
Johnson, Todd .....................36
Johnson, William E............155
Johnson, W. Robert, III........62
Johnsson, W. G ..................323
Jones, Abraham....................80
Jones, A. M. ................80, 326
Jones, Barbara E.................86
Jones, Brooker T. ...............146
Jones, Cassandra ................170
Jones, Charles H. ................67
Jones, Clifton ....................146
Jones, C. Stephen.................251
Jones, Dana ......................340
Jones, Donna .....................140
Jones, Danny .....................332
Jones, Elbert......................100
Jones, G. Daniel .................261
Jones, Greg........................195
Jones, Gregory ...................301
Jones, Jacqueline .................252
Jones, Jerry........................174
Jones, Jesse ......................170
Jones, Joyce ......................208
Jones, Judy ........................266
Jones, Juliette .....................42
Jones, Kenneth E. .........88, 326
Jones, Larry.......................196
Jones, Lindsay E. ..................92
Jones, Mark E. ...................103
Jones, Melanie ...................239
Jones, Mike .......................140

Jones, Patrick .....................104
Jones, Paul Griffin, II.........249
Jones, Ralph E....................118
Jones, Scott J......................171
Jones, Stephen.....................267
Jones, Terrence J. ................63
Jones, Tim ...................97, 340
Jones, Verity A. ..................329
Jones, Verlene.....................267
Jones, Walter D. ...................93
Jones, Wilmer....................152
Jordan, Anthony L. .............161
Jordan, Joe ........................316
Jordan, Larry W. ................307
Jordan, L. G. ......................141
Joseph, Emmanuel ...............70
Joseph, Hieromonk .............146
Joseph, Thomas....................69
Joudrey, Philip ............320, 322
Jourdain, Cheryl.................210
Jourdain, Todd....................248
Judge, Beverly ...............32, 42
Julian, James ......................125
Julien, Tom.........................121
Juliot, Brent.................101, 193
Jump, Rick .........................267
Jung, Hee-Soo .....................171
Junier, Sandra.....................245
Jupin, J. Michael .................244
Just, Donald R.....................117
Justman, James A. ...............117
Juuti, Richard C. ...................73

Kaada, Virginia ..................256
Kaguni, Samuel...................123
Kaiser, John.......................240
Kalamba, Patrice T..............103
Kalcik, Sharon K. ...............250
Kallappa, M. George...........298
Kalmanek, Edward...............32
Kalmanek, Judy ...................32
Kalmar, Laura ....................349
Kammerer, Charlene ..........173
Payne
Kanouse, Kevin S. ..............117
Kao, Monica.......................259
Kapanke, John G.................116
Kapeluck, Michael..............166
Kaplan, Clemis Eugene ......163
Karaman, Dennis G. ............87
Karanja, Benson M. ...........297
Karrott, Sandra ...................263
Karssen, Paul .....................153
Karsten, Albert ....................90
Kashdin, Linda....................254
Kashmar, Mary ...................235
Kashuck, Claire...................245
Kasimer, Sol........................58
Kauffman, Cephas...............349
Kaugers, Girts ....................134
Kautz, William ...................111
Kawimbe, Paul Jones...........61
Mulenga

Kay, James R. ....................342
Kays, Joanne ......................252
Kazanjian, Shant ..................73
Kearns, Curtis A., Jr............150
Keating, A. C. ....................201
Keaton, Jonathan D.............172
Keeler, William ...............33, 45
Keener, Lamar.......................31
Keeney, Del L. .....................91
Keeney, Mervin B. ...............91
Keeran, Keith P. .................305
Keesecker, Joseph D ............41
Keiller, James B. .................133
Keith, Raymond J. Jr .........103
Keller, Connie L. ...............359
Kelley, Charles...................308
Kelly, Arthur......................329
Kelly, Bridgette ..................359
Kelly, Doug........................150
Kelly, Francis D. .........297, 310
Kelly, Ronald D. .................176
Kelly, Sue ..........................265
Kelly, Thomas ....................250
Kelsey, James A. .................111
Kemp, Linda ......................242
Kemp, Roger........................42
Kemper, Ken ......................127
Kemper, Kenneth B. ...........302
Kemper, Nancy Jo...............243
Kendall, David W................122
Kendall, Michael.................253
Kendall, Stephen.................204
Kendrick, Deloris................125
Kennaugh, R. S. .................202
Kennebrew, Vernon..............92
Kennedy, Alric ...................254
Kennedy, Joanne .................326
Kennedy, Johnny..................72
Kennedy, Leland .................296
Kennedy-Wong, Phillip.......259
Kent, Allen ..........................68
Kent, Edgar .......................133
Kepa, Peter Mar .................129
Kerr-Wilson, Gregory K .....183
Kersey, Tay .......................106
Kersten, David ...................114
Kersten, Nicholas...............160
Kesohole, Erastus................123
Kesselheim, Don. ...............268
Kessler, Angela ...................325
Kessler, Diane C. ...............246
Ketcham, Donald ...............175
Ketli, Vahe..........................74
Keurian, Alice ....................128
Kevern, John R. ..................297
Keyes, Randy ......................174
Keys, Michael ....................116
Keyser, Judy E. ....................91
Khamis, Aprim.....................69
Khasufa, Sylvester ..............124
Khory, George......................48
Khouri, Antoun ....................69
Kibble, Alvin M. .................159

Kicanas, Gerald F.................83
Kidd, Jerry.........................119
Kidd, William B.................293
Kidwell, Gary W. ................85
Kieschnick, Gerald B.........136
Kiesey, Deborah L. ............171
Kikumoto, David ...............176
Kiley, Clete .........................35
Kilgore, Gary ....................122
Kilgore, James ...................97
Killam, Gillis ......................55
Killoren, Eileen .................235
Killpack, Jennifer...............105
Kim, Ko-Eun.....................267
Kim, Nam Soo ....................75
Kimball, John....................106
Kimbrough, Orvin..............250
Kimbrow, Terry .................298
Kimer, Stan ......................176
Kimsey, Rustin ..................110
Kind, Kerry D. ..................176
King, Arthur ......................108
King, Donald G.................159
King, Eileen ........................49
King, Elizabeth .................168
King, Eric ...........................94
King, Fred G. ......................90
King, Gordon ....................320
King, Harding ...................253
King, James R., Jr. ............173
King, Johnny .....................210
King, Robert L. .................136
King, Stephen......................22
Kinnaman, David ..............216
Kinney, John W..........312, 315
Kirchhoff, Bernard.............41
Kireopoulos, Tony..............40
Kirk, Doug ........................123
Kirk, Jennifer .....................48
Kirkland, Theodore Larry .....61
Kirkpatrick, Clifton............150
Kirkpatrick, Susan .............124
Kirn, John.........................308
Kishkovsky, Leonid 46, 49, 338
Kisia, Joseph .....................123
Kisner, Elaine....................247
Kitchens, Sidney Lee..........156
Kitui, John.........................123
Kivuya, Thomas ................124
Kjera, Timothy ..................163
Klaassen, Martin ................47
Klaus, Byron D. .................296
Klein, Ralph W..................329
Klein, Stephen...................248
Kleinfelter, Kenneth...........175
Kline, Dale ........................257
Kline, Thomas L. ...............126
Klinsing, P. David ..............90
Klusmeyer, W. Michie 111, 268
Klutz, C. H...........................69
Kneece, Brenda..................263
Knight, Keith .........55, 56, 204
Knoche, H. Gerard .............118

Knoedler, Lon ....................268
Knoth, Rick ........................330
Knowles, Louis L.................49
Knudsen, Chilton R. ...........108
Knudsen, Herbert L. ............86
Knull, Stanley ....................245
Knutson, Mark ...................259
Kobel, Jon ...........................91
Kochis, Michael ..................166
Kocian, Dorothy.................175
Kocses, Richard .................251
Koehn, Dale ................95, 191
Koehn, Gladwin .................336
Koelpin, Daniel...................178
Koepke, Donald R. ..............42
Koh, Linda .........................159
Kohlbruegge, H..................153
Kohler, Ann.........................30
Kokesch, William.................56
Kolb, Leonard R. ...............142
Kolbaba, Ginger.................335
Kolowski, Donald ................34
Kolsti, Carol.........................30
Kong, Joe ...........................89
Kong, Joseph S. ...................90
Konkel, August H. ..............320
Konsolo, Ephraim ..............123
Kooistra, Paul D.................149
Koopman, Joop ..................325
Koplow, Cordelia ................243
Kopp, Herb........................126
Koptak, Paul E....................329
Korgen, Jeffry .....................35
Korson, Gerald...................338
Kosanke, Charles G ...........312
Kostura, Carol ...................236
Kovalski, Gerald ................159
Kowalski, Kelly .................255
Krahn, Robert.....................184
Krashel, Rosemary..............350
Kraus, Gene ......................169
Krause, Henry ....................196
Kraybill, J. Nelson ..............296
Krell, Barbara.....................239
Krestrick, Robert C. ............198
Kreuger, Kurt .....................136
Krey, Philip D. W................306
Krieger, W. J. .....................153
Kring, S..............................185
Kriska, Chloe Ann ..............257
Kroeker, Irvin J. .................351
Kroeze, Nicholas V. ............305
Krog, Karen ........................91
Krueger, Delton....................27
Kruschel, Peter....................177
Krutz, C. Dana ............31, 244
Krywolap, George...............166
Kucharek, Wilma S. ............118
Kuchta, Thomas ..................136
Kuhlman, Dexter.................119
Kuhn, Robert T. ..................136
Kuliczowski, Czeslan..........148
Kun, Zolton .......................130

Kunda, Theresa E................139
Kunder, William...................210
Kunselman, James ................64
Kuntaraf, Jonathan ..............159
Kurima, Andrew H. S. .........124
Kurtz, Calvin......................262
Kurtz, Joseph E. ...................83
Kuruvila, Alexander.............49
Kutash, Ihor.......................295
Kutosi, Peter.......................124
Kuykendall, Russell E. .......190
Kvam, Roger A. ...................37
Kwan, Joseph .....................347
Kwok, Jack P......................161
Kwok, Meggy .....................52

Labrosse, G. .........................295
Lacey, Jon ...........................86
Lacey, Paul..........................22
Lachatanere, Diana .............355
Lacy, Homer, Jr. .................242
Ladd, Carol ........................248
Ladefaged, Jenny .................30
Lage, Eerika .......................194
Lahey, Raymond .................206
Laitner, Christine ...............162
Lake, Jan ...........................147
Lakey, Othal H......................89
Lallo, Cecelia .....................339
Lamarre-Vincent, David .....251
Lambert, Jerry.....................102
Lamm, Norman ..................310
Lance, Paul........................236
Lance, Rick ........................160
Land, Richard D..................160
Land, Steven J. .....96, 192, 299
Landahl, Paul R...................117
Landers, Bedford F. ............162
Landon, Dennis ...................47
Landon, Dennis L. ................85
Lane, Dan G.......................244
Lane, Gwendolyn...............170
Lane, Hardist......................239
Lanes, T. A..........................75
Lang, Kristy .........................99
Lang, Kurt ...........................99
Langdon, Adrian ..................54
Langille, Fran .....................246
Langley, Ken........................83
Langsfeld, Paul J.................310
Lansing, Steven H...............116
Lant, Cheryl C......................99
Lapsansky, Emma Jones .......35
Larade, Sharon ...........210, 361
Larkin, Michael...................132
Larmondin, Leanne .............346
Larom, Margaret ................109
Larsen, David.....................356
Larson, April Ulring............117
Larson, Duane H.................315
Larson, Rebecca S...............116
Larson, Ronald.....................78
Lassiter, Voni......................125

425

Last, Michael A. ................117
Lau, David ..........................100
Lau, Jennifer ......................35o
Laughlin, Robert ................256
Laurence, Steven B. ............261
Laurus (Archbishop)...338, 339
Lav, Iris ............................238
Lavender, Deane ................259
Lavigne, David P. ...............188
Lavuna, Joseph...................124
Law, William F., Jr. .............31
Lawrence, Caleb J.......182, 183
Lawrence, James F............313
Lawrence, Merlyn ..............168
Lawrence, William B. .........309
Lawson, Joyce....................257
Lawson, Phil ......................235
Lawton, George...................246
Lawton, Gordon..........158, 312
Lay, Bertha.........................259
Layne, Samuel A................146
Layton, Betty .....................353
Laza, Kent .........................175
Leavitt, Robert F. ...............311
Ledeboer (Reverend) .........142
Ledesma, Juanita................264
Lee, Arthur ........................266
Lee, Bill .............................85
Lee, C. R. ...........................146
Lee, Darrel D. ..............73, 332
Lee, David H.......................161
Lee, Jinwol..........................48
Lee, Linda .........................172
Lee, Nathan .......................101
Lee, Peter ..........................248
Lee, Peter J.........................111
Lee, Randall R. ............40, 116
Lee, Robert.........................298
Lee, Robert L. ......................76
Lee, Terri ...........................251
Leech, David ......................264
Leech, Robert E. ................150
Leflore, David.....................23
Legge, W. James ................259
Leggett, James D. ...............133
Lehman, Richard................254
Lehmann, Daniel J ......116, 335
Leibrecht, John J..................27
Leidel, Edwin M., Jr. .........110
Leigh, Charles......................70
Lekic, Mike ........................208
Leman, Bruce.....................341
Lemler, James ....................109
Lemming, Patrick................164
Lemon, Robert E................159
Leng, Janet...........................38
Lennick, Robert B................45
Lenoir, Regina....................152
Leonard, Bill........96, 192, 315
Leonard, Darnell ................260
Leonard, Richard ......106, 331
Leonard, Shirley .......106, 331
Leopold, Phyllis J. .............236

Leopold, Virginia ........132, 328
Leslie, David A. ..................258
Lettini, Gabriella.................23
Leung, Donna......................185
LeVan, Patte ......................336
Levy, B. Barry.....................319
Lew, Khristina......................51
Lewis, Beth A. ....................116
Lewis, Bradley ...................204
Lewis, C. A. .......................100
Lewis, Donald.....................347
Lewis, Ed ...........................121
Lewis, Greg E. ....................136
Lewis, Harry ......................211
Lewis, James W. .................220
Lewis, Ray .........................140
Lewis, Richard Allen ...........61
Lewis, Robert L. ...................71
Lewis, Robert L., Jr. .............42
Lewis, Stephen.....................94
Lewis, Vicki L.......................63
Lewis, William L. ...............105
L'Heureux, N. J., Jr....253, 255
Liebling, Mordechai..............35
Liegl, Sara .........................249
Liggett, J. D. .......................177
Light, Gordon.....................183
Lightbody, C. Stuart............191
Liimatta, Michael..................25
Likis, Betty.........................233
Lilande, Joshuah .................124
Lillback, Peter A. ................316
Lim, Jimmy ........................253
Lima, David ........................246
Lincourt, Raoul...................295
Lind, Christopher J. L.........322
Ling, Mary ...........................99
Lindgren, A. Bruce .............105
Lindhal, Kay ........................48
Lindham, Charles................252
Lindner, Eileen W. ...............40
Lindqist, Tonia I..................116
Lindsay, Emery ....................92
Lindsay, R. Rex...................161
Lingle, Mark ......................236
Linsey, Nathaniel L..............89
Liolin, Arthur E.....................64
Lipps, Robert T.....................29
Lipscomb, John B. ..............111
Lisby, Michael ............62, 342
Listecki, Jerome E. ...............83
Little, Christiane ...................93
Little, Edward S., III ..........111
Little, Jeannine...................242
Little, P. ..............................95
Little, Vanuel C...................146
Litwin, Paul........................254
Liu, Felix...........................306
Livingston, John.................153
Livingston, Michael..............40
Livingston, Michael E.132, 326
Llamoso-Songco, Annie......328
Lloyd, Roy ...........................21

Lobenstine, Clark................238
Lockard, Christopher ...........35
Locklear, Helen...................150
Lockwood, Daniel R............308
Lofquist, Les ..............131, 344
Lofton-Brook, Oliver..........208
Logsdon, Gary B................258
Lohrmann, Marcus C. ........117
Lollike, Inge Lise..................49
London, Denise.....................22
Long, Denise.......................257
Long, Sotello V. ...................87
Looper, Kirk.......................160
López, Héctor......................168
Lopoukhine, Nikita .............200
Lorentzen, Paul ....................77
Lorimer, Paul D. .................191
Lott, William R ...................141
Lotz, Linda...........................35
Loughran, James ..........34, 329
Louttit, Henry, Jr. ...............108
Love, Jan............................298
Love, Mary A...............63, 328
Love, Ralph E., Sr...............170
Love-Jones, Vivian ...............30
Loveland, Erma Jean ..........354
Lovett, Sidney.......................44
Lovingood, Vivian ..............263
Lowe, Asa ..........................133
Lowe, S. L............................94
Lowen, A. Wayne................302
Lowenthal, Robert .............266
Loy, David ..........................241
Lucco, Richard....................114
Lucero, Karina.....................22
Ludwig, Koloman K. ..........169
Ludwig, Robert A. ..............308
Luebbert, Karen .................250
Luebkeman, Kurt ................65
Luedtke, Joel ......................249
Luginbill, Betty ....................30
Luginbuhl, David..........55, 207
Luke (Father) .....................338
Luke, L. M. .........................139
Lumpkin, Ramona ..............319
Luna, Leonardo ..................103
Lundgren, Dean A...............114
Lundin, Jack .........................48
Lundquist, Stella .................249
Lundy, Sarah E.....................96
Lunich, Nedeljko ................ 338
Lupas, Liana.......................355
Lutes, Christopher...............325
Luthy, David ...............201, 348
Lutterell, Gwen ..................207
Luttrell, Bill ........................207
Lutz, James E........................67
Luz, David W. .....................158
Luzano, Christine..........32, 42
Lyght, Ernest S. .........171, 172
Lykins, Terry ......................133
Lyle, Charles ......................185
Lyle, Dennis J. ...........308, 315

Lynch, Damon, III..............257
Lyons, Arthur ......................47
Lyons, Deborah .................147
Lyons, Marsha.....................28
Lysyj, Anatol.....................166

MacAdam, Murray.............347
MacDermid, Gordon E. ......322
MacDonald, Mark.......109, 233
Machen, J. Gresham ..........146
Mack, Karen......................259
Mack, Paget .......................72
MacKenzie, Daryl.............193
MacKenzie, Margaret ..........58
Mackey, Bill F....................161
Mackin, Paddy ..................267
Macklin, Jerry .....................44
Macklin, J. W. ....................94
MacLagan, Lynn ...............245
MacMillan, Clare ...............194
MacMillan, Patricia Dwyer 260
Macnie, Peggy ..................263
MacPherson, Damian.........295
MacPherson, D. Bruce .......111
MacQueen, Kenneth G. ......322
Maddo, Robert ..................238
Madison, Carol..................330
Madison, S. C. ..................171
Maggs, Robert W., Jr. .........150
Magie, Sandra ...................315
Magnus, Brian....................210
Magnus, Paul .......................55
Magnus, Richard A., Jr. ......116
Magrill, Richard.................107
Mahe, Sally .......................48
Maher, Philip......................58
Maheras, John ...................246
Mahlman, Margaret............175
Maier, Paul L. ...................136
Main, Donald .....................261
Mains, Bill ........................186
Makarenko, William ...208, 352
Maki, Lynn I. .....................210
Malayang, José A..............168
Malcolm, Barbara ..............236
Malcolm, Matt W. R. .........164
Maldonado, Luis ................189
  Fernando Hoyos
Malenge, Zablon Isaac.......123
Maleske, A. .......................200
Malherbe, Jean-François.....322
Malinovic, Mirko ...............207
Mallinak, John ...................339
Malloy, David ....................83
Maly, Milton .............175, 325
Manahan, Ronald E. ..........302
Manes, John .......................99
Mangassarian, Silva............184
Manis, H. Lee .....................22
Manly, Frances..................254
Mann, David .....................139
Mann, Gayle......................241
Mann, Stuart.....................346

Manning, Robert ...............316
Manning, Vicki ...................40
Mannoia, Kevin W. .............33
Manon, John C....................119
Manousos, Anthony ...........331
Manseau, William .................32
Mansholt, Gerald L........... 117
Mansur, Mary.....................338
Mantha, Ray........................58
Manthei, Jim .......................30
Manz, Kevin......................168
Mapson, Charlrean B. ..........63
Marani, Samson .................123
Marceil, Christopher ..........268
Marcum, John P. .................25
Mardirossian, Moushegh .....73
Mardoian, Jack....................73
Marinaro, Eleonora V..........32
Marini, Christine .................87
Marks, Kirk .......................113
Markus, Carol O. ...............51
Marquardt, Kami L. ............258
Marrin, Patrick ..................326
Marsh, Fred........................337
Marsh, Jack .......................257
Marshall, Jay Wade............301
Marshall, Molly T. .............298
Marshall, Paul ...............55, 109
Martens, Ed.......................198
Martensen, Jean .................27
Martin, Clyde ....................175
Martin, J. Bruce .................156
Martin, J. Dwayne..............265
Martin, John A. ..................308
Martin, Joseph...................263
Martin, Marty....................329
Martin, Paul E. ...................68
Martinez, Margarita ...........118
Martinez, Joel N..................173
Martinson, Bradley ............101
Marty, Martin ....................331
Marvel, Misha....................252
Marx, Robert.......................36
Maslo, William ..................262
Mason, Debra......................46
Mason, Donald E. ...............239
Mason, Frederick A. ............32
Mason, H. Lee....................340
Mason, Larry D...................66
Mason, Linda J....................94
Massey, Frank....................123
Massey, Stephen K..............68
Mast, Gregg A....................308
Masters, Mary ...................254
Masterson, Rod..................320
Matagi-Vilitama, Joanna S....49
Mathai, Anish......................49
Mathes, James R. ...............111
Mathew, T.A......................137
Mathew, Thomson K..........309
Mathewes, Charles T..........333
Mathews, Michael..............125
Mathies, Ronald J. R............38

Matiz, Jose Ruben Garcia...189
Matoon, Gordon.................240
Matson, Louise...................248
Matsuura, Junko...................49
Matthew, Frank Sr .............139
Matthew, Lamar.................123
Matthews, Daniel Paul....32, 42
Matthews, F. Clayton .........109
Matthews, Larry.................346
Matthews, Marcus...............172
Matthews, Mary ..................63
Matthews, Victoria......33, 183
Matthewson, Alice .............122
Mattock, Terry....................266
Mattoni, Vincent ................255
Mattson, Linda ...................327
Mattox, Cynthia .................331
Matusiak, John...........145, 338
Mauney, James F. ...............118
Mauney, Patrick ...................41
Maxim (Bishop)...................158
Maximos (Metropolitan).....128
Maximus (Bishop) .............130
Maxwell, Anita...................264
Maxwell, Laurie.................235
May, David G.....................246
May, Nareth ........................89
May, Thomas R...................39
Mayan, Ralph...............56, 200
Maye, James A....................103
Maynard, J. L......................95
Mays, Rod............................14
Maze, Larry E. ...................109
Mazur, Francis X. ..............254
Mbachi, Charles..................123
Mbato, Hannington .............124
McAdam, Kerry ..................123
McAlister, John...................347
McAlister, Lorne D..............203
McAllister-Wilson,.............316
  David F.
McAnally, Ben ...................150
McBride, Larry ...................243
McCaffrey, Renée Roeder...254
McCain, Jacquelyn B..........170
McCain, Paul .....................136
McCallister, Cline ...............133
McCandless, Christopher...123,
  266
McCann, Gordon ...............345
McCann, Jeff........................46
McCardle, Jody ..................248
McClain, Gene .....................68
McClain, Rebecca ..............109
McClesky, J. Lawrence ........173
McCloskey, Pat ...................341
McCloud, E. Earl .................61
McCloud, E. Earle, Jr...........31
McClure, George..................123
McClure, Marian.................150
McCoid, David J.........33, 118
McColgin, Linda .................252
McCollum, Odell ...............170

427

McCombs, Jerry L. ...............63
McConnell, Alvester ..........171
McCool, Marilyn ...............102
McCormack, Alan ..............206
McCormick, Pat ...............304
McCown, Sue....................264
McCoy, Clinton..........150, 255
McCoy, Glenda .................265
McCoy, James E. ...........61, 62
McCoy, Myron F. ...............311
McCreary, Glenn................262
McCreary, Leroy ...............132
McCulley, Bonnie J. ............32
McCullough, John L. ...........41
McCurdy, Claire................40
McDermott, Pat................243
McDonald, Jamey S............185
McDonald, Janet ...............210
McDonald, Jeff ...............344
McDonald, Lee M.............317
McDonald, Lora................242
McDonald, Malcom ...........259
McDonald, Tim.................239
McDonough, Linda............126
McDowell, Leon A. ...........147
McFadden, Wendy ...............91
McFarland, James K. .........155
McGibbon, Carol Ann .........47
McGinnis, Pat ...............158
McGinnis, Robert S., Jr. .....135
McGlynn, Sheilagh ...........57
McGough, Nancy...............346
McGovern, Mike.................132
McGrattan, William T. .........321
McGraw, Tom ...............242
McGuire, Damaris .............255
McGuire, G. Dennis......96, 191
McHugh, Matthew ...............26
McIntire, Carl.................146
McIntosh, Kenneth W. ........265
McJunkin, James E., Jr. ........67
McKain, George E., II .........63
McKay, Ginger.................175
McKee, Joan ..................240
McKelvey, Jack M. ............111
McKenzie, Vashti Murphy....61
McKernan, Leo .................262
McKinney, Brent...............123
McKinney, G. D..................94
McKinney, William.............309
McKinnon, Patricia............350
McKnight, James E.............96
McKnight, James E., Jr.........96
McKnight, John .................22
McLarty, Alan .................169
McLaughlin, Roy L ............79
McLaughlin, Scott .............109
McLaughlin, Scott E..........300
McMahill, David................169
McManus, Robert J.............83
McMillan, John ...............322
McMillan, Susan ...............207
McMillon, Lynn ...............326

McMullen, Shawn...............334
McMurray, Robert .............146
McNair, David C..................37
McNamara, Dexter.............235
McNamara, Mary.................26
McNeil, J. E. ....................27
McNish, Mary Ellen .............22
McPhail, Paul...................199
McQueen, Arpie.................324
McSwain, Laurin M.............31
McVay, John K..................312
McVey, Kita ....................315
McWain, Bonnie ...............237
Meade, Kenneth ................87
Meador, Prentice A., Jr........323
Meagher, Timothy...............359
Mean, John D....................211
Mecham, Marilyn P............250
Medders, David S. .............317
Medenwald, Greg.................79
Medinger, Daniel L............326
Medley, A. Roy ..................66
Meek, Gary .....................25
Meier, Gordon F...................89
Meisner, Lorne.................186
Mekhsian, Sipan................337
Melbourne, Bertram...........304
Melchizedek (Mar) .....130, 187
Mellis, John....................320
Melton, David ..................297
Melton, Gordon.................219
Mendenhall, Laura S..........300
Mendez, Jose Manuel .........139
Mendoza, Salvador .............44
Menes, Nadia ...................49
Mengel, Gail ....................30
Menning, Bruce .................204
Meno, John.......................163
Menter, William ...............167
Mentzer, Steve .................260
Mercer, Amy ...................244
Mercer, Larry ..................298
Merrill, A. Roger................99
Merrill, John....................68
Meschisen, Eugene .............166
Mesner, Neil....................124
Messer, Tom ....................314
Messiah, Wilfred Jacobus .....61
Messias, Pedro .................133
Messina, Carol .................139
Methodios (Metropolitan)...128
Metzger, Laura .................243
Meunch, David.................136
Meyer, Cheryl ...................211
Meyer, Dale A .................300
Meyer, Don......................315
Meyer, Donald L.......114, 329
Meyer, Mary C..................338
Meyer, Russell L................238
Meyer, William. ...............119
Mgonja, Assah E.................49
Micevych, Paul .................166
Mich, Marvin ...................253

Michaelson, Wesley ...........204
  Granberg
Micon, Joseph ...................241
Middeke, Paul W.................136
Middendorf, Jesse C. ..........101
Middleton, Edward .............155
  Russell
Middleton, Jane Allen.........172
Miericke, Kurt A. ...............114
Mikovsky, Anthony.....148, 332
Miles, Ray ......................86
Millar, Len .....................207
Millay, James I....................326
Miller, Alan C....................169
Miller, Carol.....................238
Miller, Charles S. ...............116
Miller, Claude E. W. ..........183
Miller, David....................27, 63
Miller, G..........................95
Miller, George ...........113, 300
Miller, John U............250, 252
Miller, Joy Ann .................323
Miller, Kathleen ...............293
Miller, Keith.....................113
Miller, Kit ......................239
Miller, Lauren E.................318
Miller, Lee M ....................117
Miller, Len .....................207
Miller, Marcus J ...............306
Miller, Mark ...................169
Miller, Myron P..................311
Miller, Paul L...............79, 325
Miller, Rick ....................106
Miller, Roman J. ...............339
Miller, Steven A. ...............110
Miller, Susan Fisher............336
Miller, Ted......................239
Milliken, Paul...................264
Milliken, Richard D. ..........308
Mills, Charles ..................343
Mills, Earl E.....................105
Mills, Wes ......................184
Miloro, Frank P. ................67
Milsap, Cynthia..................47
Minch, Jack N...................335
Ming, Wayman, Jr. .............147
Minnix, Janet ...................121
Minor, Marlene .................143
Miranda, Jesse...................75
Mirchuk, Nadia .................166
Mirek, Art.........................68
Mirkovich, Joseph A............96
Miscamble, Wilson ............307
Missick, Glen ...................153
Mitchell, Belita D. ..............91
Mitchell, Christine .............54
Mitchell, James K................92
Mitchell, Lisa H. ...............38,
  247
Mitchell, Lois P.................195
Mitchem, Susan .................359
Mitrophan (Bishop)...........158
Mittman, F. Russell............169

428

Mobley, Jean .......................119
Mobley, John P. .....................86
Mock, George ....................246
Moes, D. ............................348
Moffett, Marilyn ................241
Mogabgab, John S. ............344
Mogenson, Cris ..................252
Mohler, R. Albert, Jr. .........313
Mojica, Miguel .............98, 191
Moldstad, John A. ..............118
Mollard, Bishop Tikhon.....312
Molyneux, John .................343
Moncher, Gary .............96, 192
Moncure, Rhymes H., Jr. ....172
Monroe, Bill .......................78
Monroe, Kenneth ...........61, 62
Monson, Thomas S. .............99
Montanez, Jose D. .............192
Monteith, Fred ..................210
Montgomery, Carl ..............174
  Halloway, II
Montgomery, Kathleen C....167
Montgomery, Richard .........235
Montgomery, Robert ..........233
Mood, Jacques ...................142
Moody, C. L. .......................95
Moody, Robert M. ..............111
Moon, Angelia ...................264
Moon, Hyung J. ...................89
Mooney, Paul. ....................174
Moore, Clark ......................266
Moore, Donna J. ................258
Moore, Douglas .................203
Moore, Hugh ......................240
Moore, Kenneth W. ..............86
Moore, Larry J. ..................175
Moore, Marvin ...................341
Moore, P. J. .........................10
Moore, Robert A. ..........96, 192
Moore, Willis .....................238
Moorhead, James H. ...........334
Moorjani-Vaswani, ..............48
  Shakuntala
Morales, Bernardo .............167
Morales, Lillian..................260
Mordecai, Patricia C. .........109
Moreau, Dorylas ................205
Moreno, Rene .....................113
Moretz, Lawrence ..............157
Morgan, Brent R. ...............132
Morgan, Donn F. .................299
Morgan, Gerald ..................247
Morgan, John .....................302
Morgester, Mike .................259
Morin, Darci.......................241
Morissette, Pierre ..............206
Morris, Adrienne A. ...........345
Morris, Calvin S. ................239
Morris, John ......................304
Morris, Tracy .....................350
Morrison, Susan M. ............171
Morrison, Ronald J .............89
Morrison, William C., Jr. ......86

Morrow, William..................44
Morrow, William D. ............203
Morse, Daniel R. .................154
Mortelliti, David ................187
Morton, Cindy....................241
Morton, Cristopher.............249
Morton, Darrell D. ..............116
Morton, Kama....................250
Morton, Karon ....................34
Morton, Raymond E. ..........155
Mosaad, Mohamed...............48
Moses, Tom..........................96
Mosier, Barbara..................147
Mosier, Charles R. ..............147
Mosley, Steve .....................263
Mostert, Thomas J., Jr. ........159
Moulton, Geoff ..................348
Moultrie, Henry A., II.........103
Moury, Fred.......................113
Mouw, Richard J. ..........33, 302
Mowatt, Ann ........................58
Moxham, John ...................264
Moyer, Bruce .............110, 315
Moyer, David .....................169
Mphahlele, Louis ................77
Mstyslav (Metropolitan) .....164
Mueller, Craig ....................36
Mueller, George ..................84
Mueller, Wayne D. ..............177
Mufarrij, Alexander .............69
Muganda, Baraka G. ...........159
Mukulu, Andrew ................123
Mukwanja, H. M. ...............123
Mulama, Joseph Anyonge...124
Mulder, Gary........................90
Mullan, Donald W. .......189, 351
Mullen, David G. ................116
Muller, Marilyn..................351
Mulongo, Andrew ..............124
  Namasaka
Mulvaney, Elizabeth ...........262
Munday, Robert S. .............308
Munk, D. ...........................318
Munro, Victor.....................295
Muravski, A. ......................203
Murdoch, John .....................39
Murdy, Peter.......................106
Murphy, Sue.......................239
Murphy, Thomas .........336, 340
Murphy, Tom......................139
Murphy, Warren .................269
Murray, Edward J. ..........32, 42
Murray, George W. .............299
Murray, Harold.....................57
Murray, James ....................126
Murray, James W. ...............298
Murray, Michele....................54
Murray, Sue........................253
Murray, Yolanda .................254
Musindi, Meschack ............124
Mussa, Joan..........................50
Musungu, Philip .................123
Mutoigo, Ida Kaastra ...........90

Mutti, Albert F. ...................31
Muyskens, Samuel ........38, 242
Muzingo, Cathy .................147
Mwanzi, Solomon ..............124
Myers, Jerry.........................68
Myers, John J. .....................83
Myers, Mark.......................147
Myers, Richard N. ..............253
Myers-Wirt, Cathy ..............86

Nadasdy, Dean L. ...............136
Nafzger, Samuel..................136
Nahoolewa, Connie.............265
Naik, Deepak .......................48
Naubggolan, Kalmen E. ......103
Nakonachny, John ..............166
Namasaka, Andrew .............124
Namwembe, Despina ...........48
Nance, Cynthia.....................36
Naten, Loyd L. ....................147
Nauenburg, Hilda................191
Navarre, Joy Sorensen ........248
Naylor, Susan .....................194
Neal, Carl J .......................103
Neal, Joseph C., Jr. ...............88
Neal, Ricardo .....................245
Neale, Archie .....................124
Nectaria (Nun) ...................341
Nederveen, G. ....................187
Needham, Philip..................157
Neelands, David ..................322
Neely, Constance D. ...........247
Nees, Tom ..........................102
Neevel, Mary Ann ..............268
Neff, David ..........................31
Neils, Michae J. ..................234
Nelson, Arnold C., Jr. ...........85
Nelson, Beter T. ...................72
Nelson, Christine L. .............261
Nelson, Dean W. .................116
Nelson, Elden K. ..................76
Nelson, Gart .......................188
Nelson, Jerome O. ...............114
Nelson, J. Herbert .................36
Nelson, Jodi .......................248
Nelson, Judy.......................196
Nelson, Kim Byer ...............251
Nelson, Russell M. ................98
Nelson, Saundra .................132
Nelson, Steven L. ................268
Nelson, Vernon H. ...............357
Nemkovich, Robert M. .......147,
  148, 312
Nenson, Alice......................332
Nenson, David ....................207
Nesbitt, Phyllis M. ...............51
Nesdahl, Gary .....................263
Nesmith, Virginia .................41
Netterfield, Cal....................186
Nettleton, Minot B. .............237
Neufeld, John ......................54
Neuhaus, Richard J. ............331
Newcomer, Audrey ..............24

Newell, Dernard...................47
Newhouse, Herbert ............151
Newland, Terry ...................150
Newport, Leroy...................81
Newton, Alan .......................67
Newton, Douglas M...........334
N'goma, Joyce .....................48
Ngoya, John .......................123
Ngurukiri, Renison Mbogo.103
Nguyen, Tai Anh ..................90
Nicholas (Metropolitan)......128
Nicholas, David .................312
Nicholovos, (Mar)..............137
Nichols, John D. ................192
Nichols, Terrence L..............90
Nicholson, Betty ................125
Nickleson, Isaac .................240
Nicodemus, Eugene J...........37
Nicoll, Niel...........................50
Niederauer, George H. .........83
Nielsen, Nancy....................48
Nielson, E. Kenneth.............34
Nielson, Niel .....................149
Nieto, Amelia .....................235
Nieuwsma, Virginia ...........332
Nikkel, Lynn ......................161
Niles, Dennis D..................314
Nippak, Ivar ......................196
Niswender, Joy...................252
Nix, Lan .............................263
Nixon, Samuel ...................152
Njegovan, James D. ............182
Noble, Kathy......................333
Noesner, Pam ....................268
Noffsinger, Stanley J............91
Nolan, Michael...................126
Noland, Martin...........136, 356
Nolan-Elliason, Megan .......248
Nolde, Nancy L...................261
Nolla, Ormara .....................49
Nolson, Stanley ..................116
Nordhem, Paula .................248
Nordtvedt, Joel T................306
Norlin, Dennis A...................23
Norman, Clarence ..............108
Norris, Dennis E. .................66
Norris, Jeffrey A. .................89
Norris, Larry R...................105
Norris, Richard Franklin......61
Nortness, Michal ................266
Norton, Jon .................253, 255
Norton, Larry ....................265
Norton, Timothy A........37, 342
Novak, Mark A. .................114
Novecosky, Peter ...............350
Nsofwa, Alfred...................103
Nunn, Harry, Sr..................75
Nyenzo, Evans ...................123

Oaks, Dallin H. ...................99
Oakes, Ronald L. ...............298
Oancea, David ....157, 207, 342
Oates, Lonnie F...................86

Obengerger, Glenn ..............118
Ochoa-Krueger, Ninfa........264
O'Connor, Elizabeth ..........335
Odams, John.......................245
Odegaard, Edward ..............93
Odhner, Carroll C. .............359
Odom, Elzie .......................264
O'Donnell, Frances.............359
O'Farrell, Mark T........90, 314
O'Flaherty, Edward............246
Ogilvie, Kevin A ................319
Ogles, Jerry L.....................324
Ogunmola, Matthew ...........103
O'Hara, John .......................25
O'Hara, Karen....................254
Ohl, C. Wallis, Jr. ..............111
Ohotin, Nicholas A ............157
Ojeda-Carcamo, Sergio......301
O'Keefe, Mark ...................311
Olekshy, Ovest ..................202
Olinger, Danny E. ..............337
Oliver, Juan M. C...............302
Oliver, Lon D......................24
Oliver, Willie B..................155
Olmsted, Thomas J. ............83
Olsen, Donald P. ................140
Olsen, Ron .........................210
Olson, Norman A. ..............324
Olszewski, Brian T.............325
Olubalang, Alan A. ..............68
Omland, Richard R. ...........116
O'Neill, Jerry F. .........155, 310
O'Neill, Patrick H...............301
O'Neill, Robert J................110
Oommen, Joseph.................137
Oosting, Ken ......................316
Ophoff, George ..................152
Orcino, Danilo M................103
Orewiler, Teri ....................131
Osborn, Kenneth W............159
Osborne, Brenda .................68
Osborne, Fred C..................319
Osborne, Linda...................268
Osodo, Lam Kisanya ..........123
Oswald, Laurie...................345
Ottenhoff, Don B. ..............218
Otterson, Michael...............99
Otzelberger, E. Ann............142
Oubre, Sinclair.....................36
Ouest, Jarry ........................351
Ough, Bruce R. ..................172
Oussoren, Harry .................210
Owen, David L....................309
Owen, Dean .........................50
Owen, Moses ......................139
Owen, Timothy P. ................90
Owens, C. D..........................94
Owens, Thomas M., Sr. ......342
Oyando, Gilbert Akenga .....123
Oyster, Lisa A. ...................257

Paarlberg, John....................43
Pace, Diane ........................332

Packard, George.................109
Packer, Boyd K. ...................99
Padilla, Rafael Malpica.......116
Paez, Leticia.........................51
Pagán, Samuel....................312
Pagano, Nicholas .................22
Palmberg, Glenn R.............114
Palmer, Floyd.....................259
Palmer, Gregory V..............172
Palmer, John........................75
Palmer, Michael .................310
Palmer, Paul ......................139
Palmer, Robert M................71
Palmieri, Paul ......................99
Palumbo, Billie L...............147
Pantupong, Woranut.............49
Papagermanos, Stavros H...338
Papazian, Iris.....................338
Paperini, Richard ...............307
Paprocki, Thomas ................24
Pappajohn, John .................128
Paquette, Mario...........205, 206
Parchia, Earl......................146
Parish, Donny.......................79
Park, Jeremiah J..................172
Park, Michael .....................159
Parker, George Lee ..............87
Parker, Jane .......................242
Parker, Rebecca..................313
Parker, Ronald L. ...............86
Parker, William ..................155
Parker, William J................334
Parkin, Bonnie D. ................98
Parking, Richard ................109
Parkinson, Ward .................198
Parkyn, David I ..................114
Parr, Jeb.............................267
Parrish, Walter L., II ...........67
Parrott, Rod........................236
Parrott, Steven F.................103
Parry, Walter P...................235
Parshall, Janet .....................42
Parsley, Henry N., Jr. .........109
Parson, Robert G.................203
Parsons, Gradye .................150
Parsons, Reginald...............150
Pasbrig, Robert...................177
Paslay, Mormon R ..............174
Pastukhiv, Serhij K. ...........129
Pate, Catherine ..................348
Paterakis, John ....................41
Patterson, G. E.....................94
Patterson, J. O., Jr. ..............94
Patterson, L. Dale ..............357
Patterson, Paige..................313
Patterson, Tom .....................76
Pattillo, Wesley M................40
Patton, Marcia......................66
Patton, Vince .....................342
Patzer, Jere D. ....................159
Paulding, Ta Queena ...........132
Paulsen, Jan........................159
Paulsen, Vivian ..................331

Paulson, Bob ......................329
Paup, Edward W.................173
Payiavlas, John...................128
Pavichevich, Dennis...........158
Payne, Aleta ...................... 257
Payne, James T...................155
Payne, Margaret G. ............117
Payson, Barbara .................246
Pearce, Paul.......................186
Pears, George S...................96
Pearson, Jean......................248
Pearson, John ...............29, 245
Pediso, Marlene .................124
Pediso, Steve......................124
Peifer, Elvin H. ....................81
Pelavin, Mark.......................36
Pell, Archie..........................54
Pellechia, James N......134, 200
Pelles, Rosalyn....................36
Pelley, Barry D...................203
Pember, Arlyn ......................75
Pena, Carlos F....................116
Pence, Jerry G....................177
Pendergast, Arthur J...........293
Penfield, Jack ....................237
Penner, David.....................198
Penner, Rick .......................55
Penner, Ron........................198
Pennings, Kenneth .............268
Pennywell, Clarence C........140
Pepe, Joseph A. .....................83
Peper, Mike ...........................78
Peplowski, Thaddeus S.......148
Pepper, Donald R. ................37
Pepper, Gail.......................261
Perkins, Davis ....................150
Perkins, Joseph...................295
Perkins, Larry.....................320
Perkins, William T..............307
Perkins-Hughes, Vera.........170
Perman, Lauri.....................122
Perpener, A...........................95
Perrin, Clive ......................237
Perry, Joseph N. ...................83
Perry, L. Tom .......................99
Perry, Roger ......................237
Perry, Troy D.......................175
Perschbacher, Gerald .........335
Persell, William D...............110
Persson, Bertil .....................72
Peterkin, Valerie .................237
Peters, Donald.................38, 56
Peters, Judith .....................258
Peters, Marshall ...................66
Peters, Samuel....................101
Peterson, Brian.....................32
Peterson, Cartis D ..............114
Peterson, David....................39
Peterson, Duane A. .............356
Peterson, Kathleen .............252
Peterson, Roland .................115
Peterson, Timothy ..............351
Peterson, Timothy J. ...........198

Peterson, Wendy ...................55
Petersoo, Udo..............196, 348
Petitt, Charles W. ................309
Petkau, Dave .......................319
Petrie, Lou............................78
Petro, John G. ....................297
Petrochuk, Sherrie..............257
Petroff, Valerie .....................52
Pettit, Charles W..................309
Pettit, Kim A. ......................333
Pfortmiller, Sandra .............337
Phelan, John E.....................308
Phelan, John E., Jr. .............114
Philipose, K.G. ...................137
Phillips, Annie Lee..............255
Phillips, Aubrey ..................196
Phillips, Carole....................187
Phillips, David J....................89
Phillips, Donald D. .............183
Phillips, Stephen .................105
Phillips, Sue Watlov...........248
Phipps, Ron ........................139
Pickle, Claudette .................107
Pierce, David.......................318
Pierce, Garland.....................40
Pierce, Leslie.......................106
Pierce, R. W. ......................203
Pierre, Louis Marcel .............77
Piescik, Joseph ...................237
Pihach, Dennis ....................202
Piita, Vaieli Fuiono ..............49
Pile, Gregory R. ..................115
Pimentel, Juan.....................103
Pimentel, Serafin................103
Pinkett, Leo ..........................88
Pinkston, Ron......................131
Pinson, J. Matthew..............302
Pinson, Mathew ..................140
Pipes, Carol.........................338
Pishko, Daria.......................166
Pitman, Cyrus C. J. .............183
Pitner, Kim..........................132
Pitt, Benjamin A..................146
Pittman, Wallace B., Jr........147
Pitts, Clifford R...................170
Pitts, Tyrone S.....................151
Plantinga, Cornelius, Jr. .....298
Platt, Allyson D...................246
Poandl, Robert .....................33
Poe, James............................24
Pohl, Faye ...........................43
Poirier, Jim .........................194
Poirier, Tim ........................353
Poist, William......................64
Poitier, Annette .....................49
Polasek, Joseph ...................175
Polding, M. Fred ...................89
Polite, William ....................155
Pollema, Vernon ..................154
Pollesel, Michael F .............182
Pollington, Cody....................67
Polston, Jimmy....................158
Pomeroy, Betty....................252

Pomykal, Janet....................174
Poole, Philip..........................45
Pooler, David ......................243
Poon, Abraham H..................90
Pope, Dan............................319
Pope, Deidre........................248
Pope, Janet ..........................267
Pope, Kenneth........................68
Popoff, Dmitri E. (Jim).......349
Popovich, Edward ...............124
Popp, Nathaniel..........157, 207
Porch, James M....................161
Porret, Jean.........................351
Porter, Jerry D.....................100
Porter, John ........................124
Porter, Stanley E. ................319
Porterfield, Ammoa.............327
Posey, Michael ....................131
Poss, Sue Harper.................331
Posterski, Don .......................58
Potter, Jim ..........................194
Potterveld, Riess W.............305
Powell, Christopher .............80
Powell, F. Neff ....................111
Powell, George H.................194
Powell, James L. ...................85
Powell, Jerry .......................147
Powell, Joel.........................147
Powell, Joseph ....................155
Powell, Larry ......................140
Powell, Paul W.....................302
Powell, Raymond, Sr. .........100
Powell, S. J. ...........................95
Powers, Diane .......................39
Powers, Reggie O. ..............147
Prachar, T. ..........................200
Preheim, Rich......................356
Preheim-Bartel, Dean..........240
Premawardhana, Shanta D....40
Prendergast, Terrence..........206
Presler, Titus L. ..................301
Prestol, Juan R. ...................159
Preus, Christan A. ...............136
Price, Ellen W .......................45
Price, R................................171
Primavera, Wendy...............252
Priniski, Mary .......................36
Prior, Joseph G....................311
Pritchett, Wayne .........207, 321
Privett, John E.....................183
Probus, Lawrence..................50
Proctor, Matt .......................309
Proffitt, Kevin .....................356
Propes, M. Thomas .............192
Prosser, Robert ....................107
Provance, Terry .....................43
Prudente, Karen ....................49
Pruter, Karl............................83
Pryor, Christine ...................337
Pue, Carson ...........................55
Puglisi, Amy........................262
Pugsley, John W. ...................39
Pullen, Kristy Arneson..........65

431

Pulins, Juris.........................134
Puni, Erika .........................159
Puryear, Richard ................259
Pusateri, John .....................259
Putman, Bob.........................325
Pyles, Franklin ...................190

Quackenbush, David..........187
Quay, Ronald .....................239
Quello, Julie.......................249
Quessy, Herve L.................143
Quevedo, Jose Moises ........189
  Moncada
Quick, Braaley ...................126
Quinn, John.........................200
Quinn, Michaelita ...............32
Quinn, Thomas.....................32
Quirog, Bonifacio ................48
Quispe, Benito Ramos ........103

Rabenold, Nelson...............260
Raccah, William.................318
Racine, Jacques..................322
Radius, Lesley M. ..............239
Radtke, Robert ...................109
Ragsdale, John....................111
Rainer, Thom S. .................160
Raines, James Ray ...............79
Ralston, Darwin .................257
Ramirez, Cleb Hernandez...103
Ramos, David.......................22
Ramos-Scharron,...............116
  Francis R
Ramphal, Dwarka .......147, 303
Ramsay, John .....................207
Ramseth, Mark R. ..............314
Ramsey, Ron ......................103
Rand, Lucinda Glenn..........355
Randall, Mike.....................324
Randall, R. Irene ...............250
Randels, J. Richard ............244
Rankin, Jerry A. .................160
Rankin, Nancy ...................234
Ransom, Robert ..................139
Ranum, Mary S .................116
Rasell, Edith........................35
Rasmussen, Donald R. ........67
Rassmussen, Philip ............349
Rathbun, Peter.....................21
Ratzinger, Joseph ................83
Rauser, Randal ....................54
Ravenell, Joseph P. ............251
Ray, Keith H. .....................305
Raymond, Jonathan S. ........321
Read, Glenn .......................256
Read, James .........................55
Realpe, Marcelo ..................90
Reaney, Dwayne .................200
Rebeck, Victoria A..............24
Redal, R. H. ...............106, 301
Redd, Eugene .....................146
Reddick, Lawrence L., III....89
Reddig, Jill S......................328

Reddin, George ....................79
Redekopp, Alf.............349, 360
Redhead, Bob.....................207
Reece, Scott .......................131
Reed, Jeremiah....................146
Reed, J. George...................256
Reed, Michael B. .................72
Reed, Millard .....................314
Reed, Rodger Hall, Sr..........238
Reeder, Allen R. .................340
Reese, Jack R. ....................295
Reese, John D. ....................323
Reese, Ron .........................104
Reese, Rosemary................262
Reeves, Justus Y. ...............325
Reeves, Steve .......................66
Regan, Tom ........................294
Regehr, Nancy......................57
Regier, Rob .........................55
Register, Wayne ...................30
Regnier, Julie .......................50
Rehling, Tom......................169
Reichter, Arlo R. ..................67
Reid, Gail...........................348
Reid, Sharmaine R. ............203
Reid-MacNevin, Susan ........56
Reierson, Gary B. .......248, 249
Reimer, Gerald ...................198
Reinert, Peter .....................238
Reinheimer, Larry ..............202
Reiser, Linda .....................136
Reist, L. "Gere" ................171
  Fitzgerald II
Reithmaier, Jan ...................32
Reithmaier, Paul...................32
Remalt, Theodore J. ...........337
Rempel, Ron ......................138
Rempel, Valerie...................127
Rempel-Burkholder,....340, 349
  Byron
Rendall, Joanne.....................41
Renick, Nancy......................47
Retzman, Alan....................199
Retzer, Gordon L. ...............159
Revis, Charles ......................66
Reyes, Emilio .......................21
Reyes, José, Sr. ...................193
Reynolds, Ariene................258
Reynolds, Kristine .............248
Reynolds, Paul V. ...............211
Rhéaume, Serge ...................52
Rhoads, Armen O................177
Rhoden, H. Robert ...............75
Rhodes, Arthur D........96, 191
Rhodes, Schuyler .................36
Rice, Gene D.........96, 192
Richard, Thomas M. ...........140
Richards, Carmen...............116
Richards, Jack ....................169
Richards, James G. .............321
Richards, James W. .............161
Richards, Mrs. Stephen.......186

Richardson, Adam................61
  Jefferson, Jr.
Richardson, John M. ............86
Richardson, Melvin.............257
Richardson, Ralph.......55, 195
Richardson, Wendell ............77
Richert, Jean.......................237
Riches, Leonard .................154
Richey, John R. ..................144
Richmond, Raymond, Jr. ......63
Ridings, Dean.......................31
Rieley-Goddard, ................253
  Catherine
Riemenschneider, Dan ........139
Ries, Thomas......................136
Rigali, Justin .......................83
Riggs, Ann K. ......................40
Riggs, Don R. .....................248
Riggs, Jennifer .....................41
Riley, Adele M. ....................63
Riley, E. Roy ..............116, 117
Riley, Meg............................36
Rinden, David ....................100
Rinehart, Neil.....................139
Ripp, Peggy..........................32
Ripp, Phil.............................32
Risser, Paul C. ....................132
Ritchie, Tracy.....................259
Ritts, Kerry R. ....................152
Rivera, Regina W. ................63
Rivera-Rosa, Rafael..............86
Rivers, Francis .....................23
Rivers, W. M. ......................95
Rizzo, Janice ......................341
Robben, Jerome ..................189
Robbins, Earldean V. S. ......150
Roberson, James T., Jr. .......313
Roberson, Joseph .................41
Roberts, James P., Jr............135
Roberts, Mark E. .................355
Roberts, Robert H. ...............66
Roberts, R. Philip................307
Roberts, Sharon....................22
Roberts, Tom ......................337
Robertson, C.C....................141
Robertson, Cory ...................48
Robertson, Creighton L. .....109
Robertson, Terry M............161
Robertson, William ............341
Robey, Connie....................266
Robins, Roger ....................357
Robinson, Anita ...................80
Robinson, Barbara A...........251
Robinson, Dave..................326
Robinson, David ................125
Robinson, Densimore..........142
Robinson, Ellen..................294
Robinson, Judith ................182
Robinson, Julian B........96, 192
Robinson, Kenneth N.........105
Robinson, Kenneth O., Sr. ..170
Robinson, Laurie.........342, 345
  Oswald

Robinson, Mattie A. ............345
Robinson, Paul ..................248
Robinson, Robert H ..........122
Robinson, Thomas .............265
Robinson, Thomas E. ........150
Robinson, Tommy ................80
Robinson, V. Gene .............110
Robinson-Rumble, .............333
  Beverly J.
Roblyer, Kathy ...................331
Rochon, Igumen Irenee......202
Rockwell, David ................250
Rockwood, Perry F. ...........349
Rodgers, Bob .....................160
Rodgers, Darrin............16, 332
Rodriguez, Placido .............83
Rodriguez-Villa, Jorge ........144
Roebuck, David ...96, 192, 357
  G.
Roegner, Robert .................135
Roehl, Ronald ....................101
Roehl, Shirley ....................330
Rogelstad, David................188
Rogers, Huie ........................81
Rogers, Laura M. ...............256
Rogers, Scott......................256
Rogers-Witte, Cally ....168, 169
Rogness, Matthew...............101
Rogness, Peter....................117
Rohlfs, Steven P. ...............308
Roland, David ....................113
Roland, John ......................262
Rolf, Kathy.........................240
Rolheiser, Ronald...............309
Roller, John .......................335
Rollins, Richard A. ............140
Rollins, Robert L. ..............170
Romero, Carlos ..................138
Romero, Daniel F. ..............168
Romero-Palma, Sylvestre ...110
Ronsvalle, John L. ..............217
Ronsvalle, Sylvia ...............217
Roof, Joe ...........................121
Roop, Eugene F..................297
Roozen, David A................218
Rorie, Stephen....................267
Rosario, Luis......................169
Rosco, Michael ..................328
Roscover, Norma ...............255
Rose, Donald L. .................337
Rose, J. Hugh ....................174
Rose, Jonathan ....................48
Rose, Whaid.........................99
Rosen, Janice .....................360
Rosengarten, Richard A. .....315
Roso, Henry A. ...113, 330, 332
  (Hank)
Ross, Eugene......................169
Ross, Kent..........................334
Ross, Mary Jane .................218
Ross, Nan ............................31
Ross, Patricia .....................233
Rost, Nori...........................175

Rostan, June .......................23
Rostand, Dean J. ................347
Roth, Adam ........................258
Roth, Jared D. ....................132
Roth, John D. .....................336
Rothamel, John, Jr...............142
Rottenberg, John .................27
Rottino, Kathleen................142
Rourk, David C....................96
Rourke, Marguerite .............240
Rouse, Michael ....................36
Roussin, Raymond ..............206
Rowley, Robert D., Jr..........111
Roy, Marie-Michèle ............348
Royster, Bill .......................169
Royster, Carl ........................25
Rozeboom, John A...............90
Rubeck, Dustin "Dusty" .....300
Rubin, Fred ........................103
Ruble, Randall T. ...............301
Rucker, Jaqueline P. ............259
Ruffin, Jeff .........................100
Ruge, Mark ........................200
Rumscheidt, Martin .............57
Rundbraaten, Edwin............193
Rundell, Jay .......................307
Rupe, Jolene .......................306
Rupp, Alan .........................120
Rusch, Willam G..................33
Rusche, Brian A. .........248, 249
Rush, Betty.........................257
Rush, Henry .......................235
Rush, Patricia .....................255
Rush, Robert D. .................105
Russell, Al..........................334
Russell, Dorothy .................43
Russell, Gary E. ...................90
Russell, Joseph...................155
Russell, Keith A. ................295
Rust, Harold................193, 317
Ruth, Gary............................22
Rutherford, F. Thomas ........190
Rutland, Mark ....................313
Rutzler, John ......................264
Ryan, Bridget .....................248
Ryan, James R....................236
Rydman, Philip ...................351
Ryoo, Keihwan ...................343
Ryskamp, Andrew...............90
Rystephanuk, David............202
Ryzy, Emigidiusz H. ............72

Saenz, Agnes......................245
Safari, Nelly .......................52
Salge, Carol........................241
Saliba, Philip........................69
Salico, Dale V. .....................66
Salmon, Edward L., Jr.........111
Saltzman, Russell E. ...........331
Salvas, M. Sylvain ......205, 206
Samra, Cal..........................334
Samuel, Lloyd U. .................72
Samuels, Thomas W............142

Sanchagrin, Kenneth M. .......33
Sande, Jonathan M..............123
Sanders, Bill.......................243
Sanders, Chris .....................36
Sanders, Hiram...................308
Sanders, Kay ......................243
Sanders, Robert L. .............103
Sandford, Byron.................122
Sandford, Christopher........247
Sandler, Abraham................90
Sandoval, Robert................252
Sanford, Don A. .................354
Santiago, Carlos .................132
Santiago, Felix .............98, 193
Santiago, Rolando ...............38
Saperstein, David...............229
Sapp, W. David ....................37
Sarmazian, Yessayi ...........184
Sartain, J. Peter ...................83
Sarwa, Andrzej J. ...............189
Satterfield, Ray ....................63
Satterlee, Erin S. W............343
Sauceda, Sam.....................268
Sauls, Stacy F. ....................110
Saunders, Dwight...............131
Saunders, Willard...............146
Savaloja, Timothy D. ..........300
Savas (Bishop) ...................128
Savell, Medrick...................313
Sawatzky, Leonard..............198
Sawyer, Luke .......................29
Sawyer, Rodney J...............114
Saxe, Susan ........................228
Sayre, Larry D. ....................66
Scales, Michael G. .............295
Scar, William......................236
Scarfe, Alan........................108
Scarpato, John ....................259
Schaal, David D. .................105
Schaal, Wendell J. ................37
Schaefer, Beth ....................323
Schaer, Marilyn ..................201
Schaper, Michael..................81
Schell, Steve.......................132
Schellenberg, Rick .............317
Schemmel, Wade.........169, 257
Schermerhorn, Eunic .........260
Schiemann, D.....................200
Schiemant, Donald.............125
Schierenbeck, John ............101
Schilling, Ira.......................162
Schindell, Dal.....................347
Schipper (Mr.)....................333
Schlabach, Darrel...............139
Schlatter, William R.............71
Schleicher, Andrew J. .........337
Schlemmer, Douglas............68
Schlenker, Janet .................236
Schlosser, Rick ..................234
Schmeling, G. R.........299, 335
Schmidgall, Paul ..........96, 192
Schmidt, Harry...........125, 299
Schmidt, Krystin ................123

INDEX

433

Schnase, Robert C. ............172
Schneider, Bette ................268
Schneider, Don C. ..............159
Schneider, Francis J. ..........312
Schneider, Richard ...............53
Schneider, Theodore F. .......118
Schner, Joseph G. ..............321
Schnurr, Dennis M. ..............83
Schoder-Ehri, Bill ..............122
Schoelles, Patricia A. ..........310
Schoenhals, Floyd M. .........114
Schofield, John-David ........111
Schofield-Bodt, Brian ........237
Schol, John R. ....................172
Schoonover, Wayne ............127
Schori, Katharine Jefferts ...109
Schrader, David ..................194
Schrag, James M. ...............138
Schramm, Richard W. .........324
Schreiberg, John H .............117
Schremp, James .................125
Schrock, Simon ....................79
Schrock, Wayne ...................79
Schrodt, Paul .......................23
Schubert, Jeffrey ...............136
Schueddig, Louis C. .............31
Schug, Tricia ......................267
Schulte, Gary .....................169
Schulte, Raymond ...............27
Schulter, Nancy ..................251
Schultz, Harvey ..................119
Schultz, John C. ..................295
Schultz, Raymond ................56
Schultz, Raymond L. ..........197
Schultz, Ronald ..................136
Schultz, Stephen R. ..............78
Schwarr, Carolyn ...............266
Schwartz, Beth .....................42
Schwich, Kathie Bender ......116
Scott, Alphonso ..................146
Scott, Charles G. ................147
Scott, Hopeton ...................237
Scott, Philip L. ...................144
Scott, Richard G. ..................99
Scott, W. Peter ...................210
Scruggs, Endia ...................108
Scruton, Gordon P. .............111
Scudder-Youth, Edwina ........49
Scurry, Frank P. .................298
Seaman, Ashley ....................49
Searle, Don L. ....................330
Seasoltz, R. Kevin ..............345
Seater, Robert P. ................268
Secola, Cheryl ....................248
Segall, Susan .....................267
Seide, Emmanuel ...........89, 90
Selby, Richard ....................264
Seler, Debby ......................328
Sellers, Asbury R. ..............192
Semel, Rita ..........................48
Semore, Garvis ...................306
Sene, Daniel ......................239
Senior, Donald ...................298

Seppala, Ivan M. ..................73
Seraphim (Bishop) ............. 202
Serapion (Bishop) .......107, 323
Sergeva, Yelena ..................259
Serratelli, Arthur J. ...............83
Sessions, Jim ........................35
Seville, Jack ......................169
Sewell, Don ..........................43
Shada, Doug .........................79
Shaffer, Kenneth M., Jr. ......354
Shaffer, Steve .....................120
Shah, Ajay ..........................225
Shahidi, Munirah ..................48
Shalman, Charles ................254
Shamana, Beverly J. ...........172
Shand, James J. ..................110
Shanlin, Jeff .......................205
Shannon, S. E. ....................100
Sharp, Arthur ......................139
Sharp, Bill ..........................119
Sharp, Donald .......................47
Sharp, Stephen .....................22
Sharp, Tammy .......................25
Sharpe, Conner ...................266
Sharpe, Michael .........107, 336
Shaver, Ruth .......................245
Shaw, Barbara L. ...................63
Shaw, Milton ......................134
Shaw, M. Thomas, III .........110
Shaw, Richard .....................245
Shaw, William J ..................141
Shawl, Sallie ......................266
Shea, William B. ...................37
Sheard, J. .............................94
Sheehan, Michael J. ..............83
Sheffield, Dan .....................199
Sheie, Myrna J. ...................116
Sheldon, William A. ..............92
Shellabarger, Thomas ...........36
Shelley, Marshall ................334
Shellhammer, Destiny ...........26
Shelly, Rubel ......................344
Shelton, Don W. ....................86
Shelton, Tom ........................13
Shepard, Beverley ...............123
Shepard, Morgan D. ............160
Shepherd, D. A. ...................203
Shepherd, Oscar .................132
Shepson, Bill ......................132
Shequel, Sleiman ..................69
Sherer, Ann Brookshire .......172
Sherry, Brian ........................22
Sherry, Paul ...................35, 41
Sheveland, Gerald .................78
Shibly, Othman ...................254
Shields, Janis .......................22
Shin, Jacob S ......................315
Shinachi, Enoch ..................124
Shipley, Joseph .....................87
Shipman, Joan G. ................261
Shisanya, Jonathan .............124
Shivachi, Nilson ..................124
Shlensky, Evely Laser ..........35

Shockley, Howard ...............119
Shockley, Nathan ................177
Short, Peter B. ....................210
Showers, Merle ...................254
Shreffler, Marilyn ................258
Shuman, Maryellen .............262
Sibley, Wallace J. ..........96, 192
Sickbert, Bryan W. ..............169
Sides, Richard ....................139
Sidner, Art .........................249
Sidorak, Stephen J., Jr. ........237
Siebert, Dorothy .................348
Siebert, John ........................57
Siepka, Richard W. ..............298
Sigman, Michael W. ............113
Signer, Ray ...........................48
Siker, Jeffrey S. ..................306
Sills, John F. .......................331
Silvey, James L. ....................79
Simerson, Suzanne .............248
Simiyu, Benson ...................124
Simiyu, Maurice ..................123
Simmons, Blanche ................30
Simms, John A. ...................294
Simon, Mark .......................132
Simon, Paula ......................268
Simpson, John ....................247
Simpson, Susan V. ..............126
Sinasac, Joseph ..................347
Sinclair, James H. ...............210
Sinclair, L. (Aftimios) ............72
Singh, Mandit .....................296
Singh, Manmohan ...............232
Singh, Mohinder ...................48
Singleton, Richard ..............247
Singley, Martin, III .............132
Sinkford, William .................167
Sippert, Steve .....................334
Sisk, Mark ..........................110
Sitaras, Constantine L. ........128
Sivulich, Stephen ................343
Skeene, Andrea ..................245
Skidmore, W. Chris ............243
    Benham
Skiles, Neal ..........................91
Sklba, Richard J. ...................83
Skocypec, Emil ...................166
Skrenes, Thomas A .............117
Skurla, Laurus ....................303
Skylstad, William S. ..............83
Slauter, James E. ................105
Slie, Samuel N. ...................237
Sly, Margery .......150, 355, 360
Small, Hazel .......................187
Small, Heather-Dawn ..........159
Smalley, Martha ..................356
Smedberg, Barry ................235
Smeeton, Donald D. .......96, 192
Smiley, Wayne ......................72
Smisko, Nicholas ..........67, 299
Smith, Alexei .....................236
Smith, Alycia .....................240
Smith, Andrew D. .......110, 237

434

Smith, Arthur ......................342
Smith, Autholene ................80
Smith, Brad ........................296
Smith, Bruce ......................193
Smith, Craig S......................89
Smith, Diana E......................25
Smith, Donnie W ................96
Smith, Dwayne...................103
Smith, Edward P.................296
Smith, Eric .........................139
Smith, Francis L.................146
Smith, Glenn ................55, 294
Smith, Guy H., III................76
Smith, Horace E.................146
Smith, James T...................103
Smith, Jane Orion ..............351
Smith, J. Morris .................262
Smith, Kenneth ..................352
Smith, Kenneth A...............155
Smith, Kirk Stevan.............109
Smith, Lawrence ................135
Smith, Leroy, Jr..................100
Smith, Liz...........................324
Smith, Marilyn McCann .....117
Smith, Marvin .....................80
Smith, Michael Gene..........111
Smith, Phil .........................334
Smith, R. Bruce....................54
Smith, Rebecca ..................241
Smith, Richard ...........205, 206
Smith, Robert .....................189
Smith, Robert E. ................303
Smith, Ron .........................237
Smith, Ronald ....................105
Smith, Ronald E..................316
Smith, Ron C. .....................336
Smith. Stephen ...................102
Smith, Steve .......................256
Smith, Susan J....................233
Smith, T. DeWitt ................152
Smith, Terry M....................198
Smith, Tom.........................258
Smith, T. Randall ...............265
Smith, Velma......................268
Smith, Victor P.....................92
Smith, Wallace ...................344
Smith, Wallace C. ..............309
Smith, Wayne .....................110
Smith, William L. ...............144
Smith, Zollie ........................75
Smith-Snyder, Donna..........247
Smock, Robert W. ................80
Snair, Karen .......................259
Snell, Catherine..................142
Snelson, J. E.......................327
Snow, Catherine J. .............203
Snow, Sharon .....................132
Snowman, Sharon L.............142
Snyder, Carol .....................330
Snyder, Joni........................242
Snyder, Richard D...............122
Snyder, William. .................263
Soderquist, Marilyn ............266

Solie, Daryl ........................200
Sommer, Donald .................127
Song, James .......................307
Sonnenburg, Brian ..............293
Soper, John F........................89
Sophia (Zion) (Nun) ...........347
Sorensen, Gordon H............185
Sorensen, Steven R. ............356
Soroka, Stefan......................83
Sotirios (Archbishop)..........199
Soto, Jaime...........................83
Sox, Aileen Andres .....338, 339
Spans, J. ..............................338
Sparkman, Alan...................147
Sparkman, Wayne ...............358
Sparks, Dennis D. ...............268
Sparks, William....................56
Spataro, Francis C...........72, 77
Spears, Rusty ......................236
Speas, Philip.......................305
Speer, James.........................79
Spence, Pamela.....................32
Spence, Ralph .....................183
Spencer, Archie ....................54
Spencer, Randy ...................107
Spencer, Shirley .................333
Sperzel, Ceil.......................241
Spittal, David J....................313
Spitzer, Lee ..........................66
Spleth, Richard L. ................86
Sprague, Roy.......................131
Spriggs, J. Wayne..................89
Spurgeon, Don ....................104
Spyridon (Bishop)...............130
Stafford, E. E. .....................140
Stafford, Willian S. .............312
Stahr, James A..............84, 189
Stair, Randel.......................149
Stairs, M. Jean.....................32o
Staller, Thomas ...................121
Stallings, James O..................67
Stamm, John M....................314
Standen, Michael ................256
Stanford, Alan ......................43
Stange, John .......................152
Stanley, Heidi ......................52
Stanley, Judy ......................262
Stanton, James M.................110
Stapert, Craig W...................325
Staples, Charles E................262
Stark, J. ..............................153
Starnes, Darryl B. ................63
Starr, Barbara .....................142
Stauch, Karimah...................48
Stauffer, Rick .....................119
Stavert, A. Bruce.................182
Steadman, William ..............210
Stearns, Richard ...................50
Steckbeck, Dori I. ..............354
Steele, Charles ....................36
Steenson, Jeffrey .................111
Stefanis, Anthony................128
Steib, J. Terry ......................83

Steinbacher, Wil...................33
Steinwand, Randy L.............59
Stelck, Brian .......184, 318, 322
Stella, Brigitte ....................252
Stemmle, Carol ...................243
Stenberg, Luther..................193
Stendahl, John K..................246
Stenson, Jane........................42
Stephanopoulos, Nikki........128
Stephanopoulos,..................128
  Robert G.
Stephen (Archbishop) .........164
Stephens, Mary ...................242
Stephens, Robert .................245
Stephenson, Carl H. ............211
Stephenson, Robert E..........105
Stern, George M...................261
Stetler, P. Daniel..................303
Stevens, Bruce G. ...............151
Stevens, Ruth J......................64
Stevenson, I..........................95
Stevenson, Philip T. ............177
Stewart, Betty......................124
Stewart, Danny......................86
Stewart, Dan R....................305
Stewart, Glen J......................87
Stewart, Jewelle ..................133
Stewart, Lois R....................148
Stewart, Mary C...................260
Stewart, Paul A. G., Sr......... 89
Stewart, Richard....................22
Stewart, Timothy.................152
Stewart-Rhude, Eileen ..........55
Steytler, Jessica ..................359
Stief, Ron .............................36
Stiller, Brian.................55, 324
Stimson, Eva .......................339
Stinnett, Daniel ...................186
Stinnett, J. Dwight ................66
Stinton, Rick .......................304
Stith, Betty V.........................63
Stith, Rhandi M.....................63
Stoesz, Conrad ....................360
Stokes, Thomas E. ..............354
Stoll, Christian ....................352
Stoll, Joseph ...............350, 352
Stolov, Yehuda ......................48
Stoltzfus, Margaret...............124
Stone, Barbara.....................259
Stone, Jack .........101, 102, 194
Stone, Mary Ruth.........96, 192
Stopperich, J. R...................241
Stortz, Dennis.....................136
St. Pierre, Bill .....................188
Strain, Patricia....................344
Strand, Sherri .....................136
Straub, Gregory...................109
Straughan, Gary ..................139
Strauser, AnnaMae ..............124
Strauser, Carol.....................125
Strauser, Charles Elwood.....124
Strauser, Simeon .................332
Strauss, Sandra L. ...............261

INDEX

435

Straut, Charles H., Jr. ..........252
Strawser, Craig L. .................90
Streeter, Terry.....................152
Strickland, Marshall H., I .....62
Strobel, David R. ................118
Strohmaier, Sharon E............242
Stromberg, Jean......................28
Strommen, E. Peter ............114
Strong, Robert F.................102
Stroupe, Jamie.....................339
Strout, Mark .........................320
Strout, Richard E. ...............350
Struchen, Shirley W. .......40, 45
Struck, Jane Johnson............342
Struik, Félix ........................300
Strunk, Orlo, Jr....................334
Stuart, Robert F..................238
Stuck, James R....................117
Studivant, G. W....................155
Stuehrenberg, Paul F. ...........23
Stumbo, Bruce ....................330
Stumbo, John P ....................89
Stumme-Diers, Paul W........117
Stump, Tiffany......................307
Sturtevant, Elwood...............242
Stutzman, Rose Mary...........342
Suarez, Gus .........................161
Subotic, Zivorad...................207
Suderman, Derek ..................54
Suderman, Robert ...............201
Sudhaker, Paul ....................103
Suhrheinrich, Heidi..............244
Sullivan, Anita .....................125
Sullivan, Bernard .................63
Sullivan, Don Jr ....................86
Sullivan, John......................161
Sullivan, Veronica ................34
Sumner, George R., Jr.........322
Sumners, Bill ......................353
Sundholm, James V ............114
Sure, Heng ...........................48
Sutroeter, Helga ..................255
Sutton, Edgar N. ...................66
Sutton, Ray R......................154
Svennungsen, Ann ................33
Swain, Lawrence O...............67
Swain, Thomas.............23, 147
Swan, Richard......................244
Swan, Tina ..........................251
Swank, Sandy......................242
Swanson, Douglas...............249
Swanson, Gary B. .......328, 329
Swanson, James E., Sr. .......173
Swanson, Paul R. ................114
Swanson-Nystrom, Jane K..329
Swanstrom, James...............242
Swartwood, Theresa............242
Swartz, Fred W.....................91
Swartzendruber, Loren........301
Swatkowski, Ray ..................78
Sweeney, Michael ...............300
Swenson, Kristin ..................48
Swenson, Mary Ann............173

Swidler, Leonard.................333
Swinburne, R. Douglas.........89
Swindle, Zephaniah ............165
Swing, William ....................48
Switzer, Patricia .................253
Swyers, Philip .....................157
Sydnor, Calvin H III .....61, 324
Sydow, James.....................101
Szabo, Stephen...........129, 335
Szo, Robert............................57

Tabbernee, William .............309
Taber-Hamilton, Nigel ........267
Taillon, Gerald ...........161, 188
Talbot, Lydia ......................239
Talbot, Nathan......................93
Talcott, Sarah .......................48
Talmage, Stephen S.............116
Talone, Cheryl.....................253
Tammen, Mark....................150
Tan, Hong Kia.....................175
Tandon, Atul..........................50
Tanis, Justin ........................174
Tanner, Susan W...................99
Tappen, Jerry......................268
Tarr, Rita .............................239
Taturn, Ed............................147
Taylor, Ann..........................253
Taylor, Betty P.....................264
Taylor, David F. .................249
Taylor, Don ...........................53
Taylor, Mark A ....................327
Taylor, Mark Lloyd .............312
Taylor, G. Porter..................111
Taylor, J. Glenn.....................54
Taylor, J. Graley..................266
Taylor, James .......................53
Taylor, Joyce.........................95
Taylor, L. Roy .....................149
Taylor, Mary Virginia .........173
Taylor, Steve .......................121
Taylor, Susan.......................123
Taylor, Victor ........................88
Taylor, Wayne .....................133
Taylor, Wesley M. ...............103
Teague, Peter W. .................305
Tedesco, John.......................87
Temple, Guy ........................261
Temple, Jan .........................261
Templeton, Beth ..................263
Tenold, Margo.....................234
Terry, Bill ............................133
Tesch, Walter F.....................136
Tetreau, Jerry.......................304
Thell, Barbara......................248
Thibodeau, Francois............206
Thiesen, John ......................357
Thiessen, David ..................197
Thiessen, Henry ..................198
Thistlethwaite, Susan ..........298
  Brooks
Thomann, David A...............80
Thomas, D. Karl .................184

Thomas, Dominic..................99
Thomas, Everett ..................335
Thomas, Freeman M. ..........146
Thomas, James P. ...............105
Thomas, John H. .................168
Thomas, Reginald H. ...........151
Thomas, Ronald P. ...............60
Thomas, Tenney ....................40
Thomas, Thomas.................260
Thomas, T. V. ......................191
Thomason, Jeanette...............31
Thomford, Christopher M...307
Thompson, Brice..........98, 193
Thompson, Dean K .............306
Thompson, Doug ..................264
Thompson, Else B ...............116
Thompson, Glendon G........322
Thompson, Herbert, Jr........111
Thompson, Houston.............241
Thompson, James W. ..........340
Thompson, Ken....................121
Thompson, Kenneth............265
Thompson, Leonard, Sr........66
Thomsen, Eric .....................338
Thon, Carol .........................241
Thopil, Markose..................146
Thoreson, Joel .....................356
Thorne, Leo S. ......................66
Thornton, Bobby C. .............78
Thorpe, Debbie ...................264
Thurston, Stephen J ............140
Thurton, Winston .................55
Tidwell, Dan........................119
Tiemann, Ray ......................117
Tillet, Charles......................237
Timmerman, Larry J. ..........192
Tinsley, Charles...................235
Tisdale, Delores ..................260
Tisdale, Janet.......................142
Titus, Beth...........................263
Titus, Devi...........................132
Titus, Richard C. .................233
Tizzard, Brian ......................58
Tkachuk, Rod......................202
Tolbert, Mark C..................146
Tolbert, Rosa ........................72
Tolbert, T. C., Jr. ..................72
Tolbert, T. C., Sr...................72
Tolborh, Moses ....................80
Tollefson, Rebecca J. ..........258
Tolley, S. T. ...............151, 326
Tom, Phil..............................36
Tombaugh, Richard F.........109
Tomesch, Harald .................318
Tomic, Vasilije ....................349
Tomlinson, Susanna M. ......260
Toner, Margaret...................206
Tong, Joseph .......................304
Toompuu, Marie..................185
Tooze, George ......................67
Toppins, Helen ...........123, 124
  Garay
Torok, Stefan M. .................130

436

Torrance, Iain R. ................310
Torrance, John...................185
Torrens, Gary .....................148
Tortoriello, John.................124
Torvik, John R....................114
Towne, Becky.....................334
Towns, L. Ferrell.................90
Townsend, Fred..................293
Trache, Robert G.................264
Trachian, Barkev.................314
Traftan, Margie ..................350
Trammell, Mary ..327, 332, 334
    M.
Trammell, Mary Metzner......93
Trapp, Edwin A., Jr. ............136
Trask, Thomas....................74
Trauger, Kenneth................260
Trautman, Donald W............83
Treanor, John J. ....................25
Trees, Richard ...................132
Trejo, José .........................248
Tremblay, Bernard ..............293
Tremblay, Donald...............293
Trent, Earl .........................152
Tressel, Rose .....................167
Trevino, Max A. .................159
Trevino, Yoland..................48
Triantafilou, Nicholas .126, 303
Tribett, Brenda ..................152
Trickett, David ..................304
Trine, Melinda.....................22
Tripp, Linda ........................58
Trotter, LaTonya ................48
Trotti, Melinda ..................255
Trowbridge, Constance ......267
Trowbridge, Kathleen ........245
Truett, Chris .....................140
Truss, James ......................72
Trusty, Bill .......................244
Tsapwe, Simon..................124
Tschetter, Charles...............119
Tse, James N. .....................31
Tsimbaki, Matthew .............121
Tucker, Neville...................63
Tucker, Tommy ..................243
Tune, Leslie C......................40
Tunnicliffe, Geoff ...............55
Turnage, Juleen ..................74
Turner, B. G. .....................133
Turner, Carl A. ..................146
Turner, Emil ......................160
Turner, Harvey L.................96
Turner, Rex A., Jr...............315
Tweet, Margaret ..................30
Tyler, Arlene......................152
Tyler, Robert D. .................100
Tyndall, Margaret................51
Tyrrell, Wilfred L................34
Tyson, James E. ..................146

Uchtdorf, Dieter F...............99
Uglem, Dwayne ..................317
Ugoletti, Dennis .................260
Ugolnik, Anthony................343
Ulery, Kent J......................169
Ullestad, Steven L..............117
Unruh, Ron ................196, 351
Up De Graff, Morse............149
Updegrove, John H. ............262
Uptain, Misti......................267
Upton, John V., Jr...............161
Usgaard, Harold L...............116
Utterback, J. Michael....96, 192
Uyeded-Kai, Kim................210

Valentine, Linda ...................50
Valentine, Pamela.................63
Valenzuela, Carmen ....248, 249
Vallance, James E. .............326
VanBeusekom, Hein...........135
VanBroekhoven,............67, 339
    Deborah
Van Campen, Frank .............79
Vandee, Pastor and .............186
    Mrs. Daniel
VanderMolen, Steven..153, 204
Vanderslice, Kenneth W........79
Vandervelde, George............33
Van Eyl, Christina ...............330
Vang, Timothy T. .................89
VanGelderen, Sharon ...........28
Vanhaverbeke, Sylvia Lisk ...49
Vaniber, Craig ...................119
van Laar, Erwin...................52
Van Leer, Thomas ...............248
Van Loon, Cathy.................351
Van Marter, Jerry .........24, 339
Vansen, Beatrice..................27
Van Vallenburgh, Gail........255
Vanyi, Laszlo B..................130
Vardemann, Brady J............250
Vargas, David A. ..................85
Varlaam, (Rev.) ..................145
Varley, Peter......................52
Varsberga-Paza, Anita ........134
Vasko, Rebecca ..................217
Vassiouchkine, Alexei.........202
Vaughan, Roland E. ......96, 192
Vaughn-Kelly, Sandra. ........248
Vaught, Don ......................258
Veazey, Stephen M..............105
Veech, Guthrie....................311
Veeraswamy, B....................80
Veillette, Martin .................206
Veitenhans, Michael............50
Veliko, Lydia........................31
Velozo, Ruth M...................267
Venema, Cornelius P. .........307
Verhoef, A. H. ...................142
Verigin, John J., Sr.............209
Vermillion, William............114
Vest, R. Lamar ........21, 44, 192
Vettrus, Richard .................100
Vickery, David ....................76
Victor (Metropolitan)..........129
Victorson, Vernon ..............252

Vidolo, Japheth ..................124
Viego, Alisa.........................30
Vila, Vesna .........................259
Villafane, Eldin ...................33
Villalba, Eddie .....................99
Vining, John K.............96, 192
Vinton, Samuel....................127
Visscher, J. .........................347
Vissers, John .....................320
Vlad, Mike ..........................99
Vodden, Lori ........................24
Vogel-Borne, Jonathan........124
Vonicessler, Caroline ..........264
von Rosenberg, Charles ......110
Von Wade, Melvin, Sr.........141
Voskuil, Betty.................40, 41
Voskuil, Dennis N. ..............316
Votary, Marilyn E................349
Votary, R. E. ......................200
Vree, Dale ..........................337
Vreeland, Richard ................49
Vsevolod (Archbishop).........16

Wackernagel, Betsy.............266
Wade, James........................61
Wagener, Ginny ..................236
Waggoner, Berten A............77
Waggoner, James E., Jr. ......111
Waggoner, Sara Jo .............258
Waghray, Rajyashri..............41
Wagner, Gary .....................29
Wagner, Jane ......................175
Wagner, Mark.....................309
Wagner, Norman ................146
Wagner, Rebecca................245
Waites, Bob .......................162
Wakefield, Wesley H. .186, 349
Walden, Jay ........................97
Waldner, Jacob ...................131
Walker, Alice......................343
Walker, Céleste ..................334
Walker, Diane.....................348
Walker, Frank.....................153
Walker, Gail .......................36
Walker, George ............61, 62
    Washington Carver, Sr.
Walker, Jewett L. ................63
Walker, Orris G., Jr. ...........110
Walker, Riley H. ..................66
Walker-Smith, Angelique....240
Wall, Jim ...........................147
Wallace, Peter M.................31
Wallace, Robert...................66
Wallace, Vicki ....................171
Walle, Ann..........................41
Waller, Leonora..................242
Walles, Caroline .................250
Walles, Charles A................114
Walles, Harry .....................250
Walley, Wendel ..................297
Wallis, Hope.......................254
Wallis, Jim.........................341
Walsh, Daniel......................83

INDEX

437

Walsh, Gary............................55
Walsh, Robert......................52
Walter, Bob .........................48
Walter, Ewa..........................49
Walter, Martin ...................131
Waltner, Sharon.................138
Walton, Christopher ...........343
   Walton
Wamala, Francis.................124
Wang, Karen ........................40
Wangberg, Rolf P. ..............116
Wangensteen, Peg .............249
Wanner, Janet .....................241
Ward, George ......................50
Ward, Hope Morgan...........173
Ward, Marion J. .................267
Ward, Michael, Sr. ..............68
Ward, Sarah F......................43
Warfel, Michael W. .............83
Warkie, Peter......................146
Warner, Vincent W. ...........111
Warner, Wayne ...................353
Warr, Sterling E. ................203
Warren, Cindy .....................30
Warren, David ...................126
Warren, Mike .....................328
Warren, Patty.....................233
Warrick, J. K. .....................101
Wartman, Paul...................318
Washington, Don A.............245
Wasielewski, Charles, .....67, 68
   Sr.
Wasserman, Joseph ............236
Watkins, David J.............79, 80
Watkins, Dennis W........95, 192
Watkins, Sharon R. .............85
Watson, B. Michael.............173
Watson, Robert....................99
Watt, Jonathan...................156
Watt, Neil ...........................207
Waugh, David ......................40
Wauls, Robert....................146
Wawire, Blastus .................124
Waxler, Mel.......................264
Waybright, Gregory L.........314
Waynick, Catherine M. ......110
Weakland, Rembert G.........268
Weaver, David......................41
Weaver, James...................346
Weaver, Peter D. .........171, 172
Weavill, George .................263
Webb, Robert .....................354
Webb, Suzanne.....................31
Webber, Robert D. ...............44
Webster, Gordon V.............253
Webster, Joe L....................170
Wedig, Mark E. ..................296
Weeks, Dewayne.................147
Weeks, Louis B. ..................314
Weeks, Thomas J. ...............146
Weeks, Thomas W., Sr. .......146
Weems, L. ............................94
Weigand-Buckley, Amber ...338

Weigand-Buckley, Arnold ...338
Weigley, David...................159
Weikel, Calvin...................133
Weinacht, Alan ..................123
Weinreb, Tzvi Hersh ..........230
Weinstein, Judy ..................261
Welch, Shirley......................62
Wells, Bobbi.......................328
Wells, D. L. S.......................95
Wells, D. R.........................201
Wells, Martin D..................116
Welscott, Richard........153, 204
Welsh, Robert K...........85, 325
Welty, Marcel A. ..................40
Wendland, Paul O. .............316
Wendorf, Mark.....................36
Wenthe, Dean O..................300
Werkheiser, Kevin D...........102
Wert, Rita ............................43
Wesley, John .......151, 172, 186
West, Barbara J. .................154
West, James C., Sr. .....154, 300
West, Jonathan .....................23
West, Suzy............................29
Westberg, M. Victor.............93
Westbrook, Don .................125
Westbrook, T. L....................94
Wetzel, C. Robert...............301
Wetzel, Daniel R...................90
Whalen, Paul......................243
Whalon, Pierre ...................110
Whalon, Pierre W................109
Wheaton, Keith D...............323
Wheeler, Edward L. ...........299
Wheeler, Jack ....................253
Wheeler, Roger ..................131
Whitaker, Timothy..............173
White, Alma Bridwell.........148
White, Barbara .....................38
White, Cyrus N. ...................85
White, David O. ..................236
White, Douglas ...................113
White, F. O...........................94
White, R. Fowler.................305
White, J. C............................95
White, James Emery ...........302
White, Jim ..........................249
White, J. Robert ..................161
White, K. Gordon ...............246
White, Marcus...............38, 268
White, Patricia ...................107
White, Patricia P.................329
White, R................................95
White, Raymond W..............130
White, Reid R., Jr..................63
White, Susan ......................148
White, Terry .........................31
WhiteEagle, Sheila..............249
Whitehead, Evan ................185
Whitehead, Ron ..................121
Whiten, Bennie, Jr................36
Whitener, Ray .....................244
Whitfield, D. Max ...............172

Whiting, D. Douglas .............44
Whitmore, Keith B..............110
Whitney, Dale .....................235
Whitt, Dwight Reginald......300
Whittaker, Bill....................299
Whittaker, Fermin A. ..........161
Wickmann, David L............139
Widger, Janet........................79
Wiebe, Dave .......................188
Wiebe, Henry .....................205
Wiebe, Jim ..........................191
Wiebe, Virgil........................80
Wieczerzak, Joseph.............358
Wiens, Hart ..........................52
Wieser, Walter W. ...............186
Wiesner, Gerald...................205
Wigger, Barbara ..........126, 345
Wiggins, James B. ..............254
Wiginton, Melissa ................33
Wilcox, Donald M. ..............252
Wildman, Doug...................347
Wildman, Ingrid..................196
Wiley, Galen.......................121
Wilkerson, Jack...................160
Wilkie, Owen ......................325
Wilkinson, Ed .....................342
Willemsma, Tena...................24
Williams, Annie M.................63
Williams, Arsenia................142
Williams, Bert ....328, 329, 331,
   342
Williams, Bertha .................43
Williams, Carol....................257
Williams, Cheryl Powers ....248
Williams, Connie B..............63
Williams, Dennis L...............86
Williams, Don Dixon............28
Williams, Elijah ....44, 170, 171
Williams, Elvonia ................95
Williams, Gregory...............335
Williams, Horace K. ............95
Williams, John ....................150
Williams, John P., Jr............115
Williams, Matthew................95
Williams, Michael A............66
Williams, Michelle James...174
Williams, Newell ................297
Williams, Patrick J..............309
Williams, Preston ..................61
   Warren II
Williams, Ray .....................141
Williams, Robert ................109
Williams, Ron ....................132
Williams, Roy ....................138
Williams, Sam ...................115
Williams, Warren, II..............61
Williams, W.J. ....................142
Williamson, Edward W. .......119
Williamson, Elaine..............240
Williamson, Henry M. ..........89
Williamson, Jack ..................39
Williamson, Portia Turner.....33
Williamson, Stephen ...........256

438

Williard, Laura Lee ............138
Williford, Craig ...................300
Willimon, William H. .........173
Willis, Carolyn ...................346
Willis, Mike ........................343
Wills, Richard J., Jr. ............173
Wills, Susan ........................264
Wills, Wanda Bryant ............85
Wilson, Alex V. ...................345
Wilson, Dori .......................236
Wilson, Earle L. .................. 176
Wilson, Glenna ...................262
Wilson, H. C. ......................211
Wilson, Helen Tibbs ...........233
Wilson, Holly .....................348
Wilson, Ian E. .....................360
Wilson, Jeffrey K. ...............159
Wilson, John ......................241
Wilson, Maureen ................196
Wilson, Nancy L. ................174
Wilson, Norman G. ......176, 344
Wilson, Robert ...................150
Wilson, Rod ........................321
Wilson, Ronald ............31, 105
Wiltschek, Walt ...................336
Wiltse, David A. ..................345
Wimberly, Don A. ..............111
Winbush, R. L. H. .........94, 95
Winbush, Robina ................150
Wind, James P. ......................21
Wine (Sister) ......................155
Wines, Roger ......................151
Wingender, Eric ..................318
Winger, Brian ......................209
Winger, Darrell S. ................81
Wingle, James .....................205
Winn, Robert ........................92
Winston, Mervin .................248
Winter, Linda .....................262
Winter, Roy ..........................91
Winters, Carolyn M. ...........233
Wipf, John ...........................131
Wirt, Douglas ........................86
Wirthlin, Joseph B. ...............99
Wisler, Jacob ......................144
Wissel, Saney .......................33
Wisthoff, Grace ...................257
Witczak, Michael G. ...........311
Witherspoon, Anthony ........250
Witt, Richard ......................255
Wittberg, Patricia ...............340
Woelbern, James ...................26
Wojcicki, Ted L. .................305
Wolf, Geralyn .....................111
Wolfe, Bennet .......................92

Wolfe, Dean E. .....................110
Wolfe, Thomas V ................254
Wolford, Kathryn F. ..............37
Wolfram, Donald J. .............148
Wolgemuth, Dan ...................51
Wollersheim, Gary M. .........117
Woloschak, Gayle ...............166
Womack, Anne ......................23
Wontor, Caryn ....................265
Wood, Bertice Y. ...................31
Wood, Edward W. ...............133
Wood, George O. ..................74
Wood, Maudie .....................102
Wood, Robert Stanley .........108
Wood, Susan. ......................162
Wood, Virginia ...................123
Woodbury, Clayton R. ..........67
Woodrich, Noya ..................248
Woodring, DeWayne S. ..........47
Woodruff, James .................253
Woods, Gayle ......................307
Woods, William K. ..............257
Woodson, Darryl D. .............174
Woodward, George ........... 202
Woodward, Jim ...................244
Woodworth, Rodger ...........119
Woofenden, Lee ..................338
Woolfolk, Thomas E. ..........101
Workowski, Joan ................155
Worley, Lloyd .....................135
Worthington, Melvin ............47
Wortman, Julie A. ...............344
Wright, Abraham .................31
Wright, Benny ....................266
Wright, David ..............50, 303
Wright, Frank .......................42
Wright, Harold ...................235
Wright, Hilman ..................156
Wright, Walter L. ................159
Wright, Wayne P. ........110, 238
Wright-Riggins, Aidsand F. ...67
Wruck, Demetrios E. ...........165
Wuerch, Harry ....................198
Wukwanja, Geoffrey M. .....123
Wvertele, Peggy M ............118
Wyatt, Peter ........................318
Wylie, Ken .........................239
Wynick, Karmen ..................22
Wyse, Mark ........................120

Yaldezian, John ....................74
Yanagihara, Akio ................267
Yasenka, David ...................251
Yates, Jonathan ...................142
Yeats, John .........................160

Yeglikian, Albert .................184
Yeso, Lynn ..........................259
Yessa, John ...........................22
Yi, Maria Renya ..................123
Yntema, Philip ....................201
Yoder, Grace .......................357
Yoffie, Eric H. .....................230
York, Alwyn .......................106
Yost, Wayne .......................259
Young, Lyle ..........................93
Young, Martha ....................245
Young, McKinley ............49, 61
Young, M. Norvel ...............323
Young, Ronald L. ................146
Youngren, David .................201
Yount, Diana ......................354
Yrigoyen, Charles, Jr. .........336

Zabel, Nancy ........................43
Zacharias, Carl ...................198
Zacharias, Ken ...................197
Zahl, Paul F. M. ..................314
Zain, Thomas ...............69, 183
Zakian, Chris ........................74
Zander, Vera .........................30
Zandier, Don ......................262
Zanicky, Robert ..................263
Zavalo, Gambino ..................34
Zangmeister, Pat ..................30
Zapeda, Monica ..................267
Zarling, Thomas F. ..............178
Zavitz-Bond, Jane ...............360
Zawierucha, Bazyl ..............166
Zehlaoui, Joseph ..................69
Zehr, Marvin ......................242
Zeiders, G. Edwin ...............314
Zelenitz, Myrna ..................260
Zelinsky, Daniel .........343, 344
(Heiromonk)
Zell, R. Thomas .........325, 346
Zeller, Stephanie ................108
Zelter, Barbara ...................256
Zetto, J. Jeffrey ...................263
Ziemer, Dale ........................27
Zilmer, Norman D. ...............84
Zimmerman, Phillip ...........152
Zintak, Nancy .......................31
Zipfel, Paul .........................257
Zirille, Francis M. ...............241
Zobel, Tom ...........................25
Zottoli, Carmine ...................87
Zubik, Davd A. .....................83
Zuck, Lowell ......................359
Zusevics, Deab Lauma ........134
Zylla, Phil ...........................317

INDEX

439

# Notes

# Notes

# Notes

# Notes

# Notes

# Notes

# Notes

# Notes

# Notes